CONTINUUM MECHANICS

MACMILLAN SERIES IN APPLIED MECHANICS

FRED LANDIS, EDITOR

The Analysis of Stress and Deformation
by George W. Housner and Thad Vreeland, Jr.
Analytical Methods in Vibrations by Leonard Meirovitch
Continuum Mechanics by Walter Jaunzemis
Statics of Deformable Bodies by Nils O. Myklestad

WALTER JAUNZEMIS
The Pennsylvania State University

CONTINUUM MECHANICS

THE MACMILLAN COMPANY, NEW YORK
COLLIER-MACMILLAN LIMITED, LONDON

First Printing

Library of Congress catalog card number: 67-16053

THE MACMILLAN COMPANY, NEW YORK
COLLIER-MACMILLAN CANADA, LTD., TORONTO, ONTARIO

Printed in the United States of America

PREFACE

This book grew out of lecture notes for a two-semester graduate course aimed at providing a reasonably thorough introduction to the ideas and mathematical methods of continuum mechanics. To become proficient in continuum mechanics, the student needs a good deal of groundwork, the presentation of which has been traditionally the province of graduate courses, and is also the main task of this book. The learning of the fundamentals may be, like the learning of vocabulary and grammar, hard and occasionally dull work. For this reason an attempt has been made to enliven the flood of terminologies by providing motivations or anticipating later applications. Still, the book is for those who do not dislike mathematics and for whom the subjects taken up in the first three chapters will have some appeal of their own.

Continuum mechanics is, in a manner of speaking, the common denominator of the continuum theories, of which elasticity theory and hydrodynamics are well-known instances. It is a *field theory*, in the sense that all properties of material bodies (including the regions of space in which the bodies are more or less accurately located!) appear as fields, i.e. as functions of space coordinates and time. Of course, even wave mechanics is a field theory. What sets it apart from continuum mechanics is that the fields are studied within very small domains. In continuum mechanics, on the other hand, the domains are so large as to make the macroscopic aspects of bodies virtually insensitive to the details of microstructure. If, as in statistical theories, we imagine that matter is made up of particles, then a continuum theory will assign field values (e.g., displacements) to points that may be unoccupied. But there is no harm in that, as long as the field values are correct at places that are occupied. Thus if a small portion of a body is viewed as a system of particles, then the correlation of a continuum theory with the particle picture is not unlike the problem of curve-fitting, in which a continuous curve is drawn so that it passes through the assigned points. Needless to say, if the number of particles is enormous, and their motions highly "individualistic,' then the task of devising a single function to fit all the data will be hopeless. Therefore, a continuum theory can describe, locally, only the simplest, "continuum" modes of the collective behavior of systems (e.g., mass center motion, angular momentum, homogeneous strain). By the same token, the limitation to simple modes of behavior makes it possible to devise, outright, simple theories governing these modes, so that the gross behavior of bodies can be predicted from gross observations alone.

Each theory is made up, in part, of conventions, and in part of empirical facts. In the main, the conventions determine the form of a theory. For instance, it is customary to divide the empirical laws of continuum mechanics into *physical principles*, which are the same in each theory, and *constitutive equations*, which differ from one theory to another. The approach of covering the physical principles once for all, without recourse to constitutive equations, has been also adopted in this book. An alternative approach, known as *Hamilton's principle*, has been illustrated in the context of special theories (see pp. 397–408, 421–422, 555–556). In Hamilton's principle the starting point is a constitutive potential of a body, and the form-invariance of this potential to certain "observer transformations" is now equivalent to the physical principles.

As remarked by Truesdell [177],† one may look upon Euclidean geometry, mechanics of rigid bodies, and mechanics of deformation as successive stages of a theory of material bodies. One may equally well look upon each of these stages as a constitutive model, designed with a special class of *problems* in mind. The use of a more elaborate model is an improvement in the sense that it will open to analysis certain phenomena that eluded the more idealized theory. At the same time, problems that were solvable in the more idealized theory may prove to be intractable in the improved theory. Therefore, a nonlinear theory will seldom replace the linearized theory; rather, it will complement it.

The book unavoidably falls far short of a complete coverage of continuum mechanics. In particular, the limitation of size made it necessary to omit the classical theories of hydrodynamics and plasticity. It does contain, however,

† Numbers in square brackets refer to the Bibliography.

a fair portion of details of derivations—enough, it is hoped, to make reading relatively easy. Because of the diversity of the subject matter, the level of presentation varies considerably. Two kinds of notations are used: (1) an explicit (or "scalar") notation for calculations and (2) abbreviated notations (e.g., index notation, simplified designations for derivatives and integrals). The latter describe a kind of "programming," which records ideas, derivations, and the like, while suppressing the detailed instructions for the execution of the operations. For the most part, the abbreviated notations are no more than common sense, which would be introduced sooner or later by everyone who had to deal with certain operations often enough.

The book also contains material that is needed in order to make the presentation reasonably complete, but which can be omitted in a first, or selective, reading of the book. A brief outline of the main parts of the book is as follows (additional comments will be found in the Solutions Manual).

The first chapter is devoted to operations with tensors. It is unlikely that one could, or would even want to, cover all of this material in class. In fact, correct tensor operations can be performed solely on the basis of the notational conventions introduced in Section 1. The examples on pages 39–46 can be used to form an intuitive idea of the nature of tensors. A knowledge of the properties of second rank tensors (pp. 54–73) will be also needed sooner or later. A quick glance through the remainder of the chapter (so as to become familiar with the notations) will then suffice. The presentation of tensors is fairly self-contained and unhurried so that the chapter can serve as a reference and also facilitate a review of various topics (e.g., vectors, integral transformations), if such a review is necessary.

Tensor calculus in orthogonal curvilinear coordinates (Section 6) is developed solely in terms of *physical components* (also called *anholonomic components* or *local Cartesian components*). These components are in many ways convenient, the main advantages being that each tensor is represented by one matrix only (rather than having matrices of contravariant, covariant, and mixed representations), and that all components of a tensor have the same dimension. Because tensor analysis in terms of the physical components is relatively unknown, there seemed to be a need for a thorough exposition of this subject. To avoid possible confusion, the variables that appear in the place of Christoffel symbols (they are really components of "anholonomic objects") have been named *wryness coefficients.* Except when it is advantageous to use oblique coordinate systems (as in the deformation theory of surfaces—see pp. 244–249), the formalism given in this section is perfectly adequate for any problem in spaces that are at least locally Euclidean. As a glance at the book will show, the main kinematical results and the physical principles, as well as a good many applications, are presented in the familiar setting of Cartesian coordinate systems. Therefore, in a first reading one may omit all the material involving curvilinear coordinates.

In Chapter 2, the first section deals, in effect, with the kinematics of a single particle. Although some of the finer points made in this section are not too vital, the substance of the section, including the idea of observer transformations, is basic to much of the later work. In Section 8, on the other hand, attention may be confined to mapping of material lines, surfaces, and volumes, leaving the other results until the time when they are needed. The theory of singular surfaces is first mentioned in Section 8, and appears again in other sections. It is perhaps best to deal with the entire theory in one place. (Propagation of acceleration fronts in viscoelastic media, discussed in Section 14, may serve as an application of the theory.)

The requirement for admission to the club of mechanicists is simple and inflexible: a complete grasp of the idea of a *state of stress* at a point. This idea is explored in Section 10, with particular attention to tetrahedral "free bodies" and boundary conditions for stresses. Generalizations of the classical idea of stress are taken up in Section 11, which deals with *multipolar theories* and certain classical theories cast into the mold of multipolar theories (e.g., shells considered as "Cosserat surfaces").† This branch. continuing through Section 16, stands separate from the rest of the book.

In Chapter 4 the applications are to linear theories, but the discussion of general ideas is, for the most part, not limited to small deformations or linear constitutive equations. In particular, the outline of a theory of constitutive equations (Section 14) will also serve as the starting point for the nonlinear theories of elasticity and viscoelasticity. The presentation of the linear theory of elasticity suffers, no doubt, from the usual drawbacks of a compromise, being too long for a survey, too short for adequate coverage. Rather than emphasizing the more conventional applications, the section is directed mainly toward "point imperfections," dislocations, and plasticity, and other applications suggested by problems in solid state physics. It is of course far from evident that the linear theory of elasticity can be an adequate basis for "continuum theories of point imperfections," but that is no reason why such applications should not be explored.

Sections 15 and 16 are not prerequisites for the nonlinear theories. In fact, one may proceed directly from the stress relation obtained in Section 14 to solution of problems of nonlinear elasticity (Sections 18, 19, 21).

There will be two exceptions to the use of numbered references: *The Non-Linear Field Theories of Mechanics* by C. Truesdell and W. Noll (*Enc. of Physics*, III/3, New York: Springer-Verlag (1965)) will be referred to by the

† The starred section titles indicate special material that may be omitted without affecting the continuity of the text.

abbreviation *NFTM*, and *The Classical Field Theories* by C. Truesdell and R. A. Toupin (*Enc, of Physics*, III/1, New York: Springer Verlag (1960)) will be referred to by the abbreviation *CFT*. By and large, the references listed in the Bibliography have been used in the writing of the book. No attempt has been made to give a complete bibliography. Extensive bibliographies may be found in *CFT* and *NFTM*.

It is a pleasure to acknowledge indebtedness to former students for their appreciation and forbearance; to friends and colleagues, particularly Drs. M. A. Beatty, S. C. Cowin, R. L. Fosdick, and A. C. Pipkin, who were kind enough to read and criticize the first draft of the book; to the Air Force Office of Scientific Research for its continued support, and to the publishers for their help and patience.

W. J.

CONTENTS

LIST OF SYMBOLS

The following is a list of frequently used symbols. To minimize the necessary number of letter types, some of the symbols have more than one meaning (though not in the same context). When dealing with deformations, variables associated with a reference configuration are usually denoted by majuscule letters, e.g., $dS^2 = dX_i\, dX_i$, and variables associated with the current configuration by minuscule letters, thus $ds^2 = dx_i\, dx_i$. The overbar, as in $\bar{\mathbf{T}}$, has been used throughout as an "all purpose notation" (i.e., it has no specific meaning assigned to it).

Symbol	*Meaning*
$\mathscr{P}$	particle
$\mathscr{E}$	the infinite space
$\mathscr{O}$	(Euclidean) observer
$\alpha, \beta, \gamma, \ldots$	coordinate indices in even-dimensional spaces
$i, j, k, \ldots$	indices assigned to Cartesian coordinate systems
$a, b, c, \ldots, A, B, C, \ldots$	indices assigned to orthogonal curvilinear coordinate systems
$\mathbf{1}, \delta_{ij}$	Kronecker delta
$\varepsilon_{ij}, \varepsilon_{ijk}, \ldots$	alternators
ρ, ϕ, z	cylindrical coordinates

r, θ, ϕ	spherical coordinates
θ_a, Θ_A	orthogonal curvilinear coordinates
X_i, x_i	Cartesian coordinates of a particle in the initial and final configurations, respectively (in curvilinear coordinates the corresponding designations are Θ_a and θ_a, for instance)
$\partial_i = \dfrac{\partial}{\partial x_i}, \Delta_i = \dfrac{\partial}{\partial X_i}$	differential operators
$h_{\underline{a}}^{-2} = x_{i,\underline{a}} x_{i,\underline{a}}$	(no sum over $\underline{a}$!) metric coefficients
$\partial_a = h_{\underline{a}} \dfrac{\partial}{\partial \theta_a}$	differential operator
$D = \partial_{\underline{n}} = \mathbf{n} \cdot \nabla$	gradient operator in the direction of $\mathbf{n}$
$D_m = \partial_m - n_m D$	gradient operator in a surface
t, τ	present and past instants
s	elapsed time $t - \tau$ (also, arc length)
Π, π	initial and final position vectors
$\mathbf{e}_i = \partial_i \pi$	Cartesian base vectors
$\mathbf{i}_a = \partial_a \pi$	unit base vectors in curvilinear coordinates
$Q_{ai} = \partial_a x_i$	direction cosines
$w_{cab} = \mathbf{i}_a \cdot \partial_b \mathbf{i}_c$	wryness coefficients (the counterpart of Christoffel symbols)
$v_{a;b} = \partial_b v_a + w_{cab} v_c = Q_{ai} Q_{bj} v_{i,j}$	absolute derivatives ("physical components of covariant derivatives")
$\varkappa, \chi$	configurations of a body
$F_{ij} = x_{i,j} = \Delta_j x_i$	deformation gradients
$J = \det \mathbf{F}$	determinant of $\mathbf{F}$
C, C_{ijkm}	elastic coefficients
G, G_{ijkm}	relaxation moduli
$\mathbf{U}, \mathbf{V}$	stretch tensors
$\mathbf{R} = \mathbf{V}^{-1}\mathbf{F} = \mathbf{F}\mathbf{U}^{-1}$	rotation tensor
$\left.\begin{array}{l}\mathbf{B} = \mathbf{F}\mathbf{F}^T = \mathbf{V}^2, \\ \mathbf{C} = \mathbf{F}^T\mathbf{F} = \mathbf{U}^2\end{array}\right\}$	deformation tensors (starting with Section 8)
$\mathbf{E}, \mathbf{e}$	strain tensors
$H_{im} = \Delta_m u_i$	displacement gradients

$\mathbf{P}$	tensor of intrinsic rotation
$\tilde{\mathbf{E}}, \tilde{\mathbf{R}}$	infinitesimal strains and rotations
$\mathbf{v} = \dot{\mathbf{x}}$	particle velocity
$L_{ij} = v_{i,j}$	velocity gradients
$\mathbf{D}, \mathbf{W}$	rate-of-deformation tensor, spin tensor
$\mathbf{\Sigma} = \dot{\mathbf{P}}\mathbf{P}^{-1}$	intrinsic angular velocity
$\mathbf{\Omega} = \dot{\mathbf{Q}}\mathbf{Q}^{-1}$	angular velocity defined by an orthogonal tensor $\mathbf{Q}$
ρ	mass density (if cylindrical coordinates occur, then mass density is denoted by m)
θ	temperature
η	entropy density
γ	density of entropy production
ε, k	densities of internal energy and kinetic energy
W	strain-energy density per unit volume
$\mathbf{q}$	heat flux vector
r	volume density of heat supplies
$\mathbf{t}, t_i$	stress vector
$\mathbf{T}, T_{ij}$	stress tensor
$\boldsymbol{\mu}, \mu_i$	couple stress vector
$\mathbf{M}, M_{ij}$	couple stress tensor
β_i	body couples
$\lambda = \lambda_E, \mu = \mu_E$	Lame's coefficients of elasticity
$\lambda_V = \lambda_V, \mu = \mu_V$	coefficients of viscosity
l	characteristic length
$q, \mathbf{j}$	densities of charge and current
E_i, B_i	electric field and magnetic field
D_i, H_i	electric excitation and magnetic excitation
$V, \partial V$	a region of space and its boundary
Σ	surface
$V[\ldots]$	abbreviation for volume integrals
$\partial V[\ldots], \Sigma[\ldots]$	abbreviations for surface integrals

$\partial\Sigma$	boundary curve of a surface
$\partial\Sigma[\ldots]$	abbreviations for line integrals
σ_1, σ_2	normal stress functions
τ	shearing stress function

CHAPTER **1**

INTRODUCTION TO TENSORS

To make this text reasonably self-contained, and establish a common basis of terminology and notation with the reader, this chapter is devoted to some of the mathematical requisites of continuum mechanics. The chapter is intended to be more than a mere collection of formulas; although it must fall far short of completeness, a good deal of effort has gone into trying to make the presentation systematic and readable. In particular, the main results for tensors are developed with care, while stripping away those elaborations that are not needed for the intended applications.

Continuum mechanics may appear as a fortress surrounded by the walls of tensor notation. Much of the complexity and full generality of tensor analysis is unneeded, however, for describing the physical principles. The reference space of continuum mechanics is three-dimensional and Euclidean. Therefore, tensors, and subsequently the physical principles, are introduced in the familiar setting of Cartesian coordinate systems. Tensor analysis in curvilinear coordinates is taken up at the end of this chapter. The gain in clarity and simplicity achieved by this approach outweighs, it is felt, the attendant loss of systematic ordering.

Section 1
NOTATIONS

This section contains an outline of the established notations of continuum mechanics. The preoccupation with notations will be a recurring concern, prompted not so much by an innate fussiness as by a belief that clear ideas and deductions deserve a clear mathematical representation. As our ultimate aim is for science, we shall heed the advice of Thomson and Tait [162] neither to seek nor to avoid mathematical complications; we shall strive to develop notations which permit us to see beyond mathematical minutiae to contemplate the physical facts.

A notation is a symbolic language, a means of communicating thoughts and translating ideas into mathematical equations. Ideally there should be a one-to-one correspondence between concepts and operations on the one hand, and a vast array of typographical symbols on the other hand. But the various requisites of notation often conflict, hence it becomes necessary to make compromises and tolerate ambiguities. In choosing between the virtues of brevity and clarity, however, it seems best to be on the side of the latter.

Our immediate task is to develop a clear and concise notation so that formulas and derivations would not be obscured by their sheer bulkiness. We further require that the meaning of the abbreviated expressions be readily apparent, and that their unraveling to yield fully explicit representations be possible in a straightforward manner. The *index notation* is admirably suited for our purposes because of its economy and directness. It can indeed be said to combine the compactness of *direct notation* (using vector and matrix symbols) with the explicitness of *scalar notation*.

A part of any notation is the designation of physical objects and mathematical variables by special letters, referred to as *kernel letters*. For instance, we can use v to denote speed, and θ to denote temperature. In order to complete the specification of a variable, it may be necessary to adjoin to kernel letters one or more subscripts. Italic and Greek minuscules, written as subscripts and to the right of kernel letters, will be called *indices* (or, index letters). The structure of a complete symbol is therefore as follows:

kernel A

ij indices

The number of indices is said to be the *rank* of the symbol.†

† This rank is not necessarily what is referred to as a rank of a matrix.

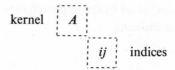

Index notation is really a scalar notation with a dash of common sense: it eliminates an inherent, even obvious repetitiousness of the scalar notation by means of two conventions. As a point of departure let us take a system of N linear equations with the coefficients $A_{11}, A_{12}, \ldots, A_{NN}$ and the variables $c_1, c_2, \ldots, c_N, x_1, x_2, \ldots, x_N$:

$$\begin{aligned} A_{11}x_1 + A_{12}x_2 + \cdots + A_{1N}x_N &= c_1, \\ A_{21}x_1 + A_{22}x_2 + \cdots + A_{2N}x_N &= c_2, \\ \cdot \quad \cdot \quad \cdot \quad \cdot \quad \cdot \quad \cdot \quad \cdot \quad \cdot \quad \cdot \quad &\cdot \quad , \\ A_{N1}x_1 + A_{N2}x_2 + \ldots + A_{NN}x_N &= c_N. \end{aligned} \tag{1.1}$$

Here N stands for an unspecified yet fixed integer; we shall not use letters reserved for indices to denote particular integers.

Let us attempt a kind of a miniaturization of the system (1.1) whereby, for instance, the left-hand sides would be replaced by one typical term in such a way that by the rules of index notation a reconstruction of the original system is possible. The basis of this simplification is the introduction of two types of indices, a *free index* that occurs *once* in every summand (summands being terms separated by plus, minus, equality, or inequality signs), and a *summation index* that occurs *twice* in a summand (but not necessarily in every summand). We shall now make these conventions precise.

Free indices

To denote a system of similar equations by a single expression, we adopt the following rule of free indices:

A free index is an index which occurs only once in each summand. We agree that a free index may take on any of its admissible values.

In a three-dimensional problem, for instance, the range of a free index is from one to three, hence an expression

$$a_k + b_k = c_k \tag{a}$$

stands for any of the following equations, $a_1 + b_1 = c_1$, $a_2 + b_2 = c_2$, $a_3 + b_3 = c_3$; whereas in a two-dimensional problem it would stand for $a_1 + b_1 = c_1$, $a_2 + b_2 = c_2$.

The letter k in (a) is the free index. It can be replaced by another letter without changing the meaning of the expression. Thus we may write (a) as $a_i + b_i = c_i$. Expressions like $a_i + b_i = c_k$ are, of course, meaningless in the framework of index notation.

If a notation is to be really useful, then we should not be unduly dogmatic about it. For instance, we shall admit numbers as exceptions to the rule of free indices by writing $a_i = 0$ in the place of $a_1 = 0$, $a_2 = 0$, $a_3 = 0$.

Let us also consider examples in which several free indices occur. In a two-dimensional problem, the expression $a_i b_j = rC_{ij}$ stands for any of the following four equations (in a three-dimensional problem it would stand for nine equations), $a_1 b_1 = rC_{11}$, $a_1 b_2 = rC_{12}$, $a_2 b_1 = rC_{21}$, $a_2 b_2 = rC_{22}$. We emphasize that, in accord with the definition of free indices, it is necessary to use different letters for the two free indices. If we write $a_i b_i = rC_{ii}$, then i is *not* a free index. Moreover, all indices of a formula must have the same range.

As another illustration we take the *condition of symmetry*,

$$U_{ij} = U_{ji}, \tag{1.2}$$

and the *condition of skew-symmetry*,

$$V_{ij} = -V_{ji}. \tag{1.3}$$

For a range of three, from (1.2) follow the nontrivial conditions $U_{12} = U_{21}$, $U_{23} = U_{32}$, $U_{31} = U_{13}$, whereas from (1.3) it follows that $V_{11} = V_{22} = V_{33} = 0$, $V_{12} = -V_{21}$, $V_{23} = -V_{32}$, $V_{31} = -V_{13}$.

Summation indices

The convention of free indices enables us to abbreviate a system of equations: if all equations are of the same form, we simply write down a typical equation carrying a free index in each of its summands. In particular, the system (1.1) can now be replaced by

$$A_{i1}x_1 + A_{i2}x_2 + \cdots + A_{iN}x_N = c_i, \tag{1.4}$$

where the range of i is from 1 to N.

Let us also attempt to shorten a given equation itself. We do this by replacing a sum with a typical member of the sum, the idea being that addition and accumulative multiplication are sufficiently familiar so that there is no need to write them out every time. Following Einstein,† we introduce a convention ("Einstein's summation convention") for a pair of repeated (or, summation) indices:

If in a term an index occurs twice, in which case it is called a summation index, then the term is to be summed with respect to this index over the range of its admissible values.

† Albert Einstein (1879–1955), who created the general theories of relativity and gravitation, was also one of the first scientists to use index notation extensively.

Naturally we can use the conventions of free and summation indices together. Thus (1.4) takes on the form

$$A_{ij}x_j = c_i, \tag{1.5}$$

where the ranges of both i (a free index) and j (a summation index) are from 1 to N. Another way of getting from (1.1) to (1.5) is to use the summation convention first: $A_{1j}x_j = c_1$, $A_{2j}x_j = c_2, \ldots, A_{Nj}x_j = c_N$, and then use the convention of free indices.

For a further example let

$$t_i = T_{ji}n_j, \tag{1.6}$$

where the range of all indices is from one to three. Then, since i is a free index, the expression (1.6) stands for

$$t_1 = T_{j1}n_j, \qquad t_2 = T_{j2}n_j, \qquad t_3 = T_{j3}n_j. \tag{b}$$

Moreover, since j is a summation index, the right-hand sides of (b) are sums of three terms. Therefore, the fully explicit form of (1.6) is given by

$$\begin{aligned} t_1 &= T_{11}n_1 + T_{21}n_2 + T_{31}n_3, \\ t_2 &= T_{12}n_1 + T_{22}n_2 + T_{32}n_3, \\ t_3 &= T_{13}n_1 + T_{23}n_2 + T_{33}n_3. \end{aligned} \tag{c}$$

It is evident that (1.6) is merely a shorthand notation for (c). Moreover, the shorthand abbreviates only the most trivial mathematical features and operations, namely, the repetitiousness of the scalar notation, and the accumulative multiplication of numbers. Admittedly time and practice are needed before one gains confidence in derivations involving forms of the type shown in (1.6). Whenever a feeling of uncertainty arises, the compacted formulas can, and should, be written out.

Since the only function of a pair of summation indices is to state that a term must be summed, it does not matter which letter is used for the summation indices. For instance, we have that

$$A_{ii} = A_{kk} = A_{11} + A_{22} + A_{33}.$$

A step that frequently occurs in derivations is the *interchange of summation indices*. The following steps are typical of the manipulations that will be performed time and again.

Let us suppose that U_{ij} is symmetric and that W_{ij} is general (or, *asymmetric*), i.e. W_{ij} is neither symmetric nor skew-symmetric. Then the double-sum

$$c = U_{ij}W_{ij} = U_{11}W_{11} + U_{12}W_{12} + \cdots + U_{21}W_{21} + U_{22}W_{22} + \cdots \tag{d}$$

can be also described by $c = U_{ji}W_{ji}$, because the order of additions in finite sums is immaterial. We say that the last form has been obtained by interchanging the summation indices i and j in (d). It is to be noted that $U_{ij}W_{ij} = U_{ji}W_{ji}$ is an *identity* regardless of the properties of U_{ij} and W_{ij}. A more elaborate way of interchanging the summation indices would be to write, first, $U_{ij}W_{ij} = U_{mn}W_{mn}$, and then let $m = j$, $n = i$. Let us now use the assumed symmetry of U_{ij}: $c = U_{ji}W_{ji} = U_{ij}W_{ji}$. Adding this to (d), we get

$$c = \frac{1}{2}U_{ij}(W_{ij} + W_{ji}) = U_{ij}W_{(ij)}. \tag{1.7}$$

where

$$W_{(ij)} = \frac{1}{2}(W_{ij} + W_{ji}) \tag{1.8}$$

is called the *symmetric part* of W_{ij}. Similarly, if V_{ij} is skew-symmetric, then

$$V_{ij}W_{ij} = V_{ij}W_{[ij]}, \tag{1.9}$$

where

$$W_{[ij]} = \frac{1}{2}(W_{ij} - W_{ji}) \tag{1.10}$$

is called the *skew-symmetric part* of W_{ij}. Evidently

$$W_{ij} = W_{(ij)} + W_{[ij]}. \tag{1.11}$$

In the current example $U_{ij} = U_{(ij)}$, $V_{ij} = V_{[ij]}$.

We also record the formulas

$$A_{(ij)}B_{[ij]} = 0, \quad C_{ij}C_{ij} = C_{(ij)}C_{(ij)} + C_{[ij]}C_{[ij]}. \tag{1.12}$$

A last remark: U_{ij}, W_{ij}, etc. stand for numbers; multiplication of numbers is commutative, hence we can write that $U_{ij}W_{ij} = W_{ij}U_{ij}$, $U_{ji}W_{ji} = W_{ji}U_{ji}$, etc.

Direct notation†

It is natural to inquire whether in reducing (1.1) to (1.5) we have exhausted all possibilities for abbreviation. Indeed we have not, for it is possible to

† Also called matrix or dyadic notation.

devise a *direct notation* which represents the ultimate in simplicity. In this notation (1.5) becomes†

$$\mathbf{Ax} = \mathbf{c}, \tag{1.13}$$

where the bold-face letters **A**, **x**, **c** signify that the equation does not relate ordinary numbers but sets of numbers.

The obvious advantage of the direct notation is that it records physical or mathematical statements in a form unencumbered by mathematical details needed only for calculations. For instance, we may interpret (1.13) to state that **c** is obtained by applying an operator **A** to **x**. Particularly in derivations, where as a rule we have no intention of carrying out calculations at intermediate stages, the direct notation enables us to present the various steps simply and economically in a kind of a *flow chart*.

It is convenient to represent the symbols **A**, **x**, **c** by ordered arrays. We illustrate these representations for a range of three:

$$\|\mathbf{A}\| = \begin{Vmatrix} A_{11} & A_{12} & A_{13} \\ A_{21} & A_{22} & A_{23} \\ A_{31} & A_{32} & A_{33} \end{Vmatrix}, \qquad \|\mathbf{x}\| = \begin{Vmatrix} x_1 \\ x_2 \\ x_3 \end{Vmatrix}, \qquad \|\mathbf{c}\| = \begin{Vmatrix} c_1 \\ c_2 \\ c_3 \end{Vmatrix}.$$

Here *the first index labels the rows, the second index labels the columns*; variables with one index are represented by a single column.‡

The operation defined by (1.5) is represented for the arrays by the familiar rule of matrix multiplication, e.g.

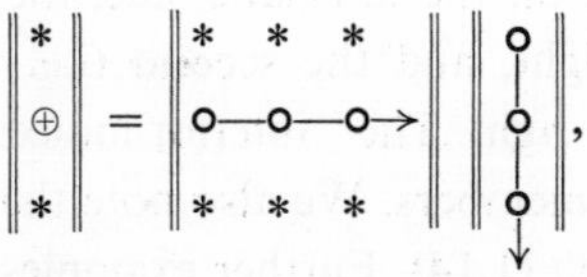

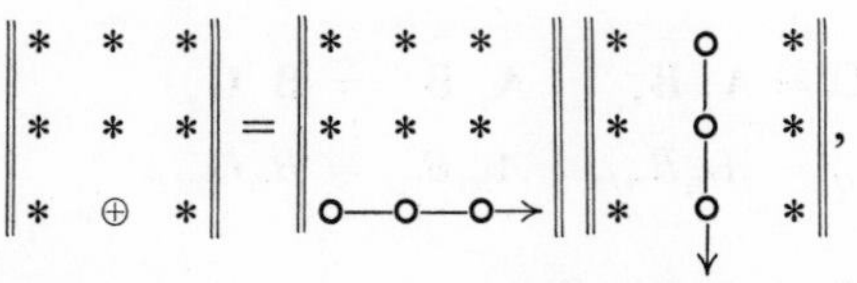

where the arrows indicate the directions in which the accumulative multiplication must progress.

† In view of the accepted notation for scalar products of vectors, e.g. $\mathbf{x} \cdot \mathbf{x} = x_i x_i$, it would have been more consistent to write (1.13) as $\mathbf{A} \cdot \mathbf{x} = \mathbf{c}$. However, because operations of the type $A_{ij}x_j$ occur very frequently, it is best to reserve the simpler notation **Ax** for them.

‡ But see (1.16).

If indices are suppressed, then operations with indices can be described only by means of special designations. We shall write $\mathbf{A}^T$, called the *transpose* of $\mathbf{A}$, for the symbol whose array is obtained by interchanging rows with columns in the array of $\mathbf{A}$. Then

$$A_{ij}^T \equiv A_{ji}, \tag{1.14}$$

and the definitions of symmetry and skew-symmetry now read $\mathbf{U} = \mathbf{U}^T$, $\mathbf{V} = -\mathbf{V}^T$.

The formula (1.6) becomes $\mathbf{t} = \mathbf{T}^T\mathbf{n}$, because $t_i = T_{ij}^T n_j = T_{ji}n_j$. But let us consider in greater detail the *rule for interpreting direct notation.*

In the case of second rank variables, the rule which translates direct notation into index notation (and vice versa) is best illustrated by the following symbolic formula:

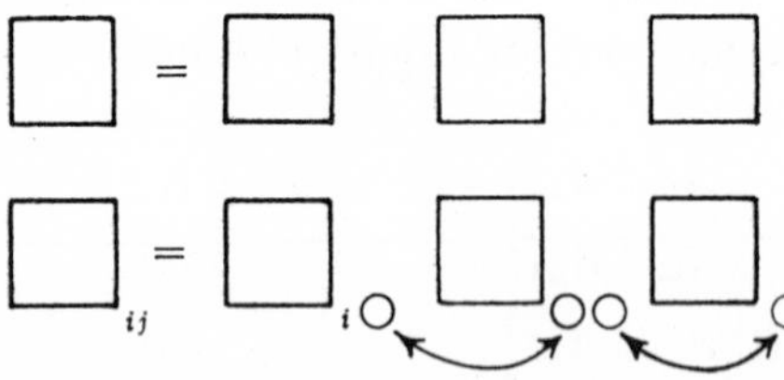

(1.15)

Here the blocks stand for any second rank variable whatever, and the joined circles indicate pairs of summation indices that connect the adjacent members. Except for the choice of the summation indices being arbitrary, the arrangement of indices in $(1.15)_2$ is completely determined: as soon as the free indices are selected on the left-hand side, the first free index goes into the first place on the right, and the second (i.e. the last) free index goes into the last place on the right. The "interior indices" are summation indices connecting the adjacent members. We also note that the transposed symbols can be eliminated through (1.14). Further examples may clarify these points:

$$\mathbf{C} = \mathbf{A}\ \mathbf{B}, \qquad \mathbf{A}\ \mathbf{B} = \mathbf{B}\ \mathbf{G},$$
$$C_{ij} = A_{im}B_{mj}, \qquad A_{im}B_{mj} = B_{ik}G_{kj},$$

$$\mathbf{F} = \mathbf{A}\ \mathbf{B}\ \mathbf{A}^T\ \mathbf{A}$$
$$F_{ij} = A_{im}B_{mn}A_{np}^T A_{pj} = A_{im}B_{mn}A_{pn}A_{pj}.$$

It must be emphasized that *the indices of a given variable follow from its place in the formula*; for instance, in the second example $\mathbf{B}$ is translated into B_{mj} on the left, into B_{ik} on the right. Conversely, in going to direct notation, *only one set of free indices, arranged in one and the same way, can be "erased."*

The foregoing convention applies also to formulas containing variables with one free index only, e.g.

$$\triangle = \square \ \triangle$$

$$\triangle_i = \square_{i\circlearrowright} \triangle_\circ$$

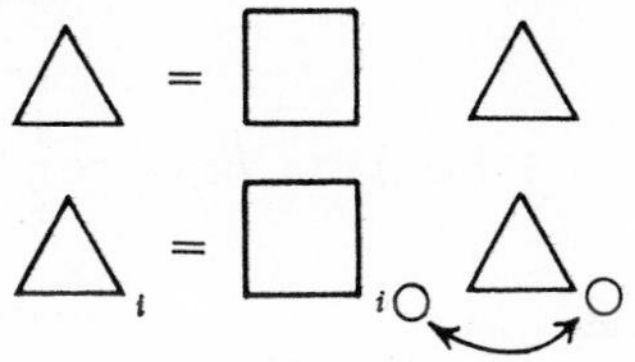

Operations that are in index notation so simple as to be trivial often require special care in direct notation. A typical case is the identity $A_{ij}x_j = x_jA_{ij}$, which says no more than that multiplication of numbers is commutative. The rule for interpreting direct notation cannot be applied here without modification, therefore, we shall translate x_jA_{ij} into $\mathbf{x}^T\mathbf{A}^T$. In index notation we simply set $x_j^T = x_j$, so that $x_j^T A_{ji}^T = x_jA_{ij}$. In direct notation, however, $\mathbf{x}^T$ stands for a row symbol, or else the rule for matrix multiplication would not apply. For instance,

$$\mathbf{c}^T = \mathbf{x}^T\mathbf{A}^T,$$

$$c_i = x_jA_{ij}, \tag{1.16}$$

$$\|c_1, c_2, c_3\| = \|x_1, x_2, x_3\| \begin{Vmatrix} A_{11} & A_{21} & A_{31} \\ A_{12} & A_{22} & A_{32} \\ A_{13} & A_{23} & A_{33} \end{Vmatrix}.$$

It is easily verified that this yields the same result as

$$\mathbf{c} = \mathbf{Ax}$$

$$c_i = A_{ij}x_j,$$

$$\begin{Vmatrix} c_1 \\ c_2 \\ c_3 \end{Vmatrix} = \begin{Vmatrix} A_{11} & A_{12} & A_{13} \\ A_{21} & A_{22} & A_{23} \\ A_{31} & A_{32} & A_{33} \end{Vmatrix} \begin{Vmatrix} x_1 \\ x_2 \\ x_3 \end{Vmatrix}.$$

There is no complete uniformity in the existing notations; one should not be surprised to find $(1.16)_1$ written as $\mathbf{c} = \mathbf{xA}^T$.

A notation is also needed for the sum of the diagonal terms of a second rank variable $\mathbf{A}$; we shall denote it by $\text{tr}\mathbf{A}$ ("trace of $\mathbf{A}$"):

$$\text{tr}\mathbf{A} = A_{kk}. \tag{1.17}$$

Then also $\text{tr}(\mathbf{AB}) = A_{im}B_{mi} = B_{mi}A_{im} = \text{tr}(\mathbf{BA})$ (even though $\mathbf{AB} \neq \mathbf{BA}$!),† $\text{tr}(\mathbf{ABC}) = A_{im}B_{mn}C_{ni}$, etc.

† Cf. p. 10.

If the rank of a variable is greater than two, then the use of direct notation is rather precarious. For instance, there is no simple way of reproducing formulas like†

$$E_{(ij)mn} = \frac{1}{2}(E_{ijmn} + E_{jimn}), \qquad E_{i(jm)n} = \frac{1}{2}(E_{ijmn} + E_{imjn}).$$

The arithmetic of forms

Our main arithmetical skills are limited to operations with individual numbers only. In the framework of index notation, however, it is necessary to work directly with *forms* that represent finite sums and systems of finite sums. For instance, let us substitute

$$m_1 = N_{11}p_1 + N_{12}p_2, \qquad m_2 = N_{21}p_1 + N_{22}p_2$$

into

$$a_1 = B_{11}m_1 + B_{12}m_2, \qquad a_2 = B_{21}m_1 + B_{22}m_2$$

obtaining

$$a_1 = B_{11}(N_{11}p_1 + N_{12}p_2) + B_{12}(N_{21}p_1 + N_{22}p_2),$$
$$a_2 = B_{21}(N_{11}p_1 + N_{12}p_2) + B_{22}(N_{21}p_1 + N_{22}p_2).$$

The same substitution is carried out correctly, and with much less effort, by using $m_k = N_{ks}p_s$ in $a_i = B_{ik}m_k$: $a_i = B_{ik}N_{ks}p_s$ (or, $\mathbf{m} = \mathbf{Np}$ into $\mathbf{a} = \mathbf{Bm}$: $\mathbf{a} = \mathbf{BNp}$!).

In expanding repeated sums it is best to proceed by stages, e.g.

$$a_2 = B_{2k}N_{ks}p_s = B_{21}N_{1s}p_s + B_{22}N_{2s}p_s = B_{21}(N_{11}p_1 + N_{12}p_2) + B_{22}(N_{21}p_1 + N_{22}p_2),$$

or equivalently, $a_2 = B_{2k}(N_{k1}p_1 + N_{k2}p_2) = B_{21}(N_{11}p_1 + N_{12}p_2) + B_{22}(N_{21}p_1 + N_{22}p_2)$.

The values of the variables being real numbers, we can deduce various properties of forms from the properties of real numbers. Thus $A_{im}B_{mj} = B_{mj}A_{im}$, because multiplication of real numbers is commutative. However, this does *not* mean that $\mathbf{AB} = \mathbf{BA}$; on the contrary, in general

$$\mathbf{AB} \neq \mathbf{BA}$$
$$A_{im}B_{mj} \neq B_{im}A_{mj}.$$

The distinction between this and the identity $A_{im}B_{mj} = B_{mj}A_{im}$ is best seen by converting the latter into direct notation: $\mathbf{AB} = (\mathbf{B}^T\mathbf{A}^T)^T$. That is, we can

† These formulas are extensions of the definition (1.8).

multiply by one and the same number B_{mj} either from the right or from the left (in $A_{im}B_{mj} \neq B_{im}A_{mj}$ the indices of **B** are different on the two sides of the equation!). In particular, starting from $(\mathbf{AB})_{ij} = A_{im}B_{mj} = B_{mj}A_{im} = B^T_{jm}A^T_{mi}$, we obtain the useful identity

$$(\mathbf{AB})^T = \mathbf{B}^T\mathbf{A}^T. \tag{1.18}$$

The operations with forms present really no difficulties provided that one possible pitfall is avoided. Namely, because the number of available index letters is limited, it becomes necessary to use the same letters as free and summation indices in different formulas. Therefore, whenever one formula is substituted into another, we must avoid obtaining index letters that are repeated three or more times in the resulting expression.

If one formula is to be substituted into another, the two formulas evidently must have an index in common. We shall call this index a *connecting index* (this enables us to state simply the subsequent *caution*). Let us consider, for instance,

$$\phi = b_n c_n, \qquad b_s = K_{sr}p_r.$$

Before substituting the second expression into the first, we either rewrite the first as $\phi = b_s c_s$, thus establishing s as the connecting index, or write the second as $b_n = K_{nr}p_r$, establishing n as the connecting index. The connecting index can be a summation index in one of the formulas, but not in both.

We now state the following *caution*:

In order that we may substitute one formula into another, the two formulas should not have summation indices or a free index and a summation index in common (*the connecting index being an exception to the last case*).

The following examples illustrate typical substitutions

Let
$$a_i = b_j C_{ji}, \tag{e}$$
$$b_j = e_i D_{ij}. \tag{f}$$

Before substituting (f) into (e), we change the summation index in (f) to k: $b_j = e_k D_{kj}$. Substituting this into (e), we get the correct result $a_i = e_k D_{kj} C_{ji}$. Had we not "overhauled" the summation index in (f), we would have obtained $a_i = e_i D_{ij} C_{ji}$. Here the index i is a free index on the left-hand side, but is repeated three times on the right-hand side. Therefore, the formula cannot be interpreted by the rules of index notation.

Let us now take

$$\phi = c_j M_{jk} n_k, \tag{g}$$
$$n_k = P_{kj} q_j. \tag{h}$$

Before substituting (h) into (g), we change the summation index in (h): $n_k = P_{kr}q_r$. Then $\phi = c_j M_{jk} P_{kr} n_r$. Again, a straight substitution of (h) into (g) would have resulted in $\phi = c_j M_{jk} P_{kj} q_j$, a formula obviously not covered by the rules of index notation.

Our failure to observe the foregoing *caution* is always signaled by the appearance of more than two repeated indices. It is then necessary to retrace a step or two, and change the summation indices as needed.

Exceptional cases

As was to be expected, or feared, there are instances, fortunately very few, in which formulas cannot be put into the conventional index notation. For the present, we shall only point out two special conventions; other cases will be dealt with as they arise.

A typical case in which index notation must be amended is illustrated by the condition $A_{11} = A_{22} = A_{33} = 0$. Here $A_{ij} = 0$ (i.e. $A_{11} = A_{22} = \cdots = A_{13} = 0$) claims too much, whereas $A_{ii} = 0 = A_{11} + A_{22} + A_{33}$ claims too little. There is really no way out but to state explicitly that in $A_{ii} = 0$ *the summation convention is suspended.* A customary notation for this is as follows:

$$A_{ii} = 0 \quad \text{(no sum)}.$$

Sometimes we shall prefer to indicate this by placing bars under the index letters (in which case the indices may be said to represent a *double-free index*), thus

$$A_{\underline{ii}} = 0.$$

Whatever the notation, the suspension of summation will be always made clear.

It is also desirable to use abbreviated notations for symbols appearing as independent variables. For instance, in the place of $h = f(A_{11}, A_{12}, A_{21}, A_{22})$ we prefer to write $h = f(A_{ij})$, or even better: $h = f(\mathbf{A})$.

Whenever a rule is adopted exceptions appear, and a notation is needed for indicating the suspension of this rule. Throughout our work we shall place the independent variables in square brackets in cases where we do *not* wish to exclude these variables from the accounting of indices for the entire expression; for example

$$f_i[a_j] = K_{ij}.$$

In particular, this notation will be used for *linear operations* (cf. Section 3).

Alternator and Kronecker delta

Two numerical symbols, defined in what follows, have proved to be extremely useful algebraic devices. The *Kronecker delta*† δ_{ij} is defined by

$$\delta_{ij} = \begin{matrix} 1 & \text{for } i = j \text{ (no sum)},\ddagger \\ 0 & \text{for } i \neq j. \end{matrix} \tag{1.19}$$

and denoted by **1** in the direct notation. From the definition it follows that δ_{ij} is symmetric; for a range of three we have the representation

$$\|\mathbf{1}\| = \begin{Vmatrix} 1 & 0 & 0 \\ 0 & 1 & 0 \\ 0 & 0 & 1 \end{Vmatrix}.$$

Let us record two special results,

$$\delta_{kk} = \text{tr}\mathbf{1} = N, \tag{1.20}$$

$$\mathbf{11} = \mathbf{1}, \qquad \delta_{im}\delta_{mj} = \delta_{ij}, \tag{1.21}$$

where N is the range of indices. In order to verify (1.21), we write $\delta_{i1}\delta_{1j} + \delta_{i2}\delta_{2j} + \delta_{i3}\delta_{3j} = \delta_{ij}$. If $i = 1$, then the second and third summands vanish, and the first summand equals unity only if also $j = 1$. Analogous reasoning for $i = 2$ and $i = 3$ then completes the proof. We have supplied then an *absolute proof* of (1.21) in the sense that the result has been verified in all possible cases. When dealing with finite sets such proofs are often possible. Thus it is easy to see that $\delta_{ij}A_{ij} = A_{ii} = \text{tr}\mathbf{A}$, $\mathbf{1A} = \mathbf{A1} = \mathbf{A}$ $(\delta_{im}A_{mj} = A_{im}\delta_{mj} = A_{ij})$, $\mathbf{1v} = \mathbf{v}$ $(\delta_{ij}v_j = v_i)$. One of the main uses of the Kronecker delta is to prevent a "branching" of formulas and derivations. Depending on whether or not certain indices are numerically equal, a formula may require two distinct representations. With the aid of the Kronecker delta, however, these representations can often be combined into one, e.g. $T_{11} = -p + 2\mu D_{11}$, ..., ..., $T_{12} = 2\mu D_{12}$, ..., ..., become $T_{ij} = -p\delta_{ij} + 2\mu D_{ij}$.

The *alternator* ε_{ijk} is defined by

$$\varepsilon_{ijk} = \begin{matrix} 1 & \text{if } ijk \text{ are an even permutation of 123} \\ -1 & \text{if } ijk \text{ are an odd permutation of 123} \\ 0 & \text{otherwise} \end{matrix} \tag{1.22}$$

† Named after the German mathematician Leopold Kronecker (1823–1891).

‡ The "no sum" convention applies, of course, only to the equation in which it is used; it does *not* prohibit a summation δ_{kk} elsewhere (cf. (1.20)). Another representation of (1.19) is as follows: $\delta_{\underline{ii}} = 1$, $\delta_{ij} = 0$ for $i \neq j$.

By a *permutation* we mean a sequence of *transpositions*, the latter being interchanges of two adjacent elements of an ordered set. In the set 123 the following distinct permutations are possible:

$$123 \quad 1\underbrace{32} \quad \underbrace{31}2 \quad 3\underbrace{21} \quad \underbrace{23}1 \quad 2\underbrace{13}$$

Here the circular arcs indicate the pairs that have been transposed relative to the preceding set.

An even or odd number of transpositions from the set 123 defines even or odd permutations of 123, respectively. Therefore, the even permutations of 123 are 123, 231, 312, whereas the odd permutations are given by 132, 321, 213. A convenient mnemonic device for the permutations of 123 is shown in Figure 1.1.

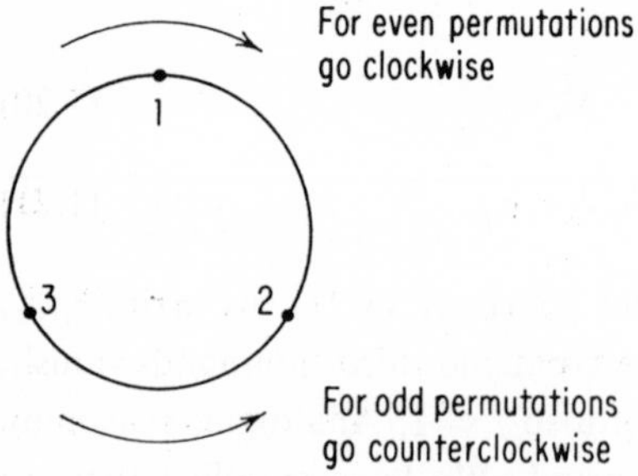

FIGURE 1.1 A mnemonic device for the permutations of 123.

An alternator $\varepsilon_{ijk\cdots n}$ of rank $N > 1$ takes on the value $+1$ or -1 depending on whether the indices $ijk\cdots n$ are an even or odd permutation of $123\cdots N$, and vanishes for other sets. In particular,

$$\varepsilon_{11} = \varepsilon_{22} = 0, \qquad \varepsilon_{12} = 1, \qquad \varepsilon_{21} = -1. \tag{1.23}$$

If $N > 3$, a mnemonic device of the type shown in Figure 1.1 is not possible. For future use we record the permutations of 1234:

$$\begin{array}{lcccccc} \textit{even} & 1234 & 1342 & 1423 & 2143 & 2314 & 2431 \\ & 3241 & 3124 & 3412 & 4321 & 4132 & 4213 \\ \textit{odd} & 1324 & 1432 & 1243 & 2134 & 2341 & 2413 \\ & 3214 & 3142 & 3421 & 4312 & 4123 & 4231 \end{array} \tag{1.24}$$

We note that whereas the definition of the Kronecker delta does not limit in any way the range of the indices, the rank of an alternator must equal the range of the indices.

With the aid of alternators it is possible to express compactly the definition of *determinants*. Let A_{ij} be a typical variable of rank two; then det**A**, the determinant of **A**, is defined by

$$\det\mathbf{A} = A_{11}A_{22}A_{33} + A_{12}A_{23}A_{31} + A_{13}A_{21}A_{32} - A_{11}A_{23}A_{32} - A_{12}A_{21}A_{33} - A_{13}A_{22}A_{31}. \tag{1.25}$$

The following, equivalent representation makes the properties of determinants more readily apparent:

$$\varepsilon_{mnp} \det\mathbf{A} = \varepsilon_{ijk}A_{im}A_{jn}A_{kp} = \varepsilon_{ijk}A_{mi}A_{nj}A_{pk}. \tag{1.26}$$

In particular

$$\det\mathbf{A} = \det\mathbf{A}^T. \tag{1.27}$$

Another, familiar representation of (1.26), in terms of bordered arrays, is as follows,

$$\varepsilon_{mnp} \det\mathbf{A} = \begin{vmatrix} A_{1m} & A_{1n} & A_{1p} \\ A_{2m} & A_{2n} & A_{2p} \\ A_{3m} & A_{3n} & A_{3p} \end{vmatrix} = \begin{vmatrix} A_{m1} & A_{m2} & A_{m3} \\ A_{n1} & A_{n2} & A_{n3} \\ A_{p1} & A_{p2} & A_{p3} \end{vmatrix}.$$

From this we can read off the following "master formula,"

$$\begin{vmatrix} A_{im} & A_{in} & A_{ip} \\ A_{jm} & A_{jn} & A_{jp} \\ A_{km} & A_{kn} & A_{kp} \end{vmatrix} = \varepsilon_{ijk}\varepsilon_{mnp} \det\mathbf{A}. \tag{1.28}$$

Setting $\mathbf{A} = \mathbf{1}$, we obtain the important identity

$$\varepsilon_{ijk}\varepsilon_{mnp} = \begin{vmatrix} \delta_{im} & \delta_{in} & \delta_{ip} \\ \delta_{jm} & \delta_{jn} & \delta_{jp} \\ \delta_{km} & \delta_{kn} & \delta_{kp} \end{vmatrix}. \tag{1.29}$$

The following special cases of (1.29) will be used frequently,

$$\begin{aligned} \varepsilon_{ijk}\varepsilon_{mnk} &= \delta_{im}\delta_{jn} - \delta_{in}\delta_{jm}, \\ \varepsilon_{ijk}\varepsilon_{mjk} &= 2\delta_{im}, \\ \varepsilon_{ijk}\varepsilon_{ijk} &= 6. \end{aligned} \tag{1.30}$$

As we shall see in the later sections, formulas of the type $c_i = \varepsilon_{ijk}a_jb_k$ are denoted by $\mathbf{c} = \mathbf{a} \times \mathbf{b}$ in the direct notation. To convert a formula $A_{ij} = \varepsilon_{ijk}v_k$ into direct notation requires a little ingenuity. We write $\mathbf{A} = \mathbf{1} \times \mathbf{v} = -\mathbf{v} \times \mathbf{1}$, and interpret this as follows, $A_{im} = -\varepsilon_{ijk}v_j\delta_{km} = -\varepsilon_{ijm}v_j = \varepsilon_{imj}v_j$.

It is a simple exercise to derive the *multiplication theorem for determinants*,

$$\det(\mathbf{AB}) = (\det\mathbf{A})(\det\mathbf{B}). \tag{1.31}$$

Namely, denoting for the moment $\mathbf{AB}$ by $\mathbf{C}$, we write $\det\mathbf{C} = \varepsilon_{ijk}C_{i1}C_{j2}C_{k3}$. But $C_{i1} = A_{im}B_{m1}$, etc., so that

$$\det(\mathbf{AB}) = \varepsilon_{ijk}A_{im}B_{m1}A_{jn}B_{n2}A_{kp}B_{p3} = \varepsilon_{mnp}\det\mathbf{A}\, B_{m1}B_{n2}B_{p3},$$

where we have used (1.26). Evidently $\det(\mathbf{AB}) = \det(\mathbf{BA})$, even though $\mathbf{AB} \neq \mathbf{BA}$.

Partial derivatives

The customary notation for partial derivatives is relatively cumbersome; we require a notation that is not only simpler but can also be incorporated into the index notation. Therefore, we adopt the following rule:

Differentiation with respect to a coordinate x_i is shown by an index i preceded by a comma. The comma does not interfere with other rules of index notation; in particular, the summation convention applies across the comma.

Let us take a number of examples. The symbol $f_{,i}$ stands for any of the partial derivatives $\partial f/\partial x_1$, $\partial f/\partial x_2$, $\partial f/\partial x_3$ (or, equivalently, $\partial f/\partial x$, $\partial f/\partial y$, $\partial f/\partial z$). The system of equations described by $T_{ji,j} = 0$ is

$$\begin{aligned} T_{xx,x} + T_{yx,y} + T_{zx,z} &= 0, \\ T_{xy,x} + T_{yy,y} + T_{zy,z} &= 0, \\ T_{xz,x} + T_{yz,y} + T_{zz,z} &= 0, \end{aligned}$$

where we have used the notations $T_{xx,x} = \partial T_{xx}/\partial x$, etc.

An alternative notation for partial derivatives with respect to x_i is as follows: $f_{,i} = \partial_i f$, thus $f_{,x} = \partial_x f$, etc., $T_{ji,j} = \partial_j T_{ji}$. The operator ∂ will be also used for describing directional derivatives (cf. Section 5).

The *Laplacian* of a function f is given by

$$\nabla^2 f = \partial_i\partial_i f = f_{,ii} = \partial_x^2 f + \partial_y^2 f + \partial_z^2 f.$$

Similarly, $\nabla^4 f = f_{,iikk}$.

Occasionally we may wish to perform differentiation with respect to Cartesian coordinates X_i different from x_i. For this operation we shall replace the comma with a *period*, and ∂_i by Δ_i, thus

$$f_{,i} = \frac{\partial f}{\partial x_i} = \partial_i f, \qquad f_{.i} = \frac{\partial f}{\partial X_i} = \Delta_i f. \tag{1.32}$$

All conventions for the comma also apply to the period. In particular, if Cartesian coordinates are independent of each other, then

$$x_{i,j} = \delta_{ij}, \qquad X_{i.j} = \delta_{ij}. \tag{1.33}$$

If x_i and X_i are functionally related, we can derive various *chain rules*, e.g.

$$\begin{aligned} f_{,i} &= f_{.m} X_{m,i}, \qquad & f_{.i} &= f_{,m} x_{m.i}, \\ x_{i.m} X_{m,j} &= \delta_{ij}, \qquad & X_{i,m} x_{m.j} &= \delta_{ij}. \end{aligned} \tag{1.34}$$

In $f_{,m}$ it is understood that f is a function of x_i, whereas in $f_{.m}$ it is understood that f is a function of X_i.

Labels; an extension of index notation

The letters of the alphabet do not always suffice for describing physical objects, particularly when we are dealing with an unspecified number of members of an aggregate. It is then natural to use *labels* ("enumerative indices"). We shall write labels as subscripts or superscripts, but always in such a way that they are readily distinguishable from indices. *The rules of index notation will not apply to labels*; in particular, a summation with respect to labels will be explicitly shown by means of a summation sign. As a rule, a label belongs to the kernel letter, so that a complete symbol is of the form

kernel A^K

ij indices

where K is a label.

In many cases we shall use underlined letters, e.g. $\underline{i}$, $\underline{i} = \underline{1}, \underline{2}, \underline{3}$, for labels. Then the following extension of index notation will apply: *if a label* $\underline{i}$ *and an index* i *occur in the same expression, then* $\underline{i}$ *and* i *take on the same numerical values* (it is understood that labels do not interfere in any way with the conventions governing the indices). Thus

$$a_i = K_{\underline{i}} b_i,$$

$$a_1 = K_{\underline{1}} b_1, \qquad a_2 = K_{\underline{2}} b_2, \qquad a_3 = K_{\underline{3}} b_3, \tag{1.35}$$

$$c = K_{\underline{i}} P_{ii} = K_{\underline{1}} P_{11} + K_{\underline{2}} P_{22} + K_{\underline{3}} P_{33}. \tag{1.36}$$

The preceding convention is primarily intended to simplify the description of diagonal arrays. For instance, if

$$\|\mathbf{K}\| = \begin{Vmatrix} K_{11} & 0 & 0 \\ 0 & K_{22} & 0 \\ 0 & 0 & K_{33} \end{Vmatrix},$$

then, letting $K_{11} = K_{\underline{1}}$, $K_{22} = K_{\underline{2}}$, $K_{33} = K_{\underline{3}}$ $(K_{\underline{ii}} = K_{\underline{i}}!)$, we can express formulas of the type $a_i = K_{ij} b_j$ more explicitly by $a_i = K_{\underline{i}} b_i$. Most of the time diagonal arrays will be written in the following abbreviated form,

$$\|\mathbf{K}\| = \operatorname{diag}(K_{11}, K_{22}, K_{33}),$$

or

$$\|\mathbf{K}\| = \operatorname{diag}(K_1, K_2, K_3).$$

If a label does not coincide with any of the index letters occurring in the same formula, then we may consider the label as a free index, keeping in mind, of course, that the range of the label may be different from the range of the indices. Moreover, a label need not occur singly, as is the case for a free index, e.g. $\mathbf{A}^K \mathbf{A}^K = \mathbf{A}^{2K}$.

The notational problems in a unified presentation of physical sciences are endless; the sympathetic reader will appreciate that, in a manner of speaking, one must take an inventory of the physical world while using only the letters of a few alphabets. It is no wonder, then, that symbols often resemble decorated Christmas trees. However, almost all of the ornamentation will consist of labels, which are quite harmless from a mathematical point of view. That is, labels are merely a way of extending the number of distinct kernel letters; they are name plates, qualifiers, reminders, etc., hence there are no mathematical operations associated with them. On the other hand, we shall come to respect indices, because they are a sure sign of mathematical complexity.

Problems

The following set of problems is designed to illustrate the conventions of the main notations. Each group of problems uses only the material of the preceding groups.

A. FREE INDEX

1. Translate the following sets of equations into index notation by using the rule of the free index.

a. $u_1 + v_1 + w_1 = r_1$
$u_2 + v_2 + w_2 = r_2$
$u_3 + v_3 + w_3 = r_3$
$u_4 + v_4 + w_4 = r_4$

b. $u_1v_1 + w_1r_1 = A_{11}$
$u_1v_2 + w_1r_2 = A_{12}$
$u_2v_1 + w_2r_1 = A_{21}$
$u_2v_2 + w_2r_2 = A_{22}$

c. $u_1v_1w_1 = A_{111}$ $\quad u_2v_1w_1 = A_{211}$ $\quad u_3v_1w_1 = A_{311}$
$u_1v_1w_2 = A_{112}$ $\quad u_2v_1w_2 = A_{212}$ $\quad u_3v_1w_2 = A_{312}$
$u_1v_1w_3 = A_{113}$ $\quad u_2v_1w_3 = A_{213}$ $\quad u_3v_1w_3 = A_{313}$
$u_1v_2w_1 = A_{121}$ $\quad u_2v_2w_1 = A_{221}$ $\quad u_3v_2w_1 = A_{321}$
$u_1v_2w_2 = A_{122}$ $\quad u_2v_2w_2 = A_{222}$ $\quad u_3v_2w_2 = A_{322}$
$u_1v_2w_3 = A_{123}$ $\quad u_2v_2w_3 = A_{223}$ $\quad u_3v_2w_3 = A_{323}$
$u_1v_3w_1 = A_{131}$ $\quad u_2v_3w_1 = A_{231}$ $\quad u_3v_3w_1 = A_{331}$
$u_1v_3w_2 = A_{132}$ $\quad u_2v_3w_2 = A_{232}$ $\quad u_3v_3w_2 = A_{332}$
$u_1v_3w_3 = A_{133}$ $\quad u_2v_3w_3 = A_{233}$ $\quad u_3v_3w_3 = A_{333}$

2. For a range of four, write out all expressions contained in the condition of symmetry, $A_{ij} = A_{ji}$, and in the condition of skew-symmetry, $B_{ij} = -B_{ji}$.

3. Show that $A_{ij} = u_iu_j$ satisfies the condition of symmetry, whereas $B_{ij} = u_iv_j - v_iu_j$ satisfies the condition of skew-symmetry. Obtain expressions for the symmetric and skew-symmetric parts of $C_{ij} = u_iv_j$.

4. If an expression contains M free indices with range from 1 to R, what is the number N of equations described by the expression?

5. Calculate the numerical values of $C_{ij} = u_iv_j$ if $u_1 = 1, u_2 = 2, u_3 = 3, v_1 = 5, v_2 = 10, v_3 = 4$.

B. SUMMATION INDEX

6. Translate the following sets of equations into index notation by using the rule of the summation index.

a. $ds^2 = g_{11}(dx_1)^2 + g_{12}\,dx_1\,dx_2 + g_{13}\,dx_1\,dx_3 + g_{21}\,dx_2\,dx_1 + g_{22}(dx_2)^2 + g_{23}\,dx_2\,dx_3 + g_{31}\,dx_3\,dx_1 + g_{32}\,dx_3\,dx_2 + g_{33}(dx_3)^2$

b. $u_1v_1 + u_2v_2 + u_3v_3 + u_4v_4 = 0$

c. $\phi = u_1v_1w_1r_1 + u_1v_1w_2r_2 + u_2v_2w_1r_1 + u_2v_2w_2r_2$

d. $dS^2 = (dX_1)^2 + (dX_2)^2 + (dX_3)^2$

e. $\phi = (u_1^2 + u_2^2 + u_3^2)(v_1^2 + v_2^2 + v_3^2)$

7. Verify (1.12). Also show that $W_{ij}u_iu_j = W_{(ij)}u_iu_j$, $B_{[ij]}u_iu_j = 0$.

8. For a range of three, write out in scalar notation the expression $\phi = A_{ij}A_{ji}$.

9. For a range of two, write out in scalar notation the following:

a. $\phi = u_k v_k A_{jj}$ **b.** $\phi = u_i v_i + w_j r_j$ **c.** $A_{kk} = p_j r_j$
d. $u_i = v_i + A_{ikk}$ **e.** $u_i v_j w_j = B_{ik} r_k$ **f.** $A_{ij} = B_{ik} C_{kn} D_{nj}$

10. Evaluate $\phi = u_i v_i + A_{kk}$ for $u_1 = 2$, $u_2 = 4$, $v_1 = 3$, $v_2 = 1$, $A_{11} = 5$, $A_{12} = 36$, $A_{21} = 10$, $A_{22} = 5$.

11. Translate the following sets of equations into index notation:

a.
$$\begin{aligned} v_1 &= A_{111} + A_{122} + A_{133} \\ v_2 &= A_{211} + A_{222} + A_{233} \\ v_3 &= A_{311} + A_{322} + A_{333} \end{aligned}$$

b.
$$\begin{aligned} A_{11} &= B_{11}C_{11} + B_{12}C_{21} \\ A_{12} &= B_{11}C_{12} + B_{12}C_{22} \\ A_{21} &= B_{21}C_{11} + B_{22}C_{21} \\ A_{22} &= B_{21}C_{12} + B_{22}C_{22} \end{aligned}$$

c.
$$\begin{aligned} u_1 &= v_1^2 w_1 + v_2^2 w_1 + v_3^2 w_1 \\ u_2 &= v_1^2 w_2 + v_2^2 w_2 + v_3^2 w_2 \\ u_3 &= v_1^2 w_3 + v_2^2 w_3 + v_3^2 w_3 \end{aligned}$$

12. For a range of three, write out in scalar notation the following:

a. $v_i = B_{ji} u_j$ **b.** $u_i = B_{ik} A_{kjj}$

13. For a range of three, obtain the scalar representations of $v_{i;j} = v_{i,j} + w_{kij} v_k$, where w_{kij} have the skew-symmetry property $w_{kij} = -w_{ikj}$. Work as though the commas and semicolons between indices were not there.

C. DIRECT NOTATION

14. If **C** is of rank two, write out in index notation the following:

$$-\mathbf{C}^3 + \mathrm{I}_C\mathbf{C}^2 - \mathrm{II}_C\mathbf{C} + \mathrm{III}_C\mathbf{1} = \mathbf{0}.$$

Here $\mathbf{C}^2 \equiv \mathbf{CC}$, $\mathbf{C}^3 \equiv \mathbf{CCC}$, and I_C, II_C, III_C are special designations of scalar coefficients (i.e. these symbols are to be left as they are).

15. Translate the following expressions into direct notation:

a. $(\mathbf{A}^2)_{ij} = A_{ik}A_{kj}$ **b.** $(\mathbf{A}^3)_{ij} = A_{ik}A_{km}A_{mj}$
c. $B_{ij} = A_{ki}A_{kj}$ **d.** $C_{ij} = A_{ik}A_{jk}$ **e.** $D_{ij} = A_{ik}A_{mk}A_{jm}$
f. $E_{kk} = A_{im}A_{jm}A_{ij}$ **g.** For a range of two, write out (a) and (b).

16. Change the following into index notation:

a. $\mathbf{G} = \mathbf{A}^T\mathbf{A}\mathbf{A}^T$ **b.** $\mathbf{A}^4 = \mathbf{AAAA}$ **c.** $\mathbf{FB} = \mathbf{BG}$
d. $\mathbf{D} = \mathbf{A}\mathbf{B}^T\mathbf{C}$ **e.** $\mathbf{B} = \mathbf{F}\mathbf{F}^T$ **f.** $\mathbf{C} = \mathbf{F}^T\mathbf{F}$
g. $\phi = \mathrm{tr}(\mathbf{AB})$ **h.** $\mu = \mathrm{tr}(\mathbf{A}^T\mathbf{B})$ **i.** $\bar{\mathbf{A}} = \mathbf{QAQ}^T$
j. $\mathbf{AB} \neq \mathbf{BA}$ **k.** $\mathrm{tr}(\mathbf{AB}) = \mathrm{tr}(\mathbf{BA})$

17. Let $\mathbf{C} = \mathbf{AB}$, $\mathbf{D} = \mathbf{A}^T\mathbf{B}$, $\mathbf{E} = \mathbf{AB}^T$, $\mathbf{F} = \mathbf{A}^T\mathbf{B}^T$, where

$$\|\mathbf{A}\| = \begin{Vmatrix} 1 & 1 & 5 \\ 6 & 2 & 3 \\ 2 & 4 & 3 \end{Vmatrix}, \qquad \|\mathbf{B}\| = \begin{Vmatrix} 3 & 3 & 1 \\ 4 & 2 & 5 \\ 2 & 6 & 1 \end{Vmatrix}$$

Calculate the arrays of **C**, **D**, **E**, **F**.

18. Let $\|\mathbf{x}^T\| = \|1, 2, 3\|$; if **A** and **B** are as in Problem 17, calculate $\mathbf{c}^T = \mathbf{x}^T\mathbf{A}^T$, $\mathbf{e} = \mathbf{Bx}$.

19. Let **A** and **B** be as in Problem 17. Calculate tr(**AB**).

D. ARITHMETIC OF FORMS

20. Substitute $u_i = B_{ij}v_j$ and $C_{ij} = p_i q_j$ into $w_m = C_{mn}u_n$.
21. Substitute $u_i = A_{ik}n_k$ into $\phi = u_k v_k$.
22. Substitute $v_i = B_{ij}A_{jkk}$ into $\phi = v_i C_{jij}$.
23. Substitute $A_{ij} = B_{ik}C_{kj}$ into $\phi = A_{mk}C_{mk}$.

E. EXCEPTIONAL CASES

24. For a range of three, write the explicit form of $f = f(A_{ij})$.
25. Write out the explicit forms of $v_i = f_i(u_j)$ for a range of three.
26. Write out the components of $A_{\underline{iikk}}$ for a range of two.
27. Write out $A_{\underline{ii}} = 0$ for a range of three.

F. ALTERNATOR AND THE KRONECKER DELTA

28. Continue and simplify wherever possible:

a. $\delta_{3k}p_k =$ b. $\delta_{3i}\delta_{ji} =$ c. $\delta_{2i}A_{ji} =$
d. $\delta_{i2}\delta_{ik}\delta_{3k} =$ e. $\delta_{i2}\delta_{i2} =$ f. $\delta_{i2}\delta_{j3}A_{ij} =$

29. For a range of three, write out in scalar notation the equations represented by

$$A_{ij} = -\varepsilon_{ijk}\,{}^{+}\!A_k, \qquad {}^{+}\!A_k = -\frac{1}{2}\varepsilon_{kij}A_{ij}.$$

30. Continue and simplify if possible:

a. $\delta_{ij}\varepsilon_{ijk} =$ b. $\delta_{ij}v_i v_j =$ c. $\varepsilon_{ijk}u_i v_j v_k =$
d. $\varepsilon_{ijk}a_i a_j a_k =$

31. Translate into index notation the following:

a. $\mathbf{QQ}^T = \mathbf{1}$ b. $\mathbf{A} = \mathbf{1A}$ c. $\mathbf{Q}^T\mathbf{Q} = \mathbf{1}$
d. $\phi = \mathrm{tr}(\mathbf{1} + \mathbf{A})$ e. $\phi = \mathrm{tr}(\mathbf{1} + \mathbf{1})$

32. Translate into index notation the following:

$$
\begin{array}{lll}
A_{111} = 0 & A_{211} = B_{31} & A_{311} = -B_{21} \\
A_{112} = 0 & A_{212} = B_{32} & A_{312} = -B_{22} \\
A_{113} = 0 & A_{213} = B_{33} & A_{313} = -B_{23} \\
A_{121} = -B_{31} & A_{221} = 0 & A_{321} = B_{11} \\
A_{122} = -B_{32} & A_{222} = 0 & A_{322} = B_{12} \\
A_{123} = -B_{33} & A_{223} = 0 & A_{323} = B_{13} \\
A_{131} = B_{21} & A_{231} = -B_{11} & A_{331} = 0 \\
A_{132} = B_{22} & A_{232} = -B_{12} & A_{332} = 0 \\
A_{133} = B_{23} & A_{233} = -B_{13} & A_{333} = 0
\end{array}
$$

33. Verify (1.24). Is there a reasonably systematic way of doing it?

34. Verify (1.30) by carrying out the summations in (1.29).

35. What are the counterparts of (1.28)–(1.30) for the alternator ε_{ij}?

36. In direct notation we denote $\varepsilon_{ijk}u_iv_jw_k$ by $[\mathbf{uvw}]$. Show that

$$[\mathbf{uvw}] = [\mathbf{vwu}] = [\mathbf{wuv}] = -[\mathbf{vuw}] = -[\mathbf{wvu}] = -[\mathbf{uwv}].$$

37. Write out in scalar notation $\phi = \varepsilon_{ijk}u_iv_jw_k$.

G. PARTIAL DERIVATIVES

38. Change $d\phi = \dfrac{\partial\phi}{\partial x}dx + \dfrac{\partial\phi}{\partial y}dy + \dfrac{\partial\phi}{\partial z}dz$ into index notation.

39. For a range of three, write out in scalar notation the following:

a. $\phi_{,ii} = 0$ **b.** $\phi_{,iikk} = 0$ **c.** $\operatorname{div}\mathbf{v} \equiv v_{i,i}$
d. $(\operatorname{curl}\mathbf{v})_i \equiv \varepsilon_{ijk}v_{k,j}$

40. Find $u_{i,i}$, $v_{j,j}$, $u_{i,j} - u_{j,i}$, $v_{i,j}$ if $u_1 = 5x_1$, $u_2 = -3x_2$. $u_3 = 7x_3$, $v_1 = 3x_1x_2$, $v_2 = 4x_2x_3$, $v_3 = 6x_3x_1$.

41. Find $\phi_{,i}$ if $\phi(\mathbf{x}) = x_1^2x_2x_3^2$.

42. Continue, and simplify wherever possible, the following:

a. $x_{k,k} =$ **b.** $(x_ix_j)_{,i} =$ **c.** $(x_ix_i)_{,k} =$ **d.** $(x_ix_j)_{,k} =$
e. $(\varepsilon_{ijk}x_jv_k)_{,m} =$ **f.** $(x_mx_mx_iA_{ij})_{,k} =$ **g.** $x_{i,j} - x_{j,i} =$

43. For a range of three, write out in scalar notation the following:

a. $x_{i.m} = \delta_{im} + u_{i.m}$ **b.** $X_{i,n} = \delta_{in} - u_{i,n}$
c. $B_{ij} = x_{i.m}x_{j.m}$ **d.** $C_{ij} = x_{m.i}x_{m.j}$
e. $2E_{ij} = u_{i.j} + u_{j.i} + u_{m.i}u_{m.j}$ **f.** Derive (e) from $2\mathbf{E} = \mathbf{C} - \mathbf{1}$ by using (d) and (a).

44. For a range of three, write out in scalar notation the following:

a. $\dot\rho + \rho v_{i,i} = 0$ **b.** $a_i = \partial v_i/\partial t + v_kv_{i,k}$
c. $T_{ji,j} + \rho b_i = \rho a_i$ **d.** $\rho\dot u + q_{i,i} = T_{ij}D_{ij}$

45. Substitute $\tilde{E}_{ij} = \frac{1}{2}(u_{i,j} + u_{j,i})$ into $T_{ij} = \lambda\delta_{ij}\tilde{E}_{kk} + 2\mu\tilde{E}_{ij}$; then substitute the resulting expression into $T_{ji,j} + \rho b_i = \rho\ddot{u}_i$. (Here λ and μ are constants.)

46. Substitute $D_{ij} = \frac{1}{2}(v_{i,j} + v_{j,i})$ into $T_{ij} = -p\delta_{ij} + 2\mu D_{ij}$, where μ is a constant. Then substitute the resulting expression into $T_{ji,j} + \rho b_i = \rho\dot{v}_i$.

47. Substitute $q_i = -k\theta_{,i}$ and $T_{ij} = -p\delta_{ij} + 2\mu D_{ij}$, where k and μ are constants, and D_{ij} is defined in Problem 46, into $\rho\dot{\varepsilon} + q_{i,i} = T_{ij}D_{ij}$.

48. For a range of two, and letting $x_1 = x$, $x_2 = y$, $X_1 = X$, $X_2 = Y$, write out the following:

a. $x_{i,j} = \delta_{ij} = x_{i.m}X_{m,j}$ **b.** $X_{i.j} = \delta_{ij} = X_{i,m}x_{m.j}$

H. LABELS

49. For a range of two, write out in scalar notation $C_{\underline{m}i\underline{m}} = Q_{\underline{m}j}\partial_i Q_{\underline{m}j}$.

50. For a range of two, write out in scalar notation the following:

a. $A = v_{\underline{m}}C_{mm}$ **b.** $u_i = F_{\underline{i}}v_i$ **c.** $A_{\underline{m}i} = B_{\underline{m}j}C_{\underline{m}ji}$

Section 2
VECTOR SPACES

Scalars, vectors, and tensors are the main algebraic tools of continuum mechanics. Of these we shall take scalars and vectors for granted, except for some rather lengthy "commentaries" on vectors which will fill out this section. Our task here will be twofold: to emphasize the generality of the vector concept, and to investigate thoroughly the existing notations for vectors. We shall use the language of abstract algebra, but, of necessity, our presentation will be informal rather than rigorous.

Operational definition of vectors

The elementary notion of vectors is that of entities that can be represented by directed line segments, and for which there exists a parallelogram law of addition. One of the most fruitful generalizations in mathematics has been the abstract approach to vectors. Here the parallelogram law is replaced by an "addition" which has the same basic properties as the parallelogram law (e.g. commutativity, associativity), but is unspecified otherwise. Even the notion of equality is replaced by the broader concept of "equivalence," which may have a different interpretation in each instance. Properties of vectors are the properties of operations postulated for vectors; in this way the vector concept represents what is common to all vectors, and no more.

What of the "definition" which states that vectors are entities with a *magnitude* and a *direction*? This is really not a definition at all but a rather incomplete description of some familiar vectors. According to it we may admit pencils as vectors, if their lengths are taken as the magnitudes, and the directions in which they point as the directions. To have an even more ludicrous example, we may consider bread as the magnitude, butter as the direction, and sandwiches as vectors. Clearly, then, the parallelogram law must be a part of the definition, or else pencils, sandwiches, and other undesirables cannot be excluded from the community of vectors. In brief, the definition of vectors must be *operational*. Then, however, it is not possible to define a single vector; rather, we consider a family of vectors $\alpha, \beta, \gamma, \ldots,$ called a *vector space*.†

With these ideas in mind, we define a vector space Γ as a set of elements $\alpha, \beta, \gamma, \ldots,$ called vectors, for which there exist two operations:‡ *addition* $\alpha + \beta$ and *magnification* (or, multiplication by a scalar) $m\alpha$.§ The operations must have the *closure property*, meaning that $\alpha + \beta$ and $m\alpha$ again belong to Γ. Moreover, we require of the addition that it be commutative and associative:

$$\alpha + \beta = \beta + \alpha, \qquad \alpha + (\beta + \gamma) = (\alpha + \beta) + \gamma, \tag{2.1}$$

that there exist a *vector zero* θ such that

$$\alpha + \theta = \alpha, \tag{2.2}$$

and that each vector α have a *negative*, $-\alpha$, such that

$$\alpha + (-\alpha) \equiv \alpha - \alpha = \theta. \tag{2.3}$$

Magnification is assumed to have the following properties:

$$\begin{gathered} m(n\alpha) = (mn)\alpha, \qquad 1\alpha = \alpha \\ (m + n)\alpha = m\alpha + n\alpha, \qquad m(\alpha + \beta) = m\alpha + m\beta. \end{gathered} \tag{2.4}$$

In the interpretation of (2.1)–(2.4) some of the postulates may come out to be completely trivial requirements. They are needed nevertheless in order to make the mathematical formulation *complete*. That is, no matter how trivial

† Also called a linear space, or, a linear vector space.

‡ Actually the equivalence relation " = " is a third operation. It must be reflexive: $\alpha = \alpha$, symmetrical: $\alpha = \beta$ implies $\beta = \alpha$, and transitive: $\alpha = \beta$ and $\beta = \gamma$ imply $\alpha = \gamma$.

§ If the scalars $m, n, p, \ldots,$ are complex numbers, then the vector space is said to be complex. In what follows the scalars will be always real numbers.

a requirement $1\alpha = \alpha$ may seem in a particular instance, in the mathematical formulation it must be either proved or postulated.

It is not difficult to show that θ and $-\alpha$ are unique, and that†

$$-\alpha = (-1)\alpha, \qquad -(m\alpha) = (-m)\alpha, \qquad m\theta = \theta, \qquad 0\alpha = \theta.$$

Another way of defining vectors is to state that their components transform under a change of coordinate systems as the differentials of coordinates. In effect, differentials of coordinates are taken as the prototypes of vector components. Our only criticism of this definition is that it is likely to be difficult to interpret. For let us suppose that someone in the color mixing trade is wondering whether his calculations could benefit from the use of vector algebra.‡ In order to decide whether colors are vectors, the definition prescribes a coordinate transformation as a test. But coordinate transformations may have little or no affinity with the characteristics of colors; for that matter, how is one going to use coordinate transformations to test whether a force is a vector or not?§ Admittedly, the foregoing definition is very convenient in cases where it is known *a priori* whether a quantity is a vector or not.

In order to illustrate the usefulness of the operational definition, let us return to the man engaged in the mixing of colors. Noting that two operations are needed, he may choose mixing as the addition. Then the properties (2.1) can be tested experimentally, and are likely to be satisfied. But the existence of a negative will present problems: how does one extract a color from a mixture? The important fact is, however, that once we have discovered certain interactions, we can test experimentally whether these interactions conform to the postulates laid down for the addition and magnification of vectors.

So as not to leave the impression that coordinate transformations will always play an unimportant role, let us add that in the study of *fields* of vectors, e.g. $\alpha = \alpha(x, y, z)$, coordinate transformations will be used frequently, and for a variety of purposes.‖ However, when it comes to defining, and grasping, the vector concept (as well as the tensor concept), the algebraic approach is not only natural but also more helpful.

We list a few examples of vector spaces, chosen so as to illustrate the

† Hints for proofs are given in Problems 1–5.

‡ A delightful parody of outlandish uses of vectors and tensors (probably aimed at Gabriel Kron's revolutionary tensor methods for describing electrical machinery) was published by J. Slepian [143]. Actually much of Slepian's criticism of vector methods concerns the use of coordinate transformations, which are only of secondary importance in the approach based on (2.1)–(2.4).

§ The customary demonstration uses a round "force table" with angles marked along the edge. Three weights attached to strings joined in a point are suspended over the edge; the parallelogram law for the equilibrium configuration can then be verified.

‖ Cf. the definition of absolute derivatives in Section 6.

generality of the vector concept. The *arithmetic N-space* R_N is the set of ordered N-tuples of real numbers:

$$\alpha = [a_1, a_2, \ldots, a_N], \qquad \beta = [b_1, b_2, \ldots, b_N], \quad \text{etc.}$$

We choose the following interpretations of equality, addition, and magnification: $\alpha = \beta$ means that $a_i = b_i$, $\gamma = \alpha + \beta$ means that $c_i = a_i + b_i$, and $m\alpha = \beta$ means that $ma_i = b_i$. Moreover, we let

$$\theta = [0, 0, \ldots, 0], \qquad -\alpha = [-a_1, -a_2, \ldots, -a_N].$$

From the properties of real numbers it follows then that the postulates (2.1)–(2.4) are satisfied.

A slightly more general example is obtained by taking the arrays of second rank variables: $\alpha = \|A_{ij}\|$, $\beta = \|B_{ij}\|$, etc., and defining the operations in the obvious way, e.g. $\alpha + \beta = \|A_{ij} + B_{ij}\|$, $m\alpha = \|mA_{ij}\|$. Actually for second rank variables it is possible to define a *multiplication* $\alpha\beta = \|A_{im}B_{mj}\|$. Therefore, since (2.1)–(2.4) do not exhaust all properties of second rank variables, we simply ignore the fact that these variables also constitute a vector space. In the same way, we ignore the fact that real numbers and complex numbers are, trivially, vectors.

Now for some less popular examples of vectors. Let $f, g, h, \ldots$, be scalar-valued functions of the scalars $x_1, x_2, \ldots, x_N$. We can identify the functions themselves with vectors, but in the present context this does not lend itself to any interesting applications. Instead, we identify the *differentials of functions* with vectors: $\alpha = df$, $\beta = dg$, $\gamma = dh$, etc. The operations are then defined as follows: $\alpha + \beta = d(f + g)$, $m\alpha = d(mf)$, $-\alpha = d(-f)$, $\theta = dc$, where c is a constant. In the same vein, let us introduce as vectors the *directional derivatives* $\alpha = \partial_{\underline{\mathrm{a}}} \equiv a_i\partial_i$, $\beta = \partial_{\underline{\mathrm{b}}} \equiv b_i\partial_i$, $\gamma = \partial_{\underline{\mathrm{c}}} \equiv c_i\partial_i$, etc., where $\partial_i = \partial/\partial x_i$. Then addition $\gamma = \alpha + \beta$ is defined by $c_i\partial_i f = a_i\partial_i f + b_i\partial_i f$, i.e. γ is that vector whose value at f is equal to the sum of the values of α and β at f. Similarly, if $\alpha = a\mu$, $\mu = m_i\partial_i$, then $\partial_{\underline{\mathrm{a}}} = a\partial_{\underline{\mathrm{m}}}$.†

If the last two examples appear a little unreasonable, we should remember that being "reasonable" is not one of the required properties of vectors; only (2.1)–(2.4) are.

Linear independence, bases

Let us now generalize the simple notions of collinearity and coplanarity of directed line segments ("arrow "). If α and β are collinear vectors, we write $\alpha = m\beta$, where m is a scalar. Similarly, if α, β, γ are coplanar, then one vector

† These properties of directional differentation are derived in Section 5.

can be expressed as a *linear combination* of the other two, e.g. $\gamma = m\alpha + n\beta$ (Figure 2.1).

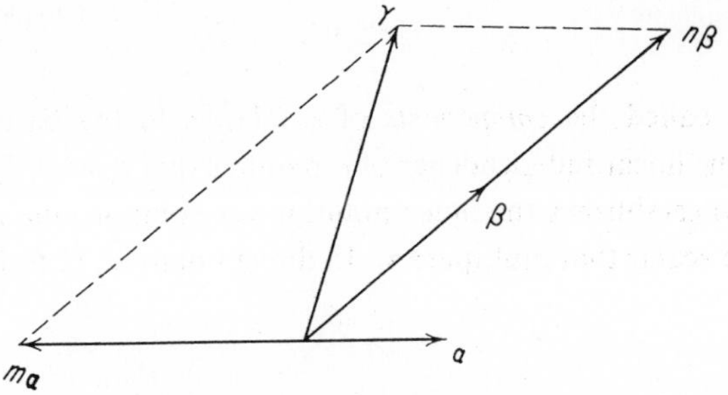

FIGURE 2.1 Coplanar vectors α, β, γ.

More generally, we say that any three coplanar vectors admit a linear relation $m\alpha + n\beta + p\gamma = \theta$ such that *not all scalars m, n, p are zero* (the trivial case $0\alpha + 0\beta + 0\gamma \equiv \theta$ must be excluded). It remains to extend this idea to cases where the number of vectors is not specified. *Definition:*

A set of N vectors $\alpha, \beta, \ldots, \phi$ is said to be *linearly dependent* if there exist N scalars $m, n, \ldots, r$, not all zero, such that

$$m\alpha + n\beta + \cdots + r\phi = \theta. \tag{2.5}$$

Otherwise the set is said to be *linearly independent*. (In what follows it will be more convenient to speak of linearly independent vectors than of linearly independent sets of vectors.)

For the time being, we shall only consider *finite-dimensional vector spaces*, defined as follows:

If a vector space Γ has a set of N linearly independent vectors, and if every set of $N + 1$ vectors of Γ is linearly dependent, then Γ is said to be N-dimensional. A set of N linearly independent vectors is called a *basis* of Γ, the vectors being referred to as *base vectors*.

Obviously some convention is now needed in order to eliminate the "and so on's" (α, β, and so on ϕ; $m\alpha + n\beta +$ and so on $+ r\phi$). Indeed, it is at this point that, in a manner of speaking, *we invent indices*. We choose for the base vectors a kernel letter, say, ε, and attach subscripts to it: ε_i. *The letters that label base vectors will be called henceforth indices, and will be subject to the conventions of index notation.* Moreover, we stipulate that the indices of any variable, e.g. v_i, A_{ij}, will have to be established by making reference to the notations ε_i for the base vectors.†

† This will be done in this section for vectors, in the next section for general tensors.

The base vectors ε_i are said to span the vector space Γ, because each vector α of Γ admits the unique (component) *representation*

$$\alpha = a_i \varepsilon_i, \tag{2.6}$$

where a_i are called the *components* of α relative to the base vectors ε_i. If $\alpha = \theta$, then the linear independence of ε_i requires that $a_i = 0$. The representation (2.6) also establishes the index notation for components: a_i is the designation of the scalar that multiplies ε_i. In direct notation, (2.6) is expressed as follows,

$$\alpha = \mathbf{a}^T \varepsilon = \|a_1, \ldots, a_N\| \begin{Vmatrix} \varepsilon_1 \\ \vdots \\ \varepsilon_N \end{Vmatrix} = \varepsilon^T \mathbf{a} = \|\varepsilon_1, \ldots, \varepsilon_N\| \begin{Vmatrix} a_1 \\ \vdots \\ a_N \end{Vmatrix}, \tag{2.7}$$

where α is now regarded as an array which consists of a single element.

To derive (2.6), we suppose that $\varepsilon_1, \ldots, \varepsilon_N$ are a basis of an N-dimensional vector space Γ. Then the set $\alpha, \varepsilon_1, \ldots, \varepsilon_N$ is linearly dependent for every vector α of Γ, or else the dimension of Γ would be at least $N + 1$. Therefore, by (2.5), there must exist a relation

$$m\alpha + m_i \varepsilon_i = \theta \tag{a}$$

with not all coefficients equal to zero. In fact, we must have that $m \neq 0$, otherwise (a) would contradict the assumed independence of ε_i. The representation (2.6) now follows from (a) by setting $a_i = -m_i/m$. To show the uniqueness of (2.6), we suppose that there exists another representation $\alpha = k_i \varepsilon_i$. Then $\alpha - \alpha = \theta = (a_i - k_i)\varepsilon_i$, and from the linear independence of ε_i it follows that $a_i = k_i$.

Let us return to the previously given examples of vector spaces. In the arithmetic N-space we can define ε_i by placing the number 1 in the ith entry and zeros elsewhere:

$$\begin{aligned} \varepsilon_1 &= [1, 0, 0, \ldots, 0], \quad \varepsilon_2 = [0, 1, 0, \ldots, 0], \ldots, \\ \varepsilon_N &= [0, 0, 0, \ldots, 1]. \end{aligned} \tag{2.8}$$

Another possible basis is obtained by placing 1's in the entries up to and including the ith entry and zeros after it: $\bar{\varepsilon}_1 = [1, 0, 0, \ldots, 0]$, $\bar{\varepsilon}_2 = [1, 1, 0, \ldots, 0], \ldots, \bar{\varepsilon}_N = [1, 1, 1, \ldots, 1]$. It is evident that (2.8), for instance, are linearly independent vectors, because from $a_i \varepsilon_i = [a_1, a_2, \ldots, a_N] = \theta$ it follows that $a_i = 0$.

In the vector space of the $N \times N$ arrays $\alpha = \|A_{ij}\|$ we may choose as base vectors ε_{ij} the arrays that have the number 1 at the intersection of the ith row and jth column and zeros elsewhere. Then $\alpha = A_{ij}\varepsilon_{ij} = \|A_{ij}\|$, hence $\alpha = \theta$ implies $A_{ij} = 0$: the base vectors so defined are linearly independent.

The differentials of scalar-valued functions of scalars admit the representations $df = f_{,i}\,dx_i$, $dg = g_{,i}\,dx_i$, etc. This immediately suggests the interpretation of coordinate differentials as base vectors: $dx_i = \varepsilon_i$; the linear independence of ε_i follows from the assumed independence of x_i. This example is rather instructive because it differs so strikingly from the usual interpretation of dx_i as *components* of vectors (i.e. scalars).†

The component representations of directional differentiations were in fact already given: $\alpha = a_i\partial_i$, where ∂_i are the base vectors.

With the aid of (2.6) it is possible to obtain the component representation of any vector operation. For instance, let the operation be $\gamma = \alpha + \beta$, and let $\alpha = a_i\varepsilon_i$, $\beta = b_i\varepsilon_i$, $\gamma = c_i\varepsilon_i$. Then $\gamma = \alpha + \beta$ is equivalent to $\varepsilon_i(a_i + b_i - c_i) = \theta$, which yields the component representation $a_i + b_i = c_i$. Consequently, addition admits the two component representations

$$\begin{aligned} \mathbf{a} + \mathbf{b} &= \mathbf{c} \\ a_i + b_i &= c_i \end{aligned} \tag{2.9}$$

(direct notation being of course merely an abbreviated index notation), and the vector representation

$$\alpha + \beta = \gamma. \tag{2.10}$$

Now, there exists another notation, deeply entrenched by long usage, in which **u**, **v**, **w**, etc. stand for *vectors*; in particular, the vector zero and the base vectors are denoted by **0** and $\mathbf{e}_i$, respectively. Then

$$\mathbf{u} = u_i\mathbf{e}_i, \tag{2.11}$$

etc. If we follow this usage, as we are going to do, then the interpretation of direct notation becomes ambiguous.‡ Thus $\mathbf{c} = \mathbf{a} + \mathbf{b}$ stands for both

† The latter is obtained by considering differentials of a vector-valued function π ("position vector"); in the notation of Section 5, $d\pi = \pi_{,i}dx_i = \mathbf{e}_i dx_i$. Thus π can be considered as the prototype of all vectors. However, a position vector need not exist in general spaces; therefore, we must seek other prototypes. Roughly speaking, every space has coordinates x_i, and there are two things that we can "do" with the coordinates: dx_i and $\partial/\partial x_i$. The differentials dx_i and the operators $\partial/\partial x_i$ actually provide a pair of "dual" bases.

‡ The ambiguity can be avoided by working with tensor components only, as is indeed frequently done. But this limitation is rather inconvenient, particularly in the case of vectors.

$c_i = a_i + b_i$ and $c_i\mathbf{e}_i = a_i\mathbf{e}_i + b_i\mathbf{e}_i$. Since one expression implies the other, the ambiguity is not particularly troublesome. However, the notation (2.6) cannot be abandoned altogether, because there are cases where the two interpretations of direct notation collide. For instance, in (2.7) we certainly cannot write $\mathbf{a} = \mathbf{e}^T\mathbf{a}$!

As a rule, one can rely on the context to suggest the appropriate interpretation of direct notation.

A basis $\mathbf{e}_1, \mathbf{e}_2, \ldots, \mathbf{e}_N$ cannot be unique, because from it we can easily construct other bases, e.g. $\mathbf{e}_1 + \mathbf{e}_2, \mathbf{e}_2, \ldots, \mathbf{e}_N$. This leads us to the notion of *basis transformations* that relate the vectors of the "old" and the "new" bases. To save time, we shall take up basis transformations only in the context of metric vector spaces.

Euclidean vector spaces

For most of the vectors encountered in applications it is possible to define a physically meaningful *magnitude* and *direction*, in which case the vector spaces are said to have a *metric*. The definitions of magnitude and direction should be operational, hence they require the existence of another operation, called the *scalar product* of vectors,† and denoted by $\mathbf{u} \cdot \mathbf{v}$. We assume that this operation is

a. symmetric $\mathbf{u} \cdot \mathbf{v} = \mathbf{v} \cdot \mathbf{u}$
b. bilinear $(m\mathbf{u} + n\mathbf{v}) \cdot \mathbf{w} = m(\mathbf{u} \cdot \mathbf{w}) + n(\mathbf{v} \cdot \mathbf{w})$
c. positive definite $\mathbf{u} \cdot \mathbf{u} \geq 0$, and $\mathbf{u} \cdot \mathbf{u} = 0$ only if $\mathbf{u} = \mathbf{0}$.

The last property characterizes *Euclidean vector spaces*; in Section 13 we shall consider the case of an *indefinite metric*: $\mathbf{u} \cdot \mathbf{u} \gtrless 0$.

The scalar products of base vectors $\mathbf{e}_i$ are denoted by g_{ij}:

$$\mathbf{e}_i \cdot \mathbf{e}_j = g_{ij} = g_{ji}. \tag{2.12}$$

Letting $\mathbf{u} = u_i\mathbf{e}_i$, $\mathbf{v} = v_j\mathbf{e}_j$, we obtain through successive applications of the property (b) the component representation of the scalar product $\mathbf{u} \cdot \mathbf{v}$:

$$\mathbf{u} \cdot \mathbf{v} = g_{ij}u_iv_j. \tag{2.13}$$

As a consequence of (c), the coefficients g_{ij} must describe *positive definite quadratic forms*,‡

$$\mathbf{u} \cdot \mathbf{u} = g_{ij}u_iu_j \geq 0, \tag{2.14}$$

† Also called the inner or dot product.
‡ Also called positive, semi-definite forms.

where equality holds only if $\mathbf{u} = \mathbf{0}$. Another consequence of the positive-definiteness of scalar products is

$$\det(g_{ij}) \neq 0. \tag{2.15}$$

Namely, if we let $y_i = g_{ij}u_j$, then $u_i y_i = 0$ holds only if $u_i = 0$. Therefore, if $\mathbf{u} \neq \mathbf{0}$, then all components y_i cannot vanish simultaneously, but this implies (2.15).

Let us also note that $\det(\mathbf{e}_i \cdot \mathbf{e}_j) = \det(g_{ij}) \neq 0$ ensures the linear independence of $\mathbf{e}_i$. For if $\mathbf{0} = a_i\mathbf{e}_i$, then $0 = a_i g_{ij}$, hence it follows that $a_i = 0$.

The magnitude $|\mathbf{u}|$ of a vector $\mathbf{u}$ is defined by

$$|\mathbf{u}| = \sqrt{\mathbf{u} \cdot \mathbf{u}}. \tag{2.16}$$

In view of (2.14), the magnitude so defined is a positive number. The positive-definiteness of the scalar product has another important consequence which we shall now derive from the identity $(\mathbf{u} + m\mathbf{v}) \cdot (\mathbf{u} + m\mathbf{v}) = m^2(\mathbf{v} \cdot \mathbf{v}) + 2m(\mathbf{u} \cdot \mathbf{v}) + (\mathbf{u} \cdot \mathbf{u})$, where m is a real number, and it is assumed that $\mathbf{u} + m\mathbf{v} \neq \mathbf{0}$. Because the left-hand side is positive, m cannot be a real root of the right-hand side. Therefore, the discriminant $(\mathbf{u} \cdot \mathbf{v})^2 - (\mathbf{u} \cdot \mathbf{u})(\mathbf{v} \cdot \mathbf{v})$ of the right-hand side is negative. The result

$$(\mathbf{u} \cdot \mathbf{v})^2 \leq (\mathbf{u} \cdot \mathbf{u})(\mathbf{v} \cdot \mathbf{v}), \tag{2.17}$$

where equality holds only when $\mathbf{u}$ and $\mathbf{v}$ are proportional, is known as the *inequality of Schwarz*.

We are now in a position to define direction; specifically, the cosine of the angle θ between vectors $\mathbf{u}$ and $\mathbf{v}$ is given by

$$\mathbf{u} \cdot \mathbf{v} = |\mathbf{u}|\,|\mathbf{v}| \cos\theta. \tag{2.18}$$

For this definition to be meaningful, the absolute value of $\mathbf{u} \cdot \mathbf{v}/|\mathbf{u}|\,|\mathbf{v}|$ cannot exceed unity; this is indeed ensured by the inequality of Schwarz.

If $\mathbf{u} \cdot \mathbf{v} = 0$ (i.e. $\cos\theta = 0$), then $\mathbf{u}$ and $\mathbf{v}$ are said to be *orthogonal*. Let us now show that, given an arbitrary set of base vectors $\mathbf{d}_i$, we can construct another set of base vectors $\mathbf{f}_i$ which are mutually orthogonal. We start by taking $\mathbf{f}_1 = \mathbf{d}_1$, $\mathbf{f}_2 = \mathbf{d}_2 + A\mathbf{f}_1$, where A is determined from the condition $\mathbf{f}_2 \cdot \mathbf{f}_1 = 0$: $A = -\mathbf{d}_2 \cdot \mathbf{f}_1/\mathbf{f}_1 \cdot \mathbf{f}_1$. The rest follows by induction: if $K - 1$ orthogonal vectors $\mathbf{f}_1, \mathbf{f}_2, \ldots, \mathbf{f}_{K-1}$ have been already determined, we let $\mathbf{f}_K = \mathbf{d}_K + A_1\mathbf{f}_{K-1} + A_2\mathbf{f}_{K-2} + \cdots + A_{K-1}\mathbf{f}_1$. The $K - 1$ conditions $\mathbf{f}_K \cdot \mathbf{f}_i = 0 = \mathbf{d}_K \cdot \mathbf{f}_i + A_{K-i}\mathbf{f}_{\underline{i}} \cdot \mathbf{f}_{\underline{i}}$ (no sum over $\underline{i}$!), $i = 1, 2, \ldots, K - 1$, then suffice for calculating the $K - 1$ coefficients.† Finally, we can construct an *orthonormal* basis, formed by mutually orthogonal unit vectors $\mathbf{e}_i$,‡ by letting

$$\mathbf{e}_i = \frac{\mathbf{f}_i}{\sqrt{\mathbf{f}_{\underline{i}} \cdot \mathbf{f}_{\underline{i}}}} \tag{2.19}$$

For orthonormal bases (2.12) reduces to

$$\mathbf{e}_i \cdot \mathbf{e}_j = \delta_{ij}, \tag{2.20}$$

in which case (2.13) reduces to

$$\mathbf{u} \cdot \mathbf{v} = \delta_{ij} u_i u_j = u_i v_i. \tag{2.21}$$

Moreover, for orthonormal bases the ith component of a vector $\mathbf{v}$ equals its projection $\mathbf{v} \cdot \mathbf{e}_i$ on the ith base vector:

$$\mathbf{v} \cdot \mathbf{e}_i = v_i. \tag{2.22}$$

It is easy to see that a set of vectors $\mathbf{e}_i$ having the property (2.20) is linearly independent: from $\mathbf{0} = v_i \mathbf{e}_i$ it follows that $\mathbf{0} \cdot \mathbf{e}_j = 0 = v_i \delta_{ij} = v_j$.

We shall use throughout only orthonormal bases.

Orthogonal transformations

Transformations between orthonormal bases are called *orthogonal transformations*. A basis transformation is defined by relations of the type

$$\bar{\mathbf{e}}_m = Q_{mi} \mathbf{e}_i, \qquad Q_{mi} = \mathbf{e}_m \cdot \mathbf{e}_i, \tag{2.23}$$

Q_{mi} being referred to as cosines in direct (since $\bar{\mathbf{e}}_m$ and $\mathbf{e}_i$ are unit vectors, it follows that $\bar{\mathbf{e}}_m \cdot \mathbf{e}_i = \cos \theta$, where θ is the angle enclosed by $\bar{\mathbf{e}}_m$ and $\mathbf{e}_i$). The condition that both bases be orthonormal requires that

$$\bar{\mathbf{e}}_m \cdot \bar{\mathbf{e}}_n = \delta_{mn} = Q_{mi} Q_{nj} \mathbf{e}_i \cdot \mathbf{e}_j = Q_{mi} Q_{ni},$$

thus

$$\begin{aligned} \mathbf{Q}\mathbf{Q}^T &= \mathbf{Q}^T\mathbf{Q} = \mathbf{1}, \\ Q_{mi} Q_{ni} &= Q_{im} Q_{in} = \delta_{mn} \end{aligned} \tag{2.24}$$

† This is the well-known *Gram-Schmidt orthogonalization process.*
‡ The magnitude of a unit vector is 1.

(note that if $\mathbf{QQ}^T = \mathbf{1}$, then also $\mathbf{Q}^T\mathbf{Q} = \mathbf{1}^T = \mathbf{1}$). The corresponding transformation formulas of vector components are now *derived* from the definition (2.23) and a *condition of invariance*, according to which all representations must be equivalent. For instance, starting from $\alpha = \bar{a}_m\bar{\mathbf{e}}_m = a_i\mathbf{e}_i$, we find that, by (2.23), $\bar{a}_m Q_{mi}\mathbf{e}_i = a_i\mathbf{e}_i$. One might be tempted to "cancel" $\mathbf{e}_i$, thus obtaining

$$\bar{\mathbf{a}} = \mathbf{Q}\mathbf{a}, \qquad \mathbf{a} = \mathbf{Q}^T\bar{\mathbf{a}} \tag{2.25}$$

(in view of (2.24), the second expression is obtained by multiplying the first from the left by $\mathbf{Q}^T$). However, although (2.25) are correct, their derivation is not, as is evident from inspection of $a_i\mathbf{e}_i = a_1\mathbf{e}_1 + a_2\mathbf{e}_2 + a_3\mathbf{e}_3$ (which of the base vectors was canceled?). The correct derivation of (2.25) rests on the linear independence of $\mathbf{e}_i$: because $(\bar{a}_m Q_{mi} - a_i)\mathbf{e}_i = \mathbf{0}$, it follows that each coefficient must vanish. As a check on the consistency of the transformation formulas, let us note that, by (2.24), $\alpha = \bar{a}_m\bar{\mathbf{e}}_m = Q_{mi}a_iQ_{mj}\mathbf{e}_j = \delta_{ij}a_i\mathbf{e}_j = a_i\mathbf{e}_i$. In matrix notation this is reproduced by $\alpha = \bar{\mathbf{a}}^T\bar{\mathbf{e}} = \mathbf{a}^T\mathbf{Q}^T\mathbf{Q}\mathbf{e} = \mathbf{a}^T\mathbf{e}$ (cf. (2.7)).

The formulas (2.23)–(2.25) are in what may be called the *conventional notation*. Here the same index letters are used for all bases; moreover, and this is very important, the order of indices is fixed as follows: *in Q_{mi} the first index belongs to the new basis, the second index to the old basis; in Q^T_{im} this ordering is reversed: the first index belongs to the old basis; the second index to the new basis.* Each pair of summation indices must belong, in a transformation formula, to the same basis. For instance, in $\mathbf{QQ}^T = \mathbf{1}$ the summation is over indices of the old basis, whereas in $\mathbf{Q}^T\mathbf{Q} = \mathbf{1}$ it is over indices of the new basis. Further, because

$$Q_{mi} = \bar{\mathbf{e}}_m \cdot \mathbf{e}_i, \qquad Q_{im} = \bar{\mathbf{e}}_i \cdot \mathbf{e}_m, \tag{2.26}$$

and thus

$$Q_{mi} \neq Q_{im}, \tag{2.27}$$

it is evident that the proper ordering of the indices must be meticulously observed.

Recalling (1.27), (1.31), we obtain

$$\det\mathbf{Q} = \pm 1. \tag{2.28}$$

An array having the properties (2.24), (2.28) is said to be *orthogonal* (or, an *orthogonal tensor*). If $\det\mathbf{Q} = \mathbf{1}$ the orthogonal transformation is called a *proper* one; in the case $\det\mathbf{Q} = -1$ it is called an *improper* orthogonal transformation. The familiar distinction between "left-handed" and "right-handed" bases is translated into the idea of *orientation*. A set of N linearly independent vectors, $\mathbf{a}, \mathbf{b}, \ldots, \mathbf{v}$ is said to define a positive or negative orientation depending on whether $\det(\mathbf{a}, \mathbf{b}, \ldots, \mathbf{v})$ is positive or negative. Because $\varepsilon_{ijk}\bar{u}_i\bar{v}_j\bar{w}_k = \varepsilon_{ijk}Q_{im}Q_{jn}Q_{kp}u_m v_n w_p = \varepsilon_{mnp}u_m v_n w_p \det\mathbf{Q}$, a basis transformation preserves the orientation only if it is a proper one.

Often it will be convenient to use the more elaborate *kernel-index notation of Schouten*, which aims at displaying a *complete* description of components. It rests on the simple agreement that, whereas a kernel letter is the name of an object, the *indices are the name of a basis* (or, identify the basis). Thus a basis $\mathbf{e}_1, \mathbf{e}_2, \ldots, \mathbf{e}_N$ may be referred to by the symbol (i), where i is a typical member of the set of indices $i, j, k, \ldots, v, w$ assigned to that basis; a typical base vector is denoted by $\mathbf{e}_i$. Another basis is referred to by the symbol (a), for instance, meaning that this basis has been assigned the set of indices $a, b, c, \ldots, g, h$; a typical base vector is then denoted by $\mathbf{e}_a$.† (Needless to say, other ways of distinguishing between different bases are possible: we can use red and blue index letters!) To distinguish the indices i and a even when formulas are written out in scalar notation, it is necessary to use different sets of numbers for these indices, e.g. $i = 1, 2, 3$, $a = \mathbf{1}, \mathbf{2}, \mathbf{3}$. To summarize, Schouten's notation not only identifies the object but also the basis used for representing it:

object	v		v	
basis		i		a

Moreover, it is possible to distinguish a *transformation of a vector*, indicated by a change of the kernel letter, e.g. $\bar{v}_i = T_{ij}v_j$, and a transformation of the basis, e.g. $v_a = Q_{ai}v_i$. In the first case it is understood that the basis remains the same, but the vector is changed. In the second case the vector remains unchanged, the changes in *components* being solely due to a change of basis.

It is a characteristic of Schouten's notation that the order of the indices in transformation coefficients is immaterial; indeed, one of the aims of this notation is to remove the need for memorizing some required order. Therefore, we can write $Q_{ai} = Q_{ia}$, but these relations do *not* express a symmetry property, because the indices i and a run through different sets of numbers. For instance, $Q_{\mathbf{2}1} = Q_{1\mathbf{2}}$ is merely an identity. We can also say that the identity $Q_{ai} = Q_{ia}$ is a consequence of the notation being completely specific: a and i mark the coefficient of $\mathbf{e}_a$ in the expansion of $\mathbf{e}_i$, so that it does not matter whether we denote this coefficient by Q_{ai} or by ${}^aQ_i$ or by ${}_iQ_a$. On the

† Cf. the statement on p. 27 that "letters that label base vectors will be called henceforth indices."

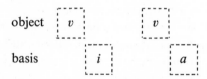

other hand, if the same index letters are used for both bases, then the indices alone cannot contain a complete specification of the coefficient. Rather, a convention is needed concerning the *order* in which the indices are written. As a rule, we shall not make use of the identity $Q_{ai} = Q_{ia}$, for the simple reason that adhering to a definite ordering of indices makes the transition to the conventional notation more straightforward. Schouten's notation has the advantage of explicitness, hence we shall use it to exhibit transformations, representations, and the like. However, this same explicitness is often the undoing of Schouten's notation, particularly in cases where the distinction between basis transformations and (equivalent) transformations of vectors themselves is irrelevant.

To compare transformations of vectors with equivalent basis transformations, let us take a transformation $a_i \to \bar{a}_i = Q_{ij}a_j$. As is evident from $\alpha = a_i\mathbf{e}_i$, $\bar{\alpha} = \bar{a}_j\mathbf{e}_j = Q_{ji}a_i\mathbf{e}_j = a_iQ^T_{i\ j}\mathbf{e}_j \equiv a_i\bar{\mathbf{e}}_i$, the same change of vector components may be obtained by holding the vector constant, but subjecting the basis to the inverse rotation $\mathbf{Q}^T$. This is illustrated below in a two-dimensional setting.

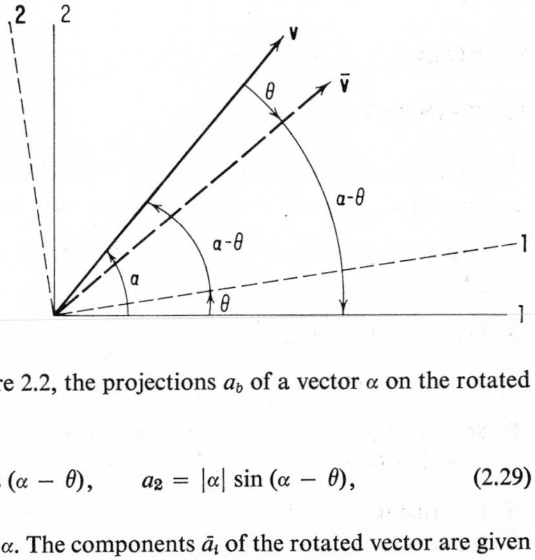

FIGURE 2.2 A basis transformation and an equivalent transformation of a vector.

As may be seen from Figure 2.2, the projections a_b of a vector α on the rotated basis are given by

$$a_1 = |\alpha| \cos(\alpha - \theta), \qquad a_2 = |\alpha| \sin(\alpha - \theta), \tag{2.29}$$

where $|\alpha|$ is the magnitude of α. The components $\bar{a}_i$ of the rotated vector are given relative to the (i) basis by

$$\bar{a}_1 = |\alpha| \cos(\alpha - \theta), \qquad \bar{a}_2 = |\alpha| \sin(\alpha - \theta). \tag{2.30}$$

The two sets of components are identical, so that we are free to use either interpretation of orthogonal transformations. The only distinction is that in (2.29) the frame is rotated *counterclockwise*, whereas in (2.30) the vector is rotated *clockwise*.

Schouten's notation is now particularly easy to use. In the case shown in Figure 2.2, the direction cosines are as follows:

$$
\begin{aligned}
Q_{11} &= \cos(\mathbf{e}_1, \mathbf{e}_1) = \cos\theta \qquad Q_{22} = \cos(\mathbf{e}_2, \mathbf{e}_2) = \cos\theta, \\
Q_{12} &= \cos(\mathbf{e}_1, \mathbf{e}_2) = \cos\left(\frac{\pi}{2} - \theta\right) = \sin\theta, \\
Q_{21} &= \cos(\mathbf{e}_2, \mathbf{e}_1) = \cos\left(\frac{\pi}{2} + \theta\right) = -\sin\theta.
\end{aligned}
\tag{2.31}
$$

Then

$$
\begin{aligned}
a_1 &= Q_{11}a_1 + Q_{12}a_2 = a_1\cos\theta + a_2\sin\theta, \\
a_2 &= Q_{21}a_1 + Q_{22}a_2 = -a_1\sin\theta + a_2\cos\theta, \\
a_1 &= Q_{11}a_1 + Q_{12}a_2 = a_1\cos\theta - a_2\sin\theta, \\
a_2 &= Q_{21}a_1 + Q_{22}a_2 = a_1\sin\theta + a_2\cos\theta.
\end{aligned}
$$

Euler is said to have remarked once that sometimes his pencil seemed to be more clever than he himself. A good notation should leave just this impression!

Problems

A. DEFINITION OF VECTORS

1. Prove the uniqueness of the zero vector (*Hint:* let $\mathbf{v} + \mathbf{0} = \mathbf{v}$, $\mathbf{v} + \bar{\mathbf{0}} = \mathbf{v}$, then let $\mathbf{v} = \bar{\mathbf{0}}$ in the first, $\mathbf{v} = \mathbf{0}$ in the second).

2. Prove the uniqueness of a negative $-\mathbf{v}$ (*Hint:* let $\mathbf{v} - \mathbf{v} = \mathbf{v} - \bar{\mathbf{v}} = \mathbf{0}$, then add $-\mathbf{v}$).

3. Show that $0\mathbf{v} = \mathbf{0}$ (*Hint:* consider $0\mathbf{v} = (0 + 0)\mathbf{v} = 0\mathbf{v} + 0\mathbf{v}$).

4. Show that $m\mathbf{0} = \mathbf{0}$ (*Hint:* consider $m\mathbf{0} = m(\mathbf{0} + \mathbf{0}) = m\mathbf{0} + m\mathbf{0}$).

5. Show that $(-1)\mathbf{v} = -\mathbf{v}$ (*Hint:* consider $\mathbf{0} = 0\mathbf{v} = (1 - 1)\mathbf{v}$). Next, show that $-(m\mathbf{v}) = (-m)\mathbf{v}$.

6. Describe tests for demonstrating that a force (e.g. a tension in a string) and the velocity of a particle are vectors.

7. Show that for two points with the plane polar coordinates (ρ_1, ϕ_1) and (ρ_2, ϕ_2) the addition $(\rho, \phi) = (\rho_1 + \rho_2, \phi_1 + \phi_2)$ does not satisfy the parallelogram law.

8. How does the parallelogram law imply the commutativity of addition? Prove the associativity of addition based on the parallelogram law.

9. Show ways of interpreting real or complex numbers as vectors.

10. Consider the addition $c = a \oplus b$ of arrows a and b, shown in the drawing below.

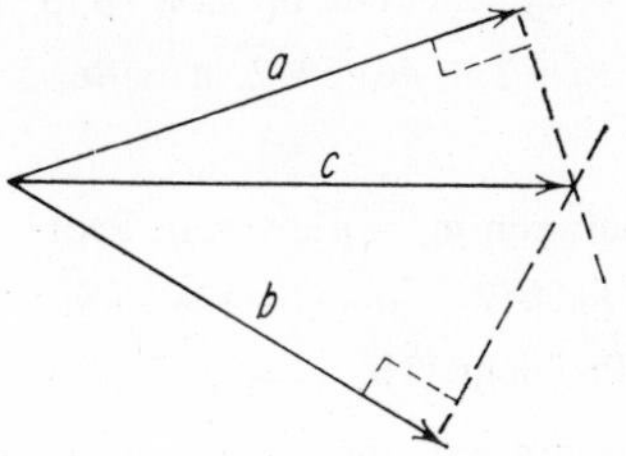

Are a, b, c vectors? *Hint:* investigate (graphically) the associative law of addition.

B. LINEAR INDEPENDENCE, BASES

11. Investigate the linear independence of

a. $3\mathbf{e}_1 + 2\mathbf{e}_2 + \mathbf{e}_3 = \mathbf{u}$,
$2\mathbf{e}_1 + 5\mathbf{e}_2 + 10\mathbf{e}_3 = \mathbf{v}$,
$9\mathbf{e}_1 + 6\mathbf{e}_2 + 3\mathbf{e}_3 = \mathbf{w}$.

b. $3\mathbf{e}_1 + 2\mathbf{e}_2 + \mathbf{e}_3 = \mathbf{u}$,
$5\mathbf{e}_1 + 6\mathbf{e}_2 + 7\mathbf{e}_3 = \mathbf{v}$,
$8\mathbf{e}_1 + 9\mathbf{e}_2 + 10\mathbf{e}_3 = \mathbf{w}$.

12. If the base vectors are as in Problem 13, calculate $\mathbf{u}, \mathbf{v}, \mathbf{w}$ defined by **(a)** Problem 11a, **(b)** Problem 11b.

13. Show that $\mathbf{e}_1 = [1, 0, 0]$, $\mathbf{e}_2 = [1, 1, 0]$, $\mathbf{e}_3 = [1, 1, 1]$ are linearly independent.

14. Show that

$$\varepsilon_{11} = \begin{Vmatrix} 1 & 0 \\ 0 & 0 \end{Vmatrix}, \quad \varepsilon_{12} = \begin{Vmatrix} 1 & 1 \\ 0 & 0 \end{Vmatrix}, \quad \varepsilon_{21} = \begin{Vmatrix} 1 & 1 \\ 1 & 0 \end{Vmatrix}, \quad \varepsilon_{22} = \begin{Vmatrix} 1 & 1 \\ 1 & 1 \end{Vmatrix}$$

are linearly independent.

15. Given that $\varepsilon_1 = [2, 1]$, $\varepsilon_2 = [0, 2]$, $\alpha = [11, 3]$, $\beta = [1, 4]$. What are the components of α and β relative to this basis?

16. Given that $\varepsilon_1 = [2, 1, 0]$, $\varepsilon_2 = [0, 1, 0]$, $\varepsilon_3 = [0, 0, 1]$, $\alpha = [1, 4, 6]$. What are the components of α relative to this basis?

17. If differentials of scalar-valued functions df, dg, etc. are considered as vectors, can you adduce component representations of them?

18. Let $\varepsilon_1 = [1, 0]$, $\varepsilon_2 = [0, 1]$, $\bar{\varepsilon}_1 = [1, 0]$, $\bar{\varepsilon}_2 = [1, 1]$. Find $\mathbf{Q}$ such that $\bar{\varepsilon}_i = Q_{ij}\varepsilon_j$.

19. Let $\varepsilon_1 = [1, 0, 0]$, $\varepsilon_2 = [0, 1, 0]$, $\varepsilon_3 = [0, 0, 1]$, $\bar{\varepsilon}_1 = [1, 0, 0]$, $\bar{\varepsilon}_2 = [1, 1, 0]$, $\bar{\varepsilon}_3 = [1, 1, 1]$. Find $\mathbf{Q}$ such that $\bar{\varepsilon}_i = Q_{ij}\varepsilon_j$.

C. EUCLIDEAN VECTOR SPACES

20. If $g_{11} = g_{22} = 2$, $g_{12} = g_{21} = 1$, obtain the component representation of the scalar product of $\mathbf{u} = u_1\mathbf{e}_1 + u_2\mathbf{e}_2$, $\mathbf{v} = v_1\mathbf{e}_1 + v_2\mathbf{e}_2$.

21. Assuming that $\mathbf{e}_i \cdot \mathbf{e}_j = \delta_{ij}$, calculate $\mathbf{u} \cdot \mathbf{v}$, $\mathbf{v} \cdot \mathbf{w}$, $\mathbf{w} \cdot \mathbf{u}$ for $\mathbf{u}, \mathbf{v}, \mathbf{w}$ given by **(a)** Problem 11a, **(b)** Problem 11b.

22. Assuming that $\mathbf{e}_i \cdot \mathbf{e}_j = \delta_{ij}$, calculate $\mathbf{m} \cdot \mathbf{n}$, $\mathbf{n} \cdot \mathbf{p}$, $\mathbf{p} \cdot \mathbf{m}$, as well as $\det(\mathbf{m}, \mathbf{n}, \mathbf{p})$, for $\mathbf{m} = 3\mathbf{e}_1/5\sqrt{2} + \mathbf{e}_2/\sqrt{2} + 4\mathbf{e}_3/5\sqrt{2}$, $\mathbf{n} = 4\mathbf{e}_1/5 - 3\mathbf{e}_2/5$, $\mathbf{p} = -3\mathbf{e}_1/5\sqrt{2} + \mathbf{e}_2/\sqrt{2} - 4\mathbf{e}_3/5\sqrt{2}$.

23. Evaluate the angles between $\mathbf{m}, \mathbf{n}, \mathbf{p}$ given in Problem 22.

24. For an orthonormal basis $\mathbf{e}_i$, calculate the angles between $\mathbf{u}, \mathbf{v}, \mathbf{w}$ given by **(a)** Problem 11a, **(b)** Problem 11b.

25. Relative to an orthonormal basis, $\mathbf{u} = \mathbf{e}_1 + 2\mathbf{e}_2 + 3\mathbf{e}_3$, $\mathbf{v} = 4\mathbf{e}_1 + 5\mathbf{e}_2 + 6\mathbf{e}_3$, $\mathbf{w} = 7\mathbf{e}_1 + 8\mathbf{e}_2 + 9\mathbf{e}_3$. Calculate the cosines of the angles between $\mathbf{u} - \mathbf{v}$, $\mathbf{v} - \mathbf{w}$, $\mathbf{w} - \mathbf{u}$.

26. If $\mathbf{u} = \mathbf{e}_1$, $\mathbf{v} = \mathbf{e}_2$, $\mathbf{w} = \mathbf{e}_3$, calculate $\det(\mathbf{u}, \mathbf{v}, \mathbf{w})$.

27. Let $\varepsilon_1 = [2, 1, 0]$, $\varepsilon_2 = [0, 2, 0]$, $\varepsilon_3 = [0, 0, 1]$. Starting with $\phi_1 = \varepsilon_1$, construct from the given basis an orthogonal basis.

28. Verify all details of the example given by (2.31).

29. Let $\mathbf{k}, \mathbf{m}, \mathbf{n}$ and $\mathbf{K}, \mathbf{M}, \mathbf{N}$ be two triples of orthonormal vectors. Show that $R_{ij} = k_iK_j + m_iM_j + n_iN_j$ is orthogonal.

Section 3
TENSOR ALGEBRA

We shall now take up the fundamental concept of a *tensor*. The motivation for this concept is intimately linked to geometry and physics, hence it is only proper to discuss first, however briefly, the purpose of the use of tensors.

Coordinate systems, observers, invariant laws

It is plausible to imagine that the idea of coordinate systems derives from our experience with relatively rigid bodies. From grids scribed on such bodies we abstract the idea of coordinate systems that are rigid (or, permanent, unchanging). The coordinate systems serve as frames of reference for recording observations, so that the terms *coordinate system* and *frame* are used interchangeably.

Along with coordinate systems there is always implied the existence of some means for determining the coordinates. In this broader sense, then, a coordinate system may be thought of as an observer, or rather, as a *representation of an observer*. By coordinate transformations we shall mean changes from one representation of an observer to another, equivalent representation of the same observer. For instance, a two-dimensional frame of reference may be represented by various grids scribed on a "rigid" plate; grids scribed on another plate will represent another observer. The correlation of two sets of frames that are in relative motion is called an *observer transformation*, in contrast to a coordinate transformation, which involves only a single observer. (Observer transformations can be also viewed as time-dependent coordinate transformations.)

From observations of physical events, recorded in various coordinate systems, we seek to extract a core of information that is *invariant* in the sense of being true in all coordinate systems. In particular, we require that physical principles be form-invariant to a change of coordinate systems; that is, the *functional form* of the principles must be the same in all coordinate systems.† Since this requirement is so basic and comprehensive, it is natural that we attempt to satisfy it in a general way, rather than verifying it in each isolated case. The manner in which the foregoing invariance requirement is automatically fulfilled rests on the representation of physical objects by tensors, the properties of tensors being such as to ensure the desired invariance. Our approach here will be very simple: *we shall define tensors without any reference to coordinate systems.* The transformation formulas connecting the component representations will be *derived* from the condition of equivalence of these representations.

Heuristic introduction of tensors

Scalars and vectors are fitted into the hierarchy of tensors by identifying scalars with tensors of rank zero, and vectors with tensors of rank one. The components of higher rank tensors have two or more indices, though we hasten to add that not every variable with indices represents a tensor.‡ This is of course only a rough identification of tensors; however, it is also true that the rules of index notation enable us to perform automatically many tensor operations even before tensors are properly defined. For instance, *addition* $A_{ij} + B_{ij}$, *composition* $B_{ij}v_k$, *contraction* B_{ii}, *transvection* (defined as composition followed by a contraction) $B_{ij}v_j$, etc. are, at least in the component representation, mere exercises in index notation. In fact, *the sole purpose of index notation is to describe correct tensor operations.* Thus $A_{ij} + C_{ijk}$ makes no sense in index notation, and, correspondingly, addition of tensors of unequal ranks is not defined. Any formula that is acceptable in index notation corresponds, except in very special circumstances (cf. the second footnote), to a possible tensor operation. Therefore, one can rely on

† The invariance to observer transformations is another matter!

‡ For instance, curvilinear coordinates θ_a and wrynesses w_{cab}, introduced in Section 6, are not tensor components. Consequently, no invariant meaning can be attached to θ_a and w_{cab}. Whether or not transformation coefficients Q_{ai} should be interpreted as tensor components is a matter of taste (cf. the discussion of intermediate components later in this section).

index notation to carry one safely through involved tensor operations long before a complete understanding of tensors has been reached. At the same time, however, it is important to develop as early as possible an intuitive grasp of tensors, so that they need not remain mere algebraic entities.

If we are to explain tensors, we could begin by saying that tensors are linear operators acting on vectors. We can express this notion more tangibly by writing as $T\bigcirc\bigcirc$ the tensor whose components are T_{ij}, the marks $\bigcirc$ indicating the two *valences* ("mouths") of the tensor which can be *saturated* by feeding vectors into them. If only one valence of a second rank tensor is saturated, then the result is a tensor of rank one (a vector). If both valences are saturated, we say that the *tensor has been saturated to a scalar*. For instance, letting I_{ij} be the inertia tensor and ω_j the angular velocity vector, we obtain the angular momentum vector H_i as a result of $\mathbf{I}$ operating on $\boldsymbol{\omega}$: $\mathbf{H} = \mathbf{I}\boldsymbol{\omega}$ ($H_i = I_{ij}\omega_j$). The fully saturated tensor, denoted by $\mathbf{I}[\boldsymbol{\omega}, \boldsymbol{\omega}]$, then yields the formula $2T = I_{ij}\omega_i\omega_j = \mathbf{I}[\boldsymbol{\omega}, \boldsymbol{\omega}]$, where T is the kinetic energy of rotation. A more graphic illustration of this sequence of steps is as follows, $I\bigcirc\bigcirc$, $H\bigcirc = I\bigcirc\textcircled{\scriptsize$\omega$}$, $2T = I\textcircled{\scriptsize$\omega$}\textcircled{\scriptsize$\omega$}$.

Now let $\mathbf{m}$ and $\mathbf{n}$ be two mutually orthogonal unit vectors. The moment of inertia about the axis of $\mathbf{n}$ will be denoted either by $\mathbf{I}[\mathbf{n}, \mathbf{n}]$ or by $I_{\underline{\mathrm{nn}}}$; similarly, $\mathbf{I}[\mathbf{m}, \mathbf{n}]$ or $I_{\underline{\mathrm{mn}}}$ will denote the product of inertia with respect to the axes of $\mathbf{m}$ and $\mathbf{n}$. Then

$$\mathbf{I}[\mathbf{m}, \mathbf{n}] = I_{\underline{\mathrm{mn}}} = I_{ij}m_i n_j, \tag{3.1}$$

$$\mathbf{I}[\mathbf{n}, \mathbf{n}] = I_{\underline{\mathrm{nn}}} = I_{ij}n_i n_j, \tag{3.2}$$

$\mathbf{I}[\mathbf{m}, \mathbf{m}] = I_{ij}m_i m_j$, and so on. The formula (3.1) is the model for all fully saturated tensors; it also shows that $\mathbf{I}$ acts *linearly* on each vector $\mathbf{m}$ and $\mathbf{n}$, and that the fully saturated tensor yields a scalar.

For another view of the tensor concept let us consider a rather typical case of the way in which tensors arise. We suppose that at a given point there exists a scalar $v_{\underline{\mathrm{n}}}$ (e.g. speed) associated with each direction at that point, the directions being described by a unit vector $\mathbf{n}$ of variable direction. We shall refer to the multiplicity of scalars $v_{\underline{\mathrm{n}}}$ as a *scalar state*. If the scalar state is but a manifestation of a vector $\mathbf{v}$ (e.g. velocity), we write

$$v_{\underline{\mathrm{n}}} = \mathbf{v}[\mathbf{n}] = v_i n_i, \tag{3.3}$$

where the square brackets are used to emphasize that $\mathbf{v}$ is a linear operator on $\mathbf{n}$. According to (3.3), the state $v_{\underline{\mathrm{n}}}$, interpreted as the totality of the scalars $v_{\underline{\mathrm{n}}}$

associated with all possible directions, is fully known if the components of **v** are known for any three mutually orthogonal directions.

Let us now consider a *vector state*: at a given point, a different vector $\mathbf{t}_{\underline{n}}$† is associated with each direction **n** (Figure 3.1). Again we can inquire whether the vectors $\mathbf{t}_{\underline{n}}$ are but a manifestation of a second rank tensor, e.g. $\mathbf{t}_{\underline{n}} = \mathbf{T}^T\mathbf{n}$ ($t_{\underline{n}i} = T_{ji}n_j$). In brief, we expect that in many cases multiplicities of scalars will exhibit the kind of coherence that will enable us to represent them by tensors.

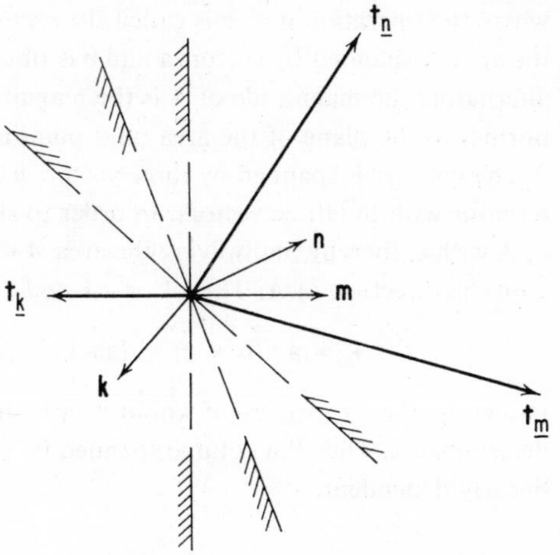

FIGURE 3.1 Elements of a vector state (**k**,**m**,**n** are unit normal vectors of the shaded planes).

Familiar examples of tensors

To find out what tensors are, it may be a good idea to try to see what they do. For this reason we shall review familiar concepts in a way that emphasizes the characteristics common to all tensors. Some of the illustrative examples will deal with tensors that will be defined precisely only in later chapters. This inconsistency is not a serious one because the requisite physical concepts are sufficiently familiar from elementary mechanics. Other examples will concern elementary concepts, e.g. vector-area, volume, moment of force, which are collected here for later reference.

We begin by interpretating the role of the alternator ε_{ijk}. We suppose that **m** and **n** are two given unit vectors, and now choose the problem of determining a unit vector **k** normal to the plane of **m** and **n**. The vector **k** is found from the conditions $\mathbf{k}\cdot\mathbf{m} = 0$, $\mathbf{k}\cdot\mathbf{n} = 0$, $\mathbf{k}\cdot\mathbf{k} = 1$, where the first two conditions state that **k** is orthogonal to both **m** and **n**, whereas the last condition states that **k** is a unit vector. Solving, we get $k_i = \varepsilon_{ijk}m_jn_k/D$, where $D^2 = (m_1n_2 - m_2n_1)^2 + (m_2n_3 - m_3n_2)^2 + (m_3n_1 - m_1n_3)^2 = 1 - (\mathbf{m}\cdot\mathbf{n})^2 = 1 - \cos^2\theta = \sin^2\theta$. Therefore,

$$\sin\theta\, k_i = \varepsilon_{ijk}m_jn_k. \tag{3.4}$$

† Cf. p. 50 concerning the notations $\mathbf{t}_{\underline{n}}$, $\mathbf{t}(\mathbf{n})$, etc.

If the vectors **m** and **n** are replaced by $\mathbf{a} = \mathbf{m}a$, $\mathbf{b} = \mathbf{n}b$, then from (3.4) it follows that

$$k_i ab \sin\theta = \varepsilon_{ijk} a_j b_k. \tag{3.5}$$

The area A spanned by **a** and **b** is given by $A = ab \sin\theta$, where θ is the angle between **a** and **b** (or, equivalently, between **m** and **n**). Therefore, (3.5) suggests the introduction of a *vector-area* **A** defined by

$$\mathbf{A} = \mathbf{a} \times \mathbf{b}, \qquad A_i = \varepsilon_{ijk} a_j b_k, \tag{3.6}$$

where the operation $\mathbf{a} \times \mathbf{b}$ is called the *vector product* of **a** and **b**. To summarize, the area **A** spanned by vectors **a** and **b** is obtained by feeding the vectors into the alternator; the magnitude of **A** is the magnitude of the area, the direction of **A** is normal to the plane of the area (and pointing away from it).

The volume V spanned by three vectors **a**, **b**, **c** is obtained by saturating the alternator with the three vectors. In order to show this, we form the scalar product of **A** with **c**, thereby multiplying the area A with the height obtained by projecting **c** on the direction of **A**. Then $V = c_i \varepsilon_{ijk} a_j b_k = \varepsilon_{kij} c_k a_i b_j$, or,†

$$V = \mathbf{a} \cdot (\mathbf{b} \times \mathbf{c}) \equiv [\mathbf{abc}] = \varepsilon_{ijk} a_i b_j c_k = \det(\mathbf{a}, \mathbf{b}, \mathbf{c}). \tag{3.7}$$

Evidently the properties of volumes are the same as the properties of 3×3 determinants. Thus the volume spanned by three vectors is zero if the vectors are linearly dependent.

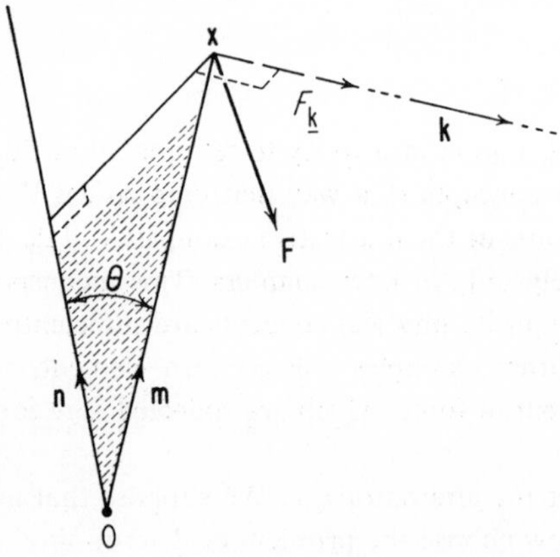

FIGURE 3.2 Variables for calculating the moment of a force about an axis.

The derivation that led to the idea of vector-area can be adapted for calculating the moment of a force **F** about an axis specified by a unit vector **n**. Let $\mathbf{x} = x_i \mathbf{e}_i$ be the point of application of the force. We construct a unit vector **m** in the direction of **x** by letting $m_i = x_i/r$, where $r = \sqrt{x_i x_i}$. Denoting by $F_{\underline{k}}$ the component of **F** perpendicular to the plane of **m** and **n**, we define the moment $M_{\underline{n}}$ of **F** about the axis of **n** by $M_{\underline{n}} = -r \sin\theta\, F_{\underline{k}}$, where θ is the angle between **m** and **n**. The quan-

† This product is called a box product, or, a triple scalar product.

tity $r \sin\theta$ is the lever arm, so that $M_{\underline{n}}$ is that action which would turn a "door" that is hinged along **n** and passes through **x** (Figure 3.2); the minus sign in $M_{\underline{n}} = -r \sin\theta\, F_{\underline{k}}$ is needed because a positive component $F_{\underline{k}}$ will produce a moment that is *clockwise* when sighting along the axis of **n** towards the origin. Using (3.4), we obtain $F_{\underline{k}} = \mathbf{F} \cdot \mathbf{k} = F_i \varepsilon_{ijk} x_j n_k / (r \sin\theta)$, thus

$$M_{\underline{n}} = \mathbf{n} \cdot (\mathbf{x} \times \mathbf{F}) = \varepsilon_{ijk} n_i x_j F_k. \tag{3.8}$$

The formula (3.8) describes a scalar state; it also suggests the introduction of a moment vector

$$\mathbf{M} = \mathbf{x} \times \mathbf{F}, \tag{3.9}$$

such that the moment about any axis **n** is the projection of **M** upon **n**:

$$M_{\underline{n}} = \mathbf{M}[\mathbf{n}] = \mathbf{M} \cdot \mathbf{n} = M_i n_i. \tag{3.10}$$

The full designation of **M** is: moment of force **F** about the point 0. If it is necessary to stress the dependence of **M** upon 0, we use the notation $\mathbf{M}^{[0]} = \mathbf{x} \times \mathbf{F}$.

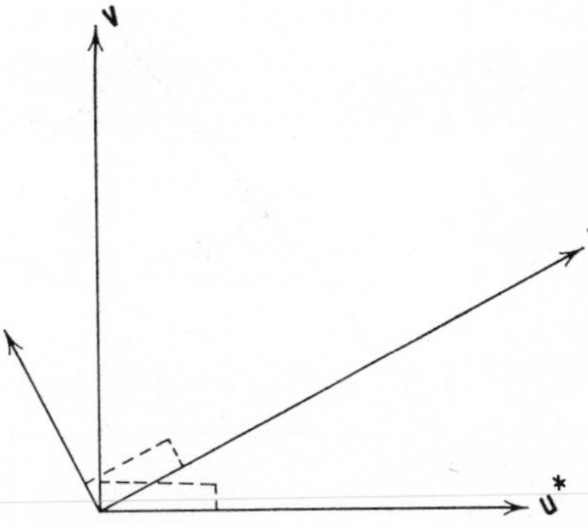

FIGURE 3.3 Reciprocal pairs of vectors in a plane.

A set of three non-coplanar vectors is often referred to as a *triad* (of vectors). For a given triad of vectors **u**, **v**, **w**, we define the *reciprocal triad* **u***, **v***, **w*** by

$$\begin{aligned} &\mathbf{u} \cdot \mathbf{u}^* = 1, \quad &\mathbf{v} \cdot \mathbf{u}^* = 0, \quad &\mathbf{w} \cdot \mathbf{u}^* = 0, \\ &\mathbf{u} \cdot \mathbf{v}^* = 0, \quad &\mathbf{v} \cdot \mathbf{v}^* = 1, \quad &\mathbf{w} \cdot \mathbf{v}^* = 0, \\ &\mathbf{u} \cdot \mathbf{w}^* = 0, \quad &\mathbf{v} \cdot \mathbf{w}^* = 0, \quad &\mathbf{w} \cdot \mathbf{w}^* = 1. \end{aligned} \tag{3.11}$$

Thus each vector of the reciprocal triad is orthogonal to two vectors of the original triad, and has a unit projection on the third. Reciprocal pairs of vectors in two dimensions are illustrated in Figure 3.3. Using (3.11) and (3.4), we obtain

$$\mathbf{u}^* = \frac{\mathbf{v} \times \mathbf{w}}{V}, \quad \mathbf{v}^* = \frac{\mathbf{w} \times \mathbf{u}}{V}, \quad \mathbf{w}^* = \frac{\mathbf{u} \times \mathbf{v}}{V}, \tag{3.12}$$

where $V = [\mathbf{uvw}]$ is the volume spanned by the triad **u**, **v**, **w**. A straight calculation shows that

$$[\mathbf{u}^*\mathbf{v}^*\mathbf{w}^*][\mathbf{uvw}] = 1. \tag{3.13}$$

To interpret second rank tensors, the inertia tensor I_{ij} is perhaps the best example. It describes the nature of distribution of mass with respect to some reference point, the diagonal components $I_{\underline{11}}$ being indicative of an average distance of the mass from that point, whereas the off-diagonal components I_{ij}, $i \neq j$, describe the unbalance of the distributed mass. In Cartesian coordinates the definitions for I_{ij} are†

$$I_{xx} = \int_D (y^2 + z^2)\,\mathrm{dm}, \ldots, \ldots, I_{xy} = -\int_D xy\,dm, \ldots, \ldots,$$

where D is the region of integration, and dm is an element of mass. In index notation we have the compact representation

$$I_{ij} = \int_D [x_k x_k \delta_{ij} - x_i x_j]\,dm. \tag{3.14}$$

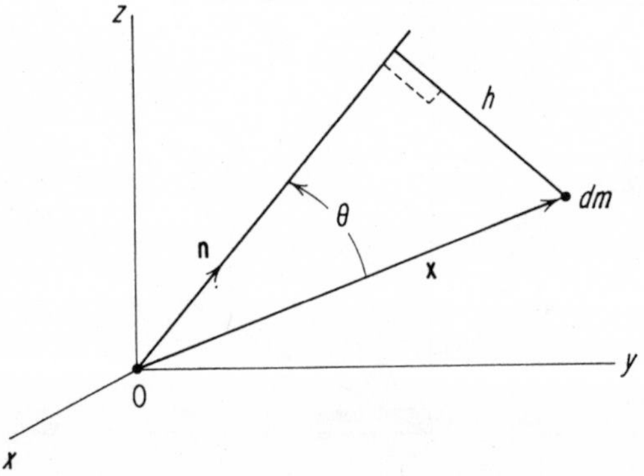

FIGURE 3.4 Variables for calculating a moment of inertia.

Let us verify the formula (3.2) by a direct calculation. As shown in Figure 3.4, the perpendicular distance h of dm from the axis of **n** is given by $h = r \sin\theta$, where $r = \sqrt{x_i x_i}$. But we also have that $r \sin\theta = |\mathbf{x} \times \mathbf{n}|$, $(\mathbf{x} \times \mathbf{n})_i = \varepsilon_{ijk} x_j n_k$. Therefore, $h^2 = |\mathbf{x} \times \mathbf{n}|^2 = \varepsilon_{ijk} x_j n_k \varepsilon_{irs} x_r n_s = x_j x_j n_s n_s - x_r n_r x_s n_s = n_r n_s (x_j x_j \delta_{rs} - x_r x_s)$, where we have used $(1.30)_1$. Thus

$$\mathbf{I}[\mathbf{n}, \mathbf{n}] = \int_D h^2\,dm = n_r n_s \int_D (x_j x_j \delta_{rs} - x_r x_s)\,dm = I_{rs} n_r n_s.$$

† The sign of products of inertia has no physical significance, hence, as is often done in elementary mechanics, we may choose the plus signs in the definitions. Then, however, the fluency of formulas such as $\mathbf{I}[\mathbf{n},\mathbf{n}] = I_{ij} n_i n_j$ would be disrupted by the appearance of minus signs there.

Stretching our imagination a little, we may think of the saturation of tensors with vectors as a measurement, or else as a thought experiment, the vectors being an *input of information.* The tensor itself is an operator which acts not unlike a computer. That is, the components I_{ij} represent a complete set of relevant data ("memory") needed to predict moments and products of inertia about any axes passing through the point in question. Consequently, a tensor is simply an effective way of organizing the relevant information about certain scalar states; the algebraic nature of tensors is such as to provide simple rules for obtaining predictions, e.g. $I_{\underline{mn}} = I_{ij}m_i n_j$ (as we shall see a little later on, this rule is but a disguised transformation formula of tensor components).

For another illustration, let us consider the *stress tensor* T_{ij} in a two-dimensional setting. We shall study this tensor with the aid of a free body diagram of a material prism, denoting by **n** the unit normal vector of the inclined face (Figure 3.5). The internal forces of a body are described by introducing a vector state of stress ("Cauchy's stress hypothesis"): at a given point in the body, to each plane specified by a unit normal vector **n** there corresponds a *stress vector* $\mathbf{t}_{\underline{n}}$ having the dimension of force per area (cf. also Figure 3.1). The totality of the stress vectors associated with all planes passing through the given point ("the state of stress at the point") is described in turn by a second rank stress tensor **T**.

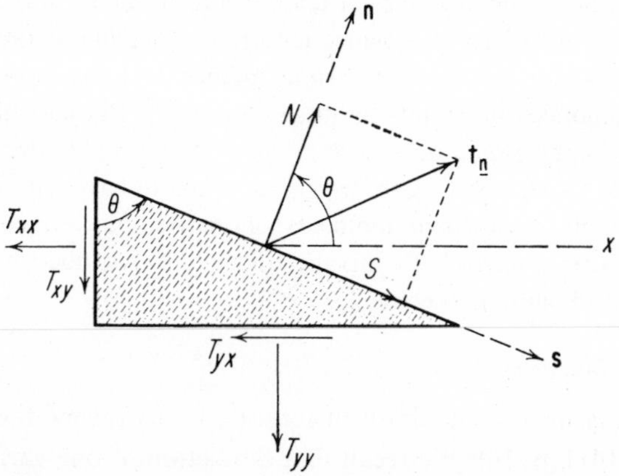

FIGURE 3.5 Stresses acting on a material prism.

The unit normal vector **n** in Figure 3.5 has the components $n_x = \cos\theta$, $n_y = \sin\theta$, whereas the unit vector **s** pointing along the inclined face has the components $s_x = \sin\theta$, $s_y = -\cos\theta$. In science it is considered bad form to point with one's finger, one uses unit vectors instead. Therefore, to find the stress vector acting on the inclined face, we feed the unit normal vector **n** into the stress tensor **T**. We then obtain the stress vector

$$t_{\underline{n}i} = T_{ji}n_j, \tag{3.15}$$

because only one valence of the stress tensor has been saturated. Conversely, (3.15) can be obtained by applying the conditions of equilibrium to the material prism, and denoting the stress vectors acting on the coordinate planes by $t_i(\mathbf{e}_j)\mathbf{e}_i = T_{ji}\mathbf{e}_i$. The conditions of equilibrium thus imply that the stress vectors $\mathbf{t}_j = \mathbf{t}(\mathbf{e}_j)$, $j = 1, 2, 3$, constitute a second rank tensor T_{ji}.

In order to obtain the *normal component* N of $\mathbf{t}_{\underline{n}}$, we feed $\mathbf{n}$ twice into $\mathbf{T}$; similarly, the *shearing component* $\mathbf{S}$ of $\mathbf{t}_{\underline{n}}$ is obtained by saturating $\mathbf{T}$ with $\mathbf{n}$ and $\mathbf{s}$: $N = \mathbf{t}_{\underline{n}} \cdot \mathbf{n} = T_{ji}n_jn_i = T_{xx}\cos^2\theta + T_{yy}\sin^2\theta + 2T_{xy}\sin\theta\cos\theta$, $S = \mathbf{t}_{\underline{n}} \cdot \mathbf{s} = T_{ji}n_js_i = (T_{xx} - T_{yy})\sin\theta\cos\theta + T_{xy}(\sin^2\theta - \cos^2\theta)$.

If we let, in turn, $\mathbf{n} = \mathbf{e}_x$ and $\mathbf{n} = \mathbf{e}_y$, then $\mathbf{t}_x = \mathbf{t}(\mathbf{e}_x) = T_{xx}\mathbf{e}_x + T_{xy}\mathbf{e}_y$, $\mathbf{t}_y = \mathbf{t}(\mathbf{e}_y) = T_{yx}\mathbf{e}_x + T_{yy}\mathbf{e}_y$. More generally, the stress vectors associated with Cartesian coordinate planes will be the rows in the array of the stress tensor:

$$\|\mathbf{T}\| = \begin{Vmatrix} T_{xx} & T_{xy} & T_{xz} \\ T_{yx} & T_{yy} & T_{yz} \\ T_{zx} & T_{zy} & T_{zz} \end{Vmatrix}.$$

Therefore, just as three numbers may constitute a vector, three vectors may constitute a second rank tensor. However, this view of second rank tensors is not always physically meaningful.

We could go on listing examples of tensors. For instance, in the study of electrical circuits we encounter inductance tensors L_{mn}, having as their components the mutual and self inductances of various meshes, and measuring the magnetic energy $L_{mn}i_mi_n$ induced in circuits by mesh currents i_k. But enough of examples; it may be more appropriate now to recall an often-repeated anecdote about the French scientist D'Alembert. A student is supposed to have complained that he, the student, could understand moments of inertia, but somehow could not believe in products of inertia. To this the advice of D'Alembert had been: "Just keep going and the faith will come."

Multilinear functions

Before taking up the definition of tensors, let us review the concept of a *function* (cf. [141], p. 16). We recall that a function of one variable has three ingredients: a *domain* X of (independent) variables x, a *range* Y of values y, and a *rule* f that associates x with y. The rule manifests itself in the way in which the variables x are paired off with the values $y = f(x)$. Therefore, f is described by the totality of the ordered pairs (x, y); symbolically, $f = \{(x, y), x \in X, y \in Y\}$. This suggests a visualization of f by means of a *graph* lying in the rectangle defined by the segments X and Y of the x and y axes, respectively.

A precise notation for functions tends to be rather cumbersome; in practice, it is customary to use simplified notations, even though this leads to some ambiguity in the interpretation of formulas. As a rule, no explicit mention is made of the domain and the range, the terms *function* and *rule* being then interchangeable. Second, the same symbol $f(x)$ denotes both the rule and the values of the function. The reason why the notation $f(x)$ is so deeply ingrained is that only few rules have names (e.g. sin, log), so that we are accustomed to expressing rules in terms of the variable x (e.g. $f(x) = x^2 + 3x$). Unfortunately, this tends to obscure the fact that a rule has nothing whatever to do with what the x is. More than that, we shall see time and again that the more general conceptions of a function require no new, unfamiliar rules. On the contrary, most of the rules will be of the simplest kind (e.g. linear correspondences!), the generalizations lying solely in the admission of general domains and ranges. Therefore, rather than having to learn a new concept of a function, one must, if anything, unlearn a narrow conception created by long familiarity with the $y = f(x)$ functions, and compounded by the use of the customary, ambiguous notations. Nothing more is needed now than to discern the notion of a rule, or correspondence, regardless of whether x and y are stresses, strain histories, or just plain numbers. While the *representation* of functions over general domains may not be easy, none of the difficulties are conceptual.

With a view to defining tensors, let us consider *linear functions.* If $f(x)$ is a linear function, then the parentheses are replaced by square brackets: $f[x]$. A linear function f is additive, $f[x + \bar{x}] = f[x] + f[\bar{x}]$, and homogeneous, $f[mx] = mf[x]$. It will be recalled that in general a function $f(x, y, z)$ is said to be homogeneous of degree N if $f(mx, my, mz) = m^N f(x, y, z)$. A linear function is homogeneous of degree 1 in each variable separately: $f[mx, ny] = mnf[x, y]$.

The case of scalar-valued functions of scalars is in fact rather confusing because both x and m are scalars, thus $mf[x] = xf[m]$. Letting $f[x] = xf[1]$, we conclude that a linear function admits the representation $f[x] = Cx$, where $C = f[1]$ is a constant. If j designates the function whose value at x is x, then $f = Cj$. The properties of linear functions can be combined into the formula

$$f[mx + n\bar{x}] = mf[x] + nf[\bar{x}]. \tag{3.16}$$

A function $f(x) = Cx + D$ is not linear, because $f(x + \bar{x}) = C(x + \bar{x}) + D \neq f(x) + f(\bar{x}) = (Cx + D) + (C\bar{x} + D)$. The square brackets are often omitted altogether, thus $y = fx$ ($\mathbf{t} = \mathbf{Tn}$!).

The generalization from linear functions to *multilinear functions* is straightforward: a multilinear function is linear with respect to each of its independent variables. We illustrate this for *bilinear functions*:

$$\begin{aligned} f[mx + n\bar{x}, u] &= mf[x, u] + nf[\bar{x}, u], \\ f[x, mu + n\bar{u}] &= mf(x, u) + nf[x, \bar{u}]. \end{aligned} \tag{3.17}$$

These expressions can be combined into one, but the resulting expression $f[mx + n\bar{x}, ru + s\bar{u}] = mrf[x, u] + msf[x, \bar{u}] + nrf[\bar{x}, u) + nsf[\bar{x}, \bar{u}]$ is less easy to read than (3.17). A bilinear function is represented by

$$f[x, u] = Cxu, \tag{3.18}$$

where C is a constant. A function $f(x, u) = Cxu + Dx + Eu$ is evidently not bilinear, e.g. $f(x, mu) = mCxu + Dx + mEu \neq mf(x, u) = mCxu + mDx + mEu$.

Since a rule f is independent of what the domain and the range may be, we can immediately extend the notion of linear functions to more general cases.† For instance, if the domain is a vector space A: $(\mathbf{a}, \mathbf{b}, \mathbf{c}, \ldots)$ and the range is a vector space U: $(\mathbf{u}, \mathbf{v}, \mathbf{w}, \ldots)$, then a linear function $\mathbf{u} = f[\mathbf{a}]$ has the property $f[m\mathbf{a} + n\mathbf{b}] = mf[\mathbf{a}] + nf[\mathbf{b}]$. Here f is a *linear vector-valued function of vectors*; ordinarily such functions are denoted by special symbols, e.g. $\mathbf{u} = \mathbf{T}[\mathbf{a}]$. In view of $\mathbf{u} \cdot \mathbf{v} = \mathbf{T}[\mathbf{a}] \cdot \mathbf{v} \equiv \mathbf{T}[\mathbf{a}, \mathbf{u}]$, $\mathbf{T}$ can be also interpreted as a *bilinear scalar-valued function* over A and U. Other, familiar examples are: $\mathbf{v} \cdot \mathbf{v}$—scalar-valued function of vectors, $\mathbf{a} \times \mathbf{u}$—vector-valued function of vectors, $\det\mathbf{T}$—scalar-valued function of tensors.

Definition of tensors; transformation formulas

After the lengthy introduction and preparations we can set down the definition of tensors right away:

Tensors are scalar-valued multilinear functions of vectors.

Let us interpret this definition in the case of second rank tensors (*bilinear functions*). We denote by

$$\mathbf{T}[\mathbf{e}_i, \mathbf{e}_j] = T_{ij} \tag{3.19}$$

the scalar values obtained by saturating the tensor $\mathbf{T}$ with the base vectors $\mathbf{e}_i$ and $\mathbf{e}_j$; a *component* T_{ij} may be referred to as the *value of* $\mathbf{T}$ *at* $\mathbf{e}_i$ *and* $\mathbf{e}_j$. In accord with the agreement introduced on p. 27, this formula defines the indices of tensor components in terms of the indices of the base vectors.

The linearity of the tensor $\mathbf{T}$ in each of its arguments is expressed as in (3.17):

$$\begin{aligned} \mathbf{T}[m\mathbf{u} + n\mathbf{v}, \mathbf{w}] &= m\mathbf{T}[\mathbf{u}, \mathbf{w}] + n\mathbf{T}[\mathbf{v}, \mathbf{w}], \\ \mathbf{T}[\mathbf{u}, m\mathbf{v} + n\mathbf{w}] &= m\mathbf{T}[\mathbf{u}, \mathbf{v}] + n\mathbf{T}[\mathbf{u}, \mathbf{w}]. \end{aligned} \tag{3.20}$$

† If the range and the domain are not sets of real numbers, the term *linear mapping* is often used in the place of *linear function*.

From (3.20) now follows the *component representation* of the fully saturated tensor:

$$\mathbf{T}[\mathbf{u}, \mathbf{v}] = T_{ij}u_i v_j \tag{3.21}$$

(cf. (3.18)). We can write, for instance, $\mathbf{T}[\mathbf{u}, \mathbf{v}] = \mathbf{T}[u_1\mathbf{e}_1 + u_2\mathbf{e}_2 + u_3\mathbf{e}_3, \mathbf{v}]$. Then, by consecutive applications of the property $(3.20)_1$, $\mathbf{T}[\mathbf{u}, \mathbf{v}] = u_1\mathbf{T}[\mathbf{e}_1, \mathbf{v}] + u_2\mathbf{T}[\mathbf{e}_2, \mathbf{v}] + u_3\mathbf{T}[\mathbf{e}_3, \mathbf{v}] = u_i\mathbf{T}[\mathbf{e}_i, \mathbf{v}]$. In the next step we let $\mathbf{v} = v_j\mathbf{e}_j$ and use $(3.20)_2$: $\mathbf{T}[\mathbf{u}, \mathbf{v}] = u_i\mathbf{T}[\mathbf{e}_i, v_j\mathbf{e}_j] = u_i v_j\mathbf{T}[\mathbf{e}_i, \mathbf{e}_j]$.

In the case of higher rank tensors the notations and procedures are the same. For instance, if $\mathbf{M}$ is a third rank tensor, then $\mathbf{M}[\mathbf{e}_2, \mathbf{e}_1, \mathbf{e}_1] = M_{211}$, etc., whereas the linearity property is illustrated by $\mathbf{M}[\mathbf{e}_1, \mathbf{e}_1 + \mathbf{e}_3, \mathbf{e}_2] = M_{112} + M_{132}$. The saturated tensor $\mathbf{M}[\mathbf{u}, \mathbf{v}, \mathbf{w}]$ is represented by $M_{ijk}u_i v_j w_k$.

It is interesting to note that a vector now wears two mantles: apart from being "itself" (i.e. a vector), it is also a tensor of rank one (i.e. a linear scalar-valued function of vectors). A vector space V^*: $(\mathbf{u}^*, \mathbf{v}^*, \mathbf{w}^*, \ldots)$ of linear scalar-valued functions over a vector space V: $(\mathbf{u}, \mathbf{v}, \mathbf{w}, \ldots)$ is called the *covector space*.† A linear function $\mathbf{u}^*$ is uniquely specified by its values $\mathbf{u}^*[\mathbf{e}_i] = \mathbf{u}_i^*$ at the base vectors of V. Then $\mathbf{u}^*[\mathbf{w}] = u_i^* w_i$ is the unique value of $\mathbf{u}^*$ at the vector $\mathbf{w}$. Now, in a *metric* space V there exists a similar operation, the scalar product $\mathbf{u}[\mathbf{w}] \equiv \mathbf{u} \cdot \mathbf{w}$, so that we may establish one-to-one correspondences $\mathbf{u}^* \to \mathbf{u}$, etc., by letting $\mathbf{u}^*[\mathbf{w}] = \mathbf{u} \cdot \mathbf{w}$. In this way the covector space becomes a replica of the vector space. Of course, this is only a formal equivalence: although a covector space of "forces" $\mathbf{F}$ is *identical in form* ("isomorphic") with a vector space of "velocities" $\mathbf{v}$ ($\mathbf{F}[\mathbf{v}] = F_i v_i =$ power, a scalar!), they are distinguishable on physical grounds. For one, all quantities in physics possess an additional characteristic: dimension!

According to (2.13), a scalar product of vectors can be interpreted as the saturated form of a *metric tensor* $\mathbf{g}$: $\mathbf{u} \cdot \mathbf{v} = \mathbf{g}[\mathbf{u}, \mathbf{v}] = g_{ij}u_i v_j$, where $g_{ij} = \mathbf{g}[\mathbf{e}_i, \mathbf{e}_j] \equiv \mathbf{e}_i \cdot \mathbf{e}_j$. In particular, $|\mathbf{u}|^2 = \mathbf{g}[\mathbf{u}, \mathbf{u}]$. For orthonormal bases $\mathbf{g} = \mathbf{1}$.

Orthogonal basis transformations are defined by

$$\mathbf{e}_a = Q_{ai}\mathbf{e}_i, \qquad \mathbf{e}_i = Q_{ai}\mathbf{e}_a \tag{3.22}$$

(cf. (2.23); (we also recall that in Schouten's notation $Q_{ai} = Q_{ia}$). The transformation formulas for tensor components then follow immediately, e.g. $T_{ab} = \mathbf{T}[\mathbf{e}_a, \mathbf{e}_b] = \mathbf{T}[Q_{ai}\mathbf{e}_i, Q_{bj}\mathbf{e}_j] = Q_{ai}Q_{bj}\mathbf{T}[\mathbf{e}_i, \mathbf{e}_j]$, or,

$$T_{ab} = Q_{ai}Q_{bj}T_{ij}. \tag{3.23}$$

† Also called the dual space or the conjugate space. V can be interpreted, in turn, as the covector space over V^*.

In the conventional notation this reads

$$\begin{aligned} \bar{\mathbf{T}} &= \mathbf{Q}\mathbf{T}\mathbf{Q}^T, & \bar{T}_{mn} &= Q_{mi}T_{ij}Q^T_{jn}. \\ \mathbf{T} &= \mathbf{Q}^T\bar{\mathbf{T}}\mathbf{Q}, & T_{ij} &= Q^T_{im}\bar{T}_{mn}Q_{nj}. \end{aligned} \tag{3.24}$$

Schouten's notation does really all the work for basis transformations, e.g. $M_{abc} = Q_{ai}Q_{bj}Q_{ck}M_{ijk}$, $E_{ijmn} = Q_{ia}Q_{jb}Q_{mc}Q_{nd}E_{abcd}$. There is no simple way of putting the preceding formula into direct notation.†

At this point it is instructive to reinterpret formulas of the type

$$\mathbf{I}[\mathbf{m}, \mathbf{n}] = I_{\underline{mn}} = I_{ij}m_i n_j. \qquad (3.1)R‡$$

Now, the orthogonal unit vectors **m** and **n** can be considered as base vectors of some orthonormal basis. Then, however, the designations **m** and **n** are "wrong": as base vectors, **m** and **n** must be labeled by letters that are the indices assigned to that basis. Therefore, let us denote **m** by $\mathbf{e}_a$ and **n** by $\mathbf{e}_b$, whereby the components of **m** and **n** are now identified with the direction cosines relating the bases (i) and (a): $\mathbf{e}_a = Q_{ai}\mathbf{e}_i$, $\mathbf{e}_b = Q_{bj}\mathbf{e}_j$. Then the saturated form is revealed as a disguised transformation formula: $\mathbf{I}[\mathbf{e}_a, \mathbf{e}_b] = I_{ab} = I_{ij}Q_{ai}Q_{bj}$.

Notations like $\mathbf{t}_{\underline{n}}$ also require explanation. Here again $\underline{n}$ is a descriptive mark, a "reminder" that **t** depends on **n**. Therefore this mark is rather like a button without a buttonhole, because we do not quite know where to put it: $\mathbf{t}_{\underline{n}}$, $\mathbf{t}(\mathbf{n})$, $\mathbf{t}^{\underline{n}}$. The reason for this difficulty lies in the designation **n** for the unit normal vector of the plane in question. We are missing an *index* here; if we write $\mathbf{e}_a$ in the place of **n**, then $\mathbf{t}_{\underline{n}}$ becomes $\mathbf{t}_a$, and $t_{\underline{n}i}$ become the *intermediate components*

$$T_{ai} = \mathbf{T}[\mathbf{e}_a, \mathbf{e}_i] = Q_{aj}T_{ji}. \tag{3.25}$$

Using the appropriate basis transformations, the intermediate components can be related to T_{ij} or T_{ab} in various ways, e.g. $T_{ib} = \mathbf{T}[\mathbf{e}_i, Q_{bj}\mathbf{e}_j] = Q_{bj}T_{ij} = \mathbf{T}[Q_{ia}\mathbf{e}_a, \mathbf{e}_b] = Q_{ia}T_{ab}$. In view of the orthonormality condition $\mathbf{e}_a \cdot \mathbf{e}_b = \delta_{ab} = Q_{ai}\mathbf{e}_i \cdot Q_{bj}\mathbf{e}_j = Q_{ai}Q_{bi}$, the direction cosines themselves can be considered as the intermediate components of the tensor δ_{ij}.

We have postponed until now any mention of a notational ambiguity which was already encountered for vectors. Specifically, a typical symbol **A** has

† But see the discussion of anisotropy in Section 14.

‡ The letter R adjoined to the number of an equation means that the equation bearing this number is being repeated. An asterisk attached to the number of an equation will mean that the equation is a modified form of the original equation (cf. (4.30), (4.30)*).

been used to denote both a tensor (i.e. a function) and its values (i.e. as an abbreviation for the components A_{ij}). It is again expedient to let this ambiguity remain, provided, however, that a precise notation is made available. Therefore, in analogy with the notation used for vectors (cf. (2.1)–(2.4)), we shall denote tensors of rank greater than one also by Greek majuscules: A, B, Δ, Σ, etc.† An alternative notation for the value of a second rank tensor A at the vectors α and β will be $A[\alpha, \beta]$; in particular, $A[\varepsilon_i, \varepsilon_j] = A_{ij}$.

Operations with tensors

The introduction of algebraic operations with tensors holds by now no surprises, because it amounts to giving names to those manipulations of indexed variables which are meaningful in the context of index notation. Naturally the definition of operations must be invariant, that is, expressed without reference to any particular representation. In most cases we shall illustrate the operations for second rank tensors only; the nature of the corresponding operations for higher rank tensors then becomes evident.

Addition is defined for tensors of the same rank. We write, for instance, $\mathbf{A}[\mathbf{u}, \mathbf{v}] + \mathbf{B}[\mathbf{u}, \mathbf{v}] = \mathbf{C}[\mathbf{u}, \mathbf{v}]$, i.e. $\mathbf{C}$ is that tensor whose value at $\mathbf{u}$ and $\mathbf{v}$ is the sum of the values of $\mathbf{A}$ and $\mathbf{B}$ at $\mathbf{u}$ and $\mathbf{v}$‡. Since the saturated tensors are scalars, the addition so defined is commutative and associative. The component representation $A_{ij} + B_{ij} = C_{ij}$ is derived as follows. Because the definition holds for *arbitrary* $\mathbf{u}$ and $\mathbf{v}$, we choose $u_1 = v_1 = 1$, $u_2 = u_3 = v_2 = v_3 = 0$, so that $A_{ij}u_iv_j + B_{ij}u_iv_j = C_{ij}u_iv_j$ implies $A_{11} + B_{11} = C_{11}$. Next, we can let $u_1 = v_2 = 1$, $u_2 = u_3 = v_1 = v_3 = 0$, and so on.

We define *magnification* by $m\mathbf{A}[\mathbf{u}, \mathbf{v}] = \mathbf{D}[\mathbf{u}, \mathbf{v}]$, i.e. $\mathbf{D}$ is that tensor whose value at $\mathbf{u}$ and $\mathbf{v}$ is m times the value of $\mathbf{A}$ at $\mathbf{u}$ and $\mathbf{v}$. Evidently $mA_{ij} = D_{ij}$. With addition and magnification so defined, tensors of like rank constitute a vector space; the vector-zero is provided by the *null-tensor* $\tilde{\mathbf{0}}$ which vanishes at all vectors: $\tilde{\mathbf{0}}[\mathbf{u}, \mathbf{v}] = 0$.

Composition of tensors is illustrated by $\mathbf{A}[\mathbf{u}, \mathbf{v}]\, \mathbf{a}[\mathbf{w}] = \mathbf{M}[\mathbf{u}, \mathbf{v}, \mathbf{w}]$ or, in the component representation, by $A_{ij}a_k = M_{ijk}$. Here the rank of the resulting tensor equals the sum of the ranks of the tensors entering into the composition. The expression $A_{ij}a_k$ is also called a *free product* (or, tensor product) of A_{ij} and a_k.§

Of particular interest to us is the representation of tensors by free products of vectors, e.g. $T_{ij} = u_iv_j$, $M_{ijk} = u_iv_jw_k$. The properties of free products are

† Most of the Greek majuscules are identical with the ordinary majuscules.

‡ Incidentally, the frequent use of the saturated forms suggests an alternative definition of tensor components as coefficients of invariant multilinear forms.

§ In the literature a free product is often designated by the symbol $\otimes$, e.g. $\mathbf{M} = \mathbf{A} \otimes \mathbf{a}$.

easily derived by using the saturated forms, e.g. $\mathbf{T}[\mathbf{a}, \mathbf{b}] = \mathbf{u}[\mathbf{a}]\mathbf{v}[\mathbf{b}]$. In particular, we have that

$$\begin{aligned}
&\text{a.} \quad \mathbf{u}(\mathbf{v} + \mathbf{w}) = \mathbf{uv} + \mathbf{uw}, \\
&\text{b.} \quad (\mathbf{u} + \mathbf{v})\mathbf{w} = \mathbf{uw} + \mathbf{vw}, \\
&\text{c.} \quad m(\mathbf{uv}) = (m\mathbf{u})\mathbf{v} = \mathbf{u}(m\mathbf{v}), \\
&\text{d.} \quad \mathbf{uv} = \tilde{\mathbf{0}} \text{ only if } \mathbf{u} = \mathbf{0} \text{ or } \mathbf{v} = \mathbf{0} \text{ or both.}
\end{aligned} \tag{3.26}$$

Introducing the representations $\mathbf{u} = u_i\mathbf{e}_i$, $\mathbf{v} = v_j\mathbf{e}_j$, we obtain

$$\mathbf{T} = \mathbf{uv} = u_i v_j \mathbf{e}_{ij}, \tag{3.27}$$

where

$$\mathbf{e}_{ij} \equiv \mathbf{e}_i\mathbf{e}_j \tag{3.28}$$

are a set of base vectors for the second rank tensors **T** interpreted as elements of a vector space. In order to see that $\mathbf{e}_{ij}$ are linearly independent, let us consider $\mathbf{A} = A_{ij}\mathbf{e}_i\mathbf{e}_j = \mathbf{a}_j\mathbf{e}_j$, where $\mathbf{a}_j = A_{ij}\mathbf{e}_i$. Since $\mathbf{e}_j \neq \mathbf{0}$, it follows that $\mathbf{A} = \tilde{\mathbf{0}}$ only if $\mathbf{a}_j = \mathbf{0}$, but that would contradict the assumed linear independence of $\mathbf{e}_i$.

If vectors and tensors are represented by ordered arrays, then the free product of vectors is performed as follows:

$$\mathbf{uv}^T = \begin{Vmatrix} u_1 \\ u_2 \\ u_3 \end{Vmatrix} \|v_1, v_2, v_3\| = \begin{Vmatrix} u_1v_1 & u_1v_2 & u_1v_3 \\ u_2v_1 & u_2v_2 & u_2v_3 \\ u_3v_1 & u_3v_2 & u_3v_3 \end{Vmatrix} = \|\mathbf{T}\|. \tag{3.29}$$

In particular, if $\mathbf{e}_1 = (1, 0, 0)$, $\mathbf{e}_2 = (0, 1, 0)$, $\mathbf{e}_3 = (0, 0, 1)$, then

$$\|\mathbf{e}_{12}\| = \begin{Vmatrix} 1 \\ 0 \\ 0 \end{Vmatrix} \|0, 1, 0\| = \begin{Vmatrix} 0 & 1 & 0 \\ 0 & 0 & 0 \\ 0 & 0 & 0 \end{Vmatrix},$$

$$\|\mathbf{e}_{31}\| = \begin{Vmatrix} 0 \\ 0 \\ 1 \end{Vmatrix} \|1, 0, 0\| = \begin{Vmatrix} 0 & 0 & 0 \\ 0 & 0 & 0 \\ 1 & 0 & 0 \end{Vmatrix} \quad \text{etc.}$$

It is not difficult to see that representation $T_{ij} = u_i v_j$ is not general enough, because then $\det\mathbf{T} = 0$. For instance, for a range of two, $\det\mathbf{T} = \varepsilon_{mn}T_{m1}T_{n2}$

$= \varepsilon_{mn}u_m v_1 u_n v_2 = 0$. In this case a sufficiently general representation is given by

$$\mathbf{T} = \mathbf{au} + \mathbf{bv}, \qquad T_{ij} = a_i u_j + b_i v_j. \tag{3.30}$$

where, in view of

$$\det\mathbf{T} = \det(\mathbf{a}, \mathbf{b}) \det(\mathbf{u}, \mathbf{v}), \tag{3.31}$$

each vector pair **a**, **b** and **u**, **v** must be linearly independent. The representation is not unique: it relates four tensor components T_{ij} to eight vector components. For a range of three we let

$$\mathbf{T} = \mathbf{au} + \mathbf{bv} + \mathbf{cw}, \qquad T_{ij} = a_i u_j + b_i v_j + c_i w_j, \tag{3.32}$$

whence it follows that

$$\det\mathbf{T} = \det(\mathbf{a}, \mathbf{b}, \mathbf{c}) \det(\mathbf{u}, \mathbf{v}, \mathbf{w}). \tag{3.33}$$

A remark concerning the interpretation of direct notation: as was emphasized on p. 8, the indices assigned to a variable are determined by the *place* that this variable occupies in a given expression. The following example should make this convention clear:

$$\mathbf{M} = \mathbf{auw} + \mathbf{wuv} + \mathbf{uav},$$
$$M_{ijk} = a_i u_j w_k + w_i u_j v_k + u_i a_j v_k,$$

The *contraction* of a tensor T_{ij} is defined by

$$\mathrm{tr}\mathbf{T} = T_{ii}. \tag{3.34}$$

In particular, if $\mathbf{T} = \mathbf{uv}$, then $\mathrm{tr}\mathbf{T} = \mathbf{u} \cdot \mathbf{v}$; evidently an equivalent definition of trace is $\mathrm{tr}(\mathbf{e}_i\mathbf{e}_j) = \mathbf{e}_i \cdot \mathbf{e}_j$. This operation decreases the rank of a tensor by two, producing a scalar from a second rank tensor. For a third rank tensor M_{ijk} the following contractions are possible: M_{iik}, M_{iji}, M_{ijj}.

To make the definition of contraction as brief as possible, we have committed the cardinal sin of using component representations. Therefore, it is now necessary to show that the operation so defined is invariant. Let us take $T_{ab} = Q_{ai}Q_{bj}T_{ij}$, for instance. Forming the contraction $T_{aa} = Q_{ai}Q_{aj}T_{ij}$, and recalling the orthonormality condition (2.24), we find that $T_{aa} = T_{ii}$.

Transvection combines composition with contraction; the result of this operation is also known as a *contracted free product*. Typical transvections are: $I_{ij}\omega_j$, $A_{im}B_{mj}$.

Evidently to reproduce transvections in terms of the representations $I = I_{ij}\mathbf{e}_i\mathbf{e}_j$, $\omega = \omega_k\mathbf{e}_k$, etc., a transvection must be interpreted as a scalar product,† subject to the following rules:

$$\mathbf{e}_k \cdot (\mathbf{e}_i\mathbf{e}_j) = (\mathbf{e}_k \cdot \mathbf{e}_i)\mathbf{e}_j = \delta_{ki}\mathbf{e}_j, \qquad (\mathbf{e}_i\mathbf{e}_j) \cdot \mathbf{e}_k = \mathbf{e}_i(\mathbf{e}_j \cdot \mathbf{e}_k) = \mathbf{e}_i\delta_{jk},$$
$$(\mathbf{e}_r \ldots \mathbf{e}_i\mathbf{e}_j) \cdot (\mathbf{e}_m\mathbf{e}_n \ldots \mathbf{e}_s) = \mathbf{e}_r \ldots \mathbf{e}_i(\mathbf{e}_j \cdot \mathbf{e}_m)\mathbf{e}_n \ldots \mathbf{e}_s = \delta_{jm}\mathbf{e}_r \ldots \mathbf{e}_i\mathbf{e}_n \ldots \mathbf{e}_s. \tag{3.35}$$

For instance, if $A = A_{ij}\mathbf{e}_i\mathbf{e}_j$ and $B = B_{mn}\mathbf{e}_m\mathbf{e}_n$, then $AB = A_{ij}\mathbf{e}_i\mathbf{e}_j \cdot B_{mn}\mathbf{e}_m\mathbf{e}_n = A_{ij}B_{mn}\mathbf{e}_i\delta_{jm}\mathbf{e}_n = A_{im}B_{mn}\mathbf{e}_i\mathbf{e}_n$.

For second rank tensors a transvection of the form $A_{ij}B_{jk}$ is particularly important. It is natural to call this operation a *multiplication*, because it possesses the closure property: multiplication of second rank tensors yields second rank tensors (by the same token, it would be misleading to refer to composition as multiplication). The algebra based on the operations of addition, magnification, and multiplication is then identical with *matrix algebra.*

With the aid of multiplication we can define (positive) integral powers $\mathbf{T}^K$ of a tensor $\mathbf{T}$ as follows:

$$\begin{aligned} \mathbf{T}^K &= \mathbf{T}^{K-1}\mathbf{T} \qquad \mathbf{T} = T T^{K-1} \\ \mathbf{T}^1 &= \mathbf{T}, \qquad \mathbf{T}^0 = \mathbf{1}. \end{aligned} \tag{3.36}$$

To define negative integral powers, we start with the *inverse*, $\mathbf{T}^{-1}$, defined by

$$\begin{aligned} \mathbf{T}^{-1}\mathbf{T} &= \mathbf{1}, \\ (\mathbf{T}^{-1})_{ij}T_{jk} &= \delta_{ik}. \end{aligned} \tag{3.37}$$

Since the operation $1/T_{ij}$ will never occur (it is not a tensor operation), the components of $\mathbf{T}^{-1}$ may be designated by T_{ij}^{-1}. A roundabout way of calculating T_{ij}^{-1} starts from the *cofactors* in the expansion of det$\mathbf{T}$. The cofactor $C_{1i} = C_{1i}(\mathbf{T})$ corresponding to the term T_{1i} is defined by det$\mathbf{T} = \varepsilon_{ijk}T_{1i}T_{2j}T_{3k} \equiv C_{1i}T_{1i}$. Thus $C_{1i} = \varepsilon_{ijk}T_{2j}T_{3k} = \frac{1}{2}(\varepsilon_{ijk}T_{2j}T_{3k} - \varepsilon_{ijk}T_{2k}T_{3j}) = \frac{1}{2}\varepsilon_{ijk}\varepsilon_{1np}T_{nj}T_{pk}$. Evidently the general formula is (cf. also Problem 24)

$$C_{mi} = \frac{1}{2}\,\varepsilon_{mnp}\varepsilon_{ijk}T_{nj}T_{pk} = (-1)^{m+i}\Delta_{mi}, \tag{3.38}$$

Where Δ_{mi} is the 2×2 determinant obtained by deleting the nth row and the ith column in det $\mathbf{C}$.

† We are again reminded that $\mathbf{I}\boldsymbol{\omega}$ is not a very consistent abbreviation of $I_{ij}\omega_j$. It would have been better to denote the latter by $\mathbf{I} \cdot \boldsymbol{\omega}$.

Next, we note that $C_{mi}T_{ri} = \frac{1}{2}\varepsilon_{mnp}\varepsilon_{ijk}T_{ri}T_{nj}T_{pk} = \frac{1}{2}\varepsilon_{mnp}\varepsilon_{rnp}\,\det\mathbf{T}$, therefore,

$$C_{mi}T_{ri} = \delta_{mr}\,\det\mathbf{T}. \tag{3.39}$$

A comparison with (3.37) now yields

$$T_{ik}^{-1} = \frac{C_{ki}}{\det\mathbf{T}}. \tag{3.40}$$

It is worth noting that $\mathbf{T}^{-1} = \mathbf{C}^T/\det\mathbf{T}$ implies $(\mathbf{T}^{-1})^T = \mathbf{C}/\det\mathbf{T}$, but $\mathbf{C}/\det\mathbf{T} = (\mathbf{T}^T)^{-1}$, i.e.

$$(\mathbf{T}^{-1})^T = (\mathbf{T}^T)^{-1}. \tag{3.41}$$

The inverse $\mathbf{T}^{-1}$ exists only if $\det\mathbf{T} \neq 0$, in which case $\mathbf{T}$ is said to be *non-singular*. Integral negative powers of non-singular tensors are defined in the usual way: $\mathbf{T}^{-2} = \mathbf{T}^{-1}\mathbf{T}^{-1}$, etc.

Let us also show that (3.37) implies

$$\mathbf{T}\mathbf{T}^{-1} = \mathbf{1}. \tag{3.42}$$

We first note that the "unit" $\mathbf{1}$ is unique. For if we assume that there exists another unit $\bar{\mathbf{1}}$ such that $\mathbf{T}\bar{\mathbf{1}} = \bar{\mathbf{1}}\mathbf{T} = \mathbf{T}$, then it follows that $\mathbf{1}\bar{\mathbf{1}} = \mathbf{1} = \bar{\mathbf{1}}$. Next, we multiply (3.37) from the left by $\mathbf{T}$, taking into account that this multiplication is associative: $\mathbf{T}(\mathbf{T}^{-1}\mathbf{T}) = (\mathbf{T}\mathbf{T}^{-1})\mathbf{T} = \mathbf{T}$. Multiplying (3.37) from the right by $\mathbf{T}^{-1}$, we obtain $(\mathbf{T}^{-1}\mathbf{T})\mathbf{T}^{-1} = \mathbf{T}^{-1}(\mathbf{T}\mathbf{T}^{-1}) = \mathbf{T}^{-1}$, which concludes the proof.

To calculate the inverse of a product $\mathbf{T} = \mathbf{RS}$, we note that $\mathbf{S}^{-1}\mathbf{R}^{-1}\mathbf{T} = \mathbf{S}^{-1}\mathbf{R}^{-1}\mathbf{RS} = \mathbf{1}$, thus

$$(\mathbf{RS})^{-1} = \mathbf{S}^{-1}\mathbf{R}^{-1}. \tag{3.43}$$

The rule expressed by (3.43) can be generalized to products of arbitrary number of second rank tensors: the inverse (transpose) of a product equals the product of the inverses (transposes) taken in reverse order.

Problems

A. FAMILIAR EXAMPLES OF TENSORS

1. Verify the derivation of (3.4) and (3.6).

2. Derive (3.12) and (3.13).

3. Derive (3.1) and (3.2).

4. Check the formulas for N and S on p. 46 by considering the conditions of equilibrium for the material prism.

B. MULTILINEAR FUNCTIONS

5. Write down a definition and a representation for a trilinear scalar-valued function of the scalar variables x, y, z.

6. Show that

a. $\sqrt{x^2 + y^2 + z^2}$ is a homogeneous function but not a linear one.
b. $f(x, y) = x^2 - xy + y^2$ is not a bilinear function.

7. Write down (in index notation) appropriate generalizations of $y = fx \equiv f[x]$ if the range and the domain of the linear function are specified by stating that the function is

a. a scalar-valued function of vectors.
b. a vector-valued function of vectors.
c. a vector-valued function of second rank tensors.
d. a scalar-valued function of second rank tensors.
e. a linear mapping of second rank tensors into second rank tensors.

C. DEFINITION OF TENSORS; TRANSFORMATION FORMULAS

8. Write down the component representations of the following fully saturated forms:

a. $\mathbf{v}[\mathbf{a}]$	**b.** $\mathbf{v}[\mathbf{v}]$	**c.** $\mathbf{T}[\mathbf{a}, \mathbf{b}]$	**d.** $\mathbf{T}[\mathbf{u}, \mathbf{u}]$
e. $\mathbf{M}[\mathbf{a}, \mathbf{b}, \mathbf{c}]$	**f.** $\mathbf{M}[\mathbf{u}, \mathbf{u}, \mathbf{w}]$	**g.** $\mathbf{E}[\mathbf{a}, \mathbf{b}, \mathbf{c}, \mathbf{u}]$	**h.** $\mathbf{E}[\mathbf{a}, \mathbf{u}, \mathbf{a}, \mathbf{u}]$

9. Express in terms of the tensor components the following:

a. $\mathbf{v}[\mathbf{e}_1]$	**b.** $\mathbf{v}[\mathbf{e}_3 + 2\mathbf{e}_2]$	**c.** $\mathbf{v}[y\mathbf{e}_1 - x\mathbf{e}_2]$
d. $\mathbf{T}[\mathbf{e}_2, \mathbf{e}_1]$	**e.** $\mathbf{T}[\mathbf{e}_3, 5\mathbf{e}_3 + 4\mathbf{e}_1]$	**f.** $\mathbf{T}[\mathbf{e}_1 + \mathbf{e}_2, \mathbf{e}_1 + \mathbf{e}_3]$
g. $\mathbf{M}[\mathbf{e}_2, \mathbf{e}_1, \mathbf{e}_1]$	**h.** $\mathbf{M}[2\mathbf{e}_2, \mathbf{e}_1 + \mathbf{e}_3, 3\mathbf{e}_2]$	**i.** $\mathbf{E}[\mathbf{e}_1, \mathbf{e}_1, \mathbf{e}_1 + \mathbf{e}_2, \mathbf{e}_1]$

10. Write down the transformation formulas from the (i) basis to the (a) basis for

a. v_a **b.** T_{aa} **c.** $I_{ab}n_b$ **d.** F_{abcde}

11. Write down the transformation formulas from the (a) basis to the (i) basis for

a. v_i **b.** v_iv_i **c.** $I_{ij}n_in_j$ **d.** F_{ijkmn}

12. Let

$$\|Q_{ai}\| = \begin{Vmatrix} \cos\alpha & \sin\alpha \\ -\sin\alpha & \cos\alpha \end{Vmatrix}.$$

Calculate $\overline{\mathbf{T}} = \mathbf{Q}\mathbf{T}\mathbf{Q}^T$ for

$$\|\mathbf{T}\| = \begin{Vmatrix} A & C \\ A & B \end{Vmatrix}.$$

13. If

$$\|\mathbf{Q}\| = \begin{Vmatrix} A & B \\ C & D \end{Vmatrix}.$$

is orthogonal, show that it can be reduced to the form given for **Q** in Problem 12.

D. OPERATIONS WITH TENSORS

14. Verify (3.26).
15. Verify (3.29).
16. Given that $\mathbf{u} = A\mathbf{e}_1 + B\mathbf{e}_3$, $\mathbf{v} = C\mathbf{e}_1 + D\mathbf{e}_2$, calculate the components of $\mathbf{T} = \mathbf{uv}$.
17. Let $\mathbf{e}_1 = (1, 0, 0)$, $\mathbf{e}_2 = (1, 1, 0)$, $\mathbf{e}_3 = (1, 1, 1)$. Calculate the base vectors $\mathbf{e}_{ij} = \mathbf{e}_i\mathbf{e}_j$.
18. Write down the possible contractions of E_{ijkm}.
19. Write down the possible transvections for

    a. A_{ij} and v_k b. A_{ij} and B_{mn}

20. Let

$$\|\mathbf{A}\| = \begin{Vmatrix} A & B \\ C & D \end{Vmatrix}.$$

Calculate $\mathbf{A}^2$ and $\mathbf{A}^3$.

21. Calculate $\mathbf{A}^{-2}$ for

    a. $\|\mathbf{A}\| = \begin{Vmatrix} 2 & 1 \\ 2 & 1 \end{Vmatrix}$ b. $\|\mathbf{A}\| = \begin{Vmatrix} 1 & 1 \\ -1 & 1 \end{Vmatrix}$.

22. Let **R** be an orthogonal tensor. Show that $\mathbf{R}^K$ is also an orthogonal tensor.
23. Let **A** be skew-symmetric, **C** symmetric, and **R** orthogonal. Show that $\mathbf{RAR}^T$ and $\mathbf{RCR}^T$ are skew-symmetric and symmetric, respectively. (Must **R** be orthogonal?)
24. From (3.38), interpret cofactors c_{mi} as 2×2 sub–determinants.

Section 4
SECOND RANK TENSORS

The mechanics of particles and rigid bodies is almost entirely a vectorial mechanics, the basic kinematical and dynamical concepts being vectors, e.g. force, velocity. An essential feature of the transition to mechanics of deformable bodies is the appearance of second rank tensors, e.g. stress, strain. For this reason the present section will be the highlight, and the conclusion, of the presentation of linear algebra.

Vector algebra is simple and widely applicable because only very few properties are postulated for vectors. By the same token, vector algebra has little to offer in the way of interesting results. In order that it be possible to derive many interesting results, the elements of a system must have more properties to begin with (i.e. they must satisfy more axioms). This is indeed the case for second rank tensors. Although they are more complex than vectors, their properties are not unfamiliar. On the contrary, we recover many algebraic properties of real numbers; it is no exaggeration to say that second rank tensors resemble scalars more than do vectors! Let us start out by exploring this similarity more fully.

Linear mappings and their algebra; the Cayley–Hamilton equation

In higher algebra we seek to generalize the algebra of real numbers.† The complex numbers still have all of the algebraic properties of real numbers, but further generalizations are possible only by omission of some of the axioms for real numbers. Thus linear associative algebras are obtained, in essence, by omitting the commutative law of multiplication. Specifically, the elements $\mathbf{A}, \mathbf{B}, \mathbf{C}, \ldots$ of a linear associative algebra satisfy the axioms for vector spaces, and possess a multiplication which is associative: $(\mathbf{AB})\mathbf{C} = \mathbf{A}(\mathbf{BC}) \equiv \mathbf{ABC}$, distributive: $\mathbf{A}(\mathbf{B} + \mathbf{C}) = \mathbf{AB} + \mathbf{AC}$, $(\mathbf{B} + \mathbf{C})\mathbf{A} = \mathbf{BA} + \mathbf{CA}$, and possesses a "principal unit" $\mathbf{1}$ such that $\mathbf{A1} = \mathbf{1A} = \mathbf{A}$. The multiplication is assumed to be invertible, so that $\mathbf{AX} = \mathbf{B}$ has a solution $\mathbf{X} = \mathbf{A}^{-1}\mathbf{B}$, except for a class of elements ("divisors of zero") that satisfy $\mathbf{AX} = \mathbf{0}$ for $\mathbf{X} \neq \mathbf{0}$.

Linear associative algebras are examples of systems which have almost all of the properties of real numbers. For instance, in the same way that fractional powers of positive numbers are again positive numbers, it is possible to define fractional powers of "positive" elements.‡

Evidently second rank tensors constitute a linear associative algebra; therefore, it is instructive to consider them, at least from time to time, not as arrays or bilinear functions but simply as "hyper-complex numbers" (also called dyads, nonions). These "numbers" can be expressed as linear combinations of the "hyper-complex units" ε_{ij}, e.g. $A = A_{ij}\varepsilon_{ij}$, the multiplication law being

$$\varepsilon_{ij}\varepsilon_{mn} = \delta_{jm}\varepsilon_{in} \tag{4.1}$$

(cf. (3.35)). It is easy to see that $\varepsilon = \varepsilon_{ii}$ ("idemfactor") has the properties of

† The algebraic properties of real numbers define an algebraic *field*. In addition, real numbers have topological properties, e.g. ordering, nearness.
‡ Cf. (4.60) *et seq.*

the principal unit: $\varepsilon_{kk}A_{ij}\varepsilon_{ij} = A_{kj}\varepsilon_{kj} = A_{ij}\varepsilon_{ij}\varepsilon_{kk} = A_{ik}\varepsilon_{ik}$. The principal unit is of course no other but the unit tensor **1**:

$$\mathbf{e}_i\mathbf{e}_i = \begin{Vmatrix} 1 \\ 0 \\ 0 \end{Vmatrix} \|1, 0, 0\| + \begin{Vmatrix} 0 \\ 1 \\ 0 \end{Vmatrix} \|0, 1, 0\| + \begin{Vmatrix} 0 \\ 0 \\ 1 \end{Vmatrix} \|0, 0, 1\| = \begin{Vmatrix} 1 & 0 & 0 \\ 0 & 1 & 0 \\ 0 & 0 & 1 \end{Vmatrix} = \mathbf{1}.$$

Let us derive a few general results concerning linear associative algebras. It will be recalled that a second rank tensor **T** may be also viewed as a *linear mapping* between vector spaces, e.g. $\mathbf{a} = \mathbf{Tu}$ (note that $\mathbf{a} \cdot \mathbf{b} = (\mathbf{Tu}) \cdot \mathbf{b} \equiv \mathbf{T}[\mathbf{u}, \mathbf{b}]$). To obtain an explicit description of **T**, we replace in the representation (3.32) the vectors **u**, **v**, **w** by the reciprocal triad **u***, **v***, **w***, thus

$$\mathbf{T} = \mathbf{au}^* + \mathbf{bv}^* + \mathbf{cw}^*. \tag{4.2}$$

Multiplying this, in turn, by **u**, **v**, **w**, then taking into account (3.11), we arrive at

$$\mathbf{a} = \mathbf{Tu}, \qquad \mathbf{b} = \mathbf{Tv}, \qquad \mathbf{c} = \mathbf{Tw}. \tag{4.3}$$

Moreover, by (3.13), (3.33),

$$\det\mathbf{T} = \frac{[\mathbf{abc}]}{[\mathbf{uvw}]}. \tag{4.4}$$

Evidently

$$\mathbf{T}^{-1} = \mathbf{ua}^* + \mathbf{vb}^* + \mathbf{wc}^*. \tag{4.5}$$

Combining (4.2) and (4.5), we obtain the following representations of **1**,

$$\mathbf{1} = \mathbf{uu}^* + \mathbf{vv}^* + \mathbf{ww}^* = \mathbf{aa}^* + \mathbf{bb}^* + \mathbf{cc}^*. \tag{4.6}$$

In (4.3) we may choose 9 of the 18 components a_i, b_i, c_i, u_i, v_i, w_i arbitrarily; that is, **T** describes only the *deformation*, so to speak, of a triad. Namely, if the 9 components u_i, v_i, w_i are given, then **T** determines the 9 components a_i, b_i, c_i. It is worth noting that if we adjoin to (4.3) another relation $\mathbf{d} = \mathbf{Tx}$, then **d** can *not* be prescribed arbitrarily. This has to do with the dimension of the space. Because **d** and **x** must be expressible as linear combinations of the other vectors, thus $\mathbf{x} = L\mathbf{u} + M\mathbf{v} + N\mathbf{w}$, $\mathbf{d} = A\mathbf{a} + B\mathbf{b} + C\mathbf{c}$, it follows from $\mathbf{d} = \mathbf{Tx}$ that $(A - L)\mathbf{a} + (B - M)\mathbf{b} + (C - N)\mathbf{c} = 0$. If the triads **a**, **b**, **c** and **u**, **v**, **w** are each linearly independent, then $A = L$,

$B = M$, $C = N$, i.e. the change of $\mathbf{x}$ is completely determined by the relations (4.3). The tensor $\mathbf{T}$ is said to define a *homogeneous deformation*, which may be visualized as a deformation of a material "matrix" in which the vectors have been imbedded, and which is determined by the deformation of any three non-coplanar vectors.

The formula (4.4) which relates the volumes spanned by $\mathbf{u}, \mathbf{v}, \mathbf{w}$ and $\mathbf{a}, \mathbf{b}, \mathbf{c}$ can be extended by considering other combinations of the vectors. Specifically, we find that

$$\begin{aligned} [\mathbf{uvw}]\,\mathrm{I}_{\mathbf{T}} &= [\mathbf{avw}] + [\mathbf{ubw}] + [\mathbf{uvc}], \\ [\mathbf{uvw}]\,\mathrm{II}_{\mathbf{T}} &= [\mathbf{abw}] + [\mathbf{avc}] + [\mathbf{ubc}], \\ [\mathbf{uvw}]\,\mathrm{III}_{\mathbf{T}} &= [\mathbf{abc}], \end{aligned} \tag{4.7}$$

where $\mathrm{I}_{\mathbf{T}}$, $\mathrm{II}_{\mathbf{T}}$, $\mathrm{III}_{\mathbf{T}}$, called the *principal invariants* of $\mathbf{T}$, are given by

$$\begin{aligned} \mathrm{I}_{\mathbf{T}} &= \mathrm{tr}\mathbf{T} = \mathrm{T}_{11} + T_{22} + T_{33}, \\ \mathrm{II}_{\mathbf{T}} &= \det\mathbf{T}\,\mathrm{tr}\mathbf{T}^{-1} = ((\mathbf{T}^{-1})_{11} + (\mathbf{T}^{-1})_{22} + (\mathbf{T}^{-1})_{33})\det\mathbf{T} \\ &= \begin{vmatrix} T_{22} & T_{23} \\ T_{32} & T_{33} \end{vmatrix} + \begin{vmatrix} T_{11} & T_{13} \\ T_{31} & T_{33} \end{vmatrix} + \begin{vmatrix} T_{11} & T_{12} \\ T_{21} & T_{22} \end{vmatrix}, \\ \mathrm{III}_{\mathbf{T}} &= \det\mathbf{T}. \end{aligned} \tag{4.8}$$

The equivalence of the expressions for $\mathrm{II}_{\mathbf{T}}$ follows from (3.40). In view of $(4.8)_3$, the relation $(4.7)_3$ is merely a restatement of (4.4). To verify $(4.7)_1$, we use (4.2) and (3.12): $T_{ii} = \mathbf{a}\cdot\mathbf{u}^* + \mathbf{b}\cdot\mathbf{v}^* + \mathbf{c}\cdot\mathbf{w}^* = ([\mathbf{avw}] + [\mathbf{bwu}] + [\mathbf{cuv}])/[\mathbf{uvw}]$. To verify $(4.7)_2$ we proceed in the same way, using (4.5), $(4.7)_3$, and (3.12).

The principal invariants of $\mathbf{T}$ are combinations of the components of $\mathbf{T}$ which are invariant to the choice of bases. This is really evident from (4.7), because the relations between the various volumes (scalars!) should be independent of the reference bases used for calculating the volumes. Therefore, the coefficients $\mathrm{I}_{\mathbf{T}}$, $\mathrm{II}_{\mathbf{T}}$, $\mathrm{III}_{\mathbf{T}}$ should come out the same for all bases. However, direct algebraic proofs of this invariance are easily obtained, e.g. $T_{ii} = Q_{ai}Q_{bi}T_{ab} = \delta_{ab}T_{ab} = T_{aa}$.

The invariants of a tensor are not unique, because any scalar function of the invariants is also an invariant. Thus in the place of the principal invariants we may use the *principal moments* $\overline{\mathrm{I}}_{\mathbf{T}}$, $\overline{\mathrm{II}}_{\mathbf{T}}$, $\overline{\mathrm{III}}_{\mathbf{T}}$, defined by

$$\begin{aligned} \overline{\mathrm{I}}_{\mathbf{T}} &= \mathrm{tr}\mathbf{T} = \mathrm{I}_{\mathbf{T}}, \qquad \overline{\mathrm{II}}_{\mathbf{T}} = \mathrm{tr}\mathbf{T}^2 = \mathrm{I}_{\mathbf{T}}^2 - 2\mathrm{II}_{\mathbf{T}}, \\ \overline{\mathrm{III}}_{\mathbf{T}} &= \mathrm{tr}\mathbf{T}^3 = \mathrm{I}_{\mathbf{T}}^3 - 3\mathrm{I}_{\mathbf{T}}\mathrm{II}_{\mathbf{T}} + 3\mathrm{III}_{\mathbf{T}}. \end{aligned} \tag{4.9}$$

We shall leave the determination of the greatest number of independent invariants until later. If it is clear from the context that the invariants are those of a tensor **T**, we omit the labels, thus $\mathrm{I} \equiv \mathrm{I}_{\mathbf{T}}$, $\mathrm{II} \equiv \mathrm{II}_{\mathbf{T}}$, $\mathrm{III} \equiv \mathrm{III}_{\mathbf{T}}$.

For linear associative algebras the existence of a principal unit has the following remarkable consequence, known as the *Cayley-Hamilton equation*:

$$\begin{aligned} \mathbf{T}^3 - \mathrm{I}\mathbf{T}^2 + \mathrm{II}\mathbf{T} - \mathrm{III}\mathbf{1} &= \tilde{\mathbf{0}}, \\ T_{im}T_{mn}T_{nj} - \mathrm{I}T_{im}T_{mj} + \mathrm{II}T_{ij} - \mathrm{III}\delta_{ij} &= 0. \end{aligned} \tag{4.10}$$

A formal proof of (4.10) can be based on the identity $\det(\mathbf{1T} - \mathbf{T1}) \equiv 0$ (cf. [85], p. 346), which we expand in the same way as we would expand $\det(\mathbf{T} - T\mathbf{1})$:

$$\begin{vmatrix} \mathbf{1}T_{11} - \mathbf{T} & \mathbf{1}T_{12} & \mathbf{1}T_{13} \\ \mathbf{1}T_{21} & \mathbf{1}T_{22} - \mathbf{T} & \mathbf{1}T_{23} \\ \mathbf{1}T_{31} & \mathbf{1}T_{32} & \mathbf{1}T_{33} - \mathbf{T} \end{vmatrix} = \tilde{\mathbf{0}}. \tag{4.10)*}$$

A less formal proof of (4.10) is lengthier. We return to (4.7), which hold for arbitrary non-coplanar vectors **u**, **v**, **w**. Comparing the coefficients of the component u_i, for instance, we find from $(4.7)_1$ that $\varepsilon_{mjk}v_jw_k(\mathrm{I}\delta_{im} - T_{im}) = \delta_{im}\varepsilon_{mjk}(T_{nj}v_nw_k + T_{nk}v_jw_n)$. Proceeding in the same manner with $(4.7)_2$, we get $\varepsilon_{ijk}(v_jw_k\mathrm{II} - T_{mj}T_{nk}v_mw_n) = T_{im}\varepsilon_{mjk}(T_{nj}v_nw_k + T_{nk}v_jw_n)$. Eliminating the common factor of the right-hand sides, we obtain after a rearrangement of terms $\varepsilon_{mjk}v_jw_k(\mathrm{I}T_{pm} - T_{pi}T_{im}) = \varepsilon_{pjk}(v_jw_k\mathrm{II} - T_{mj}T_{nk}v_mw_n)$. The equation (4.10) now follows by noting that, as a consequence of $(4.7)_3$, $\varepsilon_{pjk}T_{mj}T_{nk}v_mw_n = T_{ps}^{-1}\mathrm{III}\varepsilon_{sjk}v_jw_k$.

The main consequence of the Cayley-Hamilton equation is that a power $\mathbf{T}^K$, $K \geq 3$, can be expressed as a linear combination of $\mathbf{1}$, $\mathbf{T}$, $\mathbf{T}^2$, with coefficients depending on I, II, III only. For instance, since $\mathbf{T}^3 = \mathrm{I}\mathbf{T}^2 - \mathrm{II}\mathbf{T} + \mathrm{III}\mathbf{1}$, it follows that

$$\mathbf{T}^4 = \mathrm{I}\mathbf{T}^3 - \mathrm{II}\mathbf{T}^2 + \mathrm{III}\mathbf{T} = (\mathrm{I}^2 - \mathrm{II})\mathbf{T}^2 + (\mathrm{III} - \mathrm{I}\,\mathrm{II})\mathbf{T} + \mathrm{I}\,\mathrm{III}\,\mathbf{1}.$$

Reasoning by induction, we arrive at

$$\mathbf{T}^K = c_{\underline{0}}^K\mathbf{1} + c_{\underline{1}}^K\mathbf{T} + c_{\underline{0}}^K\mathbf{T}^2, \qquad K \geq 3, \tag{4.11}$$

where $c_{\underline{i}}^K = c_{\underline{i}}^K(\mathrm{I}, \mathrm{II}, \mathrm{III})$ are polynomial functions of the principal invariants. (K is a label in c_i^K, not an exponent).

Principal values and principal directions; the characteristic equation

We shall now begin a systematic study of second rank tensors. Our aim will be to obtain particular interpretations, as well as other, equivalent descriptions, of the information stored in the nine components of a tensor. Let us see what this task entails for vectors. A vector α is described by its components a_1, a_2, a_3, or, equivalently, in terms of the magnitude $|\alpha| = a$ and the direction $\mathbf{n}$: $\alpha = a\mathbf{n}$. In an orthonormal basis $\mathbf{k}, \mathbf{m}, \mathbf{n}$, the vector α has the following representation: $\|\bar{\alpha}\|^T = \|0, 0, a\|$. The magnitude a is an invariant of α (in fact, the only invariant of α); that is, a represents a "real" physical quantity that is found to be the same no matter what reference frame is used for its calculation. The direction $\mathbf{n}$, on the other hand, is not an invariant: the observed orientation of $\mathbf{n}$ depends on the orientation of the reference basis. To put it even more simply: *invariants are scalars*, $\mathbf{n}$ *is a vector.*

In the case of second rank tensors we again seek special directions, called the *principal directions*, and special components, called the *principal values*. Here a motivation is provided by the tensors for which the saturated forms, e.g. $c_{ij}dx_idx_j$, define the equation of an ellipsoid. An ellipsoid contains three invariant magnitudes, the lengths of its axes. Correspondingly, we expect to obtain from c_{ij} a set of three invariants, the principal values $c_{\underline{1}}, c_{\underline{2}}, c_{\underline{3}}$ (or, equivalently, $\mathrm{I_c}$, $\mathrm{II_c}$, $\mathrm{III_c}$!). The axes of the ellipsoid define the principal directions of the associated symmetric tensor. The principal directions, although an essential part of the make-up of the tensor, are not invariants, because the observed orientation of an ellipsoid depends on the orientation of the reference frame.

The precise definition of principal values and principal directions is as follows:†

A unit vector $\mathbf{n}$ is said to be a principal vector of a second rank tensor $\mathbf{T}$, and T the corresponding principal value of $\mathbf{T}$, if

$$\begin{aligned} \mathbf{Tn} &= T\mathbf{n}, \\ T_{ij}n_j &= Tn_i. \end{aligned} \tag{4.12}$$

The axis of $\mathbf{n}$ is called a *principal direction* of $\mathbf{T}$, and the plane normal to $\mathbf{n}$ a *principal plane*.

We note that the principal vectors cannot be assigned uniquely, because if $\mathbf{n}$ satisfies (4.12) then so does $-\mathbf{n}$. Also, (4.12) simply states that the axis of $\mathbf{n}$ is an *invariant direction of the tensor* $\mathbf{T}$; that is, $\mathbf{T}$ operating on $\mathbf{n}$ does not turn $\mathbf{n}$ but merely "stretches" it into $T\mathbf{n}$. Other interpretations of (4.12) will be

† Principal values are also called proper numbers, characteristic values, and eigenvalues.

obtained from the actual determination of the principal values and the principal directions.

Let us pause for a moment to note an important extension of (4.12): $\mathbf{T}^2\mathbf{n} = T\mathbf{T}\mathbf{n} = T^2\mathbf{n}$, etc.; similarly, if $\det\mathbf{T} \neq 0$, then $\mathbf{T}^{-1}\mathbf{T}\mathbf{n} = \mathbf{n} = T\mathbf{T}^{-1}\mathbf{n}$ etc. Therefore, *if* **n** *is a principal vector of a* (non-singular) *tensor* **T**, *and* T *the principal value associated with* **n**, *then* **n** *is also a principal vector of* $\mathbf{T}^K$, *and* T^K *the principal value associated with* **n**,

$$\mathbf{T}^K\mathbf{n} = T^K\mathbf{n}. \tag{4.13}$$

In order to prove that principal directions exist, it is necessary to show that $\mathbf{T}\mathbf{n} = T\mathbf{n}$ yields real solutions for **n**, the trivial solution $\mathbf{n} = \mathbf{0}$ being excluded by the normalizing condition

$$\mathbf{n} \cdot \mathbf{n} = n_i n_i = 1. \tag{4.14}$$

A nontrivial solution **n** of the homogeneous equations

$$\begin{gathered}(\mathbf{T} - T\mathbf{1})\mathbf{n} = \mathbf{0}, \\ (T_{ij} - T\delta_{ij})n_j = 0\end{gathered} \tag{4.15}$$

exists, however, only if the determinant of the coefficients vanishes:

$$\det(\mathbf{T} - T\mathbf{1}) = \begin{vmatrix} T_{11} - T & T_{12} & T_{13} \\ T_{21} & T_{22} - T & T_{23} \\ T_{31} & T_{32} & T_{33} - T \end{vmatrix} = 0. \tag{4.16}$$

Using (4.8), the expanded determinant can be put into the following form, called the *characteristic equation* of **T**,

$$-T^3 + \mathrm{I}T^2 - \mathrm{II}T + \mathrm{III} = 0, \tag{4.17}$$

where I, II, III are the principal invariants of **T**. It is a rather curious fact that, whereas the characteristic equation (4.17) is satisfied only by particular scalars T associated with **T**, the tensor **T** itself always satisfies the analogous Cayley-Hamilton equation (4.10): $-\mathbf{T}^3 + \mathrm{I}\mathbf{T}^2 - \mathrm{II}\mathbf{T} + \mathrm{III}\mathbf{1} = \tilde{\mathbf{0}}$.†

Being a cubic, the characteristic equation has certainly one real root T, and, associated with T, a principal vector **n**. The other two roots are in general complex, hence we shall continue to study (4.17) only in the special cases

† Hence the phrase "A second rank tensor satisfies its own characteristic equation."

when **T** is either orthogonal or symmetric. The case of skew-symmetric tensors is trivial; for basis transformations that are orientation-preserving, skew-symmetric tensors A_{ij} may be replaced by ("axial") vectors A_i as follows,

$$A_{ij} = -\varepsilon_{ijk}A_k, \qquad A_k = -\frac{1}{2}\varepsilon_{kij}A_{ij}. \tag{4.18}$$

Alternatively, we may let

$$A_{ij} = \varepsilon_{ijk}\alpha_k, \qquad \alpha_k = \frac{1}{2}\varepsilon_{kij}A_{ij}. \tag{4.19}$$

The reason for introducing two alternative definitions has to do with there being two versions of formulas involving cross products, e.g. $\mathbf{M} = \mathbf{x} \times \mathbf{F}$, $\dot{\mathbf{x}} = \boldsymbol{\omega} \times \mathbf{x}$ (cf. (7.46)). In any case, we have that $A_iA_i = \alpha_i\alpha_i = \frac{1}{2}A_{mn}A_{mn}$ is the only independent invariant. Moreover, from $A_{ij}n_j = An_i$ it follows that $A_{ij}n_in_j = A = 0$, but this in turn implies $A_{ij}n_j = -\varepsilon_{ijk}A_kn_j = 0$. Therefore, the direction of α is a principal direction of **A** (the corresponding principal value A being zero).

Orthogonal tensors†

An *orthogonal tensor* **R** is defined by

$$\mathbf{R}^{-1} = \mathbf{R}^T, \tag{4.20}$$

thus

$$\mathbf{R}\mathbf{R}^T = \mathbf{R}^T\mathbf{R} = \mathbf{1}, \qquad \det\mathbf{R} = \pm 1. \tag{4.21}$$

Let us recall that the characteristic equation (4.17) has at least one real root. We denote it by R, and let **n** be the associated principal vector. Multiplying together $R_{ij}n_j = Rn_i$ and $R_{ik}n_k = Rn_i$, then taking into account $(4.21)_1$, we get that $R^2 = 1$, thus

$$R = \pm 1. \tag{4.22}$$

As the next step, we transform **R** to a new basis (a) in which the base vector $\mathbf{n}_3 = Q_{3i}\mathbf{e}_i$ ($\mathbf{e}_i$ being some reference basis) is the principal vector **n** associated with the principal value R. From $R_{ij}Q_{3j} = RQ_{3i}$, $R_{b3} = R_{ij}Q_{3j}Q_{bi} = RQ_{3i}Q_{bi} = R\delta_{3b}$ we conclude that $R_{13} = R_{23} = 0$. Using this in conjunction with the orthogonality conditions $R_{a1}R_{a3} = 0$, $R_{a2}R_{a3} = 0$, we find that also R_{31}

† Orthogonal tensors were previously encountered in (2.23)–(2.31).

$= R_{32} = 0$. Consequently, in the (*a*) frame $\mathbf{R}$ has the reduced representation $\overline{\mathbf{R}}$ given by

$$\|\overline{\mathbf{R}}\| = \begin{Vmatrix} R_{11} & R_{12} & 0 \\ R_{21} & R_{22} & 0 \\ 0 & 0 & R \end{Vmatrix}.$$

The remaining orthogonality conditions contained in $(4.21)_1$ are $(R_{11})^2 + (R_{12})^2 = 1$, $R_{11}R_{21} + R_{12}R_{22} = 0$, $(R_{21})^2 + (R_{22})^2 = 1$. Together with $\det\mathbf{R} = R(R_{11}R_{22} - R_{12}R_{21}) = \pm 1$, they suggest the following representations of $\mathbf{R}$:

Case I: Pure rotation ($R = 1$, $\det\mathbf{R} = 1$)

$$\|\overline{\mathbf{R}}\| = \begin{Vmatrix} \cos\phi & -\sin\phi & 0 \\ \sin\phi & \cos\phi & 0 \\ 0 & 0 & 1 \end{Vmatrix}. \tag{4.23}$$

The particular choice $R_{11} = R_{22} = \cos\phi$, $R_{21} = -R_{12} = \sin\phi$ corresponds to a rotation through ϕ degrees about the axis of $\mathbf{n}_3$ (the rotation is counterclockwise when viewed along the axis of $\mathbf{n}_3$ towards the origin of the reference frame) (cf. the example (4.27)).

The remaining principal values of $\mathbf{R}$ are complex conjugate, $R = e^{\pm i\phi}$, so that we may speak of *the* principal plane. Evidently $\mathbf{R}$ can be reduced to the familiar matrix of plane rotations, *provided that the plane in question is the principal plane of* $\mathbf{R}$.

Case II: Rotation and reflection ($R = -1$, $\det\mathbf{R} = -1$)

$$\|\overline{\mathbf{R}}\| = \begin{Vmatrix} \cos\phi & -\sin\phi & 0 \\ \sin\phi & \cos\phi & 0 \\ 0 & 0 & -1 \end{Vmatrix}. \tag{4.24}$$

In particular, pure reflections of the x, y, and z axes, respectively, are

$$\operatorname{diag}(-1, 1, 1), \quad \operatorname{diag}(1, -1, 1), \quad \operatorname{diag}(1, 1, -1). \tag{4.25}$$

If the signs of the principal value R and of $\det\mathbf{R}$ are taken to be opposite, no new results are obtained, because the representation $\overline{\mathbf{R}}$ is then a combination of representations obtained in (4.23) and (4.25).

The reduced representations (4.23), (4.24) hold only if the reference frame

$\mathbf{n}_1, \mathbf{n}_2, \mathbf{n}_3$ is such that $\mathbf{n}_3 = \mathbf{n}$ is a principal vector. Other, equivalent representations can be obtained by re-labeling of the axes. For instance, if y axis is a principal direction, we let $\mathbf{1} \rightarrow z$, $\mathbf{2} \rightarrow x$, $\mathbf{3} \rightarrow y$, hence in the xyz frame $\mathbf{R}$ is given by

$$\|\overline{\mathbf{R}}\| = \begin{Vmatrix} \cos\phi & 0 & \sin\phi \\ 0 & 1 & 0 \\ -\sin\phi & 0 & \cos\phi \end{Vmatrix}.$$

An orthogonal tensor $\mathbf{R}$ has only one invariant, which may be taken to be the angle ϕ. If it is preferable to use invariants that are rational functions of the tensor components, then we can take†

$$\mathrm{I}_{\mathbf{R}} = \mathrm{II}_{\mathbf{R}} = 2\cos\phi \pm 1, \tag{4.26}$$

for instance. The third principal invariant is of course a constant: $\mathrm{III}_{\mathbf{R}} = \det\mathbf{R} = \pm 1$.

Let us now consider $\mathbf{R}$ as a linear mapping of vectors: $\mathbf{x} = \mathbf{R}\mathbf{X}$. We first note that $\mathbf{R}$ leaves the magnitudes of vectors unchanged: $x_i x_i = R_{ij} R_{ik} X_j X_k = R^T_{ji} R_{ik} X_j X_k = X_k X_k$. Second, if $\mathbf{R}$ is given by (4.23), there exists only one vector $\mathbf{n}$ whose *direction* is left unchanged by $\mathbf{R}$. Therefore, it is natural to interpret $\mathbf{R}$ as describing a rotation of ϕ degrees about the axis of $\mathbf{n}$. The composition of two rotations $(\phi, \mathbf{n})$ and $(\phi', \mathbf{n}')$ is described by the product of the associated orthogonal tensors: if $\mathbf{x}' = \mathbf{R}'\mathbf{x}$, $\mathbf{x} = \mathbf{R}\mathbf{X}$, then $\mathbf{x}' = \mathbf{R}'\mathbf{R}\mathbf{X}$.

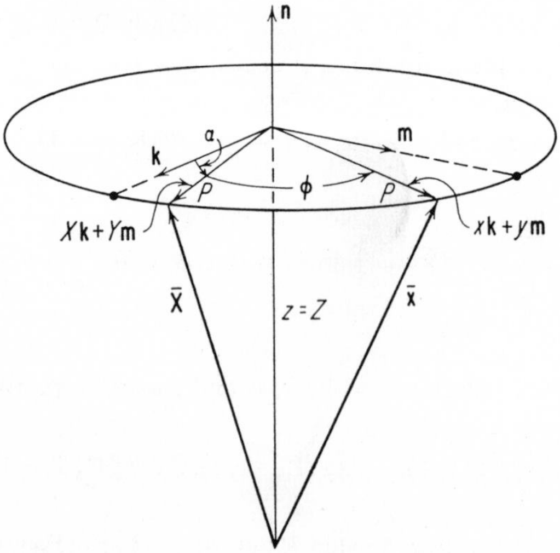

FIGURE 4.1 Finite rotation of a vector $\overline{\mathbf{X}}$ into the vector $\overline{\mathbf{x}}$.

† The values of the invariants are, of course, independent of the reference basis in which they are calculated.

Let $\mathbf{n}_1 = \mathbf{k}$, $\mathbf{n}_2 = \mathbf{m}$, $\mathbf{n}_3 = \mathbf{n}$, $\bar{\mathbf{X}} = X\mathbf{k} + Y\mathbf{m} + Z\mathbf{n}$, $\bar{\mathbf{x}} = x\mathbf{k} + y\mathbf{m} + z\mathbf{n}$. Using $\bar{\mathbf{x}} = \overline{\mathbf{R}\mathbf{X}}$ and (4.23), we obtain

$$\begin{aligned} x &= X\cos\phi - Y\sin\phi = P\cos(\alpha + \phi), \\ y &= X\sin\phi + Y\cos\phi = P\sin(\alpha + \phi), \\ z &= Z, \end{aligned} \tag{4.27}$$

where we have let $X = P\cos\alpha$, $Y = P\sin\alpha$. The finite rotation which takes $\bar{\mathbf{X}}$ into $\bar{\mathbf{x}}$ is illustrated in Figure 4.1.

Orthogonal tensors frequently occur in connection with rotations of orthonormal triads **K**, **M**, **N** into other orthonormal triads **k**, **m**, **n**. Let us collect here certain formulas which will be used time and again. Recalling (4.2), we obtain the following representation of orthogonal tensors,

$$\mathbf{R} = \mathbf{kK} + \mathbf{mM} + \mathbf{nN}, \tag{4.28}$$

so that

$$k_i = R_{ij}K_j, \qquad m_i = R_{ij}M_m, \qquad n_i = R_{ij}N_j. \tag{4.29}$$

In particular, the case of no rotation (i.e. when $\mathbf{R} = \mathbf{1}$) yields the relations

$$\delta_{ij} = K_iK_j + M_iM_j + N_iN_j = k_ik_j + m_im_j + n_in_j \tag{4.30}$$

(cf. (4.6)). If the rotation is about the axis of **N** (i.e. $\mathbf{n} = \mathbf{N}$), for instance, then (4.28) reduces to

$$\mathbf{R} = \mathbf{kK} + \mathbf{mM} + \mathbf{NN}. \tag{4.31}$$

The preceding formulas can be expressed more compactly by renaming **K**, **M**, **N** as the *director triad* $\mathbf{D}_a$, $a = \mathbf{1}, \mathbf{2}, \mathbf{3}$,† and **k**, **m**, **n** as the director triad $\mathbf{d}_a$, $a = \mathbf{1}, \mathbf{2}, \mathbf{3}$. In addition, we introduce a *common frame* of reference ("laboratory frame"), $\mathbf{e}_i$, $i = 1, 2, 3$, and let

$$\begin{aligned} \mathbf{d}_a = d_{ai}\mathbf{e}_i, \qquad \mathbf{D}_a = D_{ai}\mathbf{e}_i, \\ \mathbf{e}_i = d_{ai}\mathbf{d}_a = D_{ai}\mathbf{D}_a \end{aligned} \tag{4.32}$$

(Schouten's notation!). The direction cosines d_{ai} and D_{ai} constitute orthogonal tensors, of course. The orthonormality conditions $\mathbf{k}\cdot\mathbf{k} = 1$, $\mathbf{k}\cdot\mathbf{m} = 0$, etc. now read

$$\mathbf{d}_a\cdot\mathbf{d}_b = d_{ai}d_{bi} = \delta_{ab}, \qquad \mathbf{D}_a\cdot\mathbf{D}_b = D_{ai}D_{bi} = \delta_{ab}, \tag{4.33}$$

whereas the counterparts of (4.30) are given by

$$\mathbf{e}_i\cdot\mathbf{e}_j = \delta_{ij} = d_{ai}d_{aj} = D_{ai}D_{aj}. \tag{4.30*}$$

† The indices assigned to the director triads are a, b, c, . . . , h.

Further, the counterparts of (4.28), (4.29) are given by

$$R_{ij} = d_{ai}D_{aj}, \qquad d_{bi} = R_{ij}D_{bj}. \tag{4.34}$$

Those who prefer the conventional notation may replace $\mathbf{d}_a$, $\mathbf{D}_a$ by $\mathbf{d}_m$, $\mathbf{D}_m$, and (4.32) by $\mathbf{d}_m = Q_{mi}\mathbf{e}_i$, $\mathbf{D}_m = P_{mi}\mathbf{e}_i$, $\mathbf{e}_i = Q^T_{im}\mathbf{d}_m = P^T_{im}\mathbf{D}_m$. Then (4.33) (4.30)* become, respectively, $\mathbf{QQ}^T = \mathbf{1}$, $\mathbf{PP}^T = \mathbf{1}$, $\mathbf{1} = \mathbf{Q}^T\mathbf{Q} = \mathbf{P}^T\mathbf{P}$. Finally, (4.34) is represented by

$$\mathbf{R} = \mathbf{Q}^T\mathbf{P} \tag{4.35}$$

(the second of (4.34) is now an obvious consequence of the first: $\mathbf{R}^T = \mathbf{P}^T\mathbf{Q}$, thus $\mathbf{Q} = \mathbf{PR}^T$).

The representation (4.31) can be put into the following, equivalent form:

$$R_{ij} = N_iN_j - \varepsilon_{ijk}N_k \sin\alpha + (\delta_{ij} - N_iN_j)\cos\alpha, \tag{4.31*}$$

where α is the angle of rotation about the axis of $\mathbf{N}$. Now, $\mathbf{R}$ admits a reduced representation of the form (4.23) only if $\mathbf{N}$ belongs to the reference basis. Therefore, $\mathbf{R}$ should be represented in the director frame by

$$\|\overline{\mathbf{R}}\| = \begin{Vmatrix} \cos\alpha & -\sin\alpha & 0 \\ \sin\alpha & \cos\alpha & 0 \\ 0 & 0 & 1 \end{Vmatrix}.$$

The components in this representation are $R_{ab} \equiv D_{ai}D_{bj}R_{ij}$ (note that, by (4.34), $d_{ai}d_{bj}R_{ij} = R_{im}D_{am}R_{jn}D_{bn}R_{ij} = \delta_{mj}D_{am}R_{jn}D_{bn} = D_{am}D_{bn}R_{mn} = R_{ab}$!). Moreover, according to (4.34), this representation is equivalent to $R_{ab} = D_{ai}d_{bi}$. Multiplying this by D_{ak}, we find that, by (4.30)*,

$$d_{bk} = R_{ab}D_{ak}. \tag{4.36}$$

In the more explicit notation this reads as follows,

$$\begin{aligned} k_i &= R_{11}K_i + R_{21}M_i + R_{31}N_i = K_i\cos\alpha + M_i\sin\alpha, \\ m_i &= R_{12}K_i + R_{22}M_i + R_{32}N_i = -K_i\sin\alpha + M_i\cos\alpha, \\ n_i &= R_{13}K_i + R_{23}M_i + R_{33}N_i = N_i. \end{aligned}$$

Substituting this into (4.31), we get $R_{ij} = (K_iK_j + M_iM_j)\cos\alpha - (K_iM_j - M_iK_j)\sin\alpha + N_iN_j$. It remains to eliminate $K_iK_j + M_iM_j$ by using (4.30): $K_iK_j + M_iM_j = \delta_{ij} - N_iN_j$.

Symmetric tensors

Let **C** be a typical symmetric tensor. We again recall that the characteristic equation (4.17) has at least one real root. We denote this root by C and the associated principal vector by **n**. Next, we introduce a new basis (α), $\alpha = \underline{1}, \underline{2}, \underline{3}$, such that $\mathbf{n}_{\underline{3}} = \mathbf{n}$. Then $C_{\beta\underline{3}} = C_{\underline{3}\beta} = Q_{\beta i} Q_{\underline{3}j} C_{ij} = C Q_{\underline{3}i} Q_{\beta i} = C\delta_{\underline{3}\beta}$, hence the representation $\bar{\bar{\mathbf{C}}}$ in the (α) basis is given by

$$\|\bar{\bar{\mathbf{C}}}\| = \begin{Vmatrix} C_{\underline{11}} & C_{\underline{12}} & 0 \\ C_{\underline{21}} & C_{\underline{22}} & 0 \\ 0 & 0 & C_{\underline{33}} \end{Vmatrix}.$$

The characteristic equation $\det(\bar{\bar{\mathbf{C}}} - C\mathbf{1}) = 0$ can now be factored, and we obtain the explicit solutions

$$C_{\underline{33}} = C,$$
$$C_{\underline{1},\underline{2}} = \frac{1}{2}\left[(C_{\underline{11}} + C_{\underline{22}}) \pm \sqrt{(C_{\underline{11}} - C_{\underline{22}})^2 + 4C_{\underline{12}}C_{\underline{21}}}\,\right]. \tag{4.37}$$

From the symmetry condition $C_{\underline{12}} = C_{\underline{21}}$ it follows that the expression under the square-root consists of a sum of two squares; thus we have shown that *the principal values of symmetric second rank tensors are always real.*

Let us also show that the *principal directions associated with distinct principal values are orthogonal.* If **m** and **n** are the principal vectors associated with the principal values B and C, respectively, then, by (4.12), $C_{ik}m_k = Bm_i$, $C_{ik}n_k = Cn_i$. Starting with the first of these, we write $Bm_in_i = C_{ik}m_kn_i = C_{ki}m_in_k = C_{ik}m_in_k = Cm_in_i$, where the second step is obtained by interchanging the summation indices i and k, and the third step uses the symmetry of **C**. Thus $(B - C)\mathbf{m} \cdot \mathbf{n} = 0$, hence $B \neq C$ implies $\mathbf{m} \cdot \mathbf{n} = 0$. As is evident from the proof, this result need not be true for asymmetric tensors.

If, for instance, $C_{\underline{3}} \neq C_{\underline{1}} = C_{\underline{2}}$, then $(4.37)_2$ implies that $C_{\underline{11}} = C_{\underline{22}}$, $C_{\underline{12}} = 0$, i.e. $\mathbf{n}_{\underline{1}}$ and $\mathbf{n}_{\underline{2}}$ are principal vectors. Because these vectors were arbitrary, except for being orthogonal to $\mathbf{n}_{\underline{3}} = \mathbf{n}$, it follows that in this case any direction orthogonal to **n** is a principal direction. Finally, if all principal values are equal, then every direction is a principal direction. In any case it is possible to select an orthonormal triad of principal vectors which then defines a *principal coordinate system* (a) of **C**, $a = \mathbf{1}, \mathbf{2}, \mathbf{3}$; if the principal values of **C** are distinct, then the principal coordinate system of **C** is uniquely determined. In the (*a*) coordinate system **C** has the diagonal representation

$$\|\bar{\mathbf{C}}\| = \operatorname{diag}(C_{\underline{1}}, C_{\underline{2}}, C_{\underline{3}}). \tag{4.38}$$

Using (4.38), we can obtain particularly simple representations of the principal invariants and the principal moments:

$$\begin{aligned} \mathrm{I}_{\mathbf{C}} &= C_{\underline{1}} + C_{\underline{2}} + C_{\underline{3}}, \qquad \mathrm{II}_{\mathbf{C}} = C_{\underline{1}}C_{\underline{2}} + C_{\underline{2}}C_{\underline{3}} + C_{\underline{3}}C_{\underline{1}}, \\ \mathrm{III}_{\mathbf{C}} &= C_{\underline{1}}C_{\underline{2}}C_{\underline{3}}, \\ \bar{\mathrm{I}}_{\mathbf{C}} &= C_{\underline{1}} + C_{\underline{2}} + C_{\underline{3}}, \qquad \overline{\mathrm{II}}_{\mathbf{C}} = (C_{\underline{1}})^2 + (C_{\underline{2}})^3 + (C_{\underline{3}})^2, \\ \overline{\mathrm{III}}_{\mathbf{C}} &= (C_{\underline{1}})^3 + (C_{\underline{2}})^3 + (C_{\underline{3}})^3. \end{aligned} \tag{4.39}$$

Let us illustrate the calculation of the principal values and the principal directions for

$$\|\mathbf{C}\| = \begin{Vmatrix} -2 & 2 & 10 \\ 2 & -11 & 8 \\ 10 & 8 & -5 \end{Vmatrix}.$$

The characteristic equation is then

$$\begin{vmatrix} -2 - C & 2 & 10 \\ 2 & -11 - C & 8 \\ 10 & 8 & -5 - C \end{vmatrix} = (C - 9)(C + 9)(C + 18) = 0.$$

Substituting the principal value $C = 9$ into $C_{ij}k_j = Ck_i$, we obtain the following system of equations: $-11k_1 + 2k_2 + 10k_3 = 0$, $2k_1 - 20k_2 + 8k_3 = 0$, $10k_1 + 8k_2 - 14k_3 = 0$. Because the determinant of the coefficients vanishes (this determinant being the characteristic equation for the case when $C = 9$), there are only two linearly independent equations in the above system. For instance, adding the second equation multiplied by one-half to the last equation we get the negative of the first equation. Therefore, in the place of one of the equations it is necessary to use the condition $\mathbf{k} \cdot \mathbf{k} = 1$. This will require at some stage the extraction of a square-root, so that we shall have to choose between plus and minus signs. This means that the principal vectors cannot be assigned to the principal directions in a unique way; however, the choice of signs must be such as to make the principal coordinate system a right-handed one ($\mathbf{n}_3 = \mathbf{n}_1 \times \mathbf{n}_2$). In the present case we use the first two equations to obtain $k_1 = k_3$, $k_2 = \frac{1}{2}k_3$. Then from $\mathbf{k} \cdot \mathbf{k} = 1$ it follows that $k_3 = \pm\frac{2}{3}$. We choose the plus sign, so that **k** lies in the first octant: $\mathbf{k} = \frac{2}{3}\mathbf{e}_1 + \frac{1}{3}\mathbf{e}_2 + \frac{2}{3}\mathbf{e}_3$. In the same way we determine the principal vector **m** associated with the principal value $C = -9$, $\mathbf{m} = -\frac{2}{3}\mathbf{e}_1 + \frac{2}{3}\mathbf{e}_2 + \frac{1}{3}\mathbf{e}_3$, and the principal vector **n** associated with the principal value $C = -18$, $\mathbf{n} = -\frac{1}{3}\mathbf{e}_1 - \frac{2}{3}\mathbf{e}_2 + \frac{2}{3}\mathbf{e}_3$. If the principal vectors are renamed as follows, $\mathbf{k} = \mathbf{n}_1$, $\mathbf{m} = \mathbf{n}_2$, $\mathbf{n} = \mathbf{n}_3$, then the principal vectors can be described by

$$\mathbf{n}_a = Q_{ai}\mathbf{e}_i,$$

where
$$\|Q_{ai}\| = \frac{1}{3}\begin{Vmatrix} 2 & 1 & 2 \\ -2 & 2 & 1 \\ -1 & -2 & 2 \end{Vmatrix}.$$

Moreover, the calculation of the principal values can be viewed as the "diagonalization" of **C**:†

$$\overline{\mathbf{C}} = \mathbf{QCQ}^T,$$

$$\begin{Vmatrix} 9 & 0 & 0 \\ 0 & -9 & 0 \\ 0 & 0 & -18 \end{Vmatrix} = \frac{1}{9}\begin{Vmatrix} 2 & 1 & 2 \\ -2 & 2 & 1 \\ -1 & -2 & 2 \end{Vmatrix}\begin{Vmatrix} -2 & 2 & 10 \\ 2 & -11 & 8 \\ 10 & 8 & -5 \end{Vmatrix}\begin{Vmatrix} 2 & -2 & -1 \\ 1 & 2 & -2 \\ 2 & 1 & 2 \end{Vmatrix}.$$

It is not difficult to see that relations of the type (4.12), (4.13) are merely disguised transformation formulas. Denoting the principal vectors by $\mathbf{n}_a = Q_{ai}\mathbf{e}_i$, we rewrite $\mathbf{Cn} = C\mathbf{n}$ as follows, $C_{ij}Q_{bj} = C_{\underline{b}}Q_{bi}$, so that

$$C_{ab} = Q_{ai}Q_{bj}C_{ij} = C_{\underline{b}}Q_{ai}Q_{bi} = C_{\underline{b}}\delta_{ab} \tag{4.40}$$

(as explained on p. 17, this notation does *not* imply summation over b). Similarly,

$$C_{ij} = Q_{ib}Q_{jb}C_{\underline{b}}, \qquad C^K_{ij} = Q_{ib}Q_{jb}C^K_{\underline{b}}, \tag{4.41}$$

where b is now a summation index. One may prefer to express (4.41) in a less compact form, in which case one should return to the notations **k**, **m**, **n** for the principal vectors:

$$\mathbf{C} = C_{\underline{1}}\mathbf{kk} + C_{\underline{2}}\mathbf{mm} + C_{\underline{3}}\mathbf{nn}, \tag{4.42}$$

and
$$\mathbf{C}^K = C^K_{\underline{1}}\mathbf{kk} + C^K_{\underline{2}}\mathbf{mm} + C^K_{\underline{3}}\mathbf{nn}. \tag{4.43}$$

† This is the usual terminology of *matrix algebra*. There it is traditional to introduce matrices without any reference to coordinate systems, so that many tensor operations appear under different names, e.g. a transformation formula $\overline{\mathbf{C}} = \mathbf{QCQ}^T$ is known as a "similarity transformation."

Roughly speaking, the representations (4.42) and (4.43) are the counterpart of the representation $a_i = |\alpha| n_i$ for vectors, the principal values being the counterparts of the magnitude $|\alpha|$.

If all principal values of **C** are the same, then, by (4.30), the representation (4.42) reduces to

$$C_{ij} = C\delta_{ij}. \tag{4.44}$$

If $C_{\underline{1}} = C_{\underline{2}} = C \neq C_{\underline{3}}$, then from the identity $C_{ij} = C(k_i k_j + m_i m_j + n_i n_j) + (C_{\underline{3}} - C) n_i n_j$, and (4.30), it follows that

$$C_{ij} = C\delta_{ij} + (C_{\underline{3}} - C) n_i n_j. \tag{4.45}$$

For symmetric tensors the Cayley-Hamilton equation $\mathbf{C}^3 - \mathrm{I}\mathbf{C}^2 + \mathrm{II}\mathbf{C} - \mathrm{III}\mathbf{1} = \tilde{\mathbf{0}}$ can be derived from the characteristic equation, $C_{\underline{b}}^3 - \mathrm{I}C_{\underline{b}}^2 + \mathrm{II}C_{\underline{b}} - \mathrm{III} = 0$, by multiplying the latter with $Q_{ib}Q_{jb}$, then taking into account (4.41).

If the principal values $C_{\underline{b}}$ are positive, then the exponents in (4.43) can be arbitrary real numbers. We distinguish *positive tensors* and *positive definite tensors*; a tensor **T** is said to be positive if it has positive principal values and three linearly independent principal vectors. Positive tensors are said to be positive definite if they are also coefficients of positive definite quadratic forms. In particular, a positive *symmetric* tensor **C** is also positive definite. To prove this we merely note that in the principal coordinate system of **C** the quadratic form specified by **C** reduces to a sum of squares with the principal values $C_{\underline{b}}$ as coefficients. Therefore, the quadratic form will be positive definite if the principal values are positive, and vice versa.

We illustrate the calculation of $\sqrt{\mathbf{C}}$ for

$$\|\mathbf{C}\| = \begin{Vmatrix} 3 & 2 & 0 \\ 2 & 3 & 0 \\ 0 & 0 & 9 \end{Vmatrix}.$$

As the first step we determine the principal values and principal directions of **C**. We obtain

$$\|\bar{\mathbf{C}}\| = \begin{Vmatrix} 1 & 0 & 0 \\ 0 & 5 & 0 \\ 0 & 0 & 9 \end{Vmatrix}, \qquad \|Q_{ai}\| = \frac{1}{\sqrt{2}} \begin{Vmatrix} 1 & -1 & 0 \\ 1 & 1 & 0 \\ 0 & 0 & \sqrt{2} \end{Vmatrix}.$$

Then
$$\|\sqrt{\bar{\mathbf{C}}}\| = \begin{Vmatrix} 1 & 0 & 0 \\ 0 & \sqrt{5} & 0 \\ 0 & 0 & 3 \end{Vmatrix},$$

and
$$\sqrt{\mathbf{C}} = \mathbf{Q}^T\sqrt{\bar{\mathbf{C}}}\mathbf{Q},$$

$$\|\sqrt{\mathbf{C}}\| = \frac{1}{2}\begin{Vmatrix} \sqrt{5}+1 & \sqrt{5}-1 & 0 \\ \sqrt{5}-1 & \sqrt{5}+1 & 0 \\ 0 & 0 & 6 \end{Vmatrix}$$

$$= \frac{1}{2}\begin{Vmatrix} 1 & 1 & 0 \\ -1 & 1 & 0 \\ 0 & 0 & \sqrt{2} \end{Vmatrix}\begin{Vmatrix} 1 & 0 & 0 \\ 0 & \sqrt{5} & 0 \\ 0 & 0 & 3 \end{Vmatrix}\begin{Vmatrix} 1 & -1 & 0 \\ 1 & 1 & 0 \\ 0 & 0 & \sqrt{2} \end{Vmatrix}.$$

As a check we may use $\sqrt{\mathbf{C}}\sqrt{\mathbf{C}} = \mathbf{C}$.

Extremal properties of symmetric tensors†

In every reference basis a symmetric tensor is represented by the six scalar components. The following questions immediately come to mind: What are the algebraically largest and smallest values that the diagonal components can have, and what is the largest value that the off-diagonal components can have? The answers to these questions must be extracted from the transformation formulas.

Let us consider the diagonal components first. We suppose that the components C_{ij} are known for some reference basis (i). Then

$$N(\mathbf{n}) \equiv C_{\underline{\mathrm{nn}}} = C_{ij}n_in_j \tag{4.46}$$

describes all the diagonal components associated with all directions $\mathbf{n}$. The variables n_i are not independent, however, because they must satisfy the condition $n_in_i = 1$. Therefore, we shall seek the extrema of N by solving

$$\frac{\partial N}{\partial n_i} = 0 \tag{4.47}$$

subject to the constraint $n_in_i - 1 = 0$.

At this point it is necessary to digress to the *method of Lagrange's multipliers.*‡ Let us suppose that we wish to find the extrema of a family of curves

† A more complete discussion is given in [32].
‡ Cf. [21].

$f(x, y) = C$, subject to the constraint condition that these extrema lie on another curve $g(x, y) = 0$ (Figure 4.2).

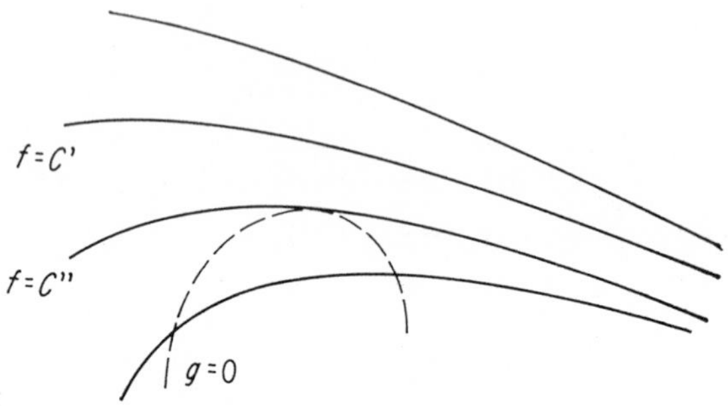

FIGURE 4.2 A maximum of curves $f(x,y) = C$, lying on the curve $g(x,y) = 0$.

Then a geometrical visualization of the problem tells us that f and g must have the same slope at the extremal point (we exclude here the points where slopes are not defined). Hence† $dy/dx = -f_{,x}/f_{,y} = -g_{,x}/g_{,y}$, or, $f_{,x}g_{,y} - f_{,y}g_{,x} = 0$. Denoting the common value of $f_{,y}/g_{,y}$ and $f_{,x}/g_{,x}$ by A, we can write that

$$f_{,i} - Ag_{,i} = 0. \tag{4.48}$$

The two coordinates of the extremal point and the Lagrange's multiplier A can now be determined by solving (4.48) in conjunction with $g(x, y) = 0$.

To find the extrema of surfaces $F(x, y, z) = C$, subject to the constraint $G(x, y, z) = 0$, we again require the equality of slopes: $F_{,x}/F_{,z} = G_{,x}/G_{,z}$, $F_{,y}/F_{,z} = G_{,y}/G_{,z}$, and therefore it follows that $F_{,i} - AG_{,i} = 0$.

Returning to (4.46), (4.47), we now consider

$$\frac{\partial}{\partial n_k}[C_{ij}n_in_j - A(n_in_i - 1)] = 0. \tag{4.49}$$

The given components C_{ij} and the Lagrange's multiplier A do not depend on **n**, hence we find from (4.49) that $C_{ik}n_k = An_i$. These conditions, together with $n_in_i = 1$, provide a system of four equations for A and n_i. But this system is the same as the equations (4.12) defining principal values and principal directions; moreover, the Lagrange's multiplier A is identical with the extremal value of the diagonal elements $C_{\underline{nn}}$: $C_{ik}n_kn_i = An_in_i = A$. If we order the principal values as follows,

$$C_{\underline{1}} \geq C_{\underline{2}} \geq C_{\underline{3}}, \tag{4.50}$$

† Cf. *op. cit.*, p. 114.

then $C_{\underline{1}}$ *is also the algebraically largest diagonal component of* **C**, *and* $C_{\underline{3}}$ *the algebraically smallest diagonal component of* **C**.

The off-diagonal components

$$S = C_{\underline{\mathrm{pq}}} = C_{ij}p_iq_j \tag{4.51}$$

can be investigated in the same way. The extrema of S, subject to the constraints $\mathbf{p}\cdot\mathbf{p} = 1$, $\mathbf{q}\cdot\mathbf{q} = 1$, $\mathbf{p}\cdot\mathbf{q} = 0$, are found from $\partial\phi/\partial p_k = 0$, $\partial\phi/\partial q_k = 0$, where $\phi = [C_{ij}p_iq_j - \frac{1}{2}P(p_ip_i - 1) - \frac{1}{2}Q(q_iq_i - 1) - Rp_iq_i]$. We get

$$C_{ik}p_k = Qq_i + Rp_i, \qquad C_{ik}q_k = Pp_i + Rq_i. \tag{4.52}$$

Multiplying the first expression by q_i and the second by p_i, then taking into account (4.51) and the symmetry of **C**, we find that $P = Q = S$. Next, multiplying the first expression by p_i and the second by q_i, we find that, by (4.46),

$$C_{\underline{\mathrm{pp}}} = C_{\underline{\mathrm{qq}}} = R \equiv \bar{N}.$$

Therefore, an equivalent representation of (4.52) is given by

$$C_{ik}(q_k + p_k) = (\bar{N} + S)(q_i + p_i), \qquad C_{ik}(q_k - p_k) = (\bar{N} - S)(q_i - p_i), \tag{4.53}$$

i.e. $\bar{N} + S$ is the principal value associated with the principal vector $(\mathbf{q} + \mathbf{p})/\sqrt{2}$, whereas $\bar{N} - S$ is the principal value associated with the principal vector $(\mathbf{q} - \mathbf{p})/\sqrt{2}$. With the ordering given by (4.50), the maximum value of S is evidently obtained by letting $\bar{N} + S = C_{\underline{1}}$, $\bar{N} - S = C_{\underline{3}}$, in which case†

$$S = \frac{1}{2}(C_{\underline{1}} - C_{\underline{3}}), \qquad \bar{N} = \frac{1}{2}(C_{\underline{1}} + C_{\underline{3}}). \tag{4.54}$$

If **k** and **n** are the principal vectors associated with $C_{\underline{1}}$ and $C_{\underline{3}}$, respectively then

$$\mathbf{q} = \frac{\mathbf{k} + \mathbf{n}}{\sqrt{2}}, \qquad \mathbf{p} = \frac{\mathbf{k} - \mathbf{n}}{\sqrt{2}}. \tag{4.55}$$

This means that the planes of maximum "shear" S are inclined at 45° to the first and third principal planes.

† These results are often derived by using a geometrical method known as the *Mohr's circles*, [125], pp 50–54.

Let **C** be again a symmetric tensor. Then in its principal coordinate system (a), $a = \underline{1}, \underline{2}, \underline{3}$, we have that $C_{\underline{12}} = C_{\underline{23}} = C_{\underline{31}} = 0$. This result suggests the following question: Does there exist a basis (i), $i = 1, 2, 3$, such that $C_{11} = C_{22} = C_{33} = 0$. The answer will be *no*, in general; but let us first introduce a name for what we are trying to find:

A symmetric second rank tensor **C** is said to describe a *state of pure shear* if there exists a basis (i) such that

$$C_{11} = C_{22} = C_{33} = 0. \tag{4.56}$$

It is not difficult to show that a necessary and sufficient condition for **C** to describe a state of pure shear is that

$$\mathrm{I}_{\mathbf{C}} = \mathrm{tr}\mathbf{C} = 0. \tag{4.57}$$

In view of this theorem a symmetric tensor **C** can be always decomposed into a *spherical part* $\mathbf{C}^S$ and a *pure shear part* $\mathbf{C}^D$ as follows†

$$\mathbf{C}^S = \frac{1}{3}\mathbf{1}\,\mathrm{tr}\mathbf{C}, \qquad \mathbf{C}^D = \mathbf{C} - \mathbf{C}^S. \tag{4.58}$$

The proof of the necessity of (4.57) is trivial: if (4.56) holds, then certainly $\mathrm{tr}\mathbf{C} = C_{11} + C_{22} + C_{33} = 0$. In order to prove the sufficiency of (4.57), we must show that whenever (4.57) holds then

$$C_{\underline{ss}} = C_{\underline{1}}(s_{\underline{1}})^2 + C_{\underline{2}}(s_{\underline{2}})^2 + C_{\underline{3}}(s_{\underline{3}})^2 = 0 \tag{4.59}$$

will have as solutions three orthonormal vectors **s**. If $C_{\underline{2}} = 0$, then these vectors are given by $s_{\underline{2}} = 1$, $s_{\underline{1}} = s_{\underline{3}} = 0$ and $s_{\underline{2}} = 0$, $s_{\underline{1}} = \pm\, s_{\underline{3}}$. If $C_{\underline{2}} \neq 0$, we write $C_{\underline{1}} = A$, $C_{\underline{2}} = B$, $C_{\underline{3}} = -(A + B)$. Since the right-hand side of (4.59) is zero, we can equally well use an orthogonal triad **u**, **v**, **w** in the place of the orthonormal vectors **s**. Then the calculations can be simplified by letting $u_{\underline{3}} = v_{\underline{3}} = w_{\underline{3}} = 1$. We note right away that $u = (1, 1, 1)$ is one solution of (4.59). The vector **v** must now be orthogonal to **u**, $v_{\underline{1}} + v_{\underline{2}} + 1 = 0$, and must satisfy (4.59), $A(v_{\underline{1}})^2 + B(v_{\underline{2}})^2 = A + B$. We obtain

$$(A + B)v_{\underline{1}} = -B + \sqrt{B^2 + A(A + B)}, \quad (A + B)w_{\underline{1}} = -B - \sqrt{B^2 + A(A + B)},$$
$$(A + B)v_{\underline{2}} = -A - \sqrt{B^2 + A(A + B)}, \quad (A + B)w_{\underline{2}} = -A + \sqrt{B^2 + A(A + B)},$$

where $\mathbf{v} \cdot \mathbf{w} = 0$ is satisfied.

† Also called the hydrostatic and deviatoric parts, respectively.

The polar representation of second rank tensors

Symmetric and orthogonal tensors have now been investigated in some detail, but so far we have found out very little about asymmetric tensors. This will be remedied by the *polar representation*,† which expresses a general second rank tensor as a product of a positive symmetric tensor with an orthogonal tensor.

Let **F** be nonsingular, i.e. det**F** $\neq 0$. Then **F** admits the unique representations

$$\mathbf{F} = \mathbf{RU} = \mathbf{VR}, \tag{4.60}$$

also referred to as the right and left decompositions of **F**, respectively, where **U** and **V** are positive symmetric tensors, and **R** is an orthogonal tensor. Evidently

$$\begin{aligned} \mathbf{U}^2 &= \mathbf{F}^T\mathbf{F} \equiv \mathbf{C}, & \mathbf{V}^2 &= \mathbf{F}\mathbf{F}^T \equiv \mathbf{B}, \\ \mathbf{V} &= \mathbf{R}\mathbf{U}\mathbf{R}^T, & \mathbf{B} &= \mathbf{R}\mathbf{C}\mathbf{R}^T. \end{aligned} \tag{4.61}$$

To derive the right decomposition $\mathbf{F} = \mathbf{RU}$, we consider **F** as a mapping that carries a vector $\mathbf{v}$ into a vector $\bar{\mathbf{v}}$: $\bar{v}_i = F_{ij}v_j$. By hypothesis det**F** $\neq 0$, hence $\bar{\mathbf{v}} = \mathbf{0}$ only if $\mathbf{v} = \mathbf{0}$. It follows then that the squared magnitude of $\bar{\mathbf{v}}$ defines a positive definite quadratic form, $|\bar{\mathbf{v}}|^2 = \bar{v}_i\bar{v}_i = F_{ij}F_{ik}v_jv_k = F^T_{ki}F_{ij}v_jv_k$, and that the coefficients $C_{ki} = F^T_{ki}F_{ij}$ constitute a positive definite (symmetric) tensor. Therefore

$$\mathbf{U} \equiv \sqrt{\mathbf{C}} \tag{4.62}$$

is well defined. We now let

$$\mathbf{R} \equiv \mathbf{F}\mathbf{U}^{-1}, \tag{4.63}$$

and verify that **R** is orthogonal: $\mathbf{R}^T\mathbf{R} = (\mathbf{F}\mathbf{U}^{-1})^T(\mathbf{F}\mathbf{U}^{-1}) = \mathbf{U}^{-1}\mathbf{F}^T\mathbf{F}\mathbf{U}^{-1} = \mathbf{U}^{-1}\mathbf{C}\mathbf{U}^{-1} = \mathbf{1}$.

To prove the uniquenes of the decomposition $\mathbf{F} = \mathbf{RU}$, we suppose that $\mathbf{F} = \mathbf{RU} = \bar{\mathbf{R}}\bar{\mathbf{U}}$. Then $\mathbf{F}^T\mathbf{F} = \mathbf{U}^2 = \bar{\mathbf{U}}^2$, hence $\mathbf{U} = \bar{\mathbf{U}}$. The uniqueness of **R** then follows from $\mathbf{RU} = \bar{\mathbf{R}}\bar{\mathbf{U}}$.

The derivation of the left decomposition is entirely analogous. We write, at first, $\mathbf{F} = \mathbf{V}\mathbf{R}^*$ because there is no reason for supposing that $\mathbf{R}^*$ is the same tensor as **R** in $\mathbf{F} = \mathbf{RU}$. However, from $\mathbf{F} = \mathbf{R}^*\mathbf{R}^{*T}\mathbf{V}\mathbf{R}^*$ and from the uniqueness of the right decomposition we can conclude that $\mathbf{R}^* = \mathbf{R}$, $\mathbf{U} = \mathbf{R}^T\mathbf{V}\mathbf{R}$.

† This name presumably derives from a rather tenuous analogy with the polar representation $z = re^{i\theta}$ for complex numbers.

The polar decomposition cannot be expressed by a formula; rather, there is only the prescribed sequence of operations: $\mathbf{F} \to \mathbf{F}^T\mathbf{F} = \mathbf{C}$, $\mathbf{U} = \sqrt{\mathbf{C}}$, $\mathbf{R} = \mathbf{F}\mathbf{U}^{-1}$. This means that, in general, the components of **U** and **R** will be transcendental functions of the components of **F**.

If **K, M, N** are the principal vectors of **U**, then, by (4.42), $U_{mj} = U_{\underline{1}}K_mK_j + U_{\underline{2}}M_mM_j + U_{\underline{3}}N_mN_j$. Let **k, m, n** be the orthonormal triad into which **K, M, N** are mapped by **R**; then, by (4.28), $R_{im} = k_iK_m + m_iM_m + n_iN_m$. Combining the two expressions, we obtain (cf. (4.2))

$$F_{ij} = R_{im}U_{mj} = U_{\underline{1}}k_iK_j + U_{\underline{2}}m_iM_j + U_{\underline{3}}n_iN_j. \tag{4.64}$$

If the two triads are denoted by $\mathbf{n}_a$, $\mathbf{N}_a$, $a = \mathbf{1, 2, 3}$, respectively, then (4.64) may be expressed as $F_{ij} = R_{im}U_{mj} = U_{\underline{a}}n_{ai}N_{aj}$, or as $\phi = F_{ij}\mathbf{e}_i\mathbf{e}_j = U_{\underline{a}}\mathbf{n}_a\mathbf{N}_a$.

Let us illustrate the polar decomposition for

$$\|\mathbf{F}\| = \begin{Vmatrix} \sqrt{3} & 1 & 0 \\ 0 & 2 & 0 \\ 0 & 0 & 1 \end{Vmatrix}.$$

Here **F** can be interpreted as a mapping which relates the initial coordinates X, Y, Z of a particle to its final coordinates x, y, z:

$$\mathbf{x} = \mathbf{F}\mathbf{X},$$

$$x = \sqrt{3}\,X + Y, \qquad y = 2Y, \qquad z = Z.$$

In view of $z = Z$, a mapping of this type can be produced in a biaxial stretching of a rubber sheet. For instance, a circle $X^2 + Y^2 = 1$ drawn on the unstretched sheet will change into the ellipse $x^2 - xy + y^2 = 3$. In a coordinate system $(\bar{x}, \bar{y})$ rotated 45° counterclockwise, this ellipse has the representation $\bar{x}^2/6 + \bar{y}^2/2 = 1$. The polar decomposition of **F** will now yield a "pure deformation" **U** and a rigid rotation **R** of the entire sheet. Under the mapping **U** two orthogonal diameters of the circle $X^2 + Y^2 = 1$ will retain their directions (principal directions of **U**!), but their lengths will change to the lengths of the axes of the ellipse.

We calculate

$$\|\mathbf{C}\| = \|\mathbf{F}^T\mathbf{F}\| = \begin{Vmatrix} 3 & \sqrt{3} & 0 \\ \sqrt{3} & 5 & 0 \\ 0 & 0 & 1 \end{Vmatrix},$$

$$\|\bar{\mathbf{C}}\| = \begin{Vmatrix} 6 & 0 & 0 \\ 0 & 2 & 0 \\ 0 & 0 & 1 \end{Vmatrix}, \qquad \|\bar{\mathbf{U}}\| = \begin{Vmatrix} \sqrt{6} & 0 & 0 \\ 0 & \sqrt{2} & 0 \\ 0 & 0 & 1 \end{Vmatrix},$$

the principal vectors $\mathbf{n}_a$ of $\mathbf{C}$ (and of $\mathbf{U}$) being given by $\mathbf{n}_a = Q_{ai}\mathbf{e}_i$,

$$\|Q_{ai}\| = \begin{Vmatrix} 1/2 & \sqrt{3}/2 & 0 \\ -\sqrt{3}/2 & 1/2 & 0 \\ 0 & 0 & 1 \end{Vmatrix}.$$

Thus $\mathbf{n}_1$ and $\mathbf{n}_2$ make an angle of 60° with the axes of x and y, respectively. Then from $U_{ij} = Q_{ia}Q_{jb}U_{ab}$ it follows that

$$\|\mathbf{U}\| = \|\mathbf{Q}^T\bar{\mathbf{U}}\mathbf{Q}\| = \frac{1}{2\sqrt{2}}\begin{Vmatrix} 3+\sqrt{3} & 3-\sqrt{3} & 0 \\ 3-\sqrt{3} & 1+3\sqrt{3} & 0 \\ 0 & 0 & 2\sqrt{2} \end{Vmatrix}.$$

Moreover, by (3.40), $\|\mathbf{U}^{-1}\| = \dfrac{1}{4\sqrt{6}}\begin{Vmatrix} 1+3\sqrt{3} & -(3-\sqrt{3}) & 0 \\ -(3-\sqrt{3}) & 3+\sqrt{3} & 0 \\ 0 & 0 & 4\sqrt{6} \end{Vmatrix}.$

Finally, $\|\mathbf{R}\| = \|\mathbf{F}\mathbf{U}^{-1}\| = \dfrac{1}{2\sqrt{2}}\begin{vmatrix} \sqrt{3}+1 & \sqrt{3}-1 & 0 \\ 1-\sqrt{3} & \sqrt{3}+1 & 0 \\ 0 & 0 & 2\sqrt{2} \end{vmatrix}.$

Therefore, $\mathbf{R}$ describes a clockwise rotation through 15°. In the case of the left decomposition $\mathbf{F} = \mathbf{VR}$ we find that

$$\|\mathbf{V}\| = \frac{1}{\sqrt{2}}\begin{Vmatrix} \sqrt{3}+1 & \sqrt{3}-1 & 0 \\ \sqrt{3}-1 & \sqrt{3}+1 & 0 \\ 0 & 0 & \sqrt{2} \end{Vmatrix}.$$

The first and second principal vectors of $\mathbf{V}$ make an angle of 45° with the axes of x and y, respectively.

To interpret $\mathbf{F} = \mathbf{RU}$, we write $\mathbf{x} = \mathbf{FX} = \mathbf{R}\bar{\mathbf{X}}$, where $\bar{\mathbf{X}} = \mathbf{UX}$. Here $\mathbf{U}$ maps the unit circle $X^2 + Y^2 = 1$ into an ellipse whose major axis is inclined at 60° to the x axis (Figure 4.3a), the axes of this ellipse coinciding with the principal directions of $\mathbf{U}$. In the second stage, $\mathbf{x} = \mathbf{R}\bar{\mathbf{X}}$ describes a clockwise rotation through 15° of this ellipse into the ellipse whose major axis is inclined at 45° to the x axis. In the case of the left decomposition $\mathbf{x} = \mathbf{FX} = \mathbf{VRX}$, the mapping $\mathbf{R}$ again describes a clockwise rotation through 15°; in particular, a vector originally inclined at 60° to the x axis will then make an angle of 45° with the axis. In the second stage the (rotated) unit circle is mapped by $\mathbf{V}$ into an ellipse whose major axis is inclined at 45° to the x axis (the 45° direction is a principal direction of $\mathbf{V}$!). No matter which decomposition is used, we find that two orthogonal diameters of the unit circle, inclined initially at 60° to the axes of x and y, respectively, will remain orthogonal. The rotation of these diameters is the rotation contained in **F**.

The two modes of decomposition are fully equivalent, differing only in the order in which we imagine the pure deformation and the rotation performed. During an actual stretching of a sheet, pure deformation and rotation will occur simultaneously, of course.

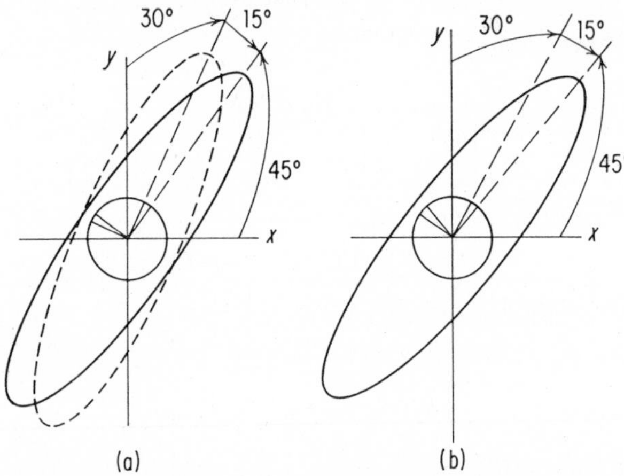

FIGURE 4.3 (a) Right decomposition of **F**: pure deformation (dashed curve) followed by a clockwise rotation through 15°. (b) Left decomposition of **F**: clockwise rotation of the circle through 15°, followed by the pure deformation **V**.

As a matter of curiosity, let us note that $\mathbf{R} = \mathbf{F}\mathbf{U}^{-1}$ implies $\det\mathbf{R} = (\det\mathbf{F})/(\det\mathbf{U})$. Now, $\det\mathbf{U} = U_{\underline{1}}U_{\underline{2}}U_{\underline{3}} > 0$; hence $\det\mathbf{R} = 1$ only if $\det F > 0$. In particular, if **F** is symmetric, but *not* positive, then $\det\mathbf{R} = F_{\underline{1}}F_{\underline{2}}F_{\underline{3}}/|F_{\underline{1}}F_{\underline{2}}F_{\underline{3}}|$.

Invariants of second rank tensors

At this point we have all the tools needed for determining the maximal number of independent invariants of second rank tensors. A symmetric tensor **S** is completely determined by its principal values $S_{\underline{b}}$ and its principal vectors $\mathbf{n}_a$, the components of **S** in any other basis (i) being given by the transformation formula $S_{ij} = Q_{ib}Q_{jb}S_{\underline{b}}$. Therefore, the maximal number of independent invariants for symmetric tensors is three. An orthogonal tensor **R** has only one invariant, which may be taken to be the angle of rotation, ϕ. The unit vector **n** specifying the axis of rotation is, of course, not an invariant of **R** (invariants are scalars). How is it then that a general second rank tensor **B**, representable by $\mathbf{B} = \mathbf{RS}$, has in general six independent invariants? The answer here is that the orientation of **n**† relative to the principal coordinate

† Here **n** is the principal vector of **R**.

system of $\mathbf{S}$ is described by the invariant direction cosines n_1, n_2, n_3 (only two of which are independent). No matter which reference basis is used for calculating the angles between $\mathbf{n}$ and the principal vectors of $\mathbf{S}$, these angles will always appear the same because they are intrinsic properties of the tensor $\mathbf{B}$. Reduced to its simplest form, our argument states that the angle between two *given* lines is invariant, whereas the angle between one line and some coordinate axis depends on the choice of the coordinate system. Thus $\mathbf{B}$ may be characterized geometrically by an ellipsoid (describing $\mathbf{S}$) impaled on an arrow (the unit vector $\mathbf{n}$), which also carries a "tag," the scalar ϕ.

If we prefer to use as invariants rational functions of the components of $\mathbf{B}$, then we may choose, in addition to the principal moment $\overline{\mathrm{I}}_B$, $\overline{\mathrm{II}}_B$, $\overline{\mathrm{III}}_B$ (defined in (4.9)), the following:

$$\overline{\mathrm{IV}}_{\mathbf{B}} = \mathrm{tr}(\mathbf{B}\mathbf{B}^T), \quad \overline{\mathrm{V}}_{\mathbf{B}} = \mathrm{tr}(\mathbf{B}^2\mathbf{B}^T), \quad \overline{\mathrm{VI}}_{\mathbf{B}} = \mathrm{tr}(\mathbf{B}^T\mathbf{B}^2\mathbf{B}^T). \qquad (4.65)$$

According to (4.64), we have that $B^2_{ij} = B_{im}B_{mj} = B_{\underline{a}}B_{\underline{b}}n_{ai}N_{am}n_{bm}N_{bj}$,

$$(\mathbf{B}^T\mathbf{B})_{ij} = B_{mi}B_{mj} = B_{\underline{a}}n_{am}N_{ai}B_{\underline{b}}n_{bm}N_{bj} = B^2_{\underline{a}}N_{ai}N_{aj},$$

$$(\mathbf{B}\mathbf{B}^T)_{ij} = B_{im}B_{jm} = B_{\underline{a}}n_{ai}N_{am}B_{\underline{b}}n_{bj}N_{bm} = B^2_{\underline{a}}n_{ai}n_{aj},$$

etc., hence it is easy to see that

$$\mathrm{tr}(\mathbf{B}^T\mathbf{B}) = \mathrm{tr}(\mathbf{B}\mathbf{B}^T),\ \mathrm{tr}(\mathbf{B}\mathbf{B}^T\mathbf{B}) = \mathrm{tr}(\mathbf{B}^T\mathbf{B}^2) = \mathrm{tr}(\mathbf{B}^2\mathbf{B}^T), \text{ etc.}$$

The invariants of $\mathbf{B}$ can be also investigated by decomposing $\mathbf{B}$ into a symmetric part $\mathbf{B}^S$ and a skew-symmetric part $\mathbf{B}^A$. The skew-symmetric part may be described in terms of the vector $b_i = \frac{1}{2}\varepsilon_{ijk}B_{jk}$, so that in the principal coordinate system of $\mathbf{B}^S$ we obtain

$$\|\mathbf{B}\| = \begin{Vmatrix} \beta_{\underline{1}} & 0 & 0 \\ 0 & \beta_{\underline{2}} & 0 \\ 0 & 0 & \beta_{\underline{3}} \end{Vmatrix} + \begin{Vmatrix} 0 & b_{\underline{3}} & -b_{\underline{2}} \\ -b_{\underline{3}} & 0 & b_{\underline{1}} \\ b_{\underline{2}} & -b_{\underline{1}} & 0 \end{Vmatrix},$$

where $\beta_{\underline{i}}$ are the principal values of $\mathbf{B}^S$. This representation suggests the following set of invariants:

$$\begin{aligned}
\mathrm{I}^*_{\mathbf{B}} &= \beta_{\underline{1}} + \beta_{\underline{2}} + \beta_{\underline{3}} \\
\mathrm{II}^*_{\mathbf{B}} &= \beta^2_{\underline{1}} + \beta^2_{\underline{2}} + \beta^2_{\underline{3}} \\
\mathrm{III}^*_{\mathbf{B}} &= \beta^3_{\underline{1}} + \beta^3_{\underline{2}} + \beta^3_{\underline{3}} \\
\mathrm{IV}^*_{\mathbf{B}} &= \mathbf{b}\cdot\mathbf{b} = b^2_{\underline{1}} + b^2_{\underline{2}} + b^2_{\underline{3}} \\
\mathrm{V}^*_{\mathbf{B}} &= \mathbf{B}^S[\mathbf{b}, \mathbf{b}] = \beta_{\underline{1}}b^2_{\underline{1}} + \beta_{\underline{2}}b^2_{\underline{2}} + \beta_{\underline{3}}b^2_{\underline{3}} \\
\mathrm{VI}^*_{\mathbf{B}} &= (\mathbf{B}^S)^2[\mathbf{b}, \mathbf{b}] = \beta^2_{\underline{1}}b^2_{\underline{1}} + \beta^2_{\underline{2}}b^2_{\underline{2}} + \beta^2_{\underline{3}}b^2_{\underline{3}}
\end{aligned}$$

Problems

A. LINEAR MAPPINGS

1. Verify (4.6).

2. Carry out in detail the derivation of (4.7).

3. Verify (4.9).

4. What kind of algebra is obtained for vectors by taking the "cross product" as the multiplication? (Is the multiplication associative? What about powers of vectors?)

5. Consider representations of the form $\mathbf{A} = A_{ij}\varepsilon_{ij}$. What is the matrix (and tensor) associated with the principal unit $\varepsilon = \varepsilon_{ii}$?

6. Express $\mathbf{T}^5$ in terms of $\mathbf{1},\mathbf{T},\mathbf{T}^2,\mathrm{I}_\mathbf{T},\mathrm{II},{}_\mathbf{T}\mathrm{III}_\mathbf{T}$.

B. ORTHOGONAL TENSORS

7. Write down the arrays of **R** representing rotations of 180° about
a. x axis **b.** y axis **c.** z axis

8. Write down the arrays of **R** representing rotations through ϕ degrees about
a. x axis **b.** y axis **c.** z axis
Also obtain the special cases corresponding to $\phi = 90°$.

9. If two reflections are combined (i.e. applied in succession), what is the resultant transformation?

10. A rotation of 90° about x axis is followed by a rotation of 180° about y axis. Calculate the array of **R** describing the resultant rotation.

11. Let A be a rotation of 90° about x axis, B a rotation of 180° about x axis, C a rotation of 90° about z axis, D a rotation of 180° about z axis. Find the array of **R** for the resultant rotation of

a. A followed by C **b.** A followed by D **c.** C followed by A
d. D followed by A **e.** B followed by C **f.** B followed by D
g. A followed by C followed by B.

C. SYMMETRIC TENSORS

12. Find the principal values and the principal vectors of **C** if

$$\text{a.}\quad \|\mathbf{C}\| = \begin{Vmatrix} 1 & \frac{3}{2} \\ \frac{3}{2} & \frac{13}{4} \end{Vmatrix} \qquad \text{b.}\quad \|\mathbf{C}\| = \begin{Vmatrix} 1 & \frac{5}{6} \\ \frac{5}{6} & \frac{61}{36} \end{Vmatrix}$$

13. In a coordinate system $Oxyz$ a tensor **C** is represented by

$$\|\mathbf{C}\| = \begin{Vmatrix} 7 & 3 & 0 \\ 3 & 7 & 4 \\ 0 & 4 & 7 \end{Vmatrix}$$

a. Show that the principal values are 12, 7, 2, and that the principal vectors are given by

$$\mathbf{k} = \frac{3\mathbf{e}_1}{5\sqrt{2}} + \frac{\mathbf{e}_2}{\sqrt{2}} + \frac{4\mathbf{e}_3}{5\sqrt{2}}, \qquad \mathbf{m} = \frac{4\mathbf{e}_1}{5} - \frac{3\mathbf{e}_3}{5},$$

$$\mathbf{n} = -\frac{3\mathbf{e}_1}{5\sqrt{2}} + \frac{\mathbf{e}_2}{\sqrt{2}} - \frac{4\mathbf{e}_3}{5\sqrt{2}}.$$

b. Continuing the preceding problem, calculate the components of $\sqrt{\mathbf{C}}$ in the *Oxyz* coordinate system.

14. Find the principal values and the principal directions of

$$\textbf{a. } \|\mathbf{C}\| = \begin{Vmatrix} 1 & 3 \\ 3 & 1 \end{Vmatrix} \qquad \textbf{b. } \|\mathbf{C}\| = \begin{Vmatrix} 3 & 1 \\ 1 & 3 \end{Vmatrix}$$

Check your results through $\overline{\mathbf{C}} = \mathbf{QCQ}^T$, in which $\overline{\mathbf{C}}$ is the diagonal representation of $\mathbf{C}$, and the rows of the orthogonal tensor $\mathbf{Q}$ are made up of the principal vectors of $\mathbf{C}$.

15. Calculate $(\mathbf{C})^{1/3}$ if

$$\|\mathbf{C}\| = \begin{Vmatrix} 3 & 1 \\ 1 & 3 \end{Vmatrix}$$

D. POLAR DECOMPOSITION

16. Obtain the polar decomposition $\mathbf{F} = \mathbf{RU}$ for

$$\textbf{a. } \|\mathbf{F}\| = \begin{Vmatrix} 1 & \frac{3}{2} \\ 0 & 1 \end{Vmatrix} \qquad \textbf{b. } \|\mathbf{F}\| = \begin{Vmatrix} 1 & \frac{8}{3} \\ 0 & 1 \end{Vmatrix}$$

17. Obtain the polar decomposition $\mathbf{F} = \mathbf{VR}$ for $\mathbf{F}$ given by

a. Problem 16a **b.** Problem 16.b.

18. For $\mathbf{F}$ given by

$$\|\mathbf{F}\| = \begin{Vmatrix} 1 & K & 0 \\ 0 & 1 & 0 \\ 0 & 0 & 1 \end{Vmatrix}$$

find **a.** the polar decomposition $\mathbf{F} = \mathbf{RU}$,

b. the polar decomposition $\mathbf{F} = \mathbf{VR}$.

Hints, checks, etc. To simplify the resulting expressions, use the substitution $K = 2 \tan \alpha$. Then

$$\|\mathbf{U}\| = \begin{Vmatrix} \cos\alpha & \sin\alpha & 0 \\ \sin\alpha & (1 + \sin^2\alpha)/\cos\alpha & 0 \\ 0 & 0 & 1 \end{Vmatrix},$$

$$\mathbf{n}_1 = \mathbf{e}_1 \cos\alpha \,/\sqrt{2(1 + \sin\alpha)} + \mathbf{e}_2\sqrt{(1 + \sin\alpha)/2},$$

$$\mathbf{n}_2 = \mathbf{e}_1 \cos\alpha \,/\sqrt{2(1 - \sin\alpha)} - \mathbf{e}_2\sqrt{(1 - \sin\alpha)/2},$$

$$\mathbf{n}_3 = \mathbf{e}_3.$$

19. Obtain the polar decomposition of

$$\|\mathbf{A}\| = \begin{Vmatrix} 0 & a \\ -a & 0 \end{Vmatrix}$$

E. INVARIANTS OF SECOND RANK TENSORS

20. Show that $\mathrm{tr}(\mathbf{T}\mathbf{T}^T\mathbf{T}\mathbf{T}^T\mathbf{T})$ can be expressed in terms of $\bar{\mathrm{I}}_{\mathbf{T}}$ through $\overline{\mathrm{VI}}_{\mathbf{T}}$ (*Hint*: note that $\mathbf{T}\mathbf{T}^T = \mathbf{C}^2$, where $\mathbf{C}$ is a symmetric tensor).

21. Let $\mathbf{F} = \mathbf{R}\mathbf{U}$, where $\mathbf{R}$ is orthogonal and $\mathbf{U}$ is positive and symmetric. Obtain the component representation of $\bar{\mathrm{I}}_{\mathbf{F}}$ through $\overline{\mathrm{VI}}_{\mathbf{F}}$ in terms of $\mathbf{R}$ and $\mathbf{U}$, and simplify them as much as possible.

Section 5
ELEMENTARY TENSOR ANALYSIS

The main purpose of this section is to record for later reference the basic integral transformations. We shall also use this occasion to review some of the ideas of analysis, although "review" is hardly the right word: the presentation here will be, of necessity, little more than a summary of notations and terminologies.

Euclidean point spaces

In mathematics by *space* we mean an infinite set of elements called *points*. There are various kinds of mathematical spaces that can be devised; the one that is motivated by our experience of the ambient space is called a *Euclidean point space*. It is rather interesting to see which of the intuitive ideas about the ambient space are carried over into mathematics, as well as to clarify the way in which it is done. Among other things, one would like to see, in a mathematical sense, just where coordinate systems, complete with base vectors $\mathbf{e}_x$, $\mathbf{e}_y$, $\mathbf{e}_z$ (or $\mathbf{i}$, $\mathbf{j}$, $\mathbf{k}$), come from. The answer will be: they are postulated. The existence of such "global" coordinate systems is in fact one of the main characteristics of Euclidean point spaces.

We shall carry out the definition of Euclidean point spaces in two stages. In the first stage we introduce the notion of an *affine point space* $\mathscr{E}_N$ as a set (*manifold*) X of points P, Q, R, ... ("places"), together with the possibility of moving from one point to another. To describe the means of getting about in the manifold X, we associate with X an N-dimensional vector space V_N of *translation vectors* $\mathbf{u}$, $\mathbf{v}$, $\mathbf{w}$, $\mathbf{p}$, ... This procedure is but a slight modification of the elementary view of vectors as directed line segments (or, point "differences"). The existence of translation vectors is one of the defining properties of Euclidean spaces. In general spaces the existence of finite translation vectors is not assumed; as it turns out, travel in such spaces is more precarious, its outcome more uncertain. (A "for instance": a captain bent on circumnavigating the globe (a curved 2-space!) steers his ship always 30° to the north. What will be the path of the ship?)

Let us now list the basic properties of affine point spaces. We assume that for any point P and any vector $\mathbf{u}$ there exists an *addition* with the properties $(P + \mathbf{u}) + \mathbf{v} = P + (\mathbf{u} + \mathbf{v})$, $P + \mathbf{u} = P$ only if $\mathbf{u} = \mathbf{0}$. Moreover, we assume that to every pair of points P and Q there corresponds a vector $\mathbf{u}$ such that $P + \mathbf{u} = Q$. It is easy to see that $P + \mathbf{u} = Q$, also written as the *point difference* $Q - P = \mathbf{u}$,† defines a unique vector $\mathbf{u}$: if $P + \mathbf{u} = P + \mathbf{v}$ then $(P + \mathbf{u}) - \mathbf{u} = P = P + (\mathbf{v} - \mathbf{u})$, thus $\mathbf{v} = \mathbf{u}$.

A *coordinate system* in $\mathscr{E}_N$ is constructed by selecting in V_N a basis (i) and in X a point 0, the *origin*. The coordinate system is then designated by $(0, \mathbf{e}_i)$, or, if an explicit reference to the origin is unnecessary, by the usual symbol (i). To each point difference $P - 0$ there corresponds a unique vector π, also called the *position vector*. Denoting by x_i the components of π, we write

$$\pi = P - 0 = x_i\mathbf{e}_i. \tag{5.1}$$

The numbers x_i are referred to as the *coordinates* of the point P in the coordinate system $(0, \mathbf{e}_i)$. The introduction of coordinates amounts to a parametrization of points, whereby a one-to-one correspondence is set up between points and N-tuples of real numbers:

$$P = P(x_1, x_2, \ldots, x_N), \qquad x_i = x_i(P). \tag{5.2}$$

In addition, if $P - 0 = x_i\mathbf{e}_i$, $Q - 0 = y_i\mathbf{e}_i$, then $Q - P = (y_i - x_i)\mathbf{e}_i$.

As a rule, we shall use for points the customary designations $\mathbf{x}, \mathbf{y}, \mathbf{z}$, etc. In direct notation $\mathbf{x}$ also stands for x_i; therefore, whenever confusion threatens, we shall revert to the designations P, Q, R, etc.

The parametrization of points also gives substance to the intuitive idea of spaces as "continua." That is, the correspondence $P \to x_1, x_1, \ldots, x_N$ establishes in point spaces a *natural topology* based on the topological properties of real numbers. Here by a topology we mean an assignment of subsets, called *neighborhoods*, to a space; for instance, a neighborhood of a point P may be defined as the set of points Q satisfying $Q = P + u_i\mathbf{e}_i$, $|u_i| < \delta$, where δ is a positive number. Neighborhoods are needed in the definitions of limits, continuity, etc. Thus if a deformation f maps points P into points $\bar{P}$, then f is continuous at P if to every neighborhood of $\bar{P}$ there corresponds a neighborhood of P. Similarly, P is a limit point of a sequence of points if a neighborhood of P contains all but a finite number of the points of the

† The addition of points is *not* defined!

sequence. These definitions are of course merely rewordings of the corresponding ε-δ definitions.

Although the natural topologies are not invariant with respect to coordinate transformations, the definitions of limits and continuity are (e.g. if $x_i \to x_i^0$, then also $x_a \to x_a^0$, where $x_a^0 = Q_{ai}x_i^0$).

It remains to make $\mathscr{E}_N$ into a Euclidean point space E_N by requiring the existence of Euclidean metric in the vector space V_N. Naturally the idea of Euclidean metric is suggested by the possibility of measuring distances in the ambient space (e.g. by means of "rigid" rods, or light signals and clocks).

The *distance function* $D(P, Q)$ of a Euclidean point space is based on the scalar product in the associated vector space V_N:

$$D(P, Q) = |Q - P| = \sqrt{(Q - P)\cdot(Q - P)} = \sqrt{(y_i - x_i)(y_i - x_i)}, \tag{5.3}$$

where we have used the representation $Q - P = (y_i - x_i)\mathbf{e}_i$. If the bases in V_N are orthonormal, then the corresponding coordinate systems in E_N are called Cartesian coordinate systems (*Cartesian frames*).

A basis transformation in V_N induces a *coordinate transformation* in E_N. If the coordinate transformation also involves a change of origin, we write $P - 0^* = (P - 0) - (0^* - 0)$; the associated component representations in frames (i) and (a) are

$$Q_{ai}x_a^* \equiv x_i^* = x_i - c_i, \quad x_a^* = x_a - c_a \equiv Q_{ai}(x_i - c_i) \tag{5.4}$$

(Schouten's notation!), where $\mathbf{Q}$ is an orthogonal tensor. A coordinate transformation is distinguished from all other mappings by two properties. First, it leaves distances unchanged: $|Q - P|^2 = (y_i - x_i)(y_i - x_i) = (y_a - x_a) \times (y_a - x_a)$ (this eliminates *deformations*). Second, the direction cosines Q_{ai} and the "translation vector" $\mathbf{c}$ appearing in (5.4) are constants, because they were "borrowed" from a single vector space. If Q_{ai} and $\mathbf{c}$ are permitted to vary with time, we speak of *rigid motions*.

The distance function determines an additional topology in the point space, e.g. a (spherical) neighborhood $N(P)$ of a point P may be defined as the set of all points Q satisfying $|Q - P| < r$ for some positive number r.

Differentiation of tensors

Let Ψ ("trident") denote point-valued or tensor-valued functions of a real variable t: $\Psi = \Psi(t)$. The derivative of Ψ with respect to t is defined in the usual way:

$$\dot{\Psi} \equiv \frac{d\Psi}{dt} = \lim_{\Delta t \to 0} \frac{\Psi(t + \Delta t) - \Psi(t)}{\Delta t}. \tag{5.5}$$

If Ψ is a point-valued function, then the right-hand side of (5.5) is, in accord with the definition of Euclidean point spaces, a vector, and $\dot{\Psi}$ is a vector-valued function. If Ψ is a tensor-valued function, then so is $\dot{\Psi}$.

Let us now consider a region V of a Euclidean point space E_3 (in the present context V may be called an *underlying space*, or, *support*). By a *field* $\Psi(P)$† we shall mean a function Ψ which is defined at all points P of V. A point-valued function of points is often referred to as a *deformation*. All of the algebraic results for tensors are valid, of course, at every point of the underlying space. We may emphasize the dependence of tensor components upon coordinates by writing algebraic relations in a notation $t_i(P) = T_{ji}(P)n_j$, for instance, but ordinarily this is not done. In the study of field properties, however, the dependence upon P may have to be shown explicitly.

The variation of a tensor field $T_{ij}(P)$ from point to point is described by the partial derivatives $\partial_k T_{ij} = T_{ij,k}$. It is easy to verify that (ordinary) *differentiation in Cartesian coordinates is an invariant operation*. Namely, applying $\partial_c = Q_{ck}\partial_k$ to $T_{ab} = Q_{ai}Q_{bj}T_{ij}$, and noting that the transformation coefficients are constants, we arrive at $\partial_c T_{ab} = Q_{ai}Q_{bj}Q_{ck}\partial_k T_{ij}$. This means that $T_{ab,c}$ and $T_{ij,k}$ represent the *same* tensor, so that it does not matter whether a tensor is differentiated in one coordinate system and then transformed to another coordinate system or differentiated outright in the other coordinate system. We can also say that a partial derivative of a tensor is, in Cartesian frames, an *absolute* quantity, or, an absolute measure of the variation of the tensor. It is represented in all Cartesian frames by the same tensor, e.g. $\mathbf{\nabla T}$.

For future reference let us record the invariance condition for ordinary differentiation:

$$\partial_j Q_{ai} = Q_{ai,j} = 0. \tag{5.6}$$

This simple formula will reappear even in general coordinates: there we shall say that *a* differentiation D_b is an invariant operation if $D_b Q_{ai} = 0$.

Introducing the *del* operator

$$\mathbf{\nabla} = \mathbf{e}_i\partial_i, \tag{5.7}$$

we can express the familiar operations *grad*, *div*, and *curl* as follows,

$$\text{grad}\phi = \mathbf{\nabla}\phi, \qquad (\text{grad}\phi)_i = \partial_i\phi = \phi_{,i}, \tag{5.8}$$

$$\text{div}\mathbf{v} = \mathbf{\nabla}\cdot\mathbf{v}, \qquad \text{div}\mathbf{v} = \partial_i v_i = v_{i,i}, \tag{5.9}$$

$$\text{curl}\mathbf{v} = \mathbf{\nabla}\times\mathbf{v}, \qquad (\text{curl}\mathbf{v})_i = \varepsilon_{ijk}\partial_j v_k = \varepsilon_{ijk}v_{k,j}. \tag{5.10}$$

† The term *field* also denotes algebraic fields (e.g. the field of real numbers), but there is little possibility of confusion.

Similarly,

$$\nabla \mathbf{v} = \mathbf{e}_i\partial_i(\mathbf{e}_j v_j) = \mathbf{e}_i\mathbf{e}_j v_{j,i}, \quad (\text{grad}\mathbf{v})_{ij} = v_{j,i}, \tag{5.11}$$

$$\nabla \cdot \mathbf{T} = \mathbf{e}_k\partial_k \cdot (\mathbf{e}_i\mathbf{e}_j T_{ij}) = \delta_{ik}\mathbf{e}_j T_{ij,k} = \mathbf{e}_j T_{kj,k}, \tag{5.12}$$
$$(\text{div}\mathbf{T})_j = T_{kj,k}.$$

In direct notation we are sometimes hard pressed to invent special symbols for the various operations (in the index notation these operations are shown explicitly, therefore no special names are needed). Thus along with the *left-gradient* $\nabla\mathbf{v}$ we must introduce a *right-gradient* $\mathbf{v}\nabla = v_i\mathbf{e}_i\mathbf{e}_j\partial_j \equiv \mathbf{e}_i\mathbf{e}_j v_{i,j}$, so that $(\mathbf{v}\nabla)_{ij} = v_{i,j}$. Along with the *left-divergence* (5.12) we introduce a *right-divergence*

$$(\mathbf{T} \cdot \nabla)_j = T_{jk,k}. \tag{5.13}$$

A *left-curl* and a *right-curl* are defined by

$$(\nabla \times \mathbf{T})_{im} = \varepsilon_{ijk}T_{km,j}, \qquad (\mathbf{T} \times \nabla)_{im} = T_{ij,k}\varepsilon_{jkm}, \tag{5.14}$$

respectively. These definitions follow from $\nabla = \mathbf{e}_i\partial_i$, $T = \mathbf{e}_j\mathbf{e}_k T_{jk}$, and $\ldots\mathbf{e}_i\mathbf{e}_j \times \mathbf{e}_k\mathbf{e}_m = \varepsilon_{pjk}\ldots\mathbf{e}_i\mathbf{e}_p\mathbf{e}_m$ (cf. (3.35)). A repeated *curl* operation, referred to as the "incompatibility operator" *Ink*, is defined by (cf. Problem 4)

$$(\text{Ink}\mathbf{T})_{im} = -(\nabla \times \mathbf{T} \times \nabla)_{im} = \varepsilon_{ijk}\varepsilon_{mnp}T_{kp,jn}. \tag{5.15}$$

The *scalar Laplacian* $\nabla^2 = \nabla \cdot \nabla$ is defined by

$$\nabla^2\phi = \text{div grad}\phi = \phi_{,ii}. \tag{5.16}$$

The *vector Laplacian* ✡† is defined by

$$✡\mathbf{v} = \text{grad div}\mathbf{v} - \text{curl curl}\mathbf{v}. \tag{5.17}$$

In Cartesian coordinates‡ this reduces to

$$✡\mathbf{v} = \mathbf{e}_i\nabla^2 v_i. \tag{5.18}$$

† This is the notation used by P. Moon and D. E. Spencer [99]. Most authors use the same symbol ∇^2 to denote both the scalar and the vector Laplacians.

‡ But see the discussion on p. 118.

Finally, we record two important identities which follow directly from the definitions of the differential operators:

$$\text{curl grad}\phi = 0, \qquad \text{div curl}\mathbf{v} = 0, \tag{5.19}$$

As is well known from modern analysis, differentiation can be defined in a very general setting. To illustrate this, let us take a tensor-valued function $\phi(\mathbf{x})$ of the points of a Euclidean space. Denoting by $\mathbf{n}$ a unit vector, we define a *directional derivative* $\partial_{\underline{\mathrm{n}}}\phi$ (in the direction of $\mathbf{n}$) by

$$\partial_{\underline{\mathrm{n}}}\phi(\mathbf{x}) = \lim_{\varepsilon \to 0} \frac{1}{\varepsilon} [\phi(\mathbf{x} + \varepsilon\mathbf{n}) - \phi(\mathbf{x})] = \frac{d}{d\varepsilon} \phi(\mathbf{x} + \varepsilon\mathbf{n})\Big|_{\varepsilon = 0}. \tag{5.20}$$

In particular, if $\mathbf{n}$ coincides with a Cartesian base vector $\mathbf{e}_i$, then the customary notation $\partial_i\phi$ is used. For instance, if $\phi(\mathbf{x}) = x^2 + y^2$, $\mathbf{n} = (\cos\alpha, \sin\alpha, 0)$, then $\partial_{\underline{\mathrm{n}}}\phi = \lim_{\varepsilon \to 0} [(x + \varepsilon\cos\alpha)^2 + (y + \varepsilon\sin\alpha)^2 - x^2 - y^2]/\varepsilon = 2(x\cos\alpha + y\sin\alpha)$.

Let us recall that in $\pi = P - 0 = x_i\mathbf{e}_i$ the origin 0 is fixed. Therefore, since the base vectors do not depend on $\mathbf{x}$,†

$$\partial_k\mathbf{e}_i = 0, \tag{5.21}$$

we have that

$$\partial_k P = \partial_k \pi = \mathbf{e}_k. \tag{5.22}$$

Here $\partial_k P$ may be referred to as a *vector-derivative* of the point function $P(\mathbf{x})$. The geometrical interpretation of (5.22) is simple enough: we consider increments of the position vector π along the x_k coordinate line, so that $\mathbf{e}_k$ is represented by a unit vector tangent to the coordinate line.

If the scalar state $\partial_{\underline{\mathrm{n}}}\phi$ exists and is continuous, then it can be described in terms of the *gradient vector* $\nabla\phi$:

$$\partial_{\underline{\mathrm{n}}}\phi = \mathbf{n} \cdot \nabla\phi, \qquad \nabla\phi = \mathbf{e}_i\partial_i\phi. \tag{5.23}$$

In the example cited above, $\nabla\phi = 2(x\mathbf{e}_x + y\mathbf{e}_y)$, $\mathbf{n} = \mathbf{e}_x\cos\alpha + \mathbf{e}_y\sin\alpha$, $\mathbf{n} \cdot \nabla\phi = 2(x\cos\alpha + y\sin\alpha)$.

A proof of (5.23) may be carried out along the following lines.‡ First, letting $\mathbf{u} = m\mathbf{n}$, where m is a scalar, we obtain from (5.20) that

$$\partial_{\underline{\mathrm{u}}}\phi(\mathbf{x}) = \lim_{\varepsilon \to 0} \frac{1}{\varepsilon} [\phi(\mathbf{x} + \varepsilon m\mathbf{n}) - \phi(\mathbf{x})] = m \lim_{m\varepsilon \to 0} \frac{1}{m\varepsilon} [\phi(\mathbf{x} + \varepsilon m\mathbf{n}) - \phi(\mathbf{x})],$$

or,

$$\partial_{\underline{m\mathrm{n}}}\phi(\mathbf{x}) = m\partial_{\underline{\mathrm{n}}}\phi(\mathbf{x}). \tag{a}$$

† The base vectors have been "borrowed" from a single vector space V_N.
‡ Noll [107], p. 68.

Since it is assumed that $\partial_{\underline{n}}\phi$ exists and is continuous, we have that $\phi(\mathbf{x} + \varepsilon\mathbf{n}) - \phi(\mathbf{x}) = \varepsilon\partial_{\underline{n}}\phi(\mathbf{x}) + \varepsilon 0(\varepsilon)$, where $0(\varepsilon) \to 0$ as $\varepsilon \to 0$. Similarly, $\phi(\mathbf{x} + \varepsilon\mathbf{k} + \varepsilon\mathbf{n}) - \phi(\mathbf{x} + \varepsilon\mathbf{k}) = \varepsilon\partial_{\underline{n}}\phi(\mathbf{x} + \varepsilon\mathbf{k}) + \varepsilon\bar{0}(\varepsilon)$. But the continuity of $\partial_{\underline{n}}\phi$ implies that $\partial_{\underline{n}}\phi(\mathbf{x} + \varepsilon\mathbf{k}) = \partial_{\underline{n}}\phi(\mathbf{x}) + \varepsilon\bar{\bar{0}}(\varepsilon)$, so that $\phi(\mathbf{x} + \varepsilon\mathbf{k} + \varepsilon\mathbf{n}) - \phi(\mathbf{x}) = \phi(\mathbf{x} + \varepsilon\mathbf{k} + \varepsilon\mathbf{n}) - \phi(\mathbf{x} + \varepsilon\mathbf{k}) + \phi(\mathbf{x} + \varepsilon\mathbf{k}) - \phi(\mathbf{x}) = \varepsilon\partial_{\underline{n}}\phi(\mathbf{x}) + \varepsilon^2\bar{\bar{0}}(\varepsilon) + \varepsilon\bar{0}(\varepsilon) + \varepsilon\partial_{\underline{k}}\phi(\mathbf{x}) + \varepsilon 0(\varepsilon)$. Thus

$$\partial_{\underline{k}+\underline{n}}\phi = \partial_{\underline{k}}\phi + \partial_{\underline{n}}\phi\,; \tag{b}$$

recalling (a), we conclude that $\partial_{\underline{n}}\phi$ is a linear transformation of $\mathbf{n}$. Consequently, there exists a vector $\nabla\phi$, called the gradient of ϕ, such that $\partial_{\underline{n}}\phi = \mathbf{n} \cdot \nabla\phi$. To emphasize that $\partial_{\underline{n}}\phi$ is a linear function of $\mathbf{n}$, we may consider the directional derivative as a *differential* $\delta\phi(\mathbf{x}|\mathbf{n})$:

$$\partial_{\underline{n}}\phi(\mathbf{x}) = \delta\phi(\mathbf{x}|\mathbf{n}). \tag{5.24}$$

In a broader view, a differential is a *linear mapping* which provides a local approximation of the function: $\phi(\mathbf{x} + \varepsilon\mathbf{n}) \approx \phi(\mathbf{x}) + \varepsilon\partial_{\underline{n}}\phi(\mathbf{x})$, $\partial_{\underline{n}}\phi = \nabla\phi[\mathbf{n}]$.

The preceding derivations are independent of the interpretations attached to $\mathbf{x}$ and $\mathbf{n}$. It is only necessary that $\mathbf{x} + \varepsilon\mathbf{n}$ be meaningful, and that convergence in the spaces of $\mathbf{x}$ and $\phi(\mathbf{x})$ can be defined. If we recall that tensors of equal rank constitute a vector space, and that any component representation introduces a natural topology into the vector space, it becomes clear that (5.20) applies equally well to tensor-valued functions of tensors. For instance, if $\mathbf{A}$ and $\mathbf{B}$ are two second rank tensors, then a routine calculation yields the result

$$\partial_{\mathbf{B}} \det\mathbf{A} = \frac{d}{d\varepsilon} \det(\mathbf{A} + \varepsilon\mathbf{B})\Big|_{\varepsilon=0} = B_{im}C_{im},$$

where C_{im} is the cofactor of A_{im}. Therefore,

$$\frac{\partial}{\partial A_{im}} \det\mathbf{A} = C_{im}, \qquad \nabla_{\mathbf{A}} \det\mathbf{A} = \mathbf{C}. \tag{5.25}$$

To investigate the vectors ∇x_i, we consider the chain rule $\nabla\phi = (\partial_i\phi)\nabla x_i$, from which it follows that $\partial_{\underline{n}}\phi = \mathbf{n} \cdot \nabla\phi = (\partial_i\phi)\mathbf{n} \cdot \nabla x_i$. In particular, if $\mathbf{n} = \mathbf{e}_1$, then $\partial_{\underline{n}}\phi = \partial_1\phi = (\partial_i\phi)\mathbf{e}_1 \cdot \nabla x_i$, which permits us to identify ∇x_i with $\mathbf{e}_i$:

$$\nabla x_i = \mathbf{e}_i. \tag{5.26}$$

Consequently, there exist two equivalent definitions of the base vectors: $\mathbf{e}_i = \partial_i P = \nabla x_i$ (note that, in orthonormal frames, $\nabla P = (\partial_i P)\nabla x_i = \mathbf{e}_i\mathbf{e}_i = \mathbf{1}!$). The formula (5.26) evidently agrees with the usual interpretation of *gradient* as a vector pointing in the direction of most rapid change of a scalar field (this is also borne out by $(\partial/\partial n_k)[n_i\partial_i\phi - \frac{1}{2}A(n_in_i - 1)] = 0$ (cf. 4.49), from which it follows that the desired unit vector $\mathbf{n}$ is in the direction of $\nabla\phi$: $\partial_k\phi = An_k$). In view of $\nabla\phi = (\partial_i\phi)\nabla x_i = (\partial_i\phi)\mathbf{e}_i$, the representation of ∇ is given by (5.7). We may interpret ∇ as a *vector-valued function of scalars*; the value of ∇ at the scalar ϕ is the gradient of ϕ:

$$\phi \xrightarrow{\nabla} \nabla\phi$$

(note the consistency of $\mathbf{e}_k = \nabla x_k = \mathbf{e}_i\partial_i x_k = \mathbf{e}_i\delta_{ik}!$). As is evident from (5.23), the vector $\nabla\phi$ can be interpreted, in turn, as a *scalar-valued function of vectors*, e.g.

$$d\mathbf{x} \xrightarrow{\nabla\phi} d\phi = \phi_{,i}\, dx_i.$$

Line, surface, and volume integrals

Before taking up the basic integral transformations, let us review integrals defined over curves, surfaces, or general regions of space. In particular, we shall sketch the reduction of such integrals to the familiar Riemann integrals of the type

$$\int \phi(u)\, du, \qquad \iint \phi(u, v)\, du\, dv, \qquad \iiint \phi(u, v, w)\, du\, dv\, dw.$$

A space curve C is described by

$$x_i = x_i(u), \tag{5.27}$$

where u is a parameter. We shall assume that the tangent of the curve is defined everywhere, so that not all $x_{i,u}$ can vanish simultaneously. In

$$x_{i,u} = \frac{dx_i}{du} \tag{5.28}$$

the subscript u is to be treated as a label; in particular, an expression $x_{i,u}x_{i,u}$ does *not* imply summation over u.

A squared infinitesimal length ds^2 of the curve C is given by

$$ds^2 = d\mathbf{x} \cdot d\mathbf{x} = x_{i,u}x_{i,u}\, du^2. \tag{5.29}$$

If C is the map of the interval D: $a \leq u \leq b$, of real numbers, then the arc length $s(C)$ of C is calculated from

$$s(C) = \int_a^b \sqrt{x_{i,u}x_{i,u}}\, du. \tag{5.30}$$

We denote by $\boldsymbol{\tau} = d\mathbf{x}/ds$ the unit tangent vectors of C, and by v_τ the projections of a vector field $\mathbf{v}$ upon C:

$$v_\tau = \mathbf{v} \cdot \boldsymbol{\tau}. \tag{5.31}$$

Then from $v_i \tau_i\, ds = v_i\, dx_i$ it follows that

$$C[\mathbf{v}] = \int_C v_\tau\, ds = \int_C v_i\, dx_i = \int_a^b v_i(u) x_{i,u}\, du. \tag{5.32}$$

The quantity $C[\mathbf{v}]$ is called the *flow* of $\mathbf{v}$ along C; its integral representations are referred to as *line integrals* of v_τ. If C is a closed curve Γ in which case it is called a *circuit*, then (5.32) is written as

$$\Gamma[\mathbf{v}] = \oint_\Gamma v_i\, dx_i, \tag{5.33}$$

and $\Gamma[\mathbf{v}]$ is called the *circulation* of $\mathbf{v}$ around Γ.

We note that in (5.32) a line integral is reduced to an ordinary integral in the variable u by an outright substitution of (5.27) into $v_i\, dx_i$. For instance, if $\mathbf{v} = x_i \mathbf{e}_i$, and C: $x = au$, $y = bu^2$, $z = cu^3$, then $v_i\, dx_i = x_i\, dx_i = (a^2 u + 2b^2 u^3 + 3c^2 u^5)\, du$.

A surface S can be described by

$$x_i = x_i(u, v), \tag{5.34}$$

where u and v are parameters ("surface coordinates"). For $u =$ const. (5.34) describe one family of space curves (lying in the surface), for $v =$ const. another. We shall assume that the unit normal vector of a surface is defined everywhere. This will mean that not all determinants Δ_i, defined by†

$$\Delta_i = \varepsilon_{ijk} x_{j,u} x_{k,v},$$

$$\Delta_x = \frac{\partial(y, z)}{\partial(u, v)} = \begin{vmatrix} \dfrac{\partial y}{\partial u} & \dfrac{\partial y}{\partial v} \\ \dfrac{\partial z}{\partial u} & \dfrac{\partial z}{\partial v} \end{vmatrix}, \ldots, \ldots, \tag{5.35}$$

can vanish simultaneously.

† Because we have used the *scalar notations* u and v for surface coordinates, rather than u_α, $\alpha = 1, 2$, both u and v are to be treated as labels in $x_{i,u} = \partial x_i/\partial u$, $x_{i,v} = \partial x_i/\partial v$.

To describe an area element $d\mathbf{a}$, we introduce the incremental vectors $d_u\pi = x_{i,u}\mathbf{e}_i\, du$ and $d_v\pi = x_{i,v}\mathbf{e}_i\, dv$ along the curves $v =$ const., $u =$ const., respectively. Then $d\mathbf{a} = d_u\pi \times d_v\pi$, in which the *orientation* of $d\mathbf{a}$ (i.e. the "positive" side of $d\mathbf{a}$) is determined by the order of $d_u\pi$ and $d_v\pi$ in the cross product.† Thus

$$da_i = \Delta_i\, du\, dv\,; \tag{5.36}$$

hence the surface area $A(S)$ of S is given by

$$A(S) = \int_D \sqrt{\Delta_i \Delta_i}\, du\, dv\,. \tag{5.37}$$

Here D is the region in the u–v plane that contains the values of u and v specifying S.

The unit normal vector $\mathbf{n}$ of $d\mathbf{a}$ is defined by

$$n_i = \frac{da_i}{da} = \frac{\Delta_i}{\sqrt{\Delta_m \Delta_m}}\,. \tag{5.38}$$

Denoting by

$$v_{\underline{n}} = \mathbf{v} \cdot \mathbf{n} \tag{5.39}$$

the components of a vector field $\mathbf{v}$ normal to S, and taking into account $v_i n_i\, da = v_i\, da_i = v_i \Delta_i\, du\, dv$, we arrive at

$$S[\mathbf{v}] = \int_S v_{\underline{n}}\, da = \int_S v_i n_i\, da = \int_D v_i(u, v)\Delta_i(u, v)\, du\, dv\,. \tag{5.40}$$

The quantity $S[\mathbf{v}]$ is called the *flux* of $\mathbf{v}$ across S. If S is a closed surface Σ, then $\Sigma[\mathbf{v}]$ is called the *efflux* of $\mathbf{v}$.

The formula (5.40) reduces a particular surface integral to a Riemann double-integral. For instance, let us consider the spherical coordinates r, θ (co-latitude) and ϕ (longitude). If $\mathbf{v} = x_i\mathbf{e}_i$ and S is a spherical surface of radius a: $x = a \sin\theta \cos\phi$, $y = a \sin\theta \sin\phi$, $z = a\cos\theta$ (D: $0 \leq \theta \leq \pi$, $0 \leq \phi \leq 2\pi$), then it readily follows that $v_i n_i\, da = a^3 \sin\theta\, d\theta\, d\phi$.

Finally, let us consider a region of space, V, described by

$$x_i = x_i(u, v, w), \tag{5.41}$$

† The orientation so defined is invariant with respect to any transformation $\bar{u} = f(u, v)$, $\bar{v} = g(u, v)$ satisfying $\dfrac{\partial(\bar{u}, \bar{v})}{\partial(u, v)} > 0$.

where u, v, w are parameters ("curvilinear coordinates"). Proceeding as before, we describe a volume element by†

$$dv = [d_u\pi, d_v\pi, d_w\pi] = J\, du\, dv\, dw, \tag{5.42}$$

where the *Jacobian* J of the mapping (5.41) is given by

$$J = \varepsilon_{ijk} x_{i,u} x_{j,v} x_{k,w}, \tag{5.43}$$

$$J = \frac{\partial(x, y, z)}{\partial(u, v, w)} = \begin{vmatrix} \dfrac{\partial x}{\partial u} & \dfrac{\partial x}{\partial v} & \dfrac{\partial x}{\partial w} \\ \dfrac{\partial y}{\partial u} & \dfrac{\partial y}{\partial v} & \dfrac{\partial y}{\partial w} \\ \dfrac{\partial z}{\partial u} & \dfrac{\partial z}{\partial v} & \dfrac{\partial z}{\partial w} \end{vmatrix}.$$

We assume that J vanishes at most at a finite number of points.

From (5.42) now follows that

$$\int_V \phi\, dv = \int_D \phi(u, v, w) J(u, v, w)\, du\, dv\, dw, \tag{5.44}$$

where D is that region in the u-v-w space that contains the values of u, v, w specifying V. In spherical coordinates, for instance, $J = r^2 \sin\theta$; hence the integral of ϕ over a sphere of radius a is given by

$$\int_V \phi\, dv = \int_0^a \int_0^\pi \int_0^{2\pi} \phi(r, \phi, \theta)\, r^2 \sin\theta\, dr\, d\theta\, d\phi.$$

Basic integral theorems

The evolution of most vector operations is closely linked to classical hydrodynamics. Although these operations are in no way limited to hydrodynamics, examples of various flows still afford the best means for visualizing them. For instance, the net flow of an incompressible fluid through a closed surface is a measure of the productivity of sources inside the surface. An integral transformation then suggests the *divergence* of velocity as a measure of source strength. Similarly, to detect a rotation ("vorticity") present in a fluid sheet, we may calculate at the boundary of the sheet the sum of the projections of the velocity on the boundary curve. An integral transformation

† The orientation of dv is determined by the order of $d_u\pi, d_v\pi, d_w\pi$.

now suggests the *curl* of velocity as a measure of the mean rotation of fluid filaments. In each case the field at the boundary is related to a differential property of the field in the interior through transformation of surface integrals into volume integrals, or of line integrals into surface integrals.

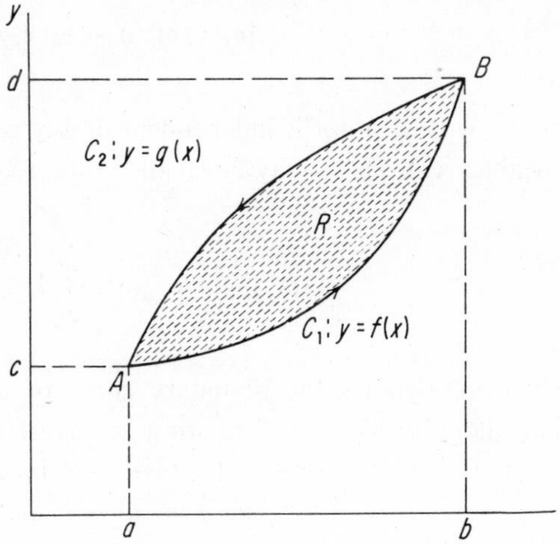

FIGURE 5.1 A convex region R for the proof of Green's transformation.

Let us first take up *Green's transformation*,

$$\oint_C \mathbf{v} \cdot d\mathbf{x} = \int_R (\text{curl}\,\mathbf{v})_z \, dx\, dy,$$
$$\oint_C (v_x\, dx + v_y\, dy) = \int_R (v_{y,x} - v_{x,y}) dx\, dy, \tag{5.45}$$

where C is the boundary of some plane region R. We agree that C is *oriented* in such a way that upon traversing C the positive side of the region R is always on the left. If $(\text{curl}\,\mathbf{v})_z = 0$, then

$$\int_{C_1} (v_x\, dx + v_y\, dy) = -\int_{C_2} (v_x\, dx + v_y\, dy)$$

(cf. Figure 5.1), which means that the path C_1 of the line integral can be "deformed" into the path C_2. The minus sign in the above expression reverses the sense indicated in Figure 5.1 for the integral along C_2.

A region is said to be x-convex (y-convex) if a line parallel to the x axis (y axis) intersects the boundary only twice. A convex plane region is both x-convex and y-convex; for such regions the proof of Green's transformation is simple, and amounts to treating double-integrals as iterated integrals. Thus in the case illustrated in Figure 5.1, we have that

$$-\int_R v_{x,y}\,dx\,dy = -\int_a^b dx \int_{f(x)}^{g(x)} v_{x,y}\,dy$$

$$= -\int_a^b dx[v_x(x, g(x)) - v_x(x, f(x))] = \oint_C v_x\,dx,$$

etc. Now, this proof is independent of any particular interpretation that the variables x, y, v_x, v_y may have; therefore, (5.45) can be equally well written as

$$\int_{\partial D} (\bar{v}_u\,du + \bar{v}_v\,dv) = \int_D (\bar{v}_{v,u} - \bar{v}_{u,v})\,du\,dv, \tag{5.46}$$

where ∂D denotes the boundary curve of a plane region D. This means that the Green's transformation is invariant to a mapping $x = x(u, v)$, $y = y(u, v)$ that changes the region R into the region D, provided that $v_i\,dx_i = v_i x_{i,u}\,du + v_i x_{i,v}\,dv \equiv \bar{v}_u\,du + \bar{v}_v\,dv$. Therefore, if we imagine R as a plane rubber sheet, then Green's transformation remains valid after R has been stretched into another planar shape D. This suggests a further generalization: we shall deform D into an (orientable) surface S bounded by the space curve ∂S, whereby the *Kelvin's transformation*†

$$\oint_{\partial S} \mathbf{v}\cdot d\mathbf{x} = \int_S \mathbf{n}\cdot \mathrm{curl}\,\mathbf{v}\,da,$$

$$\oint_{\partial S} v_i\,dx_i = \int_S \varepsilon_{ijk} n_i v_{k,j}\,da, \tag{5.47}$$

will be reduced to (5.46). Let S be defined by $x_i = x_i(u, v)$, D being the trace of S in the u–v plane. Letting $\bar{v}_u = v_i x_{i,u}$, $\bar{v}_v = v_i x_{i,v}$, we find that $\bar{v}_{v,u} - \bar{v}_{u,v} = v_{i,j}x_{j,u}x_{i,v} + v_i x_{i,vu} - v_{i,j}x_{j,v}x_{i,u} - v_i x_{i,uv}$,

thus
$$\bar{v}_{v,u} - \bar{v}_{u,v} = x_{i,u}x_{j,v}(v_{j,i} - v_{i,j}). \tag{5.48}$$

Evidently the nature of the operation is preserved: the "three-dimensional" *curl* $v_{j,i} - v_{i,j}$ induces a "two-dimensional" *curl* $\bar{v}_{v,u} - \bar{v}_{u,v}$. This is a remarkable result which is not true of differential operations in general. As a

† Commonly called the "Stokes's theorem." The history of this theorem is given by C. Truesdell in [171], Footnote 2, p. 12. The theorem holds if S is an orientable (i.e. two-sided) surface, and if both $\mathbf{v}$ and its partial derivatives are continuous.

rule, each space will have its own kind of "invariant differentiation," because this operation is related to the metric of the space. In the derivation of (5.48), on the other hand, metric concepts are really not needed; only the continuity of $x_{i,uv}$ is used.

Let us not forget to verify the reduction of (5.47) to (5.46). Namely, by (5.35), (5.36), $\varepsilon_{ijk}n_i v_{k,j}\, da = \varepsilon_{ijk}\, da_i v_{k,j} = \varepsilon_{ijk}\varepsilon_{imn} x_{m,u} x_{n,v} v_{k,j}\, du\, dv = (v_{x,u}x_{,v} - v_{x,v}x_{,u} + v_{y,u}y_{,v} - v_{y,v}y_{,u} + v_{z,u}z_{,v} - v_{z,v}z_{,u})\, du\, dv = (\bar{v}_{v,u} - \bar{v}_{u,v})\, du\, dv$.

Among more general regions we distinguish *simply connected* and *multiply connected regions*. The boundary of a simply connected region consists of a single closed curve. The boundary of a multiply connected region consists of several closed curves; we also say that there exist closed curves that are not *reducible*, i.e. cannot be contracted to a point without leaving the region. If the boundary curves do not have any irregular features (e.g. infinitely many extrema, spikes), then a region can be subdivided into convex regions by introducing pairwise canceling cuts (cf. Figure 5.2).

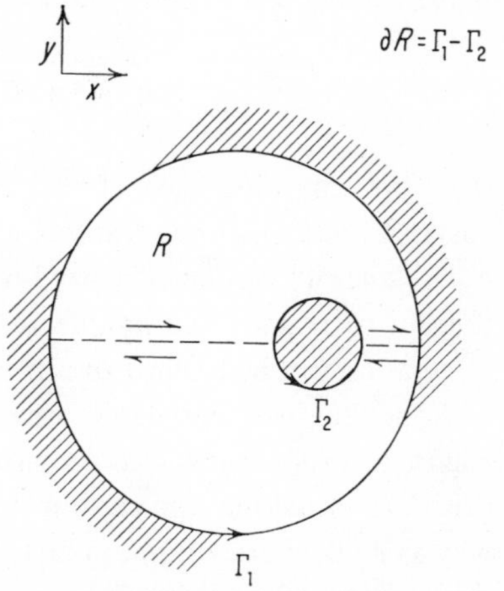

FIGURE 5.2 Decomposition of a multiply connected region into y-convex regions.

Consequently, the transformations of Green and Kelvin will also hold in general regions, provided that *the boundary is taken as consisting of all boundary curves*. In Figure 5.2 the boundary ∂R of the region R is given by $\partial R = \Gamma_1 - \Gamma_2$, where $-\Gamma_2$ indicates the reversal of the sense of Γ_2 shown in the Figure. If $\operatorname{curl}\mathbf{v} = 0$, then, by (5.47),

$$\oint_{R} \mathbf{v}\cdot d\mathbf{x} = \oint_{\Gamma_1} \mathbf{v}\cdot d\mathbf{x} - \oint_{\Gamma_2} \mathbf{v}\cdot d\mathbf{x} = 0.$$

If $\operatorname{curl}\mathbf{v} = \mathbf{0}$ and the region R is simply connected, then $\Gamma[\mathbf{v}] = 0$ on any closed curve Γ in R. This means that the line integrals of $\mathbf{v}$ are independent of the path of integration, in which case they define a point function ϕ such that $\mathbf{v} = \text{grad}\phi$.

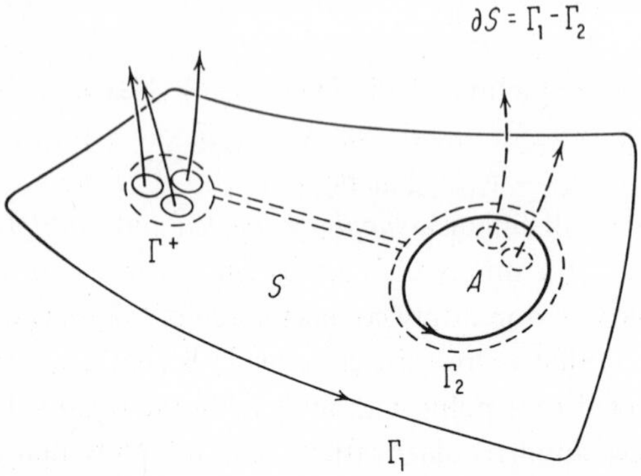

FIGURE 5.3 A drawing for a hydrodynamical interpretation of Kelvin's transformation.

In order to obtain a hydrodynamic interpretation of (5.47), let us introduce the *vorticity* $\mathbf{w} = \text{curl}\mathbf{v}$ as a measure of the mean rotation of fluid filaments. If the surface S is as shown in Figure 5.3, then

$$\int_S \mathbf{w} \cdot \mathbf{n}\, da = \Gamma_1[\mathbf{v}] - \Gamma_2[\mathbf{v}];$$

therefore, the difference of the circulations associated with the bounding curves Γ_1 and Γ_2 equals the flux of vorticity through the surface. The distributed vorticity can be visualized in terms of *vortex lines* that are everywhere tangent to $\mathbf{w}$ and, like minute tornadoes, thread the surface S. A path of integration can be likened to a rubber band: if $\text{curl}\mathbf{v} = \mathbf{0}$ over some portion of S then the path can be deformed through that portion, as is illustrated in Figure 5.3, so that it is spanned around the clusters of vortex lines only. Here it is to be noted that the cut-out A restrains a path of integration in the same way as do the vortex lines. In fact, we can imagine A filled with fluid having a distribution of vorticity $\bar{\mathbf{w}}$ that yields the correct value of the circulation around Γ_2:

$$\Gamma_2[\mathbf{v}] = \int_A \bar{\mathbf{w}} \cdot \mathbf{n}\, da.$$

Finally, let Σ be a single *closed* surface, and Γ a curve dividing Σ into surfaces S^+ and S^-. Applying (5.47) to S^+ and S^- separately, then adding the two expressions together, it follows that

$$\int_\Sigma \mathbf{n} \cdot \text{curl}\mathbf{v}\, da = 0, \qquad (5.49)$$

because the line integrals over ∂S^+ and ∂S^- have opposite senses.

We now turn to the *divergence theorem*.† Let V be a three-dimensional region with a finite boundary ∂V. Let $\mathbf{v}$ be a vector field such that both $\mathbf{v}$ and its partial derivatives are continuous; if V is not bounded, then $\mathbf{v}$ is assumed to satisfy the *regularity condition*

$$r^2 v_i \to 0 \text{ as } r \to \infty, \quad \text{where } r^2 = x^2 + y^2 + z^2.$$

Then

$$\int_{\partial V} \mathbf{v} \cdot \mathbf{n}\, da = \int_V \operatorname{div}\mathbf{v}\, dv,$$
$$\int_{\partial V} v_i n_i\, da = \int_V v_{i,i}\, dv, \tag{5.50}$$

where $\mathbf{n}$ is the unit *outward* normal vector ("outer normal") of the boundary ∂V.

For simple kinds of regions the proof of the divergence theorem is simple. For instance, if V is a parallelepiped, the proof amounts to replacing the triple-integral by iterated integrals.‡ Next, it can be shown that (5.50) holds in regions that can be continuously deformed into a parallelepiped; such regions can then be pieced together to form even more general shapes.

The divergence theorem also holds in multiply connected regions. For regions lying in a plane, or on a surface, multiple connectivity means that the boundary of the region consists of several closed curves. A three-dimensional region bounded by several closed surfaces need not be multiply connected, however. For instance, a spherical shell is simply connected, whereas a torus, having only one boundary surface, is multiply connected. A spherical shell is nevertheless an example of special regions that are said to be *periphractic*, because there exist closed surfaces that are not reducible (i.e. they cannot be contracted to a point without leaving the region). If $\operatorname{div}\mathbf{v} = 0$ in a spherical shell V bounded by the surfaces Σ_1 and Σ_2, then

$$\int_{\partial V} \mathbf{v} \cdot \mathbf{n}\, da = \int_{\Sigma_1} \mathbf{v} \cdot \mathbf{n}\, da - \int_{\Sigma_2} \mathbf{v} \cdot \mathbf{n}\, da = 0,$$

or, $\Sigma_1[\mathbf{v}] - \Sigma_2[\mathbf{v}] = 0$. Expressing the boundary as $\partial V = \Sigma_1 - \Sigma_2$ means that the normals of Σ_1 and Σ_2 would coincide if the surfaces were deformed into each other.

To obtain a hydrodynamic interpretation of (5.50), we consider flow of incompressible fluids. As shown in Figure 5.4, in a time interval dt a volume

† This theorem is also associated with the names of Gauss, Green, and Ostrogradsky.
‡ Cf. [7], pp. 348–351. Proofs for more general regions are given by O. D. Kellogg in [82], pp. 84–120.

$v_i n_i\, da\, dt$ of fluid passes through the area da. The discharge (time rate of volume flow) dQ is then given by $dQ = \mathbf{v} \cdot \mathbf{n}\, da$. Letting $q = \operatorname{div}\mathbf{v}$ be the density of the distributed sources, we obtain

$$Q = \int_{\partial V} dQ = \int_V q\, dv.$$

In effect, the formula expresses the law of conservation of mass: if there is a discharge Q through the boundary, then that amount of fluid must be supplied by sources in the interior of the region.

Kelvin's transformation and the divergence theorem are also applicable to higher rank tensors because the additional (free) indices are then only a means for treating similar expressions simultaneously, e.g.

$$\int_{\partial V} T_{ji} n_j\, da = \int_V T_{ji,j}\, dv. \tag{5.51}$$

To prove (5.51), let v_i in (5.50) be given by $v_i = T_{ij} a_j$, where $\mathbf{a}$ is a constant, arbitrary vector field.

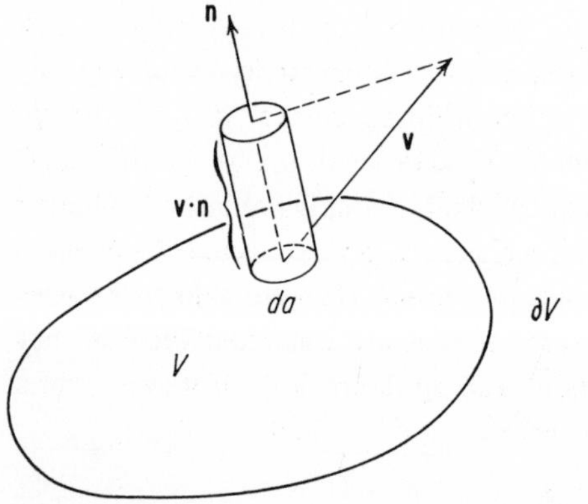

FIGURE 5.4 Variables for calculating discharge.

Problems

A. DIFFERENTIATION OF TENSORS

1. Let $\mathbf{n} = \left(\frac{3}{5}, 0, -\frac{4}{5}\right)$, $\phi(\mathbf{x}) = x^3 + 3xy^2 + z^2$. Calculate $\partial_{\underline{n}}\phi(\mathbf{x})$.

2. Let $\mathbf{n} = \left(\frac{1}{\sqrt{2}}, \frac{1}{\sqrt{2}}, 0\right)$, $\phi(\mathbf{x}) = y^2 - e^{-x}$. Calculate $\partial_{\underline{n}}\phi(\mathbf{x})$.

3. Let x_i be oblique rectilinear coordinates. Consider the base vectors $\mathbf{e}_i = \pi_{,i}$ and $\bar{\mathbf{e}}_i = \nabla x_i$, and show that they constitute reciprocal sets of vectors.

4. Show that $\nabla \times (\mathbf{T} \times \nabla) = (\nabla \times \mathbf{T}) \times \nabla$, and thus verify the definition (5.15).

5. If **T** is a second rank tensor, obtain the component representation of the "right-divergence" $\mathbf{T} \cdot \nabla$.

6. Derive (5.18) from (5.17).

7. Verify (5.19).

8. Obtain the component representation for div grad**v** and grad grad**v**.

9. If **T** is a second rank tensor, obtain the component representation for grad**T**.

B. LINE, SURFACE, AND VOLUME INTEGRALS

10. Let C be a curve given by $x = a \cos \phi$, $y = a \sin \phi$, $z = 0$, where a is constant, and $0 \leq \phi \leq 2\pi$. Evaluate $\int_C v_i \, dx_i$ for the following fields:

a. $v_x = v_y = 0$, $v_z = v =$ const.
b. $v_x = v \cos \phi$, $v_y = v \sin \phi$, $v_z = v\phi$, where v is a constant.
c. $v_x = -v \sin \phi$, $v_x = v \cos \phi$, $v_z = v\phi$, where v is a constant.

11. Let C be a curve given by $x = a \cos \phi$, $y = a \sin \phi$, $z = k\phi$, where a and k are constants, and $0 \leq \phi \leq N\pi$. Evaluate $\int_C v_i \, dx_i$ for the vector fields given in

a. Problem 10a **b.** Problem 10b **c.** Problem 10c

12. Let S be a cylinder defined by $\rho = a$, $0 \leq z \leq L$. Calculate $\int_S v_i n_i \, da$ for the vector fields given in

a. Problem 10a **b.** Problem 10b **c.** Problem 10c

13. Let S be as in Problem 12. Calculate $\int_S v_i n_i \, da$ for the following vector fields:

a. $v_\rho = v_\phi = 0$, $v_z = v =$ const.
b. $v_\rho = v \sin \theta$, $v_\phi = 0$, $v_z = v \cos \theta$, in which v is a constant, and θ is the co-latitude in spherical coordinates.

14. Let S be a spherical surface defined by $r = a$. Calculate $\int_S v_i n_i \, da$ for the vector fields given by

a. Problem 10a **b.** Problem 10b **c.** Problem 10c **d.** Problem 13a
e. $v_r = v =$ const., $v_\theta = v_\phi = 0$.

15. Let V be the solid cylinder $0 \leq \rho \leq a$, $0 \leq z \leq L$. Calculate $\int_V \phi \, dv$ for ϕ given by

a. $\phi = x$ **b.** $\phi = z$ **c.** $\phi = x^2 + y^2$

16. Let V be the solid sphere $0 \leq r \leq a$. Calculate $\int_V \phi \, dv$ for ϕ given by

a. Problem 15a **b.** Problem 15b **c.** Problem 15c

C. BASIC INTEGRAL THEOREMS

17. Let Γ be a closed rectangular path in the x–y plane, with corners at (0, 0), (0, 2), (1, 2), (1, 0). Calculate the circulation $\Gamma[\mathbf{v}]$ for the vector fields

a. $\mathbf{v} = 2\mathbf{e}_x + 3\mathbf{e}_y$ **b.** $\mathbf{v} = x^2\mathbf{e}_x + y^2\mathbf{e}_y$
c. $\mathbf{v} = y\mathbf{e}_x - x\mathbf{e}_y$ **d.** $\mathbf{v} = x^2\mathbf{e}_x - xy\mathbf{e}_y$

18. Let Γ be the ellipse $(x^2/a^2) + (y^2/b^2) = 1$. Calculate the circulation $\Gamma[\mathbf{v}]$ for the vector fields given by

a. Problem 17a **b.** Problem 17b **c.** Problem 17c **d.** Problem 17d

19. Use $v_i = T_{ij}a_j$, in which $\mathbf{a}$ is a constant vector field, to derive a Kelvin's transformation involving T_{ij}. Repeat the same for $v_i = T_{ji}a_j$.

20. If $\text{curl}\mathbf{v} = a\mathbf{e}_x + b\mathbf{e}_y + c\mathbf{e}_z$, where a, b, c are given, what is the easiest way of evaluating $\oint_C v_i\, dx_i$ where C is the unit circle in the x–y plane?

21. Let V be a cube bounded by $\Sigma: x = \pm 1$, $y = \pm 1$, $z = \pm 1$. Calculate the efflux $\Sigma[\mathbf{v}]$ for the following vector fields

a. $\mathbf{v} = \mathbf{e}_x + \mathbf{e}_y + \mathbf{e}_z$ **b.** $\mathbf{v} = x\mathbf{e}_x + y\mathbf{e}_y + z\mathbf{e}_z$

c. $\mathbf{v} = x^3\mathbf{e}_x + y^3\mathbf{e}_y + z^3\mathbf{e}_z$

22. Let V be a sphere bounded by Σ: $r = a$. Calculate the efflux $\Sigma[\mathbf{v}]$ for the vector fields given by

a. Problem 21a **b.** Problem 21b **c.** Problem 21c

Section 6
TENSOR ANALYSIS IN EUCLIDEAN SPACES*

Curvilinear coordinates

In curvilinear coordinates the tensor formalism becomes more complex. Thus a vector $\mathbf{v}$ may be represented by its *contravariant components* v^i, for which the prototypes are the increments dx^i of curvilinear coordinates x^i, or else by its *covariant components* v_i, for which the prototypes are the gradients of a scalar function ϕ: $\phi_{,i} = \partial\phi/\partial x^i$. The rule of free indices applies to superscripts and subscripts separately; the summation convention holds only if one of the repeated indices is a superscript and the other a subscript, e.g. $d\phi = \phi_{,i}\, dx^i = \phi_{,1}\, dx^1 + \phi_{,2}\, dx^2 + \phi_{,3}\, dx^3$.

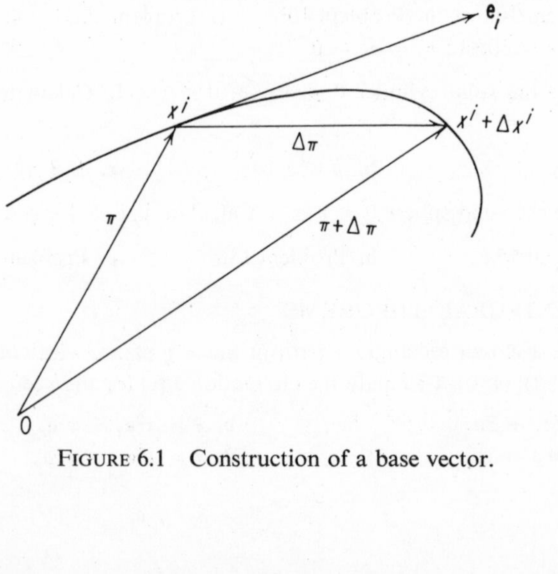

FIGURE 6.1 Construction of a base vector.

In Euclidean point spaces the (local) *natural base vectors* $\mathbf{e}_i$ are defined by

$$\mathbf{e}_i = \pi_{,i} = \frac{\partial \pi}{\partial x^i}, \tag{6.1}$$

where $\pi = P - 0$ is a position vector from the coordinate origin 0 to the point P in question. As is evident from Figure 6.1, a base vector $\mathbf{e}_i$ is tangent to the x^i coordinate line. If the base vectors are mutually orthogonal, then the system of curvilinear coordinates is said to be orthogonal. The base vectors $\mathbf{e}_i$ in curvilinear coordinates are *not*, in general, unit vectors, nor do they have the same physical dimension. This is illustrated below for plane polar coordinates.

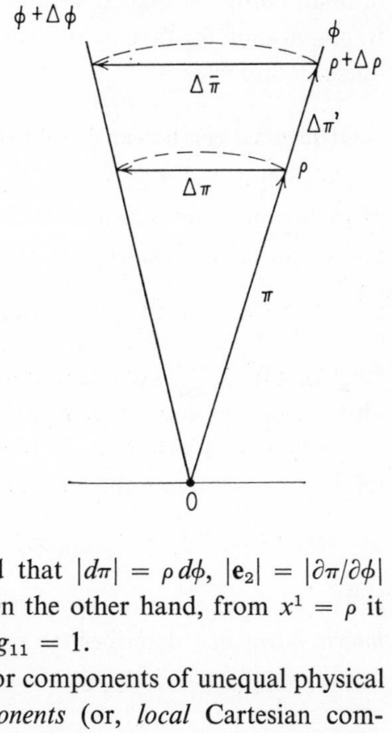

FIGURE 6.2 Increments of position vectors.

Moving along an $x^2 = \phi$ line, we find that $|d\pi| = \rho\, d\phi$, $|\mathbf{e}_2| = |\partial\pi/\partial\phi| = \rho$, $\mathbf{e}_2 \cdot \mathbf{e}_2 = g_{22} = \rho^2$, where $\rho = |\pi|$. On the other hand, from $x^1 = \rho$ it follows that $|\mathbf{e}_1| = |\partial\pi/\partial\rho| = 1$, $\mathbf{e}_1 \cdot \mathbf{e}_1 = g_{11} = 1$.

Whenever it is inappropriate to use tensor components of unequal physical dimensions, we introduce *physical components* (or, *local* Cartesian components) having the same physical dimension. Denoting by $T_{\langle ij \rangle}$ the physical components of a tensor $\mathbf{T}$, we write

$$\mathbf{T}_{\langle 11 \rangle} = \frac{T_{11}}{g_{11}}, \qquad T_{\langle 12 \rangle} = \frac{T_{12}}{\sqrt{g_{11} g_{22}}}, \tag{6.2}$$

etc. In the initial formulation of tensor analysis the contravariant-covariant algorithm and the algorithm of physical components appear side by side.†

† Cf. the celebrated memoir by G. Ricci and T. Levi-Civita [128]. Additional references to the history of tensor analysis may be found in [188].

The subsequent elaboration of tensor analysis occurred largely before tensor methods had taken a hold in physics, which probably explains why the calculus with physical components has fallen into neglect. Besides, the subscript-superscript notation seems to have an enticing symmetry, even typographical neatness, about it. However, these virtues must be weighed against the attendant dimensional inhomogeneity of tensor components. The curious neglect of tensor calculus in terms of physical components was pointed out by Truesdell [172] more than a decade ago. Because almost all of the intended applications will involve physical components only, we are going to give here a full exposition of the calculus with physical components. Moreover, we shall carry out the transition to physical components in orthogonal coordinates *directly*, that is, without recourse to the general tensor formalism. In preparation for this, let us collect the basic formulas for orthogonal curvilinear coordinates.

Orthogonal curvilinear coordinates

We shall denote Cartesian coordinates by x_i, $i = 1, 2, 3$, and a typical set of orthogonal curvilinear coordinates by θ_a, $a = 1, 2, 3$.† The two sets of coordinates are related by the transformation formulas

$$x_i = x_i(\boldsymbol{\theta}), \qquad \theta_a = \theta_a(\mathbf{x}). \tag{6.3}$$

Recalling from (6.1) the definition of the natural base vectors, the orthogonality conditions can be expressed by $\mathbf{e}_a \cdot \mathbf{e}_b = \pi_{,a} \cdot \pi_{,b} = 0$, $a \neq b$. If we let $\pi = x_i(\boldsymbol{\theta})\mathbf{e}_i$, and keep in mind that the Cartesian base vectors $\mathbf{e}_i$ are constant (cf. (5.21)), we obtain the equivalent representation

$$x_{i,a}x_{i,b} = 0, \qquad a \neq b. \tag{6.4}$$

The basis of a metric geometry is the existence of a quadratic form (the *metric form*) that describes the square of an infinitesimal arc length ds:‡

$$ds^2 = dx_i\, dx_i = \sigma_a \sigma_a, \qquad \sigma_a = \frac{d\theta_a}{h_{\underline{a}}}. \tag{6.5}$$

Here $h_{\underline{a}}$ are the *Euclidean metric coefficients* defined by

$$h_{\underline{a}}^{-1} = \sqrt{x_{i,\underline{a}}x_{i,\underline{a}}}, \qquad h_{\underline{a}} = \sqrt{\theta_{\underline{a},i}\theta_{\underline{a},i}}. \tag{6.6}$$

† It is really not consistent with Schouten's notation to use the same numbers for indices of both coordinate systems. However, we can avoid difficulties when they arise by using special notations, e.g. x, y, z for Cartesian indices, r, θ, ϕ for indices of curvilinear coordinates.

‡ The invariance of ds^2 with respect to the transformation (6.3) is, in effect, the property that defines *coordinate transformations* among the mappings described by (6.3).

The differential forms $\sigma_a = h_{\underline{a}}^{-1}\, d\theta_a = h_{\underline{a}}^{-1}\theta_{a,i}\, dx_i$ are not, in general, exact differentials. We also record the useful relation

$$\theta_{b,j} = h_{\underline{b}}^2 x_{j,b}. \tag{6.7}$$

The first of (6.6) is obtained from $ds^2 = dx_i\, dx_i = x_{i,a}x_{i,b}\, d\theta_a\, d\theta_b$ and (6.4). To verify the second of (6.6), we first prove (6.7). According to $(6.3)_1$, $x_{i,j} = \delta_{ij} = x_{i,a}\theta_{a,j}$; multiplying this by $x_{i,b}$ and taking into account (6.4), we arrive at (6.7): $x_{j,b} = x_{i,b}x_{i,a}\theta_{a,j} = h_{\underline{b}}^{-2}\theta_{\underline{b},j}$. Finally, we obtain $(6.6)_2$ from $\theta_{\underline{b},j}\theta_{\underline{b},j} = h_{\underline{b}}^4 x_{j,\underline{b}}x_{j,\underline{b}}$.

Because the transformations from Cartesian to curvilinear coordinates are nonlinear, we cannot describe the structure of a point space referred to curvilinear coordinates in terms of a single vector space (transformations in vector spaces are linear). However, the transformations of coordinate differentials are linear:

$$dx_i = x_{i,a}(\boldsymbol{\theta})\, d\theta_a, \qquad d\theta_a = \theta_{a,i}(\mathbf{x})\, dx_i. \tag{6.8}$$

For instance, if $x = \rho \cos\phi$, $y = \rho\sin\phi$, then $dx = d\rho\cos\phi - \rho\sin\phi\, d\phi$, $dy = d\rho\sin\phi + \rho\cos\phi\, d\phi$ are linear in the differentials $dx, dy, d\rho, d\phi$. Thus although $x_{i,a}(\boldsymbol{\theta})$ and $\theta_{a,i}(\mathbf{x})$ vary from point to point, at any given point the transformation formulas (6.8) are no different from $x_a = Q_{ai}x_i$, (cf. (5.4)), for instance. Consequently, a space E_3 referred to curvilinear coordinates will have *locally* the structure of a vector space V_3; for this reason the metric of V_3 is transferred, through (6.5), only to the infinitesimal increments $d\theta_a$ of curvilinear coordinates.

Actually a representation

$$ds^2 = \sigma_a\sigma_a, \qquad \sigma_a = h_{\underline{a}}^{-1}\, d\theta_a \tag{6.9}$$

of the metric form is equally valid in *Riemannian* (or, "curved") spaces. A Euclidean space is characterized by the existence of global Cartesian frames, so that Euclidean metric coefficients admit the particular representations (6.6) involving Cartesian coordinates. Riemannian metric coefficients do not have representations of the form (6.6); rather, they are assigned outright as functions of the coordinates θ_a.

Evidently the physical components of tensors can be obtained by using orthonormal bases in the place of natural bases $\mathbf{e}_a$. The orthonormal bases are, in effect, *local Cartesian bases*; they consist of mutually orthogonal unit vectors aligned with the curvilinear coordinate lines. Thus in the place of a single Cartesian frame, called a *common frame*, we shall use a specially chosen Cartesian frame at each point of the space.

The base vectors of the local Cartesian frames will be denoted by $\mathbf{i}_a$, and will have the property that

$$\mathbf{i}_a \cdot \mathbf{i}_b = \delta_{ab}. \tag{6.10}$$

In special instances more suggestive notations may be used, e.g. $\mathbf{i}_\rho$, $\mathbf{i}_\theta$, $\mathbf{i}_z$ in cylindrical coordinates, and $\mathbf{i}_r$, $\mathbf{i}_\theta$, $\mathbf{i}_\phi$ in spherical coordinates. We define $\mathbf{i}_a$ by $\mathbf{i}_a = \mathbf{e}_a/|\mathbf{e}_{\underline{a}}| = \pi_{,a}/|\pi_{,\underline{a}}|$. Then from $|\pi_{,\underline{a}}| = \sqrt{\pi_{,\underline{a}} \cdot \pi_{,\underline{a}}} = \sqrt{x_{i,\underline{a}} x_{i,\underline{a}}} = h_{\underline{a}}^{-1}$ follows

$$\mathbf{i}_a = \partial_a \pi \tag{6.11}$$

(cf. (5.22)), where the symbol ∂_a henceforth will denote the directional differentiation

$$\partial_a = h_{\underline{a}} \frac{\partial}{\partial \theta_a}. \tag{6.12}$$

Using (6.11), the orthonormality conditions (6.10) can be expressed by

$$(\partial_a x_i)(\partial_b x_i) = h_{\underline{a}} h_{\underline{b}} x_{i,a} x_{i,b} = \delta_{ab}. \tag{6.10*}$$

It may be of some interest to consider base vectors $\mathbf{e}_a^*$ that constitute the reciprocal triad of the natural basis. Recalling (5.26), we let $\nabla x_i = \mathbf{e}_i = x_{i,a} \nabla \theta_a \equiv x_{i,a} \mathbf{e}_a^*$; multiplying this by $\theta_{b,i}$, we obtain $\mathbf{e}_b^* = \theta_{b,i} \mathbf{e}_i$. Now, $\mathbf{e}_a = \pi_{,a} = x_{j,a} \mathbf{e}_j$, thus $\mathbf{e}_i = \theta_{a,i} \mathbf{e}_a$ and†

$$\mathbf{e}_b^* = \theta_{b,i} \theta_{a,i} \mathbf{e}_a = h_{\underline{b}}^2 \mathbf{e}_b. \tag{6.13}$$

Thus $\mathbf{i}_a = h_{\underline{a}} \mathbf{e}_a = h_{\underline{a}}^{-1} \mathbf{e}_a^*$,

$$|\mathbf{i}_{\underline{a}}| = \sqrt{\mathbf{e}_{\underline{a}} \cdot \mathbf{e}_{\underline{a}}^*}$$

Moreover, because $\nabla \phi = \phi_{,a} \nabla \theta_a = \phi_{,a} \mathbf{e}_a^*$, it follows that $\nabla = \mathbf{i}_a \partial_a$.

It is frequently convenient to use the *direction cosines* Q_{ai} relating the base vectors $\mathbf{e}_i$ of the common frame with the base vectors $\mathbf{i}_a$ of the local frames:

$$Q_{ai} = Q_{ia} = \mathbf{i}_a \cdot \mathbf{e}_i = \partial_a x_i = h_{\underline{a}}^{-1} \theta_{a,i}. \tag{6.14}$$

† In the usual notation, $\nabla \theta_a = \mathbf{e}_a^*$ is replaced by $\nabla \theta^a = \mathbf{e}^a$, whereas (6.13) becomes $\mathbf{e}^b = \mathbf{e}_b/\sqrt{g_{\underline{bb}}}$.

The following formulas then simply express the chain rule of differentiation:

$$\mathbf{i}_a = Q_{ai}\mathbf{e}_i, \qquad \mathbf{e}_i = Q_{ia}\mathbf{i}_a, \tag{6.15}$$

$$\partial_a = Q_{ai}\partial_i, \qquad \partial_i = Q_{ia}\partial_a, \tag{6.16}$$

$$\sigma_a = Q_{ai}\, dx_i, \qquad dx_i = Q_{ia}\sigma_a. \tag{6.17}$$

Naturally (6.15) and (6.16) agree with the condition of invariance of ∇:

$$\nabla = \mathbf{e}_i\partial_i = \mathbf{i}_a\partial_a. \tag{6.18}$$

To verify (6.14), we write $\mathbf{i}_a = \partial_a\pi = h_{\underline{a}}\,\partial\pi/\partial\theta_a = h_{\underline{a}}x_{i,a}\mathbf{e}_i = Q_{ai}\mathbf{e}_i$, and also take into account (6.7). The formulas (6.15)–(6.17) are then simple consequences of (6.14) and of the chain rule of differentiation, e.g. $\sigma_a = h_{\underline{a}}^{-1}\, d\theta_a = h_{\underline{a}}^{-1}\theta_{a,i}\, dx_i = Q_{ai}\, dx_i$.

In view of (6.15), the orthonormality conditions $\mathbf{e}_i \cdot \mathbf{e}_j = \delta_{ij}$, $\mathbf{i}_a \cdot \mathbf{i}_b = \delta_{ab}$ are equivalent to

$$Q_{ai}Q_{aj} = \delta_{ij}, \qquad Q_{ai}Q_{bi} = \delta_{ab}, \tag{6.19}$$

respectively. Because $\mathbf{Q}$ is orthogonal, we have that

$$\det\mathbf{Q} = 1, \tag{6.20}$$

and, by (6.14),

$$J = \frac{1}{h_1h_2h_3}, \tag{6.21}$$

where J is the Jacobian of the transformation from x_i to θ_a:

$$J = \frac{\partial(x, y, z)}{\partial(\theta_1, \theta_2, \theta_3)} = \det(x_{i,a}). \tag{6.22}$$

The physical components T_{ab} of a tensor $\mathbf{T}$ are defined as the components relative to the local Cartesian frames:

$$T_{ab} = \mathbf{T}[\mathbf{i}_a, \mathbf{i}_b] \tag{6.23}$$

(cf. (3.19)). Using (6.15), the components T_{ab} can be related to the components T_{ij} in the common frame through the usual transformation formulas

$$T_{ab} = Q_{ai}Q_{bj}T_{ij}, \qquad T_{ij} = Q_{ia}Q_{jb}T_{ab}. \tag{6.24}$$

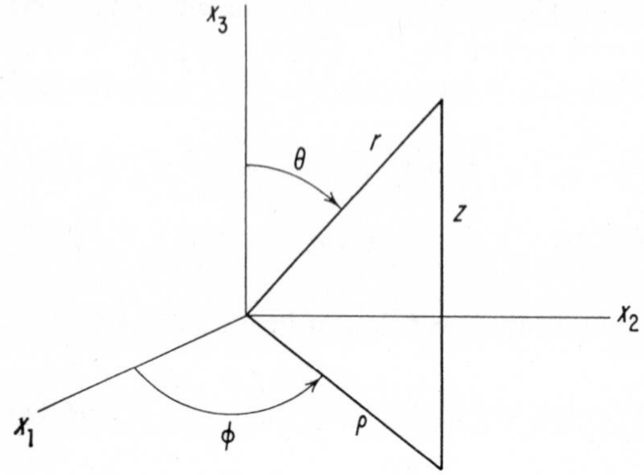

FIGURE 6.3 Cylindrical coordinates ρ,ϕ,z and spherical coordinates r,θ,ϕ. As shown, θ is a positive angle about the "ϕ axis."

If θ_a are the cylindrical coordinates ρ, ϕ, z (Figure 6.3), then $(6.3)_1$ read

$$x_1 = \rho \cos \phi, \qquad x_2 = \rho \sin \phi, \qquad x_3 = z, \tag{6.25}$$

and, by $(6.6)_1$, (6.12),

$$\begin{gathered} h_1 = h_3 = 1, \qquad h_2 = \frac{1}{\rho}, \\ \partial_\rho = \frac{\partial}{\partial \rho}, \qquad \partial_\phi = \frac{1}{\rho}\frac{\partial}{\partial \phi}, \qquad \partial_z = \frac{\partial}{\partial z}. \end{gathered} \tag{6.26}$$

Using (6.14), we find that the array of direction cosines $Q_{ai} = \partial_a x_i$ is given by

$$\|Q_{ai}\| = \begin{Vmatrix} \cos\phi & \sin\phi & 0 \\ -\sin\phi & \cos\phi & 0 \\ 0 & 0 & 1 \end{Vmatrix}, \tag{6.27}$$

where a and i label the rows and the columns, respectively.

If θ_A are the spherical coordinates r, θ, ϕ (Figure 6.3), then

$$x_1 = r \sin\theta \cos\phi, \quad x_2 = r \sin\theta \sin\phi, \quad x_3 = r\cos\theta, \tag{6.28}$$

$$\begin{gathered} h_1 = 1, \qquad h_2 = \frac{1}{r}, \qquad h_3 = \frac{1}{r \sin\theta}, \\ \partial_r = \frac{\partial}{\partial r}, \qquad \partial_\theta = \frac{1}{r}\frac{\partial}{\partial \theta}, \qquad \partial_\phi = \frac{1}{r\sin\theta}\frac{\partial}{\partial\phi}, \end{gathered} \tag{6.29}$$

$$\|Q_{Ai}\| = \|\partial_A x_i\| = \begin{Vmatrix} \sin\theta\cos\phi & \sin\theta\sin\phi & \cos\theta \\ \cos\theta\cos\phi & \cos\theta\sin\phi & -\sin\theta \\ -\sin\phi & \cos\phi & 0 \end{Vmatrix}. \tag{6.30}$$

From $\mathbf{i}_A = Q_{Ai}\mathbf{e}_i = Q_{Ai}Q_{ia}\mathbf{i}_a$ it follows that the direction cosines Q_{Aa} relating the spherical and the cylindrical frames are given by

$$Q_{Aa} = Q_{Ai}Q_{ia}. \tag{6.31}$$

If (6.31) is evaluated as a matrix product, then the array (6.27) must be transposed. Second, because ϕ is the same angle in spherical and cylindrical coordinates, we choose the order z, ρ, ϕ for the latter:

$$Q_{ia}:\quad \begin{array}{c|ccc} & z & \rho & \phi \\ \hline x & 0 & \cos\phi & -\sin\phi \\ y & 0 & \sin\phi & \cos\phi \\ z & 1 & 0 & 0 \end{array}$$

Then

$$\|Q_{Aa}\| = \begin{Vmatrix} \cos\theta & \sin\theta & 0 \\ -\sin\theta & \cos\theta & 0 \\ 0 & 0 & 1 \end{Vmatrix} \tag{6.32}$$

$$= \begin{Vmatrix} \sin\theta\cos\phi & \sin\theta\sin\phi & \cos\theta \\ \cos\theta\cos\phi & \cos\theta\sin\phi & -\sin\theta \\ -\sin\phi & \cos\phi & 0 \end{Vmatrix} \begin{Vmatrix} 0 & \cos\phi & -\sin\phi \\ 0 & \sin\phi & \cos\phi \\ 1 & 0 & 0 \end{Vmatrix}.$$

Let us also calculate in cylindrical and spherical coordinates the curvilinear components π_a of the position vector:

$$\pi_a = Q_{ai}\pi_i = Q_{ai}x_i. \tag{6.33}$$

Using (6.27), we obtain

$$\pi_\rho = \rho, \qquad \pi_\phi = 0, \qquad \pi_z = z, \tag{6.34a}$$

whereas from (6.30) we obtain

$$\pi_r = r, \qquad \pi_\theta = \pi_\phi = 0. \tag{6.34b}$$

These results are really self-evident. It is in the very nature of spherical coordinates that the r-coordinate is measured in the direction to the point in question, or, in other words, that the r-coordinate is laid off at the proper longitude ϕ and the proper co-latitude θ. Therefore, both π_ϕ and π_θ vanish. Similarly, in cylindrical coordinates the ρ-coordinate is laid off at the proper longitude ϕ, hence π_ϕ vanishes. As has been remarked before, *the curvilinear coordinates themselves are not components of a vector.*

The generalized cylindrical coordinates u, v, z are characterized by

$$ds^2 = h^{-2}(du^2 + dv^2) + dz^2, \tag{6.35}$$

where $h = h(u, v)$. Then, in scalar notation,

$$\partial_u = h\frac{\partial}{\partial u}, \qquad \partial_v = h\frac{\partial}{\partial v}, \qquad \partial_z = \frac{\partial}{\partial z}, \tag{6.36}$$

The coordinate surfaces are the planes $z =$ const. and cylinders erected over orthogonal grids of curves in the u–v plane. In the elliptic cylinder coordinates defined by

$$\begin{gathered} x_1 = c\cosh u\cos v, \quad x_2 = c\sinh u\sin v, \quad x_3 = z, \\ h^{-2} = c^2(\sinh^2 u + \sin^2 v), \end{gathered} \tag{6.37}$$

these curves are ellipses and hyperbolas. In bipolar coordinates defined by

$$\begin{gathered} u = \log\left(\frac{\rho_1}{\rho_2}\right), \qquad v = \phi_1 - \phi_2, \\ h = \frac{1}{c}(\cosh u - \cos v) \end{gathered} \tag{6.38}$$

(cf. Figure 6.4), the curves are two families of circles.

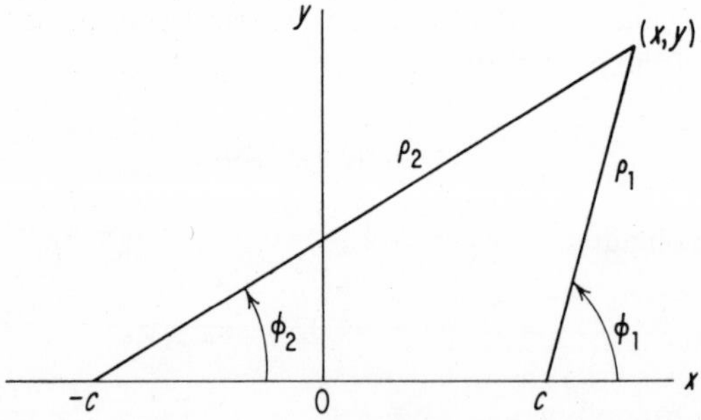

FIGURE 6.4 Parameters for the definition of bipolar coordinates.

Finally, we record the definition of parabolic cylinder coordinates:

$$x_1 = \frac{1}{2}(u^2 - v^2), \quad x_2 = uv, \quad x_3 = z, \quad h^{-2} = u^2 + v^2. \tag{6.39}$$

Absolute differentiation in orthogonal curvilinear coordinates

The difficulties with curvilinear coordinates arise from the variation of coordinate directions from point to point. As is illustrated in Figure 6.5, a constant plane vector field **v** (i.e. a field such that v_x = const., v_y = const.) will have variable components v_ρ and v_ϕ.

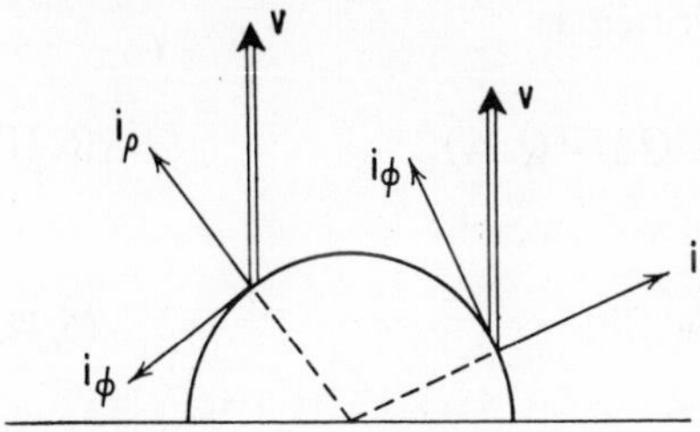

FIGURE 6.5 Constant vector field **v** and variable reference bases ($\mathbf{i}_\rho$, $\mathbf{i}_\phi$).

Hence the ordinary derivatives $v_{a,b}$ are not true measures of the variation of the vector field **v**, or, they do not represent *absolute derivatives*. Our task will now be to define and interpret absolute differentiation. Of course, there is only one *operation* of taking derivatives, namely, the operation explained in calculus courses. Consequently, the different kinds of derivatives that we shall invent will be no more than *ordinary derivatives in various preferred coordinate systems*. This is an important fact to remember: the one and only method for generating special derivatives is expressed by the "equation"

Special (or, preferred) derivative = the ordinary derivative in a special (or, preferred) coordinate system.

Let us contemplate for a moment the nature of Euclidean spaces. A common (Cartesian) frame may be called an *absolute* (or, preferred) *frame*, the existence of Cartesian frames being the very essence of Euclidean spaces. Because in a common frame ordinary differentiation is an invariant operation, we shall identify the equivalent operation in curvilinear coordinates with absolute differentiation (in Cartesian coordinates ordinary and absolute differentiations are one and the same thing). Specifically, we introduce the *absolute derivatives* $v_{a;b}$ of a vector field **v** by†

$$\partial_b \mathbf{v} = \mathbf{e}_i \partial_b v_i = \mathbf{i}_a v_{a;b} \leftrightarrow v_{a;b} = Q_{ai} Q_{bj} v_{i,j}. \tag{6.40}$$

That is, $v_{a;b}$ *and* $v_{i,j}$ *are two representations of the same tensor*, because the two sets of components are related by the transformation formula of second rank tensors. This means of course that *absolute differentiation in curvilinear coordinates is the same operation as the ordinary differentiation in Cartesian coordinates.*

† In the general tensor formalism the name would be "physical components of the covariant derivative."

It remains to derive an explicit representation of $v_{a;b}$ in which only the physical components v_a occur. The method for doing this is a standard one, and will be used whenever we are dealing with preferred frames. We note that, by (6.16), the definition (6.40) can be written as

$$v_{a;b} = Q_{ai}\,\partial_b v_i = Q_{ai}\,\partial_b(Q_{ci}v_c). \tag{6.41}$$

Therefore
$$v_{a;b} = \partial_b v_a + w_{cab}v_c, \tag{6.42}$$

where
$$w_{cab} = \mathbf{i}_a \cdot \partial_b \mathbf{i}_c = Q_{ai}\,\partial_b Q_{ci}, \tag{6.43}$$

will be called the *wryness coefficients* of the (a) frames. This name was suggested by Eriksen and Truesdell [31]; other names for w_{cab} are: Ricci's coefficients of rotation, physical components of Christoffel symbols (cf. Ericksen [32], pp. 804–805). The variables w_{cab} are not tensors but convenient auxiliary quantities.

From the orthonormality condition $(6.19)_2$ it follows that w_{cab} have the skew-symmetry property

$$w_{cab} = -w_{acb}. \tag{6.44}$$

The wryness coefficients defined by (6.43) are characteristic of a "flat space," but they are not necessarily *Euclidean* wryness coefficients. The reason for this is that we have not as yet accounted for the fact that $\mathbf{i}_a$ are the unit normal vectors of smooth coordinate surfaces defined by $\theta_a = \text{const}$. It is intuitively plausible that smooth surfaces cannot be constructed to fit any distribution of unit normal vectors $\mathbf{i}_a = Q_{ai}(\mathbf{x})\mathbf{e}_i$; i.e. unless $Q_{ai}(\mathbf{x})$ satisfy certain *integrability conditions*, the triads $\mathbf{i}_a$ will constitute a kind of a "dislocated space." Let us recall that a *lamellar* field $\mathbf{c}$ is characterized by $\mathbf{c} = \operatorname{grad}\phi$, whence it follows that $\operatorname{curl}\mathbf{c} = \mathbf{0}$. A *complex-lamellar* field is of the form $\mathbf{V} = P(\mathbf{x})\operatorname{grad}Q(\mathbf{x})$. It is easy to verify that

$$\mathbf{V} \cdot \operatorname{curl}\mathbf{V} = 0 \tag{6.45}$$

is a necessary condition for $\mathbf{V}$ to be complex-lamellar; that it is also sufficient is shown below. Now, in view of $Q_{ai} = h_{\underline{a}}^{-1}\,\theta_{a,i}$, the triad $\mathbf{i}_a$ constitutes a three-fold family of complex-lamellar vectors, so that the following must hold:

$$-A_{\underline{a}} \equiv \mathbf{i}_{\underline{a}} \cdot \nabla \times \mathbf{i}_{\underline{a}} = \varepsilon_{ijk}Q_{\underline{a}i}Q_{\underline{a}k,j} = 0. \tag{6.46}$$

Using $\varepsilon_{ijk} = \varepsilon_{bce} Q_{bi} Q_{cj} Q_{ek}$, we can rewrite (6.46) as $\varepsilon_{\underline{ace}} Q_{ek}\, \partial_c Q_{\underline{a}k} = \varepsilon_{\underline{ace}} w_{\underline{a}e\underline{c}} = 0$. Explicitly: $w_{231} = w_{213}$, $w_{312} = w_{321}$, $w_{123} = w_{132}$. Adding the first two relations and subtracting the third, then using (6.44), we obtain $w_{231} = 0$. The proofs of $w_{312} = 0$, $w_{123} = 0$ are analogous. Thus if $\mathbf{i}_a$ are the unit normal vectors of a triply orthogonal system of coordinate surfaces $\theta_a = \text{const.}$, then w_{cab} vanish whenever all indices are distinct:

$$w_{cab} = 0, \qquad a \neq b, \qquad b \neq c, \qquad c \neq a. \tag{6.47}$$

By (6.44), (6.47), the nonvanishing *Euclidean wryness coefficients* must be of the type $w_{\underline{b}a\underline{b}} = -w_{a\underline{bb}}$, $a \neq b$. Noting that, by (6.10)*, $x_{i,\underline{b}} x_{i,b\underline{a}} = -h_{\underline{b}}^{-3} h_{\underline{b},a}$, we obtain from $w_{a\underline{bb}} = h_{\underline{b}} x_{i,\underline{b}} h_{\underline{b}} (h_{\underline{a}} x_{i,a})_{,\underline{b}} = h_{\underline{b}}^2 h_{\underline{a}} x_{i,a\underline{b}} x_{i,\underline{b}}$ the result

$$w_{\underline{b}a\underline{b}} = h_{\underline{b}}^{-1}\, \partial_a h_{\underline{b}} = \partial_a \log h_{\underline{b}} = -w_{a\underline{bb}}, \; a \neq b. \tag{6.48}$$

In connection with (6.45), let us show that a field of unit vectors $\mathbf{n}(\mathbf{x})$ is normal to a surface only if

$$\begin{gathered} -A \equiv \mathbf{n} \cdot (\operatorname{curl} \mathbf{n}) = 0, \\ n_1(n_{3,2} - n_{2,3}) + n_2(n_{1,3} - n_{3,1}) + n_3(n_{2,1} - n_{1,2}) = 0, \end{gathered} \tag{6.46*}$$

where A is referred to as the *abnormality* of the vector field $\mathbf{n}$. Now, if $\mathbf{n}$ is normal to a surface $\phi(\mathbf{x}) = 0$, then $\mathbf{n}$ must be proportional to the gradient of ϕ: $n_k = \lambda \phi_{,k}$. Therefore, it follows that $(\operatorname{curl}\mathbf{n})_i = \varepsilon_{ijk} \lambda_{,j} \phi_{,k}$ and $n_i (\operatorname{curl}\mathbf{n})_i = 0$. To prove the sufficiency of (6.46), we consider the integrability of $\mathbf{n} \cdot d\mathbf{x} = n_i\, dx_i = 0$; evidently the incremental vector $d\mathbf{x}$ lies in the surface element defined locally by $\mathbf{n}$. Assuming that the coordinate system is oriented so that $n_3 \neq 0$, we write $dx_3 = f_1\, dx_1 + f_2\, dx_2$, where $f_1 = -n_1/n_3$, $f_2 = -n_2/n_3$. Consequently, the integrability condition $f_{1,2} = f_{2,1}$ is represented by $n_1 n_{3,2} - n_2 n_{3,1} + n_3(n_{2,1} - n_{1,2}) = 0$. But this condition is obtained from (6.46) by specializing $\mathbf{n}$ to be a function of the independent variables x_1 and x_2 only: $\mathbf{n}(x_1, x_2) \equiv \mathbf{n}(x_1, x_2, x_3(x_1, x_2))$. A fuller discussion of non-integrable mappings is given on pp. 334–343.

The formula (6.42) for absolute derivatives of vectors can be readily extended to higher rank tensors, e.g. $T_{ab;c} = Q_{ai} Q_{bj} Q_{ck} T_{ij,k} = Q_{ai} Q_{bj}\, \partial_c T_{ij} = Q_{ai} Q_{bj}\, \partial_c (Q_{di} Q_{ej} T_{de}) = \partial_c T_{ab} + T_{db} Q_{ai}\, \partial_c Q_{di} + T_{ae} Q_{bj}\, \partial_c Q_{ej}$, or, by (6.43),

$$T_{ab;c} = \partial_c T_{ab} + w_{eac} T_{eb} + w_{ebc} T_{ae}. \tag{6.49}$$

From inspection of (6.42) and (6.49) we can state the following rule: the absolute derivative equals the directional derivative plus a sum of terms, one for each index of the tensor, which compensate for the variation of the local bases. The first index of wryness coefficients is a summation index, the last index is the differentiation index, and the middle index is the free index which in the tensor has been replaced by the summation index. Symbolically,

$$M_{.a.;b} = \partial_b M_{.a.} + \cdots + w_{eab} M_{.e.} + \cdots. \tag{6.50}$$

All differential operations defined previously in Cartesian coordinates can be changed to curvilinear coordinates simply by replacing the *comma* with the *semicolon*. For instance,

$$\phi_{;c} = \partial_c \phi = (\text{grad}\phi)_c, \tag{6.51}$$

$$\text{div}\mathbf{v} = v_{a;a} = \partial_a v_a + w_{caa} v_c, \quad (\text{curl}\mathbf{v})_c = \varepsilon_{cab} v_{b;a}, \tag{6.52}$$

$$(\text{div}\mathbf{T})_a = T_{ba;b} = \partial_b T_{ba} + w_{ebb} T_{ea} + w_{eab} T_{be}, \tag{6.53}$$

$$\nabla^2 \phi = \phi_{;cc} \equiv (\phi_{;c})_{;c}. \tag{6.54}$$

The wryness coefficients can be related directly to the variation of the base vectors $\mathbf{i}_a$ from point to point. Starting from $\mathbf{i}_a = Q_{ai}\mathbf{e}_i$, we obtain $\partial_b \mathbf{i}_a = (\partial_b Q_{ai})\mathbf{e}_i = (\partial_b Q_{ai})(Q_{ci}\mathbf{i}_c) = -(Q_{ai}\partial_b Q_{ci})\mathbf{i}_c$; thus, in contrast to (5.21),

$$\partial_b \mathbf{i}_a = -w_{cab}\mathbf{i}_c. \tag{6.55}$$

Evidently a wryness coefficient w_{cab} describes the rate of turning of the base vector $\mathbf{i}_a$ as we progress along the θ_b coordinate line. The equivalent form

$$\mathbf{i}_{a;b} = \partial_b \mathbf{i}_a + w_{cab}\mathbf{i}_c = 0 \tag{6.56}$$

expresses an identity: the variation of $\mathbf{i}_a$ (given by $\partial_b \mathbf{i}_a$) is canceled by the term $w_{cab}\mathbf{i}_c$ that compensates for the variation of the base vectors.

Writing $\partial_b \mathbf{v} = \partial_b(v_a \mathbf{i}_a) = (\partial_b v_a)\mathbf{i}_a + v_a \partial_b \mathbf{i}_a$,† and using (6.55), we obtain after a suitable change of indices the formula

$$\partial_b \mathbf{v} = \mathbf{i}_a v_{a;b} = \mathbf{i}_a(\partial_b v_a + w_{cab} v_c). \tag{6.57}$$

The formulas (6.52) can be reproduced in the same way: $\nabla \cdot \mathbf{v} = (\mathbf{i}_b \partial_b) \cdot (\mathbf{i}_a v_a) = \mathbf{i}_b \cdot \mathbf{i}_a v_{a;b} = v_{a;a}$, $\nabla \times \mathbf{v} = (\mathbf{i}_b \partial_b) \times (\mathbf{i}_a v_a) = \mathbf{i}_b \times \mathbf{i}_a v_{a;b} = \varepsilon_{cba}\mathbf{i}_c v_{a;b}$.

† Because direct notation is not being used at the present, the notation $\mathbf{v} = v_a \mathbf{i}_a$ should cause no confusion.

Examples of absolute differentiation

The wryness coefficients are calculated from (6.48). In cylindrical coordinates the only variable metric coefficient is $h_2 = 1/\rho$ (cf. (6.26)); hence the nonvanishing wryness coefficients are

$$w_{122} = \frac{1}{\rho} = -w_{212}. \tag{6.58}$$

In spherical coordinates we obtain

$$w_{122} = w_{133} = \frac{1}{r} = -w_{212} = -w_{313}, \quad w_{233} = \frac{\cot\theta}{r} = -w_{323}. \tag{6.59}$$

In generalized cylindrical coordinates, using scalar notation,

$$w_{uvu} = h_v = -w_{vuu}, \qquad w_{vuv} = h_u = -w_{uvv},$$
$$h_v = \frac{\partial h}{\partial u}, \qquad h_v = \frac{\partial h}{\partial v}, \tag{6.60}$$

To show that $v_{i,j}$ and $v_{a;b}$ represent the same operation, we may consider the constant vector field $v_x = A$, $v_y = B$, $v_z = C$. By hypothesis, $v_{i,j} = 0$. Using (6.30), we now calculate the spherical components of $\mathbf{v}$: $v_r = Q_{ri}v_i = A\sin\theta\cos\phi + B\sin\theta\sin\phi + C\cos\theta$, $v_\theta = Q_{\theta i}v_i = A\cos\theta\cos\phi + B\cos\theta\sin\phi - C\sin\theta$, $v_\phi = Q_{\phi i}v_i = -A\sin\phi + B\cos\phi$. Evidently $v_{a,b} \neq 0$, but we can verify that $v_{a;b} = 0$. For instance, $v_{2;3} = v_{\theta;\phi} = \partial_\phi v_\theta + w_{\phi\theta\phi}v_\phi = (1/r\sin\theta)(-A\cos\theta\sin\phi + B\cos\theta\cos\phi) - (\cot\theta/r)(-A\sin\phi + B\cos\phi) = 0$.

In cylindrical coordinates the explicit forms of $v_{a;b}$ are

$$v_{\rho;\rho} = \partial_\rho v_\rho,\ v_{\rho;\phi} = \partial_\phi v_\rho - \frac{1}{\rho}v_\phi,\ v_{\rho;z} = \partial_z v_\rho,$$
$$v_{\phi;\rho} = \partial_\rho v_\phi,\ v_{\phi;\phi} = \partial_\phi v_\phi + \frac{1}{\rho}v_\rho,\ v_{\phi;z} = \partial_z v_\phi, \tag{6.61}$$
$$v_{z;\rho} = \partial_\rho v_z,\ v_{z;\phi} = \partial_\phi v_z,\ v_{z;z} = \partial_z v_z.$$

In spherical coordinates,

$$v_{r;r} = \partial_r v_r,\ v_{r;\theta} = \partial_\theta v_r - \frac{1}{r}v_\theta,\ v_{r;\phi} = \partial_\phi v_r - \frac{1}{r}v_\phi,$$
$$v_{\theta;r} = \partial_r v_\theta,\ v_{\theta;\theta} = \partial_\theta v_\theta + \frac{1}{r}v_r,\ v_{\theta;\phi} = \partial_\phi v_\theta - \frac{\cot\theta}{r}v_\phi, \tag{6.62}$$
$$v_{\phi;r} = \partial_r v_\phi,\ v_{\phi;\theta} = \partial_\theta v_\phi,\ v_{\phi;\phi} = \partial_\phi v_\phi + \frac{1}{r}v_r + \frac{\cot\theta}{r}v_\theta,$$

in generalized cylindrical coordinates

$$v_{u;u} = \partial_u v_u - h_v v_v,\ v_{u;v} = \partial_v v_u + h_u v_v,\ v_{u;z} = \partial_z v_u,$$
$$v_{v;u} = \partial_u v_v + h_v v_u,\ v_{v;v} = \partial_v v_v - h_u v_u,\ v_{v;z} = \partial_z v_v, \tag{6.63}$$
$$v_{z;u} = \partial_u v_z,\ v_{z;v} = \partial_v v_z,\ v_{z;z} = \partial_z v_z$$

To put the formulas (6.54), (6.52) into a more familiar form, let us write out (6.42) explicitly: $v_{1;1} = \partial_1 v_1 + w_{211}v_2 + w_{311}v_3$, etc., $v_{1;2} = \partial_2 v_1 + w_{212}v_2$, etc., or by (6.48),

$$\begin{aligned} v_{1;1} &= \partial_1 v_1 - v_2 \partial_2 \log h_1 - v_3 \partial_3 \log h_1, \ldots, \ldots, \\ v_{1;2} &= \partial_2 v_1 + v_2 \partial_1 \log h_2, \ldots, \ldots, \ldots, \ldots, \ldots. \end{aligned} \tag{6.64}$$

Then it follows that

$$\begin{aligned} \operatorname{div}\mathbf{v} &= h_2 h_3 \partial_1 \frac{v_1}{h_2 h_3} + h_3 h_1 \partial_2 \frac{v_2}{h_3 h_1} + h_1 h_2 \partial_3 \frac{v_3}{h_1 h_2}, \\ v_{(1;2)} &= \frac{1}{2}(v_{1;2} + v_{2;1}) = \frac{1}{2}\left[\frac{1}{h_1}\partial_2(v_1 h_1) + \frac{1}{h_2}\partial_1(v_2 h_2)\right], \end{aligned} \tag{6.65}$$

$$\ldots, \ldots, \ldots, \ldots, \ldots,$$

$$\begin{aligned} (\operatorname{curl}\mathbf{v})_1 &= v_{3;2} - v_{2;3} = h_3 \partial_2 \frac{v_3}{h_3} - h_2 \partial_3 \frac{v_2}{h_2}, \\ (\operatorname{curl}\mathbf{v})_2 &= v_{1;3} - v_{3;1} = h_1 \partial_3 \frac{v_1}{h_1} - h_3 \partial_1 \frac{v_3}{h_3}, \\ (\operatorname{curl}\mathbf{v})_3 &= v_{2;1} - v_{1;2} = h_2 \partial_1 \frac{v_2}{h_2} - h_1 \partial_2 \frac{v_1}{h_1}. \end{aligned} \tag{6.66}$$

The scalar Laplacian $\nabla^2\phi$ is obtained by letting $v_a = \partial_a \phi$ in $(6.65)_1$. The vector Laplacian ✡v = grad divv − curl curlv requires the repeated application of the operator *curl*, e.g.

$$\begin{aligned} (\operatorname{curl}\operatorname{curl}\mathbf{v})_3 &= [(\operatorname{curl}\mathbf{v})_2]_{;1} - [(\operatorname{curl}\mathbf{v})_1]_{;2} \\ &= h_2 \partial_1 \frac{1}{h_2}(\operatorname{curl}\mathbf{v})_2 - h_1 \partial_2 \frac{1}{h_1}(\operatorname{curl}\mathbf{v})_1 \\ &= h_2 \partial_1 \left(\frac{h_1}{h_2}\partial_3 \frac{v_1}{h_1} - \frac{h_3}{h_2}\partial_1 \frac{v_3}{h_3}\right) - h_1 \partial_2 \left(\frac{h_3}{h_1}\partial_2 \frac{v_3}{h_3} - \frac{h_2}{h_1}\partial_3 \frac{v_2}{h_2}\right). \end{aligned} \tag{6.67}$$

Finally, let us write out the explicit forms of (6.53) in several coordinate systems. In cylindrical coordinates the nonvanishing wryness coefficients are w_{122} and w_{212} hence the repeated summations in (6.53) reduce to at most two terms. We obtain

$$\begin{aligned} (\operatorname{div}\mathbf{T})_\rho &= \partial_\rho T_{\rho\rho} + \partial_\phi T_{\phi\rho} + \partial_z T_{z\rho} + \frac{1}{\rho}(T_{\rho\rho} - T_{\phi\phi}), \\ (\operatorname{div}\mathbf{T})_\phi &= \partial_\rho T_{\rho\phi} + \partial_\phi T_{\phi\phi} + \partial_z T_{z\phi} + \frac{1}{\rho}(T_{\rho\phi} + T_{\phi\rho}), \\ (\operatorname{div}\mathbf{T})_z &= \partial_\rho T_{\rho z} + \partial_\phi T_{\phi z} + \partial_z T_{zz} + \frac{1}{\rho} T_{\rho z}. \end{aligned} \tag{6.68}$$

In spherical coordinates the nonvanishing wryness coefficients are w_{122}, w_{133}, w_{212}, w_{313}, w_{233}, w_{323}. Again, the nonvanishing terms in the summations occurring in (6.53) can be written down by inspection. We obtain

$$\begin{aligned}
(\mathrm{div}\mathbf{T})_r &= \partial_r T_{rr} + \partial_\theta T_{\theta r} + \partial_\phi T_{\phi r} \\
&\quad + \frac{1}{r}[2T_{rr} - T_{\theta\theta} - T_{\phi\phi} + T_{\theta r}\cot\theta], \\
(\mathrm{div}\mathbf{T})_\theta &= \partial_r T_{r\theta} + \partial_\theta T_{\theta\theta} + \partial_\phi T_{\phi\theta} \\
&\quad + \frac{1}{r}[2T_{r\theta} + T_{\theta r} + (T_{\theta\theta} - T_{\phi\phi})\cot\theta], \\
(\mathrm{div}\mathbf{T})_\phi &= \partial_r T_{r\phi} + \partial_\theta T_{\theta\phi} + \partial_\phi T_{\phi\phi} \\
&\quad + \frac{1}{r}[2T_{r\phi} + T_{\phi r} + (T_{\theta\phi} + T_{\phi\theta})\cot\theta].
\end{aligned} \tag{6.69}$$

In generalized cylindrical coordinates we get

$$\begin{aligned}
(\mathrm{div}\mathbf{T})_u &= \partial_u T_{uu} + \partial_v T_{vu} + \partial_z T_{zu} \\
&\quad - h_v(T_{vu} + T_{uv}) + h_u(T_{vv} - T_{uu}), \\
(\mathrm{div}\mathbf{T})_v &= \partial_u T_{uv} + \partial_v T_{vv} + \partial_z T_{zv} \\
&\quad - h_u(T_{uv} + T_{vu}) + h_v(T_{uu} - T_{vv}), \\
(\mathrm{div}\mathbf{T})_z &= \partial_u T_{uz} + \partial_v T_{vz} + \partial_z T_{zz} \\
&\quad - h_u T_{uz} - h_v T_{vz}.
\end{aligned} \tag{6.70}$$

Further discussion of absolute differentiation

We shall collect here various special results and observations concerning absolute differentiation. First, as a rule directional derivatives do not commute; for instance, in cylindrical coordinates

$$\partial_\rho\partial_\phi - \partial_\phi\partial_\rho = \frac{\partial}{\partial\rho}\frac{1}{\rho}\frac{\partial}{\partial\phi} - \frac{1}{\rho}\frac{\partial}{\partial\phi}\frac{\partial}{\partial\rho} = -\frac{1}{\rho}\partial_\phi = w_{\phi\rho\phi}\partial_\phi.$$

More generally, using the commutativity of the ordinary derivatives, $\partial_j\partial_i = \partial_i\partial_j$, we find from $\partial_a = Q_{ai}\partial_i$, $\partial_b = Q_{bj}\partial_j$ that

$$[\partial_a, \partial_b] = \partial_a\partial_b - \partial_b\partial_a = (w_{cab} - w_{cba})\partial_c, \tag{6.71}$$

where $[\partial_a, \partial_b]$ is called the *Poisson bracket* of the directional derivatives. It is now easy to verify that, as a consequence of (6.71), the second absolute derivatives of a scalar commute:

$$\phi_{;ab} = \phi_{;ba}. \tag{6.72}$$

Let us also investigate the second derivatives of a vector. Because $v_{c;ab}$ represents the same operation as $v_{k,ij}$, and since $v_{k,ij} - v_{k,ji} = 0$, we naturally expect that

$$v_{c;ab} = v_{c;ba}. \tag{6.73}$$

However, this result does not become self-evident if we proceed in a purely formal way. Then from $v_{c;ab} = (v_{c;a})_{;b} = \partial_b v_{c;a} + w_{ecb}v_{e;a} + w_{eab}v_{c;e}$, $v_{c;ba} = (v_{c;b})_{;a} = \partial_a v_{c;b} + w_{eca}v_{e;b} + w_{eba}v_{c;e}$ follows

$$v_{c;ab} - v_{c;ba} = v_e R_{ecab}, \tag{6.74}$$

where
$$R_{ecab} = \partial_b w_{eca} - \partial_a w_{ecb} + w_{edb}w_{cda} - w_{eda}w_{cdb} + w_{ecd}(w_{dab} - w_{dba}) \tag{6.75}$$

is called the *Riemann-Christoffel curvature tensor*. It is evident that R_{ecab} is skew-symmetric in the pairs of indices *ec* and *ab*; also, recalling that the non-vanishing wryness coefficients are of the form (6.48), the last term of (6.75) can be expressed as follows:

$$w_{ecd}(w_{dab} - w_{dba}) = w_{ecb}w_{\underline{b}a\underline{b}} - w_{eca}w_{\underline{a}b\underline{a}}, \quad a \neq b, \quad c \neq e. \tag{6.76}$$

In Euclidean spaces R_{ecab} should vanish; indeed, substituting (6.43) into (6.75) we find that $R_{ecab} = 0$, which is a reminder that the definition (6.43) is characteristic of flat spaces only. If (6.75) is evaluated by using (6.48), then the vanishing of R_{ecab} can be verified only if it is made explicit that the metric coefficients are Euclidean, i.e. given by (6.6), because the representation (6.48) holds equally well in Riemannian spaces.

When dealing with curvilinear coordinates, one is always warned against confusing the scalar and vector Laplacians, defined by (5.16) and (5.17), respectively. It is really not incorrect to interpret the vector Laplacian as $\nabla^2 =$ div grad, but there is a good reason for the warning nevertheless. Let us calculate $\nabla\mathbf{v} = (\mathbf{i}_b\partial_b)(\mathbf{i}_a v_a) = \mathbf{i}_b\mathbf{i}_a v_{a;b}$, div grad$\mathbf{v} = (\mathbf{i}_c\partial_c)\cdot(\mathbf{i}_b\mathbf{i}_a v_{a;b})$; through repeated use of (6.55) we now obtain

$$\nabla^2\mathbf{v} = \mathbf{i}_a v_{a;bb} = \mathbf{i}_a \nabla^2 v_a. \tag{6.77}$$

But $(\text{✡}\mathbf{v})_a = (\text{grad div}\mathbf{v})_a - (\text{curl curl}\mathbf{v})_a = v_{b;ba} - \varepsilon_{abc}\varepsilon_{cde}v_{e;db} = v_{b;ba} - v_{b;ab} + v_{a;bb}$; hence, by (6.73), $\text{✡}\mathbf{v} = \nabla^2\mathbf{v}$. However, in a particular case the cancellation $v_{b;ba} - v_{b;ab} = 0$ may not be demonstrable in a simple way because it involves, in essence, the vanishing Riemann-Christoffel tensor. Therefore, the vector Laplacian should be calculated from (5.17), because then the *customary* representation is obtained.

Let us also consider time rates. We describe the motion of a particle by giving its coordinates as functions of time t: $x_i = x_i(t)$. The velocity $\mathbf{v}$ and acceleration $\mathbf{a}$ are then defined by $\dot{x}_i = dx_i/dt = v_i$, $a_i = \ddot{x}_i = d^2x_i/dt^2$. Following the particle, a tensor field $T_{ij}(\mathbf{x})$ appears as a function of time: $T_{ij}(t) = T_{ij}(\mathbf{x}(t))$.

The ordinary time rate yields different tensors in different coordinate systems, e.g. $\dot{v}_a = \dot{Q}_{ai}v_i + Q_{ai}\dot{v}_i$. Therefore, it is natural to seek an *absolute differentiation* $\delta/\delta t$† that has the same effect as produced by d/dt in a common frame. We first record the formula

$$v_e = h_{\underline{e}}^{-1}\dot{\theta}_e, \tag{6.78}$$

which follows from $v_e = Q_{ei}\dot{x}_i = Q_{ei}x_{i,b}\dot{\theta}_b$ and (6.14), (6.19)$_2$. In complete analogy with (6.40) we now write

$$\frac{\delta}{\delta t}T_{ab} \equiv Q_{ai}Q_{bj}\frac{d}{dt}T_{ij}, \tag{6.79}$$

i.e. the absolute time rate represents the same tensor as would be obtained by the ordinary time rate in a Cartesian frame. Proceeding in the usual way, we obtain

$$\frac{\delta}{\delta t}T_{ab} = Q_{ai}Q_{bj}\frac{d}{dt}(Q_{ci}Q_{dj}T_{cd}) = \dot{T}_{ab} + T_{cb}Q_{ai}Q_{ci,e}\dot{\theta}_e + T_{ad}Q_{bj}Q_{dj,e}\dot{\theta}_e,$$

thus

$$\frac{\delta}{\delta t}T_{ab} = \dot{T}_{ab} + w_{cae}v_eT_{cb} + w_{cbe}v_eT_{ac}.$$

The ordinary time rate of T_{ab} can be evaluated through a chain rule: $(d/dt)T_{ab} = \dot{T}_{ab} = T_{ab,e}\dot{\theta}_e = v_e\partial_eT_{ab}$, so that an alternative representation of the absolute time rate is‡

$$\frac{\delta}{\delta t}T_{ab} = T_{ab;e}v_e. \tag{6.80}$$

The components of the acceleration $\mathbf{a}$ are obtained from

$$a_b = \frac{\delta}{\delta t}v_b = \dot{v}_b + w_{cbe}v_ev_c = v_ev_{b;e}. \tag{6.81}$$

† Usually called an *intrinsic differentiation*.

‡ In kinematics of a *continuum* we shall treat the more general case $\mathbf{T} = \mathbf{T}(\mathbf{x}, t)$. Then (6.80) will be replaced by $(\delta/\delta t)T_{ab} = \partial_tT_{ab} + v_eT_{ab;e}$, where ∂_tT_{ab} denotes the time rate at a fixed $\mathbf{x}$.

For instance, in cylindrical coordinates $v_\rho = \dot{\rho}$, $v_\phi = \rho\dot{\phi}$, $v_z = \dot{z}$. Therefore, by (6.58), (6.81), $a_\rho = \ddot{\rho} - \rho\dot{\phi}^2$, $a_\phi = \rho\ddot{\phi} + 2\dot{\rho}\dot{\phi}$, $a_z = \ddot{z}$. Incidentally, we also have that $v_a = (\delta/\delta t)\pi_a$, where π_a are the curvilinear components of the position vector.

Finally, let us take up again the interpretation of the wryness coefficients. If (a) and (A) are two systems of curvilinear coordinates, then, by (6.31), $Q_{Ai} = Q_{Aa}Q_{ai}$. Substituting this into $w_{CAB} \equiv Q_{Ai}\partial_B Q_{Ci}$, we obtain

$$w_{CAB} = Q_{Cc}Q_{Aa}Q_{Bb}w_{cab} + Q_{Aa}\partial_B Q_{Ca}. \tag{6.82}$$

This expression differs from the transformation formula of third rank tensors by the "inhomogeneous" term on the right-hand side. In particular, if the (a) coordinate system is Cartesian, i.e. $w_{cab} = 0$, we recover from (6.82) the formula (6.43).

Variables satisfying a transformation formula of the type shown in (6.82) are called *geometric objects*. They are not tensors ("physical objects") because they do not represent invariant quantities; rather, geometric objects describe properties of particular coordinate systems. For instance, let us consider a particle sliding along a guide which rotates about a fixed axis. In order to reconcile the one-dimensional motion $\rho = \rho(t)$ with Newton's second law, $F = m\ddot{\rho}$, it is necessary to supplement the impressed force F' (in the direction of the ρ axis) by the "inertial force" $m\rho\dot{\phi}^2 = mw_{\rho\phi\phi}v_\phi^2$, $v_\phi = \rho\dot{\phi}$, thus

$$F' + mw_{\rho\phi\phi}v_\phi^2 = m\ddot{\rho}.$$

Problems

A. ORTHOGONAL CURVILINEAR COORDINATES

1. Verify **a.** (6.26), (6.27) **b.** (6.29), (6.30), (6.32).
2. Verify (6.34).
3. Let η, θ, ϕ be prolate spheroidal coordinates given by

$$\begin{aligned} x_1 &= a \sinh\eta \sin\theta \cos\phi, & 0 &\le \eta < \infty \\ x_2 &= a \sinh\eta \sin\theta \sin\phi, & 0 &\le \theta \le \pi \\ x_3 &= a \cosh\eta \cos\theta, & 0 &\le \phi < 2\pi \end{aligned}$$

Calculate h_a, ∂_a, and Q_{ai}. What are the surfaces of this coordinate system?

4. Let η, θ, ϕ be oblate spheroidal coordinates given by

$$\begin{aligned} x_1 &= a \cosh\eta \sin\theta \cos\phi, & 0 &\le \eta < \infty \\ x_2 &= a \cosh\eta \sin\theta \sin\phi, & 0 &\le \theta \le \pi \\ x_3 &= a \sinh\eta \cos\theta, & 0 &\le \phi < 2\pi \end{aligned}$$

Calculate h_a, ∂_a and Q_{ai}. What are the surfaces of this coordinate system?

5. Let u, v, ϕ be parabolic coordinates given by

$$x_1 = uv\cos\phi, \qquad 0 \le u < \infty$$
$$x_2 = uv\sin\phi, \qquad 0 \le v < \infty$$
$$x_3 = \frac{1}{2}(u^2 - v^2), \quad 0 \le \phi < 2\pi$$

Calculate h_a, ∂_a and Q_{ai}. What are the surfaces of this coordinate system?

B. ABSOLUTE DERIVATIVES

6. Consider orthonormal frames of vectors $\mathbf{d}_A$ defined by $\mathbf{d}_A = Q_{Ai}\mathbf{e}_i$, in which

$$\|Q_{Ai}\| = \begin{Vmatrix} \cos\alpha & \sin\alpha & 0 \\ -\sin\alpha & \cos\alpha & 0 \\ 0 & 0 & 1 \end{Vmatrix},$$

and $\alpha = \alpha(x, y)$. Calculate w_{CAB}.

7. Let θ_a be cylindrical coordinates, and consider orthonormal frames of vectors $\mathbf{d}_A$ defined by $\mathbf{d}_A = Q_{Aa}\mathbf{i}_a$, in which

$$\|Q_{Aa}\| = \begin{Vmatrix} \cos\alpha & \sin\alpha & 0 \\ -\sin\alpha & \cos\alpha & 0 \\ 0 & 0 & 1 \end{Vmatrix},$$

and $\alpha = \alpha(\rho)$. Calculate w_{CAB}.

8. Write out the explicit formulas for

   a. $M_{abc;e}$ **b.** $T_{ab;ce}$ **c.** $\phi_{;abc}$

9. Let $v_i = x_i$, hence $v_{i,j} = \delta_{ij}$. Verify $v_{a;b} = \delta_{ab}$ in

   a. cylindrical coordinates **b.** spherical coordinates

10. Verify (6.58), (6.59), (6.60).

11. Verify (6.61), (6.62), (6.63).

12. Obtain explicit formulas for grad$f$, div**b**, and curl**b** in

    a. cylindrical coordinates **b.** spherical coordinates
    c. generalized cylindrical coordinates

13. Verify **a.** (6.68) **b.** (6.69) **c.** (6.70)

14. Calculate the nonvanishing wryness coefficients for the curvilinear coordinates given in

    a. Problem 3 **b.** Problem 4 **c.** Problem 5

15. Let **T** be a symmetric second rank tensor. Write out the components of div**T** assuming that the coordinate system is the principal coordinate system of **T**.

16. Write out the explicit formulas for $(\text{div}\mathbf{T})_a$ (without, however, substituting the values of the non-vanishing wryness coefficients) in the curvilinear coordinates given by

a. Problem 3 **b.** Problem 4 **c.** Problem 5

17. Verify (6.71) and (6.72).

18. Verify (6.74) and (6.75).

19. Calculate the components of particle velocity and particle acceleration in spherical coordinates.

20. Calculate the components of particle velocity and particle acceleration in generalized cylindrical coordinates.

21. Can you interpret (6.43) as $Q_{ci;b} = 0$, thus obtaining the counterpart of (5.6)?

22. To describe toroidal shells, the following coordinates may be used. Let $x^2 + y^2 = A^2$ be the center line of the torus, and let $\phi = \tan^{-1}(y/x)$ be the angle of plane polar coordinates. In each meridional plane $\phi = \text{const.}$, let r be the distance measured from the intersection of the meridional plane with the center line, and let $M = \sin^{-1}(z/r)$ be the angle measured up from the xy plane. Calculate ∂_a, Q_{ai}, and w_{cab}. If r, M, ϕ are to be an acceptable set of coordinates, should there be some limitations on r (e.g. $r < A$)?

CHAPTER **2**

KINEMATICS

Kinematics is that branch of mechanics which deals with motions of bodies. It may be called the time-geometry of motions, and is not in any way concerned with the causes of motions. A leaf driven by the wind, an electron moving in a magnetic field, the sweeping hand of a clock, all belong to the domain of kinematics, though the forces that propel these motions are of diverse natures.

The purely kinematical aspect of motions is also the one that is directly related to our immediate physical experience, because it is built on the familiar concepts of time and position. In the same way that our everyday life is described by reference to time and position, kinematics supplies the main framework of physical sciences. For no matter how complicated the causes that we invent, their function is but to move a particle from one point to another, to change one shape of a body into another. Thus a description of nature is not only bound to kinematics, it is actually *kinematics-oriented.*

This chapter contains a brief exposition of the basic kinematical concepts. These concepts lie at the very foundations of continuum mechanics, its scope and character being determined by the nature of these concepts.

Section 7
MOTION OF PARTICLES

In what follows we shall discuss the motion of a generic "particle" of a body; the ideas associated with the motion of entire strings or layers of particles will be taken up in the next section. The concepts of motion, velocity, acceleration, transformations between moving frames, etc., are of course familiar from mechanics of discrete systems. On the other hand, the particular attention given to representations of these concepts, and to the attendant questions of invariance, is typical of continuum mechanics.

Particles, bodies, motion

Let us briefly review the description of motion of discrete particle systems. We consider a swarm of particles, illustrated in Figure 7.1. The individual particles of masses $m(\underline{n})$ are enumerated, or named, by a label $\underline{n}$, where $\underline{n} = 1, 2, \ldots, \underline{N}$. The components $x_k(\underline{n})$ of the position vector $\mathbf{x}(\underline{n})$ pointing to the $\underline{n}$th particle are functions of time; thus we shall also use the notation

$$x_k = x_k(\underline{n} \mid t). \tag{7.1}$$

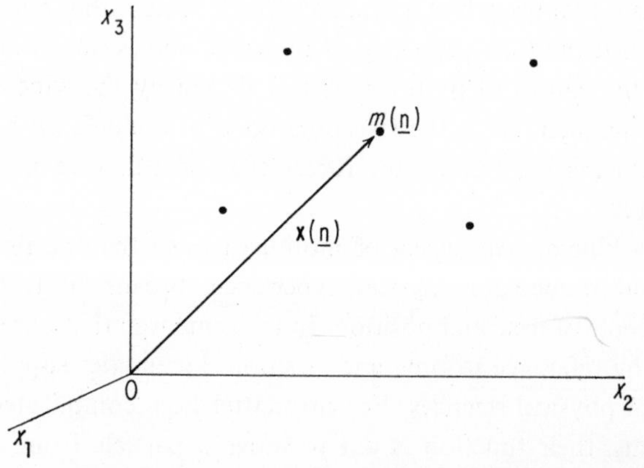

FIGURE 7.1 A discrete system of particles.

The *velocity* $\mathbf{v}$ and the *acceleration* $\mathbf{a}$ of the $\underline{n}$th particle are then defined by†

$$\begin{aligned} \mathbf{v}(\underline{n} \mid t) &= \frac{d}{dt}\mathbf{x}(\underline{n} \mid t) = \dot{\mathbf{x}}(\underline{n} \mid t), \\ \mathbf{a}(\underline{n} \mid t) &= \frac{d}{dt}\mathbf{v}(\underline{n} \mid t) = \dot{\mathbf{v}}(\underline{n} \mid t) = \ddot{\mathbf{x}}(\underline{n} \mid t), \end{aligned} \tag{7.2}$$

† Differentiation with respect to time at a fixed particle is often denoted by D/Dt.

in which, as is customary in mechanics, a superposed dot denotes *differentiation with respect to time at a fixed particle.* For the benefit of later developments, we emphasize that to obtain the velocity and acceleration of a particle, the "particle coordinate" $\underline{n}$ must be held constant during differentiation.

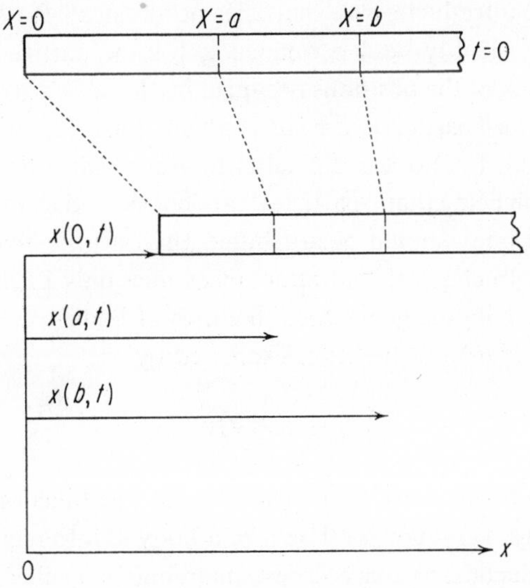

FIGURE 7.2 One-dimensional motion of a bar and material coordinates.

With a view towards describing particles of continuous bodies, let us introduce an alternative method for labeling discrete systems. At some instant t_0 a particle $\underline{n}$ is in the position $X_k = x_k(\underline{n} \mid t_0)$. Because matter is assumed to be impenetrable, only one particle can occupy $\mathbf{X}$ at the time t_0. Therefore, the particles can be labeled by their positions at time t_0: $\mathbf{x} = \mathbf{x}(\mathbf{X}, t)$. For instance, if we consider a swarm of particles (rain) falling under the influence of gravity, then the one-dimensional motion of the system can be described by $x(X, t) = X + \frac{1}{2}gt^2$, where g is the acceleration due to gravity. Each particle has been labeled by its position X at time $t = 0$, so that $x(X, t)$ *is the position at time t of that particle which at time t* $= 0$ *occupied the position X.* To illustrate the analogous procedure for continuous bodies, we suppose that a bar, aligned with the x direction, is struck at its left end (Figure 7.2). If the motion is one-dimensional, its description is of the form $x = x(X, t)$, where X is a continuous variable that labels the cross sections of the bar. We may think of X as a label for one and the same layer of "atoms": it is as though different layers were painted in different colors so that their motions could be seen. But continuous bodies really require a more deliberate approach.

The first requisite of kinematics is a *geometrical* description of bodies, In continuum theories we imagine a body as, first of all, filling out a region of space, which means that bodies possess the same *topological* features as do regions of space. Now, the topology of a space is expressed by the assignment of real numbers x_1, x_2, x_3 ("coordinates") to its points P. In quite the same way, we consider a body $\mathscr{B}$ as an infinite set of "particles" $\mathscr{P}$ which can be brought into a one-to-one correspondence with ordered triplets R_1, R_2, R_3 of real numbers. The introduction of "particle coordinates" R_1, R_2, R_3 amounts to postulating an identity, and permanence, for the particles, so that it is meaningful to speak of the positions occupied by the same particle at different instants of time. The "particles" are *not* small portions of matter. They should be no more difficult (or no less difficult!) to grasp than "points" of space, the only distinction being that "particles" are considered as moving in space. Whether or not a body should be attributed any intrinsic *geometry* is really an open question. In classical continuum mechanics only Euclidean concepts are used for describing the geometrical features of bodies.

The concept of *motion* of bodies is expressed by

$$\mathbf{x} = \boldsymbol{\chi}(\mathscr{P}, t), \tag{7.3}$$

where $\mathbf{x}$ is said to be the *place* of the particle $\mathscr{P}$.† The function $\boldsymbol{\chi}$ describes a family of mappings, varying with time t, of a body $\mathscr{B}$ into regions $V = \boldsymbol{\chi}(\mathscr{B})$ of the ambient (Euclidean) space. These mappings are called *configurations* of the body; they are not unlike photographic pictures of the body. A body is known to us only through its configurations, i.e. by what we can see. We define particle velocity and acceleration in terms of (7.3):

$$\mathbf{v} = \dot{\mathbf{x}} = \frac{d}{dt}\boldsymbol{\chi}(\mathscr{P}, t), \qquad \mathbf{a} = \ddot{\mathbf{x}} = \frac{d^2}{dt^2}\boldsymbol{\chi}(\mathscr{P}, t), \tag{7.4}$$

where, as in (7.2), the *material rate* d/dt must be executed at a fixed particle.

So far t has denoted any instant whatever. When dealing with motions, the "present" instant is usually singled out for special attention; we shall denote it by t, and let τ denote any previous instant. Frequently one also uses the *elapsed time* s, defined by

$$s = t - \tau, \tag{7.5}$$

where $0 \leq s < \infty$, $-\infty < \tau \leq t$. We now restate the definitions (7.3), (7.4) as follows:‡

$$\mathbf{x}(\tau) = \boldsymbol{\chi}(\mathscr{P}, \tau), \qquad -\infty < \tau \leq t, \tag{7.6}$$

† This terminology is due to A. S. Lodge [90].
‡ $d/d\tau$ is executed at a fixed particle $\mathscr{P}$.

$$\mathbf{v}(\tau) = \dot{\mathbf{x}}(\tau) = \frac{d}{d\tau}\boldsymbol{\chi}(\mathscr{P}, \tau), \qquad -\infty < \tau \leq t, \tag{7.7}$$

$$\mathbf{a}(\tau) = \ddot{\mathbf{x}}(\tau) = \frac{d^2}{d\tau^2}\boldsymbol{\chi}(\mathscr{P}, \tau), \qquad -\infty < \tau \leq t. \tag{7.8}$$

Equivalently, (7.6)–(7.8) may be referred to as *histories* of motion, velocity, and acceleration, respectively. For $\tau = t$ it is customary to use the simplified notations $\mathbf{x} \equiv \mathbf{x}(t)$, $\mathbf{v} \equiv \mathbf{v}(t)$, $\mathbf{a} \equiv \mathbf{a}(t)$.

To illustrate (7.6)–(7.8), we let

$$x_1(\tau) = R_1 + K(\tau)R_2, \quad x_2(\tau) = R_2, \quad x_3(\tau) = R_3. \tag{7.9}$$

Then $v_1(\tau) = \dot{K}(\tau)R_2$, $v_2(\tau) = v_3(\tau) = 0$, $a_1(\tau) = \ddot{K}(\tau)R_2$, $a_2(\tau) = a_3(\tau) = 0$.

It must be appreciated that (7.6) is only a mathematical statement of the idea of motion. Correspondingly, (7.7) and (7.8) express the derived concepts of velocity and acceleration; (7.6) is not a concrete description of motion because a method for identifying the particles has not been given. Therefore, our next task will be to discuss *the classical descriptions of motion*: the material description, and the spatial description.

The material description of motion

How can we describe, or mark, the elusive particles? There is really no other way but to identify them with their positions $\mathbf{X}$ in some reference configuration $\boldsymbol{\varkappa}$:

$$\mathbf{X} = \boldsymbol{\varkappa}(\mathscr{P}), \qquad \mathscr{P} = \boldsymbol{\varkappa}^{-1}(\mathbf{X}), \tag{7.10}$$

where X_i are called the *material coordinates* of particles (it is not necessary that a particle should ever occupy the position $\mathbf{X}$, i.e. the reference configuration can be an imagined one). The relations (7.10) need not be "real" formulas; that is, they summarize in mathematical language the statement preceding them. This is certainly an important function of mathematics: to *record* ideas or concepts, and describe their relation to other concepts. In the next paragraph we shall put two ideas together: motion, and the identification of particles.

The identification of particles with their places $\mathbf{X}$ in a reference configuration $\boldsymbol{\varkappa}$ is a perfectly natural thing to do, yet it means that we have introduced a *representation* of particles, and whenever we are dealing with representations, questions of *invariance* arise. In the present case, substituting (7.10) into (7.6), we obtain

$$\mathbf{x}(\tau) = \boldsymbol{\chi}(\mathscr{P}, \tau) = \boldsymbol{\chi}(\boldsymbol{\varkappa}^{-1}(\mathbf{X}), \tau) \equiv \boldsymbol{\chi}_{\varkappa}(\mathbf{X}, \tau). \tag{7.11}$$

To distinguish between a motion and its description, we refer to $\mathbf{x}(\tau) = \boldsymbol{\chi}_{\varkappa}(\mathbf{X}, \tau)$ as the *deformation from the configuration* $\boldsymbol{\varkappa}$. If another configuration $\bar{\boldsymbol{\varkappa}}$ is used for identifying the particles, then $\bar{\mathbf{X}} = \bar{\boldsymbol{\varkappa}}(\mathscr{P})$, $\mathscr{P} = \bar{\boldsymbol{\varkappa}}^{-1}(\bar{\mathbf{X}})$, and $\mathbf{x}(\tau) = \boldsymbol{\chi}(\bar{\boldsymbol{\varkappa}}^{-1}(\bar{\mathbf{X}}), \tau) \equiv \boldsymbol{\chi}_{\bar{\varkappa}}(\bar{\mathbf{X}}, \tau)$. The invariance condition now requires that the position of a particle be independent of how the particle was identified:

$$\mathbf{x}(\tau) = \boldsymbol{\chi}_{\varkappa}(\mathbf{X}, \tau) = \boldsymbol{\chi}_{\bar{\varkappa}}(\bar{\mathbf{X}}, \tau). \tag{7.12}$$

The condition (7.12) specifies the *transformation of mappings under changes of reference configuration.* This is in fact how transformation formulas arise: a condition of invariance to a change of representations yields a transformation formula. All of this may seem like a very fine point, and it is, yet the generality of a theory derives from just such invariance conditions.

The functional notations often tend to give a rather formidable appearance to routine changes of independent variables. Thus from $y = f(x)$, $z = g(x)$ we can obtain $x = g^{-1}(z)$ and the rather formidable looking expression $y = f(g^{-1}(z)) \equiv h(z)$. But these notations are only one more kind of mathematical "shorthand" that one must learn to *read*; as is evident from the example that follows, the actual operations are straightforward enough.

Let $\mathbf{x}(\tau) = \boldsymbol{\chi}(\mathscr{P}, \tau)$ be given by

$$x(\tau) = R_1(1 + \tau), \quad y(\tau) = R_2(1 + \tau)^2, \quad z(\tau) = R_3(1 + \tau^2). \tag{7.13}$$

For the reference configuration $\boldsymbol{\varkappa}$ we may choose the actual configuration at $\tau = 0$. Then $\mathbf{X} = \boldsymbol{\varkappa}^{-1}(\mathscr{P})$: $X = R_1$, $Y = R_2$, $Z = R_3$, and $\mathbf{x}(\tau) = \boldsymbol{\chi}_{\varkappa}(\mathbf{X}, \tau)$: $x(\tau) = X(1 + \tau)$, $y(\tau) = Y(1 + \tau)^2$, $z(\tau) = Z(1 + \tau^2)$. If $\bar{\boldsymbol{\varkappa}}$ is the actual configuration at $\tau = 1$, then $\bar{\mathbf{X}} = \bar{\boldsymbol{\varkappa}}^{-1}(\mathscr{P})$: $\bar{X} = 2R_1$, $\bar{Y} = 4R_2$, $\bar{Z} = 2R_3$ and $\mathbf{x}(\tau) = \boldsymbol{\chi}_{\bar{\varkappa}}(\bar{\mathbf{X}}, \tau)$: $x(\tau) = \frac{1}{2}\bar{X}(1 + \tau)$, $y(\tau) = \frac{1}{4}\bar{Y}(1 + \tau)^2$, $z(\tau) = \frac{1}{2}\bar{Z}(1 + \tau^2)$.

As a rule, we express the material description of motion as follows,

$$\mathbf{x}(\tau) = \boldsymbol{\chi}(\mathbf{X}, \tau), \tag{7.14}$$

reverting to the more elaborate notation (7.11) only when the distinction between the concept $\boldsymbol{\chi}$ and its representation $\boldsymbol{\chi}_{\varkappa}$ becomes vital. We assume that (7.14) is differentiable any number of times with respect to τ. The nature and the consequences of the continuity assumptions concerning the dependence of $\mathbf{x}$ upon X_1, X_2, X_3 will be discussed in the next section. For the time being we shall suppose that, in accord with the intuitive idea of continuity of deformation, the mapping $\boldsymbol{\chi}$ is a *smooth homeomorphism*, by which we mean that both $\boldsymbol{\chi}$ and its inverse $\boldsymbol{\chi}^{-1}$ are one-to-one and differentiable. A corollary of these assumptions is the *principle of impenetrability*:†

† Cf. *CFT*, p. 244.

a portion of matter can never penetrate another portion of matter.

In particular,

$$J = \det(\partial x_i/\partial X_m) > 0, \tag{7.15}$$

which means that an infinitesimal volume element cannot be deformed into a point, and vice versa (cf. (8.17)). Much of the time we use for (7.14) and its inverse,

$$\mathbf{X} = \boldsymbol{\chi}^{-1}(\mathbf{x}, \tau), \tag{7.16}$$

the simpler notations $x_i(\tau) = x_i(\mathbf{X}, \tau)$, $X_i = X_i(\mathbf{x}, \tau)$.

The assumptions about the "smoothness" of the mapping $\boldsymbol{\chi}$ are also referred to as *compatibility conditions*. They can be expressed in terms of other kinematical tensors as well, in which case one speaks of the *equations of compatibility* (cf. (15.33)).

The material description of velocity,

$$\mathbf{v}(\tau) = \mathbf{F}(\mathbf{X}, \tau), \tag{7.17}$$

and the material description of acceleration,

$$\mathbf{a}(\tau) = \dot{\mathbf{F}}(\mathbf{X}, \tau), \tag{7.18}$$

are found from

$$\mathbf{v}(\tau) = \dot{\mathbf{x}}(\mathbf{X}, \tau), \qquad \mathbf{a}(\tau) = \dot{\mathbf{v}}(\tau). \tag{7.19}$$

It is expedient to have an operator-symbol, D_τ, for material rates, thus

$$D_\tau = \left.\frac{\partial}{\partial \tau}\right|_{\mathbf{X}=\text{const.}} \tag{7.20}$$

The definitions (7.19) then read

$$\mathbf{v}(\tau) = D_\tau \mathbf{x}(\mathbf{X}, \tau), \qquad \mathbf{a}(\tau) = D_\tau \mathbf{v}(\mathbf{X}, \tau). \tag{7.21}$$

To obtain the spatial descriptions of velocity and acceleration,†

$$\mathbf{v}(t) = \mathbf{f}(\mathbf{x}, t), \qquad \mathbf{a}(t) = \dot{\mathbf{f}}(\mathbf{x}, t), \tag{7.22}$$

we use $\mathbf{X} = \boldsymbol{\chi}^{-1}(\mathbf{x}, t)$ to eliminate $\mathbf{X}$:

$$\begin{aligned} \mathbf{v}(t) &= \mathbf{F}(\mathbf{X}, t) = \mathbf{F}(\boldsymbol{\chi}^{-1}(\mathbf{x}, t), t) \equiv \mathbf{f}(\mathbf{x}, t), \\ \mathbf{a}(t) &= \dot{\mathbf{F}}(\mathbf{X}, t) = \dot{\mathbf{F}}(\boldsymbol{\chi}^{-1}(\mathbf{x}, t), t) \equiv \dot{\mathbf{f}}(\mathbf{x}, t). \end{aligned} \tag{7.23}$$

† Descriptions of the type $\mathbf{v}(\mathbf{x}, \tau)$ and $\mathbf{a}(\mathbf{x}, \tau)$ will be taken up in the next subsection.

If there is no danger of confusion, we write (7.17), (7.18) as $\mathbf{v}(\tau) = \mathbf{v}(\mathbf{X}, \tau)$, $\mathbf{a}(\tau) = \mathbf{a}(\mathbf{X}, \tau)$ and (7.22) as $\mathbf{v} = \mathbf{v}(\mathbf{x}, t)$, $\mathbf{a} = \mathbf{a}(\mathbf{x}, t)$.

To illustrate the rules for calculating velocity and acceleration, we return to (7.13) and let $\mathbf{x}(\tau) = \boldsymbol{\chi}(\mathbf{X}, \tau)$:

$$x(\tau) = X(1 + \tau), \quad y(\tau) = Y(1 + \tau)^2, \quad z(\tau) = Z(1 + \tau^2). \tag{7.24}$$

Then $v_x(\tau) = X$, $v_y(\tau) = 2Y(1 + \tau)$, $v_z(\tau) = 2Z\tau$, $a_x(\tau) = 0$, $a_y(\tau) = 2Y$, $a_z(\tau) = 2Z$. Because $\mathbf{X} = \boldsymbol{\chi}^{-1}(\mathbf{x}, t)$: $X = x/(1 + t)$, $Y = y/(1 + t)^2$, $Z = z/(1 + t^2)$, where $x_i = x_i(t)$, the spatial descriptions are given by $v_x = x/(1 + t)$, $v_y = 2y/(1 + t)$, $v_z = 2zt/(1 + t^2)$, $a_x = 0$, $a_y = 2y/(1 + t)^2$, $a_z = 2z/(1 + t^2)$.

A reference configuration of a body, and the associated material coordinates X_i, provide literally a picture of the body, or, its map, or, better yet, a "diagram"† of the body, in the same way that coordinates x_i provide a diagram of a region of space. The fields which act on a body, whether they relate to deformations, loads, or other influences, can be referred to this map, even though these fields may be associated with entirely different configurations of the body. That is, in the material description the reference configuration always remains the map of a body, and all processes are viewed, so to speak, from this map.

The spatial description of motion

We shall now take up the spatial description of motion separately. In its classical form the spatial description does not relate directly to particles but only to their velocities.‡ Consequently, a body is but a region of space endowed with physical properties; these properties belong, in a manner of speaking, to the space points. Although the idea of particles is still retained in the sense that $\mathbf{v}(\mathbf{x}, t)$ is the field of particle velocities, the viewpoint is now different. Thus a particle is said to take on the local value of the velocity field; therefore, a particle may be likened to a driver who drives, very conscientiously, at the speed indicated by highway signs (these signs constituting the spatial description of "particle" velocities!).

The spatial description is particularly appropriate in cases where a knowledge of the paths of individual particles is not needed. This may be the case, for instance, when calculating pressure distributions over wing surfaces, or finding discharges in conduits. Moreover, the mathematical problems arising in the spatial description are usually more tractable than those associated with the material description.

† Cf. *CFT*, pp. 507, 508.

‡ According to Truesdell (footnote on p. 328, *CFT*), in the early works on hydrodynamics (prior to 1760) the velocity occurred as a primitive concept unrelated to the idea of particle motion!

In the spatial description the field of particle velocities, $\mathbf{v} = \mathbf{f}(\mathbf{x}, t)$, is considered as a *primitive field*, and *not* as obtained by differentiating with respect to time some position vector (of course, the material description $x_i = x_i(\mathbf{X}, t)$ can be found by integrating $dx_i/dt = v_i(\mathbf{x}, t)$, in which case X_i will enter as constants of integration). In fact, because $\mathbf{x}$ and t are now independent variables, we have that $\partial x_i/\partial t = 0$, i.e. $\mathbf{x}$ is merely a fixed point of space, whereas in the material description it is the current place of a particle. Thus

$$\partial_t x_i = 0, \qquad D_t X_i = 0.$$

As a matter of curiosity, we note that to $D_t x_i = v_i$ there corresponds a velocity with which a space point traverses the body, $r_i = \partial_t X_i$. The chain rule $D_t X_i = 0 = X_{i,m} D_t x_m + \partial_t X_i$ then yields $r_i = -X_{i,m} v_m$.

The distinction between material and spatial descriptions is basic: in the former $\mathbf{x}$ is the dependent variable, and $\mathbf{X}$ and t the independent variables, whereas in the latter $\mathbf{v}$ is the dependent variable, and $\mathbf{x}$ and t the independent variables. The space coordinates are frequently called *Eulerian*, the material coordinates *Lagrangean*. This terminology is unfortunately incorrect, as the use of both types of coordinates in fluid mechanics goes back to Euler. The correct attribution has been given by several authors, but the complete clarification of the history of these terminologies is due to Truesdell (second footnote on page 30, [171]). Euler wrote X, Y, Z for material coordinates, and x, y, z for spatial coordinates. The literature generally follows Lagrange in using a, b, c for material coordinates.

To calculate the acceleration of a particle, we must revert momentarily to the particle picture: $\mathbf{v} = \mathbf{f}(\mathbf{x}, t) = \mathbf{f}(\mathbf{x}(\mathbf{X}, t), t)$. Now, the material rate must be executed for $\mathbf{X} = \text{const.}$, in which case $\mathbf{f}(\mathbf{x}(\mathbf{X}, t), t) = \mathbf{q}(t)$. Therefore, by $(7.19)_2$, $\mathbf{a}(t) = d\mathbf{q}(t)/dt$. For greater clarity, let us write $\mathbf{q}(t) = \mathbf{f}(\mathbf{x}(\mathbf{X}, t), \theta(t))$, where $\theta(t) = t$. Then, using the chain rule of differentiation, we get $d\mathbf{q}(t)/dt = (\partial \mathbf{f}/\partial \theta)(d\theta/dt) + (\partial \mathbf{f}/\partial x_k) D_t x_k$, or, in a more convenient notation,

$$\mathbf{a} = \dot{\mathbf{v}} = \partial_t \mathbf{v} + (\mathbf{v} \cdot \nabla)\mathbf{v}, \qquad a_i = \dot{v}_i = \partial_t v_i + v_k v_{i,k}, \tag{7.25}$$

where

$$\partial_t = \frac{\partial}{\partial t}\bigg|_{\mathbf{x}=\text{const.}} \tag{7.26}$$

is called the *local* (time) *rate*. It is understood that in $\partial_t v_i$ and in $v_{i,k}$ the independent variables are $\mathbf{x}$ and t. If the independent variables are $\mathbf{X}$ and t, then $\dot{v}_i$ stands for $D_t v_i$, of course.

Both formulas $D_t v_i$ and $\partial_t v_i + v_k v_{i,k}$ naturally yield the same value of $\mathbf{a}$, although the functional representations of **a** in the material and spatial descriptions are entirely different. Let us return to the example (7.24). Then, for instance, from $v_x = x/(1 + t)$ and (7.25) it follows that $a_x = \partial_t v_x + v_k v_{x,k} = -x/(1 + t)^2 + [x/(1 + t)][1/(1 + t)] = 0$. This agrees with the result obtained from the material description.

The chain rule expressed by (7.25) also represents the transformation of material rates from the material description to the spatial description. To exhibit this transformation more clearly, we write

$$D_t = \partial_t + \mathbf{v} \cdot \boldsymbol{\nabla}, \tag{7.27}$$

or, equivalently,

$$\dot{\Psi} = D_t \Psi = \partial_t \Psi + v_k \Psi_{,k}, \tag{7.28}$$

where Ψ ("trident") stands for a tensor of arbitrary rank. Here the following terminology is customary: *the local rate* ∂_t *is found by an observer situated at a fixed point* **x**, *the material rate* D_t *is found by an observer moving with a particle* **X**. If the observer moves with its own velocity **u**, then (7.27) becomes

$$\frac{d_{\mathbf{u}}}{dt} \equiv \partial_t + \mathbf{u} \cdot \boldsymbol{\nabla}. \tag{7.29}$$

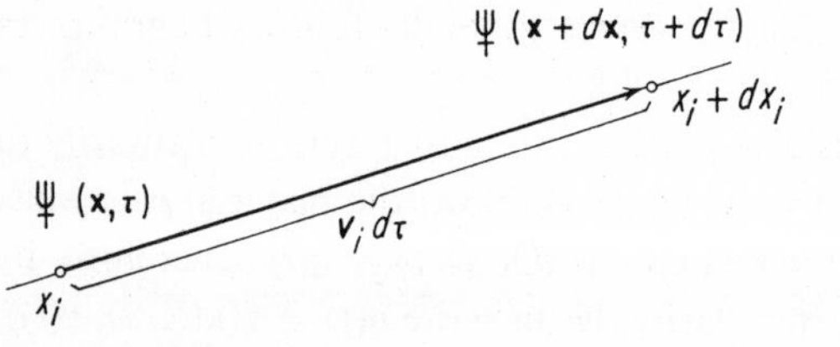

FIGURE 7.3 The change of field values Ψ found by a moving observer $\mathcal{O}$.

Let us give a proof of (7.28) that is less formal. As shown in Figure 7.3, an observer $\mathcal{O}$ attached to a particle **X** moves during the time interval dt from x_i to $x_i + dx_i$, where $dx_i = v_i\, dt$. At the instant t the observer is at x_i, and records there the field value $\Psi(\mathbf{x}, t)$. At the instant $t + dt$ the observer is at $x_i + dx_i$, and records the field value $\Psi(\mathbf{x} + d\mathbf{x}, t + dt)$. Approximating $\Psi(\mathbf{x} + d\mathbf{x}, t + dt)$ by the first three terms of the Taylor series expansion, $\Psi(\mathbf{x} + d\mathbf{x}, t + dt) \doteq \Psi(\mathbf{x}, t) + \partial_t \Psi(\mathbf{x}, t)\, dt + \Psi(\mathbf{x}, t)_{,k}\, dx_k$, we find that the observed change is $\Psi(\mathbf{x} + d\mathbf{x}, t + dt) - \Psi(\mathbf{x}, t) \doteq \partial_t \Psi\, dt + \Psi_{,k}\, dx_k$. To obtain (7.28), we only need to recall that $dx_k = v_k\, dt$.

The term $\partial_t \Psi$ is the *local rate* of the field. The term $v_k \Psi_{,k}$ is said to be the *convected rate*; it arises because the particle-bound observer moves, by virtue of its instantaneous velocity **v**, into regions of different local field values. We often borrow the language of fluid mechanics and say that Ψ is a *steady field* if the local rate vanishes, and a *uniform field* if the convected rate vanishes.

Another variant of the material description

Because particles can be labeled by their places in any configuration, we may identify material coordinates X_i with the places at the present instant: $x_i = x_i(t)$. Then, however, the description of motion reduces to an identity at time t, i.e. this choice of material coordinates is appropriate only if the past motion, rather than the present configuration, is of main interest. To explain the role of the various descriptions, we shall briefly look ahead to questions concerning the nature of mechanical behavior.

The form of kinematics is largely determined by the kind of mechanical response that is being described. The two classical theories of continuum mechanics are elasticity theory and hydrodynamics. Although we can use in these theories either of the classical descriptions of motion, from the point of view of mechanical response alone the material description is natural for elasticity theory, whereas the spatial description is natural for hydrodynamics. An elastic solid has, by definition, an exceptional reference configuration: the undistorted state. The solid can be also said to possess a "perfect memory" of the undistorted state, because it returns to this state when loads are removed. To describe this property mathematically, the undistorted state must be, first of all, marked in some way. This we do by letting the undistorted state be the reference configuration used for identifying the particles. The material coordinates X_i are then, in a manner of speaking, the footprints of the undistorted state.

A viscous fluid is at the other extreme of mechanical behavior, because its response is determined solely by the instantaneous values of the time rates of deformation. That is, viscous fluids have no memory at all, or, there are no past configurations that are special in any way.† For this reason, it is natural to use the spatial description for viscous fluids.

In continuum mechanics we also deal with materials for which the entire history of motion of each particle must be considered. If the relevant history is not of a finite duration, then there exists only one special configuration: the present one. Consequently, particles are identified with the positions which they occupy at time t:

$$\mathbf{x} = \mathbf{x}(t) = \boldsymbol{\chi}(\mathscr{P}, t), \qquad \mathscr{P} = \boldsymbol{\chi}^{-1}(\mathbf{x}, t). \tag{7.30}$$

† In a broader sense this is not true, because *initial conditions* may define a unique configuration in the past. However, a particular initial condition is a feature of a particular problem, and has nothing whatever to do with the nature of the fluid.

Substituting $(7.30)_2$ into (7.6), we arrive at

$$\mathbf{x}(\tau) = \boldsymbol{\chi}(\mathscr{P}, \tau) = \boldsymbol{\chi}(\boldsymbol{\chi}^{-1}(\mathbf{x}, t), \tau) = \boldsymbol{\chi}_{\underline{t}}(\mathbf{x}, \tau), \tag{7.31}$$

where $\boldsymbol{\chi}_{\underline{t}}$ is called the *relative deformation function* (this does seem to overwork the word "relative"; what one wants to say is that in (7.31) the reference configuration with which all other configuration are compared is the present one). In the place of (7.31) we frequently use the simpler notation

$$x_i(\tau) = x_i(\mathbf{x}, t, \tau). \tag{7.32}$$

Here $\mathbf{x}(\tau)$ is the position at time τ of that particle which at time t will occupy the position $\mathbf{x} = \mathbf{x}(t)$.

It should be appreciated that it takes four things to specify a particle: three material coordinates, and a reference configuration in which the particle is located by these coordinates. Symbolically, $\mathscr{P}$: $\{\varkappa, X_1, X_2, X_3\}$. In particular, if $\varkappa$ is the actual configuration at time t_0, we can write $\mathscr{P}$: $\{t_0, X_1, X_2, X_3\}$. Another possibility is to let $\mathscr{P}$: $\{\boldsymbol{\chi}, x_1, x_2, x_3\}$, or, equivalently, $\mathscr{P}$: $\{t, x_1, x_2, x_3\}$. Now, a material rate D_τ must be executed at a fixed particle. Therefore, in the description $\mathbf{x}(\tau) = \mathbf{x}(\mathbf{X}, \tau)$ we must hold $\mathbf{X}$ (and, of course, $\varkappa$) constant, whereas in the description $\mathbf{x}(\tau) = \mathbf{x}(\mathbf{x}, t, \tau)$ we must hold $\mathbf{x}$ *and* t constant. In the latter case, then, D_τ is defined by

$$D_\tau = \left.\frac{\partial}{\partial \tau}\right|_{\mathbf{x},\, t = \text{const.}} \tag{7.33}$$

Subject to this agreement, the definitions

$$\mathbf{v}(\tau) = D_\tau \mathbf{x}(\tau), \qquad \mathbf{a}(\tau) = D_\tau^2 \mathbf{x}(\tau) \tag{7.34}$$

remain valid regardless of which description, (7.14) or (7.32), has been used.

In the example (7.13) we now let $x = x(t)$, $y = y(t)$, $z = z(t)$. Then $\mathbf{x}(\tau) = \boldsymbol{\chi}_{\underline{t}}(\mathbf{x}, \tau)$:

$$x(\tau) = \frac{x(1 + \tau)}{1 + t}, \qquad y(\tau) = \frac{y(1 + \tau)^2}{(1 + t)^2}, \qquad z(\tau) = \frac{z(1 + \tau^2)}{1 + t^2}, \tag{7.35}$$

and $$v_x(\tau) = \frac{x}{1 + t}, \qquad v_y(\tau) = \frac{2y(1 + \tau)}{(1 + t)^2}, \qquad v_z(\tau) = \frac{2z\tau}{1 + t^2},$$

In particular, letting $t = \tau$, we obtain $v_x = x/(1 + t)$, $v_y = 2y/(1 + t)$, $v_z = 2zt/(1 + t^2)$. (Cf. the example (7.24)).

Moving frames, observer transformations, objective tensors

A familiar topic in elementary mechanics is the transformation of velocities and accelerations from one reference frame to another, moving frame. In continuum mechanics this transformation is particularly important because, recalling that each frame represents an observer (cf. the introductory remarks in Section 3), transformations between moving frames can be interpreted as *observer transformations.* It is evident that for the same theory to be used in all corners of the earth, on space platforms, etc., the theory must be properly invariant to changes of observers. Therefore, observer transformations will be a powerful tool for discovering what is invariant, or "real," in our physical experience.

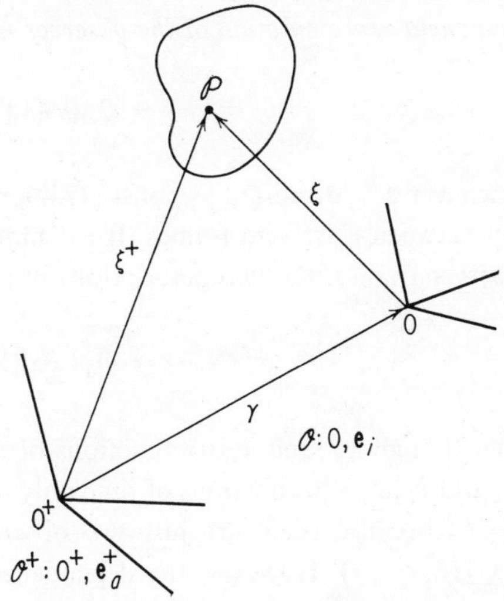

FIGURE 7.4 Observer transformation.

We consider two frames $(0, \mathbf{e}_i)$ and $(0^+, \mathbf{e}_a^+)$, representing the observers $\mathcal{O}$ and $\mathcal{O}^+$, respectively (Figure 7.4). For brevity we shall refer to the frames by the symbols (i) and (a). The relative motion of the two frames may be described by

$$c_i = c_i(\tau), \qquad \mathbf{e}_a^+(\tau) = Q_{ai}(\tau)\mathbf{e}_i, \tag{7.36}$$

(cf. also (2.23)). If $\mathscr{P}$ is a particle occupying the point P at the given instant, then its position vectors relative to the (i) and (a) frames are connected by the *observer transformation*†

$$\xi^+ = \xi + \gamma \tag{7.37}$$

(Figure 7.4), where

$$\xi^+ = P - 0^+, \qquad \xi = P - 0, \qquad \gamma = 0 - 0^+. \tag{7.38}$$

† For the sake of clarity it is preferable to use vector and tensor notations along with the component notations.

The simultaneous use of two reference frames creates a rather confusing variety of notations, because each vector may be projected on either one of the frames, e.g. $\beta = b_i\mathbf{e}_i = b_a\mathbf{e}_a^+$. In addition, we must distinguish between the observations of $\mathcal{O}$ and $\mathcal{O}^+$; this will be done by marking the latter by "+", thus $\beta^+ = b_i^+\mathbf{e}_i = b_a^+\mathbf{e}_a^+$. With these conventions in mind, we can write that

$$\begin{aligned} \xi^+ &= x_a^+\mathbf{e}_a^+ = x_i^+\mathbf{e}_i, \qquad & \xi &= x_i\mathbf{e}_i = x_a\mathbf{e}_a^+, \\ \gamma &= c_i\mathbf{e}_i = c_a^+\mathbf{e}_a^+, \qquad & Q_{ai} &= \mathbf{e}_a^+\cdot\mathbf{e}_i. \end{aligned} \tag{7.39}$$

Even though $\gamma = \gamma^+$, it will be expedient to carry along the designations c_a^+, c_i^+ (cf. (7.50) *et seq.*). From (7.37) and (7.39) we now obtain the following *component representation of the observer transformation*,

$$x_a^+(\tau) = Q_{ai}(\tau)[x_i(\tau) + c_i(\tau)]. \tag{7.40}$$

Whenever $\mathbf{c} = \mathbf{0}$ and $Q_{ai} = \text{const.}$, (7.40) reduces to a coordinate transformation between Cartesian frames. If the motion of a body is viewed from two observer frames, the two descriptions of motion are related by

$$x_a^+(\mathbf{X}, \tau) = Q_{ai}(\tau)x_i(\mathbf{X}, \tau) + c_a^+(\tau). \tag{7.40*}$$

Even though x_a^+ and x_i are functions of the material coordinates and time, Q_{ai} and c_i are still functions of time only (or, functions of time and the labels $\mathcal{O}$, $\mathcal{O}^+$) because there are just *two* observer frames: $c_i = c_i(\mathcal{O}, \mathcal{O}^+, \tau)$, $Q_{ai} = Q_{ai}(\mathcal{O}, \mathcal{O}^+, \tau)$. However, the dependence of c_i and Q_{ai} on the two labels can be suppressed, because the observer frames are distinguishable by means of the different sets of indices assigned to them.

To follow histories of particle motions, a history of observer transformation must be also prescribed, i.e. $c_i(\tau)$ and $Q_{ai}(\tau)$ must be given for $-\infty < \tau \le t$.

The mark "+" in (7.40) means of course that x_a^+ and x_i represent different vectors. We shall adhere to this notation throughout; for instance, we shall denote by T^+ a tensor observed by $\mathcal{O}^+$ (it can be represented either as T_{ab}^+ or as T_{ij}^+), and by T the corresponding observation by $\mathcal{O}$ (which can again be represented either as T_{ab} or as T_{ij}). Although $T_{ab}^+(\tau) = Q_{ai}(\tau)Q_{bj}(\tau)T_{ij}^+(\tau)$, $T_{ab}(\tau) = Q_{ai}(\tau)Q_{bj}(\tau)T_{ij}(\tau)$, the relation $T_{ab}^+(\tau) = Q_{ai}(\tau)Q_{bj}(\tau)T_{ij} = T_{ab}$ need *not* be true in general; this simple observation is indeed the whole point of this subsection. One example will suffice ((7.40) is another!): the velocities of a particle relative to two moving frames are obviously different. In fact, if the (a) frame moves together with the particle, then $v_a^+ = 0$. If equality does hold, $T_{ab}^{+}(\tau) = Q_{ai}(\tau)Q_{bj}(\tau)T_{ij}(\tau)$, then the mark "+" may be omitted, meaning that the *same tensor* T is found by both observers (the difference between the components T_{ab} and T_{ij} being solely due to the different orientations of the frames).

An observer transformation may be referred to as a *Euclidean transformation*. One of its characteristics is that time is not transformed (absolute time!); a translation of the time scale, $t^{+} = t - a$, where a is a constant, is however permitted. Second, from (7.40) it follows that, at any given instant of time,

$$d\xi^{+} = d\xi, \tag{7.41}$$

so that lengths remain invariant: $ds^2 = dx_i^{+}\,dx_i^{+} = dx_i\,dx_i$.

Let us recall the form of a typical transformation formula, e.g. $\overline{\mathbf{T}} = \mathbf{QTQ}^T$, ($T_{ab} = Q_{ai}Q_{bj}T_{ij}$). As is evident from what preceded, when dealing with component representations it is advantageous to continue to use this notation even when the direction cosines are functions of time:

$$\overline{\mathbf{T}}(\tau) = \mathbf{Q}(\tau)\mathbf{T}(\tau)\mathbf{Q}^T(\tau), \tag{7.42}$$

In particular, (7.41) admits the representations

$$\begin{aligned} d\mathbf{x} &= d\mathbf{x}^{+} = \mathbf{Q}^T\,d\overline{\mathbf{x}}^{+}, & d\overline{\mathbf{x}}^{+} &= d\overline{\mathbf{x}} = \mathbf{Q}\,d\mathbf{x}, \\ dx_i &= dx_i^{+} \equiv Q_{ia}(\tau)\,dx_a^{+}, & dx_a^{+} &= dx_a \equiv Q_{ai}(\tau)\,dx_i. \end{aligned} \tag{7.41}^*$$

Although the direction cosines entering into (7.42) are functions of time, at any given instant the formulas (7.42) are indistinguishable from a coordinate transformation. Thus $T_{ab}(\tau)$ are obtained by performing, at the instant τ, the proper component transformation from the (i) frame to the (a) frame. The distinction between (7.42) and "real" coordinate transformations becomes apparent only when we consider time rates of tensors.

We are now ready to classify tensors in regard to their behavior under observer transformations. Generalizing (7.41), we say that $P_{i\ldots n}$ is an *objective* tensor in observer transformations (or, a *Euclidean invariant*), if it obeys the transformation law

$$\begin{aligned} \Pi^{+} &= \Pi, \\ P_{a\ldots e}^{+} &= P_{a\ldots e} \equiv Q_{ai}(\tau)\ldots Q_{en}(\tau)P_{i\ldots n}, \\ P_{i\ldots n}^{+} &= P_{i\ldots n} \equiv Q_{ia}(\tau)\ldots Q_{ne}(\tau)P_{a\ldots e}. \end{aligned} \tag{7.43}$$

In this case the components $P_{a\ldots e}$ and $P_{i\ldots n}$ differ only because of the relative orientation of the observer frames; the relative *motion* of the observer frames has no effect whatever on the physical quantity represented by the objective tensor **P**. An objective tensor thus describes a quantity that is "real," because it appears the same to all observers.

If a quantity is not objective, then it is said to be "relative." *The behavior of each physical variable under observer transformations must be known* (or, postulated), or else it is not possible to use observer transformations for investigating the invariance of physical laws.

In contrast to coordinate transformations, then, observer transformations involve motion of the frames. The effect of the motion is exhibited in a pure form, so to speak, if the observer frames are aligned at the given instant. Then, by (7.43),

$$\mathbf{P}^+ = \mathbf{P}, \qquad P^+_{i\ldots n} = P_{i\ldots n}. \tag{7.44}$$

A *caution*: if differentiations with respect to time are performed, then the alignment of the frames should be made *after* the differentiation (the frames can be aligned only at one instant!).

Right now we are only concerned with particle velocity and acceleration. However, differentiation of (7.40) with respect to time will give rise to an *angular velocity* which we must now define.

The velocity field of a *rigid motion* is very simple; it can be described in terms of a translational velocity of a reference point and an angular velocity. The latter is a convenient *device* for describing the time rate of rotation about the reference point. That is, angular velocity is not the velocity of any part of the body; rather, it is an imagined arrow that enables us to calculate the velocities of all points by a simple cross-product rule. The description of a rigid motion will be obtained in the next section (cf. (8.10)). For the time being, we shall characterize rigid motion as follows. We suppose that an orthonormal triad $\mathbf{e}_a^+$ (the *body frame*) is attached to the body. If the coordinates of particles remain constant in this frame, then the motion of the body is said to be rigid. In particular, the rotation of the body, as observed in some *laboratory frame* $\mathbf{e}_i$, is described by $\mathbf{e}_a^+(t) = Q_{ai}(t)\mathbf{e}_i$. To calculate the angular velocity of the body, as observed in the laboratory frame, we take the time rate of $\mathbf{e}_a^+$, while holding $\mathbf{e}_i$ constant (i.e. we wish to obtain the angular velocity of the body *relative* to the laboratory frame). We write $\dot{\mathbf{e}}_a^+ = \dot{Q}_{ai}\mathbf{e}_i \equiv \Omega\mathbf{e}_a^+ = \Omega_{ij}\mathbf{e}_i\mathbf{e}_j \cdot \mathbf{e}_a^+$, where Ω_{ij} is the representation, in the laboratory frame, of the angular velocity of the body (observed in the laboratory frame). Thus

$$\dot{\mathbf{e}}_a^+ = \Omega\mathbf{e}_a^+, \qquad \dot{Q}_{ai} = \Omega_{ij}Q_{aj}, \qquad \Omega_{ij} = \dot{Q}_{ai}Q_{aj} = -\Omega_{ji}. \tag{7.45}$$

Because Ω_{ij} is skew-symmetric, we also have that

$$\dot{\mathbf{e}}_a^+ = \boldsymbol{\omega} \times \mathbf{e}_a^+, \qquad \dot{Q}_{ai} = \varepsilon_{ijk}\omega_j Q_{ak},$$

$$\omega_j = -\frac{1}{2}\varepsilon_{jmn}\Omega_{mn}.$$

To verify that these are indeed the conventional definitions, let us take a vector $p_a\mathbf{e}_a^+$ that is fixed in the body, i.e. $\dot{p}_a = 0$. Then the time rate of its laboratory components $p_i = Q_{ai}p_a$ is given by $\dot{p}_i = \dot{Q}_{ai}p_a = \Omega_{ij}Q_{aj}p_a$, so that

$$\dot{\mathbf{p}} = \boldsymbol{\omega} \times \mathbf{p}, \qquad \dot{p}_i = \varepsilon_{ijk}\omega_j p_k = \Omega_{ik}p_k. \tag{7.46}$$

The description of rigid motion is now obtained by letting $\mathbf{p} = \mathbf{x} - \boldsymbol{\alpha}$, where $\boldsymbol{\alpha}$ is the radius vector of the reference point. Then $\dot{\mathbf{x}} = \dot{\mathbf{p}} + \dot{\boldsymbol{\alpha}} = (\boldsymbol{\omega} \times \mathbf{p}) + \dot{\boldsymbol{\alpha}}$, or,

$$\mathbf{v} = \dot{\boldsymbol{\alpha}} + \boldsymbol{\omega} \times (\mathbf{x} - \boldsymbol{\alpha}). \tag{7.47}$$

Angular velocities can be troublesome for two reasons. First, they always come in pairs: to Ω there corresponds the angular velocity Ω^+ of the laboratory frame, as observed in the body frame (naturally we expect that $\Omega^+ = -\Omega$). Second, each angular velocity admits two representations, Ω_{ij} and $\Omega_{ab} = Q_{ai}Q_{bj}\Omega_{ij}$, Ω_{ij}^+ and $\Omega_{ab}^+ = Q_{ai}Q_{bj}\Omega_{ij}^+$. This variety is often a source of errors (mostly sign errors!). To define Ω^+, we reverse the roles of $\mathbf{e}_a^+$ and $\mathbf{e}_i$: $\dot{\mathbf{e}}_i = \dot{Q}_{ai}\mathbf{e}_a^+ \equiv \Omega^+\mathbf{e}_i = \Omega_{ab}^+\mathbf{e}_a^+\mathbf{e}_b^+ \cdot \mathbf{e}_i$, thus

$$\begin{aligned} \dot{Q}_{ai} &= \Omega_{ab}^+ Q_{bi}, \qquad \Omega_{ab}^+ = \dot{Q}_{ak}Q_{bk}, \\ \Omega_{ij}^+ &= Q_{ai}Q_{bj}\Omega_{ab}^+ = Q_{ai}\dot{Q}_{aj} = -\Omega_{ij}. \end{aligned} \tag{7.48}$$

Therefore, (7.45) can be alternatively expressed by

$$\dot{Q}_{ai} = -\Omega_{ij}^+ Q_{aj}. \tag{7.45}^*$$

In the conventional notation the variety of formulas is no less confusing. With $\mathbf{e}_a^+ \rightarrow \bar{\mathbf{e}}_m^+ = Q_{mi}\mathbf{e}_i$, $\Omega_{ab} \rightarrow \bar{\Omega}_{mn} = Q_{mi}Q_{nj}\Omega_{ij}$, etc., we obtain

$$\begin{aligned} \boldsymbol{\Omega} &= \dot{\mathbf{Q}}^T\mathbf{Q}, \qquad \Omega_{ij} = \dot{Q}_{mi}Q_{mj}. \\ \bar{\boldsymbol{\Omega}} &= \mathbf{Q}\boldsymbol{\Omega}\mathbf{Q}^T = \mathbf{Q}\dot{\mathbf{Q}}^T, \qquad \bar{\Omega}_{mn} = Q_{mi}\dot{Q}_{ni}. \end{aligned} \tag{7.49}$$

To connect (7.49) with the previously developed theory of orthogonal tensors, let us suppose that $\mathbf{D}_a$ represent the (constant) initial configuration of the directors.

Then, by (4.34), $\dot{d}_{bi} = \dot{R}_{im}D_{bm} = \dot{R}_{im}R_{jm}d_{bj}$, thus $\mathbf{\Omega} = \dot{\mathbf{R}}\mathbf{R}^{-1}$, or, by (4.33), $\Omega_{ij} = \dot{R}_{im}R_{jm} = \dot{d}_{ai}d_{aj}$. For instance, let $\mathbf{R}$ be a counter-clockwise rotation about z axis:

$$\|\mathbf{R}\| = \begin{Vmatrix} \cos\phi & -\sin\phi & 0 \\ \sin\phi & \cos\phi & 0 \\ 0 & 0 & 1 \end{Vmatrix}.$$

Then

$$\|\mathbf{\Omega}\| = \dot{\phi}\begin{Vmatrix} 0 & -1 & 0 \\ 1 & 0 & 0 \\ 0 & 0 & 0 \end{Vmatrix},$$

or, equivalently, $\|\omega\|^T = \|0, 0, \dot{\phi}\|$. The equivalence of the representations $\mathbf{\Omega} = \dot{\mathbf{Q}}^T\mathbf{Q}$ and $\mathbf{\Omega} = \dot{\mathbf{R}}\mathbf{R}^T$ serves as a reminder that the appropriate changes in the components of a vector can be induced either by a rotation of the vector, e.g. $\bar{v}_i = R_{ij}v_j$, or by the inverse rotation of the coordinate system, thus $v_a = Q_{ai}v_i$, where $\mathbf{Q} = \mathbf{R}^T$(cf. (2.29) *et seq.*).

We now return to the definition of observer transformations,

$$\xi^+(\tau) = \xi(\tau) + \gamma(\tau), \qquad x_a^+(\tau) = Q_{ai}(\tau)x_i(\tau) + c_a^+(\tau). \tag{7.50}$$

The mark "+" on the components of γ is necessary in order to distinguish, notationally, the time rates of c_a^+ and c_i at an instant when the two frames are aligned (because $c_a^+ = Q_{ai}c_i$, it follows that $\dot{c}_a^+ = \dot{Q}_{ai}c_i + Q_{ai}\dot{c}_i$; at an instant when the frames are aligned, this reduces to $\dot{c}_i^+ = \Omega_{ik}^+c_i + \dot{c}_i$). Applying the material rate to (7.50), and letting $\dot{x}_a^+ = v_a^+$, $\dot{x}_i = v_i$, we obtain

$$\dot{\xi}^+ = \dot{\xi} + \Omega^+\xi + \dot{\gamma}, \qquad v_a^+ = Q_{ai}^+(v_i + \Omega_{ij}^+x_j) + \dot{c}_a^+. \tag{7.51}$$

The particle velocity is clearly not objective, for if it were then we should get $\dot{\xi}^+ = \dot{\xi}$: $v_a^+ = Q_{ai}v_i \equiv v_a$ (cf. (7.43)). The observed velocities $\mathbf{v}^+$ and $\mathbf{v}$ differ by the translational velocity $\dot{\mathbf{c}}$ and by the velocity $\mathbf{\Omega}^+\mathbf{x}$ due to rotation of the (i) frame relative to the (a) frame. In the same way we find that acceleration is not objective:

$$a_a^+ = Q_{ai}[a_i + 2\Omega_{ij}^+v_j + (\Omega_{ij}^+ + \Omega_{ik}^+\Omega_{kj}^+)x_j] + \ddot{c}_a^+. \tag{7.52}$$

If the observer frames are aligned at the given instant, then (7.51) and (7.52) reduce to

$$v_i^+ = v_i + \Omega_{ij}^+x_j + \dot{c}_i^+, \tag{7.53}$$

$$a_i^+ = a_i + 2\Omega_{ij}^+v_j + (\dot{\Omega}_{ij}^+ + \Omega_{ik}^+\Omega_{kj}^+)x_j + \ddot{c}_i^+, \tag{7.54}$$

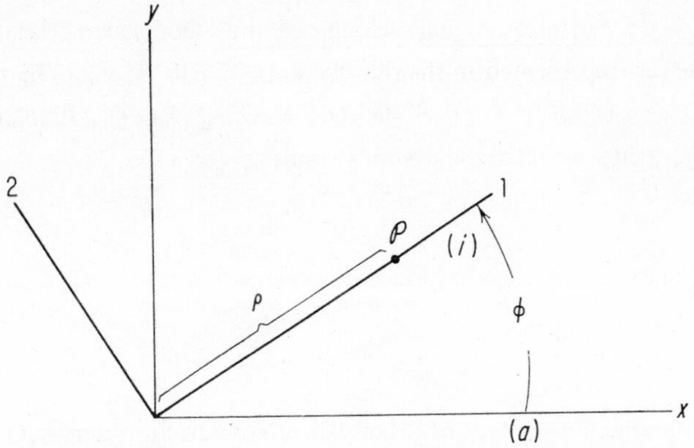

FIGURE 7.5 Motion of a particle along a rotating axis.

The results (7.53), (7.54) are the familiar formulas for motion of particles relative to moving frames. We give a simple two-dimensional illustration, in which (*a*) is considered as a fixed Cartesian frame, and (*i*) as a rotating Cartesian frame (Figure 7.5). Let $\mathscr{P}$ be a particle which moves along the "1" axis of the (*i*) frame: $x_1 = \rho$, $x_2 = 0$, $v_1 = \dot{\rho}$, $v_2 = 0$, $a_1 = \ddot{\rho}$, $a_2 = 0$. Denoting by $\omega = \Omega^+_{21} = -\Omega^+_{12} = \dot{\phi}$ the nonvanishing component of the relative angular velocity of the (*i*) frame, we obtain, by (7.51), (7.52),†

$$\begin{aligned} v_x^+ &= \dot{\rho}\cos\phi - \rho\omega\sin\phi, \qquad v_y^+ = \dot{\rho}\sin\phi + \rho\omega\cos\phi, \\ a_x^+ &= (\ddot{\rho} - \rho\omega^2)\cos\phi - (\rho\dot{\omega} + 2\omega\dot{\rho})\sin\phi, \\ a_y^+ &= (\ddot{\rho} - \rho\omega^2)\sin\phi + (\rho\dot{\omega} + 2\omega\dot{\rho})\cos\phi. \end{aligned} \tag{7.55}$$

In the (*i*) frame one observes only the velocity $\dot{\rho}$ and the acceleration $\ddot{\rho}$; the values v_a^+ and a_a^+ found by the observer (*a*) are quite different (even when the frames are aligned, i.e. $\phi = 0$ at the given instant).

For completeness let us also investigate angular velocity and angular acceleration in observer transformations. To avoid having too many kinds of indices, we may use the conventional notation in the following way. Let ε_r be a "body frame," $\mathbf{e}_i$ the first observer frame, and $\bar{\mathbf{e}}_m$ the second observer frame. The three sets of direction cosines are then defined by $\bar{\mathbf{e}}_m = Q_{mi}\mathbf{e}_i$, $\varepsilon_r = P_{ri}\mathbf{e}_i = \bar{P}_{rm}\bar{\mathbf{e}}_m$. Because the base vectors are linearly independent, we obtain from $\varepsilon_r = P_{ri}\mathbf{e}_i = \bar{P}_{rm}Q_{mi}\mathbf{e}_i$ the basic identity

$$P_{ri} = \bar{P}_{rm}Q_{mi}. \tag{7.56}$$

In accord with (7.49), we now define the following angular velocities: angular velocity of $(\bar{\mathbf{e}}_m)$ relative to $(\mathbf{e}_i)$ (represented in the $(\mathbf{e}_i)$ frame), $\Omega_{ij} = \dot{Q}^T_{im}Q_{mj}$, angular velocity of the "body axes" relative to the first observer (represented in the $(\mathbf{e}_i)$

† The requisite direction cosines Q_{ai} are listed on p. 108.

frame), $\Sigma_{ij} = \dot{P}^T_{ir} P_{rj}$, and angular velocity of the "body axes" relative to the second observer (represented in the $(\bar{\mathbf{e}}_m)$ frame!), $\bar{\Sigma}^+_{mn} = \dot{\bar{P}}^T_{mr}\bar{P}_{rn}$. The rest is now routine: $\Sigma_{ij} = (\dot{Q}^T_{im}\bar{P}^T_{mr} + Q^T_{im}\dot{\bar{P}}^T_{mr})\bar{P}_{rn}Q_{nj} = \dot{Q}^T_{im}Q_{mj} + Q^T_{im}(\dot{\bar{P}}^T_{mr}\bar{P}_{rn})Q_{nj} = \Omega_{ij} + Q^T_{im}\bar{\Sigma}^+_{mn}Q_{nj}$, thus we have the obvious result

$$\Sigma_{ij} = \Omega_{ij} + \Sigma^+_{ij}, \tag{7.57}$$

or, introducing $\Sigma_{ij} = -\varepsilon_{ijk}\sigma_k$, $\Omega_{ij} = -\varepsilon_{ijk}\omega_k$,

$$\boldsymbol{\sigma} = \boldsymbol{\sigma}^+ + \boldsymbol{\omega}. \tag{7.57)*$$

In words, the angular velocity of a body B relative to an observer O equals the sum of the angular velocity of B relative to an observer Ō and the angular velocity of Ō relative to O:

$$\boldsymbol{\omega}_{B/O} = \boldsymbol{\omega}_{B/\bar{O}} + \boldsymbol{\omega}_{\bar{O}/O}. \tag{7.58}$$

Corresponding to Σ_{ij} and Ω_{ij}, we define $\dot{\Sigma}_{ij}$ and $\dot{\Omega}_{ij}$ as angular accelerations represented in the $(\mathbf{e}_i)$ frame; similarly, to $\bar{\Sigma}_{mn}$ there corresponds an angular acceleration $\dot{\bar{\Sigma}}_{mn}$ (represented in the $(\bar{\mathbf{e}}_m)$ frame!). With (7.45)*, we readily obtain from $\Sigma_{ij} = \Omega_{ij} + Q^T_{im}\bar{\Sigma}^+_{mn}Q_{nj}$ that

$$\dot{\Sigma}_{ij} = \dot{\Omega}_{ij} + \Omega_{ir}\Sigma^+_{rj} + \dot{\Sigma}^+_{ij} + \Omega_{jr}\Sigma^+_{ir}, \tag{7.59}$$

where
$$\dot{\Sigma}^+_{ij} \equiv Q^T_{im}\dot{\bar{\Sigma}}^+_{mn}Q_{nj}. \tag{7.60}$$

It is easy to see that (7.59) is equivalent to

$$\dot{\boldsymbol{\sigma}} = \dot{\boldsymbol{\sigma}}^+ + \dot{\boldsymbol{\omega}} + (\boldsymbol{\omega} \times \boldsymbol{\sigma}^+), \tag{7.61}$$

i.e.
$$\boldsymbol{\alpha}_{B/O} = \boldsymbol{\alpha}_{B/\bar{O}} + \boldsymbol{\alpha}_{\bar{O}/O} + (\boldsymbol{\omega}_{\bar{O}/O} \times \boldsymbol{\omega}_{B/\bar{O}}),$$

where $\boldsymbol{\alpha}$ stands for angular acceleration.

Problems

A. MOTION OF PARTICLES

1. The motion of a discrete system of particles is described by $x(\underline{n} \mid t) = \underline{n}(1 + t)$, $y(\underline{n} \mid t) = \underline{n}^2(1 + t)^2$, $z(\underline{n} \mid t) = \underline{n}^3(1 + t^2)$, $\underline{n} = \underline{1}, \underline{2}, \ldots, \underline{N}$. Obtain expressions for the velocities and accelerations of the particles. What are the velocity and acceleration of the second particle at $t = 0$?
2. Consider a semi-infinite bar defined by $0 \leq X < \infty$ at $t = 0$. The one-dimensional motion of the bar is given by $x = X$ for $ct \leq X$, and $x = X + A[1 - \exp(X - ct)]$ for $ct \geq X$, where c and A are constants. What

general observations can you make concerning this motion? Let $A = 1$ and $c = 1$, and sketch the $x - t$ curves for the particles corresponding to $X = 0$, $X = 1$, and $X = 10$.

B. THE MATERIAL DESCRIPTION OF MOTION

3. Obtain the material descriptions of velocity and acceleration for the motion

$$x(\tau) = X(1 + \tau^2), \qquad y(\tau) = X\tau + Y, \qquad z(\tau) = Z.$$

Then obtain the spatial descriptions $\mathbf{v}(\mathbf{x}, t)$, $\mathbf{a}(\mathbf{x}, t)$.

4. Obtain the material descriptions of velocity and acceleration for the motion

$$x(\tau) = Xe^{-c\tau}, \qquad y(\tau) = Ye^{-c\tau}, \qquad z(\tau) = Ze^{-c\tau},$$

where c is a constant. Then obtain the spatial descriptions $\mathbf{v}(\mathbf{x}, t)$, $\mathbf{a}(\mathbf{x}, t)$.

5. Obtain the material descriptions of velocity and acceleration for the motion

$$x(\tau) = X + Y\tau^2, \quad y(\tau) = \frac{Y}{1 + \tau}, \quad z(\tau) = Z + X\tau,$$

where $\tau > -1$. Then obtain the spatial descriptions $\mathbf{v}(\mathbf{x}, t)$, $\mathbf{a}(\mathbf{x}, t)$.

6. Obtain the material and spatial descriptions of velocity and acceleration for the motion $x = X + K(t)Y$, $y = Y$, $z = Z$.

7. Obtain the material and spatial descriptions of velocity and acceleration for the motion $x = \alpha(t)X$, $y = \beta(t)Y$, $z = \gamma(t)Z$.

8. Let $x_i(\tau) = F_{ij}(\tau)X_j$, where $\det\mathbf{F} \neq 0$, and F_{ij} are functions of time only. Develop general expressions for the material descriptions of velocity and acceleration. Then obtain representations of $\mathbf{v}(\mathbf{x}, t)$, $\mathbf{a}(\mathbf{x}, t)$.

9. Calculate $\dot{\phi}(\mathbf{X}, \tau)$ if $\phi(\mathbf{X}, \tau)$ is given by

a. $\tau^3 + 2$ **b.** $X + YZ$ **c.** $X\tau^3 - YZ\tau$

In what follows x, y, z will stand for $x(t), y(t), z(t)$, respectively.

10. Calculate $\mathbf{v}(\mathbf{x}, t, \tau)$ and $\mathbf{a}(\mathbf{x}, t, \tau)$ from the descriptions of motion obtained by eliminating X, Y, Z in terms of x, y, z in

a. Problem 3 **b.** Problem 4 **c.** Problem 5 **d.** Problem 6

Check $\mathbf{v}(\mathbf{x}, t) = \mathbf{v}(\mathbf{x}, t, t)$ with $\mathbf{v}(\mathbf{X}, t)$ by using $\mathbf{x} = \boldsymbol{\chi}(\mathbf{X}, t)$.

11. Let $x(\tau) = x(1 + \tau)/(1 + t)$, $y(\tau) = y(1 + \tau)^2/(1 + t)^2$, $z(\tau) = z(1 + \tau^2)/(1 + t^2)$. Calculate $\mathbf{v}(\mathbf{x}, t, \tau)$, $\mathbf{a}(\mathbf{x}, t, \tau)$. If X_i are the particle positions at $\tau = 0$, obtain $\mathbf{x}(\tau) = \boldsymbol{\chi}(\mathbf{X}, \tau)$.

12. Consider $x(\tau) = x - (t - \tau)y$, $y(\tau) = y$, $z(\tau) = z$. Calculate $\mathbf{v}$ and $\mathbf{a}$ at time t.

C. THE SPATIAL DESCRIPTION OF MOTION

13. Calculate $\mathbf{a}(x, t)$ if

a. $v_x = x, v_y = y, v_z = z$ **b.** $v_x = y, v_y = z, v_z = x$

c. $v_x = t, v_y = t, v_z = y$ **d.** $v_x = x, v_y = t, v_z = xt$

14. Calculate $\mathbf{a}(\mathbf{x}, t)$ if $v_x = xt + yt^2$, $v_y = z - xt^3$, $v_z = z$.

15. Calculate $\mathbf{a}(\mathbf{x}, t)$ directly from (7.25) by using $\mathbf{v}(\mathbf{x}, t)$ obtained in

a. Problem 3 **b.** Problem 4 **c.** Problem 5 **d.** Problem 6

16. Calculate $\dot{\phi}(\mathbf{x}, t)$ for $\phi(\mathbf{x}, t) = xt + y$ if $\mathbf{v}(\mathbf{x}, t)$ is given by

a. Problem 13a **b.** Problem 13b **c.** Problem 13c **d.** Problem 13d

17. Let $\mathbf{V}(\mathbf{x}, t) = -y\mathbf{e}_x + x\mathbf{e}_y$. Calculate $\dot{V}_i$ if $\mathbf{v}(\mathbf{x}, t)$ is given by

a. Problem 13a **b.** Problem 13b **c.** Problem 13c **d.** Problem 13d

18. Let $\phi(\mathbf{x}, t) = x^2 + y^2$, and let an observer $\mathcal{O}$ move with the velocity $\mathbf{u} = \mathbf{e}_x + 2\mathbf{e}_y + 3\mathbf{e}_z$. What is the rate of change of ϕ found by $\mathcal{O}$ at

a. $x = y = z = 1$ **b.** $x = 0,\ y = z = 1$ **c.** $x = 1,\ y = 2,\ z = 3$

19. Consider a tank (large or small) filled with water, with a horizontal pipeline (of constant or variable diameter) connected to it. Describe the circumstances under which the flow will be

a. steady and uniform **b.** nonsteady but uniform
c. uniform but nonsteady **d.** nonsteady and nonuniform

D. MOVING FRAMES, OBSERVER TRANSFORMATIONS

20. Verify (7.51) and (7.52).

21. Verify the example (7.55).

22. Verify the derivation of (7.57) and (7.59).

23. Let (i) and (a) be two observer frames. We consider (i) as a fixed Cartesian frame, and (a) as a moving frame that is always aligned with the local directions of cylindrical coordinates ρ, ϕ, z. The origin of the (a) frame moves (in the (i) frame) as follows: $\rho = A$, $\phi = B\tau$, $z = C\tau$, where A, B, C are constants, and $\tau \geq 0$.

a. Calculate $\|\Omega_{ij}^{+}\|$ (the requisite direction cosines are given by (6.27)).
b. Let $\mathbf{v} = \mathbf{e}_z$ be a vector field observed in the (i) frame. Calculate v_a^{+} and a_a^{+}.
c. Suppose that a rigid body is rotating with a constant angular velocity Σ_{zy} about the x axis. Calculate $\|\Sigma_{ab}^{+}\|$, $\|\dot{\Sigma}_{ab}^{+}\|$.

24. Repeat the steps of the preceding problem when the (a) frame is aligned with the local directions of spherical coordinates (the requisite direction cosines are given by (6.30)), and its origin moves as follows: $r = A$, $\theta = C$, $\phi = B\tau$, where A, B, C are constants, and $\tau \geq 0$.

25. Let (i) and (a) be two Cartesian frames having a common origin and a common y axis. We consider (i) as a fixed frame, and (a) as rotating about the y axis with the constant angular velocity A. If a rigid body rotates with a constant angular velocity B about the z axis of the (a) frame, calculate the components of its angular velocity and angular acceleration in the (i) frame.

26. A sphere rotates about one axis of a fixed frame with the constant angular velocity ω. A particle is moving along a meridian of the sphere with a velocity v relative to the sphere. Develop expressions for the velocity and acceleration of the particle relative to the fixed frame.

Section 8
KINEMATICS OF DEFORMATION

In the preceding section we focused our attention upon individual particles of a body. As a consequence, the kinematical concepts were the same as in the case of discrete systems. In the present section we introduce ideas of deformation by considering bodies as consisting of strings of particles, called *material lines* (or, material filaments). Each material line consists at all times of the same particles, and can be visualized as a colored thread inserted in a body and deforming with it.

Unless one assumes that deformation is sufficiently "smooth" (i.e. differentiable as many times as is needed), there is very little that one can do, all of the main results of the deformation theory being direct consequences of the assumed smoothness. For this reason we shall permit discontinuities only on a finite set of surfaces ("surfaces of discontinuity"), whereas in the regions bounded by these surfaces all fields will be assumed to be sufficiently smooth. The kinematics of surfaces of discontinuity will be taken up in the last subsection.

Material lines, surfaces, and volumes

To make the notion of *material lines* precise, we first recall the definition of *space curves*,

$$x_i = f_i(u) \tag{8.1}$$

(cf. (5.27)), where u is a scalar parameter. This equation is a mathematical way of identifying, or marking, the points which belong to the space curve, in quite the same way that the points of curves on a blackboard are marked by chalk. The definition of material lines is no different: a material line consists of those particles whose material coordinates satisfy an equation

$$X_i = F_i(u). \tag{8.2}$$

As the scalar u ranges in some interval $u_0 \leq u \leq u_1$, a continuous material line is traced out in the reference configuration of the body, starting at the particle $\mathbf{X}(u_0)$ and ending at the particle $\mathbf{X}(u_1)$.

The particles satisfying (8.2) are mapped by a motion

$$\mathbf{x}(\tau) = \boldsymbol{\chi}(\mathbf{X}, \tau) \tag{8.3}$$

into a family of space curves,

$$x_i = \chi_i(\mathbf{F}(u), \tau) \equiv f_i(u, \tau) \tag{8.4}$$

representing the configurations of the material line. For instance, a material line $X = u$, $Y = Au^2$, $Z = 0$ is mapped by the motion $x = X + K(\tau)Y$, $y = Y$, $z = Z$ into the family of space curves $x = u + AK(\tau)u^2$, $y = Au^2$, $z = 0$. A simple visualization of the mathematical operations is as follows: we scribe a (material) line on a rubber sheet; this step is the counterpart of (8.2). Stretching of the sheet, as described by (8.3), then makes the material line appear as a sequence of space curves, described by (8.4).

Material surfaces and *material volumes* are spatial surfaces and volumes, respectively, defined in the reference configuration of the body. Thus a material surface is defined by

$$X_i = X_i(u, v) \tag{8.5}$$

(cf. (5.34)), where u, v are appropriate surface coordinates, and a material volume is defined by

$$X_i = X_i(u, v, w) \tag{8.6}$$

(cf. (5.41)), where u, v, w are curvilinear coordinates in space. The motion (8.3) now maps a material surface into a family of surfaces in space:

$$x_i = \chi_i(\mathbf{X}(u, v), \tau) = x_i(u, v, \tau). \tag{8.7}$$

Similarly, material volumes are mapped into regions of space defined by

$$x_i = \chi_i(\mathbf{X}(u, v, w), \tau) = x_i(u, v, w, \tau). \tag{8.8}$$

A material surface can be imagined in a colored sheet inserted in a body and deforming with it. The material surface consists at all times of the same particles, namely, the particles identified by (8.5). The interpretation of material volumes is analogous.

Impenetrability, continuity, compatibility

In what follows we shall suppose that every deformation $x_i(\tau) = \chi_i(X_1, X_2, X_3, \tau)$ associates only one particle X_1, X_2, X_3 with a given set of coordinates x_1, x_2, x_3 and time τ. This amounts to assuming that matter is impenetrable: at any instant τ, two particles cannot occupy the same point x_1, x_2, x_3. Moreover, we shall assume that x_i as functions of X_1, X_2, X_3 and τ are not only continuous but also differentiable as many times as is needed. As was remarked before, these smoothness assumptions are largely a matter of expediency, because without them there can be no theory. In order to reconcile the assumptions with those features of actual motion which are manifestly discontinuous, e.g. turbulence, mixing of two fluids, it is necessary to introduce additional hypotheses. Thus we may identify the smooth mapping (8.3) with a "mean motion" of a turbulent flow. Again, in the case of mixtures we may suppose that the motion of each constituent is smooth, although that of the mixture is not (a "particle" of the mixture will be made up of different "constituent particles" at different instants).† But these special interpretations belong to special theories; in kinematics, as in mathematics, we are concerned with the *form* of the theory, not its interpretation.

Because the smoothness assumption is so basic, it should not be surprising that the main theorems are, at the core, theorems of analysis. Let us recall that if a mapping $\boldsymbol{\chi}_\tau$ from X_1, X_2, X_3 to x_1, x_2, x_3 is continuous, then it maps open sets into open sets.‡ Hence it follows that, in smooth deformations, a material surface which forms the boundary of a material volume can never become a part of the interior of the volume, and, conversely, an "interior" particle of a body can never migrate into the boundary of the body. Also, an infinitesimal material neighborhood $N(\mathbf{X})$ is mapped into an infinitesimal, connected neighborhood $N(\mathbf{x})$. The most important single result is the following *approximation theorem*:§

Let $\boldsymbol{\chi}_\tau$ be a differentiable mapping of a material volume D, and let $\mathbf{X}$ be a particle belonging to a closed subset ~~of~~ E of D. Then

$$\boldsymbol{\chi}_\tau(\mathbf{X} + \Delta\mathbf{X}) \equiv \boldsymbol{\chi}(\mathbf{X} + \Delta\mathbf{X}, \tau) = \boldsymbol{\chi}_\tau(\mathbf{X}) + \mathbf{F}(\mathbf{X})\Delta\mathbf{X} + \mathbf{R}(\Delta\mathbf{X}),$$

where the *tensor of deformation gradients*, $\mathbf{F}$, is given by

$$\|\mathbf{F}\| = \|\Delta_m \boldsymbol{\chi}_\tau\| = \begin{Vmatrix} \dfrac{\partial x}{\partial X} & \dfrac{\partial x}{\partial Y} & \dfrac{\partial x}{\partial Z} \\[2ex] \dfrac{\partial y}{\partial X} & \dfrac{\partial y}{\partial Y} & \dfrac{\partial y}{\partial Z} \\[2ex] \dfrac{\partial z}{\partial X} & \dfrac{\partial z}{\partial Y} & \dfrac{\partial z}{\partial Z} \end{Vmatrix},$$

and

$$\lim_{\Delta\mathbf{X}\to 0} \frac{|\mathbf{R}(\Delta\mathbf{X})|}{|\Delta\mathbf{X}|} = 0$$

† At one and the same point there are now several "constituent particles." However, according to the principle of impenetrability, there is only one particle of each constituent at a given point.

‡ Cf. Buck [7], p. 169.

§ Cf. Buck [7], Section 5.5.

uniformly for all **X** in E. What the theorem asserts is that a small enough material neighborhood of a particle **X** is mapped by a single tensor **F**, evaluated at **X**, into its deformed configurations. That is, whereas on a large scale the mappings (8.3) will be as a rule nonlinear, their differentiability will make them *locally linear* (cf. Figure 8.1), so that one and the same tensor $\partial x_i/\partial X_m$ will map *all* infinitesimal vectors $dX = \mathbf{e}_i\, dX_i$ emanating from a point into their deformed configurations $dx = \mathbf{e}_i\, dx_i = \mathbf{e}_i(\partial x_i/\partial X_m)\, dX_m$. We write

$$\mathbf{dx} = \mathbf{F}\, d\mathbf{X}, \qquad F_{im} = x_{i,m} = \frac{\partial x_i}{\partial X_m}, \tag{8.9}$$

or, symbolically,

$$\mathscr{B}(\mathbf{X}) \xrightarrow{\mathbf{x}} V(\mathbf{x})$$

$$N(\mathbf{X}) \xrightarrow{\mathbf{F}} N(\mathbf{x})$$

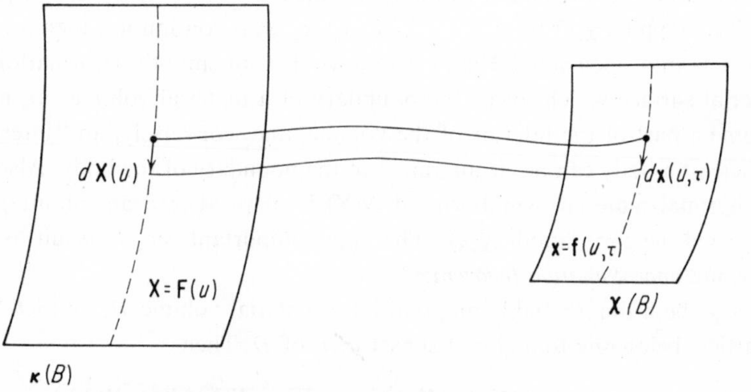

FIGURE 8.1 Mapping of a material line.

In more graphical terms, the effect of **F** upon a neighborhood $N(\mathbf{X})$ can be imagined as viewing $N(\mathbf{X})$ through a lens. The distorted image $N(\mathbf{x})$ is then a picture of the deformation of $N(\mathbf{X})$. In general **F** varies from point to point, so that each neighborhood $N(\mathbf{X})$ must be viewed through a different lens $\mathbf{F}(\mathbf{X})$.

To explain the role of **F**, it may help to recall that a differentiable function $y = f(x)$ admits in a neighborhood of any point $\bar{x}$ the linear approximation $y - \bar{y} = (x - \bar{x})\,\partial_x \bar{f}$, where $\partial_x \bar{f}$ is the value of the derivative at $\bar{x}$, and $\bar{y} = f(\bar{x})$. Similarly, the equation of a surface, $z = f(x, y)$, gives rise to a linear approximation, $z - \bar{z} = (x - \bar{x})\,\partial_x \bar{f} + (y - \bar{y})\,\partial_y \bar{f}$, the tangent plane. Evidently $z - \bar{z}$ approximates the rise in height corresponding to a displacement whose projections on the xy plane are $x - \bar{x}$ and $y - \bar{y}$. At any point $(\bar{x}, \bar{y}, \bar{z})$, the slope of the tangent plane, i.e. the gradients $\partial_x \bar{f}$, $\partial_y \bar{f}$, determines the increment $z - \bar{z}$ no matter what the displacements $x - \bar{x}$ and $y - \bar{y}$ are: these displacements merely locate various points in the same tangent plane.

The deformation of each neighborhood $N(\mathbf{X})$, as described by $\mathbf{F}(\mathbf{X})$, is said to be *homogeneous*, meaning that it is of the type $x_i = F_{ij}X_j$, where F_{ij} are at most functions of time. It is not difficult to show that a homogeneous deformation maps parallel lines into parallel lines, similar triangles into similar triangles, ellipsoids into ellipsoids, etc. Consequently, on a small scale the aspect of every (differentiable) deformation is highly regular. To exhibit a homogeneous deformation, we may take a rubber sheet with lines, circles, ellipses, etc. scribed on it, and then subject the sheet to uniaxial or biaxial stretching.

To illustrate (8.9), we choose a deformation $x = X + BXY$, $y = Y + BY^2$, $z = Z + BXY$, where B is a constant. Then

$$\|\mathbf{F}\| = \begin{Vmatrix} 1 + BY & BX & 0 \\ 0 & 1 + 2BY & 0 \\ BY & BX & 1 \end{Vmatrix}.$$

Let $d_1\mathbf{X} = (dX, 0, 0)$, $d_2\mathbf{X} = (0, dY, 0)$. At $X = 0$, $Y = 1$, Z these filaments are mapped into $d_1\mathbf{x} = \mathbf{F}(0, 1, Z)\, d_1\mathbf{X}$: $\|1 + B, 0, B\|\, dX$, $d_2\mathbf{x} = \mathbf{F}(0, 1, Z)\, d_2\mathbf{X}$: $\|0, 1 + 2B, 0\|\, dY$. At $X = 1$, $Y = 0, Z$ they are mapped into $d_1\bar{\mathbf{x}} = \mathbf{F}(1, 0, Z)\, d_1\mathbf{X}$: $\|1, 0, 0\|\, dX$, $d_2\bar{\mathbf{x}} = \mathbf{F}(1, 0, Z)\, d_2\mathbf{X}$: $\|B, 1, B\|\, dY$.

Rigid motion is a very special case of (8.9). It is easy to show that invariance of lengths, $dx_i\, dx_i = dX_i\, dX_i$, now requires that

$$x_i(\mathbf{X}, t) = \alpha_i(t) + R_{ij}(t)X_j, \tag{8.10}$$

where $\mathbf{R}$ is an orthogonal tensor. Namely, because now $\delta_{mn} = x_{i.m}x_{i.n}$, it follows that $0 = x_{i.mp}x_{i.n} + x_{i.m}x_{i.np}$. Interchanging the indices as follows, $m \to p$, $p \to n$, $n \to m$, and subtracting this from the original equation, we obtain $0 = x_{i.mp}x_{i.n} - x_{i.p}x_{i.mn}$. Interchanging p and m, and adding to the first identity, we arrive at $0 = x_{i.mp}x_{i.n}$. Since $\det(x_{i.n}) = \pm 1$, it follows that $x_{i.mp} = 0$, i.e. in rigid motions the mapping from $\mathbf{X}$ to $\mathbf{x}$ is linear.

Let us approach deformation gradients in still another way. We consider a neighborhood $N(\mathbf{X})$ of a particle $\mathbf{X}$, and let $\mathbf{Z}$ denote a typical particle of the neighborhood. The motion of the neighborhood can be represented by a Taylor series expansion of $\mathbf{x}(\mathbf{Z}, \tau)$ about $\mathbf{X}$:

$$\begin{aligned} x_i(\mathbf{Z}, \tau) &= x_i(\mathbf{X}, \tau) + (Z_m - X_m)F_{im}(\mathbf{X}, \tau) \\ &\quad + \frac{1}{2}(Z_m - X_m)(Z_n - X_n)F_{im.n}(\mathbf{X}, \tau) + \dots. \end{aligned} \tag{8.11}$$

Here $x_i(\mathbf{X}, \tau)$ describes the translation common to all particles of the neighborhood. The factors $(Z_m - X_m)$, $(Z_n - X_n)$ etc. merely identify the particles, the *deformation* of the neighborhood being characterized by $F_{im}(\mathbf{X}, \tau)$, $F_{im.n}(\mathbf{X}, \tau)$, etc. If, as is the case in the classical theories of continuum mechanics, $F_{im}(X, \tau)$ are taken as the sole measures of local deformation, then we say that the material is *simple*, or, that it has no *microstructure*. Thus microstructure is a term which refers to some kind of *inhomogeneity in the local deformation*; in Section 11 we shall briefly examine some models of microstructure and their representations. For the time being, let us only note that whereas a linear approximation $\mathbf{x}(\mathbf{Z}) - \mathbf{x}(\mathbf{X}) = \mathbf{F}(\mathbf{X})(\mathbf{Z} - \mathbf{X})$ is valid in the limit as $\mathbf{Z} \to \mathbf{X}$, a quadratic approximation of the type shown in (8.11) implies the notion of a small but *finite* neighborhood (of diameter l, say) in which deviations from linearity are noticeable.

As was remarked in the previous section, the smoothness conditions imposed on $\boldsymbol{\chi}$ may be referred to as *compatibility conditions.*

Deformation tensors

Because $\mathbf{F}$ provides a complete description of homogeneous local deformations,† it is natural to consider $\mathbf{F}$ as the primitive measure of deformation. The polar decomposition theorem, presented in Section 4, is the principal tool for studying finite deformations. According to this theorem, the tensor of deformation gradients can be represented as follows:

$$\mathbf{F} = \mathbf{RU} = \mathbf{VR} \tag{8.12}$$

(cf. (4.60)). This formula describes the decomposition of a general (local) deformation into a rotation, specified by the orthogonal *rotation tensor* $\mathbf{R}$, and a pure deformation specified by the positive, symmetric *stretch tensors* $\mathbf{U}$ and $\mathbf{V}$. For the inverse of $\mathbf{F}$ we write

$$F_{im}^{-1} = X_{i,m} = \frac{\partial X_i}{\partial x_m}, \tag{8.13}$$

and, by (3.43), $$\mathbf{F}^{-1} = \mathbf{U}^{-1}\mathbf{R}^T = \mathbf{R}^T\mathbf{V}^{-1}. \tag{8.14}$$

We call $\mathbf{U}$ the right stretch tensor, $\mathbf{V}$ the left stretch tensor. Correspondingly, $\mathbf{C} = \mathbf{F}^T\mathbf{F} = \mathbf{U}^2$ is called the right Cauchy-Green deformation tensor, $\mathbf{B} = \mathbf{F}\mathbf{F}^T = \mathbf{V}^2$ the left Cauchy-Green deformation tensor (cf. (4.61)). The two classical strain measures $\mathbf{E}$ and $\mathbf{e}$ are defined by $2\mathbf{E} = \mathbf{C} - \mathbf{1}$, $2\mathbf{e} = \mathbf{1} - \mathbf{B}^{-1}$.

From $C_{ij} = F_{im}^T F_{mj} = F_{mi}F_{mj} = x_{m.i}x_{m.j}$ it follows that $C_{11} = (\partial x/\partial X)^2 + (\partial y/\partial X)^2 + (\partial z/\partial X)^2, \ldots, \ldots, C_{12} = (\partial x/\partial X)(\partial x/\partial Y) + (\partial y/\partial X)(\partial y/\partial Y)$

† We use the term *deformation* for the time being to denote both (rigid) rotation and pure deformation.

$+ (\partial z/\partial X)(\partial z/\partial Y), \ldots, \ldots$. Introducing a displacement vector $\mathbf{u}$ through $\mathbf{x} = \mathbf{X} + \mathbf{u}$, we arrive at the "strain-displacement relations" $2E_{11} = C_{11} - 1 = 2u_{x,X} + (u_{x,X})^2 + (u_{y,X})^2 + (u_{z,X})^2, \ldots, \ldots, 2E_{12} = C_{12} = u_{x,Y} + u_{y,X} + u_{x,X}u_{x,Y} + u_{y,X}u_{y,Y} + u_{z,X}u_{z,Y}, \ldots, \ldots$. Similarly, from $\mathbf{B}^{-1} = (\mathbf{F}^T)^{-1}\mathbf{F}^{-1} = (\mathbf{F}^{-1})^T\mathbf{F}^{-1}$ (cf. (3.41)) it follows that $B_{ij}^{-1} = F_{mi}^{-1}F_{mj}^{-1} = X_{m,i}X_{m,j}$, hence† $2e_{11} = 1 - B_{11}^{-1} = 2u_{x,x} - (u_{x,x})^2 - (u_{y,x})^2 - (u_{z,x})^2, \ldots, \ldots, 2e_{12} = -B_{11}^{-1} = u_{x,y} + u_{y,x} - u_{x,x}u_{x,y} - u_{y,x}u_{y,y} - u_{z,x}u_{z,y}, \ldots, \ldots$.

Like geometry, deformation theory abounds in special theorems, concepts, and constructions. For this reason it is important to keep in mind that only the polar decomposition is basic and that the rest is only elaboration. To refresh our memory of the meaning of polar decomposition, let us return to the problem of simple shear:

$$x = X + KY, \qquad y = Y, \qquad z = Z. \tag{a}$$

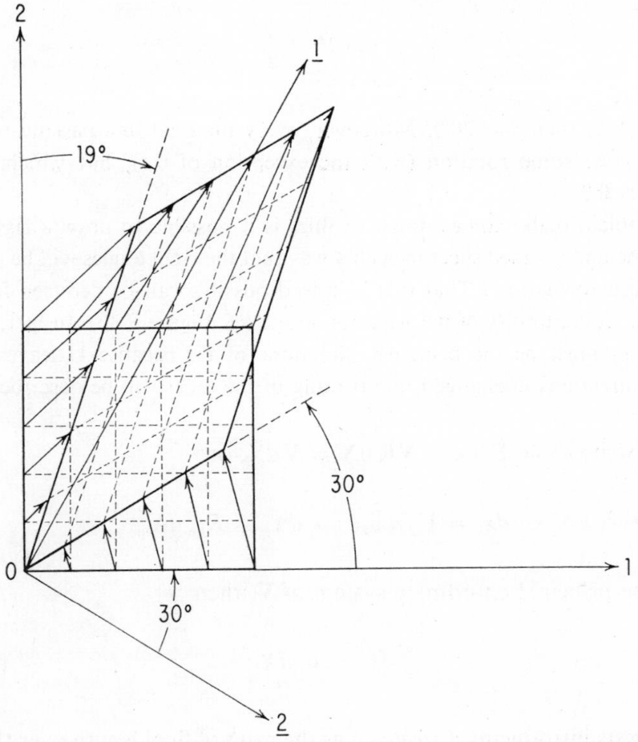

FIGURE 8.2 The pure shear deformation described by $\sqrt{\mathbf{C}}$; $0\underline{1}$ is one of the invariant directions of $\mathbf{C}$.

† Here B_{11}^{-1} stands for the "11" component of $\mathbf{B}^{-1}$.

Assuming that $K = \tan\theta = 2/\sqrt{3}$ ($\theta \approx 49°$), we find that **R** describes a clockwise rotation through 30°, and that the principal direction of **U** which lies in the first quadrant makes an angle of 60° with the x axis (Figure 8.2). The extraction of a rigid rotation **R** from the total deformation **F** is, at first, a rather elusive thing. To gain some insight into the deformation, we can draw various lines on a square of the undeformed sheet (Figure 8.3a). If we consider a diagonal and a circle on it, we obtain right away a somewhat unexpected result: in the deformed configuration the major axis of the ellipse does not lie on the diagonal. The diagonal corresponds to the material line $Y/X = 1$, hence, by (a),

$$\tan\alpha = \frac{1}{1+K}, \tag{b}$$

where $\tan\alpha = y/x$ is the slope of the diagonal in the deformed configuration. A circle $X^2 + Y^2 = a^2$ is deformed into the ellipse $x^2 - 2Kxy + (1 + K^2)y^2 = a^2$, and it is easy to see that the angle β that the major axis makes with the x axis is given by

$$\tan 2\beta = \frac{2}{K} \tag{c}$$

(if $K = 2/\sqrt{3}$, then $\beta = 30°$). Moreover, every material line passing through 0 has undergone some rotation (with the exception of $0A$), but which of these rotations is **R**?

The problem really comes down to this: is it possible to draw a right-angled cross on the undeformed sheet in such a way that the right angles will be preserved during the deformation? That this is indeed possible can be deduced from considerations of continuity of deformation alone (cf. Figure 8.3b). In fact, the lines of the cross must be the principal directions of **U**; because **U** leaves its own principal directions unchanged, the turning of the cross will be described by **R**.

Let us write $d\mathbf{x} = \mathbf{F}\, d\mathbf{X} = \mathbf{VR}\, d\mathbf{X} = \mathbf{V}\, d\bar{\mathbf{X}}$, or,

$$dx_i = V_{ij}\, d\bar{X}_j, \qquad d\bar{X}_j = R_{jm}\, dX_m. \tag{8.15}$$

If (i) is the principal coordinate system of **V**, then

$$dx_i = V_{\underline{i}}\, dX_i. \tag{8.15)*$$

This suggests introducing a *stretch* λ as the ratio of final length over the initial length,

$$\lambda_{\underline{n}} = \frac{dx}{dX}, \tag{8.16}$$

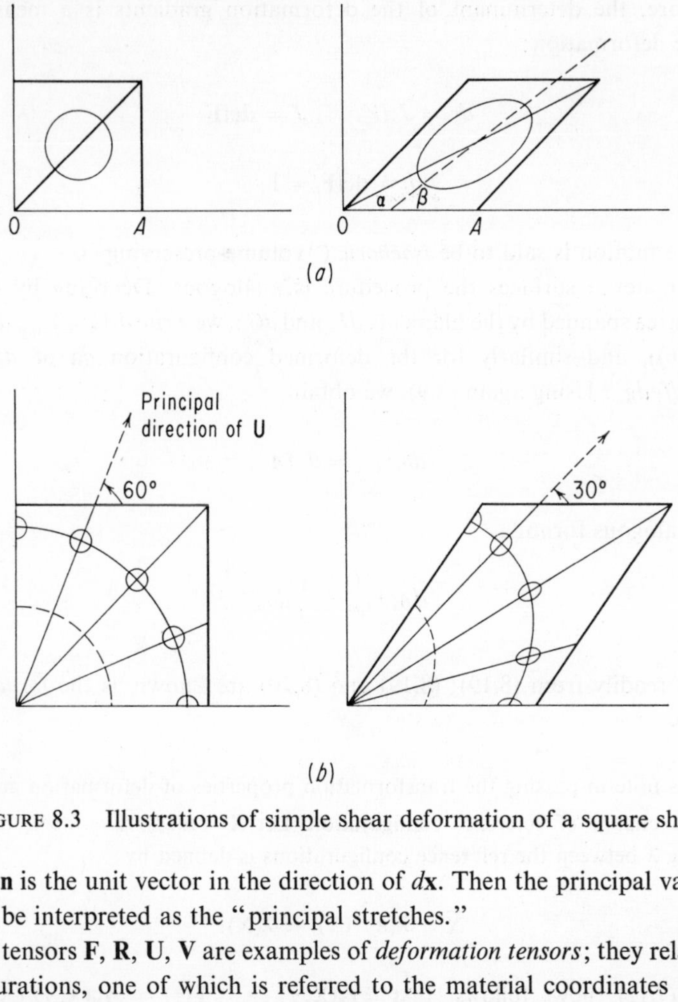

FIGURE 8.3 Illustrations of simple shear deformation of a square sheet.

where $\mathbf{n}$ is the unit vector in the direction of $d\mathbf{x}$. Then the principal values of $\mathbf{V}$ can be interpreted as the "principal stretches."

The tensors $\mathbf{F}$, $\mathbf{R}$, $\mathbf{U}$, $\mathbf{V}$ are examples of *deformation tensors*; they relate two configurations, one of which is referred to the material coordinates X_i, the other to the coordinates $x_i(\tau)$. It should be noted that if there is no deformation, then the deformation tensors reduce to the unit tensor. The strain tensors, on the other hand, reduce to zero in this case.

Let us also investigate the deformation of material volumes. If $X_i = F_i(u)$, $X_i = G_i(v)$, $X_i = H_i(w)$ are three families of material lines, then a volume element dV located at a generic particle $\mathbf{X}$ is given by $dV = \varepsilon_{mnp}\, dF_m\, dG_n\, dH_p$ (cf. (3.7)). The motion (8.3) maps the material lines into the space curves $x_i = f_i(u, \tau)$, $x_i = g_i(v, \tau)$, $x_i = h_i(w, \tau)$, and the volume element dV into its deformed configuration $dv = \varepsilon_{ijk}\, df_i\, dg_j\, dh_k$. Using (8.9) and the property (1.26) of determinants, we obtain

$$dv = \varepsilon_{ijk} x_{i,m} x_{j,n} x_{k,p}\, dF_m\, dG_n\, dH_p = \varepsilon_{mnp} \det\mathbf{F}\, dF_m\, dG_n\, dH_p = dV \det\mathbf{F}.$$

Therefore, the determinant of the deformation gradients is a measure of volume deformation:

$$dv = J\,dV, \qquad J = \det\mathbf{F}. \tag{8.17}$$

If

$$J = \det\mathbf{F} = 1, \tag{8.18}$$

then the motion is said to be *isochoric* ("volume-preserving").

For material surfaces the procedure is analogous. Denoting by $d\mathbf{A}$ the vector-area spanned by the filaments dF_n and dG_p, we write $dA_m = \varepsilon_{mnp}\, dF_n\, dG_p$ (cf. (3.6)), and similarly for the deformed configuration $d\mathbf{a}$ of $d\mathbf{A}$: $da_i = \varepsilon_{ijk}\, df_j\, dg_k$. Using again (8.9), we obtain

$$da_i x_{i,m} = J\,dA_m. \tag{8.19}$$

The analogous formula

$$dA_i X_{i,m} = \frac{1}{J}\,da_m \tag{8.20}$$

follows readily from (8.19); (8.19) and (8.20) are known as the *formulas of Nanson.*

Let us note in passing the transformation properties of deformation gradients under a change of reference configuration. Let $\mathbf{X} = \varkappa(\mathscr{P})$, $\overline{\mathbf{X}} = \bar{\varkappa}(\mathscr{P})$; then the mapping $\boldsymbol{\lambda}$ between the reference configurations is defined by

$$\overline{\mathbf{X}} = \bar{\varkappa}(\varkappa^{-1}(\mathbf{X})) \equiv \boldsymbol{\lambda}(\mathbf{X}). \tag{8.21}$$

From (7.12) now follows that $\partial\chi_\varkappa(\mathbf{X}, \tau)/\partial\mathbf{X} = \mathbf{F}(\tau) = \partial\chi_{\bar{\varkappa}}(\overline{\mathbf{X}}, \tau)/\partial\overline{\mathbf{X}}\, \partial\overline{\mathbf{X}}/\partial\mathbf{X} = \overline{\mathbf{F}}(\tau)\mathbf{G}$, thus

$$\mathbf{F} = \overline{\mathbf{F}}\mathbf{G}, \qquad \overline{\mathbf{F}} = \mathbf{F}\mathbf{G}^{-1}, \tag{8.22}$$

where

$$\mathbf{G} = \frac{\partial\overline{\mathbf{X}}}{\partial\mathbf{X}} = \frac{\partial\boldsymbol{\lambda}(\mathbf{X})}{\partial\mathbf{X}}. \tag{8.23}$$

In the example (7.13), $\overline{\mathbf{X}} = \boldsymbol{\lambda}(\mathbf{X})$: $\overline{X} = 2X$, $\overline{Y} = 4Y$, $\overline{Z} = 2Z$, and

$$\|\mathbf{F}\| = \operatorname{diag}(1 + \tau, (1 + \tau)^2, 1 + \tau^2), \ \|\mathbf{G}\| = \operatorname{diag}(2,4,2),$$

$$\|\overline{\mathbf{F}}\| = \operatorname{diag}\Big(\frac{1}{2}(1 + \tau), \frac{1}{4}(1 + \tau)^2, \frac{1}{2}(1 + \tau^2)\Big).$$

Let us recall from (7.32) the alternative description of motion whereby the current positions $\mathbf{x}$ and time t serve to identify the particles:

$$x_i(\tau) = x_i(\mathbf{x}, t, \tau). \tag{8.24}$$

As is customary, we shall use the abbreviations $x_i \equiv x_i(t)$, $\mathbf{F} \equiv \mathbf{F}(t)$, etc. With the material description (8.24) we may now associate the deformation gradients

$$\begin{aligned} \mathbf{F}_{\underline{t}}(\tau) &= \nabla \boldsymbol{\chi}_{\underline{t}}(\mathbf{x}, \tau), \\ F_{\underline{t}im}(\tau) &= x_{i,m}(\tau) = \frac{\partial x_i(\tau)}{\partial x_m}, \end{aligned} \tag{8.25}$$

Evidently $\mathbf{F}_{\underline{t}}(\tau)$ is the same type of tensor as $F_{ij}^{-1}(t) = X_{i,j}$, except that now the configuration described by $x_i(\tau)$ has replaced the configuration described by X_i; $\mathbf{F}_{\underline{t}}(\tau)$ are also referred to as "relative" deformation gradients.

In the example (7.35) we obtain diag$\{(1 + \tau)/(1 + t), (1 + \tau)^2/(1 + t)^2, (1 + \tau^2)/(1 + t^2)\} = \|\mathbf{F}_{\underline{t}}(\tau)\|$. We note that $\mathbf{F}_{\underline{t}}(t) = \mathbf{1}$, a result that is self-evident because for $\tau = t$ we have that $\mathbf{F}_{\underline{t}}(t) = \partial\mathbf{x}/\partial\mathbf{x} = \mathbf{1}$.

From $\mathbf{x}(\tau) = \boldsymbol{\chi}(\mathbf{X}, \tau)$ and $\mathbf{x} = \boldsymbol{\chi}(\mathbf{X}, t)$ we obtain the important chain rule $\partial x_i(\tau)/\partial x_j = \partial x_i(\tau)/\partial X_m \, \partial X_m/\partial x_j$, or,

$$\mathbf{F}_{\underline{t}}(\tau) = \mathbf{F}(\tau)\mathbf{F}^{-1}. \tag{8.26}$$

In particular, letting $\tau = t$,

$$\mathbf{F}_{\underline{t}}(t) = \mathbf{1}. \tag{8.27}$$

This result, together with the polar decompositions

$$\mathbf{F}_{\underline{t}}(\tau) = \mathbf{R}_{\underline{t}}(\tau)\mathbf{U}_{\underline{t}}(\tau) = \mathbf{V}_{\underline{t}}(\tau)\mathbf{R}_{\underline{t}}(\tau), \tag{8.28}$$

implies

$$\mathbf{R}_{\underline{t}}(t) = \mathbf{1}, \qquad \mathbf{U}_{\underline{t}}(t) = \mathbf{V}_{\underline{t}}(t) = \mathbf{1} \tag{8.29}$$

for the rotation tensor $\mathbf{R}_{\underline{t}}(\tau)$ and the stretch tensors $\mathbf{U}_{\underline{t}}(\tau)$ and $\mathbf{V}_{\underline{t}}(\tau)$. All of the usual definitions remain in force naturally. For instance,

$$\mathbf{C}_{\underline{t}}(\tau) = \mathbf{F}_{\underline{t}}^T(\tau)\mathbf{F}_{\underline{t}}(\tau), \qquad \mathbf{B}_{\underline{t}}(\tau) = \mathbf{F}_{\underline{t}}(\tau)\mathbf{F}_{\underline{t}}^T(\tau), \tag{8.30}$$

are the (relative) left and right Cauchy-Green deformation tensors, respectively.

The study of deformation tensors would not be complete without a reference to observer transformations. Here the results are really obvious (if one may use that word from time to time): observer motion consists of translation and rotation, hence it can only modify those kinematical tensors which also relate to translation and rotation. Consequently, deformation tensors **U, V, C, B** and strain tensors **E, e** are objective, but **F** and the rotation tensor **R** are not. A more formal approach to these equations is as follows. Recalling (7.40), we write

$$x_a^+ = Q_{ai}x_i + c_a^+, \qquad x_a^+(\tau) = Q_{ai}(\tau)x_i(\tau) + c_a^+(\tau), \tag{8.31}$$

where $Q_{ai} = Q_{ai}(t)$. Then from $F_{\underline{t}ab}^+(\tau) = \partial x_a^+(\tau)/\partial x_b^+ = \partial x_a^+(\tau)/\partial x_i(\tau)\ \partial x_i(\tau)/\partial x_j\ \partial x_j/\partial x_b^+$ it follows that

$$F_{\underline{t}ab}^+(\tau) = Q_{ai}(\tau)Q_{bj}F_{\underline{t}ij}(\tau), \tag{8.32}$$

and $$C_{\underline{t}ab}^+(\tau) = Q_{aj}Q_{bm}C_{\underline{t}jm}(\tau), \qquad B_{\underline{t}ab}^+(\tau) = Q_{aj}(\tau)Q_{bm}(\tau)B_{\underline{t}jm}(\tau). \tag{8.33}$$

Let us suppose that the reference configuration is an actual configuration corresponding to $t = t_0$. Then it is easy to see that

$$F_{ab}^+(\tau) = Q_{ai}(\tau)Q_{bj}(t_0)F_{ij}(\tau), \tag{8.34}$$

$$C_{ab}^+(\tau) = Q_{aj}(t_0)Q_{bm}(t_0)C_{jm}(\tau), \qquad B_{ab}^+(\tau) = Q_{aj}(\tau)Q_{bm}(\tau)B_{jm}(\tau).$$

For material coordinates X_i we may use one reference frame, for current coordinates $x_i(\tau)$ another. Therefore, **F** is a *double-vector* in the following sense. If $\mathbf{x}\to\mathbf{x}$, but $\mathbf{X}\to\hat{\mathbf{X}} = \mathbf{SX}$, where $\mathbf{S}^{-1} = \mathbf{S}^T$, then $\mathbf{F}\to\hat{\mathbf{F}} = \mathbf{FS}^T$ ($\hat{\mathbf{C}} = \mathbf{SCS}^T$, $\hat{\mathbf{B}} = \mathbf{B}$!), whereas if $\mathbf{X}\to\mathbf{X}$, $\mathbf{x}\to\mathbf{x}^+ = \mathbf{Qx}$, then $\mathbf{F}\to\mathbf{F}^+ = \mathbf{QF}$ ($\mathbf{B}^+ = \mathbf{QBQ}^T$, $\mathbf{C}^+ = \mathbf{C}$!).

A comparison of these transformations with (7.43) again shows that **C** and **B** are objective whereas **F** is not.

Rates of deformation

We shall now introduce kinematical variables that describe the instantaneous time rates of deformation. These variables, usually referred to as (kinematical) *rate tensors*, are not in general the time rates of the deformation tensors introduced previously. The reason for this is that deformation tensors are functions of two configurations (e.g. an "initial" and a "final" configuration), whereas rate tensors are, by definition, functions of the instantaneous configuration alone. For instance, a typical rate of deformation is the *stretching* D defined as the ratio of the material rate of a length to that length:

$$D_{\underline{n}} = \dot{\overline{dx}}/dx. \tag{8.35}$$

A typical measure of deformation is the stretch λ defined by (8.16). Because the material rate of material coordinates vanishes, $\dot{\overline{dX}} = 0$, it follows that $\dot{\lambda} = \dot{\overline{dx}}/dX = (\dot{\overline{dx}}/dx)(dx/dX)$, or,

$$D = \dot{\lambda}\lambda^{-1}. \tag{8.36}$$

Evidently the stretching D equals the material rate of stretch λ only at the instant when $\lambda = 1$.

The notation $x_i(\tau)$ for coordinates at the instant τ is not very convenient to work with; therefore, we shall use t and $x_i = x_i(t)$ instead. The derived results will hold, of course, at any instant τ, $-\infty < \tau \leq t$.

Let us first evaluate the material rate of deformation gradients, $\dot{F}_{im} = \dot{\overline{x_{i,m}}}$, where the superposed bar is used to indicate that differentiation with respect to time must be executed last. In the material description $\mathbf{X}$ and t are independent variables, so that the order of differentiations with respect to $\mathbf{X}$ and t can be interchanged: $D_t\Delta_m x_i = \Delta_m D_t x_i = v_{i.m}$. Thus

$$\dot{F}_{im} = v_{i.m} = \frac{\partial}{\partial X_m} v_i(\mathbf{X}, t). \tag{8.37}$$

Here the instantaneous velocity $\mathbf{v}$ is differentiated with respect to the coordinates X_m in the reference configuration, i.e. $\dot{F}_{im}$ is *not* a rate tensor. But the gradients of velocity with respect to the current coordinates x_i do constitute a rate tensor; it is called the *tensor of* (spatial) *velocity gradients*, L_{ij},

$$L_{ij} = v_{i,j}. \tag{8.38}$$

Changing from the material description $\mathbf{v}(\mathbf{X}, t)$ to the spatial description $\mathbf{v}(\mathbf{x}, t)$, we have the chain rule $v_{i.m}(\mathbf{X}, t) = v_{i,j}(\mathbf{x}, t)x_{j.m}$; thus by (8.37),

$$\mathbf{L} = \dot{\mathbf{F}}\mathbf{F}^{-1}, \qquad L_{ij} = v_{i.m}X_{m,j} = \dot{F}_{im}F^{-1}_{mj} \tag{8.39}$$

(cf. (8.36)). Further,

$$\dot{\overline{\mathbf{F}^{-1}}} = -\mathbf{F}^{-1}\mathbf{L}, \qquad \dot{\overline{X_{i,m}}} = -X_{i,j}v_{j,m}. \tag{8.40}$$

The tensor $\mathbf{L}$ can be looked upon as the primitive rate tensor. This is particularly suggested by the result

$$\dot{\overline{dx_i}} = L_{ij}\,dx_j = v_{i,j}\,dx_j, \tag{8.41}$$

which now takes the place of $dx_i = F_{im}\,dX_m$. To verify (8.41), we write $\dot{\overline{dx_i}} = \dot{F}_{im}\,dX_m$, and, by (8.37), $\dot{\overline{dx_i}} = v_{i,m}\,dX_m$. The rest follows from the chain rule $\dot{\overline{dx_i}} = v_{i,j}x_{j,m}\,dX_m = v_{i,j}\,dx_j$.

In the further study of $\mathbf{L}$ we shall consider separately the symmetric part

$$\mathbf{D} = \frac{1}{2}(\mathbf{L} + \mathbf{L}^T), \qquad D_{ij} = L_{(ij)} = \frac{1}{2}(v_{i,j} + v_{j,i}), \tag{8.42}$$

called the *stretching tensor* (or, rate-of-deformation tensor), and the skew-symmetric part, called the *spin tensor*:†

$$\mathbf{W} = \frac{1}{2}(\mathbf{L} - \mathbf{L}^T), \qquad W_{ij} = L_{[ij]} = \frac{1}{2}(v_{i,j} - v_{j,i}). \tag{8.43}$$

One interpretation of $\mathbf{D}$ is found from

$$\dot{\overline{ds^2}} = \dot{\overline{dx_i\,dx_i}} = 2\dot{\overline{dx_i}}\,dx_i = 2v_{i,j}\,dx_i\,dx_j = 2v_{(i,j)}\,dx_i\,dx_j:$$

$$\dot{\overline{ds^2}} = 2D_{ij}\,dx_i\,dx_j. \tag{8.44}$$

Here $\mathbf{D}$ describes the material rates of the squared lengths of all filaments $d\mathbf{x}$ emanating from a point $\mathbf{x}$ in the instantaneous configuration. In particular, if $dx_2 = dx_3 = 0$, then $\dot{\overline{ds^2}} = \dot{\overline{(dx_1)^2}} = 2\,\dot{\overline{dx_1}}\,dx_1 = 2D_{11}(dx_1)^2$, or,

$$D_{11} = \frac{\dot{\overline{dx_1}}}{dx_1} \equiv D_{\underline{1}}. \tag{8.45}$$

In words, D_{11} is the stretching of a filament aligned with the direction of $\mathbf{e}_1$ in the instantaneous configuration. The interpretations of D_{22} and D_{33} are analogous. More generally, let us relate $\mathbf{D}$ to $D_{\underline{n}}$ defined in (8.35). Starting from $dx = \sqrt{dx_i\,dx_i}$ we obtain $\dot{\overline{dx}} = D_{ij}\,dx_i\,dx_j/dx$, and

$$\frac{\dot{\overline{dx}}}{dx} = D_{\underline{n}} = D_{ij}n_in_j, \tag{8.46}$$

where $n_i = dx_i/dx$.

To interpret the shearing components of $\mathbf{D}$, we consider the scalar product of two vectors $d\mathbf{x}(1)$ and $d\mathbf{x}(2)$ making an angle θ_{12} with each other:

$$dx(1)\,dx(2)\cos\theta_{12} = dx_i(1)\,dx_i(2).$$

† In hydrodynamics it is traditional to use in the place of $\mathbf{W}$ the *vorticity vector* $\mathbf{w} = \operatorname{curl}\mathbf{v}$, thus $W_{ij} = -\frac{1}{2}\varepsilon_{ijk}w_k$. A very complete discussion of the interpretations of $\mathbf{w}$ has been given by Truesdell [171].

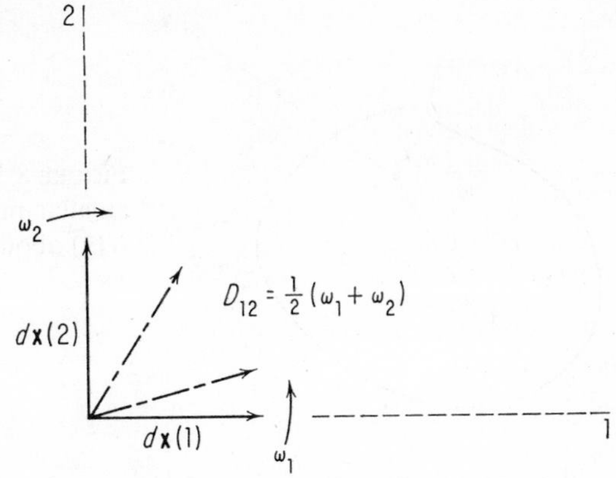

FIGURE 8.4 Interpretation of D_{12}.

Applying the material rate, then using (8.41) and (8.46), we arrive at

$$(D_{\underline{1}} + D_{\underline{2}}) \cos \theta_{12} - \dot{\theta}_{12} \sin \theta_{12} = 2D_{ij}n_i(1)n_j(2). \tag{8.47}$$

If $d\mathbf{x}(1) = \mathbf{e}_1\, dx_1$, $d\mathbf{x}(2) = \mathbf{e}_2\, dx_2$, then $\theta_{12} = \pi/2$ and

$$D_{12} = -\frac{1}{2}\dot{\theta}_{12}. \tag{8.48}$$

Therefore, D_{12} equals one half of the material rate at which the right angle θ_{12} is decreasing (cf. Figure 8.4).

The spin $\mathbf{W}$ can be interpreted in various ways as a *mean angular velocity in the medium*. It is easy enough to discern a (common) angular velocity in rigid body motions. For instance, all lines scribed on a sheet of paper will rotate with the same angular velocity as the sheet is moved about in its plane. Not so in deformations; here each "line" will have a different angular velocity. To define mean values of these angular velocities, it is necessary to obtain a local description of the velocity field. Let $N(\bar{\mathbf{x}})$ be a small neighborhood of a point $\bar{\mathbf{x}}$ (Figure 8.5). We denote the positions of particles relative to $\bar{\mathbf{x}}$ by $\mathbf{u} = \mathbf{x} - \bar{\mathbf{x}}$. We shall now calculate the angular momentum $\mathbf{H}$ of $N(\bar{\mathbf{x}})$ about the point $\bar{\mathbf{x}}$, approximating the particle velocities by the Taylor series terms

$$v_i \doteq \bar{v}_i + v_{i,j}\Big|_{\mathbf{x}=\bar{\mathbf{x}}} u_j = \bar{v}_i + \bar{D}_{ij}u_j + \bar{W}_{ij}u_j, \tag{8.49}$$

where the overbars are used to denote the (constant) values of variables at the point $\bar{\mathbf{x}}$. The neglection of the higher order terms in (8.49) limits the size of $N(\bar{\mathbf{x}})$, but does not limit the motion in any way.

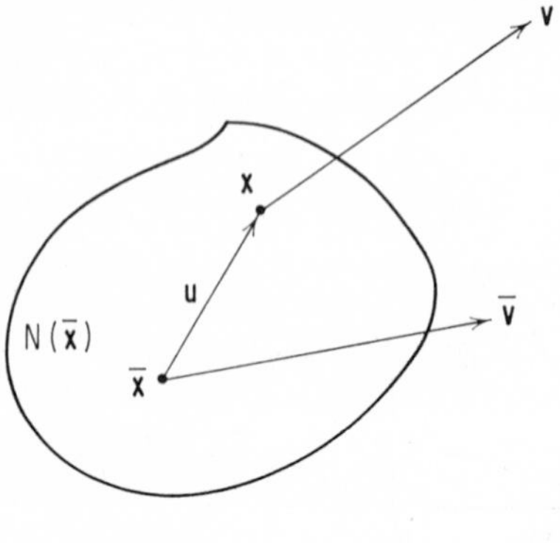

FIGURE 8.5 Variables for calculating the angular momentum of the neighborhood $N(\bar{\mathbf{x}})$ about the point $\bar{\mathbf{x}}$.

To simplify the calculation of the angular momentum $\mathbf{H} = \int(\mathbf{u} \times \mathbf{v})\, dm$, we assume that the coordinate system coincides with the principal coordinate system of $\overline{\mathbf{D}}$, and that $\bar{\mathbf{x}}$ is the mass center of $N(\bar{\mathbf{x}})$. Then the terms involving $\bar{v}_i$ drop out, and we obtain $H_1 = \int [u_2(\bar{D}_{33}u_3 - \overline{W}_{13}u_1 + \overline{W}_{32}u_2) - u_3(\bar{D}_{22}u_2 + \overline{W}_{21}u_1 - \overline{W}_{32}u_3)]\, dm$, etc. Recalling from (3.14) the definition of moments and products of inertia, we arrive at

$$H_1 = I_{23}(\bar{D}_{22} - \bar{D}_{33}) + I_{11}\overline{W}_{32} + I_{12}\overline{W}_{13} + I_{13}\overline{W}_{21}, \qquad (8.50)$$

etc. Finally, we assume that the neighborhood is spherical, i.e. $I_{ij} = 0$ for $i \neq j$. Then

$$H_1 = I_{11}\overline{W}_{32}, \ \ldots, \ \ldots. \qquad (8.51)$$

Let us now suppose that the infinitesimal material sphere is suddenly *solidified*. This requires, in principle, the introduction of new internal forces which can ensure the rigidity of the sphere. However, no *external* forces are involved, hence the angular momentum is conserved. Initially, at least, the angular velocity of the solid sphere will be exactly equal to the spin vector $\bar{\boldsymbol{\omega}}_i = -\frac{1}{2}\varepsilon_{ijk}\overline{W}_{jk}$ of the medium. The spin $\bar{\boldsymbol{\omega}}$ represents, of course, a mean value of the angular velocities of individual material filaments, because the filaments rotate relative to each other in the shearing motion described by D_{12}, D_{23}, D_{31}.

It must be also emphasized that it would be incorrect to interpret the spin as an angular velocity of particles. For one, in the classical theories a particle is completely characterized by its position, so that it is meaningless to speak of angular velocities of particles. Second, the spin is the mean angular velocity of small but *finite* elements of a medium. Thus a theorem of Cauchy† states

† [171], p. 59–62.

that the projection of $\boldsymbol{\omega}$ upon an axis $\mathbf{n}$ is the mean of the angular velocities about $\mathbf{n}$ of any two orthogonal filaments lying in the plane normal to $\mathbf{n}$. A similar interpretation, also due to Cauchy, is as follows: the projection of $\boldsymbol{\omega}$ upon any axis $\mathbf{n}$ is the mean of the angular velocities about $\mathbf{n}$ of all filaments lying in the plane normal to $\mathbf{n}$.

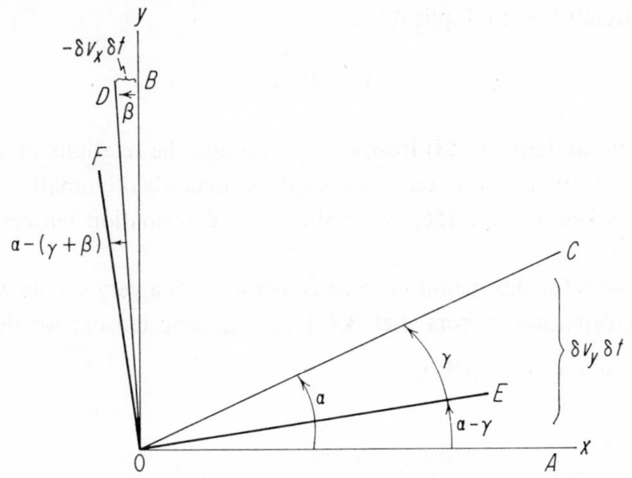

FIGURE 8.6 Drawing for the interpretation of ω_z. The segments $0A$ and $0B$ represent initial configurations, $0C$ and $0D$ the later configurations. The orthogonal axes $0E$ and $0F$ show the rigid rotation contained in the motion.

To illustrate Cauchy's theorem, we choose at a point 0 two filaments $d\mathbf{x}(1) = \varepsilon \mathbf{e}_x$ and $d\mathbf{x}(2) = \varepsilon \mathbf{e}_y$. The filaments being small, the particle velocities can be approximated by linear distributions. Moreover, because changes in lengths are irrelevant to this interpretation, we assume that, relative to the particle at 0, the velocities are at right angles to the filaments. Then, as is shown in Figure 8.6, the particles of the filament $0A$ move in the y direction, whereas the particles of the filament $0B$ move in the x direction. The infinitesimal angles α and β describing the rotations of the filaments are given by $\tan \alpha = \delta v_y \, \delta t/\varepsilon$, $\tan \beta = -\delta v_x \, \delta t/\varepsilon$, in which we have taken into account that the senses of positive v_x and of positive β are opposite. Therefore, at the instant $\delta t = 0$, $\dot{\alpha} = \delta v_y/\varepsilon = v_{y,x}$, $\dot{\beta} = -\delta v_x/\varepsilon = -v_{x,y}$, and so it follows that

$$D_{xy} = v_{(x,y)} = \frac{1}{2}(\dot{\alpha} - \dot{\beta}), \quad \omega_z = v_{[y,x]} = \frac{1}{2}(\dot{\alpha} + \dot{\beta}). \tag{8.52}$$

Thus ω_z equals the mean of the angular velocities of two orthogonal filaments in the xy plane, whereas D_{xy} is one half of the difference of the angular velocities. If $\dot{\alpha} = \dot{\beta}$, then the filaments remain orthogonal, i.e. there is no shearing present.

We note in passing that the decomposition of the basic rate tensor into a spin **W** and a rate-of-deformation **D** is additive,

$$\mathbf{L} = \mathbf{W} + \mathbf{D}, \tag{8.53}$$

but the decomposition of the basic deformation tensor **F** into a finite rotation **R** and a stretch **U** is multiplicative:

$$\mathbf{F} = \mathbf{RU}. \tag{8.54}$$

It is possible to derive (8.53) from (8.54),† though the relations between deformation tensors and rate tensors are not particularly illuminating because, as was remarked on page 156, material rates of deformation tensors are not rate tensors.

Rate tensors for the instant t can be constructed in a very simple way from relative deformation tensors. Let $\mathbf{A}_{\underline{t}}(\tau)$ be a generic tensor; we define the associated rate tensor $\dot{\mathbf{A}}_{\underline{t}}(t)$ by

$$\dot{\mathbf{A}}_{\underline{t}}(t) = \frac{\partial}{\partial \tau} \mathbf{A}_{\underline{t}}(\tau)\bigg|_{\tau = t}. \tag{8.55}$$

For instance, recalling from (8.26) and (8.39) that $\mathbf{F}_{\underline{t}}(\tau) = \mathbf{F}(\tau)\mathbf{F}^{-1}(t)$, $\mathbf{L} = \dot{\mathbf{F}}\mathbf{F}^{-1}$, we immediately obtain

$$\dot{\mathbf{F}}_{\underline{t}}(t) = \mathbf{L}. \tag{8.56}$$

This formula, combined with (8.53) and the polar decomposition (8.28), yields an attractive result: $\dot{\mathbf{F}}_{\underline{t}}(t) = \dot{\mathbf{R}}_{\underline{t}}(t)\,\mathbf{U}_{\underline{t}}(t) + \mathbf{R}_{\underline{t}}(t)\,\dot{\mathbf{U}}_{\underline{t}}(t) = \dot{\mathbf{R}}_{\underline{t}}(t) + \dot{\mathbf{U}}_{\underline{t}}(t) = \mathbf{W} + \mathbf{D}$. Therefore,

$$\dot{\mathbf{R}}_{\underline{t}}(t) = \mathbf{W}, \qquad \dot{\mathbf{U}}_{\underline{t}}(t) = \mathbf{D}. \tag{8.57}$$

Let us also derive the basic formulas for deformation rates of material volumes and surfaces. We first calculate $\dot{J} = \overset{\cdot}{\overline{\det\mathbf{F}}} = (\partial J/\partial x_{i.m})\overset{\cdot}{\overline{x_{i.m}}} = \bar{x}_{i.m}v_{i.m}$, where we have used (8.37), and $\bar{x}_{i.m}$ is the cofactor of $x_{i.m}$ in $\det\mathbf{F}$. Then $\dot{J} = v_{i,j}x_{j.m}\bar{x}_{i.m}$, hence, by (3.39),

$$\dot{J} = J\,\mathrm{div}\mathbf{v} = Jv_{i,i}. \tag{8.58}$$

† Cf. Problem 30.

Since $\dot{\overline{dV}} = 0$, from $(8.17)_1$ now follows that

$$\dot{\overline{dv}} = v_{i,i}\, dv. \tag{8.59}$$

In the same way we derive from (8.19) the formula

$$\dot{\overline{da_i}} = v_{k,k}\, da_i - da_k\, v_{k,i}. \tag{8.60}$$

The observer transformations for **L**, **W**, and **D** can be easily read off from (7.51). We find $L^+_{ab} = \partial v^+_a / \partial x^+_b = Q_{ai} Q_{bj} L_{ij} + Q_{ai} Q_{bj} \Omega^+_{ij}$. In particular, when the observer frames are aligned,

$$\mathbf{L}^+ = \mathbf{L} + \mathbf{\Omega}^+ ; \tag{8.61}$$

so that

$$\mathbf{D}^+ = \mathbf{D}, \qquad \mathbf{W}^+ = \mathbf{W} + \mathbf{\Omega}^+. \tag{8.62}$$

As was to be expected, the spin **W** is not objective: an observer can always adjust his angular velocity so that the mean angular velocity of the material neighborhood will appear to be zero. The tensor **D**, on the other hand, describes the rate at which a material sphere is deforming into an ellipsoid, so that it appears the same to all observers.

Surfaces of discontinuity†

The kinematical theory which we have developed so far is applicable in any region where the relevant variables have the necessary smoothness properties. We shall now consider the case of two such regions, R^+ and R^-, that are contiguous, and separated by a surface of discontinuity, S (Figure 8.7). On S a kinematical variable Ψ may suffer a *jump* (or, discontinuity), meaning that the one-sided limits of Ψ do not coincide on S. Thus if S is described by $g(\mathbf{x}, t) = 0$, then‡

$$\Psi^+ \equiv \lim_{\mathbf{x}^+, t^+ \to \mathbf{x}, t} \Psi(\mathbf{x}^+, t^+), \qquad \Psi^- \equiv \lim_{\mathbf{x}^-, t^- \to \mathbf{x}, t} \Psi(\mathbf{x}^-, t^-)$$

may be such that the jump $[\![\Psi]\!]$ does not vanish: $[\![\Psi]\!] \equiv \Psi^+ - \Psi^- \neq 0$.

† A very complete coverage of this subject may be found in *CFT*, Sections 172–194.

‡ The designations $\mathbf{x}^+, t^+$ have a different meaning in observer transformations, but there is little chance for confusion.

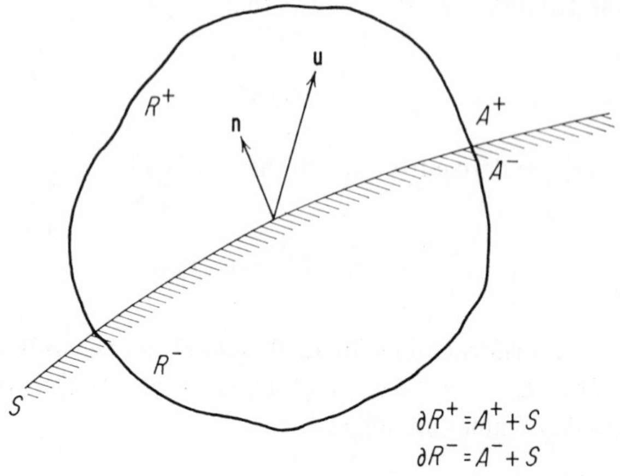

FIGURE 8.7 A region $R = R^+ + R^-$ containing a surface of discontinuity, S.

By a *wave* we ordinarily mean a certain kind of oscillating solution ("sinusoidal plane progressive wave") of a differential equation. From this point of view, however, a theory of waves is bound to be a very special one, because for the differential equations to provide a *determinate* system of equations, they must incorporate special assumptions about the constitution of a medium. The only way to obtain a general theory of waves is by characterizing a wave (or rather, a wavefront) in strictly kinematical terms, namely as a *moving surface of discontinuity*. Roughly speaking, moving surfaces of discontinuity are very steep wave fronts, produced by "impact," or by a distortion of moving disturbances which is not unlike the breaking of waves on a shore. In a particular theory it may be possible to introduce surfaces of discontinuity as mathematically convenient idealizations of thin layers in which variables undergo rapid changes. For instance, shock waves in a gas are very thin "boundary layers" in which the flow regime is viscous. Because these interpretations require a knowledge of the constitution of a medium, they cannot be pursued in the context of kinematics. A comparison of the results obtained from a study of moving singular surfaces on the one hand, and (infinitesimal) progressive plane waves on the other hand, is an intriguing problem.†

It is customary to refer to waves in which displacements are discontinuous across a surface as *zero order waves*. Thus a zero order discontinuity is one in which separation of material takes place, e.g. fracture, "dislocation." In a *first order wave* displacements remain continuous, but displacement gradients and velocities may suffer a jump. Depending on whether the jump is normal

† Cf. the discussion of wave propagation in Section 14.

or tangential to the surface of discontinuity, we speak of shock waves or vortex sheets. In *waves of order two*, displacement gradients and particle velocities are continuous, but discontinuities occur in certain components of second displacement gradients and particle acceleration. Therefore, these waves are referred to as *acceleration waves* (or, acoustic waves).

Much of the theory of surfaces of discontinuity has to do with decomposing the jump of a given variable into components normal and tangential to the surface. The resulting identities are then called *geometric conditions of compatibility* if only the spatial or material gradients of the variables are considered.

If $\mathbf{x} = \mathbf{x}(s)$ is a space curve lying in the (open) region R^+, then $d\Psi/ds$ can be evaluated through the chain rule

$$\frac{d\Psi}{ds} = \Psi_{,i}\frac{dx_i}{ds}. \tag{8.63}$$

Assuming that Ψ approaches a limit Ψ^+ on the surface of discontinuity, S, we can ask whether the chain rule remains valid for curves lying in S. According to *Hadamard's lemma*, the answer is in the affirmative, because any two points of S can be connected by a polygonal path lying in R^+. The polygonal paths then provide a means for defining the one-sided limits of the partial derivatives $\Psi_{,i}$. Thus

$$\frac{d\Psi^+}{ds} = \Psi^+_{,i}\frac{dx_i}{ds}, \qquad \frac{d\Psi^-}{ds} = \Psi^-_{,i}\frac{dx_i}{ds};$$

consequently, *the tangential derivative of the jump* $[\![\Psi]\!]$ *equals the jump of the tangential derivative*:†

$$\frac{d}{ds}[\![\Psi]\!] = \left[\!\!\left[\frac{d\Psi}{ds}\right]\!\!\right] = [\![\Psi_{,i}]\!]\frac{dx_i}{ds}. \tag{8.64}$$

Therefore, introducing the surface gradient D_i by

$$D_i = \partial_i - n_i D, \tag{8.65}$$

where

$$D = \partial_{\underline{n}} = n_k \partial_k \tag{8.66}$$

† Cf. *CFT*, p. 493.

denotes differentiation in the direction of unit normal vector $\mathbf{n}$ of S, we can express Hadamard's lemma as follows,

$$D_k[\![\Psi]\!] = [\![D_k\Psi]\!]. \tag{8.67}$$

With the notations

$$[\![\Psi]\!] = A, \qquad [\![D\Psi]\!] = [\![n_i\Psi_{,i}]\!] = B, \tag{8.68}$$

we have that, by (8.65),

$$[\![\Psi_{,i}]\!] = D_iA + n_iB; \tag{8.69}$$

moreover, if Ψ is continuous, i.e. $A = 0$, we obtain *Maxwell's theorem*:

$$[\![\Psi_{,i}]\!] = n_iB, \qquad B = [\![D\Psi]\!]. \tag{8.70}$$

If Ψ stands for a vector $\mathbf{c}$, then Maxwell's theorem yields the following formulas,

$$\begin{aligned} [\![c_{k,i}]\!] &= n_iB_k, & B_k &= [\![Dc_k]\!], \\ [\![\text{curl}\mathbf{c}]\!] &= \mathbf{n}\times\mathbf{B}, & [\![\text{div}\mathbf{c}]\!] &= \mathbf{n}\cdot\mathbf{B}. \end{aligned} \tag{8.71}$$

Finally, let us take the case where $A = B = 0$, but

$$C = [\![D^2\Psi]\!] \tag{8.72}$$

does not vanish. Then, by (8.67) and $D_jB = 0$, $D_j[\![\Psi_{,i}]\!] = 0$, it follows that

$$[\![\Psi_{,ij}]\!] = Cn_in_j. \tag{8.73}$$

This relation is a second order condition of compatibility; higher order conditions of compatibility may be derived in like manner.

Turning now to motion of surfaces of discontinuity, let us first note that a body may be viewed either in its actual configuration (i.e. the configuration $\mathbf{x} = \boldsymbol{\chi}(\mathscr{P}, t)$, where t is the present time), or in some reference configuration $\mathbf{X} = \boldsymbol{\varkappa}(\mathscr{P})$. That is, either one of these configurations is an acceptable "map" of the body, permitting us to chart the progress of the surface of discontinuity. Thus if U_α, $\alpha = 1, 2$, are surface coordinates by which the surface of discontinuity, S, is parametrized, then

$$x_i = f_i(U_\alpha, t), \qquad X_i = F_i(U_\alpha, t) \tag{8.74}$$

describe the motion of S from point to point, and from particle to particle, respectively. Eliminating the surface coordinates, we obtain the equivalent descriptions

$$g(\mathbf{x}, t) = 0, \qquad G(\mathbf{X}, t) = 0. \tag{8.75}$$

Differentiation with respect to time at a fixed point of S will be denoted by S_t, thus

$$S_t = \left.\frac{\partial}{\partial t}\right|_{U_\alpha = \text{const.}} \tag{8.76}$$

The velocity $\mathbf{u}$ of the points of S in space is then defined by

$$u_i = S_t x_i. \tag{8.77}$$

Similarly, we define an *intrinsic velocity* $\mathbf{U}$ by

$$U_i = S_t X_i. \tag{8.78}$$

Evidently $\mathbf{U}$ describes the rate at which S traverses the material medium. However, because the medium is continually deforming, and the choice of material coordinates X_i is arbitrary, $\mathbf{U}$ does not admit a direct geometrical interpretation comparable to that of $\mathbf{u}$. The *relative velocity*

$$\mathbf{V} = \mathbf{u} - \mathbf{v}, \tag{8.79}$$

on the other hand, is simply the velocity of S in the body.

To express the *condition of persistence* of a (single) surface of discontinuity, we assume, first, that the motion of the surface in space, or in the body, cannot be discontinuous (i.e. neither $\mathbf{u}$ nor $\mathbf{U}$ suffer jumps). Moreover, the motion of the body, $\mathbf{x} = \boldsymbol{\chi}(\mathbf{X}, t)$, is continuous on S, and differentiable as often as is needed in the open regions R^+ and R^-, it being understood that the one-sided limits of the derivatives of $\boldsymbol{\chi}$ need not coincide on S. With this in mind, we consider the chain rule

$$S_t = D_t + U_j \Delta_j = \partial_t + u_j \partial_j, \tag{8.80}$$

thus

$$\mathbf{u} = \left.\frac{\partial \mathbf{x}}{\partial t}\right|_{U_\alpha} = \left.\frac{\partial \boldsymbol{\chi}}{\partial \mathbf{X}}\right|_t \left.\frac{\partial \mathbf{X}}{\partial t}\right|_{U_\alpha} + \left.\frac{\partial \boldsymbol{\chi}}{\partial t}\right|_{\mathbf{X}},$$

$$\mathbf{u} = \mathbf{F}\mathbf{U} + \mathbf{v} = \mathbf{V} + \mathbf{v}. \tag{8.81}$$

If the material coordinates are identified with the current positions, then $\mathbf{F} = \mathbf{1}$ and $\mathbf{U} = \mathbf{V}$. In view of the continuity of $\mathbf{u}$ and $\mathbf{U}$, it follows that

$$[\![\mathbf{v}]\!] = -[\![\mathbf{V}]\!] = -[\![\mathbf{F}]\!]\mathbf{U}. \tag{8.82}$$

As a rule, we are only interested in changes across a surface of discontinuity. In accord with (8.75), the unit normal vectors are defined by

$$\begin{aligned} N_i &= \frac{G_{.i}}{M}, \qquad M = \sqrt{G_{.j}G_{.j}}, \\ n_i &= \frac{g_{,i}}{m}, \qquad m = \sqrt{g_{,j}g_{,j}}. \end{aligned} \tag{8.83}$$

The correspondence between $\mathbf{N}$ and $\mathbf{n}$ can be deduced from the identity $g(\mathbf{x}, t) = g(\mathbf{x}(\mathbf{X}, t), t) = G(\mathbf{X}, t)$, from which it follows that $N_m = g_{,i}x_{i.m}/M$, or,

$$N_m = \frac{m}{M} n_i x_{i.m}. \tag{8.84}$$

If $\mathbf{t}$ is a unit vector lying in the intersection of the tangent plane of S with the plane of $\mathbf{u}$ and $\mathbf{n}$, then

$$\mathbf{u} = \bar{u}\mathbf{n} + \hat{u}\mathbf{t}. \tag{8.85}$$

In quite the same way we let

$$\mathbf{U} = \bar{U}\mathbf{N} + \hat{U}\mathbf{T}. \tag{8.86}$$

Traditionally $\bar{u}$ is referred to as the *speed of displacement*, and $\bar{U}$ as the *speed of propagation*. The *relative speed of propagation* is defined by

$$\bar{V} = \mathbf{V}\cdot\mathbf{n} = \bar{u} - \bar{v}, \tag{8.87}$$

where $\bar{v} = \mathbf{v}\cdot\mathbf{n}$ is particle speed in the direction normal to S. Using (8.84), (8.81), it is easy to see that

$$\bar{V} = \frac{M}{m}\bar{U}. \tag{8.88}$$

Let us recall again that in a material description we follow the progress of a surface of discontinuity, S, in a reference configuration of the medium, the unit normal vectors of S being denoted by $\mathbf{N}$. Because the choice of reference configurations is arbitrary, the vectors $\mathbf{N}$ have no direct geometrical significance in the actual configuration.

To calculate $\bar{u}$ from the representation $(8.75)_1$, we reason that if $\mathbf{x}$ and t satisfy $(8.75)_1$, then $g(\mathbf{x} + \mathbf{u}\,dt, t + dt) = 0$ must also hold. Therefore, $S_t g = \partial_t g + \mathbf{u} \cdot \nabla g = 0$, from which it follows that

$$\bar{u} = -\frac{\partial_t g}{m}. \tag{8.89}$$

Similarly,

$$\bar{U} = -\frac{\dot{G}}{M}. \tag{8.90}$$

The identities arrived at by decomposing jumps of time rates into components normal and tangential to S are called *kinematical conditions of compatibility*. A typical example is given by (8.82); here, noting that $[\![\dot{x}_i]\!] = -[\![x_{i.m}]\!](\bar{U}N_m + \hat{U}T_m) = -\bar{U}[\![x_{i.m}N_m]\!] - \hat{U}[\![D_T x_i]\!]$ and $[\![D_T x_i]\!] = D_T[\![x_i]\!] = 0$ (cf. (8.67)), we get the "compatibility condition for first order waves":

$$[\![\dot{x}_i]\!] = -\bar{U}A_i, \qquad A_i = [\![x_{i.m}N_m]\!]. \tag{8.91}$$

At any point P of S, the jump of a variable is a function of time only: $\alpha(t) = [\![\Psi]\!]$. To connect $d\alpha/dt$ with the jump of a time rate of $\Psi(\mathbf{x}, t)$, the latter time rate must be obtained by an observer bound to P, i.e. d/dt must be interpreted inside the bracket operator as S_t defined by (8.80):

$$\frac{d}{dt}[\![\Psi]\!] = [\![\partial_t \Psi + u_i \partial_i \Psi]\!] = [\![D_t \Psi + U_i \Delta_i \Psi]\!]. \tag{8.92}$$

All kinematical compatibility conditions are found by applying S_t to given conditions of persistence. For second order waves we start from $[\![\dot{x}_i]\!] = 0$, $[\![x_{i.m}]\!] = 0$. From the first it follows that $0 = [\![\ddot{x}_i]\!] + U_j[\![\dot{x}_{i.j}]\!] = [\![\ddot{x}_i]\!] + V_k[\![\dot{x}_{i,k}]\!]$, where we have used $U_j F_{kj} = V_k$. But $[\![\dot{x}_{i,k}]\!] = D_k[\![\dot{x}_i]\!] + n_k[\![D\dot{x}_i]\!]$ (cf. (8.67)), where $[\![D\dot{x}_i]\!] = [\![\dot{x}_{i,j}]\!]n_j$. Therefore, we get the following compatibility condition for acceleration waves,

$$[\![\ddot{x}_i]\!] = -\bar{V}[\![D\dot{x}_i]\!]. \tag{8.93}$$

From $[\![x_{i.m}]\!] = 0$ we obtain in the same way

$$[\![\ddot{\mathbf{x}}]\!] = \mathbf{a}\bar{U}^2, \qquad a_k = [\![x_{k.mp}]\!]N_m N_p. \tag{8.94}$$

The *amplitude* of the acceleration wave, **s**, is defined by

$$\mathbf{s} = \frac{\bar{U}^2}{\bar{V}^2}\mathbf{a} = \frac{m^2}{M^2}\mathbf{a}, \tag{8.95}$$

so that $(8.94)_1$ can be also expressed as

$$[\![\ddot{\mathbf{x}}]\!] = \mathbf{s}\bar{V}^2. \tag*{(8.94)*}$$

If the jump of $x_{k.m}$ is zero, then, in analogy with (8.73),

$$[\![x_{k.mp}]\!] = a_k N_m N_p. \tag{8.96}$$

Eliminating **N** through (8.84), we readily obtain

$$[\![x_{k.mp}]\!] = s_k x_{i.m} x_{j.p} n_i n_j. \tag{8.97}$$

Further, starting from $[\![\dot{x}_{i.m}]\!] + U_j[\![x_{i.mj}]\!] = 0$, we find that, by (8.84), (8.88), (8.95), (8.96),

$$\begin{gathered} [\![v_{i,j}]\!] = -\bar{V}s_i n_j, \\ [\![\operatorname{div}\dot{\mathbf{x}}]\!] = -\bar{V}\mathbf{s}\cdot\dot{\mathbf{x}}, \qquad [\![\operatorname{curl}\dot{\mathbf{x}}]\!] = -\bar{V}\mathbf{s}\times\dot{\mathbf{x}}. \end{gathered} \tag{8.98}$$

Finally, it is not difficult to show that a third order wave front satisfies the jump conditions†

$$\begin{gathered} [\![x_{k.mjr}]\!] = s_k F_{pm} F_{qj} F_{sr} n_p n_q n_s, \\ [\![\ddot{x}_{i,r}]\!] = s_i \bar{V}^2 n_r. \end{gathered} \tag{8.99}$$

The study of wave motion is particularly simple for one-dimensional motions $x = x(X, t)$, where x is the position of a typical particle X of a "cross section." Deformation gradient, velocity, and acceleration are now *scalars* defined by

$$F = \frac{\partial x(X, t)}{\partial X}, \qquad v = \dot{x} = \frac{\partial x(X, t)}{\partial t}, \qquad a = \ddot{x} = \frac{\partial^2 x(X, t)}{\partial t^2}$$

Describing the motion of a (single) surface of discontinuity, S, is even simpler:

† *CFT,* Section 191.

we denote by $x = r(t)$ the position of S in space, and by $X = R(t)$ its position in a reference configuration. Thus

$$u = \frac{dr}{dt}, \qquad U = \frac{dR}{dt}, \qquad V = u - v = \frac{d}{dt}(r - x).$$

Moreover, since $r(t) = x(R(t), t)$, we have that $u = FU + v$. The compatibility condition (8.91) now reduces to $[\![\dot{x}]\!] = -U[\![F]\!]$. A simple illustration is provided by

$$x = \alpha t + \beta X, \qquad x \le r,$$

$$x = X, \qquad x \ge r,$$

$$r = R = \frac{\alpha t}{1 - \beta}.$$

Then $u = U = \alpha/(1 - \beta)$, and

$$x \le r\colon v = \alpha, \qquad F = \beta, \qquad V = \frac{\alpha\beta}{1 - \beta},$$

$$x \ge r\colon v = 0, \qquad F = 1, \qquad V = \frac{\alpha}{1 - \beta},$$

hence $[\![V]\!] = \alpha = -[\![v]\!] = U[\![F]\!]$.

Problems

A. DEFORMATION TENSORS

1. Consider a material line $X^2 + Y^2 = A^2, Z = 0$, where A is a constant. What is the image of this line under the mapping $x = X + KY$, $y = Y$, $z = Z$ (K a constant)? Determine the main geometrical features of the image.

2. For the mapping given in Problem 1, what is the image of $(X^2/A^2) + (Y^2/B^2) = 1, Z = 0$?

3. If you were given a million dollar grant to make an educational movie, models, etc. to explain kinematics of continuous bodies, what experiments, models, etc. would you choose? In particular, how would you go about demonstrating the rotation **R** contained in every motion?

4. If $dS^2 = dX_i\, dX_i$, then $dS^2 = c_{ij}\, dx_i\, dx_j =$ const. is said to describe a *strain ellipsoid.* What is its image under the deformation? How are the principal values $c_{\underline{i}}$ related to the semiaxes of the ellipsoid?

5. If $ds^2 = dx_i\, dx_i$, then $ds^2 = C_{ij}\, dX_i\, dX_j =$ const. is said to describe a *reciprocal strain ellipsoid.* What is its image under the deformation? How are the principal values $C_{\underline{i}}$ related to the semiaxes of the ellipsoid?

6. Consider the mapping $x = (b/a)X$, $y = Y$. Show that it carries the ellipse $(b^2/a^2)X^2 + Y^2 = b^2$ and the circle $X^2 + Y^2 = a^2$ into the circle $x^2 + y^2 = b^2$ and the ellipse $(a^2/b^2)x^2 + y^2 = a^2$, respectively. Also calculate the tensors **C** and **c** defined in Problem 4 and Problem 5, and sketch the circles and ellipses in question.

7. Calculate **F** for the deformation given in

a. Problem 7.3 **b.** Problem 7.4 **c.** Problem 7.5 **d.** Problem 7.6

8. Let $x = X + Ct$, $y = Y + AXY$, $z = Z + ACZ^2t$, where A and C are constants. Calculate **F**.

9. Let $x = X + KYZ$, $y = Y + KZ^2$, $z = Z + KX^2$, where K is a constant, Let $d_1\mathbf{X} = (dX, 0, 0)$, $d_2\mathbf{X} = (0, dY, 0)$, $d_3\mathbf{X} = (0, 0, dZ)$. Calculate **F**; then calculate $d_{\underline{i}}\mathbf{x} = \mathbf{F}\, d_{\underline{i}}\mathbf{X}$ at (0, 0, 0), (0, 0, 1), (0, 1, 0), (1, 0, 0).

10. Show that a homogeneous deformation maps parallel lines into parallel lines, similar triangles into similar triangles, and ellipsoids into ellipsoids.

11. For the mapping given in Problem 1, calculate **B**, **C**, **E**, and **e**.

12. Let $x = AX$, $y = BY$, $z = CZ$, where A, B, C are constants. Calculate **B**, **C**, **E**, and **e**.

13. Calculate $J = \det\mathbf{F}$ for the deformations given in

a. Problem 9 **b.** Problem 8 **c.** Problem 6

14. Let $\overline{\mathbf{X}}$ be the positions of particles at $\tau = 2$. Calculate $\mathbf{G} = \partial\overline{\mathbf{X}}/\partial\mathbf{X}$ for the deformations given in

a. Problem 7.3 **b.** Problem 7.4 **c.** Problem 7.5

d. Problem 7.6 for $K(\tau) = K\tau$.

15. Calculate the relative deformation gradients for the motions given in

a. Problem 7.3 **b.** Problem 7.4 **c.** Problem 7.5 **d.** Problem 7.6

16. Calculate $\mathbf{C}_{\underline{t}}(\tau)$ for the deformation given in Problem 7.6.

17. Let $x(\tau) = A\tau X$, $y(\tau) = B\tau Y$, $z(\tau) = C\tau Z$, where A, B, C are constants. Calculate $\mathbf{C}_{\underline{t}}(\tau)$ and $2\mathbf{E}_{\underline{t}}(\tau) = \mathbf{C}_{\underline{t}}(\tau) - \mathbf{1}$.

18. Verify the derivation of (8.33).

19. Verify the derivation of (8.34).

20. Consider the radial motion $\rho = \rho(P, t)$, $\phi = \Phi$, $z = Z$ of a cylinder $A \le P \le B$. Show that an *isochoric* motion must be of the form

$$\rho(P, t) = \sqrt{\rho^2(A, t) + P^2 - A^2}.$$

21. Consider the radial motion $r = r(R, t)$, $\theta = \Theta$, $\phi = \Phi$ of a spherical shell $A \le R \le B$. Show that an *isochoric* motion must be of the form

$$r(R, t) = \sqrt[3]{r^3(A, t) + R^3 - A^3}.$$

B. RATES OF DEFORMATION

22. Calculate $\mathbf{D}$ and $\mathbf{W}$ for the motion given in

 a. Problem 7.13 b. Problem 7.14

23. For the motion given by Problem 7.6 calculate $\mathbf{D}$ and $\mathbf{W}$ from $\mathbf{L} = \dot{\mathbf{F}}\mathbf{F}^{-1}$. Then calculate $\mathbf{F}_{\underline{t}}(\tau)$ and $\mathbf{L} = \dot{\mathbf{F}}_{\underline{t}}(t)$.

24. For the motion given in Problem 17, calculate $\mathbf{F}_{t}(\tau)$ and $\mathbf{L} = \dot{\mathbf{F}}_{\underline{t}}(t)$.

25. Obtain $\mathbf{F}_{\underline{t}}(\tau)$, then calculate $\mathbf{L} = \dot{\mathbf{F}}_{\underline{t}}(t)$ for the motion given in

 a. Problem 7.3 b. Problem 7.4 c. Problem 7.5

26. Verify (8.60).

27. Derive the observer transformation for acceleration gradients.

28. Derive the observer transformation for gradients of angular velocity.

29. Plot a typical velocity profile for the motion $v_x = ky$, $v_y = v_z = 0$, where k is a constant. By selecting suitable filaments, verify that $\mathbf{W}$ must be interpreted as the average angular velocity for a pair of filaments which are momentarily orthogonal.

30. Let $\mathbf{F} = \mathbf{R}\mathbf{U}$, $\mathbf{L} = \dot{\mathbf{F}}\mathbf{F}^{-1}$. Show that $\mathbf{W} = \dot{\mathbf{R}}\mathbf{R}^T + (\mathbf{R}\dot{\mathbf{U}}\mathbf{U}^{-1}\mathbf{R}^T)_{\underline{a}}$, $\mathbf{D} = (\mathbf{R}\dot{\mathbf{U}}\mathbf{U}^{-1}\mathbf{R}^T)_{\underline{s}}$, where $\underline{a}$ and $\underline{s}$ denote the skew-symmetric and symmetric parts, respectively.

31. Prove the theorem of Gosiewski: if $\mathbf{n}$ is a principal vector of $\mathbf{D}$, then $\dot{\mathbf{n}} = \mathbf{W}\mathbf{n}$.

CHAPTER **3**

PHYSICAL PRINCIPLES OF CONTINUUM MECHANICS

With the introduction of physical principles we leave pure mathematics behind. But even though the outlook will be different, the form of the presentation will remain the same because continuum mechanics, by its very nature as a *unified* description of deformations and forces, requires a deductive approach. So that the presentation should not seem unduly dogmatic, however, we shall digress to historical points of interest from time to time.

Like fashion, the doctrine concerning laws of nature is subject to change, each period having its *Zeitgeist*, its own spirit of times. In this utilitarian age we are embarrassed by the term *Laws of Nature*; we speak of physical principles and balance equations instead. Moreover, in each principle we discern the operation of some method of reasoning, thus recognizing the strongly subjective flavor of science. With the aid of these methods of reasoning, our experience is ordered into rational schemes, or theories. As in any other endeavor, we are also guided by common sense, aesthetic values, and various intuitive principles.† It has been said by Poincare that *simplicity* and *generality* are the chief virtues of laws of science. These virtues are nowhere more evident than in classical physics, which rests on the principles governing mass, energy, charge, linear and angular momenta, the laws of Ampere and Faraday for

† Cf. Newton's famous dictum: "We are to admit no more causes of natural things than such as may be both true and sufficient to explain their appearances. Indeed, Nature is simple and affects not the pomp of superfluous causes."

electromagnetic flux, and the idea of irreversibility. Almost everything that we can see or hear, or build, is explained by these few principles.

Mechanics was the first of physical sciences. It has supplied the language, concepts, and models for the later sciences of physics. The particular charm of mechanics, which has attracted scientists throughout the ages, may be due to the fact that the first and most notable successes of mechanics were celebrated in the study of planetary motion, surely a problem of ancient and mysterious attraction for all mankind. The unified approach to continuum mechanics is based on the recognition that the same physical principles govern every process, no matter what the constitution of bodies. Whether the substance is milk, honey, or steel, whether it is hot or cold, mass must be conserved, energy balance must add up, entropy changes must satisfy the proper limitations. Constitutive equations, of which Hooke's law of elasticity is a familiar example, can then be combined with the physical principles to yield special theories. The structure of continuum mechanics can thus be illustrated by the following drawing, which we shall call the "tree of continuum mechanics theories."

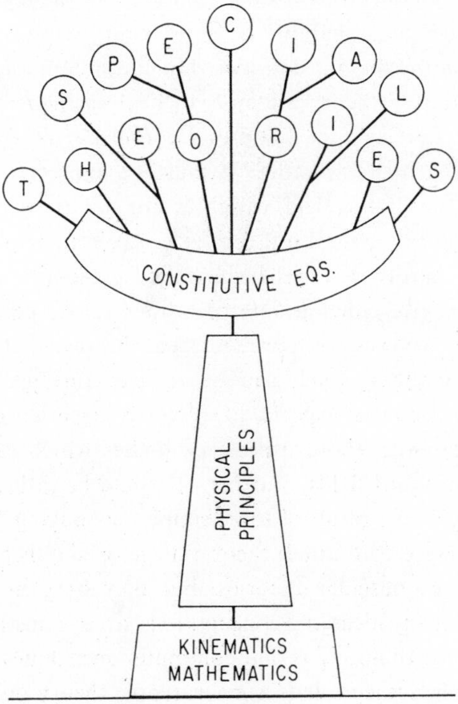

Admittedly, this visualization of continuum mechanics is, apart from being rather naive, also misleading in one respect. Rather than being safely secured to solid ground, the tree hovers over the abyss of mathematical concepts, undefinables, and unpalatable axioms. The branches are, on the other hand, secured to physical experience that is permanent and solid ground. It would be also wrong to imply that the foundations of continuum mechanics have been completed once and for all. New theories continually require additions to these foundations.

The simplicity of a verbal description of events is often deceptive, because putting it into a mathematical form may call for all the mathematical resources that we can muster. But that is the way of it; science only begins when verbal statements, visual impressions, etc., are translated into mathematical symbols and equations. Indeed, *one of the main services rendered by mathematics is to enable us to state ideas with precision.* Further, it is only through the versatility of mathematics that simple ideas can be applied to complex events.

The extent to which a physical phenomenon has been understood is reproduced in a mathematical model. Continuum mechanics is a *field theory*: here the physical variables occur as fields, or distributions, assigned to regions of space. For that matter, so is wave mechanics, but the regions in which one studies the variation of probability densities, charge clouds, and the like, are much smaller than the regions considered in continuum mechanics. Roughly speaking, a continuum theory attempts to deal *outright* with what may be interpreted as certain average quantities, or *modes of collective behavior*, associated with the microstructure. It must be appreciated, however, that such interpretations of the field variables are not particularly relevant to continuum mechanics *per se*. If a theory is a mere transcription of experience (in which case it hardly deserves being called a theory), then it should be indeed possible to give concrete interpretations for all concepts and operations. The general theories are more than that, however; at the core they are mathematical disciplines which can be related, through definite *rules of interpretation*, to isolated aspects of physical experience. In continuum mechanics we deal with those aspects of bodies which can be adequately described by continuous fields. Further, it would be rather naive to view a continuum theory as the result of some simple "averaging" of a corpuscular theory. Not only were continuum theories developed either before or largely independently of corpuscular theories, but they have also been an independent source of many ideas and concepts (e.g. stress, constitutive equations).

Another point worth noting is that continuum mechanics is not necessarily limited to gross phenomena. It is a macroscopic theory only in the sense of making predictions about finite bodies directly. Using a hierarchy of tensors (as in *multipolar continuum mechanics*), we can describe processes which take place at a point in great detail.

The rules which are supposed to connect mathematical theory with physical experience are perhaps the most elusive part of science.† But it seems that for the most part the interpretation of theories is a matter of controversy only on a philosophical level. In practice we can draw on several centuries of experience in the successful application of mathematical theories. In any case, no attempt will be made here to discuss these rules.

For each physical principle it is necessary to consider three representations, in terms of integrals, differential equations (*field equations*), and difference equations (conditions of continuity or discontinuity). The integral representation is the basic one, the others being valid in more specialized circumstances. In particular, if the field variables possess the requisite differentiability properties in some (open) region, then the field equations can be derived there from the integral representation. At the boundary of a region the integral representations can be used to express the continuity properties of variables, or, as the case may be, to obtain the appropriate *jump conditions*. The latter will be discussed in Sections 9 and 10; elsewhere it will be assumed that the fields have the necessary smoothness.

The integral representations of physical principles are all formally alike. Let ∂V be the boundary of a region V, and Ψ the field to which the physical principle refers. The physical principle is then expressed as an equation of balance,

$$\frac{d}{dt}\int_V \Psi\, dv = \int_{\partial V} i_{\underline{n}}\, da + \int_V q\, dv,$$

where q is the distribution of volume *sources*, and $i_{\underline{n}}$ is called an *influx*. For instance, Ψ may be the momentum (density) of a body, in which case $i_{\underline{n}}$ and q describe surface and body forces, respectively. Again, Ψ may be the mass density, in which case $q = 0$ and $i_{\underline{n}}$ describes the mass flux across the boundary. Of course, we may not wish to assume that mass is conserved, in which case $q \neq 0$. Then, however, it is necessary to have some information about q (this is where constitutive equations usually come in), or else the balance equation cannot be used. The general balance can be applied to various "free bodies", e.g. a tetrahedron or a thin slice, to obtain special equations. This will be illustrated in Sections 10 and 11.

Obviously the idea underlying balance equations could not be simpler: increase of Ψ equals the "supply" of Ψ. Two things help to make this bit of common sense into versatile theories: the power of mathematics, and the abstraction, from experience, of concrete models of the variables Ψ, $i_{\underline{n}}$, and q.

† Cf. the delightful discussion by J. L. Synge on pp. 103–105, [157].

Along with each physical principle, we shall specify its *form-invariance* to appropriate observer transformations. Here form-invariance will mean that balance equations as described by another, "starred" observer are of the same form,

$$\frac{d}{dt}\int_V \Psi^* \, dv = \int_{\partial V} i^*_{\underline{\mathrm{n}}} \, da + \int_V q^* \, dv,$$

although the fields Ψ, $i_{\underline{\mathrm{n}}}$, q may depend on the choice of observers. This invariance establishes classes of *equivalent observers*. Because observer transformations cannot be performed unless the transformation properties of all variables are known, the definitions of the dynamical variables must include the transformation properties with respect to changes of observers (cf. (9.18), (9.39), (9.59)).

Section 9
THE PRINCIPLES OF MECHANICS

In this section we shall set down the law of conservation of mass, and the balance equations for linear momentum, angular momentum, and energy. The balance of energy of course opens the door to thermodynamics, but no matter. The derivation of the field equations expressing the balance equations for momenta and energy will have to wait until the introduction of the stress hypothesis in the next section.

Balance of mass

According to the principle of conservation of mass, each body $\mathscr{B}$ possesses an unchanging property, called mass, which is a non-negative dimensional number, denoted by m or $m(\mathscr{B})$. We express the invariance of mass by

$$\frac{d}{dt} m(\mathscr{B}) = 0. \tag{9.1}$$

The dimension of m is denoted by M; we shall not assume M to be reducible to the kinematical dimensions L for length and T for time.†

We shall consider mass to be, like force, energy, and temperature, a *primitive* (or, undefined) *concept*, relying on special problems to provide interpretations of mass as well as methods for measuring it. For instance, the

† A possible reduction would be to write the law of gravitational attraction of point masses as follows: $F = m_1 m_2 / r^2$; then $M = L^3 T^{-2}$.

mass of a relatively rigid body can be measured with reasonable accuracy as follows. We attach the body to a spring and investigate vibratory motions; the (average) acceleration of the body will then be given by $a = -(k/m)x$, where x denotes positions of the body, k is a property of the spring, and m is a constant, additive property of the body.

In a field theory we must be able to describe the mass of any portion of a body. For this reason we introduce a point function ρ called the *mass density*. For this concept to be meaningful, we postulate two further properties for mass. First, we require that mass be *additive*, so that the masses of volume elements of a body add up to the total mass of the body. Second, and this is a characteristic assumption in continuum mechanics, we assume that mass is a continuous function of the volume.†

In any configuration $\boldsymbol{\chi}$, then, the mass distribution $\rho_{\boldsymbol{\chi}}$ induces a measure into the region $\boldsymbol{\chi}(\mathscr{B})$ which is distinct from the Euclidean volume-measure. This measure $m(\mathscr{B})$ is obtained through the additivity property by

$$m(\mathscr{B}) = \int_V dm = \int_V \rho \, dv, \tag{9.2}$$

where $V = \boldsymbol{\chi}(\mathscr{B})$ is the region occupied by the body $\mathscr{B}$, and we have used the shorter designation $\rho = \rho_{\boldsymbol{\chi}}$. Evidently m is but a single number obtained from a knowledge of the distribution of mass density $\rho(\mathbf{x}, t)$. We can recover more, and progressively finer, details of the distribution $\rho(\mathbf{x}, t)$ by going to the *moments*

$$m_i = \int_V x_i \, dm, \qquad m_{ij} = \int_V x_i x_j \, dm, \tag{9.3}$$

etc., where x_i are coordinates of the mass elements dm. In particular,

$$I_{ij} = m_{kk}\delta_{ij} - m_{ij} \tag{9.4}$$

is referred to as the *inertia tensor*, whereas the first of (9.3), when written as

$$mc_i = \int_V x_i \, dm, \tag{9.5}$$

is said to define the *mass center* $\mathbf{c}$ of the body. Replacing a distribution by one

† In a more mathematical language, we say that mass $m(\mathscr{B})$ and volume $v(\mathscr{B})$ are examples of additive set functions, the set being the body $\mathscr{B}$. Mass density at a particle $\mathscr{P}$ is the limit of $m(\mathscr{B})/v(\mathscr{B})$ as $\mathscr{B}$ tends to $\mathscr{P}$. Cf. Buck [7], pp. 99–104.

or several of its moments entails naturally a vast loss of information. However, as we shall see, these moments are all that is needed in order to express the principles of linear and angular momenta.

Let us now write the law of conservation of mass as follows,

$$\frac{d}{dt}\int_V \rho\, dv = 0. \tag{9.1}^*$$

An integral of the type (9.2) is at most a function of time, $m(\mathscr{B}, t)$. Consequently, in (9.1)* we are dealing with differentiation of a function of the single variable t: $dm(\mathscr{B}, t)/dt$. However, if d/dt is taken through the integral sign, then it must be interpreted as the material rate if V is a material volume, and as the local rate ∂_t if V is a fixed volume of space.

Let us first take the case where V is a fixed region of space ("control volume"). Then the mass contained in V need not be conserved,

$$\frac{d}{dt}\int_V \rho\, dv = \int_V (\partial_t \rho)\, dv \neq 0.$$

However, the increase of mass in V must equal the flow of mass into V:

$$\int_V (\partial_t \rho)\, dv = -\int_{\partial V} \rho \mathbf{v} \cdot \mathbf{n}\, da.$$

Here the minus sign on the right-hand side is needed because $\mathbf{n}$ is always chosen to be the *outward* normal of the boundary ∂V. Using the divergence theorem, we now obtain

$$0 = \int_V (\partial_t \rho + \operatorname{div} \rho \mathbf{v})\, dv.$$

Because this is true of any "control volume" V, it follows that

$$\partial_t \rho + \operatorname{div} \rho \mathbf{v} = 0. \tag{9.6}$$

Noting that the material rate of ρ is given by

$$\dot{\rho} = \partial_t \rho + \rho_{,i} v_i, \tag{9.7}$$

we also have that

$$\dot{\rho} + \rho v_{i,i} = 0. \tag{9.8}$$

A third representation of mass balance is obtained by introducing the *specific volume v*,

$$v = \frac{1}{\rho}. \tag{9.9}$$

Then

$$\dot{v} = v v_{i,i}. \tag{9.10}$$

If V is a material volume ("free body"), the law of conservation of mass requires that

$$\frac{d}{dt}\int_V \rho\, dv = \int_V \dot{\overline{\rho\, dv}} = 0.$$

The current configuration dv of a material volume dV is not constant with respect to material rates; in fact, because $dv = J\,dV$, $\dot{\overline{dv}} = \dot{J}\,dV = J \operatorname{div} \mathbf{v}\, dV$ (cf. (8.58)), where $J = \det(x_{i,m})$ is the Jacobian of the deformation, it follows that

$$\dot{\overline{dv}} = v_{i,i}\, dv. \tag{8.59)R}$$

Consequently, we again recover

$$\frac{dm}{dt} = 0 = \int_V (\dot{\rho} + \rho v_{i,i})\, dv.$$

In view of (8.59), the equation (9.8) can be alternatively written as

$$\dot{\overline{dm}} = \dot{\overline{\rho\, dv}} = 0. \tag{9.11}$$

Further, since (9.8) is equivalent to $\dot{\rho}J + \rho\dot{J} = 0$, we arrive at

$$\rho J = \rho_0, \tag{9.12}$$

where ρ_0 can depend on material coordinates, but not on time.

The law of conservation of mass is a "true" conservation law (the law of conservation of charge is another). Although the phrases "conservation of energy," "conservation of momentum" are often used, energy and momentum are not conserved in general; instead, the change in energy or momentum can be related to other variables through balance equations. With mass it is different: the mass of a material volume is always the same (in classical physics, that is).

To derive $\rho J = \rho_0$ directly, we note that the mass of one and the same material volume must remain constant. Let $\varkappa$ be a reference configuration, referred to the material coordinates X_i, and ρ_0 the mass density in that configuration. Then

$$m(\mathscr{B}) = \int_D \rho_0 \, dX \, dY \, dZ,$$

where $D = \varkappa(\mathscr{B})$ is the region occupied by $\mathscr{B}$ in the reference configuration. If χ is any other configuration of $\mathscr{B}$, referred to the coordinates x_i, and ρ the mass density in that configuration, then

$$m(\mathscr{B}) = \int_V \rho \, dv,$$

where $V = \chi(\mathscr{B})$. Let us now transform the last integral from the coordinates x_i to the coordinates X_i. Then, by (8.17), $dv = J\,dV = J\,dX\,dY\,dZ$; moreover, because χ is a configuration of the same body $\mathscr{B}$, the region of integration, $V = \chi(\mathscr{B})$, will change into $D = \varkappa(\mathscr{B})$. Therefore,

$$\int_D \rho_0 \, dX \, dY \, dZ = \int_D \rho J \, dX \, dY \, dZ,$$

and $\rho J = \rho_0$. Similarly, if $\rho(\tau)$ is the mass density in a configuration described by $x_i(\tau)$, then

$$\rho(\tau) J(\tau) = \rho, \tag{9.13}$$

where

$$J(\tau) = \det(x_{i,j}(\tau)). \tag{9.14}$$

A simple illustration may help to clarify matters. We consider the two-dimensional motion of a circular lamina. Then D: $X^2 + Y^2 < R^2$, ∂D: $X^2 + Y^2 = R^2$. Since

$$m = \int_V \rho \, dv = \int_{-R}^{R} dX \int_{-\Delta}^{\Delta} \rho(X, Y, t) J(X, Y, t) \, dY,$$

where $\Delta = (R^2 - X^2)^{1/2}$, it is clear that dm/dt can be evaluated by differentiating under the integral signs, provided that this differentiation be executed at constant X and Y, thus

$$\frac{dm}{dt} = 0 = \int_{-R}^{R} dX \int_{-\Delta}^{\Delta} dY \, D_t \rho J.$$

A volume-preserving motion is said to be isochoric. Then

$$J = \det\mathbf{F} = 1, \tag{8.18)R}$$

or, equivalently,

$$\dot{\rho} = 0, \qquad \operatorname{div}\mathbf{v} = 0. \tag{9.15}$$

The conservation of mass has an important consequence for integrals of the type

$$F(t) = \int_V f(\mathbf{x}, t)\, dm, \tag{9.16}$$

where f stands for an arbitrary tensor, and V is a material volume, i.e. the boundaries of V remain fixed relative to the particles. Then d/dt can be taken through the integral sign, provided that it is interpreted as the material rate under the integral sign. Taking into account (9.11), we obtain

$$\frac{dF}{dt} = \int_V \dot{f}\, dm. \tag{9.17}$$

The objectivity of mass, $m^+ = m$, or

$$\rho^+ = \rho, \tag{9.18}$$

is actually contained in the conservation law, which states, in effect, that

$$m = \int_V \rho\, dv = \int_{V^*} \rho^*\, dv^*$$

is an invariant of the motion $x_i = x_i(\mathbf{X}, t)$. That is, the value of m is the same no matter at which instant the integration is performed, provided, however, that the regions V and V^* are two configurations of the same body. This simply means that, if we imagine the trajectories of particles as wires on which the body is mounted, then the mass of the body remains unchanged as the (deforming) body slides along the trajectories. The reason why this view of the conservation law for mass is interesting is that it introduces a new type of invariance: *invariance under motion*. This invariance is evidently a much stronger requirement than invariance to coordinate transformations or observer transformations. To put it in another way, the assignment of mass is, like counting, a primitive operation that does not require any ideas of metric and time, so that the invariance of mass to observer transformations is trivially satisfied.

The balance equations for linear momentum and angular momentum

Before stating the remaining principles of mechanics, we shall review the classical measures of motion and the types of loading encountered in continuum mechanics. We begin by restating in a form appropriate to continuum mechanics some of the concepts from mechanics of discrete systems.

A basic dynamical measure of motion is the (linear) *momentum* **P** defined by

$$\mathbf{P}(t) = \int_V \mathbf{v}\, dm, \tag{9.19}$$

where $\mathbf{v}$ is the velocity of the mass element dm, and we have written $\mathbf{P}(t)$ to emphasize that **P** is at most a function of time. Evidently, by (9.16), (9.17),

$$m\dot{\mathbf{c}} = \int_V \dot{\mathbf{x}}\, dm = \int_V \mathbf{v}\, dm,$$

i.e. the momentum equals the total mass m multiplied by the velocity $\dot{\mathbf{c}}$ of the mass center:

$$\mathbf{P} = m\dot{\mathbf{c}}, \qquad \dot{\mathbf{P}} = m\ddot{\mathbf{c}}. \tag{9.20}$$

Further, from (9.19) it follows that

$$\dot{\mathbf{P}} = \int_V \mathbf{a}\, dm, \tag{9.21}$$

where $\mathbf{a} = \dot{\mathbf{v}}$ stands for particle acceleration.

A reminder concerning the notations. A superposed dot indicates a material rate, executed at a fixed particle. Because **P** and **c** are functions of time only, the material rates $\dot{\mathbf{P}}$ and $\dot{\mathbf{c}}$ are actually the ordinary derivatives $d\mathbf{P}/dt$ and $d\mathbf{c}/dt$. If d/dt is taken through the integral sign, then (V being a material volume) it must be interpreted as the material rate, e.g.

$$\dot{\mathbf{P}} = \frac{d}{dt}\mathbf{P}(t) = \int_V \left.\frac{\partial}{\partial t}\right|_{\mathbf{X}=\text{const.}} [\mathbf{v}(\mathbf{X}, t)\, dm].$$

In addition to the momentum **P**, we can again introduce the higher moments, thus

$$P_i = \int_V v_i \, dm, \quad P_{ij} = \int_V x_i v_j \, dm, \quad P_{ijk} = \int_V x_i x_j v_k \, dm, \tag{9.22}$$

etc. It turns out that a particularly important measure of motion is the *angular momentum* $\mathbf{H}^{[0]}$ about the coordinate origin, defined by $H_i^{[0]} = \frac{1}{2}\varepsilon_{ijk}P_{jk}$, i.e.

$$\mathbf{H}^{[0]} = \int_V (\mathbf{x} \times \mathbf{v}) \, dm. \tag{9.23}$$

Using again (9.16), (9.17), and the identity $\overline{\mathbf{x} \times \mathbf{v}}^{\boldsymbol{\cdot}} = (\mathbf{v} \times \mathbf{v}) + (\mathbf{x} \times \mathbf{a}) = \mathbf{x} \times \mathbf{a}$, we arrive at

$$\dot{\mathbf{H}}^{[0]} = \int_V (\mathbf{x} \times \mathbf{a}) \, dm. \tag{9.24}$$

There exists a simple relation between $\mathbf{H}^{[0]}$ and the angular momentum $\mathbf{H}^{[c]}$ about the mass center. Let us introduce the position $\bar{\mathbf{x}}$ relative to the mass center, $\mathbf{x} = \mathbf{c} + \bar{\mathbf{x}}$. Then

$$\mathbf{H}^{[0]} = \int_V [(\mathbf{c} + \bar{\mathbf{x}}) \times \mathbf{v}] \, dm = \mathbf{c} \times \int_V \mathbf{v} \, dm + \int_V (\bar{\mathbf{x}} \times \mathbf{v}) \, dm,$$

thus

$$\mathbf{H}^{[0]} = (\mathbf{c} \times \mathbf{P}) + \mathbf{H}^{[c]}. \tag{9.25}$$

Moreover, in view of $\dot{\mathbf{c}} \times \mathbf{P} = \dot{\mathbf{c}} \times m\dot{\mathbf{c}} = \mathbf{0}$, we have that

$$\dot{\mathbf{H}}^{[0]} = (\mathbf{c} \times \dot{\mathbf{P}}) + \dot{\mathbf{H}}^{[c]}. \tag{9.26}$$

A further dynamical measure of motion is the *kinetic energy* K,†

$$K = \int_V k \, dm, \tag{9.27}$$

where the *density of kinetic energy*, k, is given by

$$k = \frac{1}{2}\mathbf{v} \cdot \mathbf{v}. \tag{9.28}$$

† Kinetic energy and angular momentum were first introduced by Leibniz and Euler, respectively. According to Truesdell (*CFT*, p. 482, first footnote), the concept of linear momentum can be traced to the Middle Ages, but the complete history of this concept is not known.

Therefore, by (9.16), (9.17),

$$\dot{\mathbf{K}} = \int_V \mathbf{a} \cdot \mathbf{v} \, dm. \tag{9.29}$$

Let us write $\mathbf{x} = \mathbf{c} + \bar{\mathbf{x}}$, $\mathbf{v} = \dot{\mathbf{c}} + \bar{\mathbf{v}}$, noting that (9.5) implies

$$\int_V \bar{\mathbf{x}} \, dm = \int_V (\mathbf{x} - \mathbf{c}) \, dm = \mathbf{0}, \qquad \int_V \bar{\mathbf{v}} \, dm = \mathbf{0}.$$

Then the kinetic energy decomposes into a translational kinetic energy $\frac{1}{2}m\dot{c}^2$ and a kinetic energy of relative motion:

$$K = \frac{1}{2} m\dot{c}^2 + \frac{1}{2} \int_V \bar{\mathbf{v}} \cdot \bar{\mathbf{v}} \, dm. \tag{9.30}$$

Before proceeding to the definitions of resultant forces and moments, a few comments about forces are in order. As a rule, the idea of force is closely linked with the fundamental technique of *separation* which singles out a body $\mathscr{B}$ ("free body") for special attention, the forces representing the influences of the rest of the universe upon $\mathscr{B}$. In its full generality, force is an *undefined concept*.† An undefined concept is "explained" by listing special instances of it. Indeed, the intuitive notion of force is based largely on visualization of tensions in strings, and our ability to exert push or pull. In mathematics one is inclined to view axioms as implicit definitions of the undefined symbols. In science, of course, we not only rely on physical principles, but also on experience, intuition, and applications of the theories to give substance to what are *formally* undefined terms.

In general, forces will manifest themselves through changes in kinematical variables; using properties of bodies (e.g. mass, stiffness), we can then assign quantitative measures to the various forces. For instance, a force may be measured by the product of mass and acceleration. Naturally this does not mean that force *is* mass times acceleration. On the contrary, the fruitfulness of the concept of force derives from the possibility (at least, we assume that such a possibility exists) of determining forces by other considerations, so that Newton's second law can be used to calculate accelerations from forces, rather than the other way around.

A basic assumption underlying all continuum mechanics is that forces are *distributed*. Occasionally we introduce concentrated forces by letting the

† Truesdell in his "Baltimore Lectures" ([196], p. 94, *et seq.*) attributes a general conception of force to Newton.

load region shrink to a point while the load intensity increases in such a way that the resultant load on the region remains constant. It must be then investigated in each case whether the limiting "singular" solution exists mathematically, and is meaningful physically. Of course, the idea of concentrated loads is introduced into continuum mechanics only to obtain simple types of solutions.

As the first type of force between a body and its surroundings we consider (mechanical) surface loads. These forces act not unlike wet sand poured on a rough surface; their distribution can be visualized as a dense forest of arrows that indicate the directions and magnitudes of the loading. We characterize the distributed surface loads by *surface traction vectors* $\bar{\mathbf{t}}$. The dimensions of $\bar{\mathbf{t}}$ is $ML^{-1}T^{-2}$, or, force per unit area. Distributed body forces, e.g. weight, may be described by a vector field $\mathbf{b}$, the body force intensity per unit mass. If V is the region occupied by a body, and ∂V its boundary, then the resultant external force $\mathbf{F}$ acting on the body is defined as the surface integral over ∂V of forces $\bar{\mathbf{t}}\, da$ acting on the area elements da of the boundary, complemented by the volume integral over V of forces $\mathbf{b}\, dm$ acting on the mass elements dm of the body (Figure 9.1),

$$\mathbf{F} = \int_V \mathbf{b}\, dm + \int_{\partial V} \bar{\mathbf{t}}\, da. \tag{9.31}$$

The resultant torque $\mathbf{L}^{[0]}$ about the coordinate origin 0 is defined by

$$\mathbf{L}^{[0]} = \int_{\partial V} (\mathbf{x} \times \bar{\mathbf{t}})\, da + \int_V (\mathbf{x} \times \mathbf{b})\, dm. \tag{9.32}$$

If $\mathbf{v}$ is the velocity field of a body, and $\bar{\mathbf{t}}$, $\mathbf{b}$ the fields of surface tractions and body forces acting on the body, then the *mechanical power* (or, "rate-of-working") M of the loading is defined by

$$M = \int_{\partial V} \bar{\mathbf{t}} \cdot \mathbf{v}\, da + \int_V \mathbf{b} \cdot \mathbf{v}\, dm. \tag{9.33}$$

In 1775 Euler proposed as *two independent principles of mechanics*, applicable to finite, arbitrarily deforming bodies, the balance of linear momentum,

$$\mathbf{F} = \dot{\mathbf{P}}, \tag{9.34}$$

and the balance of angular momentum,

$$\mathbf{L}^{[0]} = \dot{\mathbf{H}}^{[0]}. \tag{9.35}$$

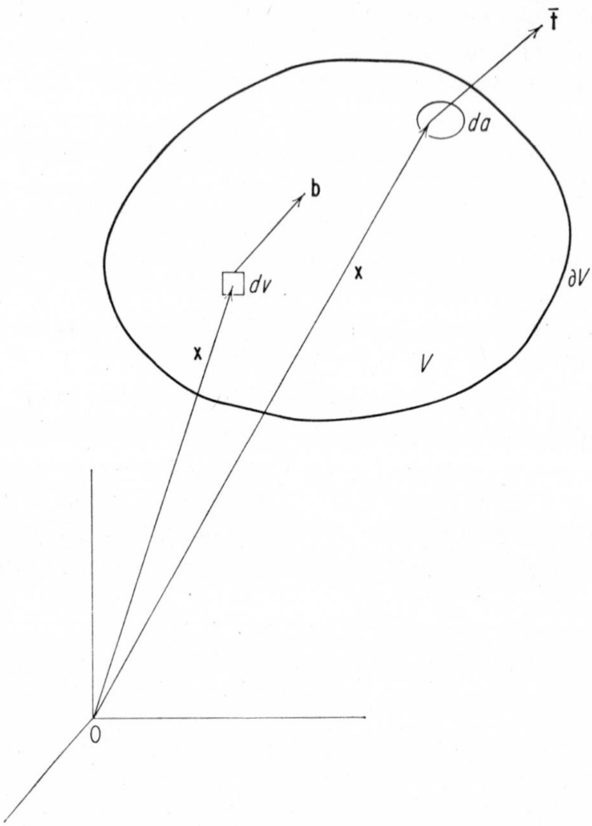

FIGURE 9.1 Surface tractions, $\bar{\mathbf{t}}$, and body forces, **b**.

Here $\dot{\mathbf{P}}$ is the time rate of linear momentum defined by (9.19), **F** is the resultant external force defined by (9.31), $\mathbf{L}^{[0]}$ and $\dot{\mathbf{H}}^{[0]}$ are the torque (about a fixed point 0 of the frame of reference) and time rate of angular momentum defined by (9.32), (9.23), respectively. Together with the balance equations for mass and energy, (9.34) and (9.35) constitute the foundation of classical mechanics.

If the reference frame is translating together with the mass center, then the form (9.35) of balance of angular momentum remains unchanged:

$$\mathbf{L}^{[c]} = \dot{\mathbf{H}}^{[c]}. \tag{9.36}$$

To verify this, we note that the resultant torque satisfies a relation similar to (9.25),

$$\mathbf{L}^{[0]} = (\mathbf{c} \times \mathbf{F}) + \mathbf{L}^{[c]}. \tag{9.37}$$

Then, by (9.26), (9.34), $\mathbf{L}^{[0]} = (\mathbf{c} \times \dot{\mathbf{P}}) + \dot{\mathbf{H}}^{[c]} = (\mathbf{c} \times \mathbf{F}) + \mathbf{L}^{[c]} = (\mathbf{c} \times \dot{\mathbf{P}}) + \mathbf{L}^{[c]}$.

From $(9.20)_2$ and (9.34) we obtain that

$$\mathbf{F} = m\ddot{\mathbf{c}}, \tag{9.38}$$

which is of the same form as Newton's second law for mass particles. The balance equations (9.34) and (9.35) are often derived from Newton's second law by subdividing a body into cells, and assuming that the mass of each cell may be concentrated at one of its points. Although it is intuitively plausible that the motion of the body will be obtained in the limit as the size of cells tends to zero, it is not at all obvious that a rigorous proof of this claim is possible, nor is this approach natural to continuum mechanics. For one, it would be necessary to make special assumptions concerning the nature of forces acting between the particles ("Newton's third law").

In the popular view of the history of mechanics, Newton's *Principia*, published in 1687, looms as the definitive formulation of mechanics. This view has been severely criticized by Truesdell (cf. [182], [179], [174]) as a gross oversimplification of the actual history, because nearly seventy years of continual search, first by Daniel and James Bernoulli, and later by Euler, were needed to obtain general equations of motion for systems and finite bodies. Because of our familiarity with simple methods for deriving these equations, this fact may be hard to grasp. However, at the time of Newton, concepts and laws which nowadays have a precise meaning or mathematical representation, e.g. internal force, "free body," "Newton's second law," were much more vague, often altogether inaccessible to mathematical analysis. Almost three centuries of practice with mechanics has sharpened the understanding to the point where one can now present in a day's work those discoveries which were wrested from experience by long and arduous researches.

As it stands, the statements of the balance equations are incomplete, because the admissible observer transformations have not been specified. Let us first introduce the notion of a *dynamical process*. The motion of a body $\mathscr{B}$ is a one-parameter family of mappings $\boldsymbol{\chi}(t)$, $-\infty < t < \infty$, of $\mathscr{B}$ into regions of the ambient space. We denote by $\{\mathbf{F}(t), \mathbf{L}^{[0]}(t)\}$, $-\infty < t < \infty$, the one-parameter family of resultant forces and torques acting on $\mathscr{B}$. A triple $\{\boldsymbol{\chi}(t), \mathbf{F}(t), \mathbf{L}^{[0]}(t)\}$, $-\infty < t < \infty$, is then said to constitute a dynamical process if it obeys the principles (9.34), (9.35). Correspondingly, an observer transformation is said to be admissible if it transforms one dynamical process into another (i.e. preserves the form of the principles of linear and angular momenta).

As part of the characterization of surface tractions and body forces, we must prescribe their transformations with changes of observers (regardless of whether or not surface tractions and body forces can be directly observed). It is plausible (at least, it becomes more plausible as we go on) that *contact forces*, and surface tractions in particular, ought to be objective, i.e. independent of the motions of observers that record them. A fuller understanding of this hypothesis requires an exploration of the various facets of constitutive equations (e.g. principle of local action, objectivity of material properties). For the time being we may adopt the attitude that, unless we are forced to assume the contrary,

$$\bar{\mathbf{t}}^+ = \bar{\mathbf{t}}. \tag{9.39}$$

Because velocities and accelerations are not objective, it is clear that the principles of linear and angular momenta can be form-invariant to arbitrary observer transformations only if the body forces are permitted to be non-objective. In view of (9.31), (9.34), and (9.39), however, the *effective body forces*

$$\bar{\mathbf{b}} = \mathbf{b} - \dot{\mathbf{v}} \tag{9.40}$$

are objective.

Following Newton, one may avoid observer transformations altogether by postulating as the frame of reference for mechanics an *absolute space* and an *absolute time*. This hypothesis is open to the criticism that absolute space and time cannot be determined. It is true, of course, that as a mathematical discipline mechanics is no more concerned with the existence of absolute space and time than is geometry with the existence of points and lines. To apply mechanics, however, there must be available rules for interpreting the concepts, coordinate systems, and time scales employed in the theory. Here we can adopt either one of two viewpoints. First, we can state that the laws of mechanics hold in *all* observer frames. In this case body forces are not objective, meaning that we may have to admit body forces ("inertial forces") which have no identifiable sources, or, at least, no sources that can be localized. For instance, we may have to assume that the entire universe is the seat of the "centrifugal forces." This interpretation of mechanics may not be to everyone's taste, therefore we list another. If mechanics is to have a practical value, then there must exist observer frames, which we shall call *inertial frames*, which fulfill the role of the absolute space to the desired degree of accuracy. Every theorem of mechanics is then, in principle, a means for testing the admissibility of a given observer frame.

The question of the observer frames, however troublesome it may be in an axiomatic presentation of mechanics, has not deterred in any way the successful application of mechanics. Suitable observer frames and time scales have been found and tested by experience, so that the use of mechanics is not beset by any doubts or difficulties.

A closer inspection of (9.34), (9.35) shows that these principles express *acceleration laws*. Therefore, observer transformations that leave accelerations invariant are of some interest. We define a *Galilean* (observer) *transformation* by

$$x_i^+ = x_i + \dot{\alpha}_i t, \tag{9.41}$$

where $\dot{\alpha}_i$ are constant (evidently no generality is gained by replacing (9.41) with $x_a^+ = Q_{ai}(x_i + \dot{\alpha}_i t)$, where Q_{ai} are constants). In this transformation the two observer frames are aligned, and translate relative to each other with a constant velocity. Thus

$$\mathbf{v}^+ = \mathbf{v} + \dot{\boldsymbol{\alpha}}, \qquad \dot{\mathbf{v}}^+ = \dot{\mathbf{v}}, \tag{9.42}$$

so that both observers measure the same acceleration. We say that acceleration is a *Galilean invariant*. The form-invariance of the balance equations for linear momentum and angular momentum now requires that body forces be Galilean invariants.† The invariance of the laws of motion with respect to a uniform translation of observer frames is called the *relativity principle of Galilei*, because Galilei has been credited with discovering the importance of acceleration. Another statement of this principle is as follows: *no purely mechanical experiments, performed in the interior of an inertial frame, can detect the uniform translation of that frame relative to another frame.*

Finally, let us note that what prevents us at the moment from applying the principles for linear and angular momenta to arbitrary "free bodies" (i.e. portions of a body) is the lack of a hypothesis concerning the internal forces. This will be remedied in the next section.

Rigid body motion

Let $\bar{\mathbf{x}}$ be the position vector from the mass center to a fixed particle of the body. Denoting by $\bar{\mathbf{v}}$ the velocity of that particle relative to the mass center, we have that

$$\bar{\mathbf{v}} = \boldsymbol{\omega} \times \bar{\mathbf{x}}. \tag{9.43}$$

† For electromagnetic forces this is only an approximation valid for particle velocities much smaller than the speed of light.

This formula enables us to obtain an explicit formula for the angular momentum about the mass center. To calculate $\bar{\mathbf{x}} \times (\boldsymbol{\omega} \times \bar{\mathbf{x}})$, we write, by (1.30), $\varepsilon_{ijk}\bar{x}_j\varepsilon_{kmn}\omega_m\bar{x}_n = \omega_n(\bar{x}_m\bar{x}_m\delta_{in} - \bar{x}_i\bar{x}_n)$; recalling the definition (9.4), and noting that in rigid motion $\boldsymbol{\omega}$ depends on time only, we obtain

$$H_i^{[c]} = I_{in}\omega_n. \tag{9.44}$$

Owing to the rotation of the body relative to the space axes, the spatial components I_{ij} of the inertia tensor are functions of time, so that, by (9.36), $L_i^{[c]} = \dot{H}_i^{[c]} = \dot{I}_{ij}\omega_j + I_{ij}\dot{\omega}_j$. Because the term $\dot{I}_{ij}$ is awkward to deal with, we introduce a *body coordinate system* defined by an orthonormal triad of vectors $\mathbf{e}_a$ fixed in the body. Then from $L_a = Q_{ai}L_i = Q_{ai}\,\dot{H}_i = \dot{\overline{(Q_{ai}H_i)}} - \dot{Q}_{ai}H_i$ it follows that, by (7.45),

$$L_a = \dot{H}_a + \varepsilon_{abc}\omega_b H_c. \tag{9.45}$$

In the body frame the components I_{ab} are constants; in particular, if the body frame coincides with the principal directions of the inertia tensor (at the mass center), then

$$H_a = I_{\underline{a}}\omega_a, \tag{9.46}$$

where $I_{\underline{a}}$ are the principal values of **I**. In this case (9.45) become the celebrated Euler's equations for rigid body rotation:

$$I_1\dot{\omega}_1 + \omega_2\omega_3(I_3 - I_2) = L_1, \ldots, \ldots. \tag{9.47}$$

We may also wish to transform (9.38) to the body frame. Writing for simplicity $\dot{\mathbf{c}} = \mathbf{v}$, we obtain $F_a = Q_{ai}F_i = Q_{ai}m\dot{v}_i = m\dot{v}_a - mv_i\dot{Q}_{ai}$, from which it follows that

$$\begin{aligned} F_a &= m(\dot{v}_a + \varepsilon_{abc}\omega_b v_c), \\ F_1 &= m(\dot{v}_1 + \omega_2 v_3 - \omega_3 v_2), \ldots, \ldots. \end{aligned} \tag{9.48}$$

If the body is rotationally symmetric about the axis of $\mathbf{e}_3$, for instance, we write $I_1 = I_2 = I$, $I_3 = J$. In this case the body may be permitted to rotate about the axis of $\mathbf{e}_3$. If $\boldsymbol{\sigma}$ is the angular velocity of the body frame (and $\boldsymbol{\omega}$ still the angular velocity of the body), then $\sigma_1 = \omega_1$, $\sigma_2 = \omega_2$, $\sigma_3 \neq \omega_3$. Replacing in (9.45) $\boldsymbol{\omega}$ by $\boldsymbol{\sigma}$, but retaining (9.46), we get

$$\begin{aligned} I\dot{\sigma}_1 + \sigma_2(J\omega_3 - I\sigma_3) &= L_1, \\ I\dot{\sigma}_2 - \sigma_1(J\omega_3 - I\sigma_3) &= L_2, \\ J\dot{\omega}_3 &= L_3. \end{aligned} \tag{9.49}$$

Similarly, (9.48) now read

$$F_a = m(\dot{v}_a + \varepsilon_{abc}\sigma_b v_c). \tag{9.50}$$

We can also approach Euler's equations by evaluating I_{ij}. Using (9.43), we readily obtain

$$\dot{I}_{ij} = \omega_m(\varepsilon_{imn}I_{nj} + \varepsilon_{jmn}I_{in}). \tag{9.51}$$

Substituting this into $\mathbf{L} = \dot{\mathbf{H}}$, we arrive at $L_i = I_{ij}\dot{\omega}_j + \varepsilon_{imn}\omega_m\omega_j I_{nj}$. These equations are formally identical with Euler's equations, but the spatial components I_{kj} are now functions of time.

Finally, let $K' = \frac{1}{2}I_{ij}\omega_i\omega_j$ be the kinetic energy of rotation. Then, by (9.51),

$$\dot{K}' = I_{ij}\dot{\omega}_i\omega_j. \tag{9.52}$$

But $L_i\omega_i = I_{ij}\dot{\omega}_j\omega_i + \varepsilon_{imn}\omega_i\omega_m\omega_j I_{nj} = I_{ij}\dot{\omega}_j\omega_i = \dot{K}'$; taking into account the analogous formula for the kinetic energy of translation, $\dot{K}'' = ma_i v_i = F_i v_i$, we obtain the energy balance for rigid body motion:

$$\dot{K} = F_i v_i + L_i\omega_i. \tag{9.53}$$

Moreover, since $L_i = \dot{H}_i$, it follows that

$$\dot{K}' = \dot{H}_i\omega_i. \tag{9.54}$$

Energy balance

We regard energy as a primitive concept, and adopt the following form for the principle of energy balance:

The time rate of energy increase in a body equals the time rate of energy supply to the body.

To clarify this statement, a few more definitions are needed.

For several reasons it is important to break up the total energy into the kinetic energy K and the internal energy E.† Thus E equals the total energy less the kinetic energy; it may consist of a heat energy, a strain energy Σ, and so on. We let

$$E = \int_V \varepsilon \, dm, \qquad \dot{E} = \int_V \dot{\varepsilon} \, dm, \tag{9.55}$$

† Two of the reasons are: internal energy is in general an undefined concept, and K is not objective, whereas E will be assumed to be objective.

where ε is the density of internal energy per unit mass, and V is the region occupied by the body. Further, we denote by P the time rate of the total energy supply (or, total power of external agencies). The energy balance then reads

$$\dot{K} + \dot{E} = P, \tag{9.56}$$

i.e. energy increase equals energy supply. It is expedient to decompose P into mechanical power M, defined by (9.33), and *non-mechanical power* Q, defined analogously by

$$Q = \int_V r\,dm + \int_{\partial V} h\,da, \tag{9.57}$$

where r is the volume distribution of sources of non-mechanical power supply, and h represents the supply of non-mechanical power across the boundary ∂V. With these notations, (9.56) can be put into the form

$$\int_V (\dot{\varepsilon} + \dot{k})\,dm = \int_V (\mathbf{b}\cdot\mathbf{v} + r)\,dm + \int_{\partial V} (\bar{\mathbf{t}}\cdot\mathbf{v} + h)\,da. \tag{9.58}$$

Green and Rivlin [51] have recently shown that the *balance equations for linear momentum and angular momentum are consequences of the form-invariance, in observer transformations, of the energy balance*. What is meant by form-invariance is, of course, that a "starred" observer will arrive at an energy balance $\dot{K}^+ + \dot{E}^+ = P^+$, where K^+, E^+, P^+ are calculated in the same way as K, E, P (i.e. using the same definitions). Naturally different observers may obtain different *values* of the variables (this is certainly true of the kinetic energy); however, the form of the energy balance is assumed to be the same for all.

To proceed in an orderly manner, let us recall that mass density is objective, and that surface tractions were assumed to be objective. In addition, we assume that density of internal energy, ε, as well as the energy supplies h and r are also objective. These assumptions express the intuitive notion that internal energy and its flux are "real" quantities that cannot be influenced in any way by the motion of the observer. (If E is the strain energy, for instance, then E is objective simply because distances between particles are not changed by an observer transformation.) Thus

$$\varepsilon^+ = \varepsilon, \qquad h^+ = h, \qquad r^+ = r; \tag{9.59}$$

further,†

$$\dot{\varepsilon}^+ = \dot{\varepsilon}, \qquad \dot{\rho}^+ = \dot{\rho}. \tag{9.60}$$

† Cf. Problem 6.

Assuming that body forces are Galilean invariants, we begin with a Galilean transformation $\mathbf{v}(\mathbf{x}, t) \to \mathbf{v}^+(\mathbf{x}, t) = \mathbf{v}(\mathbf{x}, t) + \dot{\boldsymbol{\alpha}}$, where $\dot{\boldsymbol{\alpha}}$ is a constant vector, so that $\dot{\mathbf{v}}^+ = \dot{\mathbf{v}}$. In view of the preceding assumptions, the only change occurring in (9.58) will be the replacement of v_i by $v_i + \dot{\alpha}_i$. Subtracting (9.58) from its transformed version, we are left with the difference

$$\dot{\alpha}_i\left[\int_{\partial V} t_i \, da + \int_V (b_i - \dot{v}_i) \, dm\right] = 0.$$

Because the expression in the brackets is independent of $\dot{\boldsymbol{\alpha}}$, we recover the balance of linear momentum, (9.34). Moreover, (9.39) implies that the effective body forces $\bar{\mathbf{b}} = \mathbf{b} - \dot{\mathbf{v}}$ are objective. Writing (9.58) in the form

$$\int_V \dot{\varepsilon} \, dm = \int_V (\bar{\mathbf{b}} \cdot \mathbf{v} + r) \, dm + \int_{\partial V} (\bar{\mathbf{t}} \cdot \mathbf{v} + h) \, da,$$

and performing the observer transformation $\mathbf{v}(\mathbf{x}, t) \to \mathbf{v}^+(\mathbf{x}, t) = \mathbf{v}(\mathbf{x}, t) + \boldsymbol{\Omega}(t)\mathbf{x}$, we similarly recover the balance of angular momentum, (9.35).

Balance equations at surfaces of discontinuity†

Let us recall from Section 8 the notion of a *surface of discontinuity*, S. At surfaces of discontinuity the derivations of the field equations are no longer valid; instead, the balance equations must be expressed in the form of *jump conditions.*

We shall first extend the formulas (9.16), (9.17) to the case when the region of integration contains a surface of discontinuity. Let R be a moving region bounded by a surface A, and let $\mathbf{u}$ be the velocity field of the boundary points. If

$$F(t) = \int_R \rho f \, dv, \qquad (9.16)\text{R}$$

then the time rate of F is defined as follows

$$\dot{F} = \int_R \partial_t(\rho f) \, dv + \int_A \rho f \bar{u} \, da, \qquad (9.61)$$

where

$$\bar{u} \equiv u_{\underline{n}} = u_i n_i, \qquad (9.62)$$

† Cf. *CFT*, pp. 525–529, and A. E. Green and P. M. Naghdi [50].

n being the outer normal at A. In (9.61) the first integral describes the variation of F due to the local rate of the field of ρf, whereas the second integral accounts for the change in F due to the volume swept out by the moving boundary A. In particular, if **u** equals the particle velocities, and $f = 1$, then $\dot{F} = 0$ expresses the balance of mass.

The definition (9.61) may be approached in a more elaborate way as follows. Because F is a function of time only, $\dot{F}$ is but another notation for $dF(t)/dt$. To take the differentiation through the integral sign, however, the boundary ∂R of the moving region R must remain fixed with respect to the observers measuring the time rates. This requires that we introduce an auxiliary field of observer velocities, $\mathbf{u}^*$, which is such that $\mathbf{u} = \mathbf{u}^*$ on ∂R. Then

$$\frac{dF(t)}{dt} = \int_R \frac{d^*}{dt}(\rho f\, dv), \qquad \frac{d^*}{dt} \equiv \partial_t + u_i^* \partial_i .$$

(cf. (7.29)). Because, in analogy with (8.59),

$$\frac{d^*}{dt}\, dv = u_{i,i}^*\, dv,$$

we have that
$$\frac{dF(t)}{dt} = \int_R [\partial_t(\rho f) + u_i^*(\rho f)_{,i} + u_{i,i}^* \rho f]\, dv .$$

Applying the divergence theorem to the integral of $(u_i^* \rho f)_{,i}$, we immediately obtain (9.61).

Let us now choose R to be a material volume which is traversed by a surface of discontinuity, S. Then S decomposes R into two parts, R^- and R^+, which are of the kind that was considered in (9.61). We denote the boundary ∂R of R by $A = A^- + A^+$, the boundaries of R^- and R^+ by $B^- = A^- + S$, $B^+ = A^+ + S$, respectively (Figure 8.7). The boundaries A^- and A^+ move together with the particles, whereas the points of S move with the velocities **u**, $\bar{u}$ now being called the *displacement speed* of S (it is the speed of S relative to the space, and in the direction normal to S). We denote by **n** unit vectors that are normal to S and point into R^+. Then at S the outer normals of R^+ are given by $-\mathbf{n}$, so that $\mathbf{u}^+ \cdot (-\mathbf{n}) = -\bar{u}$. Consequently,

$$\dot{F} = \int_{R^-} \partial_t(\rho f)\, dv + \int_{A^-} \rho f \bar{v}\, da + \int_S \rho f \bar{u}\, da$$
$$+ \int_{R^+} \partial_t(\rho f)\, da + \int_{A^+} \rho f \bar{v}\, da - \int_S \rho f \bar{u}\, da,$$

where $\bar{v}$ denotes the component of particle velocity normal to the boundaries. Denoting by Ψ^+ and Ψ^- the one-sided limits of Ψ on S,† we define by

$$[\![\Psi]\!] = \Psi^+ - \Psi^- \tag{9.63}$$

the *jump* of a quantity Ψ at S. We then obtain

$$\dot{F} = \int_R \partial_t(\rho f)\, dv + \int_A \rho f \bar{v}\, da - \int_S [\![\rho f]\!] \bar{u}\, da.$$

Next, we introduce the (relative) *speed of propagation*, $\bar{V}$,

$$\bar{V} = \bar{u} - \bar{v}, \tag{8.87)R}$$

which is the speed of S relative to particles located at the instant on S, and in the direction normal to itself. Then from‡

$$\begin{aligned} F = &\int_R \partial_t(\rho f)\, dv + \int_{B^+} \rho f v_i n_i\, da - \int_S [\rho f v_i]^- n_i\, da \\ &+ \int_{B^-} \rho f v_i n_i\, da + \int_S [\rho f v_i]^+ n_i\, da \\ &- \int_S [\rho f]^+ \bar{u}\, da + \int_S [\rho f]^- \bar{u}\, da \end{aligned}$$

it follows that

$$\dot{F} = \int_R \partial_t(\rho f)\, dv + \int_B \rho f \bar{v}\, da - \int_S [\![\rho f \bar{V}]\!]\, da, \tag{9.64}$$

where $B = B^+ + B^-$. One more modification is possible: in each of the open regions R^- and R^+ the variables have no discontinuities, so that the divergence theorem can be applied to the integrals over B^+ and B^-. Then

$$\dot{F} = \int_R \dot{f}\, dm - \int_S [\![\rho \bar{V} f]\!]\, da. \tag{9.65}$$

We are now in a position to apply the general balance to a thin slice enclosing a surface of discontinuity. Writing the general balance as follows,

$$\frac{d}{dt}\int_R \Psi \rho\, dv = \int_{\partial R} i_{\underline{n}}\, da + \int_R q\, dv, \tag{9.66}$$

† The mark "+" is also used in observer transformations; it is hoped that this will not create any confusion.
‡ Note that the outer normal of R^+ at S is $-\mathbf{n}$.

where Ψ is now a *density per unit mass*, we consider the limit of (9.66) as R shrinks to a portion of S. If q and $\dot{\Psi}$ are bounded in R, then it follows from (9.65) that

$$[\![\rho\Psi\overline{V}]\!] + [\![i_{\underline{n}}]\!] = 0. \tag{9.67}$$

In particular, because (9.1)* corresponds to $\Psi = 1$, $i_{\underline{n}} = 0$, the *balance of mass at a surface of discontinuity* is given by

$$[\![\rho\overline{V}]\!] = 0. \tag{9.68}$$

If the surface of discontinuity is stationary relative to the medium, i.e. $\overline{V} = 0$, then ρ must be continuous.

While we are on the subject of surfaces of discontinuity, let us record the appropriate generalizations of the basic integral transformations. When applied to the region R of Figure 8.7, the divergence theorem must be modified as follows:

$$\int_R \operatorname{div}\mathbf{b}\, dv = \int_A b_i n_i\, da - \int_S [\![b_i]\!] n_i\, da. \tag{9.69}$$

To prove this we merely have to add

$$\int_{R^\pm} \operatorname{div}\mathbf{b}\, dv = \int_{A^\pm} b_i n_i\, da \mp \int_S [b_i]^\pm n_i\, da.$$

Here, in accord with the convention that the unit normal vectors $\mathbf{n}$ of S point into R^+, the outer normal of R^+ at S is taken to be $-\mathbf{n}$.

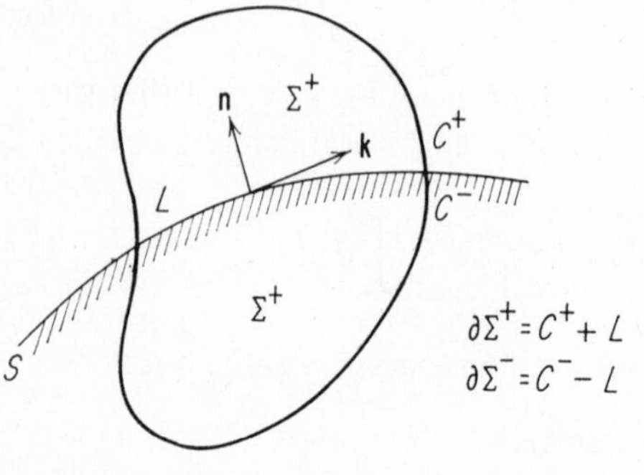

FIGURE 9.2 Variables for applying Kelvin's transformation to a plane area $\Sigma = \Sigma^+ + \Sigma^-$ containing a line of discontinuity, L (L is the intersection with a surface of discontinuity, S, of a plane containing a unit normal vector $\mathbf{n}$ of S).

To investigate the modifications that are necessary in Kelvin's transformation, we take a closed curve C that lies in a plane containing the unit normal vector $\mathbf{n}$ of the surface of discontinuity, S, and is divided by S into two branches C^+ and C^- (Figure 9.2). The intersection of the plane with S is a curve L. Now,

$$\int_\Sigma d\mathbf{a}\cdot \mathrm{curl}\mathbf{b} = \int_{\partial\Sigma} d\mathbf{x}\cdot\mathbf{b}, \qquad \partial\Sigma^+ = C^+ + L \quad \text{or} \quad \partial\Sigma^- = C^- - L,$$

therefore adding the two expressions we obtain

$$\int_\Sigma d\mathbf{a}\cdot \mathrm{curl}\mathbf{b} = \int_{\partial\Sigma} d\mathbf{x}\cdot\mathbf{b} + \int_L \mathbf{k}\cdot [\![\mathbf{b}]\!]\, ds, \tag{9.70}$$

where $\Sigma = \Sigma^+ + \Sigma^-$, $\partial\Sigma = C^+ + C^-$, and $\mathbf{k}$ is a unit tangent vector of L (such that a rotation of $\mathbf{k}$ into $\mathbf{n}$ defines a counterclockwise sense of $\partial\Sigma^+$, for instance).

If Σ is a material surface which contains no lines of discontinuity, then

$$\frac{d}{dt}\int_\Sigma b_i\, da_i = \int_\Sigma \overset{*}{b}_i\, da_i, \tag{9.71}$$

where, by (8.60), $\overset{*}{\mathbf{b}}$ is given by

$$\begin{aligned} \overset{*}{\mathbf{b}}_i &= \dot{b}_i + b_i v_{k,k} - b_k v_{i,k}, \\ \overset{*}{\mathbf{b}} &= \partial_t\mathbf{b} + \mathbf{v}\,\mathrm{div}\mathbf{b} + \mathrm{curl}(\mathbf{b}\times\mathbf{v}). \end{aligned} \tag{9.72}$$

Applying Kelvin's transformation to the integral of $\mathrm{curl}(\mathbf{b}\times\dot{\mathbf{x}})$, we obtain another variant of (9.71):

$$\frac{d}{dt}\int_\Sigma b_i\, da_i = \int_\Sigma (\partial_t b_i + v_i\,\mathrm{div}\mathbf{b})\, da_i + \int_{\partial\Sigma} d\mathbf{x}\cdot(\mathbf{b}\times\mathbf{v}). \tag{9.73}$$

Let us now return to the case shown in Figure 9.2. We assume that the velocity field of the line of discontinuity, L, is $\mathbf{u}$, and apply (9.73), in turn, to the areas bounded by $\partial\Sigma^+ = C^+ + L$ and $\partial\Sigma^- = C^- - L$ (on L the velocity field $\mathbf{v}$ must be replaced by $\mathbf{u}$!):

$$\frac{d}{dt}\int_{\Sigma^+} \mathbf{b}\cdot d\mathbf{a} = \int_{\Sigma^+} \mathbf{p}\cdot d\mathbf{a} + \int_{C^+} d\mathbf{x}\cdot(\mathbf{b}\times\mathbf{v}) + \int_L d\mathbf{x}\cdot(\mathbf{b}\times\mathbf{u})$$

$$= \int_{\Sigma^+} \mathbf{p}\cdot d\mathbf{a} + \int_{\partial\Sigma^+} d\mathbf{x}\cdot(\mathbf{b}\times\mathbf{v}) + \int_L d\mathbf{x}\cdot[\mathbf{b}\times(\mathbf{u}-\mathbf{v})],$$

$$\frac{d}{dt}\int_{\Sigma^-} \mathbf{b}\cdot d\mathbf{a} = \int_{\Sigma^-} \mathbf{p}\cdot d\mathbf{a} + \int_{\partial\Sigma^-} d\mathbf{x}\cdot(\mathbf{b}\times\mathbf{v}) - \int_L d\mathbf{x}\cdot[\mathbf{b}\times(\mathbf{u}-\mathbf{v})],$$

where $p_i = \partial_t b_i + v_i \operatorname{div}\mathbf{b}$. The line integrals over $\partial\Sigma^+$ and $\partial\Sigma^-$ can be converted into surface integrals; adding the expressions we then arrive at

$$\frac{d}{dt}\int_{\Sigma} \mathbf{b}\cdot d\mathbf{a} = \int_{\Sigma} \overset{*}{\mathbf{b}}\cdot d\mathbf{a} + \int_L \mathbf{k}\cdot[\![\mathbf{b}\times(\mathbf{u}-\mathbf{v})]\!]\, ds. \tag{9.74}$$

Problems

A. BALANCE OF MASS

1. If a motion is steady then $\partial_t\rho = 0$, in which case the mass balance becomes $\operatorname{div}\rho\mathbf{v} = 0$. This can be satisfied identically by letting $\rho\mathbf{v} = \operatorname{curl}\mathbf{A}$, where $\mathbf{A}$ is referred to as a streamfunction vector. For two-dimensional flows we let $\mathbf{A} = \mathbf{e}_z Q(x, y)$. Show that Q can be interpreted as the discharge of mass across a curve (in the xy plane), and that, in particular, $Q =$ const. defines streamlines (curves which have everywhere the same direction as the flow velocity $\mathbf{v}$).

2. Obtain the representation of the law of conservation of mass for a one-dimensional motion $x = x(X, t)$, $y = Y$, $z = Z$. (*Hint*: consider a material volume bounded by X and $X + dX$).

3. By selecting a suitable "free body," derive the representation of the law of conservation of mass for a rotationally symmetric motion $\rho = \rho(P, t)$, $\phi = \Phi$, $z = Z$.

4. By selecting a suitable "free body," derive the representation of the law of conservation of mass for a spherically symmetric motion $r = r(R, t)$, $\theta = \Theta$, $\phi = \Phi$.

5. By selecting a suitable "free body," derive the representation of the law of conservation of mass for a rotationally symmetric deformation $\rho = \rho(P)$, $\phi = \Phi$, $z = kZ$, where k is a constant.

6. Since ρ is objective, so is $\dot{\rho}$ (why?). But $\dot{\rho}$ admits the representation $\partial_t\rho + v_i\rho_{,i}$, where $\mathbf{v}$ is not objective. Show that $\partial_t\rho + \rho_{,i}v_i$ nevertheless represents an objective quantity. (*Hint*: consider

$$\left.\frac{\partial}{\partial t}\right|_{\mathbf{x}^+ = \text{const.}} = \left.\frac{\partial}{\partial t}\right|_{\mathbf{x} = \text{const.}} + \left.\frac{\partial x_i}{\partial t}\right|_{\mathbf{x}^+ = \text{const.}} \left.\frac{\partial}{\partial x_i}\right).$$

7. Is there a way of satisfying identically the balance of mass? (*Hint*: let x_i, $i = 1, 2, 3$, $x_4 = t$ and $\gamma_i = \rho v_i$, $\gamma_4 = \rho$, so that the balance of mass becomes "div" $\gamma = 0$).

8. Verify the details of the derivation of

a. (9.65) **b.** (9.69) **c.** (9.70)
d. (9.73) **e.** (9.74)

B. THE PRINCIPLES OF LINEAR AND ANGULAR MOMENTA

9. A body $\mathscr{B}$ occupies at the given instant the region V defined by $0 \leq x \leq L$, $0 \leq y \leq L$, $0 \leq z \leq L$. Let $v_x = ky$, $v_y = v_z = 0$, where k is a constant. Calculate $\mathbf{P}$, $\mathbf{H}^{[0]}$, $\mathbf{H}^{[c]}$ and K for $\mathscr{B}$, assuming that the mass density is constant.

10. A body $\mathscr{B}$ occupies at the given instant the region V defined in cylindrical coordinates by $B \leq \rho \leq A$, $-L \leq z \leq L$. If the mass density is constant, calculate $\mathbf{P}$, $\mathbf{H}^{[0]}$ and K for the motion

a. $v_\rho = v_z = 0$, $v_\rho = k\phi$ **b.** $v_\rho = v_z = 0$, $v_\phi = k/\rho$
c. $v_\rho = 0$, $v_\phi = k\rho$, $v_z = U$
(U and k are constants).

11. Let $v_i(\mathbf{x}) = \bar{v}_i + \bar{D}_{ij}x_j + \bar{W}_{ij}x_j$, where $\bar{v}_i$, $\bar{D}_{ij}$, $\bar{W}_{ij}$ are constants ($\bar{D}_{ij}$ is symmetric, and $\bar{W}_{ij}$ is skew-symmetric). Obtain general representations for $\mathbf{P}$, $\mathbf{H}^{[0]}$ and K.

12. Let V be a sphere $0 \leq r \leq A$. The spherical components of the surface tractions $\bar{\mathbf{t}}$ are given by $t_r = t_\theta = 0$, $t_\phi = k \sin\theta \sin\phi/2$, where k is a constant. Assuming that $\mathbf{b} = 0$, calculate $\mathbf{F}$ and $\mathbf{L}^{[0]}$.

13. A body $\mathscr{B}$ occupies the region V defined by $0 \leq x \leq L$, $0 \leq y \leq L$, $0 \leq z \leq L$. If the mass density is constant, calculate $\mathbf{F}$ and $\mathbf{L}^{[0]}$ for

a. $\bar{\mathbf{t}} = Ax\mathbf{e}_x$, $\mathbf{b} = B\mathbf{e}_x$ **b.** $\bar{\mathbf{t}} = Ax\mathbf{e}_y$, $\mathbf{b} = Ey^2\mathbf{e}_z$
(A, B, E are constants).

14. Consider the body and the motion described in Problem 9. Calculate the power of external forces if $\bar{\mathbf{t}}$ and $\mathbf{b}$ are given by

a. Problem 13a **b.** Problem 13b

15. Calculate $\mathbf{F}$ and $\mathbf{L}^{[0]}$ for the case described in Problem 9.

16. Calculate $\mathbf{F}$ and $\mathbf{L}^{[0]}$ for the case described in

a. Problem 10a **b.** Problem 10b **c.** Problem 10c

C. RIGID BODY MOTION

17. Give detailed derivations of (9.47) and (9.48).

18. Give detailed derivations of (9.49) and (9.50).

19. Derive (9.51), (9.52).

20. Verify that (9.54) holds.

21. Writing Euler's equations as $L_a = \overset{\circ}{H}_a$, interpret $\overset{\circ}{H}_a$ (what is the angular velocity that must be used in the definition of $\overset{\circ}{H}_a$?).

22. Integrate (9.47) in the case when $\mathbf{L} = \mathbf{0}$.

23. If $v_a = \varepsilon_{abc}\pi_b\omega_c =$ const., $\omega_c =$ const., interpret the "inertial forces" F_a defined by (9.48).

Section 10
STRESS

Introduction

To derive field equations expressing the balance of linear and angular momenta, some hypothesis concerning the nature of internal forces is needed. This hypothesis is embodied in the concept of *stress*. Although the idea of an internal pressure in fluids can be traced to the writings of Archimedes, the general concept of stress was first put forward by Cauchy in 1822.† The present decade is another milestone in the history of stress. The search for more faithful descriptions of the microstructure of materials has led to sweeping generalizations of the concept of stress and of the stress equations of motion.

The nature of internal forces is largely determined by the assumed structural models of materials. If we abandon for a moment the continuum viewpoint, then materials can be imagined as collections of particles, each of which is the seat of forces, and is in turn acted upon by forces emanating from other particles. By the internal force acting on a typical particle we mean the total force exerted on it by all other particles, that is, not only the forces due to "nearest neighbors" but also due to "next-nearest neighbors," and so on. Consequently, the view of internal forces as a kind of contact forces is not altogether accurate, except when the interparticle forces decay very rapidly with distance.

It may be of some interest to look briefly at the period just preceding Cauchy's stress hypothesis. The 1820s saw the birth of the classical linear elasticity theory, largely as a result of the discovery by Young and Fresnel of the wavelike nature of light. This discovery led to a search for models of an "aether" capable of sustaining transverse vibrations. The "elastic aether" model was based, at first, on the notion of elastic solids as systems of particles held together by central interparticle forces. In 1821 Navier submitted to the French Academy a derivation of

† Cf. Truesdell [173].

the equations governing the motion of a generic particle.† In this derivation particles are subjected to small displacements **u** that change the distances between the particles from r to $\bar{r}$. Denoting by **n** the unit vector along the line joining two particles P and Q (Figure 10.1), we obtain the approximate expressions $\bar{r} - r \doteq \mathbf{n} \cdot \delta\mathbf{u}$, where $\delta\mathbf{u}$ is the difference of the displacements of P and Q. This change in distance is assumed to induce a restoring force $\boldsymbol{\tau}$ given by $\tau = F(r)(\bar{r} - r) = F(r)n_i\,\delta u_i$, where $F(r)$ describes the variations of the inter-particle forces with distance. Then $\tau_j = \tau n_j = F(r)n_i n_j \delta u_i$; letting $\delta x_i = rn_i$, we now expand $\delta\mathbf{u}$ in a Taylor series about P, $\delta u_i = u_{i,k}rn_k + \frac{1}{2}u_{i,km}r^2 n_k n_m + \cdots$, whence it follows that $\tau_j \doteq rF(r)n_i n_j[u_{i,k}n_k + \frac{1}{2}ru_{i,km}n_k n_m]$. To find the total restoring force acting on P, we integrate (*sic*!) this over the entire space, which is the same as integrating it over a finite body provided that $F(r)$ decays rapidly enough with increasing r. In spherical coordinates, $n_x = \sin\theta\cos\phi$, $n_y = \sin\theta\sin\phi$, $n_z = \cos\theta$, $dv = r^2\sin\theta\,dr\,d\theta\,d\phi$; the terms containing odd powers of the direction cosines n_i vanish, leaving the main contribution $\tau_i = \mu(\nabla^2 u_i + 2\vartheta_{,i})$, where $\vartheta = \operatorname{div}\mathbf{u}$, and

$$\mu = \frac{2}{15}\int_0^\infty r^4 F(r)\,dr$$

is a material property. Relating $\boldsymbol{\tau}$ and the body force intensity **b** to the particle acceleration $\ddot{\mathbf{u}}$, we arrive at Navier's equations of motion for elastic bodies, $\mu(\nabla^2\mathbf{u} + 2\nabla\vartheta) + \rho\mathbf{b} = \rho\ddot{\mathbf{u}}$. These equations actually correspond to the particular value $\nu = \frac{1}{4}$ of Poisson's ratio. This defect was removed by Cauchy who replaced, in essence, $F(r)$ by a Taylor series expansion $f(\bar{r}) \doteq f(r) + (\bar{r} - r)f'(r)$ of a function $f(r)$ describing the inter-particle forces also in the undeformed state.‡

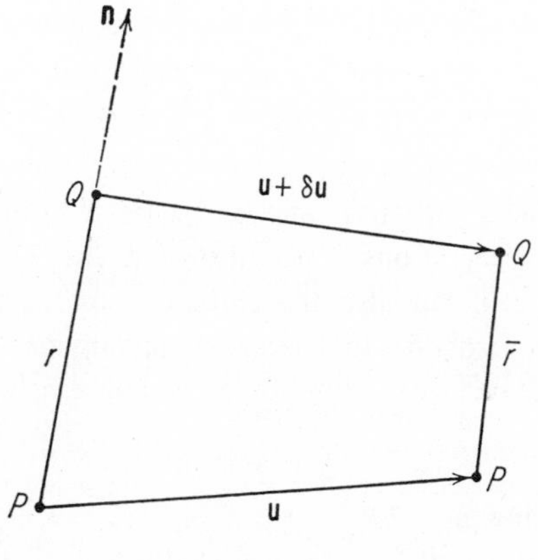

FIGURE 10.1 Displacements of particles P and Q.

† More on the history of this period, as well as references to the main works, can be found in [91] and [101].

‡ Cauchy was one of the referees of Navier's paper.

If the restoring forces are of another kind, then a new derivation of the equations of motion is needed. For instance, in fluids the force $\boldsymbol{\tau}$ is assumed to be proportional to the differences of velocities rather than to the differences of displacements.† We then obtain the Navier-Stokes equations of hydrodynamics, which resemble Navier's equations of elasticity, except that displacements are replaced on the left-hand sides by velocities. In each case the equations of motion express the physical principle for linear momentum and a constitutive property of the medium. The balance of linear momentum can be expressed, in the interior of a body, in a "pure" form only through the use of stress.

Elasticity theory was preceded in many respects by the special theories for thin rods and plates. In particular, in 1771 Euler gave the following equations of motion governing extension and bending of rods,‡

$$\frac{dT}{ds} + V\frac{d\phi}{ds} + F_{\underline{t}} = \sigma a_{\underline{t}}, \qquad \frac{dM}{ds} - V = 0,$$

$$\frac{dV}{ds} - T\frac{d\phi}{ds} + F_{\underline{n}} = \sigma a_{\underline{n}},$$

where T, V, M are tension, shearing force, and bending moment, respectively, σ is the mass density per unit length, and ϕ describes the slope of the center line. These equations express the balance of linear and angular momenta without any admixture of special assumptions concerning the material.

To derive the *boundary conditions* which must be adjoined to the field equations, Navier apparently felt that another approach was better suited. The approach he chose foreshadows the use of the "strain-energy function", which was later fully developed by G. Green. Navier considered the principle of virtual work in the following form,

$$\int_V b_i \,\delta u_i \, dm + \int_S t_i \,\delta u_i \, da = \frac{1}{4}\int_V F(r)\,\delta(\bar{r} - r)^2 \, dv,$$

where the term on the right-hand side represents the potential of the internal forces. Appropriate integrations not only yield the boundary conditions $t_i = \mu(\vartheta n_i + (u_{i,j} + u_{j,i})n_j]$, but also the equations of motion. It was Cauchy's great achievement to recognize that relations analogous to the boundary conditions are also applicable in the interior of bodies, $\mathbf{t}$ being the (internal) stress vectors.

Cauchy's stress principle

The *stress principle of Cauchy* ascribes to every imagined surface within a body interactions that are of the same kind as the distributed surface loads;

† This hypothesis is known as *Newton's law of viscosity*; its general statement is due to Stokes.

‡ Cf. the second reference cited on p. 189.

that is, forces acting across surfaces in the interior of a body are assumed to be no different from forces acting on the boundary of the body. In more precise terms, we say that the internal forces acting on one side of an imagined surface S are equivalent to a distribution of *stress vectors* $\mathbf{t}$ having the dimension of force per area (Figure 10.2).

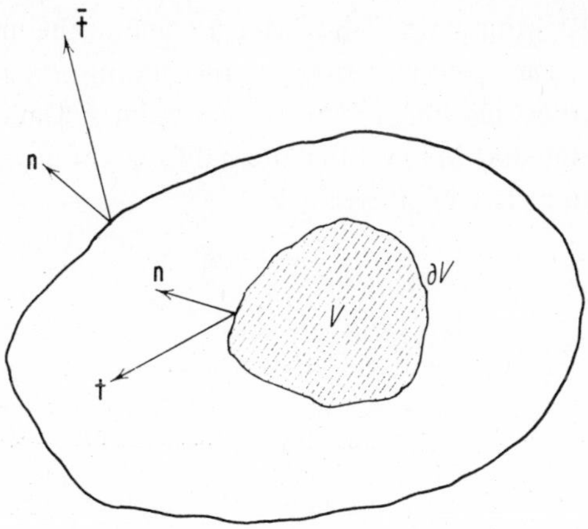

FIGURE 10.2 Surface traction $\bar{\mathbf{t}}$ and (internal) stress vector $\mathbf{t}$.

Although Cauchy's stress principle is of utter simplicity, one should not fail to appreciate its power, nor forget the simplifying assumptions inherent in it. This principle provides a description of internal forces in all situations; without it there could be no continuum mechanics as a science describing solids and fluids alike. At the same time, this principle implies that when a material volume V is removed from a body, then it is possible to maintain V in its initial state merely by applying suitably distributed forces $\mathbf{t}$ on the boundary ∂V. If the range of cohesion forces, l, although small, cannot be neglected altogether, then the notions of stress and "surface separation" must be reconsidered. Specifically, the "surface of separation" must be at first a shell of thickness l. In general, to represent the effect of the shell upon V, it will be necessary to distribute on ∂V not only stress $\mathbf{t}$ but also more complex, "multipolar" stresses, e.g. couple stresses, "hypertractions" (cf. Section 16).

Let us continue to explore the content of Cauchy's hypothesis. The most important observation concerning stress vectors is that they are defined in conjunction with the surfaces that transmit them. It is meaningless to refer merely to a "stress vector $\mathbf{t}(\mathbf{x})$ at a point $\mathbf{x}$"; rather, the plane on which $\mathbf{t}$ acts (or, equivalently, the unit normal vector $\mathbf{n}$ of that plane) must be specified. We write $\mathbf{t} = \mathbf{t}(\mathbf{x}, \mathbf{n})$, thereby emphasizing that $\mathbf{t}$ *is a function of* $\mathbf{x}$ *and* $\mathbf{n}$. To put it in another way, Cauchy's hypothesis assumes not one stress vector at each point, it assumes a *stress vector state* $\mathbf{t}(\mathbf{x}, \mathbf{n})$ such that, at one and the same point $\mathbf{x}$, there is a distinct stress vector associated with each direction $\mathbf{n}$ (thus at a point $\mathbf{x}$ there are ∞^2 stress vectors, each associated with one of the ∞^2 possible directions). Recalling from p. 41 the remarks concerning the origin of tensors, we naturally expect to find in the multiplicity of vectors $\mathbf{t}(\mathbf{x}, \mathbf{n})$ the manifestation of a *stress tensor* $\mathbf{T}(\mathbf{x})$, but that is another matter. Right now we wish to give a name to the multiplicity of stress vectors:

The totality of stress vectors $\mathbf{t}(\mathbf{x}, \mathbf{n})$ *at a fixed* $\mathbf{x}$ *and for all directions* $\mathbf{n}$ *is called the state of stress at the point* $\mathbf{x}$. Cauchy's stress principle can now be stated as follows: the internal forces at any point $\mathbf{x}$ of a body are equivalent to a state of stress.

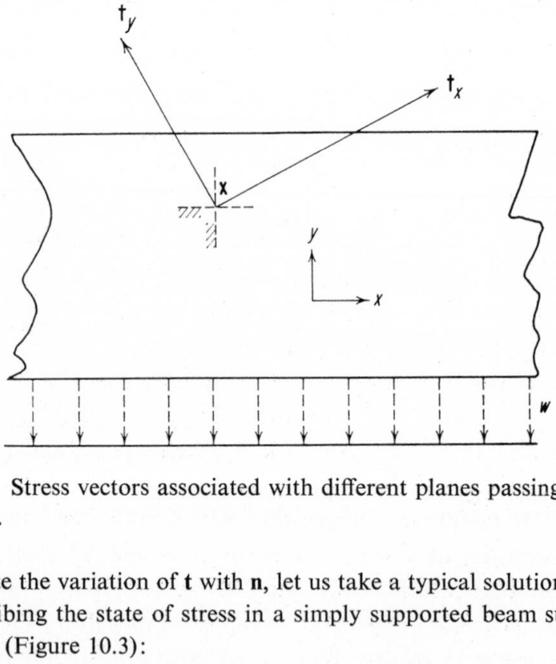

FIGURE 10.3 Stress vectors associated with different planes passing through the same point $\mathbf{x}$.

To illustrate the variation of $\mathbf{t}$ with $\mathbf{n}$, let us take a typical solution of elasticity theory, describing the state of stress in a simply supported beam subjected to a uniform load (Figure 10.3):

$$T_{xz} = T_{yz} = T_{zz} = 0, \qquad T_{xy} = -A(c^2 - y^2)x,$$

$$T_{xx} = A(L^2 - x^2)y + A\left(\frac{2}{3}y^3 - \frac{2}{5}c^2y\right), \tag{10.1}$$

$$T_{yy} = -A\left(\frac{1}{3}y^3 - c^2y + \frac{2}{3}c^3\right),$$

where $A = 3w/4c^3 = \text{const}$. As shown in Figure 10.3, at a point $\mathbf{x}$ there exists a stress vector $\mathbf{t}_x = T_{xx}\mathbf{e}_x + T_{xy}\mathbf{e}_y$ that acts on the plane $x = \text{const.}$, and a stress vector $\mathbf{t}_y = T_{yx}\mathbf{e}_x + T_{yy}\mathbf{e}_y$ that acts on the plane $y = \text{const}$. The determination of stress vectors acting on the other planes passing through **x** will be taken up in Cauchy's fundamental theorem.

The reason why the dependence of **t**(**x**, **n**) upon **n** cannot be emphasized too strongly is that our intuitive grasp of physical states derives mainly from scalar states which are a manifestation of a single vector. But while there is only one velocity vector, for instance, at each point, there is an infinity of stress vectors acting at a point. There is of course only one stress vector acting on a definite plane (i.e. at a point of a definite "free body"), but as the plane varies so does the stress vector.

At a generic point **x**, let **t**(**n**) be the stress vector acting on the plane whose normal is **n**.† It is evidently possible to represent **t**(**n**) in terms of a *normal component* N and a *shearing component* S as follows,

$$\mathbf{t}(\mathbf{n}) = \mathbf{n}N(\mathbf{n}) + \mathbf{s}S(\mathbf{n}), \tag{10.2}$$

where **s** is a unit vector perpendicular to **n** and lying in the plane of **n** and **t**(**n**). In addition, we have the representation

$$\mathbf{t}(\mathbf{n}) = t_j(\mathbf{n})\mathbf{e}_j \tag{10.3}$$

in some common frame $(\mathbf{e}_j)$. If the plane on which the stress vector acts is also a coordinate plane, e.g. $\mathbf{n} = \mathbf{e}_1$, then we shall use the *Cartesian component notation*‡

$$\mathbf{t}(\mathbf{e}_i) = \mathbf{t}_i = T_{ij}\mathbf{e}_j, \tag{10.4}$$

where

$$T_{ij} = \mathbf{t}_i[\mathbf{e}_j] \tag{10.5}$$

is the component in the direction of $\mathbf{e}_j$ of that stress vector which acts on a plane normal to $\mathbf{e}_i$ (Figure 10.4).

If the normal component N of a stress vector is a tension, then N is assigned positive values, negative values if N is a compression. For the shearing component S a sign convention is evidently not possible, because its direction can be anywhere in the plane normal to **n**. For the Cartesian components of stress vectors acting on coordinate planes the following sign convention is adopted: if the normal of the plane in question is in the positive (negative) coordinate direction, then a positive stress component acts in the positive (negative) coordinate direction. As shown in Figure 10.4, all components are positive.

† Whenever the dependence of **t** upon **x** is of no concern, we suppress it in our notations.
‡ Here our notation anticipates the subsequent derivation of a stress tensor T_{ij}. The various designations for stress vectors, **t**(**n**), $\mathbf{t}_{\underline{n}}$, etc., were previously discussed on p. 50.

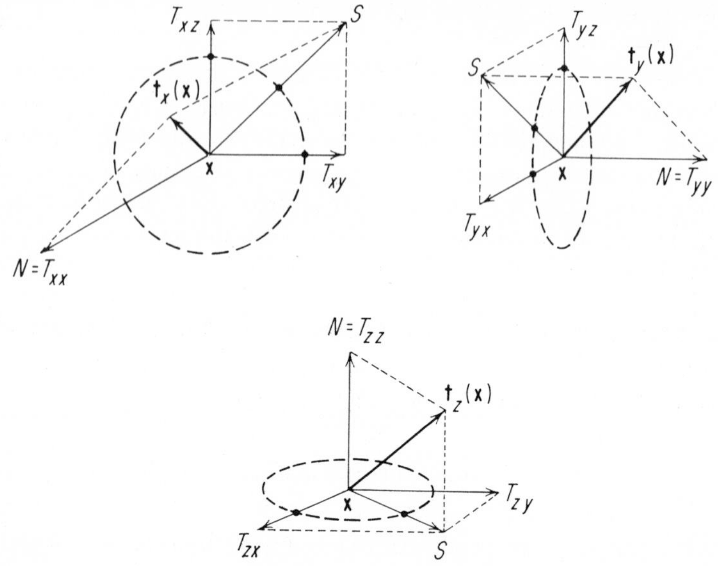

FIGURE 10.4 Stress vectors at a point **x**, and acting on the coordinate planes:

$$\mathbf{t}(\mathbf{x},\mathbf{e}_x) = \mathbf{t}_x(\mathbf{x}) = T_{xx}\mathbf{e}_x + T_{xy}\mathbf{e}_y + T_{xz}\mathbf{e}_z,$$
$$\mathbf{t}(\mathbf{x},\mathbf{e}_y) = \mathbf{t}_y(\mathbf{x}) = T_{yx}\mathbf{e}_x + T_{yy}\mathbf{e}_y + T_{yz}\mathbf{e}_z,$$
$$\mathbf{t}(\mathbf{x},\mathbf{e}_z) = \mathbf{t}_z(\mathbf{x}) = T_{zx}\mathbf{e}_x + T_{zy}\mathbf{e}_y + T_{zz}\mathbf{e}_z.$$

Let us pause for a moment in order to see what remains to be done. The task of this section is the study of internal forces, the available tools are the principles of linear and angular momenta,

$$\mathbf{F} = \dot{\mathbf{P}}, \tag{9.34)R$$

$$\mathbf{L}^{[0]} = \dot{\mathbf{H}}^{[0]}, \tag{9.35)R$$

and the stress principle of Cauchy, according to which the internal forces at any surface can be represented by stress vectors. There is really a third tool: the "free body" technique. To study the variation of $\mathbf{t}(\mathbf{x}, \mathbf{n})$ with $\mathbf{x}$ (while holding $\mathbf{n}$ fixed), or to study the variation with $\mathbf{n}$ (while holding $\mathbf{x}$ fixed), suitable "free bodies" can be devised. As the following subsections will show, three types of "free bodies" are useful: a slice (or *pill-box*) for investigating continuity properties and boundary conditions, an arbitrary portion of a body for deriving the field equations of momentum balance, and a *tetrahedon* for investigating boundary conditions as well as the general variation of **t** with **n**.

Stress tensor, boundary conditions

Let us suppose that the field of stress vectors $\mathbf{t}$ is continuous in a neighborhood $N(\mathbf{x})$ of a point $\mathbf{x}$. We choose as a "free body" a small yet finite slice of the body (contained in $N(\mathbf{x})$) as shown in Figure 10.5. To apply the principle of linear momentum, it is necessary to evaluate the integrals $\dot{\mathbf{P}} = \int \dot{\mathbf{v}}\, dm$, $\mathbf{F} = \int \mathbf{t}\, da + \int \mathbf{b}\, dm$. Now, in the limit as the thickness h of the slice tends to zero, the volume integrals will become infinitesimals of a higher order than the surface integral. Therefore, (9.34) will reduce to $\lim_{h\to 0} \int \mathbf{t}\, da = \mathbf{0}$. Because $\mathbf{t}$ is assumed to be continuous, the surface integrals can be evaluated by using the mean value theorem. Then the integrations over the faces are replaced by products of the mean values $\tilde{\mathbf{t}}$ of stresses times the area A of a face: $\tilde{\mathbf{t}}(\mathbf{x}, \mathbf{n})A + \tilde{\mathbf{t}}(\bar{\mathbf{x}}, -\mathbf{n})A$, where $\mathbf{n}$ defines a direction normal to the faces. As h tends to zero, the contributions of the edge vanish, thus leaving $\tilde{\mathbf{t}}(\mathbf{x}, \mathbf{n}) = -\tilde{\mathbf{t}}(\mathbf{x}, -\mathbf{n})$. Consequently,

$$\mathbf{t}(\mathbf{x}, \mathbf{n}) = -\mathbf{t}(\mathbf{x}, -\mathbf{n}), \tag{10.6}$$

i.e. stress vectors acting at the same point but on opposite sides of a surface are equal in magnitude and opposite in direction. This statement of the continuity property (10.6) reminds one of the usual wording of *Newton's third law*; for this reason it is worth noting that (10.6) was *derived* here from the balance of linear momentum and Cauchy's stress principle.

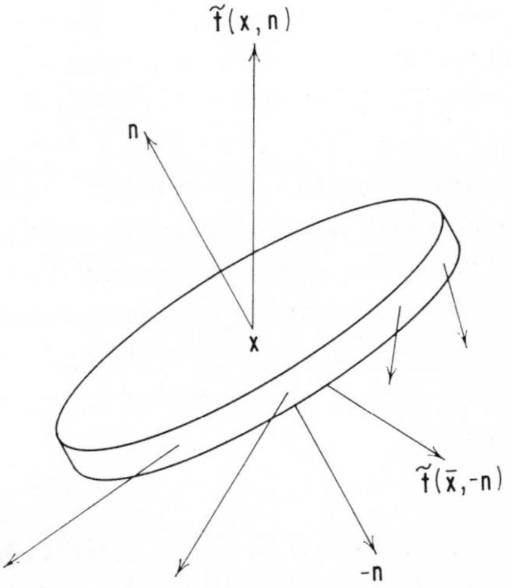

FIGURE 10.5 Diagram for the application of momentum balance to a thin slice of a body.

In the special case when one face of the slice lies in the boundary of the body, it follows from (10.6) that

$$\bar{\mathbf{t}}(\mathbf{x}, \mathbf{n}) = -\mathbf{t}(\mathbf{x}, -\mathbf{n}) \equiv \mathbf{t}(\mathbf{x}, \mathbf{n}), \tag{10.7}$$

where $\mathbf{n}$ is the outer normal at the boundary, and $\bar{\mathbf{t}}$ is the surface traction on the boundary. As can be seen from (10.7), the (internal) stresses merge, at the boundary, continuously into surface tractions, which suggests that the latter be regarded as the *boundary values of stresses*. In particular, we shall speak of *boundary condition*

$$\mathbf{t}(\mathbf{x}, \mathbf{n}) = \bar{\mathbf{t}}(\mathbf{x}, \mathbf{n}) \qquad \mathbf{x} \text{ on } S, \tag{10.8}$$

where $\mathbf{n}$ is the outer normal at the boundary S. This condition shows the manner in which external agencies influence internal forces, namely by controlling the boundary values $\bar{\mathbf{t}}$ of the internal forces.

The merging of stresses into surface tractions can be observed in the example (10.1) by letting $y \to c$ or $y \to -c$: $\mathbf{t}_y(c) = \mathbf{0}$, $\mathbf{t}_y(-c) = -w\mathbf{e}_y$. The values of $\mathbf{t}_x$ at the boundary, e.g. $T_{xx}(c) = A(L^2 - x^2)c + \frac{4}{15}Ac^3$, are not governed by boundary conditions because $\mathbf{t}_x$ does not act *on* the boundary. More about that later.

We now come to the central problem: to find a *description of the state of stress* at a point. It will be recalled that a state of stress comprises an infinity of stress vectors $\mathbf{t}(\mathbf{x}, \mathbf{n})$, one for each plane passing through $\mathbf{x}$. Are these vectors related in any way, and if so, how many vectors can be prescribed independently? For the present task the appropriate "free body" is a tetrahedron,† because we shall be concerned with the variation with $\mathbf{n}$ of $\mathbf{t}(\mathbf{x}, \mathbf{n})$ at a fixed point $\mathbf{x}$. Specifically, we shall consider a small but finite tetrahedron with one corner at $\mathbf{x}$; the tetrahedron must be small in the sense of being contained in a neighborhood $N(\mathbf{x})$ of $\mathbf{x}$ in which the field of stress vectors is assumed to be continuous. The tetrahedron is then shrunk to the point $\mathbf{x}$, whereby the balance equations for linear and angular momenta are reduced to algebraic expressions yielding the desired description of the state of stress at $\mathbf{x}$.

We state *Cauchy's fundamental theorem*:

The state of stress at a point $\mathbf{x}$ *is determined if the stress vectors associated with three mutually perpendicular planes are known at* $\mathbf{x}$ *and are continuous in a neighborhood of* $\mathbf{x}$. Moreover, if the planes in question are coordinate planes, then

$$t_i(\mathbf{x}, \mathbf{n}) = T_{ji}(\mathbf{x})n_j, \tag{10.9}$$

† In texts in which the general theory is developed, at least initially, in a two-dimensional setting, the tetrahedron is replaced by a prism whose cross section is a right triangle.

where T_{ji} are the Cartesian components of stress vectors, defined by (10.4), (10.5).

The idea of the proof is very simple: we orient a tetrahedron in such a way that the stress vectors acting on the three mutually perpendicular faces are the known ones. Then the three scalar balance equations for linear momentum suffice to determine the three unknown components $t_i(\mathbf{n})$ of the stress vector acting on the fourth face. Applying the balance of angular momentum it is easily seen that, in the limit as the tetrahedron shrinks to a point, the moments of all forces cancel.

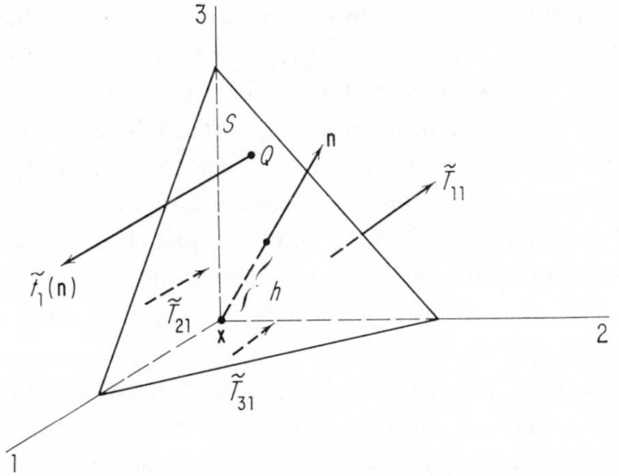

FIGURE 10.6 A tetrahedron for the proof of Cauchy's fundamental theorem. Only the x components of stress vectors are shown.

Let us illustrate the proof of (10.9) when $i = 1$. For the sake of clarity stress components in x_2 and x_3 directions have been omitted in Figure 10.6.

Let A be the area of the inclined face S, $\mathbf{n}$ the unit normal vector of S, and h the perpendicular distance from $\mathbf{x}$ to S (Figure 10.6). We shall denote by $\tilde{t}_i(\mathbf{n}), \tilde{T}_{ji}$ the mean values of $t_i(\mathbf{n})$, T_{ji} over the respective areas. In particular,

$$A\tilde{t}_1(\mathbf{n}) = \int_S t_1(\mathbf{n})\, da = At_1(Q, \mathbf{n}),$$

where as a consequence of the mean value theorem for integrals, Q lies inside S.†

The areas of the mutually perpendicular faces being An_i, the balance of linear momentum, (9.34), in the x_1 direction now reads $\tilde{t}_1(\mathbf{n})A - An_1\tilde{T}_{11} - An_2\tilde{T}_{21} - An_3\tilde{T}_{31} + (Ah/3)\rho\phi_1 = 0$, where $Ah/3$ is the volume of the tetrahedron, and $\rho\phi_1$ is the average value of body forces and inertial forces in x_1 direction. We now cancel A and let $h \to 0$. Since Q lies in S, it follows that $t_1(Q, \mathbf{n}) \to t_1(\mathbf{x}, \mathbf{n})$; the

† The continuity of stress vectors was assumed precisely for this to be the case.

same holds true also for the mean values of the Cartesian components T_{ji}: $\tilde{T}_{ji} \to T_{ji}(\mathbf{x})$. Noting that the body force term does not contribute in the limit $h \to 0$, we get $t_1(\mathbf{x}, \mathbf{n}) = T_{j1}(\mathbf{x})n_j$.

Let us discuss the various aspects of Cauchy's formula (10.9). First, we see that stress vectors depend *linearly* on $\mathbf{n}$: $t_i(\mathbf{n}) = t_i[\mathbf{n}] = T_{ji}n_j$, T_{ji} being only functions of $\mathbf{x}$. Second, because $\mathbf{n}$ and $\mathbf{t}$ are vectors, it follows that T_{ji} constitute a second rank tensor, the *stress tensor* $\mathbf{T}$.† To reinforce this interpretation of Cauchy's fundamental theorem, let us take $\mathbf{n}$ as a base vector $\mathbf{n}_b$ of another Cartesian coordinate system. Writing $\mathbf{n}_b = Q_{bj}\mathbf{e}_j$, we find from (10.9) that $T_{ji}Q_{bj} = t_i(\mathbf{n}_b) = T_{bi}$. But $t_i(\mathbf{n}_b)$ are vector components, hence we also have that $t_a(\mathbf{n}_b) = Q_{ai}t_i(\mathbf{n}_b)$, thus $T_{ji}Q_{bj}Q_{ai} = Q_{ai}T_{bi} = T_{ba}$. Consequently, $t_i(\mathbf{n}) = T_{ji}n_j$ is but another notation for the transformation formula $T_{ba} = Q_{bj}Q_{ai}T_{ji}$ of second rank tensors, i.e. Cauchy's fundamental theorem amounts to the statement that the nine Cartesian components T_{ji} of the stress vectors $\mathbf{t}_j$ acting on the coordinate planes constitute a second rank tensor. Let us note the converse of Cauchy's fundamental theorem: if (10.9) hold, then the linear momentum of an infinitesimal tetrahedron is balanced. It is also worth noting that at this point we have no way of knowing whether the tensor $\mathbf{T}$ is symmetric or not.

As a rule we look upon a stress *vector* as the primitive concept, or, as the entity which is intuitively understood. A stress *tensor*, on the other hand, is merely a tool for describing the state of stress; only the elements of that state, i.e. the stress vectors, are open to direct interpretation. Of course, such questions may be largely a matter of taste. Moreover, in other situations it is often the tensor that must be accepted outright. Typical examples of this are the strain and inertia tensors. Here our physical intuition must leap from the components directly to the tensors, because a strain vector $E_i(\mathbf{n}) = E_{ji}n_j$ and an inertia vector $I_i(\mathbf{n}) = I_{ji}n_j$, although perfectly admissible from a mathematical viewpoint, have no useful physical interpretation. Finally, let us note in passing that a tetrahedron has one "weakness": it has edges, where the unit normal vectors are not defined. When investigating the dependence of internal forces upon $\mathbf{n}$, this may be grounds for some uneasiness, since the edges are in effect singular lines. In some of the recent generalizations of classical continuum mechanics there occur situations in which a "stress" $\mathbf{h}$ is not a linear function of $\mathbf{n}$, e.g. $h_i(\mathbf{n}) = h_{kmi}n_kn_m$, or may even depend on the gradients of $\mathbf{n}$. In these cases the tetrahedral "free bodies" are not used.

Whether or not stress can be considered as directly observable, its behavior

† A heuristic interpretation of the relation between stress vectors and stress tensors was given on pp. 45–46. The related matter of "intermediate components" is discussed on p. 50.

in *observer transformations* must be formally prescribed. There is of course no way of deriving the requisite transformation properties, because stress is an invented concept, not reducible to kinematical quantities. We assume, then, as an integral part of the concept of stress its objectivity:

$$\mathbf{t}^+(\mathbf{n}) = \mathbf{t}(\mathbf{n}), \qquad \mathbf{T}^+ = \mathbf{T} \tag{10.10}$$

(cf. (9.39)). This assumption embodies our very conception of internal forces as being the dynamical response to local states of deformation. It also sets stresses apart from body forces, because the latter are in general not objective. A more special argument in favor of (10.10) can be based on the fact that internal forces are often functions of the inter-particle distances alone. Because observer transformations leave distances invariant, they cannot affect the values of internal forces.

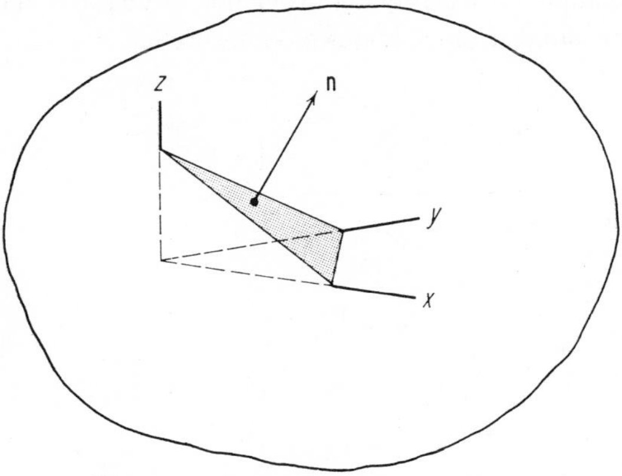

FIGURE 10.7 A material tetrahedron with one of its faces lying in the tangent plane of the boundary.

A tetrehedron can be also adapted for investigating boundary conditions. To do so, we let the inclined face fall in the tangent plane of the boundary, whereas the rest of the tetrahedron remains in the interior of the body (Figure 10.7). If the tetrahedron is shrunk to a point on the boundary, then, in accord with (10.9),

$$\bar{t}_i(\mathbf{n}) = T_{ji}n_j, \tag{10.11}$$

where $\mathbf{n}$ is the outer normal at the boundary, and $\bar{t}_i(\mathbf{n})$ the prescribed surface tractions. Here T_{ji} are components of *stress vectors acting at the boundary but not on it* (the stress vectors $\mathbf{t}_j$ act on the coordinate planes which define the remaining three faces of the finite tetrahedron). However, in view of $t_i(\mathbf{n}) = T_{ji}n_j$, it follows that (10.11) are nothing but a restatement of the boundary conditions (10.8). That is, stress vectors acting on various planes passing through a point are related by the requirements of momentum balance of a tetrahedron, so that a boundary condition on $t_i(\mathbf{n})$ is equivalent to a boundary condition on the combination $T_{ji}n_j$ of the Cartesian components of the stress tensor. But the latter view only tends to create confusion; we prefer to keep the matter of boundary conditions simple: *boundary conditions apply only to stress vectors acting on the tangent plane of the boundary.* If $\mathbf{x}$ is a point on the boundary, and $\mathbf{n}$ the outer normal at $\mathbf{x}$, then $\mathbf{t}(\mathbf{x}, \mathbf{n})$ can be prescribed, but any other stress vector $\mathbf{t}(\mathbf{x}, \bar{\mathbf{n}})$ cannot be prescribed.

The distinction between stress vectors acting on the boundary, and stress vectors acting at the boundary, but not on it, is very important, because the former are external loads that can be controlled directly by external agencies, whereas the latter are internal forces that are determined by the complete set of field equations and boundary conditions. To clarify this distinction further, it is not a bad idea to look hard at some familiar distributions of stress vectors.

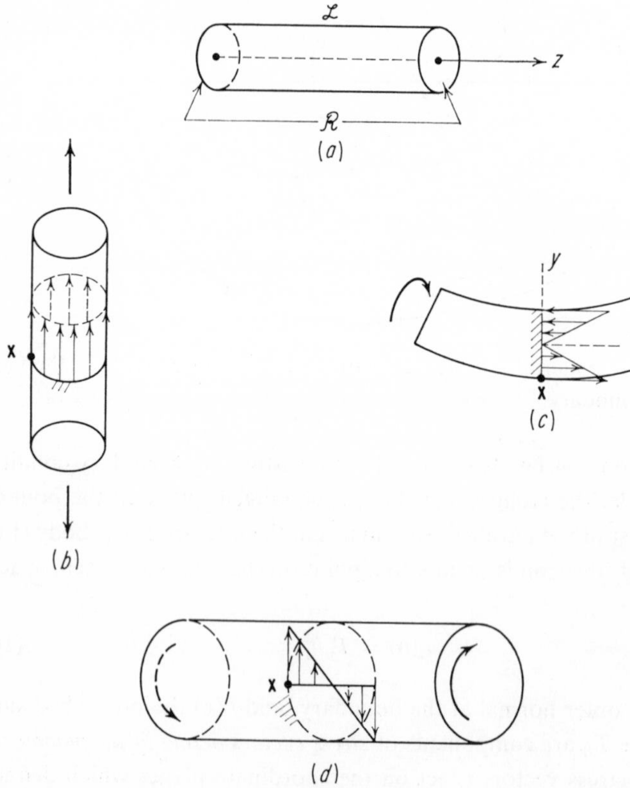

FIGURE 10.8 (*a*) Notation for the boundaries of a prismatic body. (*b–d*) Stress distribution for extension, pure bending, and torsion of a circular cylinder.

For each of the circular cylinders shown in Figure 10.8, the arrow drawn at the boundary point $\mathbf{x}$ represents an internal stress vector, and *not* a surface traction. In the cases (b) and (c) the arrows at $\mathbf{x}$ represent tensions acting on the transverse cross sections; in the case (d) the arrow at $\mathbf{x}$ represents a shearing stress acting on the transverse cross section. In fact, the lateral boundary $\mathscr{L}$ has been assumed here to be a *stress free boundary*. Using a cylindrical coordinate system, we can express this by†

$$T_{\rho\rho} = T_{\rho\phi} = T_{\rho z} = 0, \tag{10.12}$$

or, equivalently, by $t_i(\mathbf{i}_\rho) = T_{\rho i} = 0$. At the end sections $\mathscr{R}$ the surface tractions are prescribed as follows: in the case (b),

$$T_{zz} = \frac{P}{A} = \text{const.}, \qquad T_{z\rho} = T_{z\phi} = 0, \tag{10.13}$$

in the case (c),

$$T_{zz} = -\frac{My}{I}, \frac{M}{I} = \text{const.}, \qquad T_{z\rho} = T_{z\phi} = 0, \tag{10.14}$$

in the case (d),

$$T_{z\phi} = \frac{M\rho}{J}, \frac{M}{J} = \text{const.}, \qquad T_{zz} = T_{z\rho} = 0. \tag{10.15}$$

In general, stress boundary conditions are given only over a portion B_T of the total boundary S; we shall call B_T a *traction boundary*. Another possible boundary condition would be to prescribe the movements of particles which lie in a *displacement boundary* B_u.

Stress equations of motion, energy balance

To derive the field equations expressing the balance of linear and angular momenta, we choose as a "free body" an arbitrary portion V of the region occupied by a body at some instant of time. We denote by $\mathbf{n}$ the outer normal of the boundary ∂V of V (Figure 10.2).

The balance equations (9.34), (9.35) can be applied to any portion of a body provided that a description of the internal forces is available. According to Cauchy's principle, the resultant force acting on the "free body" is given by

$$F_i = \int_{\partial V} t_i(\mathbf{n})\, da + \int_V b_i\, dm,$$

† At a fixed point the distinction between directions $\mathbf{i}_\rho$, $\mathbf{i}_\phi$, $\mathbf{i}_z$ of cylindrical coordinates and Cartesian coordinate directions $\mathbf{e}_x$, $\mathbf{e}_y$, $\mathbf{e}_z$ is a purely notational one, that is, we can equally well write $\mathbf{t}(\mathbf{i}_\rho) = \mathbf{t}_\rho = T_{\rho\rho}\mathbf{i}_\rho + T_{\rho\phi}\mathbf{i}_\phi + T_{\rho z}\mathbf{i}_z$, etc.

where $\mathbf{t}(\mathbf{n})$ are the (internal) stress vectors acting on the surface of separation. We now use $t_i(\mathbf{n}) = T_{ji}n_j$ and apply the divergence theorem to the surface integral:

$$F_i = \int_V (T_{ji,j} + \rho b_i)\, dv.$$

Then the balance equation (9.34) becomes

$$\int_V (T_{ji,j} + \rho b_i - \rho \dot{v}_i)\, dv = 0.$$

Assuming that the integrands are continuous in every region V, we obtain the *Cauchy's equations*

$$T_{ji,j} + \rho b_i = \rho \dot{v}_i. \tag{10.16}$$

To derive the field equations expressing the balance of angular momentum, we proceed in the same way. In view of (10.9), the expression (9.32) for the resultant external torque may be written as

$$L_i^{[0]} = \int_{\partial V} \varepsilon_{ijk} x_j T_{mk} n_m\, da + \int_V \varepsilon_{ijk} x_j b_k\, dm.$$

Applying the divergence theorem to the surface integrals, we find that (9.35) reduces to

$$\int_V [\varepsilon_{imk} T_{mk} + \varepsilon_{ijk} x_j (T_{mk,m} + \rho b_k - \rho \dot{v}_k)]\, dm = 0.$$

Taking into account (10.16) we see that *the balance of angular momentum is satisfied only if the stress tensor is symmetric*:

$$T_{ij} = T_{ji}. \tag{10.17}$$

The equations (10.16), (10.17) are also referred to as the *stress equations of motion*. They express the balance of linear and angular momenta in a "pure" form, because no special assumptions about the nature of the bodies have been made.† In particular, (10.16) and (10.17) hold also for rigid bodies, but

† Strictly speaking this is not true, because it has been assumed that internal forces are describable in terms of stress vectors. However, no special assumptions were made concerning the "mechanical properties," such as elasticity or viscosity.

there the problem would remain indeterminate: because no additional equations are available for rigid bodies, we are left with only 3 equations for the 9 unknowns T_{ij}, v_i.

To obtain a differential representation of the energy balance, we let $\bar{t}_i = T_{ji}n_j$ in (9.58), then use the divergence theorem to convert $v_i T_{ji} n_j \, da$ into $(v_{i,j}T_{ji} + v_i T_{ji,j})\, dv$. Cancelling the terms which make up the vanishing expression (10.16), we arrive at the following reduced form of the energy balance,

$$\int_V \dot{\varepsilon}\, dm = \int_V (\rho r + v_{i,j}T_{ji})\, dv + \int_{\partial V} h\, da. \tag{10.18}$$

Let us now choose V to be an infinitesimal tetrahedron, in which case the volume integrals are infinitesimals of a higher order than the surface integral, thus leaving

$$\int_{\partial V} h\, da = 0. \tag{10.19}$$

If the area of the face associated with the normal $\mathbf{n}$ is A, then the areas of the faces that are parallel to the coordinate planes are given by An_i. Recalling that h is a flux in the direction of $-\mathbf{n}$, we denote by h_i the fluxes in the coordinate directions ("Cartesian component notation"!). Then, by (10.19) and the mean value theorem, $hA + h_1An_1 + h_2An_2 + h_3An_3 = 0$, thus†

$$-h(\mathbf{n}) = h_i n_i. \tag{10.20}$$

This proves that h_i constitute a vector (i.e. $h(\mathbf{n})$ is a scalar state). To obtain the classical representation of the energy balance, it remains to substitute (10.20) back into (10.18), and apply the divergence theorem to the surface integral. We obtain

$$\rho\dot{\varepsilon} + \operatorname{div}\mathbf{h} - \rho r = T_{ji}v_{i,j}. \tag{10.21}$$

In view of the symmetry of $\mathbf{T}$, this can be also written as

$$\rho\dot{\varepsilon} + \operatorname{div}\mathbf{h} - \rho r = T_{ij}D_{ij}. \tag{10.22}$$

Jump conditions

At a surface of discontinuity, S, the balance equations introduced in this section must be replaced by appropriate *jump conditions*. A model of these

† To avoid the minus sign in (10.20), we should replace h by $-h$ in (10.18).

transformations is provided by (9.66), (9.67). Thus while the energy balance (9.56) still holds, to evaluate $\dot{K}$ and $\dot{E}$ we must take into account (9.65). Let us take as the region R a thin slice containing S in its interior. In the limit as the thickness of the slice tends to zero we shall be left with

$$- [\![\rho(\varepsilon + k)\overline{V}]\!] = [\![t_i v_i + h]\!], \tag{10.23}$$

where k is the density of kinetic energy, and ε is the density of internal energy. In Galilean transformations $\mathbf{v} \to \mathbf{v} + \dot{\boldsymbol{\alpha}}$, the (relative) speed of propagation, $\overline{V}$, remains the same, hence we find from (10.23) that

$$[\![\rho\overline{V}]\!] = 0, \qquad (9.68)\text{R}$$

$$[\![\rho v_i \overline{V} + t_i(\mathbf{n})]\!] = 0. \tag{10.24}$$

To summarize, across the surface of discontinuity the jump conditions for mass and linear momentum are given by (9.68) and (10.24), respectively, whereas (10.23) represents the energy balance.

If the surface of discontinuity is stationary relative to the medium, then $\overline{V} = 0$, so that (10.24) reduces to

$$[\![t_i(\mathbf{n})]\!] = 0. \tag{10.25}$$

This reduction also holds at any surface of discontinuity satisfying $[\![\mathbf{v}]\!] = \mathbf{0}$. It should be noted that jump conditions impose no limitations on stress vectors acting at a surface of discontinuity but not *on* it. For instance, if two bodies are bonded together, or held together in any other way (e.g. as in a shrink fit), then the stresses acting on planes normal to the surface of contact may suffer an arbitrary jump (cf. Figure 10.9).

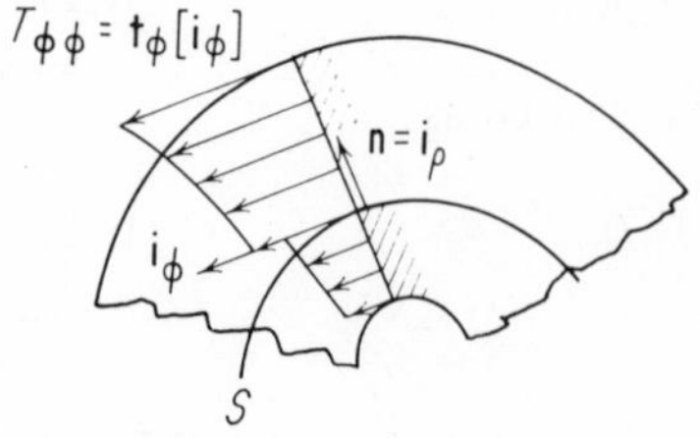

FIGURE 10.9 Discontinuity of "tangential" stresses $T_{\phi\phi}$ at the junction of two bodies.

According to (10.24), we also have that $[\![\rho\bar{v}\overline{V}]\!] = -[\![\overline{T}]\!]$,where $\bar{v} = v_{\underline{\mathrm{n}}}$, $\overline{T} = T_{ij}n_i n_j$. Because $[\![\bar{v}]\!] = -[\![\overline{V}]\!]$, it follows that $[\![\overline{T} - \rho\overline{V}^2]\!] = 0$. Writing

$[\![\overline{T}]\!] = \rho^+(\overline{V}^+)^2 - \rho^-(\overline{V}^-)^2 = (\rho^-\overline{V}^-)^2/\rho^+ - \rho^-(\overline{V}^-)^2 = -(\rho^-/\rho^+)(\overline{V}^-)^2[\![\rho]\!] = -\overline{V}^-\overline{V}^+[\![\rho]\!]$, we arrive at the *Rankine-Hugoniot equation*

$$\overline{V}^+\overline{V}^- = -\frac{[\![\overline{T}]\!]}{[\![\rho]\!]}. \tag{10.26}$$

Evidently in a compression shock the normal pressure $-\overline{T}$ must increase.

To reduce the energy balance (10.23), we let $\mathbf{v} = \bar{v}\mathbf{n} + \hat{v}\mathbf{s}$, where $\mathbf{s}$ is a unit vector lying in the surface of discontinuity. Then $t_i v_i = \overline{T}\bar{v} + \hat{T}\hat{v}$, $\hat{T} = T_{ji}n_j s_i$ being the shearing component, in the direction of $\mathbf{s}$, of the stress vector $\mathbf{t}(\mathbf{n})$ acting on S. With $\bar{v} = \bar{u} - \overline{V}$, $[\![\bar{u}]\!] = 0$ and $[\![\bar{v}]\!] = -[\![\overline{V}]\!]$, we now have that $[\![\overline{T}\bar{v} + \hat{T}\hat{v} + h]\!] = -\rho^\pm\overline{V}^\pm[\![\varepsilon + \tfrac{1}{2}\overline{V}^2 + \tfrac{1}{2}\hat{v}^2 - \bar{u}\overline{V}]\!]$. The term $[\![\overline{T}\bar{v}]\!]$ can be eliminated as follows. We start with the identity $[\![\overline{T}\bar{v}]\!] = \bar{u}[\![\overline{T}]\!] - [\![\overline{T}\overline{V}]\!] = \bar{u}[\![\overline{T}]\!] - [\![(1/\rho)\overline{T}\rho\overline{V}]\!]$, and, by (9.68), (10.26), obtain

$$[\![\overline{T}\bar{v}]\!] = -\bar{u}\rho^\pm\overline{V}^\pm[\![\bar{v}]\!] - \rho^\pm\overline{V}^\pm\left[\!\!\left[\frac{\overline{T}}{\rho}\right]\!\!\right] = \bar{u}\rho^\pm\overline{V}^\pm[\![\overline{V}]\!] - \rho^\pm\overline{V}^\pm\left[\!\!\left[\frac{\overline{T}}{\rho}\right]\!\!\right],$$

so that the energy balance (10.23) reduces to

$$-\rho^\pm\overline{V}^\pm\left[\!\!\left[\varepsilon + \frac{1}{2}\overline{V}^2 - \frac{\overline{T}}{\rho} + \frac{1}{2}\hat{v}^2\right]\!\!\right] = [\![h + \hat{T}\hat{v}]\!]. \tag{10.27}$$

If S is neither a shock nor a vortex sheet, then (10.27) yields *Fourier's condition*

$$[\![h(\mathbf{n})]\!] = 0. \tag{10.28}$$

In gas dynamics we assume that stress is spherical, $\mathbf{T} = -p(\rho)\mathbf{1}$. Because at a shock front $[\![\hat{v}]\!] = 0$, (10.28) then reduces to

$$-\left[\!\!\left[\varepsilon + \frac{p}{\rho} + \frac{1}{2}\overline{V}^2\right]\!\!\right] = \frac{[\![h]\!]}{\rho^\pm\overline{V}^\pm}. \tag{10.29}$$

Problems

A. STRESS TENSOR, BOUNDARY CONDITIONS

1. Calculate and plot the surface tractions on a sphere, a cube, and a tetrahedron if (*a*) $T = -p\mathbf{1}$ (*b*) $Tij = a = \text{const}$.
2. Consider the following typical solution of elasticity theory in cylindrical coordinates, describing the state of stress in a circular cylinder subject to internal pressure p and external pressure q (it is assumed that an elongation or

shortening of the cylinder is prevented): $\mathbf{t}(\mathbf{i}_\rho) \equiv \mathbf{t}_\rho = \mathbf{i}_\rho T_{\rho\rho}$, $\mathbf{t}(\mathbf{i}_\phi) \equiv \mathbf{t}_\phi = \mathbf{i}_\phi T_{\phi\phi}$, $\mathbf{t}(\mathbf{i}_z) \equiv \mathbf{t}_z = \mathbf{i}_z T_{zz}$,

$$T_{\rho\rho} = -\left[p\left(\frac{b^2}{\rho^2} - 1\right) + q\left(\frac{b^2}{a^2}\right)\left(1 - \frac{a^2}{\rho^2}\right)\right]\Big/\Delta,$$

$$T_{\phi\phi} = \left[p\left(\frac{b^2}{\rho^2} + 1\right) - q\left(\frac{b^2}{a^2}\right)\left(1 + \frac{a^2}{\rho^2}\right)\right]\Big/\Delta,$$

$$T_{zz} = 2\nu\,\frac{pa^2 - qb^2}{b^2 - a^2},$$

$$\Delta = \frac{b^2}{a^2} - 1, \qquad a \le \dot{\rho} \le b,$$

where ν is a material property (*Poisson's ratio*). Make a sketch of the cylinder, and investigate the limits of $\mathbf{t}_\rho$ and $\mathbf{t}_\phi$ as $\rho \to a$ or $\rho \to b$ (which of these stress vectors becomes a surface traction?). Also, calculate and sketch the stress vector $\mathbf{t}(\mathbf{n})$ for

a. $\rho = a = 1, \quad \mathbf{n} = \dfrac{1}{\sqrt{2}}\mathbf{i}_\rho + \dfrac{1}{\sqrt{2}}\mathbf{i}_\phi \quad (\text{let } b = 2)$

b. $\rho = b = 2, \quad \mathbf{n} = \dfrac{1}{\sqrt{2}}\mathbf{i}_\rho - \dfrac{1}{\sqrt{2}}\mathbf{i}_\phi \quad (\text{let } a = 1)$

3. Let $T_{xx} = (3P/2c^3)(L - x)y$, $T_{xy} = -(3P/4c)(1 - y^2/c^2)$, $T_{yy} = T_{xz} = T_{yz} = T_{zz} = 0$, and consider the parallelepiped $-h \le z \le h$, $-c \le y \le c$, $0 \le x \le L$. Determine the distribution of surface tractions on each of the six boundaries of the body (because the solution is a two-dimensional one, a sketch in the xy plane is sufficient).

4. Repeat the calculations of the preceding problem for the stress field given in (10.1).

5. Let $T_{rr} = A[1 - 2p(2 - \nu)/(1 - 2\nu)]$, $T_{\theta\theta} = Ap^2(1 + p)$,

$$T_{\phi\phi} = \frac{A(p^2 + p - 1)}{1 + p}, \qquad T_{r\theta} = \frac{Apq}{1 + p}, \qquad T_{r\phi} = T_{\theta\phi} = 0,$$

where $p = \cos\theta$, $q = \sin\theta$, $A = P(1 - 2\nu)/2\pi r^2$ (P, ν are constants), and consider a body occupying the region $r > r_0$, $z > 0$ (i.e. the boundary consists of $z = 0$, $r_0 \le r < \infty$ and $r = r_0$, $0 \le \theta \le \pi/2$, $0 \le \phi \le 2\pi$).

a. Determine the distribution of surface tractions.
b. Calculate the load $\mathbf{F}$ acting on the boundary.

6. Let $T_{\rho\phi} = T_{\phi\phi} = T_{\rho z} = T_{\phi z} = T_{zz} = 0$, $T_{\rho\rho} = -P\cos\phi/\rho(\alpha + \frac{1}{2}\sin 2\alpha)$, and consider a body occupying the region $-h \le z \le h$, $\rho \ge \rho_0$, $-\alpha \le \phi \le \alpha$ (P, α, h are constants).

a. Determine the distribution of surface tractions.
b. Calculate the load $\mathbf{F}$ acting on the boundary.

7. Let $T_{\rho z} = T_{\phi z} = T_{zz} = 0$, $T_{\rho\rho} = -(3+\nu)P\cos\phi/4\pi\rho$, $T_{\phi\phi} = (1-\nu)P\cos\phi/4\pi\rho$, $T_{\rho\phi} = (1-\nu)P\sin\phi/4\pi\rho$, and consider a body occupying the region $-h \le z \le h$, $\rho \ge \rho_0$, $-\pi \le \phi \le \pi$ (P, h, ν are constants).

   a. Determine the distribution of surface tractions.

   b. Calculate the load **F** acting on the boundary.

8. In the example (10.13), show that $T_{zz} = P/A$, all other T_{ij} being equal to zero, is a solution satisfying the boundary conditions $t_i(\mathbf{n}) = 0$ on the lateral boundary.

9. Repeat the preceding problem when

   a. $T_{zz} = -\dfrac{My}{I}$, all other $T_{ij} = 0$.

   b. $T_{zx} = -\dfrac{Mx}{J}$, $T_{zy} = \dfrac{My}{J}$, all other $T_{ij} = 0$.

B. STRESS EQUATIONS OF MOTION

10. Verify the derivation of Navier's equations of elasticity, given in the Introduction. How will the result be affected if $F(r)$ is replaced by $f(\bar{r}) \doteq f(r) + (\bar{r} - r)f'(r)$. How would you go about deriving the equations of motion of a viscous fluid?

11. Show that the stress equations of motion are satisfied by the stresses given by

    a. Problem 2 **b.** Problem 3 **c.** Problem 9a **d.** Problem 9b

12. Consider $T_{xx} = 4x$, $T_{xy} = 6x - 4y$, $T_{yy} = -6y + 4x$, $T_{xz} = T_{yz} = T_{zz} = 0$. Do these stresses satisfy the equations of equilibrium? Sketch the variation of the surface tractions on the body for which the cross section is shown in the drawing.

13. Let $T_{xx} = -Ay$, $T_{zz} = 0 = T_{xz} = T_{yz}$,

$$T_{yy} = \left[\frac{P}{\tan\alpha} - \frac{2A}{\tan^3\alpha}\right]x + \left[\frac{A}{\tan^2\alpha} - P\right]y,$$

$$T_{xy} = -\frac{Ax}{\tan^2\alpha}.$$

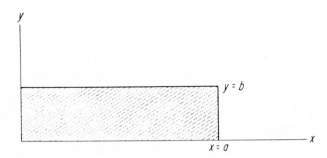

Considering P as a body force, do these stresses satisfy the equations of equilibrium? Sketch the surface tractions acting on the body shown below.

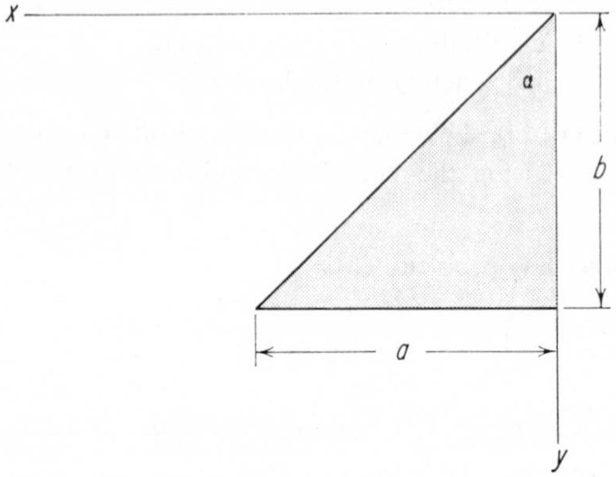

14. Let T_{ij} be a two-dimensional state of stress, by which we mean that $T_{zx} = T_{zy} = T_{zz} = 0$. In the absence of body forces the stress equations of equilibrium are identically satisfied by letting

$$T_{xx} = \frac{\partial^2 F}{\partial y^2}, \qquad T_{yy} = \frac{\partial^2 F}{\partial x^2}, \qquad T_{xy} = -\frac{\partial^2 F}{\partial x \partial y},$$

where F is referred to as the Airy's stress function. What problem is solved by $F = C[\rho^2(\alpha - \phi) + \rho^2 \sin\phi \cos\phi - \rho^2 \cos^2\phi \tan\alpha]$, where ρ, ϕ are plane polar coordinates, C, α are constants, and the cross section of the prismatic body is bounded by $y = 0$ and $\phi = \alpha$? (Determine the nature and the distribution of the surface tractions).

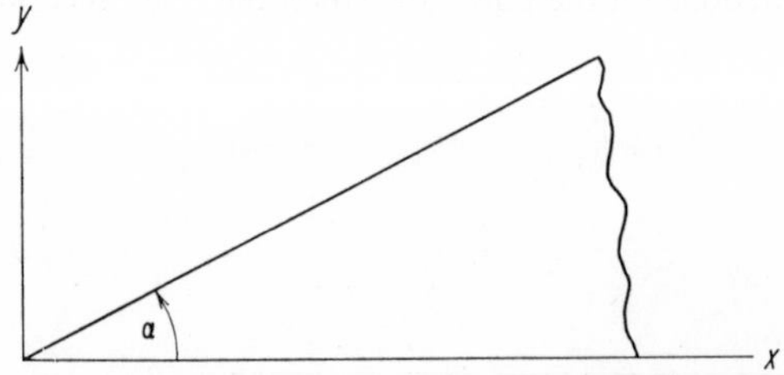

15. Let the body occupy the infinite half-space $y \geq 0$. What problem is solved by the Airy's function

$$F = \frac{P}{2\pi}\left\{(x^2 + y^2)\tan^{-1}\frac{y}{x} - xy\right\}?$$

16. Verify the derivation of (10.21).

C. JUMP CONDITIONS

17. Derive (10.29) from (9.58).

18. Derive (10.24) from (10.23).

Section 11
MULTIPOLAR MEDIA*†

So far the geometrical model of a body has been a "continuum" of particles, the only geometrical property of a particle being its position. A closer look at materials will naturally reveal grains, crystals, complex molecules, and other topological features of the arrangement of matter that are not taken into account by the geometrical model of the classical theories. If an observer is far enough removed from a huge organic molecule, he will see the molecule as a point, a "particle." But a theory that strips away all the geometrical characteristics of a molecule, save the position of its mass center, may also fail to explain the finer aspects of mechanical behavior. In the framework of multipolar continuum mechanics, a molecule may be represented by a "deformable particle" that is a true replica of a deformable body, possessing its own internal strains ("microstrains"). These strains represent certain types of *collective behavior* of the sub-particles that constitute the molecule, e.g. homogeneous deformation of the molecule. We hasten to add that the particular model of fat particles is as helpful in some ways as it is misleading in others. The added kinematical tensors can be given a variety of interpretations, but it is best to explore them in the context of special theories.

It goes without saying that theories of multipolar continuum mechanics are very specialized. They supply a more faithful description of the microstructure of materials, but by the same token each of these theories can be expected to apply only to a small class of materials. The classical continuum mechanics (which may be called *monopolar continuum mechanics* in the present context), on the other hand, describes only those macroscopic features of motion which are shared by all substances; consequently, it more than makes up in breadth of application what it lacks in depth of perception.

The theories of multipolar continuum mechanics are still in a state of growth, so that an orderly presentation of these theories is not possible. Therefore, we can do no more than survey the ideas found in the current literature (cf. *CFT*, p. 548, [30], [49], [96], [170]).

Some models of microstructure

Examples of microstructure that are instructive (though not necessarily realistic), are afforded by particles $\mathscr{P}$ that are revealed, upon further magnification, to be true replicas of finite bodies or systems of "sub-particles" P. The mass and the coordinates of a typical sub-particle will be denoted by m_P

† In special instances multipolar media are also referred to as oriented media, media with microstructure, materials of grade N, Cosserat continua, structured continua.

and x_{Pi}, where P is a *label*. In particular, summation over P from 1 to N will be indicated by the symbol **S**. Thus the total mass of $\mathscr{P}$ is $m = \mathbf{S}m_P$, and its mass center is defined in the usual way:

$$m\mathbf{c} = \mathbf{S}m_P\mathbf{x}_P. \tag{a}$$

In a passage to a continuum of particles $\mathscr{P}$, $\mathbf{c}$ is replaced by the continuous variable $\mathbf{x}$.

Let us now look at the second moments of mass, as seen by an observer whose vision is keener than the vision of a "macroscopic observer": $\mathbf{S}m_Px_{Pi}x_{Pj}$. Introducing the relative positions $\bar{\mathbf{x}}_P = \mathbf{x}_P - \mathbf{c}$ of sub-particles, we find that, in view of (a),

$$\mathbf{S}m_Px_{Pi}x_{Pj} = mc_ic_j + \mathbf{S}m_P\bar{x}_{Pi}\bar{x}_{Pj}. \tag{b}$$

It is evident that $(9.3)_2$ corresponds only to the first term of the right-hand side of (b). Consequently, if microstructure is to be accounted for, then (9.3) should be replaced by relations of the type†

$$m_i = \int_V x_i\,dm + \int_V \alpha_i\,dm,$$

$$m_{ij} = \int_V x_ix_j\,dm + \int_V (x_i\alpha_j + \alpha_ix_j)\,dm + \int_V \beta_{ij}\,dm,$$

etc., where α_i is referred to as *vector polarization*, β_{ij} as *tensor polarization*, and so on. In the present example the vector polarization vanishes, but the tensor polarization does not. In mechanics of rigid bodies, a body is specified in terms of the "mass-center particle" and the "polarization tensor" I_{ij}.

The various dynamical measures of motion can be investigated along the same lines. For instance, taking into account that $m\dot{\mathbf{c}} = \mathbf{S}m_P\mathbf{v}_P$, $\mathbf{S}m_P\bar{\mathbf{v}}_P = \mathbf{0}$, we obtain

$$\mathbf{S}m_Px_{Pi}v_{Pj} = mc_i\dot{c}_j + \mathbf{S}m_P\bar{x}_{Pi}\bar{v}_{Pj}. \tag{c}$$

A continuum theory will describe only certain simple modes of the internal motions, e.g. "homogeneous stretching"

$$\bar{v}_{Pj} = v_{jk}\bar{x}_{Pk}, \tag{d}$$

† Cf. the work of Dahler and Scriven [30].

where v_{jk} may be referred to as *dipolar velocities* (they are the counterparts of the velocity gradients $v_{i,j}$ describing the rates of deformation of what could be imagined as a network of lines connecting the mass centers of $\mathscr{P}$). Then (c) reduces to

$$\mathbf{S}m_P x_{Pi} v_{Pj} = m c_i \dot{c}_j + m_{ik} v_{jk}, \qquad m_{ik} = \mathbf{S}m_P \bar{x}_{Pi} \bar{x}_{Pk}, \tag{e}$$

whereas the kinetic energy is decomposed as follows,

$$\frac{1}{2}\mathbf{S}m_P v_{Pi} v_{Pi} = \frac{1}{2} m \dot{c}_i \dot{c}_i + \frac{1}{2} m_{jk} v_{ij} v_{ik}. \tag{f}$$

If the internal motions are described in greater detail, e.g. $\bar{v}_{Pi} = v_{ij}\bar{x}_{Pj} + v_{ijk}\bar{x}_{Pj}\bar{x}_{Pk} + \ldots$, then the representations of the dynamical measures must be modified accordingly.

The preceding formulas become particularly neat if the particles $\mathscr{P}$ are assumed to be "rigid," so that v_{ij} in (d) is replaced by an *intrinsic angular velocity* $\Sigma_{ij} = -\frac{1}{2}\varepsilon_{ijk}\sigma_k$:

$$\bar{v}_{Pi} = \Sigma_{ij}\bar{x}_{Pj}. \tag{d)*$$

Then the angular momentum $h_k = \frac{1}{2}\varepsilon_{ijk}\mathbf{S}m_P x_{Pi} v_{Pj}$ is given by

$$\mathbf{H} = m(\mathbf{c} \times \dot{\mathbf{c}}) + m\boldsymbol{\eta}, \tag{g}$$

where

$$\boldsymbol{\eta} = \mathbf{i}\boldsymbol{\sigma} \tag{h}$$

is the density of *intrinsic angular momentum*, and $i_{jk} = (m_{rr}\delta_{jk} - m_{jk})/m$ is the *intrinsic inertia tensor*.

Particles that are replicas of a rigid body are traditionally called *oriented particles*, and a continuum of oriented particles a *Cosserat continuum*. This particular interpretation of Cosserat continua is of course not binding; what matters is that aside from a velocity field $\mathbf{v}(\mathbf{x}, t)$ there exists now another, independent field of kinematical variables $\boldsymbol{\Sigma}(\mathbf{x}, t)$. The orientations are described by a field of orthogonal tensors $\mathbf{Q}$ (so that $\boldsymbol{\Sigma} = \dot{\mathbf{Q}}^T\mathbf{Q}$), or, equivalently, by triads of unit vectors (*directors*) $\mathbf{d}_a(\mathbf{x}, t)$, $a = 1, 2, 3$. A few additional models of microstructure are illustrated below.

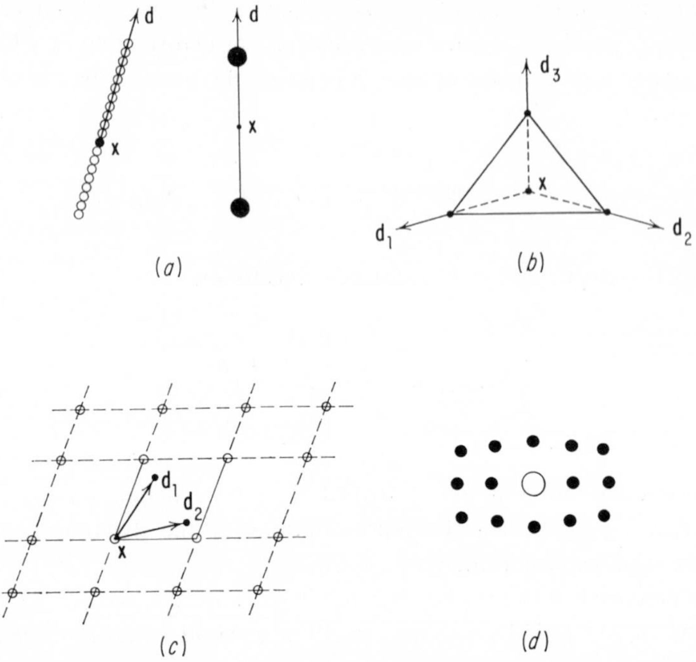

FIGURE 11.1 Models of microstructure: (*a*) Elongated molecules, (*b*) Oriented particle ("grain"), (*c*) Unit cell of a lattice, (*d*) Inclusion in a lattice.

Rod-like or dumb-bell molecules (Figure 11.1a) are particular instances of oriented particles. For a typical "particle," we select a reference point **X**, located at **x**, and adjoin to it a director **d** that is attached to **X** and accounts for the orientation and stretching of the molecule. If the stretching is negligible, then **d** can be taken as a unit vector: **d** = **n**. The motion of points **X** is described in the usual way: $x_i = x_i(\mathbf{X}, \tau)$. The additional variables $d_i(\mathbf{X}, \tau)$ constitute, so to speak, a superstructure erected over the classical continuum model.

Examples in which the number of directors is neither one nor three are not difficult to find. For instance, we can identify "particles" with unit cells in a crystalline lattice (Figure 11.1c). The motion $x_i = x_i(\mathbf{X}, \tau)$ then refers to the mean displacements of the cells, whereas the microdeformation, which has to do with the displacements of atoms within a cell, is described in terms of the directors $\mathbf{d}_A$, $A = 1, 2, \ldots, N$. In particular, the microdeformation may be locally homogeneous, so that all directors $\mathbf{D}_A$ of a cell are mapped by a single tensor x_{im} into their final configurations $\mathbf{d}_A$: $d_{Ai} = x_{im}D_{Am}$. Here x_{im} describe in general "incompatible" deformations in the sense that x_{im} need not be gradients of a vector field in the way that $F_{im} = x_{i,m}$ are. This means that, as a rule, microdeformations cannot be pieced together to form a smooth and one-valued displacement field (microdeformations of this type have been conjectured as a model of martensite transformations, cf. [191]).

The idea of microdeformation can be also used to describe inclusions within a lattice, e.g. foreign atoms (Figure 11.1d). Here the effect of an inclusion may be similar to that of a "double-force."†

Along with the resultant force $\mathbf{F} = \mathbf{S}\mathbf{F}_P$, we introduce the moments $F_{ij} = \mathbf{S}F_{Pi}\bar{x}_{Pj}$, $F_{ijk} = \mathbf{S}F_{Pi}\bar{x}_{Pj}\bar{x}_{Pk}$, etc., also referred to as *multipolar forces*. With $\bar{v}_{Pi} = v_{ij}\bar{x}_{Pj} + v_{ijk}\bar{x}_{Pj}\bar{x}_{Pk} + \ldots$, these forces are obtained as coefficients in the expansion of the mechanical power,

$$M = \mathbf{S}F_{Pi}v_{Pi} = F_i\dot{c}_i + F_{ij}v_{ij} + F_{ijk}v_{ijk} + \cdots. \tag{i}$$

The vector $\beta_k = -\frac{1}{2}\varepsilon_{kij}F_{ij}$ is the counterpart of *distributed couples* in the continuum theories.

The behavior of an ensemble of particles can be deduced from the basic laws governing a single particle. In particular, there may exist modes of collective behavior which obey fairly simple laws. The motion of the mass center is a case in point; assuming that $\mathbf{F}_P = m_P\ddot{\mathbf{x}}_P$, we readily obtain $\mathbf{F} = m\ddot{\mathbf{c}}$, the common translation $\mathbf{c}$ being the simplest mode of collective behavior. Moreover, if the forces $\mathbf{F}_P$ are decomposed into internal forces (exerted from within $\mathscr{P}$) and external forces (exerted from without $\mathscr{P}$), then, subject to suitable assumptions (e.g. "Newton's third law"), it follows that $\mathbf{F}$ is the resultant of external forces only. In this case the motion $\mathbf{c} = \mathbf{c}(t)$ is independent of any "constitutive equations" describing the nature of the internal forces. To determine more complex modes of behavior, it is necessary, as a rule, to prescribe these constitutive equations. For instance, a good many cosmological problems have to do with the collective behavior of gravitating particles (nebulae!). What is nowadays called in physics the "N-body problem" deals with similar problems, but the particles are atoms, ions, and so on. In contrast, the method of continuum mechanics is to formulate outright the laws that govern simple types of collective behavior. A correlation of some of the "N-body problems" with theories of multipolar continuum mechanics is an exciting prospect for the future.‡

Multipolar velocities, body forces, and stresses

In multipolar continuum mechanics the emphasis lies on kinematical variables even more so than in classical continuum mechanics. Each member

† The construction of double-forces is illustrated on pp. 229, 230.

‡ The correspondence between lattice theories and continuum theories of elasticity is briefly reviewed in Section 16.

of a set of basic kinematical variables assigned to a body represents a characteristic mode of motion. The corresponding multipolar stresses are far more difficult to visualize; one is often inclined to consider them as mere names for expressions involving kinematical tensors and certain "material properties." As was illustrated in the preceding subsection, in particular instances each multipolar velocity has a definite interpretation. However, right now such interpretations serve no other purpose than to give an idea of what the theory is about, because the general form of the balance equations for multipolar media must be the same for any interpretation of multipolar velocities. The only thing that must be known about multipolar velocities is their behavior in observer transformations. Thus we may consider multipolar velocities $V_{ij}, V_{ijk}, \ldots$ that are modeled after the velocity gradients $v_{i,j}, v_{i,jk}, \ldots$, so that the observer transformations are given by $V_{ij}^+ \to V_{ij} + \Omega_{ij}^+$, $V_{ijk}^+ \to V_{ijk}, \ldots$. Alternatively, recalling from (8.56) that

$$\frac{\partial}{\partial \tau} x_{i,m}(\tau)\bigg|_{\tau=t} = v_{i,m} = L_{im},$$

we may define multipolar velocities $v_{im} = v_{im}(t)$, $v_{imn} = v_{imn}(t), \ldots$, by

$$v_{im} = \frac{\partial}{\partial \tau} \phi_{im}(\tau)\bigg|_{\tau=t}, \tag{11.1}$$

etc., the deformation tensors $\phi_{im}, \phi_{imn}, \ldots$, being modeled after $\partial x_i(\tau)/\partial x_m$, $\partial^2 x_i(\tau)/\partial x_m \partial x_n$, where $\mathbf{x}$ stands for $\mathbf{x}(t)$ (even though $x_{i,m}(t) = \delta_{im}$, $x_{i,mn}(t) = 0, \ldots$, we do *not* assume that the same is true of $\phi_{im}, \phi_{imn}, \ldots$). Thus, in analogy with (8.32), we assume that

$$\phi_{ab}^+(\tau) = Q_{ai}(\tau) Q_{bm} \phi_{im}(\tau), \qquad \phi_{abc}^+(\tau) = Q_{ai}(\tau) Q_{bm} Q_{cn} \phi_{imn}(\tau),$$
$$\phi_{ab,c}^+(\tau) = Q_{ai}(\tau) Q_{bm} Q_{ck} \phi_{im,k}(\tau), \tag{11.2}$$

etc., where $\mathbf{Q} = \mathbf{Q}(t)$. From these it follows that

$$\begin{aligned} v_{ab}^+ &= Q_{ai} Q_{bm} (v_{im} + \Omega_{ij}^+ \phi_{jm}), \\ v_{abc}^+ &= Q_{ai} Q_{bm} Q_{cn} (v_{imn} + \Omega_{ij}^+ \phi_{jmn}), \\ v_{ab,c}^+ &= Q_{ai} Q_{bm} Q_{ck} (v_{im\ k} + \Omega_{ij}^+ \phi_{jm,k}), \end{aligned} \tag{11.3}$$

etc. From the multipolar velocities we can construct objective variables as follows,

$$\beta_{im} \equiv v_{im} + L_{ji} \phi_{jm}, \qquad \beta_{im|k} \equiv v_{im,k} + L_{ji} \phi_{jm,k}, \tag{11.4}$$

etc.

To simplify the appearance of formulas, we shall confine our attention for the most part to *dipolar media*, in which case the kinematical variables are v_i and a dipolar velocity. To be specific, let us choose the latter to be v_{ij}, so that the density of kinetic energy is given by

$$k = \frac{1}{2} v_i v_i + \frac{1}{2} a_{mn} v_{im} v_{in} \tag{11.5}$$

(cf. (f)). The term $\frac{1}{2}a_{mn}v_{im}v_{in}$ can be interpreted by introducing "micro-coordinates" π_i such that $\dot{\pi}_i = v_{im}\pi_m$. Then $\frac{1}{2}\dot{\pi}_i\dot{\pi}_i = \frac{1}{2}a_{mn}v_{im}v_{in}$, where $a_{mn} = \pi_m\pi_n$ characterizes the arrangement of the "micromasses"; it is, in essence, equivalent to a tensor introduced by Ericksen [29] for describing macromolecules. Moreover,

$$\dot{a}_{mn} = v_{mk}a_{kn} + v_{nk}a_{km}. \tag{11.6}$$

The study of stress can be approached either from a synthetic viewpoint or from a formal viewpoint. In the synthetic method we begin with the ordinary concept of force, and then proceed to construct couples, double-forces, etc. in the same way that electric dipoles, quadrupoles, etc. are constructed from point charges. There are no simple interpretations of the more complex forces, and any particular interpretation is likely to involve special assumptions about the microstructure. For instance, if a material is viewed as an aggregate of small yet deformable particles, then within each particle there are "microstresses" M_{kij} which are the counterparts of the stresses T_{ij} associated with the macrodeformation. In general we should admit an entire hierarchy of forces: (monopolar) body forces b_i, (monopolar) stresses T_{ij}, dipolar body forces b_{ij}, dipolar stresses M_{kij}, and so on.

Roughly speaking, vectors of stress and of couple stress are the counterparts of concentrated forces and couples. To illustrate the synthetic method, let us recall the familiar construction of concentrated couples from concentrated forces. We consider pairs of anti-parallel forces, each of magnitude $1/h$, where h is the distance between the points of application of the forces. In Figure 11.2 three constructions are illustrated separately, but it is understood that they can be performed simultaneously at the same point. We denote by $q_x(h, 0, 0)$ a unit force acting in the x direction, with the point of application at $x = h$, $y = z = 0$; in other cases the same type of notation applies. Then

$$q_{x,x} = \lim_{h \to 0} \frac{1}{h} [q_x(h, 0, 0) - q_x(0, 0, 0)],$$

for instance, defines a *double-force without moment*. Evidently this quantity is obtained by letting the points of application of the pair of forces tend together (i.e. $h \to 0$), while the magnitudes of the forces become infinite as $1/h$. An example of a *double-force with moment* is given by

$$q_{x,y} = \lim_{h \to 0} \frac{1}{h} [q_x(0, h, 0) - q_x(0, 0, 0)].$$

Similarly
$$q_{y,x} = \lim_{h \to 0} \frac{1}{h} [q_y(h, 0, 0) - q_y(0, 0, 0)].$$

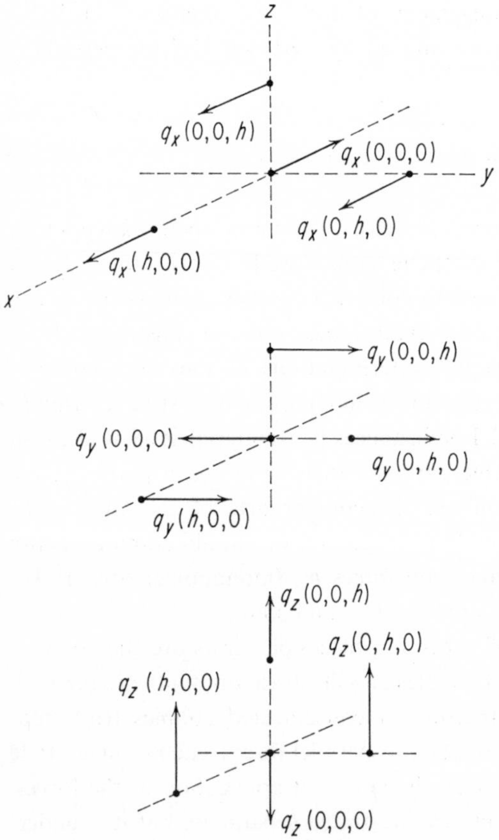

FIGURE 11.2 Diagrams showing the construction of concentrated double-forces.

The moment of $q_x(0, h, 0)/h$ and $q_x(0, 0, 0)/h$ about the z axis is -1, whereas the moment of $q_y(h, 0, 0)/h$ and $q_y(0, 0, 0)/h$ about the z axis is 1, so that one may be tempted to write $q_{x,y} = -q_{y,x}$; but then we might as well set $q_{x,x}$ equal to zero, because statically it is a "zero." The point is of course that static equivalence, defined on the basis of effects produced in a *rigid body*, is not the appropriate criterion in continuum mechanics. Here $q_{x,x}$ is not a "zero," because it produces nonvanishing stresses. Similarly, $q_{x,y}$ and $-q_{y,x}$ are two distinct double-forces that happen to have the same moment. It is in fact not difficult to imagine experiments in which finite, "almost concentrated" double-forces are applied in the manner of $q_{x,y}$ and $q_{y,x}$ to the surface of a body. Our intuition then tells us that there will be a definite directional effect associated with each force pair. However, we can *define* a (pure) couple $B_{[xy]}$ by $B_{[xy]} = \frac{1}{2}(q_{x,y} - q_{y,x})$.

Naturally in continuum mechanics we deal with volume and surface distribution of forces, couples (e.g. $B_{[xy]} = b_{[xy]}\,dv$), double-forces, and so on. In the case of multipolar stresses the plane of action must be also specified; for instance, on a plane whose normal is in the z direction there may exist dipolar stresses M_{zxx}, M_{zxy}, M_{zyx}, M_{zxz}, etc. The couple stresses $M_{z[ij]}$ are then defined by

$$M_{z[ij]} = \frac{1}{2}(M_{zij} - M_{zji}). \tag{11.7}$$

The components M_{zxx}, $M_{z(xy)}$, etc. do not occur in the classical theory. The Cartesian components M_{zij} are illustrated in Figure 11.3.

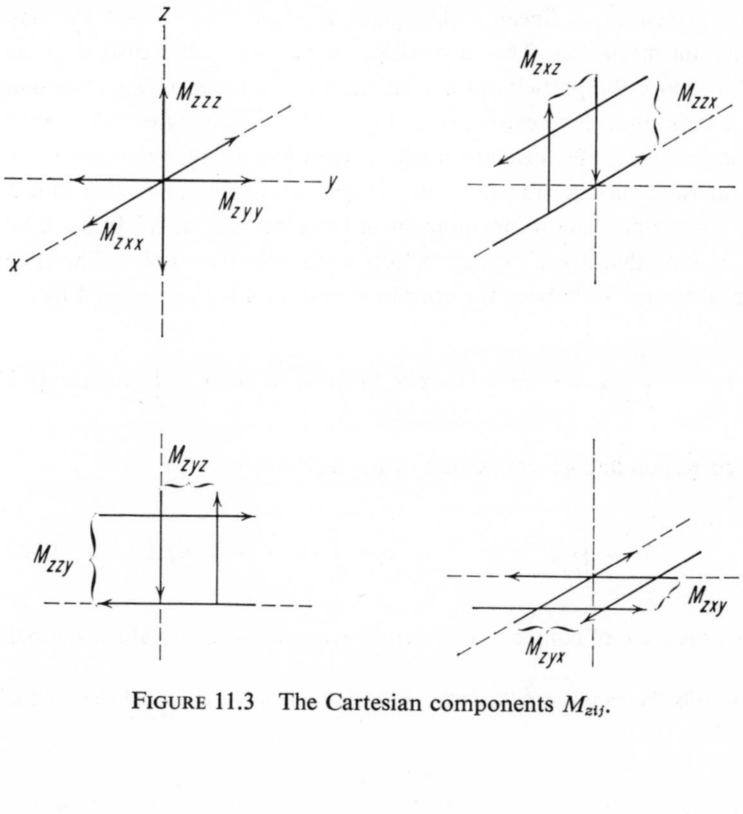

FIGURE 11.3 The Cartesian components M_{zij}.

To provide a background for the formal method, we recall that in Lagrange's equations of dynamics the generalized forces Q_i are defined by the requirement that their products with the corresponding generalized velocities $\dot{q}_i$ add up to the instantaneous power P of the external agencies: $P = Q_i\dot{q}_i$. The formal approach to multipolar stresses is similar.† That is, the mechanical power of body forces and stresses is given by

$$M = \int_V (b_i v_i + b_{ij} v_{ij})\, dm + \int_{\partial V} (t_i v_i + m_{ij} v_{ij})\, da, \qquad (11.8)$$

where m_{ij} are the dipolar surface tractions. Physical interpretations of stresses and body forces can be obtained directly from (11.8). For instance, if v_{11} is of the same nature as the component D_{11} of the stretching tensor, then, assuming that v_{11} is the only mode of deformation which is present, we obtain from (11.8) the interpretation of m_{11} as a double-force without moment. As the complexity of the kinematical tensors increases, the interpretations of the associated multipolar stresses become less tangible. As in the case of Cauchy's stress, we shall assume that *multipolar stresses are objective*.

Balance equations

The principles of linear and angular momenta round out the classical continuum mechanics. They also suffice for a theory of Cosserat continua. In this theory the particles of a medium may be interpreted as "oriented," in the sense that there exists an intrinsic angular velocity $\boldsymbol{\sigma}$ and an intrinsic inertia tensor i_{mn}. We extend Cauchy's stress hypothesis by assuming that in general each surface transmits also *couple stress vectors* $\boldsymbol{\mu}$; the dimension of $\boldsymbol{\mu}$ is force per length (or, moment of force per unit area). In addition, we may assume that a *body couple* $\boldsymbol{\beta}$ acts at each interior point. The resultant external torque $\mathbf{L}^{[0]}$ about the coordinate origin 0 is then defined by

$$\mathbf{L}^{[0]} = \int_{\partial V} (\mathbf{x} \times \mathbf{t})\, da + \int_V (\mathbf{x} \times \mathbf{b})\, dm + \int_{\partial V} \boldsymbol{\mu}\, da + \int_V \boldsymbol{\beta}\, dm. \qquad (9.32)^*$$

The corresponding generalization of the mechanical power is

$$M = \int_{\partial V} (\mathbf{t} \cdot \mathbf{v} + \boldsymbol{\mu} \cdot \boldsymbol{\sigma})\, da + \int_V (\mathbf{b} \cdot \mathbf{v} + \boldsymbol{\beta} \cdot \boldsymbol{\sigma})\, dm. \qquad (9.33)^*$$

The presence of couple stress vectors evidently does not affect the balance

† Ordinarily the term *generalized stresses* is used only in the theory of rods and shells.

of linear momentum. Applying the balance of angular momentum, (9.35), to a thin slice and invoking the previous arguments, we arrive at $\lim_{h\to 0}\left[\int \boldsymbol{\mu}\, da + \int (\mathbf{x} \times \mathbf{t})\, da\right] = \mathbf{0}$. Therefore, by (10.6), $\boldsymbol{\mu}(\mathbf{x}, \mathbf{n}) = -\boldsymbol{\mu}(\mathbf{x}, -\mathbf{n})$. Again, if one face of the slice lies in the boundary of the body, then $\bar{\boldsymbol{\mu}}(\mathbf{x}, \mathbf{n}) = -\boldsymbol{\mu}(\mathbf{x}, -\mathbf{n}) = \boldsymbol{\mu}(\mathbf{x}, \mathbf{n})$, so that $\bar{\boldsymbol{\mu}}$ can be regarded as the boundary values of the couple stresses $\boldsymbol{\mu}$. Applying the balance of angular momentum to a tetrahedron, we get

$$\mu_i(\mathbf{n}) = M_{ji}n_j, \tag{11.9}$$

where $M_{ji} = \mu_i(\mathbf{e}_j)$ are the Cartesian components of the couple stress tensor.

The appropriate generalizations of kinetic energy and angular momentum are

$$\begin{aligned} k &= \frac{1}{2}\mathbf{v} \cdot \mathbf{v} + \frac{1}{2}\boldsymbol{\eta} \cdot \boldsymbol{\sigma}, \\ \mathbf{H}^{[0]} &= \int_V (\mathbf{x} \times \mathbf{v})\, dm + \int_V \boldsymbol{\eta}\, dm, \end{aligned} \tag{11.10}$$

where $\eta_m = i_{mn}\sigma_n$ is referred to as the (density of) *intrinsic angular momentum.* To obtain the differential form of the balance of angular momentum, we substitute (11.9), $(11.10)_2$ into (9.35), then use (10.16), thus arriving at the *Cosserat's equations*

$$M_{ji,j} + \rho\beta_i + \varepsilon_{ijk}T_{jk} = \rho\dot{\eta}_i. \tag{11.11}$$

Evidently the vanishing of intrinsic angular momentum, couple stresses, and body couples requires that the stress tensor $\mathbf{T}$ be symmetric. On the basis of statistical theory, Grad [46] has shown that $\boldsymbol{\eta} = R^2\boldsymbol{\sigma}$, where $\boldsymbol{\sigma}$ is the intrinsic angular velocity of particles, and R is a radius of gyration of particles.

Because stresses as well as couple stresses are assumed to be objective, it follows from (11.11) that the *effective body couples* $\bar{\boldsymbol{\beta}}$, defined by $\bar{\boldsymbol{\beta}} = \boldsymbol{\beta} - \dot{\boldsymbol{\eta}}$, are objective, although neither $\boldsymbol{\beta}$ nor $\boldsymbol{\eta}$ is objective.

The relations (10.9), (11.9), together with the equations of motion, can now be used to convert the energy balance (9.56) into the following differential form,

$$\begin{aligned} \rho\dot{\varepsilon} + h_{i,i} - \rho r &= T_{(ij)}D_{ij} + T_{[ij]}\Psi_{ij} + M_{ji}\sigma_{i,j} \\ &= T_{ji}(L_{ij} - \Sigma_{ij}) + M_{ji}\sigma_{i,j}, \end{aligned} \tag{11.12}$$

where

$$\Psi_{ij} = \Psi_{[ij]} = \Sigma_{[ij]} - W_{ij} \tag{11.13}$$

is the difference between the angular velocity $\Sigma_{[ij]}$ of a particle and (local) mean angular velocity of material lines. The terms on the right-hand side of (11.12) are said to represent the *stress power*. If $\Psi_{ij} = 0$, i.e. the particles rotate with the (local) mean angular velocity of material lines, then the stress power of $T_{[ij]}$ vanishes. We say that in this case $T_{[ij]}$ are *workless constraint forces* (not unlike stresses in a rigid body). Similarly, $T_{(ij)}$ and M_{ji} are workless constraint forces if $D_{ij} = 0$ and $\sigma_{i,j} = 0$, respectively. This sheds some light on the role of the various types of stresses. For instance, if we suppose that oriented particles represent rough grains, then M_{ji} may be interpreted as frictional couples resisting the relative rotation of the grains.

As with couples, the sign convention for couple stresses is interpreted in conjunction with a right-hand rule. Thus a moment M_{xz}, acting on a plane whose normal is the positive x direction, is positive if it is counterclockwise when sighted along the positive z axis towards the origin. Because the moment of a force $\mathbf{F}$ can have either of the representations $M_{[ij]} = x_i F_j - x_j F_i$, $M_k = \frac{1}{2}\varepsilon_{kij} M_{[ij]} = \varepsilon_{kij} x_i F_j$, we can denote the Cartesian components of couple stress vectors alternatively by

$$\begin{aligned} M_{k[ij]} &= \varepsilon_{pij} M_{kp}, \quad M_{kp} = \tfrac{1}{2}\,\varepsilon_{pij} M_{k[ij]}, \\ M_{k[xy]} &= M_{kz}, \quad M_{k[yz]} = M_{kx}, \quad M_{k[zx]} = M_{ky}. \end{aligned} \tag{11.14}$$

If we introduce additional multipolar stresses, then it is also necessary to set up additional balance equations governing the multipolar stresses. But these equations will be, in effect, constitutive equations! To choose a definite *form* for these equations, and for the ensuing theories, we may adopt either *Hamilton's principle* (discussed in Section 16), or one form or another of a *principle of virtual work*.

As a rule, the principle of virtual work makes use of virtual, or imagined, motions that are introduced as a kind of *thought experiment* whereby a body is made to reveal its laws of motion. Consequently, the virtual motions must be characteristic of the geometrical and physical constitution of the body. For instance, in Cosserat continua we may consider rigid motions, characterized by $v_{i,j} - \Sigma_{ij} = 0$, $\sigma_{i,j} = 0$, where $\Sigma_{ij} = -\varepsilon_{ijk}\sigma_k$. For such motions the energy balance reduces to the following version of the principle of virtual work: in a rigid motion of a body, the work of external forces and torques equals the change of the kinetic energy. Namely, if the motion is rigid, then there exists an observer frame in which the body is at rest, so that $\dot{\varepsilon} = 0$. Because ε is objective, $\dot{\varepsilon} = 0$ must hold in all observer frames, thus

$$\int_V \dot{k}\, dm = \int_V (\mathbf{b}\cdot\mathbf{v} + \boldsymbol{\beta}\cdot\boldsymbol{\sigma})\, dm + \int_{\partial V} (\mathbf{t}\cdot\mathbf{v} + \boldsymbol{\mu}\cdot\boldsymbol{\sigma})\, da.$$

We may now use the method of Lagrange's multipliers, whereby the restriction to rigid motions is removed by adding to the right-hand side the volume integral of $-T_{ji}(v_{i,j} - \Sigma_{ij}) - M_{ji}\sigma_{i,j}$, where $-T_{ji}$ and $-M_{ji}$ are now interpreted as Lagrange's multipliers. Routine integrations by parts, followed by the observer transformations $v_i \to v_i + \dot{\alpha}_i$ and $v_{i,j} \to v_{i,j} + \Omega_{ij}$, $\Sigma_{ij} \to \Sigma_{ij} + \Omega_{ij}$ then yield both the boundary conditions and the field equations. The general method of Green and Rivlin [49] is in fact to assume that *the energy balance is form-invariant for all observer transformations.* We shall illustrate this method in the case of a dipolar medium.

Following Green and Rivlin, we postulate for dipolar media the following energy balance,

$$\int_V (\dot{\varepsilon} + \dot{k})\, dm = \int_V (r + b_i v_i + \bar{b}_{ij} v_{ij})\, dm + \int_{\partial V} (t_i v_i + t_{ij} v_{ij} - h)\, da. \qquad (11.15)$$

For reasons of convenience, we have introduced the effective body forces $\bar{b}_{ij} = b_{ij} - a_{mj}\dot{v}_{im} - \frac{1}{2}\dot{a}_{mj}v_{im}$, so that $\dot{k}$ now stands for $v_i\dot{v}_i$. Performing a Galilean transformation, we readily obtain the balance of linear momentum, (9.34). When applied to a tetrahedron, (9.34) reduces to $t_i(\mathbf{n}) = T_{ji}n_j$; the energy balance then simplifies to

$$\int_V \dot{\varepsilon}\, dm = \int_V (\rho r + \bar{b}_{ij} v_{ij} + T_{ji} v_{i,j})\, dv + \int_{\partial V} t_{ij} v_{ij}\, da - \int_{\partial V} h\, da. \qquad (11.16)$$

To establish the existence of a dipolar stress tensor, we apply (11.16) to a tetrahedron. Should the stresses depend also on the curvature of surfaces of separation, e.g. $t_{ij} = t_{ij}(\mathbf{n}, \nabla\mathbf{n})$, then tetrahedral "free bodies" cannot be used, because a sharp edge is in effect a singular line (cf. Section 16). Assuming that that is not the case, we obtain from (11.16) the boundary condition

$$\bar{t}_{ij} v_{ij} - \bar{h} = 0, \qquad (11.17)$$

where

$$\bar{t}_{ij} = t_{ij} - T_{kij} n_k, \qquad \bar{h} = h - h_i n_i. \qquad (11.18)$$

If h, t_{ij} are not assumed to be linear functions of $\mathbf{n}$, the subscript k in $h(\mathbf{e}_k)$, $t_{ij}(\mathbf{e}_k)$ is not necessarily a tensor index. However, because it will be necessary to sum over contributions $n_k h(\mathbf{e}_k)$, $n_k t_{ij}(\mathbf{e}_k)$ arising from the coordinate planes of a tetrahedron, it is expedient to retain the summation convention, thus $n_k h(\mathbf{e}_k) = n_k h_k$, $n_k t_{ij}(\mathbf{e}_k) = n_k T_{kij}$. The ordinary stress tensor is an exception; here the balance of linear momentum implies $t_i(\mathbf{n}) = t_i[\mathbf{n}]$, so that i is indeed a tensor index.

Once h is eliminated in (11.16) through (11.17), (11.18), the energy balance becomes

$$\rho\dot{\varepsilon} + h_{i,i} - \rho r = T_{ji}v_{i,j} + \overline{T}_{ij}v_{ij} + T_{kij}v_{ij,k},$$

where
$$\overline{T}_{ij} \equiv T_{kij,k} + \rho\bar{b}_{ij}. \tag{11.19}$$

Subsequently performing a general observation transformation $v_{ij}^{+} = v_{ij} + \Omega_{im}^{+}\phi_{mj}$, $v_{ij,k}^{+} = v_{ij,k} + \Omega_{im}^{+}\phi_{mj,k}$, we obtain

$$T'_{im} = T'_{mi}, \tag{11.20}$$

where
$$T'_{im} \equiv T_{im} - \overline{T}_{ij}\phi_{mj} - T_{kij}\phi_{mj,k}. \tag{11.21}$$

To recover from (11.20) the Cosserat's equations (11.11), we let

$$M_{kim} = -\tfrac{1}{2}T_{kij}\phi_{mj}, \qquad \beta_{im} = -\tfrac{1}{2}\bar{b}_{ij}\phi_{mj} \tag{11.22}$$

(the factor $-\frac{1}{2}$ arises from a comparison of $t_{ij}v_{ij}$ with $\mu_i\sigma_i = -\frac{1}{2}\mu_i\varepsilon_{ijk}\Sigma_{jk} = -\frac{1}{2}m_{jk}\Sigma_{jk}$). Then (11.21) can be put into the form

$$M_{kim,k} + \rho\beta_{im} + \tfrac{1}{2}T_{im} = \tfrac{1}{2}T'_{im}. \tag{11.21*}$$

In particular, (11.20) is identical with the Cosserat's equations. Evidently in multipolar continua the balance of angular momentum, $T'_{im} = T'_{mi}$, gives rise to a rather complicated expression, because then $T'_{im} = T_{im} - \overline{T}_{ij}\phi_{mj} - \overline{T}_{ijk}\phi_{mjk} - \cdots - \overline{T}_{kij}\phi_{mj,k} - T_{kijp}\phi_{mjp,k} - \cdots$. Moreover, the additional balance equations $T_{kij,k} + \rho\bar{b}_{ij} = \overline{T}_{ij}$ require the knowledge of $\overline{T}_{ij}$ through appropriate constitutive equations.

A representation of the energy balance which is automatically form-invariant in all observer transformations is given by

$$\rho\dot{\varepsilon} + h_{i,i} - \rho r = T'_{im}D_{im} + \overline{T}_{ij}\beta_{ij} + T_{kij}\beta_{ij|k}, \tag{11.23}$$

where $D_{im} = \frac{1}{2}(v_{i,m} + v_{m,i})$, and β_{ij}, $\beta_{ij|k}$ are the objective variables defined in (11.4).

To illustrate the method of Green and Rivlin, let us consider *mixtures of two monopolar media*† (mixtures of more than two constituents can also be investigated by the method outlined here, but the notations become rather unwieldy). We consider a mixture of two monopolar constituents C and $\overline{C}$;

† Green and Naghdi [52].

variables relating to $\bar{C}$ will be denoted by barred letters. For each constituent the usual description of motion is assumed to hold:

$$x_i = x_i(\mathbf{X}, t), \qquad \bar{x}_i = \bar{x}_i(\bar{\mathbf{X}}, t). \tag{11.24}$$

Thus

$$v_i = \frac{\partial}{\partial t} x_i \bigg|_{\mathbf{X}=\text{const.}}, \qquad \bar{v}_i = \frac{\partial}{\partial t} \bar{x}_i \bigg|_{\bar{\mathbf{X}}=\text{const.}}. \tag{11.25}$$

When dealing with mixtures the spatial description is more appropriate; in particular, we shall consider a fixed region of space, V ("control volume"), bounded by a surface S, and assume that at the given instant

$$x_i = \bar{x}_i, \tag{11.26}$$

so that

$$\partial_m = \frac{\partial}{\partial x_m} = \frac{\partial}{\partial \bar{x}_m}. \tag{11.27}$$

Material rates D_t, $\bar{D}_t$, following the constituents C, $\bar{C}$, respectively, are defined by

$$D_t = \partial_t + v_m \partial_m, \qquad \bar{D}_t = \partial_t + \bar{v}_m \partial_m. \tag{11.28}$$

In addition, we introduce the total mass density p, and the mean velocity $\mathbf{w}$ by

$$p = \rho + \bar{\rho}, \qquad p\mathbf{w} = \rho\mathbf{v} + \bar{\rho}\bar{\mathbf{v}}, \tag{11.29}$$

and define a mean material rate, indicated by a superposed dot, by

$$\dot{f} = \partial_t f + w_m \partial_m f. \tag{11.30}$$

Then it is easy to see that

$$\rho D_t f + \bar{\rho} \bar{D}_t f = p\dot{f}. \tag{11.31}$$

We now postulate the following form of the energy balance,

$$\begin{aligned} \int_V [\partial_t(p\varepsilon) + \partial_t(\rho k) + \partial_t(\bar{\rho}\bar{k})\, dv &= -\int_S (pw_i\varepsilon + \rho v_i k + \bar{\rho}\bar{v}_i\bar{k}) n_i \, da \\ &+ \int_V (pr + \rho b_i v_i + \bar{\rho}\bar{b}_i\bar{v}_i)\, dv + \int_S (t_i v_i + \bar{t}_i \bar{v}_i - h)\, da. \end{aligned} \tag{11.32}$$

The density of kinetic energy has been decomposed into the parts k and $\bar{k}$, but a corresponding decomposition of the internal energy density ε would amount to a special assumption. The quantity h not only accounts for heat flux but also for energy transport due to chemical reactions.

Applying the divergence theorem to the first integral on the right hand side, we can reduce (11.32) to the form

$$\int_V (p\dot{\varepsilon} + M\varepsilon + \mu k + \bar{\mu}\bar{k})\, dv = \int_V (pr + \rho B_i v_i + \bar{\rho}\bar{B}_i\bar{v}_i)\, dv + \int_S (t_i v_i + \bar{t}_i\bar{v}_i - h)\, da,$$

where

$$M = \dot{p} + pw_{i,i} = \mu + \bar{\mu}, \quad \mu = D_t\rho + \rho v_{i,i}, \quad \bar{\mu} = \bar{D}_t\bar{\rho} + \bar{\rho}\bar{v}_{i,i}, \tag{11.33}$$

and $B_i = b_i - a_i$, $\bar{B}_i = \bar{b}_i - \bar{a}_i$ are the effective body force densities. From a Galilean transformation now follows, in a routine way, that

$$M = \dot{p} + pw_{i,i} = 0, \tag{11.34}$$

and that

$$\int_V (\rho B_i + \bar{\rho}\bar{B}_i - \mu v_i - \bar{\mu}\bar{v}_i)\, dv + \int_S (t_i + \bar{t}_i)\, da = 0. \tag{11.35}$$

Applying (11.35) to a tetrahedron, we obtain

$$t_i(\mathbf{n}) + \bar{t}_i(\mathbf{n}) = (T_{ji} + \bar{T}_{ji})n_j. \tag{11.36}$$

Substituting this back into (11.35), we arrive at the equations of motion expressing the balance of linear momentum,

$$(T_{ji} + \bar{T}_{ji})_{,j} + \rho b_i + \bar{\rho}\bar{b}_i = \partial_t(\rho v_i) + \partial_j(\rho v_i v_j) + \partial_t(\bar{\rho}\bar{v}_i) + \partial_j(\bar{\rho}\bar{v}_i\bar{v}_j). \tag{11.37}$$

The term $\partial_j(\rho v_i v_j)$ represents *efflux* of the momentum of C (by divergence theorem, the term can be changed into $\rho v_i v_j n_j$, where $\mathbf{n}$ is the outer normal), i.e. $\partial_t(\rho v_i) + \partial_t(\rho v_i v_j)$ is the net increase of the momentum of C in the control volume V. According to (11.37), then, the net increase of momentum within V equals the sum of the resultant body force and the divergence of the partial stresses T_{ji} and $\bar{T}_{ji}$. Because chemical reactions are permitted, the masses of the constituents are not conserved separately, but the total mass is conserved with respect to the mean motion.

In order to obtain further reductions of the energy balance, we let $t_i v_i + \bar{t}_i \bar{v}_i = \frac{1}{2} v_i(t_i + \bar{t}_i) + \frac{1}{2} \bar{v}_i(t_i + \bar{t}_i) + \frac{1}{2}(t_i - \bar{t}_i)(v_i - \bar{v}_i)$, and introduce the same type of substitution also for the body force terms. Then, using (11.36), (11.37), we get

$$\int_V (\rho\dot{\varepsilon} - \rho r)\, dv = \frac{1}{2}\int_V (T_{ji} + \bar{T}_{ji})(v_i + \bar{v}_i)_{,j} - \int_S h\, da \tag{11.38}$$
$$+ \frac{1}{2}\int_V (\rho B_i - \bar{\rho}\bar{B}_i)(v_i - \bar{v}_i)\, dv + \frac{1}{2}\int_S (t_i - \bar{t}_i)(v_i - \bar{v}_i)\, da.$$

If V is a tetrahedron, then it follows that

$$\pi_i(v_i - \bar{v}_i) - (h - h_i n_i) = 0, \tag{11.39}$$

where

$$\pi_i = \frac{1}{2}[(t_i - \bar{t}_i) - (T_{ji} - \bar{T}_{ji})n_j]. \tag{11.40}$$

Elimination of h in (11.38) now yields

$$\rho\varepsilon + h_{i,i} - \rho r = T_{ji}v_{i,j} + \bar{T}_{ji}\bar{v}_{i,j} + T_i(v_i - \bar{v}_i), \tag{11.41}$$

where

$$T_i = \frac{1}{2}(T_{ji} - \bar{T}_{ji})_{,j} + \frac{1}{2}(\rho B_i - \bar{\rho}\bar{B}_i). \tag{11.42}$$

Finally, applying a general observer transformation to (11.41) we can conclude that $(T_{ji} + \bar{T}_{ji})\Omega^+_{ij} = 0$, thus

$$T_{[ij]} = \bar{T}_{[ij]}. \tag{11.43}$$

Therefore, the energy balance reduces to

$$\rho\dot{\varepsilon} + h_{i,i} - \rho r = T_{ij}D_{ij} + \bar{T}_{ij}\bar{D}_{ij} + T_i(v_i - \bar{v}_i) - T_{[ij]}(W_{ij} - \bar{W}_{ij}). \tag{11.44}$$

To summarize, the balance equation for mass is given by (11.34), for linear momentum by (11.37), for angular momentum by (11.43), and for energy by (11.44). The stress power terms in (11.44) are indicative of the dynamical response described by the stresses. Thus $T_{[ij]}$ may be interpreted as a reaction to the "angular velocity of diffusion," $W_{ij} - \bar{W}_{ij}$.

Thin rods and shells

When dealing with thin rods and shells it is expedient to devise simplified theories in which the smallness of a particular dimension has been used to obtain approximations of the actual state of deformation. This task is by no means an easy one. For one, there are many ways in which approximations can be introduced. Second, the consistency of the various orders of approximation must be established. A brief review of a subject that is quite formidable does not seem possible. However, it may be of some interest to view rods and shells as concrete examples of one- and two-dimensional media with microstructure, the latter being of course the material around some "center line" or "middle surface." Rather than applying the synthetic method (which is probably the best method for theories of rods and shells), we shall use this opportunity to illustrate more formal methods in what is a relatively familiar setting.

In a "zero-order theory" of rods we replace a rod by a filament that offers no resistance to bending or twist. To develop the theory from the ground up, we shall have to obtain a few results from the differential geometry of space curves. To make the presentation reasonably short, most of the details of derivations will be omitted.

We denote by s and S, respectively, the arc lengths in the final and initial configurations of a space curve. The two configurations are described by $x_i = f_i(s, t)$, $X_i = F_i(S)$. In addition, we require the knowledge of the "intrinsic motion": $s = \phi(S, t)$. With the aid of the latter, we can locate one and the same particle S in both configurations: $X_i = F_i(S)$, $x_i = f_i(\phi(S, t), t) \equiv \bar{F}_i(S, t)$. We shall use the notations

$$\hat{\Psi} = \frac{\partial}{\partial s} \Psi \bigg|_{t = \text{const.}}, \qquad \dot{\Psi} = \frac{\partial}{\partial t} \Psi \bigg|_{S = \text{const.}}.$$

The *differential description* of a space curve is given by the *formulas of Frenet-Serret*,

$$\hat{\boldsymbol{\sigma}} = \kappa \boldsymbol{\nu}, \qquad \hat{\boldsymbol{\nu}} = -\kappa \boldsymbol{\sigma} + \tau \boldsymbol{\beta}, \qquad \hat{\boldsymbol{\beta}} = -\tau \boldsymbol{\nu}, \tag{11.45}$$

where κ is curvature, τ is torsion, and the tangent vector $\boldsymbol{\sigma}$, the (principal) normal vector $\boldsymbol{\nu}$, and the binormal vector $\boldsymbol{\beta}$ constitute an orthonormal triad (*Frenet triad*). To derive (11.45), we start with $\boldsymbol{\sigma} = \hat{\mathbf{x}}$, then let $\hat{\boldsymbol{\sigma}} = \kappa \boldsymbol{\nu}$ (noting that $\boldsymbol{\sigma} \cdot \boldsymbol{\sigma} = 1$, $\boldsymbol{\sigma} \cdot \hat{\boldsymbol{\sigma}} = 0$), $\boldsymbol{\beta} = \boldsymbol{\sigma} \times \boldsymbol{\nu}$, and so on.

The velocity field $v_i = \dot{x}_i$ of a space curve can be related to the field of angular velocities $\bar{\boldsymbol{\omega}}$ of the Frenet triads. To obtain $\bar{\boldsymbol{\omega}}$ from $\dot{\boldsymbol{\sigma}} = \bar{\boldsymbol{\omega}} \times \boldsymbol{\sigma}$, etc., we must evaluate $\dot{\boldsymbol{\sigma}}$, $\dot{\boldsymbol{\nu}}$, $\dot{\boldsymbol{\beta}}$. Writing $\sigma_i = (1/\lambda)\partial x_i/\partial S$, where the *stretch* $\lambda = ds/dS$ is a measure of intrinsic deformation, and noting that in material rates the order of differentiation with respect to t and S can be interchanged, we obtain $\dot{\boldsymbol{\sigma}} = -D\boldsymbol{\sigma} + \hat{\mathbf{v}}$, where

$$D = \dot{\lambda}\lambda^{-1} = \boldsymbol{\sigma} \cdot \hat{\mathbf{v}} \tag{11.46}$$

(cf. (8.39)). Next, writing $\boldsymbol{\nu} = (1/\kappa\lambda)\partial\boldsymbol{\sigma}/\partial S$, we obtain $\kappa\dot{\boldsymbol{\nu}} = \boldsymbol{\beta}\boldsymbol{\beta}\cdot\hat{\hat{\mathbf{v}}} - \kappa\boldsymbol{\sigma}\boldsymbol{\nu}\cdot\hat{\mathbf{v}}$. Here we have used (11.46) to eliminate $\partial D/\partial s$, and $\dot{\boldsymbol{\nu}}\cdot\boldsymbol{\nu} = 0$ to eliminate $\dot{\kappa}$ through

$$\dot{\kappa} = -2D\kappa + \boldsymbol{\nu}\cdot\hat{\hat{\mathbf{v}}}. \tag{11.47}$$

Finally, the formula $\dot{\boldsymbol{\beta}} = -\boldsymbol{\sigma}\boldsymbol{\beta}\cdot\hat{\mathbf{v}} - \rho\boldsymbol{\nu}\boldsymbol{\beta}\cdot\hat{\hat{\mathbf{v}}}$ is readily found by differentiating $\boldsymbol{\sigma}\cdot\boldsymbol{\beta} = 0$, $\boldsymbol{\nu}\cdot\boldsymbol{\beta} = 0$.

For the interpretation of multipolar velocities, it is of some interest to note that, by (11.47), the second velocity gradients determine the time rate of curvature of a material line (as is evident from (11.46), the first gradients determine the stretching). The time rate of torsion is related to the third velocity gradients.

It is now easy to show that the representation of $\overline{\boldsymbol{\omega}}$ in the Frenet triads is given by

$$\begin{aligned} \overline{\omega}_3 &= \overline{W}_{21} = \nu_i\dot{\sigma}_i = \nu_i\hat{v}_i, \\ \overline{\omega}_2 &= \overline{W}_{13} = \sigma_i\dot{\beta}_i = -\beta_i\hat{v}_i, \\ \overline{\omega}_1 &= \overline{W}_{32} = \beta_i\dot{\nu}_i = \rho\beta_i\hat{\hat{v}}_i. \end{aligned} \tag{11.48}$$

A motion is rigid if the velocities of neighboring points differ by $d\mathbf{v} = \overline{\boldsymbol{\omega}} \times \boldsymbol{\sigma}\, ds$, and if the angular velocity does not depend on s. The conditions for rigid motion are thus

$$\hat{v}_i - \varepsilon_{ijk}\overline{\omega}_j\sigma_k = 0, \qquad \hat{\overline{\omega}}_j = 0. \tag{11.49}$$

A motion is merely inextensional if $D = \hat{v}_i\sigma_i = 0$.

To derive the equations of motion, we let $dm = \rho\, ds$ be a mass element, $\mathbf{b}\, dm$ the line load per length ds, and denote by t^A, t^B the "surface tractions" (i.e. end loads) acting at the endpoints A and B of a filament. Assuming that non-mechanical power is zero, and that the motion is inextensional, the time rate of internal energy can be set equal to zero. As in the case of Cosserat continua, we may now generate boundary conditions and equations of motion from

$$\int_A^B \dot{k}\, dm = \int_A^B (\rho\mathbf{b}\cdot\mathbf{v} - TD)\, ds + \mathbf{t}\cdot\mathbf{v}\Big|_A^B,$$

where $\dot{k} = v_i\dot{v}_i$, and $-T$ is the Lagrange's multiplier associated with $D = 0$. Integrating by parts according to $T\sigma_i\hat{v}_i = (\partial/\partial s)(T\sigma_i v_i) - v_i(\partial/\partial s)T\sigma_i$, and subsequently performing a Galilean transformation $v_i \to v_i + \dot{\alpha}_i$, we arrive at

$$\dot{\alpha}_i \int_A^B \left(\frac{\partial}{\partial s} T\sigma_i + \rho b_i - \rho \dot{v}_i \right) ds + \dot{\alpha}_i (t_i - T\sigma_i) \Big|_A^B = 0.$$

Therefore, $$\mathbf{t} = T\boldsymbol{\sigma} \text{ at } A \text{ or } B,$$

and $$\hat{T}\sigma_i + \kappa T \nu_i + \rho b_i = \rho \dot{v}_i .$$

In Frenet triads the equations of motion are

$$\begin{aligned} \hat{T} + \rho b_\sigma &= \rho(\dot{v}_\sigma - [\mathbf{v}, \bar{\boldsymbol{\omega}}, \boldsymbol{\sigma}]), \\ \kappa T + \rho b_\nu &= \rho(\dot{v}_\nu - [\mathbf{v}, \bar{\boldsymbol{\omega}}, \boldsymbol{\nu}]), \\ b_\beta &= \dot{v}_\beta - [\mathbf{v}, \bar{\boldsymbol{\omega}}, \boldsymbol{\beta}], \end{aligned} \tag{11.50}$$

where we have used $\dot{v}_i \sigma_i = \dot{v}_\sigma - v_i \dot{\sigma}_i = \dot{v}_\sigma - v_i \varepsilon_{ijk} \bar{\omega}_j \sigma_k$, etc. The differential form of the energy balance can now be expressed as follows,

$$\rho \dot{\varepsilon} + \hat{h} - \rho r = TD. \tag{11.51}$$

Let us now seek a "first-order theory" that will also account for resistance to shear, bending, and torsion. A "rod" must now have some lateral dimension; if this dimension is small, then we may assume that a cross section does not deform, and lies in the plane of $\boldsymbol{\nu}$ and $\boldsymbol{\beta}$. The geometrical model of a rod is now a *filament of oriented particles* (the Frenet triads describing the orientations)! We may also refer to this model as a (*one-dimensional*) *Cosserat continuum with constrained rotations*, because the rotations are already determined by the shape of the center line. This is not yet a satisfactory model, because it would fail to account for the torsional resistance of a straight rod. For this reason we orient the cross sections by another field of *director triads* $\mathbf{d}_a$, $a = 1, 2, 3$, which are such that $\mathbf{d}_1 = \boldsymbol{\sigma}$, but $\mathbf{d}_2$ is rotated by an angle ϕ from $\boldsymbol{\nu}$. The angular velocity of the director triads, $\boldsymbol{\omega}$, is then given by $\omega_1 = \bar{\omega}_1 + \dot{\phi}$, $\omega_2 = \bar{\omega}_2$, $\omega_3 = \bar{\omega}_3$.

The problem of defining a center line of a rod is by no means a trivial one. If the rod is considered at first as a three-dimensional body, then it may be possible to base this definition on certain statical calculations (e.g. "neutral fibre"). The method that we shall use here rests on the decomposition of kinetic energy into translational and rotational energies. We describe the location of a typical mass particle (S, Y, Z) of the rod by $x_i(S, Y, Z) = x_i + Yd_{2i}(S) + Zd_{3i}(S)$, where $x_i = x_i(S)$ stand for the coordinates of the center line. Because deformation of cross sections is neglected, the coordinates Y and Z are independent of time. The velocity of the particle is then given by $v_i(S, Y, Z) = v_i + (Yd_{2j} + Zd_{3j})W_{ij}$. Next, we take *averages* over a cross section Q, defined by

$$\bar{f} = \frac{1}{\mu}\int_Q f\,d\mu,$$

where μ denotes mass density in the cross section. Assuming that the center line passes through the centroids of cross sections, we obtain $\bar{v}_i(S, Y, Z) = v_i$. The average magnitude of velocities can be characterized by the average of $\frac{1}{2}\mathbf{v}(S, Y, Z) \cdot \mathbf{v}(S, Y, Z)$. Assuming that $\mathbf{d}_2$ and $\mathbf{d}_3$ are (centroidal) principal vectors of the inertia tensor of the cross section, we obtain $k = \frac{1}{2}v_i v_i + \frac{1}{2}r_{\underline{a}}^2\omega_a\omega_a$ where

$$r_1^2 = \frac{1}{\mu}\int_Q (Y^2 + Z^2)\,d\mu, \quad r_2^2 = \frac{1}{\mu}\int_Q Z^2\,d\mu, \quad r_3^2 = \frac{1}{\mu}\int_Q Y^2\,d\mu$$

are the principal radii of gyration of the cross section. Equivalently, $k = \frac{1}{2}v_i v_i + \frac{1}{2}i_{mn}\omega_m\omega_n$.

The conditions for rigid motion are now $\hat{v}_i - \varepsilon_{ijk}\omega_j\sigma_k = 0$, $\hat{\omega}_j = 0$. Denoting by $-T_i$ and $-M_i$ the associated Lagrange's multipliers, we obtain in a routine way the boundary conditions $\mathbf{t} = \mathbf{T}$, $\boldsymbol{\mu} = \mathbf{M}$, and the field equations $\hat{\mathbf{T}} + \rho\mathbf{b} = \rho\dot{\mathbf{v}}$, $\hat{\mathbf{M}} + \rho\mathbf{l} + (\boldsymbol{\sigma} \times \mathbf{T}) = \rho\dot{\boldsymbol{\eta}}$. Here $\eta_m = i_{mn}\omega_n$, $\boldsymbol{\mu}$ is an end couple, and $\mathbf{l}$ is the line distribution of couples. Using identities of the type

$$\begin{gathered} \hat{T}_i\sigma_i = \hat{T}_\sigma - \kappa T_\nu, \qquad \hat{T}_i\beta_i = \hat{T}_\beta + \tau T_\nu, \\ \hat{T}_i\nu_i = \hat{T}_\nu + \kappa T_\sigma - \tau T_\beta, \end{gathered} \tag{11.52}$$

the equations of motion can be represented in the Frenet triads. The equations of motion are fully general, because the internal force $\mathbf{T}$ and the internal moment $\mathbf{M}$ are now vectors.

It is interesting to note that equilibrium problems are "statically determinate," there being six equations for the six components of $\mathbf{T}$ and $\mathbf{M}$. Statically determinate problems are a rarity in continuum mechanics.

Finally, the energy balance reduces to

$$\rho\dot{\varepsilon} + \hat{h} - \rho r = T_\sigma D + M_i\hat{\omega}_i. \tag{11.53}$$

This shows that, in a one-dimensional Cosserat continuum with constrained rotations, the shearing forces T_ν and T_β are *workless constraint forces*. These forces maintain the cross sections at right angles to the center line. If the rotations are not constrained, so that $\omega_1 \neq \bar{\omega}_1$, $\omega_2 \neq \bar{\omega}_2$, $\omega_3 \neq \bar{\omega}_3$, then the equations of motion remain the same, but the energy balance becomes

$$\rho\dot{\varepsilon} + \hat{h} - \rho r = T_\sigma D - T_\nu(\omega_3 - \bar{\omega}_3) + T_\beta(\omega_2 - \bar{\omega}_2) + M_i\hat{\omega}_i. \quad (11.53)^*$$

The theory now accounts even for some average shear deformation of rods (whereby the center line would become inclined to the cross sections).

In a "second-order theory" we might allow the directors to deform (cf. Ericksen and Truesdell [31]), so that $d_{ai} = x_{im}D_{am}$, x_{im} being a measure of the "microstrains." It is difficult to say whether such a theory is needed; after all, if the deformations of a rod must be known in great detail, then one might as well consider the rod as a three-dimensional body.

The same methods can be equally well applied to thin shells. That is, starting with perfectly flexible membranes, we may proceed to two-dimensional Cosserat continua, with or without constrained rotations, and if need be go as far as two-dimensional dipolar continua. Surfaces are, however, a nuisance, because they require a more complicated tensor formalism than is needed in one-dimensional or three-dimensional problems. For one, it is often expedient to use oblique surface coordinates; for this reason we shall write tensor indices also as superscripts (it being understood that the rule of free indices applies to subscripts and superscripts separately), and use the summation convention only if one of the repeated indices is up, the other down.

We denote surface coordinates in the initial configuration by U^α, $\alpha = 1, 2$, in the final configuration by u^α. The two configurations of a surface are then described by $x_i = f_i(\mathbf{u}, t)$, $X_i = F_i(\mathbf{U})$. The equations of intrinsic motion are $u^\alpha = \phi^\alpha(\mathbf{U}, t)$; with the aid of these we can write $x_i = f_i(\mathbf{u}(\mathbf{U}, t), t) \equiv \bar{F}_i(\mathbf{U}, t)$. The natural basis in the final configuration is defined by $\mathbf{e}_\alpha = \partial\pi/\partial U^\alpha = \pi_{,\alpha}$; if $\mathbf{e}_i$ are a Cartesian basis of the ambient space, then

$$\mathbf{e}_\alpha = x_{i,\alpha}\mathbf{e}_i. \quad (11.54)$$

The vectors of the reciprocal basis are denoted by $\mathbf{e}^\alpha$; note that $\mathbf{e}^\alpha = \nabla U^\alpha$ (cf. (5.26) *et seq.*) is in a direction normal to $U^\alpha = \text{const}$. The "covariant representation" of the surface metric is defined by

$$a_{\alpha\beta} = \mathbf{e}_\alpha \cdot \mathbf{e}_\beta = x_{i,\alpha}x_{i,\beta}. \quad (11.55)$$

We shall denote by a the determinant $a_{11}a_{22} - a_{12}^2$. If we write

$$\mathbf{e}^\beta = a^{\beta\alpha}\mathbf{e}_\alpha, \quad (11.56)$$

then, in view of $\mathbf{e}_\rho \cdot \mathbf{e}^\beta = \delta_\rho^\beta$, it follows that

$$\mathbf{e}^\beta \cdot \mathbf{e}^\rho = a^{\beta\rho}, \qquad a^{\beta\alpha}a_{\alpha\gamma} = \delta_\gamma^\beta, \quad (11.57)$$

i.e. the "contravariant representation" of the surface metric, $a^{\beta\alpha}$, is the inverse of the covariant representation. Further, from (11.56) it follows that the metric tensor can be used to "raise or lower the indices," e.g. $T_{\alpha\beta} = \mathbf{T}[\mathbf{e}_\alpha, \mathbf{e}_\beta] = a_{\alpha\gamma}\mathbf{T}[\mathbf{e}^\gamma, \mathbf{e}_\beta] = a_{\alpha\gamma}T^\gamma{}_\beta = a_{\alpha\gamma}a_{\beta\rho}T^{\gamma\rho}$.

The unit normal vector of a surface, $\mathbf{n}$, is defined by $\mathbf{n} = (\mathbf{e}_1 \times \mathbf{e}_2)/|\mathbf{e}_1 \times \mathbf{e}_2|$. Because $|\mathbf{e}_1 \times \mathbf{e}_2|^2 = a$, we can write

$$\mathbf{n} = \frac{\mathbf{e}_1 \times \mathbf{e}_2}{\sqrt{a}}. \tag{11.58}$$

A vector $\mathbf{v} = v_i\mathbf{e}_i$ can be equally well represented by $\mathbf{v} = v_\alpha\mathbf{e}^\alpha + v\mathbf{n}$, $v_\alpha = v_i x_{i,\alpha}$ being the surface components, and $v = v_i n_i$ the normal component. It is to be noted that the 2×3 matrix $x_{i,\alpha}$ does not have an inverse, i.e. surface components alone cannot determine the whole vector. If $v = 0$, in which case $\mathbf{v}$ is said to be a *surface vector*, then

$$v_i = x_{i,\alpha}v^\alpha. \tag{11.59}$$

Similarly, if A_{ij} is a surface tensor, then $A_{\underline{nn}} = A_{\underline{n}\alpha} = A_{\alpha\underline{n}} = 0$, and $A_{ij} = x_{i,\alpha}x_{j,\beta}A^{\alpha\beta}$.

The curvature of a surface determines the rate of turning of the unit normal vector as we progress along the surface. The gradients of $\mathbf{n}$ have no component along $\mathbf{n}$, because $n_i n_i = 1$ requires that $n_i n_{i,\alpha} = 0$. Therefore, we can write

$$\mathbf{n}_{,\alpha} = -k_{\alpha\beta}\mathbf{e}^\beta, \tag{11.60}$$

where

$$k_{\alpha\beta} = k_{\beta\alpha} = -n_{i,\alpha}x_{i,\beta} = n_i x_{i,\alpha\beta}. \tag{11.61}$$

To evaluate the gradients of the base vectors, we consider $\mathbf{e}_{\alpha,\beta} = x_{i,\alpha\beta}\mathbf{e}_i = x_{i,\alpha\beta}(\mathbf{n}n_i + x_{i,\rho}\mathbf{e}^\rho)$, thus

$$\mathbf{e}_{\alpha,\beta} = a^\gamma_{\alpha\beta}\mathbf{e}_\gamma + k_{\alpha\beta}\mathbf{n}, \tag{11.62}$$

where

$$a^\gamma_{\alpha\beta} = a^{\gamma\rho}a_{\alpha\beta\rho}, \quad a_{\alpha\beta\rho} = \frac{1}{2}(a_{\rho\beta,\alpha} + a_{\alpha\rho,\beta} - a_{\alpha\beta,\rho}) = x_{i,\alpha\beta}x_{i,\rho}. \tag{11.63}$$

Evidently the counterparts of the formulas of Frenet-Serret are (11.60), (11.62), called the *equations of Gauss and Weingarten.* They are identical in content with the equations $\partial_b\mathbf{i}_a = -w_{cab}\mathbf{i}_c$ used for curvilinear coordinates in three dimensions (cf. Section 6), except that now no derivatives in the direction of $\mathbf{i}_3 \to \mathbf{n}$ occur, and, $\mathbf{n}$ being a preferred direction, the gradients of $\mathbf{n}$ and the normal components $w_{3ab} \to k_{\alpha\beta}$ are recorded separately. In particular,

$$\mathbf{v}_{,\beta} = (v^\alpha \mathbf{e}_\alpha + v\mathbf{n})_{,\beta} = \mathbf{e}_\alpha(v^\alpha{}_{|\beta} - vk^\alpha_\beta) + \mathbf{n}(v_{,\beta} + v^\alpha k_{\alpha\beta}) \tag{11.64}$$

where

$$v^\alpha{}_{|\beta} = v^\alpha_{,\beta} + a^\alpha_{\gamma\beta}v^\gamma \tag{11.65}$$

is referred to as the *intrinsic derivative of* $\mathbf{v}$ *on the surface* (it is an invariant operation with respect to transformations of the surface coordinates). Even when $\mathbf{v}$ is a surface vector, $\mathbf{v}_{,\beta}$ is not the same as $\mathbf{e}_\alpha v^\alpha{}_{|\beta}$; the latter, being an intrinsic derivative, takes no account of the curvature.

Except for a few lemmas, we are finished with tensor analysis. First, the condition that ordinary differentiation of scalars be invariant, thus $(v^\alpha v_\alpha)_{|\beta} = (v^\alpha v_\alpha)_{,\beta}$, yields the complementary formula

$$v_{\alpha|\beta} = v_{\alpha,\beta} - a^\alpha_{\gamma\beta}v_\gamma. \tag{11.65)*$$

Next, it is easy to verify that $a_{\alpha\beta|\gamma} = a_{\alpha\beta,\gamma} - a^\rho_{\alpha\gamma}a_{\rho\beta} - a^\rho_{\beta\gamma}a_{\alpha\rho} = 0$, and similarly $a^{\alpha\beta}{}_{|\gamma} = 0$. Further,

$$(\sqrt{a})_{,\beta} = a^\alpha_{\alpha\beta}\sqrt{a}. \tag{11.66}$$

The last item is the *divergence theorem on a surface.* Let $\sigma_i = \acute{x}_i$ be a unit tangent vector of the boundary ∂S: $x_i = x_i(s)$ of a surface S. A unit vector $\mathbf{m}$ that is normal to ∂S and lies in the tangent plane of S is defined by $\mathbf{m} = \boldsymbol{\sigma} \times \mathbf{n}$. We wish to show that

$$\int_{\partial S} \mathbf{f} \cdot \mathbf{m}\, ds = \int_S f^\alpha{}_{|\alpha}\, da. \tag{11.67}$$

With $\sigma_j\, ds = \acute{x}_j\, ds = x_{j,\beta}\acute{U}^\beta\, ds = x_{j,\beta}\, dU^\beta$, $m_i = \varepsilon_{ijk}\sigma_j n_k$, $f_i = f^\alpha x_{i,\alpha} + fn_i$, we obtain $\mathbf{f} \cdot \mathbf{m}\, ds = f^\alpha \varepsilon_{ijk}x_{i,\alpha}x_{j,\beta}n_k\, dU^\beta = f^1\sqrt{a}\, dU^2 - f^2\sqrt{a}\, dU^1$. Applying the Green's transformation (5.46), and taking into account (11.66), we arrive at (11.67). Turning now to time rates, we first evaluate $\dot{\mathbf{e}}_\alpha = \dot{x}_{i,\alpha}\mathbf{e}_i = v_{i,\alpha}\mathbf{e}_i$. From $v_i = vn_i + v^\mu x_{i,\mu}$, $\mathbf{e}_i = x_{i,\rho}\mathbf{e}^\rho + n_i\mathbf{n}$ it follows after a routine calculation that

$$\begin{aligned} \dot{\mathbf{e}}_\alpha &= \mathbf{e}^\mu(v_{\mu|\alpha} - vk_{\mu\alpha}) + \mathbf{n}(k_{\mu\alpha}v^\mu + v_{,\alpha}). \\ 2D_{\alpha\beta} &= \dot{a}_{\alpha\beta} = v_{\alpha|\beta} + v_{\beta|\alpha} - 2k_{\alpha\beta}v, \\ \dot{\mathbf{n}} &= -\,\mathbf{e}^\alpha(k_{\mu\alpha}v^\mu + v_{,\alpha}). \end{aligned} \tag{11.68}$$

The spin tensor $\overline{\mathbf{W}}$ is given by $\frac{1}{2}(v_{i,j} - v_{j,i})$; its surface components are $\frac{1}{2}(v_{\alpha,\beta} - v_{\beta,\alpha})$, whereas the other components can be obtained from $\dot{n}_i = \overline{W}_{ij}n_j$. Thus

$$\begin{aligned} \overline{W}_{21} &= \tfrac{1}{2}(v_{2,1} - v_{1,2}), \\ \overline{W}_{32} &= k_{12}v^1 + k_{22}v^2 + v_{,2} = n_i v_{i,2}. \\ \overline{W}_{13} &= -k_{11}v^1 - k_{21}v^2 - v_{,1} = -n_i v_{i,1}. \end{aligned} \tag{11.69}$$

In a membrane theory we consider only the conditions of inextensibility: $D_{\alpha\beta} = 0$. The tensor of Lagrange's multipliers, $T^{\alpha\beta}$, is symmetric, so that $T^{\alpha\beta}D_{\alpha\beta} = T^{\alpha\beta}(v_{\beta|\alpha} - vk_{\alpha\beta})$. But $v_{\beta|\alpha} - vk_{\alpha\beta} = x_{i,\beta}v_{i,\alpha} = x_{i,\beta}(vn_i + v^\rho x_{i,\rho})_{,\alpha}$, which enables us to write $T^{\alpha\beta}D_{\alpha\beta} = T^\alpha{}_i\, v_{i,\alpha}$. The rest is quite analogous to the derivation of (11.50), (11.51), thus

$$\int_S \dot{k}\, dm = \int_S \mathbf{b}\cdot\mathbf{v}\, dm + \int_{\partial S} \mathbf{t}\cdot\mathbf{v}\, da - \int_S T^\alpha{}_i\, v_{i,\alpha}\, da,$$

where $\mathbf{b}$ are the distributed loads on the surface, and $\mathbf{t}$ are the line loads acting on the boundary ∂S. Because $v_{i,\alpha} = v_{i|\alpha}$, the integration by parts can be based on $T^\alpha{}_i v_{i|\alpha} = (T^\alpha{}_i v_i)_{|\alpha} - T^\alpha{}_{i|\alpha}v_i$. The condition of Galilean invariance then yields the boundary conditions $T^\alpha{}_i m_\alpha = t_i$ as well as the field equations $T^\alpha{}_{i|\alpha} + \rho b_i = \rho\dot{v}_i$. Recalling that $T^{\alpha\beta}$ is a surface tensor, thus $T^\alpha{}_i = T^{\alpha\beta}x_{i,\beta}$, we find that $\mathbf{t}$ must lie in the tangent plane of the surface, and that

$$T^\alpha{}_\beta m_\alpha = t_\beta. \tag{11.70}$$

The surface components of acceleration are $\dot{v}_i x_{i,\beta} = \dot{v}_\beta - v_i v_{i,\beta} = \dot{v}_\beta - k_{,\beta}$, whereas the normal component is given by $\dot{v}_i n_i = \dot{v} - v_i \overline{W}_{ij}n_j = \dot{v} + \overline{W}_{\underline{n}\alpha}v^\alpha$. Further, $T^\alpha{}_i n_i = 0$ implies that $T^\alpha{}_{i|\alpha}n_i = T^{\alpha\beta}k_{\alpha\beta}$, and, in view of $x_{i,\rho}x_{i|\beta\alpha} = 0$ (cf. $(11.63)_2$), $T^\alpha{}_{i|\alpha}x_{i,\beta} = T^\alpha{}_{\beta|\alpha}$. Therefore, the equations of motion are

$$\begin{aligned} T^\alpha{}_{\beta|\alpha} + \rho b_\beta &= \rho(\dot{v}_\beta - k_{,\beta}), \\ T^{\alpha\beta}k_{\alpha\beta} + \rho b &= \rho(\dot{v} + \overline{W}_{\underline{n}\alpha}v^\alpha), \end{aligned} \tag{11.71}$$

whereas the energy balance can be reduced to

$$\rho\dot{\varepsilon} + h^\alpha{}_{|\alpha} - \rho r = T^{\alpha\beta}(v_{\beta|\alpha} - vk_{\alpha\beta}). \tag{11.72}$$

The next stage is a two-dimensional Cosserat continuum with constrained rotations. As in the case of rods, it can be shown that the velocities of the middle surface are mean velocities of the shell (provided that the mass centers of the fibres lie in the middle surface), and that the average value of $\frac{1}{2}\mathbf{v}(\mathbf{U}, Z) \cdot \mathbf{v}(\mathbf{U}, Z)$ is given by

$$k = \frac{1}{2} v_i v_i + \frac{1}{2} i_{mn} \bar{\omega}_m \bar{\omega}_n,$$

where i_{mn} is the inertia tensor of the fibres mounted on the middle surface. The conditions for rigid motion are now $v_{i|\alpha} - \varepsilon_{ijk}\bar{\omega}_j x_{k,\alpha} = 0$, $\bar{\omega}_{j,\alpha} = 0$; we introduce the associated Lagrange's multipliers $-T^\alpha{}_i$, $-M^\alpha{}_j$, and proceed as before. We then obtain a fully general set of equations of motion,

$$\begin{aligned} T^\alpha{}_{i|\alpha} + \rho b_i &= \rho \dot{v}_i, \\ M^\alpha{}_{i|\alpha} + \rho l_i + \varepsilon_{ijk} x_{j,\alpha} T^\alpha{}_k &= \rho \dot{\eta}_i. \end{aligned} \tag{11.73}$$

The boundary conditions are

$$T^\alpha{}_i m_\alpha = t_i, \qquad M^\alpha{}_i m_\alpha = \mu_i, \tag{11.74}$$

where $\boldsymbol{\mu}$ denotes the line distribution of couples acting along the edge ∂S. With a little work, the energy balance can be put into the form

$$\rho \dot{\varepsilon} + h^\alpha_{|\alpha} - \rho r = T^{\alpha\beta} D_{\alpha\beta} + M^{\alpha\beta}(\bar{\omega}_{\beta|\alpha} - \bar{\omega} k_{\alpha\beta}) + M^\alpha(\bar{\omega}_{,\alpha} + k_{\alpha\beta}\bar{\omega}^\beta), \tag{11.75}$$

where $e_{\alpha\beta} = \sqrt{a}\,\varepsilon_{\alpha\beta}$, and $M^\alpha = M^\alpha{}_i n_i$ (M^α is usually set equal to zero in shell theories.) Evidently the skew-symmetric part of the membrane stresses, $T^{[\alpha\beta]}$, as well as the shearing forces $T^\alpha = T^\alpha{}_i n_i = T^\alpha{}_{\underline{n}}$ are workless constraint forces.

For a Cosserat surface with unconstrained rotations† the equations of motion remain the same, but the shearing forces now do work. The difference between the angular velocity of directors and that of a membrane element, $\boldsymbol{\psi} = \boldsymbol{\omega} - \bar{\boldsymbol{\omega}}$, is a new kinematical variable. It seems plausible to assume that $\psi = 0$ (i.e. the angular velocity of director triads about $\mathbf{n}$ is equal to the angular velocity $\bar{\omega}_{\underline{n}}$ of the supporting membrane element). Then the only term added to the energy balance (11.75) is $e_{\alpha\beta}T^\alpha\psi^\beta$. The next generalization would be some variant of a "dipolar surface."‡

In general coordinates the components of a tensor do not necessarily have

† Cf. Guenther [58].
‡ Cf. Cohen and DeSilva [197].

the same dimensions (cf. also the introductory remarks in Section 6). To obtain *physical components* of like dimension, the natural base vectors must be replaced by unit vectors, thus

$$\mathbf{i}_\alpha = h_{\underline{\alpha}}\mathbf{e}_\alpha, \qquad \mathbf{i}^\alpha = h^{\underline{\alpha}}\mathbf{e}^\alpha, \tag{11.76}$$

where

$$h_{\underline{\alpha}} = \frac{1}{\sqrt{a_{\underline{\alpha\alpha}}}}, \qquad h^{\underline{\alpha}} = \frac{1}{\sqrt{a^{\underline{\alpha\alpha}}}}. \tag{11.77}$$

In orthogonal coordinates $h_{\underline{\alpha}} = 1/h^{\underline{\alpha}}$, otherwise not. It seems that there is little to be gained by singling out a particular set of components as *the* physical components. Rather, one may be content to put each representation into a dimensionally homogeneous form. A fairly good case can be made for using the (contravariant physical) components $v^{\langle\alpha\rangle}$ defined by

$$\mathbf{v} = v^\alpha\mathbf{e}_\alpha \equiv v^{\langle\alpha\rangle}\mathbf{i}_\alpha, \qquad v^{\langle\alpha\rangle} = \frac{v^\alpha}{h_{\underline{\alpha}}}, \tag{11.78}$$

as well as the (covariant physical) components $v_{\langle\langle\alpha\rangle\rangle}$ defined by

$$\mathbf{v}\cdot\mathbf{i}_\alpha \equiv v_{\langle\langle\alpha\rangle\rangle}, \qquad v_{\langle\langle\alpha\rangle\rangle} = v_\alpha h_{\underline{\alpha}} \tag{11.79}$$

(this does not exhaust all possibilities, as we may choose $\mathbf{v}\cdot\mathbf{i}^\alpha$, etc.). Each tensor component can then be expressed in terms of physical components, e.g. $T^{\alpha\beta} = h_{\underline{\alpha}}h_{\underline{\beta}}\tau^{\alpha\beta}$, $T^\alpha_\beta = \tau^\alpha_\beta h_{\underline{\alpha}}/h_{\underline{\beta}}$. However, because the scale factors $h_{\underline{\alpha}}$, $h^{\underline{\alpha}}$ are not constant, additional terms will appear in differential equations (the most serious disadvantage of oblique coordinate systems is, however, the multiplicity of representations for each tensor).

Problems

A. MULTIPOLAR MEDIA

1. Consider a two-dimensional state of dipolar stress such that M_{kij} vanishes whenever any index equals three. Sketch the dipolar stresses acting on a square element lying in the $x_1 - x_2$ plane.
2. Consider the motions $\dot{x} = \alpha x$, $\dot{y} = \beta y$, $\dot{z} = \gamma z$ and $\dot{x} = ky$, $\dot{y} = \dot{z} = 0$ (α, β, γ, k are constants), for instance; can you interpret the normal and the shearing components of the stress tensor $\mathbf{T}$ from the stress power term $T_{ij}D_{ij}$ alone ($\mathbf{D}$ is the rate-of-deformation tensor)?

3. Consider a medium with a director $\mathbf{d}$ at each of its points. Derive the equations of balance for linear and angular momenta, and reduce the energy balance as far as possible.

B. RODS AND SHELLS

4. Derive (11.45).

5. Derive (11.47), (11.48).

6. Following the method outlined in the text, derive the equations of motion of a Cosserat rod with unconstrained rotations. Represent these equations as well as the energy balance in the Frenet triads.

7. Following the method outlined in the text, derive (11.68), (11.69).

8. Following the method outlined in the text, derive the equations of motion of a Cosserat surface with unconstrained rotations, and obtain a reduced form of the energy balance.

9. Consider a flat membrane referred to the coordinates X and Y. The membrane is maintained under large extensions given by $T_{ij} = T\delta_{ij}$. It is then acted upon by a pressure $p = \rho b$, the resulting deflections being so small that the changes in the tensions can be neglected: $k_{\underline{1}} + k_{\underline{2}} = -p/T$. The small deformations of the membrane can be described by $\mathbf{x} = X\mathbf{e}_x + Y\mathbf{e}_y + w(X, Y)\mathbf{e}_z$, where the gradients $\partial w/\partial X$ and $\partial w/\partial Y$ are assumed to be small. Then $ds^2 = d\mathbf{x} \cdot d\mathbf{x} \approx (dX)^2 + (dY)^2$, $\mathbf{e}_1 = \partial \mathbf{x}/\partial X = \mathbf{e}_x + \mathbf{e}_z\, \partial w/\partial X$, etc. and $k_{11} = \mathbf{e}_z \cdot \partial \mathbf{e}_1/\partial X = \partial^2 w/\partial X^2$, $k_{22} = \partial^2 w/\partial Y^2$, $k_{12} = \partial^2 w/\partial X \partial Y$. (Note that if the product of the slopes, $\partial w/\partial X\, \partial w/\partial Y$, is small, then $\mathbf{e}_1 \cdot \mathbf{e}_2 \approx 0$; however, $\partial^2 w/\partial X \partial Y$ need not be small, because $\mathbf{e}_1$ and $\mathbf{e}_2$ are not the principal vectors of $\mathbf{k}$). Thus show that

$$\nabla^2 w = -\frac{p}{T}.$$

10. Consider infinitesimal deflections of a thin, elastic plate. Neglecting membrane stresses, show that the equations of equilibrium require that $T^{\alpha}_{|\alpha} = -\lambda$, where λ is the intensity of normal loads per unit area. Introduce the conventional bending stresses $B^{\alpha}{}_{\rho} = e_{\rho\beta} M^{\alpha\beta}$, and show that the equations of equilibrium also require $T_{\rho} = B^{\alpha}{}_{\rho|\alpha}$, so that $B^{\alpha\rho}{}_{|\alpha\rho} = -\lambda$. Now let $B^{\alpha\rho} = Bk^{\alpha\rho}$ where B is the (constant) bending stiffness. Evaluating $k_{\alpha\beta}$ as in the preceding problem, show that

$$\nabla^4 w = -\frac{\lambda}{B}.$$

Section 12
THERMODYNAMICS

The cornerstones of thermodynamics are the balance of energy ("first law of thermodynamics") and the concept of *entropy*. A theory derives its generality, in part, from the use of undefined concepts, special theories being a result of special interpretations of these concepts. In a general theory of thermodynamics, then, energy, temperature, and entropy are undefined concepts. Naturally some of the energies are well known, as are thermometers, but we think no more of defining temperature by a thermometer than defining force as push or pull.† To counter Poincare's well-known criticism ([123], p. 127) that the law of conservation of energy now reduces to a statement "there is something which remains constant," we can only point to the hypothesis, certainly justified by past experience, that in concrete situations there will be ways of determining *a priori* the quantities that appear in the general theory as undefined concepts.

Statistical mechanics and continuum mechanics are of course very far apart, but this need not always remain so. Therefore, it may be worthwhile to mention briefly the kind of interpretations of temperature and entropy that are used in statistical mechanics. Here temperature is a measure of "thermal agitation"; in particular, as this agitation dies down, temperature approaches a lower bound (*absolute temperature* corresponds to the choice of zero for the lower bound). The heat content depends not only on temperature but also on the specific heats, which characterize the number and the kinds of thermal agitations. Putting it rather inexactly, as heat is withdrawn from a system, our knowledge of the configuration of the system (e.g. locations of particles) increases; it may even happen that the decrease of thermal agitation will permit the internal forces to establish some degree of ordering in the system. If we interpret disorder as a complete lack of knowledge about the actual configuration, then an increase of "information" may be described by a decrease of "configurational entropy." For instance, assuming that there are P_0 configurations, and that the system may be in any one of P_1 configurations, a possible measure of "information" is given by‡ $I_1 = k \log (P_0/P_1) = H_0 - H_1$, where k is a constant, and H is the entropy. This view of entropy may be of some relevance to the multipolar continuum theories.

Homogeneous deformations§

Much of classical thermodynamics has to do with *homogeneous processes*, in which all variables are functions of time only. There is then no need to introduce densities of internal energy and entropy; rather, we may work with the total internal energy E and the total entropy H. We denote the

† This point and others are forcefully made by Truesdell in the last of his "Baltimore Lectures" [196] (cf. also the forthcoming work [199]).
‡ L. Brillouin (cf. [198]).
§ The presentation here follows, in substance, that of Truesdell [199].

mechanical power by M, and the rate of heat supply by Q. The energy balance (9.56) then reads

$$\dot{K} + \dot{E} = M + Q. \tag{12.1}$$

Because temperature cannot be decreased below a certain absolute minimum, we define an "absolute" temperature θ, measured in any system of units, by choosing its greatest lower bound to be zero. We also recall that in any admissible deformation the determinant of the deformation gradients $\mathbf{F}$ cannot vanish; thus each thermodynamic process must satisfy the conditions

$$\theta \geq 0, \qquad \det\mathbf{F} \neq 0. \tag{12.2}$$

The entropy H describes, roughly speaking, the quality of internal energy, as it is a measure of heat contained in the internal energy. To explain what is formally an undefined concept, we must resort to special cases. For instance, if a process obeys a thermodynamic constitutive equation of the form $E = E(H, \ldots)$, then $E = E(H)$ means that all of internal energy is heat, whereas $E = E(H, \det\mathbf{F})$ (recall that $\det\mathbf{F} = v/v_0$!) means that the internal energy consists of both heat and energy of volume deformation. Similarly, we write $E = E(\mathbf{F}, H)$ if a body is capable of storing both heat and (elastic) strain energy. A more specific interpretation of entropy can be deduced from the second law of thermodynamics. Let us define an *internal dissipation*, D, by

$$D = \theta\dot{H} - Q; \tag{12.3}$$

the ratio of D to θ is called the *internal entropy production*, I, thus

$$I = \frac{D}{\theta} = \dot{H} - \frac{Q}{\theta}. \tag{12.4}$$

The second law of thermodynamics can be expressed in the following form, referred to as the *Clausius-Duhem inequality*,

$$D = \theta\dot{H} - Q \geq 0. \tag{12.5}$$

We interpret $\theta\dot{H}$ as the *heating*, i.e. as the time rate of change of the heat content of a body. If $D = 0$, then the process is said to be *reversible*, otherwise *irreversible*. In reversible processes $\dot{H} = Q/\theta$, so that one may view entropy as a parameter that orders heating processes in a very special way, namely according to the ratio of heat supply to the temperature at which the heat exchange occurs. Processes in which $Q = 0$, thus $\dot{H} \geq 0$, are said to be *adiabatic*, whereas processes in which $\dot{H} = 0$, thus $Q \leq 0$, are said to be *isentropic*. Evidently the second law does *not* require that entropy must increase; in fact, in reversible processes the withdrawal of heat means a lowering of entropy: $\theta\dot{H} = Q < 0$. What the second law does require is that the *internal production of entropy must be positive*, so that heating can never be less than the rate of heat supply.

With the statement of the second law of thermodynamics, the foundations of thermodynamics are now completed. To discover what the main implications of the second law are, it is convenient to have another form of this law. In the present context, $\dot{K}$ and M occur only in the combination

$$L = M - \dot{K}, \tag{12.6}$$

which is the excess of mechanical power over the time rate of kinetic energy. We can eliminate Q in (12.5) by using the energy balance, $\dot{E} - L = Q$. The expression

$$D = \theta\dot{H} + L - \dot{E} \geq 0 \tag{12.7}$$

is then called the *reduced dissipation inequality*. Further, if we define a *free energy* ψ by

$$\psi = E - \theta H, \tag{12.8}$$

then (12.7) takes on the form

$$L - \dot{\psi} \geq \dot{\theta} H. \tag{12.9}$$

A (homogeneous) thermodynamic process is described by a set of functions $\theta(t)$, $L(t)$, $E(t)$, $Q(t)$, $H(t)$, $B_K(t)$, $K = 1, 2, \ldots, N$. The process is said to be *admissible* if it meets the following conditions: the restrictions (12.2), the balance equations for mass, momentum, and energy, and the reduced dissipation inequality (12.7). To remove the limitations imposed by the balance equations, we suppose that mass, body forces, and heat supply Q are determined from the balance equations for mass, momentum, and energy, respectively. Of course this conflicts with the usual procedure of considering the body forces and Q as being given *a priori*. In the present context, however, the usual procedure is inappropriate. What it comes down to is this: we should like to investigate, from a purely thermodynamic point of view, various "comparison states" $\{\theta, L, E, Q, H, B_K\}$; so as to make these states dynamically and energetically possible, we assume that appropriate body forces and heat supplies can be "turned on" at will. That this may be difficult to do in practice is of no consequence, because we are seeking to determine the *processes that are prohibited on thermodynamic grounds alone.*

To summarize, as far as the balance equations are concerned, every process is a possible one. What does limit a thermodynamic process is the Clausius-Duhem inequality. An inequality cannot be satisfied by solving for one variable in terms of the others; moreover, because the heat supply is determined, in principle, from the energy balance, it cannot be adjusted so as to permit arbitrary variations of θ and $\dot{H}$. Therefore, the Clausius-Duhem inequality is a restriction on the variation of entropy.

In a particular theory, defined by its *constitutive equations*, the Clausius-Duhem inequality will reduce to an inequality involving the independent variables, e.g. $\theta(t)$, $\mathbf{F}(t)$, and certain coefficients arising from the constitutive equations. Should the Clausius-Duhem inequality be a restriction on the constitutive equations, or on the independent variables? It is difficult to imagine that a body would accommodate one assignment of $\theta(t)$, $\mathbf{F}(t)$, but not another; in any case, this would go against the very idea of variables that can be controlled independently. Therefore, we shall assume that *the Clausius-Duhem inequality is a restriction on constitutive equations, i.e. it must be satisfied identically, for any assignment of independent variables.*

To illustrate the ramifications of the Clausius-Duhem inequality, let us choose the constitutive equations $\psi = \psi(\theta, B_K)$, $H = H(\theta, B_K)$, $L = -\mathbf{S}T_K(\theta, \mathbf{B})\dot{B}_K$, where $\mathbf{S}$ denotes summation over K from 1 to N. Substituting these into (12.9), we obtain $\dot{\theta}(H + \partial_\theta\psi) + \mathbf{S}\dot{B}_K(T_K + \partial_{B_K}\psi) \le 0$. We now consider a process $\theta(t) = \bar{\theta} + \alpha(t - \bar{t})$, $B_K(t) = \bar{B}_K + \beta_K(t - \bar{t})$, where α, β_K, $\bar{\theta}$, $\bar{B}_K$, and $\bar{t}$ are constants. The interval $t - \bar{t}$ is chosen so small that (12.2) hold throughout the interval. Moreover, because the Clausius-Duhem inequality must hold throughout the interval, it will also hold in the limit as $t \to \bar{t}$. But then we have that $\alpha C + \mathbf{S}C_K\beta_K \le 0$, where C, C_K are independent of α, β_K. Therefore, the inequality is satisfied identically only if the coefficients vanish, thus

$$H = -\partial_\theta\psi, \qquad T_K = -\partial_{B_K}\psi. \tag{12.10}$$

According to the Clausius-Duhem inequality, then, the constitutive equations for ψ, H, and L cannot be assigned independently, because the constitutive equation for ψ determines all the others. Moreover, the processes governed by these constitutive equations are reversible.

If L is given by $L = -\mathbf{S}T_K\dot{B}_K - \mathbf{S}T_{KL}\dot{B}_K\dot{B}_L$ (double-summation over K and L being understood), then the term $\mathbf{S}T_{KL}\dot{B}_K\dot{B}_L$ must be added to the previous inequality. Again, at any instant the independent variables and their time rates can be assigned independently, so that the inequality is of the form $\alpha_i x_i + \alpha_{ij} x_i x_j \leq 0$ (summations from 1 to N), the coefficients α_i, α_{ij} being constants. If we let $x_i = \lambda c_i$, where c_i are constants, then $\lambda(c_i\alpha_i) + \lambda^2(c_i c_j \alpha_{ij}) \leq 0$, which can be satisfied for all λ only if, separately, $c_i\alpha_i = 0$, $c_i c_j \alpha_{ij} \leq 0$. Thus $\alpha_i = 0$, whereas α_{ij} must be the coefficients of a negative, semi-definite form. In this way we find that (12.10) are now complemented by the condition

$$D = L - \dot{\psi} - \dot{\theta} H = -\mathbf{S} T_{KL} \dot{B}_K \dot{B}_L \geq 0, \tag{12.11}$$

i.e. the free energy does not determine all other constitutive equations, because the coefficients T_{KL} can be assigned independently (to satisfy the Clausius-Duhem inequality, these coefficients must define a negative, semi-definite quadratic form).

Nonhomogeneous processes

The same laws govern homogeneous and non-homogeneous processes, but in the latter case it is necessary to obtain field representations of the laws. To this end, we introduce the entropy density per unit mass, η, so that

$$H = \int_V \eta \, dm. \tag{12.12}$$

The time rate of heat supply is represented by

$$Q = -\int_{\partial V} \mathbf{q} \cdot \mathbf{n} \, da + \int_V r \, dm, \tag{12.13}$$

where r is the distribution of heat sources through the volume V, $\mathbf{q}$ is the heat flux vector, and $\mathbf{n}$ denotes outward-directed unit normal vectors at the boundary ∂V (thus $-\mathbf{q} \cdot \mathbf{n}$ represents flow *into* V). We define the *production of entropy*, Γ, by

$$\Gamma = \dot{H} + \int_{\partial V} \frac{1}{\theta} \mathbf{q} \cdot \mathbf{n} \, da - \int_V \frac{r}{\theta} \, dm. \tag{12.14}$$

We adopt the second law of thermodynamics in the form of a principle of non-negative entropy production, expressed by the *Clausius-Duhem inequality*

$$\Gamma \geq 0. \tag{12.15}$$

According to (9.67), at a surface of discontinuity this reduces to

$$\left[\!\left[\rho\eta\overline{V} - \frac{1}{\theta}\mathbf{q}\cdot\mathbf{n} \right]\!\right] \leq 0. \tag{12.16}$$

Away from surfaces of discontinuity we can let

$$\Gamma = \int_V \gamma \, dm. \tag{12.17}$$

Then, because (12.15) is to hold for any part of a body, it follows that

$$\gamma = \dot{\eta} + \frac{1}{\rho}\operatorname{div}\left(\frac{\mathbf{q}}{\theta}\right) - \frac{r}{\theta} \geq 0. \tag{12.18}$$

In view of (12.12), (12.14), γ can be decomposed as follows,

$$\begin{gathered} \gamma = \gamma_l + \gamma_c, \\ \gamma_l = \dot{\eta} + \frac{1}{\rho\theta}\operatorname{div}\mathbf{q} - \frac{r}{\theta}, \qquad \gamma_c = -\frac{1}{\rho\theta^2}\mathbf{q}\cdot\operatorname{grad}\theta, \end{gathered} \tag{12.19}$$

where γ_l and γ_c are called, respectively, the *local entropy production* and the *entropy flux* (associated with heat flux). In the place of γ_l we may introduce the *internal dissipation* δ defined by

$$\delta = \rho\theta\gamma_l = \rho\theta\dot{\eta} + q_{i,i} - \rho r. \tag{12.20}$$

If ψ denotes the *free energy*, thus

$$\psi = \varepsilon - \theta\eta, \tag{12.21}$$

then δ can be expressed as follows,

$$\delta = w - \rho\eta\dot{\theta} - \rho\dot{\psi}, \tag{12.22}$$

where w is the rate of working of internal forces. In monopolar media,

$$w = T_{ji}v_{i,j} = \operatorname{tr}(\mathbf{TL}). \tag{12.23}$$

To show that (12.22) is the same as (12.20), we eliminate $\dot{\varepsilon}$ in $\rho\dot{\psi} = \rho\dot{\varepsilon} - \rho\dot{\theta}\eta - \rho\theta\dot{\eta}$ through the energy balance $\rho\dot{\varepsilon} = -q_{i,i} + \rho r + w$.

The two parts of entropy production, γ_l and γ_c, correspond to dissipation of mechanical energy into heat and entropy transport associated with heat flux, respectively. In particular, $\gamma_c \geq 0$ is the familiar requirement that heat flux should be in a direction opposite to the temperature gradient (i.e. that heat should flow from hotter regions to colder regions). However, instead of assuming $\gamma_c \geq 0$ outright, it is more instructive to explore this inequality in the context of particular kinds of thermo-mechanical response.

For multipolar media the Clausius–Duhem inequality (12.18) is left unchanged; for a mixture of two monopolar media it is replaced by

$$\int_V \rho\dot{\eta}\, dv + \int_{\partial V} \frac{1}{\theta}\mathbf{q} \cdot \mathbf{n}\, da \geq 0, \tag{12.24}$$

where $\mathbf{q}$ denotes the heat flux.

The Clausius–Duhem inequality again imposes limitations on the constitutive equations. This will be taken up in Section 14.

Problems

1. Consider homogeneous processes, and assume a constitutive equation $E = E(p, V)$, where p is a pressure, and V is a volume. Using the energy balance $dE = -pdV + \Delta B$, where ΔB denotes the heat supply, define entropy by $dH = \Delta B/\theta = (dE + pdV)/\theta$, where $1/\theta$ is an integrating factor. Are H and θ so defined essentially unique? *Hints*: note that $\theta\, \partial H/\partial V = p + \partial E/\partial V$, $\theta\, \partial H/\partial p = \partial E/\partial p$. From these obtain $\partial\theta/\partial p\, \partial H/\partial V - \partial\theta/\partial V\, \partial H/\partial p = 1$, and eliminating the derivatives of H, $(\partial E/\partial V + p)\partial A/\partial p - \partial E/\partial p\, \partial A/\partial V = 1$, where $A = \log\theta$. Because $E = E(p, V)$ is assumed to be known, the last equation can be solved. Let θ_0 be a solution, and let $\bar{\theta}$ be a solution of the associated homogeneous equation. Show that then $\theta = \theta_0 f(\bar{\theta})$ is the general solution. What additional hypotheses are needed to specify f (such as $f(\bar{\theta}) = \text{const.}$)? Verify that the differential equation is the condition for

$$H = H_0 + \int_{p_0,V_0}^{p,V} dH$$

to be independent of the path of integration.

2. Let $E = E(H, V)$, and $p = -\partial E/\partial V$, $\theta = \partial E/\partial H$. Define a free energy $F(\theta, V) = E(H(\theta, V), V) - \theta H(\theta, V)$; show that $p = -\partial F/\partial V$, $H = -\partial F/\partial\theta$.

3. Continuing the preceding problem, define a Gibbs free energy $G(p, \theta) = F + pV = E - \theta H + pV$. Show that $\partial G/\partial\theta = -H$, $\partial G/\partial p = V$.

Section 13
ELECTROMAGNETISM, LORENTZ TRANSFORMATIONS, RELATIVITY*

To round out classical physics, we shall record here the basic ideas of electromagnetism. To do this in so short a space requires a departure from the customary, more deliberate method in which the notions of electric and magnetic fields are introduced through particular examples or motivated by basic experiments. The formal approach to electromagnetism is not without advantages; aside from its economy, it exhibits the foundations of electromagnetism with a clarity that may be lost otherwise.

The physical principles of electromagnetism are embodied in the *Maxwell's equations*. The proper setting of Maxwell's equations is a four-dimensional *space-time* in which there exist preferred, "inertial" observer frames, the correlation of their data being described by *Lorentz transformations*.

Lorentz transformations, simultaneity, relativity†

Considering the importance of length and time in physics, our attitude towards measuring them is (or rather, *was* until the time of Einstein) surprisingly vague. It is taken for granted that length and time can be measured anywhere, anytime, with any desired accuracy, provided that one takes enough pains. But "rigid" rods are not really available, nor can they be transported to distant nebulae. If we wish to specify clear operational methods for measuring length and time, then we must provide tools that are more practical, and more perfect, than the "rigid" rods. Fortunately such tools exist: light signals (or radar) and accurate clocks. Nowadays it is not at all difficult to accept the relevance of a "theory of communications" in which the only tools are clocks and devices for sending and receiving radar signals. Let us take a contemporary example: three spaceships traveling in the solar system. To determine their relative motions, the spaceships send and return, receive and record, various signals, it being understood that the source of each signal can be identified on the basis of some code (wavelength, number of "beeps," etc.). In order to extract information from the received signals, a theory is needed, the *k-calculus of Bondi*.‡ This calculus is in effect the basis of the (special) *theory of relativity*, which is the body of results obtained from Lorentz (observer) transformations, the latter being consequences of a strictly operational approach to measurement of positions and times. When

† A thorough presentation of these subjects is given by J. L. Synge [158].
‡ Cf. [6], pp. 375–459.

approached in this way, relativity theory loses all the mystery that seems to have surrounded it for half a century.

There remains perhaps one question: why *must* we insist on the operational approach; why not use an "idealized" signal speed $c' = \infty$, in which case all relativistic effects would vanish? After all, we usually have no compunctions about using "rigid" rods and other idealizations. But a "rigid" rod is a useful measuring device only for motions that are large compared to the actual deformations of massive metallic bodies.† Similarly, in cases where velocities are comparable to the highest attainable signal speed, the operational approach is a guide in selecting the concepts that are meaningful.

Let us illustrate right away a possible operational approach. We consider two observers A and B who can send and return (i.e. reflect) light signals. The light signals are assumed to travel with a constant speed, c, the speed of light *in vacuo*. To synchronize their clocks, A sends a signal at time t_1 and notes that the signal returns from B at time t_2 (both readings t_1 and t_2 are according to A's clock). A now notifies B (through mail, for instance) that at the time of reception the reading on B's clock should have been

$$t_B = t_1 + \frac{1}{2}(t_2 - t_1) = \frac{1}{2}(t_2 + t_1). \tag{13.1}$$

B adjusts his clock, and the procedure is repeated once more in order to make the scaling of the clocks equal. In addition, A assigns to B a distance r_B through

$$r_B = \frac{c}{2}(t_2 - t_1). \tag{13.2}$$

The constancy of the signal speed c is, of course, a basic prerequisite for the usefulness of this method.

It is to be noted that A can only measure $t_2 - t_1$; therefore, inherent in (13.1), (13.2) is the assumption that the travel times of the signal from A to B, and from B to A, are the same. Evidently this cannot be so if A is moving and B is at rest. But because only relative velocities are admissible, A cannot tell whether he is moving or B is moving. Consequently, the interpretation of data according to (13.1), (13.2) (i.e. when A *imagines* himself to be at rest) is perfectly natural to A. If B flashes at $\bar{t}_1$ and receives the reflected flash at $\bar{t}_2$ (both times according to B's clock), then B will assign to A at the instant $\bar{t}_A = \frac{1}{2}(\bar{t}_2 + \bar{t}_1)$ the distance $\bar{r}_A = c(\bar{t}_2 - \bar{t}_1)/2$.

† As is to be expected, deformations of metallic bodies are measured by optical interference methods and not by comparing the bodies with "rigid" standards, although the latter procedure is quite acceptable for highly deformable substances such as rubber.

In the case of signals transmitted by material media (e.g. sound waves in a column of air or steel) it is not unusual to find that the signal speed is independent of the velocity of the source. However, the speeds with which a signal and a receiver approach each other are additive. But for light the situation is quite different. The mechanism of propagation of light is of another kind, because light is propagated also in a vacuum; in fact, matter only hinders the propagation of light. Second, in the absence of a known absolute space, only the relative velocity of two observers A and B can be meaningful, i.e. it is not possible to distinguish between the cases where A is moving and B is stationary and vice versa. Thus if the speed of light is independent of the motion of the source, then it must be also independent of the motion of the receiver. In brief, *the speed of light is independent of the relative velocity between the source and the receiver.*

Even though moving clocks can be synchronized, a relative motion will affect the intervals at which flashes from one station are received at another. This is known as the *Doppler effect*. If A flashes at intervals of T seconds, then observer B moving relative to A will "see" the flashes at intervals of KT seconds, the distortion factor K being a function of the relative velocity and of the signal speed. Conversely, if B flashes every T seconds, then A receives the flashes KT seconds apart. Moreover, $K < 1$ if A and B are approaching each other, $K > 1$ if they are receding from each other.

Let us imagine three observers, denoted by A, B, C. We denote the distortion factors associated with the pairs AB, AC, BC by K, k^+, k, respectively:

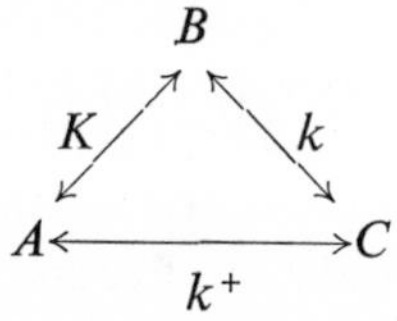

If A flashes every T seconds, the flashes are seen by B at intervals of KT seconds, by C at intervals of k^+T seconds. We now suppose that B also flashes whenever it receives a flash from A. The flashes from B are then received by C at intervals of $k(KT) = kKT$ seconds. In particular, if A, B, and C are *collinear*, with B between A and C, then the flashes from B travel together with the flashes which reached B from A, thus $k(KT) = k^+T$, or

$$kK = k^+. \tag{13.3}$$

If A and C remain at a fixed distance from each other, thus $k^+ = 1$, then

$$K = \frac{1}{k} \tag{13.4}$$

This means that the Doppler effect is not "symmetric"; depending on whether two observers are moving together or moving apart (with the same relative speed), the distortion factor is k' or $1/k'$.

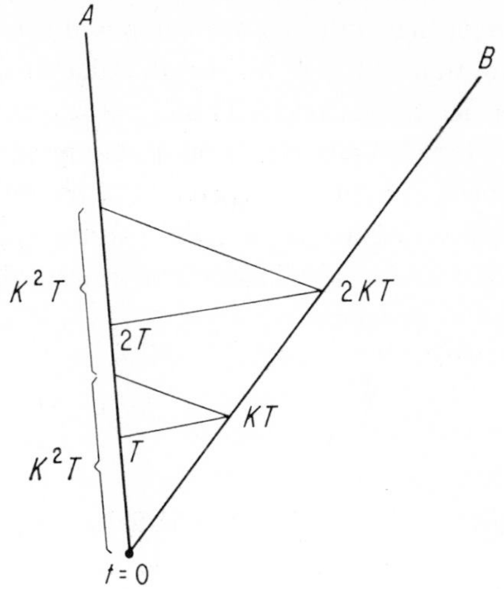

FIGURE 13.1 Scheme of signals sent and received by observers A and B.

The formula (13.3) is actually the relativistic observer transformation for velocities. Suppose that A and B coincide at $t = 0$, and that A flashes every T seconds. Then A receives the reflected flashes at intervals of $K(KT) = K^2T$ seconds (Figure 13.1), or, at the instants $t_0 = 0$, $t_2 = K^2T$, $t_4 = 2K^2T$, etc. (the first flash (at $t = 0$) is reflected instantaneously, whereas the second flash, emitted at $t_1 = T$, is received back at $t_2 = K^2T$, and so on). Then, by (13.1), (13.2),

$$t_B = \frac{T}{2}(1 + K^2), \qquad r_B = c\frac{T}{2}(K^2 - 1).$$

The (constant) relative velocity V of A and B is defined by

$$\frac{V}{c} = \frac{r_B}{ct_B} = \frac{K^2 - 1}{K^2 + 1}. \tag{13.5}$$

Thus

$$K = \sqrt{\frac{1 + \beta}{1 - \beta}}, \tag{13.6}$$

where $\beta = V/c$. Let us describe the relative velocities of the pairs AC, BC by $\alpha^+ = U^+/c$, $\alpha = U/c$, respectively. Then, by (13.3),

$$\alpha^+ = \frac{k^{+2} - 1}{k^{+2} + 1} = \frac{k^2K^2 - 1}{k^2K^2 + 1} = \frac{\alpha + \beta}{1 + \alpha\beta}. \tag{13.7}$$

If $\alpha\beta \ll 1$, we recover from (13.7) the Galilean transformation (9.42). In contrast to Galilean transformations, (13.7) was obtained on the basis of explicit operations involving signals which propagate at a finite speed (and independently of relative motion of observers). At any one point, particle velocities are of course composed according to the parallelogram law. The formula (13.7) is, on the other hand, the (Lorentz) observer transformation which relates velocities of a particle as seen by two observers.

The formula (13.7) fits perfectly with the empirical observation that the speed of light is independent of the relative velocity between a source and a receiver. Namely, a light particle (*photon*) which moves with the speed $U = c\ (\alpha = 1)$ in the $x - t$ frame will also move with the speed c in the $x^+ - t^+$ frame:

$$\alpha^+ = \frac{1 + \beta}{1 + \beta} = 1.$$

Second, if V and U both equal c, i.e. $\alpha = \beta = 1$, then

$$\alpha^+ = \frac{1 + 1}{1 + 1} = 1,$$

hence there is no observer frame in which a photon is at rest.

Because light interacts with matter, its propagation in material media is a complex phenomenon. Ordinarily the speed of light relative to the medium is denoted by c/n, where n is the *index of refraction*. If the medium is moving with a speed V, then V is added to c/n in accord with (13.7):

$$\frac{c^+}{n} = \frac{c/n + V}{1 + cV/nc^2} \doteq \frac{c}{n} + V\left(1 - \frac{1}{n^2}\right). \tag{13.8}$$

To derive the Lorentz transformation, we consider two observers, A and B, and a moving point P, where it is assumed that A, B, and P are collinear.† According to (13.1), (13.2), if A assigns to P at the instant T the coordinate X, then the signal from A to P was emitted by A at $t_1 = T - (X/c)$, and received back by A at $t_2 = T + (X/c)$. Similarly, if B assigns to P at the instant T^+ the coordinate X^+, then the times of emission and reception at B are $t_1^+ = T^+ - (X^+/c)$ and $t_2^+ = T^+ + (X^+/c)$, respectively. Now let us suppose that A and B start their clocks at the instant when B passes A (moving towards P). To help the book-keeping of intervals, we may assume that A and B flash at this instant, but these flashes have nothing to do with locating

† Cf. Bondi, pp. 398–400, *op. cit.*

P. To locate P, A sends a signal at $t_1 = T - (X/c)$. This signal overtakes B at $t_1^+ = T^+ - (X^+/c) = K[T - (X/c)]$, and on the leg from B to P serves also as a signal sent from B to P. The signal returns from P to B at $t_2^+ = T^+ + (X^+/c)$; because the flashes of B at $t_0^+ = 0$ and t_2^+ would be seen at A an interval Kt_2^+ apart, it follows that $T + (X/c) = K[T^+ + (X^+/c)]$ (cf. Figure 13.2). Thus

$$T^+ - \frac{X^+}{c} = K\left(T - \frac{X}{c}\right), \qquad T^+ + \frac{X^+}{c} = \frac{1}{K}\left(T + \frac{X}{c}\right).$$

Solving for X^+ and T^+, we get $X^+ = AX + BcT$, $T^+ = AT + (B/c)X$, where we have used (13.6), and

$$\begin{aligned} A &= \frac{1}{2}\left(\frac{1}{K} + K\right) = W = \frac{1}{\sqrt{1-\beta^2}}, \qquad \beta = \frac{V}{c}, \\ B &= \frac{1}{2}\left(\frac{1}{K} - K\right) = -W\beta, \end{aligned} \tag{13.9}$$

V being the speed of B relative to A. Consequently,

$$X^+ = W(X - \beta cT), \qquad T^+ = W\left(T - \frac{\beta X}{c}\right). \tag{13.10}$$

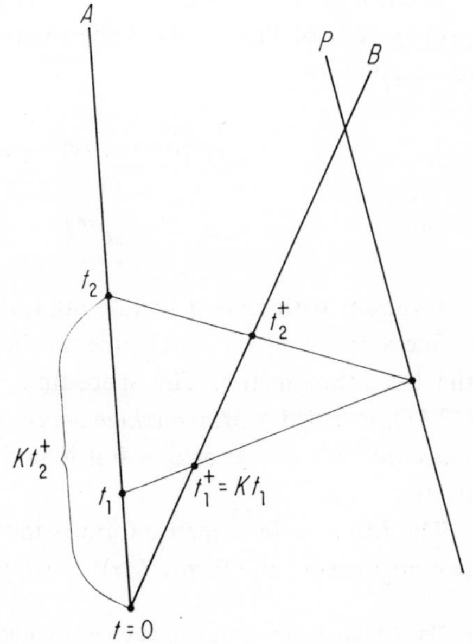

FIGURE 13.2 Collinear observers A, B, P. Signals sent by A at $t = 0$, $t = t_1$ are received by B at $t^+ = 0$, t_1^+. Signals sent by B at $t = 0$, $t = t_2^+$ are received by A at $t = 0$, t_2.

One of the numerous consequences of Lorentz transformation is that *simultaneity of events is a relative concept.* For instance, if two events at X_A^+, T_A^+ and X_B^+, T_B^+ are simultaneous in the "starred" frame, i.e. $T_A^+ = T_B^+$, then they need not be simultaneous in another frame:

$$T_A - T_B = \frac{V}{c^2}(X_A - X_B).$$

"Relativity" is, then, a consequence of the operational approach. Although each observer uses the same methods for making measurements, the values obtained by different observers need not agree. Quantities and concepts that are customarily regarded as absolute, e.g. "actual length," simultaneity, now become relative. If light were not available, so that communications would be possible only by touch or sound, then the relativity of things and appearances would be a natural part of our experience.

Because Lorentz transformations coincide in the limit as $\beta = V/c \to 0$ with Galilean transformations, the natural way of reconciling mechanics and electromagnetism is to make mechanics also Lorentz-invariant ("relativistic mechanics"). Fortunately the main applications of electromagnetism in continuum mechanics (e.g. deformation of dielectrics, magnetohydrodynamics) concern particle velocities that are negligible compared to the speed of light, so that the distinction between the two types of invariance is practically negligible.

According to (13.10), $(X^+)^2 - c^2(T^+)^2 = X^2 - c^2T^2$, i.e. the speed of propagation of light is the same relative to both observers A and B. The quadratic form

$$\phi = g_{\alpha\beta}\, dx^\alpha\, dx^\beta = (dx)^2 + (dy)^2 + (dz)^2 - c^2(dt)^2, \tag{13.11}$$

where†

$$\|g_{\alpha\beta}\| = \|g^{\alpha\beta}\| = \text{diag}(1, 1, 1, -1), \tag{13.12}$$

is invariant with respect to Lorentz transformations, so that it can serve to define a metric of the space-time, in the same way that $ds^2 = dx_i\, dx_i$ defines the Euclidean metric. The space-time, complemented by the metric form (13.11), is called a *Minkowskian space.* If $\phi > 0$, the vector $d\mathbf{x}$ is said to be *space-like*, for $\phi < 0$ or $\phi = 0$ it is said to be *time-like* or *light-like*, respectively.

The Minkowskian metric form is indefinite, in fact, it is the difference of two positive definite forms, $(dx)^2 + (dy)^2 + (dz)^2$ and $c^2(dt)^2$. So as to assign

† The subscript-superscript notation was outlined on p. 102 (cf. also p. 244).

a real value to the *separation* ds of two events (ds being the counterpart of distance in Euclidean geometry), we define ds by

$$ds^2 = e\phi = eg_{\alpha\beta}\,dx^\alpha\,dx^\beta, \tag{13.13}$$

where $e = 1$ for space-like separation

$e = -1$ for time-like separation

The Lorentz transformations can be also derived quite formally from the condition of invariance of (13.11). That is, repeating the steps used in the derivation of (8.10), we find that the separation remains invariant in a general transformation $X^\alpha = X^\alpha(x^1, x^2, x^3, x^4)$ only if the transformation is of the form

$$X^\alpha = L^\alpha{}_\beta\, x^\beta, \tag{13.14}$$

where the Lorentz matrix $\mathbf{L}$ is orthogonal,

$$L_{\alpha\beta}L^{\alpha\mu} = \delta^\mu_\beta, \qquad L_{\alpha\beta}L^{\mu\beta} = \delta^\mu_\alpha, \tag{13.15}$$

so that the inverse transformation is given by

$$x^\alpha = L_\mu{}^\alpha X^\mu. \tag{13.16}$$

As always, the raising and lowering of indices is done with the metric tensor, e.g. $g_{\lambda\mu}L^\lambda{}_\alpha = L_{\mu\alpha}$, $g^{\rho\beta}L^\mu{}_\beta = L^{\mu\rho}$, $g_{\alpha\beta}g^{\rho\beta} = \delta^\rho_\alpha$. In view of (13.12), however, the various representations are, except in one case, identical: $L_{11} = L^1{}_1 = L_1{}^1 = L^{11}, L_{12} = L_1{}^2 = L^1{}_2 = L^{12}$, etc. whereas $L_{i4} = -L^{i4}, L_{4i} = -L^{4i}$, $i = 1, 2, 3$ (but $L_{44} = -L_4{}^4 = L^{44}$). In the case of a vector $\mathbf{V}$ the two representations V_α and V^β are related by $V_\alpha = g_{\alpha\beta}V^\beta$, thus $V_1 = V^1$, $V_2 = V^2$, $V_3 = V^3$, $V^4 = -V_4$, and $\mathbf{V}\cdot\mathbf{V} = g_{\alpha\beta}V^\alpha V^\beta = V_\alpha V^\alpha = (V^1)^2 + (V^2)^2 + (V^3)^2 - (V^4)^2$.

The 16 components of a Lorentz matrix must satisfy 10 orthogonality conditions, thus leaving 6 degrees of freedom. This freedom permits us to align the space axes of two observers (no such alignment of time axes is possible, because transformations of the space axes of a given observer are made possible by there being more than one space axis). In this way we obtain (cf. (13.10))

$$\begin{gathered} \mathbf{x}^+ = \mathbf{L}\mathbf{x}, \\ x^+ = W(x - \beta\tau), \quad y^+ = y, \quad z^+ = z, \quad \tau^+ = W(\tau - \beta x), \end{gathered} \tag{13.17}$$

$$\|\mathbf{L}\| = \|L^{\alpha}{}_{\beta}\| = \begin{Vmatrix} W & 0 & 0 & -W\beta \\ 0 & 1 & 0 & 0 \\ 0 & 0 & 1 & 0 \\ -W\beta & 0 & 0 & W \end{Vmatrix}, \tag{13.18}$$

where $\tau = ct$ (this is time measured in *light-centimeters*), and $V = c\beta$ is the speed of the $(\mathbf{x}^+)$ frame in the $(\mathbf{x})$ frame.

Let us note that not only is the separation invariant to Lorentz transformations, but that, $\mathbf{L}$ being an orthogonal tensor, these transformations can be formally interpreted as rotations in the four-dimensional space-time. If we require that all physical principles be form-invariant to Lorentz transformations, then the simplest way of meeting this requirement is to recast the basic equations in terms of *four-tensors* which have components on space axes as well as on the time axis. That is, Lorentz transformations are identified with orthogonal coordinate transformations in space-time, so that the desired Lorentz-invariance is automatically fulfilled by virtue of all quantities being represented by four-tensors (the invariance with respect to coordinate transformations of a "three-space" is fulfilled in a similar way, i.e. through the use of appropriate "three-tensors"). The change of mechanics into (Lorentz-invariant) relativistic mechanics is of course a vast undertaking, and many questions remain unresolved so far. For instance, what is to become of Euclidean observer transformations, which, in contrast to Galilean transformations, involve time-dependent rotations of the space axes of observers?

To give an example of the insights gained by a transition to the world of space-time, we take up again the relativistic composition of velocities, (13.7). Along with the "non-relativistic" velocities $U^i = dx^i/dt$, $i = 1, 2, 3$, we can define four-vector velocities as follows. A time-like separation $ds^2 = c^2\,dt^2 - (dx^2 + dy^2 + dz^2)$ now plays the role of time increments; we write

$$ds = \frac{d\tau}{w}, \qquad w^{-2} = 1 - \frac{\mathbf{U}\cdot\mathbf{U}}{c^2}, \tag{13.19}$$

where $d\tau = c\,dt$. The *four-velocity* u^α is defined by $u^\alpha = dx^\alpha/ds$, so that

$$u^1 = \frac{w}{c}U^1, \ldots, \ldots, u^4 = w. \tag{13.20}$$

Let w^+ be the component $(u^4)^+$, and let W be as defined in (13.9). With the aid of (13.3), and using the definitions corresponding to (13.6), we obtain

$$\frac{w^+}{Ww} = 2\,\frac{(k^+)^2 + 1}{(k^2 + 1)(K^2 + 1)} = 1 + \alpha\beta, \tag{13.21}$$

where $\alpha = U/c$, $\beta = -V/c$. In one-dimensional motions, then, it is easy to see from (13.18) that the Lorentz transformation $(u^+)^1 = L^1{}_1 u^1 + L^1{}_4 w$ is identical with (13.7), whereas the transformation of the time-like component, $w^+ = L^4{}_1 u^1 + L^4{}_4 w$, reduces to (13.21). That is, in terms of the four-velocities, the composition (13.7) is simply a linear (Lorentz) transformation of the velocity components, whereas in terms of "ordinary" velocities this transformation is nonlinear (i.e. the ordinary velocities do not even behave as vectors in this observer transformation).

In analogy with component transformations in a three space, we define Lorentz transformations of a four-tensor $F^{\alpha\beta}$ by

$$(F^{\mu\pi})^+ = L^\mu{}_\alpha L^\pi{}_\beta F^{\alpha\beta}. \tag{13.22}$$

Similarly,

$$F^+_{\mu\pi} = L_\mu{}^\alpha L_\pi{}^\beta F_{\alpha\beta}, \tag{13.23}$$

where

$$\|\mathbf{L}^{-1}\| = \|L_\mu{}^\alpha\| = \begin{Vmatrix} W & 0 & 0 & W\beta \\ 0 & 1 & 0 & 0 \\ 0 & 0 & 1 & 0 \\ W\beta & 0 & 0 & W \end{Vmatrix}. \tag{13.24}$$

Maxwell's equations

Charge distributions play a dual role in field theories. On the one hand, a charge distribution q is looked upon as the cause of a field $\mathbf{D}$, while on the other hand q can be also interpreted as the divergence of the field, i.e. $q = \operatorname{div}\mathbf{D}$. From the second point of view, Maxwell's equations assert the existence, or nonexistence, of certain kinds of charges. However, the divergence of a three-vector is not Lorentz-invariant, which means that $q = \operatorname{div}\mathbf{D}$ is not a properly invariant statement. Now, the determination of the amount of charge can be imagined as a "counting" of charged particles; but counting is a simple operation that should not require the ideas of metric, Lorentz transformations, and so on. Therefore, let us take a four-dimensional space that has no other properties than the topology induced by a parametrization of its points by the coordinates x^α, $\alpha = 1, 2, 3, 4$. In particular, because a metric is not assumed, no coordinate can be interpreted as being space-like or time-like. With no more than this, we shall be able to express a general form of Maxwell's equations.

What we need now are some invariant differential operators. Evidently the ordinary derivatives will not do, for if we consider coordinate transformations $\bar{x}^\mu = \bar{x}^\mu(x^\alpha)$, and the associated tensor transformations, e.g. $\bar{V}^\mu = \bar{x}^\mu_{,\alpha} V^\alpha$, then it is easy to see that the ordinary derivatives will not transform as tensors. An operation that does turn out to be invariant is the *cyclic divergence* of a skew-symmetric tensor $F_{\alpha\beta}$, defined by

$$(\mathrm{Div}\overline{\mathbf{F}})_{\alpha\beta\gamma} = F_{\alpha\beta,\gamma} + F_{\beta\gamma,\alpha} + F_{\gamma\alpha,\beta}. \tag{13.25}$$

We shall call $F_{\alpha\beta}$ the *vacuum field.* With the identification

$$\begin{aligned} F_{41} &= E_1, & F_{32} &= B_1, \\ F_{42} &= E_2, & F_{13} &= B_2, \\ F_{43} &= E_3, & F_{21} &= B_3, \end{aligned} \tag{13.26}$$

where $\mathbf{E}$ is called the *electric vector*, and $\mathbf{B}$ the *magnetic vector*, we now find that

$$F_{\alpha\beta,\gamma} + F_{\beta\gamma,\alpha} + F_{\gamma\alpha,\beta} = 0 \tag{13.27}$$

are equivalent to the first set of Maxwell's equations,

$$\underset{\text{e.u.}}{\mathrm{curl}\mathbf{E}} + \underset{\text{m.u.}}{\partial_\tau \mathbf{B}} = \mathbf{0}, \qquad \mathrm{div}\mathbf{B} = 0. \tag{13.28}$$

Here $\partial_\tau = (1/c)\partial_t$, and e.u., m.u. indicate the use of (rationalized) electrostatic and magnetostatic units (these units are defined in the next subsection). We may interpret (13.27) as an assertion of the nonexistence of magnetic charges; its representation is valid in any four-dimensional coordinate system, and for any motion of the medium.

The presence of matter will modify the vacuum field, which leads us to introduce the *total field* $W_{\alpha\beta}$. The second set of Maxwell's equations asserts the existence of electric charges, so that we must also introduce a current four-vector $\mathbf{j}$, somewhat along the lines of $[J^1, J^2, J^3, q]$, where $\mathbf{J}$ is the ordinary current vector. But there is a difficulty: the cyclic divergence of $W_{\alpha\beta}$ defines a third rank tensor, thus

$$W_{\alpha\beta,\gamma} + W_{\beta\gamma,\alpha} + W_{\gamma\alpha,\beta} = j_{\alpha\beta\gamma}. \tag{13.29}$$

To obtain a less awkward representation of the current, we proceed as follows. Let $\varepsilon^{\alpha\beta\gamma\varepsilon}$ be the alternator; then

$$\varepsilon^{\lambda\mu\pi\sigma} = \bar{x}^{\lambda}_{,\alpha}\bar{x}^{\mu}_{,\beta}\bar{x}^{\pi}_{,\gamma}\bar{x}^{\sigma}_{,\delta}\,\frac{\varepsilon^{\alpha\beta\gamma\delta}}{\det(\bar{x}^{\lambda}_{,\alpha})}$$

expresses the familiar rule for evaluating determinants. Owing to the factor $1/\det(\bar{x}^{\lambda}_{,\alpha})$, the alternator is not a tensor; we say that it is a *relative tensor*. Let us now multiply (13.29) by $\frac{1}{6}\varepsilon^{\alpha\beta\gamma\delta}$, and use the definitions

$$w^{\gamma\delta} = \frac{1}{2}\varepsilon^{\alpha\beta\gamma\delta}W_{\alpha\beta}, \qquad j^{\delta} = \frac{1}{6}\varepsilon^{\alpha\beta\gamma\delta}j_{\alpha\beta\gamma} \tag{13.30}$$

(the quantities so defined are relative tensors!). Then (13.29) becomes

$$(\mathrm{div}\mathbf{w})^{\beta} = w^{\alpha\beta}{}_{,\alpha} = j^{\beta}. \tag{13.31}$$

Moreover, from the skew-symmetry of $w^{\alpha\beta}$ there follows the *law of conservation of charge*,

$$\mathrm{div}\mathbf{j} = j^{\alpha}{}_{,\alpha} = 0. \tag{13.32}$$

To obtain the second set of Maxwell's equations, we use the identifications

$$\begin{aligned} w^{14} &= D_1, & w^{32} &= H_1, \\ w^{24} &= D_2, & w^{13} &= H_2, \\ w^{34} &= D_3, & w^{21} &= H_3, \end{aligned} \tag{13.33}$$

where **D** is called the *electric excitation*, and **H** is called the *magnetic excitation*. Then, by (13.31),†

$$\underset{\text{m.u.}}{\mathrm{curl}\mathbf{H}} - \underset{\text{e.u.}}{\partial_\tau \mathbf{D}} = \underset{\text{m.u.}}{\mathbf{J}}, \qquad \mathrm{div}\mathbf{D} = q, \tag{13.34}$$

where

$$\mathbf{j} = (\mathbf{J}, q) \tag{13.35}$$

(it is customary to express in this way the "extension" of a three-vector **J** to a four-vector **j**). We also write‡

$$\mathbf{D} = \mathbf{E} + \mathbf{P}, \qquad \mathbf{H} = \mathbf{B} - \mathbf{M}, \tag{13.36}$$

and refer to **P** and **M** as *polarization* and *magnetization*, respectively.

† Upon seeing Maxwell's equations (13.28), (13.34) for the first time, Boltzmann is said to have exclaimed "Was it a god who wrote these lines!" One wonders what Boltzmann's reaction would have been to the forms (13.27) and (13.31).

‡ The unsymmetric choice of signs is traditional.

In the relations (13.26), (13.33) the indices do not occur in a symmetric way; in particular, the index 4, which corresponds in the special theory of relativity to time-like components, is a preferred one. The preferred role of an index cannot be invariant to general coordinate transformations, which means that in replacing $F_{\alpha\beta}$, $w^{\alpha\beta}$ by the vectors **E**, **D**, **B**, **H** the Maxwell's equations have lost their natural invariance. We could assume that (13.28), (13.34) hold in an absolute space ("aether") only, but the notion of an absolute space always turns out to be untenable. Instead, we require that all theories be form-invariant to a certain class of observer transformations. In relativistic theories these are the Lorentz transformations (Einstein's principle of relativity).† How do Lorentz transformations fit into a general, four-dimensional space? To answer this, we first recall that a metric describes some invariant property of a space. Further, in a three-space with the metric form $ds^2 = g_{ij} dx^i\, dx^j \geq 0$ there exist, at least locally, coordinates x_i such that $ds^2 = \delta_{ij}\, dx_i\, dx_j$, i.e. the metric is locally Euclidean. Because separation, rather than distance, is an invariant of Lorentz transformations, we now require that the general space which provided a setting for (13.27), (13.31) be locally Minkowskian. That is, there must exist, at least locally, coordinates x^1, x^2, x^3, x^4 such that the separation $ds^2 = g_{\alpha\beta}\, dx^\alpha\, dx^\beta$ is represented by $ds^2 = (dx^1)^2 + (dx^2)^2 + (dx^3)^2 - (dx^4)^2$. Moreover, the invariance of separation requires that the local coordinate transformations (i.e. the relations between coordinate differentials) be identical with Lorentz transformations. In the large, the variation of $g_{\alpha\beta}$ may be such as to describe a "curved space" that accounts intrinsically for gravitational attraction; this is indeed the case in what is referred to as the general theory of relativity (a curious name for a relativistic, general theory of gravitation!).‡

Because electromagnetism is Lorentz-invariant, so is the speed of propagation of electromagnetic fields. Thus the relativity principle incorporates in a natural way the empirical fact that the speed of light is the same for all observers, and its value *in vacuo* is the highest attainable signal speed. According to the general relativity theory, gravitational fields can decrease the

† This principle can be worded in the same way as the relativity principle of Galilei (cf. p. 191): no mechanical or electromagnetical experiments, performed in the interior of an inertial frame, can detect the uniform translation of that frame relative to another inertial frame.

‡ In this connection one hears time and again the phrase that geometry has now become a part of physics. It is difficult to see how one could possibly mean that. To quote Poincare [123]: "If geometry were an experimental science, it would not be an exact science. . . . The axioms of geometry are therefore neither synthetic *a priori* intuitions nor experimental facts. They are conventions. . . . What, then, are we to think of the question: is Euclidean geometry true? It has no meaning. We might as well ask if the metric system is true, and if the old weights and measures are false; if Cartesian coordinates are true and polar coordinates false. One geometry cannot be more true than another; it can be only more convenient."

speed of propagation of light, as well as changing the direction of light rays (e.g. bending of light rays that pass near the sun). But this is only of interest in cosmological theories.

As is evident from (13.26), (13.33), the space-time formulation favors the assignment of the same dimension to **E**, **D**, **B**, **H** (although the units of **E** and **D** may be electrostatic, those of **B** and **H** magnetostatic). Second, from (13.27) it follows that $\bar{\mathbf{F}}$ is the *curl* of a four-vector $\bar{\boldsymbol{\phi}}$, called the charge potential:

$$F_{\alpha\beta} = \phi_{\alpha,\beta} - \phi_{\beta,\alpha}. \tag{13.37}$$

Letting $\bar{\boldsymbol{\phi}} = (\mathbf{A}, -\varnothing)$, we find that (13.37) are equivalent to

$$\mathbf{E} = -\operatorname{grad}\varnothing - \partial_\tau \mathbf{A}, \qquad \mathbf{B} = \operatorname{curl}\mathbf{A}. \tag{13.38}$$

Ordinarily one chooses potentials that satisfy the Lorentz gauge condition

$$\operatorname{div}\boldsymbol{\phi} = 0. \tag{13.39}$$

The space-time formulation of electromagnetism enables us to obtain with ease the familiar transformation properties of the field vectors. For instance, from $\mathbf{j}^+ = \mathbf{L}\mathbf{j}$ it follows that $J_1^+ = W(J_1 - \beta q)$, $J_2^+ = J_2$, $J_3^+ = J_3$, $q^+ = W(q - \beta J_1)$. If we allow the direction of the relative velocity **V** to be arbitrary, and assume that $W \doteq 1$, we obtain the Galilean transformations

$$q^+ \doteq q, \qquad \mathbf{J}^+ \doteq \mathbf{J} - \boldsymbol{\beta} q, \qquad \boldsymbol{\beta} = \frac{\mathbf{V}}{c} \tag{13.40}$$

(if **J** is measured in electrostatic units, then $J_1^+ = W(J_1 - Vq) \doteq J_1 - Vq$, but $q^+ = W(q - VJ_1c^{-2}) \doteq q$). The interpretation of (13.40) is simple: if the charges are at rest in the $x^+ - t^+$ frame, then in the $x - t$ frame there exists a current $\mathbf{J} = \boldsymbol{\beta} q$, where $\mathbf{V} = c\boldsymbol{\beta}$ is the observed velocity of the $x^+ - t^+$ frame.

The transformations (13.23) yield the relations $F_{12}^+ = W(F_{12} + \beta F_{42})$, $F_{13}^+ = W(F_{13} + \beta F_{43})$, $F_{14}^+ = F_{14}$, $F_{23}^+ = F_{23}$, $F_{24}^+ = W(F_{24} + \beta F_{21})$, $F_{34}^+ = W(F_{34} + \beta F_{31})$. Therefore, by (13.26),

$$\begin{aligned} E_1^+ &= E_1, \quad E_2^+ = W(E_2 - \beta B_3), \quad E_3^+ = W(E_3 + \beta B_2), \\ B_1^+ &= B_1, \quad B_2^+ = W(B_2 + \beta E_3), \quad B_3^+ = W(B_3 - \beta E_2). \end{aligned} \tag{13.41}$$

With $W \doteq 1$, and for arbitrary direction of the relative velocity, we get the Galilean transformations

$$\mathbf{E}^+ \doteq \mathbf{E} + (\boldsymbol{\beta} \times \mathbf{B}), \qquad \mathbf{B}^+ \doteq \mathbf{B} \tag{13.42}$$

($\mathbf{E}^+$ is often called the *electromotive force*). Transforming $w^{\alpha\beta}$ according to (13.22), we get

$$\mathbf{D}^+ \doteq \mathbf{D}, \qquad \mathbf{H}^+ \doteq \mathbf{H} - (\boldsymbol{\beta} \times \mathbf{D}). \tag{13.43}$$

If only electrostatic units are used, then, for instance, $E_2^+ = W(E_2 - \beta c B_3) \doteq E_2 - VB_3$, whereas $cB_2^+ = W(cB_2 + \beta E_3)$ reduces to $B_2^+ \doteq B_2$.

Finally, let us suppose that the starred frame is one in which a charged particle is instantaneously at rest. We define the (Lorentz) force acting on the particle by $\mathbf{f}^+ = q^+\mathbf{E}^+$; then in another frame this force is given by

$$\mathbf{f} \doteq q\mathbf{E} + (\mathbf{J} \times \mathbf{B}), \qquad \mathbf{J} = q\boldsymbol{\beta}, \tag{13.44}$$

$\mathbf{V} = c\boldsymbol{\beta}$ being the observed velocity of the starred frame. With $q_{\text{e.u.}}/q_{\text{m.u.}} = c$, we can obtain from $\mathbf{f}_{\text{dynes}} = q_{\text{e.u.}}\mathbf{E}_{\text{e.u.}} + q_{\text{e.u.}}(\mathbf{v}_{cm} \times \mathbf{B}_{\text{e.u.}}) = q_{\text{m.u.}}\mathbf{E}_{\text{m.u.}} + q_{\text{m.u.}}(\mathbf{v}_{cm} \times \mathbf{B}_{\text{m.u.}})$ ratios of units for other variables, e.g. $B_{\text{m.u.}} = cB_{\text{e.u.}}$.

To obtain integral representations of Maxwell's equations, we consider a material surface S bounded by a material curve C. Denoting now by

$$\boldsymbol{\beta} = \frac{\mathbf{v}}{c}$$

the dimensionless particle velocities, we obtain

$$\oint_C \mathbf{E}^+ \cdot d\mathbf{x} = -\frac{d}{d\tau}\int_S \mathbf{B} \cdot d\mathbf{a} \quad \text{(Faraday's law of induction)} \tag{13.45}$$

$$\oint_C \mathbf{H}^+ \cdot d\mathbf{x} = \frac{d}{d\tau}\int_S \mathbf{D} \cdot d\mathbf{a} + \int_S \mathbf{j}^+ \cdot d\mathbf{a} \quad \text{(Ampère's law)} \tag{13.46}$$

To verify (13.45), for instance, we write, by (8.60),

$$\frac{d}{dt}\int_S \mathbf{B} \cdot d\mathbf{a} = \int_S \overline{B_i\, da_i}^{\,\cdot} = \int_S da_i(\dot{B}_i + B_i v_{k,k} - v_{i,k}B_k).$$

The reduction to $(13.28)_1$ now follows by applying the Kelvin's transformation to the left-hand side of (13.45).

If S is a surface enclosing a region V, then, by (13.45), (13.46)

$$\int_S \mathbf{B} \cdot d\mathbf{a} = 0 \quad \text{(nonexistence of magnetic charge)}, \tag{13.47}$$

$$\int_S \mathbf{D} \cdot d\mathbf{a} = \int_V q\, dv \quad \text{(existence of electric charge)}. \tag{13.48}$$

The conservation of charge,

$$\underset{\text{e.u.}}{\partial_\tau q} + \underset{\text{m.u.}}{\operatorname{div}\mathbf{J}} = 0, \tag{13.49}$$

is a consequence of Maxwell's equations, as can be verified by applying *div* to the first of (13.34), and ∂_τ to the second. Historically, the introduction of the *displacement current* $\partial_\tau \mathbf{D}$ must have been motivated, in part, by the need to reconcile the "pre-Maxwell equations"

$$\operatorname{curl}\mathbf{E} + \partial_\tau \mathbf{B} = \mathbf{0}, \qquad \operatorname{div}\mathbf{B} = 0, \tag{13.28)R}$$

$$\operatorname{curl}\mathbf{H} = \mathbf{J}, \qquad \operatorname{div}\mathbf{D} = q \tag{13.50}$$

with the conservation of charge.

The integral representations can be adapted for the derivation of *boundary conditions* and *jump conditions* across a surface of discontinuity, S. First, by (13.28), (13.47), and (9.69),

$$\mathbf{n} \cdot [\![\mathbf{B}]\!] = 0, \tag{13.51}$$

where $\mathbf{n}$ is a unit normal vector of S. If there exists a surface charge density σ, we obtain from (13.48) in the same way that

$$\mathbf{n} \cdot [\![\mathbf{D}]\!] = \sigma. \tag{13.52}$$

Next, combining (13.45) with (9.74), we arrive at $\mathbf{k} \cdot [\![-\mathbf{E} - (\boldsymbol{\beta} \times \mathbf{B}) + (\mathbf{B} \times (\boldsymbol{\alpha} - \boldsymbol{\beta}))]\!] = 0$, where $\mathbf{k}$ is a unit tangent vector of S, and $\boldsymbol{\alpha} = \mathbf{u}/c$ is the dimensionless velocity field of the surface of discontinuity. If S is a material surface, e.g. a boundary, then $\boldsymbol{\alpha} = \boldsymbol{\beta}$, so that

$$\mathbf{n} \times [\![\mathbf{E} + (\boldsymbol{\beta} \times \mathbf{B})]\!] = \mathbf{0}. \tag{13.53}$$

That is, only the normal component of $\mathbf{E} + (\boldsymbol{\beta} \times \mathbf{B})$ can suffer a jump. If S is not a material surface, then

$$\mathbf{n} \times [\![\mathbf{E} + (\bar{\boldsymbol{\alpha}} \times \mathbf{B})]\!] = \mathbf{0}, \qquad \bar{\boldsymbol{\alpha}} = \bar{\alpha}\mathbf{n}, \tag{13.54}$$

where $\bar{\alpha}$ is the displacement speed of S.

Turning to (13.46), we apply (9.70) to the left-hand side. Then

$$\mathbf{k} \cdot [\![\mathbf{H} - (\boldsymbol{\alpha} \times \mathbf{D})]\!] = \mathbf{m} \cdot (\mathbf{i} - \sigma\boldsymbol{\beta}), \tag{13.55}$$

where $\mathbf{i}$ is the density of surface current, and $\mathbf{k}$, $\mathbf{m}$, $\mathbf{n}$ are a right-handed triad of unit vectors. If there is no surface charge or surface current, then

$$\mathbf{n} \times [\![\mathbf{H}]\!] + \boldsymbol{\alpha}[\![\mathbf{D}]\!] = \mathbf{0}. \tag{13.56}$$

At boundaries that do not move,

$$\begin{aligned} \mathbf{n} \times [\![\mathbf{H}]\!] &= \mathbf{0}, \qquad \mathbf{n} \times [\![\mathbf{E}]\!] = \mathbf{0}, \\ \mathbf{n} \cdot [\![\mathbf{B}]\!] &= 0, \qquad \mathbf{n} \cdot [\![\mathbf{D}]\!] = \sigma. \end{aligned} \tag{13.57}$$

Dot-multiplying $(13.34)_1$ with $\mathbf{E}$, and $(13.28)_1$ with $\mathbf{H}$, and noting that $E_i\varepsilon_{ijk}H_{k,j} - H_i\varepsilon_{ijk}E_{k,j} = -\varepsilon_{ijk}(E_jH_k)_{,i} = -\text{div}(\mathbf{E} \times \mathbf{H})$, we arrive at

$$-\text{div}\mathbf{p} = \mathbf{E} \cdot \partial_\tau \mathbf{D} + \mathbf{H} \cdot \partial_\tau \mathbf{B} + \mathbf{E} \cdot \mathbf{J}, \tag{13.58}$$

where $\mathbf{p}$, called the *Poynting's vector*, is given by

$$\mathbf{p} = \mathbf{E} \times \mathbf{H}. \tag{13.59}$$

Integration of (13.58) over a region V now yields *Poynting's theorem*:

$$\int_V (\mathbf{E} \cdot \partial_\tau \mathbf{D} + \mathbf{H} \cdot \partial_\tau \mathbf{B})\, dv = \int_{\partial V} \mathbf{p} \cdot d\mathbf{a} - \int_V \mathbf{E} \cdot \mathbf{J}\, dv. \tag{13.60}$$

Because $\mathbf{p} \cdot d\mathbf{a} = n_i\varepsilon_{ijk}E_jH_k\,da$, where $\mathbf{n}$ is a unit normal vector of ∂V, it follows that the normal components of $\mathbf{E}$ and $\mathbf{H}$ drop out of $\mathbf{p} \cdot d\mathbf{a}$, thus $\mathbf{p} \cdot d\mathbf{a} = E_{||}H_{||} \sin\theta\, da$, where θ is the angle between the projections $E_{||}$ and $H_{||}$ of $\mathbf{E}$ and $\mathbf{H}$ upon ∂V.

The equation (13.60) resembles an energy balance, the integral of $\mathbf{p} \cdot d\mathbf{a}$ representing the *efflux of electromagnetic energy*, whereas the integral of $-\mathbf{E} \cdot \mathbf{J}$ (*Joule power*) represents a loss of electromagnetic energy (the energy being transformed into thermal and mechanical energies). However, it must be kept in mind that rather than being a separate principle, (13.60) was derived from Maxwell's equations. Second, the localization of electromagnetic energy and its flux is still a matter of some controversy, because it appears that in some cases $\mathbf{p} = \mathbf{E} \times \mathbf{H}$ cannot be interpreted as the density of energy flux (cf. [78], p. 52).

Charges and currents, the elastic dielectric

Charge may be determined by means of Coulomb's law,

$$F = K\frac{QQ'}{r^2}, \tag{13.61}$$

which is a consequence of the general equations of electromagnetism. In (13.61) F is the force between two charged bodies that are small compared to the distance r separating them. If K is taken to be a dimensional coefficient, then we can assign to charge a new dimension which is not reducible to the mechanical dimensions of mass, length, and time. This is indeed done in the Giorgi system (also called the *QMKS* system). We prefer to choose $K = 1/(4\pi)$ instead, in which case charge is measured in (rationalized) electrostatic units in the c.g.s. system, the dimension of charge being $M^{1/2}L^{3/2}T^{-1}$ (cr. [113], Appendix I).

Our reason for preferring the (rationalized) *Gaussian system of units* (electrical units for charge and electric field, magnetic units for currents and magnetic field) is that it makes the transition to the four-dimensional formulation natural. Other than that, it may be preferable to use the Giorgi system because the use of basic laws for eliminating dimensions is generally frowned upon. For instance, we do not (except in astronomy and potential theory!) use Newton's law of gravitation,

$$F = K\frac{MM'}{r^2}, \tag{13.61)*$$

to express the dimension of mass as L^3T^{-2} by setting the gravitational constant K equal to a pure number. There is, however, no general agreement as to the importance that one should attach to dimensions. The matter of units is often overemphasized, it seems to us: are the units of the Giorgi system so rewarding as to compensate for the cluttering up of simple formulas with certain factors ε_0, μ_0? In actual applications one is likely to use *natural units* anyway; thus for studying free fall the unit of acceleration would be g.

Currents can be measured, in principle, on the basis of the Biot-Savart formula, which is another consequence of the basic equations of electromagnetism. Thus if $d\mathbf{F}$ is the force exerted on a current filament $J\mathbf{m}\,ds$ by another filament $J^*\mathbf{m}^*ds^*$ located at $\mathbf{r}$ relative to $J\mathbf{m}\,ds$, $\mathbf{m}$ and $\mathbf{m}^*$ being unit vectors in the directions of the filaments, then

$$d\mathbf{F} = \frac{(J\,ds)(J^*\,ds^*)}{4\pi r^3}\,[-\mathbf{m}^*(\mathbf{r}\cdot\mathbf{m}) + \mathbf{r}(\mathbf{m}\cdot\mathbf{m}^*)]. \tag{13.62a}$$

Conversely, the force exerted on $J^*\mathbf{m}^*ds^*$ is given by

$$d\mathbf{F}^* = \frac{(J\,ds)(J^*\,ds^*)}{4\pi r^3}\,[\mathbf{m}(\mathbf{r}\cdot\mathbf{m}^*) - \mathbf{r}(\mathbf{m}\cdot\mathbf{m}^*)] \tag{13.62b}$$

(note that $d\mathbf{F}$ and $d\mathbf{F}^*$ are not collinear!). The (rationalized) magnetostatic unit is then based on the c.g.s. system. The experimentally determined ratio of the electrostatic and magnetostatic units of charge equals $c = 3.10^{10}$ cm sec^{-1}, the speed of light *in vacuo*.

If $\mathbf{v}$ is the velocity field of charged particles, then the associated convection current is defined by $\mathbf{J}_{\text{e.u.}} = q_{\text{e.u.}}\mathbf{v}$. But because $q_{\text{e.u.}}/q_{\text{m.u.}} = c$, we also have that $\mathbf{J}_{\text{m.u.}} = q_{\text{e.u.}}\boldsymbol{\beta}$, where $\boldsymbol{\beta} = \mathbf{v}/c$.

Electromagnetism has really been the first "multipolar theory",† in the sense that here questions relating to the "microstructure" of charge distributions have always been crucial. That is, while the equations governing the electric and magnetic fields can be stated in fully general terms, the specification of what is meant by charges and currents introduces constitutive assumptions, based on considerations of microstructure, at the very outset. In view of the great diversity of conduction phenomena, e.g. drift of ions in gases or "free electrons" in metals, change of "polarization" of molecules of a dielectric, this branching of electromagnetism into specialized theories can hardly be avoided.

Let us follow along the lines of thought first indicated in Section 9. The total charge of a body which occupies a region V is given by

$$Q = \int_V q\, dv + \int_{\partial V} \sigma\, da, \tag{13.63}$$

where q is the volume distribution of *free charges* (e.g. ions, free electrons), and σ is a surface distribution of free charges. The latter can describe the density of the "boundary layer" of free charges, for instance. However, σ can be also used to describe the distortion in the arrangement of bound charges which occurs naturally at free boundaries (due to charges being attracted or repelled from one side only, so to speak). If this distortion occurs within a narrow boundary layer, then the layer can be replaced by a charge distribution σ over the boundary.

We now proceed to the first moments, making allowance for a *polarization*, $\mathbf{P}$, of the volume distribution of charges, as well as a polarization $\boldsymbol{\sigma}$ of the surface distribution of charges:

$$Q_i = \int_V x_i q\, dv + \int_{\partial V} x_i \sigma\, dv + \int_V P_i\, dv + \int_{\partial V} \sigma_i\, da.$$

In view of the identity $P_i = x_{i,j}P_j = (x_i P_j)_{,j} - x_i P_{j,j}$, we have that

$$Q_i = \int_V x_i q^*\, dv + \int_{\partial V} (x_i \sigma^* + \sigma_i)\, da,$$

where
$$q^* = q - \text{div}\mathbf{P}, \qquad \sigma^* = \sigma + P_i n_i \tag{13.64}$$

† The very term *multipolar* having been coined to describe charge multipoles (e.g. dipoles, quadrupoles, etc.).

may be referred to as the *true* distributions of volume and surface charges. One can illustrate the difference between q and q^* in various ways, although explanations based on particular models tend to be rather labored. Thus one could say that $q\,dv$ is not the actual charge within a volume element dv, because using q amounts to "concentrating" the charges of a molecule at one of its points. The neglect of polarization will cause a certain error, owing to the inclusion of charges that are really outside of dv. In particular, if V' is a region, and there are no true surface charges on $\partial V'$, then $\sigma = -\mathbf{P}\cdot\mathbf{n}$, so that, according to (13.63), the surface integral of $-\mathbf{P}\cdot\mathbf{n}$ corrects this error. Whenever charges are summed up over the entire body, we get the same result regardless of whether we use q and σ, or q^* and σ^*, in (13.63).

But why stop at a vector polarization? Indeed, the literature is not lacking in examples of more general multipolar theories.† If we go one step further, and define second moments as volume integrals of $x_i x_j q + (x_i P_j + x_j P_i) + P_{ij}$, with similar contributions from the bounding surface, then, with the aid of the identities $P_{ij} = \frac{1}{2}(x_i P_{kj} + x_j P_{ki})_{,k} - \frac{1}{2}(x_i x_j P_{mk,m})_{,k} + \frac{1}{2}x_i x_j P_{mk,mk}$, $(x_i x_j P_k)_{,k} = x_i x_j P_{k,k} + x_j P_i + x_i P_j$, we obtain a reduced representation similar to that for Q_i, with

$$\begin{aligned} q^* &= q - \operatorname{div}\mathbf{P}^*, \qquad & P_i^* &= P_i - \frac{1}{2}P_{mi,m}, \\ \sigma_i^* &= \sigma_i + P_{ki}n_k, \qquad & \sigma^* &= \sigma + P_i^* n_i. \end{aligned} \tag{13.65}$$

The distribution q^* of charge density not only accounts for the vector polarization P_i, but also for the tensor polarization P_{ij} ("electric quadrupole moment").

Free charges may give rise to a *convection current* $\bar{\mathbf{J}} = q\mathbf{v}$ moving with the mean velocity of the medium, or a *conduction current* $\mathbf{C} = q'\mathbf{u}$ which moves relative to the material matrix (e.g. motion of free electrons in a metallic conductor). Because $\mathbf{C}$ is but another type of a convection current, we may speak of the total convection current $\mathbf{J} = \bar{\mathbf{J}} + \mathbf{C}$. To describe the conservation of charge in the presence of currents produced by displacements of bound charges, a plausible starting point is

$$\frac{d}{dt}\int_V q\,dv = -\int_{\partial V} \mathbf{C}\cdot d\mathbf{a},$$

V being a material volume. Because, by (8.60),

$$\begin{aligned} \frac{d}{dt}\int_V q\,dv &= \frac{d}{dt}\int_V (q^* + \operatorname{div}\mathbf{P}^*)\,dv = \frac{d}{dt}\int_V q^*\,dv + \frac{d}{dt}\int_{\partial V} P_i^*\,da_i \\ &= \int_V (\partial_t q^* + \operatorname{div} q^*\mathbf{v})\,dv + \int_{\partial V} (\dot{P}_i^* + P_i^* v_{k,k} - P_k^* v_{i,k})\,da_i, \end{aligned}$$

† Cf. [22], [137], [39].

the balance of charge can be reduced to $\partial_t q^* + \text{div}\mathbf{J}^* = 0$, where $\mathbf{J}^* = \mathbf{J} + \partial_t\mathbf{P}^* + \text{curl}(\mathbf{P}^* \times \mathbf{v})$ (note that $\dot{P}_i^* + P_i^* v_{k,k} - P_k^* v_{i,k} = \partial_t P_i^* + [\text{curl}(\mathbf{P}^* \times \mathbf{v})]_i + v_i \,\text{div}\mathbf{P}^*$). However, the polarization of the distribution of currents calls for an additional term, the magnetization current $\mathbf{J}_M = \text{curl}\mathbf{M}$, where $\mathbf{M}$ is the density of magnetization (or, density of "magnetic dipoles"). Thus

$$\partial_t q^* + \text{div}\mathbf{J}^* = 0, \qquad \mathbf{J}^* = \mathbf{J} + \mathbf{J}_P + \text{curl}\mathbf{M}, \tag{13.66}$$

where

$$\mathbf{J}_P = \partial_t\mathbf{P}^* + \text{curl}(\mathbf{P}^* \times \mathbf{v}) \tag{13.67}$$

is referred to as the *polarization current*.

To "explain" the origin of $\mathbf{J}_M$, let us take the usual model of a "particle" $\mathscr{P}$ that consists of sub-particles located at $x_{Ki} = c_i + \bar{x}_{Ki}$, and carrying charges Q_K. Denoting summation over the label K by $\mathbf{S}$, we have that $Q = \mathbf{S}Q_K$, $Q_i = \mathbf{S}x_{Ki}Q_K = c_iQ + P_i$, $Q_{ij} = \mathbf{S}x_{Ki}x_{Kj}Q_K = c_ic_jQ + c_iP_j + c_jP_i + P_{ij}$, where $P_i = \mathbf{S}\bar{x}_{Ki}Q_K$, $P_{ij} = \mathbf{S}\bar{x}_{Ki}\bar{x}_{Kj}Q_K$. The moments of the distribution of currents are introduced in the same way: $J_i = \mathbf{S}v_{Ki}Q_K = \dot{c}_iQ + \dot{P}_i$, $J_{ij} = \mathbf{S}x_{Ki}v_{Kj}Q_K = c_iJ_j + \dot{c}_jP_i + M_{ij}$, where $M_{ij} = \mathbf{S}\bar{x}_{Ki}\bar{v}_{Kj}Q_K$ describes the polarization of the distribution of currents. It is not difficult to show that $M_{(ij)} = \frac{1}{2}\dot{P}_{ij}$, i.e. the symmetric part is wholly determined by the time rate of the electric quadrupoles. The skew-symmetric part, on the other hand, must be carried along separately; in view of the identity $M_{[ij]} = \frac{1}{2}(x_iM_{[kj]})_{,k} - \frac{1}{2}(x_jM_{[ki]})_{,k} - \frac{1}{2}x_iM_{[kj],k} + \frac{1}{2}x_jM_{[ki],k}$, we can incorporate the last two terms into $x_{[i}J_{j]}$ as the currents $\mathbf{J}_M = \text{curl}\,\mathbf{M}$, $M_i = -\frac{1}{2}\varepsilon_{ijk}M_{[jk]}$.

Incidentally, one should seek in the preceding relations the exact counterparts of $(13.66)_2$, etc., because here we are dealing with charges and currents, not their densities.

The Lorentz force $\mathbf{F} = \mathbf{S}Q_K\mathbf{E}(\mathbf{x}_K) + \mathbf{S}Q_K\mathbf{v}_K \times \mathbf{B}(\mathbf{x}_K)$ can be evaluated by expanding $\mathbf{E}(\mathbf{x}_K)$ and $\mathbf{B}(\mathbf{x}_K)$ in a Taylor series about $\mathbf{c}$. Then

$$F_i = QE_i + E_{i,j}P_j + \varepsilon_{imn}J_mB_n + \cdots \tag{13.68}$$

If we introduce the identity $E_{i,j}P_j = (E_iP_j)_{,j} - E_iP_{j,j}$, and assume that the term $(E_iP_j)_{,j}$ is "transformed away" into a surface integral, then we can write $F_i = Q^*E_i - \cdots$, where $Q^* = Q - \text{div}\mathbf{P}$.

To illustrate the manner in which electromagnetism blends with mechanics and thermodynamics, let us consider the theory of the *Maxwell-Lorentz dielectric*.† Here it is assumed, first, that free charges and magnetic dipoles are absent, thus

$$q^* = -\text{div}\mathbf{P}, \qquad \mathbf{J} = \mathbf{J}_P. \tag{13.69}$$

† Cf. [39], [168].

Letting $\mathbf{D} = \mathbf{E} + \mathbf{P}$, we find from Maxwell's equations that $\text{curl}\mathbf{H} - \partial_\tau \mathbf{E} = \partial_\tau \mathbf{P}$. This suggests the further assumption $\mathbf{H} = \mathbf{B} - (\mathbf{P} \times \boldsymbol{\beta})$, so that the first of (13.34) reduces

$$\text{curl}\mathbf{B} - \partial_\tau \mathbf{E} = \mathbf{J}_P. \tag{13.70}$$

The Lorentz force is given by $\mathbf{f} = -\mathbf{E}\,\text{div}\mathbf{P} + (\mathbf{J}_P \times \mathbf{B})$. But $\mathbf{J}_P = \partial_\tau \mathbf{P} + \text{curl}(\mathbf{P} \times \mathbf{B}) = \overset{*}{\mathbf{P}} - \boldsymbol{\beta}\,\text{div}\mathbf{P}$, where

$$\overset{*}{P}_i = \partial_\tau P_i + P_{i,j}\beta_j + P_i\beta_{k,k} - P_j\beta_{i,j}. \tag{13.71}$$

Therefore,

$$\mathbf{f} = -\mathbf{E}^+\,\text{div}\mathbf{P} + (\overset{*}{\mathbf{P}} \times \mathbf{B}), \qquad \mathbf{E}^+ = \mathbf{E} + (\boldsymbol{\beta} \times \mathbf{B}). \tag{13.72}$$

The Joule power $\mathbf{J}_P \cdot \mathbf{E}$ can be transformed as follows. Writing $\mathbf{J}_P \cdot \mathbf{E} = (\overset{*}{\mathbf{P}} - \boldsymbol{\beta}\,\text{div}\mathbf{P}) \cdot (\mathbf{E}^+ - (\boldsymbol{\beta} \times \mathbf{B})) = \overset{*}{\mathbf{P}} \cdot \mathbf{E}^+ - \boldsymbol{\beta} \cdot \mathbf{E}^+\,\text{div}\mathbf{P} + \boldsymbol{\beta} \cdot (\boldsymbol{\beta} \times \mathbf{B})\,\text{div}\,\mathbf{P} - \overset{*}{\mathbf{P}} \cdot (\boldsymbol{\beta} \times \mathbf{B})$, and noting that $\boldsymbol{\beta} \cdot (\boldsymbol{\beta} \times \mathbf{B}) = 0$, whereas $-\overset{*}{\mathbf{P}} \cdot (\boldsymbol{\beta} \times \mathbf{B}) = \boldsymbol{\beta} \cdot (\overset{*}{\mathbf{P}} \times \mathbf{B})$, we obtain

$$\mathbf{J}_P \cdot \mathbf{E} = \overset{*}{\mathbf{P}} \cdot \mathbf{E}^+ + \mathbf{f} \cdot \boldsymbol{\beta}, \qquad \boldsymbol{\beta} = \frac{\mathbf{v}}{c}. \tag{13.73}$$

The Lorentz force shows up in the equations of motion, $T_{ji,j} + \rho b_i = \rho \dot{v}_i$, as part of the body force $\rho\mathbf{b}$. In the energy balance $\rho\dot{\varepsilon} + q_{i,i} - \rho r = T_{ji}v_{i,j}$, the supply of nonmechanical energy, ρr, must now include the fraction $\overset{*}{\mathbf{P}} \cdot \mathbf{E}^+$ of the Joule power.

Problems

A. RELATIVITY

1. How does the relative motion of two observers affect the wavelengths of the received signals?
2. The speed of light was first estimated in 1675 by Roemer from the observed periods of the moons of Jupiter. For about half of the year Jupiter moves away from the earth, and approaches the earth during the other half. How can the Doppler effect associated with the observed periods be used to calculate the speed of light?
3. ("Clock paradox").† Consider three collinear observers A, B, C, and assume B and C move towards A with the same relative speed. Also assume that

† Cf. Bondi, p. 391, *op. cit.*

initially C is farther from A than is B, so that B first meets A, then C, and finally C meets A. Let T be the interval, according to A's clock, between the meetings of A with B and C. Calculate a corresponding interval T' from measurements made by B and C (e.g. assuming that A and B set their clocks at zero when they meet, and C adjusts his clock to agree with B's clock when B and C meet).

B. MAXWELL'S EQUATIONS

4. Using a coordinate transformation, show that (13.25) is an invariant operation.

5. Show that the divergence in (13.31) is an invariant operation.

6. Show that Maxwell's equations in vacuo are satisfied by letting $\mathbf{E} = -\text{grad}\phi - \partial_\tau \mathbf{A}$, $\mathbf{B} = \text{curl}\mathbf{A}$, provided that ϕ and $\mathbf{A}$ satisfy the wave equation.

7. Supposing that true magnetic charges and magnetic currents may exist, can you conjecture the modifications required in Maxwell's equations?

8. Derive (13.45), (13.46) from Maxwell's equations.

9. Verify the derivations of (13.42), (13.43).

10. Let $\bar{\mathbf{G}} = (\mathbf{f}, -\mathbf{J}\cdot\mathbf{E})$, where $\mathbf{f}$ is defined by (13.44). Show that *in vacuo*

$$G_\lambda = \partial_\mu M^\mu_\lambda, \tag{a}$$

where

$$M^\mu_\lambda = -F_{\lambda\alpha}F^{\mu\alpha} + \frac{1}{4}\delta^\mu_\lambda F_{\alpha\beta}F^{\alpha\beta}$$

is sometimes referred to as the tensor of electromagnetic energy. *Hints*: Use $\text{div}\mathbf{F} = \mathbf{J}$ (cf. (13.31)) to eliminate $\mathbf{J}$ in (a). Then obtain $F^{\beta\gamma}\partial_\beta F_{\alpha\gamma} = \frac{1}{2}F^{\beta\gamma}(\partial_\beta F_{\alpha\gamma} + \partial_\gamma F_{\beta\alpha})$, and using (13.27), eliminate the terms in the parentheses. Show that $\mathbf{M}$ is symmetric, and admits the representation

$$\|M^\mu_\lambda\| = \begin{Vmatrix} p_{11} & p_{12} & p_{13} & p_1 \\ p_{21} & p_{22} & p_{23} & p_2 \\ p_{31} & p_{32} & p_{33} & p_3 \\ p_1 & p_2 & p_3 & \sigma \end{Vmatrix}$$

where the *electromagnetic energy* σ is given by $\sigma = M_{44} = \frac{1}{2}(\mathbf{E}\cdot\mathbf{E} + \mathbf{B}\cdot\mathbf{B})$, the *electromagnetic momentum* $\mathbf{p}$ is given by $\mathbf{p} = \mathbf{E}\times\mathbf{B}$, and the *Maxwell's stress tensor* p_{ij} is given by $p_{11} = E_1^2 + B_1^2 - \sigma, \ldots, \ldots, p_{12} = -E_1E_2 - B_1B_2, \ldots, \ldots$.

CHAPTER 4

LINEAR THEORIES OF CONTINUUM MECHANICS

In what follows we shall survey the main linear theories of continuum mechanics. This will be done for two reasons. First, we wish to illustrate the application of the theory developed so far. Second, the solutions obtained for the linear theories will serve as a basis for comparison with the solutions of the nonlinear theories.

It goes without saying that a reasonably complete presentation of the topics mentioned in this chapter would require a separate treatise for each of them. In the space available here we can only sketch some of the physical and mathematical aspects of the theories.

From time to time we shall require the knowledge of certain results from *potential theory*. A brief summary of potential theory is given in Appendix I at the end of the book. As a rule, we shall not dwell upon those problems of continuum mechanics which can be reduced to problems of potential theory (this means that the greater part of hydrodynamics, namely the theory of flows that are isochoric and irrotational, will be left out).

Section 14
CONSTITUTIVE EQUATIONS

The system of equations describing the physical principles is, in general, under-determined, i.e. the physical principles alone do not suffice to determine the behavior of bodies. To make the problems determinate, it is necessary to introduce *constitutive equations* which define various *types of response*. Now, one of the key words in continuum mechanics is *invariance*; in the same way that we use tensors to extract information that is invariant to coordinate transformations, we must formulate constitutive equations so as to make them invariant to choice of kinematical variables, reference configurations, and so on. In this way a mathematical theory of constitutive equations takes shape, a theory in which we cannot hide behind words but must set down as mathematical operations what were at the outset perhaps vague, intuitive notions about material properties, bits of common sense, and the like. In the main, mathematics will serve only to *record* exactly the extent to which a problem has been understood. The rarified atmosphere of abstract deliberations may leave us temporarily breathless, but there is no other way if we wish to obtain general results.

The *representation* of constitutive equations is of course much simpler if the constitutive equations are assumed to be linear. However, when dealing with the *ideas* expressed by constitutive equations, there is nothing to be gained by introducing representations, linear or nonlinear. For this reason we shall first develop the constitutive equations pertinent to this chapter in a kind of "flow chart" of ideas, leaving the theory of representation until later.

Determinism, local action, equipresence

A new subject always requires some new vocabulary. We first recall the usual convention of denoting the present time by t, and the past times by τ, thus $-\infty < \tau \leq t$. The elapsed time $s = t - \tau$ is a positive quantity: $0 \leq s < \infty$. Let us take temperature θ as a typical independent variable. Its history at a generic particle $\mathbf{X}$ is the totality of the values $\theta(\mathbf{X}, t - s)$ for $0 \leq s < \infty$. Whenever we are dealing with no more than one particle at a time, the dependence of θ upon $\mathbf{X}$ need not be shown explicitly.

A *fixed* history $\theta(t - s)$, $0 \leq s < \infty$, is a family of functions that depend on one parameter, the present time t. We shall denote these functions by θ^t, their values being of course given by $\theta^t(s) = \theta(t - s)$. Finally, the functions that describe histories of entire temperature fields will be denoted by $\theta^t(\cdot)$; the value of $\theta^t(\cdot)$ at a particle $\mathbf{X}$ is the temperature history at $\mathbf{X}$, namely the function $\theta^t = \theta^t(\mathbf{X})$. As a rule we shall assume that $\theta^t(\mathbf{Z})$ may be approximated in a neighborhood $|\mathbf{Z} - \mathbf{X}| < \delta$ by N terms of Taylor series expansion (*approximation of grade N*),

$$\theta^t(\mathbf{Z}) = \theta^t(\mathbf{X}) + (Z_i - X_i)\theta^t_{.i}(\mathbf{X}) + \frac{1}{2}(Z_i - X_i)(Z_j - X_j)\theta^t_{.ij}(\mathbf{X}) + \cdots \tag{14.1}$$

With the vocabulary out of the way, we can now take up the formulation of constitutive equations. A constitutive equation must express, first of all, some form of the idea of *determinism*. Determinism has always been, in one form or another, an integral part of the natural sciences. It is ordinarily understood to imply that the past determines the future,† and in its most audacious form was expressed by the French celestial mechanicist and mathematician P. S. Laplace: "Given for one instant an intelligence which could comprehend all the forces by which nature is animated and the respective situation of the beings who compose it—an intelligence sufficiently vast to submit these data to analysis—it would embrace in the same formula the movements of the greatest bodies of the universe and those of the lightest atom; for it, nothing would be uncertain, and the future, as the past, would be present in its eyes."‡ In continuum mechanics we adopt a much more modest version of determinism, requiring only that *the past should determine the present*. Taking the stress **T** as a typical dependent variable, and the histories of motion $\boldsymbol{\chi}^t(\cdot)$, temperature $\theta^t(\cdot)$, . . ., as the dependent variables, we write

$$\mathbf{T} = \mathbf{G}(\boldsymbol{\chi}^t(\cdot), \theta^t(\cdot), \ldots, \mathbf{X}, t), \tag{14.2}$$

where $\mathbf{T} = \mathbf{T}(t)$. Material properties are described, in general, by functions, of which the *response function* **G** in (14.2) is a typical example. The explicit dependence of **G** upon **X** allows for "inhomogeneity" of the body, whereas the explicit dependence upon t allows for an "ageing". For *fixed* histories $\boldsymbol{\chi}^t(\cdot)$, $\theta^t(\cdot)$, . . ., stress is a function of t (and **X**) only (the value of t identifies a particular instant of history as the "present" one).

It is customary to refer to functions as *functionals* whenever some of the independent variables are fields, e.g. histories $\theta^t(\mathbf{X})$ at a particle, space fields $\theta(\cdot)$, or histories of space fields, $\theta^t(\cdot)$. Thus we say that in

$$T_{ij} = G_{ijkm}(0)E_{km}(t) + \int_0^\infty \dot{G}_{ijkm}(s)E^t_{km}(s)ds$$

stress is a (linear) functional of strain **E**, meaning that it is a (linear) function of the strain history $\mathbf{E}^t$. An older way of writing functionals, due to Vito Volterra (cf. [206]), is of the form

$$\mathbf{T} = \left[\mathop{\mathbf{E}(t - s)}_{s=0}^{s=\infty}\right]\cdot$$

† This is also called the condition of "non-retroactivity".
‡ Cf. [80], p. 252.

For typographical convenience, we suppress the "dummy variable" s; this is like denoting an integral by $\int f$, which may not be convenient for calculations, but otherwise is just as legitimate as the designation f' for the derivative.

To exclude "actions at-a-distance" from constitutive equations, we adopt a *principle of local action.* According to this principle, the response at a particle $\mathbf{X}$ is determined if the conditions are known for an arbitrarily small neighborhood of $\mathbf{X}$. We shall leave approximations of the type (14.1) for grades higher than one until Section 16. Materials corresponding to approximations of grade one will be referred to as *simple materials* (here the adjective "simple" only indicates the absence of a microstructure). For these materials, assuming that the response functional is at least continuous, we obtain reduced constitutive equations of the form

$$\mathbf{T} = \mathbf{G}(\boldsymbol{\chi}^t, \mathbf{F}^t, \theta^t, \mathbf{h}^t, \ldots, \mathbf{X}, t, d\mathbf{X}) \tag{14.3}$$

(to conserve letters, we have kept on the designation $\mathbf{G}$), where $\mathbf{h}$ is a convenient symbol for temperature gradients:

$$h_i = \frac{\partial \theta}{\partial X_i}. \tag{14.4}$$

The differentials $d\mathbf{X}$ arising from the approximations $\boldsymbol{\chi}^t(\mathbf{X} + d\mathbf{X}) = \boldsymbol{\chi}^t(\mathbf{X}) + \mathbf{F}^t(\mathbf{X})\, d\mathbf{X}$, etc., naturally belong to the domain of the response functional. However, let us now introduce a local basis $\mathbf{H}_i$, $i = 1, 2, 3$, so that $dX = dX_i\mathbf{H}_i$. Any mapping of dX into $d\hat{X} = d\hat{X}_i\mathbf{H}_i$, where

$$d\hat{X}_i = S_{ij}\, dX_j, \tag{14.5}$$

may be also described by holding the components dX_i unchanged, and subjecting the base vectors to the mapping

$$\hat{\mathbf{H}}_i = S_{ij}^T\mathbf{H}_j \tag{14.6}$$

(cf. (4.2) *et seq.*), thus $d\hat{X} = S_{ij}\, dX_j\mathbf{H}_i = dX_j\hat{\mathbf{H}}_j$. Because the "local" coordinates of the particles that belong to the neighborhood of $\mathbf{X}$ may be assumed to remain the same in all reference configurations, there is no need to retain an explicit dependence of $\mathbf{G}$ upon all $d\hat{\mathbf{X}}$. Therefore, we write

$$\mathbf{T} = \mathbf{G}(\boldsymbol{\chi}^t, \mathbf{F}^t, \theta^t, \mathbf{h}^t, \ldots, \mathbf{X}, t, \mathbf{H}_i). \tag{14.7}$$

The explicit dependence of $\mathbf{G}$ upon $\mathbf{H}_i$ is often replaced by an implicit dependence, particularly when there is no need to introduce more than one reference configuration. For instance, if $\mathbf{K}$ is the reference configuration "spanned" by $\mathbf{H}_i$, we may write $\mathbf{G}(\ldots, \mathbf{H}_i) = \mathbf{G}_{\mathbf{K}}(\ldots)$.

As the last of the general rules, we record Truesdell's *principle of equipresence*, which states that if an independent variable is present in one constitutive equation, then it should be present in all, unless its presence contradicts other principles or known properties (e.g. material symmetry), or is excluded by some type of linearization. This principle is a valuable guide in the formulation of *general* constitutive equations; it reminds us that, at the core, mechanical, thermal, and electromagnetic phenomena are but particular manifestations of one process, so that if the coupling between these phenomena is neglected, then there should be a reason for it. For instance, if we adjoin to (14.7) a constitutive equation for the free energy ψ, then at the outset the independent variables should be the same: $\psi = \psi(\boldsymbol{\chi}^t, \mathbf{F}^t, \theta^t, \mathbf{h}^t, \ldots, \mathbf{X}, t, \mathbf{H}_i)$.

If the domain of the response functionals contains no histories, thus

$$\begin{aligned} \mathbf{T} &= \mathbf{g}(\boldsymbol{\chi}, \mathbf{F}, \theta, \mathbf{h}, \ldots, \mathbf{X}, t, \mathbf{H}_i), \\ \psi &= \psi(\boldsymbol{\chi}, \mathbf{F}, \theta, \mathbf{h}, \ldots, \mathbf{X}, t, \mathbf{H}_i), \ldots, \end{aligned} \tag{14.8}$$

where $\mathbf{T} = \mathbf{T}(t)$, $\mathbf{F} = \mathbf{F}(t)$, etc., we speak of a *quasi-elastic response*. As noted by Wang and Bowen [215], for *fixed* histories of deformation, temperature, etc., the constitutive equation $(14.8)_1$ is fully equivalent to (14.7), because the dependence on a history θ^t may be written as $\mathbf{G}(\bar{\theta}^t, \theta, \ldots)$, where $\bar{\theta}^t$ is now the *restriction* of the history to the open interval $0 < s < \infty$; then

$$\mathbf{G}(\theta^t, \ldots)\Big|_{\bar{\theta}^t, \ldots = \text{const.}} = \mathbf{g}(\theta, \ldots)$$

(cf. the remark following (14.66)). However, whereas $\mathbf{G}$ in (14.7) is a material property that determines the stress for any choice of histories, the response function $\mathbf{g}$ is a property of a particle $\mathbf{X}$ having experienced a particular history (i.e. the dependence of $\mathbf{g}$ upon history is *implicit*). If this history is replaced by another, then $\mathbf{g}$ must be replaced by another response function. This of course says no more than that in materials with "memory," defined by equations of the form (14.7), the instantaneous response is quasi-elastic, and depends on the histories experienced by the materials. To describe materials that have an instantaneously viscous response, one may generalize (14.8) by including $\dot{\mathbf{F}}$ among the independent variables.†

† Wang and Bowen [215].

It remains to investigate various conditions that must be fulfilled by constitutive equations. Of these, the condition that a constitutive equation must not contradict the physical principles can be applied only in the context of special theories. The Clausius-Duhem inequality, on the other hand, can be applied directly to constitutive equations. The remaining conditions involve transformations of reference frames and reference configurations. By a coordinate transformation we shall mean a change from one common, Cartesian frame to another. Thus if $x_i(\tau)$ is the place of a particle at time τ, and X_i its place in a reference configuration (the particle need not actually occupy $\mathbf{X}$, i.e. the reference configuration may be an imagined one), then a coordinate transformation is described by $x_i(\tau) \to x^*_m(\tau) = Q_{mi}x_i(\tau)$, $X_i \to X^*_m = Q_{mi}X_i$. Correspondingly, $T^*_{mn} = Q_{mi}T_{ij}Q_{nj}$, $F^*_{mn} = Q_{mi}F_{ij}Q_{nj}$, and so on. Let us take a constitutive equation $\mathbf{T} = \mathbf{f}(\mathbf{F})$. Then the equivalence of $T_{ij} = f_{ij}(\mathbf{F})$ and $T^*_{ij} = f^*_{ij}(\mathbf{F}^*)$ amounts to the condition $T^*_{ij} = Q_{im}Q_{jn}f_{mn}(\mathbf{F}) = f^*_{ij}(\mathbf{QFQ}^T)$, i. e. the condition that all representations of a single observer be equivalent requires that the component functions transform according to

$$\mathbf{Qf(F)Q}^T = \mathbf{f}^*(\mathbf{QFQ}^T). \tag{14.9}$$

In particular, if all representations of the function are identical, thus $\mathbf{f}^* = \mathbf{f}$, or,

$$\mathbf{Qf(F)Q}^T = \mathbf{f}(\mathbf{QFQ}^T), \tag{14.10}$$

then $\mathbf{f}$ is said to be an *isotropic function.* Correspondingly, we say that the material property described by $\mathbf{f}$ is isotropic, because from $\mathbf{T} = \mathbf{f}(\mathbf{F})$ it follows that $\mathbf{T}^* = \mathbf{QTQ}^T = \mathbf{Qf(F)Q}^T = \mathbf{f}(\mathbf{QFQ}^T) = \mathbf{f}(\mathbf{F}^*)$, i.e. the constitutive equation has the same form in all coordinate systems. A more explicit definition of isotropy will be given later on (cf. (14.34) *et seq.*).

An isotropic function is, then, "insensitive" to the choice of coordinate systems; if the independent variable is represented in a frame (i), then so will be the value of an isotropic function. To illustrate more general isotropic functions, let $\mathbf{A}$ be a second rank tensor, and $\mathbf{a}$ a vector. Then $\mathbf{v} = \mathbf{h}(\mathbf{A}, \mathbf{a})$ is a vector-valued isotropic function, and $\mathbf{T} = \mathbf{f}(\mathbf{A}, \mathbf{a})$ a tensor-valued isotropic function, if

$$\mathbf{Qh}(\mathbf{A}, \mathbf{a}) = \mathbf{h}(\mathbf{QAQ}^T, \mathbf{Qa}), \qquad \mathbf{Qf}(\mathbf{A}, \mathbf{a})\mathbf{Q}^T = \mathbf{f}(\mathbf{QAQ}^T, \mathbf{Qa}). \tag{14.11}$$

Examples of isotropic functions are easy to find; thus, $\mathbf{a} \cdot \mathbf{v}$ is a scalar-valued isotropic function of the vectors $\mathbf{a}$ and $\mathbf{v}$, $\mathbf{T} = \text{const. } e^{\mathbf{A}}$ is a tensor-valued isotropic function of the tensor $\mathbf{A}$. To construct an example of "anisotropic" functions, let $\mathbf{n}$ be a fixed unit vector. Then $f(\mathbf{a}) = \mathbf{a} \cdot \mathbf{n}$ is a scalar-valued, "anisotropic" function of the vector $\mathbf{a}$. Thus in a coordinate system in which $\mathbf{n} = \mathbf{e}_2, f(\mathbf{a}) = a_2$, whereas in a coordinate system in which $\mathbf{n} = \mathbf{e}_3$ we have that $f(\mathbf{a}) = a_3$, i.e. the rule varies from one coordinate system to another. Less trivial examples are given by the anisotropic stress-strain relations (cf. (14.46)*).

Regarding the representations $T_{ij} = f_{ij}(A_{km})$, it is important to note that the component functions f_{ij} do *not* constitute a second rank tensor. In general $\mathbf{f}$ is merely a tensor-valued function of tensors, e.g. $\mathbf{T} = \mathbf{f}(\mathbf{A}) = \text{const. } \mathbf{e}^{\mathbf{A}}$. *Linear* functions are an exception; for instance, the coefficients f_{ijkm} in $T_{ij} = f_{ijkm}A_{km}$ represent a tensor of rank four.

Material objectivity and material symmetry

Because there is nothing more to be learned from coordinate transformations, let us leave the common frame out of the picture. In its place, we introduce two sets of Cartesian frames; one for describing the current configuration (x_i), the other for describing the reference configuration (X_i). The tensor of deformation gradients can then be interpreted as a *double-vector*, that is, although the same indices will be assigned to all frames, it is understood that the material coordinates X_i will remain unchanged in any observer transformation

$$\bar{x}_m^+(\tau) = Q_{mi}(\tau)x_i(\tau) + \bar{c}_m^+(\tau) \tag{14.12}$$

(cf. (7.40)). Here the mark "+" identifies the variables recorded by the "starred" observer (*any* variable represented in the "starred" observer frame is marked by an overbar). In view of what has been said, an observer transformation of deformation gradients is given by

$$F_{im}^+(\tau) = Q_{ij}(\tau)F_{jm}(\tau). \tag{14.13}$$

This is a basic result: *in observer transformations the deformation gradients transform as vectors.* A like result will hold for *symmetry transformations*

$$d\hat{X}_i = S_{ij}\, dX_j \qquad \text{(14.5)R}$$

(cf. (14.21)).

The idea that material properties are something "real," or inherent to a body, is expressed by the *principle of material objectivity*, according to which *material properties are invariant to observer transformations.* Let us illustrate right away the use of this principle. We consider a block of mass m; if the block is attached to a vertical spring, the spring will elongate by an amount $\delta = mg/k$, where g is the acceleration of free fall, and k is a property of the spring. If the support of the spring moves upward with an acceleration a, a different elongation δ' will be observed. To what should we attribute the change of elongation: to a change of m, a change of k, or a change of motion? The answer is, "of course," $\delta' = m(a + g)/k$. That is, we assume that the material property k is not affected by the (accelerated!) motion. In this light the principle of material objectivity appears as a particular *interpretation* of the experiment. It is clear that some principle, or convention, of this kind is needed, or else the experiments would not tell us anything.

In any constitutive equation the translation $\boldsymbol{\chi}(\mathbf{X}, \tau)$ can be "transformed away" by selecting an observer that moves with the particle $\mathbf{X}$. According to the principle of material objectivity, a response function $\mathbf{g}$ is the same for all observers,

$$\mathbf{g} = \mathbf{g}^+ . \tag{14.14}$$

Therefore, if stress is independent of $\boldsymbol{\chi}(\mathbf{X}, \tau)$ in one observer frame, then it must be independent of $\boldsymbol{\chi}(\mathbf{X}, \tau)$ in all observer frames. It is worth noting that in a mixture of two constituents C and $\bar{C}$ the *relative* velocity $\bar{\mathbf{v}} - \mathbf{v}$ cannot be transformed away, so that it does qualify as an independent variable in the constitutive equations.

To continue, let us take a constitutive equation $\mathbf{T} = \mathbf{g}(\mathbf{F})$. Recalling (14.13), and that stress is assumed to be objective, $\bar{\mathbf{T}}^+ = \bar{\mathbf{T}} = \mathbf{QTQ}^T$, we have that $\mathbf{QTQ}^T = \mathbf{Qg}(\mathbf{F})\mathbf{Q}^T = \mathbf{g}(\mathbf{QF})$, thus

$$\mathbf{Qg}(\mathbf{F})\mathbf{Q}^T = \mathbf{g}(\mathbf{QF}). \tag{14.15}$$

What we have found is that *in observer transformations* (i.e. when $\mathbf{F}$ is transformed as a vector!) *the response function* $\mathbf{g}$ *is an isotropic function* (cf. (14.11)). This condition, imposed by material objectivity, can be fulfilled once for all. We start with the polar decomposition $\mathbf{F} = \mathbf{RU}$, where $\mathbf{R}$ is an orthogonal tensor, and $\mathbf{U}$ is a positive symmetric tensor. An observer transformation $\mathbf{F} \to \mathbf{QF}$ changes $\mathbf{R}$ into $\mathbf{R}^+ = \mathbf{QR}$, but $\mathbf{U}$ is invariant to observer transformations. We now select a special observer by letting $\mathbf{Q} = \mathbf{R}^T$. Then (14.15) reduces to $\mathbf{g}(\mathbf{F}) = \mathbf{Rg}(\mathbf{U})\mathbf{R}^T$. Again, because $\mathbf{g}$ does not depend on $\mathbf{R}$ in one observer frame, it is independent of $\mathbf{R}$ in all observer frames. Therefore, the elastic "stress-strain relation" $\mathbf{T} = \mathbf{g}(\mathbf{F})$ admits the reduced representation

$$\mathbf{T} = \mathbf{Rg}(\mathbf{U})\mathbf{R}^T. \tag{14.16}$$

Moreover, $\mathbf{g}$ as a function of $\mathbf{U}$ is an isotropic function in all observer transformations by virtue of $\mathbf{U}$ being "insensitive" to observer transformations!

The representation (14.16) is a striking result. For one, it shows that the response function can be determined from tests involving pure deformations alone, because the effect of a rotation is merely to rotate the stress vectors, e.g. $\bar{\mathbf{T}} = \mathbf{QTQ}^T = (\mathbf{QR})\mathbf{g}(\mathbf{U})(\mathbf{QR})^T$. In the linear theory of elasticity we replace $\mathbf{R}$ by $\mathbf{1} + \tilde{\mathbf{R}}$, and $\mathbf{U}$ by $\mathbf{1} + \tilde{\mathbf{E}}$, where $\tilde{\mathbf{R}}$ describes the infinitesimal rotations, and $\tilde{\mathbf{E}}$ is the infinitesimal strain tensor. With $g_{ij}(\mathbf{1} + \tilde{\mathbf{E}}) \approx T^0_{ij} + C_{ijkm}\tilde{E}_{km}$, the stress-strain relation then becomes

$$T_{ij} = T^0_{ij} + \tilde{R}_{im}T^0_{mj} - T^0_{im}\tilde{R}_{mj} + C_{ijkm}\tilde{E}_{km}, \tag{14.17}$$

T^0_{ij} being the *initial stress*.

Evidently the reduction of $\mathbf{T} = \mathbf{g}(\mathbf{F})$ is not affected if $\mathbf{g}$ depends on any number of additional variables that are insensitive to observer transformations. In particular, let S be the set of independent variables θ, $\mathbf{h}$, $\mathbf{X}$, t, $\mathbf{H}_i$. Because temperature is assumed to be objective, we can write that

$$\mathbf{T} = \mathbf{R}\tilde{\mathbf{g}}(\mathbf{U}, S)\mathbf{R}^T, \tag{14.18}$$

where $\tilde{\mathbf{g}}$ is automatically an isotropic function in all observer transformations. Similarly, for the free energy ψ, the heat flux $\mathbf{q}$ and the entropy η we obtain the reduced constitutive equations

$$\psi = \tilde{\psi}(\mathbf{U}, S), \qquad \mathbf{q} = \mathbf{R}\tilde{\mathbf{q}}(\mathbf{U}, S), \qquad \eta = \tilde{\eta}(\mathbf{U}, S). \tag{14.19}$$

If stress depends on the history $\mathbf{F}^t$, then we must also introduce a history of observer transformations, $\mathbf{Q}^t$. With $\mathbf{Q}^t(0) = \mathbf{Q}(t) \equiv \mathbf{Q}$, we now consider $\mathbf{QTQ}^T = \mathbf{QG}(\mathbf{F}^t)\mathbf{Q}^T = \mathbf{G}(\mathbf{Q}^t\mathbf{F}^t)$. As before, we let $\mathbf{Q}(t - s) = \mathbf{R}^T(t - s)$, thus arriving at

$$\mathbf{T} = \mathbf{RG}(\mathbf{U}^t)\mathbf{R}^T. \tag{14.20}$$

If one of a pair of observers views a body in a mirror, then the observer transformation will be a *roto-reflection*, combining a rotation and a reflection. Because an intrinsic orientation may be one of the properties of a material, it is not altogether clear what the consequences of admitting roto-reflections as observer transformations would be.

The idea underlying the principle of material objectivity is of course not new. In fact, it may have seemed so self-evident to the writers of some decades ago that it is barely mentioned. Thus in Love's treatise on elasticity theory

([91], p. 92) it is stated: "The property of recovery of an original size and shape is the property that is termed *elasticity*. The changes of size and shape are expressed by specifying *strains*." In Lamb's "Hydrodynamics" ([216], p. 1) we find: ". . . tangential forces are not called into play so long as the fluid moves as a solid body, but only whilst a change of shape of some portion of mass is going on, . . ." But many readers must have felt at a loss as to how these observations could be understood more fully, or expressed more explicitly. Besides, theories that violate the principle of material objectivity have been proposed in the past; as a rule, they were later abandoned as not being fruitful. In any case, observer transformations alone should remind us that a choice must be made: mechanical response must be assumed to be either objective or non-objective.

The principle of material objectivity is actually known by several names. The name used by Noll [106] at one time is the *principle of isotropy of space.* Curiously enough, this name seems to fit Rivlin's interpretation of material objectivity [217], but Rivlin speaks of "form-invariance under rotation of the physical system." On the other hand, Oldroyd [111], who was the first to state this principle explicitly, avoids rotations altogether by using "convected" coordinate systems that move and deform with a body to formulate constitutive equations. Truesdell, who had coined the term "material objectivity," now seems to prefer "material frame-indifference."

Let $N(\mathscr{P})$ be a neighborhood of a particle $\mathscr{P}$. By a *local reference configuration* of $\mathscr{P}$ we mean an assignment of material coordinates $d\mathbf{X}$ to the particles of the neighborhood, whereby $\mathscr{P}$ corresponds to $\mathbf{0}$. When formulating constitutive equations it is unimportant whether or not the local reference configurations can be joined smoothly into a reference configuration $\boldsymbol{\varkappa}$ for the whole body. That is, in order to test the response of a small portion of a body, we consider this portion separately (or, as "cut out" from the body). If the response of all portions is elastic, for instance, then the body is elastic, even though the portions may be joined together so as to produce a state of self-stress that cannot be relieved by a compatible deformation of the whole body.

As a rule, the response of a solid to a deformation will depend on the initial state of the solid. For instance, if a strain E measured from the natural state produces a stress $T = E^2$, then the function that describes the stress increment $\bar{T}$ produced by a strain $\bar{E}$ measured from the deformed configuration $E = C$ will be different: $\bar{T} = T - T^0 = 2\bar{E}C + \bar{E}^2$ (it should be noted, however, that because $T^0 = C^2$, $E = \bar{E} + C$, the total stress, T, comes out to be the same, i.e. the response function will depend on how the total deformation E is broken up into an initial deformation C and a superposed deformation $\bar{E}$, but the stress will depend only on the total deformation from the natural state).

Therefore, if the response to deformations from a (local) reference configuration $\mathbf{K}$ is described by $\mathbf{g}$, then the response to deformations from a (local) reference configuration $\hat{\mathbf{K}}$ will be described by another function $\hat{\mathbf{g}}$.

If the stress vanishes in a reference configuration $\mathbf{K}$, thus $\mathbf{T}^0 = \mathbf{g}(\mathbf{1}) = \mathbf{0}$, then $\mathbf{K}$ is called a *natural state*; it may be imagined as the state of a small fragment after it has been "cut out" from the body, thereby permitting it to relax its stress. As part of a continuous body, a fragment will not be in general in its natural state, because a lack of fit among the fragments that make up the body will have to be corrected by the application of suitable initial stresses. That is, the deformation, $\mathbf{F}$, from an initial configuration of a body is, in general, only a part of the total deformation, $\mathbf{M} = \mathbf{F}\boldsymbol{\phi}$, of its elements from their natural states. Denoting the latter by $\mathbf{R}$, we have the following diagram:

$$\begin{array}{ccc} \mathbf{R} & \xrightarrow{\mathbf{F}\boldsymbol{\phi}} & d\mathbf{x} \\ & \boldsymbol{\phi}\searrow \qquad \nearrow\mathbf{F} & \\ & d\mathbf{X} & \end{array}$$

Now let $\mathbf{f}$ describe the response to deformations from the natural state: $\mathbf{T} = \mathbf{f}(\mathbf{F}\boldsymbol{\phi})$. A function of $\mathbf{F}\boldsymbol{\phi}$ is certainly a function of $\mathbf{F}$ and $\boldsymbol{\phi}$, so that we can write $\mathbf{T} = \mathbf{g}'(\mathbf{F}, \boldsymbol{\phi})$. In the place of $\boldsymbol{\phi}$, we can use a material frame $\mathbf{H}_i$ to characterize the local reference configuration, i.e. we can write $\mathbf{T} = \mathbf{g}(\mathbf{F}, \mathbf{H}_i)$. If another reference configuration $d\hat{X}_i = S_{ij}\, dX_j$ is chosen (or, equivalently, if we let $\mathbf{H}_i \to \hat{\mathbf{H}}_i = \mathbf{H}_j S_{ji}$), then, because the final configuration is held fixed, $dx_i = F_{im}\, dX_m = \hat{F}_{im}\, d\hat{X}_m$, thus

$$\hat{\mathbf{F}} = \mathbf{F}\mathbf{S}^{-1}. \tag{14.21}$$

For the same total deformation $\mathbf{F}\boldsymbol{\phi} = \hat{\mathbf{F}}\hat{\boldsymbol{\phi}}$, the stress must be the same: $\mathbf{T} = \mathbf{g}(\mathbf{F}, \mathbf{H}_i) = \mathbf{g}(\hat{\mathbf{F}}, \hat{\mathbf{H}}_i)$. We now absorb, in a manner of speaking, the dependence upon the reference configurations into the response function. Then from one function $\mathbf{g}$ we get two, namely $\mathbf{g}(\mathbf{F}) \equiv \mathbf{g}(\mathbf{F}, \mathbf{H}_i)$ and $\hat{\mathbf{g}}(\hat{\mathbf{F}}) = \mathbf{g}(\hat{\mathbf{F}}, \hat{\mathbf{H}}_i)$. Thus invariance of stress to change of local reference configurations yields the transformation law

$$\mathbf{T} = \mathbf{g}(\mathbf{F}) = \hat{\mathbf{g}}(\mathbf{F}\mathbf{S}^{-1}) \tag{14.22}$$

for response functions (we may also interpret (14.22) as stating that stress is independent of how the particles were labeled).

For an elastic body there are two properties: mass density ρ, and a response function $\mathbf{g}$. If a body consists of the same material, then for any two material neighborhoods $N(\mathbf{X})$ and $N(\hat{\mathbf{X}})$ there exist reference configurations $\mathbf{K}$ and $\hat{\mathbf{K}}$, respectively, in which the properties of the neighborhoods are identical:

$$\rho = \hat{\rho}, \qquad \mathbf{g} = \hat{\mathbf{g}}. \tag{14.23}$$

If there exists a compatible reference configuration $\varkappa$ for the whole body such that the response function $\mathbf{g}_\varkappa$ is the same at each point, then the body is said to be *homogeneous*. Whereas ρ and $\mathbf{g}$ are material properties, inhomogeneity, if it exists, is a *property of the body* as a whole, i.e. it has to do with the manner in which the material neighborhoods are pieced together.

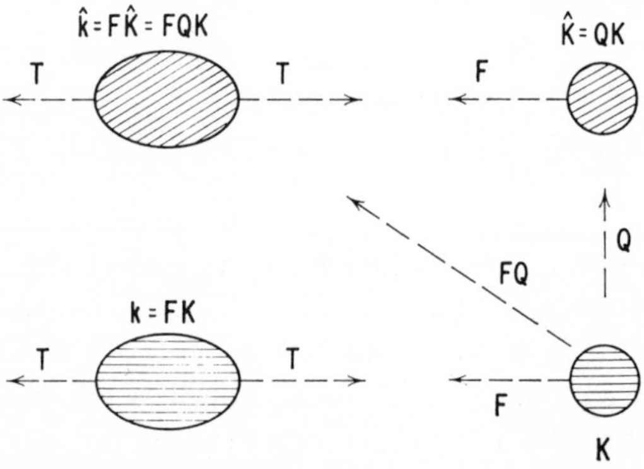

FIGURE 14.1 A schematic representation of a test for isotropy.

There is another reason for our preoccupation with reference configurations. Namely, the mapping from a local reference configuration $\mathbf{K}$ to another local reference configuration $\hat{\mathbf{K}}$ can be interpreted as an actual experiment that will show how the response of a "test specimen" is affected by that particular deformation. For instance, let us consider two reference configurations that differ by a rigid rotation $\mathbf{Q}$: $d\hat{\mathbf{X}} = \mathbf{Q}\, d\mathbf{X}$; then $\mathbf{g} = \hat{\mathbf{g}}$ is really the condition of isotropy! More generally, let us suppose that at a particle $\mathscr{P}$ the material properties are the same in two distinct configurations $\mathbf{K}$ and $\hat{\mathbf{K}}$. Then, by (14.22), (14.23), $\mathbf{g}(\mathbf{F}) = \mathbf{g}(\mathbf{F}\mathbf{S}^{-1})$, where $\mathbf{S}$ must be *unimodular*, i.e. $\det\mathbf{S} = 1$ (because $\rho = \hat{\rho}$ must hold!). For convenience, let us write $\mathbf{S}^{-1} = \mathbf{H}$, thus

$$\mathbf{g}(\mathbf{F}) = \mathbf{g}(\mathbf{F}\mathbf{H}), \tag{14.24}$$

where $\mathbf{H}$ represents a (unimodular) mapping that can be performed on a "test specimen" without affecting its response (cf. Figure 14.1). The mappings

H that leave a response function **g** invariant are said to constitute the *isotropy group*† of the response function. The various types of response may now be classified according to the types of isotropy groups. For instance, a fluid is understood to have no preferred reference configurations (thus if we take a half-filled glass of water, then tilt it, we do not think of the water in the tilted glass as "deformed," or different in any way from what it was initially). With this in mind, we may define fluids by stating that their isotropy group is the full unimodular group (all mappings **H** satisfying $\det\mathbf{H} = 1$). An elastic fluid must satisfy material objectivity, $\mathbf{Q}\mathbf{g}(\mathbf{F})\mathbf{Q}^T = \mathbf{g}(\mathbf{QF})$, as well as (14.24) for any unimodular mapping **H**. If we take **H** to be an orthogonal tensor $\mathbf{Q}^T$, so that $\mathbf{g}(\mathbf{F}) = \mathbf{g}(\mathbf{FQ}^T)$, $\mathbf{g}(\mathbf{QF}) = \mathbf{g}(\mathbf{QFQ}^T)$, then it follows that **g** is an isotropic function, i.e. all elastic fluids are isotropic. Moreover, with $\mathbf{H} = \mathbf{F}^{-1}\det\mathbf{F}$, we have that $\mathbf{g}(\mathbf{F}) = \mathbf{g}(\mathbf{1}\det\mathbf{F})$, $\mathbf{QTQ}^T = \mathbf{Qg}(\mathbf{1}\det\mathbf{F})\mathbf{Q}^T = \mathbf{g}(\mathbf{1}\det\mathbf{F}) = \mathbf{T}$, i.e. **T** must be an isotropic tensor. Therefore, in view of $\det\mathbf{F} = \rho_0/\rho$, we can describe elastic fluids by

$$\mathbf{T} = -p(\rho)\mathbf{1}. \tag{14.25}$$

More generally, if a material possesses a (local) reference configuration **K** such that the isotropy group $\mathscr{g}$ is either the orthogonal group $\mathscr{o}$, or contains $\mathscr{o}$ as a subgroup, then the material is said to be isotropic, and **K** is said to be an *undistorted state*. If the isotropy group is the orthogonal group $\mathscr{o}$, or a subgroup of $\mathscr{o}$, then the material is said to be an elastic *solid*; it is isotropic in the former case, anisotropic (or, aelotropic) in the latter case. The isotropy group of a fluid is the full unimodular group.

To summarize, the response of a material to a deformation from any of its undistorted states is the same. In solids these states are related by rotations (i.e. a deformation will affect, in general, the response of a solid), whereas in fluids they can differ by any isochoric deformation.

The idea of classifying materials on the basis of their isotropy groups is a counterpart of the celebrated *Klein's Erlanger Program*, which proposed the study of geometrical objects on the basis of invariants of groups of transformations. Indeed, we can view Euclidean geometry, rigid body mechanics, and continuum mechanics as successive stages of a theory of material objects.‡ In Euclidean geometry we study the invariants of the groups of translations and rotations; for instance, a rotation of an isosceles triangle through 120° or 240° yields a configuration that is indistinguishable from the original one. Similarly, in deformable bodies there may exist deformations **H** that leave the response unchanged.

† The idea of a *group* is explained briefly in Appendix II.
‡ Cf. Truesdell [177].

A broad indication of the types of response may be obtained from dimensional analysis. For instance, to put a constitutive equation $\mathbf{T} = \mathbf{f}(\mathbf{F}, \dot{\mathbf{F}}, \Delta_j\mathbf{F}, \ldots)$ into a nondimensional form, we need a material property with the dimension of stress, a material time τ, and a material length ℓ. These properties may be thought of as characterizing, respectively, the elasticity, the viscosity, and the microstructure of the material. A combination of elasticity and viscosity gives rise to a stress relaxation ("viscoelasticity"), whereas a combination of elasticity and microstructure gives rise to boundary layer effects and dispersion of waves (cf. Section 16).

Viscous response

A shearing motion $x = X + K(t)Y$, $y = Y$, $z = Z$ serves well to illustrate the difference between elasticity and fluidity. In elastic solids, to an applied stress $S = T_{xy}$ there will correspond an equilibrium configuration defined by $K = S/\mu_E$ (in general, the elastic modulus μ_E will be a function of K). In particular, a line $X = 0$ marked on the undeformed configuration of a membrane lying in the xy plane will have undergone a rotation through an angle θ given by $K = \tan\theta$. In a viscous fluid, on the other hand, there is no stress required to maintain a fixed (isochoric!) deformation from the initial state. Stress is needed only to maintain flow, thus $S/\mu_V \sim \dot{K}$, where $\dot{K} = \partial v_x/\partial_y$. Because we can "undo" any isochoric deformation, there is no loss of generality if $\dot{K}$ is evaluated when $K = 0$, in which case $\dot{K} = \dot{\theta}$. Summarizing, in elastic solids a constant shearing stress will produce an angular *displacement* of the line $X = 0$, whereas in viscous fluids it will produce an angular *velocity* of this line. Therefore, as long as the stress is maintained, a fluid will flow. If the stress is removed, then so is the deformation of an elastic solid; in a viscous fluid the removal of stress merely causes the motion to stop (i.e. the deformation remains).

The idea of viscous response is embodied in the *principle of Stokes* (1845),

$$\mathbf{T} = -p\mathbf{1} + \mathbf{f}(\mathbf{D}), \qquad \mathbf{f}(\mathbf{0}) = \mathbf{0},$$

where the pressure term $-p\mathbf{1}$ describes the state of stress in fluids at rest, and $\mathbf{D}$ is the symmetric part of the velocity gradients $L_{ij} = v_{i,j}$. It is easy to see that the more general equation $\mathbf{T} = -p\mathbf{1} + \mathbf{f}(\mathbf{L})$ must reduce to the principle of Stokes. We first recall the observer transformation $\overline{\mathbf{L}}^+ = \mathbf{QDQ}^T + \mathbf{Q}(\mathbf{W} + \boldsymbol{\Omega}^+)\mathbf{Q}^T$ (cf. (8.61)), where $\boldsymbol{\Omega}^+$ is the angular velocity of the new frame. Letting $\boldsymbol{\Omega}^+ = -\mathbf{W}$, we obtain $\mathbf{T}^+ = -p\mathbf{1} + \mathbf{f}(\mathbf{D}^+)$; therefore, a dependence of stress upon the spin tensor would contradict the principle of material objectivity. Moreover, because $\overline{\mathbf{T}}^+ = \mathbf{QTQ}^T$, $\overline{\mathbf{D}}^+ = \mathbf{QDQ}^T$, it follows that $\mathbf{f}$

is an isotropic function: $\mathbf{Qf(D)Q}^T = \mathbf{f(QDQ}^T)$; i.e. *the principle of Stokes defines isotropic fluids only.*

Let us recall that if $\mathbf{T} = \mathbf{f(F)}$, then the principle of material objectivity does *not* require $\mathbf{f}$ to be an isotropic function: $\mathbf{Qf(F)Q}^T = \mathbf{f(QF)}$. We seem to have been saved by the breadth of one $\mathbf{Q}$, so to speak, but far from being accidental, the distinction is very basic. Namely, the transformation formula $\mathbf{F}^+ = \mathbf{QF}$ is typical of deformation tensors, which have only one "foot" in the current configuration (and, correspondingly, $\mathbf{T} = \mathbf{f(F)}$ describes solids), whereas the transformation formula $\bar{\mathbf{D}}^+ = \mathbf{QDQ}^T$ is typical of objective rate tensors, which stand with both feet in the current configuration.

General (i.e. nonlinear) isotropic functions are merely an extension of the idea of linear isotropic functions (isotropic tensors!). The components of an isotropic tensor are the same in all coordinate systems, e.g. $M_{ij\,\dots} = \bar{M}_{ij\,\dots}$. In the case of an isotropic function $\mathbf{f}$ the *forms* of the component function $f_{ij\dots}$ are the same in all coordinate systems: $f_{ij\dots} = \bar{f}_{ij\dots}$. For instance, let $\mathbf{j}^K$ be a function whose value at a second rank tensor $\mathbf{D}$ is given by $\mathbf{D}^K$. Then various isotropic functions $\mathbf{f}$ can be defined by power series of the type

$$\mathbf{f} = \sum_{K=0}^{\infty} C_K \mathbf{j}^K, \qquad \mathbf{f(D)} = \sum_{K=0}^{\infty} C_K \mathbf{D}^K,$$

where C_K are constants. The Cayley-Hamilton equation, (4.10), can now be used to eliminate all powers $\mathbf{D}^K$, $K \geqslant 3$. Because the invariants $\mathrm{I}_\mathbf{D}$, $\mathrm{II}_\mathbf{D}$, $\mathrm{III}_\mathbf{D}$ occur as coefficients in the Cayley-Hamilton equation, the coefficients f_i of the reduced representation of $\mathbf{f}$ will be functions of these invariants. In this way we arrive at the following explicit form of Stokes's principle, known as the *Reiner-Rivlin equation*:†

$$\mathbf{T} = -p\mathbf{1} + f_0\mathbf{1} + f_1\mathbf{D} + f_2\mathbf{D}^2, \tag{14.26}$$

the response coefficients f_i being functions of $\mathrm{I}_\mathbf{D}$, $\mathrm{II}_\mathbf{D}$, $\mathrm{III}_\mathbf{D}$.

Evidently the ratio f_2/f_1 has the dimension of time, so that a Reiner–Rivlin fluid may be said to possess a characteristic time T_N. To put (14.26) into a nondimensional form, we need a second material constant, e.g. a "natural viscosity" μ_N, where $[\mu_N] = ML^{-1}T^{-1}$. The ratio $E_N = \mu_N/T_N$ is then of the dimension of stress, i.e. E_N is a "natural elasticity." But although dimensional analysis can give us a glimpse into the nature of a response, it does not tell us very much. For instance, while a characteristic time may correspond to certain "memory" effects, e.g. stress relaxation in viscoelastic fluids, no such

† A more general derivation is given in the text preceding (17.15).

effects are contained in (14.26). Similarly, although the "natural elasticity" may manifest itself in a "dilatancy" which gives rise to a swelling of simple shearing flows, it is not an elasticity of the kind encountered in viscoelastic fluids. The nonlinearity of (14.26) is primarily linked to the sensitivity of a fluid to magnitudes of shear rates. However, to make a statement that shear rates are large, or small, meaningful, a fluid must be ascribed a material constant k_N, *the natural shear rate*. The constitutive equation can then be made nondimensional as follows: $\mathbf{T}/\mu_N k_N \sim \mathbf{f}(\mathbf{D}/k_N)$. A linearization that neglects $\mathbf{D}^2/k_N^2$ amounts to the assumption that, for the given fluid, the natural "unit" of shearing, k_N, is so large that all flows appear as being at small shear rates. In this connection it is interesting to compare (14.26) with a stress-strain relation $\mathbf{T} = g_0\mathbf{1} + g_1\mathbf{E} + g_2\mathbf{E}^2$. Because strain is dimensionless, we can say that a linearization requires that strains be small. However, velocity and velocity gradients are not dimensionless, so that it makes no sense to say that they are small, i.e. a linearization of (14.26) requires that it be first made nondimensional.

It should be added that the equation (14.26) has not been found so far to be an accurate description of any "Non-Newtonian" flow phenomena; rather, the deviations from linear response appear to require the introduction of higher "strain rates," e.g. $A_{ij}^{(2)} \equiv v_{i,j} + v_{j,i} + 2v_{m,i}v_{m,j}$. More about that in Chapter 6.

If the viscous response is *linear*, then $\mathbf{f}$ must be an isotropic tensor, thus

$$\mathbf{T} = -p\mathbf{1} + \lambda\mathbf{1}\,\mathrm{tr}\mathbf{D} + 2\mu\mathbf{D}, \qquad (14.26)^*$$

where the coefficients of viscosity, $\lambda = \lambda_V$ and $\mu = \mu_V$, are now constants. However, so as to include the effect of compressibility, we should permit p to depend on ρ and θ, so that (14.26)* is strictly speaking not a linear constitutive equation.

To complete the specification of the thermo-mechanical response, we should adjoin to (14.26)* a constitutive equation for heat flux, and a constitutive equation for the density of internal energy, $\varepsilon = \varepsilon(\eta, v)$, where η and v are the entropy density and the specific volume, respectively. Then the local production of entropy is given by $\theta\rho\gamma_\ell = (\pi - p)D_{ii} + \lambda D_{ii}D_{jj} + 2\mu D_{ij}D_{ij}$, where $\pi = -\partial\varepsilon/\partial v$ is the *thermodynamic pressure*.

The condition that γ_ℓ be positive requires that $\mu \geqslant 0$, $3\lambda + 2\mu \geqslant 0$, and that p equals the thermodynamic pressure π:

$$p = \pi = -\frac{\partial\varepsilon}{\partial v}.$$

To see this, we consider isochoric motions, $D_{ii} = 0$. Then it follows that

$\mu \geqslant 0$. Next, taking $\mathbf{D} = D\mathbf{1}$, we arrive at $(\pi - p)D + (3\lambda + 2\mu)D^2 \geqslant 0$. If λ, μ, p, π are independent of D, then this condition can be satisfied in all cases only if $\pi = p$, $3\lambda + 2\mu \geqslant 0$.

Evidently the stress tensor can be uniquely resolved into a portion $-p\mathbf{1}$ doing work which is always mechanically recoverable, and the *extra stress* $\mathbf{S} = \mathbf{T} + p\mathbf{1}$ the work of which is always dissipated. Moreover, the following form of the entropy balance holds for compressible and incompressible fluids alike: $\rho\theta\dot{\eta} + q_{i,i} = \mathrm{tr}(\mathbf{SD})$. It should be noted, however, that the thermodynamic pressure is not in general equal to the mean pressure $\bar{p} = -T_{kk}/3$. If incompressibility is assumed, then p is arbitrary, and, because of $\mathrm{tr}\mathbf{D} = 0$, must be identified with $\bar{p}$.

Whenever $\varepsilon = \varepsilon(\eta, v)$ is given, the energy balance can be cast into the form of a *heat transfer* equation. Namely, inverting $\theta = \partial\varepsilon(\eta, v)/\partial\eta$ to yield $\eta = f(\theta, v)$, we now find that, with $\mathbf{q} = -k\,\mathrm{grad}\theta$, the energy balance (10.22) is of the form $\rho\theta\dot{\theta}\partial_\theta f - k\nabla^2\theta = -\theta D_{kk}\partial_v f + \lambda D_{ii}D_{jj} + 2\mu D_{ij}D_{ij}$. In particular, let us suppose that ε can be approximated by the polynomial $\varepsilon = \varepsilon_0 + \theta_0(\eta - \eta_0) - \pi_0(v - v_0) + \frac{1}{2}[A(\eta - \eta_0)^2 + 2B(\eta - \eta_0)(v - v_0) + C(v - v_0)^2]$, where $\varepsilon_0, \theta_0, \eta_0, \pi_0, v_0, A, B, C$ are constants. Then $\rho\dot{\varepsilon} \doteq \rho c_v\dot{\theta} - c_v B D_{ii}$, where c_v, the *specific heat at constant volume*, is defined by

$$c_v = \left.\frac{\partial\varepsilon}{\partial\theta}\right|_{v=\mathrm{const.}} \doteq \frac{\theta_0}{A}.$$

The corresponding approximation of (10.22) is now given by

$$\rho c_v\dot{\theta} - k\nabla^2\theta = Bc_v D_{ii} + \lambda D_{ii}D_{jj} + 2\mu D_{ij}D_{ij}.$$

What makes hydrodynamics difficult is that we are dealing with motions, not equilibrium. Even when a linear constitutive equation is assumed, the equations of motion,

$$-p_{,i} + \mu\nabla^2 v_i + (\lambda + \mu)v_{k,ki} + \rho b_i = \rho(\partial_t v_i + v_k v_{i,k}), \qquad (14.27)$$

known as the *Navier–Stokes equations*, remain nonlinear, owing to the presence of the convective acceleration $v_k v_{i,k}$. It is therefore necessary, as a rule, to seek further simplifications. Thus whenever possible we consider the effects of *compressibility* and *viscosity* separately, i.e. we deal either with inviscid flows, $\mathbf{T} = -p(\rho, \theta)\mathbf{1}$, or with isochoric flows, $\mathbf{T} = -p\mathbf{1} + 2\mu\mathbf{D}$, where p is an arbitrary pressure. As a matter of fact, most of the known solutions have been obtained for flows that are both inviscid and incompressible! In any case, it must be kept in mind that the applicability of a constitutive equation depends as much on the kinematical properties of a flow as it does on the mechanical properties of the fluid. The flow of glycerine is inviscid if velocity gradients are small enough, i.e. $\mu\mathbf{D} \approx \mathbf{0}$, whereas the flow of air in a "boundary-layer" is viscous. A meaningful assessment of the effects of viscosity and compressibility requires the definition of appropriate dimensionless numbers.

Elastic anisotropic solids

To illustrate how the symmetry properties of a material are incorporated into its constitutive equation, we shall consider a "stress-strain relation"

$$T_{ij} = C_{ijkm}E_{km}. \tag{14.28}$$

We assume that $\mathbf{T}$ and $\mathbf{E}$ are symmetric tensors, from which it follows that $C_{ijkm} = C_{jikm} = C_{ijmk}$, so that the number of distinct coefficients is decreased from 81 to 36. This enables us to devise a *simplified notation* for C_{ijkm}, in which the index pairs ij and km are each replaced by single subscripts as follows: $11 \to 1$, $22 \to 2$, $33 \to 3$, $23, 32 \to 4$, $31, 13 \to 5$, $12, 21 \to 6$. This convention can be also used to identify components of stress and strain by means of a single subscript. However, $T_{ij} = C_{ijkm}E_{km}$ is not transformed into $T_A = C_{AB}E_B$, $A, B = 1, 2, \ldots, 6$, unless the replacement is made according to $E_{11} \to E_1, \ldots, \ldots, E_{21} = 2E_6, \ldots, \ldots$. As a rule, the abbreviated notations are unsuited for calculations.

To simplify matters, let us assume that (14.28) describes nondissipative processes in a medium with a constitutive equation $\varepsilon = \varepsilon(\mathbf{F}, \eta)$ for the density of internal energy. If the internal dissipation is to vanish, then, by (12.21), (12.22), $\delta = w - \rho\eta\dot{\theta} - \rho\dot{\psi} = w - \rho\dot{\eta}\theta - \rho\dot{\varepsilon} = 0$, where $w = T_{ji}L_{ij}$. Thus in isentropic processes we can identify ε with a strain-energy density Σ, whereas in isothermal processes Σ can be identified with the free energy $\psi = \varepsilon - \eta\theta$. It is often more convenient to use W, the strain-energy density per unit volume in the reference configuration:

$$W = \rho_0\Sigma. \tag{14.29}$$

Then, with $\rho\dot{\varepsilon} = (\rho/\rho_0)\dot{W} = (1/J)(\partial W/\partial F_{im})\dot{F}_{im}$ and $\dot{F}_{im} = L_{ij}F_{jm}$, we obtain

$$T_{ij} = \frac{1}{J}\frac{\partial W}{\partial F_{im}}F_{jm}. \tag{14.30}$$

The strain-energy density must be objective, thus $\overline{W}(\mathbf{F}) = \overline{W}(\mathbf{QF})$, from which it follows that $\overline{W}(\mathbf{F}) = \overline{W}(\mathbf{U})$, and, in view of $\mathbf{F}^T\mathbf{F} = \mathbf{C} = \mathbf{U}^2$,

$$\overline{W}(\mathbf{F}) = W(\mathbf{C}). \tag{14.31}$$

As a function of **C**, the strain-energy density is automatically objective, because **C** is insensitive to observer transformations (if $\mathbf{F}^+ = \mathbf{QF}$, then $\mathbf{C}^+ = \mathbf{F}^T\mathbf{Q}^T\mathbf{QF} = \mathbf{C}$!). It is a simple exercise to show that the objectivity of W implies the objectivity of the stress. Combining (14.30), (14.31), we obtain

$$T_{ij} = \frac{2}{J}\frac{\partial W}{\partial C_{km}} F_{ik}F_{jm} \doteq \frac{\partial W}{\partial E_{ij}}, \tag{14.30*}$$

the last expression being valid in the limit of infinitesimal deformations (cf. Section 15). If initial stresses are present, then **F** in the linearized equations must be replaced by $\mathbf{1} + \tilde{\mathbf{H}}$. In particular, if $W \doteq W^0 + T^0_{ij}E_{ij} + \frac{1}{2}W_{ijkm}\tilde{E}_{ij}\tilde{E}_{km}$, then, with $\tilde{\mathbf{H}} = \tilde{\mathbf{E}} + \tilde{\mathbf{R}}$, $C_{ijkm} = W_{ijkm} - \delta_{km}T^0_{ij} + \delta_{i(k}T^0_{m)j} + \delta_{j(k}T^0_{m)i}$, we recover from (14.30)* the stress-strain relation (14.17). In what follows we shall assume that there are no initial stresses.

In the linear theory there are now at most 21 distinct elastic coefficients, because

$$W = \frac{1}{2} C_{ijkm}E_{ij}E_{km}, \qquad C_{ijkm} = C_{kmij}. \tag{14.32}$$

The condition that the strain-energy density be positive, semi-definite, imposes certain restrictions on C_{ijkm}. In view of (14.32), the tensor of elasticity can be considered as a symmetric second rank tensor in a space of six dimensions. It is not difficult to see that the principal values of a symmetric tensor are real regardless of the range of the indices. Let us suppose that a principal value and the corresponding principal vector are complex: $C = a + ib$, $n_k = \alpha_k + i\beta_k$. Then $\bar{C} = a - ib$, $\bar{n}_k = \alpha_k - i\beta_k$ are also a principal value and the corresponding principal vector. Because $C \neq \bar{C}$, and the tensor is symmetric, it follows that $\mathbf{n}\cdot\bar{\mathbf{n}} = 0 = \alpha_k\alpha_k + \beta_k\beta_k$, so that $\alpha_k = 0$, $\beta_k = 0$. This contradicts the assumption that **n** is not a zero-vector. Therefore, we can state that the strain energy is positive definite if the principal invariants of **C** (interpreted as a second rank tensor) are positive. In order to see this, it is only necessary to consider (14.32) referred to the principal coordinate system of **C**.

Additional reductions of the number of distinct elastic coefficients are possible only if a body possesses *material symmetries*. The idea of material symmetry carries with it the picture of some sort of a structure which enables one to tell whether or not a small specimen has been rotated ($d\hat{\mathbf{X}} = \mathbf{S}\,d\mathbf{X}$, $\det\mathbf{S} = 1$), and whether it is being viewed directly or in a mirror (in the latter case $d\hat{\mathbf{X}} = \mathbf{S}\,d\mathbf{X}$, $\det\mathbf{S} = -1$). This structure manifests itself in the existence of (local) *material frames* $\mathbf{H}_i$, $i = 1, 2, 3$, that are intrinsic to the material. A *symmetry operation* $\mathbf{S}$ transforms one material frame into another, equivalent material frame. The class of symmetry operations defines the *anisotropy* of a body.

In solids symmetry operations are rotations and roto-reflections (rotations viewed in a mirror), so that $\det\mathbf{S} = \pm 1$, and, by (14.21), $\hat{\mathbf{F}} = \mathbf{F}\mathbf{S}^T$. Let us now recall (14.16): $\mathbf{T} = \mathbf{R}\mathbf{g}(\mathbf{U})\mathbf{R}^T$. Before applying the symmetry operation, we introduce a modified response function $\mathbf{f}$ by $\mathbf{g}(\mathbf{U}) = \mathbf{U}\mathbf{f}(\mathbf{C})\mathbf{U}$, where $\mathbf{C} = \mathbf{U}^2 = \mathbf{F}^T\mathbf{F}$. Then

$$\mathbf{T} = \mathbf{F}\mathbf{f}(\mathbf{C})\mathbf{F}^T. \tag{14.33}$$

If $\mathbf{S}$ is indeed a symmetry operation of the material, then the stress $\mathbf{T}$ will be the same regardless of whether a deformation $\mathbf{F}$ is applied to the original specimen or to the rotated specimen: $\mathbf{T} = \mathbf{F}\mathbf{f}(\mathbf{C})\mathbf{F}^T = \hat{\mathbf{F}}\mathbf{f}(\hat{\mathbf{C}})\hat{\mathbf{F}}^T$. Because $\hat{\mathbf{F}} = \mathbf{F}\mathbf{S}^T$, $\hat{\mathbf{C}} = \mathbf{S}\mathbf{C}\mathbf{S}^T$, we arrive at the following representation of the condition of material symmetry: $\mathbf{F}\mathbf{S}^T\mathbf{f}(\mathbf{S}\mathbf{C}\mathbf{S}^T)\mathbf{S}\mathbf{F}^T = \mathbf{F}\mathbf{f}(\mathbf{C})\mathbf{F}^T$. Therefore,

$$\mathbf{f}(\mathbf{S}\mathbf{C}\mathbf{S}^T) = \mathbf{S}\mathbf{f}(\mathbf{C})\mathbf{S}^T. \tag{14.34}$$

Conversely, if (14.34) holds, then stress is unaffected by symmetry operations applied to the undeformed specimens. We say that *the elastic response* $\mathbf{f}$ *is an isotropic function in all symmetry operations.* For linear functions this condition becomes

$$f_{pqrs} = S_{ip}S_{jq}S_{kr}S_{ms}f_{ijkm}, \tag{14.35}$$

and $\mathbf{f}$ is called an *isotropic tensor relative to* $\mathbf{S}$. In quite the same way we conclude that the strain-energy function must be form-invariant to all symmetry operations: $W(\mathbf{C}) = W(\mathbf{S}\mathbf{C}\mathbf{S}^T)$. In the approximation $W = W^0 + T^0_{ij}E_{ij} + \frac{1}{2}W_{ijkm}E_{ij}E_{km}$, this invariance now requires not only that W_{ijkm} satisfy (14.35), but that also $\mathbf{T}^0 = \mathbf{S}\mathbf{T}^0\mathbf{S}^T$, i.e. the initial stress in the undistorted state must be invariant to the symmetry operations.

If there are no preferred (material) frames, we speak of *elastic isotropy*; in this case *the elastic coefficients are the same in all coordinate systems*:

$$\bar{C}_{ijkm} = Q_{ip}Q_{jq}Q_{kr}Q_{ms}C_{pqrs} = C_{ijkm}. \tag{14.36}$$

Consequently, the elastic tensor $\mathbf{C}$ is a fourth rank isotropic tensor.

Every scalar is obviously an isotropic tensor of rank zero (this need not be true of scalar-valued *functions* of tensors!). It is easy to see that there are no isotropic vectors. A vector $\mathbf{v}$ obeys a transformation formula of the type

$\bar{\mathbf{v}} = \mathbf{Q}\mathbf{v}$; if $\mathbf{v}$ is assumed to be isotropic, then, in addition, $\bar{\mathbf{v}} = \mathbf{v}$, thus $Q_{ij}v_j = v_i$. Let $\mathbf{Q}$ be a rotation of 180° about z axis: $\mathbf{Q} = \text{diag}\,(-1, -1, 1)$. Then the conditions $Q_{ij}v_j = v_i$ are $v_1 = -v_1$, $v_2 = -v_2$, $v_3 = v_3$, i.e. $\mathbf{v}$ must be of the form $\|\mathbf{v}\|^T = \|0, 0, v\|$. A similar rotation about x axis (or y axis) will show that the remaining component must vanish too. However, *anisotropic vectors* do exist; for instance, if only rotations about z axis are permitted, then $\|0, 0, v\|$ represents a "transversely isotropic" vector.

A general method for constructing isotropic tensors is provided by a representation theorem of Cauchy. A scalar-valued function ϕ of vectors is said to be an *isotropic function* if, given any orthogonal tensor $\mathbf{Q}$,

$$\phi(\mathbf{u}, \mathbf{v}, \mathbf{w}, \ldots) = \phi(\mathbf{Q}\mathbf{u}, \mathbf{Q}\mathbf{v}, \mathbf{Q}\mathbf{w}, \ldots), \tag{14.37}$$

i.e. the value of ϕ is independent of the coordinate system in which the vectors $\mathbf{u}, \mathbf{v}, \mathbf{w}, \ldots$ are represented. The theorem of Cauchy now states that a scalar-valued function of vectors $\mathbf{v}_1, \mathbf{v}_2, \ldots, \mathbf{v}_M$ is isotropic if it depends on the scalar products $\mathbf{v}_A \cdot \mathbf{v}_B$ only, where the labels $A, B \ldots$ may take on the values $1, 2, \ldots, M$.

If ϕ is a scalar-valued function of vectors, then its value is the same regardless of the coordinate system in which it is calculated: $\phi(\mathbf{u}, \mathbf{v}, \mathbf{w}, \ldots) = \phi^*(\mathbf{u}^*, \mathbf{v}^*, \mathbf{w}^*, \ldots)$, where $\mathbf{u}^* = \mathbf{Q}\mathbf{u}$, $\mathbf{v}^* = \mathbf{Q}\mathbf{v}$, etc. What the theorem asserts is that, if ϕ is an *isotropic* function, then the functional dependence is the same too: $\phi = \phi^*$.

To prove the theorem, we consider another set of M vectors $\mathbf{u}_A$ such that

$$\mathbf{v}_A \cdot \mathbf{v}_B = \mathbf{u}_A \cdot \mathbf{u}_B. \tag{a}$$

The vectors $\mathbf{v}_A$ can be renumbered in such a way that $\mathbf{v}_1, \mathbf{v}_2, \mathbf{v}_3$ form a basis of the set $\mathbf{v}_1, \mathbf{v}_2, \ldots, \mathbf{v}_M$.† Then

$$\begin{vmatrix} \mathbf{v}_1 \cdot \mathbf{v}_1 & \mathbf{v}_1 \cdot \mathbf{v}_2 & \mathbf{v}_1 \cdot \mathbf{v}_3 \\ \mathbf{v}_2 \cdot \mathbf{v}_1 & \mathbf{v}_2 \cdot \mathbf{v}_2 & \mathbf{v}_2 \cdot \mathbf{v}_3 \\ \mathbf{v}_3 \cdot \mathbf{v}_1 & \mathbf{v}_3 \cdot \mathbf{v}_2 & \mathbf{v}_3 \cdot \mathbf{v}_3 \end{vmatrix} \neq 0$$

(cf. (2.15) *et seq.*), and by (a), the corresponding set $\mathbf{u}_1, \mathbf{u}_2, \mathbf{u}_3$ is also linearly independent. According to (4.2), (4.3), there exists a mapping $\mathbf{Q}$ such that $\mathbf{u}_1 = \mathbf{Q}\mathbf{v}_1$, $\mathbf{u}_2 = \mathbf{Q}\mathbf{v}_2$, $\mathbf{u}_3 = \mathbf{Q}\mathbf{v}_3$, and $[\mathbf{u}_1, \mathbf{u}_2, \mathbf{u}_3] = [\mathbf{v}_1, \mathbf{v}_2, \mathbf{v}_3]\det\mathbf{Q}$. Moreover, it follows from (a) that $\mathbf{Q}$ is orthogonal.

† Here we specialize the proof given in section 11, *NFTM*, to three-dimensional vector spaces.

It remains to show that

$$\mathbf{u}_A = \mathbf{Q}\mathbf{v}_A \tag{b}$$

holds for *all* vectors of the two sets. To this end, we make use of the (unique!) representations $\mathbf{v}_A = \alpha_A\mathbf{v}_1 + \beta_A\mathbf{v}_2 + \gamma_A\mathbf{v}_3$, $A > 3$. Then, using (a), we find from $\mathbf{v}_A \cdot \mathbf{v}_1 = \alpha_A\mathbf{v}_1 \cdot \mathbf{v}_1 + \beta_A\mathbf{v}_2 \cdot \mathbf{v}_1 + \gamma_A\mathbf{v}_3 \cdot \mathbf{v}_1 = \mathbf{u}_A \cdot \mathbf{u}_1 = \alpha_A\mathbf{u}_1 \cdot \mathbf{u}_1 + \beta_A\mathbf{u}_2 \cdot \mathbf{u}_1 + \gamma_A\mathbf{u}_3 \cdot \mathbf{u}_1$ that $\mathbf{u}_A = \alpha_A\mathbf{u}_1 + \beta_A\mathbf{u}_2 + \gamma_A\mathbf{u}_3$, $A > 3$. Therefore, (b) are satisfied whenever (a) hold good. But if (b) are satisfied, then $\phi(\mathbf{v}_1, \mathbf{v}_2, \ldots, \mathbf{v}_M) = \phi(\mathbf{u}_1, \mathbf{u}_2, \ldots, \mathbf{u}_M)$, so that, in view of (a), the isotropic function can depend only on the scalar products.

A scalar-valued function ϕ of vectors which obeys (14.37) is said to be *hemitropic* if $\mathbf{Q}$ is restricted to be a proper rotation (i.e. $\det\mathbf{Q} = 1$). Then $[\mathbf{u}_A, \mathbf{u}_B, \mathbf{u}_C] = [\mathbf{v}_A, \mathbf{v}_B, \mathbf{v}_C]\det\mathbf{Q} = [\mathbf{v}_A, \mathbf{v}_B, \mathbf{v}_C]$ must be also satisfied, from which it follows that a hemitropic function ϕ depends on the vectors through the scalar products $\mathbf{v}_A \cdot \mathbf{v}_B$ *and* the box products $\mathbf{v}_A \cdot (\mathbf{v}_B \times \mathbf{v}_C)$.

Isotropic tensors are *multilinear* isotropic functions of vectors. For instance, an isotropic tensor of rank two must be a bilinear function of vectors **a** and **b**, say, so that $\mathbf{I}[\mathbf{a}, \mathbf{b}] = Aa_ib_i = A\delta_{ij}a_ib_j$, where A is a constant. Thus **I** is a multiple of the unit tensor: $I_{ij} = A\delta_{ij}$. If the rank is an odd number, then a tensor can be at most hemitropic, e.g. $\mathbf{H}[\mathbf{a}, \mathbf{b}, \mathbf{c}] = A\mathbf{a} \cdot (\mathbf{b} \times \mathbf{c}) = A\varepsilon_{ijk}a_ib_jc_k$, thus $H_{ijk} = A\varepsilon_{ijk}$. But the alternator is not invariant to reflections.

Next, from $Aa_ib_ic_jd_j + Ba_ic_ib_jd_j + Ca_id_ib_jc_j = a_ib_jc_kd_m(A\delta_{ij}\delta_{km} + B\delta_{ik}\delta_{jm} + C\delta_{im}\delta_{kj})$, we conclude that isotropic tensors of rank four are represented by

$$I_{ijkm} = A\delta_{ij}\delta_{km} + B\delta_{ik}\delta_{jm} + C\delta_{im}\delta_{kj}, \tag{14.38}$$

where A, B, C are constants. Similarly, for isotropic tensors of rank six we obtain

$$\begin{aligned} I_{ijkmnp} = {} & A_1\delta_{ij}\delta_{km}\delta_{np} + A_2\delta_{ij}\delta_{kn}\delta_{mp} + A_3\delta_{ij}\delta_{kp}\delta_{nm} + A_4\delta_{ik}\delta_{jm}\delta_{np} \\ & + A_5\delta_{ik}\delta_{jn}\delta_{mp} + A_6\delta_{ik}\delta_{jp}\delta_{nm} + A_7\delta_{im}\delta_{kj}\delta_{np} + A_8\delta_{im}\delta_{kn}\delta_{jp} \\ & + A_9\delta_{im}\delta_{kp}\delta_{nj} + A_{10}\delta_{in}\delta_{km}\delta_{jp} + A_{11}\delta_{in}\delta_{kj}\delta_{mp} + A_{12}\delta_{in}\delta_{kp}\delta_{jm} \\ & + A_{13}\delta_{ip}\delta_{km}\delta_{nj} + A_{14}\delta_{ip}\delta_{kn}\delta_{mj} + A_{15}\delta_{ip}\delta_{kj}\delta_{mn}. \end{aligned} \tag{14.39}$$

The fifteen terms evidently correspond to all the combinations of pairs of indices taken from the set *ijkmnp*.

The preceding results would seem to imply that the specification of an isotropic tensor of rank $2K$ requires $(2K - 1)(2K - 3)\cdots 3\cdot 1 = P$ constants (each vector **a**, say, can be paired with any of the $2K - 1$ other vectors; to each pair, e.g. $a_i b_i$, we adjoin a third vector **c** that in turn can be paired with any of the remaining $2K - 3$ vectors, and so on). Unfortunately this is not true in general: for $K \geqslant 4$ it is possible to show that some of the conditions of isotropy result in linear relations between the constants. Using group-theoretic methods, Racah [126] has shown that the correspondence between rank, R, and the number of independent constants, P, is as follows:

R	0	1	2	3	4	5	6	7	8	9	10
P	1	0	1	1	3	6	15	36	91	232	603

For instance, a hemitropic tensor of rank five is given by†

$$H_{ijkmn} = A\delta_{jk}\varepsilon_{imn} + B\delta_{jm}\varepsilon_{ikn} + C\delta_{jn}\varepsilon_{imk} + D\delta_{mk}\varepsilon_{ijn} + E\delta_{nk}\varepsilon_{imj} + F\delta_{mn}\varepsilon_{ijk}, \tag{14.40}$$

whereas from the inspection of $\varepsilon_{ijk}a_i b_j c_k d_m e_m$ we would be led to believe that there are 10 independent constants. In this case the relations between the components are of the type $H_{23111} = H_{23122} + H_{23212} + H_{23221}$, etc.

Substituting $C_{ijkm} = A\delta_{ij}\delta_{km} + B\delta_{ik}\delta_{jm} + C\delta_{im}\delta_{kj}$ into (14.28), we obtain the linear isotropic law

$$T_{ij} = \lambda E_{kk}\delta_{ij} + 2\mu E_{ij}, \quad 2\mu E_{ij} = T_{ij} - \frac{\lambda}{3\lambda + 2\mu} T_{kk}\delta_{ij}, \tag{14.41}$$

where $\lambda = A$, $2\mu = B + C$. In the general case we define the inverse of C_{ijkm} as follows. Letting

$$E_{km} = C^{-1}_{kmrs} T_{rs}, \tag{14.42}$$

we find that $T_{ij} = C_{ijkm}C^{-1}_{kmrs}T_{rs}$, $C_{ijkm}C^{-1}_{kmrs}T_{rs} - \frac{1}{2}(T_{ij} + T_{ji}) = [C_{ijkm}C^{-1}_{kmrs} - \frac{1}{2}(\delta_{ir}\delta_{js} + \delta_{jr}\delta_{is})]T_{rs} = 0$, so that

$$C_{ijkm}C^{-1}_{kmrs} = \frac{1}{2}(\delta_{ir}\delta_{js} + \delta_{jr}\delta_{is}). \tag{14.43}$$

It should be noted that the "unit tensor" $\bar{\delta}_{ijkm} = \frac{1}{2}(\delta_{ik}\delta_{jm} + \delta_{jk}\delta_{im})$ is represented by $\|\bar{\delta}_{ijkm}\| = \text{diag}(1, 1, 1, \frac{1}{2}, \frac{1}{2}, \frac{1}{2})$, the subscripts of the diagonal elements being 1111, 2222, 3333, 2323, 3131, 1212. Along with $\bar{\delta}_{ijkm}$ we can

† Caldonazzo [8].

introduce another "unit tensor" $\|\delta_{ijkm}\| = \|\delta_{ik}\delta_{jm}\| = \text{diag}(1, 1, 1, 1, 1, 1)$. Evidently $\bar{\delta}_{ijkm} = \frac{1}{2}(\delta_{ijkm} + \delta_{jikm})$, i.e. the appearance of $\bar{\delta}_{ijkm}$ in (14.43) reflects the symmetry $C_{ijkm} = C_{jikm}$ of the elastic coefficients. The symmetries of $\bar{\delta}_{ijkm}$ are $\bar{\delta}_{ijkm} = \bar{\delta}_{jikm} = \bar{\delta}_{ijmk} = \bar{\delta}_{kmij}$.

Among the various symmetry operations in solids we distinguish rotations, satisfying $\det\mathbf{S} = 1$, and reflections, or combined rotations and reflections ("roto-reflections"), satisfying $\det\mathbf{S} = -1$. In particular, a material property is said to be *centro-symmetric* if the inversion $-\mathbf{1}$ is one of the symmetry operations. If $-\mathbf{1}$ is not a symmetry operation, then the material possesses an *intrinsic orientation*, that is, the screw-sense of (intrinsic) material frames of reference, $\mathbf{H}_1$, $\mathbf{H}_2$, $\mathbf{H}_3$, is a characteristic of the material.†

The symmetry operation $\underset{N}{A}$ which corresponds to an *N-fold axis of symmetry*, A, is a rotation about A through the angle $2\pi/N$. For instance, if z axis is a two-fold axis of symmetry, then

$$\underset{2}{z} = \text{diag}(-1, -1, 1). \tag{14.44}$$

Evidently the two symmetry operations $-\mathbf{1}$ and $\underset{2}{z}$ imply symmetry with respect to reflections in the xy plane, because $-\mathbf{1}\underset{2}{z} = \text{diag}(1, 1, -1) \equiv \underset{z}{E}$. Materials which do not admit $\underset{z}{E}$ can again be thought of as having an intrinsic orientation, e.g. we may imagine the infinitesimal material filaments to have the "structure" of a rope, or a helical spring, so that a filament and its image in a mirror would have opposite orientations.

In crystal physics a basic hypothesis is the *principle of Fr. Neumann*,‡ according to which the *crystal symmetries constitute the most complete description of the geometric constitution of crystals*. Consequently, the symmetry group of a given material property must include the crystal group. That is, a material property may be invariant to more, but not fewer, symmetry operations than are contained in the appropriate crystal group. A constitutive equation relating two second rank tensors, e.g. $A_{ij} = M_{ijkm}B_{km}$, is a case in point. Because $\mathbf{A} = (-\mathbf{1})\mathbf{A}(-\mathbf{1})$, etc., the property $\mathbf{M}$ is centro-symmetric even if the crystal is not. Therefore, in elasticity theory we may disregard the symmetry operation $-\mathbf{1}$.

The basic approach to the study of the anisotropic tensors C_{ijkm} requires a knowledge of the theory of polynomial bases,§ hence we shall illustrate here

† Materials with a center of symmetry are also called "holohedral," those without a center of symmetry, "hemihedral."

‡ Cf. [109], p. 20–24.

§ Cf. Appendix II.

a direct method of reduction of the constitutive equation. If **S** is a symmetry operation of the material, then, because

$$C_{pqrs} = \bar{C}_{pqrs} = S_{pi}S_{qj}S_{rk}S_{sm}C_{ijkm}, \tag{14.45}$$

$$\begin{aligned} \bar{C}_{pqrs} &= S_{pi}(S_{rk}C_{ijkm}S^T_{ms})S^T_{jq}, \\ \bar{\mathbf{C}}_{pq} &= S_{pi}(\mathbf{S}\mathbf{C}_{ij}\mathbf{S}^T)S^T_{jq}, \\ \bar{\mathbf{C}} &= \mathbf{S}(\mathbf{S}\mathbf{C}\mathbf{S}^T)\mathbf{S}^T, \end{aligned}$$

we only need to know the transformation properties for one of the index-pairs, km, for instance; the reduction can then be carried out by inspection. Let us suppose that the z axis is a two-fold axis of symmetry, so that **S** is given by (14.44). We now consider a "model" transformation

$$\underset{2}{z}\mathbf{B}\underset{2}{z}^{-1} = \begin{Vmatrix} B_{11} & B_{12} & -B_{13} \\ B_{12} & B_{22} & -B_{23} \\ -B_{13} & -B_{23} & B_{33} \end{Vmatrix}.$$

Thus $B_{11} \to B_{11}$, $B_{22} \to B_{22}$, $B_{33} \to B_{33}$, $B_{12} \to B_{12}$, $B_{13} \to -B_{13}$, $B_{23} \to -B_{23}$; in terms of the abbreviated notation, this amounts to the "index transformation" $1 \to 1$, $2 \to 3$, $3 \to 3$, $4 \to -4$, $5 \to -5$, $6 \to 6$. Consequently, $C_{16} \to C_{16}$, but $C_{14} \to -C_{14}$, etc. In this way we conclude that $C_{14} = C_{24} = C_{34} = C_{15} = C_{25} = C_{35} = C_{46} = C_{56} = 0$, thus obtaining the matrix **C** appropriate to monoclinic crystals. These crystals have three preferred directions such that one of them (here identified with the z axis) is orthogonal to the other two; the latter need not be mutually orthogonal.

The symmetry operations for *cubic crystals* are

$$\underset{4}{x} = \begin{Vmatrix} 1 & 0 & 0 \\ 0 & 0 & -1 \\ 0 & 1 & 0 \end{Vmatrix}, \quad \underset{4}{y} = \begin{Vmatrix} 0 & 0 & 1 \\ 0 & 1 & 0 \\ -1 & 0 & 0 \end{Vmatrix}, \quad \underset{4}{z} = \begin{Vmatrix} 0 & -1 & 0 \\ 1 & 0 & 0 \\ 0 & 0 & 1 \end{Vmatrix}.$$

Of these only two are needed because, for instance $\underset{4}{y} = \underset{4}{z}\,\underset{4}{x}\,\underset{4}{z}^{-1}$. Proceeding as before, we consider the "model transformations"

$$\underset{4}{z}\mathbf{B}\underset{4}{z}^{-1} = \begin{Vmatrix} B_{22} & -B_{12} & -B_{23} \\ -B_{12} & B_{11} & B_{13} \\ -B_{23} & B_{13} & B_{33} \end{Vmatrix}, \qquad \underset{4}{x}\mathbf{B}\underset{4}{x}^{-1} = \begin{Vmatrix} B_{11} & -B_{13} & B_{12} \\ -B_{13} & B_{33} & -B_{23} \\ B_{12} & -B_{23} & B_{22} \end{Vmatrix}.$$

The first transformation requires that $1 \to 2$, $2 \to 1$, $3 \to 3$, $4 \to 5$, $5 \to -4$,

$6 \to -6$, so that $C_{14} = C_{25} = -C_{14} = 0$, $C_{11} = C_{22}$, etc. The second transformation requires that $1 \to 1$, $2 \to 3$, $3 \to 2$, $4 \to -4$, $5 \to 6$, $6 \to -5$, thus $C_{13} = C_{12}$, $C_{45} = -C_{46} = -C_{45} = 0$, etc. In this way we arrive at

$$\|\mathbf{C}\| = \begin{Vmatrix} C_{11} & C_{12} & C_{12} & 0 & 0 & 0 \\ C_{21} & C_{11} & C_{12} & 0 & 0 & 0 \\ C_{21} & C_{21} & C_{11} & 0 & 0 & 0 \\ 0 & 0 & 0 & C_{44} & 0 & 0 \\ 0 & 0 & 0 & 0 & C_{44} & 0 \\ 0 & 0 & 0 & 0 & 0 & C_{44} \end{Vmatrix}. \tag{14.46}$$

Thus if a strain-energy function is assumed to exist, then there are only three distinct coefficients: C_{11}, C_{12}, and C_{44}. For the strain energy to be positive definite, it is necessary that $C_{44} > 0$, $C_{11} - C_{12} > 0$, $C_{11} + 2C_{12} > 0$. This can be seen by decomposing strains into $\vartheta = \text{tr}\mathbf{E}$ and deviatoric strains ε_{ij}: $\frac{1}{3}\vartheta^2(C_{11} + 2C_{12}) + (C_{11} - C_{12})(\varepsilon_{11}^2 + \varepsilon_{22}^2 + \varepsilon_{33}^2) + C_{44}(\varepsilon_{23}^2 + \varepsilon_{31}^2 + \varepsilon_{12}^2) > 0$.

To convert the representation (14.46) into index notation, we start with the term $2\mu E_{ij}$, $\mu = C_{44}$. Because the coefficient C_{44} is absent in the relation between normal stresses and strains, we also introduce a term $E_{\underline{aa}}\delta_{ai}\delta_{aj}$ (summation over a from one to three!).† With $\lambda = C_{12}$, $2\alpha = C_{11} - C_{12} - 2\mu$, we then have that $T_{ij} = \lambda\vartheta\delta_{ij} + 2\mu E_{ij} + 2\alpha E_{\underline{aa}}\delta_{ai}\delta_{aj}$. More generally, if $\mathbf{e}_i$ is any Cartesian coordinate system, and $\mathbf{H}_a = H_{ai}\mathbf{e}_i$ the representation of an intrinsic material basis, then

$$T_{ij} = \lambda\vartheta\delta_{ij} + 2\mu E_{ij} + 2\alpha E_{\underline{aa}} H_{ai} H_{aj}, \tag{14.46*}$$

where $E_{\underline{aa}} = E_{km} H_{\underline{a}k} H_{\underline{a}m}$.

The reductions are somewhat more laborious if the symmetry operations are of the type $\underset{3}{z}$ or $\underset{6}{z}$, because then in the place of simple "index transformations" we obtain linear relations between tensor components.

Transverse isotropy is a *continuous group* of material symmetries, all directions perpendicular to a vector $\mathbf{h}$ being equivalent. It is not one of the crystal symmetries, but may be found in materials with a laminated structure.

Because any rotation about the axis of $\mathbf{h}$ is a symmetry operation, we may use the following method of reduction. If a scalar-valued function of vectors, $\phi(\mathbf{a}, \mathbf{b}, \mathbf{c}, \mathbf{d})$, is "transversely isotropic," then it can depend not only on the isotropic invariants $\mathbf{a} \cdot \mathbf{a}$, $\mathbf{a} \cdot \mathbf{b}$, etc., but also on the invariants associated with

† Thomas [218].

rotations about the axis of $\mathbf{h}$: $\mathbf{h}\cdot\mathbf{a}$, $\mathbf{h}\cdot\mathbf{b}$, $\mathbf{h}\cdot\mathbf{c}$, $\mathbf{h}\cdot\mathbf{d}$. Therefore, the saturated form of a transversely isotropic *tensor* will be a linear combination of the terms $\mathbf{a}\cdot\mathbf{b}\ \mathbf{c}\cdot\mathbf{d}$, $\mathbf{a}\cdot\mathbf{c}\ \mathbf{b}\cdot\mathbf{d}$, $\mathbf{a}\cdot\mathbf{d}\ \mathbf{b}\cdot\mathbf{c}$ and $\mathbf{h}\cdot\mathbf{a}\ \mathbf{h}\cdot\mathbf{b}\ \mathbf{c}\cdot\mathbf{d}$, $\mathbf{h}\cdot\mathbf{b}\ \mathbf{h}\cdot\mathbf{c}\ \mathbf{d}\cdot\mathbf{a}$, $\mathbf{h}\cdot\mathbf{c}\ \mathbf{h}\cdot\mathbf{d}\ \mathbf{a}\cdot\mathbf{b}$, $\mathbf{h}\cdot\mathbf{d}\ \mathbf{h}\cdot\mathbf{a}\ \mathbf{b}\cdot\mathbf{c}$, $\mathbf{h}\cdot\mathbf{a}\ \mathbf{h}\cdot\mathbf{c}\ \mathbf{b}\cdot\mathbf{d}$, $\mathbf{h}\cdot\mathbf{b}\ \mathbf{h}\cdot\mathbf{d}\ \mathbf{c}\cdot\mathbf{a}$, $\mathbf{h}\cdot\mathbf{a}\ \mathbf{h}\cdot\mathbf{b}\ \mathbf{h}\cdot\mathbf{c}\ \mathbf{h}\cdot\mathbf{d}$. Taking into account the symmetries $C_{ijkm} = C_{jikm} = C_{ijmk}$, we arrive at†

$$C_{ijkm} = \lambda\delta_{ij}\delta_{km} + \mu(\delta_{ik}\delta_{jm} + \delta_{im}\delta_{kj}) + \alpha(\delta_{ij}h_k h_m + \delta_{km}h_i h_j)$$
$$+ \beta(\delta_{ik}h_j h_m + \delta_{jk}h_i h_m + \delta_{im}h_j h_k + \delta_{jm}h_i h_k) + \gamma h_i h_j h_k h_m, \quad (14.47)$$

where λ, μ, α, β, γ are the elastic coefficients (the isotropic case corresponds to $\alpha = \beta = \gamma = 0$). If $\mathbf{h} = \mathbf{e}_3$, then $h_i = \delta_{i3}$.

To illustrate symmetry operations in a more general context, we consider the following constitutive equations,

$$T_{ij} = C_{ijkm}E_{km} + S_{ijk}P_k + \alpha_{ij}\theta, \qquad E_i = S_{jki}E_{kj} + A_{im}P_m + p_i\theta, \quad (14.48)$$

where $\mathbf{E}$ is the electric vector, $\mathbf{P}$ is the polarization, and θ is the temperature. The coupling of the mechanical, thermal, and electrical variables gives rise to host of names, e.g. pyro-electricity, piezo-electricity, etc.,‡ but we shall not go into that. Depending on the symmetries of the material, one or more of the effects may be absent. Thus from the invariance of a vectorial property $\mathbf{p}$ to a symmetry operation $\mathbf{Q}$, namely $\mathbf{p} = \mathbf{Qp}$, we conclude that $\mathbf{p} = \mathbf{0}$ in centro-symmetric materials. On the other hand, a property that is represented by a second rank tensor is automatically centro-symmetric. To illustrate the possible reductions of second rank tensors, we consider the symmetry operations of cubic crystals. Then it is easy to verify that

$$\boldsymbol{\alpha} = \underset{4}{x}\boldsymbol{\alpha}\underset{4}{x}^{-1} = \underset{4}{z}\boldsymbol{\alpha}\underset{4}{z}^{-1}$$

requires $\boldsymbol{\alpha}$ to be of the form $\alpha\mathbf{1}$. That is, cubic crystals are isotropic with regard to properties described by second rank tensors.

Properties represented by third rank tensors are of course present only in materials without a center of symmetry. Writing $S_{ijk} \to \mathbf{S}_k$, $Q_{kp}(\mathbf{QS}_p\mathbf{Q}^T) = \mathbf{S}_k$, we can use simultaneously the transformations of a vector and a

† Note that although terms like $\varepsilon_{ijk}h_i a_j b_k$ are invariant to rotations about the axis of $\mathbf{h}$, they fail to have the symmetries of $\mathbf{C}$ (cf. also the discussion of transverse isotropy in Appendix II).

‡ A classification of the various effects may be found in Nye's book [109], for instance.

second rank tensor to obtain the desired reduction. For instance, if $\mathbf{Q}$ is the monoclinic symmetry operation diag$(-1, -1, 1)$, we have that

$$\begin{Vmatrix} v_1 \\ v_2 \\ v_3 \end{Vmatrix} \to \begin{Vmatrix} -v_1 \\ -v_2 \\ v_3 \end{Vmatrix}, \quad \begin{Vmatrix} T_{11} & T_{12} & T_{13} \\ T_{21} & T_{22} & T_{23} \\ T_{31} & T_{32} & T_{33} \end{Vmatrix} \to \begin{Vmatrix} T_{11} & T_{12} & -T_{13} \\ T_{21} & T_{22} & -T_{23} \\ -T_{31} & -T_{32} & T_{33} \end{Vmatrix}.$$

Thus $S_{111} \to -S_{111}$, $S_{131} \to S_{131}$, hence $S_{111} = 0$ but $S_{131} \neq 0$, and so on. In this way we arrive at the following table of coefficients,

$$\begin{matrix} \underline{S}_{ij}\text{:} & 0 & 0 & 0 & S_{\underline{4}1} & S_{\underline{5}1} & 0 \\ & 0 & 0 & 0 & S_{\underline{4}2} & S_{\underline{5}2} & 0 \\ & S_{1\underline{3}} & S_{2\underline{3}} & S_{3\underline{3}} & 0 & 0 & S_{\underline{6}3} \end{matrix} \tag{14.49}$$

Here the first two indices have been replaced by a single subscript in the usual way.

Linear viscoelasticity

In what follows we shall sketch the linear theory of viscoelasticity, not as a special case of the nonlinear theory, but in a way that is closer to its past history.

Elastic solids can be said to possess a perfect memory of their natural (or, undistorted) states, whereas viscous fluids exhibit no memory at all, no tendency to recoil. Correspondingly, the stresses in elastic solids vanish if the deformation vanishes, whereas in viscous fluids the stresses vanish (except for a hydrostatic pressure p) whenever the motion stops. This distinction can be made explicit also by introducing the idea of a *relaxation time* τ, which describes the time rate at which stresses decay when the deformation is held constant (i.e. after the motion has stopped). For elastic solids we set $\tau = \infty$, whereas for viscous fluids $\tau = 0$. It is natural to view elasticity and viscosity as the endpoints of a continuous spectrum of viscoelastic behavior exhibiting some elasticity of shape as well as some fluidity. In particular, the response of a solid will show an increasing fluidity as the temperature is raised, or, equivalently, as the period of observation is lengthened. In a broader view, then, we can say with Heraclitus that "panta rhei"—everything flows.†

† The founders of the Society of Rheology, Marcus Reiner and E. C. Bingham, chose "panta rhei" as the motto of the Society. At the Fourth International Congress on Rheology, Marcus Reiner proposed a dimensionless *Deborah number*, D, defined by $D =$ (time of relaxation)/(time of observation); elastic and viscous responses then correspond to $D = \infty$ and $D = 0$, respectively. Reiner's delightful after-dinner talk is reprinted in *Physics Today*, Jan. 1964.

One avenue of approach to viscoelasticity is by outright *superposition of elastic and viscous responses*. Let us first note that in pure shear the stress-strain relation $T_{ij} = 2\mu_E E_{ij}$, $i \neq j$, and the viscous law $T_{ij} = 2\mu_V D_{ij}$, $i \neq j$, are each of the form

$$T = 2\mu_E e, \qquad T = 2\mu_V d. \tag{14.50}$$

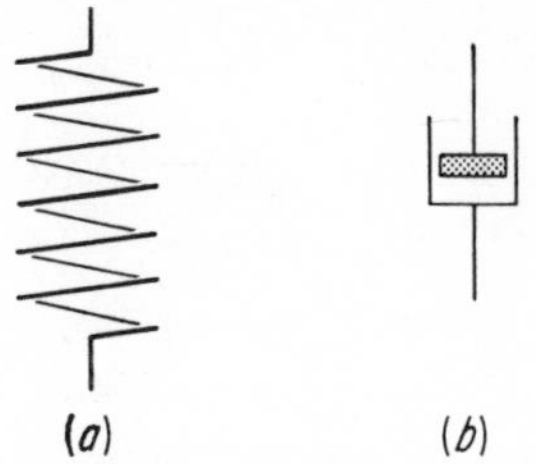

FIGURE 14.2 Constitutive models for (a) elasticity, (b) viscosity.

For simplicity, then, we can illustrate the superposition of elasticity and fluidity by means of the one-dimensional equations (14.50), and use "constitutive models" for visualizing these equations. A constitutive model is a kind of picture showing the essence of the tensorial constitutive equations, and of the physical idea embodied in them (Figure 14.2). Elasticity being synonymous with "springiness," we shall use a spring as the mental picture of an elastic solid. This model conveys to us at a glance the main features of elasticity: (a) to each load there corresponds a definite deformation, (b) upon removal of loads a body returns to its undeformed configuration. As a constitutive model of fluidity we shall use a "dashpot." Again, this model expresses simply the main idea that flow will continue as long as forces act on the system. Needless to say, constitutive models should not be used in situations for which they were not intended, e.g. derivations of general results. Rather, the function of constitutive models is merely to *suggest* various extensions of elasticity and fluidity.

We shall confine the discussion to infinitesimal deformations, in which case $D_{ij} \approx \partial_t E_{ij} \approx \dot{E}_{ij}$ (cf. (15.16)). In the place of $(14.50)_2$ we can then write $T = 2\mu_V \dot{e}$.

Let us begin with a *Maxwell fluid*; as shown in Figure 14.3, its constitutive model consists of a spring and a dashpot joined in series. Evidently this model represents a fluid, because the flow in the dashpot will continue for as long as a force is applied. Moreover, a change in loading will be accompanied by an instantaneous elastic response, because the deformation of the spring is not hampered by the presence of the dashpot. To derive the appropriate constitutive equation, we observe that the force T in the spring and in the dashpot is the same, whereas the deformation e_E in the spring and the deformation e_V in the dashpot are additive: $\dot{e} = \dot{e}_E + \dot{e}_V$. Then, by (14.50),

$$2\mu_E \dot{e} = \dot{T} + \frac{1}{\tau} T, \qquad \tau = \frac{\mu_V}{\mu_E}. \tag{14.51}$$

To allow for ageing, we might let the *relaxation time* τ be a function of t.

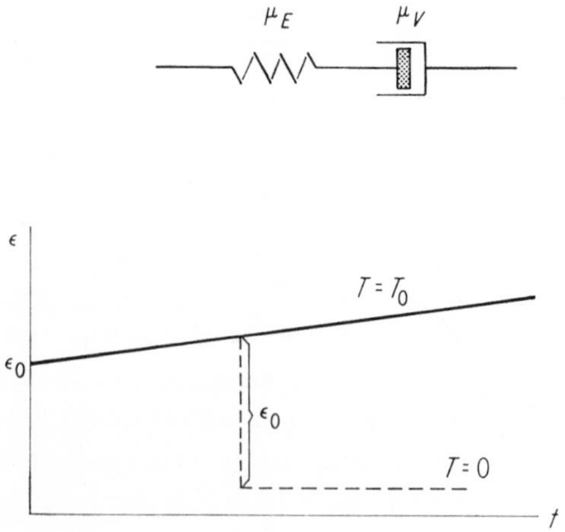

FIGURE 14.3 Constitutive model and creep curve for a Maxwell fluid.

The equation $2\mu_E \dot{e} = \dot{T} + (1/\tau)T$ is typical of rate theories, in which constitutive equations are in effect differential equations. But the mechanical response described by a differential equation may be strongly influenced by the assigned initial values of stresses. Indeed, as has been demonstrated by Bernstein [3], depending on the initial conditions the responses described by one and the same rate equation can be so diverse as to make it implausible that they could belong to the same material. Consequently, it is felt that a theory of the rate-type does not characterize a single material, but, rather, describes a type of behavior which may be common to various materials. Of course this does not lessen the practical value of the rate-type theories.

One of the standard experiments is the *creep test*, in which a specimen is subjected to a constant load T_0 for a long period of time. In view of the long duration of the test (for concrete slabs measurements have been obtained for periods up to twenty years), the application and removal of the load can be considered to be instantaneous, even though they require a finite time in practice in order that unwanted vibrations be prevented. For a constant load $T = T_0$ the equation (14.51) reduces to $2\mu_E \dot{e} = T/\tau$, and the solution is $e = e_0 (1 + t/\tau)$, $T_0 = 2\mu_E e_0$. Because the instantaneous response of the

Maxwell fluid is elastic, the constant of integration has been set equal to the elastic strain e_0.

After unloading (14.51) reads $2\mu_E\dot{e} = 0$, thus $e = \text{const.}$, i.e. a *permanent deformation* has been produced. To evaluate this constant, we again note that the instantaneous response is elastic, so that upon unloading the strain will decrease by an amount equal to the elastic strain e_0. Therefore, if the load is applied at $t = 0$ and removed at $t = t_0$, then

$$e = e_0\left(1 + \frac{t}{\tau}\right), \qquad 0 < t < t_0,$$

$$e = \frac{e_0 t_0}{\tau}, \qquad t > t_0.$$

The Maxwell model predicts creep curves of the form $e = Tf(t)$. The function $f(t)$ is the same for all stress levels; in particular, if the stress is doubled, the ordinates in Figure 14.3 are multiplied by a factor two, without changing the shapes of the creep curves. It is with respect to this separation of the influences of stress and time that experimental data deviate most frequently from the predictions based on the linear viscoelastic model (14.51): for equally spaced stress levels the creep curves are not equally spaced. Nevertheless, the general linear viscoelasticity theory has a number of useful applications; in the case of concrete the linear theory appears to be valid for loads up to 30 percent of the ultimate load (cf. [138]).

Another basic experiment is the *relaxation test* in which the specimen is kept at a constant strain e_0 for long periods of time. Then (14.51) reduces to $\dot{T} + T/\tau = 0$, and the solution is given by $T = T_0 \exp(-t/\tau)$, $T_0 = 2\mu_E e_0$. From this result we can interpret the relaxation time τ as the interval in which the initial stress T_0 is decreased by the factor $\underline{e}^{-1}$. Needless to say, creep and relaxation tests are but two aspects of the same property of viscoelasticity, characterized by the material property τ.

If the spring and the dashpot are joined in parallel (Figure 14.4), we obtain a *Kelvin solid.* An inspection of the constitutive model shows that the deformations of the spring and the dashpot are equal: $\dot{e}_E = \dot{e}_V = \dot{e}$, whereas the forces in the spring and the dashpot are additive, $T = T_E + T_V$, so that

$$\frac{T}{2\mu_E} = \dot{e} + \frac{e}{\tau}. \tag{14.52}$$

It is important to note that the instantaneous response of a Kelvin solid is fluid-like, because the presence of the dashpot inhibits any sudden displacements of the spring. Therefore, this model may be said to represent "delayed elastic response."

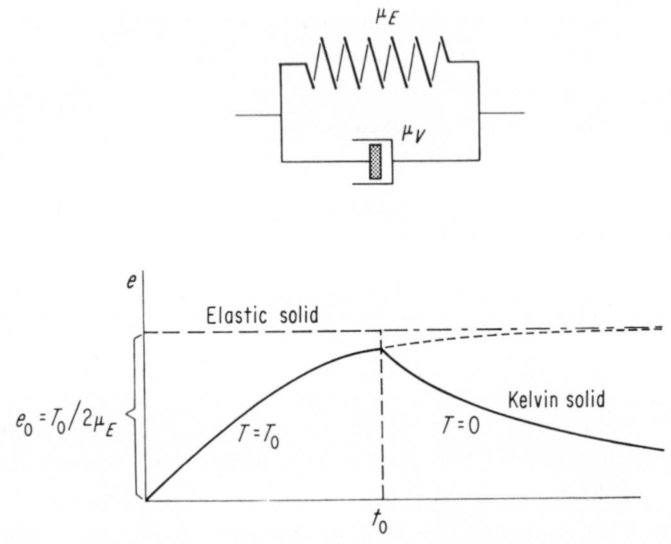

FIGURE 14.4 Constitutive model and creep curve for a Kelvin solid.

A creep test followed by unloading at $t = t_0$ is described by (cf. Figure 14.4)

$$e = e_0\left[1 - \exp\left(-\frac{t}{\tau}\right)\right], \qquad 0 < t < t_0,$$

$$e = e_0\left[\exp\left(-\frac{t - t_0}{\tau}\right) - \exp\left(-\frac{t}{\tau}\right)\right], \quad t > t_0,$$

where $T_0 = 2\mu_E e_0$. Evidently the creep curves are again of the form $e = Tf(t)$. After unloading, the deformation of a Kelvin solid tends to zero. The model may be used to describe some dissipative processes in an essentially elastic body, e.g. internal damping which becomes noticeable if vibrations are observed for long periods of time or at elevated temperatures. That the Kelvin solid describes a dissipative medium can be verified by calculating the energy W dissipated in the dashpot during a complete loading-unloading cycle:

$$W = \int_0^\infty T_V \dot{e}_V \, d\tau = 2\mu_V \int_0^\infty \dot{e}^2 \, d\tau = T_0 e_0\left[1 - \exp\left(-\frac{t_0}{\tau}\right)\right].$$

A spring-dashpot assembly also suggests the idea of a *variable reference configuration* R that would serve to describe the evolution of the "inelastic" deformation, the elastic part of the total deformation being expressed in terms of strains measured from R. Following Eckart [26], we decompose the total strain E_{ij} into a strain of elastic deformation, p_{ij}, and a strain of inelastic deformation, r_{ij}, thus $E_{ij} = p_{ij} + r_{ij}$. The total rate-of-deformation, D_{ij}, is decomposed in the same way, $\dot{E}_{ij} = D_{ij} = \dot{p}_{ij} + \dot{r}_{ij}$. In addition, we assume that the density of internal energy, ε, is a function of p_{ij}, the specific volume v (if p_{ij} are not the total strains, then v can be varied independently of p_{ij}), and the entropy density η. The quantity $\sigma_{ij} = \rho \partial\varepsilon/\partial p_{ij}$ will be referred to as the "elastic stress." Letting $\theta = \partial\varepsilon/\partial\eta$, $\pi = -\partial\varepsilon/\partial v$, where θ is the absolute temperature, and π the thermodynamic pressure, we find that the energy balance now reads $\rho\dot{\varepsilon} = \sigma_{ij}\dot{p}_{ij} - \pi D_{ii} + \rho\theta\dot{\eta} = -\text{div}\mathbf{q} + T_{ij}D_{ij}$. Therefore, the Clausius-Duhem inequality governing the production of entropy is given by

$$\rho\theta\gamma = \rho\theta\dot{\eta} + \text{div}\left(\frac{\mathbf{q}}{\theta}\right) = -\frac{1}{\theta}\mathbf{q}\cdot\text{grad}\,\theta + T_{ij}D_{ij} + \pi D_{ii} - \sigma_{ij}\dot{p}_{ij} \geq 0. \qquad (14.53)$$

The terms on the right-hand side of (14.53) suggest various types of constitutive equations that conform to the condition of positive entropy production, e.g. $\mathbf{q} = -k\,\text{grad}\,\theta$, $k > 0$. Admittedly, this is like putting a cart before a horse, because thermodynamics cannot tell us what the material is like (i.e. a constitutive equation should be formulated first, and the limitations imposed by $\gamma \geq 0$ investigated later). However for once let us not be dogmatic about that, and take the motivations where we can find them. Specifically, to satisfy

$$(T_{ij} + \pi\delta_{ij})D_{ij} - \sigma_{ij}\dot{p}_{ij} = V_{ij}D_{ij} + \sigma_{ij}\dot{r}_{ij} \geq 0, \qquad (14.54)$$

where $\mathbf{V} = \mathbf{T} + \pi\mathbf{1} - \boldsymbol{\sigma}$ is a deviatoric "viscous stress," we choose

$$V_{ij} = \lambda_V D_{kk}\delta_{ij} + 2\mu_V D_{ij}, \qquad \mu_V \geq 0, \qquad 3\lambda_V + 2\mu_V \geq 0,$$
$$\dot{r}_{ij} = \lambda_R\sigma_{kk}\delta_{ij} + 2\mu_R\sigma_{ij}, \qquad \mu_R \geq 0, \qquad 3\lambda_R + 2\mu_R \geq 0.$$

We illustrate the further reduction for deviatoric components only. Denoting these components by $\bar{\mathbf{T}}$, $\bar{\boldsymbol{\sigma}}$, $\bar{\mathbf{V}}$, $\bar{\mathbf{p}}$, $\bar{\mathbf{r}}$, $\bar{\mathbf{D}}$, we have that $\bar{\mathbf{T}} = \bar{\boldsymbol{\sigma}} + \bar{\mathbf{V}}$, $\bar{\boldsymbol{\sigma}} = 2\mu_E\bar{\mathbf{p}}$, $\bar{\mathbf{V}} = 2\mu_V\bar{\mathbf{D}}$, $\dot{\bar{\mathbf{r}}} = 2\mu_R\bar{\boldsymbol{\sigma}}$, so that $4\mu_E\mu_R\bar{\mathbf{T}} = 2\mu_E\dot{\bar{\mathbf{r}}} + 8\mu_E\mu_V\mu_R\bar{\mathbf{D}}$, $\dot{\bar{\mathbf{T}}} = 2\mu_E\dot{\bar{\mathbf{p}}} + 2\mu_V\dot{\bar{\mathbf{D}}}$, and

$$\dot{\bar{\mathbf{T}}} + 4\mu_E\mu_R\bar{\mathbf{T}} = 2\mu_E(1 + 4\mu_R\mu_V)\bar{\mathbf{D}} + 2\mu_V\dot{\bar{\mathbf{D}}}. \qquad (14.55)$$

This equation can be represented by a "Jeffreys model" consisting of a Maxwell element (μ_E, $\mu_V' = \mu_R$) in parallel with a dashpot (μ_V). From the Jeffreys model we recover Maxwell's fluid by letting $\mu_V = 0$, $\mu_R = 1/\bar{\mu}_V$, and Kelvin's solid by letting $\mu_R = 0$.

It is worth noting that (14.54) may suggest theories other than viscoelasticity theory. For instance, we may consider *thermoplasticity* (cf. [87]); in that case the plastic deformation is assumed to be isochoric: $r_{ii} = 0$, so that $v = v_0(1 + p_{ii})$, i.e. v cannot be introduced as an independent variable. This means that π is absent from the entropy inequality: $T_{ij}\dot{r}_{ij} + (T_{ij} - \sigma_{ij})\dot{p}_{ij} \geq 0$. If we identify $\boldsymbol{\sigma}$ with the total stress $\mathbf{T}$, and let $\mathbf{T} = -p\mathbf{1} + \mathbf{S}$, where $\mathbf{S}$ is the deviatoric stress, then the entropy inequality reduces to $S_{ij}\dot{r}_{ij} \geq 0$. Now, because the constitutive equation governing $\mathbf{S}$ is already prescribed, the inequality can be satisfied in only one way: by choosing a suitable constitutive equation $\dot{\mathbf{r}} = \mathbf{f}(\mathbf{S}, \dot{\mathbf{S}})$ for the plastic strain rates.

Adding a Maxwell fluid and a Kelvin solid in series we obtain a constitutive model, designated by $K - M$, which gives rise to creep curves that are more representative of the experimentally obtained curves. Naturally we can continue adding springs and dashpots to constitutive models, although the usefulness of this procedure rapidly diminishes because there is no way of determining uniquely the number and arrangement of springs and dashpots necessary to represent a given mechanical response. If the simple models of Maxwell and Kelvin are not satisfactory, then we must seek generalizations in a more rational manner. For instance, we may construct a constitutive model from N Maxwell elements joined in parallel. Then the deformation is the same in each element, whereas, the forces are additive. Denoting the relaxation time and the elastic modulus μ_E of the Kth element by τ_K and μ_K, respectively we can describe the decay of stress in a stress relaxation test by $T(t) = 2e_0\mathbf{S}\mu_K \exp(-t/\tau_K)$, where $\mathbf{S}$ indicates summation over K from 1 to N. The stresses in the individual Maxwell elements are not, of course, observable quantities; they are only introduced in the initial stage of derivation. It is now natural to pass to the limit $N \rightarrow \infty$:

$$T(t) = 2e_0 \int_0^\infty \mu(\tau) \exp\left(-\frac{t}{\tau}\right) d\tau.$$

A *stress relaxation function* $G(t)$ is then defined by $G(t) = T(t)/e_0$, and replaces the individual Maxwell elements. However, whereas the Maxwell elements are described by differential equations that can be equally well applied to variable strains $e(t)$, the stress relaxation function was obtained as a particular solution corresponding to a *constant* strain. Therefore, it is necessary to adopt a principle of superposition, also known as *Boltzmann's principle*, according to which an increment of strain, $de(\tau)$, produces an increment of stress, $dT(t) = de(\tau)G(t - \tau)$, that is independent of the values of strain outside of the interval $(\tau, \tau + d\tau)$. With the notation

$$A * B = \int_{-\infty}^{t} A(t - \tau)B(\tau)\, d\tau \tag{14.56}$$

(often referred to as a "convolution" (integral) of A and B), we can express Boltzmann's principle as follows,

$$T = G * \dot{e} = G(0)e + \dot{G} * e, \tag{14.57}$$

where we have set $G(\infty)e(-\infty) = 0$.

The *creep function* J is introduced in a similar way:

$$e = J * \dot{T}. \tag{14.58}$$

Moreover, either one of the functions determines the other. For instance, assuming that stress and strain vanish up to time $t = 0$, and applying the Laplace transformation to (14.57), (14.58), we obtain $1 = p^2\bar{J}(p)\bar{G}(p)$, from which it follows that

$$t = \int_0^\infty G(t - \tau)J(\tau)\,d\tau, \qquad t > 0.$$

If the mechanical response is linear, and the response functionals satisfy certain smoothness conditions, then the general constitutive equations

$$T_{ij} = G_{ijkm} * \dot{E}_{km}, \qquad E_{ij} = J_{ijkm} * \dot{T}_{km} \tag{14.59}$$

can be rigorously derived.† These equations are further limited by one form or another of a *principle of fading memory*. For instance, to express the idea that the current stress is more affected by strains in recent past than by strains in distant past, we can require that if the deformation is held constant from some instant t_0 on, then, as $t \to \infty$, the stress should approach a constant value which is independent of the strain history in the domain $-\infty < \tau < t_0$. More generally, the property of fading memory can be expressed by postulating a *norm*, or "recollection", of strain histories, $|\mathbf{E}|_h$, which is weighted in favor of recent past, e.g.

$$|\mathbf{E}|_h^2 = \int_0^\infty |\mathbf{E}(t - s)|^2 h^2(s)\,ds. \tag{14.60}$$

Here $|\mathbf{E}(t - s)|^2 = E_{ij}(t - s)\,E_{ij}(t - s)$, and the weight function $h(s)$ must be positive, monotonically decreasing with s, and satisfy $h(0) = 1$. The weight function $h(s)$ itself is not assumed to be a material property, but its existence is.

† Gurtin and Sternberg [65], Meixner [93]. Media with instantaneously viscous response are not included in (14.59)!

For large deformations, the constitutive equations (14.59) violate the principle of material objectivity (because then the linearized strains are not objective tensors). For this reason we are going to leave viscoelastic fluids out of the picture right now. One could, of course, use the finite strains $2\mathbf{E} = \mathbf{C} - \mathbf{1}$; however, a more systematic approach, outlined in Chapter 6, suggests other deformation tensors.

In isotropic materials the relaxation moduli G_{ijkm} and the creep compliances J_{ijkm} must be isotropic tensors, e.g. $G_{ijmn}(t) = \lambda(t)\delta_{ij}\delta_{mn} + \mu(t)(\delta_{im}\delta_{jn} + \delta_{jm}\delta_{in})$. Then

$$T_{ii} = G_2 * \dot{E}_{ii}, \qquad G_2 = 3\lambda + 2\mu, \tag{14.61}$$

whereas the deviatoric stresses, $\mathbf{S} = \mathbf{T} - \frac{1}{3}\mathbf{1}\,\mathrm{tr}\mathbf{T}$, and the deviatoric strains, $\boldsymbol{\epsilon} = \mathbf{E} - \frac{1}{3}\mathbf{1}\,\mathrm{tr}\mathbf{E}$, are related by

$$S_{ij} = G_1 * \dot{\epsilon}_{ij}, \qquad G_1 = 2\mu. \tag{14.62}$$

Because the tensors of stress and strain are symmetric, the relaxation moduli have the symmetries $G_{ijkm}(t) = G_{jikm}(t) = G_{ijmk}(t)$ (the same is of course true of the creep compliances). The condition

$$G_{ijkm}(t) = G_{kmij}(t) \tag{14.63}$$

is evidently satisfied in the isotropic case, but it is not obvious why it should hold in general. As pointed out by Rogers and Pipkin [135], it is instructive to determine the special cases of (14.63) which are satisfied because of material symmetries alone. For instance, in the particular case of transverse anisotropy characterized by rotational symmetry about z axis and reflectional symmetry in all planes passing through the z axis, (14.63) reduces to the single condition $G_{1133} = G_{3311}$ (cf. (B.18)). This condition can be tested experimentally by the following simple arrangement. As shown in Figure 14.5, two identical strips A and B, sufficiently thin to justify a plane stress approximation of the problem, are bonded together in such a way that the axis of symmetry, x_3, is in the plane of A, and normal to the plane of the bond, whereas in B it is along the thickness dimension. Except in the vicinity of the bonding surface, a stress $\sigma = T_{33}$ will give rise to $E_{22} = J_{2233}\sigma = J_{1133}\sigma$ in A; similarly, a stress $\sigma = T_{22}$ will produce a strain $E_{33} = J_{3322}\sigma = J_{3311}\sigma$ in B (cf. (B.18)). Thus if $J_{1133} \neq J_{3311}$, then the thickening of A and B will show an asymmetry, and, correspondingly, the bonding surface will be curved.

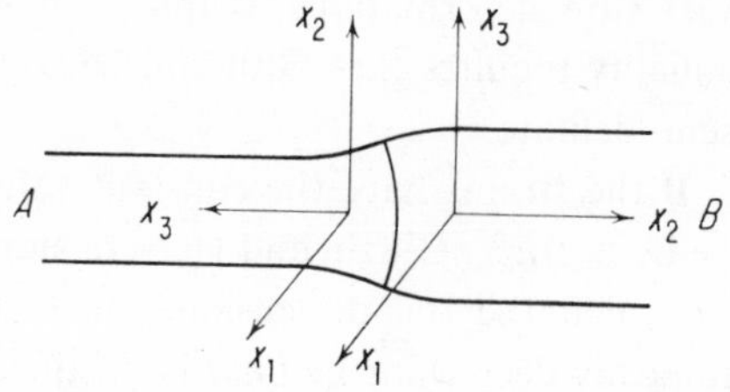

FIGURE 14.5 Arrangement for a test of the condition $G_{1133} = G_{3311}$.

To investigate the condition that work must be done to deform a viscoelastic body from its virgin state, let us consider strain histories that vanish on $-\infty \leq \tau \leq 0$. Following Gurtin and Herrera [64], we say that the constitutive equation is *dissipative* if the work up to time t, $w(t)$, satisfies

$$w(t) = \int_0^t T_{ij}(u)\dot{E}_{ij}(u)\, du \geq 0, \qquad 0 \leq t < \infty. \tag{14.64}$$

A constitutive equation is said to be *strongly dissipative* if equality holds only for a strain history that is identically zero. We now introduce a scaling of strain history, $\mathbf{E}^{(\alpha)}$, defined by

$$\mathbf{E}^{(\alpha)}(\tau) = \mathbf{E}(\alpha\tau). \tag{14.65}$$

Thus if $\mathbf{E}^{(\alpha)}(\bar{t}) = \mathbf{E}(t)$, then $\bar{t} = t/\alpha$, so that $\mathbf{E}^{(\alpha)}$ takes longer to reach the value $\mathbf{E}(t)$ if $\alpha < 1$ (*retarded history*), and less time if $\alpha > 1$ (*accelerated history*). The stress $\mathbf{T}^{(\alpha)}$ associated with a strain history $\mathbf{E}^{(\alpha)}$ is given by

$$\mathbf{T}^{(\alpha)}(u) = \int_0^u \mathbf{G}(u - \tau)\dot{\mathbf{E}}^{(\alpha)}(\tau)\, d\tau.$$

Noting that $\dot{\mathbf{E}}^{(\alpha)}(\tau) = \partial_\tau \mathbf{E}^{(\alpha)}(\tau) = \alpha\partial_{\alpha\tau}\mathbf{E}(\alpha\tau) \equiv \alpha\dot{\mathbf{E}}(\alpha\tau)$, we readily obtain

$$\mathbf{T}^{(\alpha)}\left(\frac{u}{\alpha}\right) = \int_0^u \mathbf{G}\left(\frac{u}{\alpha} - \frac{\xi}{\alpha}\right)\dot{\mathbf{E}}(\xi)\, d\xi, \qquad w^{(\alpha)}\left(\frac{t}{\alpha}\right) = \int_0^t T_{ij}^{(\alpha)}\left(\frac{u}{\alpha}\right)\dot{E}_{ij}(u)\, du.$$

If $\mathbf{G}$ and $\mathbf{E}$ satisfy certain smoothness conditions, it can be shown that†

$$\lim_{\alpha\to\infty} \mathbf{T}^{(\alpha)}\left(\frac{u}{\alpha}\right) = \mathbf{G}(0)\mathbf{E}(u), \qquad \lim_{\alpha\to 0} \mathbf{T}^{(\alpha)}\left(\frac{u}{\alpha}\right) = \mathbf{G}(\infty)\mathbf{E}(u),$$

where $\mathbf{G}(0) = \mathbf{G}(\mathbf{x}, 0)$ may be referred to as the *instantaneous elasticity tensor*, and $\mathbf{G}(\infty) = \mathbf{G}(\mathbf{x}, \infty)$, if it exists, as the *equilibrium elasticity tensor*. Thus (14.59) describes a viscoelastic response that in very rapid deformations, or

† Gurtin and Herrera, p. 238, *op. cit.*

very slow deformations, is approximately elastic. Further, the dissipation inequality requires that $\mathbf{G}(0)$ and $\mathbf{G}(\infty)$ (if it exists) be symmetric and positive semi-definite.

If the strains have the constant values E_{ij}^0 from $t = 0$ onward, then $T_{ij}(t) = G_{ijkm}(t)E_{km}^0$. Gurtin and Herrera show that the usual assumption according to which the one-dimensional relaxation function is positive and monotonically decreasing can *not* be justified by the dissipation inequality.

Leaving theory aside for a while, let us digress to a few mathematical aspects of the determination of relaxation and compliance functions. To keep the notations simple, we shall discuss the one-dimensional case only. In isotropic media this entails no loss of generality, because the constitutive equations governing deviatoric components and hydrostatic components of tensors are exactly of the form of the one-dimensional equation.

To determine a material constant may not be much of a problem, but to determine a material *function*, e.g. $G(t)$, is another matter. For the sake of illustration let us again suppose that the strain history vanishes for $-\infty < \tau \leq 0$, so that

$$T(t) = \int_0^t G(t - \tau)\dot{E}(\tau)\, d\tau .$$

If the stress and strain are known (i.e. have been measured) in the entire interval $0 \leq t < \infty$, then $G(t)$ can be obtained right away, at least formally. For instance, applying a Laplace transformation to the constitutive equation, we arrive at $\bar{G}(p) = \bar{T}(p)/p\bar{E}(p)$, where p is the transformation parameter, and the transformed variables have been marked by overbars. The inverse Laplace transformation will now yield $G(t)$. Experiments of very long duration may be inconvenient, therefore, it is a matter of practical importance to show that the infinite interval $0 \leq t < \infty$ can be replaced by the infinite range of frequencies, $0 < \omega < \infty$, to which the material is subjected. With this in mind, we consider *steady-state oscillations*, maintained by a suitable forcing function acting over the boundary, which are of the form $E = \varepsilon \sin \omega t$. Substituting this into (14.57), we obtain $T/\varepsilon = (E_0 + E_1) \sin \omega t + E_2 \cos \omega t$, where

$$E_0 = G(0),$$

$$E_1 = \int_0^\infty \dot{G}(s) \cos \omega s\, ds = -E_0 + \omega \int_0^\infty G(s) \sin \omega s\, ds, \tag{14.66}$$

$$E_2 = -\int_0^\infty \dot{G}(s) \sin \omega s\, ds = \omega \int_0^\infty G(s) \cos \omega s\, ds$$

may be referred to as the *static modulus*, the *dynamic modulus* ($E_1 + E_0$ being the *storage modulus*), and the *loss modulus*, respectively. It will be noted that, because the strain history is fixed, the response turns out to be quasi-elastic: $T = f(E, t) = E(E_0 + E_1 + E_2 \cot \omega t)$. A more convenient description of the stress is given by $T/\varepsilon = A \sin(\omega t + \phi)$, $A^2 = (E_0 + E_1)^2 + E_2^2$, $\tan \phi = E_2/(E_0 + E_1)$. Similarly, an oscillating stress field $T = \tau \sin \omega t$ will give rise to the strain field $E/\tau = \bar{A} \sin(\omega t + \bar{\phi})$, $\bar{A}^2 = (J_0 + J_1)^2 + J_2^2$, $\tan \bar{\phi} = J_2/(J_0 + J_1)$, where the compliances are defined in the same way as the moduli E_0, E_1, E_2. Because the two processes $T/\varepsilon = A \sin(\omega t + \phi)$, $E = \varepsilon \sin \omega t$, and $E/\tau = \bar{A} \sin(\omega t + \bar{\phi})$, $T = \tau \sin \omega t$, are indistinguishable to the material, we should be able to make the two descriptions identical. Let us write $E/\tau = \bar{A} \sin(\omega \bar{t} + \bar{\phi})$, $T = \tau \sin \omega \bar{t}$, where $\omega \bar{t} + \bar{\phi} = \omega t$ and $\tau \bar{A} = \varepsilon$. Then the strain fields coincide; for stresses to be also the same, we must require further that $\omega \bar{t} \equiv \omega t - \bar{\phi} = \omega t - \phi$, $\tau = A\varepsilon = A\bar{A}\tau$, thus $\bar{\phi} = -\phi$, $\bar{A} = 1/A$. These conditions can be expressed as

$$J^* = \frac{1}{E^*} \tag{14.67}$$

by introducing a complex modulus $E^* = (E_0 + E_1) + iE_2$ and a complex compliance $J^* = (J_0 + J_1) + iJ_2$.

Because $E_s/\omega \equiv (E_0 + E_1)/\omega$ and the *dynamic viscosity* $\eta = E_2/\omega$ are Fourier transforms, we can invert them, thus obtaining

$$G(t) = \frac{2}{\pi} \int_0^\infty \frac{E_s(\omega)}{\omega} \sin \omega t \, d\omega = \frac{2}{\pi} \int_0^\infty \frac{E_2(\omega)}{\omega} \cos \omega t \, d\omega. \tag{14.68}$$

Therefore, $G(t)$, and similarly $J(t)$, can be determined by measuring either $E_s(\omega)$ or $E_2(\omega)$ in steady-state vibration problems. The practical problems, in experimentation as well as in mathematics, are, however, not inconsiderable.

Let us also recall from p. 314 that the relaxation function corresponding to a distribution of Maxwell elements in parallel is of the form

$$G(t) = \int_0^\infty \mu(\tau) \exp\left(-\frac{1}{\tau}\right) d\tau. \tag{14.69}$$

If we represent a general function $G(t)$ in the same way, then $\mu(\tau)$ is said to describe the *relaxation spectrum* of the material. The correspondence (14.69) can be changed into a Laplace transformation by letting $p = 1/\tau$, $p^{-2}\mu(1/p) \equiv M(p)$. Then

$$G(t) = \int_0^\infty M(p) e^{-pt} \, dp, \tag{14.70}$$

p being referred to as the relaxation frequency. Various formulas connecting G and M can be derived,† e.g.

$$E_s(\omega) = \int_0^\infty M(u)\frac{\omega^2}{\omega^2 + u^2}\,du, \qquad E_2(\omega) = \int_0^\infty M(u)\frac{\omega u}{\omega^2 + u^2}\,du. \tag{14.71}$$

Similar relations exist between J and the retardation spectrum N. Schematically,

$$\begin{array}{ccccc}
E_s, E_2 & \xleftrightarrow[\text{transformation}]{\text{Fourier}} & G & \xleftrightarrow[\text{transformation}]{\text{Laplace}} & M \\
\updownarrow \scriptstyle(14.67) & & & & \\
J_s, J_2 & \xleftrightarrow[\text{transformation}]{\text{Fourier}} & J & \xleftrightarrow[\text{transformation}]{\text{Laplace}} & N
\end{array}$$

The relations between G and J, or M and N, are of the form of integral equations.

It is well known that viscoelasticity is very sensitive to temperature changes. The behavior of glass is a case in point. At room temperatures, glass is very much like a brittle elastic solid; as the temperature is raised, glass changes gradually (i.e. without there being a critical temperature) into a viscous fluid. So far a concrete representation of nonisothermal laws has been obtained only in the case of isotropic, "thermorheologically simple" materials.‡ Here the temperature-dependence of viscoelastic response is incorporated through the interesting hypothesis that, rather than reading the "indifferent" time of a laboratory clock, the material reads its own clock. The *material time* ξ is given by a constitutive equation of the form

$$\xi(\mathbf{x}, t) = \int_0^t \phi[\theta(\mathbf{x}, \tau)]\,d\tau, \tag{14.72}$$

where ϕ is a positive, monotonically increasing function of temperature, so that a fixed interval Δt is mapped into progressively longer intervals $\Delta\xi$ as the temperature is raised. In nonisothermal processes, then, (14.61) and (14.62) are replaced by

$$\begin{aligned}
T_{ii}(t) &= \int_{-\infty}^t G_2[\xi(t) - \xi(\tau)][\dot{E}_{ii}(\tau) - 3\alpha\dot{\theta}(\tau)]\,d\tau, \\
S_{ij}(t) &= \int_{-\infty}^t G_1[\xi(t) - \xi(\tau)]\dot{e}_{ij}(\tau)\,d\tau,
\end{aligned} \tag{14.73}$$

† They have been summarized by Gross [57].
‡ Morland and Lee, [100].

where α is the coefficient of thermal expansion, and the dependence upon $\mathbf{x}$ has not been shown explicitly. Evidently stress is, in general, a nonlinear functional of temperature-history; moreover, if the temperature field is inhomogeneous, then so are the fields of the relaxation moduli.

Most of the solutions in linear viscoelasticity theory concern problems in which acceleration is neglected (*quasi-static problems*). These can be reduced to equivalent boundary value problems of elastostatics with the aid of a Laplace transformation, for instance, which removes the time-dependence of variables, so that the equations governing the transformed problem will have the same structure as the equations of elastostatics.† Moreover, if (14.63) holds, then we shall obtain Green's elasticity, otherwise Cauchy's elasticity. In this connection it is interesting to note that Betti's reciprocal theorem (15.55), can be extended to linear viscoelasticity only if (14.63) holds.‡ In the presence of temperature fields, a Laplace transformation with respect to the laboratory time cannot be performed, because $G(\xi(\mathbf{x}, t), t)$ is now a function of another function of time. If on the other hand the laboratory time is eliminated altogether, then the equations of equilibrium become

$$\frac{\partial T_{ji}(\mathbf{x}, \xi)}{\partial x_j} + \frac{\partial T_{ji}(\mathbf{x}, \xi)}{\partial \xi}\frac{\partial \xi}{\partial x_j} = 0,$$

so that the correspondence with elastostatics is lost again.

Propagation of viscoelastic waves

Recently Coleman, Gurtin, Herrera [13], and Varley [186] have developed a complete theory for the propagation of surfaces of discontinuity in nonlinearly viscoelastic materials. For the time being we shall only record a few of their interesting results concerning one-dimensional acceleration waves in *linearly* viscoelastic bodies. To do so, it is necessary to recall from Section 8 the relevant jump conditions. Velocity and deformation gradient will be assumed to be continuous, thus $[\![\dot{x}]\!] = 0$, $[\![F]\!] = 0$. The persistence of these conditions requires that

$$\frac{d}{dt}[\![\dot{x}]\!] = [\![S_t\dot{x}]\!] = [\![\ddot{x} + U\,\partial_X\dot{x}]\!] = 0,$$

$$\frac{d}{dt}[\![F]\!] = [\![S_tF]\!] = [\![\dot{F} + U\,\partial_XF]\!] = 0,$$

$$S_t = \left.\frac{\partial}{\partial t}\right|_{X=\text{const.}} + U\frac{\partial}{\partial X}, \qquad U = \frac{dR}{dt},$$

† This and other methods are described in the review articles by Rogers [136] and Sternberg [219]. Green's elasticity and Cauchy's elasticity are explained in the text accompanying (15.54).

‡ Gurtin and Sternberg [66].

where $X = R(t)$ is the location of the surface of discontinuity, S, in the reference configuration. Thus

$$[\![\ddot{x}]\!] = U^2[\![\partial_X F]\!] \tag{14.74}$$

(cf. (8.94)); similarly, if $\alpha(t) = [\![\ddot{x}]\!]$ is the jump of acceleration, then

$$\frac{d\alpha}{dt} = [\![S_t \ddot{x}]\!] = [\![\dddot{x}]\!] + U[\![\ddot{F}]\!]. \tag{14.75}$$

Next, we turn to the constitutive equation, which is assumed to be of the form

$$T(X, t) = G(0)\gamma(X, t) + \int_0^\infty \dot{G}(s)\gamma(X, t - s)\, ds, \tag{14.76}$$

where $\gamma = F - 1 = \partial w/\partial X$, $w = x - X$. The equation of motion is given by $\partial T/\partial X = \rho_0 \ddot{x}$, where ρ_0 is the mass density in the reference configuration. Consequently,

$$[\![\partial_X T]\!] = \rho_0 [\![\ddot{x}]\!].$$

and, by (14.76),

$$[\![\partial_X T]\!] = G(0)\, [\![\partial_X F]\!].$$

Namely, at any particle $\bar{X}$ the gradient of F is discontinuous only at the instant $\bar{\tau} = t - \bar{s}$ satisfying $\bar{X} = R(t - \bar{s})$, so that the *integrals* of $\partial_X \gamma^+(t-s)$ and $\partial_X \gamma^-(t - s)$ are the same. Combining the last two expressions, we obtain

$$\rho_0 [\![\ddot{x}]\!] = G(0)\, [\![\partial_X F]\!].$$

Comparing this with (14.74), we obtain

$$U^2 = \frac{G(0)}{\rho_0}. \tag{14.77}$$

To deal with

$$\rho_0 [\![\dddot{x}]\!] = [\![\partial_X \dot{T}]\!],$$

we consider

$$\frac{\partial \dot{T}}{\partial X} = G(0)\frac{\partial \dot{F}}{\partial X} + \int_0^\infty \dot{G}(s)\frac{\partial^2 F(X, t - s)}{\partial X\, \partial t}\, ds.$$

Performing an integration by parts, we obtain

$$\frac{\partial \dot{T}}{\partial X} = G(0)\frac{\partial \dot{F}}{\partial X} + \dot{G}(0)\frac{\partial F}{\partial X} + \int_0^\infty \ddot{G}(s)\,\frac{\partial F(X, t-s)}{\partial X}\,ds,$$

whence it follows that

$$[\![\partial_X \dot{T}]\!] = \rho_0[\![\ddot{x}]\!] = G(0)\,[\![\partial_X \dot{F}]\!] + \dot{G}(0)\,[\![\partial_X F]\!]. \tag{14.78}$$

To eliminate $[\![\ddot{F}]\!]$ in (14.75), we recall that $\alpha = [\![\ddot{x}]\!] = -U[\![\dot{F}]\!]$, thus

$$\frac{d\alpha}{dt} = -U[\![S_t\dot{F}]\!] = -U[\![\ddot{F}]\!] - U^2\,[\![\partial_X \dot{F}]\!]$$

(note that $U = \text{const.}!$), and, by (14.75), (14.78),

$$\frac{d\alpha}{dt} = [\![\dddot{x}]\!] + U[\![\ddot{F}]\!] = U^2\,[\![\partial_X \dot{F}]\!] + \frac{\dot{G}(0)}{\rho_0}\,[\![\partial_X F]\!] + U[\![\ddot{F}]\!].$$

Adding, we obtain

$$2\frac{d\alpha}{dt} = \frac{\dot{G}(0)}{\rho_0}\,[\![\partial_X F]\!] = \frac{\dot{G}(0)}{\rho_0 U^2}\,\alpha,$$

$$\text{or} \quad \alpha = \alpha_0 e^{-\mu t}, \qquad \mu = -\frac{\dot{G}(0)}{2G(0)}. \tag{14.79}$$

Thus we have the explicit result that the jump of acceleration waves is wholly determined by the two moduli $G(0)$ and $\dot{G}(0)$. It is natural to expect that

$$G(0) > 0, \qquad \dot{G}(0) \leq 0, \tag{14.80}$$

so that the *attenuation* μ would come out positive. The first of these inequalities is equivalent to the condition that the speed U be real, or that the relaxation law be dissipative in the sense of (14.64). As shown by Gurtin and Herrera,† the last condition also requires that $G(t) \leq G(0)$ $(0 < t < \infty)$, which means that (14.80) are always satisfied by dissipative relaxation laws.

To explore the relation between acceleration fronts and infinitesimal plane

† Theorem 4.2 in [64].

waves, let us express the equation of motion in terms of the displacement $w = x - X$:

$$\rho_0 \ddot{w} = G(0) \frac{\partial^2 w}{\partial X^2} + \int_0^\infty \dot{G}(s) \frac{\partial^2 w(X, t - s)}{\partial X^2} ds.$$

We now choose a *damped sinusoidal progressive wave* of the form

$$w = Ae^{-\mu X} \cos \omega \left(t - \frac{X}{c}\right),$$

where A is the (constant) *amplitude*, and ω, c, and μ are, respectively, the *frequency*, the *speed*, and the *attenuation* of the wave. Substituting this into the equation of motion, and setting the coefficients of $\cos \omega(t - X/c)$ and $\sin \omega(t - X/c)$ separately equal to zero, we obtain the following conditions, $\rho_0 \omega^2 c^2 + (\mu^2 c^2 - \omega^2)(E_0 + E_1) - 2\mu\omega c E_2 = 0$, $2\mu\omega c(E_0 + E_1) + (\mu^2 c^2 - \omega^2)E_2 = 0$, where E_0, E_1, E_2 are defined in (14.66). For a given ω, we obtain

$$\mu(\omega) = \frac{\omega}{c(\omega)} \tan \frac{\phi(\omega)}{2}, \qquad \tan \phi(\omega) = \frac{E_2}{E_0 + E_1},$$

$$\rho_0 c^2(\omega) = \frac{\sqrt{(E_0 + E_1)^2 + E_2^2}}{\cos^2 [\phi(\omega)/2]}. \tag{14.81}$$

Evidently viscoelastic media are *dispersive*, i.e. the speeds of propagation depend on the frequency: $c = c(\omega)$. If the storage modulus $E_0 + E_1$ vanishes, then the medium cannot propagate any waves.

Using known properties of Fourier transformations, we can conclude that†

$$\lim_{\omega \to \infty} E_1 = 0, \qquad \lim_{\omega \to \infty} E_2 = 0,$$

$$\lim_{\omega \to \infty} \omega E_1 = 0, \qquad \lim_{\omega \to \infty} \omega E_2 = -\dot{G}(0).$$

Consequently,

$$c_\infty^2 \equiv \lim_{\omega \to \infty} c^2(\omega) = \frac{G(0)}{\rho_0} = U^2, \tag{14.82}$$

$$c_\infty \mu_\infty \equiv \lim_{\omega \to \infty} c(\omega)\mu(\omega) = -\frac{\dot{G}(0)}{2G(0)} = \mu, \tag{14.83}$$

† Cf. [150], p. 11.

where μ is the attenuation of acceleration fronts. The limiting values c_∞ and μ_∞ may be called the *ultrasonic speed* and the *ultrasonic attenuation*, respectively. With this we have established that the propagation and attenuation of acceleration fronts and ultrasonic plane waves are the same.

Consequences of the Clausius-Duhem inequality

As was noted in Section 12, the Clausius–Duhem inequality must be satisfied identically (i.e. for all admissible processes) by any set of constitutive equations. To illustrate the consequences of the Clausius–Duhem inequality, let us consider a quasi-elastic response defined by $\mathbf{T} = \hat{\mathbf{T}}(S)$, $\mathbf{q} = \hat{\mathbf{q}}(S)$, $\eta = \hat{\eta}(S)$, $\psi = \hat{\psi}(S)$, where the symbols $\mathbf{T}$, $\hat{\mathbf{q}}$, $\hat{\eta}$, $\hat{\psi}$ denote *functions* having as values the stress $\mathbf{T}$, the heat flux $\mathbf{q}$, the entropy density η, and the free energy ψ, respectively, and S stands for the set of variables $\mathbf{F} = \mathbf{F}(t)$, $\theta = \theta(t)$, $h_i = \partial\theta/\partial X_i$, and t. The Clausius–Duhem inequality, (12.18), can be expressed as $\delta - (1/\theta)\,\mathbf{h}\cdot\mathbf{q} \geq 0$, where δ is given by $\delta = w - \rho\eta\dot{\theta} - \rho\dot{\psi}$, $w = T_{ji}v_{i,j} = \text{tr}(\mathbf{TL})$. Substituting

$$\dot{\psi} = \frac{\partial\hat{\psi}}{\partial F_{ij}}\dot{F}_{ij} + \frac{\partial\hat{\psi}}{\partial\theta}\dot{\theta} + \frac{\partial\hat{\psi}}{\partial h_i}\dot{h}_i + \partial_t\hat{\psi}, \qquad \dot{F}_{ij} = L_{im}F_{mj},$$

into the inequality, we can now obtain the conditions that are *necessary* by taking special choices of the fields $\mathbf{F}$ and θ. By the same reasoning that led to (12.10), we find that $\hat{\psi}$ is independent of $\mathbf{h}$, and that the free energy function determines both the stress relation and the entropy relation, thus

$$T_{mi} = \rho F_{mj}\frac{\partial\hat{\psi}(\mathbf{F}, \theta, t)}{\partial F_{ij}}, \qquad \eta = -\frac{\partial\hat{\psi}(\mathbf{F}, \theta, t)}{\partial\theta}, \qquad \mathbf{q} = \hat{\mathbf{q}}(\mathbf{F}, \theta, \mathbf{h}, t). \tag{14.84}$$

With these relations, the Clausius–Duhem inequality reduces to

$$\delta + \rho\theta\gamma_c = -\rho\partial_t\psi - \frac{1}{\theta}\mathbf{q}\cdot\text{grad}\,\theta \geq 0. \tag{14.85}$$

Evidently (14.84) and (14.85) are also *sufficient* to satisfy the Clausius–Duhem inequality.

If $\partial_t\psi = 0$, then (14.85) requires that† $f(\mathbf{u}) \equiv \mathbf{u}\cdot\hat{\mathbf{q}}(\mathbf{F}, \theta, \mathbf{u})$ is never positive, and $f(\mathbf{0}) = 0$. Therefore, f has a maximum at $\mathbf{u} = \mathbf{0}$. Because $\partial f/\partial u_i = \hat{q}_i + u_k(\partial\hat{q}_k/\partial u_i)$, it follows that

$$\hat{\mathbf{q}}(\mathbf{F}, \theta, \mathbf{0}) = \mathbf{0}, \tag{14.86}$$

† *NFTM*, p. 356.

i.e. heat flux vanishes whenever the temperature gradient does (Pipkin and Rivlin [220]). If $\theta = \text{const.}$, then the variation of ψ can be interpreted as the variation of a strain energy, otherwise not.

To account for viscous effects, we may include $\dot{\mathbf{F}}$ among the independent variables. This makes the derivations a little more intricate. We begin with the observation that, except for the limitations (12.2), $\mathbf{F}$ and θ can be assigned arbitrary values. Further, if we let $\theta(\mathbf{X}) = a(t) + b_i(t)(X_i - \bar{X}_i)$, so that $\theta(\bar{\mathbf{X}}) = a(t)$, $g_i = b_i(t)$, each of the functions $a(t)$, $b_i(t)$ (and, similarly, $F_{ij}(t)$) may be defined by power series of the form $f(t) = \alpha + \beta(t - \bar{t}) + \gamma(t - \bar{t})^2/2 + \cdots$, where the constants $\alpha, \beta, \gamma, \ldots$ are arbitrary. Therefore, at any instant $\bar{t}$ we can not only prescribe $\mathbf{F}$, θ, and $\mathbf{h}$, but also $\dot{\mathbf{F}}$, $\ddot{\mathbf{F}}$, $\dot{\theta}$, and $\dot{\mathbf{h}}$. The Clausius-Duhem inequality can be put into either of the forms $A + B_i\dot{\mathbf{h}}_i \geq 0$, $C + C_{ij}\ddot{F}_{ij} \geq 0$, where A and B_i are independent of $\dot{h}_i$, and C and C_{ij} are independent of $\ddot{F}_{ij}$. Because $\dot{h}_i$ and $\ddot{F}_{ij}$ can be assigned independently of the other variables, it follows that ψ cannot depend on $\dot{\mathbf{F}}$ and $\mathbf{h}$. In this way we recover $(14.84)_2$, whereas $(14.84)_1$ is replaced by

$$T_{mi} = \rho F_{mj} \frac{\partial \hat{\psi}(\mathbf{F}, \theta, t)}{\partial F_{ij}} + \hat{T}_{mi}(\mathbf{F}, \dot{\mathbf{F}}, \theta, \mathbf{h}, t). \tag{14.87}$$

Further, the Clausius–Duhem inequality reduces to

$$\operatorname{tr}(\mathbf{VL}) - \frac{1}{\theta}\mathbf{q} \cdot \operatorname{grad}\theta - \rho\partial_t\psi \geq 0, \tag{14.88}$$

where $\mathbf{V} = \hat{\mathbf{T}}(\mathbf{F}, \mathbf{F}, \theta, \mathbf{h}, t)$ may be referred to as the "viscous stress". We define *thermodynamic equilibrium* by

$$h_i = 0, \qquad \dot{F}_{ij} = 0, \qquad \partial_t\psi = 0. \tag{14.89}$$

In this case the viscous stress can be shown to vanish,† so that the *equilibrium stress* $\mathbf{T}^0 = \mathbf{T}(\mathbf{F}, \mathbf{0}, \theta, \mathbf{0}, t)$ is given by $(14.84)_1$. A possible proof would be to expand $\mathbf{V}$ and $\mathbf{q}$ about $\dot{\mathbf{F}} = \mathbf{0}$, then use $\dot{\mathbf{F}} = \alpha\mathbf{A}(t)$, and reason from $B\alpha^2 + C\alpha \geq 0$ that $B = 0$, $C = 0$.

Another, very striking application of the Clausius–Duhem inequality is a theorem of Gurtin [221] which concerns the reduction of constitutive equations involving space functionals: $\mathbf{T} = \hat{\mathbf{T}}(\theta(\cdot), \boldsymbol{\chi}(\cdot))$, $\psi = \hat{\psi}(\theta(\cdot), \boldsymbol{\chi}(\cdot))$, etc. (cf. (14.2)). Gurtin shows that, except for $\mathbf{q}$, the constitutive equations must reduce to $\mathbf{T} = \hat{\mathbf{T}}(\theta, \mathbf{F})$, $\psi = \hat{\psi}(\theta, \mathbf{F})$, etc. Thus if internal forces are de-

† Coleman and Mizel [14].

scribed in terms of a symmetric, second rank stress tensor only, then this stress tensor cannot depend on the higher gradients $\nabla\mathbf{F}$, $\nabla\nabla\mathbf{F}$, etc., of deformation (this is not true, however, if multipolar stresses are admitted).

Problems

1. Consider a stress relation $T_{ij} = f_{ij}(\mathbf{H})$, where $H_{im} = \Delta_m u_i$ are displacement gradients. Is it possible to apply observer transformation, and, if so, what is the reduced form of the stress relation?
2. Consider $T_{ij} = f_{ij}(\mathbf{L}, \mathbf{R})$, where $L_{ij} = v_{i,j}$ are the (spatial) velocity gradients, and $\mathbf{R}$ is the rotation tensor obtained in the polar decomposition $\mathbf{F} = \mathbf{RU}$. What can be found out by applying the observer transformations to this constitutive equation?
3. By the method outlined in the text, derive (14.39).
4. Give a detailed derivation of
   a. (14.46) b. (14.49)
5. How will the creep and relaxation experiments be affected if τ in (14.51) is given by $\tau = \tau_0 \exp(\alpha t)$, where τ_0 and α are constants.
6. To investigate the possibility of acceleration waves in viscous fluids, derive the requisite jump conditions for second derivatives of velocity (cf. (8.93) *et seq.*), then apply these conditions to the Navier-Stokes equations (14.27) (assume incompressibility).
7. Verify in detail the derivation of (14.81)–(14.83).

Section 15
LINEAR ELASTICITY THEORY

Introduction

We shall give here a kind of birds-eye view of elasticity theory by reducing it to its barest essentials. More than that, we are going to show that the method of elasticity theory is the same as that used in elementary strength of materials.

We begin in elementary fashion, by describing the distinction between *statics* and mechanics of deformable bodies. In statics we may be expected to solve the following problems. A (relatively) rigid block is attached to two wires having initially the same length L (Figure 15.1a). We are required to find the tensions T_1 and T_2. Applying the equations of equilibrium,

$$F = 0, \qquad M^{[0]} = 0, \tag{a}$$

we obtain the solution

$$T_1 = T_2 = \frac{W}{2}. \tag{b}$$

The solution of the problem turns out to be a very simple matter: the result (b) is obtained from the equations of equilibrium alone. This is typical of statics.

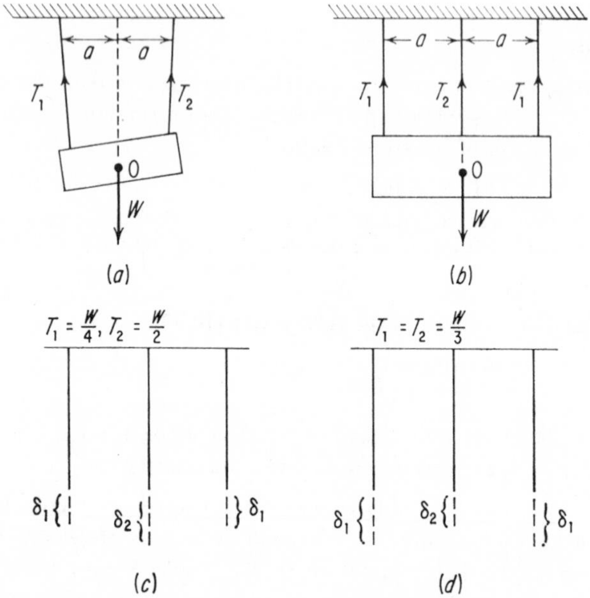

FIGURE 15.1 Statically determinate and indeterminate problems.

Actually both wires will stretch and become inclined when the load is applied In the solution this was neglected: the moment arms and the components of the tensions were calculated from the configuration as it was before the load was applied. The error thus introduced is in many cases very small because the deformations are small. For instance, a mild steel rod, 6 ft. long and with a cross section of 1 square inch, will elongate only 0.1 inch when subjected to the near-breaking load of 40,000 lbs.

The equations of equilibrium hold, of course, regardless of whether or not a body is assumed to be rigid. The application of these equations is, however, greatly simplified if deformations are neglected, because then calculations can be based on the known undeformed shape.

We soon discover that the rigid body model does not go very far: no matter how small the deformations are, they have to be taken into account in some way in order to obtain solutions. To illustrate this, we suppose that a rigid block is now attached to three equidistant wires having initially the same length L (Figure 15.1b). Although the number of unknowns has increased to three, the number of equilibrium equations remains the same. We find from (a) that $T_1 = T_3$, $T_1 + T_2 + T_3 = W$, hence

$$2T_1 + T_2 = W. \tag{c}$$

We have arrived at a *paradox of statics*—there are infinitely many "statically admissible" solutions of the problem!

We say that the preceding problem is *statically indeterminate*. Obviously statical indeterminacy is the rule rather than an exception: after all, one can go on adding wires. Moreover, this indeterminacy is not a paradox of nature (there are no such things) but a limitation of the rigid body model. The rigid body is the simplest model of material bodies; it is used whenever possible because it leads to the simplest kind of mathematics. The limits of applicability of this model are marked by the appearance of paradoxa (of statics), i.e. by problems that remain unsolvable as long as this model is retained. (If one is tempted to set $T_1 = T_2 = W/3$, one should also consider the case where the middle wire is made of steel, whereas the other two are rubber bands. Would the assumed result make sense?)

If we drop the assumption of rigidity, then it is possible to use experimental data concerning the dependence of loads upon deformations (*constitutive equations*). Assuming in the present problem that the side wires are identical, we write

$$T_1 = k_1\delta_1, \qquad T_2 = k_2\delta_2, \tag{d}$$

where δ is the elongation of a wire, and k is a (constant) *material property*.

Although we have gained two more equations, the problem still remains unsolvable because there are also two additional unknowns, δ_1 and δ_2. But let us look at two typical, statically admissible solutions: (1) $T_1 = W/4$, $T_2 = W/2$, (2) $T_1 = T_2 = W/3$. We calculate the corresponding elongations from (d), thus obtaining deformations of the type shown in Figure 15.1 c, d. In general neither of the assumed solutions will be correct, because they will produce *incompatible deformations*, that is, deformations that are incompatible with the constraint imposed by the rigid block. In fact, the symmetry of the suspension requires that

$$\delta_1 = \delta_2. \tag{e}$$

This condition may be called the *equation of compatibility of deformations*. Using (c), (d), (e) simultaneously, we now obtain

$$T_1 = \frac{Wk_1}{2k_1 + k_2}, \qquad T_2 = \frac{Wk_2}{2k_1 + k_2}.$$

The correct solution satisfies not only equations of equilibrium but also the condition of compatibility for deformations: it is both statically and kinematically admissible.

Let us note that although the deformations were taken into account through (e), they were still neglected in deriving (c). This is a characteristic of small deformation theories. It is vital to understand, however, that no matter how small the deformations are the *distribution* of the deformations holds the clue to the solution. For instance, if $\delta_1 = \varepsilon$, $\delta_2 = 2\varepsilon$, where ε is as small as you wish, the smallness of the elongations is quite irrelevant at this point. What matters is that one is twice the other, so that the tensions will also be (for linearly elastic bodies) in the ratio of two to one. On the other hand, as far as the equations of equilibrium are concerned, the smallness of deformations permits us to base the calculations on the undeformed shape of the body.

The solution of the three-wire problem, trivial as it may seem, contains all the features of elasticity theory. Let us consider the extension of a bar. It is clear that the statical indeterminacy is now infinite (curiously enough the term "statically indeterminate" is usually reserved for cases in which the redundancy is finite). If we visualize the stress vector at each point of a cross section as being exerted by an infinitesimal wire filament, then we would need infinitely many such filaments to represent a stress distribution.

How does one solve the stress problem in elasticity theory? In the same way as before: by using simultaneously the equations of equilibrium, constitutive equations (*Hooke's law*), and the equations of compatibility of deformations. Thus there is no difference in method, although the mathematical form of the equations does change. In particular, in the place of forces and elongations we use stresses T_{ij}, strains $\tilde{E}_{ij}$, and displacements u_i. Also, what were before algebraic relations may now appear as partial differential equations. For the conditions of equilibrium the correspondence is as follows:

$$F = 0 \leftrightarrow T_{ji,j} + \rho b_i = 0$$

$$M^{[0]} = 0 \leftrightarrow T_{ij} = T_{ji}$$

From the point of view of mathematics, Hooke's law is the definition of a class of materials (or, a model of mechanical response). From a physical viewpoint it is an idealization of experimental results obtained for certain ranges of loading and environmental conditions. For linearly elastic, isotropic bodies Hooke's law is given by

$$E\tilde{E}_{ij} = (1 + \nu)T_{ij} - \nu\delta_{ij}T_{kk}, \tag{15.1}$$

where E is called Young's modulus and ν is called Poisson's ratio; E and ν are related to Lame's coefficients λ and μ as follows,

$$\lambda = \frac{E\nu}{(1 + \nu)(1 - 2\nu)}, \qquad \mu = \frac{E}{2(1 + \nu)},$$
$$E = \mu\frac{3\lambda + 2\mu}{\lambda + \mu}, \qquad \nu = \frac{\lambda}{2(\lambda + \mu)}. \tag{15.2}$$

Both E and ν can be found from a tension test, E being a measure of stiffness,

$$E\tilde{E}_{xx} = T_{xx}, \tag{f}$$

and ν a measure of lateral contraction,

$$E\tilde{E}_{yy} = E\tilde{E}_{zz} = -\nu T_{xx}. \tag{g}$$

The maximum shearing stress τ is given by $\frac{1}{2}T_{xx}$, the maximum shearing strain γ by $\frac{1}{2}\tilde{E}_{xx}(1 + \nu)$ (cf. $(4.54)_1$); thus, by (*f*), $E\gamma = (1 + \nu)\tau$. In view of the assumed isotropy this relation is the same for all planes, so that $E\tilde{E}_{ij} = (1 + \nu)T_{ij}$ for $i \neq j$. The general formula (15.1) is now obtained by a superposition of the special formulas: $E\tilde{E}_{xx} = T_{xx} - \nu(T_{yy} + T_{zz}), \ldots, \ldots, E\tilde{E}_{xy} = (1 + \nu)T_{xy}, \ldots, \ldots$.

It remains to investigate the nature of compatibility conditions. Again, for any statically admissible stress distribution T_{ij} the corresponding strains $\tilde{E}_{ij}$ can be calculated from Hooke's law, (15.1). It will then be found, in general, that the deformed volume elements fail to fit perfectly. To characterize compatible strains, we introduce a field of *displacement vectors* $\mathbf{u}$ defined by

$$\mathbf{u} = \mathbf{x} - \mathbf{X}, \tag{15.3}$$

where $\mathbf{x}$ and $\mathbf{X}$ are, respectively, the final and initial positions of a particle. *Compatible strains* are then defined by the *strain-displacement relations*

$$\tilde{E}_{ij} = \frac{1}{2}(u_{i,j} + u_{j,i}), \tag{15.4}$$

that is, compatible strains are derivable from a continuous and differentiable vector field $\mathbf{u}$. In addition, the displacements must be one-valued functions of position. It will be recalled that many-valued functions can be made into one-valued functions by restricting suitably their domains. For instance, if ϕ is the angle in plane polar coordinates, then a function $u_\phi = \phi$ is many-valued and continuous. Restricted to the interval $0 \leq \phi < 2\pi$, this function is one-valued, but has a discontinuity at $\phi = 0$.

The conditions of equilibrium,

$$T_{ji,j} = 0,$$

Hooke's law

$$E\tilde{E}_{ij} = (1 + \nu)T_{ij} - \nu\delta_{ij}T_{kk}, \tag{15.1)R$$

and the strain-displacement relations,

$$\tilde{E}_{ij} = \tfrac{1}{2}(u_{i,j} + u_{j,i}), \tag{15.4)R$$

constitute the *fundamental system* of equations of linear, isotropic, isothermal elastostatics. This system provides 15 equations for the 15 unknowns T_{ij}, $\tilde{E}_{ij}$ and u_i.

The solution of problems of elasticity theory is not an easy matter, hence it is natural to investigate the possibility of devising simpler theories by making additional assumptions. For instance, to estimate the safe load on a beam, a method that utilizes partial differential equations is too cumbersome, and perhaps accurate to a degree that is unnecessary. The simplified theories are usually collected under the heading of "Strength of Materials." Here, as a rule, special types of (compatible) deformations are assumed. Thus for the extension, bending, and torsion of prismatic bodies one assumes that the transverse cross sections remain plane and merely translate or rotate during a deformation. These assumptions are suggested by simple experiments; in many cases they approximate the actual deformations very closely. Once a type of deformation has been assumed, the nature of the distribution of strains (and also of stresses) follows immediately. The magnitudes of the stresses are then found by considering equilibrium of portions of the body.

Linearized strains and rotations, equations of compatibility

The linear theory of elasticity deals only with small deformations. Now, unless a quantity is dimensionless, it makes no sense to say that it is small: the numerical value of a dimensional quantity can be made as large as we wish by choosing the units small enough. The dimensionless variables that come to mind are of course the displacement gradients. Therefore, we let

$$\mathbf{R} = \mathbf{1} + \tilde{\mathbf{R}}, \qquad \mathbf{U} = \mathbf{1} + \tilde{\mathbf{E}}, \tag{15.5}$$

where the *linearized rotation tensor* $\tilde{\mathbf{R}}$ and the *linearized strain tensor* $\tilde{\mathbf{E}}$ are small in the following sense. We define the *magnitude* of a second rank tensor $\mathbf{T}$ by

$$|\mathbf{T}| = \sqrt{\operatorname{tr}(\mathbf{T}\mathbf{T}^T)}. \tag{15.6}$$

Further, a tensor $\mathbf{T}$ is said to be *of the order of* ε^N, written as $O(\varepsilon^N)$, if $|\mathbf{T}|\varepsilon^{-N}$ remains bounded as $\varepsilon \to 0$. In terms of these notations the linearized strains and rotations are characterized by

$$|\tilde{\mathbf{E}}| = O(\varepsilon), \qquad |\tilde{\mathbf{R}}| = O(\varepsilon), \tag{15.7}$$

where $\varepsilon \ll 1$. The actual value of ε at which it may be possible to replace a solution of nonlinear elasticity theory by the corresponding solution of the linearized theory will depend of course on the desired accuracy as well as on the nature of the particular problem. In practice $|\tilde{\mathbf{E}}|$ will be limited by the magnitude of the possible elastic strains (which is of the order of 1.10^{-3} in metals), but no such limitation exists for $|\tilde{\mathbf{R}}|$.

It is now possible to obtain various approximations based on (15.7). We shall use from time to time the symbol " $\doteq$ " to emphasize that an equality holds if higher order terms in ε are neglected. For instance, from $\mathbf{R}\mathbf{R}^T = \mathbf{1} = \mathbf{1} + \tilde{\mathbf{R}} + \tilde{\mathbf{R}}^T + O(\varepsilon^2)$ it follows that

$$\tilde{\mathbf{R}}^T \doteq -\tilde{\mathbf{R}}, \tag{15.8}$$

i.e. whereas a finite rotation tensor is orthogonal, *the linearized rotation tensor is skew-symmetric.* Similarly, $\mathbf{F} = \mathbf{1} + \tilde{\mathbf{R}} + \tilde{\mathbf{E}} + O(\varepsilon^2)$, thus

$$\mathbf{F} = \mathbf{1} + \mathbf{H} \doteq \mathbf{1} + \tilde{\mathbf{R}} + \tilde{\mathbf{E}}, \tag{15.9}$$

so that the linearized strains and rotations are the symmetric and skew-symmetric parts of the tensor of displacement gradients, $\mathbf{H}$:

$$\tilde{\mathbf{E}} = \frac{1}{2}(\mathbf{H} + \mathbf{H}^T), \qquad \tilde{\mathbf{R}} = \frac{1}{2}(\mathbf{H} - \mathbf{H}^T). \tag{15.10}$$

The geometric interpretations of $\tilde{\mathbf{E}}$ and $\tilde{\mathbf{R}}$ are entirely analogous to the interpretations of stretching $\mathbf{D}$ and spin $\mathbf{W}$, respectively† (e.g. $\tilde{E}_{xy}$ is one-half of the decrease of an originally right angle formed by segments parallel to x and y axes, whereas a diagonal component $\tilde{E}_{\underline{ii}}$ describes a change of a length $L_{\underline{i}}$, originally aligned with the x_i direction, divided by that length). Moreover, because $u_{i.j} = u_{i,k}x_{k.j} = u_{i,k}(\delta_{kj} + u_{k.j})$, we have that

$$H_{ij} = u_{i.j} \doteq u_{i,j}. \tag{15.11}$$

The preceding formula is characteristic of small deformation theories, in which no distinction need be made between the independent variables X_i and x_i. This can be made more precise as follows ([222], pp. 148–149). By the mean value theorem, $f(\mathbf{x}) = f(\mathbf{X} + \mathbf{u}) = f(\mathbf{X}) + u_i\partial_i\bar{f}$, where $\partial_i\bar{f}$ are the gradients evaluated at some point in the range between $\mathbf{X}$ and $\mathbf{x}$. If $|u_i\partial_i\bar{f}/f(\mathbf{X})| \ll 1$, then $\mathbf{u}$ is said to be *infinitesimal with respect to the function* f, and $f(\mathbf{x}) \approx f(\mathbf{X})$. Thus, in a manner of speaking, $\mathbf{u}$ itself can be large, and satisfy $f(\mathbf{x}) \approx f(\mathbf{X})$, if the variation of f from point to point is very small; conversely, if the variation of f is rapid, then $\mathbf{u}$ must be very small for $f(\mathbf{x}) \approx f(\mathbf{X})$ to hold. We say this "in a manner of speaking," because $\mathbf{u}$, being a dimensional quantity, may not be characterized as small, or large. What is true is that $u_i\partial_i\bar{f}$ and $f(\mathbf{X})$ have the same dimension, so that their ratio is a dimensionless number which *may* be assumed to be small. In the linearized elasticity theory the displacements are assumed to be infinitesimal with respect to stresses, body forces and surface tractions, and displacements themselves. Then boundary conditions and equations of motion can be applied to the undeformed shape of a body, e.g. $T_{ji,j} = T_{ji.k}X_{k,j} = T_{ji.k}(\delta_{kj} - u_{k,j}) \doteq T_{ji.j}$.

For small deformations the Jacobian of deformation can be approximated as follows,

$$J = \det\mathbf{F} = \det(\mathbf{1} + \mathbf{H}) = 1 + \vartheta, \qquad \vartheta = \tilde{E}_{kk} = \operatorname{div}\mathbf{u}. \tag{15.12}$$

† Cf. Section 8.

The law of conservation of mass, (9.12), then reduces to the equivalent forms

$$\rho(1 + \vartheta) = \rho_0, \qquad \vartheta = \frac{v - v_0}{v_0}, \tag{15.13}$$

where $v = 1/\rho$.

In massive bodies the rotations are small whenever the strains are small, but in thin bodies large displacements and rotations can occur even though the strains are small (a simple example is the bending of a thin sheet into a cylinder). These cases belong to the theory of rods and shells; they are not a part of the linear theory of elasticity.

To approximate material rates, we consider $\dot{f}(\mathbf{X}, t)$ as the limit of $[f(\mathbf{x} - \mathbf{u}, t + dt) - f(\mathbf{x} - \mathbf{u}, t)]/dt$. If $\mathbf{u}$ is small with respect to f, then $\dot{f} \approx \partial_t f - u_i \partial_i \partial_t f$. Thus if $\mathbf{u}$ is also small with respect to $\partial_t f$, then

$$\partial_t f \approx \dot{f}. \tag{15.14}$$

In what follows we shall assume that $\mathbf{u}$ is small with respect to velocities $\mathbf{v} = \dot{\mathbf{u}}$, velocity gradients $v_{i,j}$, and accelerations $\dot{\mathbf{v}} = \ddot{\mathbf{u}}$:

$$\mathbf{v} = \dot{\mathbf{u}} \approx \partial_t \mathbf{u}, \qquad \dot{\mathbf{v}} = \ddot{\mathbf{u}} \approx \partial_t^2 \mathbf{u}. \tag{15.15}$$

and

$$\dot{\tilde{\mathbf{E}}} \approx \partial_t \tilde{\mathbf{E}} \approx \mathbf{D}, \qquad \dot{\tilde{\mathbf{R}}} \approx \partial_t \tilde{\mathbf{R}} \approx \mathbf{W}. \tag{15.16}$$

The compatibility of deformation can be characterized in several ways. A deformation $\mathbf{x} = \mathbf{X} + \mathbf{u} = \boldsymbol{\chi}(\mathbf{X}, t)$ is compatible if the functions χ_i (hence also u_i and $v_i = \dot{x}_i$) are one-valued and continuous. Here, then, the compatibility can be verified by inspection. With other kinematical tensors the situation may be different. Recalling (15.4), for instance, we note that, if $\tilde{\mathbf{E}}$ is given, then (15.4) is an over-determined system of six equations for the three components u_i. Therefore, a one-valued and continuous displacement field will exist only if $\tilde{E}_{ij}$ satisfy appropriate compatibility conditions (*integrability conditions*).

The conventional derivation of the compatibility conditions for strains is well known;† therefore, it may be more interesting to investigate these conditions in the context of finite deformations. We start with a common (Cartesian) frame $\mathbf{e}_i$ with the (invariant!) metric $\mathbf{e}_i \cdot \mathbf{e}_j = \delta_{ij}$. The length of a material segment joining the points $\mathbf{X}$ and $\mathbf{X} + d\mathbf{X}$ is then given by $dS^2 = \delta_{ij}\, dX_i\, dX_j$. If the endpoints of the segment are moved to $\mathbf{x}$ and $\mathbf{x} + d\mathbf{x}$, respectively, then

† It is outlined in Problem 2 of this section.

its length if given by $ds^2 = \delta_{ij}\, dx_i\, dx_j$. Let us suppose that ds is the natural length of the segment $d\mathbf{X}$; we write $ds^2 = C_{ij}\, dX_i\, dX_j$, where C_{ij} may be referred to as the *material metric*. The difference between the material metric and the space metric defines the strain, $2\mathbf{E} = \mathbf{C} - \mathbf{1}$, thus $ds^2 - dS^2 = 2E_{ij}\, dX_i\, dX_j$. The equations of compatibility will state the conditions under which it is possible to "relax" the strains by a global, differentiable deformation $x_i = x_i(\mathbf{X}, t)$, so that $d\mathbf{X} \to d\mathbf{x}$ will change each length to the natural length: $\delta_{ij}\, dX_i\, dX_j \to \delta_{ij}\, dx_i\, dx_j = ds^2$. If $x_i = x_i(\mathbf{X}, t)$ indeed exists, then $C_{ij} = x_{m.i}x_{m.j}$; conversely, with $\mathbf{C} = \mathbf{F}^T\mathbf{F}$, we can say that $\mathbf{F}$ must be a gradient, thus

$$F_{ij.k} - F_{ik.j} = 0. \tag{15.17}$$

As is the case with all integrability conditions, (15.17) *are sufficient only in simply connected regions* (for instance, according to Kelvin's transformation, if the *curl* of a vector field vanishes, then the *flow integral* of the vector field will define a one-valued function only if the region is simply connected). Whether sufficient or not, the conditions (15.17), or $C_{ij} = x_{m.i}x_{m.j}$, are not what we want, because we should like to obtain differential equations involving $\mathbf{C}$ alone, which will then tell us whether the representation $C_{ij} = x_{m.i}x_{m.j}$ is at all possible. To derive these equations, we must differentiate and manipulate $C_{ij} = x_{m.i}x_{m.j}$ until there is nothing left on the right-hand side.

We begin by introducing a "three index strain"

$$C_{ijk} = \frac{1}{2}(C_{jk.i} + C_{ik.j} - C_{ij.k}) = C_{jik}. \tag{15.18}$$

If the deformation $\mathbf{C}$ is compatible, then it follows right away that $C_{ijk} = x_{m.k}x_{m.ij}$. It is easy to see that C_{ijk} are, in essence, strain gradients; specifically,

$$C_{i(jk)} = E_{jk.i}, \qquad \frac{1}{2}\,\varepsilon_{rjk}C_{i[jk]} = \varepsilon_{rjk}E_{ik.j}. \tag{15.19}$$

To continue, we introduce a "four index strain"

$$C_{imjk} = C_{ijm.k} - C_{ikm.j} + C_{rs}^{-1}(C_{ikr}C_{mjs} - C_{ijr}C_{mks}), \tag{15.20}$$

also referred to as the Riemann-Christoffel curvature tensor, $R_{imjk}^{[C]}$, associated with $\mathbf{C}$. Substituting $C_{ijm} = x_{p.m}x_{p.ij}$ into (15.20), we find that $C_{imjk} = 0$; therefore, (15.20) are the *necessary* conditions for the compatibility of $\mathbf{C}$.

In simply connected regions they are also sufficient conditions, but the proof must draw upon the theory of differential equations.†

If strains are small, then, with $C_{ijm} = E_{mj.i} + E_{im.j} - E_{ij.m}$, and neglecting products of strain gradients, we obtain from (15.20) that $E_{mj.ik} - E_{mk.ij} + E_{ik.mj} - E_{ij.mk} = 0$. By inspection, it is seen that this expression is skew-symmetric in jk, and in im, and symmetric with respect to exchange of jk and im. Therefore, a complete set of compatibility equations is given by

$$\begin{aligned}(\mathrm{Ink}\tilde{\mathbf{E}})_{im} &= \varepsilon_{ijk}\varepsilon_{mnp}\tilde{E}_{jn,kp} = 0,\\ 2\tilde{E}_{12,12} &= \tilde{E}_{11,22} + \tilde{E}_{22,11}, \ldots, \ldots,\\ \tilde{E}_{11,23} &= (\tilde{E}_{12,3} - \tilde{E}_{23,1} + \tilde{E}_{31,2})_{,1}, \ldots, \ldots.\end{aligned} \tag{15.21}$$

Using the identity (1.29), we obtain the equivalent representation

$$\begin{aligned}(\mathrm{Ink}\tilde{\mathbf{E}})_{im} = \delta_{im}\nabla^2\tilde{E}_{kk} - \delta_{im}\tilde{E}_{jk,jk} + \tilde{E}_{ik,mk}\\ + \tilde{E}_{km,ki} - \nabla^2\tilde{E}_{im} - \tilde{E}_{kk,im} = 0.\end{aligned} \tag{15.21*}$$

If the strains are compatible, that is, (15.4) hold, then the compatibility equations are identically satisfied: $\varepsilon_{ijk}\varepsilon_{mnp}\tilde{E}_{jn,kp} = \frac{1}{2}\varepsilon_{ijk}\varepsilon_{mnp}(u_{j,nkp} + u_{n,jkp}) = 0$.

It is possible to establish certain analogies between vector fields and fields of second rank tensors. The operator *curl* may be said to measure the "incompatibility" (or, *vorticity*) of a vector field $\mathbf{v}$, in the sense that if $\mathrm{curl}\mathbf{v} = \mathbf{0}$, then, in simply connected regions, there will exist a one-valued scalar potential ϕ such that $\mathbf{v} = \mathrm{grad}\phi$. Similarly, if $\mathrm{Ink}\mathbf{E} = 0$, then, in simply connected regions, there will exist a one-valued vector field $\mathbf{u}$ such that $\tilde{E}_{ij} = (\mathrm{Def}\mathbf{u})_{ij} \equiv \frac{1}{2}(u_{i,j} + u_{j,i})$. In particular, Ink Def$\mathbf{u}$ = 0 may be considered as a counterpart of the identity curl gradϕ = 0. Another pair of analogous identities is given by div curl$\mathbf{v}$ = 0 and div Ink$\tilde{\mathbf{E}}$ = 0. The representation $\mathbf{v} = \mathrm{grad}\phi + \mathrm{curl}\mathbf{c}$ suggests the following representation of symmetric second rank tensors:

$$\tilde{\mathbf{E}} = \mathrm{Def}\mathbf{u} + \mathrm{Ink}\mathbf{B}, \tag{15.22}$$

where $\mathbf{B}$ is a symmetric tensor. There is no loss in generality if we assume that $\mathrm{div}\mathbf{B} = 0$ (because $\mathrm{Ink}\mathbf{B} = \mathrm{Ink}(\mathbf{B} + \mathrm{Def}\mathbf{a})$, the null-potential Def$\mathbf{a}$ can be chosen so as to satisfy a suitable gauge condition for $\overline{\mathbf{B}} = \mathbf{B} + \mathrm{Def}\mathbf{a}$). Then Ink Ink$\mathbf{B}$ $= \nabla^4\mathbf{B} = \mathrm{Ink}\tilde{\mathbf{E}}$, and, by (A.22),

$$8\pi\mathbf{B} = -\int R\,\mathrm{Ink}\tilde{\mathbf{E}}\,dv. \tag{15.23a}$$

† Cf. [89], pp. 242–246.

The identity $\nabla^2 = \text{grad div} - \text{curl curl}$ for vectors corresponds to the identity $\nabla^4 = \text{Def}(2\nabla^2 - \text{grad div})\text{div} + \text{Ink Ink}$ for symmetric second rank tensors. With this in mind, we calculate $(2\nabla^2 - \text{grad div})\text{div}\tilde{\mathbf{E}} = \nabla^4\mathbf{u}$,† from which it follows that

$$8\pi\mathbf{u} = -\int R(2\nabla^2 - \text{grad div})\, \text{div}\tilde{\mathbf{E}}\, dv. \tag{15.23b}$$

When $\text{div}\tilde{\mathbf{E}} = 0$, the vector potential must be determined from

$$\nabla^2\text{div}\mathbf{u} = 0, \quad \nabla^2\mathbf{u} = -\nabla\text{div}\mathbf{u}. \tag{15.24}$$

In contrast to (15.17), the integrability conditions $C_{imjk} = 0$ do not involve the rotation $\mathbf{R}$ obtained in the polar decomposition of $\mathbf{F}$ (the reason for eliminating $\mathbf{R}$ is that it does not appear in Hooke's law!). We eliminated $\mathbf{R}$ by forming $\mathbf{C} = \mathbf{F}^T\mathbf{F} = \mathbf{U}^2$ (the procedure applicable to the linearized equations is outlined in Problem 2), which resulted in a much more complicated form of the integrability conditions. In the remainder of this subsection we shall explore the connection between (15.17) and $C_{imjk} = 0$, with a view to interpreting the incompatibility measure associated with (15.17) as a "source" of the incompatibility of strains. It should be added that the material that follows is not needed for elasticity theory itself; rather, it is a starting point for certain extensions of elasticity theory (e.g. "continuum theory of dislocations").

If strains are incompatible, then C_{imjk} are of course one measure of incompatibility. The *dislocation density* α_{ijm}, defined by

$$\alpha_{ijm} = F_{rm}(F_{ri,j} - F_{rj,i}) = \alpha_{[ij]m} \tag{15.25}$$

(cf. (15.17)) is another. To obtain a geometric interpretation of (15.25), let us integrate $d\mathbf{x} = \mathbf{F}d\mathbf{X}$ along a polygonal path consisting of the segment $d_1X_i = dF_i(u)$ of a space curve $X_i = F_i(u)$, followed by a segment $d_2X_i = dG_i(v)$ of another space curve $X_i = G_i(v)$. A point $X_k^0 + d_1X_k$ is then mapped into $x_k^0 + d_1x_k = x_k^0 + F_{ki}d_1X_i$, whereas $X_k^0 + d_1X_k + d_2X_k$ is mapped into $x_k^0 + d_1x_k + d_2x_k + d_1d_2x_k = x_k^0 + F_{ki}d_1X_i + F_{ki}d_2X_i + F_{ki,j} \times d_2X_id_1X_j$. The integration is independent of the path that is chosen (i.e. defines a point function $x_k = x_k(\mathbf{X})$) only if the same increment of dx_k is obtained along a path consisting (in the undeformed configuration) of d_2X_j followed by d_1X_j. This yields the integrability condition $d\beta_k \equiv (d_2d_1x_k - d_1d_2x_k) = (F_{ki,j} - F_{kj,i})d_1X_id_2X_j = 0$. Like dx_k, the discrepancy $d\beta_k$ is associated with the deformed configuration; however, in analogy with $dX_m = F_{mk}^{-1}\, dx_k$, we may associate with $d\beta_k$ a vector $d\bar{\beta}_m = F_{mk}^{-1}\, d\beta_k$ in the undeformed configuration. In the present context it is more convenient to use

† Kunin [223]. The completeness of representations of second rank tensors has been investigated by Gurtin [62] (cf. also Carlson [224]).

the vector $C_{mr}d\bar{\beta}_m = F_{kr}\, d\beta_k$ (in general tensor notation, $d\bar{\beta}_m$ would be a "contravariant" representation, so that, lowering the index with the material metric C_{mr}, we should obtain a "covariant" representation). Thus with $\alpha_{ijm} = \varepsilon_{ijk}\alpha_{km}$, $dA_k = N_k\, dA = \varepsilon_{ijk}d_1X_i d_2X_j$, and replacing $d\beta_k$ by a *Burgers vector* $B_m = F_{rm}d\beta_r/dA$, we have that

$$B_m = \alpha_{km}N_k. \tag{15.26}$$

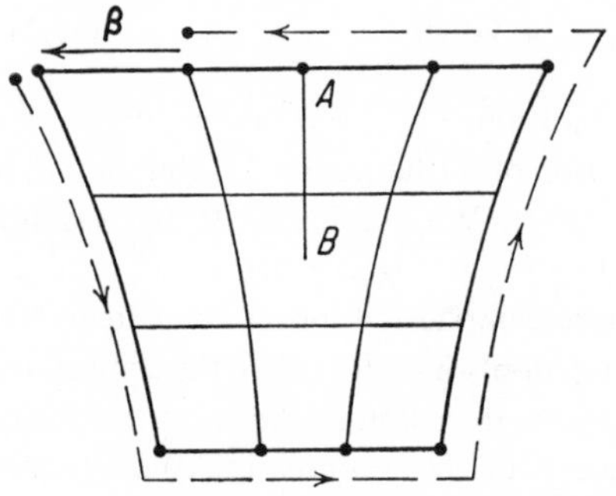

FIGURE 15.2 A visualization of a discrepancy **β** associated with a non-integrable mapping.

To summarize, a "perfect" parallelogram, spanned by the vectors $d_1\mathbf{X}$ and $d_2\mathbf{X}$, is mapped by the incompatible deformation $\mathbf{F}$ into an "imperfect" parallelogram, the sides of which do not close (cf. Figure 15.2). As a rule, this is interpreted to mean that the parallelogram is intersected by surfaces of discontinuity of deformation ("slip surfaces"). In the context of elasticity theory, we assume that deformations $d\mathbf{x} = \mathbf{F}d\mathbf{X}$ from an initial configuration are compatible, but that deformations $d\mathbf{X} = \boldsymbol{\phi}d\boldsymbol{\xi}$ from a natural state (cf. the diagram on p. 291) need not be compatible. For instance, we may interpret $\boldsymbol{\phi}$ as the local deformation during a "manufacturing" process. If the material grains remain elastic, then the total stress will be a function of the total deformation $\mathbf{M} = \mathbf{F}\boldsymbol{\phi}$. Because now $\alpha_{ijm} = 0$, we shall find that the dislocation density associated with $\mathbf{M}$ is given by

$$A_{ijm} = M^{-1}_{rm}(M^{-1}_{ri,j} - M^{-1}_{rj,i}) = F^{-1}_{km}F^{-1}_{pi}F^{-1}_{qj}\phi^{-1}_{rk}(\phi^{-1}_{rp,q} - \phi^{-1}_{rq,p}).$$

The interpretation of (15.26) is the same as for the state of stress (cf. (10.9)). In particular, $B_m[\mathbf{e}_k] = \alpha_{km}$, i.e. α_{km} are the components of the Burgers vectors associated with (infinitesimal) circuits lying in the coordinate planes. The diagonal components describe the density of "screw dislocations" (**B** normal to the plane of the circuit), whereas the off-diagonal components describe the density of "edge dislocations" (**B** in the plane of the circuit).†

† Numerous illustrations of the various types of dislocations in crystals may be found in the literature on solid state physics (cf. [192]).

The edge of a surface of discontinuity of deformation is referred to as a *dislocation line*; correspondingly, one may interpret (15.26) as describing the "flux" of dislocation lines through a surface element, thus $B_m\,dA = \alpha_{km}\,dA_k$. For instance, given a surface element dA_1, the existence of a Burgers vector $(B, 0, 0)$ is attributed to the density α_{11} of screw dislocation lines threading the surface element. Because α_{km} is a function of position, the character of a dislocation line may change from point to point.

We may describe incompatible deformations in terms of $\mathbf{C} = \mathbf{F}^T\mathbf{F}$ and α_{ijm}. However, because $\mathbf{F}$ determines both $\mathbf{C}$ and α_{ijm}, they must be connected by a differential equation. We shall derive this equation in a somewhat roundabout way. Let us recall that a mapping $dX = \mathbf{e}_i\,dX_i \rightarrow dx = \mathbf{e}_i\,dx_i = \mathbf{e}_i F_{im}\,dX_m$ may be "transferred" from the components to the base vectors: $dx = dX_m(\mathbf{e}_i F_{im}) \equiv \mathbf{E}_m\,dX_m$, thus

$$\mathbf{E}_m = \mathbf{e}_i F_{im}, \qquad \mathbf{e}_i = \mathbf{E}_m F^{-1}_{mi}. \tag{15.27}$$

In this view the material coordinates X_i define a coordinate system that is "convected" with the material, i.e. it is imbedded in the material, and moves and deforms with it. If the field $\mathbf{F}$ is given, then $\mathbf{E}_m$ are defined everywhere. Therefore, the integrability conditions $\mathbf{E}_{m.ij} - \mathbf{E}_{m.ji} = 0$ must be satisfied. With this in mind, we introduce the *material connection*

$$\omega_{ijm} = \mathbf{E}_m \cdot \mathbf{E}_{i.j}\ (= F_{rm}F_{ri.j}), \qquad 2\omega_{[ij]m} = \alpha_{ijm} \tag{15.28}$$

(cf. the definition of wryness coefficients in Section 6). With $C_{ij} = \mathbf{E}_i \cdot \mathbf{E}_j$, $C_{ij.m} = \omega_{imj} + \omega_{jmi}$, we then readily obtain

$$C_{ijm} = \omega_{ijm} - h_{ijm}, \qquad h_{ijm} = \frac{1}{2}(\alpha_{ijm} - \alpha_{mij} + \alpha_{jmi}). \tag{15.29}$$

Further, from $\alpha_{ijm} = -\alpha_{jim}$ it follows that $h_{ijm} = -h_{mji}$ (as well as $h_{[ij]m} = h_{m[ij]}$), so that we may replace h_{ijm} by

$$h_{pj} \equiv \frac{1}{2}\,\varepsilon_{imp}h_{ijm} = \alpha_{pj} - \frac{1}{2}\,\delta_{pj}\alpha_{kk}. \tag{15.30}$$

The conditions $\mathbf{E}_{m.ij} - \mathbf{E}_{m.ji} = 0$ require that the four index strain based on the connection ω_{ijm} must vanish. Introducing

$$\omega_{imjk} = \omega_{ijm.k} - \omega_{ikm.j} + C^{-1}_{rs}(\omega_{ikr}\omega_{mjs} - \omega_{ijr}\omega_{mks}),$$

and similar definitions for C_{imjk}, h_{imjk}, we obtain that, by (15.29), $\omega_{imjk} = 0$ reduces to

$$\varepsilon_{pjk}[C_{imjk} + h_{imjk} + C_{rs}^{-1}(C_{ikr}h_{mjs} + h_{ikr}C_{mjs})] = 0. \qquad (15.31)$$

In this representation of the compatibility conditions it is plausible to interpret the dislocation density as a source of the incompatibility of strains.

In the linearized theory all products are neglected, so that (15.31) becomes $\varepsilon_{pjk}C_{ijm.k} + \varepsilon_{pjk}h_{ijm.k} = 0$, where $C_{ijm.k} = E_{mj.ik} + E_{im.jk} - E_{ij.mk}$. In the product with ε_{pjk}, the middle term drops away, and the remaining two terms are skew-symmetric in i and m (so is h_{ijm}!). Therefore, we can write

$$\frac{1}{2}\varepsilon_{rmi}\varepsilon_{pjk}C_{ijm.k} = (\text{Ink}\tilde{\mathbf{E}})_{rp} = \varepsilon_{pjk}\Delta_k\left(\alpha_{rj} - \frac{1}{2}\delta_{rj}\alpha_{nn}\right),$$

where we have used (15.30). The left-hand side is symmetric in r and p; therefore, the product of ε_{rps} with the right-hand side must vanish. This gives rise to the compatibility equations

$$\alpha_{km.k} = 0 \qquad (15.32)$$

(because a dislocation line cannot end in the interior of a body, the conditions (15.32) are needed to permit the interpretation of α_{km} as describing the flux of dislocation lines). The remaining equations are then

$$(\text{Ink}\tilde{\mathbf{E}})_{rp} = \frac{1}{2}(\varepsilon_{pjk}\alpha_{rj.k} + \varepsilon_{rjk}\alpha_{pj.k}) \equiv \eta_{rp} \qquad (15.33)$$

($\text{Ink}\tilde{\mathbf{E}} = (\boldsymbol{\alpha} \times \boldsymbol{\nabla})^S$, where S designates the symmetric part).

To linearize the compatibility conditions (15.25), we let $\mathbf{F} = \mathbf{1} + \mathbf{H} = \mathbf{1} + \tilde{\mathbf{E}} + \tilde{\mathbf{R}}$, from which it follows that $\alpha_{km} = \frac{1}{2}\varepsilon_{kij}\alpha_{ijm} = \varepsilon_{kij}\tilde{E}_{mi.j} + \varepsilon_{kij}\tilde{R}_{mi.j}$. With $\phi_k = -\frac{1}{2}\varepsilon_{kij}\tilde{R}_{ij}$, we now obtain

$$\alpha_{km} = k_{mk} - \delta_{km}k_{jj} + \varepsilon_{kij}\tilde{E}_{mi.j}, \qquad k_{mk} = \phi_{k.m}. \qquad (15.34)$$

The compatibility conditions $\alpha_{km} = 0$ now state that strains and rotations cannot be assigned independently; rather, because $\alpha_{km} = 0$ implies $k_{jj} = 0$, we must have that $k_{mk} = \varepsilon_{kji}\tilde{E}_{im.j}$. The equivalent compatibility conditions (15.21) are, in effect, obtained by eliminating the rotation gradients k_{km}. If the deformation is compatible, i.e. $\tilde{E}_{ij} = u_{(i,j)}$ and $\phi = \frac{1}{2}\text{curl}\mathbf{u}$, then, as may be verified from (15.34), α_{km} vanish identically.

We have by no means exhausted all the facets of incompatibility. For instance, let us suppose that $\mathbf{E}_m$ constitute the (intrinsic) material bases that define the symmetry properties of a material. We may not always wish to assume that the local crystallographic directions are exactly known, or are without a certain misalignment. Then $\mathbf{E}_m = \mathbf{e}_i F_{im}$ should be replaced by relations $d\mathbf{E}_m = \Omega_{mij}\, dX_i \mathbf{E}_j$ that are not exact differential forms (i.e. a basis $\mathbf{E}_j$ given at some point cannot be "spread" in a unique way through the entire space).

The deeper we penetrate into the problem of deformation, the more helpful it becomes to use the ideas of differential geometry. Because "incompatibility" describes, in part, the geometric make-up of a body, it is plausible to view the body as a point space that is more general than the ambient space in which the body is placed. A point space is described first of all by establishing a correspondence between its points P and the points of one or several "coordinate spaces," the latter being in effect ordered sets of real numbers, $[R_1, R_2, R_3]$. By the introduction of coordinates we impart to point spaces the coherence and continuity implicit in the concept of space; in particular, a point space can be explored along paths that are the images of curves drawn in the coordinate space. This "parametrization" of point spaces does not define any geometrical structure, any more than the introduction of material coordinates would define a particular geometry in material bodies. To have a concrete example, let us imagine various marks (e.g. colored dots, lines) made on a rubber sheet. These marks identify once for all certain material points, but do not in any way describe the actual configuration of the sheet (the sheet may be stretched, made into a torus, and so on). A parametrized point is merely like a peg on which one can hang tensors describing the geometry of the space.

In a manner of speaking, we build general spaces in the same way that we would build polycrystalline materials: by piecing together tiny Euclidean fragments (crystals). The spaces are then *locally Euclidean*, each neighborhood being literally a small fragment of a Euclidean space, complete with a (local) reference frame. The Euclidean fragments may fit together smoothly, like the scales of a fish, to make up a manifold that has a highly regular aspect in the large. On the other hand, the arrangement of the fragments may have flaws ("dislocations"), so as to make the global aspect non-Euclidean. Let us make these ideas more explicit.

One of the characteristics of Euclidean point spaces is the existence of finite position vectors π, such that $d\pi = \mathbf{e}_i\, dx_i$, $\mathbf{e}_i = \pi_{,i}$. In locally Euclidean spaces we should obviously settle for less, assuming only the existence of infinitesimal vectors $d(\pi) = \varepsilon_i\, d(\xi)_i$. Here the symbol $d(\,)$ is used to emphasize that neither $d(\pi)$ nor $d(\xi)_i = B_{ij}\, dx_j$ need be exact differentials. (Even though ε_i need not be orthonormal, we shall continue to use Cartesian tensor notation.) As examples of local bases we mention the differential operators $\partial/\partial\xi \equiv B_{mi}^{-1}\,\partial_m$, and tangent vectors of curves that are images of coordinate lines drawn in the coordinate spaces. Again, it must be appreciated that this procedure merely identifies the curves and the local base vectors. The *metric* assigned to the base vectors, as well as the *connection* that relates bases of neighboring points, must be introduced separately.

The rules for constructing a general space (polycrystalline material!) are embodied in the *equations of structure*,

$$d\pi = \varepsilon_i\, d\xi_i, \qquad d\varepsilon_k = \Omega_{km}\varepsilon_m = \Omega_{kim}\, dx_i\varepsilon_m. \tag{15.35}$$

In addition, we assume that a metric exists, so that $\varepsilon_i \cdot \varepsilon_j = \gamma_{ij}$. The magnitudes of vectors being scalars, it is possible to compare them even though the vectors $d\pi$ may be located at different points. Not so for *directions* of vectors. The only way of interpreting a statement that two vectors $\mathbf{v}(P)$ and $\mathbf{v}(Q)$ are parallel is to refer them to the local bases, requiring that the components be identical, thus $\mathbf{v}(P) = v_i\varepsilon_i(P)$, $\mathbf{v}(Q) = v_i\varepsilon_i(Q)$. However, this definition of parallelism is in general not invariant to coordinate transformations, which is to say that the space does not admit an *absolute* (or, distant) *parallelism*. For instance, if we identify ε_i with $\partial/\partial\xi_i$ (in which case a representation $v_i\varepsilon_i$ amounts to a kind of directional differentiation associated with $\mathbf{v}$), then a coordinate transformation $\bar{\xi}_i = \bar{\xi}_i(\boldsymbol{\xi})$ will induce a basis transformation $\varepsilon_i = \partial\bar{\xi}_k/\partial\xi_i\, \partial/\partial\bar{\xi}_k = \partial\bar{\xi}_k/\partial\xi_i\, \bar{\varepsilon}_k$, and the transformed vector components will no longer be equal: $\bar{v}_k(P) = v_i\, \partial\bar{\xi}_k(P)/\partial\xi_i \neq \bar{v}_k(Q) = v_i\, \partial\bar{\xi}_k(Q)/\partial\xi_i$. If an absolute parallelism exists, then either $\partial\bar{\xi}_k/\partial\xi_i = \text{const.}$, in which case the coordinates are Cartesian (i.e. the space is Euclidean), or else there exist local bases that are invariant ("insensitive") to coordinate transformations. The local bases then represent a kind of superstructure erected over the point space, thereby making a three-dimensional point space into a six-dimensional *frame-space*.

If the connection is integrable, then a basis $\varepsilon_i(P)$ given at some point P can be spread through the entire space in a unique way, thus defining a field $\varepsilon_i(\mathbf{x}) = \mathbf{e}_j A_{ji}(\mathbf{x})$, where $\mathbf{e}_j$ are Cartesian base vectors. Moreover, the mappings of $\mathbf{e}_j$ into ε_i, and dx_j into $d\xi_i$, can be combined into one, so that the resultant mapping may be attributed to the components alone, $d\xi = \mathbf{e}_j(A_{ji}B_{ik}\, dx_k) \equiv \mathbf{e}_j\, d\xi_j$, or "transferred" to the base vectors, $d\xi = (\mathbf{e}_j A_{ji} B_{ik})\, dx_k \equiv \varepsilon_k\, dx_k$.

The local bases ε_i define an "intrinsic parallelism"; thus a vector field $\mathbf{v}$ is "parallel in the frame space" if its projections on the local bases are the same everywhere. The geometry associated with this notion of parallelism may be referred to as a *natural geometry*. For instance, if we seek a natural geometry of crystalline materials, then it is plausible to consider the lines of crystallographic directions as the skeleton of the material and of its natural geometry. These lines are taken to be "parallel" because in the intrinsic description there is no way of telling that they are not. The natural geometry has been likened to the geometry used by inhabitants of an old town: distances are measured in blocks (no matter how long each block is), and the streets are taken to be two families of parallel lines. In this geometry it is quite possible that a parallelogram of "equal" sides will fail to close by an amount $\boldsymbol{\beta}$ ("Burgers vector"), as shown in Figure 15.2.

Basic equations, uniqueness of solutions, boundary conditions

The fundamental system of equations of linear, isothermal elasticity theory consists of the stress equations of motion,

$$T_{ji,j} + \rho b_i = \rho \dot{v}_i, \qquad T_{ij} = T_{ji}, \tag{15.36}$$

Hooke's law

$$T_{ij} = C_{ijkm}\tilde{E}_{km},$$

and the strain-displacement relations

$$\tilde{E}_{ij} = \tfrac{1}{2}(u_{i,j} + u_{j,i}). \tag{15.4)R}$$

If the elastic response is isotropic, then Hooke's law reduces to

$$T_{ij} = \lambda\vartheta\delta_{ij} + 2\mu\tilde{E}_{ij}. \tag{15.37}$$

In accord with the linearization inherent in the present theory, the mass density ρ in (15.36) is set equal to the density ρ_0 of the undeformed body. In this way the balance of mass is simply bypassed (if need be, the infinitesimal changes of mass density can be calculated from (15.13)). We also recall that $(15.36)_1$ can be replaced by $T_{ji.j} + \rho b_i = \rho \dot{v}_i$, or what amounts to the same thing, by $T_{ji,j} + \rho b_i = \rho \partial_t v_i$.

Let us begin by exploring the isotropic law (15.37). In the absence of heat sources and heat flux, the balance of energy, (10.22), reduces to $\rho\dot{\varepsilon} = T_{ij}\dot{\tilde{E}}_{ij}$, which permits us to identify ε with *strain energy*. Thus, by (15.37), (15.16),

$$W = \frac{1}{2}T_{ij}\tilde{E}_{ij} = \frac{1}{2}(\lambda\vartheta^2 + 2\mu\tilde{E}_{ij}\tilde{E}_{ij}) = \frac{1}{2E}[(1+\nu)T_{ij}T_{ij} - \nu T_{ii}T_{jj}], \tag{15.38}$$

where W is referred to as the strain-energy function (or, stored-energy function). Evidently

$$T_{ij} = \frac{\partial W}{\partial \tilde{E}_{ij}}; \tag{15.39}$$

in this formula the shearing strains $\tilde{E}_{ij}$ and $\tilde{E}_{ji}$ are considered as independent, even though they are numerically equal. If the equalities $\tilde{E}_{12} = \tilde{E}_{21}, \ldots, \ldots$, are used to eliminate three of the shearing strains, then (15.39) are replaced by

$$T_{ij} = \frac{\partial W}{\partial \tilde{E}_{ij}} \quad \text{for } i = j, \qquad T_{ij} = \frac{1}{2}\frac{\partial W}{\partial \tilde{E}_{ij}} \quad \text{for } i \neq j, \tag{15.39)*}$$

where now shearing strains $\tilde{E}_{ij}$ and $\tilde{E}_{ji}$ are treated as being identical.

For isotropic bodies W depends only on the invariants of strain: $W = W(\mathrm{I}, \mathrm{II}, \mathrm{III})$, where I, II, III are the principal invariants of $\tilde{\mathbf{E}}$. For *linear* isotropic bodies, however,

$$W = \frac{\lambda + 2\mu}{2}\,\mathrm{I}^2 - 2\mu\mathrm{II}. \tag{15.40}$$

Let us now introduce a mean tension $T = \frac{1}{3}T_{ii}$. Then, by (15.37),

$$T = k\vartheta, \qquad k = \frac{3\lambda + 2\mu}{3} = \frac{E}{3(1 - 2\nu)}, \tag{15.41}$$

where k is called the *bulk modulus*. The deviatoric stresses S_{ij} and the deviatoric strains ε_{ij}, defined according to (4.58), are related as follows,

$$S_{ij} = 2\mu\varepsilon_{ij}. \tag{15.42}$$

Moreover, the strain energy decomposes into a strain energy of volumetric deformation, W_V, and a strain energy of distortion, W_D:

$$\begin{aligned} W_V &= \frac{1}{2}T\vartheta = \frac{k}{2}\vartheta^2 = \frac{T^2}{2k}, \\ W_D &= \frac{1}{2}S_{ij}\varepsilon_{ij} = \mu\varepsilon_{ij}\varepsilon_{ij} = \frac{1}{4\mu}S_{ij}S_{ij}. \end{aligned} \tag{15.43}$$

If the medium is incompressible, then $\mathrm{tr}\tilde{\mathbf{E}} = 0$, and (15.37) is replaced by

$$T_{ij} = -p\delta_{ij} + 2\mu\tilde{E}_{ij}, \tag{15.44}$$

where p is an arbitrary (hydrostatic) pressure. One may look upon $-p\delta_{ij}$ as the limit of $\lambda\delta_{ij}\mathrm{tr}\tilde{\mathbf{E}}$ as $\mathrm{tr}\tilde{\mathbf{E}} \to 0$ and $\lambda \to \infty$ (i.e. as $\nu \to \frac{1}{2}$).

The equations (15.37) when taken alone merely define a particular kind of linear response. To define a linearly *elastic* response, we must adjoin to (15.37) certain inequalities that are needed to satisfy various basic requirements, e.g. uniqueness of solutions, existence of real wave speeds. Thus we may find it necessary to require that the strain-energy density be *positive, semi-definite*, i.e. $W \geq 0$, and $W = 0$ only if $\tilde{\mathbf{E}} = \mathbf{0}$. According to (15.43), this amounts to requiring that

$$\mu > 0, \qquad 3\lambda + 2\mu > 0, \tag{15.45}$$

or, equivalently,

$$E > 0, \qquad -1 < \nu < \tfrac{1}{2}. \tag{15.45*}$$

Some of the inequalities may be interpreted as *plausibility requirements* which exclude the kinds of behavior that would run counter to our intuitive idea of elasticity. For instance, let us take uniaxial extension of prismatic bodies of constant cross-sectional area; we then obtain the following solution of the fundamental system (cf. Figure 15.3a):

$$\begin{aligned} T_{zz} &= T, \quad T_{xx} = T_{xy} = T_{xz} = T_{yy} = T_{yz} = 0, \\ Eu_x &= Tx, \quad Eu_y = -\nu Ty, \quad Eu_z = -\nu Tz, \end{aligned} \tag{15.46}$$

where T is a constant.

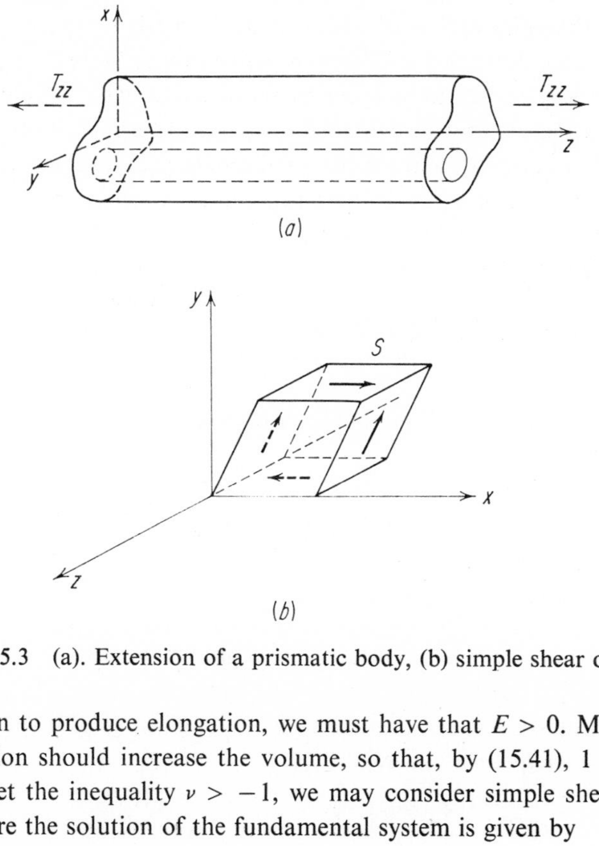

FIGURE 15.3 (a). Extension of a prismatic body, (b) simple shear of a cube.

For tension to produce elongation, we must have that $E > 0$. Moreover, a mean tension should increase the volume, so that, by (15.41), $1 - 2\nu > 0$. To interpret the inequality $\nu > -1$, we may consider simple shear (Figure 15.3b). Here the solution of the fundamental system is given by

$$\begin{aligned} T_{xy} &= S, \quad T_{xx} = T_{xz} = T_{yy} = T_{yz} = T_{zz} = 0, \\ \mu u_x &= Sy, \quad u_y = u_z = 0, \end{aligned} \tag{15.47}$$

S being the constant shear stress. If the shear deformation is to follow the applied force, then $\mu > 0$, thus $\nu > -1$, must hold.

Because the inequalities round out the definition of elastic response, the reasons for adopting them must be simple, general, and unquestionable. In this connection it is interesting to note the *empirical inequalities*

$$E > 0, \qquad 0 < \nu < \frac{1}{2}. \tag{15.48}$$

In the mathematical theory of elasticity the second inequality is ignored as being unnecessarily restrictive. That is, although we do not expect to find materials that would expand laterally when put under tension, nothing is gained by assuming Poisson's ratio to be positive, because it turns out that uniqueness theorems can be proved, real wave speeds exist, etc., even when Poisson's ratio is permitted to take on negative values. More than that, we do not wish to rely on scattered experiments to tell us what elasticity is. The domain of a theory must be delimited once for all through investigations of consistency, uniqueness, and the like, and should not be subject to continual revision to accommodate the latest experimental information.

To obtain the limitations on elastic coefficients arising from problems in the propagation of elastic waves we first relate stresses to displacement gradients,

$$T_{ij} = \lambda u_{k,k}\delta_{ij} + \mu(u_{i,j} + u_{j,i}). \tag{15.49}$$

Substituting these expressions into (15.36), we arrive at the *displacement equations of motion*,

$$\mu\nabla^2 u_i + (\lambda + \mu)u_{k,ki} + \rho b_i = \rho\partial_t^2 u_i. \tag{15.50}$$

We now let†

$$\mathbf{u} = \operatorname{grad}\phi + \operatorname{curl}\mathbf{c}, \qquad \mathbf{b} = \operatorname{grad}\varnothing + \operatorname{curl}\boldsymbol{\beta}, \tag{15.51}$$

where $\mathbf{c}$ satisfies the gauge condition $\operatorname{div}\mathbf{c} = 0$. Then (15.50) splits into the equation for *dilatational waves*,

$$c_D^2\nabla^2\phi + \varnothing = \partial_t^2\phi, \qquad c_D = \sqrt{(\lambda + 2\mu)/\rho}, \tag{15.52}$$

and the equation for *shear waves*,

$$c_S^2\nabla^2\mathbf{c} + \boldsymbol{\beta} = \partial_t^2\mathbf{c}, \qquad c_S = \sqrt{\mu/\rho}. \tag{15.53}$$

† The completeness of *Lame's representation* $(15.51)_1$ was first proved by Duhem (cf. Sternberg [227]).

If we require that the wave speeds c_D and c_S be real, then $\mu > 0$ and $\lambda + 2\mu > 0$ must hold. It is worth noting that these conditions are already contained in (15.45) (if λ is greater than $-\frac{2}{3}\mu$, then it is certainly greater than -2μ).

There are two versions of anisotropic elasticity, depending on whether or not the existence of a strain-energy function is assumed. In the first case, referred to as *hyperelasticity* (or, *Green's elasticity*), the stress-strain relation is generated by $T_{ij} = \partial W/\partial \tilde{E}_{ij} = C_{ijkm}\tilde{E}_{km}$. Therefore, in view of $C_{ijkm} = \partial T_{ij}/\partial \tilde{E}_{km} = \partial^2 W/\partial \tilde{E}_{km}\partial \tilde{E}_{ij} = \partial^2 W/\partial \tilde{E}_{ij}\partial \tilde{E}_{km} = \partial T_{km}/\partial \tilde{E}_{ij}$, it follows that

$$C_{ijkm} = C_{kmij}. \tag{15.54}$$

In the second case, referred to as *Cauchy's elasticity*, the stress-strain relation is again given by $T_{ij} = C_{ijkm}\tilde{E}_{km}$, but the condition (15.54) need not be satisfied. Let us note in passing that the existence of a strain-energy function is equivalent to *Betti's reciprocal theorem*:†

$$\int_V \bar{\mathbf{b}} \cdot \mathbf{u}^* \, dm + \int_{\partial V} \mathbf{t} \cdot \mathbf{u}^* \, da = \int_V \bar{\mathbf{b}}^* \cdot \mathbf{u} \, dm + \int_{\partial V} \mathbf{t}^* \cdot \mathbf{u} \, da, \tag{15.55}$$

where $\bar{\mathbf{b}}, \bar{\mathbf{b}}^*$ denote effective body forces, and $\mathbf{u}, \mathbf{u}^*$ are, respectively, solutions of $C_{jikm}u_{k,mj} + \rho\bar{b}_i = 0$, $C_{jikm}u^*_{k,mj} + \rho\bar{b}^*_i = 0$, $\mathbf{t}$ and $\mathbf{t}^*$ being the associated surface tractions. To see this, we consider the identity $C_{ijkm}u_{k,mj}u^*_i = (C_{ijkm}u_{k,m}u^*_i)_{,j} - C_{ijkm}u_{k,m}u^*_{i,j}$, and note that $(C_{ijkm}u_{k,m}u^*_i)_{,j} = (T_{ij}u^*_i)_{,j}$ can be converted by means of the divergence theorem into a surface integral of $T_{ij}n_ju^*_i = t_iu^*_i$. We thus arrive at the *Betti's identity*

$$\int_V \bar{b}_iu^*_i \, dm + \int_{\partial V} t_iu^*_i \, da = \int_V C_{ijkm}u_{k,m}u^*_{i,j} \, dv. \tag{15.56}$$

Betti's reciprocal theorem asserts that, on the left-hand side, $\mathbf{u}, \mathbf{b}, \mathbf{t}$ can be interchanged with $\mathbf{u}^*, \mathbf{b}^*, \mathbf{t}^*$. But then it must be also true that $C_{ijkm}u_{k,m}u^*_{i,j} = C_{ijkm}u^*_{k,m}u_{i,j}$, or, $C_{ijkm} = C_{kmij}$.

To include the effect of thermal expansion into the stress-strain relation, we may start from an expansion of the internal energy about a state corresponding to the values $\tilde{\mathbf{E}} = \mathbf{0}$, $\theta = \theta_0$, $\eta = \eta_0$ of strains, temperature, and entropy density, respectively: $W = W_0 + T^0_{ij}\tilde{E}_{ij} + \rho\theta_0(\eta - \eta_0) + \frac{1}{2}[C_{ijkm}\tilde{E}_{ij}\tilde{E}_{km} - 2C_{ijkm}\tilde{E}_{ij}A_{km}(\eta - \eta_0) + A^2(\eta - \eta_0)^2]$. Then

$$\begin{aligned} \Delta T_{ij} &= T_{ij} - T^0_{ij} = C_{ijkm}\tilde{E}_{km} - C_{ijkm}A_{km}(\eta - \eta_0), \\ \rho\Delta\theta &= \rho(\theta - \theta_0) = -C_{ijkm}\tilde{E}_{ij}A_{km} + A^2(\eta - \eta_0), \end{aligned} \tag{15.57}$$

† Cf. [183].

where C_{ijkm} are referred to as the *isentropic* (elastic) coefficients. The specific heat at constant deformation, K_E, is defined by

$$K_E = \left.\frac{\partial \varepsilon}{\partial \theta}\right|_{\tilde{\mathbf{E}}=\text{const.}} = \theta \frac{\partial \eta}{\partial \theta} = \frac{\rho \theta_0}{A^2}. \tag{15.58}$$

Introducing the density of free energy, $\psi(\tilde{\mathbf{E}}, \theta) = \varepsilon(\tilde{\mathbf{E}}, \eta(\tilde{\mathbf{E}}, \theta)) - \theta\eta(\tilde{\mathbf{E}}, \theta)$, we obtain from $T_{ij} = \rho\partial\psi/\partial\tilde{E}_{ij}$ the alternative stress relation

$$T_{ij} = C_{ijkm}\tilde{E}_{km} - \beta_{ij}(\theta - \theta_0), \quad \beta_{ij} = \frac{K_E}{\theta_0} C_{ijkm}A_{km}, \tag{15.59}$$

where the *isothermal* coefficients $\bar{\bar{C}}_{ijkm}$ are given by

$$\bar{\bar{C}}_{ijkm} = C_{ijkm} - \frac{\theta_0}{\rho K_E} \beta_{ij}\beta_{km}. \tag{15.60}$$

In the isotropic case $\qquad \beta_{ij} = \alpha(3\lambda + 2\mu)\delta_{ij}, \qquad$ (15.61)

α being the coefficient of thermal expansion.

With $\partial\varepsilon/\partial\eta = \theta$, $\rho\partial\varepsilon/\partial\tilde{E}_{ij} = T_{ij}$, the energy balance (with $r = 0$) reduces to $\rho\theta\dot{\eta} + q_{i,i} = 0$. Letting $\mathbf{q} = -k \operatorname{grad}\theta$, $k > 0$, and noting that, by (15.57), (15.58), (15.59), $\rho\theta_0\dot{\eta} = \rho K_E\dot{\theta} + \theta_0\beta_{ij}\dot{\tilde{E}}_{ij}$, we arrive at the *heat conduction equation*

$$\rho K_E\partial_t\theta - k\nabla^2\theta = -\theta_0\beta_{ij}\partial_t\tilde{E}_{ij} \tag{15.62}$$

(here $\dot{\theta} \approx \partial_t\theta$, $\dot{\tilde{E}}_{ij} \approx \partial_t\tilde{E}_{ij}$). The term $\theta_0\beta_{ij}\partial_t\tilde{E}_{ij}$ (*thermoelastic coupling*) is ordinarily negligible. But if elastic vibrations are observed over long periods of time, this term may manifest itself as an internal damping.

To discover what manner of boundary conditions will yield properly posed problems, we proceed to investigate the uniqueness of solutions. Our starting point is the energy balance

$$\dot{K} + \dot{U} = \int_S t_i v_i \, da + \int_V b_i v_i \, dm,$$

together with the restrictions which ensure that the strain-energy density is positive semi-definite. If $\mathbf{T}'$, $\mathbf{u}'$ and $\mathbf{T}''$, $\mathbf{u}''$ are two solutions of the fundamental system, then so is the difference $\mathbf{T} = \mathbf{T}' - \mathbf{T}''$, $\mathbf{u} = \mathbf{u}' - \mathbf{u}''$, except that $\mathbf{T}$, $\mathbf{u}$ now correspond to zero body force (more generally, because of the linearity of the fundamental system a *principle of superposition holds*: a linear combination of solutions is again a solution). Therefore, the energy balance applied to $\mathbf{T}$, $\mathbf{u}$ becomes

$$\int_S t_i v_i \, da = \dot{K} + \dot{U}. \tag{15.63}$$

We are going to show that if $\mathbf{T}'$, $\mathbf{u}'$ and $\mathbf{T}''$, $\mathbf{u}''$ satisfy the same set of certain *initial and boundary conditions*, then the kinetic and internal energies of the difference solution vanish: $K = 0$, $U = 0$. Now, if the left-hand side of (15.63) vanishes, then $\dot{K} + \dot{U} = 0$, $K + U = \text{const.}$ To make the constant equal to zero, we assume that the two solutions satisfy the same initial conditions at time $t = 0$:

$$\begin{aligned} \mathbf{u}'(\mathbf{x}, 0) &= \mathbf{u}''(\mathbf{x}, 0) = \mathbf{u}^*(\mathbf{x}), \qquad \mathbf{x} \text{ in } V + S, \\ \dot{\mathbf{u}}'(\mathbf{x}, 0) &= \dot{\mathbf{u}}''(\mathbf{x}, 0) = \mathbf{v}^*(\mathbf{x}), \qquad \mathbf{x} \text{ in } V + S, \end{aligned} \tag{15.64}$$

where $\mathbf{u}^*(\mathbf{x})$ and $\mathbf{v}^*(\mathbf{x})$ are given functions. Then the difference solution satisfies $K + U = 0$ at $t = 0$, hence $K + U = 0$ at any other instant. But U cannot be negative; therefore, K and U must vanish separately, so that the solutions $\mathbf{T}'$, $\mathbf{u}'$ and $\mathbf{T}''$, $\mathbf{u}''$ must remain identical.

The types of boundary conditions for which the solutions are unique are now obtained from inspection of $t_i v_i = (t_i' - t_i'')(\dot{u}_i' - \dot{u}_i'') = 0$. This condition is equivalent to

$$(t_{\underline{n}}' - t_{\underline{n}}'')(u_{\underline{n}}' - u_{\underline{n}}'') + (\mathbf{t}_{\underline{s}}' - \mathbf{t}_{\underline{s}}'')\cdot(\mathbf{u}_{\underline{s}}' - \mathbf{u}_{\underline{s}}'') = 0, \tag{15.65}$$

where the labels $\underline{n}$ and $\underline{s}$ mark the normal and shearing components (the latter being, of course, tangential to the boundary). Evidently (15.65) can be satisfied in four ways: (1) $\mathbf{t}' = \mathbf{t}''$, (2) $\mathbf{u}' = \mathbf{u}''$ (hence $\dot{\mathbf{u}}' = \dot{\mathbf{u}}''$), (3) $t_{\underline{n}}' = t_{\underline{n}}''$, $u_{\underline{s}}' = u_{\underline{s}}''$, (4) $t_{\underline{s}}' = t_{\underline{s}}''$, $u_{\underline{n}}' = u_{\underline{n}}''$. In view of this, it is customary to classify the boundary value problems of elasticity theory into the following four groups:

(1) *The traction problem*

The entire boundary S is a *traction boundary* B_T on which the surface tractions take on the prescribed values $\bar{\mathbf{t}}$:

$$\mathbf{t}(\mathbf{n}) = \bar{\mathbf{t}} \text{ on } S = B_T.$$

(2) *The displacement problem*

The entire boundary S is a displacement boundary B_u on which displacements take on the prescribed values $\bar{\mathbf{u}}$:

$$\mathbf{u} = \bar{\mathbf{u}} \text{ on } S = B_u.$$

(3) *The mixed problem*

$$S = B_T + B_u$$

$$\mathbf{t}(\mathbf{n}) = \bar{\mathbf{t}} \text{ on } B_T, \qquad \mathbf{u} = \bar{\mathbf{u}} \text{ on } B_u.$$

(4) *The mixed-mixed problems*

$$t_{\underline{n}} = \bar{t}_{\underline{n}}, \qquad u_{\underline{s}} = \bar{u}_{\underline{s}} \text{ on } B_{Tu},$$
$$t_{\underline{s}} = \bar{t}_{\underline{s}}, \qquad u_{\underline{n}} = \bar{u}_{\underline{n}} \text{ on } B_{uT}.$$

In general a boundary value problem can be a combination of all four types: $S = B_T + B_u + B_{Tu} + B_{uT}$. Then stress vectors are prescribed over B_T, displacement vectors are prescribed over B_u, normal stresses and shearing displacements are prescribed over B_{Tu}, and shearing stresses and normal displacements are prescribed over B_{uT}. For instance, let us take an elastic half-space acted upon by a circular rigid die, the contact area being lubricated. The boundary outside of the contact area is a stress-free boundary B_T: $\mathbf{t}(\mathbf{n}) = \mathbf{0}$ on B_T. If the displacement of the die is prescribed, then the contact area C is a B_{uT} boundary: $u_{\underline{n}} = \bar{u}_{\underline{n}}$, $t_{\underline{s}} = 0$. In cases where the force P exerted by the die is prescribed the situation is more complex; we can let $C = B_T$, but $\bar{t}_{\underline{n}}$ are given only indirectly by

$$P = \int_C \bar{t}_{\underline{n}}\, da.$$

If the contact between the rigid die and the half-space is perfectly rough, then several new possibilities arise, e.g. $C = B_u$.

In some cases the hypothesis of the uniqueness theorem can be considerably weakened. Thus Gurtin and Toupin [61] have proved the uniqueness of the displacement boundary value problem under the condition that C_{ijkm} be *semi-strongly elliptic*:

$$C_{ijkm} U_i U_k V_j V_m \geq 0, \tag{15.66}$$

where **U** and **V** are arbitrary vectors. To see that $C_{ijkm}\tilde{E}_{ij}\tilde{E}_{km} \geq 0$ implies (15.66), we merely let $\tilde{E}_{ij} = U_i V_j$. The converse is not true, because $U_i V_j$ does not define a general second rank tensor (cf. (3.27) *et seq.*) The condition (15.66) ensures the existence of real wave speeds. In the isotropic case it reduces to

$$c_S^2 = \frac{\mu}{\rho} \geq 0, \qquad c_D^2 = 2c_S^2 \frac{1-\nu}{1-2\nu} \geq 0,$$

or, equivalently, to

$$\mu \geq 0, \qquad -\infty < \nu < \frac{1}{2}, \qquad 1 \leq \nu < \infty$$

(cf. [60]). Namely, the ratio $(1 - \nu)/(1 - 2\nu)$ is negative only in the interval $\frac{1}{2} < \nu < 1$, so that solutions are unique whenever the wave speeds are real. If $\nu < -1$, then $\mu = E/2(1 + \nu) \geq 0$ requires that E be negative! As was remarked before, even though we do not expect to find such materials, we do not adopt inequalities if nothing is gained by doing so.

To apply elasticity theory, or any other theory for that matter, we must face the fact that not all boundary conditions are exactly known. For instance, the tractions at the built-in end of a cantilever beam are really unknown (at least, they cannot be determined without solving a far more complex problem involving both the beam and the supporting wall), although it is possible to calculate the resultants of these tractions from the conditions of equilibrium of the entire beam. The vanishing of the surface tractions on some of the lateral faces of the beam is of course a precise boundary condition. Further, even if the true boundary conditions were known everywhere, the corresponding problem may be too difficult to solve, so that it becomes necessary to explore the possibility of using boundary conditions that are statically equivalent (in the sense of having the same force and couple resultants) but simpler. The original boundary condition and the "relaxed" boundary condition then differ by a *self-equilibrated loading*. It seems natural to expect that a relaxation of boundary conditions will be justified if the load region in question is small compared to some characteristic dimension, e.g. distance from the load region; however, the shape of the body may be an important factor.

The use of relaxed boundary conditions goes back a century, to Saint-Venant's study of the torsional resistance of cylinders twisted by couples applied to the end sections. To estimate the torsional resistance, Saint-Venant chose a simple form of solution, which corresponds to a special way of applying the couples, the hypothesis being that the torsional resistance will not be significantly changed if the end sections are subjected to different, but statically equivalent, loadings. As was noted before, a hypothesis of this kind must be invoked in almost every application of elasticity theory. It is customary to consider such hypotheses as instances of a *principle of Saint-Venant*, although no clear statement of this principle is possible; it is easier to speak of the *problem* of Saint-Venant, instead, namely the study of the influence of self-equilibrated loadings.† This is perhaps the main open problem of linear elasticity theory. Needless to say, the sensitivity of solutions to changes in boundary data has important ramifications in all branches of physics. It is of particular concern in elasticity theory because here the mathematical boundary conditions are quite complex and require information that is often practically unobtainable.

As long as only the stress resultants are prescribed on some load region L, the problem does not have a unique solution, i.e. there will exist a *class* of solutions, each corresponding to some exact boundary conditions that yield the prescribed stress resultants on L. To invoke the principle of Saint-Venant is to say that all solutions belonging to that class are equivalent. The question now is this: are there any criteria for selecting a "representative" solution? Of course, one will prefer a simple solution to a complicated one; however, because Saint-Venant's principle is but a hypothesis, the investigation of other criteria is by no means without interest (cf. the discussion of Saint-Venant's torsion problem).

The linear theory of elasticity is the best-developed branch of continuum mechanics, and has served in many ways as a model for other theories. For this reason we are going to continue to explore elasticity theory with some care.

Methods of solution

The solutions of linear elasticity theory must satisfy the conditions of equilibrium and compatibility, and Hooke's law. From a mathematical viewpoint the last requirement is trivial, Hooke's law being merely a linear transformation from stresses to strains. Therefore, the methods are aimed at satisfying equilibrium and compatibility. Now, it is a general characteristic of all methods that some of the requirements are satisfied automatically by special representations of the solutions, while the remaining conditions provide the requisite differential equations. Thus it is not surprising that the main methods of elasticity theory are as follows: (a) the *displacement function method*, in which compatibility is satisfied trivially (i.e. by inspection), the differential equations for the displacement functions being the conditions of

† The main investigations of the problem of Saint-Venant are due to von Mises [97], Sternberg [156], Keller [81], Toupin [166], and Knowles [212].

equilibrium, and (b) the *stress function method*, which satisfies equilibrium conditions automatically, the differential equations for the stress functions being the compatibility conditions.

The fundamental system of equations is not convenient for solving problems; it is replaced by different systems in each of the two methods. In the method of displacement functions, the displacement equations of equilibrium,

$$\mu\nabla^2 u_i + (\lambda + \mu)u_{k,ki} + \rho b_i = 0 \tag{15.67}$$

(cf. (15.50)), provide three equations for the three unknowns u_i (stresses and strains can be *subsequently* calculated from (15.4) and (15.37)). The solution of (15.67) can be reduced to more familiar types of differential equations by letting

$$2\mu\mathbf{u} = \text{grad}(\phi + \mathbf{x}\cdot\boldsymbol{\psi}) - 4(1 - \nu)\boldsymbol{\psi}, \tag{15.68}$$

where ϕ, $\boldsymbol{\psi}$ may be called the Papkovich-Neuber (displacement) functions. The conditions of equilibrium then read

$$\nabla^2\phi = -\frac{\rho\mathbf{x}\cdot\mathbf{b}}{2(1-\nu)}, \qquad \nabla^2\boldsymbol{\psi} = \frac{\rho\mathbf{b}}{2(1-\nu)}. \tag{15.69}$$

Moreover, it can be shown that the representation (15.68) is *complete* in the sense that every solution of (15.67) is expressible in this form.†

The foregoing remarks should not mislead us to think that elasticity theory can be reduced to potential theory.‡ In fact, the main value of (15.68), (15.69) lies in what one may call "theoretical" applications rather than in the solution of specific problems. The difficulties in elasticity theory stem from the complexity of the boundary conditions which are quite unlike the simple types of boundary conditions occurring in potential theory. For instance, if $S = B_T$, the boundary conditions on the displacements are

$$t_i = T_{ji}n_j = [\lambda u_{k,k}\delta_{ij} + \mu(u_{i,j} + u_{j,i})]n_j \tag{15.70}$$

(cf. (15.49)). Evidently using the representation (15.68) will give rise to even more complicated boundary conditions. Thus while the solution of the relevant differential equations is usually a simple matter (e.g. by separation of

† Eubanks and Sternberg [40].

‡ Note that, in the absence of body forces, the term $B = \mathbf{x}\cdot\boldsymbol{\psi}$ in (15.68) is biharmonic (i.e. $\nabla^4 B = 0$, but $\nabla^2 B \neq 0$). Therefore, the displacements in isotropic elastostatics are biharmonic functions. This can be also seen from (15.67); namely, because $\nabla^2 u_{k,k} = 0$, applying ∇^2 to (15.67) we obtain $\nabla^4 u_i = 0$.

variables), to satisfy the boundary conditions a certain amount of intelligent guessing is indispensable.

The stress function method makes use of the identities div Ink**G** = 0, Ink Def**a** = 0. In the absence of body forces, the stress equations of equilibrium are identically satisfied by letting

$$\mathbf{T} = \mathrm{Ink}\mathbf{G}, \qquad \mathbf{G} = \mathbf{G}^T, \tag{15.71}$$

where **G** is called a *stress function tensor*. Moreover, $\mathbf{G}^0$ = Def**a** play the role of null-tensors, because $\mathbf{T}^0 = \mathrm{Ink}\mathbf{G}^0 = \mathbf{0}$. From the existence of null-tensors it follows that **G** can be made to satisfy various gauge conditions, e.g. div**G** = 0.

It is not difficult to see that the representation (15.71) is, in general, not complete.† Namely, **T** = Ink**G** is a *totally self-equilibrated* stress field in the sense that its resultant force and moment vanish on any closed surface. In particular, because the boundary of a periphractic region consists of several closed surfaces, (15.71) is complete only if the resultant force and moment vanish on each boundary. To verify this, let us write

$$T_{mi} = \varepsilon_{mpn}A_{in,p}, \qquad A_{in} = -\varepsilon_{ijk}G_{nj,k} \tag{15.72}$$

(incidentally, $(15.72)_1$ satisfies $T_{mi,m} = 0$ for *any* tensor A_{in}; however, the symmetry condition $T_{im} = T_{mi}$ is then rather inconvenient: $A_{mm,k} - A_{mk,m} = 0$, so that it is expedient to satisfy it by adopting $(15.72)_2$). Omitting body forces, we now calculate the resultant force and moment acting on a surface S (cf. (9.31), (9.32)):

$$F_i = \int_S \varepsilon_{mpn}A_{in,p}\,da_m, \qquad L_i = \int_S \varepsilon_{ijk}x_j\varepsilon_{mrs}A_{ks,r}\,da_m \tag{15.73}$$

(in plane problems we assume that the only nonvanishing components of **A** are $A_{13}(x, y) = F_{,y}$, $A_{23}(x, y) = -F_{,x}$; taking as S a cylinder of unit height, erected over a curve $x = x(s)$, $y = y(s)$, so that $da = ds$, we arrive at (15.101)). By Kelvin's transformation,

$$F_i = \int_{\partial S} A_{im}\,dx_m, \quad L_i = \int_{\partial S} \varepsilon_{ijk}x_jA_{km}\,dx_m + \int_S \bar{A}_{mi}\,da_m, \tag{15.74}$$

where $\bar{A}_{mi} = A_{mi} - \delta_{mi}A_{kk}$. If S is a closed surface, in which case $\partial S = 0$, then F_i vanish whether we like it or not (L_i vanish too, but less obviously).

† A complete representation has been given by Gurtin [62].

Of course, if S is the entire boundary, in which case it is reducible to a point without passing outside of the body, then $F_i = 0$, $L_i = 0$ are precisely the "compatibility conditions" that the external loads must satisfy to keep the body in equilibrium. In this case, then, the representation (15.71) is complete. If the region is periphractic, and if F_i and L_i do not vanish on each of the boundaries, then the terms $\text{Def}\mathbf{a} - \frac{1}{2}\mathbf{1}\,\text{div}\mathbf{a}$, where $\nabla^2\mathbf{a} = \mathbf{0}$, must be added to (15.71). Rather unavoidably, the discussion that follows will have to be confined to the representation (15.71).

It remains to express the conditions of compatibility in terms of $\mathbf{F}$. If $\text{Ink}\tilde{\mathbf{E}} = \boldsymbol{\eta}$ (cf. (15.33)), where $\boldsymbol{\eta}$ is a measure of the incompatibility of the strains, then, using (15.1) and (15.21)*, we arrive at

$$\nabla^2 T_{im} + \frac{1}{1+\nu}(T_{rr,mi} - \delta_{im}\nabla^2 T_{rr}) = -2\mu\eta_{im}. \qquad (15.75)$$

When $\boldsymbol{\eta} = \mathbf{0}$, these equations are known as the *Beltrami-Michell stress equations of compatibility*; they can be expressed as follows,

$$\nabla^2 T_{kk} = 0, \qquad \nabla^2 T_{im} + \frac{1}{1+\nu} T_{kk,mi} = 0. \qquad (15.75)^*$$

Introducing the modified stress functions $\bar{\mathbf{G}}$ by

$$G_{ij} = 2\mu\left(\bar{G}_{ij} + \frac{\nu}{1-\nu}\,\delta_{ij}\bar{G}_{kk}\right), \qquad \text{div}\bar{\mathbf{G}} = 0, \qquad (15.76)$$

(note that now $\text{div}\mathbf{G} \neq 0$), we find that

$$T_{im} = -2\mu\left[\nabla^2\bar{G}_{im} + \frac{1}{1-\nu}(\bar{G}_{kk,mi} - \delta_{im}\nabla^2\bar{G}_{kk})\right] \qquad (15.77)$$

and that

$$\nabla^4\bar{G}_{ij} = \eta_{ij}, \qquad \nabla^4 G_{ij} = 2\mu\left(\eta_{ij} + \frac{\nu}{1-\nu}\,\delta_{ij}\eta_{kk}\right), \qquad (15.78)$$

The stress function method also suffers from the defect that in multiply connected regions $\nabla^4\mathbf{G} = \mathbf{0}$ is not a sufficient condition for the existence of one-valued and differentiable displacements. So far the use of the stress function method has been confined almost entirely to plane problems or torsion problems for prismatic bars. If we assume that $\partial_z \mathbf{G} = \mathbf{0}$, then (15.71) reduce to

$$T_{11} = F_{,22}, \qquad T_{22} = F_{,11}, \qquad T_{12} = -F_{,12}, \tag{15.79}$$

$$T_{31} = \mu\alpha\phi_{,2}, \qquad T_{32} = -\mu\alpha\phi_{,1}, \tag{15.80}$$

$$T_{33} = G_{11,22} + G_{22,11} - 2G_{12,12}, \tag{15.81}$$

where $F = G_{33}$ is called *Airy's stress function*, and $\mu\alpha\phi = G_{23,1} - G_{31,2}$ is called *Prandtl's stress function*. The factor $\mu\alpha$, where α is a constant ("unit angle of twist"), has been introduced for reasons of convenience.

The two-dimensional problems characterized by (15.79) fall into problems of *plane strain* and problems of *plane stress*. Let us use the letters $\alpha, \beta, \ldots$ for indices that have a range from one to two only. A state of plane strain is then defined by

$$u_\alpha = u_\alpha(x, y), \qquad u_3 = 0, \tag{15.82}$$

so that

$$T_{\alpha\beta} = \lambda\tilde{E}_{\gamma\gamma}\delta_{\alpha\beta} + 2\mu\tilde{E}_{\alpha\beta}, \qquad T_{3\alpha} = 0, \qquad T_{33} = \nu T_{\alpha\alpha}. \tag{15.83}$$

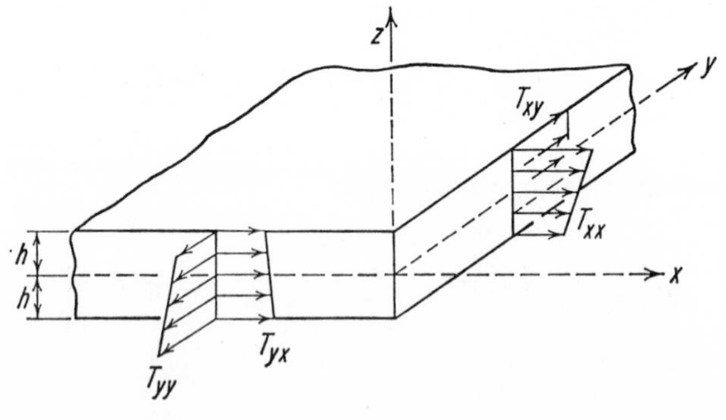

FIGURE 15.4 Drawing for the definition of plane stress solutions.

For thin bodies bounded by the planes $z = \pm h$, the exact solutions can be approximated by *plane stress* solutions expressed in terms of the thickness averages (cf. Figure 15.4)

$$\hat{\mathbf{T}} = \frac{1}{2h}\int_{-h}^{h} \mathbf{T}\, dz, \qquad \hat{\mathbf{u}} = \frac{1}{2h}\int_{-h}^{h} \mathbf{u}\, dz.$$

The plane stress solutions are only appropriate if there are no loads on the lateral surfaces, $T_{3\alpha} = 0$, $z = \pm h$, and when the edge loads have no z components. Then the first two equations of equilibrium reduce to $\hat{T}_{xx,x} + \hat{T}_{yx,y} = 0$, $\hat{T}_{xy,x} + \hat{T}_{yy,y} = 0$. To make the two-dimensional formulation self-contained, we further assume that $T_{33} = 0$. Then $\tilde{E}_{33}$ can be eliminated from Hooke's law, thus

$$\hat{T}_{\alpha\beta} = \frac{2\mu\lambda}{\lambda + 2\mu}\hat{\tilde{E}}_{\gamma\gamma}\delta_{\alpha\beta} + 2\mu\hat{\tilde{E}}_{\alpha\beta}, \qquad \hat{\tilde{E}}_{33} = -\frac{\lambda}{\lambda + 2\mu}\hat{\tilde{E}}_{\gamma\gamma}, \tag{15.84}$$

i.e. plane strain solutions become formally plane stress solutions by replacing λ with $2\mu\lambda/(\lambda + 2\mu)$. It will be recalled that in multiply connected regions the compatibility condition $\nabla^4 F = 0$ fails to ensure the one-valuedness of the displacements. This means that the calculation and inspection of displacements cannot be avoided.

To summarize, then, the two main methods of linear elastostatics are (in the absence of body forces) as follows:†

The method of

displacement functions	stress functions
$2\mu\mathbf{u} = \nabla(\phi + \mathbf{x}\cdot\boldsymbol{\psi}) - 4(1-\nu)\boldsymbol{\psi}$	$\mathbf{T} = \mathrm{Ink}\,\mathbf{G}$

automatically satisfies the conditions of

compatibility	equilibrium

whereas the differential equations

$\nabla^2\phi = 0, \quad \nabla^2\boldsymbol{\psi} = \mathbf{0}$	$\nabla^4\mathbf{G} = \mathbf{0}$

represent the conditions of

equilibrium	compatibility

To discover the problems that have relatively simple solutions, a *semi-inverse approach* is perhaps the best method. Here we start with an assumed form of solutions, or assume certain properties for the solutions outright, and then determine, in effect, the problems in which field equations and boundary conditions can be satisfied by the assumed form of solutions (this is the main

† Each of the methods actually has several variants. As was noted in the text, the stress function method shown above may not be general enough. A somewhat analogous pair of methods will be found in the study of isochoric, irrotational flows (cf. p. 567).

method of the nonlinear theories, because there a "frontal" attack on the nonlinear field equations has little chance of success). This method works particularly well for incompressible media, because it is much easier to satisfy field equations and boundary conditions with an assumed form of solution if there is an adjustable parameter, the arbitrary hydrostatic pressure p, available. To illustrate this, let us consider the plane strain problem of the inflation of a cylindrical tube with the cross section $A \leq P \leq B$ in the undeformed configuration. The motion is assumed to be purely radial. The form of the solution is then determined by the condition of incompressibility: $\rho^2 - \rho_A^2 = P^2 - A^2$; in particular, if the position ρ_A of the inner wall is known, then the position of the outer wall, ρ_B, is given by $\rho_B^2 = \rho_A^2 + B^2 - A^2$. Either ρ_A or $T_{\rho\rho}$ at ρ_A may be taken as the parameter that controls the deformation.

With $\mathbf{S} = p\mathbf{1} + \mathbf{T}$, and assuming that $T_{\rho\phi} = T_{\phi z} = T_{z\rho} = 0$, and that normal stresses depend only on ρ, we find from (6.68) that there is only one condition of equilibrium, $-\partial_\rho p + \partial_\rho S_{\rho\rho} + \rho^{-1}(S_{\rho\rho} - S_{\phi\phi}) = 0$. Because p is not determined by the constitutive equation, we can now determine it from the condition of equilibrium,

$$p = S_{\rho\rho} - \int_\rho^{\rho_B} \frac{1}{u}(S_{\rho\rho} - S_{\phi\phi})\, du,$$

where the constant of integration has been chosen so as to satisfy the boundary condition $T_{\rho\rho} = 0$ at $\rho = \rho_B$. We have now satisfied the condition of equilibrium and the boundary condition, as well as the condition that the deformation must be compatible and isochoric, without even mentioning the constitutive equation! Of course, the actual values of stresses cannot be determined without knowing what the constitutive equation is; moreover, the constitutive equation must be consistent with the assumptions about the state of stress. Still, there is no point in assuming that the deformation is small, therefore, let us write $\mathbf{T} = -p\mathbf{1} + \mu\mathbf{B}$ (*Neo-Hookean material*), $\mathbf{B} = \mathbf{F}\mathbf{F}^T$, so that for small deformations $\mathbf{B} \doteq \mathbf{1} + 2\tilde{\mathbf{E}}$, $\mathbf{T} = -p\mathbf{1} + 2\mu\tilde{\mathbf{E}}$. How to calculate the curvilinear components of $\mathbf{F}$? The initial Cartesian coordinates X_m may be related to the initial cylindrical coordinates Θ_b by the transformation formulas $dX_m = X_{m.b}\, d\Theta_b \equiv Q_{mb}\, d\Theta_b/H_{\underline{b}}$, where $H_2 = 1/P$, $H_1 = H_3 = 1$; similarly, the final Cartesian coordinates x_i and the final cylindrical coordinates θ_a may be related through $dx_i = x_{i,a}\, d\theta_a \equiv q_{ia}\, d\theta_a/h_{\underline{a}}$, where $h_2 = 1/\rho$, $h_1 = h_3 = 1$. From the chain rule

$$\frac{\partial x_i}{\partial X_m} = \left(\frac{\partial x_i}{\partial \theta_a}\right)\left(\frac{\partial \theta_a}{\partial \Theta_b}\right)\left(\frac{\partial \Theta_b}{\partial X_m}\right)$$

it then follows that (recall (6.7)!)

$$F_{ab} = q_{ia}F_{im}Q_{mb} = \frac{H_{\underline{b}}}{h_{\underline{a}}}\frac{\partial \theta_a}{\partial \Theta_b}. \tag{15.85}$$

The rest is now routine: $\mathbf{F} = \text{diag}(P/\rho, \rho/P, 1)$ (where we have used $d\rho/dP = P/\rho$), $\mathbf{B} = \text{diag}(P^2/\rho^2, \rho^2/P^2, 1) = \mathbf{S}/\mu$, so that it only remains to carry out a simple integration to evaluate p.

Whenever exact solutions are too difficult to obtain, we have to settle for approximate solutions. We shall outline here the idea behind the two classical variational methods for the mixed boundary value problem, not with the intent of going into the construction of approximate solutions, but because this will give us an opportunity to consider certain *potentials* that characterize the response of an entire "system" comprising a body and the loads that it carries.

As a rule, it is not difficult to satisfy either equilibrium or compatibility; therefore, we may attempt to construct approximate solutions from *statically admissible states* and *kinematically admissible states.* A statically admissible state is any stress field that satisfies the stress boundary condition on B_T, and the conditions of equilibrium (the strains calculated from Hooke's law need not be compatible); a kinematically admissible state is any one-valued and differentiable displacement field that satisfies the displacement boundary conditions on B_u (the stresses calculated from Hooke's law need not satisfy the conditions of equilibrium). In either case, we must define a potential, and a "variation" (i.e. a set of comparison states). Let us suppose that a potential Φ depends, among other things, on certain parameters α_m (one is tempted to think of α_m as "generalized coordinates," but that is not always appropriate, because α_m may stand for loads as well). The variation of Φ with α_m is described by the "generalized force"†

$$F_m = -\frac{\partial \Phi}{\partial \alpha_m}. \tag{15.86}$$

The vanishing of F_m indicates an extremum of Φ, i.e. an "equilibrium configuration."

Even when α_m are displacements of some kind, one should guard against interpreting F_m automatically as actual forces, nor should the variation of α_m be considered as an actual (possibly "quasi-static") process. A variation of α_m may be no more than a "thought experiment"; in particular, it may

† Again, this designation may not always be appropriate.

amount to a comparison of two equilibrium states that cannot be connected by any elastic process, so that F_m is merely a measure of the energy available for the actual, inelastic process.

The variational principles are just as easily stated in a form valid for finite deformations. However, it is then expedient to replace the Cauchy stress T_{ij} by the (first) *Piola-Kirchhoff stress* $\tilde{T}_{ij}$ defined by

$$\tilde{T}_{ji} = JF_{jk}^{-1}T_{ki} = \frac{\partial W}{\partial F_{ij}} \tag{15.87}$$

(cf. (14.30)), where $J = \det\mathbf{F}$. It should be noted that the Piola-Kirchhoff stress is not symmetric, because $T_{ij} = T_{ji}$ only requires that $F_{ik}\tilde{T}_{km} = F_{mk}\tilde{T}_{ki}$. The advantage of the Piola-Kirchhoff stress is that it refers the internal forces to area elements in one and the same reference configuration of the body. Namely, let da_i and dA_i be the current and the reference configurations, respectively, of a material surface element. Denoting by $d\mathbf{f}$ the resultant force acting on area element da, we define $\tilde{\mathbf{T}}$ by $df_k = t_k(\mathbf{n})\,da = T_{jk}n_j\,da = T_{jk}\,da_j = \tilde{t}_k(\mathbf{N})\,dA = \tilde{T}_{jk}N_j\,dA = \tilde{T}_{jk}\,dA_j$. Using the formulas of Nanson, (8.19), (8.20), we now obtain the first of (15.87). To express the equations of motion in terms of the Piola-Kirchhoff stress, we need the *Euler-C. Neumann identities*

$$(JX_{i,j})_{.i} = 0, \qquad \left(\frac{1}{J}x_{i.j}\right)_{,i} = 0. \tag{15.88}$$

These identities can be verified by a direct calculation. For instance, let us consider $(JX_{i,j})_{.i} = J_{.i}X_{i,j} + JX_{i,jk}x_{k.i} = \bar{x}_{mn}x_{m.ni}X_{i,j} + JX_{i,jk}x_{k.i}$, where $\bar{x}_{mn}$ denote the cofactors of $x_{m.n}$ in $\det(x_{i,m})$. Next, differentiating $x_{m.q}X_{q,r} = \delta_{mr}$ with respect to X_p, then multiplying the resulting expression by $x_{r.n}$, we arrive at $x_{m.np} = -x_{r.n}x_{m.q}x_{s.p}X_{q,rs}$. The first of (15.88) is now readily verified by substituting $x_{m.np}$ into the expression for $(JX_{i,j})_{.i}$. The proof of $(15.88)_2$ is analogous.

In view of (15.87) and (15.88), we now have that $T_{ji,j} = J^{-1}x_{j.k}\tilde{T}_{ki,j} = J^{-1}\tilde{T}_{ki.k}$. Therefore, multiplying the stress equations of motion by J, and taking into account the mass balance $\rho J = \rho_0$, we obtain

$$\tilde{T}_{ki.k} + \rho_0 b_i = \rho_0 \ddot{x}_i. \tag{15.89}$$

Let us take up the kinematically admissible states first. To define a "variation," we introduce a family of deformations $\mathbf{x} = \mathbf{x}(\mathbf{X}, \alpha)$, each satisfying the displacement boundary conditions on B_u. Rather than working with derivatives with respect to α, it is notationally more convenient to use the operator

$\delta = \delta\alpha\, \partial/\partial\alpha$. Because X_i and α are assumed to be independent variables, it follows that $\delta\Delta_j = \Delta_j\delta$; similarly, δ commutes with integration with respect to X_i. To construct a potential, we start with the variation of the total strain energy, δE. Because the requisite integrals will be only a part of a "flow chart," we shall use abbreviated designations for them. Specifically, a volume integral (in the reference configuration) of W over a region V will be denoted by $V[W]$, whereas surface integrals (again in the reference configuration) over the boundary ∂V will be denoted by expressions of the form $\partial V[t_i\, \delta x_i]$. Thus, with $W = W(\mathbf{F})$, we have that $\delta E = V[\delta W] = V[\tilde{T}_{ji}\, \delta F_{ij}] = V[\tilde{T}_{ji}\Delta_j\, \delta x_i] = \partial V[\tilde{T}_{ji}N_j\, \delta x_i] - V[\tilde{T}_{ji.j}\, \delta x_i]$, where we have used the divergence theorem, and $\mathbf{N}$ denotes the outward unit normal vectors of ∂V. By hypothesis, $\delta x_i = 0$ on B_u, so that $\delta E = B_T[\tilde{t}_i\, \delta x_i] - V[\tilde{T}_{ji.j}\, \delta x_i]$, where $\tilde{t}_i = \tilde{T}_{ji}N_j$. Even when the stresses satisfy the conditions of the equilibrium, thus $\tilde{T}_{ji.j} = 0$, the variation δE does not vanish. However, if E is replaced by the potential†

$$\Phi = E - B_T[\bar{t}_i x_i], \tag{15.90}$$

where $\bar{t}_i$ are the given boundary values of the Piola-Kirchhoff stresses, then, because the exact solution must satisfy also $\tilde{t}_i = \bar{t}_i$ on B_T, it follows that Φ has an extremum at the exact solution. Conversely, if a kinematically admissible solution is to satisfy $\delta\Phi = 0$, then $\tilde{T}_{ji.j} = 0$ in V, $\tilde{t}_i = \bar{t}_i$ on B_T must hold. To investigate this extremum, we consider $\delta^2\Phi = V[\delta\tilde{T}_{ji}\delta F_{ij} + \tilde{T}_{ji}\delta^2 F_{ij}] - B_T[\bar{t}_i\delta^2 x_i]$. For the exact solution we obtain

$$\delta^2\Phi = V[A_{jikm}\delta F_{ij}\delta F_{km}], \qquad A_{jikm} = \frac{\partial^2 W}{\partial F_{ij}\, \partial F_{km}}. \tag{15.91}$$

Thus if $A_{jikm}\delta F_{ij}\delta F_{km}$ is a positive definite form for any tensor $\delta\mathbf{F}$, then Φ will have a minimum at the exact solution. In the linear theory E is given by $E = V[\frac{1}{2}T_{ij}E_{ij}]$, and it is easy to show that if the strain-energy function is positive definite, then the minimum of Φ occurs *only* at the exact solution (hence the theorem that *among all kinematically admissible states the exact solution is characterized by a minimum of the potential* Φ).

The term $B_T[\bar{t}_i x_i]$ does *not* represent work done at the boundary (this work will depend, in general, on the nature of the loading process); rather, it is a "potential energy" of the loads acting on B_T. A variation of this potential energy equals the work done by the Piola-Kirchhoff stresses $\bar{t}_i$ (held fixed in the reference configuration!). It is perhaps helpful to draw an analogy with thermodynamics. Starting from $\varepsilon = \varepsilon(\eta, v)$, $-p = \partial\varepsilon/\partial v$, we introduce the

† Because $\delta x_i = \delta u_i$, where $u_i = x_i - X_i$, the surface integral could have been taken as $B_T[\bar{t}_i u_i]$.

enthalpy $h(\eta, p) = \varepsilon + pv$, so that $\delta h = \theta\, \delta\eta + v\, \delta p$. Again, the term pv is not work done; instead, we consider enthalpy as a thermodynamic potential that is appropriate for describing certain processes. In the same way, Φ is a potential that is appropriate for characterizing kinematically admissible states.

In the variational method based upon statically admissible states, the strain-energy density must be replaced by the complementary energy

$$H(\mathbf{T}) = W - \tilde{T}_{ji}F_{ij}, \tag{15.92}$$

and the potential Φ by the complementary potential

$$\Psi = V[H] - B_u[\bar{x}_i \bar{t}_i], \tag{15.93}$$

where $\bar{x}_i$ are the prescribed positions on B_u. Further, from $\partial H/\partial \tilde{T}_{ij} = \tilde{T}_{mk}\, \partial F_{km}/\partial \tilde{T}_{ij} - F_{ji} - \tilde{T}_{mk}\, \partial F_{km}/\partial \tilde{T}_{ij}$ we obtain the counterpart of (15.87),

$$F_{ji} = -\frac{\partial H}{\partial \tilde{T}_{ij}}. \tag{15.94}$$

The variations of $\delta\tilde{T}_{ij}$ must be statically admissible, i.e. they must satisfy the subsidiary conditions $\delta\tilde{T}_{ji.j} = 0$. To remove this restriction, we add $-A_i\,\delta T_{ji.j}$ to δH ($-A_i$ being Lagrange's multipliers), thus $\delta\Psi = V[-F_{ij}\,\delta\tilde{T}_{ji} - A_i\,\delta\tilde{T}_{ji.j}] - B_u[\bar{x}_i\,\delta\bar{t}_i]$. Integrating by parts, we obtain $\delta\Psi = V[(A_{i.j} - F_{ij})\,\delta\tilde{T}_{ji}] - B_u[(\bar{x}_i - A_i)\,\delta\bar{t}_i]$, where we have set $N_j\,\delta\tilde{T}_{ji} = \delta\bar{t}_i$ on B_u. Therefore, $\delta\Psi = 0$ yields the compatibility conditions $A_{i.j} - F_{ij} = 0$ as well as the boundary conditions $\bar{x}_i = A_i$ on B_u. It should be appreciated that F_{ij} calculated from (15.94) will not be in general gradients. However, the compatibility conditions require them to be gradients (also note that the Lagrange's multipliers associated with the exact solution are no other than the places x_i in the deformed configuration!). We eliminate $A_{i.j}$ through $A_{i.[jk]} = 0$, so that, by (15.94), the compatibility conditions become

$$\Delta_j \frac{\partial H}{\partial \tilde{T}_{ki}} = \Delta_k \frac{\partial H}{\partial \tilde{T}_{ji}}. \tag{15.95}$$

Again, in the linear theory it can be shown that if the strain-energy function is positive definite, then *among all statically admissible states the exact solution is characterized by a minimum of the potential* Ψ.

There are also methods which provide upper and lower bounds on the quantities that are being approximated. Of these we mention the "hypercircle method" of Prager and Synge (cf. [159]). As is to be expected, this method requires the simultaneous use of kinematically admissible states and statically admissible states.

Illustrative examples

The torsion problem still continues to attract attention, mainly in connection with studies of the principle of Saint-Venant. Let us consider a prismatic bar aligned with the z direction (cf. Figure 15.3a). The boundary C of its constant cross section is described by $x = x(s)$, $y = y(s)$, so that the outward normals $\mathbf{n}$ of C are given by $n_x = dy/ds$, $n_y = -dx/ds$. In the torsion problem we assume that the mantle of the prismatic bar is free of surface tractions, and that the ends are subjected to a stress distribution which has a resultant moment M, but no resultant force. Saint-Venant's solution of the torsion problem may be characterized by

$$T_{xx} = T_{yy} = T_{zz} = T_{xy} = 0,$$

$$T_{xz} = \mu\alpha\phi_{,y}, \qquad T_{yz} = -\mu\alpha\phi_{,x},$$

where $$\nabla^2\phi = -2, \qquad \phi = \text{const. on } C. \tag{15.96}$$

Here $(15.96)_2$ describes the boundary condition that the mantle be free of surface tractions, $T_{ji}n_j = 0$: $T_{zx}n_x + T_{zy}n_y = \mu\alpha(\phi_{,y}\,dy/ds + \phi_{,x}\,dx/ds) = \mu\alpha\,d\phi/ds$ on C. If the cross section is simply connected, then the constant value of ϕ on C may be set equal to zero. The differential equation $(15.96)_1$ expresses the condition of compatibility.

The specification of stress resultants alone does not suffice to obtain a unique solution, so that there remains the question as to why Saint-Venant's solution should be singled out among all solutions corresponding to the same boundary condition on the mantle, and the same "relaxed" boundary condition (i.e. boundary condition specifying only the stress resultants on the ends). The answer is that Saint-Venant's solution is the simplest one, and, except in the vicinity of the ends, may be expected to approximate the other solutions rather closely, the last assertion being interpreted as an instance of the principle of Saint-Venant. Quite recently Sternberg and Knowles [205] have shown that, among all solutions of the relaxed torsion problem, Saint-Venant's solution furnishes an absolute minimum of the strain energy.

Concerning $(15.96)_1$, we note that from the compatibility conditions (15.21) it follows right away that $\nabla^2\phi = \text{const}$. In order to verify that (15.96) is indeed the condition of compatibility, let us calculate the displacements. By hypothesis, $\tilde{E}_{xx} = \tilde{E}_{yy} = \tilde{E}_{zz} = \tilde{E}_{xy} = 0$, so that $u_z = u_z(x, y)$, $u_x = yh(z)$, $u_y = -xh(z)$. Next, from $T_{zx} = \mu\alpha\phi_{,y} = \mu(u_{z,x} + u_{x,z})$, $T_{zy} = -\mu\alpha\phi_{,x} = \mu(u_{z,y} + u_{y,z})$ it follows that $h'(z)$ is a constant; as it turns out it should be denoted by $-\alpha$. The displacements $u_x = -\alpha yz$, $u_y = \alpha xz$ are evidently one-valued, but the one-valuedness of u_z requires that

$$\oint_{C'} du_z = 0, \tag{15.97}$$

where C' is any closed curve lying in the cross section. Letting $du_z = u_{z,x}\,dx + u_{z,y}\,dy = \alpha[(y + \phi_{,y})\,dx - (x + \phi_{,x})\,dy]$, and using Kelvin's transformation in (15.97) we readily recover (15.96).

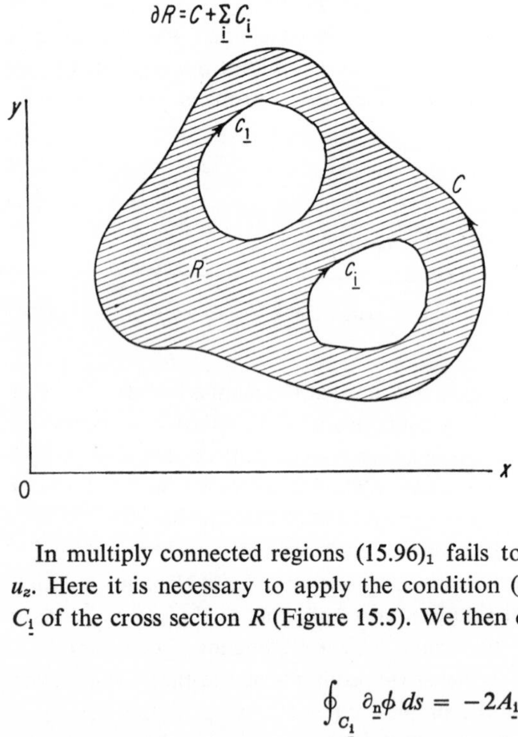

FIGURE 15.5 Notations for a multiply connected cross section R.

In multiply connected regions $(15.96)_1$ fails to ensure the one-valuedness of u_z. Here it is necessary to apply the condition (15.97) to each boundary curve $C_{\underline{i}}$ of the cross section R (Figure 15.5). We then obtain

$$\oint_{C_{\underline{i}}} \partial_{\underline{n}}\phi\, ds = -2A_{\underline{i}}, \tag{15.98}$$

where $A_{\underline{i}}$ is the area of the region enclosed by $C_{\underline{i}}$ (because ϕ is not defined in this region, Kelvin's transformation cannot be applied to the integral on the left). The conditions (15.98), together with $\phi = \pi_{\underline{i}}$ on $C_{\underline{i}}$, now replace $(15.96)_2$. The constants $\pi_{\underline{i}}$ ("periods") must be obtained as part of the solution; the constant value of ϕ on the outer boundary C may be set equal to zero.

The torque M transmitted by a cross section is given by

$$M = \int_R (xT_{zy} - yT_{zx})\,da = -\mu\alpha \int_R (x\phi_{,x} + y\phi_{,y})\,da.$$

In particular, because the torsion of a circular cylinder is solved by $\phi = \frac{1}{2}(a^2 - x^2 - y^2)$, M is then given by $M = \mu\alpha J$ where J is the polar moment of inertia of the cross section. Another expression for M follows by using the identity $2\phi - (x\phi)_{,x} - (y\phi)_{,y} = -x\phi_{,x} - y\phi_{,y}$, and noting that (cf. Figure 15.5)

$$\int_{\partial R} \cdots = \oint_C \cdots + \sum_{\underline{1}} \oint_{C_{\underline{1}}} \cdots = \oint_C \cdots - \sum_{\underline{1}} \oint_{C_{\underline{1}}} \cdots.$$

Therefore, carrying out the appropriate Kelvin's transformation, we obtain

$$M = 2\mu\alpha V, \qquad V = \int_R \phi\, da + \sum_{\underline{1}} \pi_{\underline{1}} A_{\underline{1}},$$

where we have also used (15.98). In words, the torque M is proportional to the volumes enclosed by the "torsion surface" $\phi(x, y) = z$ and pairs of plane areas bounded by $C_{\underline{1}}$ and separated by the distances $\pi_{\underline{1}}$.

The torsion surface ϕ can serve as a means for visualizing the stresses acting on the cross section. If we imagine ϕ plotted as a surface over R, $z = \phi(x, y)$, then the *contour lines* of ϕ are obtained by intersecting it with the planes $z =$ const.: $\phi(x, y) =$ const. Along a contour line, then, $d\phi = \phi_{,x}\, dx + \phi_{,y}\, dy = 0$, therefore, by (15.80), $dy/dx = T_{zy}/T_{zx}$. This means that the contour lines of ϕ are also the *trajectories of stress* (i.e. lines that are everywhere tangential to the stress vectors $\mathbf{t}_z = \mathbf{e}_x T_{zx} + \mathbf{e}_y T_{zy}$). Second, the magnitude of a stress vector is proportional to the maximum slope of ϕ at that point:

$$S = \sqrt{T_{zx}^2 + T_{zy}^2} = \mu\alpha\, |\nabla\phi|.$$

The foregoing results can be elucidated by means of an analogy between the torsion problem and the *membrane theory*. We consider a membrane which is subjected to a large initial tension T, so that changes of tension due to small deflections are negligible. The small deflections w of the membrane are governed by

$$\nabla^2 w = -\frac{p}{T} \tag{15.99}$$

(cf. problem 9 in Section 11), where p is the pressure acting on the membrane. To establish the analogy, we introduce the scaling $\phi \leftrightarrow 2Tw/p$, and assume that the membrane is spanned over a plate in which the cut-out portion is of the same shape as the outer boundary C of the cross section undergoing torsion. Because $-\partial_{\underline{n}} w$ represents the (small) slopes of the membrane, the counterpart of (15.98),

$$-T \oint_{C_{\underline{1}}} \partial_{\underline{n}} w\, ds = pA_{\underline{1}},$$

is a condition of equilibrium between the pressure force acting on $A_{\underline{1}}$ and the resultant of the tensions acting along the edge of $A_{\underline{1}}$. This means that the membrane analogy for torsion of multiply connected prismatic bars can be realized by placing weightless (i.e. counter-balanced) horizontal plates over the holes of a cross section. The action of the membrane itself will determine the heights $z = \pi_{\underline{1}}$ of the plates. Any change of these heights will affect the slopes (stresses!) of the membrane; if $\pi_{\underline{1}}$ are assigned arbitrarily, then forces will be needed to hold the plates in their positions (correspondingly, in the torsion problem the displacements will be many-valued).

In one variant of the plasticity theory it is assumed that in a fully plastic cross section, $S =$ const. and equal to some yield stress. Hence there exists a *sand-hill analogy*, that is, the torsion surface ϕ can be modeled by pouring dry sand over the cross section.

Elasticity theory is rather remarkable in that solutions of many nontrivial problems turn out to be relatively simple. Indeed, the practical value of elasticity theory derives primarily from the fact that through these solutions, and through the concepts of stress and strain, it has provided a complete framework for a rational approach to various design problems. In what follows we shall illustrate the particularly important effect of a *stress concentration* produced by an abrupt change of shape.

We consider a rectangular plate with a circular hole in it; the problem is then to find the stresses near the hole as the plate is put into tension. To simplify the problem, we assume the dimensions of the plate to be much larger than the radius a of the hole, so that the plate can be treated as being of infinite extent.† The prescribed conditions at infinity are then $T_{xx} = T$, $T_{xy} = T_{yy} = 0$; in plane polar coordinates they become

$$T_{\rho\rho} = \frac{T}{2}(1 + \cos 2\phi), \quad T_{\phi\phi} = \frac{T}{2}(1 - \cos 2\phi), \quad T_{\rho\phi} = -\frac{T}{2}\sin 2\phi,$$

$$\rho \to \infty,$$

where we have used (6.27) and the appropriate transformation formulas $T_{ab} = Q_{ai}Q_{bj}T_{ij}$. The boundary conditions are $T_{\rho\rho} = T_{\rho\phi} = 0$, $\rho = a$.

Let us take plane strain solution $u \equiv u_\rho(\rho, \phi)$ $v \equiv u_\phi(\rho, \phi)$, $w \equiv u_z = 0$ (to obtain the corresponding plane stress solution, replace λ by $2\mu\lambda/(\lambda + 2\mu)$). Using Hooke's law and the definitions $\tilde{E}_{\rho\rho} = u_{\rho;\rho} = \partial u/\partial\rho$, $\tilde{E}_{\phi\phi} = u_{\phi;\phi} = (\partial v/\partial\phi + u)/\rho$, $E_{\rho\phi} = \frac{1}{2}(u_{\rho;\phi} + u_{\phi;\rho}) = (\partial u/\partial\phi - v + \rho\partial v/\partial\rho)/2\rho$, we obtain the stress-displacement relations

$$T_{\rho\rho} = \lambda\vartheta + 2\mu\frac{\partial u}{\partial\rho}, \quad T_{\phi\phi} = \lambda\vartheta + 2\mu\left(\frac{1}{\rho}\frac{\partial v}{\partial\phi} + \frac{u}{\rho}\right),$$

$$T_{\rho\phi} = \mu\left(\frac{1}{\rho}\frac{\partial u}{\partial\phi} - \frac{v}{\rho} + \frac{\partial v}{\partial\rho}\right).$$

† This is known as the *problem of Kirsch*.

Substituting these into (6.68), we obtain the following displacement equations of equilibrium,

$$\nabla^2 u - \frac{u}{\rho^2} - \frac{2}{\rho^2}\frac{\partial v}{\partial \phi} + \frac{1}{1-2\nu}\frac{\partial \vartheta}{\partial \rho} = 0, \quad \vartheta = \text{div}\mathbf{u} = \frac{\partial u}{\partial \rho} + \frac{u}{\rho} + \frac{1}{\rho}\frac{\partial v}{\partial \phi}$$

$$\nabla^2 v - \frac{v}{\rho^2} + \frac{2}{\rho^2}\frac{\partial u}{\partial \phi} + \frac{1}{1-2\nu}\frac{1}{\rho}\frac{\partial \vartheta}{\partial \phi} = 0. \tag{15.100}$$

It is best to break up the solution into two by considering the rotationally symmetric part $u = u(\rho)$, $v = 0$ separately. For u to be a solution of (15.100), it must be of the form $u = A\rho + B\rho^{-1}$ (this is Lame's solution which can be used to describe thick-walled cylinders, shrink fits, and so on). Taking into account the conditions at infinity and the boundary condition, we now obtain

$$u = \frac{T}{4\mu}\rho(1-2\nu) + \frac{a^2}{\rho^2}, \qquad v = 0,$$

$$T_{\rho\rho} = \frac{T}{2}\left(1 - \frac{a^2}{\rho^2}\right), \quad T_{\phi\phi} = \frac{T}{2}\left(1 + \frac{a^2}{\rho^2}\right), \quad T_{\rho\phi} = 0.$$

Next, we let $u = C\rho^n \cos 2\phi$, $v = D\rho^n \sin 2\phi$. Substituting these into (15.100), we arrive at two linear, homogeneous equations for C and D; setting the determinant of the coefficients equal to zero, we find that the possible values of n are $1, -1, -3$ (correspondingly, C and D each can have three values). The evaluation of the C's and D's is now a routine matter. We record only the final result

$$T_{\rho\rho} = \frac{T}{2}\left[1 - \frac{a^2}{\rho^2} + \left(1 - 4\frac{a^2}{\rho^2} + 3\frac{a^4}{\rho^4}\right)\cos 2\phi\right],$$

$$T_{\phi\phi} = \frac{T}{2}\left[1 + \frac{a^2}{\rho^2} - \left(1 + 3\frac{a^4}{\rho^4}\right)\cos 2\phi\right],$$

$$T_{\rho\phi} = -\frac{T}{2}\left(1 + 2\frac{a^2}{\rho^2} - 3\frac{a^4}{\rho^4}\right)\sin 2\phi.$$

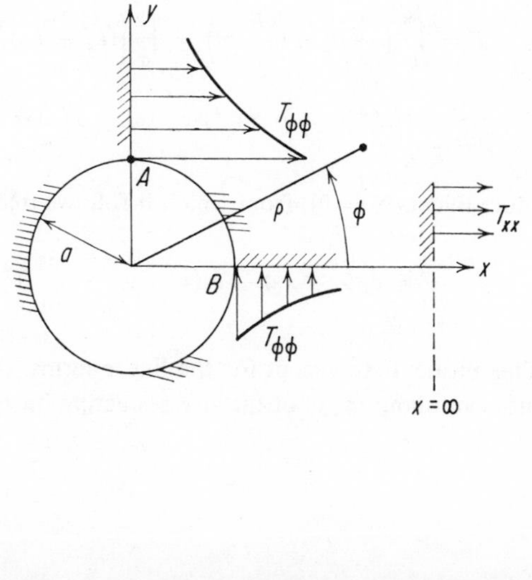

FIGURE 15.6 Drawing for the problem of Kirsch.

For $\rho = a$, $\phi = \pi/2$ (point A in Figure 15.6) we have that $T_{\phi\phi} = 3T$, i.e. the *stress concentration factor* is 3. Also, at $\rho = a$, $\phi = 0$ (point B in Figure 15.6) the stress $T_{\phi\phi}$ is compressive: $T_{\phi\phi} = -T$. In thin sheets this may create a local buckling.

From the preceding problem we can proceed to another, more complicated problem in which the hole is filled with a material with the different properties $\bar{\lambda}$ and $\bar{\mu}$. The two bodies are assumed to be bonded together, which is expressed by the continuity conditions $u = \bar{u}$, $v = \bar{v}$ for $\rho = a$. Moreover, the boundary conditions $\mathbf{t}_\rho = \mathbf{0}$ are replaced by the continuity conditions $T_{\rho\rho} = \bar{T}_{\rho\rho}$, $T_{\rho\phi} = \bar{T}_{\rho\phi}$ for $\rho = a$. One observation concerning the actual solution of the problem is important. The form of the "exterior" solution (in the region $\rho \geq a$) will be the same as in the preceding problem. For the "interior" solution (in the region $\rho \leq a$), however, we can only use the functions $\bar{u} = \bar{A}\rho$, $\bar{v} = 0$ and $\bar{u} = \bar{C}\rho\cos 2\phi$, $\bar{v} = D\rho \sin 2\phi$, because the negative powers of ρ would lead to infinite stresses and displacements at the origin.

In many plane problems the Airy's stress function F is a particularly convenient tool. To facilitate the use of F, we should relate it directly to the surface tractions. Let us consider the resultant forces

$$L_x = \int_0^s t_x \, du, \qquad L_y = \int_0^s t_y \, du$$

acting on one side of a plane curve $x = x(s)$, $y = y(s)$. In view of (15.79), we have that $t_x = T_{xx}n_x + T_{yx}n_y = (d/ds)F_{,y}$, $t_y = T_{xy}n_x + T_{yy}n_y = -(d/ds)F_{,x}$, thus $L_x = F_{,y} + c_1$, $L_y = -F_{,x} + c_2$, and

$$L_{\underline{s}} \equiv L_x \frac{dx}{ds} + L_y \frac{dy}{ds} = -\partial_{\underline{n}} F + c_1 \frac{dx}{ds} + c_2 \frac{dy}{ds}. \tag{15.101}$$

Thus at the endpoint (x, y) of the curve the normal derivative $\partial_{\underline{n}} F$ equals, except for the constant terms, the projection of $\mathbf{L}$ upon the tangent of the curve at (x, y). Next, we consider

$$F = \int_0^{\mathbf{x}} \left(\frac{\partial F}{\partial x} d\xi + \frac{\partial F}{\partial y} d\eta \right) = \int_0^s \left[(c_2 - L_y) \frac{d\xi}{du} + (L_x - c_1) \frac{d\eta}{du} \right] du$$

$$= c_2(x - x_0) - c_1(y - y_0) + yL_x(s) - xL_y(s) + \int_0^s (\xi t_y - \eta t_x)\, du$$

(note that $\mathbf{L}(0) = 0$), from which it follows that

$$F = c_2(x - x_0) - c_1(y - y_0) + \int_0^s [(\xi - x)t_y - (\eta - y)t_x]\, du.$$

This means that, except for the linear terms, the value of F at (x, y) equals the moment about (x, y) of the stresses acting on the curve.

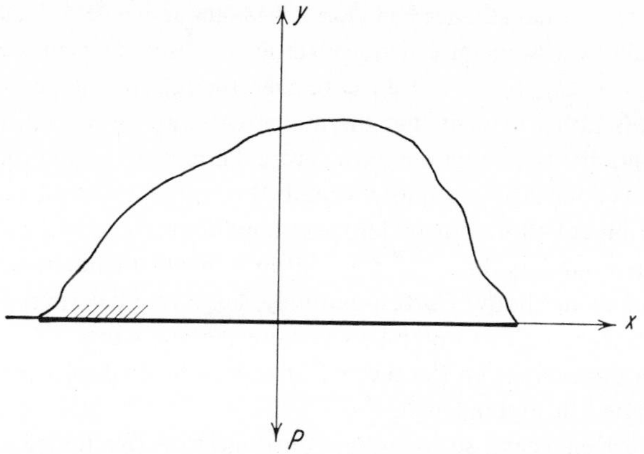

FIGURE 15.7 Concentrated load acting on a half-plane.

We illustrate the use of these interpretations for the case of a normal concentrated load acting on the half-plane $y \geq 0$ (Figure 15.7). Evidently $L_s = 0$ on the boundary curve $y = 0$, hence also $\partial F/\partial y = 0$ at $y = 0$. The moment of the loads is zero when $x < 0$ (and $y = 0$), xP when $x > 0$. This suggests that we try $F = (P/\pi)(\pi - \phi)x$ (note that F is biharmonic!). However, the condition $\partial F/\partial y = 0$ at $y = 0$ is then not satisfied, but this is easily taken care of by using the modified solution $F = (P/\pi)(\pi x - \phi x + y)$. Actually the linear terms can be omitted because they do not yield any stresses; thus $F = -(P/\pi)x\phi$.

In curvilinear coordinates we use $F_{;ab} = (\partial_a F)_{;b} = \partial_b \partial_a F + w_{cab}\partial_c F$ to express (15.79) as

$$
\begin{aligned}
T_{11} &= F_{;22} = \partial_2\partial_2 F + w_{122}\partial_1 F,\\
T_{22} &= F_{;11} = \partial_1\partial_1 F + w_{211}\partial_2 F,\\
-T_{12} &= F_{;21} = \partial_1\partial_2 F + w_{121}\partial_1 F
\end{aligned}
$$

(note that, by (6.72), $F_{;21} = F_{;12}$). In particular, in plane polar coordinates we get

$$
T_{\rho\rho} = \frac{1}{\rho}\frac{\partial F}{\partial \rho} + \frac{1}{\rho^2}\frac{\partial^2 F}{\partial \phi^2}, \qquad T_{\phi\phi} = \frac{\partial^2 F}{\partial \rho^2},
$$
$$
-T_{\rho\phi} = \frac{\partial}{\partial \rho}\left(\frac{1}{\rho}\frac{\partial F}{\partial \phi}\right). \tag{15.102a}
$$

In general cylindrical coordinates (cf. (6.36), (6.60))

$$
\begin{aligned}
T_{uu} &= h^2\frac{\partial^2 F}{\partial v^2} + h\left(h_v\frac{\partial F}{\partial v} - h_u\frac{\partial F}{\partial_u}\right),\\
T_{vv} &= h^2\frac{\partial^2 F}{\partial u^2} + h\left(h_u\frac{\partial F}{\partial u} - h_v\frac{\partial F}{\partial_v}\right),\\
-T_{uv} &= h^2\frac{\partial^2 F}{\partial u \partial v} + h\left(h_u\frac{\partial F}{\partial v} + h_v\frac{\partial F}{\partial u}\right).
\end{aligned} \tag{15.102b}
$$

The study of thermal stresses has always been an active field, most of the work being directed towards uncoupled, quasi-static problems in which accelerations are neglected, $T_{ij,j} = \bar{\bar{C}}_{ijkm}u_{k,mj} - \beta_{ij}\theta_{,j} = 0$, even though the temperature may vary with time. It is rather evident that thermal stresses are produced, in essence, by temperature gradients, so that the most severe thermal stress conditions will occur when a body is quenched or rapidly heated. It is in the nature of solutions of the heat conduction equation that under these conditions there will exist for a short period a thin boundary layer of material at a much higher temperature than the remainder of the body. Correspondingly, large thermal stresses will exist in the boundary layer; in fact one might venture the guess that $T_{ij} = -\beta_{ij}(\theta - \theta_0)$ represents an upper limit on the thermal stresses, obtained only if the heating of the boundary is "instantaneous".

The other extreme case, so to speak, concerns stress-free temperature distributions. Then, in isotropic bodies, $\tilde{E}_{ij} = -\alpha(\theta - \theta_0)\delta_{ij}$. Substituting these strains into the compatibility equations (15.21), we easily find that the only stress-free temperature distributions are $\theta = ax + by + cz$, where a, b, c are constants. In problems of plane stress or plane strain, however, the only compatibility condition is $\tilde{E}_{11,22} + \tilde{E}_{22,11} = 2\tilde{E}_{12,12}$; therefore, in simply connected regions, a solution of $\nabla^2\theta = 0$ will produce no stresses.

Wave propagation

One of the best ways of exploring the nature of mechanical response is to consider the propagation of waves. Here by a *wave* we shall either mean a moving surface of discontinuity ("wave-front"), or a carrier of oscillatory disturbances, also referred to as (infinitesimal) *plane sinusoidal progressive wave*. These two types of waves need not be the same, of course, but the manner in which they propagate will be the same (in linear elasticity theory, that is).

To get a feel of the subject, one might start with one-dimensional motions $x = x(X, t)$. The deformation gradient, particle velocity, and particle acceleration are then *scalars* defined by

$$F = \frac{\partial(X,t)}{\partial X}, \qquad v = \dot{x} = \frac{\partial x(X,t)}{\partial t}, \qquad a = \ddot{x} = \frac{\partial^2 x(X,t)}{\partial t^2}.$$

Because u in the present context stands for the displacement speed of moving surfaces of discontinuity, we shall denote displacements of particles by $w = x - X$.

To visualize a one-dimensional motion, we may think of a cylindrical rod which is constrained laterally by a rigid, frictionless guide. The relevant material properties are then the mass density ρ and the effective Young's modulus $E = C_{1111}$. The balance of mass is given by $\rho F = \rho_0$, where ρ_0 is the mass density in a reference configuration.

Assuming that the pressure $p = -T_{11}$ and the compressive strain $\varepsilon = 1 - F$ are related by $p = E\varepsilon$, we find that the equation of motion is given by $\partial F/\partial X = \ddot{x}/c^2$, $c^2 = E/\rho_0$, or, in terms of the displacement w, by

$$\frac{\partial^2 w}{\partial X^2} = \frac{\ddot{w}}{c^2}. \tag{a}$$

It is easy to see (applying the Laplace transformation to (a), for instance) that if a semi-infinite bar is subjected to the pressure pulse

$$p = \begin{cases} p_0, & 0 < t < 2\tau \\ 0, & t > 2\tau \end{cases}$$

at the end $X = 0$, then the solution $p(X, t)$ will be p_0 for $X/c < t < X/c + 2\tau$, and 0 for $t < X/c$ or $t > X/c + 2\tau$. That is, at any instant t the portion $c(t - 2\tau) < X < ct$ is uniformly compressed, the remainder of the bar being undeformed. The zone of compression traverses the material with the speed c; moreover, the *shape of the "pressure pulse" remains unchanged* as it travels down the bar.

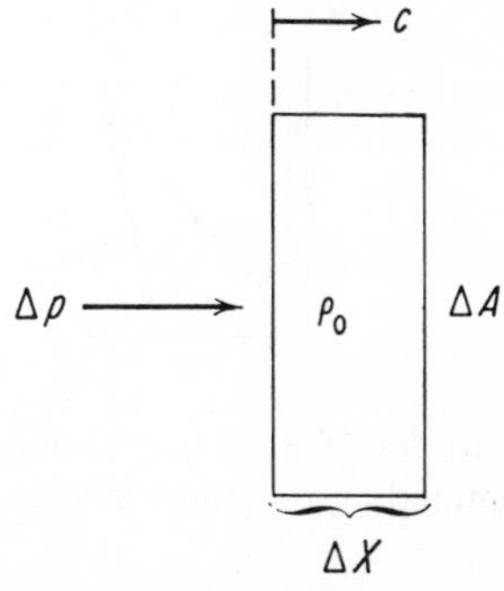

FIGURE 15.8 A diagram for the derivation of (b).

It is more instructive to derive the main features of one-dimensional waves from first principles. To this end, let us write down the balance of impulse and momentum for the generic volume element shown in Figure 15.8. We assume that the volume element is about to be overtaken by a pressure pulse Δp, travelling with a speed c relative to the medium ahead of the wave front. The increment in velocity, Δv, induced by the pressure pulse is then given by $A\,\Delta p\,\Delta X/c = A\,\Delta X \rho_0\,\Delta v$, where A is the cross-sectional area, thus

$$\Delta v = \frac{\Delta p}{\rho_0 c}. \tag{b}$$

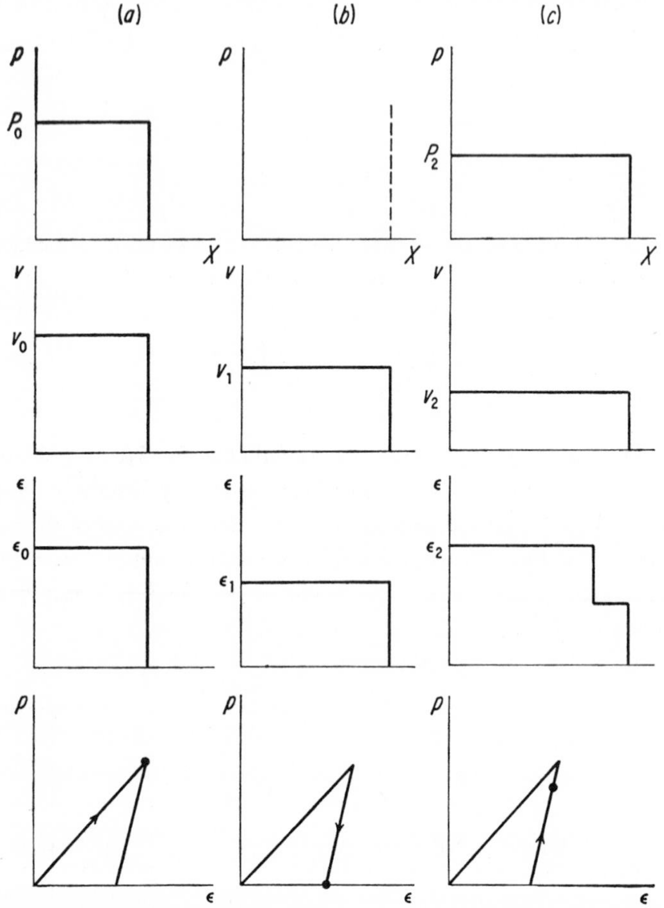

FIGURE 15.9 Distribution of pressure, velocity, and strain during a loading-unloading-reloading sequence.

To make the problem a little less trivial, let us suppose that upon unloading the Young's modulus, $\bar{E}$, is larger than the Young's modulus in loading, E. Correspondingly, unloading waves will travel with a speed $\bar{c} = (\bar{E}/\rho_0)^{1/2}$ that is greater than the speed of loading waves, c. In a way these assumptions take us outside of elasticity theory, but that is unimportant, because we only wish to illustrate the application of (b).

As before, we consider a semi-infinite bar subjected to a pressure pulse of magnitude p_0 and duration 2τ. The loading wave imparts to the material a strain $\varepsilon_0 = p_0/E$ and a velocity $v_0 = p_0/\rho_0 c$. At $t = 2\tau$ an unloading wave starts from the left end, and overtakes the loading wave (Figure 15.9b) at the instant $t = 2\tau\bar{c}/(\bar{c} - c)$. The unloading wave leaves behind a residual velocity v_1 and a residual strain given by $v_1 = v_0 - p_0/\rho_0\bar{c} = v_0(1 - c/\bar{c})$, $\varepsilon_1 = \varepsilon_0 - p_0/\bar{E} = \varepsilon_0(1 - c^2/\bar{c}^2)$.

From the point where the unloading wave overtakes the loading wave a weakened loading wave continues to move to the right with the velocity c (because it moves into unstrained material), and a reloading wave of the same strength begins to move to the left with the velocity $\bar{c}$. The strength p_2 of these waves is determined from the continuity condition for the particle velocity in the wake of these two waves. The loading wave imparts a velocity $v_2 = p_2/\rho_0 c$ to the material, whereas the reloading wave, moving into a region having the particle velocity v_1, changes this velocity to v_2, $v_2 = v_1 - p_2/\rho_0\bar{c}$. Equating these expressions, we find that $p_2 = p_0(1 - c/\bar{c})/(1 + c/\bar{c})$, and $v_2 = v_0(1 - c/\bar{c})/(1 + c/\bar{c})$. The weakened loading wave imparts a strain $p_2/E = \varepsilon_0(1 - c/\bar{c})/(1 + c/\bar{c})$ to the material, whereas the reloading wave adds an increment of strain $p_2/\bar{E} = \varepsilon_0(c^2/\bar{c}^2)(1 - c/\bar{c})/(1 + c/\bar{c})$ to the residual strain ε_1. When the reloading wave has reached the left end of the bar, the distributions of pressure, velocity, and strain are as shown in Figure 15.9c, and the steps of the preceding calculation can be repeated. It will then be found that, every time the unloading wave overtakes the loading wave, the velocity and pressure are decreased by the factor $K = (1 - c/\bar{c})/(1 + c/\bar{c})$.† The distribution of the residual strains will resemble a stairway-function; moreover, because a reloading wave is reflected at the left end as an unloading wave of the same strength, the subsequent reloading-unloading cycles will not affect the distribution of residual strains in the wake of the loading wave (although a new "step" in the distribution curve is created every time that unloading wave overtakes the loading wave).

A disturbance of the form $u = A \sin \omega[t - (X/c)]$ is said to be a sinusoidal progressive wave with the amplitude A, angular frequency ω, and phase velocity c. The distance between two stations differing in phase by 2π is the wave length λ. Thus from $2\pi + \omega[t - (X/c)] = \omega\{t - [(X - \lambda)/c]\}$ it follows that $\omega/c = 2\pi/\lambda = k$, where k is called the *wave number*. A constant phase of the oscillation is described by $\omega\{[R(t)/c] - t\} = \text{const.}$, where $X = R(t)$ is the locus of that phase. Consequently, $\dot{R} = c$ is the (constant) speed of propagation of a phase. The phase velocity, and the velocities of particles (e.g. $v = \dot{w} = A\omega \sin \omega[t - (X/c)]$) set in motion by the wave, are of course quite different things. The particles oscillate about their equilibrium positions, hence their velocities too are sinusoidal in time.

Plane waves may be represented as the real parts of expressions of the type $\mathbf{u} = \mathbf{a}\Delta$, where $\mathbf{a} = \boldsymbol{\alpha} + i\boldsymbol{\beta}$ is a complex amplitude, and $\Delta = \exp[i\omega(\mathbf{s}\cdot\mathbf{x}$

† Taylor [161].

$- t)]$. Here $\mathbf{s} = \mathbf{n}/c$ is a *slowness vector*, pointing in the direction of propagation, $\mathbf{n}$. If $\boldsymbol{\alpha}$ and $\boldsymbol{\beta}$ are parallel, then the wave is linearly polarized; if $\boldsymbol{\alpha}$ and $\boldsymbol{\beta}$ are equal in magnitude but perpendicular in direction, then the wave is circularly polarized. In the other cases the polarization is elliptical. Then the real part of $\mathbf{u}$ may be expressed as follows, $u_x = \alpha_x \cos\phi - \beta_x \sin\phi$, $u_y = \alpha_y \cos\phi - \beta_y \sin\phi$, where $\cos\phi$ is the real part of Δ, and the xy plane is perpendicular to $\mathbf{n}$. To locate the semi-axes b_1, b_2 of the ellipse, we consider

$$\frac{d}{d\phi}(u_x^2 + u_y^2) = 0,$$

obtaining $\tan 2\phi = -2\boldsymbol{\alpha}\cdot\boldsymbol{\beta}/(\boldsymbol{\alpha}\cdot\boldsymbol{\alpha} - \boldsymbol{\beta}\cdot\boldsymbol{\beta})$. Substituting this into $u_x^2 + u_y^2$, we arrive at

$$b_1^2,\ b_2^2 = \frac{1}{2}\mathbf{a}\cdot\mathbf{a}^* \pm \frac{1}{2}\{(\mathbf{a}\cdot\mathbf{a})(\mathbf{a}^*\cdot\mathbf{a}^*)\}^{1/2},$$

where $\mathbf{a}^* = \boldsymbol{\alpha} - i\boldsymbol{\beta}$. For a linearly polarized wave $\boldsymbol{\beta} = m\boldsymbol{\alpha}$, so that $b_2^2 = 0$, $b_1^2 = (1 + m^2)\boldsymbol{\alpha}\cdot\boldsymbol{\alpha}$. There is no loss of generality if we set $m = 0$ (this amounts to choosing a particular phase of the wave), so that we may characterize plane waves by

$$u_k = A_k \exp[i\omega(\mathbf{s}\cdot\mathbf{x} - t)], \tag{15.103}$$

where the amplitude vector A_k is now real.

Let us now investigate the variation of $\mathbf{s}$ with $\mathbf{n}$. The propagation of waves is influenced both by the boundary conditions and the material properties. So as to isolate the influence of the latter, we consider waves in an unbounded medium. In small deformation theory no distinction need be made between the independent variables $\mathbf{x}$ and $\mathbf{X}$; thus from $T_{ij,j} = \rho\ddot{u}_i$ we obtain the displacement equations of motion:

$$C_{ijkm}u_{k,mj} = \rho\partial_t^2 u_i. \tag{15.104}$$

Next, substituting (15.103) into (15.104), we arrive at a linear system of equations for the amplitudes A_k:

$$M_{ik}A_k = 0, \qquad M_{ik} = \rho\delta_{ik} - C_{ijkm}s_j s_m. \tag{15.105}$$

The existence of nontrivial solutions A_k now requires that $D(\mathbf{s}) \equiv \det\mathbf{M} = 0$. The linear system (15.105) determines only the ratios of the amplitudes; the actual magnitudes of A_k have no effect on $c(\mathbf{n})$.

An equivalent set of equations is obtained as follows. We define the *acoustic tensor* $\mathbf{Q}(\mathbf{n})$ by

$$Q_{ik}(\mathbf{n}) = C_{jikm} n_j n_m. \tag{15.106}$$

Then, by (15.105),

$$Q_{ik}(\mathbf{n}) A_k = \rho c^2(\mathbf{n}) A_i, \tag{15.105*}$$

i.e. the squared speed of propagation in the direction of $\mathbf{n}$ is, except for the factor ρ, a principal value of the acoustic tensor. The amplitude vector $\mathbf{A}$ is, except for a normalization factor, the principal vector associated with $c(\mathbf{n})$. The axis of $\mathbf{A}$ is said to be an acoustic axis.

In the isotropic case, $Q_{ik}(\mathbf{n}) = (\lambda + \mu) n_i n_k + \mu \delta_{ik}$, and, by (15.105)* $\rho c^2 A_i = \mu A_i + (\lambda + \mu) n_i \mathbf{A} \cdot \mathbf{n}$. If the wave is *longitudinal*, then $\mathbf{A} = m\mathbf{n}$, where m is a constant, from which it follows that $c^2 = c_L^2 = (\lambda + 2\mu)/\rho$. *Transverse waves* are defined by $\mathbf{A} \cdot \mathbf{n} = 0$, in which case $c^2 = c_T^2 = \mu/\rho$. Evidently isotropic media permit longitudinal and transverse waves to propagate in any direction $\mathbf{n}$. This is not so in anisotropic media.

It is easy to see that transverse waves correspond to isochoric (or, shearing motions), whereas longitudinal waves correspond to dilatational ("distortionless") motions. An isochoric motion obeys $\operatorname{div}\mathbf{u} = 0$, so that, by (15.103), $\operatorname{div}\mathbf{u} = \partial_k A_k \exp[i\omega(s_i x_i - t)] = (i\omega/c) A_k n_k \exp[i\omega(\mathbf{s} \cdot \mathbf{x} - t)] = 0$ requires that $\mathbf{A} \cdot \mathbf{n} = 0$. Similarly, from $\operatorname{curl}\mathbf{u} = \mathbf{0}$ we find that $\mathbf{A} = m\mathbf{n}$.

From (15.105)* it follows that $\rho c^2 = Q_{ik}(\mathbf{n}) A_i A_k / |\mathbf{A}|^2$, so that the wave speeds are real if the symmetric part of $\mathbf{Q}(\mathbf{n})$ is a positive tensor, or, equivalently, if C_{ijkm} satisfy the *strong-ellipticity condition*

$$C_{ijkm} A_i n_j A_k n_m > 0, \tag{15.107}$$

where $\mathbf{n}$ and $\mathbf{A}$ are arbitrary vectors. This condition is certainly satisfied if a strain-energy function exists and is positive definite, i.e. C_{ijkm} satisfy the *strong convexity condition*

$$C_{ijkm} \mu_{ij} \mu_{km} > 0, \tag{15.108}$$

where $\boldsymbol{\mu}$ is any tensor (because we shall be concerned with oscillations, C_{ijkm} must be interpreted as the isentropic elastic coefficients). To see that (15.108) implies (15.107), we let $\mu_{ij} = A_i n_j$; the converse is not true, because $A_i n_j$ cannot represent a *general* second rank tensor. In the isotropic case (15.108) is given by $\mu > 0$, $3\lambda + 2\mu > 0$, whereas (15.107) is given by $\mu > 0$, $\lambda + 2\mu > 0$.

In what follows we shall assume that (15.108) is satisfied thus ensuring that the characteristic equation $\det(\rho c^2\delta_{ik} - C_{ijkm}n_jn_m) = 0$ has three real, positive roots c_1, c_2, and c_3.

The equation $D(\mathbf{s}) = 0$ defines a sixth-degree surface S, called the *slowness surface*, in the space of coordinates s_1, s_2, s_3. A ray drawn from the origin, and in the direction of $\mathbf{n}$, will intersect S at three points, at distances $1/c_1$, $1/c_2$ and $1/c_3$ from the origin, where c_1, c_2, c_3 are the speeds of propagation in the direction of $\mathbf{n}$. The *velocity surface* is constructed by laying off the distances c_1, c_2, c_3 from the origin.

Rather than solving the characteristic equation directly, we can proceed as follows.† Because principal values are also *extremal values* we consider $\mathbf{Q}(\mathbf{B}, \mathbf{n}) \equiv C_{ijkm}B_in_jB_kn_m$, where $\mathbf{B}$ is an arbitrary unit vector. The vectors $\mathbf{B}$ for which $\mathbf{Q}$ has stationary values are then found from

$$\frac{\partial}{\partial B_p}[C_{ijkm}B_in_jB_kn_m - \phi(B_kB_k - 1)] = 0$$

(cf. (4.49)), where ϕ is the Lagrange's multiplier associated with the condition $B_kB_k = 1$. We get $C_{ijkm}n_jn_mB_k = \phi B_i$, i.e. $\phi = C_{ijkm}B_in_jB_kn_m$ is in fact the stationary value of $\mathbf{Q}(\mathbf{B}, \mathbf{n})$. A comparison of this with (15.105)* now shows that, as was to be expected, the stationary values $\mathbf{Q}(\mathbf{B}, \mathbf{n})$ are given by ρc_1^2, ρc_2^2, ρc_3^2, and that the corresponding vector $\mathbf{B}$ is in the direction of the amplitude vector $\mathbf{A}$.

For transverse isotropy,

$$\mathbf{Q}(\mathbf{B}, \mathbf{n}) = \mu + \beta(\mathbf{h}\cdot\mathbf{n})^2 + (\lambda + \mu)(\mathbf{B}\cdot\mathbf{n})^2 + [\beta + \gamma(\mathbf{h}\cdot\mathbf{n})^2](\mathbf{B}\cdot\mathbf{h})^2 + 2(\alpha + \beta)(\mathbf{h}\cdot\mathbf{n})(\mathbf{B}\cdot\mathbf{h})(\mathbf{B}\cdot\mathbf{n}). \quad (15.109)$$

It is readily seen that one of the stationary values is obtained by letting $\mathbf{B}$ be orthogonal to $\mathbf{h}$ and $\mathbf{n}$; we get $\rho c_1^2 = \mu + \beta(\mathbf{h}\cdot\mathbf{n})^2$. In the space of coordinates $s_i = n_i/c_1$, we have that $r^2 = s_is_i = 1/c_1^2$, so that the first sheet of the slowness surface is given by $\rho = r^2(\mu + \beta\cos^2\theta)$, where $\cos\theta = \mathbf{h}\cdot\mathbf{n}$. This equation describes a spheroid; namely, the curves $\theta =$ const. are the circles $r =$ const., whereas letting $r = x$, $r\cos\theta = z$ we obtain the ellipsoid $\mu x^2 + \beta z^2 = \rho$. All transverse waves in planes normal to $\mathbf{h}$ propagate with the speed c_1. In isotropic bodies (i.e. when $\alpha = \beta = \gamma = 0$) the spheroid reduces to the sphere $r^2 = 1/c_1^2 = \rho/\mu$, c_1 being the speed of propagation of shear waves.

To determine the remainder of the slowness surface, we let‡ $\mathbf{B} = H\mathbf{h} + N\mathbf{n}$,

† Here we follow Synge [160].
‡ Note that a wave with amplitude in the direction of $\mathbf{B}$ is neither longitudinal nor transverse.

where H and N are constants. Then $\mathbf{B} \cdot \mathbf{B} = 1$ yields the condition $H^2 + N^2 + 2HN\mathbf{h} \cdot \mathbf{n} = 1$, and $\mathbf{B} \cdot \mathbf{n} = H\mathbf{h} \cdot \mathbf{n} + N$, $\mathbf{B} \cdot \mathbf{h} = H + N\mathbf{h} \cdot \mathbf{n}$, $\mathbf{Q}(\mathbf{B}, \mathbf{n}) = \mu + \beta(\mathbf{h} \cdot \mathbf{n})^2 + KH^2 + 2LHN + MN^2$, where

$$K = (\lambda + \mu)(\mathbf{h} \cdot \mathbf{n})^2 + [\beta + \gamma(\mathbf{h} \cdot \mathbf{n})^2] + 2(\alpha + \beta)(\mathbf{h} \cdot \mathbf{n})^2,$$

$$L = (\lambda + \mu)\mathbf{h} \cdot \mathbf{n} + [\beta + \gamma(\mathbf{h} \cdot \mathbf{n})^2]\mathbf{h} \cdot \mathbf{n} + (\alpha + \beta)\mathbf{h} \cdot \mathbf{n}[1 + (\mathbf{h} \cdot \mathbf{n})^2],$$

$$M = (\lambda + \mu) + [\beta + \gamma(\mathbf{h} \cdot \mathbf{n})^2](\mathbf{h} \cdot \mathbf{n})^2 + 2(\alpha + \beta)(\mathbf{h} \cdot \mathbf{n})^2.$$

The values of $\mathbf{B}$ which make $\mathbf{Q}(\mathbf{B}, \mathbf{n})$ stationary are found from

$$\frac{\partial}{\partial H} [\mathbf{Q}(\mathbf{B}, \mathbf{n}) - \psi(H^2 + N^2 + 2HN\mathbf{h} \cdot \mathbf{n} - 1)] = 0,$$

$$\frac{\partial}{\partial N} [\mathbf{Q}(\mathbf{B}, \mathbf{n}) - \psi(H^2 + N^2 + 2HN\mathbf{h} \cdot \mathbf{n} - 1)] = 0,$$

where ψ is a Lagrange's multiplier. Carrying out the indicated differentiations, we arrive at $KH + LN = \psi(H + N\mathbf{h} \cdot \mathbf{n})$, $LH + MN = \psi(H\mathbf{h} \cdot \mathbf{n} + N)$. If we multiply the first by H and the second by N, and take into account $H^2 + N^2 + 2HN\mathbf{h} \cdot \mathbf{n} = 1$, then it follows that

$$\psi = \rho c^2 - \mu - \beta(\mathbf{h} \cdot \mathbf{n})^2.$$

Further, the existence of nontrivial solutions for H and N requires that the determinant of the coefficients vanish:

$$\psi^2 \sin^2\theta - \psi(K + M - 2L \cos \theta) + (KM - L^2) = 0, \qquad (15.110)$$

where $\cos \theta = \mathbf{h} \cdot \mathbf{n}$. This equation, together with the preceding one, defines the remainder of the slowness surface. For isotropy,

$$K = (\lambda + \mu) \cos^2\theta, \quad L = (\lambda + \mu) \cos \theta, \quad M = \lambda + \mu,$$

$$KM = L^2 = 0, \quad K + M - 2L \cos \theta = (\lambda + \mu) \sin^2\theta,$$

so that the solutions of (15.110) are $\psi = 0$ or $\psi = \lambda + \mu$. The surface defined by (15.110) then reduces to two spheres, $r^2 = 1/c_2^2 = \rho/\mu$, and $r^2 = 1/c_3^2 = \rho/(\lambda + 2\mu)$, corresponding to the propagation of shear waves and dilatational waves, respectively.

These results point out a curious degeneracy of the isotropic response: the speed of propagation of shear waves, $c = \sqrt{\mu/\rho}$, is a double-root of the characteristic equation. In anisotropic media, however, there exist two distinct shear waves with mutually perpendicular amplitude vectors.

Singular solutions, inhomogeneity, interaction of elastic singularities

In what follows we shall extend the method of potential theory, as outlined in Appendix I, to the theory of linear, isotropic elasticity. Let $\mathscr{E}$ be the entire space and $R = |\mathbf{x} - \boldsymbol{\xi}|$ the distance between a "source point" $\boldsymbol{\xi}$ and a "field point" $\mathbf{x}$. Then the basic singular solution (the *Green's function*) of $\nabla^2 U = 0$ is $1/R$. We may also interpret $1/R$ as the solution of $\nabla^2 U + 4\pi\delta(\mathbf{x} - \boldsymbol{\xi}) = 0$, where the *Dirac's delta function* $\delta(\mathbf{x} - \boldsymbol{\xi})$ describes a point source. The same ideas can be applied to the displacement function method of elasticity theory. The counterpart of ∇^2 is then $D_{ik} = C_{ijkm}\partial_j\partial_m$; because the isotropic coefficients are given by $C_{ijkm} = \lambda\delta_{ij}\delta_{km} + \mu(\delta_{ik}\delta_{jm} + \delta_{im}\delta_{jk})$, it follows that $D_{ik} = \mu\delta_{ik}\nabla^2 + (\lambda + \mu)\partial_i\partial_k$, and thus $D_{ik}u_k + \rho b_i = 0$ reproduces the displacement equations of equilibrium, (15.67).

We now seek singular solutions of $D_{ik}u_k = 0$; again, rather than assuming that body forces are absent, but the solution must have a singular point, we may introduce a body force that is a multiple of the Dirac's delta function (a concentrated force!). By substitution, it is easy to verify that the *Kelvin–Somigliana tensor* U_{kj}, defined by

$$4\pi\mu U_{kj} = \frac{1}{R}\delta_{kj} - \frac{1}{4(1-\nu)}R_{,kj}, \tag{15.111}$$

satisfies $D_{ik}U_{kj} = 0$. Evidently $U_{kj} = U_{jk}$; moreover, U_{kj} become infinite as $1/R$ at the source point, i.e. when $R = 0$. The dimension of U_{kj} is length per force, which means that in a superposition formula $u_i = U_{ij}F_j$ the coefficients F_j should have the dimension of force (we also note the obvious extensions $u_i = U_{ij,k}F_{jk}$, $u_i = U_{ij,km}F_{jkm}$, etc., where F_{jk}, F_{jkm} are force dipoles and quadrupoles, respectively). For a fixed index j, the functions U_{jk} are said to define the *Kelvin state* S_j: $(\mathbf{u}_j, \mathbf{T}_j)$. The stresses T_{mkj}, calculated from Hooke's law, are given by

$$T_{kmj} = c\left[2\mu\delta_{km}\partial_j\frac{1}{R} + 2(1-\nu)\delta_{kj}\partial_m\frac{1}{R} + 2(1-\nu)\delta_{mj}\partial_k\frac{1}{R} - \partial_k\partial_m\partial_j R\right],$$

$$c = \frac{1}{8\pi(1-\nu)}. \tag{15.112}$$

It is easy to verify that S_j has the following properties:

(1) Except at the origin, $R = 0$, S_j is a regular solution in $\mathscr{E}$, corresponding to $\mathbf{b} = \mathbf{0}$. In particular, $\mathbf{u} = O(R^{-1})$, $\mathbf{T} = O(R^{-2})$ as $R \to \infty$.

(2) If Σ is any closed surface surrounding the origin, and $\mathbf{t}_j$ is the surface traction of S_j on that side of Σ which faces the origin, then

$$\int_{\Sigma} \mathbf{t}_j \, da = \mathbf{e}_j. \tag{15.113}$$

(3) $\mathbf{T} = O(R^{-2})$ as $R \to 0$.

That is, U_{kj} is the kth component of the displacement at $\mathbf{x}$, produced by a concentrated unit force located at $\boldsymbol{\xi}$ and acting in the direction of $\mathbf{e}_j$. It can be shown that the properties (1), (2), (3) determine Kelvin's solution uniquely.† The interesting fact here is that unless the order of the singularity is prescribed, e.g. $\mathbf{T} = O(R^{-2})$ as $R \to 0$, one cannot make the solution unique because other, self-equilibrated singular solutions of a higher order are not excluded.

To construct the Kelvin states directly, we may consider a sequence of regions V_K converging to some fixed point. With each region we associate a body force field $\mathbf{b}_K$ such that $\mathbf{b}_K = \mathbf{0}$ outside of V_K, and $V_K[\rho \mathbf{b}_K] = \mathbf{L} = \text{const.}$ The requisite displacement potentials ϕ and $\boldsymbol{\psi}$ are given by (15.69). Subject to the conditions that the body forces are bounded and sufficiently smooth, the limiting solution for $V_K \to 0$ is independent of the particular choice of the body force fields, and is given by $\phi = 0$, $\boldsymbol{\psi} = -c\mathbf{L}/R$.

For later reference we record here the explicit description of S_z (r, θ, ϕ are spherical coordinates based at the singularity):

$$\phi = 0, \quad \boldsymbol{\psi} = -\mathbf{e}_z \frac{c}{r}, \quad u_\phi = 0, \quad T_{r\phi} = T_{\theta\phi} = 0,$$

$$2\mu u_r = 4(1 - \nu)c\,\frac{\cos\theta}{r}, \quad 2\mu u_\theta = -(3 - 4\nu)c\,\frac{\sin\theta}{r}, \tag{15.114}$$

$$T_{r\theta} = (1 - 2\nu)c\,\frac{\sin\theta}{r^2}, \qquad T_{rr} = -2(2 - \nu)c\,\frac{\cos\theta}{r^2},$$

$$T_{\theta\theta} = T_{\phi\phi} = (1 - 2\nu)c\,\frac{\cos\theta}{r^2}.$$

Evidently the singularity cannot be inside the material medium. Rather, we suppose that a small material neighborhood containing the singular point is removed. This introduces, in effect, a new boundary Σ. According to the principle of Saint-Venant, at a distance which is large compared to the radius of Σ it is unimportant how the resultant force $\mathbf{e}_z$ is distributed over Σ.

If S is a solution of the fundamental system, we can construct derived

† Sternberg and Eubanks [155].

solutions through differentiation; formally, $S_m \equiv S_{,m}$. Moreover, if S is generated by the displacement potentials ϕ and $\boldsymbol{\psi}$, then S_m is generated by

$$\phi_m = \phi_{,m} + \psi_m, \qquad \psi_{im} = \psi_{i,m}. \tag{15.115}$$

This follows by differentiating (15.68): $2\mu u_{i,m} = \phi_{,im} + \psi_{i,m} + \psi_{m,i} + x_k\psi_{k,im} - 4(1 - \nu)\psi_{i,m} = (\phi_{,m} + \psi_m)_{,i} + (x_k\psi_{k,m})_{,i} - 4(1 - \nu)\psi_{i,m}$. In particular, from the Kelvin's solution S_i we may construct the *doublet states* $S_{im} = S_{i,m}$. For these states the following terminology is used:

$i = m$... double-force without moment, in the direction $\mathbf{e}_i$

$i \neq m$... double-force in the direction of $\mathbf{e}_i$, with a moment about an axis forming a right-handed triad with the axes of $\mathbf{e}_m$ and $\mathbf{e}_i$.

We note that there is no reason why the doublet states should be symmetric in the labels i and m. The construction of typical doublet states is illustrated in Figure 15.10.

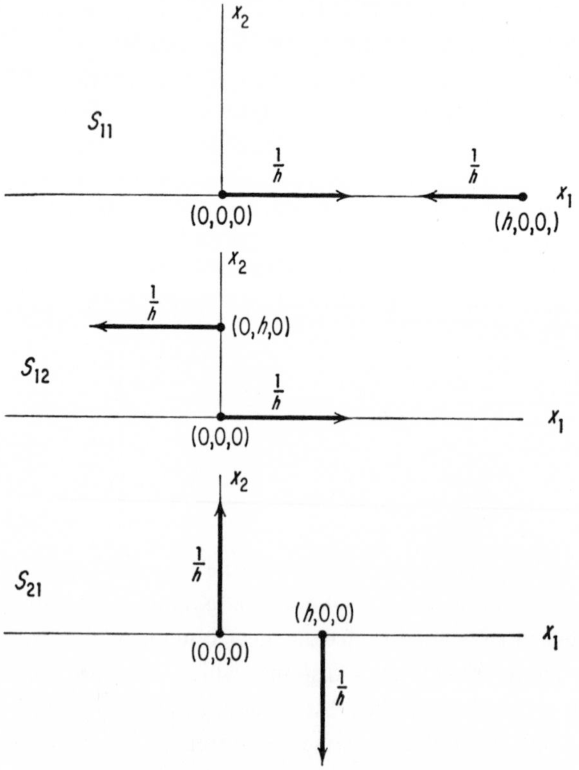

Figure 15.10 Construction of doublet states $S_{i,m}$.

The doublet states S_{im} have the following properties: $\mathbf{u} = O(r^{-2})$, $\mathbf{T} = O(r^{-3})$ as $r \to \infty$, $\mathbf{T} = O(r^{-3})$ as $r \to 0$, and

$$\mathbf{e}_k \cdot \int_\Sigma \mathbf{x} \times \mathbf{t}_{im}\, da = -\varepsilon_{kim},$$

where Σ is a closed surface surrounding the origin, and $\mathbf{t}_{im}$ is a stress vector on the side of Σ facing the origin. Because there are several doublet states, the foregoing properties do *not* define a particular doublet state uniquely.

A further doublet state is the "center of compression", S_0, defined by $S_0 = S_{11} + S_{22} + S_{33}$. Using (15.111), it can be shown that the representation of S_0 is given by

$$\phi = 2(1 - 2\nu)\frac{c}{r}, \quad \boldsymbol{\psi} = \mathbf{0}, \quad \mu u r = -c(1 - 2\nu)r^{-2}, \quad u_\theta = u_\phi = 0,$$
$$T_{rr} = 4c(1 - 2\nu)r^{-3}, \quad T_{\theta\theta} = T_{\phi\phi} = -\frac{1}{2}T_{rr}, \quad T_{r\theta} = T_{r\phi} = 0. \tag{15.116}$$

From centers of compression we can construct, in turn, other singular solutions, e.g. by distributing centers of compression along line segments. In particular, a "half-line of compression," S^z, is defined by

$$S^z(P) = \int_0^\infty S_0(P, \zeta)\, d\zeta,$$

where $S_0(P, \zeta)$ is the state at a point P due to a center of compression at the point $x = y = 0$, $z = -\zeta$. A straightforward integration of (15.116) now yields

$$S^z : \phi = \log(r + z), \qquad \boldsymbol{\psi} = \mathbf{0}. \tag{15.117}$$

Combining (15.117) with the Kelvin state S_z (cf. (15.114)), it is possible to obtain *Boussinesq's solution*, B, for a half-space subjected to a normal, concentrated force at the origin:

$$B = 4(1 - \nu)S_z - \frac{1}{2\pi}(1 - 2\nu)S^z. \tag{15.118}$$

Boussinesq's solution, together with the method of superposition, can be used to solve any problem involving normal tractions on the plane bounding a half-space.

To derive the counterpart of Green's fourth identity, (A.7), we take a region V and apply Betti's reciprocal theorem to states u_i and U_{ij}. The field point $\mathbf{x}$ at which u_i are to be evaluated is also taken as the singularity of U_{ij}, thus $U_{ij}(R)$, $R = |\mathbf{x} - \boldsymbol{\xi}|$. To make the volume integrals of U_{ij} proper, we exclude from V a spherical neighborhood of $\mathbf{x}$, the boundary of which is denoted by Σ. Then U_{ij} are well behaved in the region V^+ with the boundary $\partial V^+ = \partial V + \Sigma$. According to (15.55), $V^+[\rho b_i U_{ij}] + \partial V^+[t_i U_{ij}] = \partial V^+[t_{ij} u_i]$, where t_{ij} are the surface tractions produced by S_j. Because $da = R^2 \sin\theta\, d\theta\, d\phi$, it follows that $\Sigma[t_i U_{ij}] \to 0$ as $\Sigma \to \mathbf{x}$. To evaluate the limit of $\Sigma[T_{ij} u_i]$, we let $n_m = -\partial_m R$, $t_{kj} = T_{mkj} n_m$, so that, by (15.112), $t_{ij} = cR^{-2}[2(1 - \nu)\delta_{ij} + 3(n_i n_j - \frac{1}{3}\delta_{ij})]$. In $\Sigma[t_{ij} u_j]$, we may choose Σ small enough to permit a Taylor series expansion of u_i about $\mathbf{x}$. It is then easy to see that only the term $u_i(\mathbf{x})$ of the series will contribute to the integral as $\Sigma \to \mathbf{x}$. Similarly, it may be verified that $\Sigma[R^{-2}(n_i n_j - \frac{1}{3}\delta_{ij})] = 0$, thus $\Sigma[t_{ij} u_j] \to u_i(\mathbf{x})$. In this way we obtain the *formulas of Somigliana*,

$$u_i = V[\rho b_j U_{ij}] + \partial V[t_i U_{ij}] - \partial V[t_{ij} u_i] \tag{15.119}$$

(cf. (A.7)). These formulas permit us to calculate u_i everywhere if the boundary values of u_i and t_i are given. As indicated by the uniqueness theorem, however, it should be enough to know the boundary values of u_i alone, or of t_i alone. This means that U_{ij} must be replaced by a Green's tensor $G_{ij} = U_{ij} + U'_{ij}$, in which U'_{ij} are regular solutions in V, and on ∂V satisfy either $U_{ij} + U'_{ij} = 0$ or $t_{ij} + t'_{ij} = 0$. In this way the determination of u_i is reduced to what may be a simpler problem of finding U'_{ij}.

The singularities that arise naturally in the displacement function method are (concentrated) forces, force doublets, and so on. The stress function method shows us the other face of elasticity theory: here the basic singularities are "concentrated incompatibilities" (cf. $\nabla^4\bar{\mathbf{G}} = \boldsymbol{\eta}$!), namely dislocation lines.

To see that dislocation lines cannot end in the interior of a body, we only need to recall

$$\alpha_{km,k} = 0, \tag{15.32)R}$$

or else consider $\mathrm{Ink}\tilde{\mathbf{E}} = \boldsymbol{\eta}$, thus $\mathrm{div}\boldsymbol{\eta} = 0$. Let us suppose that the dislocation density is concentrated inside a cylindrical tube centered on a space curve C: $\xi_i = \xi_i(s)$. We have in mind the case where the cross-sectional area A is constant and very small. Therefore, let us also suppose that the dislocation lines are normal to the cross section; then $\alpha_{ij} = \sigma_i b_j$, where $\sigma_i = d\xi_i/ds$ denotes the unit tangent vectors of the center line, and b_j stands for the density of Burgers vectors. Evidently $\alpha_{ij}\sigma_i = b_j$, whereas $\alpha_{ij} n_i = 0$ for any vector $\mathbf{n}$ satisfying $\mathbf{n} \cdot \boldsymbol{\sigma} = 0$. Let V be a portion of the tube set off by two cross sections A_1 and A_2. Starting from (15.32), and applying the divergence theorem, we obtain $V[\alpha_{ij,i}] = 0 = \partial V[\sigma_i n_i b_j] = A_1[b_j] - A_2[b_j]$, because $\mathbf{n} \cdot \boldsymbol{\sigma} = 0$ on the mantle. This means that *the resultant Burgers vector is conserved*:

$$B_j = \int_A b_j \, dA = \text{const.}$$

Now let y_{ij} be the right-curl of the dislocation density: $y_{ij} = \alpha_{im}\varepsilon_{mkj}\partial_k$. Then, by (15.33), η_{ij} is the symmetric part of y_{ij}. Correspondingly, we let G_{ij} be the symmetric part of a tensor X_{ij} defined by $\nabla^4 X_{ij} = y_{ij}$ (cf. $(15.78)_1$). According to (A.22), the solution for a single dislocation line is given by

$$8\pi X_{ij} = -\int_C R\varepsilon_{mkj}\bar{\partial}_k\alpha_{im}\, ds,$$

where $R = |\mathbf{x} - \boldsymbol{\xi}|$, and $\bar{\partial}_k = \partial/\partial\xi_k$. Integrating by parts, and noting that $B_j = \text{const.}$, $\bar{\partial}_k R = -\partial_k R$, we obtain *Kroener's formula*,

$$\mathbf{G} = \mathbf{X}^S, \qquad 8\pi X_{ij} = B_m\varepsilon_{mjk}\partial_k \int_C R\, d\xi_i. \tag{15.120}$$

A particular case in which (15.120) can be integrated in a closed form is the straight dislocation line $\xi = \eta = 0$, $\zeta = \zeta(s)$. For an edge dislocation (i.e. when $B_3 = 0$), the stresses can then be found from the Airy function $F = -A\partial_2\rho^2 \log \rho$, $A = \mu B/4\pi(1 - \nu)$.† Solutions of this form have their uses in conventional boundary value problems too. For instance, let us consider a cylinder in which the material between two neighboring meridional planes has been removed. If the cylinder is closed, and the faces bonded together, then a state of self-stress will be induced. Moreover, the displacement u_ϕ will be discontinuous at the junction, because the contact faces were separated by a gap before the deformation, thus $u_\phi = \text{const.}\ \rho\phi$.

For a screw dislocation $\mathbf{B} = \mathbf{e}_3 B$ we obtain from (15.120) that

$$u_1 = u_2 = 0, \qquad u_3 = \frac{B\phi}{2\pi}. \tag{15.121}$$

If the dislocation line is moving in the x direction with a uniform speed V, then the appropriate solution is

$$u_1 = u_2 = 0, \qquad u_3 = \left(\frac{B}{2\pi}\right)\tan^{-1}\frac{By}{x - Vt}, \tag{15.122}$$

† Cf. [84], p. 74.

where $\beta^2 = 1 - V^2/c^2$, and $c^2 = \mu/\rho$ is the squared speed of shear waves. The resemblance of this formula to Lorentz transformations (cf. (13.10)) suggests that, in this case, c is an intrinsic signal speed.

We shall conclude the presentation of linear elasticity theory with a few applications that are motivated by the problems of solid state physics. In this field there is available a vast amount of information about the microstructure of materials. However, very little of this information has been expressed in terms of field-theoretic concepts, and that modest beginning has been largely modeled on the linear theory of elasticity. Although it is clear that the linear theory of elasticity is too special, and limited, to provide the basic laws from which the collective behavior of various "lattice imperfections" could be deduced,† it can be useful nevertheless in predicting the long-range effects of dislocations, lattice, vacancies, interstitial atoms, and the like. In any case, solid state physics has created a fresh outlook and interest in some classical problems of elasticity.‡

In the discussion that follows we shall draw mainly upon Eshelby's investigations of forces on elastic singularities [225]. By "force" we shall mean a gradient of the type defined in (15.86). As was noted previously, these forces are not "real" in the sense that they are no more than a way of characterizing the dependence of some potential energy upon parameters that may specify the positions of dislocations, inhomogeneities, and so on. As in thermostatics, each comparison state will be an equilibrium configuration, i.e. each stress field T_{ij} will satisfy $T_{ij,i} = 0$; therefore, invoking the divergence theorem, we can conclude that each region V of a body will be in equilibrium: $V[T_{ij,i}] = 0 = \partial V[t_i]$. Thus a "force" defined by (15.86) is only a measure of the energy available for the actual (as a rule, inelastic) process connecting the comparison states.

As the first example let us take a body in a state of initial stress, T^I_{ij}. We assume that the initial stress is induced solely by a distribution of singularities, i.e. the boundary ∂V of the body is free of surface tractions: $T^I_{ij}n_j = t^I_i = 0$ on ∂V. In general, it will not be possible to express the initial strains $\tilde{E}^I_{ij}$ as gradients of a displacement field. However, we can extract a compatible part by letting $T^I_{ij} = T^\infty_{ij} + \bar{T}_{ij}$, $\tilde{E}^I_{ij} = E^\infty_{ij} + \bar{E}_{ij}$, where T^∞_{ij}, E^∞_{ij} represent the solution for a body that fills out the entire space. Because $t^\infty_i = T^\infty_{ji}n_j$ will not vanish on ∂V, the "complementary solution" $\bar{T}_{ij}$, $\bar{E}_{ij}$ must satisfy the boundary conditions $\bar{t}_i = -t^\infty_i$ on ∂V. Moreover, because $\bar{E}_{ij}$ are strains produced by surface loading, they will be compatible: $\bar{E}_{ij} = \bar{u}_{(i,j)}$. If the

† But note Eshelby's apt remark that such a theory "suffers from the disadvantage that its limitations are more immediately obvious than are those of other approximate methods" ([225], p. 80).

‡ Survey of this field, as well as numerous references, may be found in [84], [228], [229].

singularities that give rise to the initial stress are concentrated at a point ξ_i, then T_{ij}^{∞}, E_{ij}^{∞} will be functions of $R = |\mathbf{x} - \boldsymbol{\xi}|$ and gradients of R only. For a distribution of singularities, we may choose a reference point α_i, and let ξ_i be expressed as $\xi_i = \alpha_i + s_i$. Then R can be expanded about α_i: $R(\mathbf{x} - \boldsymbol{\xi}) = R(\mathbf{x} - \boldsymbol{\alpha}) - s_i\partial_i R(\mathbf{x} - \boldsymbol{\alpha}) + \cdots$. A variation of α_i, with s_i held fixed, now amounts to a rigid displacement of the entire distribution of singularities. In this case, the fields T_{ij}^{∞}, E_{ij}^{∞} will vary with $x_i - \alpha_i$ only: $T_{ij}^{\infty} = T_{ij}^{\infty}(\mathbf{x} - \boldsymbol{\alpha})$, $E_{ij}^{\infty} = E_{ij}^{\infty}(\mathbf{x} - \boldsymbol{\alpha})$. In the complementary solution, on the other hand, the dependence of α_i is not restricted in any way: $\bar{T}_{ij} = \bar{T}_{ij}(\mathbf{x}, \boldsymbol{\alpha})$, $\bar{u}_i = \bar{u}_i(\mathbf{x}, \boldsymbol{\alpha})$.

In what follows we shall assume that the sources of self-stress can be enclosed by a surface S lying in V. This assumption is expedient for two reasons. First, it permits us to assume the existence of displacements u_i in the region bounded by ∂V and S,† thus making the definition of $\Phi = E - \partial V[t_i u_i]$ meaningful. Second, it is possible to perform a rigid translation of the entire distribution of sources of self-stress, without these sources coming to the boundary ∂V, or even passing out of the body.

Let us obtain a few lemmas about energies of interaction. We shall assume that a strain-energy function exists, thus $C_{ijkm} = C_{kmij}$. Then, for any states T'_{ij}, E'_{ij} and T''_{ij} E''_{ij}, the identity $T'_{ij}E''_{ij} = T''_{ij}E'_{ij}$ will hold. Further, for any stress T'_{ij} that is equilibrated (thus $T'_{ij,i} = 0$), and any strain field E''_{ij} that is compatible (thus $E''_{ij} = u''_{(i,j)}$), the divergence theorem will convert a volume integral of $T'_{ij}E''_{ij}$ into a surface integral:

$$V[T'_{ij}u''_{i,j}] = \partial V[t'_i u''_i]. \tag{15.123}$$

With these lemmas, and noting that $t_i^I = 0$ on ∂V, we readily obtain

$$E^I = E^{\infty} + \partial V\left[\frac{1}{2}\, t_i^{\infty}\bar{u}_i\right], \qquad E^{\infty} = V\left[\frac{1}{2}\, T_{ij}^{\infty}E_{ij}^{\infty}\right]. \tag{15.124}$$

To ensure the existence of E^I, we must assume that the sources of self-stress are *distributed*, so that T_{ij}^{∞} and E_{ij}^{∞} remain finite everywhere. However, the *variation* of E^I is well defined even in the presence of concentrated singularities. Namely, because T_{ij}^{∞}, E_{ij}^{∞} are functions of $x_i - \alpha_i$ only, we can evaluate $\partial E^{\infty}/\partial\alpha_m$ by holding the singularities fixed, and displacing instead the boundary by $-dx_m$. The strain energies E^{∞} contained in V and in the displaced region V' will then cancel *exactly* on the overlap of V and V', thus leaving only the contribution $-\partial V[n_m W^{\infty}]$.

The superposition of two states T'_{ij}, E'_{ij} and T''_{ij}, E''_{ij} gives rise to a strain

† The displacements may not be one-valued, however.

energy of interaction, $W^* = \frac{1}{2}(T'_{ij}E''_{ij} + T''_{ij}E'_{ij}) = T'_{ij}E''_{ij} = T''_{ij}E'_{ij}$. In particular, let T'_{ij}, E'_{ij} be produced solely by sources of self-stress contained in a region V' (so that in $V'' = V - V'$ the displacements u'_i are defined), and let T''_{ij}, E''_{ij} be produced solely by sources of self-stress contained in the region V'' (so that in V' the displacements u''_i are defined). Then, writing $E^* = V'[T'_{ij}u''_{i,j}] + V''[T''_{ij}u'_{i,j}]$, we obtain

$$E^* = \partial V'[t'_iu''_i - t''_iu'_i]. \tag{15.125}$$

Moreover, with $t'_i = \bar{t}_i + t^\infty_i$, $u'_i = \bar{u}_i + u^\infty_i$, and noting that $\partial V'[n_j(\overline{T}_{ji}u''_i - T''_{ji}\bar{u}_i)] = V'[\overline{T}_{ji}E''_{ij} - T''_{ji}\overline{E}_{ij}] = 0$, we have that

$$E^* = \partial V'[t^\infty_iu''_i - t''_iu^\infty_i]. \tag{15.125)*$$

If, instead, T''_{ij}, E''_{ij} are produced solely by surface tractions $t''_i = T''_{ji}n_j$ acting on ∂V, then $E^* = V[T'_{ij}u''_{i,j}] = \partial V[t'_iu''_i] = 0$, because, by hypothesis, $t'_i = 0$ on ∂V. That is, *there is no strain energy of interaction between loads and sources of self-stress*. In $\Phi = E - \partial V[t_iu_i]$, on the other hand, the term $-\partial V[t''_iu'_i]$ represents a potential energy of interaction.

Because exact solutions of elasticity theory are not easy to come by, it is important that we obtain for the various "forces" representations that require no more information than is actually needed. Thus instead of using T^I_{ij}, u^I_i we may be able to get by with the knowledge of T^∞_{ij}, u^∞_i only (these being, in effect, the definition of a source of self-stress!). To find such "reduced" representations, a good deal of insight and ingenuity is needed.

Anticipating the form of the subsequent results, we introduce

$$P_{jm} = W\delta_{jm} - T_{ij}u_{i,m}, \tag{15.126}$$

referred to by Eshelby as the *Maxwell tensor of elasticity*, and the "force"

$$F_m = \Sigma[n_jP_{jm}], \tag{15.127}$$

where Σ is a closed surface that may or may not be the boundary ∂V. If there are no sources of self-stress, then $F_m = 0$. Namely, if C_{ijkm} are constant, u_i defined everywhere in V, and the associated stresses satisfy $T_{ji,j} = 0$, then $P_{jm,j} = \frac{1}{2}T_{ij,m}E_{ij} + \frac{1}{2}T_{ij}E_{ij,m} - T_{ij}E_{ij,m} = \frac{1}{2}C_{ijrs}E_{rs,m}E_{ij} - \frac{1}{2}C_{ijrs}E_{rs}E_{ij,m} = 0$, thus

$$P_{jm,j} = 0. \tag{15.128}$$

From (15.128) we can also conclude that the value of F_m is independent of the particular shape of Σ, i.e. Σ may be deformed arbitrarily through any region that does not contain sources of self-stress. With this in mind, we shall assume that

$$F_m^\infty = \Sigma\left[n_j\left(\frac{1}{2}\, T_{ik}^\infty u_{i,k}^\infty \delta_{jm} - T_{ij}^\infty u_{i,m}^\infty\right)\right] = 0 \qquad (15.129)$$

(this requires that, as Σ tends to infinity, the density of strain energy should decrease as r^{-3}). We shall now verify (15.127) in various special cases.

Let T_{ij}^I, E_{ij}^I be produced solely by sources of self-stress, i.e. $t_i^I = 0$ on ∂V. Then $\Phi = E = E^\infty - \partial V[\frac{1}{2}\bar{t}_i\bar{u}_i]$, and $F_m^I = -\partial E/\partial\alpha_m$. In view of $V[\partial W^\infty/\partial\alpha_m] = -V[\partial_m W^\infty]$, an integration by parts will yield $-\partial E^\infty/\partial\alpha_m = \partial V[n_m W^\infty]$. To evaluate the second contribution, we first note that if u_i', u_i'' are displacements that are defined everywhere in V, and correspond to equilibrated stresses T_{ij}', T_{ij}'', then, as may be verified by applying the divergence theorem,

$$\partial V\left[n_j\left(T_{ji}'\frac{\partial u_i''}{\partial\alpha_m} - u_i'\frac{\partial T_{ji}''}{\partial\alpha_m}\right)\right] = -V\left[E_{ij}'E_{rs}''\frac{\partial C_{ijrs}}{\partial\alpha_m}\right]. \qquad (15.130)$$

We now put E_{ij}' and E_{ij}'' equal to $\bar{E}_{ij}$, and let $C_{ijkm} = \text{const}$. We then obtain $\partial V[n_m T_{ij}^\infty \bar{E}_{ij}] = V[(T_{ij}^\infty \bar{E}_{ij})_{,m}] = \partial V[n_j(T_{ij}^\infty{}_{,m}\bar{u}_i + T_{ij}^\infty \bar{u}_{i,m})]$, and similarly $\partial V[n_m\bar{W}] = V[\bar{W}_{,m}] = \partial V[n_j\bar{u}_{i,m}\bar{T}_{ij}]$. Finally, we note that $n_j(T_{ij}^\infty + \bar{T}_{ij}) = 0$ on ∂V, as well as $n_j\partial\bar{T}_{ji}/\partial\alpha_m = -n_j\partial T_{ji}^\infty/\partial\alpha_m = n_j T_{ji,m}^\infty$. With $W^I = W^\infty + \bar{W} + T_{ij}^\infty\,\bar{E}_{ij}$, it follows that

$$F_m^I = \partial V[n_m W^I]. \qquad (15.131)$$

Recalling that $t_i^I = 0$ on ∂V, we see that (15.131) conforms to the representation (15.127). It is customary to refer to F_m^I as the "image force," because it is induced by the presence of a free boundary. That is, in a body occupying the entire space, we may think of a surface ∂V as having been made free of tractions by a suitable distribution of sources outside of V, so that F_m^I would be, in effect, the force exerted by these sources upon the sources in V.

For an example, let us take a center of dilatation located in the half-space $z \geq 0$ at $(0, 0, c)$. In cylindrical coordinates, the displacements are† $u_\phi = 0$, $u_\rho = \rho[R_1^{-3} + (3 - 4\nu)R_2^{-3} - 6z(z + c)R_2^{-5}]$, $u_z = (z - c)R_1^{-3} - (3 - 4\nu) \times (z + c)R_2^{-3} - 6z(z + c)^2R_2^{-5} + 2zR_2^{-3}$, where $R_1^2 = \rho^2 + (z - c)^2$, $R_2^2 = \rho^2 + (z + c)^2$. At the free surface $z = 0$, the density of strain energy comes out to be $W = (4/\mu)(1 - \nu)[2(1 + \nu)R^{-6} - 6(1 + \nu)\rho^2R^{-8} + 9\rho^4R^{-10}]$,

† Mindlin and Cheng [226].

where $R^2 = \rho^2 + c^2$. With $dA = \pi\, d\rho^2 = \pi\, dR^2$, and noting that $n_z = -1$, we readily find from (15.131) that $F_z^I = -3(1 - \nu)/\mu c^4$, i.e. the boundary "attracts" the center of dilatation.

Let us now suppose that a self-stressed body is subjected to surface loads, which give rise to the additional displacements u_i^L and stresses T_{ij}^L. The latter satisfy $T_{ji,j}^L = 0$ in V, and $T_{ji}^L n_j = t_i^L$ on ∂V. Noting that there is no strain energy of interaction between loads and sources of self-stress, and that T_{ij}^L, u_i^L are independent of the parameters α_m that specify the location of the sources of self-stress, we obtain $-\partial\Phi/\partial\alpha_m = -\partial E^I/\partial\alpha_m + \partial V[t_i^L\, \partial u_i^I/\partial\alpha_m] = F_m^I + F_m^L$, where

$$F_m^L = \partial V\left[t_i^L \frac{\partial u_i^I}{\partial \alpha_m}\right]. \tag{15.132}$$

For the center of dilatation buried in the half-space, we obtain

$$F_z^L = -4\pi(1 - \nu)\frac{\partial}{\partial c}\int_A d\rho^2(\rho T_{\rho z}^L - cT_{zz}^L)R^{-3}, \tag{15.133}$$

where A is the load region.

A center of dilatation may serve as a simple model for an interstitial atom; therefore, it is of some interest to calculate the volume change induced by the creation of a center of dilatation. The basic formula is obtained by substituting $u_i^* = x_i$, $T_{ij}^* = 3k\delta_{ij}$, $t_i^* = 3kn_i$, $b_i^* = 0$ into Betti's theorem, (15.55), thus $3k\Delta V = V[f_i x_i] + \partial V[t_i x_i]$, where $\Delta V = E_{ii}$, and f_i describe body force density per unit volume. We note that if $f_i = 0$, $t_i = 0$, then there is no volume change, even though the body might be in a state of self-stress T_{ij}. Now let V be a portion of an infinite medium. We assume that V contains a center of dilatation, which, for convenience, is taken to be at the coordinate origin. Then $u_i^\infty = Ax_i/r^3$, $T_{ij}^\infty = 2\mu u_{i,j}^\infty$, and the volume change ΔV^∞ is produced by the movements u_i^∞ of the boundary ∂V. With $n_i = x_i/r$, we readily obtain $\Delta V^\infty = \partial V[n_i u_i^\infty] = 4\pi A$. To clear the boundary ∂V of surface tractions, so that V would become an unconstrained body, we superpose on u_i^∞ the displacements $\bar{u}_i$ produced by the surface tractions $\bar{t}_i = -t_i^\infty$. Again, with $n_j = x_j/r$, we arrive at $3k\Delta\bar{V} = \partial V[\bar{t}_i x_i] = -2\mu\, \partial V[n_j x_i u_{i,j}^\infty] = 16\pi\mu A$, or,

$$\Delta V = \Delta V^\infty + \Delta\bar{V} = 4\pi A\gamma, \qquad \gamma = \frac{3(1 - \nu)}{1 + \nu}. \tag{15.134}$$

If there are N centers of dilatation in V, then, neglecting their interaction, we obtain the volume change $\Delta V = 4\pi NA\gamma$.

At distances that are large compared to the extent of an inclusion, the effect of the inclusion may be similar to that of a center of dilatation. However, inclusions are also *inhomogeneities*, in which the elastic coefficients take on different values. Correspondingly, the "force" on inclusions will be given in part by (15.132), and in part by another term arising from the inhomogeneity. To be specific, we assume that the inhomogeneity is confined to an open region enclosed by a surface Σ. Inside of this region we let $C_{ijkm} = C_{ijkm}(\mathbf{x} - \boldsymbol{\alpha})$, $C'_{ijkm} = C_{ijkm}(\mathbf{x} - \boldsymbol{\alpha} - \Delta\boldsymbol{\alpha})$. We further assume that there are no sources of self-stress, so that the deformation produced by surface tractions t_i can be described by a displacement field u_i. Thus $W = \frac{1}{2}\,\partial V[t_i u_i] = -\Phi$, $W' = \frac{1}{2}\,\partial V[t_i u'] = -\Phi'$, where primes mark the quantities associated with the elastic coefficients C'_{ijkm}. Because T_{ij} and T'_{ij} must satisfy the same boundary condition, we have that $V[(T_{ij} - T'_{ij})E_{ij}] = \partial V[n_j(T_{ij} - T'_{ij})u_i] = 0$, where u_i, E_{ij} may be replaced by u'_i, E'_{ij}. This permits us to write $-\Delta\Phi = \Delta W = \frac{1}{2}V[T'_{ij}E'_{ij} - T_{ij}E_{ij}]$ as $\Delta W = \frac{1}{2}V[T_{ij}E'_{ij} - T'_{ij}E_{ij}]$. Dividing this by $\Delta\alpha_m$, we obtain, in the limit as $\Delta\alpha_m \to 0$, $F_m = \partial W/\partial\alpha_m = \frac{1}{2}V[C_{ijkp,m}E_{ij}E_{kp}]$. An integration by parts then yields

$$F_m = \partial V[n_j P_{jm}]. \tag{15.135}$$

Recalling that $P_{jm,j} = 0$, we can replace ∂V by Σ in (15.135). Moreover, if V itself is a portion of a body that is in a state of self-stress owing to sources distributed outside of V, then (15.135) gives the "force" exerted by these sources on the inhomogeneity.

Returning to (15.132), let us obtain several equivalent representations. As a rule, the complementary solution $\bar{u}_i$ is not known, so that we should like to eliminate it from (15.132). This is easily done if the material is homogeneous, i.e. the right-hand side of (15.130) vanishes. Because $T^I_{ji}n_j = 0$ on ∂V, we may add $-\partial V[n_j u^L_i\, \partial T^I_{ji}/\partial\alpha_m]$ to (15.132). Invoking (15.130), we then arrive at

$$F^L_m = \partial V\left[t^L_i \frac{\partial u^\infty_i}{\partial\alpha_m} - u^L_i \frac{\partial t^\infty_i}{\partial\alpha_m}\right] \tag{15.136}$$

($\partial/\partial\alpha_m$ may be replaced by $-\partial_m$!). The divergence of the integrand vanishes, so that the boundary ∂V can be replaced by any surface S that still envelops all the sources of self-stress. Thus $T^L_{ji,j} = 0$ in V implies that $T^L_{ji,j} = 0$ also on a reduced boundary. In the expression for F^L_m, the integral of $u^L_i T^\infty_{ij,m} = (u^L_i T^\infty_{ij})_{,m} - u^L_{i,m}T^\infty_{ij}$ can be modified by letting $\partial V[n_j(u^L_i T^\infty_{ij})_{,m}] = V[(E^L_{ij}T^\infty_{ij})_{,m}] = \partial V[n_m E^L_{ij}T^\infty_{ij}]$. With $E^L_{ij}T^\infty_{ij} = \frac{1}{2}(E^L_{ij}T^\infty_{ij} + E^\infty_{ij}T^L_{ij})$, we then obtain $F^L_m = \partial V[n_j(\frac{1}{2}T^L_{ik}E^\infty_{ik}\delta_{jm} - T^L_{ij}u^\infty_{i,m} + \frac{1}{2}T^\infty_{ik}E^L_{ik}\delta_{jm} - T^\infty_{ij}u^L_{i,m})]$. Adding this to (15.129) and $F^I_m = \partial V[n_j(\bar{u}_i T^\infty_{ij,m} - \overline{T}_{ij}u^\infty_{i,m})]$, and taking into account

(15.130) (with $C_{ijkp,m} = 0$), we find that $F_m = F_m^L + F_m^I = \partial V[n_j P_{jm}]$, where $T_{ij} = T_{ij}^L + T_{ij}^I$, $u_i = u_i^L + u_i^I$.

To obtain still another form of (15.136), we consider a surface S spanned over a closed curve ∂S. On ∂S, we have that $dx_j = \sigma_j\, ds$, where σ_j denotes the field of unit tangent vectors of ∂S; the abbreviated notation for line integrals of $f\, dx_j$ will be $\partial S[f\sigma_j]$. We shall need the following version of Kelvin's transformation,

$$S[n_j(w_{j,m} - w_{i,i}\delta_{jm})] = -\varepsilon_{mij}\, \partial S[w_i\sigma_j] \tag{15.137}$$

(to derive it, apply Kelvin's transformation to $\partial S[A_{mj}\sigma_j]$, then let $A_{mj} = \varepsilon_{mij}w_i$). If S is a closed surface, then the line integral on the right vanishes, except when w_i are discontinuous along a curve C lying in S. In that case

$$S[n_j(w_{j,m} - w_{i,i}\delta_{jm})] = -\varepsilon_{mij}C[[\![w_i]\!]\sigma_j]. \tag{15.137*}$$

With $u_i^L T_{ij,m}^\infty = w_{j,m} - u_{i,m}^L T_{ij}^\infty$, $w_j = u_i^L T_{ij}^\infty$, and $T_{ij}^L u_{i,m}^\infty = w_{j,m} - T_{ij,m}^L u_i^\infty$, $w_j = T_{ij}^L u_i^\infty$, we then obtain from (15.136) and (15.137) that

$$F_m^L = \partial V[n_j(u_i^\infty T_{ij,m}^L - u_{i,m}^L T_{ij}^\infty)] + \varepsilon_{mij}C[T_{ki}^L[\![u_k^\infty]\!]\, dx_j]. \tag{15.138}$$

Let us take again a center of dilatation, located at the coordinate origin: $u_i^\infty = Ax_i/r^3$, $T_{ij}^\infty = 2\mu\, \partial_j u_i^\infty$. The surface S can now be shrunk to an arbitrarily small sphere about the coordinate origin, which permits us to expand the load stresses and displacements in a Taylor series: $u_i^L = u_i^L(0) + x_k u_{i,k}^L(0) + \cdots$, etc. With $n_j = x_j/r$, the integrals in (15.138) are readily evaluated, yielding

$$F_m^L = -\frac{12\pi A(1 - \nu)p_{,m}^L}{1 + \nu}, \qquad p^L = -\frac{T_{kk}^L}{3}. \tag{15.139}$$

Evidently the actual shape of the body, ∂V, is unimportant. "Forces" on dislocations are perhaps a more appropriate application for (15.138). In two-dimensional problems, with dislocation lines parallel to the z axis, we choose ∂V to be a cylinder of unit height, and radius r. Then C is a unit length of a generator of the cylinder, and $\varepsilon_{mij}C[T_{ki}^L[\![\Delta u_k^\infty]\!]\sigma_i] = \varepsilon_{mi3}T_{ik}^L b_k$, where $b_k = [\![\Delta u_k^\infty]\!]$ is the Burgers vector of the dislocation line. To exclude other lines of singularities (e.g. a line of centers of dilatation), we set down the additional condition

$$\lim_{r=0} r u_i^\infty = 0. \tag{15.140}$$

Then, expanding T_{ij}^L, u_i^L in Taylor series about $r = 0$, and taking into account (15.140), we obtain $F_m^L = u_{i,m}^L(0)\,\partial V[T_{ji}^\infty n_j] + \varepsilon_{mi3}T_{ki}^L b_k$. But the first term is zero because the dislocation line is in equilibrium, so that

$$F_1^L = T_{k2}^L b_k, \qquad F_2^L = -T_{k1}^L b_k. \tag{15.141}$$

This agrees with the *formula of Peach and Koehler*

$$F_m^L = \varepsilon_{jkm}\sigma_j T_{ki}^L b_i, \tag{15.142}$$

which gives the force on a unit length of an arbitrary, curved dislocation line. To derive (15.142), we might apply (15.125)* to a closed surface drawn around a surface spanned by a dislocation loop.†

Problems

A. COMPATIBILITY

1. Let $\tilde{E}_{xx} = a + b(x^2 + y^2) + x^4 + y^4$, $\tilde{E}_{yy} = \alpha + \beta(x^2 + y^2) + x^4 + y^4$, $\tilde{E}_{xy} = A + Bxy(x^2 + y^2 - c^2)$, $\tilde{E}_{yz} = \tilde{E}_{zx} = \tilde{E}_{zz} = 0$, where a, b, c, A, B, α, and β are constants. Show that the strains are compatible if $B = 2$, $b + \beta + 2c^2 = 0$. Assuming these conditions to hold, calculate the displacements u_x, u_y, u_z.

2. Investigate the integrability of

$$v_i(C, \mathbf{x}) = \bar{v}_i + \int_C L_{ij}\, ds_j \equiv \bar{v}_i + C[L_{ij}\, ds_j], \tag{a}$$

where C is a curve joining points $\bar{\mathbf{x}}$ and $\mathbf{x}$, and $\bar{\mathbf{v}}$ denotes the value of $\mathbf{v}$ at the fixed point $\bar{\mathbf{x}}$. *Hints*: Denote the symmetric part of $\mathbf{L}$ by $\mathbf{D}$, and the skew-symmetric part of $\mathbf{L}$ by $\mathbf{W}$. If (a) defines a single-valued function, then $L_{ij,k} = L_{ik,j}$, or, equivalently,

$$D_{ij,k} - D_{ik,j} + W_{ij,k} - W_{ik,j} = 0. \tag{b}$$

Adding to (b) two of its cyclic permutations, obtain $W_{ij,k} + W_{jk,i} + W_{ki,j} = 0$, and $W_{ij,k} = D_{ik,j} - D_{jk,i}$. With this, and the identity $C[W_{ij}\, ds_j] = (x_j - \bar{x}_j)\overline{W}_{ij} + C[(x_j - s_j)W_{ij,k}\, ds_k]$, show that

$$\begin{aligned} v_i(\mathbf{x}) &= \bar{v}_i + (x_j - \bar{x}_j)\overline{W}_{ij} + C[M_{ik}(\mathbf{x}, \mathbf{s})\, ds_k], \\ M_{ik}(\mathbf{x}, \mathbf{s}) &= D_{ik} + (x_j - s_j)(D_{ik,j} - D_{jk,i}), \end{aligned} \tag{c}$$

where $\mathbf{x}$ occurs as a parameter, i.e. $\mathbf{D} = \mathbf{D}(\mathbf{s})$, and derivatives of $\mathbf{D}$ are taken with respect to $\mathbf{s}$.

† Eshelby [225], p. 124. Cf. also Problem 14.

Now invoke the Kelvin's transformation to show that $\mathbf{v}$ defined by (c) is one-valued and differentiable, *in a simply-connected region,* if

$$D_{ik,jm} - D_{jk,im} - D_{im,jk} + D_{jm,ik} = 0. \tag{d}$$

Further, show that if (d) hold, then from (c) it follows that

$$D_{ij} = \frac{1}{2}(v_{i,j} + v_{j,i}), \qquad W_{ij} = \frac{1}{2}(v_{i,j} - v_{j,i}).$$

Finally, show that there are only six distinct compatibility equations, given by

$$\begin{aligned}(\text{Ink}\mathbf{D})_{im} &\equiv \varepsilon_{ijk}\varepsilon_{mnp}D_{jn,kp} = 0,\\ 2D_{12,12} &= D_{11,22} + D_{22,11}, \ldots, \ldots,\\ D_{11,23} &= (-D_{23,1} + D_{31,2} + D_{12,3})_{,1}, \ldots, \ldots.\end{aligned} \tag{e}$$

B. TYPICAL PROBLEMS

3. Verify that substitution of (15.68) into displacement equations of equilibrium reduces them to (15.69).

4. Consider an equilateral triangle with vertices located in the xy plane at $(-2a, 0)$, $(a, \pm\sqrt{3}a)$. If the triangle represents the cross section of a prism, show that the torsion problem (15.96) is solved by

$$\phi = (x - a)\left(\frac{y^2}{2a} - \frac{x^2}{6a} - \frac{2x}{3} - \frac{2a}{3}\right),$$

   Let $a = 1$, and sketch the contour lines corresponding to $\phi = \frac{1}{2}$ and $\phi = \frac{1}{12}$.

5. Let R: $-a \leq x \leq a$, $-b \leq y \leq b$ be the cross section of a prismatic body. To solve the problem of torsion by couples applied to the end sections, consider the variation of

$$\Psi(S^+) = E(S^+) - \int_{B_u} \mathbf{t}^+ \cdot \mathbf{u}^* \, da,$$

   where $\mathbf{u}^*$ are the displacements prescribed on B_u. Consider the end sections as B_u, and let $\mathbf{u} = \mathbf{0}$ for $z = 0$, $u_x = u_x^* = -\alpha Ly$, $u_y = u_y^* = \alpha Lx$ for $z = L$. Taking $\phi = c(x^2 - a^2)(y^2 - b^2)$ show that the optimization procedure will yield $c = 5/4(a^2 + b^2)$. Obtain expressions for the moment transmitted by a cross-section, as well as for the maximum stress.

6. Verify the property (15.113) of Kelvin's solution.

7. Derive (15.116) from Kelvin's solution. Then obtain (15.117) from (15.116).

8. If $u_r = f(r)$, $u_\theta = u_\phi = 0$, then the solution is said to have *polar symmetry.* Show that then $T_{rr} = \{2\mu/(1 - 2\nu)\}\{(1 - \nu)f' + 2\nu f/r\}$, $T_{\theta\theta} = T_{\phi\phi} = 2\mu(\nu f' + f/r)/(1 - 2\nu)$, $T_{r\theta} = T_{\theta\phi} = T_{\phi r} = 0$, and $b_r = g(r)$, $b_\theta = b_\phi = 0$. Moreover, if $b_r = 0$, then $f(r) = c_1 r + c_2 r^{-2}$. Obtain and discuss the solution for a spheri-

cal shell under uniform surface pressures ("Lame's problem"): $r = a$, $T_{rr} = -q$, $r = b$, $T_{rr} = -p$.
Also consider the case of a solid sphere ($a = 0$) under uniform external pressure. What are the stresses then?

9. Solve the problem of a spherical inclusion (with elastic coefficients $\nu_1, \mu_1,$) in an infinite medium under hydrostatic pressure q at ∞. The elastic coefficients of the infinite medium are ν_2, μ_2. Discuss physically significant aspects of the solution.

10. If $u_\rho = u_\rho(\rho, z)$, $u_\phi = u_\phi(\rho, z)$, $u_z = u_z(\rho, z)$, then the solution is said to have axisymmetry about z axis. In particular, *torsionless* axisymmetry corresponds to $u_\phi = 0$. As a counterpart of the problem of Kirsch, determine the stress concentration at a spherical cavity of an infinite medium subjected to uniaxial tension $T_{zz} = T$ at infinity. *Hint*: consider combinations of $S_0: \phi = H_0$, $\psi = 0$, $S_1: \phi = 0, \psi = H_1$, $S_2: \phi = H_2, \psi = 0$, where $\boldsymbol{\Psi} = \mathbf{e}_z\Psi$, and H_0, H_1, H_2 are spherical harmonics given by

$$H_0 = \frac{1}{r}, \qquad H_1 = \frac{\partial}{\partial z} H_0 = -\frac{\cos\theta}{r^2},$$

$$H_2 = \frac{\partial^2}{\partial z^2} H_0 = \frac{3\cos^2\theta - 1}{r}.$$

The solution should be $S = c_0 S_0 + c_1 S_1 + c_2 S_2$, where $c_2 = a^5 T/2(7 - 5\nu)$, $c_0 = (6 - 5\nu)a^3 T/2(7 - 5\nu)$, $c_1 = 5a^3 T/2(7 - 5\nu)$,

11. (A long problem). Generalize the problem of Kirsch to the case where the region $\rho \leq a$ is filled by a material with different properties. At $\rho = a$ the two materials are bonded together. (Can the stress concentration shift into the material occupying $\rho \leq a$?)

12. A thick-walled steel cylinder occupying the region $0 \leq z \leq L$, $A \leq \rho \leq B$ contains a lead core (in the region $\rho \leq A$, that is). The core is being compressed by means of rigid plungers which move in the z direction, and just fit the opening $0 \leq \rho \leq A$. If the force exerted by a plunger is 5000 lb, and $A = 2$ in, $B = 3$ in, find the maximum shearing stresses in the steel mantle and in the lead core (use any handbook values for the material properties). *Hint*: This is a plane strain situation, which, as may be verified, holds, with suitable modifications, not only when $u_z = 0$, but also when $\tilde{E}_{zz} =$ const. A "good" solution should have no net force acting on the rims $z = 0$, $z = L$ of the steel mantle!

13. ("Shrink fit"). A cylinder $b - \varepsilon \leq \rho \leq c$ is to be shrunk onto a cylinder $a \leq \rho \leq b$. This can be done by heating the first cylinder until its inner radius becomes b. Assuming that both cylinders are made of the same material, express the "residual pressure" p_0 between the cylinders in terms of ε (p_0 is the pressure between cylinders after the assembly has cooled). Suppose that the assembly is now subjected to an "explosion pressure" p, and that the strength criterion is based on maximum allowable shearing stress

q. Choose p_0 (or, equivalently, ε) such that the maximum shearing stress is the same in both cylinders. Finally, minimize the value of q by obtaining the optimal value of b. Verify that $p = [(c - a)/c]q$, whereas for a single tube

$$p = \frac{c^2 - a^2}{2c^2} q.$$

14. Consider an infinite plate with an elliptical hole. In elliptic cylinder coordinates u, v the boundary is given by $(x/\sinh u_0)^2 + (y/\cosh u_0)^2 = 1$. If the stresses at infinity are $T_{xx} = T, T_{xy} = T_{yy} = 0$, show that the Airy's stress function must be of the form

$$F = \frac{T}{8}\{1 + \cosh 2u + 2Au + 2Ce^{-u} \sinh u + (-\cosh 2u - 1 + 2Be^{-2u} + 2Ce^{-u} \sinh u) \cos 2v\}.$$

Evaluate A, B, C from the boundary conditions $\partial F/\partial u = 0$, $\partial F/\partial v = 0$ on $u = u_0$ (what do these conditions represent?), and show that the maximum stress occurs $v = \pi/2$, $u = u_0$. Compare the stress concentration with that obtained in the problem of Kirsch; what happens when the ellipse degenerates into a crack?

15. Calculate thermal stresses in a ring $A \leq \rho \leq B$ if the inner boundary is heated to a temperature θ_0, while the outer boundary remains at the initial temperature $\theta = 0$ (here θ is *not* the absolute temperature).

16. Encouraged by one's success in the determination of slowness surfaces in transversely isotropic media, one may want to tackle cubic crystals. While the same method is applicable, no neat results can be obtained, except for very special directions. The reader may want to investigate this problem far enough to see the truth of these remarks (Added in proof: see Thomas [218]).

17. Following the method outlined in the text, give a detailed derivation of **a.** (15.141) **b.** (15.139) **c.** (15.134).

Section 16
MULTIPOLAR THEORIES

Continuum theories for discrete systems

It has been stated several times by now that continuum mechanics describes certain "continuum modes" of the motion of material bodies. A more faithful description of bodies will require more elaborate, "multipolar" continuum theories. It is no exaggeration to say that the main difficulty lies not in the development of general theories but in their application. The assurance that any problem done in elasticity theory will be done better in a generalized elasticity theory is not enough. Surely the improvements must be weighed against the greater intractability of the general theories, so that, rather than being content to add second-order corrections to solutions that are known to be adequate, we should look for effects that have eluded the classical theories altogether. That is, every successful theory has a number of impressive exhibits, so to speak, problems for which it provides a simple and satisfactory solution. For instance, linear elastostatics provides a theory of stress concentrations. In a "lattice theory" of elasticity, however, one does not talk about stress concentrations; instead, a great deal of fuss is made about dispersion of waves, frequency versus wavelength curves, surface effects, and so on. To justify a generalized continuum theory of elasticity, then, we must be able to provide simpler methods for some of the problems that are important in the lattice theories. In what follows we shall outline, very superficially, a few concrete examples of the correspondence between lattice and continuum theories of elasticity.

By a lattice we shall mean an orderly arrangement of particles, defined by a *basis* that consists of one or several particles, and one or more *lattice vectors* that generate the entire lattice by translations of the basis. For simplicity, we shall confine the discussion to one-dimensional lattices, also called *chains*. The basis of a simple chain is a single particle; the lattice vector, now a segment a, then defines the periodicity of the lattice. Variables attached to particles will carry particle labels $M, N, \ldots$ as subscripts, and summation over labels will be indicated by **S** (if summation is over one of several labels only, then that label will be placed under **S**).

The initial coordinates of particles are given by $X_N = aN$, the current ones by $x_N = X_N + u_N$. We assume that the strain energy is a function of the displacements, and admits a Taylor series expansion about the initial, equilibrium state. Then, with $W^0 = 0$, we have that

$$W = \frac{1}{2}\mathbf{S}C_{MN}u_M u_N + \frac{1}{6}\mathbf{S}C_{MNP}u_M u_N u_P + \ldots, \tag{16.1}$$

where the coefficients are derivatives of W with respect to displacements, evaluated in the initial state. We shall keep only the first term in (16.1) (this is known as the "harmonic approximation"). The force on the Mth particle is defined by

$$F_M = -\frac{\partial W}{\partial u_M} = -\underset{N}{\mathbf{S}}\, C_{MN}u_N; \tag{16.2}$$

it must vanish when the motion is a rigid displacement $u_N = u$, thus

$$\underset{N}{\mathbf{S}}C_{MN} = 0. \tag{16.3}$$

Consequently, F_M can be expressed as follows,

$$F_M = \underset{N}{\mathbf{S}}C_{MN}(u_M - u_N). \tag{16.2)*$$

To obtain a correspondence with the theory of elasticity, we choose the homogeneous deformation $u = HX$, so that

$$u_N = HX_N = aHN. \tag{16.4}$$

Comparing the harmonic approximation of W with $W = \frac{1}{2}EH^2$, we now obtain

$$E = \frac{a^2}{2V}\mathbf{S}\, C_{MN}MN,$$

where V is the volume of a unit cell.

As soon as we take deformations that are not homogeneous, the exact correspondence between the lattice theory and the continuum theory is lost. This is particularly so for plane waves

$$u = A\cos(kX - \omega t). \tag{16.5}$$

Let us recall that the speed, c, of a phase $\phi = kX - \omega t$ is given by ω/k; a phase difference of 2π corresponds, at any instant, to the wavelength λ, thus $2\pi = k\lambda$, or,

$$k = \frac{2\pi}{\lambda}, \qquad c = \frac{\omega}{k} = \frac{\omega\lambda}{2\pi}. \tag{16.6}$$

In the continuum theory, substituting (16.5) into $\partial T/\partial X = \rho_0\ddot{u}$, we find that

$$c = \frac{\omega}{k} = \sqrt{\frac{E}{\rho_0}}, \tag{16.7}$$

i.e. all frequencies are propagated at the same speed, which means that the continuum is not dispersive.

In the lattice theory, assuming nearest-neighbor interactions only, a "free body diagram" of a generic particle will yield the equation of motion

$$m\ddot{u}_N = \alpha(u_{N+1} - 2u_N + u_{N-1}), \tag{16.8}$$

where α is the force constant in the lattice. Substituting (16.5) into (16.8), we now obtain $m\omega^2 = 2k(1 - \cos ak) = 4\alpha\sin^2(ka/2)$, thus

$$\omega = 2\sqrt{\frac{\alpha}{m}}\sin\frac{ka}{2}. \tag{16.9}$$

The wave motion is now dispersive. A correspondence with the continuum theory exists only for *long waves*, i.e. when $k \to 0$; then $\omega^2/k^2 \to \alpha a^2/m$.

Next, let us suppose that the basis of the lattice is a pair of particles, with masses m and M, respectively. For the two kinds of displacements we choose $u_{2N} = A\cos(2Nak - \omega t)$ and $U_{2N+1} = B\cos[(2N+1)\alpha k - \omega t]$; substitution of these into $m\ddot{u}_{2N} = \alpha(U_{2N+1} - 2u_{2N} + U_{2N-1})$ and $M\ddot{U}_{2N+1} = \alpha(u_{2N+2} - 2U_{2N+1} + u_{2N})$ leads to the linear system $2\alpha A\cos ak + B(M\omega^2 - 2\alpha) = 0$, $A(m\omega^2 - 2\alpha) + 2\alpha B\cos ak = 0$. Therefore, non trivial solutions for A and B will exist only if

$$\omega^2 = \frac{\alpha}{\mu}\left[1 \pm \left(1 - \frac{4\mu^2}{mM}\sin^2 ak\right)^{1/2}\right] \tag{16.10}$$

where $\mu = mM/(m + M)$. In the ω–k diagram there are now two branches. On the "acoustic branch," ω becomes proportional to k as $k \to 0$ (this limit being the counterpart of the solution obtained in the continuum theory), whereas on the "optic branch" ω approaches a constant as $k \to 0$. In the latter case we find that $mA = -MB$, i.e. the two sets of particles move in opposite directions.

We can also define lattice strains (or rather, extensions) $E_{MN} = u_M - u_N$ and the associated stresses (i.e. tensions)

$$T_{MN} = \frac{\partial W}{\partial E_{MN}}.$$

If we take a chain of three particles, and let $W = \frac{1}{2}\alpha(E_{32}^2 + E_{21}^2)$, then

$$F_2 = -\frac{\partial W}{\partial u_2} = \frac{\partial W}{\partial E_{32}} - \frac{\partial W}{\partial E_{21}} = T_{32} - T_{21}$$

(this is a counterpart of $T_{ji,j} = -f_i$). The condition of equilibrium, $F_2 = 0$, is satisfied whenever $E_{32} = E_{21} =$ const. But then it may seem that, by (16.1), (16.2), W must vanish too. However, noting that αE_{32} and αE_{21} must equal the applied tension T, we have that

$$W = \frac{T}{2}[(u_3 - u_2) + (u_2 - u_1) = \frac{1}{2}(Tu_3 - Tu_1),$$

which corresponds to $W = \frac{1}{2}\partial V[t_i u_i]$.

Perhaps the first generalization of the classical continuum theory of elasticity that comes to mind is a theory of *materials of grade two*. In this theory a "particle" is a replica of a finite body undergoing the simple deformation $x(X, t) = A(t) + (X - \bar{X})B(t)$, where $A(t)$ is the location of a reference point $\bar{X}$. The associated velocity field is given by $v = \dot{A} + (X - \bar{X})\dot{B} = \dot{A} + (x - A)\dot{B}/B$; if $\bar{X}$ is the mass center of the body, then the kinetic energy splits into a kinetic energy of translation, $\frac{1}{2}m\dot{A}^2$, and a kinetic energy of internal motion, $\frac{1}{2}mi^2(\dot{B}^2/B^2)$, where i is a radius of gyration about the mass center: $mi^2 = \int dm(x - A)^2$. With this in mind, we assume that in materials of grade two the density of kinetic energy is given by

$$K = \frac{1}{2}\rho_0[v^2 + i(v')^2], \qquad v' = \frac{\partial v}{\partial X}. \tag{16.11}$$

The transition from monopolar theories to multipolar theories is not unlike the transition from the mechanics of a particle, based on Newton's second law, to a "Lagrangean mechanics" of systems. Namely, whereas linear and angular momenta are specific variables, the use of generalized (i.e. unspecified) momenta will introduce into the theory an abstract part that is only concerned with the *form* of the equations of motion, the boundary conditions, and the initial conditions. This abstract part is embodied in some principle that provides a method for generating the necessary equations. The method works well enough if "friction" is not present, because the (constitutive) potentials for conservation (e.g. strain-energy function), being state functions, are more easy to describe than potentials for dissipation (e.g. Rayleigh's dissipation function). The most commonly used method is *Hamilton's principle*, which is often presented as a kind of ultimate law, but would be perhaps better described as a kind of ultimate notation. In particular, if one is inclined to attribute a deeper significance to Hamilton's principle being an extremum principle, one should also note that this may be no more than a consequence of the basic equations being second-order differential equations.†

In Hamilton's principle we assume, first of all, the existence of a constitutive potential ("Lagrangean density") L. If it is possible to separate out a density of kinetic energy, K, then we can write $L = K - W$. The use of Hamilton's principle always entails some lengthy manipulations, integrations by parts, and the like. These operations, however lengthy, are only the trivial part of the principle; the important part is the *selection of independent variables and invariance properties.* It will be recalled that the balance equations for linear and angular momenta are equivalent to invariance of the energy balance to observer transformations.‡ By hypothesis, Hamilton's principle is form-invariant to all "variations" $\delta x_i, \ldots$ defined over the set of comparison states. Consequently, to each invariance property of L there will now correspond a balance equation. However, because the kinetic energy is now a part of the constitutive potential L, we cannot speak of invariance of L to observer *motions*. Therefore, we should only postulate the invariance of L to *Euclidean displacements* $x_i^+ = Q_{ij}x_j + c_i$, where Q_{ij}, c_i are constants.§ In particular, the invariance of L to the observer transformation $x_i \dashrightarrow x_i + c_i$ requires that (condition of "homogeneity of space"!)

$$\frac{\partial L}{\partial x_i} = 0. \tag{16.12}$$

This condition is, in fact, the balance equation for linear momentum (cf. (16.16) *et seq.*). The balance equation for angular momentum is equivalent to invariance of L to rotational displacements $x_i \to Q_{ij}x_j$, where Q_{ij} are constants (condition of "isotropy of space"!). Finally, the invariance of L to a translation $t \dashrightarrow t + \text{const.}$ of the time scale yields a balance equation for energy,

$$\frac{\partial L}{\partial t} = 0 \tag{16.13}$$

(cf. (16.20)).

Because Hamilton's principle is a method, not a formula, there is no simple way of recording it. To give a rough indication of its form, let us consider a region V with the boundary ∂V, and a time interval $I: t_0 < t < t_1$, the "boundary" of I consisting of the instants t_0 and t_1. The domain of the solutions is the four-dimensional region $V \times I$, with the "boundaries" $\partial V \times I$, $V \times \partial I$, and possibly

† An illustration of the correspondence between differential equations and variational principles is given in Appendix I.

‡ Cf. Green and Rivlin's derivation of the balance equations for linear and angular momenta, outlined on pp. 194–195.

§ Cf. Toupin [170], p. 93.

$\partial V \times \partial I$. We shall again denote integrals of $f dV$ over V by $V[f]$, and integrals of $f_i N_i \, dA$ over ∂V by $\partial V[f_i N_i]$. In addition, an integral of $f \, dt$ over I will be denoted by $I[f]$, with the understanding that $\partial I[f] = f(t_1) - f(t_0)$. The usual form of Hamilton's principle can then be described as follows,

$$\delta\Phi = IV[\delta L] + I\,\partial V[\alpha] + V\,\partial I[\beta] + \partial V\,\partial I[\gamma] = 0, \tag{16.14}$$

where α, β, γ characterize the nature of "external" agencies, e.g. surface tractions, initial conditions. As particular instances of Φ we may mention the elastic potentials (15.90), (15.93).

For materials of grade two, we let $L = K(v, v') - W(u', u'')$, where K is given by (16.11). Anticipating the results of the subsequent derivation, we define a (polarized) stress T^*, a hyperstress H, a (polarized) momentum p^*, and a hypermomentum q:

$$\begin{gathered} H = \frac{\partial W}{\partial u''}, \qquad T^* = \frac{\partial W}{\partial u'} - \frac{\partial H}{\partial X}, \\ q = \frac{\partial L}{\partial v'}, \qquad p^* = p - \frac{\partial q}{\partial X}, \qquad p = \frac{\partial L}{\partial v}. \end{gathered} \tag{16.15}$$

It is important to note that if v is given throughout a region V, then so is v'; therefore, the initial conditions on q can be prescribed only on ∂V. Hamilton's principle now reads as follows: $IV[\delta L + b\,\delta u + B\,\delta u'] + I\,\partial V[\bar{T}\delta u + \bar{H}\,\delta u'] - V\,\partial I[\bar{p}\,\delta u] - \partial V\,\partial I[\bar{q}\,\delta u] = 0$, where B is the dipolar body force, and overbars mark the given initial and boundary values of variables. Because $\delta u' = \partial_X\,\delta u$, $\delta v = D_t\,\delta u$, etc., the variations $\delta u'$, δv are not independent in V. On the other hand, δu and $\delta u'$ are assumed to be independent on ∂V; this expresses the idea that the boundary of a body of grade two is really a thin shell, so that $\delta u'$ is precisely the virtual deformation of this shell. To express all variations in V in terms of δu, it is now necessary to perform a series of routine integrations by parts, e.g. $IV[q\,\delta v'] = IV[D_t q \delta u'] - IV[\delta u' \dot{q}] = V\partial I[q \delta u'] - IV[\delta u' \dot{q}] = V\,\partial I[\partial_X q\,\delta u] - V\,\partial I[\delta u\, q'] - IV[\partial_X\,\delta u\,\dot{q}] + IV[\delta u\,\partial_X \dot{q}] = \partial V\,\partial I[q \delta u] - V\,\partial I[q'\,\delta u] - I\partial V[\dot{q}\,\delta u] + IV[\delta u\,\partial_X \dot{q}]$. In this way we obtain the equation of motion,†

$$\frac{\partial}{\partial X}(T^* - B + \dot{q}) + b = \dot{p} \text{ in } V \times I, \tag{16.16}$$

the boundary conditions

$$H = \bar{H}, \qquad T^* - B + \dot{q} = \bar{T} \text{ on } \partial V \times I, \tag{16.17}$$

and the "end conditions"

$$q = \bar{q} \text{ on } \partial V \times \partial I, \qquad p - q' = \bar{p} \text{ on } V \times I. \tag{16.18}$$

† Cf. [233].

An equivalent statement of (16.16), $(16.17)_2$ is given by

$$\frac{\partial \hat{T}}{\partial X} + b = \dot{p} \text{ in } V \times I, \qquad \hat{T} = \bar{T} \text{ on } V \times I,$$

$$\hat{T} = T^* - B + \dot{q} = -\frac{\partial L}{\partial u'} + \frac{\partial}{\partial X}\frac{\partial L}{\partial u''} + \frac{\partial}{\partial t}\frac{\partial L}{\partial v'} - B, \tag{16.19}$$

where $\hat{T}$ may be referred to as the "effective stress".

Had we assumed that $L = L(u', u'', v, v', x, t)$, then $\partial L/\partial x$ would appear on the right-hand side of (16.16). To show that $\partial_t L = 0$ implies a balance equation for energy, let us define an energy density U by $U = -L + pv + qv'$. Thus if $K = \frac{1}{2}(pv + qv') = \frac{1}{2}\rho_0(v^2 + i(v')^2)$, then $U = K + W$. Taking into account (16.15), we now obtain that $\dot{U} = -\partial_t L + Tv' + Hv'' + \dot{p}v + \dot{q}v'$, where $T = -\partial L/\partial u'$. By the usual integrations by parts, and by (16.16), (16.17), it follows that

$$V[\dot{U}] = -V[\partial_t L] + V[bv + Bv'] + \partial V[\bar{T}v + \bar{H}v'], \tag{16.20}$$

i.e. $\partial_t L = 0$ implies a balance of energy. It should be noted, however, that because heat flux is not accounted for, the present theory can apply to adiabatic conditions only. As the strain-energy function we now take

$$W = T^0 u' + lH^0 u'' + \frac{1}{2}E(u')^2 + lCu'u'' + \frac{l^2}{2}D(u'')^2, \tag{16.21}$$

where l is a characteristic length of the material, and T^0, M^0 are initial stresses. The generalization of the continuum theory now permits us to compare it with a lattice theory that accounts also for next-nearest neighbor interactions. In this theory the equations of motion are

$$m\ddot{u}_N = \alpha(u_{N+1} - 2u_N + u_{N-1}) + \beta(u_{N+2} - 2u_N + u_{N-2}). \tag{16.21}$$

Moreover, because surface tractions must represent the same kind of action as internal forces (the surface may be an imagined one!), loads applied to the boundary will not only affect the last particle of the chain, but also the next-to-last one. The last two particles are, in effect, the "boundary"; therefore, the boundary conditions are of the form

$$\begin{aligned} m\ddot{u}_{K-1} &= \alpha(u_K + u_{K-2} - 2u_{K-1}) + \beta(u_{K-3} - u_{K-1}) + P_2, \\ m\ddot{u}_K &= \alpha(u_{K-1} - u_K) + \beta(u_{K-2} - u_K) + P_1, \end{aligned} \tag{16.22}$$

where P_1 and P_2 are the external forces acting on the particles K and $K - 1$, respectively.

Substituting a plane wave solution $u = \cos(kX - \omega t)$ into (16.21), we arrive at $m\omega^2 = 2\alpha(1 - \cos ak) + 2\beta(1 - \cos ak)$, which, although more general than (16.9), is not essentially different from it. In the continuum theory, with $H = H^0 + lCu' + l^2 Du''$, $T = T^0 + Eu' - l^2 Du'''$, the equation of motion becomes

$$E\partial_X^2 u - l^2 D\partial_X^4 = \rho_0 \partial_t^2 u - i\partial_X^2 \partial_t^2 u,$$

where, as is necessary in a linear theory, we have neglected the variation of the moment of inertia, i. The plane wave solution now yields the condition $k^2(E + l^2 Dk^2) = \omega^2(\rho_0 + ik^2)$, thus

$$c = \frac{\omega}{k} = \sqrt{\frac{E + l^2 Dk^2}{\rho_0 + ik^2}}. \tag{16.23}$$

For long waves, i.e. as k tends to zero, we recover for c the classical result (16.7). The "short wave" limit of c is $\sqrt{l^2 D/i}$, the medium being now dispersive for all $k \neq 0$. Of course, we still have only the "acoustic branch" in the ω–k diagram.

Whenever there exists a material property with the dimension of length, we expect not only dispersion of waves but also "boundary layer effects." The latter may be exhibited in simple static problems involving a free boundary.† To illustrate this, we take an infinite slab of thickness $2h$. The x axis is perpendicular to the slab, the free surfaces being at $x = \pm h$. In the absence of body forces, the equation of equilibrium, $\partial T/\partial X = 0$, and the boundary condition $T = 0$ on $x = \pm h$ require that $T = T^0 + Eu' - l^2 Du''' = 0$. This is solved by $u = A_1(\cosh kX - 1) + A_2 \sinh kX - T^0 X/E$, where $k^2 = E/Dl^2$. The constants A_1 and A_2 are found from the remaining boundary conditions $H = 0$, $x = \pm h$. Thus

$$A_1 = -A^2 \frac{lkD}{C}, \qquad A_2 = \frac{(C/k)(H^0 - CT^0/E)}{(C^2 - l^2k^2D^2)\cosh kh}.$$

The linear term $u = -T^0 X/E$ represents the classical solution, whereas the exponential functions may describe a deformation that decays very rapidly with distance from the free boundary. The boundary layer effect vanishes if both $T^0 = 0$ and $H^0 = 0$. However, even though it is reasonable to assume that T^0 vanishes in the natural state, the same need not be true of H^0 (cf. the remarks on p. 405).

In the lattice theory a counterpart of the foregoing solution is obtained by substituting $u_N = A_1 \sinh \lambda N + B_1 N$ into (16.21), (16.22) (with accelerations neglected, of course). Then, by (16.21), $\cosh \lambda = -(\alpha + 2\beta)/2\beta$, the constants A_1 and B_1 being obtained from (16.22).

As will be seen in the three-dimensional theories, the vanishing of H^0 may be required by conditions of material symmetry. In that case, the boundary layer effects will be present only in theories based on materials of grade three or higher. The requisite generalizations are straightforward, e.g. for materials of grade three the stress is defined by $T = \partial W/\partial u' - \partial_X \partial W/\partial u'' + \partial_X^2 \partial W/\partial u'''$.

Elastic materials of grade N

When the ideas outlined in the preceding subsection are applied to three-dimensional problems, the only essential generalization occurs in the boundary conditions. The reason for this generalization is as follows. On a boundary ∂V we may prescribe not only the variations δx_i, but also their normal derivatives

† Toupin and Gazis [234].

$D\,\delta x_i$, $D^2\,\delta x_i$, etc., where $D = N_j\Delta_j$, **N** being the outward unit normal vectors of ∂V; that is, the boundary is, in materials of grade N, really a "boundary layer," and $D\,\delta x_i$, $D^2\,\delta x_i$, etc. describe its virtual deformations. The surface derivatives $D_j\,\delta x_i$, where $D_j = \Delta_j - N_j D$, cannot be prescribed independently, because they are determined by the values of δx_i on ∂V. Therefore, if a term like $\Delta_j\,\delta x_i = D_j\,\delta x_i - N_j D\,\delta x_i$ occurs in a surface integral, then the part $D_j\,\delta x_i$ must be eliminated (the surface derivatives $D_j\,\delta x_i$ have no counterpart in the one-dimensional theory!). The method for doing this is outlined below.

Let Σ be a surface, dA an area element of Σ, and dS an increment of arc length along the boundary curve $\partial\Sigma$ of Σ. We shall write $\Sigma[f]$ for the surface integral of $f\,dA$, and $\partial\Sigma[f]$ for the line integral of $f\,dS$. Then†

$$\Sigma[N_j D_i f] = \Sigma[f(K_{ij} - N_i N_j K_{mm})] + \partial\Sigma[M_i N_j f], \tag{16.24}$$

where f stands for any tensor,

$$K_{ij} = K_{ji} = -D_i N_j \tag{16.25}$$

are the spatial components of the curvature tensor of Σ (cf. (11.60)), and **M** are vectors that complement the unit tangent vectors $\boldsymbol{\Sigma}$ of $\partial\Sigma$ and the unit normal vectors **N** of Σ to orthonormal triads: $M_i = \varepsilon_{imp}\Sigma_m N_p$. Namely, let us consider

$$J_{ij} = \int M_i N_j f\,dS = \int \varepsilon_{imp} N_p N_j f\,dX_m,$$

where $dX_m = \Sigma_m\,dS$. According to Kelvin's transformation, J_{ij} is equivalent to a surface integral of $N_k\varepsilon_{krm}(\varepsilon_{imp}N_pN_jf)_{,r} = -N_i(N_kN_jf)_{,k} + N_k(N_kN_jf)_{,i}$. Introducing $\Delta_j = D_j + N_jD$, we find that the integrand reduces to $-N_iD_k \times (N_kN_jf) + N_kD_i(N_kN_jf) = -N_iN_jfD_kN_k + D_i(N_jf)$, from which it is easy to verify (16.24). If Σ is a closed surface without edges, and f is a continuous field, then the line integral in (16.25) vanishes (because $\partial\Sigma = 0$!). If, however, a closed surface is pieced together from smooth surface elements Σ in such a way that edges are formed on which M_iN_jf suffer discontinuity, then the line integrals of $[\![M_iN_jf]\!]$ will remain. Thus we are reminded again that in the present case Σ must be viewed as a thin shell; like a crease in a shell, an edge in a boundary surface must be treated as a line of singularities.

Following Toupin [170], let us consider static problems for hyperelastic materials of grade two, in which case the strain-energy density W, referred

† Cf. Toupin [169], p. 401.

to unit volume in the reference configuration, is a function of $F_{im} = x_{i.m}$, $F_{im.n} = x_{i.mn}$: $W = W(F_{im}, F_{im.n})$. To derive the boundary conditions and the equations of equilibrium, Toupin starts from the following version of Hamilton's principle $V[\delta W - f_i\, \delta x_i] - \partial V[t_i\, \delta x_i + h_i\, D\delta x_i] = 0$. Here all variables are referred to the reference configuration; f_i are body forces per unit volume, t_i and h_i are, respectively, surface tractions and hypertractions. We write $\delta W = \tilde{T}_{mi}\, \delta x_{i.m} + H_{mni}\, \delta x_{i.mn}$, where

$$\tilde{T}_{mi} = \frac{\partial W}{\partial x_{i.m}}, \qquad H_{mni} = \frac{\partial W}{\partial x_{i.mn}}, \tag{16.27}$$

H_{mni} being the *hyperstress tensor*. The polarization of the Piola-Kirchhoff stress $\tilde{T}_{mi}$ is defined by

$$\tilde{T}^*_{mi} = \tilde{T}^*_{mi} - \Delta_n H_{nmi}\,. \tag{16.28}$$

Because δx_i, $\delta x_{i.m}$, $\delta x_{i.mn}$ cannot be prescribed independently in V, there now follow the usual integrations by parts. In particular, from $H_{mni}\, \delta x_{i.mn} = \Delta_n(\delta x_{i.m} H_{mni}) - \Delta_m(\delta x_i \Delta_n H_{mni}) + \delta x_i \Delta_m \Delta_n H_{mni}$, we see that the first term on the right-hand side will lead to a surface integral $\partial V[N_n H_{mni}\, \delta x_{i.m}]$. We now let $\delta x_{i.m} = \Delta_m\, \delta x_i = N_m D\, \delta x_i + D_m\, \delta x_i$ and $-N_n H_{mni} D_m\, \delta x_i = -N_n D_m(H_{mni}\, \delta x_i) + N_n\, \delta x_i D_m H_{mni}$; in view of (16.25) (with $\partial\Sigma = 0$), this is the same as $-H_{mni}\, \delta x_i(K_{mn} - N_m N_n K_{rr}) + N_n\, \delta x_i D_m H_{mni}$. Therefore, the vanishing of the surface integral will yield the following boundary conditions,

$$h_i = H_{NNi}, \qquad t_i = \tilde{T}^*_{Ni} - S_m H_{mNi}, \tag{16.29}$$

where $H_{NNi} = H_{mni} N_m N_n$, $H_{mNi} = H_{mni} N_n$, $\tilde{T}^*_{Ni} = \tilde{T}^*_{mi} N_m$, and the surface operator S_m is defined by

$$S_m = D_m + N_m K_{rr}\,. \tag{16.30}$$

Finally, the vanishing of the volume integral requires that

$$\tilde{T}^*_{mi.m} + f_i = 0. \tag{16.31}$$

The boundary conditions show a radical departure from the boundary conditions $t_i = T_{ji} n_j$ of the classical theory. For one, the hypertractions $h_i(\mathbf{N})$ are not linear functions of **N**. Second, the surface tractions t_i depend not only on **N** but also on the surface gradients of **N**, i.e. at the boundary, or on an imagined "surface of separation", stresses will depend on the curvature of the surface. It is worth recalling that for inextensible deformations of a space curve the time rate of the curvature κ is proportional to the second velocity gradients of the points of the curve (cf. (11.47)). In the same way, the dependence of stress upon the second gradients $x_{i.mn}$ will correspond, in part, to a dependence upon curvatures of material surfaces.

To derive the balance equation for angular momentum, we let $x_i^+ = Q_{ij}x_j$, $F_{im}^+ = Q_{ij}F_{jm}$, $F_{im.n}^+ = Q_{ij}F_{jm.n}^+$, where $\mathbf{Q}$ depends on a continuous parameter ϕ. Then the invariance of W to any rotation of a body can be expressed by $\dot{W} = \dot{Q}_{ij}x_{j.m}\,\partial W/\partial x_{i.m}^+ + \dot{Q}_{ij}x_{j.mn}\,\partial W/\partial x_{i.mn}^+ = 0$ (cf. (19.1) *et seq.*), where a superposed dot indicates a derivative with respect to ϕ. In particular, if we choose $Q_{ij} = \delta_{ij}$, $\dot{Q}_{ij} = \Omega_{ij} = -\Omega_{ji}$, then it follows that

$$\varepsilon_{kij}\left(\frac{\partial W}{\partial x_{i.m}}\,x_{j.m} + \frac{\partial W}{\partial x_{i.mn}}\,x_{j.mn}\right) = 0. \tag{16.32}$$

Substituting $\delta x_i = \Omega_{ij}x_j + c_i$, $D\,\delta x_i = \Omega_{ij}x_{j.k}N_k \equiv \Omega_{ik}\bar{N}_k$ into Hamilton's principle, and bearing in mind that W must remain unchanged in this virtual displacement, we shall find that the external loads must satisfy the following "compatibility conditions" (they are of course the conditions of equilibrium for the material volume V): $V[f_i] + \partial V[t_i] = 0$, $V[\mathbf{x} \times \mathbf{f}] + \partial V[(\mathbf{x}\times\mathbf{t}) + (\bar{\mathbf{N}} \times \mathbf{h})] = \mathbf{0}$. In the classical theory these conditions would be applied to a tetrahedral "free body"; this is not possible here, because the edges of a tetrahedron make it a singular "free body" (cf. (16.29)!).

With a little work, we can also obtain the Cosserats' moment equation. In analogy with (15.87), we define the stress tensors

$$T_{ij}^* = \frac{1}{J}\,F_{im}\tilde{T}_{mj}^*, \qquad \tfrac{1}{2}M_{kji} = \frac{1}{J}\,F_{kn}F_{jm}H_{nmi}, \tag{16.33}$$

where $J = \det\mathbf{F}$. Now, by (16.28), $JT_{ji}^* = F_{jm}\,\partial W/\partial F_{im} + F_{jm.n}\,\partial W/\partial F_{im.n} - \Delta_n F_{jm}H_{nmi}$. The last term can be also written as $\tfrac{1}{2}\Delta_n(F_{jm}JF_{nk}^{-1}F_{mr}^{-1}M_{kri}) = -\tfrac{1}{2}\Delta_n(JF_{nk}^{-1}M_{kji})$. In view of the identity $(15.88)_1$, this simplifies to $-M_{kji,k}$, so that $JT_{ji} = (F_{jm}\partial W/\partial F_{im} + F_{jm.n}\,\partial W/\partial F_{im.n}) - \tfrac{1}{2}JM_{kji,k}$. According to (16.32), however, the expression in parentheses must be symmetric in i and j. Therefore, as a consequence of the strain-energy function having been assumed to be independent of rotations of the body, we recover the moment balance

$$\tfrac{1}{2}M_{k[ij],k} + T_{[ij]} = 0 \tag{16.34}$$

(cf. (11.11)).

To satisfy the condition that the strain-energy function be invariant to rotations of a body, we proceed in the usual way. Thus, with $\mathbf{F} = \mathbf{RU}$, $\mathbf{Q} = \mathbf{R}^T$, we have that $\overline{W}(F_{im}, \Delta_n F_{im}) = \overline{W}(U_{im}, R_{ji}\Delta_n F_{jm}) \equiv W(C_{im}, F_{ji}\Delta_n F_{jm})$, where $\mathbf{C} = \mathbf{F}^T\mathbf{F} = \mathbf{U}^2$. In view of $F_{rm}\Delta_j F_{ri} = x_{r.m}x_{r.ij} = C_{ijm} = E_{mj.i} + E_{im.j} - E_{ij.m}$ (cf. (15.19)), where $2E_{im} = C_{im} - \delta_{im}$, the strain-energy function depends only on strains and their gradients. In the linear theory, we assume the following expansion of the strain-energy density per unit volume of the reference configuration:

$$W = \mu(W^0 + T^0_{ij}E_{ij} + lH^0_{ijk}E_{ij.k} + \frac{1}{2}C_{ijkm}E_{ij}E_{km}$$
$$+ lD_{ijkmp}E_{ij}E_{km.p} + \frac{l^2}{2}F_{ijkmpr}E_{ij.k}E_{mp.r}), \quad (16.35)$$

where μ is a characteristic elastic modulus, and l is a characteristic length. The representation (16.35) may be considered as an exact description of some materials, or as an approximate description of all elastic materials of grade two (valid whenever $|\mathbf{E}| \ll 1$, $l\,|\text{grad}\mathbf{E}| \ll 1$). Evidently $\mu\mathbf{T}^0$ and $\mu l\mathbf{H}^0$ are the initial stress and hyperstress, respectively, whereas $\mu\mathbf{C}$ is the tensor of elastic moduli. Toupin and Gazis† refer to $\mu l\mathbf{D}$ as the rotary tensor, and $\mu l^2\mathbf{F}$ as the tensor of hyperelastic moduli. We assume that the material is *elastically homogeneous* in the sense that there exists at least one reference configuration in which the coefficients occurring in (16.35) are constants. This property of the coefficients will be preserved in any mapping $X_i \to \overline{X}_i = G_{ij}X_j$ with constant coefficients G_{ij}. Because $\mathbf{F} = \overline{\mathbf{F}}\mathbf{G}$, it follows that $\mathbf{C} = \mathbf{F}^T\mathbf{F} = \mathbf{G}^T\overline{\mathbf{F}}^T\overline{\mathbf{F}}\mathbf{G} = \mathbf{G}^T\overline{\mathbf{C}}\mathbf{G}$, thus $2\mathbf{E} = \mathbf{C} - \mathbf{1} = \mathbf{G}^T\overline{\mathbf{C}}\mathbf{G} - \mathbf{1} = \mathbf{G}^T(\overline{\mathbf{C}} - \mathbf{1})\mathbf{G} + 2\mathbf{A}$, where $2\mathbf{A} = \mathbf{G}^T\mathbf{G} - \mathbf{1}$ is the strain associated with $\mathbf{G}$. Bearing in mind that G_{ij} are constant, we obtain

$$\frac{\partial E_{ij}}{\partial X_k} = G_{mi}G_{nj}G_{pk}\frac{\partial \overline{E}_{mn}}{\partial \overline{X}_p}. \quad (16.36)$$

The coefficients of the strain-energy function thus transform according to $W^0 \to W^0 + T^0_{ij}A_{ij} + \frac{1}{2}C_{ijkm}A_{ij}A_{km}$, $T^0_{ij} \to \overline{T}^0_{ij} + \overline{C}_{ijkm}A_{km}$, $H^0_{ijk} \to \overline{H}^0_{ijk} + \overline{D}_{ijkmp}A_{mp}$, $C_{ijkm} \to \overline{C}_{ijkm}$, $F_{ijkmnp} \to \overline{F}_{ijkmnp}$, where overbars mark variables obtained by transformations of the type shown in (16.36). If the initial stress $\mathbf{T}^0$ is small, then there exists a local reference configuration in which $\overline{\mathbf{T}}^0 = \mathbf{0}$. Then, however, the strain $\mathbf{A}$ is fixed, so that in general the initial hyperstress $\overline{\mathbf{H}}^0$ need not vanish.

† *Op. cit.*

The linearized stress relations obtained by Toupin and Gazis are

$$\frac{1}{\mu} T_{ij} = T^0_{ij} + T^0_{jk} u_{i,k} + C_{ijkm} u_{k,m} + l(D_{ijkmp} - D_{kmijp}) u_{k,mp} - l^2 F_{ijkmnp} u_{m,np},$$

$$\frac{1}{\mu l} H_{kji} = H^0_{jki} + H^0_{kjm} u_{i,m} + D_{mnkji} u_{m,n} + l F_{mnpkji} u_{m,np}.$$

In the one-dimensional problem of an infinite slab with faces $\mathbf{N} \cdot \mathbf{X} = \pm L/2$ free of surface tractions it is readily found that the displacement field is of the form $u = A \cosh k\mathbf{N} \cdot \mathbf{X} + B \sinh k\mathbf{N} \cdot \mathbf{X} + C\mathbf{N} \cdot \mathbf{X} + D$, where A, B, C, D, k are constants. Toupin and Gazis then use the same type of displacement field to solve the problem of a finite chain with nearest and next-nearest neighbor interactions. This particular example provides a model for surface effects in a plate cut from a block of crystalline material.

It will be recalled that the material coefficients must be invariant to the symmetry operations $\mathbf{S}$, e.g. $T^0_{ij} = S_{im} S_{jn} T^0_{mn}$, $H^0_{ijk} = S_{im} S_{jn} S_{kp} H^0_{mnp}$. Thus initial hyperstress can be present only in materials without a center of symmetry. Therefore, to investigate the effects associated with $\mathbf{H}^0$, one must either go to hemitropic materials, or to crystals without a center of symmetry, or else go to materials of grade three (in which case there will exist an initial stress tensor of rank four). In the latter case the strain-energy function depends on $x_{i,m}$, $x_{i,mn}$, $x_{i,mnp}$. A linear theory of elastic materials of grade three has been recently developed by Mindlin [235]. A brief outline of this theory follows.

In the derivations that follow we shall need (16.24) and a variant of the divergence theorem on a surface, (11.67). To derive the latter, we consider a surface Σ spanned over a closed curve $\partial\Sigma$, and denote by $\boldsymbol{\Sigma}$ the unit tangent vectors of $\partial\Sigma$. The sense of $\boldsymbol{\Sigma}$ is chosen so that the unit vectors $\mathbf{M} = \boldsymbol{\Sigma} \times \mathbf{N}$ point away from Σ. Now let $\mathbf{f}$ be any tensor; because the divergence theorem will operate only on one index of $\mathbf{f}$, we shall write f_i for $f_{\ldots i}$, and f for $\mathbf{f} \cdot \mathbf{N}$. To prove that

$$\partial\Sigma[f_i M_i] = \Sigma[D_i f_i + f K_{ii}], \tag{16.37}$$

we write $\partial\Sigma[f_i M_i] = \partial\Sigma[f_i \varepsilon_{ijk} \Sigma_j N_k]$, and use Kelvin's transformation. With $A_j = \varepsilon_{ijk} f_i N_k$, the resulting integral is

$$\Sigma[N_p \varepsilon_{pmj}(N_m D + D_m) A_j] = \Sigma[N_p \varepsilon_{pmj} D_m A_j],$$

from which it is easy to verify (16.37).

Omitting the body force terms, Hamilton's principle for elastic materials of grade three is as follows: $V[\delta W] = \partial V[t_i \, \delta x_i + h_i \, D\delta x_i + p_i \, D^2 \delta x_i]$. The polarization of the Piola-Kirchhoff stress will now be given by $\tilde{T}^*_{mi} = \tilde{T}_{mi} - \Delta_n H^*_{nmi}$, where H^*_{nmi} is itself a polarization of the previously introduced hyperstress:

$$H^*_{nmi} = H_{nmi} - \Delta_p P_{pnmi}, \qquad P_{pnmi} = \frac{\partial W}{\partial x_{i.mnp}}. \tag{16.38}$$

The terms that were absent in the theory for materials of grade two will stem from $V[P_{pnmi} \, \delta x_{i.mnp}] = \partial V[N_p \, \delta x_{i.mn} P_{pmni}] - V[\delta x_{i.mn} \Delta_p P_{pnmi}]$. The last term on the right-hand side is absorbed by the polarizations of stress and hyperstress; the evaluation of the first term requires a good deal of work. To evaluate $\partial V[N_p(D_n \, \delta x_{i.m}) P_{pnmi}] = \partial V[D_n N_p \, \delta x_{i.m} P_{pnmi}] - \partial V[\delta x_{i.m} D_n N_p P_{pnmi}]$, we invoke (16.37), thus obtaining $-\partial V[\delta x_{i.m} S_n N_p P_{pnmi}]$. With $\delta x_{i.m} = D_m \, \delta x_i + N_m D \, \delta x_i$, and using again (16.37), this can be reduced to

$$-\partial V[N_m(D \, \delta x_i) S_n N_p P_{pnmi}] + \partial V[\delta x_i S_m S_n N_p P_{pnmi}].$$

The evaluation of $\partial V[N_p N_n (D \, \delta x_{i.m}) P_{pnmi}]$ is more intricate. First, we suppose that the boundary ∂V is described by $X_i = X_i(U_\alpha)$, where U_α, $\alpha = 1, 2$, are orthogonal surface coordinates. To show that $DN_i = 0$, we consider a family of parallel surfaces $\bar{X}_i = \bar{X}_i(U_\alpha, \zeta) = X_i(U_\alpha) + \zeta N_i(U_\alpha)$ in the vicinity of ∂V. In this vicinity, U_α and ζ define an orthogonal coordinate system in space. We let $\mathbf{N} = \mathbf{i}_3$, $D = \partial_3$, so that, by (6.55), $D\mathbf{N} = \partial_3 \mathbf{i}_3 = -w_{133}\mathbf{i}_1 - w_{233}\mathbf{i}_2$. Therefore, it remains to show that $w_{133} = w_{233} = 0$ (in spherical coordinates the directions normal to the closed coordinate surfaces are $\mathbf{i}_1$, and, correspondingly, $w_{211} = w_{311} = 0$). Now, by (11.60), $dN_i = -K_{\alpha\beta} X_{i,\beta} \, dU_\alpha$, so that $d\bar{X}_i = (\delta_{\alpha\beta} - \zeta K_{\alpha\beta}) X_{i,\beta} \, dU_\alpha + d\zeta \, N_i$. From this it follows that $H_3 = 1$, $w_{313} = \partial_1 \log H_3 = 0$, $w_{323} = \partial_2 \log H_3 = 0$. But if $DN_i = 0$, then $\Delta_m N_i = D_m N_i = -K_{im}$ and $D\Delta_m = N_s \Delta_s \Delta_m = N_s \Delta_m \Delta_s = \Delta_m N_s \Delta_s - (\Delta_m N_s)\Delta_s = \Delta_m D + K_{ms} D_s = N_m D^2 + D_m D + K_{ms} D_s$ (note that $K_{ms} N_s = 0$ because curvature is a surface tensor). Consequently, the second contribution to the boundary conditions can be written as

$$\begin{aligned} &\partial V[N_p N_n N_m (D^2 \, \delta x_i) P_{pnmi}] + \partial V[N_p N_n (D_m D \, \delta x_i) P_{pnmi}] \\ &\qquad + \partial V[N_p N_n K_{ms} (D_s \, \delta x_i) P_{pnmi}]. \end{aligned}$$

The last two terms can be again reduced by the method that was used before.

Noting that, by (16.37), $\partial V[D_s K_{ms}] = 0$, we thus obtain from Hamilton's principle the following boundary conditions,

$$\begin{aligned} p_i &= N_p N_n N_m P_{pnmi}, \\ h_i &= N_n N_m H^*_{nmi} - N_m S_n N_p P_{pnmi} - S_m N_n N_p P_{pnmi}, \qquad (16.39) \\ t_i &= N_m \tilde{T}^*_{mi} - S_m N_n H^*_{nmi} + S_m S_n N_p P_{pnmi} - K_{ms} D_s N_n N_p P_{pnmi}. \end{aligned}$$

The equations of equilibrium are given by

$$\Delta_m \tilde{T}^*_{mi} = 0. \qquad (16.31)^*$$

Evidently the boundary conditions are quite complicated; they become even more complicated if the boundary has edges (cf. the Appendix in [235]). But the theory is perhaps not meant for the solution of routine boundary value problems. The other function of a theory, namely to provide rational explanations of various phenomena, may be far more important. Thus Mindlin's theory can account for surface tension in isotropic materials.

A special case of the linear theory of grade two materials is obtained by assuming that the strain-energy function depends on the *curl* of strains, given by $\varepsilon_{ijk} E_{km,j} = \phi_{i,m}$, $\boldsymbol{\phi} = \frac{1}{2}\text{curl}\mathbf{u}$, rather than on all gradients of strain. The resulting "theory of elasticity with couple stresses" has received a good deal of attention in the recent literature.† The geometric model underlying this theory may be interpreted as a "Cosserat continuum with constrained rotations." Setting the intrinsic angular velocity equal to the mean angular velocity $\boldsymbol{\omega}$ of the material lines, we find from (11.12) that $T_{[ij]}$ does no work. Therefore, the constitutive equation only specifies $T_{(ij)} = \lambda E_{kk}\delta_{ij} + 2\mu E_{ij}$, and the balance of angular momentum is taken as the definition of the skew-symmetric part of stress: $\varepsilon_{ijk} T_{[jk]} = -M_{ji,j}$. Further, because $\text{div}\boldsymbol{\phi} = 0$, the scalar $\text{tr}\mathbf{M}$ also does no work, so that the constitutive equation for couple stresses determines only the deviatoric part $M^D_{ji} = A\phi_{j,i} + B\phi_{i,j}$. To obtain the appropriate boundary conditions, we may investigate the uniqueness of solutions, using the method outlined in the preceding section (cf. (15.63) *et seq.*) Assuming that the densities of strain energy and kinetic energy are positive definite, we shall find at first that the boundary conditions must specify one member from each pair $t_i v_i$ and $\mu_i \omega_i$. However, in $T_{ji} n_j v_i$ we must now eliminate $T_{[ji]}$, and in $M_{ji} n_j \omega_i$ we must not only eliminate $\text{tr}\mathbf{M}$ but also the component $\boldsymbol{\omega} \cdot \mathbf{n} = \frac{1}{2}(v_{2,1} - v_{1,2})$ (cf. $(11.69)_1$), where the indices 1 and 2 now refer

† Cf. Muki and Sternberg [103].

to surface coordinates on the boundary ∂V. With $\mu = M_{ji}n_jn_i$, we obtain by Kelvin's transformation that $\Sigma[\mu\omega] = \frac{1}{2}\varepsilon_{ijk}\Sigma[v_{k,j}\mu n_i] = \frac{1}{2}\partial\Sigma[\mu\hat{v}] - \frac{1}{2}\varepsilon_{ijk}\Sigma[n_i\mu_{,j}v_k]$, where $\hat{v}$ is the projection of velocity upon the curve $\partial\Sigma$. Introducing curvilinear coordinates θ_a, $a = 1, 2, 3$ such that $\mathbf{n} = \mathbf{i}_3$, the last term becomes $-\frac{1}{2}\Sigma[M_{33;1}v_2 - M_{33;2}v_1]$. If the boundary ∂V consists of smooth surfaces Σ that are joined along curves $\partial\Sigma$ on which M_{33} is discontinuous, then $\frac{1}{2}\partial\Sigma[M_{33}\hat{v}]$ will give rise to an additional boundary condition. Eliminating $\varepsilon_{abc}T_{[bc]} = -M_{ba;b}$ from the boundary conditions, and noting that $M_{ba;b} - M_{33;a} = M^D_{ba;b} - M^D_{33;a}$, we finally conclude that boundary conditions must specify one member from each of the following sets,

$$T_{33}u_3,\ p_{31}u_1,\ p_{32}u_2,\ M_{31}\phi_1,\ M_{32}\phi_2 \text{ on } \Sigma, \tag{16.40}$$

where

$$p_{31} = T_{(31)} - \frac{1}{2}M^D_{a2;a} + \frac{1}{2}M^D_{33;2},$$

$$p_{32} = T_{(32)} + \frac{1}{2}M^D_{a1;a} - \frac{1}{2}M^D_{33;1},$$

and one member of $[\![M_{33}]\!]\hat{u}$ on edges $\partial\Sigma$. In this theory a finite circular cylinder is not a "nice" body because of the edges at the intersections of the mantle with the cross sections.

One does not have to look very far to find tangible examples of microstructure. For one, elastic shells can be viewed as two-dimensional elastic continua with a microstructure that relates to the thickness aspect of shells. Another reason why a brief look at shells might be interesting is that deformation theory of "subspaces" (e.g. curves, surfaces) splits into *intrinsic* and *extrinsic* parts. The former is, in essence, the same as the deformation theory of three-dimensional continua (although the metric of subspaces need no longer be Euclidean). The extrinsic part is, on the other hand, a new feature, because it deals with the imbedding of subspaces. As in Section 11, our aim will not be to review the existing theories; we merely wish to see what it takes to build such theories.

Because the deformed shape of a surface is neither simple nor given *a priori*, it is expedient to use in the surface material coordinate systems U^α, $\alpha = 1, 2$ (also called convected, or imbedded, coordinate systems) defined by grids scribed on the initial configuration, and deforming together with the surface. Material coordinates are of course familiar quantities by now, but not *material coordinate systems*. That is, so far the approach has been to single out a particular configuration of a body, and to introduce in this configuration the positions of particles as their material coordinates. In this way material lines and surfaces are marked once for all; however, we have not used material coordinate systems as frames of reference at other stages of deformation, when material lines form in general oblique, curvilinear coordinate nets. To clarify the difference between spatial and material representations of deformation theory, we note that in the former a mapping $d\Pi = \mathbf{e}_i\, dX_i \to d\pi = \mathbf{e}_i dx_i$ is "applied" to the components of material filaments, the Cartesian base vectors $\mathbf{e}_i$ being held fixed. In the material representation the mapping is "transferred" to the base vectors, $\mathbf{E}_j = \mathbf{e}_i F_{ij}$ (cf. (15.27)), thus $d\Pi = \mathbf{e}_i\, dX_i \to d\pi = \mathbf{e}_i F_{ij}\, dX_j = \mathbf{E}_j\, dX_j$, and the (material) components dX_j of a filament remain unchanged. Further, $C_{ij} = \mathbf{E}_i \cdot \mathbf{E}_j$ (a deformation tensor!) becomes the metric tensor of the coordinate system X_i imbedded in the deformed body. The (metric) strain is simply the difference of the material metrics: $2E_{ij} = \mathbf{E}_i \cdot \mathbf{E}_j - \mathbf{e}_i \cdot \mathbf{e}_j = C_{ij} - \delta_{ij}$. The "three-index strains" are constructed from material Christoffel symbols, e.g.

$$
\begin{aligned}
J_{ijm} &= \frac{1}{2}(C_{mj.i} + C_{im.j} - C_{ij.m}) = x_{r.m}x_{r.ij}, \\
J_{i(jm)} &= E_{jm.i}, \quad -\frac{1}{2}\varepsilon_{kmj}J_{ijm} = \varepsilon_{kmj}E_{ij.m}.
\end{aligned}
\tag{16.41}
$$

Let $x_i = x_i(U^\alpha, t)$, $X_i = X_i(U^\alpha)$ stand, respectively, for the current and initial configurations of a surface. Variables in the initial configuration will be denoted by majuscule kernel letters, those in the current configuration by minuscule kernel letters. In particular, we shall write $a_{\alpha\beta} = x_{i,\alpha}x_{i,\beta}$ for the current metric tensor (rather than $C_{\alpha\beta} = x_{i,\alpha}x_{i,\beta}$). The definitions and notations introduced in Section 11 (cf. (11.54)–(11.63)) apply, of course, also to the initial configuration, thus $A_{\alpha\beta} = X_{i,\alpha}X_{i,\beta}$, $K_{\alpha\beta} = N_i X_{i,\alpha\beta}$. Intrinsic derivatives in the undeformed configuration will bear the mark $||$, thus $x_{i|\alpha\beta} = x_{i,\alpha\beta} - a^{\rho}_{\alpha\beta}x_{i,\rho}$, $x_{i\|\alpha\beta} = x_{i,\alpha\beta} - A^{\rho}_{\alpha\beta}x_{i,\rho}$. It is important to note that $n_i x_{i|\alpha\beta} = n_i x_{i\|\alpha\beta} = n_i x_{i\|\alpha\beta} = k_{\alpha\beta}$ (a deformation tensor now!), whereas $x_{i,\gamma}x_{i|\alpha\beta} = 0$, $x_{i,\gamma}x_{i\|\alpha\beta} = a_{\alpha\beta\gamma} - A^{\rho}_{\alpha\beta}a_{\rho\gamma}$.

An elastic surface Σ is characterized by a strain-energy function $W = W(x_{i,\alpha})$. We write $\Sigma[T^\alpha{}_i\, \delta x_{i,\alpha}] - \Sigma[f_i\, \delta x_i] - \partial\Sigma[t_i\, \delta x_i] = 0$, where $T^\alpha{}_i = \partial W/\partial x_{i,\alpha}$, f_i are "body forces" per unit area of reference configuration, and t_i are edge tractions. With $\delta x_{i,\alpha} = (\delta x_i)_{,\alpha} = (\delta x_i)_{\|\alpha}$, and (11.67), we readily obtain

$$
T^\alpha{}_{i\|\alpha} + f_i = 0 \text{ in } \Sigma, \qquad T^\alpha{}_i M_\alpha = t_i \text{ on } \partial\Sigma, \tag{16.42}
$$

where $\mathbf{M} = \mathbf{\Sigma} \times \mathbf{N}$, $\mathbf{\Sigma}$ being a unit tangent vector of the boundary curve $\partial\Sigma$. The requirement that W be form-invariant to observer transformations $x_i \to Q_{ij}(t)x_j + c_i(t)$ is met by taking W as a function of $a_{\alpha\beta} = x_{i,\alpha}x_{i,\beta}$ (note that $n_i x_{i,\alpha} = 0$), or, what amounts to the same thing, as a function of $E_{\alpha\beta} = \frac{1}{2}(a_{\alpha\beta} - A_{\alpha\beta})$. Then it follows that $T^\alpha{}_i = x_{i,\mu}\,\partial W/\partial E_{\mu\alpha}$, so that $T^\alpha{}_i n_i = 0$, and

$$T^\alpha{}_\beta = T^\alpha{}_i x_{i,\beta} = \frac{\partial W}{\partial E_{\mu\alpha}}\, a_{\mu\beta}. \tag{16.43}$$

If the material is isotropic, then W must be invariant to transformations of surface coordinates, which means that W depends only on those combinations of the components $E_{\alpha\beta}$ which are isotropic invariants (of the two-dimensional orthogonal group), e.g. $W = W(\bar{\mathrm{I}}, \bar{\mathrm{II}})$, where $\bar{\mathrm{I}} = E^\alpha{}_\alpha$, $\bar{\mathrm{II}} = E^\alpha{}_\beta E^\alpha{}_\beta$. For small strains, to obtain the linear Hooke's law, we set $a_{\mu\beta}$ equal to $A_{\mu\beta}$ in (16.43), and assume $W = \frac{1}{2}(\lambda\bar{\mathrm{I}}^2 + 2\mu\bar{\mathrm{II}})$.

To appreciate the difficulty of the theory, one should look at the strain-displacement relations. We let $x_i = X_i + u_i$, $u_i = uN_i + u^\rho X_{i,\rho}$ so that $u_{i,\alpha} = u_{,\alpha}N_i - uK_\alpha{}^\rho X_{i,\rho} + u^\rho{}_{,\alpha}X_{i,\rho} + u^\rho X_{i,\rho\alpha}$. The normal component of the last two terms is $u^\rho K_{\rho\alpha}$ (cf. (11.61)), whereas the surface components are given by $u^\beta{}_{\|\alpha}$. Thus $u_{i,\alpha} = u_{,\alpha}N_i + u^\rho K_{\rho\alpha}N_i - uK_\alpha{}^\rho X_{i,\rho} + u^\rho{}_{\|\alpha}X_{i,\rho}$; in the principal coordinate system of $K_{\alpha\beta}$,

$$\begin{aligned} 2E_{\alpha\beta} &= u_{\alpha\|\beta}\left(1 + \frac{u}{R_{\underline{\alpha}}}\right) + u_{\beta\|\alpha}\left(1 + \frac{u}{R_{\underline{\beta}}}\right) + u^\rho{}_{\|\alpha}u_{\rho\|\beta} \\ &\quad + \left(\frac{2u}{R_{\underline{\alpha}}} + \frac{u^2}{R^2_{\underline{\alpha}}}\right)\delta_{\alpha\beta} + u_{,\alpha}u_{,\beta} - u_{,\alpha}\frac{u^\beta}{R_{\underline{\beta}}} - u_{,\beta}\frac{u^\alpha}{R_{\underline{\alpha}}} + \frac{u^\alpha u^\beta}{R_{\underline{\alpha}}R_{\underline{\beta}}}, \end{aligned} \tag{16.44}$$

where we have let $K_{\alpha\beta} = -\delta_{\alpha\beta}/R_{\underline{\alpha}}$. If the surface is initially flat, then $K_{\alpha\beta} = 0$.

To illustrate the specification of initial configurations, let us take a torroidal membrane, the center line of which lies in the xy plane, and is of radius C. The meridional circles are given by $\phi =$ const.; we denote by R the radius of these circles, and by M the angle measured along a meridional circle (from the xy plane up). Then the membrane is described by

$$X = (C + R\cos M)\cos\phi, \quad Y = (C + R\cos M)\sin\phi, \quad Z = R\sin M. \tag{16.45}$$

The nonvanishing components of $A_{\alpha\beta} = X_{i,\alpha}X_{i,\beta}$ are then $A_{\phi\phi} = (C + R\cos M)^2 = 1/A^{\phi\phi}$, $A_{MM} = 1/R^2 = 1/A^{MM}$, and the nonvanishing Christoffel symbols are $A^M_{\phi\phi} = (CR^{-1} + \cos M)\sin M$, $A^\phi_{\phi M} = -\sin M/(CR^{-1} + \cos M)$. With $A = R(C + R\cos M)$, $N_i = \varepsilon_{ijk}X_{j,\phi}X_{k,M}/A$, we obtain $N_1 = \cos\phi\cos M$, $N_2 = \sin\phi\cos M$, $N_3 = \sin M$. From these, and (16.45), it follows that $-K_{\phi\phi} = N_{1,\phi}X_{,\phi} + N_{2,\phi}Y_{,\phi} + N_{3,\phi}Z_{,\phi} = (C + R\cos M)$

cos M, and, similarly, that $K_{\phi M} = 0$, $K_{MM} = -R$. We are now ready to use (16.44); thus for axisymmetric deformations we may substitute $u = u(M)$, $u_M = v(M)$ into (16.44).

For elastic shells ("elastic surfaces of grade two") we write $W = W(x_{i,\alpha}, x_{i\|\alpha\beta})$. Because X_i and U^α are held constant in the variations considered in Hamilton's principle, it follows that $\delta A^\rho_{\alpha\beta} = 0$, and $\delta x_{i\|\alpha\beta} = (\delta x_i)_{\|\alpha\beta}$. Therefore, starting with $\Sigma[T^\alpha{}_i\delta x_{i,\alpha} + H^{\alpha\beta}{}_i\,\delta x_{i\|\alpha\beta} - f_i\,\delta x_i - B^\alpha{}_i\,\delta x_{i,\alpha}] - \partial\Sigma[t_i\,\delta x_i + h_i\,D\delta x_i] = 0$, where $H^{\alpha\beta}{}_i = \partial W/\partial x_{i\|\alpha\beta}$ (note that $x_{i\|\alpha\beta} = x_{i\|\beta\alpha}$), and $D = M^\alpha\,\partial/\partial U^\alpha$ is a surface differentiation normal to $\partial\Sigma$, we obtain

$$*T^\alpha{}_{i\|\alpha} + *f_i = 0 \text{ in } \Sigma,$$

$$*T^\alpha{}_i = T^\alpha{}_i - H^{\alpha\beta}{}_{i\|\beta}, \qquad *f_i = f_i - B^\alpha{}_{i\|\alpha},$$

$$h_i = M_\alpha M_\beta H^{\alpha\beta}{}_i, \qquad t_i = M_\alpha *T^\alpha{}_i - \frac{d}{dS}\,M_\alpha\Sigma_\beta H^{\alpha\beta}{}_i \text{ on } \partial\Sigma.$$

To make W objective, we again replace the independent variables $x_{i,\alpha}$ by the "spatially isotropic" tensor $E_{\alpha\beta}$. Similarly, $x_{i\|\alpha\beta}$ may be replaced by the "spatially isotropic" tensors

$$k_{\alpha\beta} = n_i x_{i\|\alpha\beta}, \qquad E_{\alpha\beta\gamma} = x_{i,\gamma}x_{i\|\alpha\beta} = \frac{1}{2}\,(E_{\gamma\beta\|\alpha} + E_{\alpha\gamma\|\beta} - E_{\alpha\beta\|\gamma}). \tag{16.46}$$

The classical shell theory does not allow for a dependence of W upon the strain-gradients $E_{\alpha\beta\gamma}$ (this dependence would give rise to self-equilibrated hyperstresses). Even so, because stresses now depend on two kinds of strains, $E_{\alpha\beta}$ and $k_{\alpha\beta}$, the number of response coefficients will exceed the number of elastic properties found in Hooke's law, for instance. Of course, we know that some of the new properties are really geometric properties of shells; thus a "material length" l may be identified with the thickness $2h$ of a shell. Still, to obtain an explicit representation of the strain-energy function, a specific model for the "microstructure" is needed. In the classical theories a shell is considered, at first, as a three-dimensional body, and subsequently an averaging over the thickness is carried out.† This method is outlined below.

Let us mark a typical point of a shell by its surface coordinates U^α and a "normal coordinate" ζ. In *Kirchhoff's model*, a point originally located at $X_i(U^\alpha) + \zeta N_i(U^\alpha)$ will move to a position $\xi_i(U^\alpha, \zeta) = x_i(U^\alpha) + \zeta n_i(U^\alpha)$, i.e. a

† Cf. Hamel [67], pp. 159–162.

shell consists of a membrane and its unit normal vectors; the points of the shell are all strung up on the unit normal vectors. Then

$$ds^2 = d\xi_i\, d\xi_i = \gamma_{\alpha\beta}\, dU^\alpha\, dU^\beta + (d\zeta)^2,$$
$$\gamma_{\alpha\beta} = a_{\alpha\beta} - 2\zeta k_{\alpha\beta} + \zeta^2 k_{\alpha\rho} k_\beta{}^\rho. \tag{16.47}$$

With the analogous definition for $\Gamma_{\alpha\beta}$, we have that

$$dS^2 = \Gamma_{\alpha\beta}\, dU^\alpha\, dU^\beta + (d\zeta)^2 \tag{16.48}$$

in the initial configuration. For isotropic materials the strain-energy function can depend only on the isotropic invariants of $\gamma_{\alpha\beta}$: $W = W(\mathrm{I}, \mathrm{II})$. We may now base the stress relations on the average strain-energy function

$$\overline{W} = \frac{1}{2h} \int_{-h}^{h} W(\mathrm{I}, \mathrm{II})\, d\zeta. \tag{16.49}$$

In this way we would obtain a "three constant" (e.g. E, ν, h) linear theory. It would be of interest to explore a "six constant" theory in which W depends on h and the five simultaneous invariants of $a_{\alpha\beta}$ and $k_{\alpha\beta}$.

The geometric model of the preceding theory is a "Cosserat surface with constrained rotations." A general Cosserat surface would be described by

$$\xi_i(U^\alpha, \zeta) = x_i(U^\alpha) + \zeta d_i(U^\alpha), \tag{16.50}$$

where the directors **d** differ from the unit normal vectors **n** by a small rotation (cf. [58], [54]). In particular, $d_i x_{i,\alpha}$ would then account for an average shearing of the top face of a shell relative to its bottom face (note that $n_i x_{i,\alpha} = 0$!).

Oriented materials

If we look for ways of grouping together various multipolar theories, then, along with materials of grade N, we can discern the notion of "oriented materials." By "orientation" we mean here a type of microstructure that usually (but not always) exhibits a directionality. We describe this microstructure in terms of M directors $\mathbf{d}_a$ (if $M = 3$, a subscript $\underline{a}$ may be interpreted as an index, otherwise it is a label; in any case, the summation convention over $\underline{a}$ repeated as a subscript and a superscript will be retained). If the deformation of directors is *locally homogeneous*, then all directors are mapped by a single function ϕ_{im} from their initial states $\mathbf{D}_a$ into their current states:

$$d_{ai} = \phi_{im} D_{am}, \qquad D_{ai} = \phi_{im}^{-1} d_{am}. \tag{16.51}$$

In particular, with $\phi_{im} = F_{im}$ we obtain a slight generalization of materials of grade N (an explicit dependence upon $\mathbf{D}_a$ introduces a kind of "directional inhomogeneity"). As a point of departure, we shall take the classical theory of *Cosserat continua*, in which it is assumed that $M = 3$, and that the directors constitute orthonormal triads, so that one may also speak of continua with "oriented particles". The motion of directors is then described by $d_{ai}(\mathbf{X}, t) = P_{im}(\mathbf{X}, t)D_{am}(\mathbf{X})$, where $\mathbf{P}$ is an orthogonal tensor. The special case $\mathbf{P} = \mathbf{R}$ ("Cosserat continua with constrained rotations"), where $\mathbf{R}$ is obtained in the polar decomposition $\mathbf{F} = \mathbf{RU}$, belongs actually to the theory of materials of grade two.

It is too early to tell whether the theories of Cosserat continua will have any striking applications. As in all theories of microstructure, there will be a material property with the dimension of length, so that we shall be able to give some account of boundary layer effects and dispersion of waves. In a broader view, we may look upon Cosserat continua as models of continua undergoing (locally) *incompatible rotations.* We assume that the mappings $d\mathbf{X} \to d\mathbf{x} = \mathbf{F}\,d\mathbf{X}$ are compatible, as before, because if they are not, then we cannot calculate the final shape of a body from its initial shape, and vice versa. That is, even though the deformation may be, locally, less than "perfect", there is a gross change of shape that we ought to be able to describe. This is in fact done through the mapping $\mathbf{x} = \mathbf{x}(\mathbf{X}, t)$; at the same time, the interpretations of particles $\mathbf{X}$ and their places $\mathbf{x}$ become more elusive, because $\mathbf{x} = \mathbf{x}(\mathbf{X}, t)$ describes some kind of mean motion that is not unlike the mean motion of a turbulent flow, for instance. The "incompatibility" is carried along separately; it is described by the tensor field $\mathbf{P}(\mathbf{X}, t)$.

As a rule, the invariance of constitutive equations calls for deformation measures that are invariant to observer transformations. Thus from $F_{im} = \partial x_i/\partial X_m$ we construct $\mathbf{C} = \mathbf{F}^T\mathbf{F} = \mathbf{C}^+$, although $\mathbf{F}^+ = \mathbf{QF}$. The directors are assumed to be objective, so that $d_{ai}^+ = Q_{ij}d_{aj}$; because the initial states $\mathbf{D}_a$ are not affected by observer transformations, it follows that (obviously!) the rotation tensor $\mathbf{P}$ is not objective: $d_{ai}^+ = Q_{ij}P_{jm}D_{am}$, $P_{im}^+ = Q_{ij}P_{jm}$. However, the "relative" strain

$$\mathbf{\Gamma} = \mathbf{P}^{-1}\mathbf{F} = (\mathbf{P}^{-1}\mathbf{R})\mathbf{U} \tag{16.52}$$

will be objective. Finally, because the rotation gradients $P_{im.k}^+ = Q_{ij}P_{jm.k}$ are not objective, we replace them by the objective tensors

$$K_{kij} = -K_{ikj} = P_{mk}P_{mi.j}. \tag{16.53}$$

To obtain linearized strains and rotation gradients, we let $\mathbf{F} = \mathbf{1} + \tilde{\mathbf{E}}$

$+ \tilde{\mathbf{R}}$, $\mathbf{P} = \mathbf{1} + \tilde{\mathbf{P}}$ where $\tilde{\mathbf{E}}$ is the (symmetric) linearized strain tensor, and $\tilde{\mathbf{R}}$ and $\tilde{\mathbf{P}}$ are skew-symmetric tensors describing, respectively, the mean rotation of a material neighborhood and the "intrinsic" rotation. In the place of $\tilde{\mathbf{R}}$ and $\tilde{\mathbf{P}}$ we can use the infinitesimal angles

$$\phi_k = -\frac{1}{2}\,\varepsilon_{kij}\tilde{R}_{ij} = \frac{1}{2}(\mathrm{curl}\,\mathbf{u})_k, \qquad \alpha_k = -\frac{1}{2}\,\varepsilon_{kij}\tilde{P}_{ij}. \tag{16.54}$$

The "asymmetric strain" $\mathbf{A}$ corresponds to $\mathbf{\Gamma} - \mathbf{1}$:

$$A_{ij} = \tilde{E}_{ij} + \varepsilon_{ijk}\psi_k, \qquad \boldsymbol{\psi} = \boldsymbol{\alpha} - \boldsymbol{\phi}. \tag{16.55}$$

Another form of (16.55) is given by

$$A_{ij} = u_{i,j} - \tilde{P}_{ij} = u_{i,j} - \varepsilon_{jik}\alpha_k. \tag{16.55*}$$

In plane problems we have that

$$\begin{aligned} A_{xx} &= u_{x,x}, \qquad A_{yy} = u_{y,y}, \qquad A_{[xy]} = \psi, \\ A_{yx} &= u_{y,x} - \alpha, \qquad A_{xy} = u_{x,y} + \alpha, \end{aligned} \tag{16.56}$$

where $\alpha = \alpha_z$, $\psi = \psi_z$.

The linearized rotation gradients are given by $K_{kij} \doteq \delta_{mk}\tilde{P}_{mi.j} = \tilde{P}_{ki.j} \doteq \tilde{P}_{ki,j}$, so that we can equally well use

$$K_{mj} = \alpha_{m,j}, \qquad K_{mj} = -\tfrac{1}{2}\,\varepsilon_{mki}K_{kij}. \tag{16.57}$$

Let us derive the compatibility conditions for $\mathbf{A}$ and $\mathbf{K}$ (cf. Problem 2 of the preceding section). For brevity, line integrals of integrands of the form $f_i\,d\xi_i$, taken over a curve C joining the points $\bar{\mathbf{x}}$ and $\mathbf{x}$, will be denoted by $C[f_i\,d\xi_i]$. Thus, starting from $\alpha_i = \bar{\alpha}_i + C[K_{ij}\,d\xi_j]$, we obtain the compatibility conditions

$$I_{ki} \equiv \varepsilon_{kmn}K_{in,m} = 0. \tag{16.58}$$

Next, we investigate the integrability of $u_i = \bar{u}_i + C[A_{ij}\,d\xi_j] + \varepsilon_{jik}C[\alpha_k\,d\xi_j]$. Integrating by parts in the last term, we get $C[\alpha_k\,d\xi_j] = (x_j - \bar{x}_j)\alpha_k(\mathbf{x}) - C[(\xi_j - \bar{x}_j)\alpha_{k,p}\,d\xi_p]$, thus $u_i = u_i + \varepsilon_{jik}(x_j - \bar{x}_j)\alpha_k(\mathbf{x}) + C[A_{ij}\,d\xi_j - \varepsilon_{pik}(\xi_p - \bar{x}_p)\alpha_{k,j}\,d\xi_j]$. Applying Kelvin's transformation to the integral, we arrive at compatibility conditions that, by (16.58), can be expressed as follows:

$$\begin{aligned} J_{ki} &= \varepsilon_{kmj}(A_{ij,m} - \varepsilon_{mir}K_{rj}) \\ &= \varepsilon_{kmj}A_{ij,m} + \delta_{ki}K_{mm} - K_{ki} = 0. \end{aligned} \tag{16.59}$$

It is easy to verify that, by virtue of their definitions, I_{ki} and J_{ki} satisfy

$$I_{ki,k} = 0, \qquad J_{ki,k} + \varepsilon_{imn}I_{mn} = 0. \tag{16.60}$$

But (16.60) is also the form of the stress equations of equilibrium (cf. (10.16) and (11.11)) in the absence of body forces and body couples. Therefore, (16.58) and (16.59) suggest the following representations in terms of stress functions:†

$$T_{ki} = \varepsilon_{kmn}Z_{in,m}, \qquad M_{ki} = \varepsilon_{kmj}G_{ij,m} + \delta_{ki}Z_{mm} - Z_{ki}. \tag{16.61}$$

Further, because **A** defined by (16.55), and **K** defined by $(16.57)_1$, will yield $\mathbf{I} = 0$, $\mathbf{J} = 0$, we may define *null stress-function tensors* by $G^0_{ik} = U_{i,k} - \varepsilon_{kin}\Phi_n$, $Z^0_{ij} = \Phi_{i,j}$.

The stress functions are directly related to the resultant loads and couples acting on a surface Σ. We write $F_i = \Sigma[t_i]$, where $\mathbf{t} = \mathbf{t}(\mathbf{n})$, and let $t_i = T_{ji}n_j = \varepsilon_{jmn}Z_{in,m}n_j$. Then, by Kelvin's transformation,

$$F_i = \partial\Sigma[Z_{ik}\,dx_k]. \tag{16.62}$$

The resulting couple **L** acting on Σ is obtained in the same way (cf. (9.32)*), $L_k = \Sigma[\mu_k + \varepsilon_{kij}x_it_j] = \Sigma[M_{rk}n_r + \varepsilon_{kij}x_iT_{rj}n_r] = \Sigma[(\varepsilon_{rmj}G_{kj,m} + \delta_{rk}Z_{mm} - Z_{rk} + \varepsilon_{kij}x_i\varepsilon_{rmn}Z_{jn,m})n_r] = \Sigma[\varepsilon_{rmj}G_{kj,m}n_r + \varepsilon_{rmn}(\varepsilon_{kij}x_iF_{jn})_{,m}n_r]$. Applying Kelvin's transformation, we now obtain

$$L_k = \partial\Sigma[(G_{kj} + \varepsilon_{kin}x_iZ_{nj})\,dx_j]. \tag{16.63}$$

If the couple stresses vanish, then $\varepsilon_{kmj}G_{ij,m} + \delta_{ik}Z_{mm} - Z_{ki} = 0$ must hold. To solve for **Z** in terms of **G**, we must let $i = k = r$: $Z_{mm} = -\frac{1}{2}\varepsilon_{rmj}G_{rj,m}$. Then $Z_{ik} = \varepsilon_{imj}G_{kj,m} - \frac{1}{2}\delta_{ik}\varepsilon_{rmj}G_{rj,m}$, and by (16.61),

$$T_{ki} = \varepsilon_{irj}\varepsilon_{kmn}G_{nj,rm} - \tfrac{1}{2}\varepsilon_{nrj}\varepsilon_{kmi}G_{nj,rm}. \tag{16.64}$$

In particular, if **G** is assumed to be symmetric, we recover the usual formula

† The completeness of the stress functions methods in dipolar theories has been investigated by Carlson [224].

$\mathbf{T} = \text{Ink}\mathbf{G}$. This result suggests a modification of the stress functions, whereby $\mathbf{Z}$ is replaced by $\bar{Z}_{ik} = \varepsilon_{imj}G_{kj,m} - \frac{1}{2}\delta_{ik}\varepsilon_{rmj}G_{rj,m} + Y_{ik}$, so that (16.61) reduce to

$$M_{ki} = -Y_{ki},$$
$$T_{ki} = \varepsilon_{kmn}Y_{in,j} + \varepsilon_{irj}\varepsilon_{kmn}G_{nj,rm} - \tfrac{1}{2}\varepsilon_{nrj}\varepsilon_{kmi}G_{nj,rm}. \tag{16.65}$$

In plane problems, assuming that none of the stress functions depend on z, and that the only nonvanishing component of $\mathbf{G}$ is $F = G_{33}$, we obtain

$$T_{xx} = F_{,yy} - Y_{,xy}, \quad T_{yy} = F_{,xx} + Y_{,xy}, \quad M_{xz} = Y_{,x},$$
$$T_{xy} = -F_{,xy} - Y_{,yy}, \quad T_{yx} = -F_{,xy} + Y_{,xx}, \quad M_{yz} = Y_{,y}. \tag{16.66}$$

where we have let $Y_{13} = -Y_{,1}$, $Y_{23} = -Y_{,2}$.

The models of mechanical response that occur in classical continuum mechanics can of course be applied to Cosserat continua. In particular, we may develop theories of elastic Cosserat solids, viscous Cosserat fluids, and viscoelastic Cosserat materials. Moreover, the various possibilities are now far more numerous, owing to the presence of additional kinematical variables. Thus we may consider a material that responds elastically to the strains $\tilde{E}_{ij}$, but shows a viscous response to rotation gradients. For this reason we shall merely sketch, without any attempt at completeness, much less rigor, some of the ideas that readily come to mind.

Let us recall from (12.20) that, in the absence of radiative heating, the internal dissipation δ is given by $\delta = \rho\theta\dot{\eta} + \text{div}\mathbf{q}$, where $\mathbf{q}$ is the heat flux vector, and η is the entropy density. Further, by (11.12), the balance of energy can be written as

$$\rho\dot{\varepsilon} + \text{div}\mathbf{q} = w, \qquad w = T_{ji}(v_{i,j} - \Sigma_{ij}) + M_{ji}\sigma_{i,j}, \tag{16.67}$$

where the intrinsic angular velocity of particles is denoted by $\boldsymbol{\sigma}$, or by $\Sigma_{ij} = -\varepsilon_{ijk}\sigma_k$, whichever is more convenient. We may characterize incompressible Cosserat fluids first of all by the thermodynamic constitutive equation $\varepsilon = \varepsilon(\eta)$. With $\theta = \partial\varepsilon/\partial\eta$, the condition of positive entropy production becomes $\delta = w \geq 0$. Now, the constitutive equations of classical hydrodynamics are $T_{[ij]} = 0$, $M_{ji} = 0$, $T_{(ij)} = -p\delta_{ij} + 2\mu D_{ij}$. A plausible generalization of these equations is as follows,†

$$T_{(ij)} = -p\delta_{ij} + 2\mu D_{ij}, \qquad T_{[ij]} = \gamma(\Sigma_{ij} - W_{ij}),$$
$$M_{ji} = \alpha\delta_{ji}\sigma_{k,k} + 2\beta\sigma_{i,j}, \tag{16.68}$$

† Cf. [77].

where α, β, γ, μ are constants (it should be noted that the ratios of α and β to μ and γ have the dimension of length). The inequality $\delta > 0$ now requires that $\mu > 0$, $\gamma > 0$, $\beta > 0$, $3\alpha + 2\beta > 0$. Constitutive equations that are, in essence, the same as (16.68) have been derived by Grad [46] on the basis of statistical methods.

While there are guides for obtaining general theories (e.g. the "principle of equipresence"), one is always hard put to justify special theories of the kind exhibited in (16.68). To justify (16.68), we may, lacking any other guide, choose to take the suggestive forms of the stress power terms in (16.67) rather literally. That is probably the same as using an idea which Hamel ([67], p. 73) attributes to Lagrange, and calls it a *Befreiungsprinzip* ("principle of the relaxation of constraints"); we say that a stress depends, in the first place, on that kinematical variable which it inhibits in a rigid body motion.

Substituting (16.68) into (10.16), (11.11), we obtain the following generalization of the Navier-Stokes equations,

$$\begin{aligned} -p_{,i} + \mu\nabla^2 v_i + \gamma\varepsilon_{ijk}\psi_{k,j} &= \rho\dot{v}_i, \\ 2\beta\nabla^2(\omega_m + \psi_m) + \alpha\psi_{k,km} - 2\gamma\psi_m &= 0, \end{aligned} \tag{16.69}$$

where $\boldsymbol{\omega} = \frac{1}{2}\,\text{curl}\mathbf{v}$, and $\boldsymbol{\psi} = \boldsymbol{\sigma} - \boldsymbol{\omega}$ may be interpreted as a mean angular velocity of particles relative to the material lines.

Before considering boundary value problems, it is necessary to assume an additional boundary condition to be used in conjunction with the "no slip" condition $\mathbf{v} = \mathbf{0}$. Judging from some experimental evidence, fluid molecules tend to line up at boundaries;† therefore, setting the absolute angular velocity $\boldsymbol{\sigma}$ there equal to zero may be reasonable, at least in certain instances.

The second-order effects considered here are likely to be important only near boundaries and for thin films, so that a study of the boundary layer equations associated with (16.69) may be of some interest. Perhaps a more promising application of (16.69) would be to fluids carrying suspensions of particles.

The interaction of Cosserat fluids with electric fields has been investigated by Condiff and Dahler [20].

If the internal energy depends on η and $\boldsymbol{\Gamma}$, then, with $\dot{\boldsymbol{\Gamma}} = \mathbf{P}^{-1}(\mathbf{L} - \boldsymbol{\Sigma})\mathbf{F}$, and assuming that

$$T_{ji} = \frac{1}{J} P_{ik} \frac{\partial W}{\partial \Gamma_{km}} F_{jm} \approx \frac{\partial W}{\partial A_{ij}}, \tag{16.70}$$

we obtain that $\delta = M_{ji}\sigma_{i,j}$. We may adjoin to (16.70) the viscous law M_{ji}

† Cf. [72].

$= L\sigma_{k,k}\delta_{ji} + 2M\sigma_{i,j}$, thus arriving at a response that is elastic with regard to the deformations A_{ij}, and viscous with regard to the gradients of intrinsic angular velocity. These constitutive equations might provide a possible model for granular media with viscous friction forces between the grains (cf. Oshima [112]).

Finally, let us consider a quasi-elastic response governed by $W = W(\eta, \mathbf{\Gamma}, \mathbf{K}_j)$, where $\mathbf{K}_j = \mathbf{P}^T\Delta_j\mathbf{P}$ (cf. (16.53)). Because $\dot{\mathbf{P}} = \mathbf{\Sigma}\mathbf{P}$, $\dot{\mathbf{P}}^T = \mathbf{P}^T\mathbf{\Sigma}^T = -\mathbf{P}^T\mathbf{\Sigma}$, it follows that $\dot{\mathbf{K}}_j = (-\mathbf{P}^T\mathbf{\Sigma})\Delta_j\mathbf{P} + \mathbf{P}^T\Delta_j(\mathbf{\Sigma}\mathbf{P}) = \mathbf{P}^T(\Delta_j\mathbf{\Sigma})\mathbf{P}$, i.e.

$$\dot{K}_{kij} = P_{mk}P_{ni}\Sigma_{mn,p}F_{pj}. \tag{16.71}$$

Therefore, by $(16.57)_2$, $\dot{K}_{rj} = -\frac{1}{2}\varepsilon_{rki}\Sigma_{mn.j}P_{mk}P_{ni} = \frac{1}{2}\varepsilon_{ski}\Sigma_{mn.j}(P_{qr}P_{qs})P_{mk}P_{ni} = -\frac{1}{2}\varepsilon_{qmn}\Sigma_{mn.j}P_{qr}$, or,

$$\dot{K}_{rj} = P_{qr}\sigma_{q,p}F_{pj} \approx \sigma_{r,j}. \tag{16.72}$$

From the condition that the internal dissipation be zero we obtain again (16.70), and, in addition,

$$M_{ji} = \frac{1}{J}F_{jk}\frac{\partial W}{\partial K_{mk}}P_{im} \approx \frac{\partial W}{\partial \alpha_{i,j}}. \tag{16.73}$$

To write out linear stress relations, we can either start from an approximation of W that is quadratic in the strains, or make use of the representation theorems given in Appendix II. In any case, because second rank tensors are centro-symmetric, but third rank tensors are not, it follows that, in a medium with a center of symmetry, couple stresses $M_{ji} = \frac{1}{2}\varepsilon_{ikm}M_{j[km]}$ cannot depend on the strains A_{ij}, and, similarly, stresses T_{ji} cannot depend on the rotation gradients K_{jr}. Next, if we assume that $\mathbf{T} = \mathbf{f}(\mathbf{A})$, then, by (B.20), $\mathbf{T} = \lambda\mathbf{1}\,\mathrm{tr}\mathbf{A} + 2\mu\mathbf{A}$, $T_{(ij)} = \lambda\tilde{E}_{kk}\delta_{ij} + 2\mu\tilde{E}_{ij}$, $T_{[ij]} = -2\mu\psi_{ij}$, where $\psi_{ij} = \tilde{P}_{ij} - \tilde{R}_{ij}$. If, on the other hand, we assume that $\mathbf{T} = \mathbf{f}(\tilde{\mathbf{E}}, \boldsymbol{\psi})$, then it follows from (B.20) that

$$T_{(ij)} = \lambda\tilde{E}_{kk}\delta_{ij} + 2\mu\tilde{E}_{ij}, \qquad T_{[ij]} = 2\gamma\psi_{ij}, \tag{16.74}$$

i.e. the response to the strains ψ_{ij} is governed by a separate modulus γ. The stress relations (16.74) are the commonly accepted ones (cf. also the remark following (16.49)).

The same question arises when we consider the constitutive equation for $\mathbf{M}$. Starting with $\mathbf{M} = \mathbf{f}(\mathbf{K})$, we obtain $M_{ij} = A\delta_{ij}\alpha_{k,k} + 2B\alpha_{j,i}$. If $\mathbf{M}$ is assumed to depend on the symmetric and skew-symmetric parts of $\mathbf{K}$ separately, then

$$M_{ij} = A\delta_{ij}\alpha_{k,k} + 2B\alpha_{j,i} + 2C\alpha_{i,j}. \tag{16.75}$$

A stress relation of this form has been in fact calculated by Hehl and Kroener [71] by averaging internal forces produced by sets of discrete dislocations.

In plane problems we let $\mathbf{u} = \mathbf{e}_x u(x, y) + \mathbf{e}_y v(x, y)$, $P_{xy} = -P(x, y)$, thus

$$
\begin{aligned}
T_{xx} &= \lambda\left(\frac{\partial u}{\partial x} + \frac{\partial v}{\partial y}\right) + 2\mu\frac{\partial u}{\partial x}, \qquad T_{yy} = \mu\left(\frac{\partial u}{\partial x} + \frac{\partial v}{\partial y}\right) + 2\mu\frac{\partial v}{\partial y}, \\
T_{xy} &= \mu\left(\frac{\partial u}{\partial y} + \frac{\partial v}{\partial x}\right) - \gamma\left(\frac{\partial u}{\partial y} - \frac{\partial v}{\partial x}\right) - 2\gamma P, \qquad M_{xz} = 2\bar{B}\frac{\partial P}{\partial x}, \\
T_{yx} &= \mu\left(\frac{\partial u}{\partial y} + \frac{\partial v}{\partial x}\right) + \gamma\left(\frac{\partial u}{\partial y} - \frac{\partial v}{\partial x}\right) + 2\gamma P, \qquad M_{zy} = 2\bar{B}\frac{\partial P}{\partial y}.
\end{aligned}
\tag{16.76}
$$

The components $M_{zx} = 2B\,\partial P/\partial x$, $M_{zy} = 2B\,\partial P/\partial y$ do not affect the plane problem. Substituting (16.76) into the stress equations of equilibrium, we obtain

$$
\begin{aligned}
&\mu\nabla^2 u + (\lambda + \mu)\frac{\partial \vartheta}{\partial x} + 2\gamma\frac{\partial}{\partial y}(P - R) = 0, \\
&\mu\nabla^2 v + (\lambda + \mu)\frac{\partial \vartheta}{\partial y} - 2\gamma\frac{\partial}{\partial x}(P - R) = 0, \\
&\bar{B}\nabla^2 P = 2\gamma(P - R), \qquad R = \frac{1}{2}\left(\frac{\partial v}{\partial x} - \frac{\partial u}{\partial y}\right), \qquad \vartheta = \frac{\partial u}{\partial x} + \frac{\partial v}{\partial y},
\end{aligned}
\tag{16.77}
$$

where $\nabla^2 = \partial_x^2 + \partial_y^2$.

If a material is hemitropic (or, by another name, hemihedral), in which case its symmetry operations are rotations, but *not* reflections, then (16.74), (16.75) become considerably more general. In particular, stress may depend on the rotation gradients, so that hemitropic Cosserat solids are characterized by

$$
\begin{aligned}
T_{(ij)} &= \lambda\tilde{E}_{kk}\delta_{ij} + 2\mu\tilde{E}_{ij} + I\alpha_{(i,j)} + J\delta_{ij}\operatorname{div}\boldsymbol{\alpha}, \\
T_{[ij]} &= 2\gamma\psi_{ij} + D\alpha_{[i,j]}, \\
M_{(ij)} &= A\delta_{ij}\operatorname{div}\boldsymbol{\alpha} + (B + C)\alpha_{(i,j)} + F\tilde{E}_{ij} + G\delta_{ij}\tilde{E}_{kk}, \\
M_{[ij]} &= (C - B)\alpha_{[i,j]} + H\psi_{ij}.
\end{aligned}
\tag{16.78}
$$

For Cosserat media with constrained rotations, constitutive equations for crystals of cubic and hexagonal symmetry have been obtained by C. L. Huang [76].

To investigate wave motion, we start from

$$(\mu + \gamma)u_{i,kk} + (\lambda + \mu - \gamma)u_{k,ki} + 2\gamma\varepsilon_{ijk}\alpha_{k,j} = \rho\ddot{u}_i,$$
$$2B\alpha_{i,kk} + (A + 2C)\alpha_{k,ik} - 4\gamma\left(\alpha_i - \frac{1}{2}\varepsilon_{ijk}u_{k,j}\right) = \rho\dot{\eta}_i \tag{16.79}$$

(cf. (11.11)). Because it is difficult to say what the intrinsic angular momentum $\boldsymbol{\eta}$ should be, one is tempted to neglect it. Rather than do that, let us assume a representation $\eta_i = i_{ij}\sigma_j \approx i_{ij}\dot{\alpha}_j$, (cf. the discussion on p. 225), where i_{ij} represent an intrinsic moment of inertia. But in that case $\dot{\boldsymbol{\eta}}$ will be a nonlinear function of $\boldsymbol{\sigma}$. To obtain a linear theory, we have no choice but to neglect these nonlinear terms, thus writing $\dot{\eta}_i \approx i_{ij}\ddot{\alpha}_j$. Let us now substitute the plane wave solutions.

$$u_i = u_i^0 \cos[k(ct - \mathbf{x}\cdot\mathbf{n})], \qquad \alpha_i = \alpha_i^0 \sin[k(ct - \mathbf{x}\cdot\mathbf{n})]$$

into (16.79). Because u_i^0, α_i^0 are assumed to be constants, we have that

$$\partial_k u_i = kn_k u_i^0 \sin[k(ct - \mathbf{x}\cdot\mathbf{n})], \qquad \partial_i\alpha_i = -kn_i\alpha_i^0 \cos[k(ct - \mathbf{x}\cdot\mathbf{n})],$$

etc. In this way (16.79) reduce to

$$[(\mu + \gamma - \rho c^2)\delta_{ik} + (\lambda + \mu - \gamma)n_i n_k]u_k^0 + \frac{2\gamma}{k}\varepsilon_{ijk}n_j\alpha_k^0 = 0,$$
$$\left[(2B\delta_{ik} - \rho c^2 i_{ik}) + (A + 2C)n_i n_k + \frac{4\gamma}{k^2}\delta_{ik}\right]\alpha_k^0 - \frac{2}{k}\gamma\varepsilon_{ijk}n_j u_k^0 = 0. \tag{16.80}$$

In order that nontrivial solutions u_k^0, α_k^0 would exist, the determinant of the coefficients must vanish. The resulting secular equation then determines the speeds of propagation, c, associated with the direction of propagation, $\mathbf{n}$. Without going into the details, we can see right away that c will depend on the frequency ω of the wave, i.e. *an elastic Cosserat solid is dispersive.* The dispersion persists even if set $i_{ik} = 0$ or $\gamma = \mu$. Further, it can be shown that transverse waves will have an "optic" branch.

In the recent history of multipolar continuum mechanics the main contributors have been Ericksen [37], Mindlin [94], [95], [96], Green and Rivlin [49], and Toupin [169], [170]. The development and exploration of the linear theories is largely the work of Mindlin. Each author seems to prefer a different set of kinematical variables; thus Toupin [170] starts with $L = L(F_{im}, \mathbf{d}_a, \mathbf{d}_{a.m}, \dot{\mathbf{d}}_a, \mathbf{X})$, and obtains from Hamilton's principle the field equations

$$\tilde{T}_{ji.j} + f_i - \dot{p}_i = 0, \qquad \tilde{M}^a_{ji.j} + \beta^a_i - \dot{q}^a_i = \frac{\partial L}{\partial d_{ai}},$$

the boundary conditions

$$\tilde{T}_{ji}N_j = \tilde{t}_i, \qquad \tilde{M}^a_{ji}\,N_j = \tilde{\mu}^a_i,$$

and the "end conditions"

$$p_i = \bar{p}_i, \qquad q^a_i = \bar{q}^a_i, \qquad t = t_0 \text{ or } t = t_1,$$

where

$$p_i = \frac{\partial L}{\partial \dot{x}_i}, \qquad q^a_i = \frac{\partial L}{\partial \dot{d}_{ai}}, \qquad \tilde{T}_{ji} = -\frac{\partial L}{\partial x_{i.j}}, \qquad \tilde{M}^a_{ji} = -\frac{\partial L}{\partial d_{ai.j}}.$$

Mindlin's approach, when extended to finite deformations, runs along the following lines. With $W = W(F_{im}, \phi^{-1}_{im}\,F_{mj}, \phi_{im.k})$, and assuming that the variations δx_i and $\delta\phi_{im}$ are independent, we obtain from Hamilton's principle that

$$\Delta_m(\tilde{T}_{mi} + \tilde{\Pi}_{mi}) + f_i = 0, \quad \Delta_k M_{kim} + \tilde{\Pi}_{ji}A_{mj} + \Phi_{im} = 0,$$

where Φ_{im} are dipolar body forces, and

$$A_{pj} = \phi^{-1}_{pr}F_{rj}, \quad \tilde{\Pi}_{mi} = \phi^{-1}_{ji}\frac{\partial W}{\partial A_{jm}}, \quad M_{kim} = \frac{\partial W}{\partial \phi_{im.k}}.$$

Specifically, Mindlin obtains†

$$\partial_j(\tau_{ji} + \sigma_{ji}) = \rho\ddot{u}_i, \qquad \partial_i\mu_{ijk} + \sigma_{jk} = \rho a_{km}\ddot{\psi}_{jm},$$

$$\tau_{ij} = \frac{\partial W}{\partial \tilde{E}_{ij}} = \tau_{ji}, \qquad \sigma_{ij} = \frac{\partial W}{\partial \gamma_{ij}}, \qquad \mu_{ijk} = \frac{\partial W}{\partial k_{ijk}}. \tag{16.81}$$

Assuming that the strain-energy density W is a quadratic polynomial in the strains, Mindlin arrives at the following linear stress relations,

$$\begin{aligned}
\tau_{ij} &= \lambda\delta_{ij}\tilde{E}_{kk} + 2\mu\tilde{E}_{ij} + g_1\delta_{ij}\gamma_{kk} + 2g_2\gamma_{(ij)},\\
\sigma_{ij} &= g_1\delta_{ij}\tilde{E}_{kk} + 2g_2\tilde{E}_{ij} + b_1\delta_{ij}\gamma_{kk} + b_2\gamma_{ij} + b_3\gamma_{ji},\\
\mu_{ijk} &= a_1(k_{mmi}\delta_{jk} + k_{kmm}\delta_{ij}) + a_2(k_{mmj}\delta_{ik} + k_{mkm}\delta_{ij}) + a_3k_{mmk}\delta_{ij}\\
&\quad + a_4k_{imm}\delta_{jk} + a_5(k_{jmm}\delta_{ik} + k_{mkm}\delta_{ij}) + a_8k_{mjm}\delta_{ik}\\
&\quad + a_{10}k_{ijk} + a_{11}(k_{kij} + k_{jki}) + \alpha_{13}k_{ikj} + \alpha_{15}k_{kji},
\end{aligned}$$

† We have taken some liberties with the multipolar acceleration term.

where $\boldsymbol{\psi} = \boldsymbol{\phi} - \mathbf{1}$, $k_{jik} = \partial_j\psi_{ik}$, $\gamma_{ij} = \partial_i u_j - \psi_{ij}$. Substituting these into the stress equations of motion, we obtain the "displacement equations of motion" for u_i and ψ_{ij}. The various modes of motion have been extensively investigated by Mindlin. Thus one may consider micro-vibrations $u_i = 0$, $\psi_{ij} = A_{ij} \exp{(i\omega t)}$, or plane wave solutions for both the macro- and micromotions. In the latter case it is possible to group the twelve equations of motion into separate sets, e.g. "shear optical I":

$$(a_{10} + a_{13})\partial_1\partial_1\psi_{(23)} - (b_2 + b_3)\psi_{(23)} = \text{const.}\, \ddot{\psi}_{(23)}.$$

It is not unlikely, however, that a satisfactory description of dispersion of waves will be obtained only in the context of an electro-mechanical theory, and that the purely mechanical theories of microstructure will have to seek applications elsewhere (e.g. in the description of composite materials which are made so as to enhance the good qualitities of the composites, and suppress the poor qualities).

While modern continuum mechanics has accomplished a great deal in explaining the behavior of polymer solutions, and rubberlike materials under finite deformation, it has contributed little to a more accurate description of the response of metals. Indeed, there are those who say that linear elasticity theory, complemented by a simple plasticity theory, covers all that can be described by a continuum theory of metals: as soon as one looks deeper, a metal is revealed to be of such complexity as to defy any analysis other than a strictly local one (i.e. a "solid state physics" theory). Such controversial questions have usually a way of resolving themselves so that neither the optimists nor the pessimists are found to be wholly correct. In any case, attempts at "continuum theories of dislocations," for instance, have not been lacking. These attempts have often led to differential-geometric concepts of generalized spaces, never to return, so it seems, to metals. At the risk of belaboring the obvious, it ought to be said that a Riemannian geometry alone does not suffice to formulate a plasticity theory, any more than Euclidean geometry would suffice to formulate an elasticity theory. Constitutive equations are needed, and it is here that often theories that start from a broad geometric basis either stop or make very specialized assumptions. This does not happen by choice, of course; the kind of phenomena that one wishes to describe, e.g. plastic flow caused by moving dislocations, have remained intractable for a good many years now. It is perhaps unfair, and too easy, to criticize the groping of dislocationists towards a deeper theory of plasticity; it should be remembered that dislocations are there, waiting to be described by a continuum theory.

We may consider elasto-plastic response as an elastic response from a variable, plastically deforming reference configuration. Although the total deformation $d\mathbf{x} = \mathbf{F}\,d\mathbf{X}$ is assumed to be compatible, the plastic deformation $d\boldsymbol{\xi} = \boldsymbol{\phi}\,d\mathbf{X}$ and the elastic deformation $d\mathbf{x} = \mathbf{F}\boldsymbol{\phi}^{-1}\,d\boldsymbol{\xi}$ separately are incompatible. The dislocation density associated with $\boldsymbol{\phi}$ is a measure of this incompatibility (cf. (15.25) *et seq.*). In the linear theory we let $\boldsymbol{\phi} = \mathbf{1} + \tilde{\boldsymbol{\phi}}$, from which it follows that

$$\alpha_{km} = \varepsilon_{ijk}\phi_{mi,j}.$$

To describe the motion of dislocations through a material medium, we may introduce a *tensor of dislocation movement*, V_{ijk}† (cf. Mura [104], Fox [234]). Here the first, second, and third subscripts refer to the directions of movement, dislocation lines, and the associated Burgers vectors, respectively. We assume that $V_{ijk} = -V_{jik}$, so that a dislocation line moving along itself will have no effect upon the dislocation density. To set up a balance equation for dislocation density, we consider a material surface S, and denote by $\mathbf{n}$ the unit normal vectors of S. The unit tangent vectors of the boundary curve ∂S will be denoted by $\boldsymbol{\sigma}$. With $\mathbf{m} = \boldsymbol{\sigma} \times \mathbf{n}$, we now write

$$\frac{d}{dt}\int_S \alpha_{ji}\,da_j = -\int_{\partial S} m_k V_{kji} n_j\,ds + \int_S \pi_{ji}\,da_j,$$

where π_{ji} describes the sources of dislocations. Using the skew-symmetry of V_{kji}, we readily obtain

$$\overset{*}{\alpha}_{ki} = \varepsilon_{kjm} V_{mi,j} + \pi_{ki},$$

where $V_{kji} = \varepsilon_{kjr} V_{ri}$, and the asterisk marks the convected derivative defined by (13.71). The selection of suitable constitutive equations relating stresses (and π_{ij}) to F_{im}, ϕ_{im}, and V_{ijk} remains an open problem.

Problems

1. Verify the derivation of (16.10).
2. Verify the derivation of (16.16)–(16.20).
3. Derive (16.23).
4. Investigate the torsion problem for a circular cylinder made of a "Cosserat material with constrained rotations." The lateral boundary is stress free, whereas suitable forces and couples, or displacements and rotations, can be applied to the end sections.

† The tensor V_{ijk} may be of the form $V_{ijk} = V_i \alpha_{jk}$, where V denotes the velocity field of the moving dislocations. Cf. [84], p. 26.

5. Can you relate the stress functions appearing in (16.66) to loads and moments of loads?

6. Investigate rectilinear flow in a channel $-h \leq y \leq h$ for the Cosserat fluid (16.68).

7. Show that the solutions (16.80) admit an "optic" branch.

8. Assume the material to be hemitropic, i.e. isotropic with respect to all directions, but possessing an inherent screw-sense. Consider a semi-infinite body occupying the region $x \geq 0$, and assume the following deformation field:† $u_y = u_z = 0$, $u_x = u(x)$, $\psi_{zx} = \psi_{xy} = 0$, $\psi_{yz} = \psi(x)$. As the constitutive equations we take (16.78), the equation for $M_{(ij)}$ being complemented by the initial stress term $h_0\delta_{ij}$, where h_0 is a constant. With these assumptions, the equations of equilibrium reduce to $(\lambda + 2\mu)u'' + 2a\psi'' = 0$, $au''B\psi'' - 2\gamma\psi = 0$, where $a = I + J$, whereas the condition that the boundary $x = 0$ be free of tractions is given by $(\lambda + 2\mu)u' + 2a\psi' = 0$, $au' - B\psi' = -h_0$. Eliminating u in the equations of equilibrium, obtain

$$\left(1 - l^2\frac{d^2}{dx^2}\right)\psi = 0, \qquad l^2 = \frac{1}{\gamma}\left(-\frac{B}{2} + \frac{a^2}{\lambda + 2\mu}\right).$$

The boundary condition on ψ is given by $l^2\psi' = -h_0/2\gamma$. Show that the solution is

$$\psi = h_0\frac{1}{2\gamma l}\exp\left(-\frac{x}{l}\right), \qquad u = -h_0\frac{a}{(\lambda + 2\mu)\gamma\lambda}\exp\left(-\frac{x}{l}\right).$$

Is there anything interesting about this solution? Investigate the dislocation density $\alpha_{mk} - \frac{1}{2}\delta_{km}\alpha_{ii}$.

† Weitsman, Y., [193].

CHAPTER **5**

ELASTICITY

Like Latin in the humanities, elasticity theory has always been a classical education for mechanicists. This is also true in nonlinear continuum mechanics, perhaps even more so than in the domain of linear theories, because nonlinear elasticity theory provides a basis for a deeper understanding of general mechanical behavior. The linear theory is in many ways too degenerate; in the limit of infinitesimal deformations too many basic distinctions, effects, and difficulties vanish.

The modern era of the nonlinear theory spans by now two decades; its first developments were profoundly influenced by the researches of Reiner and Rivlin, particularly by Rivlin's discovery of important exact solutions for incompressible materials.† A definitive exposition of the current status of the nonlinear elasticity theory is given in Truesdell and Noll's treatise *The Non-Linear Field Theories of Mechanics*. Our goals here are modest, the exposition, of necessity, rather superficial. It is hoped that this chapter will be of value to all those who would like to benefit from a contact with the nonlinear theory; however, the presentation has not been "simplified" to a point where it would fail to provide a bridge to current literature.

† A selection of important publications from this period has been reprinted in [230], Vol. IV.

Section 17
ELASTIC RESPONSE

The stress relation

We recall from Section 14 that elastic response is defined by a *stress relation* $\mathbf{T} = \mathbf{g}(\mathbf{F})$, where $F_{im} = \partial x_i/\partial X_m$ are deformation gradients connecting the current configuration $\mathbf{x}$ with a reference configuration $\mathbf{X}$. The response function $\mathbf{g}$ depends on the choice of reference configurations (this says no more than that the response depends on the "initial" state). Thus if a local reference configuration $d\mathbf{X}$ is changed to $d\hat{\mathbf{X}} = \mathbf{S}d\mathbf{X}$, then $\mathbf{g}$ is changed to a function $\hat{\mathbf{g}}$ satisfying $\mathbf{g}(\mathbf{F}) = \hat{\mathbf{g}}(\mathbf{F}\mathbf{S}^{-1})$ (cf. (14.22)). The isotropy group of a material is the group of unimodular transformations $\mathbf{H} = \mathbf{S}^{-1}$ that do not affect its response: $\mathbf{g}(\mathbf{F}\mathbf{H}) = \mathbf{g}(\mathbf{F})$; the reference configurations in which $\mathbf{g}(\mathbf{F}\mathbf{H}) = \mathbf{g}(\mathbf{F})$ holds are called *undistorted states.* For elastic solids the "symmetry operations" $\mathbf{H}$ constitute either the orthogonal group (isotropy) or one of its subgroups (anisotropy).

Now let $d\bar{\mathbf{X}} = \mathbf{G}\, d\mathbf{X}$ be any transformation of the reference configuration. With $\mathbf{g}(\mathbf{F}) = \bar{\mathbf{g}}(\bar{\mathbf{F}})$, where $\bar{\mathbf{F}} = \mathbf{F}\mathbf{G}^{-1}$, and assuming that $d\mathbf{X}$ describe an undistorted state, thus $\mathbf{g}(\mathbf{F}) = \mathbf{g}(\mathbf{F}\mathbf{H})$, we have that $\mathbf{g}(\mathbf{F}) = \mathbf{g}(\mathbf{F}\mathbf{H}) = \bar{\mathbf{g}}(\mathbf{F}\mathbf{G}^{-1}) = \bar{\mathbf{g}}(\mathbf{F}\mathbf{H}\mathbf{G}^{-1})$, or, $\bar{\mathbf{g}}(\bar{\mathbf{F}}) = \bar{\mathbf{g}}(\bar{\mathbf{F}}\bar{\mathbf{H}})$, where

$$\bar{\mathbf{H}} = \mathbf{G}\mathbf{H}\mathbf{G}^{-1}. \tag{17.1}$$

That is, (17.1) describes the transformation of the elements of an isotropy group in a change of local reference configurations. To investigate the undistorted configurations of elastic solids, we replace in (17.1) $\mathbf{H}$ by an orthogonal tensor $\mathbf{S}$: $\bar{\mathbf{S}}\mathbf{G} = \mathbf{G}\mathbf{S}$. Because $\mathbf{G}$ admits the polar decomposition $\mathbf{G} = \mathbf{P}\mathbf{Y}$, where $\mathbf{P}$ is orthogonal, and $\mathbf{Y}$ is positive and symmetric, we can write $\bar{\mathbf{S}}\mathbf{G} = \mathbf{G}\mathbf{S}$ as follows, $(\bar{\mathbf{S}}\mathbf{P})\mathbf{Y} = (\mathbf{P}\mathbf{S})(\mathbf{S}^T\mathbf{Y}\mathbf{S})$. The uniqueness of this polar decomposition now implies that $\bar{\mathbf{S}} = \mathbf{P}\mathbf{S}\mathbf{P}^T$, and

$$\mathbf{Y} = \mathbf{S}\mathbf{Y}\mathbf{S}^T. \tag{17.2}$$

The first relation can be regarded as a coordinate transformation (or, in the language of group theory, a *similarity transformation*). Consequently, regardless of which undistorted state is used as a frame of reference, the symmetry operations will constitute the same *type* of a group. In fact, if this were not so, then we would not be justified in classifying elastic solids on the basis of their isotropy groups. We interpret (17.2) as a condition that *the stretch tensor* $\mathbf{Y}$ *of* $\mathbf{G}$ *must commute with* $\mathbf{S}$:

$$\mathbf{Y}\mathbf{S} = \mathbf{S}\mathbf{Y}. \tag{17.3}$$

As in the linear theory, the inversion $\mathbf{S} = -\mathbf{1}$ is always an admissible symmetry operation for elastic materials: $\mathbf{g}(\mathbf{FS}) = \mathbf{STS} = \mathbf{T} = \mathbf{g}(\mathbf{F})$. As it turns out, this means that in the place of 32 crystal classes we only have to deal with the 11 classes. The symmetry operations restrict, through (17.3), the stretch tensors $\mathbf{Y}$ relating the undistorted configurations of a solid. The stress on undistorted configurations, $\mathbf{T}^0 = \mathbf{g}(\mathbf{1})$, must obey the analogous restriction:

$$\mathbf{ST}^0 = \mathbf{T}^0\mathbf{S}. \tag{17.4}$$

To derive (17.4), we recall that material objectivity requires

$$\mathbf{Q}\mathbf{g}(\mathbf{F})\mathbf{Q}^T = \mathbf{g}(\mathbf{QF}) \qquad (14.15)\text{R}$$

to hold for all orthogonal tensors $\mathbf{Q}$ and all deformation gradients $\mathbf{F}$. If we now identify $\mathbf{Q}$ with a symmetry operation $\mathbf{S}$, then $\mathbf{S}\mathbf{g}(\mathbf{F})\mathbf{S}^T = \mathbf{g}(\mathbf{SF})$. But this must hold for all $\mathbf{F}$, particularly when $\mathbf{F}$ is replaced by $\mathbf{FS}^T$. With $\mathbf{g}(\mathbf{FS}^T) = \mathbf{g}(\mathbf{F})$, we then obtain

$$\mathbf{S}\mathbf{g}(\mathbf{F})\mathbf{S}^T = \mathbf{g}(\mathbf{SFS}^T), \tag{17.5}$$

i.e. *the response function is isotropic to all symmetry operations* (cf. (14.34)). To obtain (17.4), we let $\mathbf{F} = \mathbf{1}$: $\mathbf{S}\mathbf{g}(\mathbf{1})\mathbf{S}^T = \mathbf{ST}^0\mathbf{S}^T = \mathbf{g}(\mathbf{1}) = \mathbf{T}^0$. For instance, in the triclinic class we have that $\mathbf{S} = \mathbf{1}$, i.e. there are no symmetry operations really. Because $\mathbf{1}$ commutes with every tensor, every configuration is undistorted. By the same token, we cannot extract any information from the fact that a triclinic solid is in an undistorted state. The more symmetry operations a material has, the more we know about its undistorted states. Monoclinic symmetry is characterized by a rotation $\mathbf{S} = \text{diag}(-1, -1, 1)$ through 180° about the axis of $\mathbf{n}$. It is then easy to see that $\mathbf{T}^0 = \mathbf{ST}^0\mathbf{S}^T$ holds only if $\mathbf{T}^0$ is of the form

$$\|\mathbf{T}^0\| = \begin{Vmatrix} T^0_{11} & T^0_{12} & 0 \\ T^0_{21} & T^0_{22} & 0 \\ 0 & 0 & T^0_{33} \end{Vmatrix},$$

i.e. $\mathbf{n}$ is a principal vector of $\mathbf{T}^0$. The same observation applies to $\mathbf{Y}$. In the rhombic class we permit rotations through 180° about the axes of a material frame $\mathbf{k}, \mathbf{m}, \mathbf{n}$, hence it follows that $\mathbf{T}^0$ must be diagonal in the $\mathbf{k}, \mathbf{m}, \mathbf{n}$ reference frame. In the cubic class, $\mathbf{T}^0$ must not only be diagonal, its principal values must be equal (rotations through 90° amount to interchanging the principal values). Finally, for transverse isotropy any rotation about the axis of $\mathbf{n}$ must commute with $\mathbf{T}^0$, or, leave the principal directions of $\mathbf{T}^0$ invariant. This can only happen if any direction perpendicular to $\mathbf{n}$ is a principal direction of $\mathbf{T}^0$, in which case, by (4.45), $\mathbf{T}^0 = -p\mathbf{1} + q\mathbf{nn}$.

An undistorted state will be called a *natural state* if it corresponds to zero stress. Unless stated otherwise, it will be understood that response functions are referred to a natural state.

Isotropy

The assumption of isotropy permits us to obtain many specific results, or interpretations, so that it is expedient to derive at this point a representation of the isotropic stress relation. Because now any rotation qualifies as a symmetry operation, we can combine the isotropy property (17.5) with the reduced stress relation

$$\mathbf{T} = \mathbf{R}\mathbf{g}(\mathbf{U})\mathbf{R}^T, \tag{14.16)R}$$

obtaining right away the isotropic stress relation

$$\mathbf{T} = \mathbf{g}(\mathbf{V}), \tag{17.6}$$

where $\mathbf{V} = \mathbf{RUR}^T = (\mathbf{FF}^T)^{1/2}$. The rotation $\mathbf{R}$ has now been completely eliminated from the constitutive equation. In general the components of the stretch tensor $\mathbf{V}$ are not rational functions of the deformation gradients, so that we prefer to use

$$\mathbf{B} = \mathbf{V}^2 = \mathbf{FF}^T, \qquad B_{ij} = x_{i,m}x_{j,m} \tag{17.7}$$

instead. Then

$$\mathbf{T} = \mathbf{f}(\mathbf{B}), \tag{17.8}$$

where $\mathbf{f}$ is defined by $\mathbf{g}(\mathbf{V}) = \mathbf{f}(\mathbf{V}^2)$.

For the most part we shall confine our investigations to *strictly elastic solids* for which

(1) there exists a natural state,

(2) the response functions, when taken relative to the natural state, are *invertible*, i.e.

$$\mathbf{V} = \mathbf{g}^{-1}(\mathbf{T}), \qquad \mathbf{B} = \mathbf{f}^{-1}(\mathbf{T}) \tag{17.9}$$

exist.

Let us now show that the isotropic stress relation admits the representation

$$\mathbf{T} = c_0\mathbf{1} + c_1\mathbf{B} + c_2\mathbf{B}^2, \tag{17.10}$$

where the response coefficients $c_{\underline{i}}$ are general functions of the principal invariants I, II, III of $\mathbf{B}$. It is customary to designate the response coefficients $c_{\underline{i}}$ by Hebrew letters, but for calculations we tend to prefer notations that seem less elaborate. To prove (17.10), we must start from the isotropy property $\mathbf{QTQ}^T = \mathbf{Qf(B)Q}^T = \mathbf{f}(\mathbf{QBQ}^T)$. Let us denote by barred symbols the representations of $\mathbf{B}$ and $\mathbf{T}$ in the principal coordinate system of $\mathbf{B}$, thus

$$\bar{\mathbf{T}} = \mathbf{f}(\bar{\mathbf{B}}). \tag{17.11}$$

We now perform a rotation $\mathbf{Q}$ through 180° about the x axis: $\mathbf{Q} = \text{diag}(1, -1, -1)$. Then $\mathbf{Q}\bar{\mathbf{B}}\mathbf{Q}^T = \bar{\mathbf{B}}$, and from (17.11) it follows that $\mathbf{Q}\bar{\mathbf{T}}\mathbf{Q}^T = \mathbf{f}(\mathbf{Q}\bar{\mathbf{B}}\mathbf{Q}^T) = \mathbf{f}(\bar{\mathbf{B}}) = \bar{\mathbf{T}}$. Therefore, the components of $\bar{\mathbf{T}}$ also should not be affected by the rotation $\mathbf{Q}$. Comparing

$$\|\mathbf{Q}\bar{\mathbf{T}}\mathbf{Q}^T\| = \begin{Vmatrix} \bar{T}_{11} & -\bar{T}_{12} & -\bar{T}_{13} \\ -\bar{T}_{21} & \bar{T}_{22} & \bar{T}_{23} \\ -\bar{T}_{31} & \bar{T}_{32} & \bar{T}_{33} \end{Vmatrix}, \qquad \|\bar{\mathbf{T}}\| = \begin{Vmatrix} \bar{T}_{11} & \bar{T}_{12} & \bar{T}_{13} \\ \bar{T}_{21} & \bar{T}_{22} & \bar{T}_{23} \\ \bar{T}_{31} & \bar{T}_{32} & \bar{T}_{33} \end{Vmatrix},$$

we conclude that $\bar{T}_{12} = \bar{T}_{21} = \bar{T}_{13} = \bar{T}_{31} = 0$. A similar rotation about the y axis will yield the conditions $\bar{T}_{23} = \bar{T}_{32} = 0$. Thus we have shown that *if two symmetric tensors are related by an isotropic function then the principal directions of these tensors coincide.* Therefore, by (17.11), the principal values $T_{\underline{a}}$ of stress are functions of the principal values $B_{\underline{a}}$ of deformation:

$$T_{\underline{a}} = f_{\underline{a}}(B_1, B_2, B_3). \tag{17.12}$$

If the principal values of $\mathbf{B}$ are permuted, then the corresponding principal values of $\mathbf{T}$ will be permuted in the same way. To see this, we observe that a permutation of the principal values may be accomplished by an orthogonal transformation, and, because the principal directions of $\mathbf{T}$ and $\mathbf{B}$ coincide, the induced permutations in $\mathbf{T}$ and $\mathbf{B}$ will be identical.

As the final step, we express (17.12) in the form

$$T_{\underline{a}} = c_0 + c_1 B_{\underline{a}} + c_2 B_{\underline{a}}^2, \tag{17.13}$$

where the multipliers c_0, c_1, c_2 are, of course, functions of B_1, B_2, B_3 (this amounts to replacing the three functions $f_{\underline{a}}$ by another set of three functions c_0, c_1, and c_2). The relations (17.13) constitute three linear equations for c_0, c_1, c_2, the determinant Δ of the coefficients being

$$\Delta = \begin{Vmatrix} 1 & B_1 & B_1^2 \\ 1 & B_2 & B_2^2 \\ 1 & B_3 & B_3^2 \end{Vmatrix}.$$

We first assume that the principal values of **B** are distinct; then $\Delta \neq 0$, and a solution for c_0, c_1, c_2 exists. In particular, we have the result

$$c_0 = \frac{1}{\Delta}\begin{Vmatrix} T_1 & B_1 & B_1^2 \\ T_2 & B_2 & B_2^2 \\ T_3 & B_3 & B_3^2 \end{Vmatrix}.$$

A permutation of B_1, B_2, B_3 does not change c_0, hence we can conclude that c_0, and, similarly c_1 and c_2, are *symmetric functions* of B_1, B_2, B_3. But a symmetric function of N variables can be expressed in terms of N (rationally) independent combinations of these variables.† In the present case we may choose

$$\mathrm{I} = B_1 + B_2 + B_3, \quad \mathrm{II} = B_1B_2 + B_2B_3 + B_3B_1, \quad \mathrm{III} = B_1B_2B_3 \tag{17.14}$$

as the new variables, and thus consider c_0, c_1, c_2 as scalar functions of the principal invariants.

Multiplying (17.13) by $Q_{ia}Q_{ja}$, and summing over a, we find that, by (4.41),

$$\begin{aligned} \mathbf{T} &= c_0\mathbf{1} + c_1\mathbf{B} + c_2\mathbf{B}^2, \\ T_{ij} &= c_0\delta_{ij} + c_1B_{ij} + c_2B_{im}B_{mj}. \end{aligned} \tag{17.15}$$

If two principal values of **B** coincide, then (17.15) may be replaced by $\mathbf{T} = c_0\mathbf{1} + c_1\mathbf{B}$, because there are only two distinct functions $f_{\underline{a}}$ in (17.12). When all principal values are equal, then $\mathbf{T} = c_0\mathbf{1}$.

It must be emphasized that (17.15) is the representation of a *general* isotropic function, and not merely of an isotropic polynomial function, because the dependence of c_0, c_1 and c_2 on the invariants of **B** was not limited in any way. If, however, c_0, c_1, and c_2 are polynomial functions of B_1, B_2, B_3,

† Cf. Appendix II.

then they are also polynomial functions of I, II, III (this follows from the fundamental theorem on symmetric functions, proved in Appendix II).

A *linear* isotropic function **f** is evidently represented by

$$\mathbf{T} = \lambda \mathbf{1}\, \mathrm{tr}\mathbf{B} + 2\mu \mathbf{B}, \tag{17.16}$$

where λ and μ are constants.

Writing the Cayley-Hamilton equations as $\mathbf{B}^3 = \mathrm{I}\mathbf{B}^2 - \mathrm{II}\mathbf{B} + \mathrm{III}\mathbf{1}$, we obtain

$$\mathbf{B}^2 = \mathrm{I}\mathbf{B} - \mathrm{II}\mathbf{1} + \mathrm{III}\mathbf{B}^{-1}, \tag{17.17}$$

so that an equivalent form of (17.15) is given by

$$\mathbf{T} = \delta \mathbf{1} + \alpha \mathbf{B} + \gamma \mathbf{B}^{-1}, \tag{17.18}$$

where
$$\delta = c_0 - \mathrm{II}c_2, \qquad \alpha = c_1 + \mathrm{I}c_2, \qquad \gamma = \mathrm{III}c_2. \tag{17.19}$$

An incompressible material can undergo only isochoric motions, in which case $\rho = \rho_0$, and the balance of mass requires that $J = \det\mathbf{F} = 1$, or, equivalently, $\mathrm{III} = \det\mathbf{B} = 1$. Further, a hydrostatic pressure will produce no deformation at all, which means that the stress relation becomes *indeterminate* to the extent that a hydrostatic pressure p can be added to stress without affecting the deformation (although the stress relation leaves the pressure p unspecified, in a given problem either the field equations or the boundary conditions, or both, will provide a means for determining p). Now, if p is arbitrary, then so is $-p\mathbf{1} + c_0\mathbf{1}$, i.e. there is no loss of generality if c_0 is absorbed into p. Consequently, the isotropic stress relation for incompressible elastic solids can be expressed as

$$\mathbf{T} = -p\mathbf{1} + \alpha \mathbf{B} + \gamma \mathbf{B}^{-1}, \tag{17.20}$$

where α and γ are functions of the invariants I and II only.

Even with the assumption of incompressibility a complete solution of many interesting problems is not possible, which makes it necessary to turn to constitutive equations that are special but nevertheless retain the basic characteristics of nonlinearly elastic response. Here the best known example is the *Mooney-Rivlin material* defined by

$$\mathbf{T} = -p\mathbf{1} + \mu\left(\frac{1}{2} + \beta\right)\mathbf{B} - \mu\left(\frac{1}{2} - \beta\right)\mathbf{B}^{-1}, \tag{17.21}$$

μ and β now being *constants*. An equivalent representation is given by

$$\mathbf{T} = -p\mathbf{1} + \mu\left[\frac{1}{2}(1 + \mathrm{I}) + \beta(1 - \mathrm{I})\right]\mathbf{B} - \mu\left(\frac{1}{2} - \beta\right)\mathbf{B}^2. \tag{17.21}^*$$

It is not difficult to see that this material possesses a strain-energy function

$$W = \frac{1}{2}\mu\left[\left(\frac{1}{2} + \beta\right)(\mathrm{I} - 3) + \left(\frac{1}{2} - \beta\right)(\mathrm{II} - 3)\right],$$
$$\mu > 0, \qquad -\frac{1}{2} \leq \beta \leq \frac{1}{2}, \tag{17.22}$$

where the inequalities imposed on the constants μ and β are such as to make W a positive semi-definite quantity (note that $W = 0$ at $\mathbf{B} = \mathbf{1}$). Namely, with $\mathbf{B} = \mathbf{F}\mathbf{F}^T$, $\dot{\mathbf{F}} = \mathbf{L}\mathbf{F}$, where $\mathbf{L}$ is the tensor of velocity gradients, and $\mathrm{tr}(\mathbf{B}\mathbf{L}) = \frac{1}{2}\,\mathrm{tr}(\mathbf{L}\mathbf{B} + \mathbf{B}\mathbf{L}^T) = \frac{1}{2}\,\mathrm{tr}\dot{\mathbf{B}}$, etc., we readily obtain from (17.21) that $\mathrm{tr}(\mathbf{T}\mathbf{L}) = \dot{\mathbf{W}} = \partial W/\partial F_{ij}\,L_{ik}F_{kj}$. Because at any given instant the velocity gradients $\mathbf{L}$ can be assigned independently of the deformation gradients $\mathbf{F}$, it follows that

$$T_{ij} = \frac{\partial W}{\partial F_{im}}\,F_{jm} \tag{17.23}$$

(cf. (14.30)). The special case $\beta = \frac{1}{2}$ defines *Neo-Hookean materials*; the stress relation is then given by

$$\mathbf{T} = -p\mathbf{1} + \mu\mathbf{B}. \tag{17.24}$$

In view of $B_1B_2B_3 = 1$, we can write that

$$\frac{2W}{\mu} = \left(\frac{1}{2} + \beta\right)\left(B_1 + B_2 + \frac{1}{B_1B_2} - 3\right) + \left(\frac{1}{2} - \beta\right)\left(\frac{1}{B_1} + \frac{1}{B_2} + B_1B_2 - 3\right).$$

To show that the assumed limitations on μ and β indeed make W positive, we may consider the partial derivatives of W with respect to B_1 and B_2. It is then easy to see that an extremum exists for $B_1 = B_2 = 1$, and that it is a minimum, because all second derivatives of W are positive.

Restrictions on the constitutive equations

As in the linearized theory, it is necessary to investigate the restrictions, or "plausibility requirements," that must be imposed on the response function.

However, although the required properties of elastic response are as simple physically as they were in the linear theory, they will not lead to simple or manageable expressions in terms of the functions of invariants occurring in the nonlinear stress relation.† Among the various conditions we distinguish *static inequalities*, and inequalities related to wave propagation, uniqueness, and stability of solutions. The conditions that would ensure the existence of real wave speeds, for instance, cannot be interpreted wholly as restrictions on the elastic response; rather, they will also involve the state of deformation. To put it in another way, the questions concerning uniqueness, stability, and wave propagation relate to particular *problems*, or types of deformation. The static inequalities, on the other hand, express plausibility requirements that one might expect to be satisfied for *all* deformations. As *empirical inequalities* for isotropic media one may take‡

$$\delta \leq 0, \qquad \alpha > 0, \qquad \gamma \leq 0. \tag{17.25}$$

For isotropic media, the various restrictions can be expressed in a common, principal coordinate system of stress and deformation **B**. Let us denote by T_a a principal value of the stress tensor, and by V_a a principal stretch in the same direction.§ Sometimes it is more appropriate to use the *principal forces* f_a. Taking a unit cube in the reference configuration, with faces that are the principal planes of deformation (and stress), and noting that a stretch is equal to the final length divided by the initial length, we conclude that the deformed cuboid will have the side lengths V_1, V_2, V_3. The principal forces are thus related to the principal stresses by

$$f_1 = V_2V_3T_1, \qquad f_2 = V_3V_1T_2, \qquad f_3 = V_1V_2T_3. \tag{17.26}$$

A typical plausibility condition is the *T–E* (*tension-extension*) inequality, which requires that tension produce extension when the lateral faces are held fixed, thus $(\bar{f}_a - f_a)(\bar{V}_a - V_a) > 0$, $\bar{V}_b = V_b$ for $b \neq a$, where overbars mark the changed values of f_a and V_a. In the linear theory this condition reduces to $\lambda + 2\mu > 0$.

In studies of wave propagation and uniqueness, the *B–E* (*Baker-Ericksen*) inequality

$$(T_a - T_b)(V_a - V_b) > 0, \qquad a \neq b \tag{17.27}$$

† A very complete discussion of the various restrictions is given in *NFTM*, Sections 51–53.
‡ Cf. Truesdell and Toupin [175], p. 11.
§ In what follows the subscripts *a, b, c, . . .* will be considered as *labels*.

is often significant. It states that the greater principal stress should occur in the direction of the greater principal stretch. In the linear theory it is given by $\mu > 0$.

It would be desirable, of course, to combine the various static inequalities into a single, general inequality, so that the special inequalities would appear as physical interpretations of this inequality.

To obtain more explicit results, let us turn to the simplest stress relation, namely that of a Mooney-Rivlin material. In a principal coordinate system, then, $T_1 + p = \mu B_1$, $T_2 + p = \mu B_2$, $T_3 + p = \mu B_3$. If the deformation $\mathbf{B}$ is given, then the stress $\mathbf{T}$ is indeterminate to the extent of a hydrostatic pressure p. On the other hand, as shown by Rivlin [231], a given stress will determine a unique value of p from the condition $\mu^3 \det\mathbf{B} = \mu^3 = p^3 + (T_1 + T_2 + T_3)p^2 + (T_1T_2 + T_2T_3 + T_3T_1)p + T_1T_2T_3$. Being a cubic, this equation certainly has one real solution for p. If another solution exists, then, for the same state of stress, the stress relations require that B_1, B_2, B_3 be all increased (decreased) if this solution is larger (smaller) than the first. But a like change of all stretches is impossible because of $B_1B_2B_3 = 1$. Therefore, only one real solution for p exists which means that to each state of stress there corresponds a unique deformation $\mathbf{B}$.

In the present case, (17.26) reduces to $f_1 = T_1/V_1$, $f_2 = T_2/V_2$, $f_3 = T_3/V_3$, and the stress relations can be replaced by the force-stretch relations $V_1f_1 + p = \mu V_1^2$, $V_2f_2 + p = \mu V_2^2$, $V_3f_3 + p = \mu V_3^2$. As shown by Rivlin, these relations are uniquely invertible only if one or more forces are negative (i.e. compressive), or, if all are positive, then $f_1f_2f_3 < \mu^3$ holds. Thus if $f_1f_2f_3 > \mu^3$ then the deformation may depend on the sequence in which the loads are applied. Indeed, if a cube is subjected to triaxial tensions of equal magnitude, then it is not altogether implausible that, deforming the cube first into a "plate" by means of biaxial tensions, the application of the third tension to a now much greater area will not change the shape of the plate very much, whereas a simultaneous application of the three tensions would produce an entirely different deformation.

Propagation of acceleration fronts†

It is possible to learn a great deal about elastic response by investigating the propagation of second-order surfaces of discontinuity, also referred to as *acceleration fronts*, or acceleration waves. Although no exact solutions exhibiting such waves are known, there can be no doubt that results obtained from the conditions governing the propagation of acceleration fronts are

† The theory of small waves in prestrained bodies will be discussed in Section 21. The material given in this subsection is taken from Truesdell [184], [185], and Toupin and Bernstein [165].

relevant. It should be also recalled that in the linear theories of elasticity and viscoelasticity the correspondence between infinitesimal plane waves and acceleration fronts is well understood.†

Let S be a surface of discontinuity, and let us suppose that deformation gradients **F** and particle velocities $\dot{\mathbf{x}}$ are continuous at S, but that their derivatives are not. Then, according to (8.94)*, (8.97),

$$[\![\ddot{x}_i]\!] = \overline{V}^2 s_i, \qquad [\![x_{k,mj}]\!] = s_k F_{pm} F_{qj} n_q n_p, \tag{17.28}$$

where **s** is the amplitude of the acceleration front, **n** is a unit normal vector of S, and $\overline{V}$ is the speed of propagation, in the direction of **n**, of S relative to the particles that are at the moment located on S. In particular, if $\bar{u}$ is the speed, in the direction of **n**, of S relative to a space frame, then $\overline{V} = \bar{u} - \dot{\mathbf{x}} \cdot \mathbf{n}$ (cf. (8.87)). With

$$A_{jikm} = \frac{\partial \tilde{T}_{ji}}{\partial F_{km}}, \tag{17.29}$$

where $\tilde{\mathbf{T}}$ is the Piola-Kirchhoff stress defined by (15.87), the equations of motion, (15.89), now read

$$A_{jikm} F_{km,j} + \rho_0 b_i = \rho_0 \ddot{x}_i. \tag{17.30}$$

According to (17.28), at an acceleration front the equations of motion will reduce to

$$[Q_{ik}(\mathbf{n}) - \rho_0 \overline{V}^2 \delta_{ik}] s_k = 0, \tag{17.31}$$

where

$$Q_{ik}(\mathbf{n}) = C_{qikp} n_q n_p, \qquad C_{qikp} = A_{jikm} F_{qj} F_{pm}. \tag{17.32}$$

In the linear theory, C_{qikp} reduce to the *constant* elastic coefficients C_{qikp}. In general the *acoustic tensor* **Q**(**n**) is not symmetric; if, however, it happens to be symmetric, and positive, then its quadric is called *Fresnel's ellipsoid* (or, the ellipsoid of polarization). To obtain an alternative representation of C_{qikp}, we start from $T_{ji} = (1/J) F_{jp} \tilde{T}_{pi}, J F_{rm}\, \partial T_{ji}/\partial F_{km} = -\delta_{rk} F_{jp} \tilde{T}_{pi} + \delta_{jk} F_{rp} \tilde{T}_{pi} + C_{ijkr}$, from which it follows that‡

$$Q_{ik}(\mathbf{n}) = B_{jikr} n_j n_r, \qquad B_{jikr} = \frac{\partial T_{ji}}{\partial F_{km}} F_{rm}. \tag{17.32*}$$

Truesdell refers to (17.31) as the *Fresnel-Hadamard theorem*.§ It asserts that amplitude **s** of an acceleration front traveling in the direction of **n** must be a principal vector of the acoustic tensor. The speed of propagation, $\overline{V}$, is the

† Cf. Section 14.
‡ This definition of B_{jikr} is different from that given by Truesdell.
§ P. 267 of the first reference.

corresponding principal value, i.e. it is determined by the characteristic equation

$$\det[Q_{ik}(\mathbf{n}) - \rho_0 \overline{V}^2 \delta_{ik}] = 0. \tag{17.33}$$

In this generality there is of course no assurance that positive roots $\overline{V}^2$ will exist; all that can be said is that *if* they exist, then they are given by (17.33).

According to (14.16), (15.87), a stress relation satisfying material objectivity is given by

$$\tilde{\mathbf{T}} = \mathbf{k}(\mathbf{C})\mathbf{F}^T, \tag{17.34}$$

where $\mathbf{C} = \mathbf{U}^2 = \mathbf{F}^T\mathbf{F}$, and $\sqrt{\mathbf{C}}\,\mathbf{k}(\mathbf{C})\sqrt{\mathbf{C}} = J\mathbf{g}(\mathbf{U})$, $J^2 = \det\mathbf{C}$. Therefore, with

$$\frac{\partial F_{ir}}{\partial F_{km}} = \delta_{ik}\delta_{rm}, \qquad \frac{\partial C_{pq}}{\partial F_{km}} = \delta_{pm}F_{kp} + \delta_{qm}F_{kp}, \tag{17.35}$$

we obtain
$$A_{jikm} = \delta_{ik}k_{jm} + \frac{\partial k_{jr}}{\partial E_{mp}} F_{ir}F_{kp}. \tag{17.36}$$

The corresponding representation of $C_{qikp} = A_{jikm}F_{qj}F_{pm}$ now raises the possibility that the speeds of propagation may depend on the local rotations **R** which enter through $\mathbf{F} = \mathbf{RU}$. To show that this is not so, let us introduce $\overline{Q}_{nr} \equiv F_{ni}^{-1}Q_{ik}F_{kr}$, $\bar{n}_r \equiv n_k F_{kr}$. Then, by (17.36),

$$\begin{aligned} \overline{Q}_{nr} &= D_{nrpq}(\mathbf{C})\bar{n}_p\bar{n}_q, \\ D_{nrpq}(\mathbf{C}) &= \delta_{nr}k_{pq} + C_{rm}\frac{\partial k_{qn}}{\partial E_{pm}}. \end{aligned} \tag{17.37}$$

The characteristic equation now becomes $(\overline{\mathbf{Q}} - \rho_0\overline{V}^2\mathbf{1})\mathbf{U}^{-1}(\mathbf{R}^T\mathbf{s}) = \mathbf{0}$, from which it follows that the speeds of propagation are independent of the local rotation **R**. The *acoustic axes*, defined by the principal vectors **s** of the acoustic tensor, will in general depend on **R**.

Much more explicit results can be obtained if the elastic response is isotropic. To obtain a representation of $Q_{ik}(\mathbf{n})$, we first derive by a routine though lengthy calculation the following formulas,

$$F_{rm}\frac{\partial}{\partial F_{km}} B_{ji} = \delta_{jk}B_{ri} + \delta_{ik}B_{rj}, \qquad F_{rm}\frac{\partial \mathrm{I}}{\partial F_{km}} = 2B_{rk},$$

$$F_{rm}\frac{\partial}{\partial F_{km}}(\mathbf{B}^2)_{ji} = \delta_{jk}(\mathbf{B}^2)_{ri} + B_{rj}B_{ki} + B_{ri}B_{kj} + \delta_{ik}(\mathbf{B}^2)_{rj}, \tag{17.38}$$

$$F_{rm}\frac{\partial \mathrm{II}}{\partial F_{km}} = 2\mathrm{I}B_{rk} - 2(\mathbf{B}^2)_{rk}, \qquad F_{rm}\frac{\partial \mathrm{III}}{\partial F_{km}} = 2\delta_{rk}\mathrm{III}.$$

In addition, we introduce the operator

$$M_{rk} = B_{rk}\frac{\partial}{\partial \mathrm{I}} + (\mathrm{I}B_{rk} - B_{rm}B_{mk})\frac{\partial}{\partial \mathrm{II}} + \mathrm{III}\delta_{rk}\frac{\partial}{\partial \mathrm{III}}. \tag{17.39}$$

If $\mathbf{n}$ is a principal vector of $\mathbf{B}$, thus $\mathbf{Bn} = B\mathbf{n}$, then

$$n_r M_{rk} = Bn_k M, \quad M = \frac{\partial}{\partial \mathrm{I}} + (\mathrm{I} - B)\frac{\partial}{\partial \mathrm{III}} + \frac{\mathrm{III}}{B}\frac{\partial}{\partial \mathrm{III}}. \tag{17.40}$$

Using these results, and (17.15), we now obtain

$$C_{ijkr} = c_1(\delta_{jk}B_{ri} + \delta_{ik}B_{rj}) + c_2(\delta_{jk}B^2_{ri} + B_{rj}B_{ki} + B_{ri}B_{kj} + \delta_{ik}B^2_{rj}) + 2\delta_{ji}M_{rk}c_0 + 2B_{ji}M_{rk}c_1 + B^2_{ji}M_{rk}c_2, \tag{17.41}$$

where $B^2_{ri} = B_{rm}B_{mi}$, etc.

As noted by Truesdell,† in general a wave front propagates into a medium possessing three sets of special directions: the material frames $\mathbf{H}_a$ that, together with the symmetry operations, define the anisotropy of the medium, the principal directions of stress, and the principal directions of deformation. An isotropic medium, however, has no preferred directions, and the principal directions of stress and deformation coincide (hence they can be referred to as *the* principal directions). The acoustic axes can now be influenced only by these principal directions, and the direction of propagation, $\mathbf{n}$. This leads us to expect that if $\mathbf{n}$ is a principal direction, i.e. $\mathbf{Tn} = T\mathbf{n}$, $\mathbf{Bn} = B\mathbf{n}$, where T and B are the principal values associated with $\mathbf{n}$, then *the acoustic axes will coincide with the principal directions.* A wave front propagating along a principal direction is called a *principal wave*.

Indeed, letting $\mathbf{Bn} = B\mathbf{n}$, we find that

$$\frac{1}{JB}Q_{ik}(\mathbf{n}) = (\delta_{ik} + n_i n_k)c_1 + (B\delta_{ik} + 2Bn_i n_k + B_{ki})c_2 + 2(Mc_0 + BMc_1 + B^2Mc_2)n_i n_k. \tag{17.42}$$

Consequently, $Q_{ik}(\mathbf{n})$ is of the form $Q_{ik}(\mathbf{n}) = a\delta_{ik} + bB_{ik} + cn_i n_k$. From this it follows, first, that $Q_{ik}(\mathbf{n})n_k = (a + bB + c)n_i$, i.e. $\mathbf{n}$ is also a principal vector of $\mathbf{Q}(\mathbf{n})$. Similarly, if $\mathbf{m}$ is another principal vector of $\mathbf{B}$, so that $\mathbf{Bm} = \bar{B}\mathbf{m}$, $\mathbf{m}\cdot\mathbf{n} = 0$, then $Q_{ik}(\mathbf{n})m_k = (a + b\bar{B})m_i$. Moreover, because the

† [184], p. 264.

principal vectors of **B** are orthogonal,† it follows that the amplitude vectors of principal waves are either parallel or perpendicular to the direction of propagation, i.e. *every principal wave is either longitudinal or transverse.*

Replacing **s** by **n** in (17.31), we find that the speed of a longitudinal wave, V_L, propagating in the direction of **n**, is given by

$$\frac{\rho}{2B} V_L^2 = \frac{Q_{ik}(\mathbf{n})n_i n_k}{2BJ} = c_1 + 2Bc_2 + Mc_0 + BMc_1 + B^2Mc_2, \tag{17.43}$$

where $B = B_{ik}n_i n_k$. With $T_{\underline{a}} = c_0 + c_1 B_{\underline{a}} + c_2 B_{\underline{a}}^2$, it is easy to see that ρV_L^2 can be also expressed by

$$\rho V_L^2 = 2\frac{\partial T}{\partial \log B}, \tag{17.44}$$

where $T = T_{ij}n_i n_j$ is the principal stress associated with **n**. There are at least nine principal waves (there are infinitely many if not all principal values of **B** are distinct), so that it pays to introduce more systematic notations. Let us designate by $\mathbf{n}_1$ the direction of propagation, and let $\mathbf{n}_1$, $\mathbf{n}_2$, $\mathbf{n}_3$ constitute an orthonormal triad. The principal values of **B** and **T** are labeled accordingly, e.g. $T_1 = \mathbf{T}[\mathbf{n}_1, \mathbf{n}_1]$, $B_2 = \mathbf{B}[\mathbf{n}_2, \mathbf{n}_2]$. The speeds of longitudinal principal waves are denoted by V_{11}, V_{22}, V_{33}, whereas the speed of a transverse principal wave that is propagating in the direction of $\mathbf{n}_1$, and whose amplitude vector is in the direction of $\mathbf{n}_2$, is denoted by V_{12}. Then (17.44) can be written as

$$\rho V_{11}^2 = 2\frac{\partial T_1}{\partial \log B_1}. \tag{17.44*}$$

To calculate V_{12}, we replace **s** in (17.31) by $\mathbf{n}_2$, thus

$$Q_{ik}(\mathbf{n}_1)n_{2i}n_{2k} = \rho_0 V_{12}^2 = JB_1[c_1 + (B_1 + B_2)c_2], \tag{17.45}$$

and

$$\rho V_{12}^2 = B_1 \frac{T_1 - T_2}{B_1 - B_2}, \qquad \rho(V_{12}^2 - V_{13}^2) = B_1(B_2 - B_3)c_2. \tag{17.46}$$

From this we can draw several conclusions. First, if $B_2 = B_3$, then every

† If two principal values, $B(\mathbf{m}) = B_{ij}m_i m_j$ and $B(\overline{\mathbf{m}}) = B_{ij}\overline{m}_i\overline{m}_j$ coincide, then every direction in the plane spanned by **m** and $\overline{\mathbf{m}}$ is a principal direction. Correspondingly, in this plane the direction of propagation of principal waves is unrestricted. If $\mathbf{B} = B\mathbf{1}$, then every wave front is a principal wave.

direction perpendicular to $\mathbf{n}_1$ is a principal direction of $\mathbf{B}$, and, correspondingly, any amplitude vector perpendicular to $\mathbf{n}_1$ is possible; the speeds of all transverse waves propagating in the direction of $\mathbf{n}_1$ are equal. If $c_2 < 0$, and $B_2 \neq B_3$, then the amplitude of the faster wave is in the direction of the lesser principal stretch.

To summarize what has been obtained so far, we can say that in isotropic media the acoustic tensor has three real acoustic axes, but the speeds of longitudinal principal waves are real only if each principal stress is a monotonically increasing function of the corresponding principal stretch when other principal stretches are held constant, whereas the speeds of transverse principal waves are real only if the greater principal stress corresponds to the greater principal stretch. The last condition is in fact the *B–E* inequality (17.27).

In anisotropic media, we conclude from $Q_{ik}(\mathbf{n})m_i m_k = C_{qikp}n_q n_p m_i m_k$ that the speeds of propagation are real provided that, first, there exist real acoustic axes, and second, C_{qikp} obey the *strong-ellipticity (S–E) condition*

$$C_{qikp}n_q n_p m_i m_k > 0. \tag{17.47}$$

Because this condition relates only to the symmetric part of the acoustic tensor, $Q_{ik}(\mathbf{n})m_i m_k = Q_{(ik)}(\mathbf{n})m_i m_k$, it does not imply that the acoustic axes are real. However, any second rank tensor has at least one real principal vector. Therefore, given any direction of propagation, $\mathbf{n}$, the *S–E* inequality implies the existence of at least one real amplitude and speed of propagation; in isotropic media the acoustic axes were shown to be real, hence the *S–E* condition implies that all speeds of propagation of the principal waves are real.

Let us now consider the propagation of acceleration fronts in isotropic media subjected to the hydrostatic stress $\mathbf{T} = -p(\rho)\mathbf{1} = (c_0 + c_1 B + c_2 B^2)\mathbf{1}$. Longitudinal and transverse principal waves can now propagate in every direction. The common speed of the transverse waves is, by (17.45),

$$V_T^2 = \frac{B^{5/2}}{\rho_0}(c_1 + 2Bc_2). \tag{17.48}$$

To derive a similar formula for the common speed of longitudinal waves, V_L, we first note that

$$\frac{d}{dB} = 3\frac{\partial}{\partial \mathrm{I}} + 6B\frac{\partial}{\partial \mathrm{II}} + 3B^2\frac{\partial}{\partial \mathrm{III}}, \qquad \frac{d\rho}{dB} = -\frac{3}{2}\rho_0 B^{-5/2}. \tag{17.49}$$

Then, as may be seen from (17.43),

$$V_L^2 = \frac{dp}{d\rho} + \frac{4}{3}\frac{B^{5/2}}{\rho_0}(c_1 + 2Bc_2). \tag{17.50}$$

From (17.48), (17.50) it follows that

$$V_L^2 = \frac{4}{3}V_T^2 + \frac{dp}{d\rho}; \tag{17.51}$$

in the linear theory we have that $dp/d\rho = (3\lambda + 2\mu)/3\rho_0$, and (17.51) reduces to the identity $\lambda + 2\mu = \frac{4}{3}\mu + \lambda + \frac{2}{3}\mu$.

A knowledge of the nine speeds of propagation of principal waves suffices to determine c_0, c_1, c_2 as functions of I, II, III. From the formula giving the speeds of transverse waves, we obtain right away

$$c_1 = \rho\frac{(B_2 - \mathrm{I})V_{12}^2 - (B_3 - \mathrm{I})V_{13}^2}{B_1(B_2 - B_3)}, \qquad c_2 = \rho\frac{V_{12}^2 - V_{13}^3}{B_1(B_2 - B_3)}. \tag{17.52}$$

In addition, a number of *compatibility conditions* between the wave speeds can be derived, e.g. $B_2V_{12}^2 = B_1V_{21}^2$.† Once c_1 and c_2 are determined, we can calculate c_0 by solving the equations $A_1 \equiv (\rho/2B_1)V_{11}^2 - c_1 - 2B_1c_2 - B_1M_1c_1 - B_1^2M_1c_2 = M_1c_0, \ldots, \ldots,$ where $M_1 = \partial/\partial\mathrm{I} + (\mathrm{I} - B_1)\partial/\partial\mathrm{II} + (\mathrm{III}/B_1)\partial/\partial\mathrm{III}$, etc., as follows

$$\begin{aligned}
\Delta\frac{\partial c_0}{\partial \mathrm{I}} &= A_1B_1^2(B_2 - B_3) + A_2B_2^2(B_3 - B_1) + A_3B_3^2(B_1 - B_2),\\
-\Delta\frac{\partial c_0}{\partial \mathrm{II}} &= A_1B_1(B_2 - B_3) + A_2B_2(B_3 - B_1) + A_3B_3(B_1 - B_2),\\
\Delta\frac{\partial c_0}{\partial \mathrm{III}} &= A_1(B_2 - B_3) + A_2(B_3 - B_1) + A_3(B_1 - B_2),\\
\Delta &= (B_1 - B_2)(B_2 - B_3)(B_3 - B_1).
\end{aligned} \tag{17.53}$$

Then $$c_0 = \int\left(\frac{\partial c_0}{\partial \mathrm{I}}\,d\mathrm{I} + \frac{\partial c_0}{\partial \mathrm{II}}\,d\mathrm{II} + \frac{\partial c_0}{\partial \mathrm{III}}\,d\mathrm{III}\right).$$

If the medium is *hyperelastic* then $A_{jikm} = \partial^2 W/\partial F_{ij}\partial F_{km} = A_{mkij}$, from which it follows that the acoustic tensor $\mathbf{Q}(\mathbf{n})$ is symmetric for *all* $\mathbf{n}$, i.e. all

† Cf. [184], p. 278.

acoustic axes are real. Bernstein has shown that the converse is also true: if $Q_{ik}(\mathbf{n}) = Q_{ki}(\mathbf{n})$ for arbitrary $\mathbf{n}$, then the response is hyperelastic.† For isotropic response we obtain, writing $(17.32)_1$ in the principal coordinate system of stress and deformation

$$Q_{12}(\mathbf{n}) = J\left[2B_2 \frac{\partial T_1}{\partial B_2} + \frac{T_1 - T_2}{B_1 - B_2} B_1\right] n_1 n_2,$$

$$Q_{21}(\mathbf{n}) = J\left[2B_1 \frac{\partial T_2}{\partial B_1} + \frac{T_2 - T_1}{B_2 - B_1} B_2\right] n_2 n_1.$$

If the wave front is not a principal wave, then $n_1 \neq 0$, $n_2 \neq 0$, so that necessary and sufficient conditions for the existence of a strain-energy function are

$$T_2 - T_1 = 2B_2 \frac{\partial T_1}{\partial B_2} - 2B_1 \frac{\partial T_2}{\partial B_1}, \ldots, \ldots. \tag{17.54}$$

It is difficult to tell just what is implied by the existence of a strain-energy function. Therefore, whenever little or nothing is gained by assuming that a strain-energy function exists, it seems best not to make this assumption. An attempt to find general conditions under which a strain-energy function would exist would take us far afield. The mention of energy opens the door to thermodynamics, and in thermodynamics we must start with the density of internal energy. If we can assume that $\varepsilon = \varepsilon(\mathbf{F}, \eta)$, then $\rho_0 \varepsilon$ can be identified with W in isentropic processes; similarly, $\rho_0(\varepsilon - \eta\theta)$ can be identified with W in isothermal processes (cf. the remarks on p. 298). In these cases, then, the assumption that W exists has been merely replaced by other assumptions.

Using (17.38), we readily find the stress relation for isotropic hyperelastic solids is given by

$$\mathbf{T} = \frac{2}{J}[\mathrm{III}\, W_3 \mathbf{1} + (W_1 + \mathrm{I}\, W_2)\mathbf{B} - W_2 \mathbf{B}^2], \tag{17.15)*$$

where W_1, W_2, W_3 are the derivatives of W with respect to I, II, III, respectively.

It is of some interest to investigate the propagation of acceleration fronts in the context of a "second-order theory" of isotropic elasticity. We are then able to see the manner in which the nonlinear theory *begins* to deviate from the linear theory.

† Cf. [184], p. 288.

Following Truesdell, we introduce, along with the infinitesimal strain tensor $\tilde{\mathbf{E}}$, the finite strain tensor $2\mathbf{E} = \mathbf{C} - \mathbf{1}$, $\mathbf{C} = \mathbf{F}^T\mathbf{F}$. Because $\mathbf{B}$ and $\mathbf{C}$ have the same principal values $V_{\underline{a}}^2$, we can write, denoting by $\delta_{\underline{a}}$ the (relative) elongation $V_{\underline{a}} - 1$, $2E_1 = C_1 - 1 = (1 + \delta_1)^2 - 1$, thus $E_1 = \delta_1 + \frac{1}{2}\delta_1^2, \ldots, \ldots$, whereas $\tilde{E}_1 = \delta_1, \ldots, \ldots$ Further, the invariants of strain are $\mathrm{I} = \delta_1 + \delta_2 + \delta_3$, $\widetilde{\mathrm{II}} = \delta_1\delta_2 + \delta_2\delta_3 + \delta_3\delta_1$, $\mathrm{I} = \tilde{\mathrm{I}} + \frac{1}{2}(\delta_1^2 + \delta_2^2 + \delta_3^2)$. The appropriate stress relation is taken to be, in the principal coordinate system,

$$\begin{aligned}\frac{T_1}{\mu} &= \frac{\lambda}{\mu}\left[\tilde{\mathrm{I}} + \frac{1}{2}(\delta_1^2 + \delta_2^2 + \delta_3^2) + (2\delta_1 + \delta_1^2)\right] \\ &\quad + [\alpha_3\tilde{\mathrm{I}}^2 + \alpha_4(\delta_1\delta_2 + \delta_2\delta_3 + \delta_3\delta_1)] + \alpha_5\tilde{\mathrm{I}}\delta_1 + \alpha_6\delta_1^2, \qquad (17.55) \\ &\quad \ldots, \ldots,\end{aligned}$$

where λ, μ, α_3, α_5, α_6 are constants. Noting that $\rho(1 + \tilde{\mathrm{I}}) \doteq \rho_0$ to within terms of the order of $\delta_{\underline{a}}^2$, and that

$$2B_1\frac{\partial T_1}{\partial B_1} = (1 + \delta_1)\frac{\partial T_1}{\partial \delta_1},$$

we readily obtain from $\rho V_{11}^2 = 2B_1\, \partial T_1/\partial B_1$ that

$$\begin{aligned}\frac{1}{\mu}\rho_0 V_{11}^2 &= \frac{\lambda}{\mu} + 2 + \left(\frac{\lambda}{\mu} + 2 + 2\alpha_3 + \alpha_4 + \alpha_5\right)\tilde{\mathrm{I}} \\ &\quad + \left(\frac{2\lambda}{\mu} + 4 - \alpha_4 + \alpha_5 + 2\alpha_6\right)\delta_1 \qquad (17.56)\end{aligned}$$

to within terms of the order of $\delta_{\underline{a}}^2$. Similarly, $\rho V_{12}^2 = B_1(T_1 - T_2)/(B_1 - B_2)$ yields the approximation

$$\frac{1}{\mu}\rho_0 V_{12}^2 = 1 + 2\delta_1 + \left(1 + \frac{1}{2}\alpha_5\right)\tilde{\mathrm{I}} + \frac{1}{2}\alpha_6(\delta_1 + \delta_2). \qquad (17.57)$$

The conditions (17.54) for the existence of a strain-energy function now reduce, via the relation

$$\alpha_4 + \alpha_5 = 2\left(\frac{\lambda}{\mu} - 1\right), \qquad (17.58)$$

the number of independent constants from 6 to 5. In terms of the wave speeds, (17.58) becomes†

$$\left(\frac{\partial}{\partial \delta_1} - \frac{\partial}{\partial \delta_2}\right) V_{11}^2 - 4\frac{\partial}{\partial \delta_1} V_{12}^2 + \frac{6\mu}{\rho_0} = 0. \qquad (17.59)$$

† [184], p. 291.

As before, the elastic response can be determined from a knowledge of the wave speeds,† e.g.

$$\frac{1}{2}\alpha_6 = \frac{(\rho_0/\mu)(V_{12}^2 - V_{13}^2)}{\delta_2 - \delta_3}. \tag{17.60}$$

Problems

1. Express the strain-energy function (17.22) as $W = W(B_1, B_2)$. Sketch W as a surface over the $B_1 - B_2$ plane, and investigate the extrema of W.

2. Assuming that all second derivatives of $x_i = x_i(\mathbf{X}, t)$ are continuous, show that a third-order wave front satisfies the jump conditions

$$[\![x_{k,mjr}]\!] = s_k F_{pm} F_{qj} F_{sr} n_q n_p n_s, \qquad [\![\ddot{x}_{i,r}]\!] = s_i \overline{V}^2 n_r.$$

Differentiating (17.30) with respect to x_n, and noting that $F_{ij,k}$ are now continuous, obtain the following condition of propagation,

$$s_k(A_{jlkm} F_{rn}^{-1} F_{qj} F_{pm} F_{sr} n_q n_p n_s - \rho_0 \overline{V}^2 \delta_{ik} n_n) = 0,$$

which immediately reduces to (17.31). The same procedure can be applied to wave fronts of order N, thus obtaining *Truesdell–Ericksen's first theorem of equivalence*: the propagation of surfaces of discontinuity of all orders $N \geq 2$ is governed by the condition (17.31).

3. Derive (17.36), (17.37) from (17.34).

4. Verify in detail the derivation of (17.38)–(17.42).

5. Starting from (17.42), derive (17.44), (17.46), (17.48), (17.51).

6. Derive (17.52), (17.53).

Section 18
SOME EXACT SOLUTIONS OF ISOTROPIC ELASTICITY

We shall now take up some of the exact solutions of isotropic elasticity, and discuss in detail the mechanical behavior described by these solutions. As a rule, the solutions are found by what is called the *semi-inverse method.* Here the idea is to assume simple types of deformations, usually well known from the linearized theory; the corresponding stresses are then obtained from the stress relation. The next step is to investigate whether the stresses satisfy the equations of equilibrium or, as the case may be, to determine the limitations imposed by these equations upon the assumed forms of solutions. It

† [184], p. 286.

then remains to calculate the surface tractions necessary to maintain the assumed deformation. By and large one expects of a "good" solution that the surface tractions will correspond to reasonable loading conditions (better yet, that the surface tractions are of a kind that can be reproduced in laboratory).

For any assumed deformation the mass density ρ can be calculated from the law of conservation of mass. In particular, if body forces and accelerations are absent, we may ignore ρ altogether.

If a solution is to be completely general, then the response function must remain unspecified in the same way that the *values* of E and ν, for instance, remain unspecified in the linear theory. Evidently it will not be possible in general to satisfy the equations of equilibrium if the stresses are, in effect, unknown. That explains why incompressible materials play such an important role in the nonlinear theory, because the unspecified pressure p can be used, so to speak, as a wild card to meet various requirements.

The main purpose of the nonlinear theory is to predict, and explain, the basic characteristics of elastic response. Even though we cannot expect to be able to solve large numbers of routine boundary value problems of the kind considered in the linear theory, the formulation of meaningful boundary conditions is nevertheless an important task. In the *displacement boundary conditions* the deformed shape of the boundary ∂V is prescribed at all times. Thus if ∂V_R is the boundary of the body in its reference configuration, then

$$\mathbf{x} = \bar{\mathbf{x}}(\mathbf{X}, t) \tag{18.1}$$

is given for all t, and all $\mathbf{X}$ in ∂V_R. To this we adjoin the *initial conditions*

$$\mathbf{x}(\mathbf{X}, 0) = \mathbf{x}^*(\mathbf{X}) \text{ in } V. \tag{18.2}$$

The problem is then to determine $\mathbf{x} = \boldsymbol{\chi}(\mathbf{X}, t)$ in the interior of the body. The *stress boundary conditions* are more difficult to deal with, because they refer to unknown deformed configurations. In fact, what is now needed is the knowledge of surface tractions $\mathbf{t}_S$ acting on every possible shape S of the boundary:† $\mathbf{t}_S = \mathbf{M}(S)$, such that $\mathbf{t}_S(\mathbf{X}, t) = \mathbf{T}_S(\mathbf{X}, t)\mathbf{n}_S$, where $\mathbf{n}_S$ is a unit normal vector of S, are the required surface tractions when S is the shape of the boundary. If the boundary is stress-free, then we have the simple condition $\mathbf{t}_S = \mathbf{0}$. A boundary condition of pressure is given by

$$\mathbf{t}_S = -p(\mathbf{X}, t)\mathbf{n}_S, \qquad \mathbf{X} \text{ in } S.$$

† Noll ([105], p. 98) puts it this way: "The mapping **M** describes a sort of a priori strategy which tells us what force to apply for every conceivable motion of the body. In other words, the mapping **M** is a description of the action of the environment on the body under all conceivable circumstances."

As in the linear theory, a *mixed boundary condition* prescribes stresses on a part B_T of the boundary, and displacements on the part $B_u = \partial V - B_T$ of the boundary.

In view of problems such as eversion of a cylindrical tube, it is clear that one cannot expect in general a *global uniqueness* of solutions, particularly in stress boundary value problems, although uniqueness corresponding to a specific loading process may be possible. The question of uniqueness will be briefly discussed in Section 21 in connection with superposition of small deformations upon large.

Unless stated otherwise, the solutions given below will describe *static* configurations.

Homogeneous deformations

In *homogeneous deformations* all measures of deformation and rotation are constant throughout the body, so that the stresses are constant too:

$$\operatorname{div}\mathbf{T} = 0. \tag{18.3}$$

Consequently, homogeneous deformations can be maintained in equilibrium by means of surface tractions alone (i.e. no body forces are needed).

Let us take as the first example a *simple extension*† defined by

$$x = \lambda VX, \qquad y = \lambda VY, \qquad z = VZ, \tag{18.4}$$

where V is the constant stretch in the z direction, and the undetermined coefficient λ describes the lateral contraction. Evidently $\mathbf{B} = \mathbf{F}\mathbf{F}^T$ is a diagonal tensor given by

$$\mathbf{B} = \operatorname{diag}(\lambda^2 V^2, \lambda^2 V^2, V^2). \tag{18.5}$$

Substituting this into (17.18), we obtain

$$\begin{gathered} T_{xx} = T_{yy} = \delta + \alpha\lambda^2 V^2 + \gamma\lambda^{-2} V^{-2}, \\ T_{zz} = \delta + \alpha V^2 + \gamma V^{-2}, \qquad T_{xy} = T_{yz} = T_{zx} = 0, \end{gathered} \tag{18.6}$$

where the coefficients are functions of the invariants

$$\mathrm{I} = V^2(1 + 2\lambda^2), \qquad \mathrm{II} = \lambda^2 V^4 (2 + \lambda^2), \qquad \mathrm{III} = \lambda^4 V^6. \tag{18.7}$$

† Cf. (15.46).

To clear the lateral faces from the tractions T_{xx} and T_{yy}, λ must be chosen such that

$$\delta + \alpha\lambda^2 V^2 + \gamma\lambda^{-2} V^{-2} = 0. \tag{18.8}$$

It is not obvious what, if any, condition is imposed on the response functions by assuming that (18.8) has a positive root λ^2. For if $T_{xx} \neq 0$, then, assuming that V is increased to its final value while holding $\lambda V = 1$, and that T_{xx} is a *continuous* function of deformation, we conclude that if T_{xx} is positive at any value of λV, then it will remain positive even when $\lambda V \to 0$, while V is being held fixed. The body would thus "disappear," with work being continually extracted from it by T_{xx}. In any case we shall assume that a positive root λ^2 of (18.8) exists.

The case of *uniform dilatation* is obtained by setting $\lambda = 1$, in which case (18.6) reduce to

$$p \equiv -\frac{1}{3} T_{kk} = \kappa(V), \tag{18.9}$$

$$\kappa(V) = \delta(3V^2, 3V^4, V^6) - V^2\alpha(3V^2, 3V^4, V^6) - V^{-2}\gamma(3V^2, 3V^4, V^6). \tag{18.10}$$

From (18.9), (18.10) we can conclude that the elastic response in compression differs from that in dilatation, because the condition of equality, $\kappa(V) = -\kappa(1/V)$ need not be satisfied in general.

Simple shear is a particularly important problem because the solution exhibits the fundamental traits of nonlinear elasticity. With

$$x = X + KY, \qquad y = Y, \qquad z = Z, \tag{18.11}$$

we obtain

$$\|\mathbf{B}\| = \begin{Vmatrix} 1 + K^2 & K & 0 \\ K & 1 & 0 \\ 0 & 0 & 1 \end{Vmatrix}, \tag{18.12}$$

and

$$\mathrm{I} = \mathrm{II} = 3 + K^2, \qquad \mathrm{III} = 1. \tag{18.13}$$

Further, by (3.40),

$$\|\mathbf{B}^{-1}\| = \begin{Vmatrix} 1 & -K & 0 \\ -K & 1 + K^2 & 0 \\ 0 & 0 & 1 \end{Vmatrix}. \tag{18.14}$$

The constitutive equations (7.18) now read

$$\|\mathbf{T}\| = T_{zz}\begin{Vmatrix} 1 & 0 & 0 \\ 0 & 1 & 0 \\ 0 & 0 & 1 \end{Vmatrix} + \hat{\mu}K\begin{Vmatrix} 0 & 1 & 0 \\ 1 & 0 & 0 \\ 0 & 0 & 0 \end{Vmatrix} + \alpha K^2\begin{Vmatrix} 1 & 0 & 0 \\ 0 & 0 & 0 \\ 0 & 0 & 0 \end{Vmatrix} + \gamma K^2\begin{Vmatrix} 0 & 0 & 0 \\ 0 & 1 & 0 \\ 0 & 0 & 0 \end{Vmatrix}, \tag{18.15}$$

where $T_{zz} = \delta + \alpha + \gamma$, and

$$\hat{\mu}(K^2) = \alpha(3 + K^2, 3 + K^2, 1) - \gamma(3 + K^2, 3 + K^2, 1). \tag{18.16}$$

In particular, we have that

$$\frac{T_{xy}}{K} = \hat{\mu}(K^2). \tag{18.17}$$

From $2\mathbf{e} = \mathbf{1} - \mathbf{B}^{-1}$ and (18.14) now follows that

$$e_{xy} = \frac{K}{2}. \tag{18.18}$$

Neglecting K^2 in (18.16), we find that, by (18.17), (18.18), the quantity $\hat{\mu}(0)$ equals the modulus of shear, μ, in the linear theory:

$$T_{xy} \doteq 2\hat{\mu}(0)e_{xy}. \tag{18.19}$$

In the present context, $\hat{\mu}(K^2)$ may be referred to as the *secant modulus*, and $\partial T_{xy}/\partial K$ as the *tangent modulus*.

Because $\hat{\mu}(K^2)$ is an even function of K, T_{xy} is an odd function of K. Therefore, if $\hat{\mu}$ admits a series expansion about $K = 0$, then T_{xy} for small K will be given by

$$T_{xy} \doteq \mu K + AK^3 + \cdots, \tag{18.20}$$

i.e. *in simple shear the deviation from the linear theory will be proportional to K^3 rather than K^2.*

The principal values of **B** are the squared principal stretches: $B_{\underline{i}} = V_{\underline{i}}^2$. Diagonalizing (18.12), we obtain

$$B_1 = 1 + \frac{K^2}{2} + K\sqrt{1 + \frac{K^2}{4}} = \frac{1}{B_2},$$

$$B_2 = 1 + \frac{K^2}{2} - K\sqrt{1 + \frac{K^2}{4}} = \frac{1}{B_1}, \qquad (18.21)$$

$$B_3 = 1.$$

The principal stresses $T_{\underline{a}}$ are given by

$$T_{\underline{a}} = \delta + \alpha B_{\underline{a}} + \gamma B_{\underline{a}}^{-1}. \qquad (18.22)$$

Combining (18.22) with (18.21), we get $T_1 - T_2 = 2K\hat{\mu}(K^2)\sqrt{(1 + \frac{1}{4}K^2)}$, or

$$\hat{\mu}(K^2) = (T_1 - T_2)(V_1^2 - V_2^2). \qquad (18.23)$$

The stretches are by definition positive, thus $V_1 + V_2 > 0$; therefore, we can conclude that $\hat{\mu}(K^2) > 0$ whenever the *B–E* inequalities hold.

Let us now consider the normal stresses in greater detail. From the explicit formulas

$$T_{xx} = T_{zz} + \alpha K^2, \quad T_{yy} = T_{zz} + \gamma K^2, \quad T_{zz} = \delta + \alpha + \gamma \qquad (18.24)$$

it is possible to draw several conclusions. First of all, the normal stresses are evidently even functions of K. To make the deviation from the linear theory more explicit, we assume that the response functions can be expanded in Taylor series about $K = 0$:

$$\alpha(3 + K^2, 3 + K^2, 1) = \alpha(3, 3, 1) + K^2\left(\frac{\partial\alpha}{\partial \mathrm{I}} + \frac{\partial\alpha}{\partial \mathrm{II}}\right)\bigg|_{K=0},$$

etc. The stresses vanish in the natural state $K = 0$, i.e.

$$\delta(3, 3, 1) + \alpha(3, 3, 1) + \gamma(3, 3, 1) = 0, \qquad (18.25)$$

so that, in the limit as K tends to zero, the normal stresses are approximated by formulas of the type

$$T_{xx} \doteq [C + \alpha(3, 3, 1)]K^2, \quad T_{yy} \doteq [C + \gamma(3, 3, 1)]K^2, \qquad (18.26)$$

$$T_{zz} \doteq CK^2. \tag{18.27}$$

From (18.24), (18.16), (18.17) it is clear that simple shear cannot be produced by a shearing stress alone, because if the normal stresses vanish then $\delta = \alpha = \gamma = 0$, but then the shearing stress also will vanish. In the limit as $K \to 0$ we do recover the solution (15.47) of the linearized theory, because T_{xy} is proportional to K but the normal stresses are proportional to K^2. At the same time, the linearized theory fails to give so much as an indication of the nature of nonlinear elastic response: *the deviation from linearity between shearing stress and shearing strain is a third-order effect* (i.e. proportional to K^3), *but a second-order effect exists, and is related to normal stresses.*† The "normal stress effect" will be found in all nonlinear theories.

Let us note from (18.24) the result $T_{xx} - T_{yy} = \hat{\mu}K^2$. The quantity $\hat{\mu}$ can be eliminated through (18.17), thus

$$T_{xx} - T_{yy} = KT_{xy}.$$

This relation holds for isotropic elastic solids only, but for such solids it is a *universal relation* because the response functions do not appear in it. Moreover, it is readily apparent that *the normal stresses cannot be equal.*

If the necessary normal stresses are not provided, a shearing stress will produce a dilatation or compression of a specimen, depending on the sign of the mean stresses. This result was conjectured by Kelvin, and is called the *Kelvin effect.* The existence of unequal pressures in simple shear is called the *Poynting effect.* The solution of the simple shear problem provides an *indirect* explanation of the Kelvin effect; that is, we assume that if certain geometric constraints are removed from the body, then the nature of the subsequent deformation can be ascertained from a knowledge of the stresses that were needed to maintain the constraints (e.g. in the absence of a required tensile force, the body would contract in the direction of this force).

It is more instructive to deal with the normal stress N and the shearing stress S acting on the inclined faces of a sheared cube rather than consider there the Cartesian components T_{xy} and T_{xx} of the stress vectors (Figure 18.1). To calculate N and S, we first note that, by (18.11), the inclined faces are described by $X = x - KY = x - Ky = \text{const.}$; therefore, the slope of these faces is given by $dy/dx = 1/K$. Denoting by $\boldsymbol{\tau}$ a unit vector along the inclined faces, we write $\boldsymbol{\tau} = \tau_x \mathbf{e}_x + \tau_y \mathbf{e}_y$, where $\tau_y/\tau_x = 1/K$. From $\boldsymbol{\tau} \cdot \boldsymbol{\tau} = 1$ we then obtain

$$\tau_x = \frac{\pm K}{\sqrt{1 + K^2}}, \qquad \tau_y = \frac{\pm 1}{\sqrt{1 + K^2}}. \tag{18.28a}$$

† A very complete analysis of the simple shear problem is given in Section 54, *NFTM.*

Moreover, if $\mathbf{n}$ is a unit vector normal to the inclined faces, then it follows from $\mathbf{n}\cdot\boldsymbol{\tau} = 0$ that

$$n_x = \frac{+1}{\sqrt{1 + K^2}}, \qquad n_y = \frac{\pm K}{\sqrt{1 + K^2}}. \tag{18.28b}$$

Substituting (18.28) into $N = T_{ij}n_in_j$, $S = T_{ij}n_i\tau_j$, we now obtain

$$(1 + K^2)N = T_{xx} + K^2T_{yy} - 2KT_{xy},$$

$$(1 + K^2)S = K(T_{xx} - T_{yy}) + (1 - K^2)T_{xy}.$$

In view of $T_{xx} - T_{yy} = KT_{xy}$, these are equivalent to

$$S = \frac{T_{xy}}{1 + K^2}, \qquad N = T_{yy} - KS. \tag{18.29}$$

Thus $N = 0$ is possible, but $N = T_{yy}$ is not. Therefore the Poynting effect still remains in evidence.

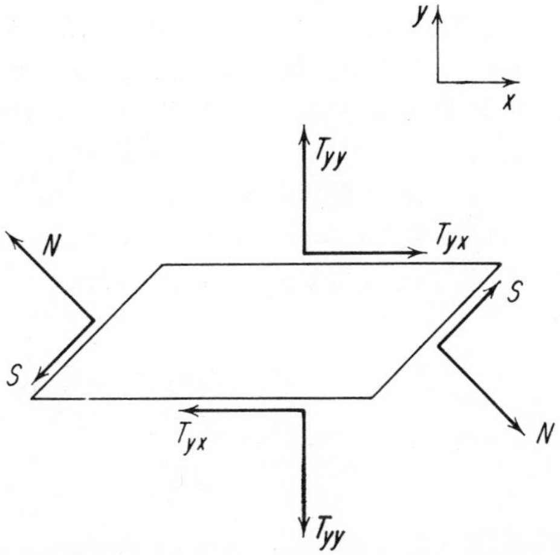

FIGURE 18.1 Stresses on the faces of a sheared cube.

For incompressible bodies the stress relation is made indeterminate by the presence there of an arbitrary pressure p. Of course, as long as stress boundary conditions are present, there is nothing arbitrary about p in a given *problem*. Thus from a mathematical point of view it is very convenient to have the arbitrary pressure p available, because now we have in effect one less boundary condition to cope with.

Returning to the problem of simple extension, we write, in accord with (17.20), $T_{xx} = T_{yy} = -p + \alpha\lambda^2V^2 + \gamma\lambda^{-2}V^2$, $T_{zz} = -p + \alpha V^2 + \gamma V^{-2}$. The condition of incompressibility, III = 1, now yields $\lambda^2 = V^{-3}$. The boundary conditions $T_{xx} = T_{yy} = 0$ are satisfied by letting $p = \alpha V^{-1} + \gamma V$, thus

$$T_{zz} = \alpha(V^2 - V^{-1}) + \gamma(V^{-2} - V). \tag{18.30}$$

If we define the principal force f_3 by

$$f_3 = \lambda^2 V^2 T_{zz} = V^{-1} T_{zz}, \tag{18.31}$$

then (18.30) takes on the form of a *force-stretch relation*

$$f_3 = (V - V^{-2})(\alpha - V^{-1}\gamma), \tag{18.30*}$$

where α and γ are functions of the invariants

$$\mathrm{I} = \frac{2 + V^3}{V}, \qquad \mathrm{II} = (2 + V^{-3})V.$$

Finally, let us investigate the *biaxial stretching* of an incompressible sheet of initial thickness $2h_0$. We assume a homogeneous deformation of the form $x = V_1 X$, $y = V_2 Y$, $z = V_3 Z$, so that the condition of incompressibility is given by $V_1 V_2 V_3 = 1$. Because $\mathbf{B} = \mathrm{diag}(V_1^2, V_2^2, V_3^2)$, the stresses given by (17.20) are as follows: $T_{xx} = -p + \alpha V_1^2 + \gamma V_1^{-2}$, $T_{yy} = -p + \alpha V_2^2 + \gamma V_2^{-2}$, $T_{zz} = -p + \alpha V_3^2 + \gamma V_3^{-2}$. In order that the lateral faces $Z = \pm h_0$ be free of tractions, p must be such that $T_{zz} = 0$; then

$$\begin{aligned} T_{xx} &= \left(V_1^2 - \frac{1}{V_1^2 V_2^2}\right)(\alpha - V_2^2\gamma), \\ T_{yy} &= \left(V_2^2 - \frac{1}{V_2^2 V_1^2}\right)(\alpha - V_1^2\gamma), \end{aligned} \tag{18.32}$$

where α, γ are functions of the invariants

$$\mathrm{I} = V_1^2 + V_2^2 + V_1^{-2}V_2^{-2}, \quad \mathrm{II} = V_1^{-2} + V_2^{-2} + V_1^2 V_2^2. \tag{18.33}$$

The principal forces f_1 and f_2, measured per unit length of the edge in the undeformed configuration, are defined by (cf. (17.26))

$$f_1 = 2h_0 V_2 V_3 T_{xx} = \frac{2h_0 T_{xx}}{V_1}, \qquad f_2 = 2h_0 V_3 V_1 T_{yy} = \frac{2h_0 T_{yy}}{V_2}.$$

The results (18.15) for simple shear apply also to incompressible materials, except that the response function δ should be replaced by the arbitrary pressure p. In particular, choosing p so as to satisfy $T_{zz} = 0$, we find that

$$T_{xx} = \alpha K^2, \qquad T_{yy} = \gamma K^2,$$

whereas the relation $T_{xy} = (\alpha - \gamma)K$ remains unchanged.

Although the Kelvin effect is absent in incompressible bodies, the Poynting effect may exhibit a great variety.

In connection with the problem of simple shear, Truesdell has recently investigated the possibility of what may be called a "material instability".† Assuming incompressibility, we introduce a strain-energy function $\overline{W}(K^2) = W(3+K^2, 3+K^2)$, and note that the secant modulus $\hat{\mu}$ can be written as

$$\hat{\mu} = \frac{T_{xy}}{K} = 2\left(\frac{\partial W}{\partial \mathrm{I}} + \frac{\partial W}{\partial \mathrm{II}}\right) = 2\frac{\partial \overline{W}}{\partial K^2}.$$

If $\overline{W}$ has a maximum at some K, then the material will lose its ability to resist shear in a state of equilibrium, i.e. a *flow in shear* will occur.

Following Truesdell, let us consider the following generalization of the Mooney-Rivlin equation.

$$\mathbf{T} = -p\mathbf{1}+\mu\left[\frac{1}{2} + \beta - \frac{1}{\gamma}(\mathrm{I} - 3)\right]\mathbf{B}-\mu\left(\frac{1}{2} - \beta\right)\mathbf{B}^{-1}, \qquad (18.34)$$

thus $$W = \frac{1}{2}\mu\left[\left(\frac{1}{2} + \beta\right)(\mathrm{I} - 3) - \frac{1}{2\gamma}(\mathrm{I} - 3)^2\right] + \frac{1}{2}\mu\left(\frac{1}{2} - \beta\right)(\mathrm{II} - 3).$$

If $\gamma > 0$, then it follows from

$$\hat{\mu} = \mu\left(1 - \frac{K^2}{\gamma}\right), \qquad W = \frac{1}{2}\mu\left(K^2 - \frac{K^4}{2\gamma}\right)$$

that a *collapse in shear*, $dT_{xy}/dK = 0$, will occur at $K^2 = \gamma/3$, and before the condition $K^2 = \gamma$ for flow in shear is reached.

Remarks on experimental determination of response functions‡

Each solution can serve, in principle, as the basis for experimental determination of the response functions. Some of the conditions (e.g. simple shear)

† This investigation is to appear in the Proceedings of the Eleventh International Congress on Applied Mechanics (Munich 1964).

‡ A survey of experimental data is given in [208].

are difficult to reproduce experimentally, whereas others, notably the simple extension test, are easy to perform but yield insufficient evidence. For incompressible materials, our task is to determine the functions $\alpha(\mathrm{I}, \mathrm{II})$ and $\gamma(\mathrm{I}, \mathrm{II})$; thus there are essentially four unknown functions to be found. In the extension test there is only one deformation variable, which means that I and II cannot be varied separately. Moreover, the functions α and γ are not separable (cf. (18.30)*). It is altogether instructive to note that the response functions occur in each solution in different combinations; clearly, then, experiments involving deformations for which exact solutions are not known are unlikely to give basic information: one simply does not know what is being measured in such experiments.

A series of biaxial tests alone would suffice to determine the functions α and γ. The classical experiments by Rivlin and Saunders [134] on rubber were in fact of this type. Assuming that $V_1 \neq V_2$, we can invert (18.32) to read

$$\begin{aligned} \alpha &= A\left(\frac{V_1^2 T_{xx}}{B} - \frac{V_2^2 T_{yy}}{C}\right), \\ \gamma &= A\left(\frac{T_{xx}}{B} - \frac{T_{yy}}{C}\right), \end{aligned} \tag{18.35}$$

where $$A = \frac{V_1^2 V_2^2}{V_1^2 - V_2^2}, \qquad B = V_1^4 V_2^2 - 1, \qquad C = V_2^4 V_1^2 - 1.$$

The right-hand sides in (18.35) are measurable quantities; therefore, the problem reduces to the determination of values of V_1 and V_2 such that either I or II remains constant. Such values are found by setting I or II equal to constants in (18.33), and then expressing V_1 in terms of V_2, for instance. The results obtained by this method can be extended, or checked, through experiments based on other known solutions. Thus it appears that the determination of response functions of incompressible materials would require only time and effort, but that there would be no basic difficulties encountered. For compressible materials we require α, γ, δ as functions of I, II, III; thus the increase in complexity is great. The available exact solutions should certainly suffice for the design of a satisfactory testing program. However, the "curve-fitting" of the experimental data is very difficult; in fact, it is probably necessary to make some assumptions about the form of the response functions outright.

As in the case of other idealizations, the drawbacks attendant to the assumption of incompressibility must be weighed against the analytical results made possible by this assumption. It is indeed a happy circumstance that many vulcanized rubbers are very nearly incompressible!

Solutions in curvilinear coordinates

Let us now investigate typical cases of non-homogeneous deformations, described in orthogonal curvilinear coordinate systems. If the response functions are general, then it is not possible, as a rule, to verify that the conditions of equilibrium are satisfied. For this reason we shall limit the problems to incompressible materials.

We refer the natural state to the curvilinear coordinates Θ_A, the final state to the curvilinear coordinates θ_a. The curvilinear components of the infinitesimal vectors dx_i and dX_i are given by $\sigma_a = Q_{ai}\, dx_i = h_{\underline{a}}^{-1}\, d\theta_a$ and $\Sigma_A = Q_{Ai}\, dX_i = H_{\underline{A}}^{-1}\, d\Theta_A$, respectively. Then

$$\sigma_a = F_{aA}\Sigma_A, \tag{18.36}$$

where
$$F_{aA} = Q_{ai}F_{im}Q_{Am} = \left(\frac{H_{\underline{A}}}{h_{\underline{a}}}\right)\frac{\partial \theta_a}{\partial \Theta_A} \tag{18.37}$$

are the curvilinear components of the deformation gradients. To verify (18.37), let $Q_{ai} = h_{\underline{a}}^{-1}\theta_{a,i}$, $F_{im} = x_{i,m}$, $Q_{Am} = H_{\underline{A}}X_{m,A}$ (cf. (6.14)). The definitions of deformation tensors remain the same, e.g. $\mathbf{B} = \mathbf{F}\mathbf{F}^T$.

One of the classical problems of nonlinear elasticity theory is the *combined extension and torsion* of a solid cylinder. Let ρ, ϕ, z be the cylindrical coordinates in the deformed configuration of a particle that is located in the natural state by the cylindrical coordinates P, Φ, Z. We shall explore the simple deformations described by

$$\rho = AP, \qquad \phi = \Phi + DZ, \qquad z = FZ, \tag{18.38}$$

where A, D, F are constants. As a result of incompressibility, $v = \pi\rho^2 z = \pi A^2 P^2 FZ = \pi P^2 Z = V$, so that $A^2 = 1/F$. Noting that $h_1 = h_3 = H_1 = H_3 = 1$, $H_2 = 1/P$, $h_2 = 1/P$, we find that

$$\|\mathbf{F}\| = \begin{Vmatrix} A & 0 & 0 \\ 0 & A & D\rho \\ 0 & 0 & F \end{Vmatrix}, \qquad \|\mathbf{B}\| = \begin{Vmatrix} A^2 & 0 & 0 \\ 0 & A^2 + D^2\rho^2 & FD\rho \\ 0 & FD\rho & F^2 \end{Vmatrix}, \tag{18.39}$$

and

$$\mathrm{I} = F^2 + 2F^{-1} + D^2\rho^2, \quad \mathrm{II} = 2F + F^{-2} + D^2\rho^2F^{-1}, \quad \mathrm{III} = 1. \tag{18.40}$$

Further, by (3.40),

$$\|\mathbf{B}^{-1}\| = \begin{Vmatrix} F & 0 & 0 \\ 0 & F & -D\rho \\ 0 & -D\rho & F^{-2} + D^2\rho^2F^{-1} \end{Vmatrix}.$$

The stresses associated with the deformation (18.38) are now calculated from (17.20); we obtain

$$\begin{aligned} T_{\rho\rho} &= -p + \alpha F^{-1} + \gamma F, \qquad T_{\rho\phi} = T_{\rho z} = 0, \\ T_{\phi\phi} &= -p + \alpha(F^{-1} + D^2\rho^2) + \gamma F, \\ T_{zz} &= -p + \alpha F^2 + \gamma(F^{-2} + D^2\rho^2F^{-1}), \\ T_{\phi z} &= FD\rho\,\mu(F), \qquad \mu(F) = \alpha - F^{-1}\gamma. \end{aligned} \tag{18.41}$$

Because the deformation is not homogeneous, the equations of equilibrium are not satisfied automatically. As is evident from (18.40), (18.41), the stresses are functions of ρ only. Then it is easy to see that the last two equations of (6.68) reduce to $\partial p/\partial z = 0$, $\partial p/\partial \phi = 0$, i.e. $p = p(\rho)$. There remains the condition of equilibrium in the radial direction,

$$\frac{d}{d\rho} T_{\rho\rho} + \frac{1}{\rho}(T_{\rho\rho} - T_{\phi\phi}) = 0. \tag{18.42}$$

Substituting from the stress relations for $T_{\rho\rho}$, $T_{\phi\phi}$, we arrive at a differential equation governing p:

$$-\frac{dp}{d\rho} + \frac{1}{F}\frac{d\alpha}{d\rho} + F\frac{d\gamma}{d\rho} - D^2\rho\alpha = 0.$$

Therefore, the condition (18.42) is satisfied by letting

$$p = \frac{\alpha}{F} + F\gamma - D^2 \int^{\rho} u\alpha(u)\,du + \text{const.}$$

The lower limit of integration is chosen so as to make the lateral boundary free of surface tractions (note that $T_{\rho\phi}$ and $T_{\rho z}$ vanish identically):

$$T_{\rho\rho} = 0, \qquad \rho = \rho_0 \tag{18.43}$$

(the radius ρ_0 of the deformed cylinder is related to the radius P_0 of the undeformed cylinder by $\rho_0 = P_0/\sqrt{F}$). The boundary condition (18.43) is evidently satisfied by letting

$$T_{\rho\rho} = -D^2 \int_{\rho}^{\rho_0} u\alpha(u)\, du; \tag{18.44}$$

the remaining stresses are then given by

$$\begin{aligned} T_{\phi\phi} &= T_{\rho\rho} + D^2\rho^2\alpha, \qquad T_{\phi z} = FD\rho\, \mu(F), \\ T_{zz} &= T_{\rho\rho} + \left(F^2 - \frac{1}{F}\right)\mu(F) + D^2 \frac{\rho^2}{F}\gamma. \end{aligned} \tag{18.45}$$

To calculate the resultant torque M and the resultant normal force N transmitted by a cross section, we consider the identity

$$\pi \int_0^{\rho_0} T_{\rho\rho}\, d(\rho^2) = \pi\rho^2 T_{\rho\rho}\Big|_0^{\rho_0} - \pi D^2 \int_0^{\rho_0} \rho^3\alpha\, d\rho = -\pi D^2 \int_0^{\rho_0} \rho^3\alpha\, d\rho,$$

where we have taken into account (18.44) and the boundary condition (18.43). Then

$$N = 2\pi \int_0^{\rho_0} \rho T_{zz}\, d\rho = 2\pi\left(F^2 - \frac{1}{F}\right) \int_0^{\rho_0} \mu(F)\rho\, d\rho - \pi D^2 \int_0^{\rho_0} \left(\alpha - \frac{2}{F}\gamma\right)\rho^3\, d\rho, \tag{18.46}$$

whereas $$M = 2\pi \int_0^{\rho_0} \rho^2 T_{z\phi}\, d\rho = 2\pi DF \int_0^{\rho_0} \mu(F)\rho^3\, d\rho. \tag{18.47}$$

The resultants M and N must be applied at the end sections to maintain the assumed deformation.

If we set $D = 0$, then T_{zz} reduces to the solution (18.30) for simple extension. To obtain *pure torsion*, we let $F = 1$; then

$$T_{\phi\phi} = T_{\rho\rho} + D^2\rho^2\alpha, \quad T_{zz} = T_{\rho\rho} + D^2\rho^2\gamma, \quad T_{\phi z} = D\rho\, \hat{\mu}(D^2\rho^2), \tag{18.48}$$

where $\mu(1) = \hat{\mu}(D^2\rho^2)$ is now the secant modulus defined by (18.16), and $T_{\rho\rho}$ is still given by (18.44). Moreover,

$$N = -\pi D^2 \int_0^{\rho_0} (\alpha - 2\gamma)\rho^3\, d\rho, \quad M = 2\pi D \int_0^{\rho_0} \hat{\mu}(D^2\rho^2)\rho^3\, d\rho. \tag{18.49}$$

Comparing (18.48) with (18.15), (18.17), we find that the shear response in pure torsion and in simple shear is identical. Moreover, because $N \sim D^2$, we can conclude that, in the absence of the axial force N, the elongation of a twisted cylinder will be proportional to the square of the twist D; this is the classical statement of Poynting's effect. The fact that torsion has been found to produce only elongation suggests the introduction of an *empirical inequality*

$$\alpha - 2\gamma > 0. \tag{18.50}$$

Then (18.50) and (18.49) imply $N < 0$.

As is clear from (18.47), the shear resistance to combined extension and torsion is affected by the stretch F. This dependence can be made more explicit in the limiting case $D \to 0$. We set

$$\mathrm{I} \doteq F^2 + 2F^{-1} = \text{const.}, \quad \mathrm{II} \doteq 2F + F^{-2} = \text{const.},$$

and obtain the limiting results

$$\lim_{D\to 0} \frac{M}{D/F} = \frac{1}{2}\pi P_0^4 \mu(F) \equiv \tau(F), \tag{18.51}$$

$$\lim_{D\to 0} N = N_0 = \pi P_0^2\left(F - \frac{1}{F^2}\right)\mu(F). \tag{18.52}$$

The modulus of the linearized theory is then given by

$$\tau(1) = \frac{1}{2}\pi P_0^4 \hat{\mu}(0) = \frac{1}{2}\pi P_0^4[\alpha(3, 3) - \gamma(3, 3)]. \tag{18.53}$$

In the absence of definite knowledge of the response functions α and γ it cannot be determined whether extension will soften an incompressible material or not. Taking the ratio of (18.51) and (18.52), however, we obtain the interesting formula of Rivlin:†

$$\frac{N_0 P_0^2}{\tau(F)} = 2\left(F - \frac{1}{F^2}\right). \tag{18.54}$$

This shows that the ratio of N_0 to $\tau(F)$ increases with F.‡

† Because the response function does not occur in (18.54), this limiting formula is another universal relation for isotropic elastic solids.

‡ A fuller exploration of the problem of combined torsion and extension is given in Section 57 of *NFTM*.

For a Mooney-Rivlin material we have that $\mu(F) = \mu[(\beta + \frac{1}{2}) + (F^{-1})(\beta - \frac{1}{2})]$, so that extension decreases the torsional resistance, whereas shortening increases it.

As the next example we take up the bending of a block into an annular wedge. Here it is convenient to describe the initial configuration in the Cartesian coordinates X, Y, Z, and the final configuration in the cylindrical coordinates ρ, ϕ, z. The appropriate plane deformation is then described by

$$\rho = \sqrt{2AX}, \qquad \phi = BY, \qquad z = \frac{Z}{AB}, \tag{18.55}$$

where the constants A and B have been introduced in such a way that the incompressibility condition $dX\,dY\,dZ = \pi\rho\,d\phi\,d\rho\,dz$ is automatically fulfilled. Making use of (18.37), we obtain

$$\begin{aligned} \|\mathbf{F}\| &= \operatorname{diag}\left(\frac{A}{\rho}, B\rho, \frac{1}{AB}\right), \\ \|\mathbf{B}\| &= \operatorname{diag}\left(\frac{A^2}{\rho^2}, B^2\rho^2, \frac{1}{A^2B^2}\right), \\ \|\mathbf{B}^{-1}\| &= \operatorname{diag}\left(\frac{\rho^2}{A^2}, \frac{1}{B^2\rho^2}, A^2B^2\right), \end{aligned} \tag{18.56}$$

and

$$\mathrm{I} = A^2\rho^{-2} + B^2\rho^2 + \frac{1}{A^2B^2}, \quad \mathrm{II} = A^2B^2 + \rho^2A^{-2} + \frac{1}{B^2\rho^2}. \tag{18.57}$$

Then, by (17.20), $T_{\rho\rho} = -p + \alpha A^2\rho^{-2} + \gamma\rho^2A^{-2}$, $T_{\phi\phi} = -p + \alpha B^2\rho^2 + \gamma B^{-2}\rho^{-2}$, $T_{zz} = -p + \alpha A^{-2}B^{-2} + \gamma A^2B^2$,

or,

$$\begin{aligned} T_{\phi\phi} - T_{\rho\rho} &= \alpha\left(B^2\rho^2 - \frac{A^2}{\rho^2}\right) + \gamma\left(\frac{1}{B^2\rho^2} - \frac{\rho^2}{A^2}\right), \\ T_{zz} - T_{\rho\rho} &= \alpha\left(\frac{1}{A^2B^2} - \frac{A^2}{\rho^2}\right) + \gamma\left(A^2B^2 - \frac{\rho^2}{A^2}\right). \end{aligned} \tag{18.58}$$

From the condition of equilibrium, (18.42), now follows that

$$T_{\rho\rho} = \int_{\rho_1}^{\rho} \left[\left(B^2u - \frac{A^2}{u^3}\right)\alpha + \left(\frac{1}{B^2u^3} - \frac{u}{A^2}\right)\gamma\right] du. \tag{18.59}$$

The choice of the lower limit of integration enables us to satisfy the boundary condition $T_{\rho\rho} = 0$, $\rho = \rho_1$. The analogous boundary condition for the surface $\rho = \rho_2$ cannot be satisfied in a general manner unless some simplifying assumptions are made about the response function (e.g. assuming a Mooney-Rivlin material†). This kind of difficulty is typical in the nonlinear theories; we have little control over the stress boundary conditions because they are largely determined by the assumed deformation field. As the result (18.59) seems to indicate, the bending of a block into a circular wedge cannot be accomplished by end loads and couples alone. Conversely, a beam subjected to end loads and couples only will not be bent into a circular shape.

Let us take up two more classes of problems in which considerable progress has been made. These are the problems in cylindrical and spherical coordinates such that the stresses depend on the radial coordinates only. In cylindrical coordinates we let‡

$$\rho = \rho(P), \qquad \phi = \Phi, \qquad z = Z. \tag{18.60}$$

The isochoric expansion of a tube bounded by the cylinders $P = A$ and $P = B$ in the natural state is then given by

$$\rho^2(P) - \rho^2(A) = P^2 - A^2 \tag{18.61}$$

so that

$$\rho' = \frac{d\rho}{dP} = \frac{P}{\rho}. \tag{18.62}$$

Then

$$\mathbf{F} = \operatorname{diag}\left(\frac{P}{\rho}, \frac{\rho}{P}, 1\right), \text{ etc.,}$$

$$\mathrm{I} = \mathrm{II} = 1 + \frac{P^2}{\rho^2} + \frac{\rho^2}{P^2}, \qquad \mathrm{III} = 1, \tag{18.63}$$

and, by (17.20)

$$T_{\rho\rho} = -p + \frac{P^2}{\rho^2}\alpha + \frac{\rho^2}{P^2}\gamma, \tag{18.64}$$

$$T_{\phi\phi} = -p + \frac{\rho^2}{P^2}\alpha + \frac{P^2}{\rho^2}\gamma, \qquad T_{zz} = -p + \alpha + \gamma.$$

Because

$$T_{\rho\rho} - T_{\phi\phi} = \left(\frac{P^2}{\rho^2} - \frac{\rho^2}{P^2}\right)\mu(\rho)$$

† Cf. Problem 3.
‡ More general cases are given in Section 57 of *NFTM*.

where $\mu(\rho) = \alpha\,(\mathrm{I}, \mathrm{II}) - \gamma\,(\mathrm{I}, \mathrm{II})$, the equilibrium condition (18.42) as well as the boundary condition $T_{\rho\rho} = 0$, $\rho = \rho(B)$, can be satisfied by letting

$$T_{\rho\rho} = \int \left[\frac{P^2(u)}{u^3} - \frac{u}{P^2(u)}\right] \mu(u)\, du. \tag{18.65}$$

From this formula we can calculate the pressure $\bar{p} = -T_{\rho\rho}|_{\rho=\rho(A)}$ necessary to increase the inner radius from A to $\rho(A)$. Conversely, if $\bar{p}$ is given, then (18.65) serves to determine $p(A)$. To obtain explicit formulas, however, special assumptions about the response coefficients must be made.

A cylindrical tube can be turned inside out (*eversion*). A general solution of the eversion problem is not available, but let us see how much can be done. First, we must replace (18.61) by

$$\rho^2(A) - \rho^2(P) = P^2 - A^2. \tag{18.66}$$

Second, if the boundary $\rho = \rho(A)$ is also free of tractions, then

$$T_{\rho\rho}|_{\rho=\rho(A)} = 0, \tag{18.67}$$

where $T_{\rho\rho}$ is given by (18.65). Finally, we may require the vanishing of the resultant force acting on the end,

$$2\pi \int_{\rho(A)}^{\rho(B)} \rho T_{zz}\, d\rho = 0,$$

where

$$T_{zz} = T_{\rho\rho} + \left(1 - \frac{P^2}{\rho^2}\right)\alpha + \left(1 - \frac{\rho^2}{P^2}\right)\gamma. \tag{18.68}$$

It may not be possible in general to find a value $\rho(A)$ such that (18.67) and (18.68) are satisfied.

We can also consider portions of the tubes, bounded by the planes ϕ = const. Then it is a matter of straight calculation to obtain the forces on the edges.

Let us outline briefly the corresponding problem in spherical coordinates. We write $r = r(R)$, $\theta = \Theta$, $\phi = \Phi$, where $r^3(R) - r^3(A) = R^3 - A^3$ holds for the expansion of spherical shells, whereas $r^3(A) - r^3(R) = R^3 - A^3$ holds in the case of eversion.† Then

$$\mathbf{B} = \operatorname{diag}\left(\frac{R^4}{r^4}, \frac{r^2}{R^2}, \frac{r^2}{R^2}\right),$$

$$\mathrm{I} = 2\frac{r^2}{R^2} + \frac{R^2}{r^4}, \qquad \mathrm{II} = 2\frac{R^2}{r^2} + \frac{r^4}{R^4}, \qquad \mathrm{III} = 1,$$

† The eversion of a spherical shell requires that a plug be cut out, and reinserted after the eversion.

and
$$T_{rr} = -p + \frac{R^2}{r^4}\alpha + \frac{r^4}{R^4}\gamma,$$

$$T_{\theta\theta} = T_{\phi\phi} = -p + \frac{r^2}{R^2}\alpha + \frac{R^2}{r^2}\gamma.$$

The equation of equilibrium in the radial direction now reads

$$\frac{d}{dr}T_{rr} + \frac{1}{r}(2T_{rr} - T_{\theta\theta} - T_{\phi\phi}) = 0;$$

it is satisfied whenever

$$T_{rr} = -\int^r (2T_{rr} - T_{\theta\theta} - T_{\phi\phi})\frac{du}{u}.$$

The lower limit can again be chosen so as to make one of the boundaries $r =$ const. free of stress.

To obtain a better idea of the potential difficulty of the nonlinear theory, a look at the problem of a torus might suffice. Let the initial radius of the center line of a torus be C. We assume that this center line lies in the xy plane; then the plane polar coordinates Φ mark the meridional cross sections. As the remaining two coordinates we take, in each meridional cross section, the radial distance R measured from C, and the angle Ψ measured from the xy plane up. Thus $X = (C + R\cos\Psi)\cos\Phi$, $Y = (C + R\cos\Psi)\sin\Phi$, $Z = R\sin\Psi$. A routine calculation now yields $H_R = 1$, $H_\Psi = 1/R$, $H_\Phi = 1/P$, where $P = C + R\cos\Psi$, and that the nonvanishing wryness coefficients are

$$W_{R\Psi\Psi} = \frac{1}{R}, \qquad W_{\Phi R\Phi} = \frac{\cos\Psi}{P}, \qquad W_{\Phi\Psi\Phi} = \frac{\sin\Psi}{P}. \tag{18.69}$$

If we consider axisymmetric deformations only, then $r = r(R, \Psi)$, $\phi = \Phi$, $\psi = \psi(R, \Psi)$, and

$$\|\mathbf{F}\| = \left\| \begin{matrix} \dfrac{\partial r}{\partial R} & 0 & \dfrac{1}{R}\dfrac{\partial r}{\partial \Psi} \\ 0 & \dfrac{\rho}{P} & 0 \\ r\dfrac{\partial \psi}{\partial R} & 0 & \dfrac{r}{R}\dfrac{\partial \psi}{\partial \Psi} \end{matrix} \right\|, \tag{18.70}$$

where $\rho = c + r\cos\psi$. If we now calculate stresses, and then look at the equations of equilibrium, then it becomes clear that no progress can be made without further simplifying assumptions, e.g. $R/C << 1$.† If the thickness of the cylinder is small compared to C, then of course the cylinder may be considered as a torroidal shell, or membrane (cf. Section 16).

Reinforcement by networks of inextensible cords

The study of forces and deformations in idealized textiles made up of inextensible filaments uses much the same ideas, and the same language, as finite deformation theory of elasticity. For this reason, and because in many applications the networks of inextensible cords are imbedded in elastic materials, we shall briefly review this subject.‡

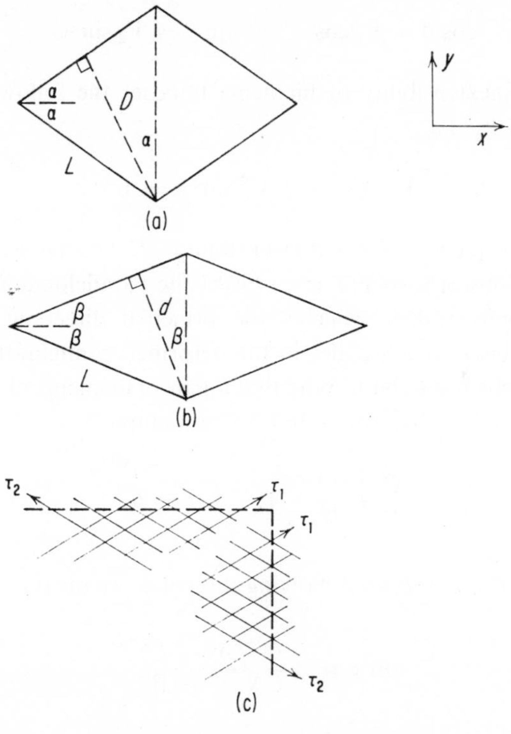

FIGURE 18.2 Deformations and forces in a plane network of inextensible cords: (a) undeformed parallelogram of cords, (b) deformed parallelogram of cords, (c) cord tensions τ_1, τ_2 intersecting coordinate planes.

We begin by considering a plane network formed by two families of straight, inextensible, perfectly flexible filaments. The filaments are assumed to form

† Cf. Kydoniefs and Spencer [232].

‡ We shall follow, in the main, a survey article by Rivlin [133]. A rather complete coverage of the subject, as well as the relevant references, can be found in [48].

a regular pattern of parallelograms, the side lengths of the parallelograms, L, being constant, i.e. it is assumed that the points at which the filaments cross permit no relative motion of the filaments. We denote by α and β the magnitudes of the angles measured from the x axis to the filaments in the undeformed and deformed configurations of the network, respectively. If D and d are the initial and final spacings of the filaments, respectively, then $D = L \sin 2\alpha$, $d = L \sin 2\beta$ (cf. Figure 18.2a, b). Even though the filaments are assumed to be inextensible, the *network* can be easily deformed; in fact, it can be deformed without applying any forces. If V_1 and V_2 are the stretches of the network in the x and y directions, then, as may be seen from Figure 18.2a, b,

$$\cos \beta = V_1 \cos \alpha, \qquad \sin \beta = V_2 \sin \alpha. \tag{18.71}$$

Therefore, the inextensibility of filaments imposes the following condition on the stretches V_1, V_2,

$$V_1^2 \cos^2 \alpha + V_2^2 \sin^2 \alpha = 1. \tag{18.72}$$

Another consequence of the inextensibility of the filaments is that the principal directions of $\mathbf{C} = \mathbf{F}^T\mathbf{F}$ must bisect the parallelogram angles in the undeformed configuration, whereas the principal directions of $\mathbf{B} = \mathbf{F}\mathbf{F}^T = \mathbf{R}\mathbf{C}\mathbf{R}^T$ must bisect these angles in the deformed configuration. To prove this rather obvious result, let us note that a pair of filaments of length L must lie in the deformed configuration on a "strain ellipse"

$$\frac{\bar{x}^2}{A^2} + \frac{\bar{y}^2}{B^2} = 1, \qquad A \neq B,$$

where $\bar{x} = L \cos \phi$, $\bar{y} = L \sin \phi$. Solving this for ϕ, we obtain

$$\sin \phi = \pm \frac{B}{L} \sqrt{\frac{A^2 - L^2}{A^2 - B^2}},$$

i.e. the filaments must be located symmetrically with respect to the diameters of the ellipse. Thus in any plane deformation, homogeneous or nonhomogeneous, we can imagine that, locally, the bisectors of the parallelogram angles are rotated by the rotation tensor $\mathbf{R}$, after which the filaments are sheared, by the stretch tensor $\mathbf{V}$, symmetrically with respect to the bisectors.

If a sheet of incompressible, isotropic material is subjected to uniaxial extension, then the axial and lateral deformations must be as follows,

$$x = VX, \qquad y = Y/\sqrt{V}, \qquad z = Z/\sqrt{V}. \tag{18.73}$$

The stretches $V_1 = V$, $V_2 = 1/\sqrt{V}$ will not satisfy in general the equation of constraint, (18.72), which governs the deformations of the network of inextensible filaments. Therefore, a uniaxial extension of a sheet that is reinforced by a network of inextensible filaments will give rise to stresses between the material matrix and the network.

To be able to treat a reinforced sheet as a "continuum," we assume that the filaments are spaced closely enough to justify the replacement of the individual tensions τ_1, τ_2 that reside in the two families of filaments by average tensions n_{ij} having the dimension of force per length. Let us recall (18.71), and note from Figure 18.2a, b that $d/\cos\beta = V_2 D/\cos\alpha$, $2L\sin\beta = 2LV\sin\alpha = V_2 D/\cos\alpha$. Then, with the aid of Figure 18.2c, we obtain $n_{xx} = (\tau_1 + \tau_2)(\cos\beta)/(d/\cos\beta)$, $n_{xy} = (\tau_1 - \tau_2)(\sin\beta)/(d/\cos\beta)$, $n_{yy} = (\tau_1 + \tau_2)(\sin\beta/2L)\cos\beta$, or

$$n_{xx} = (\tau_1 + \tau_2)\frac{V_1\cos^2\alpha}{V_2 D}, \qquad n_{yy} = (\tau_1 + \tau_2)\frac{V_2\sin^2\alpha}{V_1 D},$$

$$n_{xy} = n_{yx} = (\tau_1 - \tau_2)\frac{\sin\alpha\cos\alpha}{D}.$$

Let T_{ij} be the stresses produced in the elastic material of imbedding by the deformation $B_{ij} = V_i^2\delta_{ij}$. Then, evaluating p from $T_{33} = 0$, and making use of the condition of incompressibility, $V_1V_2V_3 = 1$, we find that the nonvanishing (elastic) stresses are $T_{11} = (V_1^2 - V_3^2)(\alpha - V_2^2\gamma)$, $T_{22} = (V_2^2 - V_3^2) \times (\gamma - V_1^2\gamma)$. Next, we replace T_{11}, T_{22} by the average tensions

$$\begin{aligned} t_{11} &= 2h_0V_3T_{11} = 2h_0V_3(V_1^2 - V_3^2)(\alpha - V_2^2\gamma), \\ t_{22} &= 2h_0V_3T_{22} = 2h_0V_3(V_2^2 - V_3^2)(\alpha - V_1^2\gamma), \end{aligned} \tag{18.74}$$

where $2h_0$ is the thickness of the undeformed sheet.† The total average tension, **s**, is then given by

$$\begin{aligned} s_{xx} &= n_{xx} + t_{xx} = (\tau_1 + \tau_2)\frac{V_1\cos^2\alpha}{V_2 D} + 2h_0V_3T_{xx}, \\ s_{yy} &= n_{yy} + t_{yy} = (\tau_1 + \tau_2)\frac{V_2\sin^2\alpha}{V_1 D} + 2h_0V_3T_{yy}, \\ s_{xy} &= n_{xy} = (\tau_1 - \tau_2)\frac{\sin\alpha\cos\alpha}{D}. \end{aligned} \tag{18.75}$$

† The dimension h_0 must be small, or else the deformations of the network and the elastic sheets bonded to it would not be the same.

For uniaxial extension we have that $s_{xy} = s_{yy} = 0$, so that $\tau_1 = \tau_2 = \tau$, and, by $(18.75)_2$,

$$\tau = \frac{Dh_0}{V_2^2}\frac{(V_2^2 - V_3^2)(\alpha - V_1^2\gamma)}{\sin^2\alpha}. \tag{18.76}$$

The filaments can support only a tension $\tau > 0$. Assuming that the empirical inequalities (17.25) are satisfied, i.e. $\alpha > 0, \gamma \leq 0$, it follows that $V_2^2 - V_3^2 < 0$ must hold, or else the network will be unable to carry any loads. Using (18.72) and $V_3 = 1/V_1V_2$, we can readily verify that

$$\begin{aligned} &V_1^2 \sin^2\alpha\,(1 - V_1^2\cos^2\alpha)(V_2^2 - V_3^2) \\ &= (V_1^6 - 1)\left(\cos^2\alpha - \frac{1}{V_1^2 - V_1 + 1}\right)\left(\cos^2\alpha - \frac{1}{V_1^2 + V_1 + 1}\right). \end{aligned} \tag{18.77}$$

Now, because $1 - V_1^2\cos^2\alpha = 1 - \cos^2\beta = \sin^2\beta > 0$, or,

$$\frac{1}{V_1^2} > \cos^2\alpha, \tag{18.78}$$

we have that

$$\frac{1}{V_1^2 - V_1 + 1} > \cos^2\alpha$$

whenever $V_1 > 1$. Consequently, to make $V_2^2 - V_3^2$ negative, it is necessary that

$$\cos^2\alpha > \frac{1}{V_1^2 + V_1 + 1}. \tag{18.79}$$

If $V_1 > 1$, then the right-hand side is always less than $\frac{1}{3}$; this means that in the range $\frac{1}{3} \leq \cos^2\alpha \leq 1$ any stretch V_1 (which does not violate the inextensibility condition (18.78)!) will induce tensions in the filaments. In the range $0 < \cos^2\alpha < \frac{1}{3}$ tensions will occur only when the stretch is large enough to satisfy (18.79).

The tension

$$\begin{aligned} n_{xx} = \frac{2h_0V_1}{V_2}\,[(1 - c^2 + V_3^4(c^2V_1^2 - V_2^2))\alpha \\ - (V_2^2 - V_1^2c^2 + V_3^4(c^2V_1^4 - V_2^4))\gamma], \end{aligned} \tag{18.80}$$

where $c = \cot\alpha$, is a measure of the stiffening produced by the imbedded network.

Special motions†

Problems involving motion are of course far more difficult than problems of statics. However, if the material is assumed to be isotropic and incompressible, then certain explicit results can be easily obtained for motions that are highly symmetrical.

As the first example let us take the radial oscillations of a cylindrical tube which in its undeformed configuration occupies the region $0 \le Z \le L$, $A \le P \le B$. Purely radial motions are described by $\rho = \rho(P, t)$, $\phi = \Phi$, $z = Z$, from which it follows that $\mathbf{F} = \text{diag}(\rho', \rho/P, 1)$, where $\rho' = \partial\rho/\partial P$. Because the mass density m is assumed to be constant, the condition of incompressibility, $\det\mathbf{F} = 1$, can be integrated right away to yield

$$\rho^2 - a^2 = P^2 - A^2, \tag{18.81}$$

or, $\rho^2 - b^2 = P^2 - B^2$, where $a = a(t) = \rho(A, t)$, $b = b(t) = \rho(B, t)$ are the positions at time t of the inner and outer boundaries, respectively. Evidently $\rho' = P/\rho$, so that $\mathbf{F}$ can be represented by

$$\|\mathbf{F}\| = \text{diag}\left(\frac{P}{\rho}, \frac{\rho}{P}, 1\right). \tag{18.82}$$

From (18.81) we also find that the radial velocity $v = \dot{\rho}$ and acceleration $\dot{v} = \ddot{\rho}$ are given by

$$v = \frac{a\dot{a}}{\rho}, \qquad \dot{v} = \frac{\dot{a}^2 + a\ddot{a}}{\rho} - \frac{(a\dot{a})^2}{\rho^2}, \qquad \dot{a} = \frac{da(t)}{dt}. \tag{18.83}$$

The isotropic stress relations corresponding to (18.82) are

$$T_{\rho\phi} = T_{\phi z} = T_{z\rho} = 0, \qquad T_{\rho\rho} = -p + \alpha\frac{P^2}{\rho^2} + \gamma\frac{\rho^2}{P^2},$$

$$T_{\phi\phi} = -p + \alpha\frac{\rho^2}{P} + \gamma\frac{P^2}{\rho^2}, \qquad T_{zz} = -p + \alpha + \gamma.$$

Noting that the extra stresses $\mathbf{S} = \mathbf{T} + p\mathbf{1}$ are functions of P and t only, we can conclude from the equations of motion in ϕ and z directions that p

† A much more complete discussion of this topic can be found in *NFTM*, Sections 61 and 62.

$= p(P, t)$, or, equivalently, $p = p(\rho, t)$. The equation of motion in ρ direction is satisfied by letting

$$p = K(t) + \alpha \frac{P^2}{\rho^2} + \gamma \frac{\rho^2}{P^2} + \int^{\rho} \mu(u) \left(\frac{P^2(u)}{u^3} - \frac{u}{P^2(u)} \right) du$$

$$- m \int^{\rho} \left(\frac{\dot{a}^2 + a\ddot{a}}{u} - \frac{(a\dot{a})^2}{u^3} \right) du,$$

where
$$\mu(u) = \alpha(\mathrm{I}, \mathrm{II}) - \gamma(\mathrm{I}, \mathrm{II}),$$

$$\mathrm{I} = \mathrm{II} = 1 + \frac{P^2(u)}{u^2} + \frac{u^2}{P^2(u)},$$

or, equivalently,

$$\mathrm{I} = \mathrm{II} = 1 + \frac{u^2 - c^2}{u^2} + \frac{u^2}{u^2 - c^2}, \qquad c^2 = a^2 - A^2.$$

The radial stress $T_{\rho\rho}$ is then given by

$$T_{\rho\rho}(\rho, t) = -\bar{K}(t) - \int^{\rho} \mu(u) \left(\frac{u^2 - c^2}{u^3} - \frac{u}{u^2 - c^2} \right) du$$
$$+ m \left[(\dot{a}^2 + a\ddot{a}) \log \rho + \frac{(a\dot{a})^2}{2\rho^2} \right], \tag{18.84}$$

$\bar{K}(t)$ being an arbitrary function of time. If we take the lower limit of integration to be $a(t)$, and introduce the boundary condition $T_{\rho\rho}(a, t) = -p_1(t)$, then (18.84) takes on the alternative form

$$T_{\rho\rho}(\rho, t) = -p_1(t) - \int_a^{\rho} \mu(u) \left(\frac{u^2 - c^2}{u^3} - \frac{u}{u^2 - c^2} \right) du.$$

If $T_{\rho\rho}(b, t) = -p_2(t)$ is also given, then

$$p_1(t) - p_2(t) = -\int_a^{b} \mu(u) \left(\frac{u^2 - c^2}{u^3} - \frac{u}{u^2 - c^2} \right) du \tag{18.85}$$

serves to determine $a(t)$ (note that $b^2 = a^2 - A^2 + B^2$). The actual solution will require in general the use of numerical methods. The converse problem of finding $p_1(t) - p_2(t)$ from $a(t)$ is evidently simpler. In the case of a Mooney-Rivlin material, $\mu(u)$ reduces to a constant μ, so that

$$p_1(t) - p_2(t) = \mu\left(\log\left[\frac{1 - \dfrac{c^2}{b^2}}{1 - \dfrac{c^2}{a^2}}\right]^{1/2} + \frac{c^2}{2a^2} - \frac{c^2}{2b^2}\right),$$

The motion of spherical shells can be investigated along the same lines.† Isochoric radial motions of a shell defined by $A \leq R \leq B$ are described by $r^3 - a^3 = R^3 - A^3$, $\theta = \Theta$, $\phi = \Phi$, where $a = a(t) = r(A, t)$. Then

$$\|\mathbf{F}\| = \operatorname{diag}\left(\frac{R^2}{r^2}, \frac{r^2}{R^2}, \frac{r^2}{R^2}\right),$$

$$v = \dot{r} = \frac{a^2\dot{a}}{r^2}, \quad \dot{v} = \ddot{r} = \frac{2a\dot{a}^2 + a^2\ddot{a}}{r^2} - \frac{2(a^2\dot{a})^2}{r^5}.$$

Wang [190] has investigated a thin shell approximation corresponding to $r^3 - a^3 = (r - a)(r^2 + a^2) = a\delta(r^2 + a^2) \approx 2a^3\delta$, and, similarly, $R^3 - A^3 \approx 2A^3\Delta$.

Problems

1. If you were given a large grant to determine the response functions of an isotropic elastic material, what experiments would you use, how would you go about determining the dependence of the response functions on the strain invariants, etc., if **a**. the material is incompressible; **b**. the material is compressible.
2. Solve the problem (18.38) of combined torsion and extension for a Mooney-Rivlin material. Investigate the influence of one loading upon the stiffness relative to the other loading.
3. Solve the bending problem (18.55) for a Mooney-Rivlin material. It should now be possible to clear the top and bottom surfaces of radial stresses.
4. Investigate the eversion of a spherical shell made of a Mooney-Rivlin material. Is it possible to clear the boundaries of surface tractions?
5. Following the outline of the problem (18.81)–(18.85), investigate radial motions of a spherical shell made of a Mooney-Rivlin material. Explore the simplifications that arise if the shell is assumed to be thin.
6. Verify (18.69), (18.70), obtain the Cauchy stress $\mathbf{T}$ from (17.20), and write out the stress equations of equilibrium for $\mathbf{T}$. What simplifications are possible if $R/C \ll 1$. Investigate the limiting case $R/C \to 0$.

† Cf. [83], [190].

7. Investigate the inflation of a cylinder, described by $\rho = \rho(P)$, $\phi = \Phi$, $z = FZ$ (use (17.20)). What simplifications are obtained by using the Mooney-Rivlin stress relation?

8. Investigate the inflation of a spherical shell, described by $r = r(R)$, $\theta = \Theta$, $\phi = \Phi$ (use (17.20)). What simplifications are obtained by using the Mooney-Rivlin stress relation?

9. It is at first not a little surprising that, as noted by Fosdick [43], *a deformation with a constant strain invariants need not be homogeneous.* An example of such deformations has been given by Singh and Pipkin [142],

$$\rho = AP, \qquad \phi = B \log \frac{P}{P_0} + C\Phi, \qquad z = \frac{Z}{A^2C},$$

where A, B, C are constants (P_0 is an inessential constant, introduced so as to make B dimensionless). Interpret this solution; in particular, note that, because the components of $\mathbf{F}$ are constant in cylindrical coordinates, so are the components of $\mathbf{R}$ and $\mathbf{B}$. What can you say about the orientations of the "strain ellipsoids"? Show that the equations of equilibrium can be satisfied by letting

$$p = (S_{\rho\rho} - S_{\phi\phi}) \log \rho + 2S_{\rho\phi} + p_0,$$

where p_0 is an arbitrary constant, and $\mathbf{S} = p\mathbf{1} + \mathbf{T}$. This means that the deformation is *controllable* in the sense that it can be maintained by means of surface tractions alone.

Section 19
PROBLEMS IN ANISOTROPIC ELASTICITY

There is a large body of work on nonlinear anisotropic elasticity. Here we can do no more than solve a few typical problems. For the most part it is expedient to assume that the stress relation is derivable from a strain-energy function W, because the representations of W for all cases of crystal symmetry have been determined by Smith and Rivlin [144].

Transverse isotropy†

By a transverse isotropy we mean, first of all, that a body in its undistorted states has a rotational symmetry about a fixed axis. There is no loss of generality if this axis is taken to be the z axis of the coordinate system. As was noted in Appendix II, there are several kinds of transverse isotropy, depending on whether or not certain reflections are permitted as additional symmetry operations. However, because second rank tensors are automatically "centro-

† Here we follow Erickson and Rivlin [33].

symmetric," it follows that elastic response is restricted only by the condition of rotational symmetry.

To derive a representation of the strain-energy function W, let us recall that, according to the principle of material objectivity, the dependence of W upon deformation gradients must be expressible in terms of the combination $\mathbf{C} = \mathbf{F}^T\mathbf{F}$ (cf. (14.31)). Moreover, if $\mathbf{S}$ is a symmetry operation, then W must be form-invariant to $\mathbf{S}: W(\mathbf{C}) = W(\mathbf{SCS}^T)$ (cf. (14.34) *et seq.*). Now, rotational symmetry is described by a *continuous group* of elements that depend on a continuous parameter $\phi: \mathbf{S} = \mathbf{S}(\phi)$. Consequently, the restriction imposed on W can be expressed by $W(\mathbf{S}(\phi)\mathbf{CS}^T(\phi)) = W(\mathbf{S}(\phi + d\phi)\mathbf{CS}^T(\phi + d\phi))$, or, by†

$$\dot{W} = \frac{\partial W}{\partial \bar{C}_{ij}} (\dot{S}_{ik}C_{km}S^T_{mj} + S_{ik}C_{km}\dot{S}^T_{mj}) = 0, \tag{19.1}$$

where $\bar{\mathbf{C}} = \mathbf{SCS}^T$, and a superposed dot indicates a derivative with respect to ϕ. Writing $\dot{\mathbf{S}} = \dot{\mathbf{S}}\mathbf{S}^T\mathbf{S} = \mathbf{\Omega S}$, $\dot{\mathbf{S}}^T = \mathbf{S}^T\mathbf{S}\dot{\mathbf{S}}^T = -\mathbf{S}^T\mathbf{\Omega}$, where $\mathbf{\Omega} = \dot{\mathbf{S}}\mathbf{S}^T = -\mathbf{S}\dot{\mathbf{S}}^T$ is a skew-symmetric tensor, we readily obtain that

$$W = 2\Omega_{ir}\bar{C}_{rj}\frac{\partial W}{\partial \bar{C}_{ij}} = 0. \tag{19.2}$$

Because this relation must hold for all $\mathbf{C}$, the overbar may be omitted. Recalling that $\mathbf{S}$ is to represent a rotation about z axis, i.e. $\mathbf{\Omega}$ is of the form $\Omega_{ir} = \text{const.}\ \varepsilon_{3ir}$, we arrive at the following condition of invariance:

$$C_{2j}\frac{\partial W}{\partial C_{1j}} = C_{1j}\frac{\partial W}{\partial C_{2j}}. \tag{19.3}$$

That is, the form-invariant function W is obtained by solving the differential equation

$$C_{12}\left(\frac{\partial W}{\partial C_{22}} - \frac{\partial W}{\partial C_{11}}\right) + (C_{11} - C_{22})\frac{\partial W}{\partial C_{12}} + C_{13}\frac{\partial W}{\partial C_{23}} - C_{23}\frac{\partial W}{\partial C_{13}} = 0. \tag{19.4}$$

It is evident right away that W may be an arbitrary function of C_{33}. The dependence of W upon the remaining components of $\mathbf{C}$ can be determined by introducing new variables as follows,

$$C_{11} = A_1 + A_2\cos A_3, \qquad C_{22} = A_1 - A_2\cos A_3, \tag{19.5}$$
$$C_{12} = A_2\sin A_3, \qquad C_{13} = A_4\cos A_5, \qquad C_{23} = A_4\sin A_5,$$

† The need to assume that W is a differentiable function of $\mathbf{C}$ is a drawback of the method. Other than that, however, the method, and the result (19.2), are quite interesting.

where A_2 and A_4 are positive. Then (19.4) reduces to $2\,\partial W/\partial A_3 + \partial W/\partial A_5 = 0$, so that $W = W(C_{33}, A_1, A_2, A_3 - 2A_5, A_4)$. As may be seen from (19.5), W cannot depend on $A_3 - 2A_5$ when either $A_2 = 0$ or $A_4 = 0$. To make W a one-valued function of the components C_{ij} that enter into $A_3 - 2A_5$, it is necessary for W to be periodic, with the period 2π, in $A_3 - 2A_5$. Therefore, we may assume that W depends on $A_3 - 2A_5$ through $\cos(A_3 - 2A_5)$ (the centro-symmetry of second rank tensors requires that the function be *even*). From these observations it follows that W can be expressed as a function of the invariants C_{33}, $C_{11} + C_{22} = 2A_1$, $(C_{11} - C_{22})^2 + 4C_{12}^2 = 4A_2^2$, $(C_{11} - C_{22})(C_{13}^2 - C_{23}^2) + 4C_{12}C_{23}C_{31} = 2A_2A_4^2\cos(A_3 - 2A_5)$, $C_{13}^2 + C_{23}^2 = A_4^2$. An equivalent set of invariants is given by the "isotropic invariants"

$$\mathrm{I} = \mathrm{I}_{\mathbf{B}} = \mathrm{I}_{\mathbf{C}}, \quad \mathrm{II} = \mathrm{II}_{\mathbf{B}} = \mathrm{II}_{\mathbf{C}}, \quad \mathrm{III} = \mathrm{III}_{\mathbf{B}} = \mathrm{III}_{\mathbf{C}}, \tag{19.6a}$$

complemented by $A_4^2 = C_{13}^2 + C_{23}^2 \equiv \mathrm{IV}, \qquad C_{33} \equiv \mathrm{V}.$ (19.6b)

Denoting by W_1, W_2, W_3, W_4, W_5, the derivatives of W with respect to I, II, III, IV, V, respectively, we have that, by (14.30),

$$\begin{aligned} T_{ij} &= \frac{1}{J} F_{ik} \frac{\partial W}{\partial F_{jk}} \\ &= \frac{1}{J} F_{ik} \left(W_1 \frac{\partial \mathrm{I}}{\partial F_{jk}} + W_2 \frac{\partial \mathrm{II}}{\partial F_{jk}} + W_3 \frac{\partial \mathrm{III}}{\partial F_{jk}} + W_4 \frac{\partial \mathrm{IV}}{\partial F_{jk}} + W_5 \frac{\partial V}{\partial F_{jk}} \right). \end{aligned}$$

To obtain a more explicit representation, we use (17.38) and

$$\begin{aligned} F_{ik} \frac{\partial C_{33}}{\partial F_{jk}} &= 2N_{ij}, \qquad F_{ik} \frac{\partial}{\partial F_{jk}} (C_{13}^2 + C_{23}^2) = 2M_{ij}, \\ N_{ij} &= F_{i3}F_{j3}, \qquad M_{ij} = C_{\alpha 3}(F_{i\alpha}F_{j3} + F_{j\alpha}F_{i3}). \end{aligned} \tag{19.7}$$

where α takes on the values 1 and 2, summation over repeated α being understood. According to the Cayley-Hamilton theorem, $\mathrm{I}\mathbf{B} - \mathbf{B}^2 = \mathrm{II}\mathbf{1} - \mathrm{III}\mathbf{B}^{-1}$, so that the stress relation can be written as follows,

$$\mathbf{T} = \frac{2}{J}[(\mathrm{II}W_2 + \mathrm{III}W_3)\mathbf{1} + W_1\mathbf{B} - \mathrm{III}W_2\mathbf{B}^{-1} + W_4\mathbf{M} + W_5\mathbf{N}]. \tag{19.8}$$

If the medium is incompressible, in which case III must equal unity, (19.8) is replaced by

$$\mathbf{T} = -p\mathbf{1} + 2(W_1\mathbf{B} - W_2\mathbf{B}^{-1} + W_4\mathbf{M} + W_5\mathbf{N}). \tag{19.9}$$

The subsequent discussion will be confined to incompressible media.

The problems and their solutions are very much the same as in the isotropic case; therefore, a mere outline of the solutions will suffice. As the first example let us take uniaxial extension: $x = X/\sqrt{V}$, $y = Y/\sqrt{V}$, $z = VZ$. Then $\mathbf{M} = \mathbf{0}$, and the only nonvanishing component of $\mathbf{N}$ is $N_{33} = V^2$. We now use the conditions $T_{xx} = T_{yy} = 0$ to obtain $p = 2[W_1(1/V) - W_2V]$; the axial stress T_{zz} is then given by

$$T_{zz} = 2V\left[\left(V - \frac{1}{V^2}\right)\left(W_1 + \frac{1}{V}W_2\right) + W_5V\right]. \tag{19.10}$$

Letting $W_5 = 0$, $2W_1 = \alpha$, $2W_2 = -\gamma$, we recover the isotropic solution (18.30).*

Because (19.10) is one equation connecting three response functions W_1, W_2, W_5, it cannot provide a means for determining any one of them. The situation is not much better in biaxial stretching of a sheet whose middle surface lies in the xy plane (z being as always the axis of symmetry). The deformation is described by $x = V_1X$, $y = V_2Y$, $z = V_3Z$, where the stretches must satisfy the incompressibility condition $V_1V_2V_3 = 1$. Setting $T_{zz} = 0$, we obtain $p = 2(W_1V_3^2 - W_2V_3^{-2} + W_5V_3^2)$, and

$$T_{\underline{\alpha\alpha}} = 2[(V_{\underline{\alpha}}^2 - V_3^2)W_1 - (V_{\underline{\alpha}}^{-2} - V_3^{-2})W_2 - W_5V_3^2]. \tag{19.11}$$

Again we have less equations than response functions. Moreover, there are only two independent stretches, which means that the invariants $\text{I} = V_1^2 + V_2^2 + V_3^2$, $\text{II} = V_1^2V_2^2 + V_2^2V_3^2 + V_3^2V_1^2$, $\text{V} = V_3^2$ cannot be varied independently. It will be recalled that in the isotropic case the corresponding equations, (18.32), sufficed to determine the response functions from measurements of forces and deformations.

To illustrate non-homogeneous deformations, let us take combined extension and torsion of a circular cylinder (aligned with the axis of symmetry): $\rho = AP$, $\phi = \Phi + DZ$, $z = FZ$, where $A^2 = 1/F$. Along with (18.39) we shall also need the vector $\|F_{i3}\|^T = \|0, D\rho, F\|$. The tensors $\mathbf{B}$ and $\mathbf{B}^{-1}$ have been calculated already ((18.39) *et seq.*); therefore, it remains to calculate $\mathbf{C} = \mathbf{F}^T\mathbf{F}$, $\mathbf{M}$ and $\mathbf{N}$. We obtain right away

$$\|\mathbf{C}\| = \begin{Vmatrix} A^2 & 0 & 0 \\ 0 & A^2 & AD\rho \\ 0 & AD\rho & F^2 + D^2\rho^2 \end{Vmatrix},$$

$$\|\mathbf{N}\| = \begin{Vmatrix} 0 \\ D\rho \\ F \end{Vmatrix} \|0, D\rho, F\| = \begin{Vmatrix} 0 & 0 & 0 \\ 0 & D^2\rho^2 & FD\rho \\ 0 & FD\rho & F^2 \end{Vmatrix}.$$

Finally, from $M_{ij} = AD\rho(F_{i2}F_{j3} + F_{j2}F_{i3})$ it follows that

$$\|\mathbf{M}\| = AD\rho(\|F_{i2}\|\,\|F_{j3}\|^T + \|F_{j2}\|\,\|F_{i3}\|^T)$$
$$= D\rho\begin{Vmatrix} 0 & 0 & 0 \\ 0 & 2F^{-1}D\rho & 1 \\ 0 & 0 & 0 \end{Vmatrix}.$$

According to (19.9), the stresses are as follows,

$$\begin{aligned} T_{\rho\rho} &= -p + 2\left(\frac{1}{F}W_1 - FW_2\right), \qquad T_{\rho\phi} = T_{\rho z} = 0, \\ T_{\phi\phi} &= T_{\rho\rho} + 2D^2\rho^2\left(W_1 + W_5 + \frac{2}{F}W_4\right), \\ T_{zz} &= T_{\rho\rho} + 2\left(F^2 - \frac{1}{F}\right)\left(W_1 + \frac{1}{F}W_2\right) + 2\left(F^2W_5 - \frac{1}{F}D^2\rho^2W_2\right), \\ T_{\phi z} &= 2D\rho[F(W_1 + W_5) + W_2 + W_4], \end{aligned} \tag{19.12}$$

where W_1, W_2, W_4, W_5 are functions of

$$\mathrm{I} = F^2 + \frac{2}{F} + D^2\rho^2, \qquad \mathrm{II} = 2F + \frac{1}{F^2} + \frac{D^2\rho^2}{F},$$
$$\mathrm{IV} = \frac{D^2\rho^2}{F}, \qquad V = F^2 + D^2\rho^2.$$

For a given deformation, we have that

$$\frac{dW}{d\rho^2} = W_1D^2 + W_2\frac{D^2}{F} + W_4\frac{D^2}{F} + W_5D^2, \quad D^2\left(W_1 + W_5 + \frac{2}{F}W_4\right)$$
$$= \frac{dW}{d\rho^2} + \frac{D^2}{F}(W_4 - W_2), \quad D[F(W_1 + W_5) + W_2 + W_4] = \frac{F}{D}\frac{dW}{d\rho^2},$$

so that, by (19.12),

$$T_{\rho\rho} - T_{\phi\phi} = 2\rho^2\frac{dW}{d\rho^2} + \frac{2}{F}D^2\rho^2(W_4 - W_2), \tag{19.13}$$

$$T_{\phi z} = \frac{2F}{D}\rho\frac{dW}{d\rho^2}. \tag{19.14}$$

To satisfy the equation of equilibrium, we proceed as in the isotropic case, obtaining

$$T_{\rho\rho} = 2D^2 \int^{\rho} u\left(W_1 + W_5 + \frac{2}{F} W_4\right) du \tag{19.15}$$

(cf. (18.44)). Because $T_{\rho\phi}$ and $T_{\rho z}$ vanish identically, the boundary condition $\mathbf{t}_\rho = T_{\rho\rho}\mathbf{i}_\rho + T_{\rho\phi}\mathbf{i}_\phi + T_{\rho z}\mathbf{i}_z = \mathbf{0}$, $\rho = a$, where a is the radius of the deformed cylinder, is satisfied by taking a to be the lower limit of integration in (19.15). Then, in view of (19.13), we can write

$$T_{\rho\rho}(\rho) = W(\rho) - W(a) + \frac{D^2}{F} \int_{a^2}^{\rho^2} [W_4(s) - W_2(s)]\, ds. \tag{19.16}$$

Similarly, by (19.14), the torque M transmitted by a cross section is given by

$$M = 2\pi \int_0^a \rho^2 T_{\rho\phi}\, d\rho = 2\pi \frac{F}{D} [a^2 W(a) - \int_0^{a^2} W(s)\, ds]. \tag{19.17}$$

The axial force N transmitted by a cross section can be calculated from

$$N = 2\pi \int_0^a \rho T_{zz}\, d\rho. \tag{19.18}$$

The simultaneous inflation and extension of a tube of circular cross section, with steady rotation thrown in for good measure, is described by

$$\rho^2 = \frac{P^2}{F} + B, \qquad \phi = \Phi + \omega t, \qquad z = FZ, \tag{19.19}$$

where ω is the constant angular velocity. Thus

$$\begin{gathered} \mathbf{M} = \mathbf{0}, \qquad \|\mathbf{F}\| = \operatorname{diag}\left(\frac{P}{\rho F}, \frac{\rho}{P}, F\right), \\ \|\mathbf{B}\| = \|\mathbf{C}\| = \operatorname{diag}\left(\frac{P^2}{\rho^2 F^2}, \frac{\rho^2}{F^2}, F^2\right), \\ \|\mathbf{B}^{-1}\| = \operatorname{diag}\left(\frac{\rho^2 F^2}{P^2}, \frac{P^2}{\rho^2}, \frac{1}{F^2}\right), \end{gathered} \tag{19.20}$$

whereas $N_{33} = F^2$ is the only nonvanishing component of $\mathbf{N}$. The nonvanishing stresses are

$$
\begin{aligned}
T_{\rho\rho} &= -p + 2\left(W_1 \frac{P^2}{\rho^2 F^2} - W_2 \frac{\rho^2 F^2}{P^2}\right), \\
T_{\phi\phi} &= -p + 2\left(W_1 \frac{\rho^2}{P^2} - W_2 \frac{P^2}{\rho^2}\right), \\
T_{zz} &= -p + 2(W_1 F^2 - W_2 F^{-2} + W_5 F^2).
\end{aligned} \tag{19.21}
$$

We choose the pressure p so as to satisfy the equation of motion,

$$
\frac{d}{d\rho} T_{\rho\rho} + \frac{1}{\rho}(T_{\rho\rho} - T_{\phi\phi}) = -m\rho\omega^2,
$$

(m denotes the constant mass density). Denoting by a and b, respectively, the inner and outer radii of the deformed tube, we then obtain

$$
\begin{aligned}
T_{\rho\rho}(a) = T_{\rho\rho}(b) &+ \frac{1}{2} m\omega^2(b^2 - a^2) \\
&+ 2\int_a^b (W_1 + W_2 F^2)\left(\frac{Fu^2 - B}{F^2 u^2} - \frac{u^2}{Fu^2 - B}\right)\frac{du}{u}.
\end{aligned} \tag{19.22}
$$

If $T_{\rho\rho}(a) = T_{\rho\rho}(b) = 0$, then one must be able to choose the parameters F and B so that (19.22) holds.

In the bending of a block, described by

$$
\rho = \sqrt{2AX}, \qquad \phi = BY, \qquad z = \frac{Z}{AB}, \tag{18.53)R
$$

the tensor of deformation gradients is again diagonal, hence a solution is not too difficult to obtain.†

Remarks on the determination of response functions

No matter to what type of anisotropy the elastic response of a body belongs, it is possible to maintain the body in a state of homogeneous deformation by means of surface tractions alone (i.e. without having to introduce rather special kinds of body forces). Namely, if $x_i = F_{ij}X_j$, where F_{ij} are constants, then the stress components will be constant too, and thus trivially satisfy the equations of equilibrium. Let us denote by $I_1, I_2, \ldots, I_M$ the elements of the

† Ericksen and Rivlin, pp. 297–300, *op. cit.*

appropriate polynomial basis in $\mathbf{C} = \mathbf{F}^T\mathbf{F}$. Then, by (15.87), the Piola-Kirchhoff stress is given by

$$\tilde{T}_{ji} = \sum_{K=1}^{M} \frac{\partial W}{\partial I_K} \left(\frac{\partial}{\partial C_{rs}} I_K \right) (\delta_{rj} F_{is} + \delta_{sj} F_{ir}). \tag{19.23}$$

The derivatives $\partial I_K(\mathbf{C})/\partial C_{rs}$ are known quantities as soon as the symmetry group is specified, so that we may look upon (19.23) as a means for calculating $W_K = \partial W/\partial I_K$ from the measurements of forces $\tilde{T}_{ji}$ and deformations F_{ij}. There are only six independent equations in (19.23), as may be seen by writing it in the equivalent form

$$T_{ik} = \frac{1}{J} \sum_{K=1}^{M} W_K \left(\frac{\partial}{\partial C_{rs}} I_K \right) (F_{kr} F_{is} + F_{ks} F_{ir})$$

(cf. (15.87)). For transverse isotropy, M equals 5, so that the determination of W_K, and subsequently $W(I_1, T_2, \ldots, I_K)$, is possible, at least in principle (in practice the difficulties in measuring all components of $\mathbf{T}$ and $\mathbf{F}$ may be very great). For crystals, on the other hand, the number of invariants exceeds 6; therefore, a determination of W is not possible unless all but six of the invariants are eliminated by means of the existing syzygies. But this will make W in general a many-valued function,† so that unless some simplifying features exist the determination of W is likely to be next to impossible.

A more modest task, although by no means an easy one, is to approximate the strain-energy function by a polynomial of degree 3 in the strains. Let us recall from (17.34) that $\tilde{\mathbf{T}} = \mathbf{k}(\mathbf{C})\mathbf{F}^T$, and introduce the expansion

$$k_{ij} = c_{ijkm} E_{km} + c_{ijkmnp} E_{km} E_{np}, \tag{19.24}$$

where $2\mathbf{E} = \mathbf{C} - \mathbf{1}$, and the *elasticities* c_{ijkm}, c_{ijkmnp} have the symmetry properties

$$\begin{gathered} c_{ijkm} = c_{jikm} = c_{ijmk}, \\ c_{ijkmnp} = c_{jikmnp} = c_{ijmknp} = c_{ijkmpn} = c_{ijnpkm}. \end{gathered} \tag{19.25}$$

In the literature c_{ijkmnp} are usually referred to as third-order elastic constants (because in the expansion of W they occur as coefficients of terms of third degree in strains). These coefficients provide in many instances a means of

† Cf. the remarks on p. 576.

obtaining information about certain aspects of microstructure, e.g. "anharmonic effects" in the lattice theory of crystals, from measurements of "macroscopic" quantities.

The measurement of wave speeds and amplitudes is perhaps the best method for obtaining c_{ijkm}, c_{ijkmnp}. According to (17.31), the amplitudes of waves must be multiples of the principal directions, $\mathbf{D}_a$, of the acoustic tensor $\mathbf{Q}(\mathbf{n})$, the principal values associated with $\mathbf{D}_a$ being $\rho_0 \overline{V}^2_{\underline{a}}$. If a strain-energy function exists, then $\mathbf{Q}$ is symmetric, and admits the representation $Q_{ik} = \rho_0 \overline{V}^2_{\underline{a}} D_{ai} D_{ak}$ (cf. (4.41)). Thus for any direction of propagation, $\mathbf{n}$, Q_{ik} can be calculated if the wave speeds and the directions of amplitudes are known. Now let us suppose that the deformation depends continuously on a scalar parameter λ; in particular, λ may stand for hydrostatic pressure. Indicating differentiations with respect to λ by primes, we obtain from $\rho_0 \overline{V}^2_{\underline{a}} = Q_{ik} D_{\underline{a}i} D_{\underline{a}k}$ that $\rho_0(\overline{V}^2_{\underline{a}})' = Q'_{ik} D_{\underline{a}i} D_{\underline{a}k} + 2Q_{ik} D_{\underline{a}i} D'_{\underline{a}k}$. Because $Q_{ik} D_{\underline{a}k} = \rho_0 \overline{V}^2_{\underline{a}} D_{\underline{a}i}$ and $D_{\underline{a}i} D'_{\underline{a}i} = 0$, it follows that

$$\rho_0(\overline{V}^2_{\underline{a}})' = D_{\underline{a}i} D_{\underline{a}k} F_{mn} \frac{\partial Q_{ik}}{\partial F_{mn}}. \tag{19.26}$$

These relations may be used to calculate the higher-order elasticities. The details of the actual calculations are not easy.†

Let us recall from (17.37) the modified acoustic tensor $\bar{Q}_{nr}(\bar{n}) = D_{nrpq}\bar{n}_p\bar{n}_q$, where

$$D_{nrpq}(\mathbf{C}) = \delta_{nr} k_{pq} + C_{rm} \frac{\partial k_{qn}}{\partial E_{pm}},$$

and $\bar{n}_i$ denote directions of propagation "convected" into the undeformed state (note that $n_i dx_i \equiv \bar{n}_i dX_i$ implies $n_i F_{ij} = \bar{n}_j$). With (19.24), (19.25), we obtain $D_{nrpq} = \delta_{nr}(c_{pqij}E_{ij} + c_{pqijsu}E_{ij}E_{su}) + C_{mr}(c_{qnpm} + 2c_{qnpmij}E_{ij})$. Consequently,

$$D^0_{nrpq} = D_{nrpq}\Big|_{\mathbf{C}=\mathbf{1}} = c_{qnpr}, \tag{19.27}$$

$$\frac{\partial D_{nrpq}}{\partial E_{ij}}\Big|_{\mathbf{C}=\mathbf{1}} = \delta_{nr} c_{pqij} + \delta_{ir} c_{qnpj} + \delta_{jr} c_{qnpi} + 2c_{qnprij}.$$

To calculate 36 coefficients c_{ijkm} from measurements of $\bar{Q}^0_{ij}(\bar{n}) = D^0_{ijkm}\bar{n}_k\bar{n}_m$, it is necessary to consider 6 distinct directions of propagation, $\bar{\mathbf{n}}_K$, $K = 1, 2,$

† Cf. [164], [92], [163]. Isotropic materials were dealt with in Section 17.

..., 6 (here K is a *label*). We assume that these directions are such that the tensors $P_{Kij} = \bar{n}_{Ki}\bar{n}_{Kj}$ are linearly independent, i.e.

$$\sum_K A_K P_{Kij} = 0$$

for all i and j only if $A_K = 0$. Then it is possible to construct an inverse set of tensors R_{Kij} (P_{Kij} itself does not have an inverse because $\det \mathbf{P}_K = 0$), defined by

$$\sum_K P_{Kij} R_{Kmn} = \tfrac{1}{2}(\delta_{im}\delta_{jn} + \delta_{in}\delta_{jm}).$$

For instance, $$\sum_K P_{Kij} R_{K11} = \delta_{i1}\delta_{j1}, \qquad i, j = 1, 2, 3,$$

provides 6 equations for R_{K11}. By $(19.27)_1$, $\bar{Q}^0_{ij} = c_{mikj} P_{Kmk}$; therefore,

$$\sum_K \bar{Q}^0_{ij} R_{Kpq} \equiv H_{ipjq} = \tfrac{1}{2}(c_{piqj} + c_{qipj}). \tag{19.28}$$

This is solved by $$c_{mikj} = H_{imjk} + H_{mijk} - H_{kmji}. \tag{19.29}$$

The data H_{ijkm} must satisfy two sets of compatibility conditions, arising from $c_{ijkm} = c_{ijmk}$, and from the condition that c_{ijkm} be independent of the particular choice of $\bar{\mathbf{n}}_K$.†

Finally, we remark that, as will be shown in Section 21, the propagation of acceleration fronts is governed by the same equations as the propagation of (infinitesimal) progressive plane waves in homogeneously deformed media. Because there are no known solutions that would exhibit acceleration fronts, the determination of the elasticities must be in fact based on experiments involving plane waves in homogeneously prestrained bodies.

Problems

1. Investigate bending, defined by (18.55), of a block of transversely isotropic, incompressible material (assume that z axis is the axis of symmetry).
2. Verify the derivation of (B.29) in Appendix II, and write out the constitutive equations for typical stress components. How do these relations compare with what would be obtained for a hyperelastic material?
3. Obtain the polynomial basis of the strain-energy function for the anisotropy referred to as cubic I. *Hints*: The symmetry operations are

$$\underset{4}{z}, \underset{4}{x}, \underset{4}{y} = \underset{4}{z}\,\underset{4}{x}\,\underset{4}{z}^{-1}.$$

Then $$\underset{2}{z} = \underset{4}{z}\,\underset{4}{z}, \qquad \underset{2}{x} = \underset{4}{x}\,\underset{4}{x}, \quad \underset{2}{y} = \underset{4}{y}\,\underset{4}{y}$$

† Toupin and Bernstein [165].

are also symmetry operations, which means that, rather than starting from $\sum (C_{11}, C_{22}, C_{33}, C_{12}, C_{23}, C_{31})$, we can start from the representation $\sum = \sum (C_{11}, C_{22}, C_{33}, C_{12}^2, C_{23}^2, C_{31}^2, C_{12}, C_{23}, C_{31})$ obtained in the rhombic case. From inspection of

$$\underset{4}{x}\,\mathbf{C}\,\underset{4}{x^{-1}}, \qquad \underset{4}{y}\,\mathbf{C}\,\underset{4}{y^{-1}}, \qquad \underset{4}{z}\,\mathbf{C}\,\underset{4}{z^{-1}}$$

(cf. the "model transformations" on p. 305), it is easy to see that cubic symmetry requires invariance with respect to the following permutations:

	C_{11}	C_{22}	C_{33}	C_{12}^2	C_{23}^2	C_{31}^2
$\underset{4}{x}$	C_{11}	C_{33}	C_{22}	C_{31}^2	C_{23}^2	C_{12}^2
$\underset{4}{y}$	C_{33}	C_{22}	C_{11}	C_{23}^2	C_{12}^2	C_{31}^2
$\underset{4}{z}$	C_{22}	C_{11}	C_{33}	C_{12}^2	C_{31}^2	C_{23}^2

In terms of indices, these permutations are described by $11 \to 22 \to 33 \to 11$, $31 \to 23 \to 12 \to 31$. The appropriate invariants are now $I_1 = C_{12}C_{23}C_{31}$ and the set of invariants given by $(B.14)$:

$$K_1 = C_{11} + C_{22} + C_{33}, \qquad\qquad K_2 = C_{22}C_{33} + C_{33}C_{11} + C_{11}C_{22},$$

$$K_3 = C_{11}C_{22}C_{33}, \qquad\qquad\qquad K_4 = C_{23}^2 + C_{31}^2 + C_{12}^2,$$

$$K_5 = C_{31}^2 C_{12}^2 + C_{12}^2 C_{23}^3 + C_{23}^2 C_{31}^2, \qquad K_6 = C_{23}^2 C_{31}^2 C_{12}^2,$$

$$K_7 = C_{22}C_{12}^2 + C_{33}C_{23}^2 + C_{11}C_{31}^2, \qquad K_8 = C_{31}^2 C_{33} + C_{12}^2 C_{11} + C_{23}^2 C_{22},$$

$$K_9 = C_{33}C_{22}^2 + C_{11}C_{33}^2 + C_{22}C_{11}^2, \qquad K_{10} = C_{12}^2 C_{31}^4 + C_{23}^2 C_{12}^4 + C_{31}^2 C_{23}^4,$$

$$K_{11} = C_{11}C_{31}^2 C_{12}^2 + C_{22}C_{12}^2 C_{23}^2 + C_{33}C_{23}^2 C_{31}^2,$$

$$K_{12} = C_{23}^2 C_{22}C_{33} + C_{31}^2 C_{33}C_{11} + C_{12}^2 C_{11}C_{22},$$

$$K_{13} = C_{11}C_{22}C_{31}^2 + C_{22}C_{33}C_{12}^2 + C_{33}C_{11}C_{23}^2,$$

$$K_{14} = C_{23}^2 C_{31}^2 C_{22} + C_{31}^2 C_{12}^2 C_{33} + C_{12}^2 C_{23}^2 C_{11}.$$

Omitting the redundant element K_6, we have a polynomial basis consisting of I_1, K_1 to K_5, and K_7 to K_{14}.

Section 20
SOME NONMECHANICAL EFFECTS OF FINITE DEFORMATIONS

The representations of nonlinear constitutive equations, developed at first in the context of mechanical theories, have been also applied to heat conduction, and electromagnetic theories in general. The examples given below are chosen so as to illustrate the influence of finite deformations upon thermal and electromagnetic phenomena.

Conduction of heat and electricity

Let $\mathbf{h} = \partial\theta/\partial\mathbf{X}$ denote temperature gradients, and $\mathbf{q}$, $\mathbf{T}$, η be the heat flux, stress, and entropy density, respectively. We assume the following constitutive equations,

$$T_{mi} = \rho F_{mj}\frac{\partial\hat{\psi}}{\partial F_{ij}}, \qquad \eta = -\frac{\partial\hat{\psi}}{\partial\theta}, \qquad \mathbf{q} = \hat{\mathbf{q}}(\mathbf{F}, \theta, \mathbf{h}) \tag{20.1}$$

(cf. (14.74)), where the free energy $\psi = \varepsilon - \eta\theta$ is a function of θ and $\mathbf{F}$. If there are no distributed sources of heat, the energy balance (10.22) reduces to

$$\gamma_\iota = \dot{\eta} + \frac{1}{\rho\theta}\operatorname{div}\mathbf{q} = 0.$$

In particular, we may consider *steady heat flow in a body held at a fixed deformation.* Then, because particles do not move, i.e. $\dot{\eta} = \partial_t\eta$, and the flow is assumed to be steady, it follows that

$$\operatorname{div}\mathbf{q} = 0. \tag{20.2}$$

As noted by Pipkin and Rivlin,† if one assumes that the flow of electricity is governed by the constitutive equation

$$\mathbf{j} = \mathbf{j}(\mathbf{F}, \mathbf{E}), \tag{20.3}$$

where $\mathbf{E}$ is the electric field vector, then steady currents in bodies held at a constant deformation obey the same equations as do steady heat flows. Namely, because the relevant field equations are now given by

$$\operatorname{div}\mathbf{j} = 0, \qquad \operatorname{curl}\mathbf{E} = \mathbf{0}$$

(cf. (13.28), (13.49)), we can let $\mathbf{E} = -\operatorname{grad}\phi$, thus obtaining the correspondence

$$\begin{gathered} \theta \leftrightarrow -\phi, \qquad \mathbf{h} \leftrightarrow -\mathbf{E}, \qquad \mathbf{q} \leftrightarrow \mathbf{j}, \\ \mathbf{q}\cdot\mathbf{h} \le 0 \leftrightarrow \mathbf{j}\cdot\mathbf{E} \ge 0. \end{gathered} \tag{20.4}$$

† [220]. Cf. also *NFTM*, p. 388.

In view of this correspondence, the solutions obtained by Pipkin and Rivlin ([116], [119]) for electrical conduction in deformed bodies can equally well serve as examples of heat flow in deformed bodies.

We assume that the constitutive equation (20.3) is materially objective, thus $\mathbf{j}^+ = \mathbf{Qj} = \mathbf{Q}\hat{\mathbf{f}}(\mathbf{F}, \mathbf{E}) = \hat{\mathbf{f}}(\mathbf{QF}, \mathbf{QE})$, where $\mathbf{Q}$ is an arbitrary orthogonal tensor. Letting $\mathbf{F} = \mathbf{RU}$, $\mathbf{Q} = \mathbf{R}^T$. we now obtain $\mathbf{j} = \mathbf{R}\hat{\mathbf{f}}(\mathbf{U}, \mathbf{R}^T\mathbf{E})$. Consequently, if we define a new response function $\mathbf{f}$ by $\hat{\mathbf{f}}(\mathbf{U}, \mathbf{E}) = \mathbf{Uf}(\mathbf{U}^2, \mathbf{UE})$, then

$$\mathbf{j} = \mathbf{Ff}(\mathbf{C}, \boldsymbol{\epsilon}), \tag{20.5}$$

where

$$\boldsymbol{\epsilon} = \mathbf{F}^T\mathbf{E}, \qquad \mathbf{C} = \mathbf{U}^2 = \mathbf{F}^T\mathbf{F}. \tag{20.6}$$

Having satisfied material objectivity, we now turn to the conditions imposed on $\mathbf{f}$ by material symmetries.† If $\mathbf{S}$ is a symmetry operation of the response function $\mathbf{f}$, then, with $\mathbf{F} \to \mathbf{FS}^T$, it follows that $\mathbf{j} = \mathbf{FS}^T\mathbf{f}(\mathbf{SCS}^T, \mathbf{S}\boldsymbol{\epsilon}) = \mathbf{Ff}(\mathbf{C}, \boldsymbol{\epsilon})$, i.e. $\mathbf{f}$ must be an isotropic function with respect to $\mathbf{S}$:

$$\mathbf{f}(\mathbf{SCS}^T, \mathbf{S}\boldsymbol{\epsilon}) = \mathbf{Sf}(\mathbf{C}, \boldsymbol{\epsilon}). \tag{20.7}$$

Following the method outlined in Appendix II, a representation of $\mathbf{f}$ can be obtained by constructing first a form-invariant polynomial $F = m_i f_i$, where $\mathbf{m}$ is an arbitrary vector. Assuming that the isotropy group of $\mathbf{f}$ is the orthogonal group, we find that the polynomial invariants in $\boldsymbol{\epsilon}$ and $\mathbf{C}$ are of the form

$$I = I_{ij\ldots m\ldots pqrs}\varepsilon_i\varepsilon_j\ldots\varepsilon_m\ldots C_{pq}C_{rs}\ldots,$$

where the coefficients are isotropic tensors expressible as free products of Kronecker deltas. Consequently, the invariants are of the form

$$\mathrm{tr}\mathbf{C}^{M+1}, \qquad \varepsilon_i C_{ij}^M \varepsilon_j, \qquad M = 0, 1, 2. \tag{20.8}$$

Similarly, the invariants J that also depend, linearly, on $\mathbf{m}$ are given by

$$m_i\varepsilon_i, \qquad m_i C_{ij}\varepsilon_j, \qquad m_i C_{ij} C_{jk}\varepsilon_k. \tag{20.9}$$

Therefore, because $F = m_i f_i$ is a linear, isotropic, scalar-valued function of $\mathbf{m}$, we have that

$$F = P_1 m_i\varepsilon_i + P_2 C_{ij} m_i\varepsilon_j + P_3 C_{ij} C_{jk} m_i \varepsilon_k, \tag{20.10}$$

† It should be noted that, in the context of thermoelasticity, the isotropy groups of the stress relation $\mathbf{T} = \hat{\mathbf{T}}(\mathbf{F}, \theta)$ and of the heat conduction law $\mathbf{q} = \mathbf{q}(\mathbf{F}, \theta, \mathbf{h})$ need not be the same.

where P_1, P_2, P_3 depend on the invariants (20.8). In view of $f_i = \partial F/\partial m_i$, $\mathbf{f}$ is given by

$$\mathbf{f} = (P_1\mathbf{1} + P_2\mathbf{C} + P_3\mathbf{C}^2)\boldsymbol{\epsilon}. \tag{20.11}$$

Finally, recalling (20.5), (20.6), we arrive at

$$\mathbf{j} = (Q_1\mathbf{1} + Q_2\mathbf{B} + Q_3\mathbf{B}^2)\mathbf{E}, \qquad \mathbf{B} = \mathbf{F}\mathbf{F}^T, \tag{20.12}$$

where we have used the Cayley-Hamilton theorem to eliminate $\mathbf{B}^3$, and Q_1, Q_2, Q_3 are functions of

$$\mathrm{tr}\mathbf{B}, \quad \mathrm{tr}\mathbf{B}^2, \quad \mathrm{tr}\mathbf{B}^3, \quad B_{ij}E_iE_j, \quad B_{ij}B_{jk}E_iE_k, \quad E_iE_i. \tag{20.13}$$

The case when $(20.12)_1$ is linear in $\mathbf{E}$ (i.e. when the coefficients depend only on $\mathrm{tr}\mathbf{B}$, $\mathrm{tr}\mathbf{B}^2$, $\mathrm{tr}\mathbf{B}^3$) is referred to as *ohmic conduction*. Except when there is no deformation, i.e. when $\mathbf{B} = \mathbf{1}$, $(20.12)_1$ is of the form $j_i = A_{ij}E_j$, so that deformation of conductors entails an *apparent* loss of isotropy.

Let us take a conductor in the shape of a tube of circular cross section. A simultaneous stretching and twisting of the tube is described by

$$\rho = \rho(P), \qquad \phi = \Phi + DZ, \qquad z = FZ$$

(cf. (18.38)), where D and F are constants, and $\rho, \phi, z, P, \Phi, Z$ denote final and initial cylindrical coordinates, respectively. Then

$$\|\mathbf{F}\| = \begin{Vmatrix} \dfrac{d\rho}{dP} & 0 & 0 \\ 0 & \dfrac{\rho}{P} & D\rho \\ 0 & 0 & F \end{Vmatrix};$$

assuming incompressibility, $\det\mathbf{F} = 1$, we obtain $\rho^2 - a^2 = (P^2 - A^2)/F$, where a and A denote, respectively, the final and initial values of the inner radius. If $E_\rho = E_\phi = 0$, $E_z = E$, then (20.12) yields

$$\begin{aligned} j_\rho = 0, \quad j_\phi &= Fv[Q_2 + (u^2 + v^2 + F^2)Q_3]E, \\ j_z &= [Q_1 + Q_2F^2 + F^2(F^2 + v^2)Q_3]E, \end{aligned} \tag{20.14}$$

where $u = \rho/P$, $v = D\rho$. Evidently $\mathrm{div}\mathbf{j} = 0$ is satisfied. Unless $Q_2 = Q_3 = 0$, *the paths of conduction are helices.* Because curl$\mathbf{H} = \mathbf{j}$, the component j_ϕ produces an axial magnetic field

$$H_z = -\int^\rho j_\phi \, d\rho .$$

Elastic dielectrics†

The theory of the elastic Maxwell-Lorentz dielectrics was sketched in Section 13. In this theory the electromagnetic equations

$$\text{curl}\mathbf{E} + \partial_\tau \mathbf{B} = \mathbf{0}, \qquad \text{div}\mathbf{B} = 0 \qquad (13.28)\text{R}$$

remain unchanged. Free charges and magnetic dipoles are assumed to be absent, i.e. $q = 0$, $\mathbf{j} = \mathbf{0}$, so that

$$q^* = -\text{div}\mathbf{P}, \qquad \mathbf{j}^* = \mathbf{J}_P = \partial_\tau \mathbf{P} + \text{curl}(\mathbf{P} \times \bar{\mathbf{v}})$$

(cf. (13.65)–(13.67)). Further, it is assumed that

$$\mathbf{H} = \mathbf{B} - (\mathbf{P} \times \bar{\mathbf{v}}), \qquad (20.15)$$

in which case (13.34) reduce to

$$\text{curl}\mathbf{B} - \partial_\tau \mathbf{E} = \mathbf{J}_P . \qquad (13.70)\text{R}$$

With the definition

$$\overset{*}{P}_i = \partial_\tau P_i + P_{i,j}\bar{v}_j + P_i \bar{v}_{k,k} - P_j \bar{v}_{i,j}, \qquad (13.71)\text{R}$$

the body force is represented by

$$\mathbf{f} = -\mathbf{E}^+ \,\text{div}\mathbf{P} + (\overset{*}{\mathbf{P}} \times \mathbf{B}), \qquad \mathbf{E}^+ = \mathbf{E} + (\bar{\mathbf{v}} \times \mathbf{B}). \quad (13.72)\text{R}$$

For electromagnetic variables we shall use the notations

$$\dot{\mathbf{E}} \equiv \frac{1}{c}\frac{\partial}{\partial t}\mathbf{E}, \quad \text{etc.};$$

† The presentation here follows Toupin [168] (but see also [38], [25]).

as before, $\bar{\mathbf{v}} = \mathbf{v}/c$. To these equations we adjoin the balance of linear momentum,

$$T_{ji,j} - E_i^+ \operatorname{div}\mathbf{P} + (\overset{*}{\mathbf{P}} \times \mathbf{B})_i = \rho \dot{v}_i, \tag{20.16}$$

and the balance of energy,

$$\rho \dot{\varepsilon} + \operatorname{div}\mathbf{q} = T_{ij}v_{i,j} + \overset{*}{\mathbf{P}} \cdot \mathbf{E}^+ \tag{20.17}$$

(cf. (13.73)).

Rather than starting from the constitutive equations $\mathbf{T} = \mathbf{T}(\mathbf{F}, \mathbf{P})$, $\mathbf{E}^+ = \mathbf{E}^+(\mathbf{F}, \mathbf{P})$,† we shall proceed as in hyperelasticity, and use the internal energy density as a constitutive potential: $\varepsilon = \bar{\Sigma}(\mathbf{F}, \mathbf{P})$. Material objectivity then requires that $\bar{\Sigma}(\mathbf{F}, \mathbf{P}) = \bar{\Sigma}(\mathbf{QF}, \mathbf{QP})$, or, with $\mathbf{Q} = \mathbf{R}^T$, $\bar{\Sigma}(\mathbf{F}, \mathbf{P}) = \bar{\Sigma}(\mathbf{U}, \mathbf{R}^T\mathbf{P})$. This suggests that we introduce a modified polarization vector $\mathbf{\Pi}$ by

$$\mathbf{P} = \frac{1}{J}\mathbf{F\Pi}, \tag{20.18}$$

where $J = \det\mathbf{F}$, and the new function Σ is defined by $\Sigma(\mathbf{C}, \mathbf{\Pi}) = \bar{\Sigma}(\mathbf{U}, J\mathbf{U\Pi})$, $\mathbf{C} = \mathbf{U}^2 = \mathbf{F}^T\mathbf{F}$. The representation

$$\varepsilon = \Sigma(\mathbf{C}, \mathbf{\Pi}) \tag{20.19}$$

then automatically satisfies the condition of material objectivity.

Next, we consider a symmetry operation $\mathbf{F} \to \hat{\mathbf{F}} = \mathbf{FS}^T$, $\det\mathbf{S} = 1$. Then $\hat{\mathbf{C}} = \mathbf{SCS}^T$, $J^{-1}\hat{\mathbf{\Pi}} = \hat{\mathbf{F}}^{-1}\mathbf{P} = \mathbf{SF}^{-1}\mathbf{P} = J^{-1}\mathbf{S\Pi}$, from which it follows that Σ must be an isotropic function with respect to $\mathbf{S}$: $\Sigma(\mathbf{C}, \mathbf{\Pi}) = \Sigma(\mathbf{SCS}^T, \mathbf{S\Pi})$. In particular, if the symmetry operations constitute the orthogonal group, then the polynomial basis of Σ is given by

$$\operatorname{tr}\mathbf{C}^{M+1}, \qquad \Pi_i C_{ij}^M \Pi_j, \qquad M = 0, 1, 2. \tag{20.20}$$

To derive the constitutive equations, we make use of the Clausius-Duhem inequality. Specifically, requiring that the internal dissipation δ, defined by (12.22), be zero, we arrive at

$$\rho\dot{\Sigma} = T_{ij}v_{i,j} + \frac{1}{J}\mathbf{E}^+ \cdot \mathbf{F}\dot{\mathbf{\Pi}}, \tag{20.21}$$

† This approach is used by Singh and Pipkin [236].

where we have taken into account the identity

$$\overset{*}{\mathbf{P}} = \frac{1}{J}\mathbf{F}\dot{\mathbf{\Pi}}. \tag{20.22}$$

If (20.21) is to hold in all processes $(\mathbf{F}, \mathbf{\Pi})$, then it follows that

$$T_{ik} = \rho \frac{\partial \Sigma}{\partial F_{ij}} F_{kj}, \qquad E_k = \rho_0 \frac{\partial \Sigma}{\partial \Pi_j} F_{jk}^{-1}, \tag{20.23}$$

where $\rho_0 = J\rho$ is the mass density in the initial configuration. The first of these can be also written as

$$T_{ik} = \rho \frac{\partial \Sigma}{\partial E_{mn}} F_{im} F_{kn}, \tag{20.24}$$

where $2E_{mn} = C_{mn} - \delta_{mn}$. According to Toupin, $(20.23)_2$ may be interpreted as an equation of molecular equilibrium,

$$E_i^+ + {}_LE_i = 0, \tag{20.25}$$

where

$${}_LE_i = -\rho_0 \frac{\partial \Sigma}{\partial \Pi_j} F_{ji}^{-1} \tag{20.26}$$

is the *local field.* Toupin then suggests the following generalization of (20.25),

$$\mathbf{E}^+ + {}_L\mathbf{E} + \mathbf{G} \times \overset{*}{\mathbf{P}} = \mathbf{0}, \tag{20.27}$$

where the *gyration vector* $\mathbf{G}$ is characterized by a constitutive equation $\mathbf{G} = \mathbf{G}(\mathbf{F}, \mathbf{P}, \mathbf{E}, \mathbf{B})$. Because $\mathbf{G} \times \overset{*}{\mathbf{P}}$ is perpendicular to $\overset{*}{\mathbf{P}}$, this generalization leaves the energy balance (20.17) unchanged.

Using (20.18), (20.22), and the identities (15.88), the equations of motion can be transformed into

$$\tilde{T}_{ji,j} - E_i^+ \Pi_{j,j} + \dot{\Pi}_m \varepsilon_{ijk} F_{jm} B_k = \rho_0 \dot{v}_i, \tag{20.28}$$

where $\tilde{\mathbf{T}}$ is the Piola-Kirchhoff stress, defined by

$$\tilde{T}_{ji} = \frac{\partial W}{\partial F_{ij}}, \qquad W = \rho_0 \Sigma$$

(cf. (15.87)). Solutions of various problems, particularly for equilibrium states, may be found in the recent literature (e.g. [79]).

Following Toupin, let us consider the *superposition of small deformations and weak fields on large deformations and strong fields.* We shall mark the variables evaluated in the intermediate configuration by a superscript 0. We assume that the intermediate configuration is a state of equilibrium, so that

$$\tilde{T}^0_{ji.j} - {}^0E_i^+ \Pi^0_{j.j} = 0.$$

Subtracting this from (20.28), we obtain

$$(\delta \tilde{T}_{ji})_{.j} - \Pi^0_{j.j}\delta E_i^+ - (\delta \Pi_j)_{.j}{}^0E_i^+ + \varepsilon_{ijk}\overline{\delta \Pi_m}^{\bullet} F^0_{jm} B^0_k = \rho_0 \ddot{u}_i,$$

where $\mathbf{u}$ is the displacement from the intermediate position $\boldsymbol{\xi}(\mathbf{X})$ to the final position $\mathbf{x}(\mathbf{X}, \mathbf{t})$. Dividing by $J^0 = \det \mathbf{F}^0$, using (15.88), and noting that $\rho_0 = \rho J = \rho^0 J^0$, we arrive at

$$\frac{1}{J^0}(\delta \tilde{T}_{ji})_{.j} - \delta E_i^+ \bar{\partial}_j P_j^0 - {}^0E_i^+ \bar{\partial}_j p_j + \varepsilon_{ijk} \overset{*}{p}_j B^0_k = \rho^0 \ddot{u}_i,$$

where $\bar{\partial}_j = \partial/\partial \xi_j$, and

$$\mathbf{p} = \frac{1}{J^0}\mathbf{F}^0\, \delta\boldsymbol{\Pi} \tag{20.29}$$

(cf. (20.18)). Moreover, invoking again (15.88), we have that

$$\frac{1}{J^0}(\delta \tilde{T}_{ji})_{.j} = \frac{1}{J^0} F^0_{pj}\, \bar{\partial}_p\, \delta \tilde{T}_{ji} \equiv \bar{\partial}_p \sigma_{pi},$$

where

$$\sigma_{pi} = \frac{1}{J^0} F^0_{pj}\, \delta \tilde{T}_{ji}. \tag{20.30}$$

The equations of motion can now be written as

$$\bar{\partial}_j \sigma_{ji} - \delta E_i^+ \bar{\partial}_j P_j^0 - {}^0E_i^+ \bar{\partial}_j p_j + \varepsilon_{ijk} \overset{*}{p}_j B^0_k = \rho^0 \ddot{u}_i. \tag{20.31}$$

It remains to derive explicit representations of σ_{pi} and δE_i^+. Noting that

$$\tilde{T}_{ji} = \frac{\partial W}{\partial E_{mj}} F_{im}, \qquad T_{ki} = \frac{1}{J}\frac{\partial W}{\partial E_{mn}} F_{km} F_{in},$$

and letting

$$\delta F_{km} = (\bar{\partial}_j u_k) F^0_{jm} \equiv H_{kj} F^0_{jm}, \qquad H_{kj} = u_{k.j}, \tag{20.32}$$

we obtain

$$\sigma_{pi} = T^0_{ps}H_{is} + L_{piks}H_{ks} + S_{pir}p_r, \tag{20.33}$$

where

$$L_{piks} = \frac{\partial^2 W^0}{\partial E_{jr}\,\partial E_{qm}} F^0_{pj}F^0_{ir}F^0_{kq}F^0_{sm}, \tag{20.34}$$

$$S_{pir} = \frac{\partial^2 W^0}{\partial E_{jm}\,\partial \Pi_s} F^0_{pj}F^0_{im}(\mathbf{F}^0)^{-1}_{sr}, \tag{20.35}$$

and

$$T^0_{ps} = \frac{\partial W^0}{\partial E_{mn}} F^0_{pm}F^0_{sn}. \tag{20.36}$$

The vectors **E** and **B** can undergo variations $\delta'\mathbf{E} = \mathbf{e}$, $\delta'\mathbf{B} = \mathbf{b}$ even in the absence of deformations; therefore, the total variations are given by

$$\delta E_i = e_i + u_j\bar{\partial}_j E^0_i, \qquad \delta B_i = b_i + u_j\bar{\partial}_j B^0_i. \tag{20.37}$$

In the limit of small displacements, then,

$$\delta E^+_i = e_i + u_j\bar{\partial}_j E^0_i + \varepsilon_{ijk}\dot{u}_j B^0_k. \tag{20.38}$$

In analogy with (20.37), we let $\delta P_i = u_j\bar{\partial}_j P_i + \delta(J^{-1}F_{ij}\Pi_j)$. With

$$\delta\left(\frac{1}{J}F_{ij}\right) = \frac{\partial}{\partial F_{km}}\left(\frac{1}{J}F_{ij}\right)\delta F_{km} = -\frac{1}{J}F_{ij}H_{rr} + \frac{1}{J}H_{ir}F_{rj},$$

we obtain

$$\delta P_i = p_i + u_j\bar{\partial}_j P^0_i - P^0_i H_{rr} + H_{ij}P^0_j. \tag{20.39}$$

Recalling that the rate $\overset{*}{\mathbf{P}}$ compensates for the deformation of the body, we set

$$\delta\overset{*}{P}_i = \dot{p}_i. \tag{20.40}$$

To obtain a representation of the incremental form of (20.27), we introduce the inverse of the polarizability tensor $\boldsymbol{\chi}$ by

$$\chi^{-1}_{ij} = \frac{\rho_0^2}{\rho^0}\frac{\partial^2\Sigma}{\partial\Pi_m\,\partial\Pi_n}(\mathbf{F}^0)^{-1}_{mi}(\mathbf{F}^0)^{-1}_{nj}. \tag{20.41}$$

Neglecting the variation of **G**, thus $\delta(\mathbf{G} \times \overset{*}{\mathbf{P}}) = \mathbf{G} \times \dot{\mathbf{p}}$, we arrive at

$$e_i + u_j\bar{\partial}_j E_i^0 + \varepsilon_{ijk}\dot{u}_j B_k^0 + {}_Le_i + \varepsilon_{ijk}G_j\dot{p}_k = 0, \tag{20.42}$$

where the increment of the local field, ${}_L\mathbf{e}$, is given by

$${}_Le_i = -S_{pmi}H_{mp} - \chi_{mi}^{-1}p_m + {}_LE_m^0 H_{mi}. \tag{20.43}$$

The linearization of the remaining equations is straightforward. Thus (13.28) reduce to

$$\text{curl}\mathbf{e} + \dot{\mathbf{b}} = 0, \qquad \text{div}\mathbf{b} = 0, \tag{20.44}$$

whereas, by (20.39), $\text{div}(\mathbf{E} + \mathbf{P}) = 0$ becomes

$$\text{div}\mathbf{e} = -(p_i + u_j P_{i,j}^0 + u_{i,j}P_j^0 - u_{j,j}P_i^0)_{,i}. \tag{20.45}$$

Finally, because $\mathbf{J}_P = \overset{*}{\mathbf{P}} - \bar{\mathbf{v}}\,\text{div}\mathbf{P}$, we find from (13.70) that

$$\text{curl}\mathbf{b} - \dot{\mathbf{e}} - \dot{\mathbf{p}} + \bar{\mathbf{v}}\,\text{div}\mathbf{P}^0 = \mathbf{0}. \tag{20.46}$$

The field equations (20.31), (20.44)–(20.46), together with the constitutive equations (20.33), (20.43), make up Toupin's linearized theory. The classical linear theory of piezoelectricity is obtained by neglecting **G**, and assuming that initially stress, electric field, and polarization vanish. The basic equations are then

$$\rho_0\ddot{u}_i = \sigma_{pi,p},$$

$$\text{curl}\mathbf{B} - \dot{\mathbf{E}} - \dot{\mathbf{P}} = \mathbf{0}, \qquad \text{div}(\mathbf{E} + \mathbf{P}) = 0,$$

$$\text{curl}\mathbf{E} + \dot{\mathbf{B}} = \mathbf{0}, \qquad \text{div}\mathbf{B} = 0,$$

and $$\sigma_{pi} = L_{piks}\tilde{E}_{ks} + S_{pik}P_k, \qquad E_i = S_{mni}\tilde{E}_{mn} + \chi_{im}^{-1}p_m.$$

In isotropic media the constitutive potential Σ depends on the isotropic invariants $\text{tr}\mathbf{E}$, $\text{tr}\mathbf{E}^2$, $\text{tr}\mathbf{E}^3$, $\Pi_i\Pi_i$, $\Pi_iE_{ij}\Pi_j$, $\Pi_iE_{ij}^2\Pi_j$. If $\mathbf{\Pi}^0 = \mathbf{0}$ in the prestrained configuration, then it is not difficult to see that

$$\boldsymbol{\chi} = A_0\mathbf{1} + A_1\mathbf{B}^0 + A_2(\mathbf{B}^0)^2, \tag{20.47}$$

where $\mathbf{B} = \mathbf{F}\mathbf{F}^T$, and A_0, A_1, A_2 depend on $\text{tr}\mathbf{E}$, $\text{tr}\mathbf{E}^2$, $\text{tr}\mathbf{E}^3$ only. Because the dielectric tensor $\mathbf{K} = \mathbf{1} + \boldsymbol{\chi}$ will have, in general, unequal principal values, the material will be birefringent i.e. exhibit the photoelastic effect (cf. Problem 2).

Problems

1. Give a detailed derivation of (20.14).

2. ("Birefringence.") Anisotropy of the relation between E_i and P_i gives rise to double refraction (*birefringence*) of light, whereby two images of the same object are seen when looking through a transparent plate. This anisotropy may be a material property, as is the case in crystals, or may be induced into isotropic materials by deformation (cf. (20.47)). The latter effect is nonlinear, because S_{ijk} are then functions of strains; it is called the *photoelastic effect.*

   To account for double refraction, investigate the propagation of linearly polarized plane light waves in media with negligible conductivity and permeability. Then $\mathbf{j} = \mathbf{0}$, $\mathbf{B} = \mathbf{H}$, and the relevant field equations are

$$\partial_\tau \mathbf{B} + \operatorname{curl}\mathbf{E} = \mathbf{0}, \qquad \partial_\tau \mathbf{D} - \operatorname{curl}\mathbf{B} = \mathbf{0}. \tag{a}$$

With $\mathbf{E} = \mathbf{E}^0\Delta$, $\mathbf{B} = \mathbf{B}^0\Delta$, where $\Delta = \exp\,[ik(\tau - r^{-1}\mathbf{x} \cdot \mathbf{N})]$, $\tau = ct$, $\mathbf{E}^0$ and $\mathbf{B}^0$ are constants, $\mathbf{N}$ is a unit vector in the direction of propagation, and r is the ratio of the phase velocity to the speed of light in a vacuum (it is the inverse of the index of refraction, n), obtain from (a) that

$$\mathbf{B} = \frac{1}{r}(\mathbf{N} \times \mathbf{E}), \qquad \mathbf{D} = -\frac{1}{r}(\mathbf{N} \times \mathbf{B}). \tag{b}$$

Further, by $r^2\mathbf{D} = -\mathbf{N} \times (\mathbf{N} \times \mathbf{E})$, show that

$$r^2 D_i = E_i - N_i \mathbf{E} \cdot \mathbf{N}. \tag{c}$$

Next, assume a constitutive equation $D_i = \varepsilon_{ij}E_j$, where $\varepsilon_{ij} = \varepsilon_{ji}$ is the dielectric tensor. Show that, in the principal coordinate system of ε_{ij}, $(r_1^2 - r^2)D_1 = N_1\mathbf{N} \cdot \mathbf{E}, \ldots, \ldots$, where $r_{\underline{1}}^{-2}$ are the principal values of ε_{ij}. Thus obtain from $\mathbf{D} \cdot \mathbf{N} = 0$ that

$$\frac{N_1^2}{r_1^2 - r^2} + \frac{N_2^2}{r_2^2 - r^2} + \frac{N_3^2}{r_2^3 - r^2} = 0 \tag{d}$$

Now verify that to each direction $\mathbf{N}$ there will correspond, in general, two distinct speeds of propagation, p and q. Show that from

$$D_1 : D_2 : D_3 = \frac{N_1}{r_1^2 - r^2} : \frac{N_2}{r_2^2 - r^2} : \frac{N_3}{r_3^2 - r^2}$$

it follows that

$$\mathbf{D}' \cdot \mathbf{D}'' = \frac{\mathbf{N}\cdot\mathbf{E}'\,\mathbf{N}\cdot\mathbf{E}''}{m^2 - p^2}\left[\frac{N_1^2}{r_1^2 - p^2} - \frac{N_1^2}{r_1^2 - q^2} + \frac{N_2^2}{r_2^2 - p^2} - \frac{N_2^2}{r_2^2 - q^2} + \frac{N_3^2}{r_3^2 - p^2} - \frac{N_3^2}{r_1^2 - q^2}\right],$$

where $\mathbf{D}'$, $\mathbf{E}'$ correspond to p, and $\mathbf{D}''$, $\mathbf{E}''$ correspond to q. Note that because p and q satisfy (d) separately, $\mathbf{D}'$ is perpendicular to $\mathbf{D}''$ whenever $p \neq q$, i.e. the amplitudes of the two linearly polarized waves are perpendicular.

A common arrangement for the observation of double refraction is as follows. Linearly polarized light may be produced by passing the light through a polarizing filter. Two "crossed" polarizing filters, i.e. two polarizing filters with their polarizing axes set perpendicularly, make up a *polariscope.* Evidently a polariscope acts like an opaque body. If, however, a transparent body is inserted between the two filters, and if this body rotates the plane of polarization (defined by $\mathbf{N}$ and $\mathbf{E}^0$, say), then some light will get through the polariscope. If the body is a crystal plate, then the incident ray will split into two rays. The speeds of propagation of the two rays will be in general different; correspondingly, the amplitude vectors of the rays will be perpendicular. After passage through the second filter, the amplitude vectors of the two rays will be aligned with the polarizing axis of the second filter, but there will now be a phase difference ε. To calculate ε, let the thickness of the plate be d, and denote by M_1 and M_2 the numbers of wave lengths spanning d. Then $M_1 = d/\lambda_1 = dn_1/\lambda$, $M_2 = d/\lambda_2 = dn_2/\lambda$, where $\lambda = \omega/c$ is the wave length in a vacuum, and n_1, n_2 are the refractive indices associated with the two rays. Consequently, the phase difference is given by $\varepsilon = 2\pi d(n_1 - n_2)/\lambda$. A wave $v = a\cos\phi$ emerging from the first filter will split upon entering the crystal plate into two waves with mutually perpendicular amplitude vectors, e.g. $X = a\cos\phi\sin\theta$, $Y = a\cos\phi\cos\theta$. The waves emerging from the plate will be $X' = a\cos(\phi + \varepsilon)\sin\theta$, $Y = a\cos\phi\cos\theta$, say, so that after passing through the second filter (whose polarizing axis is perpendicular to that of the first filter!), we should obtain the single wave

$$u = X'\cos\theta - Y\sin\theta = -\frac{a}{4}\sin 2\theta\sin\left(\phi + \frac{\varepsilon}{2}\right)\sin\frac{\varepsilon}{2}.$$

Suppose that $\theta \neq 0$, $\theta \neq \pi/2$, i.e. that the amplitude vector of the incident beam does not lie along either of the polarizing axes of the crystal plate. Then the beam will be extinguished whenever the phase difference is a multiple of 2π, thus whenever $d = N\lambda/(n_1 - n_2)$, where N is an integer. In particular, placing a crystal wedge into the polariscope we should observe equally spaced dark bands.

An isotropic, unstrained plate placed into the polariscope will prevent any light from getting through. A homogeneous straining of the plate, on the other hand, will make the plate optically anisotropic, so that some light will be transmitted. As is shown in works on photoelasticity, the phase difference ε is proportional to the maximum shearing stress, so that, as the strain is increased, the illumination of the plate will change continuously between light and dark. In particular, inhomogeneous straining will give rise to patterns of dark and light fringes.

Section 21

SMALL DEFORMATIONS SUPERPOSED ON FINITE DEFORMATIONS

In this section we shall formulate a *linearized theory of small deformations superposed on finite deformations*. This theory provides a natural extension of the classical, linear theory of elasticity, as the initial configuration need no longer be undeformed. It also establishes a basis for discussing initial stress problems, stability of finite deformations, and propagation of weak waves in prestrained bodies.

Elastic response of prestrained bodies

We consider a finite motion of a particle $\mathbf{X}$ to an intermediate position $\boldsymbol{\xi}$, and assume that the motion from $\boldsymbol{\xi}$ to the final position $\mathbf{x}$ is small, meaning that the corresponding displacement vector $\mathbf{u}$ and its gradients are small in the sense explained on p. 333. We shall mark variables associated with the intermediate configuration by a superscript 0. Thus, with

$$\mathbf{x} = \boldsymbol{\xi} + \mathbf{u}, \tag{21.1}$$

we obtain

$$\delta\mathbf{F} \equiv \mathbf{F} - \mathbf{F}^0 = \mathbf{H}\mathbf{F}^0, \tag{21.2}$$

where

$$F^0_{im} = \frac{\partial \xi_i}{\partial X_m}, \qquad H_{im} = \frac{\partial u_i}{\partial \xi_m} \tag{21.3}$$

(note that $\partial u_i/\partial \xi_j = \partial u_i/\partial x_k(\delta_{kj} + \partial u_k/\partial \xi_j) \approx \partial u_i/\partial x_j$). According to (15.87), (17.34), the stress relation can be written as follows,

$$\mathbf{T} = \frac{1}{J}\mathbf{F}\mathbf{k}(\mathbf{C})\mathbf{F}^T = \mathbf{F}\mathbf{f}(\mathbf{C})\mathbf{F}^T, \qquad \mathbf{f}(\mathbf{C}) = \frac{\mathbf{k}(\mathbf{C})}{\sqrt{\det\mathbf{C}}}. \tag{21.4}$$

We may define the *incremental stress relation* by

$$\delta T_{ij} = T_{ij} - T_{ij}^0 \doteq \left.\frac{\partial T_{ij}}{\partial F_{km}}\right|_{\mathbf{F}^0} \delta F_{km}, \tag{21.5}$$

where $\mathbf{T}^0 = \mathbf{F}^0\mathbf{f}(\mathbf{C}^0)(\mathbf{F}^0)^T$. Let

$$E_{prmk} = E_{prkm} = \frac{\partial f_{pr}}{\partial E_{km}}, \tag{21.6}$$

where $2\mathbf{E} = \mathbf{C} - \mathbf{1}$. Unless stated otherwise, it will be understood that $\mathbf{E}$ is evaluated at $\mathbf{C}^0$. Using (17.35), we readily obtain

$$\delta T_{ij} = \tilde{R}_{ik}T_{kj}^0 - T_{ik}^0\tilde{R}_{kj} + L_{ij}[\tilde{\mathbf{E}}], \tag{21.7}$$

$$\begin{aligned} L_{ij}[\tilde{\mathbf{E}}] &= \tilde{E}_{ik}T_{kj}^0 + T_{ik}^0\tilde{E}_{kj} + \bar{E}_{ijkm}\tilde{E}_{km}, \\ \bar{E}_{ijkm} &= F_{ip}^0F_{jq}^0E_{pqrs}F_{kr}^0F_{ms}^0, \end{aligned} \tag{21.8}$$

where $\tilde{\mathbf{E}}$ and $\tilde{\mathbf{R}}$ are the linearized strains and rotations based on $H_{im} = \partial u_i/\partial \xi_m$.

If the initial deformation vanishes, i.e. $\mathbf{F}^0 = \mathbf{1}$, $\mathbf{T}^0 = \mathbf{0}$, then $\delta T_{ij} = T_{ij} = \bar{E}_{ijkm}\tilde{E}_{km} = C_{ijkm}\tilde{E}_{km}$ is the linear Hooke's law. Comparing this with (21.8), we see that the response of a prestrained body to additional, infinitesimal deformations differs from (14.28) in two ways. First, *the stress increments are influenced by the infinitesimal rotation* $\tilde{\mathbf{R}}$. Second, the effective elasticities depend not only on material properties but also on the initial deformation.

To determine the cases in which $\delta\mathbf{T}$ is independent of the incremental rotation $\tilde{\mathbf{R}}$, let us suppose that $\mathbf{T}^0$ and $\tilde{\mathbf{R}}$ are represented in the principal coordinate system of $\mathbf{T}^0$, e.g. $\mathbf{T}^0 = \text{diag}(A, B, C)$,

$$\|\tilde{\mathbf{R}}\| = \left\| \begin{matrix} 0 & \alpha & \beta \\ -\alpha & 0 & \gamma \\ -\beta & -\gamma & 0 \end{matrix} \right\|.$$

Then it is easy to verify that the vanishing of $\tilde{\mathbf{R}}\mathbf{T}^0 - \mathbf{T}^0\tilde{\mathbf{R}}$ means that

(a) $\alpha = \beta = \gamma = 0$ if $A \neq B, B \neq C, C \neq A$

(b) $\beta = \gamma = 0$ (α arbitrary) if $A = B \neq C$

(c) α, β, γ arbitrary if $A = B = C$.

Thus, in particular, if the initial stress is hydrostatic (i.e. $A = B = C$), then $\delta\mathbf{T}$ is independent of the incremental rotation $\tilde{\mathbf{R}}$.

For anisotropic materials it is expedient to assume that a strain-energy function exists. By (15.87), the isotropic stress relation is then

$$\mathbf{T} = \frac{2}{J}\,[(\mathrm{II}W_2 + \mathrm{III}W_3)\mathbf{1} + W_1\mathbf{B} - \mathrm{III}W_2\mathbf{B}^{-1}]; \tag{21.9}$$

if the material is incompressible, we set $J = \sqrt{\mathrm{III}} = 1$, and replace $2(\mathrm{II}W_2 + \mathrm{III}W_3)$ by $-p$.

With (21.8), (15.87), the incremental stress relation for hyperelastic materials is given by

$$\delta\mathbf{T} = -\mathbf{T}^0\,\mathrm{tr}\tilde{\mathbf{E}} + \tilde{\mathbf{R}}\mathbf{T}^0 - \mathbf{T}^0\tilde{\mathbf{R}} + \mathbf{L}[\tilde{\mathbf{E}}], \qquad E_{ijkm} = \frac{1}{J^0}\frac{\partial^2 W}{\partial E_{ij}\,\partial E_{km}}. \tag{21.10}$$

Let us recall that any deformation $\mathbf{F}^0 = \mathbf{R}^0\mathbf{U}^0$ such that $\mathbf{U}^0$ commutes with the symmetry operations $\mathbf{S}$ will map one undistorted state into another (cf. (17.1) *et seq.*). Because, trivially, $\mathbf{U}^0\mathbf{1} = \mathbf{1}\mathbf{U}^0$, it follows that, after a hydrostatic compression $\mathbf{F}^0 = -V\mathbf{1}$, the coefficients $\bar{E}_{ijkm}$ will have the same symmetries as the coefficients C_{ijkm} that describe the response from a natural state. For instance, if the material is transversely isotropic about z axis, and $F_{ij} = -V\delta_{ij}$, we obtain†

$$\begin{aligned}\bar{E}_{ijkm} = V^4[&A\delta_{ij}\delta_{km} - B(\delta_{ik}\delta_{jm} + \delta_{im}\delta_{jk}) + C(\delta_{ij}\delta_{3k}\delta_{3m}\\ &+ \delta_{km}\delta_{3i}\delta_{3j}) + \tfrac{1}{2}W_5\,(\delta_{3i}\delta_{3k}\delta_{jm} + \delta_{3i}\delta_{3m}\delta_{jk}\\ &+ \delta_{3j}\delta_{3k}\delta_{im} + \delta_{3j}\delta_{3m}\delta_{ik}) + W_{44}\delta_{3i}\delta_{3j}\delta_{3k}\delta_{3m}],\end{aligned}$$

where $A = W_{11} + 4V^2W_{12} + 2V^4W_{13} + 4V^4W_{22} + V^8W_{33} + W_2 + V^2W_3$, $B = \frac{1}{2}(W_2 + V^2W_3)$, $C = W_{14} + 4V^2W_{24} + 2V^4W_{34}$. As a comparison with (14.47) will show, $\bar{E}_{ijkm}$ is still a transversely anisotropic tensor.

The incremental stress relations for isotropic materials are relatively simple. We recall

$$M_{rk} = B_{rk}\frac{\partial}{\partial\mathrm{I}} + (\mathrm{I}B_{rk} - B^2_{rk})\frac{\partial}{\partial\mathrm{II}} + \mathrm{III}\delta_{rk}\frac{\partial}{\partial\mathrm{III}}; \tag{17.39}R$$

in the principal coordinate system of $\mathbf{B}$,

$$M_{rk} = B_{\underline{r}}\delta_{rk}M_{\underline{r}}, \qquad M_{\underline{r}} = \frac{\partial}{\partial\mathrm{I}} + (\mathrm{I} - B_{\underline{r}})\frac{\partial}{\partial\mathrm{II}} + \frac{\mathrm{III}}{B_{\underline{r}}}\frac{\partial}{\partial\mathrm{III}}. \tag{21.11}$$

† Cf. [24].

Then, by (17.18), (21.5), and (17.38),†

$$\delta T_{ij} = 2H_{mk}(\delta_{ij}M_{km}\delta + B_{ij}M_{km}\alpha + B_{ij}^{-1}M_{km}\gamma) + (H_{ik}B_{kj} + B_{ik}H_{jk})\alpha - (H_{ki}B_{kj}^{-1} + H_{kj}B_{ki}^{-1})\gamma, \quad (21.12)$$

where all coefficients are evaluated at $\mathbf{B}^0 = \mathbf{F}^0(\mathbf{F}^0)^T$, and the superscript 0 on $\mathbf{B}$ has been omitted. In the principal coordinate system of $\mathbf{B}^0$, (21.12) simplifies to

$$\delta T_{ij} = \alpha_{\underline{ki}}\tilde{E}_{kk}\delta_{ij} + \beta_{\underline{ji}}H_{ij} + \beta_{\underline{ij}}H_{ji}, \quad (21.13)$$

where

$$\alpha_{\underline{ki}} = 2B_{\underline{k}}(M_{\underline{k}}\delta + B_{\underline{i}}M_{\underline{k}}\alpha + B_{\underline{i}}^{-1}M_{\underline{k}}\gamma), \qquad \beta_{\underline{ij}} = \alpha B_{\underline{i}} - \gamma B_{\underline{j}}^{-1}. \quad (21.14)$$

Further, in $\tilde{\mathbf{R}}\mathbf{T}^0 - \mathbf{T}^0\tilde{\mathbf{R}}$ only terms containing normal stresses remain. We obtain, for instance, $\delta T_{12} = \tilde{R}_{12}(T_{22}^0 - T_{11}^0) + \alpha\tilde{E}_{12}(B_1 + B_2) - \gamma\tilde{E}_{12}(B_1^{-1} + B_2^{-1})$; in view of $T_{22}^0 - T_{11}^0 = (B_2 - B_1)\alpha + (B_2^{-1} - B_1^{-1})\gamma$, it follows that

$$\delta T_{12} = u_{1,2}(B_2\alpha - B_1^{-1}\gamma) + u_{2,1}(B_1\alpha - B_2^{-1}\gamma). \quad (21.15)$$

If the initial stress is hydrostatic, so that $\mathbf{B}^0 = B\mathbf{1}$, then (21.13) takes on the same form as the Hooke's law,

$$\delta T_{ij} = \bar{\lambda}\delta_{ij}\tilde{E}_{kk} + 2\bar{\mu}\tilde{E}_{ij}, \quad (21.16)$$

where the *effective moduli* $\bar{\lambda}$ *and* $\bar{\mu}$ are given by

$$\bar{\mu} = B\alpha(\mathrm{I}, \mathrm{II}, \mathrm{III}) - B^{-1}\gamma(\mathrm{I}, \mathrm{II}, \mathrm{III}),$$
$$\bar{\lambda} = 2B(M\delta + BM\alpha + B^{-1}M\gamma)$$
$$= 2B\left[\frac{\partial\delta}{\partial\mathrm{I}} + 2B\frac{\partial\delta}{\partial\mathrm{II}} + B^2\frac{\partial\delta}{\partial\mathrm{III}} + B\frac{\partial\alpha}{\partial\mathrm{I}} + 2B^2\frac{\partial\alpha}{\partial\mathrm{II}} + B^3\frac{\partial\alpha}{\partial\mathrm{III}} + \frac{1}{B}\frac{\partial\gamma}{\partial\mathrm{I}} + 2\frac{\partial\gamma}{\partial\mathrm{II}} + B\frac{\partial\gamma}{\partial\mathrm{III}}\right]. \quad (21.17)$$

Consequently, if the initial stress is hydrostatic, then the response to additional small deformations is linearly elastic, with the effective elastic coefficients depending on the initial state of deformation.

† Cf. also Problem 1.

Let us derive a more compact form of (21.17). To do so, we first write, by (17.18),

$$-p = \delta(3B, 3B^2, B^3) + B\alpha(3B, 3B^2, B^3) + B^{-1}\gamma(3B, 3B^2, B^3). \tag{21.18}$$

Next, we note the identity $\rho = \exp(\log \rho)$, from which it follows that $d\rho/d(\log \rho) = \rho$, or,

$$\frac{d}{d(\log \rho)} = \rho \frac{d}{d\rho}.$$

In a deformation $\mathbf{B}^0 = B\mathbf{1}$ the balance of mass is given by $\rho B^{3/2} = \rho_0$; therefore

$$\rho \frac{d}{d\rho} = \rho \frac{dB}{d\rho} \frac{d}{dB} = -\frac{2}{3} B \frac{d}{dB}.$$

Applying the operator $d/d(\log \rho)$ to (21.18), and taking into account

$$\frac{\partial \mathrm{I}}{\partial B} = 3, \quad \frac{\partial \mathrm{II}}{\partial B} = 6B, \quad \frac{\partial \mathrm{III}}{\partial B} = 3B^2,$$

we arrive at

$$\frac{dp}{d(\log \rho)} = 2B\left[\frac{\partial \delta}{\partial \mathrm{I}} + 2B\frac{\partial \delta}{\partial \mathrm{II}} + B^2\frac{\partial \delta}{\partial \mathrm{III}} + \frac{1}{3}\alpha - \frac{1}{3B^2}\gamma \right.$$
$$\left. + B\left(\frac{\partial \alpha}{\partial \mathrm{I}} + 2B\frac{\partial \alpha}{\partial \mathrm{II}} + B^2\frac{\partial \alpha}{\partial \mathrm{III}}\right) + B^{-1}\left(\frac{\partial \gamma}{\partial \mathrm{I}} + 2B\frac{\partial \gamma}{\partial \mathrm{II}} + B^2\frac{\partial \gamma}{\partial \mathrm{III}}\right)\right].$$

Comparison with (21.17) then yields

$$\bar{\lambda} = \frac{d\tilde{p}}{d(\log \rho)} - \frac{2}{3}\bar{\mu}, \tag{21.19}$$

where $p = \tilde{p}(\rho)$ is obtained by eliminating B between (21.18) and $\rho B^{3/2} = \rho_0$.

The equations (21.13), (21.14) clearly show that in a deformed configuration the isotropic response is different from the isotropic response $T_{ij} = \lambda u_{k,k}\delta_{ij} + \mu(u_{i,j} + u_{j,i})$ from a natural state. In (21.13) the normal stresses depend only on the normal strains, but through the array of nine coefficients in the place of two coefficients λ and μ. The shearing strains are paired only with the shearing stresses acting in the same plane, but the stresses also depend on the infinitesimal rotations; moreover, the response coefficients are distinct from the coefficients relating normal stresses and strains. Thus we may speak of a *quasi-anisotropic response*. The loss of isotropy is, of course, only apparent; the total deformation is governed by the elastic law (17.18). The quasi-anisotropic law (21.13) was obtained by decomposing the total deformation into finite and infinitesimal parts, i.e. its form is a particular feature of the representation rather than expressing a change in material properties.

For incompressible media the incremental stress relation is given by

$$\delta \mathbf{T} = -\delta p \mathbf{1} + \tilde{\mathbf{R}}\mathbf{T}^0 - \mathbf{T}^0\tilde{\mathbf{R}} + \mathbf{L}[\tilde{\mathbf{E}}], \qquad \bar{E}_{ijkm} = F^0_{ip}F^0_{jq}\frac{\partial^2 W}{\partial E_{pq}\,\partial E_{rs}}F^0_{kr}F^0_{ms} \tag{21.20}$$

in general, and by

$$\delta T_{ij} = -\delta p\, \delta_{ij} + \beta_{\underline{ji}} H_{ij} + \beta_{\underline{ij}} H_{ji} \tag{21.21}$$

if the response is isotropic.

Static problems

To investigate the boundary conditions and the equations of equilibrium for the incremental stresses, it is convenient to introduce a stress tensor $\hat{\mathbf{T}}$ that is analogous to the Piola-Kirchhoff stress $\tilde{\mathbf{T}}$, except that $\hat{\mathbf{T}}$ is referred to the intermediate configuration. Thus, in accord with (15.87),

$$\hat{T}_{jk} = \hat{J}\xi_{j,m}T_{mk}, \qquad \hat{J} = \det\left(\frac{\partial x_i}{\partial \xi_j}\right). \tag{21.22}$$

For small displacements $u_i = x_i - \xi_i$, (21.22) is approximated by

$$\begin{aligned} \hat{J} &= 1 + \operatorname{tr}\mathbf{H}, \\ \hat{T}_{jk} &= T_{jk} + T_{jk}\operatorname{tr}\mathbf{H} - H_{jm}T_{mk}, \end{aligned} \tag{21.23}$$

where $H_{jm} = \partial u_j/\partial \xi_m \doteq \partial u_j/\partial x_m$, $T_{mk} = T^0_{mk} + \delta T_{mk}$. From

$$\frac{\partial T^0_{ji}}{\partial \xi_j} + \rho^0 b^0_i = 0, \qquad \frac{\partial \hat{T}_{ji}}{\partial \xi_j} + \rho^0 b_i = 0$$

(cf. (15.89)), we then obtain

$$\frac{\partial}{\partial \xi_j}\delta T_{ji} - H_{jm}\frac{\partial}{\partial \xi_j}T^0_{mi} + \rho^0[b_i - b^0_i(1 + \operatorname{tr}\mathbf{H})] = 0. \tag{21.24}$$

If the initial deformation is homogeneous, so that T^0_{mi} = const., and if the body forces are constant, then (21.24) simplify to

$$\frac{\partial}{\partial \xi_j} \delta T_{ji} - \rho^0 b_i^0 \operatorname{tr}\mathbf{H} = 0. \tag{21.25}$$

The stress boundary conditions that go with either set of equilibrium equations follow from $\delta t_k = (\hat{T}_{jk} - T^0_{jk})n^0_j$, where $\mathbf{n}^0$ are the unit normal vectors of the intermediate configuration ∂V^0 of the boundary. With (21.23), we get

$$\delta t_k = n^0_j \delta T_{jk} + n^0_j T^0_{jk} \operatorname{tr}\mathbf{H} - n^0_j H_{jm} T^0_{mk}. \tag{21.26}$$

To illustrate the foregoing theory, let us investigate the *superposition of small twists upon large extensions.*† The combined torsion and extension problem discussed in Section 18 was formulated only for circular cylinders of incompressible material. The solution outlined here will be applicable to arbitrary prismatic bars of compressible material.

In simple extension the only nonvanishing stress is (cf. (18.6), (18.8))

$$T^0_{zz} = (1 - \lambda^2)(\alpha V^2 - \gamma\lambda^{-2}V^{-2}),$$

where α and γ are functions of the invariants $\mathrm{I} = V^2(1 + 2\lambda^2)$, $\mathrm{II} = \lambda^2 V^4(2 + \lambda^2)$, $\mathrm{III} = \lambda^4 V^6$. We now superpose a torsion described by

$$u_1 = -Dyz, \qquad u_2 = Dxz, \qquad u_3 = D\phi(x, y) \tag{21.27}$$

(cf. (15.96) *et seq.*), where ϕ is called the *warping function.* Because $H_{11} = H_{22} = H_{33} = 0$, it follows from (21.13) that $\delta T_{11} = \delta T_{22} = \delta T_{33} = 0$. Further, $\delta T_{12} = 0$ and

$$\frac{\delta T_{zx}}{D} = \mu(V)(\lambda^2\phi_{,x} - y), \qquad \frac{\delta T_{yz}}{D} = \mu(V)(\lambda^2\phi_{,y} + x),$$
$$\mu(V) = V^2\alpha - \lambda^{-2}V^{-2}\gamma. \tag{21.28}$$

The only nontrivial condition of equilibrium is $\delta T_{zx,x} + \delta T_{zy,y} = 0$, so that ϕ is governed by the equation

$$\phi_{,xx} + \phi_{,yy} = 0. \tag{21.29}$$

† Cf. *NFTM*, pp. 264–267.

Using (21.26), we find that the only nontrivial boundary condition is $\delta t_3 = n_1^0 \delta T_{13} + n_2^0 \delta T_{23} - n_1^0 H_{13} T_{33}^0 - n_2^0 H_{23} T_{33}^0 = 0$, from which it follows that

$$(\phi_{,x} - y)n_x + (\phi_{,y} + x)n_y = 0. \tag{21.30}$$

It is easy to verify that the warping function $\Phi(X, Y)$ describing torsion of the undeformed body obeys the same type of equations, thus $\Phi_{,XX} + \Phi_{,YY} = 0$, $(\Phi_{,X} - Y)N_X + (\Phi_{,Y} + X)N_Y = 0$. Because the homogeneous deformation $\xi = \lambda V X$, $\eta = \lambda V Y$ does not affect the shape of the cross sections, we conclude that the warping function ϕ can be obtained from Φ by the scaling

$$\phi = \lambda^2 V^2 \Phi\left(\frac{x}{\lambda V}, \frac{y}{\lambda V}\right). \tag{21.31}$$

The axial force N is found from

$$N = \iint_A T_{zz}\, dx\, dy = (1 - \lambda^2)\mu(V)A = (1 - \lambda^2)\mu(V)A_0\lambda^2 V^2, \tag{21.32}$$

where A and A_0 are the final and initial cross-sectional areas, respectively. Similarly, the torque M is given by

$$\begin{aligned} M &= \iint_A (xT_{zy} - yT_{zx})\, dx\, dy = D\mu(V)\bar{J}, \\ \bar{J} &= \iint_A (x^2 + y^2 + \lambda^2 x\phi_{,y} - \lambda^2 y\phi_{,x})\, dx\, dy. \end{aligned} \tag{21.33}$$

In analogy with the linearized theory, we call $\tau(V) = \bar{J}\mu(V)$ the *torsional rigidity*. The torsional rigidity of the undeformed body is denoted by $\tau(1)$, thus

$$\tau(1) = \bar{J}_0\mu(1), \quad \bar{J}_0 = \iint_{A_0} (X^2 + Y^2 + X\Phi_{,Y} - Y\Phi_{,X})\, dX\, dY. \tag{21.34}$$

From these it follows that†

$$\tau(V) = \frac{M}{D} = \mu(V)\lambda^4 V^4[I_0 - \lambda^2(I_0 - \bar{J}^0)], \tag{21.35}$$

† Green and Shield [200].

where I_0 is the polar moment of inertia of the undeformed cross section. For incompressible media, $\lambda^2 = V^{-3}$ and

$$V^5\tau(V) = \mu(V)[V^3 I_0 - (I_0 - \bar{J}^0)]. \tag{21.36}$$

Except for circular cylinders, i.e. when $I_0 = \bar{J}^0 = \frac{1}{2}\pi R^4$, a compression

$$V^3 = \frac{I_0 - \bar{J}^0}{I_0} = 1 \tag{21.37}$$

may exist at which the torsional resistance vanishes! Of course, this does not mean that a cylinder can be twisted at will because the linearized solution is applicable only to small twists. For an elliptic cylinder, $I_0 = \frac{1}{4}\pi ab(a^2 + b^2)$ and $\bar{J}^0 = \pi a^3 b^3/(a^2 + b^2)$,† so that $V^3 = (a^2 - b^2)^2/(a^2 + b^2)^2$; if we choose $a = 4$, $b = 1$, then $V \approx 0.92$.

In curvilinear coordinates the incremental stress relations (21.12) must be replaced by

$$\begin{aligned}\delta T_{ab} &= 2u_{e;c}(\delta_{ab}M_{ce}\delta + B_{ab}M_{ce}\alpha + B_{ab}^{-1}M_{ce}\gamma) \\ &\quad + (u_{a;c}B_{cb} + B_{ac}u_{b;c})\alpha - (u_{c;a}B_{cb}^{-1} + B_{ca}^{-1}u_{c;b})\gamma.\end{aligned} \tag{21.12)*}$$

Correspondingly, the equations of equilibrium are

$$(\delta T_{ba})_{;b} - u_{b;c}T^0_{ca;b} = 0, \tag{21.24)*}$$

where we have omitted the body force terms. To illustrate the use of these equations, let us consider small extensions of a finitely twisted circular cylinder.

The required solution can be, of course, obtained as a limiting case of (18.41) for small extensions. Specifically, we let $F = 1 + e$, the axial strain e being small in the sense that $F^2 \doteq 1 + 2e$, $1/F \doteq 1 - e$, etc. Assuming for simplicity a Mooney-Rivlin material, we readily obtain that

$$\begin{aligned}\delta T_{\rho\rho} &= \frac{D^2}{2}\mu e\left(\frac{1}{2} + \beta\right)(A^2 - P^2), \qquad \delta T_{\rho\phi} = \delta T_{\rho z} = 0,\\ \delta T_{\phi\phi} &= \frac{D^2}{2}\mu e\left(\frac{1}{2} + \beta\right)(A^2 - 3P^2), \qquad \delta T_{\phi z} = D\mu\beta e P,\\ \delta T_{zz} &= 3\mu e + \delta T_{\rho\rho} + 2D^2\mu e P^2\left(\frac{1}{2} - \beta\right).\end{aligned} \tag{21.38}$$

† Cf. [91], p. 323.

In particular, the axial force N is related to the axial force $N_0 = 3\pi\mu e A^2$ which is found in the absence of torsion by

$$\frac{N}{N_0} = 1 + \frac{D^2A^2}{23}(1 - \beta). \tag{21.39}$$

In view of the limitation $-\frac{1}{2} \leq \beta \leq \frac{1}{2}$ imposed on Mooney-Rivlin materials, it follows that torsion always stiffens the axial resistance of a cylinder. For a general elastic response it is not possible to arrive at this simple conclusion.

In the present case the incremental stress relation (21.21) reduces to

$$\begin{aligned} \delta T_{ab} &= -\delta p\,\delta_{ab} + \mu\left(\frac{1}{2} + \beta\right)(u_{a;c}B_{cb} + B_{ca}u_{b;c}) \\ &\quad + \mu\left(\frac{1}{2} - \beta\right)(u_{c;a}B_{cb}^{-1} + B_{ac}^{-1}u_{c;b}), \end{aligned} \tag{21.40}$$

where $B_{ab}^{-1} \equiv (\mathbf{B}^{-1})_{ab}$. Introducing the incremental deformation

$$u_\rho = -\frac{eP}{2}, \qquad u_\phi = 0, \qquad u_z = eZ,$$

and recalling that $w_{122} = -w_{212} = 1/P$, we obtain, for instance,

$$\begin{aligned} \delta T_{\phi z} &= \mu\left[\left(\frac{1}{2} + \beta\right)(u_{\phi;a}B_{az} + B_{a\phi}u_{z;a}) + \left(\frac{1}{2} - \beta\right)(u_{a;\phi}B_{az}^{-1} + B_{\phi a}^{-1}u_{a;z})\right] \\ &= \mu\left[\left(\frac{1}{2} + \beta\right)\left(-\frac{e}{2}DP + eDP\right) + \left(\frac{1}{2} - \beta\right)\left(\frac{e}{2}DP - eDP\right)\right]. \end{aligned}$$

In this way we arrive at

$$\begin{aligned} &\delta T_{\rho\rho} = -\mu e - \delta p, \qquad \delta T_{\rho\phi} = \delta T_{\rho z} = 0, \\ &\delta T_{\phi\phi} = \delta T_{\rho\rho} - D^2\mu e\left(\frac{1}{2} + \beta\right)P^2, \qquad \delta T_{\phi z} = D\mu\beta e P, \\ &\delta T_{zz} = 3\mu e + \delta T_{\rho\rho} + 2D^2\mu e\left(\frac{1}{2} - \beta\right)P^2, \end{aligned} \tag{21.41}$$

The equations of equilibrium now yield the following conditions: $\partial_\phi p = 0$, $\partial_z p = 0$, and

$$\frac{\partial}{\partial P}\delta T_{\rho\rho} + w_{212}\delta T_{\phi\phi} + w_{122}\delta T_{\rho\rho} - P^{-2}u_\rho(T^0_{\rho\rho} - T^0_{\phi\phi}) - \left(\frac{\partial}{\partial P}T^0_{\rho\rho}\right)\left(\frac{\partial}{\partial P}u_\rho\right) = 0.$$

The last equation reduces to

$$-\frac{d}{dP}\,\delta p + \frac{1}{P}\,(\delta T_{\rho\rho} - \delta T_{\phi\phi}) = 0,$$

from which it follows that

$$\delta p = -\mu e + \frac{D^2}{2}\,\mu e\left(\frac{1}{2} + \beta\right)(P^2 - A^2), \tag{21.42}$$

where the constant of integration has been chosen so as to clear the lateral boundary $P = A$ of surface tractions: $\delta T_{\rho\rho} = 0$, $P = A$ (note that $\delta T_{\rho\phi}$ and $\delta T_{\rho z}$ vanish identically). It is now easy to verify that the solution (21.41), (21.42) agrees with (21.38).

Waves in prestrained bodies

We assume that the intermediate configuration is one of static, homogeneous deformation. In the absence of body forces, we then have that, by (15.89), $\tilde{T}^0_{ji.j} = 0$. Similarly, $\tilde{T}_{ji.j} = \rho_0 \ddot{u}_i$; with $\tilde{T}_{ji} = \tilde{T}^0_{ji} + A^0_{jikm}\,\delta F_{km} = \tilde{T}^0_{ji} + A^0_{jikm} H_{kp} F^0_{pm}$, where A^0_{jikm} are as given by (17.29), we obtain

$$A^0_{jikm}\,\frac{\partial^2 u_k}{\partial \xi_r\,\partial \xi_s}\,F^0_{rm}F^0_{sj} = \rho_0\,\frac{\partial^2 u_i(\boldsymbol{\xi}, t)}{\partial t^2},$$

or, by $(17.32)_2$,

$$C_{sikr}\,\frac{\partial^2 u_k}{\partial \xi_r \partial \xi_s} = \rho_0 \ddot{u}_i, \qquad C_{sikr} = A^0_{jikm} F^0_{rm} F^0_{sj}. \tag{21.43}$$

The plane wave solutions

$$u_i = a_i \cos[k(\boldsymbol{\xi}\cdot\mathbf{n} - ct)], \qquad k = \frac{\omega}{c},$$

now reduce (21.43) to a characteristic equation that is of the same form as (17.31), namely

$$[Q_{ik}(\mathbf{n}) - \rho_0 c^2(\mathbf{n})\delta_{ik}]a_k = 0, \tag{21.44}$$

where $Q_{ik}(\mathbf{n}) = C_{qikp} n_q n_p$. This means of course that the laws governing the propagation of (infinitesimal) plane waves on the one hand, and acceleration fronts on the other hand, are the same. The two types of waves need not be identical, however. For one, the theory of acceleration fronts does not limit in any way the shape of the waves or the state of deformation. At the same time, there are no known solutions that would exhibit such waves.

There is no reason why the speeds of propagation, $c(\mathbf{n})$, should be always real: a plane wave may not be able to propagate even though the medium is prestrained homogeneously. As the squared speed of propagation approaches zero, a progressive wave becomes a *standing wave*; beyond that, i.e. when $c^2 = -A^2$, it seems that the inability of the medium to transmit the incoming energy will give rise to an increase of the amplitude of the standing wave, thus

$$u_i = a_i(t) \sin(k\mathbf{n} \cdot \mathbf{x}). \tag{21.45}$$

The equations of motion now yield $(k^2 Q_{ik}(\mathbf{n}) + \rho_0 \delta_{ik} \partial_t^2) a_i = 0$. Assuming that, for instance, $Q_{11} = -\rho_0 A^2$, $Q_{12} = Q_{13} = 0$, we obtain

$$\ddot{a}_1 = A^2 k^2 a_1, \qquad a_1 = C_1 e^{Akt} + C_2 e^{-Akt}.$$

Of course, the plane wave solution is limited to small amplitudes only; however, it is natural to conclude that *the underlying homogeneous deformation is unstable whenever* $c^2 < 0$.† In this case we expect a small disturbance to throw the medium into a state of finite nonhomogeneous deformation. It can be shown that, in general, plane acceleration fronts propagating into an isotropic elastic medium in a state of homogeneous deformation either become infinite in a finite time or decay to zero in an infinite time.‡

The theory of superposition of small deformations upon large lends itself also to an investigation of *surface waves* in prestrained elastic bodies.§

In contrast to general motions $\mathbf{u} = \mathbf{u}(\mathbf{x}, t)$, in plane waves the variables $\mathbf{x}$ and t occur in the special combination ("phase")

$$\phi(\mathbf{x}, t) = k(\mathbf{n} \cdot \mathbf{x} - ct);$$

in particular, $\phi =$ const. describes what one may consider as a (plane) wave front. If the initial strains are not homogeneous, then the equations of motion, $A_{jikm} F_{km.j} = \rho_0 \ddot{x}_i$, cannot be satisfied by plane waves (because A_{jikm} are now functions of $\mathbf{X}$ and t). Instead, we must use the analogous method of

† Hayes and Rivlin [69].

‡ W. A. Green [56]. The analogous problem when the material is characterized by a hypoelastic equation of state is considered by E. Varley and J. Dunwoody [187] (cf. also [13]).

§ Hayes and Rivlin [68].

simple waves, $x_i = x_i(\alpha)$, where α is now a general function of $\mathbf{X}$ and t: $\alpha = G(\mathbf{X}, t)$.† We shall indicate differentiation with respect to α by a prime (and, as always, differentiation with respect to t at constant $\mathbf{X}$ by a superposed dot), thus $F_{im} = x_i'(\partial\alpha/\partial X_m)$, $v_i = x_i'\dot{\alpha}$, and

$$\dot{\alpha}F'_{im} = \frac{\partial\alpha}{\partial X_m} v_i'. \tag{21.46}$$

For any choice of $\mathbf{F} = \mathbf{F}(\alpha)$, $\mathbf{v} = \mathbf{v}(\alpha)$, (21.46) provides a system of partial differential equations for the determination of $\alpha = G(\mathbf{X}, t)$. But the equations of motion will impose restrictions on the choice of $\mathbf{F}(\alpha)$ and $\mathbf{v}(\alpha)$. Let $\mathbf{N}$ be the unit normal vectors of a simple wave $G(\mathbf{X}, t) = \text{const.}$ (viewed in the reference configuration of the body), and $\overline{U}$ its speed of propagation. Then, by (8.90),

$$v_k' N_m + \overline{U} F'_{km} = 0. \tag{21.46)*}$$

With this relation, and taking into account (8.84), (8.88), we find from $A_{jikm}F'_{km}\Delta_j G = \rho_0 v_i' \dot{G}$ that

$$[Q_{ik}(\mathbf{n}) - \rho_0 \overline{V}^2 \delta_{ik}]v_k' = 0, \tag{21.47}$$

where $\mathbf{n}$ are the unit normal vectors of the current configuration $\alpha = g(\mathbf{x}, t)$ of a simple wave, and $\overline{V} = \mathbf{u}\cdot\mathbf{n} - \mathbf{v}\cdot\mathbf{n}$ is the relative speed of propagation. Recalling (17.31), we conclude that simple waves propagate in the same way as acceleration fronts.

A simple wave may be also described by $t = h(\mathbf{x}, \alpha)$, where $\mathbf{x}$ and α are now considered as independent, so that $t' = \partial h/\partial\alpha$. Let L be some function of α; if a simple wave is given by $L(\alpha) = n_i(\alpha)x_i - \overline{V}(\alpha)t$, then $t' = x_i(n_i/\overline{V})' - (L/\overline{V})'$, and from $\partial_t v_i = v_i'\partial_t\alpha = v_i'/t'$ it follows that

$$\partial_t v_i = -v_i'\left[\left(\frac{L}{\overline{V}}\right)' - x_j\left(\frac{n_j}{\overline{V}}\right)'\right]^{-1}. \tag{21.48}$$

If the simple wave is moving into a homogeneously deformed region, then (21.48) describes the particle acceleration induced by the passage of the wave front.‡

† Varley [201].
‡ Varley, *op. cit.*, p. 322.

Stability

The theory of small deformations superposed on large is a valuable tool for investigating questions of stability, uniqueness, and propagation of waves.† The theory of partial differential equations and variational methods provide other avenues of approach. The determination of the extent to which the resulting criteria overlap remains largely an open problem.

According to the intuitive notion of stability, a small disturbance will produce only a small departure from a stable equilibrium configuration. In particular, a disturbance may induce small oscillations about the equilibrium configuration, or even become damped out, depending on the nature of the forces that act on the body. Let us mark by subscripts 0 and 1, respectively, variables referred to an equilibrium configuration and another configuration selected as follows. We imagine a body jolted out of its equilibrium configuration by a disturbance which imparts the kinetic energy K_0 to the body. Initially, then, the total energy is $E_0 + K_0$, where E_0 is the strain energy in the equilibrium configuration. Denoting by W_{01} the work done by external forces in the passage from state 0 to state 1, we obtain from the energy balance that $\Delta E = E_1 - E_0 = W_{01} - \Delta K$, where $\Delta K = K_1 - K_0$. The condition

$$\Delta E > W_{01} \tag{21.49}$$

(i.e. $\Delta K < 0$) then characterizes a stable equilibrium in the sense that a body can depart from the equilibrium configuration only at the expense of the kinetic energy obtained from the disturbance. If the amount of this kinetic energy is small, then so will be the departure from the equilibrium configuration. These heuristic observations lead us to consider variation of the potential ("enthalpy")

$$J = \int_V W\,dV - \int_{B_T} \mathbf{w} \cdot \tilde{\mathbf{t}}\,dA \tag{21.50}$$

(cf. (15.90)), where W is the density of strain energy per volume of the undeformed configuration, $\tilde{t}_i = \tilde{T}_{ji}N_j$ is the stress vector referred to the undeformed configuration, and $\mathbf{w} = \mathbf{x} - \mathbf{X}$ is the displacement vector. It is difficult to assess the variation of the second integral, except in the case of *dead loading*, i.e. when $\delta\tilde{t}_i = 0$. The other possibilities will not be considered here.

† References to this extensive field may be found in [1], [34], [74], [114], and *NFTM*, Sections 72 and 89.

Let $\mathbf{x} = \mathbf{X} + \mathbf{w} = \boldsymbol{\xi} + \mathbf{u}$, where $\mathbf{u}$ is a field of (small) "kinematically admissible" displacements, and let the initial deformation remain fixed, so that $\delta\mathbf{w} \equiv \mathbf{u}$. The strain-energy function W can be expanded in a Taylor series, thus

$$\Delta W = W(\mathbf{F}) - W(\mathbf{F}^0) = \frac{\partial W}{\partial H_{ij}} H_{ij} + \frac{1}{2}\frac{\partial^2 W}{\partial H_{ij}\partial H_{km}} H_{ij}H_{km};$$

in view of the chain rule $\partial F_{rs}/\partial H_{ij} = \delta_{ri}F^0_{js}$ (cf. (21.2)), this is the same as $\Delta W = \delta W + \delta^{(2)}W + \cdots$, where

$$\delta W = \frac{\partial W}{\partial F_{rs}} H_{rj}F^0_{js} = \tilde{T}^0_{sr}H_{rj}F^0_{js},$$

$$\delta^{(2)}W = \frac{1}{2}\frac{\partial^2 W}{\partial F_{rs}\partial F_{pn}} H_{rm}F^0_{ms}H_{pj}F^0_{jn} = \frac{1}{2} A^0_{srpn}H_{rm}F^0_{ms}H_{pj}F^0_{jn}.$$

If $\delta\mathbf{w}$ vanishes on the displacement boundary B_u, and $\mathbf{\tilde{t}}$ take on the prescribed values $\mathbf{\bar{t}}$ on the traction boundary B_T, then, as was shown on p. 361, $\delta J = 0$. Therefore, the stability criterion $\Delta J > 0$ will involve the second variation $\delta^{(2)}J$. Noting that the second variation of the surface integral in (21.50) vanishes, we can express the stability criterion as follows,

$$\int_V C^0_{mrpj}\frac{\partial u_r}{\partial \xi_m}\frac{\partial u_p}{\partial \xi_j}\, dV > 0, \qquad C^0_{mrpj} = A^0_{srpn}F^0_{ms}F^0_{jn}. \tag{21.51}$$

If $\partial V = B_u$, then (21.51) is known as *Hadamard's criterion.*

Truesdell† has shown that Hadamard stability implies at each point the strong ellipticity condition (17.47). This condition ensures the existence of real wave speeds; in fact, one may look upon it as a *local* stability criterion, whereas (21.51) represents a *global* stability criterion. This interpretation of strong ellipticity condition is reinforced by the findings of the preceding subsection, in which it was shown that inability to propagate waves may result in a build-up of the amplitudes of standing waves, thus providing a mechanism whereby a small disturbance can induce a finite change in the underlying deformation. However, it should be noted that (17.47) is *necessary* for stability, not sufficient. If (17.47) is not satisfied, then instability is *possible*, but whether or not it actually occurs is determined by the boundary conditions. For instance, because the "buckling" of a body is largely controled by the boundary conditions, it is evident that only global criteria, which take

† *NFTM*, Section 89.

boundary conditions into account, can give us a means for predicting instability. To clarify this point, let us consider Euler buckling:

$$EI\frac{d^2y}{dx^2} + Py = 0.$$

Characteristic functions that represent "standing waves" are given by

$$y = A \sin kx, \qquad k = \sqrt{\frac{P}{EI}}. \tag{21.52}$$

Consequently, as long as P is positive, a standing wave solution is possible. Once we introduce boundary conditions $y(0) = y(L) = 0$, however, a solution of the form (21.52) is possible only if $P \geq \pi^2 EI/L^2$. The same situation may occur in nonlinear elasticity theory. If we substitute standing wave solutions (which may be said to represent "internal buckling") into the equations of equilibrium, we obtain expressions for the wave numbers. For the wave numbers to be real, the loading and the response functions must satisfy certain conditions. A case of internal buckling has been exhibited by Biot [5]; however, Biot's formulation of the theory of small deformations superposed on large appears to differ in some details from the theory used by others. In any case, the search for examples of internal buckling is made very difficult by the variety of possible boundary conditions, and by the fact that the usual plausibility requirements and other inequalities do not provide enough information to decide whether the resulting conditions on response functions can be satisfied or not.

Let us investigate the possibility of internal buckling in isotropic materials subjected to hydrostatic pressure. The equations of equilibrium are then $\bar{\mu}\nabla^2 u_i + (\bar{\lambda} + \bar{\mu})u_{k,ik} = 0$, the effective moduli $\bar{\lambda}$ and $\bar{\mu}$ being given by (21.17), (21.19). Substituting $u_i = A_i \sin k_1 x \sin k_2 y \sin k_3 z$ into the equations of equilibrium, we obtain a linear homogeneous system of equations in A_1, A_2, A_3. If nontrivial solutions are to exist, the determinant of the coefficients must vanish. Specifically, we must have that

$$(k_1^2 + k_2^2 + k_3^2)^3 \bar{\mu}^2(\bar{\lambda} + 2\bar{\mu}) = 0. \tag{21.53}$$

Because the wave numbers k_1, k_2, k_3 must be real, it follows that either one of the conditions $\bar{\mu} = 0$, $\bar{\lambda} + 2\bar{\mu} = 0$ must hold. The first of these becomes $\alpha V^4 = \gamma$, where V is the stretch. This condition contradicts the empirical inequalities (17.25). The condition $\bar{\lambda} + 2\bar{\mu} = 0$ yields a transcendental equation in V which is difficult to assess because it involves the response functions in a complicated manner. If a speed of propagation vanishes, then, by (17.33), $\det(Q_{ik}) = 0$, where $Q_{ik} = B_{jikr}n_jn_r$, and B_{jikr} are given by $(17.32)_2^*$. In contrast to (21.53), the resulting condition $f(V_1, V_2, V_3, k_1, k_2, k_3) = 0$ does not in general separate into functions of deformation and coefficients of response.† Certain types of internal buckling can be seen right away to violate the *B–E* inequalities (17.27), but no general conclusions about internal buckling seem possible at this time.

One expects naturally to find a connection between stability and uniqueness of solutions describing small deformations superposed on large. Ericksen and Toupin‡ have shown that Hadamard stability implies uniqueness of the displacement boundary value problem, but not of the stress boundary value problem.

In the context of thermoelasticity, Ericksen [203] has investigated the following kinetic definition of necessary conditions for stability. A static solution (*rest solution*) must satisfy the condition $\theta =$ const. and appropriate boundary conditions, which we shall take to be

$$x_i = \bar{x}_i \text{ on } B_u, \qquad \bar{t}_i = \bar{t}_i \text{ on } B_T. \tag{21.54}$$

Following Ericksen, let us now take as a *disturbance* any solution defined in some interval $t_0 \leq t < t_1$. By a *transient* we shall mean a solution that coincides with the disturbance for $t < t_1$, and for $t \geq t_1$ satisfies the boundary conditions (21.54) and the condition that the boundary $\delta V = B_u + B_T$ be insulated, thus

$$\mathbf{q} \cdot \mathbf{n} = 0 \quad \text{on} \quad \partial V. \tag{21.55}$$

If every such transient converges to the rest solution at $t \to \infty$, then the rest solution will be said to be *stable with respect to the disturbance*. To derive the *necessary condition* for this, we integrate the energy balance of the transient from t_1 to ∞, taking into account the fixed boundary conditions (21.54), (21.55). We then obtain

$$V[\rho(\varepsilon - \hat{\varepsilon} - \hat{k})] + B_T[\bar{t}_i u_i] = 0, \quad u_i = \hat{x}_i - x_i, \tag{21.56}$$

where carets mark the transient solution at t_1, and the plain symbols refer to the rest solution. The other necessary condition follows from (21.55), (12.14), (12.15):

$$V[\rho\eta] \geq V[\rho\hat{\eta}]. \tag{21.57}$$

† Cf. [24].
‡ [34], [36].

With $\psi = \varepsilon - \theta\eta$, and recalling that $\theta =$ const., thus $V[\rho\theta\eta] \geq V[\rho\theta\hat{\eta}]$, we can replace (21.56) by the inequality

$$V[\rho(\hat{\varepsilon} - \theta\hat{\eta} + \hat{k} - \psi)] - B_T[\bar{t}_i u_i] \geq 0. \qquad (21.56)^*$$

Hypoelasticity and plasticity

To describe elastic response without introducing the assumption of a natural state, it seems plausible to consider constitutive equations that relate time rates of stress and deformation. Therefore, we shall begin with a digression to *objective time rates of tensors.*

As we have had occasion to remark before, there is only one *operation* of differentiation. Each of the numerous "rates" is but a particular representation, obtained by choosing a particular (or, preferred) reference frame. Let us take a vector $\mathbf{h} = h_i\mathbf{e}_i = h_a\mathbf{i}_a$, where $(\mathbf{e}_i)$ is a Cartesian frame, and $(\mathbf{i}_a)$ are local orthonormal frames of a system of orthogonal curvilinear coordinates. Because $\dot{\mathbf{e}}_i = 0$, but $\dot{\mathbf{i}}_a = (\partial_b \mathbf{i}_a)v_b = -w_{cab}\mathbf{i}_c v_b$ (cf. (6.78)), it follows that

$$\dot{\mathbf{h}} = \mathbf{e}_i\dot{h}_i = \mathbf{i}_a \frac{\delta}{\delta t} h_a,$$
$$\dot{h}_i = \partial_t h_i + v_j h_{i,j}, \qquad \frac{\delta}{\delta t} h_a = \partial_t h_a + v_b h_{a;b}. \qquad (21.58)$$

Along with the "absolute rate" $\dot{\mathbf{h}}$, we can construct numerous "intrinsic rates" by singling out special kinds of components. For instance, the body itself may serve as a (deforming!) reference frame in which case the components of $\mathbf{h}$ that are "seen" by the body may be defined, locally, by $\mathbf{h} \cdot d\mathbf{x}$. The material rate of the scalar $\mathbf{h} \cdot d\mathbf{x}$ then defines a *convected rate* $\overset{\Delta}{h}_i$:

$$\dot{\overline{h_i\, dx_i}} \equiv \overset{\Delta}{h}_i\, dx_i, \qquad \overset{\Delta}{h}_i = \dot{h}_i + v_{k,i}h_k. \qquad (21.59)$$

If $\mathbf{h}$ is projected on the infinitesimal vector-areas $d\mathbf{a}$, then, by (8.60),

$$\dot{\overline{h_i\, da_i}} \equiv \overset{*}{h}_i\, da_i, \qquad \overset{*}{h}_i = \dot{h}_i + h_i v_{k,k} - v_{i,j}h_j \qquad (21.60)$$

(cf. (13.71)). For scalars the analogous definition is

$$\dot{\overline{dv}} \equiv \overset{*}{f}\, dv, \qquad \overset{*}{f} = \dot{f} + f v_{k,k}. \qquad (21.61)$$

Now let g_i be some vector field satisfying $\overset{\triangle}{g}_i = 0$. Then another type of convected rates, $\overset{\triangledown}{h}_i$, may be defined as follows

$$\overline{h_i g_i}^{\bullet} \equiv \overset{\triangledown}{h}_i g_i, \qquad \overset{\triangledown}{h}_i = \dot{h}_i - v_{i,k} h_k. \tag{21.62}$$

Further, a *co-rotational rate* $\overset{\circ}{h}_i$ (found by a Euclidean observer rotating with the mean angular velocity of the medium) is defined by

$$\overset{\circ}{h}_i = \frac{1}{2}(\overset{\triangle}{h}_i + \overset{\triangledown}{h}_i) = \dot{h}_i - W_{ik} h_k. \tag{21.63}$$

The extension of these definitions to tensors of higher rank is straightforward, e.g.

$$\begin{aligned} \overset{\triangle}{A}_{ij} &= \dot{A}_{ij} + v_{k,i} A_{kj} + v_{k,j} A_{ik}, \\ \overset{\triangledown}{A}_{ij} &= \dot{A}_{ij} - v_{i,k} A_{kj} - v_{j,k} A_{ik}, \\ \overset{\circ}{A}_{ij} &= \dot{A}_{ij} - W_{ik} A_{kj} - W_{jk} A_{ik}. \end{aligned} \tag{21.64}$$

With a view towards constitutive equations, we should also find out which of the rates will preserve the objectivity of a tensor. If **A** is an objective tensor, then $A^+_{ab} = A_{ab} = Q_{ai}(t)Q_{bj}(t)A_{ij}$. Taking the material rate of this, and using $\dot{Q}_{ai} = \Omega_{ij} Q_{aj}$ (cf. (7.45)) to eliminate the time rates of direction cosines, we obtain

$$\dot{A}^+_{ab} = \Omega_{im} Q_{am} Q_{bj} A_{ij} + \Omega_{jm} Q_{ai} Q_{bm} A_{ij} + Q_{ai} Q_{bj} \dot{A}_{ij}. \tag{21.65}$$

Evidently the material rate of an objective tensor is not objective. It is easy to see that any tensor **M** satisfying $\mathbf{M}^+ = \mathbf{M} - \mathbf{\Omega}$ will do for constructing objective time rates of **A**, for if $\Omega_{ij} = M_{ij} - Q_{ai}(t)Q_{bj}(t)M^+_{ab}$, then (21.65) becomes

$$MA^+_{ab} = MA_{ab} = Q_{ai}(t)Q_{bj}(t)A_{ij}, \quad MA_{ij} \equiv \dot{A}_{ij} + M_{ki} A_{kj} + M_{kj} A_{ik}.$$

Identifying **M** with **L** or **W**, we recover the definitions (21.64).

To describe elastic response without resorting to the notion of a natural state, Truesdell proposed in 1953 a theory of *hypoelasticity*, with constitutive equations of the form

$$MT_{ij} = H_{ijkm}(\mathbf{T}) D_{km}, \tag{21.66}$$

where M stands for any one of the possible time rates. The response functions H_{ijkm} have the dimension of stress, so that the flow is "elastic," and not viscous. Because a constitutive equation should be invariant to the choice of time rates, and because the various rates $M\mathbf{T}$ differ by terms that are linear in $\mathbf{T}$, it follows that H_{ijkm} should be at least of degree one in $\mathbf{T}$. As was remarked on p. 310, a theory of the rate-type will describe, in general, a type of behavior rather than a definite material. Moreover, the response defined by (21.66) is isotropic. To see that, let us take $\mathring{\mathbf{T}} = H(\mathbf{T})\mathbf{D}$, for instance; then $\mathring{\mathbf{T}}^+ = \mathbf{Q}\mathring{\mathbf{T}}\mathbf{Q}^T = H(\mathbf{QTQ}^T)\mathbf{QDQ}^T$, $\mathring{\mathbf{T}} = \mathbf{Q}^T H(\mathbf{QTQ}^T)\mathbf{QD}$, i.e. H is an isotropic function of stress.

Whereas some metals are cooperative to the extent that they remain elastic almost until rupture, others exhibit a "plastic range" in which large deformations occur with little or no increase in the loads. If the plastic flow occurs at a constant stress, the material is said to be *perfectly plastic*, otherwise *strain-hardening*. Most of the terminology and ideas for the post-elastic range stem from simple tests involving uniaxial extension, or torsion, or a combination of both. To predict from simple experiments the plastic behavior under more general loadings we need first of all a "theory of yielding."

It can be shown that the response predicted by (21.66) is in many ways similar to elastic-plastic flow.† However, the classical theory of plasticity proceeds along somewhat different lines. The total strain is decomposed into elastic strain p_{ij} and a plastic strain r_{ij}; neither p_{ij} nor r_{ij} need be compatible, even if the total strain is. The onset of plastic flow is characterized by a *yield condition*, e.g. the von Mises condition

$$f(\mathbf{S}) = S_{ij}S_{ij} - k^2 = 0, \tag{21.67}$$

where $\mathbf{S}$ is the deviatoric stress. One can attempt to describe the entire range of elastic-plastic response in terms of a single constitutive equation, but that would not be very practical: the "easy" elastic range is then lost, having been incorporated into the general, nonlinear equation. Therefore, the elastic strains are related to stresses by Hooke's law, whereas the constitutive equation for the plastic strains ("flow rule") is of the form

$$\dot{r}_{ij} = \begin{matrix} 0 & \text{for unloading} \\ f(\mathbf{S}, \mathbf{r})\dot{S}_{ij} & \text{for loading} \end{matrix}$$

(thus we must also specify what is meant by loading and unloading). The bifurcation of the constitutive equation for r_{ij} may seem inelegant, but then discontinuous functions are inelegant (they are described by a "story" rather

† Cf. *NFTM*, pp. 415–426.

than by a single formula). To obtain an elegant description of irreversible processes, we should have to introduce response *functionals*. The irreversibility is then guaranteed, because we cannot reverse a history any more than we can reverse the direction of time.† In plasticity theory we look for more elementary descriptions, obtained by introducing *irreversible parameters*, i.e. time-like parameters which, by hypothesis, keep on increasing. Thus a "hysteresis curve" $A = f(B)$ may turn out to be a two-dimensional projection of a relation $A = g(B, t)$, so that, because time is irreversible, a loading branch cannot be retraced even when the variation of B is reversed. In general, we expect that a process will have its own, intrinsic time ξ. Roughly speaking, in elastic deformations a material does not "age," so that the material clock stands still. In plastic deformations, on the other hand, the material clock is running. Moreover, experience shows that "plastic life" is of a finite duration.

Let us choose for ξ a *strain-hardening parameter*

$$\xi = \int_0^t (\dot{r}_{ij}\dot{r}_{ij})^{1/2}\, d\tau,$$

and let the yield condition be of the form $f(\mathbf{S}, \theta, \xi) = F(\mathbf{S}) - H(\theta, \xi)$, where θ denotes temperature. The notion of strain-hardening is expressed by assuming that $\partial H/\partial\xi \geq 0$. Further, we define loading by $f = 0, \dot{f} = 0, \dot{\xi} > 0$, or, equivalently, by

$$\frac{\partial f}{\partial S_{ij}}\dot{S}_{ij} + \frac{\partial f}{\partial \theta}\dot{\theta} > 0.$$

As the flow rule that goes with (21.67) we may take

$$\dot{r}_{ij} = \frac{S_{ij}}{\dfrac{\partial H}{\partial \xi}|\mathbf{S}|}\left(\frac{\partial f}{\partial S_{km}}\dot{S}_{km} + \frac{\partial f}{\partial \theta}\dot{\theta}\right). \tag{21.68}$$

From inspection of (21.68) we see that isothermal processes in perfectly plastic materials may be also described by

$$S_{ij} = 2\mu_P D_{ij},$$

† That it is possible to *imagine* the direction of time reversed is quite beside the point: we never assume that time might be running backwards in a given process. As the basis for assuming the directionality of time we may take the existence of finite signal speeds (i.e. a signal is always received "after" it has been sent).

where μ_P depends, in general, upon the states of stress and strain at the point, and the material has been assumed to be incompressible in the plastic range. Collecting the equations of the von Mises theory for perfectly plastic materials, we have

$$T_{ij,j} = 0, \qquad S_{ij}S_{ij} - k^2 = 0,$$
$$S_{ij} = \mu_P(v_{i,j} + v_{j,i}), \qquad D_{kk} = 0,$$

altogether 11 equations for the 11 unknowns S_{ij}, p, μ_P, and v_i. Evidently it is not possible to have μ_P = const., because then an overdetermined system would result (the reason for that being the presence of the yield condition, which has no counterpart in elasticity theory or hydrodynamics).

In plane problems we have that $v_x = v_x(x, y)$, $v_y = v_y(x, y)$, $v_z = 0$, thus $D_{zx} = D_{zy} = D_{zz} = 0$. Then $S_{zx} = S_{zy} = S_{zz} = 0$, $T_{zz} = \frac{1}{2}(T_{xx} + T_{yy})$, and the yield condition can be reduced to $(T_{xx} - T_{yy})^2 + 4T_{xy}^2 = 4k^2$. The remaining equations of the fundamental system are now

$$T_{xx,x} + T_{xy,y} = 0, \qquad T_{xy,x} + T_{yy,y} = 0, \tag{21.69}$$

$$S_{xx} = 2\mu_P v_{x,x}, \qquad S_{xy} = \mu_P(v_{x,y} + v_{y,x}) \qquad S_{yy} = 2\mu_P v_{y,y}, \tag{21.70}$$
$$v_{x,x} + v_{y,y} = 0.$$

The general solution of (21.69) is given in terms of Airy's stress function F by $T_{xx} = \partial^2 F/\partial y^2$, $T_{yy} = \partial^2 F/\partial x^2$, $T_{xy} = -\partial^2 F/\partial x\, \partial y$. Moreover, from $T_{xx} = S_{xx} - p$, $T_{yy} = S_{yy} - p$ and $S_{xx} + S_{yy} = 0$ it follows that

$$-2p = \frac{\partial^2 F}{\partial x^2} + \frac{\partial^2 F}{\partial y^2}, \qquad S_{xx} = \frac{1}{2}\left(\frac{\partial^2 F}{\partial y^2} - \frac{\partial^2 F}{\partial x^2}\right) = -S_{yy}. \tag{21.71}$$

Finally, the yield condition may be written in the form

$$\left(\frac{\partial^2 F}{\partial x^2} - \frac{\partial^2 F}{\partial y^2}\right)^2 + 4\left(\frac{\partial^2 F}{\partial x \partial y}\right)^2 = 4k^2. \tag{21.72}$$

In principle, we can determine the general solution of (21.72), and, if the boundary is a traction boundary, solve the stress problem right then and there. Thus the existence of a yield condition leads to a class of *statically determinate solutions*. As a rule the boundary will be in part a displacement boundary; moreover, the compatibility of displacements should be verified in any case.

To satisfy the condition of incompressibility, we introduce a stream-function Q such that $v_x = -\partial Q/\partial y$, $v_y = \partial Q/\partial x$. Then the flow relations (21.70) reduce to

$$\frac{\partial^2 F}{\partial x^2} - \frac{\partial^2 F}{\partial y^2} = 4\mu_P \frac{\partial^2 Q}{\partial x\,\partial y}, \quad \frac{\partial^2 Q}{\partial x^2} - \frac{\partial^2 Q}{\partial y^2} = -\frac{1}{\mu_P}\frac{\partial^2 F}{\partial x\,\partial y}. \tag{21.73}$$

These equations may now be used to determine μ_P and Q, assuming that F was determined from (21.72).

If x and y are principal directions, then $(21.73)_2$ simplifies to $\partial^2 Q/\partial x^2 - \partial^2 Q/\partial y^2 = 0$, so that the "characteristics" are inclined at $\pm 45°$ to the principal axes. Therefore, the directions of maximum shear are the characteristics of the mathematical problem.†

The extreme mathematical difficulties inherent in the problems of plasticity are obvious. Added to these difficulties is the fact that, at any instant, some portions of the body will be elastic, and others plastic, the determination of the elastic-plastic interfaces being a part of the problem. To circumvent the last difficulty, we may consider only the stage at which the body is "fully plastic" (which usually corresponds to a "collapse" of some sort). A further simplification is to neglect the deformations prior to the body becoming fully plastic. As in elasticity theory, we can construct approximate solutions out of kinematically or statically admissible solutions, but the variational methods will now deal with dissipation rather than storage of energy. Specifically, with the dissipation function $D = \mu_P(v_{i,j}v_{i,j} + v_{i,j}v_{j,i})$, we obtain $\partial D/\partial v_{km} = S_{km}$ and $\delta D = S_{km}\,\delta v_{k,m} = S_{km}(\delta v_k)_{,m}$. If the stresses satisfy the conditions of equilibrium, and the velocities satisfy $\operatorname{div}\mathbf{v} = 0$ and the boundary conditions on the velocity boundary B_v, then an integration by parts yields $V[\delta D] = B_T[\bar{t}_i\,\delta v_i]$ (note that $\delta\mathbf{v}$ should vanish on B_v). This suggests a variational method based on minimizing $V[D] - B_T[\bar{t}_i v_i]$, where $\bar{t}_i$ are the prescribed surface tractions, and $\mathbf{v}$ is a kinematically admissible velocity field.

Problems

1. Derive (21.12) by the more elaborate method of expanding the response functions, and $\mathbf{B}$ and $\mathbf{B}^{-1}$, about the intermediate configuration. Neglecting quadratic terms in displacement gradients, show that $\mathbf{B} = \mathbf{B}^0 + \mathbf{H}\mathbf{B}^0 + \mathbf{B}^0\mathbf{H}^T$, $\mathbf{B}^{-1} = (\mathbf{B}^0)^{-1} - \mathbf{H}^T(\mathbf{B}^0)^{-1} - (\mathbf{B}^0)^{-1}\mathbf{H}$, $\mathrm{I} = \mathrm{I}^0 + 2\,\mathrm{tr}(\mathbf{H}\mathbf{B}^0)$, $\mathrm{II} = \mathrm{II}^0 + 2\mathrm{I}^0\,\mathrm{tr}(\mathbf{H}\mathbf{B}^0) - 2\,\mathrm{tr}[\mathbf{H}(\mathbf{B}^0)^2]$, $\mathrm{III} = \mathrm{III}^0 + 2\mathrm{III}\,\mathrm{tr}\mathbf{H}$, and $\alpha = \alpha^0 + 2\,\mathrm{tr}(\mathbf{H}\mathbf{B}^0)\,\partial\alpha/\partial\mathrm{I}$

† A brief exposition of the theory of characteristics may be found in [125] (cf. also [24]).

$+ 2[\mathrm{I}^0 \operatorname{tr}(\mathbf{HB}^0) - \operatorname{tr}(\mathbf{H}(\mathbf{B}^0)^2)]\ \partial\alpha/\partial\mathrm{II} + 2\mathrm{III}^0 \operatorname{tr}\mathbf{H}\ \partial\alpha/\partial\mathrm{III}$, etc. With $\mathbf{A}_1 = \mathbf{1}\ \partial\delta/\partial\mathrm{I} + \mathbf{B}\ \partial\alpha/\partial\mathrm{I} + \mathbf{B}^{-1}\ \partial\gamma/\partial\mathrm{I}$, etc. show that

$$\mathbf{T} = \mathbf{T}^0 + 2\operatorname{tr}\tilde{\mathbf{E}}\mathbf{B}\,\mathbf{A}_1 + 2(\mathrm{I}\operatorname{tr}\tilde{\mathbf{E}}\mathbf{B} - \operatorname{tr}\tilde{\mathbf{E}}\mathbf{B}^2)\mathbf{A}_2$$

$$+ 2\mathrm{III}\operatorname{tr}\tilde{\mathbf{E}}\,\mathbf{A}_3 + (\mathbf{GB} + \mathbf{BG}^T)\alpha - (\mathbf{G}^T\mathbf{B}^{-1} + \mathbf{B}^{-1}\mathbf{G})\gamma.$$

2. Verify in detail the derivation of (21.38)–(21.42).

3. Following the method indicated in text, derive (21.53).

4. Following the method indicated in text, derive (21.64).

5. Apply the material time rate to the stress relation of elasticity theory, and investigate the conditions under which the resulting expression will reduce to the hypoelastic stress relation (consider isotropy and anisotropy separately).

6. Consider the hypoelastic stress relation $\dot{\mathbf{T}} = \mathbf{WT} - \mathbf{TW} + (2\mu + \gamma_1 \operatorname{tr}\mathbf{T})\mathbf{D} + \gamma_3\mathbf{1}\operatorname{tr}(\mathbf{DT}) + \frac{1}{2}\gamma_4(\mathbf{TD} + \mathbf{DT})$ (cf. *CFT*, p. 405), where $\mu, \gamma_1, \gamma_3, \gamma_4$ are constants, and $\mathbf{W}$ is the spin tensor. For the motion $x = X + ctY$, $y = Y$, $z = Z$, where c is a constant, assume that $T_{xz} = T_{yz} = 0$, and obtain an (integrated) expression for T_{xy}. (*Hint:* Obtain a differential equation $\ddot{T}_{xy}$ + const. $T_{xy} = 0$.)

CHAPTER **6**

VISCOELASTICITY

This chapter is the last leg of the symbolic journey:

Linear elasticity theory (stress a linear function of the infinitesimal strain **E**):	→	Linear viscoelasticity theory (stress a linear functional of **E**):
$T_{ij} = C_{ijkm}E_{km}$		$T_{ij} = \int_{-\infty}^{t} G_{ijkm}(t - \tau)\dot{E}_{km}(\tau)\, d\tau$
↓		↓
Nonlinear elasticity theory (stress a nonlinear function of deformation **F**):	→	Nonlinear viscoelasticity theory (stress a nonlinear functional of the history $\mathbf{F}(t - s)$):
$\mathbf{T} = \mathbf{g}(\mathbf{F})$		$\mathbf{T} = [\mathbf{F}(t \overset{s=\infty}{\underset{s=0}{-}} s)]$

The domain of response functions is now an infinite vector space ("Hilbert space"), so that the representation theory requires a great deal of mathematical groundwork (an outline of this theory is given by Rivlin in two survey articles on viscoelasticity, [237] and [238]). For this reason the presentation here will be in the main heuristic.

Section 22
SIMPLE MATERIALS

The general theory of materials with memory originated in the work of Green and Rivlin [53] and Noll [106]. Subsequent investigations, notably by Wang [204], have added valuable insights. We shall take, of necessity, the most direct path to the main results of the theory.

Constitutive equations

A viscoelastic material need not have a preferred configuration. To allow for this, it is expedient to express a history $\mathbf{F}(t - s)$, $0 \leq s < \infty$ of deformation gradients from a configuration $\boldsymbol{\varkappa}(\mathbf{X})$ by the chain rule (8.26):

$$\mathbf{F}(\tau) = \mathbf{F}_{\underline{t}}(\tau)\mathbf{F}: \frac{\partial x_i(\tau)}{\partial X_m} = \frac{\partial x_i(\tau)}{\partial x_j}\frac{\partial x_j}{\partial X_m}, \tag{22.1}$$

where $\mathbf{x} \equiv \mathbf{x}(t)$, $\mathbf{F} \equiv \mathbf{F}(t)$. A function of the product $\mathbf{F}_{\underline{t}}(\tau)\mathbf{F}$ certainly defines a function of $\mathbf{F}_{\underline{t}}(\tau)$ *and* $\mathbf{F}$; therefore, we can write the general definition of simple materials as follows,

$$\mathbf{T} = \mathbf{J}(\mathbf{F}_{\underline{t}}(\tau), \mathbf{F}) \tag{22.2}$$

(cf. (14.7)). Roughly speaking, the dependence of $\mathbf{J}$ upon $\mathbf{F}$ is a "spring," the dependence upon $\mathbf{F}_{\underline{t}}(\tau)$ a "generalized dashpot." An observer transformation $x_i^+(\tau) = Q_{ij}(\tau)x_j(\tau)$, $x_i^+ = Q_{ij}x_j$, where $Q_{ij} \equiv Q_{ij}(t)$, will yield the condition $\mathbf{T} = \mathbf{Q}^T\mathbf{J}(\mathbf{Q}(\tau)\mathbf{F}_{\underline{t}}(\tau)\mathbf{Q}^T, \mathbf{QF})\mathbf{Q}$. With $\mathbf{Q}(\tau) = \mathbf{R}^T\mathbf{R}_{\underline{t}}^T(\tau)$, thus $\mathbf{Q} = \mathbf{R}^T$, we obtain the reduced constitutive equation

$$\mathbf{T} = \mathbf{RJ}(\mathbf{R}^T\mathbf{U}_{\underline{t}}(\tau)\mathbf{R}, \mathbf{U})\mathbf{R}^T \tag{22.3}$$

(cf. (14.20)). A more convenient form will be

$$\mathbf{T} = \mathbf{RK}(\mathbf{R}^T\mathbf{C}_{\underline{t}}(\tau)\mathbf{R}, \mathbf{C})\mathbf{R}^T, \tag{22.4}$$

where $\mathbf{C}_{\underline{t}} = \mathbf{U}_{\underline{t}}^2 = \mathbf{F}_{\underline{t}}^T\mathbf{F}_{\underline{t}}$, $\mathbf{C} = \mathbf{U}^2 = \mathbf{F}^T\mathbf{F}$. Either one of the representations (22.3), (22.4) satisfy the condition of material objectivity automatically, because the independent variables are now insensitive to observer transformations, e.g. $\mathbf{F}^+ = \mathbf{QF}$, $\mathbf{F}_{\underline{t}}^+(\tau) = \mathbf{Q}(\tau)\mathbf{F}_{\underline{t}}(\tau)\mathbf{Q}^T$ imply $\mathbf{C}^+ = \mathbf{C}$, $(\mathbf{R}^T)^+\mathbf{C}_{\underline{t}}^+(\tau)\mathbf{R}^+ = \mathbf{R}^T\mathbf{C}_{\underline{t}}(\tau)\mathbf{R}$. A symmetry operation $d\hat{\mathbf{X}} = \mathbf{S}^T d\mathbf{X}$, on the other hand, does not affect $\mathbf{C}_{\underline{t}}(\tau)$, but sends $\mathbf{C}$ into $\mathbf{SCS}^T$, and $\mathbf{R}$ into $\mathbf{RS}^T$. The invariance of stress to symmetry operations applied to the specimen now requires that **K** be an "isotropic function with respect to **S**":

$$\mathbf{SK}(\mathbf{R}^T\mathbf{C}_{\underline{t}}(\tau)\mathbf{R}, \mathbf{C})\mathbf{S}^T = \mathbf{K}(\mathbf{SR}^T\mathbf{C}_{\underline{t}}(\tau)\mathbf{RS}^T, \mathbf{SCS}^T). \tag{22.5}$$

In particular, if the material is isotropic, in which case **S** may be any orthogonal tensor, then **K** must be an isotropic function, and (22.4) reduces to

$$\mathbf{T} = \mathbf{K}(\mathbf{C}_{\underline{t}}(\tau), \mathbf{B}), \tag{22.6}$$

where $\mathbf{B} = \mathbf{FF}^T = \mathbf{RCR}^T$. Following Noll, we characterize *simple fluids* by admitting as symmetry operations all mappings **S** such that $\det\mathbf{S} = 1$. Then it follows that, by hypothesis, *simple fluids are isotropic*; moreover, by the reasoning that led to (14.25) we conclude that the constitutive equation of simple fluids must reduce to

$$\mathbf{T} = \mathbf{K}(\mathbf{C}_{\underline{t}}(\tau), \rho). \tag{22.7}$$

It is worth recalling at this point the ingredients of a function:

$$\text{domain} \xrightarrow{\text{rule}} \text{range}$$

It is convenient, though not necessary, to have a terminology that indicates the nature of the domain of a function. Thus a *functional* is a function whose domain consists of histories. Therefore, we may describe (22.7) by saying that stress is a function of the density, and a functional of deformation (the rules may be the same, e.g. stress may depend linearly on ρ and $\mathbf{C}_{\underline{t}}(t - s)$!). When dealing with constitutive equations of the form (22.7), an independent variable that is not a history will merely play the role of a parameter.

Of the results of nonlinear continuum mechanics, perhaps the most astonishing one is the discovery that not a few problems can be solved without specifying the response beyond what is stated in (22.7). How can that be possible? The answer is not far to seek: we must consider very simple flow histories! A complicated response function operating on a simple history may then result in a quite manageable stress relation. This suggests right away that we should investigate *steady flows*, because the histories of these flows are independent of the current time t (i.e. regarded as functions of the elapsed time s, these histories are the same at each instant t). But that is not enough: to obtain a single stress relation for the entire flow region, the histories must be of the same form at all points of the region! That is of course a very severe limitation on the geometry of flows; however, it turns out that many flows that are important in experimentation ("viscometric flows") do satisfy this limitation.

To be specific, let us suppose that $\mathbf{F}_{\underline{t}}(t - s)$ is independent of t, thus

$$\mathbf{F}_{\underline{t}}(t - s) = \mathbf{F}_{\underline{t}-\underline{r}}(t - r - s) = \mathbf{M}(s), \quad \mathbf{M}(0) = \mathbf{1}, \tag{22.8}$$

in which case $\mathbf{F}_{\underline{t}}(t - s)$ may be called a *constant history*. Then the response functional $\mathbf{J}$ will reduce to a *function*; symbolically, $\mathbf{T} = \mathbf{f}(\mathbf{M}, \mathbf{F})$. By listing $\mathbf{M}$ among the independent variables we mean to say that the value of stress still depends on what $\mathbf{M}$ is, e.g. given that $g(x) = Ax + Bx^2$, the linear functional $J[g] = \int g(x)\, dx$ will be a function of A and B, thus $J[g] \equiv f(A, B)$.

Following Wang,† let us show that constant histories admit a very simple representation. We start from

$$\frac{\partial x_i(t - r - s)}{\partial x_j} = \frac{\partial x_i(t - r - s)}{\partial x_m(t - r)} \frac{\partial x_m(t - r)}{\partial x_j},$$

$$\mathbf{F}_{\underline{t}}(t - r - s) = \mathbf{F}_{\underline{t}-\underline{r}}(t - r - s)\mathbf{F}_{\underline{t}}(t - r);$$

by (22.8), we now obtain $\mathbf{M}(r + s) = \mathbf{M}(s)\mathbf{M}(r)$. This equation is solved by $\mathbf{F}_{\underline{t}}(t - s) = \mathbf{M}(s) = \exp(-s\mathbf{A})$, where $\mathbf{A}$ is independent of s and t. The condition of material objectivity broadens, in effect, the class of deformations for which the reduction of (22.7) is possible, for if $\mathbf{T}$ corresponds to a constant history $\mathbf{F}_{\underline{t}}(t - s)$, then the stress associated with the "rotated" history $\mathbf{Q}(t - s)\mathbf{F}_{\underline{t}}(t - s)\mathbf{Q}^T$ will be given by $\mathbf{QTQ}^T$. Therefore, a reduction is possible whenever $\mathbf{F}_{\underline{t}}(t - s) = \mathbf{Q}(t - s)[\exp(-s\mathbf{A})]\mathbf{Q}^T$. This representation can be put into the form

$$\mathbf{F}_{\underline{t}}(t - s) = \bar{\mathbf{Q}}(s) \exp(-s\bar{\mathbf{A}}), \tag{22.9}$$

where

$$\bar{\mathbf{A}} = \mathbf{QAQ}^T, \quad \bar{\mathbf{Q}}(s) = \mathbf{Q}(t - s)\mathbf{Q}^T, \quad \bar{\mathbf{Q}}(0) = \mathbf{1}.$$

To obtain (22.9), we note that the exponential function is isotropic: $\mathbf{Q} \exp(-s\mathbf{A})\mathbf{Q}^T = \exp(-s\mathbf{QAQ}^T)$, as may be verified by expanding $\exp(-s\mathbf{A})$ in a power series.

† *Op. cit.*

Motions described by (22.9) were called *motions with constant stretch history* by Noll, and *substantially stagnant motions by* Coleman. For these motions we have that

$$\underset{-}{\mathbf{C}}_t(t - s) = \exp(-s\bar{\mathbf{A}}^T)\exp(-s\bar{\mathbf{A}}) \tag{22.10}$$

(note that this cannot be written as $\exp[-s(\bar{\mathbf{A}}^T + \bar{\mathbf{A}})]$, for that would imply that the product of the matrices $\exp(-s\bar{\mathbf{A}}^T)$ and $\exp(-s\bar{\mathbf{A}})$ is commutative). In general, the time rates of a tensor $\underset{-}{\mathbf{C}}_t(t - s)$, evaluated at $s = 0$, are known as the *Rivlin-Ericksen tensors* $\mathbf{A}_K$ (here K is a label):

$$\mathbf{A}_K(t) = (-1)^K \frac{d^K}{ds^K}\underset{-}{\mathbf{C}}_t(t - s)\bigg|_{s=0} \tag{22.11}$$

(cf. (8.55)). With (8.27), (8.56), we readily obtain

$$A_{1ij} = v_{i,j} + v_{j,i}, \quad A_{2ij} = \dot{v}_{i,j} + \dot{v}_{j,i} + 2v_{m,i}v_{m,j}.$$

Recalling from (21.59), $(21.64)_1$ the definition of convected derivatives, we can also write

$$\overset{\triangle}{\mathbf{1}} = \mathbf{A}_1, \qquad \overset{\triangle}{\mathbf{A}}_K = \mathbf{A}_{K+1},$$

or, equivalently

$$D_t^K(ds^2) = A_{Kij}dx_idx_j.$$

If, in particular, $\underset{-}{\mathbf{C}}_t(t - s)$ is given by (22.10), we obtain from (22.11) the recurrence formulas $\mathbf{A}_1 = \bar{\mathbf{A}}^T + \bar{\mathbf{A}}$, $\mathbf{A}_K = \bar{\mathbf{A}}^T\mathbf{A}_{K-1} + \mathbf{A}_{K-1}\bar{\mathbf{A}}$ ($K = 2, 3, \ldots$). Wang now proves that, *in motions with constant stretch history*, $\underset{-}{\mathbf{C}}_t(t - s)$ *is uniquely determined by the first three Rivlin-Ericksen tensors* $\mathbf{A}_1$, $\mathbf{A}_2$, $\mathbf{A}_3$. The proof given by Wang is elementary,† and for that reason somewhat lengthy, hence it will not be reproduced here. According to Wang's theorem, then, for motions with constant stretch history the constitutive equation (22.4) reduces to

$$\mathbf{T} = \mathbf{R}\mathbf{f}(\mathbf{R}^T\mathbf{A}_1\mathbf{R}, \mathbf{R}^T\mathbf{A}_2\mathbf{R}, \mathbf{R}^T\mathbf{A}_3\mathbf{R}, \mathbf{C})\mathbf{R}^T, \tag{22.12}$$

whereas (22.7) reduces to

$$\mathbf{T} = \mathbf{f}(\mathbf{A}_1, \mathbf{A}_2, \mathbf{A}_3, \rho). \tag{22.13}$$

† It makes use of the recurrence formulas, and the lemma stated on p. 493.

Here **f** is a *function* (in the sense explained below (22.7)), and all variables are evaluated at the current instant t.

By *viscometric flows* we mean flows that satisfy (22.13) and

$$\bar{\mathbf{A}}^2 = \mathbf{0}, \tag{22.14}$$

where $\bar{\mathbf{A}}$ may be a function of t (it is independent of t in steady viscometric flows).

From the point of view of dimensional analysis, viscoelasticity is characterized by two dimensional properties: an elasticity (with the dimension of stress) and a material time. Examples of the various kinds of viscoelasticity are a Maxwell fluid (cf. (14.51) *et seq.*) and a Kelvin solid (cf. (14.52) *et seq.*). A Maxwell fluid exhibits an instantaneously elastic response, and a stress relaxation. For a Kelvin solid the instantaneous response is viscous, and there is no stress relaxation. A simple material is, in effect, a generalization of a Maxwell fluid. If the response functional is discontinuous (as when it contains Dirac's delta or its derivatives), then (22.6) can also account for instantaneously viscous response. An equivalent formulation, which does not require the response functional to be discontinuous, would be to write

$$\mathbf{T} = \mathbf{K}(\mathbf{C}_{\underline{t}}(\tau), \mathbf{B}, \mathbf{A}_1, \mathbf{A}_2, \ldots), \tag{22.6*}$$

where **T** is a *function* of the Rivlin-Ericksen tensors. The discussion that follows will be confined to (22.6), i.e. to materials that exhibit an instantaneously elastic response.

Stress relaxation may be interpreted as the fading of a material's memory of past deformations. This property can be incorporated into the constitutive equation in several ways. Thus we may suppose that the memory span, m, is finite, in which case (22.4) is replaced by

$$\mathbf{T} = \mathop{\mathbf{J}}_{s=0}^{s=m} (\mathbf{F}_{\underline{t}}(t - s), \mathbf{F}).$$

Coleman and Noll† have described a continuously fading memory by introducing the idea of a magnitude, or "recollection," of deformation histories which is weighted in favor of the recent history (cf. (14.60)). Continuity of the response functional then implies that two histories of nearly the same magnitudes (i.e. two histories that have been nearly identical in the *recent* past) will yield nearly identical values of a stress. Therefore, if a deformation is constant from $t = 0$ on, thus $\mathbf{G}(s) = \mathbf{0}$ if $0 \leq s \leq t$, and $\mathbf{G}(s) = \mathbf{C}_{\underline{t}}(t-s) - \mathbf{1}$

† Cf. [16].

if $s > t$, then the property of fading memory will imply that, as $t \to \infty$, the stress approaches an equilibrium stress $\mathbf{T}^\infty$ that is independent of the history during $-\infty < \tau < 0$. The manner of convergence does depend on that history. In particular, if we consider a strain impulse described by $x_i(\tau) = X_i$, $\tau < 0$, and $x_i(\tau) = x_i(\mathbf{X})$, $\tau > 0$, thus

$$\mathbf{C}_{\underline{t}}(\tau) = \begin{matrix} \mathbf{B}^{-1} & \text{if } \tau < 0, \\ \mathbf{1} & \text{if } \tau > 0, \end{matrix} \tag{22.15}$$

where $B_{ij} = x_{i,m}x_{j,m}$, then it follows from (22.4) that the response functional depends on $(\mathbf{C}^{-1} - \mathbf{1})H(s - t)$, $t > 0$, where H is the Heaviside step function (cf. (22.25)). Because H is constant for $t > 0$, the value of the response functional is determined by the constant tensor $\mathbf{C}$, and by the elapsed time since the strain impulse, t, thus

$$\mathbf{T}^\infty = \mathbf{R}\mathbf{f}(\mathbf{C}, t)\mathbf{R}^T$$

(cf. (14.8) *et seq.*).

The reason why motions with constant stretch history are tractable is that the histories are so simple as to leave the response virtually dormant. By the same token, a study of these motions will tell us little about the response in general (as described by $\mathbf{K}$). Owing to the complexity of the response functional, however, it is not possible to study very general motions. Instead, we must look for deformation histories that, while not constant, still have some simplifying features that permit us to approximate the response functional in some way. It is clear that the approximation theories must lean heavily upon the fading of a material's memory.

To approximate $\mathbf{K}(\mathbf{C}_{\underline{t}}(t - s))$, we can either expand $\mathbf{C}_{\underline{t}}(t - s)$ in a series, or expand $\mathbf{K}$ in a series, or do both. To obtain useful results, in the first case a great deal of smoothness must be assumed for the history, whereas $\mathbf{K}$ need be no more than continuous. In the second case, no smoothness conditions are placed on the history, but $\mathbf{K}$ must be "differentiable." For instance, recalling from (14.65) the notion of a *retarded history*, we write

$$\mathbf{C}_{\underline{t}}^{(\alpha)}(t - s) \equiv \mathbf{C}_{\underline{t}}(t - \alpha s) \approx \mathbf{S}\mathbf{A}_K(t)(\alpha s)^K, \quad \alpha < 1, \tag{22.16}$$

where $\mathbf{S}$ indicates summation over K from 1 to M. By considering progressively more retarded flows, we obtain from $\mathbf{T}^{(\alpha)} = \mathbf{K}(C_{\underline{t}}^{(\alpha)}(t - s))$ approximations of the type shown in (22.26). It has been shown by Truesdell [181] that the desired approximations are not difficult to get if one assumes that the memory span is finite. Before outlining Truesdell's method, let us note that the assumption of a finite memory span permits us to approximate a deformation history in various ways, e.g. by a Fourier series. However, to obtain reasonably explicit results, we must resort to a Taylor series expansion about $s = 0$. But then the relevant portion of the history must be sufficiently smooth, so that jumps of the kind considered in (22.15) are excluded. More than that, a Taylor series describes a function on the basis of data taken from an arbitrarily small range of the function, i.e. "almost" at the same instant that a motion stops the Taylor series expansion about $s = 0$ will vanish too. Therefore, the stress relaxation will be "almost" instantaneous.

To put constitutive equations into a dimensionless form, there must exist a material property with the dimension of stress, and another material property with the dimension of time. Because the dimension of viscosity is $ML^{-1}T^{-1}$, we can also choose as the material properties a *natural viscosity* μ_N and a *natural time* τ_N. To define τ_N and μ_N in terms of the response functional we may use any of the available exact solutions (cf. (22.38)). Evidently the choice of τ_N and μ_N is by and large arbitrary, but that is unimportant here.

Let us now write the constitutive equation in a dimensionless form,

$$\frac{\tau_N}{\mu_N}\mathbf{T} = \frac{\tau_N}{\mu_N}\mathbf{J}(\mathbf{G}(s), \mathbf{B}) \equiv \mathbf{\Phi}(\mathbf{G}(\sigma), \mathbf{B}),$$

where
$$\mathbf{G}(s) = \mathbf{C}_{\underline{t}}(t - s) - \mathbf{1} \tag{22.17}$$

may be referred to as *strain history*, and $\sigma = s/\tau_N$ is the dimensionless elapsed time. For fluids $\mathbf{B}(t)$ is replaced by the mass density $\rho(t)$; in any case, tensors that do not depend on the elapsed time play no role in the approximation of response functionals. This allows us to use the simpler notation $(\tau_N/\mu_N)\mathbf{T} = \mathbf{\Phi}(\mathbf{G}(\sigma))$. We now assume that the material's memory of a class H of strain histories $\mathbf{H}(\sigma)$ is, when referred to the dimensionless time σ, of a finite span S. The response functional is then said to be *obliviating* (in the class H), and can be approximated by a functional $\mathbf{M}$ that is defined only on the interval $0 \leq \sigma \leq S$ (i.e. $0 \leq s \leq S\tau_N$) of histories. With $\mathbf{H}(\sigma) = \mathbf{G}(\sigma\tau_N) = \mathbf{G}(s)$, then, $\mathbf{\Phi}(\mathbf{G}(\sigma\tau_N)) \approx \mathbf{M}(\mathbf{G}(s))$. We now consider a sequence of fluids with progressively smaller natural times τ_N, while holding the natural viscosity μ_N, the deformation history $\mathbf{G}(s)$, and the dimensionless response functional $\mathbf{\Phi}$ fixed. This will yield the same approximation as the method of Coleman and Noll, which is based on the retardation of the flows of one and the same fluid. If τ_N is sufficiently small, then the (finite) memory span S will be mapped into a small interval $s = \sigma\tau_N < \delta$ in which the following approximation of $\mathbf{G}(s)$ is valid:

$$\mathbf{G}(s) = \mathbf{G}(\sigma\tau_N) \approx \mathbf{S}\frac{(-1)^K}{K!}\sigma^K\tau_N^K\mathbf{A}_K$$

(cf. (22.16)). If $\mathbf{\Phi}$ is obliviating, and if τ_N is small enough, we can use simultaneously the approximations for $\mathbf{\Phi}$ and $\mathbf{G}(s)$, and thus find that in the limit as $\tau_N \to 0$ the general constitutive equation of a fluid can be approximated by

$$\mathbf{T} + p\mathbf{1} = \frac{\mu_N}{\tau_N} \mathbf{f}(\tau_N \mathbf{A}_1, \tau_N^2 \mathbf{A}_2, \ldots, \tau_N^M \mathbf{A}_M), \tag{22.18}$$

where $\mathbf{f}$ is an isotropic function. If $\mathbf{f}$ is at least M times continuously differential at $\tau_N = 0$, then it can be approximated by a polynomial function, thus

$$\mathbf{T} + p\mathbf{1} \approx \mu_N \, \mathbf{S} \tau_N^{K-1} \mathbf{F}_K(\mathbf{A}_1, \mathbf{A}_2, \ldots, \mathbf{A}_M), \tag{22.19}$$

where $\mathbf{F}_K$ is an isotropic polynomial with dimensionless coefficients. The constitutive equation (22.18) is said to define a *Rivlin-Ericksen fluid of grade M*. For $M = 2$ it reads

$$\mathbf{T} = -p\mathbf{1} + \mu \mathbf{A}_1 + \alpha \mathbf{A}_2 + \beta \mathbf{A}_1^2, \tag{22.20}$$

where μ, α, β are constants.

The asymptotic nature of the approximation (22.19) can be given a more tangible interpretation if τ_N is measured in units of time that are characteristic of the period of observation, t_0, in which case τ_N may be identified with a *Deborah number* D_N defined as the ratio of the natural time to the time of observation.† That is, the Rivlin-Ericksen fluids describe simple fluids for $t_0 \gg \tau_N$.

The assumption of a finite memory, described by a natural time τ_N, can be used in another way to obtain a special theory of fluids. As in the theory of Eckart, outlined in Section 14, we may interpret viscoelasticity as an elastic response from a variable reference configuration. The variable reference configuration may be identified with the actual configuration at time $\tau^* = t - \tau_N$, in which case one speaks of *a fluid with convected elasticity*.‡ A material with convected elasticity is defined as follows,

$$\mathbf{T} = \mathbf{g}(\mathbf{F}, \mathbf{F}(\tau^*)). \tag{22.21}$$

Introducing the observer transformations $\mathbf{T}^+ = \mathbf{Q}\mathbf{T}\mathbf{Q}^T$, $d\mathbf{x}^+ = \mathbf{Q}\, d\mathbf{x}$, $d\mathbf{x}^+(\tau^*) = \mathbf{Q}^* d\mathbf{x}(\tau^*)$, where $\mathbf{Q}^* = \mathbf{Q}(\tau^*)$, we can express the material objectivity of (22.21) by $\mathbf{Q}\mathbf{g}(\mathbf{F}, \mathbf{F}(\tau^*))\mathbf{Q}^T = \mathbf{g}(\mathbf{Q}\mathbf{F}, \mathbf{Q}^*\mathbf{F}(\tau^*))$. Further, the invariance of $\mathbf{g}$

† Cf. the footnote on p. 308.
‡ Truesdell and Wang [205].

to a symmetry transformation $d\mathbf{X} \to \mathbf{H}d\mathbf{X}$ is expressed by $\mathbf{g}(\mathbf{F}, \mathbf{F}(\tau^*)) = \mathbf{g}(\mathbf{FH}, \mathbf{F}(\tau^*)\mathbf{H})$. If the substance is a fluid, then $\mathbf{H}$ may be any unimodular mapping; in particular, we can choose $\mathbf{H} = |\det\mathbf{F}(\tau^*)|\mathbf{F}^{-1}(\tau^*)$. But then it follows that $\mathbf{T} = \bar{\mathbf{g}}(\bar{\mathbf{F}}, \rho^*)$, where

$$\bar{F}_{im} = \frac{\partial x_i}{\partial x_m(\tau^*)}, \qquad \rho^* = \rho(\tau^*), \tag{22.22}$$

and we have used $\rho_0 = \rho^*\det\mathbf{F}(\tau^*)$. Because $\bar{\mathbf{F}}^+ = \mathbf{Q}\bar{\mathbf{F}}\mathbf{Q}^{*T}$, material objectivity now requires that $\mathbf{Q}\bar{\mathbf{g}}(\bar{\mathbf{F}}, \rho^*)\mathbf{Q}^T = \bar{\mathbf{g}}(\mathbf{Q}\bar{\mathbf{F}}\mathbf{Q}^{*T}, \rho^*)$. Letting $\mathbf{Q}^* = \mathbf{Q}$, we conclude that, as was to be expected, $\bar{\mathbf{g}}$ is an isotropic function. Therefore, $\mathbf{T} = \bar{\mathbf{g}}(\bar{\mathbf{F}}, \rho^*) = \bar{\mathbf{g}}(\bar{\mathbf{F}}\mathbf{Q}^{*T}\mathbf{Q}, \rho^*)$; if we now introduce the polar decomposition $\bar{\mathbf{F}} = \bar{\mathbf{V}}\bar{\mathbf{R}}$, and let $\bar{\mathbf{R}} = \mathbf{Q}^T\mathbf{Q}^*$, then it follows that $\mathbf{T} = \bar{\mathbf{g}}(\bar{\mathbf{F}}, \rho^*) = \bar{\mathbf{g}}(\mathbf{V}, \rho^*)$, or,

$$\mathbf{T} = \mathbf{f}(\bar{\mathbf{B}}, \rho^*),$$

$$\bar{\mathbf{B}} = \bar{\mathbf{F}}\bar{\mathbf{F}}^T, \qquad \bar{B}_{ij} = \frac{\partial x_i}{\partial x_m(\tau^*)}\frac{\partial x_j}{\partial x_m(\tau^*)}. \tag{22.23}$$

Response functionals too can be approximated by Taylor polynomials. To interpret derivatives of functionals, we recall that the definition (5.20) is really quite general, because there is nothing to prevent us from applying it to functionals too:

$$\delta\mathbf{J}(\mathbf{C}^t \mid \mathbf{D}^t] = \frac{d}{d\varepsilon}\mathbf{J}(\mathbf{C}^t + \varepsilon\mathbf{D}^t)\bigg|_{\varepsilon=0} \tag{22.24}$$

(cf. (5.24)), where $\mathbf{C}^t$ stands for the function with the values $\mathbf{C}^t(s) = \mathbf{C}(t - s)$, and $\mathbf{D}^t$ is a function with the values $\mathbf{D}^t(s) = \mathbf{D}(t - s)$. Of course, for (22.24) to be meaningful, it must be possible to define convergence in the space of histories. This may be done by using a "distance" defined by (14.60), or else by using the "natural topology"† of the histories. Different definitions of convergence will yield approximations that differ in certain respects, but the appearance of much of the approximation theory is little changed if one definition of convergence is replaced by another.

If the differential $\delta\mathbf{J}$ exists and is continuous, then, as was shown in Section 5, it is a *linear functional* of the incremental history $\mathbf{D}^t$. In contrast to the familiar representations $\delta\phi(\mathbf{x}|\mathbf{n}] = \mathbf{n}\cdot\nabla\phi$, however, we now have that

$$\delta\mathbf{J}(\mathbf{C}^t \mid \mathbf{D}^t] = \int_0^\infty \mathbf{G}(s)\mathbf{D}^t(s)\,ds,$$

† Cf. p. 85.

where $\mathbf{G}(s)$ depends on $\mathbf{C}^t$: $\mathbf{G}(s) \equiv \mathbf{G}(\mathbf{C}^t(s), s)$. Rather than proving that linear functionals admit a representation of this kind, we shall have to be content with the following, heuristic argument.† Let us take a linear functional J of functions f defined on some interval $a \leq x \leq b$. If x is the limit point of a sequence of points x_N, then, assuming that f is continuous, $\lim f(x_N) = f(x)$. Similarly, if f is the limit of a sequence of functions f_N, then, assuming that J is a continuous functional, $\lim J[f_N] = J[f]$. Now let $H(x' - x)$ be the Heaviside step function, thus

$$H(x' - x) = \begin{matrix} 1 \text{ if } x' > x \\ 0 \text{ if } x' < x \end{matrix}. \tag{22.25}$$

We introduce a subdivision $a = x_0 < x_1 < x_2 \ldots < x_N = b$ of the domain of f, and define a piecewise constant function f_N by

$$f_N(x) = \sum_{R=1}^{N} \bar{f}_R [H(x_R - x) - H(x_{R-1} - x)],$$

where $\bar{f}_R$ is some value of f in the interval $x_{R-1} \leq x \leq x_R$. Denoting the value of J at $H(x' - x)$ by $\phi(x')$, and invoking the linearity of J, we obtain

$$J[f_N] = \sum_{R=1}^{N} \bar{f}_R[\phi(x_R) - \phi(x_{R-1})].$$

Because J is also assumed to be continuous, in the limit $N \to \infty$ this formula becomes

$$J[f] = \int_a^b f(x)\, d\phi(x).$$

By the same kind of reasoning we should find that multilinear, continuous functionals are represented by multiple integrals, e.g. a bilinear functional $J[f, g]$ is of the form

$$J[f, g] = \int_a^b \int_a^b dx\, dy\, k(x, y) f(x) g(y).$$

If we set $f = g$, there results a quadratic functional. Therefore, we can write a Taylor polynomial of $\mathbf{K}(\mathbf{C}^t + \mathbf{D}^t)$ as follows,

$$\mathbf{K}(\mathbf{C}^t + \mathbf{D}^t) = \mathbf{K}(\mathbf{C}^t) + \delta\mathbf{K}(\mathbf{C}^t \mid \mathbf{D}^t] + \delta^2\mathbf{K}(\mathbf{C}^t \mid \mathbf{D}^t) + \cdots,$$

where $\delta^2\mathbf{K}(\mathbf{C}^t \mid \mathbf{D}^t) \equiv \delta^2\mathbf{K}(\mathbf{C}^t \mid \mathbf{D}^t, \mathbf{D}^t]$.

† Cf. [206], pp. 16, 17. A rigorous theory may be found in [10].

To illustrate differentiation of functionals, let us write $(14.59)_1$ as follows,

$$\mathbf{J}[\mathbf{E}^t, \mathbf{E}] = \mathbf{G}(0)\mathbf{E} + \int_{-\infty}^{t} \dot{\mathbf{G}}(t - \tau)\mathbf{E}(\tau)\, d\tau,$$

where $\mathbf{E} = \mathbf{E}(t)$. Evidently the history $\mathbf{E}(t - s)$, $0 \leq s < \infty$, can be replaced in $\mathbf{J}[\mathbf{E}^t, \mathbf{E}]$ by its *restriction* on the open interval $0 < s < \infty$, because the value of the integral is not going to be affected by a change of $\mathbf{E}(\tau)$ at the single point $\tau = t$. With this in mind, we find that $\partial_{\mathbf{E}}\mathbf{J}[\mathbf{E}^t, \mathbf{E}] = \mathbf{G}(0)$. Here $\mathbf{G}(0)$ may be referred to as the *instantaneous tangent modulus*. Similarly, differentiating $\mathbf{J}[\mathbf{E}^t, \mathbf{E}]$ with respect to the strain history, while holding the current strain $\mathbf{E}$ fixed, we obtain

$$\delta\mathbf{J}[\mathbf{E}^t, \mathbf{E} \mid \mathbf{E}'] = \int_{-\infty}^{t} \mathbf{G}(t - \tau)\mathbf{E}'(\tau)\, d\tau.$$

This result came out to be independent of the history $\mathbf{E}^t$, but that was so only because $\mathbf{J}$ was a linear functional at $\mathbf{E}^t$. To provide a more typical example of derivatives of functionals, let us take the constitutive equation of a *second-order incompressible fluid*,

$$\mathbf{T} + p\mathbf{1} = \int_0^\infty \mu(s)\mathbf{G}(s)\, ds + \int_0^\infty\int_0^\infty [\alpha(s_1, s_2)\mathbf{G}(s_1)\mathbf{G}(s_2) + \beta(s_1, s_2)\mathbf{G}(s_2)\,\mathrm{tr}\mathbf{G}(s_1)]ds_1 ds_2, \tag{22.26}$$

where $\mathbf{G}(s) = \mathbf{C}_t(t - s) - \mathbf{1}$. Denoting the right-hand side of (22.26) by $\mathbf{J}(\mathbf{G})$, we can write that, by a routine application of (22.24),

$$\delta\mathbf{J}(\mathbf{G} \mid \mathbf{H}] = \int_0^\infty \mu(s)\mathbf{H}(s)\, ds + \int_0^\infty\int_0^\infty [\alpha(s_1, s_2)(\mathbf{G}(s_1)\mathbf{H}(s_2) + \mathbf{H}(s_1)\mathbf{G}(s_2)) + \beta(s_1, s_2)(G(s_2)\mathrm{tr}\mathbf{H}(s_1) + \mathbf{H}(s_2)\mathrm{tr}\mathbf{G}(s_1))]ds_1 ds_2.$$

Differentiating once more, we obtain

$$\delta^2\mathbf{J}(\mathbf{G} \mid \mathbf{I}, \mathbf{H}] = \int_0^\infty\int_0^\infty [\alpha(s_1, s_2)(\mathbf{I}(s_1)\mathbf{H}(s_2) + \mathbf{H}(s_1)\mathbf{I}(s_2)) + \beta(s_1, s_2)(\mathbf{I}(s_2)\,\mathrm{tr}\mathbf{H}(s_1) + \mathbf{H}(s_2)\,\mathrm{tr}\mathbf{I}(s_1))]ds_1 ds_2.$$

The same result could have been obtained by applying to (22.26) the definition of a second derivative,

$$\delta^2\mathbf{J}(\mathbf{G} \mid \mathbf{I}, \mathbf{H}] = \frac{\partial^2}{\partial\eta\,\partial\varepsilon}[\mathbf{J}(\mathbf{G} + \varepsilon\mathbf{H} + \eta\mathbf{I})\,|_{\varepsilon=0,\eta=0}.$$

The last operation is of course the same as

$$\delta^2 f(x, y \mid \Delta x, \Delta y] = \frac{\partial^2}{\partial\varepsilon\,\partial\eta} f(x + \varepsilon\,\Delta x, y + \eta\,\Delta y)\bigg|_{\substack{\varepsilon=0\\ \eta=0}} = \frac{\partial^2 f}{\partial x\,\partial y}\Delta x\,\Delta y.$$

The only difficulty is the lack of elementary functions, e.g. x^N, xy, on which one can practice differentiation (over the domain of histories, these elementary rules are described by multiple integrals). What it comes down to is that differentiation is an operation to be executed according to its definition, rather than by memorizing a handful of formulas.

If we are prepared to differentiate functionals as fearlessly as we differentiate "ordinary" functions, we can apply the ideas of the classical theories of thermodynamics and wave propagation to materials with memory. We shall outline in a one-dimensional setting a few of the results obtained by Coleman [12], and Coleman and Gurtin [13].

Whenever a history and its value at $s = 0$ (e.g. $F^t(s)$ and $F \equiv F(t) = F^t(0)$) are both listed as independent variables, it is understood that the history is a restriction on the open interval $0 < s < \infty$. In that case, the limit as $s \to 0$ of a continuous history need not coincide with its value at $s = 0$. In a stress relation $T = J(F^t, \theta^t, F, \theta)$, the stress is an "ordinary" function of temperature θ and deformation gradient F, but a functional of their histories. Therefore, we can introduce the "ordinary" partial derivatives $\partial_F J = \partial J/\partial F$ (evaluated at fixed F^t, θ^t, and θ) and $\partial_\theta J = \partial J/\partial\theta$ (evaluated at fixed F^t, θ^t, and F). Along with these, we have the partial derivatives

$$\delta_F J(F^t, \theta^t, F, \theta \mid \Delta F^t] = \frac{d}{d\varepsilon} J(F^t + \varepsilon\,\Delta F^t, \theta^t, F, \theta)\bigg|_{\varepsilon=0},$$

$$\delta_\theta J(F^t, \theta^t, F, \theta \mid \Delta\theta^t] = \frac{d}{d\varepsilon} J(F^t, \theta^t + \varepsilon\,\Delta\theta^t, F, \theta)\bigg|_{\varepsilon=0}.$$

Further, we may introduce a total differential as follows. If $T = J(F^t, F)$, for instance, and $\Delta F = H$, then $dJ = \partial_F J(F^t, F)H + \delta_F J(F^t, F \mid H^t]$, or,

$$dJ = EH(t) + \int_0^\infty \frac{dG(s)}{ds} H^t(s)\,ds,$$

where both E and dG/ds depend on F^t and F. With $F = 1 + H$, $T \approx J(1^t, 1) + dJ(1^t, 1 \mid H^t, H]$, we can now obtain linear viscoelasticity as a "first approximation". For economy of writing, the set of independent variables F^t, θ^t, F, θ will be often denoted by M. With these definitions in mind, let us investigate the limitations imposed by the Clausius-Duhem inequality upon the constitutive equation $T = J(M, h)$ for stress, $\psi = P(M, h)$ for free energy, $\eta = N(M, h)$ for entropy, and $q = Q(M, h)$ for heat flux, h being the temperature gradient $\partial\theta/\partial X$. Starting with (12.22), and noting that now $\dot{\psi} = (\partial_F P)\dot{F} + (\partial_\theta P)\dot{\theta} + (\partial_h P)\dot{h} + \delta_F P(M, h \mid \dot{F}^t] + \delta_\theta P(M, h \mid \dot{\theta}^t]$, we again obtain that T, ψ, and η are independent of h, and that

$$T = \rho F \partial_F P, \qquad \eta = -\partial_\theta P \tag{22.27}$$

(cf. (14.84)), $\qquad \delta = -\rho\delta_F P(M \mid \dot{F}^t] - \rho\delta_\theta P(M \mid \dot{\theta}^t]$

(cf. (12.11)); in the derivation we assume $\dot{F}(t)$ and $\dot{F}^t(s) = \dot{F}(t - s) = -\partial F(t - s)/\partial s$ independent of each other (and similarly for $\dot{\theta}(t)$ and $\dot{\theta}^t(s)$). Coleman has shown that for motions that are sufficiently slow, or sufficiently fast, (22.27) reduce to the stress and entropy relations given in (14.84). That is, (14.84) may hold for *all* motions in certain "perfect" materials; they also hold for special motions (particularly, equilibrium) of all simple materials.

The investigation of acceleration fronts, begun in Section 14, can now be extended to nonlinear viscoelasticity. We recall that any jump at a surface of discontinuity, S, is a function of time only, thus $[\![\psi]\!] = f(t)$. To represent $df(t)/dt$ in terms of ψ, we must interpret d/dt, when applied inside the brackets, as $S_t = D_t + U\partial_X$, where $U = dR/dt$, and $X = R(t)$ is the location of S in the body. We then obtain the "master formula"

$$\dot{f} = \frac{d}{dt}[\![\psi]\!] = [\![\dot{\psi}]\!] + U[\![\partial_X \psi]\!].$$

If S is an acceleration front, then, by definition, x, $\dot{x}$, F, and θ are continuous at S. Therefore, $[\![\dot{x}]\!] + U[\![\dot{F}]\!] = 0$, $[\![\dot{F}]\!] + U[\![\partial_X F]\!] = 0$, $[\![\dot{\theta}]\!] + U[\![\partial_X \theta]\!] = 0$, thus

$$[\![\ddot{x}]\!] = -U[\![\dot{F}]\!] = U^2[\![\partial_X F]\!]. \tag{i}$$

Letting $a(t) = [\![\ddot{x}]\!]$, we obtain $\dot{a} = [\![\dddot{x}]\!] + U[\![\dot{F}]\!]$; however, from (i) it follows that $\dot{a} = -\dot{U}[\![\dot{F}]\!] - U[\![\ddot{F}]\!] - U^2[\![\partial_X \dot{F}]\!]$. Adding the two expressions we get

$$2\dot{a} - \frac{a}{U}\dot{U} = [\![\dddot{x}]\!] - U^2[\![\partial_X \dot{F}]\!]. \tag{ii}$$

The equation of motion, $\partial_X T = \rho_0 \ddot{x}$, gives us $\partial_X \dot{T} = \rho_0 \dddot{x}$, therefore, (ii) can be expressed as follows,

$$2\dot{a} = \frac{a}{U}\dot{U} + \frac{1}{\rho_0}[\![\partial_X \dot{T}]\!] - U^2[\![\partial_X \dot{F}]\!].$$

If $T = J(F^t, F)$, then

$$\frac{\partial T}{\partial X} = (\partial_F J)\frac{\partial F}{\partial X} + \delta_F J(F^t, F \,|\, \partial_X F^t]$$

$$\frac{\partial \dot{T}}{\partial X} = (\partial_F J)\frac{\partial \dot{F}}{\partial X} + (\partial_F^2 J)\frac{\partial F}{\partial X}\dot{F} + \delta_F \partial_F J(F^t, F \mid \dot{F}^t]\frac{\partial F}{\partial X}$$

$$+\partial_F \delta_F J(F^t, F \,|\, \partial_X F^t]\dot{F} + \delta_F^2 J(F^t, F \,|\, \partial_X F^t, \dot{F}^t] + \delta_F J(F^t, F \,|\, \partial_X \dot{F}^t].$$

As noted in Section 14, a jump in the histories $\partial_X F^t$ and $\dot{F}^t$ occurs only at one point (X, s), therefore, there is no jump in the *integrals* of $\partial_X F^t$ and $\dot{F}^t$. Thus

$$[\![\partial_X \dot{T}]\!] = E[\![\partial_X \dot{F}]\!] + \tilde{E}[\![\dot{F}\partial_X F]\!] + (A + G')[\![\partial_X F]\!] + B[\![\dot{F}]\!],$$

$$E = \partial_F J, \quad \tilde{E} = \partial_F^2 J, \quad A = \delta_F \partial_F J(F^t, F \mid \dot{F}^t], \quad B = \partial_F \delta_F J(F^t, F|\partial_X F^t],$$

and $G' \equiv G'(0)$ is defined by the representation

$$\delta_F J(F^t, F \mid H^t] = \int_0^\infty H^t(s)\, G'(s)\, ds,$$

all coefficients being evaluated at $X = R$. Together with (ii), this yields

$$\dot{a} = -\mu a + \beta\, [\![\dot{F}\partial_X F]\!]$$

$$\mu = -\frac{\dot{U}}{2U} + \frac{1}{2\rho_0 U}\left(B - \frac{G' + A}{U}\right), \quad \beta = \frac{\tilde{E}}{2\rho_0},$$

where we have used (i) and $U^2 = E/\rho_0$. The last result is obtained from $[\![\partial_X T]\!] = E[\![\partial_X F]\!] = \rho_0[\![\ddot{x}]\!] = \rho_0 U^2[\![\partial_X F]\!]$ (cf. (i)). If an acceleration wave propagates into a medium held at a fixed deformation $x(X, t - s) = F_0 X + X_0$, so that $F^t(s) = F_0$ = const., then it follows that E = const., $\tilde{E}$ = const., $G'(0)$ = const., and $A = B = 0$. Because $\dot{F} = \partial_X F = 0$ for $X > R(t)$, we also have that $[\![\dot{F}\,\partial_X F]\!] = \dot{F}^- \,\partial_X F^- = [\![\dot{F}]\!]\,[\![\partial_X F]\!] = -a^2/U^3$, and the differential equation for $a(t)$ reduces to

$$\dot{a} = -\mu a + \frac{\mu}{\lambda}a^2,$$

where $\mu = -G'(0)/2E = \text{const.}$, $\lambda = G'(0)U/E = \text{const.}$ Integrating, Coleman and Gurtin obtain the explicit formula

$$a(t) = a(0)\frac{\lambda}{(\lambda - a(0))\exp(\mu t) + a(0)}.$$

If $G'(0) = 0$ (as is the case for elastic materials), then

$$a(t) = \frac{a(0)}{1 + \nu a(0)t}, \qquad \nu = \frac{\tilde{E}}{2EU}.$$

Starting with the constitutive equations of thermomechanics of simple materials, we should find that the only change in the amplitude equation is an additional term $(U\alpha^2\theta + \phi\alpha)/2\rho_0 Uk$ in μ, where $\alpha = \partial_\theta T$, $\phi = \partial_F q$, and $k = -\partial_h q$.

Linearly viscoelastic response of isotropic solids may be defined by†

$$\mathbf{T} = \mathbf{h}(\mathbf{B}) + \int_0^\infty \mathbf{g}(\mathbf{B}, s, \mid \mathbf{G}(s)]\, ds. \tag{22.28}$$

To obtain the equations of classical viscoelasticity theory, we should carry out a consistent linearization of (22.28). With $\mathbf{u} = \mathbf{x} - \mathbf{X}$, $\mathbf{H} = \mathbf{F} - \mathbf{1}$, we introduce as a measure of smallness the quantity $\varepsilon = |\mathbf{H}| = \sqrt{u_{i.m}u_{i.m}}$, i.e. the displacement gradients $\mathbf{H}$ are taken to be of the order of $\varepsilon \ll 1$. Noting that $\mathbf{F} = \mathbf{1} + \mathbf{H} = \mathbf{1} + O(\varepsilon)$, we arrive at $\mathbf{F}^{-1} = \mathbf{1} - \mathbf{H} + O(\varepsilon^2) = \mathbf{1} + O(\varepsilon)$, $\mathbf{F}_{\underline{t}}(\tau) = \mathbf{F}(\tau)\mathbf{F}^{-1} = (\mathbf{1} + \mathbf{H}(\tau))(\mathbf{1} - \mathbf{H}) = \mathbf{1} + \mathbf{H}(\tau) - \mathbf{H}$, and $\mathbf{C}_{\underline{t}}(\tau) = \mathbf{F}_{\underline{t}}^T(\tau)\mathbf{F}_{\underline{t}}(\tau) = \mathbf{1} + 2[\tilde{\mathbf{E}}(\tau) - \tilde{\mathbf{E}}]$. Because $\mathbf{B} = \mathbf{F}\mathbf{F}^T = \mathbf{1} + 2\tilde{\mathbf{E}}$, we can write, with $\mathbf{h}(B) = \mathbf{L}(\tilde{\mathbf{E}})$,

$$\mathbf{T} = \mathbf{L}(\tilde{\mathbf{E}}) + 2\int_0^\infty \mathbf{g}(\mathbf{1}, s)[\tilde{\mathbf{E}}(t - s) - \tilde{\mathbf{E}}]\, ds.$$

An equivalent form of this is obtained by introducing the stress relaxation function $\mu(s)$: $\dot{\mu}(s) = d\mu(s)/ds = 2g(\mathbf{1}, s)$. Then

$$\begin{aligned}\mathbf{T} = \{(\lambda + \bar{\lambda}(0))\,\mathrm{tr}\tilde{\mathbf{E}} + \int_0^\infty \dot{\bar{\lambda}}(s)\,\mathrm{tr}\tilde{\mathbf{E}}(t - s)\, ds\}\mathbf{1}\\ + 2(\mu + \bar{\mu}(0))\tilde{\mathbf{E}} + 2\int_0^\infty \dot{\bar{\mu}}(s)\tilde{\mathbf{E}}(t - s)\, ds,\end{aligned} \tag{22.29}$$

† Coleman and Noll [15]. (Cf. also Lianis and DeHoff [239]).

where λ and μ are material constants (Lame's coefficients of elasticity), and $\bar{\lambda}$ and $\bar{\mu}$ are *material functions.* The coefficients $\lambda + \bar{\lambda}(t)$ and $\mu + \bar{\mu}(t)$ then may be interpreted as the time-dependent Lame's coefficients for the stress relaxation from a strain impulse at time $t = 0$.

In a second-order theory of incompressible, viscoelastic solids the extra stress $\mathbf{S} = \mathbf{T} + p\mathbf{1}$ is given by† $\mathbf{S}_1 + \mathbf{S}_2$, where

$$\mathbf{S}_1 = \int_{-\infty}^{t} K_1(t - \tau)\dot{\mathbf{E}}(\tau)\, d\tau,$$

$$\mathbf{S}_2 = \int_{-\infty}^{t}\int_{-\infty}^{t} K_2(t - \tau_1, t - \tau_2)[\dot{\mathbf{E}}(\tau_1)\dot{\mathbf{E}}(\tau_2) + \dot{\mathbf{E}}(\tau_2)\dot{\mathbf{E}}(\tau_1)]\, d\tau_1\, d\tau_2. \tag{22.30}$$

For fluids we cannot assume deformations to remain small; instead, the approximate constitutive equations must be interpreted as asymptotic cases which describe flows that are either very slow or very fast. As was noted on p. 524, the Rivlin-Ericksen fluids are an appropriate model when the ratio of relaxation time to time of observation is small. If the period of observation is shorter than the relaxation time, i.e. for rapid deformations, the response of a simple fluid will be, in effect, elastic.‡ Specifically, if we assume a fluid to be at rest for $\tau < 0$, and undergoing a deformation for $\tau > 0$, then, expanding $\mathbf{G}(s)$ in a Taylor series about $s = 0$, we obtain from (22.11) and (22.26) that

$$\mathbf{T} + p\mathbf{1} = \sum_K (-1)^K P_K \mathbf{A}_K + \sum_K\sum_L (-1)^{K+L} P_{KL}(\mathbf{A}_K\mathbf{A}_L + \mathbf{A}_L\mathbf{A}_K) + \ldots,$$

where

$$P_K = \frac{1}{K!}\int_0^t \mu(s)s^K\, ds,$$

$$P_{KL} = \frac{1}{K!L!}\int_0^t\int_0^t ds_1\, ds_2 \alpha(s_1, s_2)s_1^K s_2^L.$$

In contrast to (22.19), the coefficients are now functions of time (which tend to constant values as time increases). In flows of complex geometry (e.g. at the entrance to a pipe), a material volume may undergo rapid deformations during one interval, and slow deformations the rest of the time. Therefore, the response of the volume element will have to be approximated differently at different stages of flow.

Through the researches of Rivlin and his co-workers, there have emerged

† Cf. A. C. Pipkin [207].
‡ Cf. Metzner, White, and Denn [240].

during the last decade representations of functional constitutive equations, a theory of small deformations superimposed on large, a functional theory of plasticity, as well as a functional theory of multipolar media. Much of this work awaits further exploration. A survey of constitutive equations of the kind shown in (22.27), (22.30) is given in [207].

Recently Bernstein, Kearsley, and Zapas [4] have proposed an approximation of the general constitutive equation which appears to represent accurately a wide range of experimental data. If we imagine for a moment that a viscoelastic substance is made up of long, "elastic" chains that are bonded together at various points (so as to constitute an elastic network), then it is plausible, at least for the sake of motivating the theory, to assume that during deformation the bonds are broken in many places, and subsequently new bonds are formed. That is, a deformation is, in part, elastic (i.e. structure-preserving), and, in part, inelastic. The assumption is, then, that the response to a deformation gradient $F_{ij}(t, \tau) = \partial x_i(t)/\partial x_j(\tau)$, $\tau \leq t$, is elastic, in the sense that the stress increment is given by

$$\Delta T_{ij}(t, \tau) = 2 \frac{\partial W}{\partial F_{ik}(t, \tau)} F_{jk}(t, \tau),$$

for instance, but that $\Delta T_{ij}(t, \tau)$ decays with increasing $t - \tau$, because the structure that existed at time τ gradually vanishes. To this end, it is assumed that $W = W(\mathbf{F}(t, \tau), t - \tau)$, and that the stress relation is of the form (cf. [209])

$$T_{ij} = -p\delta_{ij} + 2\int_{-\infty}^{t} \left[\frac{\partial W}{\partial \mathrm{I}} B_{ij}(t, \tau) - \frac{\partial W}{\partial \mathrm{II}} B_{ij}^{-1}(t, \tau)\right] d\tau, \qquad (22.31)$$

where I, II are the invariants of $\mathbf{B} = \mathbf{F}\mathbf{F}^T$, and for brevity we have assumed that the material is incompressible (thus III = 1). In a homogeneous deformation $x = \lambda X$, $y = Y/\sqrt{\lambda}$, $z = Z/\sqrt{\lambda}$, we have that

$$\mathrm{I} = \frac{\lambda^2(t)}{\lambda^2(\tau)} + 2\frac{\lambda(\tau)}{\lambda(t)}, \qquad \mathrm{II} = 2\frac{\lambda(t)}{\lambda(\tau)} + \frac{\lambda^2(\tau)}{\lambda^2(t)},$$

and

$$\sigma(t) = T_{11} - T_{22} = \int_{-\infty}^{t} \left[\frac{\lambda^2(t)}{\lambda^2(\tau)} - \frac{\lambda(\tau)}{\lambda(t)}\right] h\, d\tau,$$

$$h = 2\left[\frac{\partial W}{\partial \mathrm{I}} + \frac{\lambda(t)}{\lambda(\tau)} \frac{\partial W}{\partial \mathrm{II}}\right].$$

In a single-step stress relaxation such that $\lambda(t) = 1$ for $t < 0$ and $\lambda(t) = \lambda = \text{const.}$ for $t \geq 0$,

$$\sigma(t) = \left(\lambda^2 - \frac{1}{\lambda}\right)H(\lambda, t), \qquad \frac{\partial H}{\partial t} \equiv -h.$$

Bernstein, Kearsley, and Zapas have also given the constitutive equations for non-isothermal conditions. It is not obvious, however, in what way their equations fit into the general scheme of thermomechanics.

Viscometric flows

In contrast to elasticity theory, fluid mechanics offers a much more limited class of problems that can be solved, because equilibrium problems, which constitute the main body of elasticity theory, are of little interest in fluid mechanics. Here one must deal with motions, and thus come to grips with the rather intractable acceleration terms occurring in the equations of motion. However, considerable progress can be made by assuming incompressibility, in which case the constitutive equation is of the form

$$\mathbf{T} = -p\mathbf{1} + \mathbf{K}(\mathbf{G}(s)), \qquad \mathbf{G}(s) \equiv \mathbf{C}_{\underline{t}}(t - s) - \mathbf{1}.$$

Steady flows are a source of simple deformation histories because a steady flow, by definition, does not change from one instant to another. Therefore, let us consider steady rectilinear flows that are described in some Cartesian frame by $\dot{x} = 0$, $\dot{y} = v(x)$, $\dot{z} = 0$. The orientation of coordinate axes relative to the flow is such as to make easy the comparison with Couette flow (described in cylindrical coordinates). The history of the steady motion is then

$$x(\tau) = x, \qquad y(\tau) = y - vs, \qquad z(\tau) = z, \qquad -\infty < \tau \leq t, \tag{22.32}$$

where $s = t - \tau$ is the elapsed time, and $x(t) = x$, $y(t) = y$, $z(t) = z$. The present time t is a fixed but unspecified parameter. The deformation gradients $F_{\underline{t}ij}(\tau) = \partial x_i(\tau)/\partial x_j$ are given by

$$\mathbf{F}_{\underline{t}}(t - s) = \mathbf{1} - ks\mathbf{N}, \qquad k = \frac{dv}{dx} = 2D_{12}, \tag{22.33}$$

where

$$\|\mathbf{N}\| = \begin{Vmatrix} 0 & 0 & 0 \\ 1 & 0 & 0 \\ 0 & 0 & 0 \end{Vmatrix}. \tag{22.34}$$

The tensor $\mathbf{N}$ is *nil-potent* in the sense that $\mathbf{N}^K = \mathbf{0}$, $K \geq 2$. The flow is viscometric, because

$$\mathbf{G}(s) = -\mathbf{A}_1 s + \mathbf{A}_2 \frac{s^2}{2}, \tag{22.35}$$

where

$$\mathbf{A}_1 = k(\mathbf{N} + \mathbf{N}^T), \quad \mathbf{A}_2 = 2k^2\mathbf{M}, \quad \mathbf{M} = \mathbf{N}^T\mathbf{N} = \operatorname{diag}(1, 0, 0), \tag{22.36}$$

and $\mathbf{A}_K = \mathbf{0}$, $K \geq 3$. The response functional $\mathbf{K}$ over the deformation histories (22.35) defines a *function* of the shear rate k and of the constant tensor $\mathbf{N}$; thus in effect $\mathbf{K}(\mathbf{G}(s))$ reduces to a function of k only,

$$T_{ij} = -p\delta_{ij} + f_{ij}(k). \tag{22.37}$$

We are now going to use the property of isotropy to show that the response functions f_{13} and f_{23} vanish.

Let us consider

$$\mathbf{Q}\mathbf{G}(s)\mathbf{Q}^T = -(\alpha k s)\mathbf{Q}\left(\frac{1}{\alpha}\mathbf{N} + \frac{1}{\alpha}\mathbf{N}^T\right)\mathbf{Q}^T + (\alpha^2 k^2 s^2)\mathbf{Q}\frac{1}{\alpha^2}\mathbf{M}\mathbf{Q}^T.$$

The constant factor α will be used to test the parity of the response functions. Right now we let $\alpha = 1$ and $\mathbf{Q} = \operatorname{diag}(-1, -1, 1)$. Then, as may be directly verified, $\mathbf{Q}\mathbf{N}\mathbf{Q}^T = \mathbf{N}$, $\mathbf{Q}\mathbf{M}\mathbf{Q}^T = \mathbf{M}$, and $\mathbf{Q}\mathbf{G}(s)\mathbf{Q}^T = \mathbf{G}(s)$. Because the response functional is isotropic, the stress tensor must enjoy the same invariance: $\mathbf{Q}\mathbf{T}\mathbf{Q}^T = \mathbf{T}$. But

$$\|\mathbf{Q}\mathbf{T}\mathbf{Q}^T\| = \begin{Vmatrix} T_{11} & T_{12} & -T_{13} \\ T_{21} & T_{22} & -T_{23} \\ -T_{31} & -T_{32} & T_{33} \end{Vmatrix},$$

which means that the matrix of stresses associated with the motion (22.32) must be of the form

$$\|\mathbf{T}\| = \begin{Vmatrix} T_{11} & T_{12} & 0 \\ T_{21} & T_{22} & 0 \\ 0 & 0 & T_{33} \end{Vmatrix}.$$

If the fluid is incompressible, then among the four stresses occurring in this matrix only the shearing stress and the differences of the normal stresses are determined by material response. This leads us to introduce a *shear stress function* $\tilde{\tau}$ and two *normal stress functions* $\tilde{\sigma}_{\underline{1}}$ as follows:

$$T_{12} = \tilde{\tau}(k),$$
$$T_{11} - T_{33} = \tilde{\sigma}_1(k), \quad T_{22} - T_{33} = \tilde{\sigma}_2(k). \tag{22.38}$$

The *viscosity function* $\eta(k) = \tilde{\tau}(k)/k$ evidently describes an "effective shear modulus."

The stress power $M = T_{ij}D_{ij}$ is given in the present case by $k\tilde{\tau}(k)$. Because this term represents the rate of dissipation of kinetic energy, we require that $M = k\tilde{\tau}(k) \geq 0$.

To establish the parity of the response functions, we choose $\alpha = -1$ and $\mathbf{Q} = \text{diag}(-1, 1, -1)$. Then it can be verified $\mathbf{QNQ}^T = -\mathbf{N}$, $\mathbf{QMQ}^T = \mathbf{M}$, and

$$\|\mathbf{QTQ}^T\| = \begin{Vmatrix} T_{11} & -T_{12} & 0 \\ -T_{12} & T_{22} & 0 \\ 0 & 0 & T_{33} \end{Vmatrix}.$$

This means that $\tilde{\tau}$ and $\tilde{\sigma}_{\underline{1}}$ must be, respectively, odd and even functions of the rate of shear:

$$\tilde{\tau}(-k) = -\tilde{\tau}(k), \qquad \tilde{\sigma}_{\underline{1}}(-k) = \tilde{\sigma}_{\underline{1}}(k). \tag{22.39}$$

The preceding derivations also remain valid if $\mathbf{N}$ is a function of time t, provided that $\mathbf{N}$ satisfies the condition $\mathbf{N}^3 = \mathbf{0}$.

The constitutive equation of incompressible fluids specifies only the extra stress $\mathbf{S} = \mathbf{T} + p\mathbf{1}$. In the present case the extra stresses predicted by the constitutive equations are arbitrary functions of x. However, this arbitrariness is considerably decreased by the limitations imposed by the equations of motion. Omitting the body force term, we can write $\text{div}\mathbf{S} - \text{grad}p = \rho\dot{\mathbf{v}}$. Because the motion (22.32) is without acceleration, the equations of motion reduce to $\partial_x S_{xx} + \partial_y T_{xy} - \partial_x p = 0$, $\partial_x T_{xy} + \partial_y S_{yy} - \partial_y p = 0$, $\partial_z S_{zz} - \partial_z p = 0$. The extra stresses being functions of x only, we conclude from the last equation that $p = p(x, y)$. From the first we get $S_{xx} = p + f(y)$, whereas $\partial_x T_{xy} - \partial_y p = 0$ requires that

$$p = -ay + g(x). \tag{22.40}$$

Therefore,

$$T_{xy} = -ax + q, \qquad T_{xx} = ay + b,$$
$$T_{yy} = ay + m(x), \qquad T_{zz} = ay + n(x). \tag{22.41}$$

The arbitrary functions $m(x)$ and $n(x)$ can be eliminated in terms of normal stress functions:

$$T_{yy} = ay + b + \tilde{\sigma}_2(k) - \tilde{\sigma}_1(k), \quad T_{zz} = ay + b - \tilde{\sigma}_1(k). \qquad (22.42)$$

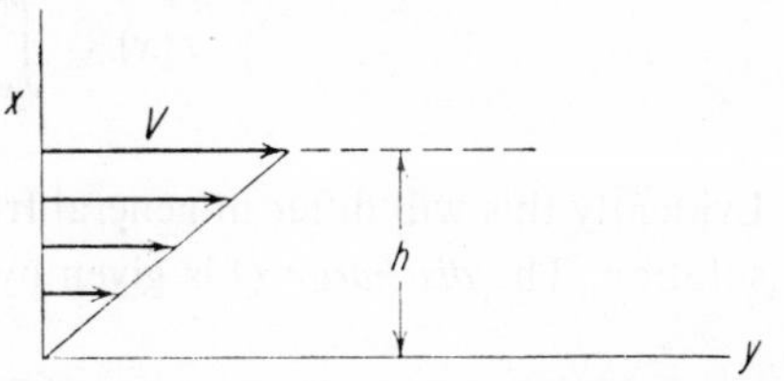

FIGURE 22.1 Simple shearing flow.

Let us now investigate two rectilinear flows: one in which the fluid is moved by dragging a plate with a velocity V on top of a channel of depth h (Figure 22.1), and another in which the fluid is moved through a conduit of depth $2h$ by supplying a pressure head a.

In the first case we assume that the pressure head is zero, because the motion is maintained by dragging the top layer with the velocity V. Then T_{yy} does not vary with y, i.e. $a = 0$. The boundary conditions for the velocity field are $v(0) = 0$, $v(h) = V$. Also, we now have that

$$T_{xy} = q = \text{const.} = \tilde{\tau}(k). \qquad (22.43)$$

Integrating $k = dv/dx = \tilde{\tau}^{-1}(q) = \text{const.}$, we obtain

$$v(x) = \frac{V}{h}x, \qquad k = \frac{V}{h}. \qquad (22.44)$$

Two of the results agree with the classical theory: the shearing stress is constant, and the velocity profile is straight. However, the relation between T_{xy} and the rate of shear is now nonlinear: $T_{xy} = \tilde{\tau}(k)$. Moreover, in contrast to nonlinearly viscous flow governed by $\mathbf{T} = -p\mathbf{1} + \alpha\mathbf{D} + \beta\mathbf{D}^2$, the normal stresses T_{xx} and T_{yy} are unequal (except in the special case $\tilde{\sigma}_1 = \tilde{\sigma}_2$).

The flow through a conduit $-h \leqslant x \leqslant h$ is evidently symmetric with respect to the y axis, so that the speed v is an even function of x. In particular, the boundary conditions on v are $v(h) = v(-h) = 0$. We now invert $T_{xy} = -ax + q = \tilde{\tau}(k)$ to read $k = dv/dx = \tilde{\tau}^{-1}(-ax + q)$. Because $\tilde{\tau}$ is an odd function of its argument, and k in the present case is an odd function of x, it follows that $q = 0$:

$$k = \frac{dv}{dx} = -\tilde{\tau}^{-1}(ax). \qquad (22.45)$$

We cannot set $a = 0$ here, of course, because a pressure head is needed to maintain the motion.

The velocity profile is obtained from

$$v(x) = \int_x^h \tilde{\tau}^{-1}(au)\, du.$$

Evidently this will differ in general from the parabolic profile of the classical solution. The *discharge* Q is given by

$$Q = \int_{-h}^h v(x)\, dx = \int_{-h}^h dx \int_x^h \tilde{\tau}^{-1}(au)\, du$$
$$= h\int_{-h}^h \tilde{\tau}^{-1}(au)\, du + \int_{-h}^h x\tilde{\tau}^{-1}(ax)\, dx.$$

Because $\tilde{\tau}$ is an odd function of its argument, the first term on the right-hand side vanishes, leaving

$$Q(a) = \frac{2}{a^2}\int_0^{ah} u\tilde{\tau}^{-1}(u)\, du.$$

Differentiating with respect to a, we arrive at

$$\tilde{\tau}^{-1}(ah) = \frac{1}{2ah^2}\frac{d}{da}\,[a^2Q(a)]. \tag{22.46}$$

This relation can be used to determine the shear stress function $\tilde{\tau}$ by measuring experimentally the discharge Q as a function of the pressure head a. A similar formula will be obtained also for pipe flow which is achieved more easily in experimentation.

The swelling of a fluid jet as it emerges from a conduit is called *Merrington's effect*. To obtain a qualitative explanation of this effect, let us evaluate the constant b in (22.41) from the balance of forces in the direction of flow. This can be done only in a very rough way; for one, we must assume that at the exit the stresses are very nearly the same as predicted by (22.41). Denoting by p_0 the atmospheric pressure, we obtain

$$-p_0 2h = \int_{-h}^h T_{yy}\, dx = 2bh + \int_{-h}^h [\tilde{\sigma}_2(k) - \tilde{\sigma}_1(k)]\, dx,$$

where we have chosen $y = 0$ at the exit. Introducing a pressure $P_{xx} = -T_{xx}$, we find that the excess pressure $P = P_{xx} - p_0$ over the atmospheric pressure is given by

$$P = \frac{1}{2h}\int_{-h}^{h} [\tilde{\sigma}_2(k) - \tilde{\sigma}_1(k)]\, dx.$$

Now, a problem involving the unconstrained jet is far too difficult to solve, so that we can only infer the actual behavior from the sign of the excess pressure P. If $P > 0$, there should be a swelling of the jet after it leaves the conduit, whereas $P < 0$ should correspond to a thinning. A jet of water shows a contraction; moreover, normal stress effects have not been observed in water. Therefore, if a liquid jet is found to swell, then it is reasonable to conclude that the normal stress functions do not vanish, and that $\tilde{\sigma}_2 - \tilde{\sigma}_1 > 0$. For pipe flow this inequality will be replaced by the weaker inequality $2\tilde{\sigma}_2 - \tilde{\sigma}_1 > 0$.

Helical flows, in which fluid particles move along circular helices, can occur in a gap separating two co-axial cylinders which rotate and translate relative to each other. Two of the basic experiments correspond to special cases of helical flows: flow in a circular pipe (*Poiseuille flow*), and plane flow between rotating cylinders (*Couette flow*).

Let $\rho(\tau)$, $\phi(\tau)$, $z(\tau)$ be the cylindrical coordinates of a particle at the instant $\tau \leq t$, and let ρ, ϕ, z be the cylindrical coordinates of the same particle at the present time t. We consider steady helical flows defined by

$$\rho(\tau) = \rho, \quad \phi(\tau) = \phi - s\omega(\rho), \quad z(\tau) = z - su(\rho). \tag{22.47}$$

The relative deformation gradients are defined by

$$F_{\underset{-}{t}ab}(\tau) = \frac{h_{\underline{b}}}{h_{\underline{a}}(\tau)} \frac{\partial \theta_a(\tau)}{\partial \theta_b}$$

(cf. (18.37)), thus, with $\omega'(\rho) = d\omega/d\rho$, $u'(\rho) = du/d\rho$,

$$\mathbf{F}_{\underset{-}{t}}(\tau) = \mathbf{1} - \gamma s\bar{\mathbf{N}}, \quad \gamma = \sqrt{\rho^2\omega'^2 + u'^2}, \tag{22.48}$$

$$\|\bar{\mathbf{N}}\| = \begin{Vmatrix} 0 & 0 & 0 \\ \alpha & 0 & 0 \\ \beta & 0 & 0 \end{Vmatrix}, \qquad \alpha = \frac{\rho\omega'}{\gamma}, \qquad \beta = \frac{u'}{\gamma}.$$

Evidently $\alpha^2 + \beta^2 = 1$.

Let us now show that at each point it is possible to find a local frame $\mathbf{d}_a$, $a = 1, 2, 3$, in which the flows (22.47) are indistinguishable from the rectilinear flows governed by the three viscometric functions $\tilde{\tau}$, $\tilde{\sigma}_1$ and $\tilde{\sigma}_2$ (i.e. if we imagine a rectilinear flow subdivided into small regions, then the contention is that the helical flows (22.47) are but another way of stringing together the same regions). For this to be true, the tensor $\bar{\mathbf{N}}$ must be reducible to the tensor $\mathbf{N}$ defined by (22.34), thus $\bar{\mathbf{N}} = \mathbf{QNQ}^T$. The appropriate orthogonal tensor $\mathbf{Q}$ is given by

$$\|\mathbf{Q}\| = \begin{Vmatrix} 1 & 0 & 0 \\ 0 & \alpha & \beta \\ 0 & -\beta & \alpha \end{Vmatrix}.$$

Consequently, the base vectors $\mathbf{d}_a$ are defined by $\mathbf{d}_1 = \mathbf{i}_\rho$, $\mathbf{d}_2 = \alpha\mathbf{i}_\phi + \beta\mathbf{i}_z$, $\mathbf{d}_3 = -\beta\mathbf{i}_\phi + \alpha\mathbf{i}_z$. In analogy with $\bar{\mathbf{N}} = \mathbf{QNQ}^T$, the representation $\bar{\mathbf{T}}$ of stresses in cylindrical coordinates is given by

$$\|\bar{\mathbf{T}}\| = \|\mathbf{QTQ}^T\| = \begin{Vmatrix} T_{11} & \alpha T_{12} & -\beta T_{12} \\ \alpha T_{12} & \alpha^2 T_{22} + \beta^2 T_{33} & -\alpha\beta(T_{22} - T_{33}) \\ -\beta T_{12} & -\alpha\beta(T_{22} - T_{33}) & \beta^2 T_{22} + \alpha^2 T_{33} \end{Vmatrix}.$$

The stress relations now follow from $T_{12} = \tilde{\tau}(\gamma)$, $T_{11} - T_{33} = \tilde{\sigma}_1(\gamma)$, $T_{22} - T_{33} = \tilde{\sigma}_2(\gamma)$,

$$\begin{aligned} T_{\rho\phi} &= \alpha\tilde{\tau}(\gamma), \quad T_{\rho z} = -\beta\tilde{\tau}(\gamma), \quad T_{\phi z} = -\alpha\beta\tilde{\sigma}_2(\gamma), \\ T_{\rho\rho} - T_{zz} &= \tilde{\sigma}_1(\gamma) - \beta^2\tilde{\sigma}_2(\gamma), \quad T_{\phi\phi} - T_{zz} = (\alpha^2 - \beta^2)\tilde{\sigma}_2(\gamma). \end{aligned} \tag{22.49}$$

We mention in passing two more flows that are, locally, simple shearing flows: "plate and cone flow" $r(\tau) = r$, $\theta(\tau) = \theta$, $\phi(\tau) = \phi - \omega(\theta)s$ (cf. (22.63) *et seq.*), and torsional flow

$$\rho(\tau) = \rho, \ \phi(\tau) = \phi - \omega(z)s, \ z(\tau) = z,$$

$$[\![\mathbf{F}_{\underline{t}}]\!] = \begin{Vmatrix} 1 & 0 & 0 \\ 0 & 1 & -\gamma s \\ 0 & 0 & 1 \end{Vmatrix}, \ \gamma = \rho\omega'(z)$$

(cf. Problem 8).

For Poiseuille flow ($\omega = 0$, $\alpha = 0$), the nonvanishing stresses are

$$T_{\rho z} = -\tilde{\tau}(\gamma), \qquad \gamma = \frac{du}{d\rho},$$
$$T_{\rho\rho} - T_{zz} = \tilde{\sigma}_1(\gamma) - \tilde{\sigma}_2(\gamma), \qquad T_{\phi\phi} - T_{zz} = -\tilde{\sigma}_2(\gamma), \tag{22.50}$$

whereas for Couette flow ($u = 0$, $\beta = 0$) they are

$$T_{\rho\phi} = \tilde{\tau}(\gamma), \qquad \gamma = \rho\frac{d\omega}{d\rho},$$
$$T_{\rho\rho} - T_{zz} = \tilde{\sigma}_1(\gamma), \qquad T_{\phi\phi} - T_{zz} = \tilde{\sigma}_2(\gamma). \tag{22.51}$$

As in rectilinear motion, the stresses are determined in part by the equations of motion,

$$\partial_\rho S_{\rho\rho} + \frac{1}{\rho}(S_{\rho\rho} - S_{\phi\phi}) - \partial_\rho p = -m\rho\omega^2,$$
$$\partial_\rho T_{\rho\phi} + \frac{2}{\rho}T_{\rho\phi} - \partial_\phi p = 0, \quad \partial_\rho T_{\rho z} + \frac{1}{\rho}T_{\rho z} - \partial_z p = 0,$$

where mass density is now denoted by m. From inspection of these equations we can conclude that p must be of the form

$$p = az + e\phi + n(\rho), \tag{22.52}$$

where a and e are constants. Moreover, the second and third equations can be integrated right away to yield

$$T_{\rho\phi} = \frac{c}{\rho^2} + \frac{e}{2}, \qquad T_{\rho z} = \frac{b}{\rho} + \frac{a\rho}{2}, \tag{22.53}$$

where b and c are constants of integration. Because $T_{\rho\rho} - T_{\phi\phi} = \tilde{\sigma}_1 - \alpha^2\tilde{\sigma}_2$, the first equation of motion is satisfied by letting

$$T_{\rho\rho} = \int \frac{1}{\rho}(\alpha^2\tilde{\sigma}_2 - \tilde{\sigma}_1 - m\rho^2\omega^2)\,d\rho + f(\phi,z),$$

thus, by (22.52),

$$T_{\rho\rho} = \int \frac{1}{\rho}(\alpha^2\tilde{\sigma}_2 - \tilde{\sigma}_1 - m\rho^2\omega^2)\,d\rho - az - e\phi + \text{const.} \tag{22.54}$$

We also note that, by (22.49), (22.53),

$$\bar{\tau}(\gamma) = \sqrt{T_{\rho\phi}^2 + T_{\rho z}^2} \equiv \delta(\rho), \qquad \delta(\rho) = \sqrt{\left(\frac{c}{\rho^2} + \frac{e}{2}\right)^2 + \left(\frac{b}{\rho} + \frac{a\rho}{2}\right)^2}. \tag{22.55}$$

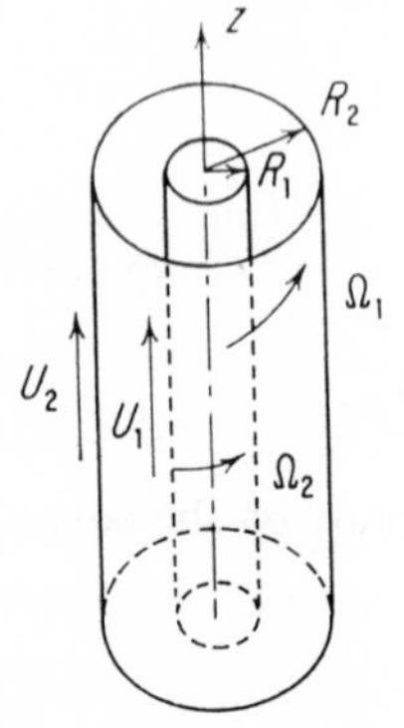

FIGURE 22.2 Assembly of cylinders for producing helical flows.

A helical flow can be produced by an assembly of two moving cylinders, illustrated in Figure 22.2. The outer cylinder $\rho = R_2$ rotates with an angular velocity Ω_2 and translates with a velocity U_2; for the inner cylinder $\rho = R_1$ these velocities are denoted by Ω_1 and U_1. The fluid contained between the cylinders must then obey the kinematical boundary conditions

$$u(R_1) = U_1, \quad u(R_2) = U_2, \quad \omega(R_1) = \Omega_1, \quad \omega(R_2) = \Omega_2.$$

In the special case

$$R_1 = 0, \quad R_2 = R, \quad U_1 = U_2 = 0, \quad \Omega_1 = \Omega_2 = 0 \tag{22.56}$$

of Poiseuille flow, the continuity of stresses at $\rho = 0$ requires that $b = c = 0$; moreover, $e = 0$ must hold in order that $T_{\rho\rho}$ be one-valued. Therefore, by (22.53), (22.55),

$$T_{\rho z} = \delta(\rho) = \frac{a\rho}{2} = \bar{\tau}(\gamma). \tag{22.57}$$

As is evident from $\partial p/\partial z = a$, the constant $H \equiv -a$ is the pressure head. Writing $\gamma = du/d\rho = -\bar{\tau}^{-1}(H\rho/2)$, we obtain the velocity profile and the discharge from

$$u(\rho) = \int_\rho^R \bar{\tau}^{-1}\left(\frac{Hw}{2}\right) dw, \qquad Q(H) = \pi \int_0^R \rho^2 \bar{\tau}^{-1}\left(\frac{H\rho}{2}\right) d\rho.$$

Inverting the last formula, we obtain

$$\tilde{\tau}^{-1}\left(\frac{HR}{2}\right) = \left(\frac{1}{\pi H^2 R^3}\right)\frac{d}{dH}\,[H^3 Q(H)]. \tag{22.58}$$

Measurements of discharge Q as a function of the pressure head H can thus serve to determine the shear stress function $\tilde{\tau}$. An investigation of Merrington's effect now suggests the inequality

$$2\tilde{\sigma}_2 - \tilde{\sigma}_1 > 0. \tag{22.59}$$

A direct test of (22.59) would be to measure $p_0 + T_{\rho\rho}$ at the wall of a pipe.

In the Couette flow the paths are concentric circles, the pressure head is set equal to zero, $a = 0$, and also $U_1 = U_2 = 0$. The constant e must again vanish in order that $T_{\rho\rho}$ be one-valued; moreover, because $T_{\rho z}$ now vanishes, we also have that $b = 0$ (cf. (22.53)). Thus

$$T_{\rho\phi} = \tilde{\tau}(\gamma) = \frac{c}{\rho^2} = \delta(\rho), \qquad \gamma = \rho\frac{d\omega}{d\rho}. \tag{22.60}$$

The constant c is found by evaluating the torque M transmitted across any surface $\rho = $ const.:

$$M = \int_0^{2\pi} \rho^2 T_{\rho\phi}\, d\phi = 2\pi c. \tag{22.61}$$

The Couette flow can be used to determine the difference $\tilde{\sigma}_2 - \tilde{\sigma}_1$ of normal stress functions by measuring the differences of the radial stresses:

$$T_{\rho\rho}(R_2) - T_{\rho\rho}(R_1) = \int_{R_1}^{R_2} \frac{1}{\rho}(\hat{\sigma}_2 - \hat{\sigma}_1 - m\rho^2\omega^2)\, d\rho,$$

$$\hat{\sigma}_{\underline{1}} = \hat{\sigma}_{\underline{1}}(\delta) \equiv \tilde{\sigma}_{\underline{1}}(\tilde{\tau}^{-1}(\delta)).$$

If $(R_2 - R_1)/R_1 \ll 1$, then the following approximation holds

$$T_{\rho\rho}(R_2) - T_{\rho\rho}(R_1) \doteq \frac{R_2 - R_1}{R_1}(\hat{\sigma}_2 - \hat{\sigma}_1 - mR_1^2\Omega_1^2).$$

The climbing of fluids along rotating cylinders is referred to as *Weissenberg's effect*; this effect can be interpreted as a manifestation of the normal stress functions. In linearly viscous fluids the immersion of a rotating cylinder will produce rather an opposite effect, as illustrated by Rankine's combined vortex flow (cf. Problem 5).

From the properties of Couette flow it is possible to obtain a qualitative explanation of Weissenberg's effect. Here the clue is the variation of the normal pressure $N = -T_{zz}$ necessary to maintain the Couette flow. Using (22.51) and the equations of motion, we get

$$T_{zz} = \int_{R_1}^{\rho} \frac{1}{w}(\tilde{\sigma}_2 - \tilde{\sigma}_1 - mw^2\omega^2)\,dw - \tilde{\sigma}_1 + g,$$

$$\frac{dN}{d\rho} = m\rho\omega^2(\rho) - \frac{1}{\rho}(\tilde{\sigma}_2 - \tilde{\sigma}_1) + \frac{d}{d\rho}\tilde{\sigma}_1.$$

If the normal stress functions vanish, then $dN/d\rho = m\rho\omega^2 > 0$. Because the pressure required to maintain the movement of particles in horizontal planes increases with ρ, a *free* surface will tend to rise with increasing ρ, i.e. we can conclude that $dN/d\rho < 0$ is possible only if normal stress functions are present.

The normal stress effect is basic to all nonlinear theories, yet the ways in which it appears in the descriptions of elasticity and fluidity are different. Recalling, for instance, the results for simple shear, $T_{xx} = \alpha K^2$, $T_{yy} = \gamma K^2$, $T_{xy} = (\alpha - \gamma)K$ (cf. (18.15)), we note that the normal stress effect is present in *all* elastic solids, and vanishes in infinitesimal deformations for *all* solids. For fluids, on the other hand, the normal stress effect is governed by separate material functions (cf. (22.51)). Therefore, it is quite possible that the normal stresses may vanish, $\tilde{\sigma}_1 = \tilde{\sigma}_2 = 0$, in *some* fluids regardless of the nature of motion.

As was noted before, the difference of the normal stress functions can be obtained by measuring the difference $T_{\rho\rho}(R_2) - T_{\rho\rho}(R_1)$ in Couette flow. The complete determination of the normal stress functions requires another test; here several possibilities exist. One can base the experiment on certain approximate solutions, e.g. flow between a plate and a rotating cone, or else consider the Poiseuille flow between two concentric cylinders. Then, by (22.53),

$$T_{\rho z} = \delta(\rho) = \frac{b}{\rho} - \frac{H\rho}{2} = \tilde{\tau}(\gamma),$$

and the velocity profile is given by

$$u(\rho) = \int_{R_1}^{\rho} \tilde{\tau}^{-1}\left(\frac{b}{w} - \frac{Hw}{2}\right) dw.$$

The additional constant b is to be determined from the condition

$$u(R_2) = \int_{R_1}^{R_2} \tilde{\tau}^{-1}\left(\frac{b}{\rho} - \frac{H\rho}{2}\right) d\rho = 0.$$

Moreover,
$$T_{\rho\rho}(R_2) - T_{\rho\rho}(R_1) = -\int_{R_1}^{R_2} \frac{1}{\rho}\,\tilde{\sigma}_1\, d\rho.$$

In all of the foregoing problems, we recover the solutions of classical hydrodynamics by setting the normal stress functions equal to zero, and identifying the viscosity function $\eta = \tau(k)/k$ with a constant μ, the coefficient of viscosity.

Rivlin-Ericksen fluids

In 1955 Rivlin and Ericksen proposed, for incompressible fluids, constitutive equations of the type

$$\mathbf{T} = -p\mathbf{1} + \mathbf{f}(\mathbf{A}_1, \mathbf{A}_2, \ldots, \mathbf{A}_N). \qquad (22.62)$$

As was shown in the first subsection, the constitutive equations (22.62) may turn out to be exact if the flow is very simple (e.g. steady viscometric flow), or else they may provide approximations that are valid when the memory of a fluid is sufficiently short or the rate of deformation sufficiently slow.†

Let us first explore "fluids of grade two", defined by

$$\mathbf{T} = -p\mathbf{1} + \mu\mathbf{A}_1 + \alpha\mathbf{A}_2 + \beta\mathbf{A}_1^2, \qquad (22.20)\text{R}$$

where μ, α, β are constants (thus, in viscometric flows, $\tilde{\tau}(k) = \mu k$, $\tilde{\sigma}_1 = (\beta + 2\alpha)k^2$, $\tilde{\sigma}_2 = \beta k^2$). It is difficult to say whether there is a significant range of shear rates such that the linear equation $\mathbf{T} = -p\mathbf{1} + \mu\mathbf{A}_1$ is not adequate, yet terms involving $\mathbf{A}_1^3$, $\mathbf{A}_1^2\mathbf{A}_2$, $\mathbf{A}_3$, etc., are negligible. Nor can one expect in general that conclusions reached on the basis of (22.20) will remain valid as one goes to fluids of grade three or higher. However, it stands to reason that an investigation of the consequences of (22.20) may yield valuable insights.

Let us consider the flow in a region bounded by a cone $\theta = \theta_0$ and a plate

† Cf. also the discussion on p. 524.

$\theta = 0$ ("cone and plate flow").† We assume $r(\tau) = r$, $\theta(\tau) = \theta$, $\phi(\tau) = \phi - \omega(\theta)s$, so that $v_\theta = v_r = 0$, $v_\phi = r \sin\theta\, \omega(\theta)$,

$$\|\mathbf{C}_t(\tau)\| = \begin{Vmatrix} 1 & 0 & 0 \\ 0 & 1 + k^2s^2 & -ks \\ 0 & -ks & 1 \end{Vmatrix}, \qquad k(\theta) = \sin\theta \frac{d\omega(\theta)}{d\theta}. \tag{22.63}$$

The nonvanishing components of the Rivlin-Ericksen tensors are $(\mathbf{A}_1)_{23} = k$, $(\mathbf{A}_2)_{22} = 2k^2$, $(\mathbf{A}_1^2)_{22} = (\mathbf{A}_1^2)_{33} = k^2$, and the stresses are given by $T_{rr} = -p$, $T_{\theta\theta} = -p + (\beta + 2\alpha)k^2$, $T_{\phi\phi} = -p + \beta k^2$, $T_{r\theta} = T_{r\phi} = \mu k$. The equations of motion reduce to

$$-\partial_r p - \frac{2}{r}(\beta + \alpha)k^2 = -mr\sin^2\theta\, \omega^2(\theta), \quad \mu\partial_\theta k + \frac{2\cot\theta}{r}\mu k - \partial_\phi p = 0.$$

$$-\partial_\theta p + (\beta + 2\alpha)\partial_\theta k^2 + \frac{2\cot\theta}{r}\alpha k^2 = -mr\sin\theta\cos\theta\, \omega^2(\theta).$$

An exact solution of the equations of motion does not exist; neglecting inertia, we obtain from the second equation that

$$k = \omega'(\theta)\sin\theta = \frac{c}{\sin^2\theta}.$$

As the boundary conditions on ω we may take $\omega = \Omega$ for $\theta = \theta_0$, $\omega = 0$ for $\theta = \pi/2$. The last and the first equations of motion yield, respectively,

$$p = \frac{1}{2}(2\beta + 3\alpha)\frac{c^2}{\sin^4\theta} + f(r),$$

$$p = \frac{c^2}{\sin^4\theta}\left[\frac{1}{2}(2\beta + 3\alpha) - 2(\beta + \alpha)\log r\right] + \text{const.},$$

which enables us to write

$$\frac{\partial T_{\theta\theta}}{\partial \log r} = 2(\beta + \alpha)\frac{c^2}{\sin^4\theta}.$$

To obtain a further simplification, we assume that the gap separating the cone and the plate is very small:

$$\theta = \frac{\pi}{2} - \psi, \qquad 0 \le \psi \le \psi_0, \qquad \psi_0 \ll 1.$$

† This is one of the flows demonstrated by Dr. H. Markovitz in his film on rheological fluids.

Then
$$\frac{d\omega}{d\theta} = -\frac{d\omega}{d\psi} = \frac{c}{\cos^3\psi} \approx c, \qquad \omega = -c\psi + \Omega_0,$$

where $c = -(\Omega_1 - \Omega_0)/\psi_0$. Finally,

$$\frac{\partial T_{\theta\theta}}{\partial \log r} \approx 2(\beta + \alpha)c^2.$$

If the fluids of grade two are regarded as fluids with convected elasticity (cf. (22.21) *et seq.*), then, in a rectilinear shearing flow $x = x(\tau^*)$, $z = z(\tau^*)$, $y = y(\tau^*) + s^*kx(\tau^*)$, where $s^* = t - \tau^*$ is the natural time lapse, and k is a constant, we shall obtain $T_{yy} - T_{xx} = ks^*T_{xy}$, so that

$$s^* = -\frac{2\alpha}{\mu}. \tag{22.64}$$

Because s^* is positive (i.e. stress must depend on the deformation from a past configuration), we can conclude that $\alpha < 0$.

We conclude this subsection with a summary of Pipkin's investigations of oscillatory flows of Rivlin-Ericksen fluids in tubes of arbitrary cross section.† We assume that the pressure variation in a straight tube aligned with the z direction is given by

$$p = -az\cos\omega t + aLP(x, y, t), \tag{22.65}$$

where a is the pressure drop over some length L of the tube. Further, we introduce dimensionless variables, and dimensionless numbers R and E, as follows,

$$\bar{x}_i = \frac{1}{L}x_i, \quad \bar{t} = \omega t, \quad \bar{v}_i = \frac{\mu}{aL^2}v_i, \quad \bar{S}_{ij} = \frac{1}{aL}S_{ij},$$

$$R = \frac{\rho L^2\omega}{\mu}, \qquad E = \frac{aL}{\mu\omega} = R\frac{a}{\rho L\omega^2},$$

where $\mathbf{S} = p\mathbf{1} + \mathbf{T}$ are the deviatoric stresses and R is a Reynolds number. As is often done, we subsequently omit the superposed bars on the dimensionless variables, e.g. $S_{zx} = v_{z,x} + v_{x,z}$, etc. It will be convenient to use Greek subscripts with the range from one to two, so that $\mathbf{v} = v_\alpha\mathbf{e}_\alpha + w\mathbf{e}_z$, etc. Assuming that $\mathbf{v}$ does not depend on z, the condition of incompressibility then reads

$$v_{\alpha,\alpha} = v_{x,x} + v_{y,y} = 0, \tag{22.66}$$

† [118], [122].

whereas the equations of motion are given by

$$\begin{aligned} \partial_t v_\alpha + E v_\beta v_{\alpha,\beta} &= \frac{1}{R}(-P_{,\alpha} + S_{\beta\alpha,\beta}), \\ \partial_t w + E v_\alpha w_{,\alpha} &= \frac{1}{R}(\cos t + S_{z\alpha,\alpha}). \end{aligned} \tag{22.67}$$

If, in particular, $v_\alpha = 0, P = 0$, then the equations of motion reduce to $R\,\partial_t w = \cos t + w_{,\alpha\alpha}$. Taking w to be the real part of a function $A\exp(it)$, we find that

$$A_{,\alpha\alpha} - iRA = -1, \tag{22.68}$$

or, with $A = A^+ + iA^-$, $A^+_{,\alpha\alpha} + RA^- = -1$, $A^-_{,\alpha\alpha} = RA^+$.

The constitutive equation of Rivlin-Ericksen fluids is of the form

$$\frac{\mathbf{S}}{\mu} = \sum_K B_K \mathbf{A}_K + \sum_K \sum_L B_{KL}(\mathbf{A}_K \mathbf{A}_L + \mathbf{A}_L \mathbf{A}_K) + \cdots,$$

where the dots stand for products of degree three and higher in $\mathbf{A}_K$. To obtain a dimensionless form, we introduce a characteristic time τ (which may be interpreted as a natural time τ_N), and let

$$\varepsilon = \omega\tau, \quad \mathbf{A}_K = \omega^{K-1}\frac{aL}{\mu}\bar{\mathbf{A}}_K, \quad B_K = \tau^{K-1}\bar{B}_K, \quad B_{KL} = \tau^{K+L-1}\bar{B}_{KL};$$

again, we subsequently omit the superposed bars. Neglecting terms that are of degree two or higher in E, we get

$$\mathbf{S} = \sum_K B_K \varepsilon^{K-1}\mathbf{A}_K + E\sum_K\sum_L B_{KL}\varepsilon^{K+L-1}(\mathbf{A}_K\mathbf{A}_L + \mathbf{A}_L\mathbf{A}_K). \tag{22.69}$$

For fluids of grade two we have that $\mathbf{S} = \mathbf{A}_1 + \varepsilon(\alpha\mathbf{A}_2 + E\beta\mathbf{A}_1^2)$. Because $A_{2ij} = \partial_t(v_{i,j} + v_{j,i}) + E(v_m A_{1ij,m} + v_{m,i}A_{1mj} + v_{m,j}A_{1im})$, etc., it follows that in the limit $E \to 0$ (e.g. when the pressure gradient decreases to zero, while ω is held constant) we obtain an equation of finite, linear, viscoelastic response,

$$S_{ij} = S(\partial_t)(v_{i,j} + v_{j,i}), \qquad S(\partial_t) = \sum_K B_K \varepsilon^{K-1}\partial_t^{K-1}. \tag{22.70}$$

If the variable pressure P and the velocity field $\mathbf{v}$ are independent of z, then the equations of motion are

$$R\,\partial_t v_\alpha = -P_{,\alpha} + S(\partial_t)v_{\alpha,\beta\beta}, \quad R\,\partial_t w = \cos t + S(\partial_t)w_{,\alpha\alpha}.$$

If we set w equal to the real part of $W\exp(it)$, then W must satisfy

$$S(i\varepsilon)W_{,\alpha\alpha} - iRW = -1. \tag{22.71}$$

Here
$$S(i\varepsilon) = \sum_K B_K(i\varepsilon)^{K-1} = |S|\exp(-i\delta)$$

is a dimensionless complex viscosity. Comparing (22.71) with (22.68), we obtain the following *correspondence principle*: if $w(x, y, iR)$ is the solution of a Newtonian flow (i.e. when $\varepsilon = 0$), then the corresponding linearly viscoelastic flow is given by

$$W = S^{-1}(i\varepsilon)w\left[x, y, i\,\frac{iR}{S(i\varepsilon)}\right]. \tag{22.72}$$

It was shown by Ericksen in 1956 that flows of viscoelastic fluids in pipes of noncircular cross sections will not be in general rectilinear.† Since then the problem of "secondary flows" has been investigated by means of various perturbation methods.‡ In particular, we may interpret (22.69) as the Rivlin-Ericksen equation in the limit of small values of ε. This suggests a linearization of the flow problem by neglecting consistently terms of the order of ε^2. Anticipating that the secondary velocities and pressure will be small, we write

$$w = \overline{w} + \varepsilon W, \qquad P = \varepsilon Q, \qquad v_\alpha = \varepsilon V_\alpha,$$

where $\overline{w}$ is the velocity of linearly viscous flow. Then $A_{\underline{1}\alpha\beta} = \varepsilon(V_{\alpha,\beta} + V_{\beta,\alpha})$, $A_{\underline{1}3\alpha} = \overline{w}_{,\alpha} + \varepsilon W_{,\alpha}$, whereas $A_{\underline{1}33} = 0$. Because $\mathbf{A}_1^2$ and $\mathbf{A}_2$ are multiplied in (22.69) by ε, we only need to consider the terms that do not contain ε, thus $A_{\underline{2}\alpha\beta} \approx 2E\overline{w}_{,\alpha}\overline{w}_{,\beta}$, $A_{\underline{2}3\alpha} \approx \partial_t\overline{w}_{,\alpha}$, $A^2_{\underline{1}\alpha\beta} \approx \overline{w}_{,\alpha}\overline{w}_{,\beta}$, $A^2_{\underline{1}33} \approx \overline{w}_{,\alpha}\overline{w}_{,\alpha}$, whereas $A_{\underline{2}33} \approx 0$, $A^2_{\underline{1}3\alpha} \approx 0$. Therefore, by (22.69),

$$\begin{aligned} S_{\alpha\beta} &= \varepsilon(V_{\alpha,\beta} + V_{\beta,\alpha} + E\gamma\overline{w}_{,\alpha}\overline{w}_{,\beta}), \quad \gamma = 2\alpha + \beta, \\ S_{3\alpha} &= \overline{w}_{,\alpha} + \varepsilon(W_{,\alpha} + \alpha\,\partial_t\overline{w}_{,\alpha}), \quad S_{33} = \varepsilon E\beta\overline{w}_{,\alpha}\overline{w}_{,\alpha}. \end{aligned} \tag{22.73}$$

Equating the coefficients of ε^0 and ε^1 in the stress equations of motion, we now obtain

$$\begin{aligned} R\,\partial_t\overline{w} &= \cos t + \overline{w}_{,\alpha\alpha} \\ R(\partial_t\overline{w} + EV_\alpha\overline{w}_{,\alpha}) &= W_{,\alpha\alpha} + \alpha\,\partial_t\overline{w}_{,\alpha\alpha}. \end{aligned} \tag{22.74}$$

† [35].

‡ References to these investigations may be found in [117]. Descriptions and pictures of observed secondary flows are given in [45].

The first of these is the equation of the linear theory; the second equation will determine the axial velocity of perturbation, W, once the transverse velocities of perturbation, V_α, have been found. The latter are governed by

$$R\partial_t V_\alpha = -Q_{,\alpha} + V_{\alpha,\beta\beta} + \gamma E(\overline{w}_{,\alpha}\overline{w}_{,\beta})_{,\beta}. \tag{22.75}$$

Once the classical problem (22.74) has been solved, (22.75) and the continuity equation $\partial_x V_x + \partial_y V_y = 0$ provide three equations for determining V_x, V_y, and Q. Pipkin has examined these equations in some detail.

The limiting case $E \to 0$ may be combined with $R \gg 1$ (as when ω is very large) to obtain an approximation for the "boundary layer" at the wall of the tube. In the boundary layer, we let x be in a direction along the wall, and y in a direction normal to the wall. Neglecting in (22.68) the derivatives with respect to x, we obtain

$$w = (iR)^{-1} - (iR)^{-1}\exp[-(iR)^{1/2}y],$$

which satisfies $w = 0$ at $y = 0$, and $w \to 1/iR$ as $yR^{1/2} \to \infty$. Thus, by (22.72),

$$W = (iR)^{-1} - (iR)^{-1}\exp[-(iR/S)^{1/2}y],$$

where $S = S(i\varepsilon)$. The quantity R/S may be thought of as a *viscoelastic Reynolds number.*

Problems

A. NEWTONIAN FLUIDS

1. Assuming incompressibility and linearly viscous response, derive from the stress equations of motion the Navier-Stokes equations

$$-\frac{1}{\rho}p_{,i} + \nu\nabla^2 v_i + b_i = \partial_t v_i + v_k v_{i,k},$$

where p is pressure, ρ is density, and $\nu = \mu/\rho$ is the *kinematic viscosity.* If the density of internal energy is a function of temperature alone, show that, with $c = \partial\varepsilon/\partial\theta$, and $\mathbf{q} = -k\,\mathrm{grad}\theta$, the energy balance reduces to the heat transfer equation

$$\dot{\theta} - \kappa\nabla^2\theta = \frac{2\nu}{c}D_{ij}D_{ij},$$

where $\kappa = k/\rho c$ is the *diffusivity.*

2. Show that $v_x = Ky$, $v_y = v_z = 0$ is a solution of the Navier-Stokes equations obtained in Problem 1. What is the associated steady-state solution of the heat transfer equation?

3. (*Bernoulli's equation*). Introduce the vorticity $\mathbf{w} = \operatorname{curl}\mathbf{v}$, and show that $\dot{\mathbf{v}} = \partial_t\mathbf{v} + \operatorname{grad}\frac{1}{2}\mathbf{v}\cdot\mathbf{v} - (\mathbf{v}\times\mathbf{w})$. Assuming that $\mathbf{b} = -\operatorname{grad}\Omega$, express the Navier-Stokes equations of Problem 1 as follows,

$$\partial_t\mathbf{v} + (\mathbf{w}\times\mathbf{v}) = -\operatorname{grad}H - \nu\operatorname{curl}\mathbf{w},\ H = \Omega + \frac{p}{\rho} + \frac{v^2}{2}.$$

In the language of hydraulics, H is the "total head", p/ρ is the "pressure head", and $v^2/2$ is the "velocity head". Show that, if the flow is steady, and $\operatorname{curl}\mathbf{w} = \mathbf{0}$, then $H = \text{const.}$ holds on streamlines (curves everywhere tangent to velocity vectors).

4. Consider one-dimensional flow of incompressible fluids through tubes of constant cross section R. Starting with the trial solution $v_x = v_y = 0$, $v_z = v(x, y, z)$ (with the boundary condition $v = 0$ on ∂R), show that v is governed by

$$\frac{\partial^2 v}{\partial x^2} + \frac{\partial^2 v}{\partial y^2} = -\alpha, \qquad \alpha = -\frac{1}{\mu}\frac{dp}{dz} = \text{const.}$$

In particular, obtain the solution for elliptic cross sections, compare the mean velocity with the maximum velocity, and obtain the matrix of the stress tensor. Can you establish an analogy with the torsion problem in elasticity theory?

5. (*Rankine's combined vortex*). In plane polar coordinates, consider a "vortex flow" $v_\rho = 0$, $v_\phi = A/\rho$ (A is a constant) in the region $\rho \geq a$, and a rigidly rotating core in $\rho \leq a$ (what is the mean angular velocity at a point of each region?). Show that Bernoulli's equation for the vortex flow is

$$\frac{p}{m} + gz + \frac{A^2}{2\rho^2} = C,$$

where C is a constant, and m denotes the mass density. The free surface is defined by $p = 0$. Next, show that Bernoulli's equation for the core is

$$\frac{p}{m} + gz - \frac{\omega^2\rho^2}{2} = D,$$

where D is a constant. Fit the two solutions together by requiring that at $\rho = a$ the velocities and the free surfaces be continuous. Sketch the shape of the free surface.

Note that the core may be replaced by a cylindrical rod without affecting the flow in the outer region. Is it reasonable to say that the solution approximates a flow obtained by draining the fluid through an orifice at the bottom of the container?

B. VISCOELASTIC FLUIDS

6. If you were given a grant to determine the viscometric functions of a fluid, what experiments would you use, and how would you calculate the viscometric functions from the experimental data?

7. Consider unsteady simple shearing flows $v_y = v_z = 0$, $v_x = v(y, t)$ of a Rivlin-Ericksen fluid of grade two. Show that the equations of motion can be satisfied by letting

$$p = (\beta + 2\alpha)\left(\frac{\partial v}{\partial y}\right)^2 + xm(t) + n(t),$$

$$\alpha \frac{\partial^3 v}{\partial y^2 \partial t} + \mu \frac{\partial^2 v}{\partial y^2} - \rho \frac{\partial v}{\partial t} = m(t).$$

With $m(t) = 0$, $\alpha = \bar{\alpha}\tau_N$, where $\bar{\alpha}$ is dimensionless, show that the solution corresponding to the boundary condition $v = V \cos \omega t$ on $y = 0$ is given by

$$v(y, t) = Ve^{-ay}\cos(\omega t - by),$$

where
$$a = \left[\frac{\rho}{2\bar{\alpha}\tau_N\mu}\left(\frac{\xi}{(1 + \xi^2)^{1/2}} + \frac{\xi^2}{1 + \xi^2}\right)\right]^{1/2},$$

$$b = \left[\frac{\rho}{2\bar{\alpha}\tau_N\mu}\left(\frac{\xi}{(1 + \xi^2)^{1/2}} - \frac{\xi^2}{1 + \xi^2}\right)\right]^{1/2}, \qquad \xi = \bar{\alpha}\tau_N\omega.$$

The coefficients a and b are positive, whereas according to (22.64) the dimensionless variable ξ is negative. As $\bar{\alpha} \to 0$, the values of a and b approach monotonically the classical value $k = (\rho\omega/2\mu)^{1/2}$.

8. For a Rivlin-Ericksen fluid of grade two, consider a steady torsional flow in a region $0 \le \rho \le R$, $0 \le z \le L$. The boundaries $z = 0$ and $z = L$ are assumed to rotate about the z axis with angular velocities Ω_0 and Ω_1, respectively (how can this flow be produced, approximately, in laboratory?). The flow is assumed to be of the form $v_\rho = v_z = 0$, $v_\phi = \rho\omega(z)$. Investigate the conditions arising from the equations of motion, and show that $\omega = cz + b$, $k = c\rho$, $b = \Omega_0$, $c = d\omega/dz = (\Omega_1 - \Omega_0)/L$. The equations of motion cannot be satisfied exactly; in particular, $\partial_z T_{zz} = 0$ contradicts $\partial_\rho p = -\beta\rho c^2 + m\rho(cz + b)^2$, where m is the mass density. Neglecting the inertia, evaluate the total force N that must be exerted on the top plate.

9. Using (22.74), (22.75), investigate the secondary flows in a pipe of elliptical cross section.

Section 23
ANISOTROPIC FLUIDITY

We have neglected so far the study of fluid-like behavior that is not isotropic. This far-flung subject is not easily summarized; therefore, we shall confine the discussion to those theories which have as a common denominator a vector field describing a microstructure that results in some kind of anisotropy. For the most part, we shall follow the work of Ericksen.†

Anisotropic fluids

To account for the existence of a distribution of elongated "particles" (even polymer chains) within a fluid, it is plausible to introduce as an added kinematical variable a vector field $\mathbf{n}(\mathbf{x}, t)$. If the orientations of the elongated particles may exhibit a long-range order, then, along with n_i, we should also include the gradients $n_{i,j}$ among the independent variables. For the time being, however, we shall rule out this possibility. The additional constitutive equations will be similar to (11.19), i.e. they will combine a constitutive assumption with the equations of "micromotion". Rather than deriving them (cf. Leslie [210]), we can just as well set down, outright, general relations of the form $\ddot{\mathbf{n}} = \mathbf{h}(\mathbf{n}, \dot{\mathbf{n}}, \mathbf{D})$, where $D_{ij} = v_{(i,j)}$. To simplify matters somewhat, we assume that the inertia of micromotion, as described by $\ddot{\mathbf{n}}$, is negligible, so that the constitutive equations are of the form

$$\overset{\circ}{n}_i = \dot{n}_i - W_{ij}n_j = g_i(\mathbf{n}, \mathbf{D}), \quad W_{ij} = v_{[i,j]}. \tag{23.1}$$

We assume that the internal forces are described by the Cauchy stress alone. If the density of intrinsic angular momentum is defined to be $\mathbf{n} \times \dot{\mathbf{n}}$, then from the balance of angular momentum it follows that $T_{ij} - T_{ji} = \rho(n_i\ddot{n}_j - n_j\ddot{n}_i)$. Therefore, the neglection of $\ddot{\mathbf{n}}$ permits us to assume that the stress tensor is symmetric. A simple model of incompressible "transversely isotropic" fluids is now given by

$$\mathbf{T} = -p\mathbf{1} + \mathbf{f}(\mathbf{D}, \mathbf{n}). \tag{23.2}$$

Because there is no reason to assume that the vectors $\mathbf{n}$ are not objective, it follows from the condition of material objectivity that $\mathbf{f}$ must be an isotropic function of $\mathbf{D}$ and $\mathbf{n}$: $\mathbf{QTQ}^T = -p\mathbf{1} + \mathbf{f}(\mathbf{QDQ}^T, \mathbf{Qn})$. If we assume that $\mathbf{f}$ is a polynomial function, and that stress is invariant to reflections $\mathbf{n} \to -\mathbf{n}$, then $\mathbf{f}$ can depend on $\mathbf{n}$ only through the combination $\mathbf{N} = \mathbf{nn}$. According to (B.23), then, a stress relation that is linear in $\mathbf{D}$ is given by

$$\begin{gathered} \mathbf{T} = -\not{p}\mathbf{1} + 2\mu\mathbf{D} + (\mu_1 + \mu_2 D)\mathbf{N} + 2\mu_3(\mathbf{DN} + \mathbf{ND}), \\ D = D_{ij}n_in_j, \qquad N_{ij} = n_in_j, \end{gathered} \tag{23.3}$$

† Cf. [28], [29], [30] (here one may also find further references, particularly to Frank and Oseen's work on liquid crystals).

μ, μ_1, μ_2, μ_3 being at most functions of $\text{tr}\mathbf{N} = \mathbf{n} \cdot \mathbf{n}$. Green† has explored a variant of this theory in which $N_{ij} = R_{\underline{a}i} R_{\underline{a}j}$, where $\mathbf{R}$ is the rotation tensor obtained in the polar decomposition of deformation gradients, and $\mathbf{H}_{\underline{a}}$ is a preferred direction in the reference configuration.

According to (23.3), the equilibrium stress $-p\mathbf{1} + \mu_1\mathbf{N}$ need not be a hydrostatic pressure. In particular, we may interpret $\mu_1\mathbf{N}$ as an apparent yield stress, so that the behavior described by (23.3) resembles that of a *Bingham plastic*. Further, a vector $\mathbf{n}$ of variable magnitude can be interpreted as a deformation measure, describing the elongation of coiled polymer chains, for instance. In that case the dependence of stress upon $\mathbf{n}$ represents an elasticity of the fluid (i.e. the fluid is viscoelastic in some sense). To obtain a purely viscous response, we should set

$$n_i n_i = 1\,. \tag{23.4}$$

A form of (23.1) that is compatible with (23.4) is then given by

$$\overset{\circ}{\mathbf{n}} = \lambda(\mathbf{D}\mathbf{n} - D\mathbf{n}) \tag{23.5}$$

(cf. (21.63)). If we adjoin to (23.3) the constitutive equations $\eta = \eta(\theta)$, $\psi = \psi(\theta)$ for entropy and free energy, then the condition of non-negative entropy production requires that $\eta = -\partial\psi/\partial\theta$, and

$$\text{tr}(\mathbf{TD}) = 2\mu\,\text{tr}\mathbf{D}^2 + \mu_1 D + \mu_2 D^2 + 4\mu_3\,\text{tr}(\mathbf{D}^2\mathbf{N}) \geq 0\,.$$

The last condition can be satisfied for any motion by imposing suitable restrictions on μ, μ_2, μ_3, but the coefficient μ_1 must be set equal to zero (because the sign of $D = D_{ij}n_i n_j$ is not definite). With $\mu_1 = 0$, the stress that can exist in a fluid at rest reduces to a hydrostatic pressure. To avoid having to set μ_1 equal to zero, we must either drop (23.4) (in which case $\psi = \psi(\theta, \text{tr}\mathbf{N})$, and a second term proportional to D may arise from $\dot{\psi}$), or else assume some kind of discontinuous behavior of μ_1, e.g. $\mu_1 > 0$ for $D \geq 0$, $\mu_1 < 0$ for $D < 0$.

Some idea about the influence of the velocity field $\mathbf{v}$ upon $\mathbf{n}$ can be gained by considering the flows $v_x = 2ay$, $v_y = 2bx$, $v_z = 0$, where a and b are constants. Then the only nonvanishing components of $\mathbf{D}$ and $\mathbf{W}$ are $D_{xy} = a+b$, $W_{xy} = a - b$. With $\mathbf{n} = \mathbf{n}(t)$, the equations of motion are satisfied, provided that $p = -2ab(x^2 + y^2) + \text{const.}$ Therefore, the problem reduces to the integration of (23.4), (23.5). One finds that for low values of $(a - b)/(a + b)$ the vectors $\mathbf{n}$ make a fixed angle with the streamlines, whereas at higher values

† Cf. [211].

the elongated particles would perform a tumbling motion. Instabilities occurring in Couette flow have been explored by Verma, Leslie, and Ericksen (cf. Ericksen [242]).

Liquid crystals

The anisotropy of crystals is an indication of a definite long-range order of the arrangement of matter. When a crystal is melted, we expect this long-range order to disappear, that is, we expect the melt to be an isotropic, viscous fluid. However, there may exist a third, intermediate phase (*meso-phase*) that is fluid-like, but retains a certain anisotropy. This phase, also called a *liquid crystal*, calls for a generalization of the existing theories of fluids.†

It is customary to fit a new theory into the pattern that emerges from Hamilton's principle. We should be permitted by now to omit the details of the integrations by parts, and concentrate on the basic assumptions and their consequences. For the density of kinetic energy we choose $k = \frac{1}{2}\mathbf{v}\cdot\mathbf{v} + \frac{1}{2}\dot{\mathbf{n}}\cdot\dot{\mathbf{n}}$. Further, we introduce a constitutive potential $W = W(\rho, n_i, n_{i,j}, \theta)$, which may be interpreted as the free energy. The variations δx_i, δn_i, $\delta\theta$ are assumed to be independent. To evaluate $\delta\rho$, we start from $\delta(\rho J) = \delta\rho_0 = 0$, thus $\delta\rho = -\rho$ (cofactor F_{ij})$(\delta F_{ij})/J = -\rho F_{ji}^{-1}\,\Delta_j\delta x_i$, or,

$$\delta\rho = -\rho(\delta x_i)_{,i}. \tag{23.6}$$

Similarly, from $F_{rk}F_{km}^{-1} = \delta_{rm}$, $\delta F_{km}^{-1} = -F_{kr}^{-1}(\delta x_r)_{,m}$, and $\delta n_{i,m} = \delta(n_{i.k}F_{km}^{-1})$ we find that

$$\delta n_{i,m} = (\delta n_i)_{,m} - n_{i,k}(\delta x_k)_{,m}. \tag{23.7}$$

In view of (23.6), (23.7), the form of δW suggests the definition of an elastic stress

$$T_{ki}^{E} = -\rho^2\frac{\partial W}{\partial\rho}\delta_{ki} - \rho\frac{\partial W}{\partial n_{j,k}}n_{j,i}, \tag{23.8}$$

and the definition of an elastic microstress

$$\tau_{ki}^{E} = \rho\frac{\partial W}{\partial n_{i,k}}. \tag{23.9}$$

† A classification and description of liquid crystals may be found in Gray [213]; there it is also pointed out that organic substances, e.g. muscle tissue, body fluids, have properties similar to those of liquid crystals. To appreciate the scope and variety of the researches into biomechanics, the reader may consult Part 4 of reference [241].

To these definitions we adjoin

$$A_i^E = \rho \frac{\partial W}{\partial n_i}. \tag{23.10}$$

We characterize dissipation by

$$\delta D = T_{ji}^D(\delta x_i)_{,j} + \tau_{ji}^D(\delta n_i)_{,j} + A_i^D \, \delta n_i + B \, \delta\theta, \tag{23.11}$$

where the dissipative stress T_{ji}^D, and similarly A_i^D, and B are assumed to be functions of $v_{i,j}$, n_i, $\dot{n}_i$, θ, and $\dot{\theta}$. In contrast to W, a dissipation function D need not exist (i.e. in general only δD is defined). The motivation for (23.11) stems from the observation that the Navier-Stokes equations of hydrodynamics can be obtained from Hamilton's principle by letting $W = W(\rho)$ and $\dot{D} = \lambda(v_{i,i})^2 + \mu(v_{i,j}v_{i,j} + v_{i,j}v_{j,i})$, so that $\delta D = \lambda v_{i,i}(\delta x_j)_{,j} + \mu[v_{i,j}(\delta x_i)_{,j} + v_{j,i}(\delta x_i)_{,j}] = \dot{D} \, \delta t$. With $\mathbf{T} = \mathbf{T}^E + \mathbf{T}^D$, the equations of motion are then

$$T_{ji,j} + \rho b_i = \rho \dot{v}_i.$$

The equations of "micromotion" are

$$(\tau_{ji}^E + \tau_{ji}^D)_{,j} + \beta_i + A_i^E + A_i^D = \rho \ddot{n}_i, \tag{23.12}$$

where β_i are body forces associated with the microstructure. It is worth noting that (23.12) are, in essence, constitutive equations.

We write the energy balance as follows, $V[\rho(\dot{\varepsilon} + \dot{k} - r)] = V[\rho b_i v_i + \beta_i \dot{n}_i] + \partial V[t_i v_i + \tau_i \dot{n}_i + h]$, where

$$\tau_i = (\tau_{ji}^E + \tau_{ji}^D) n_j.$$

The differential form of this is $\rho\dot{\varepsilon} + \operatorname{div}\mathbf{q} - \rho r = T_{ji}v_{i,j} + \tau_{ji}\dot{n}_{i,j} - A_i\dot{n}_i$. Performing an observer transformation $\mathbf{x} \to \mathbf{Q}(t)\mathbf{x}$, $\mathbf{n} \to \mathbf{Q}(t)\mathbf{n}$, we obtain the balance equation for angular momentum,

$$\Omega_{ij}(T_{ji} + \tau_{ki}n_{j,k} - A_i n_j) = 0, \quad \Omega_{ij} = -\Omega_{ji}.$$

To put this into a more familiar form, we introduce a multipolar stress M_{kij} by

$$\tfrac{1}{2}M_{kji} = \tau_{kj} n_i, \tag{23.13}$$

and interpret $M_{k[ij]}$ as a *couple stress*. Then it is easy to see that the balance of angular momentum becomes

$$\tfrac{1}{2}M_{k[ji],k} + \beta_{[i}n_{j]} + T_{[ij]} = \rho \ddot{n}_{[i}n_{j]}, \tag{23.14}$$

which agrees with the Cosserats equations (11.11). Finally, the balance of angular momentum can be used to express the energy balance as follows,

$$\rho\dot{\varepsilon} + \mathrm{div}\,\mathbf{q} - \rho r = T_{ji}v_{(i,j)} + \tfrac{1}{2}M_{k[ij]}\,W_{ij,k} + \tau_{ji}\mathring{n}_{i,j} - (A_i^E + A_i^D)\mathring{n}_i. \quad (23.15)$$

There seems to be much less confidence in the dynamic equations than in the static equations (which involve the elastic stresses only). Therefore, almost every aspect of the continuum theory of liquid crystals awaits further exploration.

Wang [214] has investigated what may be called *simple liquid crystals* (or, *subfluids*). His starting point is the constitutive equation for simple materials, $\mathbf{T} = \mathbf{J}(\mathbf{F}(\tau), \mathbf{F})$. For the isotropy group of the material Wang chooses a dilatation group that consists of unimodular stretch tensors and reflections in three linearly independent directions. Thus if $\mathbf{H}_a$, $a = 1, 2, 3$ is a set of preferred directions, then $\mathbf{S}$ is a symmetry operation only if

$$S_{mi}H_{ai} = S_{\underline{a}}H_{am}, \qquad S_1S_2S_3 = 1.$$

It turns out that there are 14 types of subfluids. Wang has been able to extend to subfluids a good many results obtained in the theory of simple fluids.

APPENDIX I

ELEMENTS OF POTENTIAL THEORY AND THE METHOD OF GREEN'S FUNCTIONS

The nature of the boundary value problems that we can attack in continuum mechanics depends on the kind of mathematical tools that we are prepared to use. In fact, the solution of boundary value problems is largely a mathematical discipline, concerned as it is with the development of special techniques aimed at special problems. Classical physics abounds in mathematical problems of the type

$$\nabla^2 U = f, \tag{A.1}$$

where f is a known function, and U must satisfy appropriate boundary conditions. It is often possible to solve such problems by simple techniques, e.g. separation of variables. To discover the general properties of the solutions U, we turn to a general method called *potential theory*.

As a rule, it is expedient to have two notations, or "languages," in mathematics: an explicit notation for use in calculations, and an abbreviated notation that may be used to record ideas, derivations, and so on. Thus we shall use freely abbreviations of the form

$$V[f] = \int_V f\,dv, \qquad \partial V[v_i n_i] = \int_{\partial V} v_i n_i\,da$$

(the integrals *are* linear functions of the integrands!). Here ∂V denotes the boundary of an open region V. Further, if $\mathbf{n}$ are the unit, outward-directed normal vectors of ∂V, we shall denote $\mathbf{n}\cdot\nabla = \partial_{\underline{n}}$ by D.

Potential theory

At the basis of potential theory lies the divergence theorem which we can write in the following three versions, known as *Green's first, second,* and *third identities:*

$$V[U\nabla^2 G] + V[\nabla U \cdot \nabla G] = \partial V[U\,DG], \tag{A.2}$$

$$V[U\nabla^2 G - G\nabla^2 U] = \partial V[U\,DG - G\,DU], \tag{A.3}$$

$$V[U\nabla^2 U] + V[|\nabla U|^2] = \partial V[U\,DU]. \tag{A.4}$$

To derive the first identity, we let $v_i = UG_{,i}$ in the divergence theorem (5.60), and note that $(UG_{,i})_{,i} = U_{,i}\,G_{,i} + UG_{,ii}$. The second identity then follows by interchanging U and G in the first, and subtracting the resulting expression from the first identity. To obtain the third identity, we let $U = G$ in the first identity.

The third identity is used for proving *uniqueness theorems*. For instance, if U_1 and U_2 satisfy the same differential equation (A.1) and take on the same values $\bar{U}$ on the boundary, then, applying (A.4) to $U = U_1 - U_2$, we conclude that $|\nabla U| = 0$. Therefore, $U_1 - U_2 = c$, where c is a constant. However, on the boundary $U_1 = U_2 = \bar{U}$, hence $c = 0$.

The divergence theorem is at the foundation of potential theory, but the proper beginning of potential theory is the *Green's fourth identity*. In order to derive it, we choose G in the second identity (A.3) to be a *Green's function* with the properties

(1) $G = \dfrac{1}{R} + A$, where $R = \sqrt{(x-\xi)^2 + (y-\eta)^2 + (z-\zeta)^2}$,

(2) $\nabla^2 A = 0$, and A has no singularities in V (i.e. the only singularity of G is at $R = 0$).

Here R is the distance between a fixed yet unspecified point $P(x, y, z)$ (the *field point*) and a variable point $Q(\xi, \eta, \zeta)$ (the *source point*) (Figure A.1). We note that

$$\partial_x R = -\partial_\xi R, \qquad \partial_y R = -\partial_\eta R, \qquad \partial_z R = -\partial_\zeta R. \tag{A.5}$$

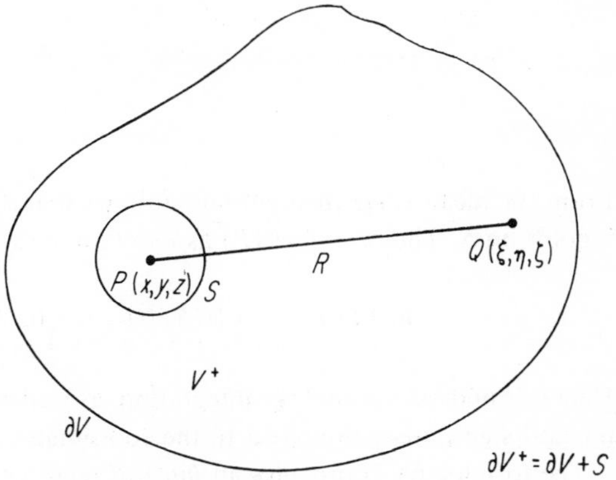

FIGURE A.1 Region V^+ for the derivation of Green's fourth identity.

Moreover, the Laplacian of $1/R$, calculated with respect to either set of variables, vanishes (except at P where $R = 0$). Therefore, the same is true of G:

$$\nabla^2 G = 0 \quad \text{for } R \neq 0. \tag{A.6}$$

The function A in G will be later used to adjust the boundary values of G. For the time being it only matters that A is well-behaved in V and satisfies there $\nabla^2 A = 0$.

Because the volume integrals in (A.3) are now improper, we must first exclude a small spherical neighborhood centered at P. We denote the radius of this neighborhood by ε, and its boundary by S. The boundary of the new region V^+ is then $\partial V^+ = \partial V + S$ (Figure A.1). In V^+ we have that $\nabla^2 G = 0$ everywhere, so that (A.3) becomes

$$-\int_{V^+} G\nabla^2 U\, dv = \int_S [U\, DG - G\, DU]\, da + \int_{\partial V} [U\, DG - G\, DU]\, da. \tag{a}$$

Denoting the surface integral over S by J, we proceed to evaluate it in the limit as $\varepsilon \to 0$. As may be seen from Figure A.2, on S we have that $R = \varepsilon$, $DG = -\partial G/\partial R = \varepsilon^{-2} - \partial A/\partial R$. On the other hand, the area element da can be expressed as $\varepsilon^2 \sin\theta\, d\theta\, d\phi$. In the limit as $\varepsilon \to 0$, then, the nonvanishing part of J is given by

$$J \doteq \frac{1}{\varepsilon^2}\int_S U\, da. \tag{b}$$

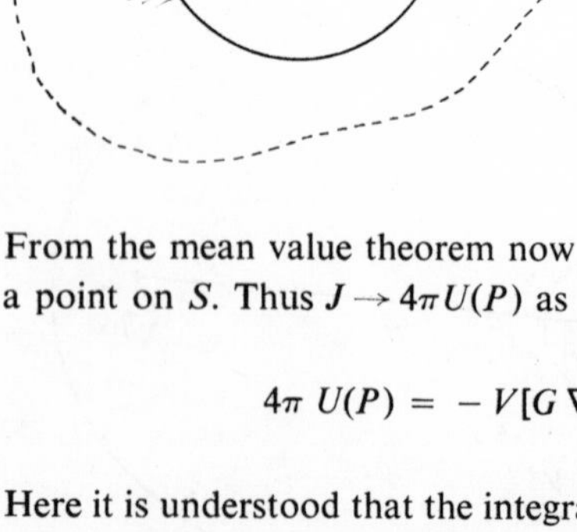

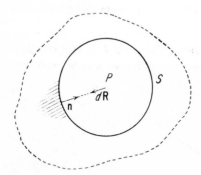

FIGURE A.2 Further detail for the derivation of Green's fourth identity.

From the mean value theorem now follows that $J \doteq \varepsilon^{-2} 4\pi\varepsilon^2 U(Q_0)$, where Q_0 is a point on S. Thus $J \to 4\pi U(P)$ as $\varepsilon \to 0$, and (a) reduces to the fourth identity

$$4\pi\, U(P) = -V[G\,\nabla^2 U] + \partial V[G\, DU - U\, DG]. \tag{A.7}$$

Here it is understood that the integration, as well as the differentiations under the integral signs, are with respect to the coordinates ξ, η, ζ of the variable point Q.

The formula (A.7) provides an *integral representation* for U. If the differential equation is of the form $\nabla^2 U = f$, where f is given, and if the boundary values of both U and its normal derivative DU are given on ∂V, then the values of U at any point P in V can be calculated from (A.7), provided of course that the Green's function G is also known. Thus we have arrived at the last stage: the selection of special kinds of Green's functions. However, one observation can be made right now: if discontinuities are present in the boundary values, they will not propagate into the interior. Namely, as is evident from (A.7), the boundary values, continuous or not, are integrated, hence what matters is only the total value of the surface integral. This property is shared by all solutions of elliptic differential equations.†

Let us suppose that A satisfies also the boundary condition $A = -1/R$ on ∂V. Then $G = 0$ on ∂V, and (A.7) reduces to

$$4\pi U(P) = -\int_V G\nabla^2 U\, dv - \int_{\partial V} U\, DG\, da, \tag{A.8}$$

where G is now called *Green's function of the first kind.* The function U is said to be a solution of the *Dirichlet problem*‡

$$\nabla^2 U = f \quad \text{in } V, \quad U = \bar{U} \quad \text{on } \partial V. \tag{A.9}$$

Defining *Green's function of the second kind* by $DA = -D(1/R)$ on ∂V (i.e. $DG = 0$ on ∂V), we can reduce (A.7) to

$$4\pi U(P) = -\int_V G\nabla^2 U\, dv + \int_{\partial V} G\, DU\, da. \tag{A.10}$$

The function U is said to be a solution of the *Neumann problem*

$$\nabla^2 U = f \quad \text{in } V, \qquad DU = \bar{h} \quad \text{on } \partial V. \tag{A.11}$$

Functions satisfying $\nabla^2 U = 0$ are said to be *harmonic*.

The existence of Green's functions can be proved,§ so that we have the following result:

If U satisfies $\nabla^2 U = f$ in the (open) region V, then on the boundary ∂V it is possible to prescribe U or the normal derivative DV, but *not* both, because the knowledge of U alone on ∂V suffices for determining U in V from (A.8), whereas the knowledge of DU alone on ∂V suffices for determining U in V from (A.10).

The potential-theoretic method reduces the determination of U to the ostensibly simpler problem of finding Green's functions for the particular region. For our purposes the main value of the formulas (A.8) and (A.10) lies in pointing out the admissible types of boundary conditions.

† Cf. the remarks following (d).
‡ Evidently A is also a solution of the Dirichlet problem.
§ Cf. Kellogg [82].

If V is the entire space $\mathscr{E}$, in which case there are no boundaries, then the "particular solution"

$$4\pi U(P) = -\int_{\mathscr{E}} \frac{f(Q)}{R(P, Q)}\, dv_Q \tag{A.12}$$

is also the general solution of $\nabla^2 U = f$. We say that $1/R$ is the Green's function for the infinite space; it can be variously interpreted as the gravitational potential of a point mass, electric potential of a point charge, and so on. As is evident from (A.8) and (A.10), the presence of boundaries can modify the potentials.

If a function f is defined and integrable over a region V, then

$$4\pi U(P) = -\int_V \frac{f(Q)}{R(P, Q)}\, dv_Q \tag{A.13}$$

is called the *Newtonian potential* of f. The potential U satisfies the conditions

$$\begin{aligned} \nabla^2 U &= f \quad \text{for } P \text{ inside } V, \\ \nabla^2 U &= 0 \quad \text{for } P \text{ outside } V. \end{aligned} \tag{A.14}$$

The first of these merely restates the fact that (A.13) is a particular solution. For P outside of V the integral is a proper one (i.e. $R \neq 0$), hence from $\nabla^2(1/R) = 0$ it follows that $\nabla^2 U = 0$. It can be also shown that, if $\mathbf{F} = \nabla U$ is the gradient of a Newtonian potential, then†

$$4\pi \mathbf{F} = 4\pi\, \nabla U = -\int_V f \nabla \frac{1}{R}\, dv. \tag{A.15}$$

This means that the representation (A.13) can be differentiated *once* under the integral sign.

For an illustration let us consider the Dirichlet problem for the half-space V: $z > 0$. Then $\nabla^2 U = f$ in V, and $U(x, y, 0) = \bar{U}(x, y)$ on ∂V: $z = 0$. The appropriate Green's function is given by

$$G = \frac{1}{R_1} - \frac{1}{R_2}, \tag{A.16}$$

i.e. $A = -1/R_2$, where the distances R_1 and R_2 are shown in Figure A.3. Introducing

$$\rho^2 = (x - \xi)^2 + (y - \eta)^2, \tag{A.17}$$

we have the representations $R_1^2 = \rho^2 + (z - \zeta)^2$, $R_2^2 = \rho^2 + (z + \zeta)^2$. The outer normals at ∂V are in the negative z direction, thus $D = -\partial/\partial\zeta$, and

$$-\left. DG\right|_{\partial V} = \left.\frac{\partial G}{\partial \zeta}\right|_{\zeta = 0} = 2z(\rho^2 + z^2)^{-3/2}.$$

† Cf. Kellogg, O. D., *op. cit.*, pp. 150–152.

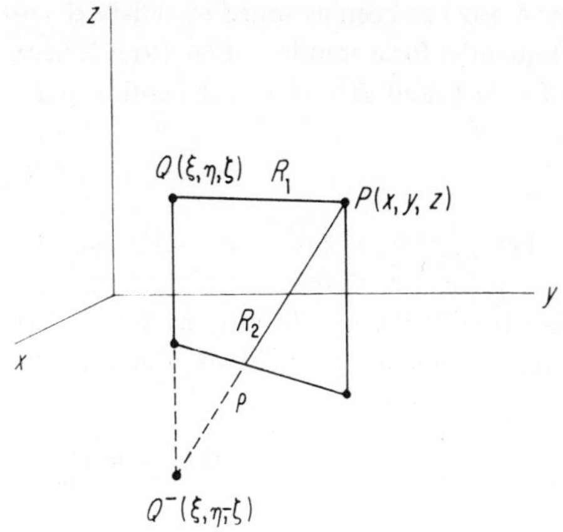

FIGURE A.3 Variables for the Green's function of a half-space.

Therefore, by (A.8),

$$4\pi U(x, y, z) = -\int_0^\infty d\zeta \int_{-\infty}^\infty d\xi \int_{-\infty}^\infty d\eta G(x, y, z; \xi, \eta, \zeta) f(\xi, \eta, \zeta)$$
$$+ 2z \int_{-\infty}^\infty d\xi \int_{-\infty}^\infty d\eta \bar{U}(\xi, \eta)(\rho^2 + z^2)^{-3/2}. \tag{A.18}$$

For two-dimensional problems the following modifications must be made in (A.8), (A.10): the factor 4π is replaced by 2π, and in G the singular function $1/R$ is replaced by $\log 1/\rho$ (the definition of A is modified accordingly).

The same methods apply also to the solutions of

$$\nabla^4 U = f. \tag{A.19}$$

If $f = 0$, then U is said to be *biharmonic*. Letting $G = \nabla^2 W$ in (A.3), we obtain

$$V[U \nabla^4 W - \nabla^2 W \nabla^2 U] = \partial V[U D\nabla^2 W - \nabla^2 W DU]. \tag{c}$$

Interchanging U and W in this expression, then subtracting the result from (c), we arrive at

$$V[U \nabla^4 W - W \nabla^4 U] = \partial V[U D\nabla^2 W - \nabla^2 W DU - W D\nabla^2 U + \nabla^2 U DW]. \tag{A.20}$$

The appropriate Green's function is now of the form $G = R + A$, where A has no singularities in V and satisfies $\nabla^4 A = 0$. Because $\nabla^2 R = 2/R$, it follows that $\nabla^4 G = 0$ except where $R = 0$. The subsequent steps are the same as in the derivation of (A.7). We obtain

$$8\pi U(P) = - V[G \nabla^4 U] + \partial V[\nabla^2 G DU - U D\nabla^2 G], \tag{A.21}$$

where G has been assumed to satisfy $G = 0$, $DG = 0$ on the boundary ∂V. Consequently, for a solution of (A.19) it is necessary to prescribe the boundary values of *both* U and DU. If V is the entire space $\mathscr{E}$, then (A.21) reduces to

$$8\pi U(P) = -\mathscr{E}[f(Q)\, R(P, Q)]. \tag{A.22}$$

Let $\rho_1^2 = (x - \xi)^2 + (y - \eta)^2$, $\rho_2^2 = (x - \xi)^2 + (y + \eta)^2$. For a half-plane $y > 0$ the Green's function of the first kind is given by $G = \log(\rho_2/\rho_1)$, the Green's function of the second kind by $G = -\log(\rho_1\rho_2)$. As can be readily verified, the Green's function of the (two-dimensional) biharmonic equation is given by

$$G = -\log\frac{\rho_1}{\rho_2} - \frac{2y(y + \eta)}{\rho_2^2}. \tag{A.23}$$

Let us briefly consider a general *linear* equation of second order: $\mathbf{L}U = A_{ij}U_{,ij} + A_iU_{,i} + AU$. Here the coefficients A, A_i, $A_{ij} = A_{ji}$ may depend upon the coordinates x_i, but not on the function U. To obtain the counterpart of (A.3), we associate with $\mathbf{L}$ the *adjoint* differential operator $\mathbf{M}$ defined as follows: $\mathbf{M}G = (A_{ij}G)_{,ij} - (A_iG)_{,i} + AG$. Forming $G\mathbf{L}U$, then "shifting" the differentiations from U to G, e.g. $A_iU_{,i}G = (A_iUG)_{,i} - (A_iG)_{,i}U$, we readily find that $G\mathbf{L}U - U\mathbf{M}G = S_{i,i}$, where $S_i = A_{ij}GU_{,j} - U(A_{ij}G)_{,j} + A_iUG$. The divergence theorem now yields

$$V[G\mathbf{L}U - U\mathbf{M}G] = \partial V[S_in_i]. \tag{d}$$

If $\mathbf{M} = \mathbf{L}$, then the differential equation is said to be *self-adjoint*. In this case the conditions $A_{ij,ij} = A_{i,i}$ and $A_{ij,j} = A_i$ must be satisfied. Evidently Laplace's equation is self-adjoint, because there $A_{ij} = \delta_{ij}$, $A_i = 0$.

Depending on whether a quadratic form with the coefficients A_{ij} is positive definite, zero, or negative definite, the differential operator $\mathbf{L}$ is said to be elliptic, parabolic, or hyperbolic. For elliptic equations the array A_{ij} can be reduced to a diagonal form: $\bar{A}_{ij} = \alpha_{\underline{i}}\,\delta_{ij}$. In particular, if the coefficients are constants, then α_i can be absorbed into the coordinates by a scaling, thereby reducing the elliptic equations to Laplace's equation. In the hyperbolic case the method of singularities must be modified, because isolated singularities can no longer occur.†

A slightly different approach to the generalization of Green's identities starts from $G\mathbf{L}U + \Lambda = P_{i,i}$, $U\mathbf{M}G + \Lambda = Q_{i,i}$, where $\Lambda = U_{,i}(A_{ij}G)_{,j} + U(A_iG)_{,i} - AUG$, $P_i = G(A_{ij}U_{,j} + A_iU)$, $Q_i = U(A_{ij}G)_{,j}$. Then $V[G\mathbf{L}U + \Lambda] = \partial V[P_in_i]$, $V[U\mathbf{M}G + \Lambda] = \partial V[Q_in_i]$. In particular, if we consider variations δU, δG of U, G, and assume that δU, δG and the variations of the derivatives of U and G vanish on the boundary, then $\delta V[\Lambda] = -V[\delta G\,\mathbf{L}U] - V[G\mathbf{L}\,\delta U]$. The last term can be replaced by using (d), thus $\delta V[\Lambda] = -V[\delta G\,\mathbf{L}U] - V[\delta U\,\mathbf{M}G]$. Consequently, the variational condition $\delta V[\Lambda] = 0$ implies the differential equations $\mathbf{L}U = 0$

† Cf. [151], pp. 52–54.

and $\mathbf{M}G = 0$. For instance, if $\mathbf{L} = \mathbf{M} = \nabla^2$, then, letting $U = G = \phi$, we have that $\Lambda = \phi_{,i}\phi_{,i} = |\mathrm{grad}\phi|^2$.

Vector fields

For the study of a vector field $\mathbf{v}$ in the large the following *Stokes's representation* is fundamental:

$$\mathbf{v} = \mathrm{grad}\phi + \mathrm{curl}\mathbf{c}. \tag{A.24}$$

To prove (A.24), we first introduce the Newtonian potential $\mathbf{a}$ associated with the given vector field $\mathbf{v}$:

$$4\pi\mathbf{a}(P) = -\int_V \mathbf{v}(Q)R^{-1}(P, Q)\, dv_Q. \tag{A.25}$$

Here the region V that carries the vector field has been assumed to be bounded. The representation (A.24) remains valid also for infinite regions provided that $\mathbf{v}$ approaches a constant field as the distance r from the coordinate origin tends to infinity.†

We now define a scalar potential ϕ and a vector potential $\mathbf{c}$ by‡

$$\phi = \mathrm{div}\mathbf{a}, \qquad \mathbf{c} = -\mathrm{curl}\mathbf{a}. \tag{A.26}$$

Then indeed $\mathrm{grad}\phi + \mathrm{curl}\mathbf{c} = \mathrm{grad\ div}\mathbf{a} - \mathrm{curl\ curl}\mathbf{a} = \mathbf{v} = \nabla^2\mathbf{a}$. The explicit representations of ϕ and $\mathbf{c}$ are

$$4\pi\phi = -\int_V \frac{1}{R}\,\mathrm{div}\mathbf{v}\, dv + \int_{\partial V} \frac{1}{R}\,\mathbf{v}\cdot\mathbf{n}\, da, \tag{A.27}$$

$$4\pi\mathbf{c} = \int_V \frac{1}{R}\,\mathrm{curl}\mathbf{v}\, dv - \int_{\partial V} \frac{1}{R}(\mathbf{v}\times\mathbf{n})\, da. \tag{A.28}$$

If V is the entire space $\mathscr{E}$, then the surface integrals are omitted:

$$4\pi\phi = -\int_{\mathscr{E}} \frac{1}{R}\,\mathrm{div}\mathbf{v}\, dv, \qquad 4\pi\mathbf{c} = \int_{\mathscr{E}} \frac{1}{R}\,\mathrm{curl}\mathbf{v}\, dv. \tag{A.29}$$

In verifying (A.27), (A.28) it is necessary to distinguish clearly between the coordinates x_i of the field point P and the coordinates ξ_i of the variable point of integration, Q. We shall use the notations $\bar{\partial}_i = \partial/\partial\xi_i$, $\partial_i = \partial/\partial x_i$, $\overline{\nabla} = \mathbf{e}_i\bar{\partial}_i$, $\nabla = \mathbf{e}_i\partial_i$. Recalling from (A.5) that $\nabla R = -\overline{\nabla}R$, we obtain

$$4\pi\phi = 4\pi\nabla\cdot\mathbf{a}(P) = -\int \mathbf{v}(Q)\cdot\nabla R^{-1}(P, Q)\, dv_Q$$
$$= \int \mathbf{v}(Q)\cdot\overline{\nabla}R^{-1}(P, Q)\, dv_Q.$$

† Gurtin [63].
‡ Cf. [115], pp. 186–189.

The formula (A.27) now follows by using the identity $v_i\bar{\partial}_i R^{-1} = \bar{\partial}_i(v_i R^{-1}) - R^{-1}\bar{\partial}_i v_i$ and applying the divergence theorem to the first term of the right-hand side. For **c** we proceed in the same way:

$$4\pi\mathbf{c} = -4\pi\nabla \times \mathbf{a}(P) = -\int \mathbf{v}(Q) \times \bar{\nabla}R^{-1}(P, Q)\, dv_Q.$$

To obtain (A.28), we use the identity $\varepsilon_{ikj}v_k\bar{\partial}_j R^{-1} = A_{ij,j} - \varepsilon_{ikj}v_{k,j}R^{-1}$, where $A_{ij} = \varepsilon_{ikj}v_k R^{-1}$.

There is no loss of generality if the vector potential **c** is assumed to satisfy the *gauge condition*

$$\operatorname{div}\mathbf{c} = 0. \tag{A.30}$$

Namely, the representation (A.24) is not affected if **c** is replaced by $\bar{\mathbf{c}} = \mathbf{c} + \operatorname{grad} f$. We now determine the scalar function f from $\nabla^2 f = -\operatorname{div}\mathbf{c}$, thus $\operatorname{div}\bar{\mathbf{c}} = \operatorname{div}\mathbf{c} + \nabla^2 f = 0$.

The special case when $\operatorname{div}\mathbf{v} = 0$ requires that, by (A.24), $\nabla^2\phi = 0$. If it is possible to set ϕ equal to zero, so that

$$\mathbf{v} = \operatorname{curl}\mathbf{c}, \tag{A.31}$$

then **v** is said to be a *solenoidal* vector field. Solenoidal vector fields satisfy the condition

$$\Omega[S] = \int_S \mathbf{v} \cdot \mathbf{n}\, da = 0 \tag{A.32}$$

for every closed reducible surface S (this follows from the divergence theorem and from the identity div curl**c** = 0).

Let us consider another possibility: $\operatorname{curl}\mathbf{v} = \mathbf{0}$. Assuming that the gauge condition (A.30) is satisfied, we find from (A.24) that $\operatorname{curl}\mathbf{v} = \operatorname{curl}\operatorname{curl}\mathbf{c} = -\nabla^2\mathbf{c} = \mathbf{0}$. If it is possible to set **c** equal to zero, so that

$$\mathbf{v} = \operatorname{grad}\phi, \tag{A.33}$$

then **v** is said to be a *lamellar* vector field. In this case **v** must satisfy the condition

$$\Gamma[C] = \oint_C \mathbf{v} \cdot d\mathbf{x} = 0 \tag{A.34}$$

for every closed reducible circuit C (this follows from Kelvin's transformation and from the identity curl gradϕ = **0**).

The decomposition of **v** into a lamellar part $\mathbf{L} = \operatorname{grad}\phi$ and a solenoidal part $\mathbf{S} = \operatorname{curl}\mathbf{c}$ is unique except for a vector-constant. To show this, we let $\mathbf{v} = \mathbf{L} + \mathbf{S} = \bar{\mathbf{L}} + \bar{\mathbf{S}}$, whence it follows that $\operatorname{div}(\mathbf{L} - \bar{\mathbf{L}}) = 0$, $\operatorname{curl}(\mathbf{S} - \bar{\mathbf{S}}) = \mathbf{0}$. Because, by definition, $\operatorname{curl}\mathbf{L} = \operatorname{curl}\bar{\mathbf{L}} = \mathbf{0}$, $\operatorname{div}\mathbf{S} = \operatorname{div}\bar{\mathbf{S}} = 0$, the proof is complete.

A vector field $\mathbf{v}$ such that $\text{div}\mathbf{v} = 0$ and $\text{curl}\mathbf{v} = \mathbf{0}$ is said to be *harmonic*, because then $\nabla^2\mathbf{v} = \mathbf{0}$. In this case one may use either of the representations $\mathbf{v} = \text{grad}\phi$ and $\mathbf{v} = \text{curl}\mathbf{c}$. To obtain vector fields other than $\mathbf{v} = \text{const.}$, we consider *singular* harmonic vector fields. This theory encompasses much of electrostatics, magnetostatics, and dynamics of isochoric, irrotational fluid flows. In the latter case, the use of the alternative representations $\mathbf{v} = \text{grad}\phi = \text{curl}\mathbf{c}$ may be summarized as follows (cf. the displacement function and stress function methods described in Section 15):

The introduction of

velocity potential ϕ	streamfunction $\mathbf{c}$

identically satisfies the condition of

irrotationality ($\text{curl}\mathbf{v} = \mathbf{0}$)	incompressibility ($\text{div}\mathbf{v} = 0$)

whereas

$\nabla^2\phi = 0$	$\nabla^2\mathbf{c} = \mathbf{0}$

represents the condition of

incompressibility	irrotationality

Many-valuedness indicates the presence of

vortex lines	point sources

because

circulation is the period of ϕ	efflux is the period of $\mathbf{c}$

If a vector field $\mathbf{c}$ is *circulation-preserving*, then, by (8.60),

$$\overset{*}{\mathbf{c}} = \partial_t\mathbf{c} - \text{curl}(\mathbf{v} \times \mathbf{c}) + \mathbf{v}\,\text{div}\mathbf{c} = \mathbf{0},$$

where $\mathbf{v}$ is the particle velocity. Using Lagrange's identity

$$\dot{\mathbf{v}} = \partial_t\mathbf{v} + \text{grad}\,\tfrac{1}{2}v^2 - (\mathbf{v} \times \mathbf{w}),$$

where $\mathbf{w} = \text{curl}\mathbf{v}$ is the vorticity, we obtain

$$\text{curl}\dot{\mathbf{v}} = \partial_t\mathbf{w} - \text{curl}(\mathbf{v} \times \mathbf{w}) = \overset{*}{\mathbf{w}}$$

(note that $\text{div}\mathbf{w} = 0$). For circulation-preserving velocity fields,

$$\Gamma = \int_S \mathbf{w}\cdot d\mathbf{a} = \text{const.},$$

and therefore

$$\overset{*}{\mathbf{w}} = \text{curl}\dot{\mathbf{v}} = \mathbf{0}.$$

The trajectories of a vector field **c** are also called its vector lines. If $x_i = x_i(u, t)$ is the equation of a vector line, then

$$\mathbf{V} = \frac{\partial \mathbf{x}(u, t)}{\partial t}$$

is the velocity of the points of the vector line. The equations of vector lines must satisfy

$$\mathbf{c} \times \frac{\partial \mathbf{x}(u, t)}{\partial t} = \mathbf{0}.$$

If this condition persists in time, then it follows that

$$\varepsilon_{ijk} c_j (c_m V_{k,m} - \partial_t c_k - c_{k,m} V_m) = 0.$$

If, in particular, the vector lines are also material lines, in which case $\mathbf{V} = \mathbf{v}$, then

$$\varepsilon_{ijk} c_j (c_m v_{k,m} - \dot{c}_k) = 0.$$

Letting $\mathbf{c} = \mathbf{w}$, we now obtain a basic result of hydrodynamics: *if* curl$\dot{\mathbf{v}} = \mathbf{0}$, *then vortex lines are material, and the motion is circulation-preserving.*†

Finally, let us note that

$$\mathbf{T} = \mathbf{a}\mathbf{u}^* + \mathbf{b}\mathbf{v}^* + \mathbf{c}\mathbf{w}^* \qquad (4.2)\mathrm{R}$$

may be used to obtain, with the aid of (A.24), decompositions of tensor fields. Because **T** describes only the deformation of a vector triad, there is no loss of generality if we replace **u**, **v**, **w** by $\mathbf{e}_1$, $\mathbf{e}_2$, $\mathbf{e}_3$, respectively. With $\mathbf{a} = \mathrm{grad}\phi + \mathrm{curl}\mathbf{A}$, $\mathbf{b} = \mathrm{grad}\psi + \mathrm{curl}\mathbf{B}$, $\mathbf{c} = \mathrm{grad}\theta + \mathrm{curl}\mathbf{C}$, we then obtain

$$\mathbf{T} = \mathbf{e}_i \mathbf{e}_m (u_{m,i} + \varepsilon_{ijk} M_{km,j}),$$

where

$$\mathbf{u} = \phi \mathbf{e}_1 + \psi \mathbf{e}_2 + \theta \mathbf{e}_3,$$

$$M_{k1} = A_k,\ M_{k2} = B_k,\ M_{k3} = C_k.$$

To obtain representations similar to (15.22), we should let $\mathbf{M} = \mathbf{N} \times \nabla$. If $\mathbf{T} = \nabla \mathbf{u}$ is possible, but **u** is many-valued, then there exist "dislocations lines," etc., etc.

† A fairly complete survey of the theory of vector fields may be found in [32]. The theory of circulation-preserving motions is given in [171].

APPENDIX **II**

ELEMENTS OF HIGHER ALGEBRA

By algebra we have meant, so far, *linear* algebra, i.e. the algebra of vectors and tensors. But the respresentation theory of functions of tensors also requires some knowledge of "nonlinear" algebra, or, to call it by its right name, *higher algebra.* This is a branch of mathematics that has been rather neglected of late, owing to one's discovery of the great value and versatility of linear algebra. However, the tortuous path of science is such that one never quite knows which books will have to be dusted off next. With the growing interest in nonlinear constitutive equations, higher algebra has become again an active field.

In what follows we shall review those theorems of higher algebra which are immediately applicable to representations of isotropic and anisotropic responses.

Polynomials, symmetric functions, the fundamental theorem on symmetric functions

A polynomial $P(\alpha)$ in the single variable α is a linear combination of positive, integral powers of α: $P(\alpha) = c_0 + c_1\alpha + \cdots + c_N\alpha^N$. According to the fundamental theorem of algebra, $P(\alpha) = 0$ has N roots; thus if $P(\alpha)$ is a *null-polynomial* such that $P(\alpha) = 0$ for all α, then each coefficient c_i must vanish.† Two polynomials are equal if their difference is a null-polynomial (i.e. if their coefficients are the same).

More generally, a polynomial in the variables $\alpha_1, \alpha_2, \ldots, \alpha_N$ is an expression of the type

$$P(\boldsymbol{\alpha}) = c_0 + c_1\alpha_1^{\alpha_1} \cdots \alpha_N^{\nu_1} + \cdots + c_M\alpha_1^{\alpha_M} \cdots \alpha_N^{\nu_M}.$$

† Unless stated otherwise, subscripts are not to be interpreted as tensor indices.

As before, $P(\boldsymbol{\alpha})$ is a null-polynomial only if each coefficient c_i vanishes. Polynomials that are invariant to arbitrary permutations $\pi(1)\pi(2)\ldots\pi(N)$ of the subscripts $12\ldots N$ of $\alpha_1, \alpha_2, \ldots, \alpha_N$, thus $P(\alpha_1, \alpha_2, \ldots, \alpha_N) = P(\alpha_{\pi(1)}, \alpha_{\pi(2)}, \ldots, \alpha_{\pi(N)})$, are said to be *symmetric polynomials.* Typical examples of symmetric polynomials are the *elementary symmetric functions*

$$\begin{aligned}
\sigma_1 &= \alpha_1 + \alpha_2 + \cdots + \alpha_N, \\
\sigma_2 &= \alpha_1\alpha_2 + \alpha_1\alpha_3 + \cdots + \alpha_1\alpha_N \\
&\quad + \alpha_2\alpha_3 + \cdots + \alpha_2\alpha_N \\
&\quad\quad + \cdot \quad \cdot \quad \cdot \quad \cdot \quad \cdot \\
&\quad\quad\quad + \alpha_{N-1}\alpha_N, \\
&\cdot \quad \cdot \quad \cdot \quad \cdot \quad \cdot \quad \cdot \quad \cdot \quad \cdot \quad \cdot \quad \cdot, \\
a_N &= \alpha_1\alpha_2\ldots\alpha_N,
\end{aligned}$$

and the power functions†

$$\begin{aligned}
p_1 &= \alpha_1 + \alpha_2 + \cdots + \alpha_N, \cdots, \\
p_2 &= \alpha_1^2 + \alpha_2^2 + \cdots + \alpha_N^2.
\end{aligned} \tag{B.2}$$

The fundamental theorem on symmetric polynomials asserts that *a symmetric polynomial can be expressed as a polynomial in* σ_i:

$$P(\boldsymbol{\alpha}) = \Pi(\sigma_1, \sigma_2, \ldots, \sigma_N). \tag{B.3}$$

As remarked by Weyl,‡ that a function of $\alpha_1, \alpha_2, \ldots, \alpha_N$ is also a function of $\sigma_1, \sigma_2, \ldots, \sigma_N$ is obvious. However, it is not at all obvious that a symmetric polynomial in $\alpha_1, \alpha_2, \ldots, \alpha_N$ is again a *polynomial* in $\sigma_1, \sigma_2, \ldots, \sigma_N$. We shall prove this theorem by induction.

We first take a symmetric polynomial in two variables: $P(\alpha, \beta) = P(\beta, \alpha)$. The elementary symmetric functions are then $\sigma_1 = \alpha + \beta, \sigma_2 = \alpha\beta$, so that $\beta = \sigma_1 - \alpha$. The polynomial $P(\alpha, \beta) = P(\alpha, \sigma_1 - \alpha)$ can be arranged according to powers of α: $P(\alpha, \sigma_1 - \alpha) = c_0 + c_1\alpha + \cdots + c_K\alpha^K$, where c_i depend on σ_1 and on the coefficients of the original polynomial $P(\alpha, \beta)$. In particular, if the coefficients of $P(\alpha, \beta)$ are integers, then so are c_i.

We now consider $F(x) = c_0 + c_1x + \cdots + c_Kx^K$, $f(x) = (x - \alpha)(x - \beta) = x^2 - \sigma_1x + \sigma_2$. The function $F(x)$ can be expressed as follows, $F(x) = Q(x)f(x) + A + Bx$, where the "quotient" $Q(x)$ is of degree $K - 2$, and the coefficients of the remainder term $A + Bx$ are polynomial (or, *rational*) functions of σ_1 and

† If x_1, x_2, x_3 denote the principal values of a symmetric tensor of rank two, then σ_i are the principal invariants ($\sigma_1 = \text{I}, \sigma_2 = \text{II}, \sigma_3 = \text{III}$), whereas p_i are the principal moments ($p_1 = \overline{\text{I}}, p_2 = \overline{\text{II}}, p_3 = \overline{\text{III}}$).

‡ [194], p. 30.

σ_2 only. If the coefficients of $P(\alpha, \beta)$ are integers, then so are the coefficients of the polynomials $A(\sigma_1, \sigma_2)$, $B(\sigma_1, \sigma_2)$. Letting $x = \alpha$, thus $f(x) = 0$, we obtain $P(\alpha, \beta) = A + B\alpha$. Similarly, letting $x = \beta$, we obtain $P(\alpha, \beta) = A + B\beta$. Therefore, as a consequence of the symmetry of $P(\alpha, \beta)$, it follows that $B = 0$.

If the theorem has been proved for $N - 1$ variables $\alpha_2, \alpha_3, \ldots, \alpha_N$, then a symmetric polynomial $P(\alpha_1, \alpha_2, \ldots, \alpha_N)$ can be arranged as follows,

$$P(\alpha_1, \alpha_2, \ldots, \alpha_N) = P_0 + P_1\alpha_1 + \cdots + P_\mu \alpha_1^\mu, \quad \mu > N, \tag{a}$$

where the coefficients are symmetric polynomials in $\alpha_2, \alpha_3, \ldots, \alpha_N$. But then they are expressible in terms of the elementary symmetric functions $\bar{\sigma}_1, \bar{\sigma}_2, \ldots, \bar{\sigma}_{N-1}$ of the variables $\alpha_2, \alpha_3, \ldots, \alpha_N$. Because $\bar{\sigma}_1 = \sigma_1 - \alpha_1$, $\bar{\sigma}_2 = \alpha_1\sigma_1 + \alpha_1^2$, etc., the coefficients can be expressed also as polynomials in $\alpha_1, \sigma_1, \sigma_2, \ldots, \sigma_{N-1}$. Therefore, an equivalent representation of (a) is $P(\alpha_1, \alpha_2, \ldots, \alpha_N) = A_0 + A_1\alpha_1 + \cdots + A_M\alpha_1^M$, where A_i are polynomials in $\sigma_1, \sigma_2, \ldots, \sigma_{N-1}$.

As in the case of two variables, we introduce $F(x) = A_0 + A_1x + \cdots + A_Mx^M$, $f(x) = (x - \alpha_1)(x - \alpha_2)\ldots(x - \alpha_N) = x^N - \sigma_1x^{N-1} + \sigma_2x^{N-2} - \cdots + (-1)^N\sigma_N$, and consider $F(x) = Q(x)f(x) + C(x)$, where $C(x) = C_0 + C_1x + \cdots + C_{N-1}x^{N-1}$, the coefficients C_i being polynomials in $\sigma_1, \sigma_2, \ldots, \sigma_N$. Letting $x = \alpha_1$, we obtain $F(\alpha_1) = P(\alpha_1, \alpha_2, \ldots, \alpha_N) = C(\alpha_1)$. However, in view of the symmetry of P, we must have that $P(\alpha_1, \alpha_2, \ldots, \alpha_N) = C(\alpha_i)$, $i = 1, 2, \ldots, N$. But this amounts to requiring that $C_{N-1}x^{N-1} + \cdots + C_0 - P(\alpha_1, \alpha_2, \ldots, \alpha_N) = 0$ has N roots. Because the degree of $C(x)$ is $N - 1$, it follows that $C(x)$ is a null-polynomial, so that

$$P(\alpha_1, \alpha_2, \ldots, \alpha_N) = C_0(\sigma_1, \sigma_2, \ldots, \sigma_N). \tag{B.4}$$

To summarize, the elementary symmetric functions $\sigma_1, \sigma_2, \ldots, \sigma_N$ constitute a *polynomial basis* (also referred to as an *integrity basis*), in the sense that each symmetric polynomial is expressible as a polynomial in $\sigma_1, \sigma_2, \ldots, \sigma_N$. Now, one always associates with bases two properties: independence, and uniqueness of representation. In the present context the independence of $\sigma_1, \sigma_2, \ldots, \sigma_N$ means the absence of a *polynomial relation* $R(\sigma_1, \sigma_2, \ldots, \sigma_N) = 0$. The proof that R must be a null-polynomial follows again by induction.† Namely, if $R(\sigma) = 0$ for any σ, then R is a null-polynomial. Next, recalling that $\sigma_1 = \bar{\sigma}_1 + \alpha_1$, $\sigma_2 = \bar{\sigma}_2 + \alpha_1\bar{\sigma}_1, \ldots, \sigma_N = \alpha_1\bar{\sigma}_{N-1}$, we obtain from $R(\sigma_1, \sigma_2, \ldots, \sigma_N) = 0$ by setting $\alpha_1 = 0$ that $R(\bar{\sigma}_1, \bar{\sigma}_2, \ldots, \bar{\sigma}_{N-1}, 0)$. If $\bar{\sigma}_1, \bar{\sigma}_2, \ldots, \bar{\sigma}_{N-1}$ are independent, then it follows that R has the property $R(x, y, \ldots, z, 0) = 0$; hence also $R(\sigma_1, \sigma_2, \ldots, \sigma_{N-1}, 0) = 0$. This means that R is of the form $R(\sigma_1, \sigma_2, \ldots, \sigma_N) = \sigma_N R^{(1)}(\sigma_1, \sigma_2, \ldots, \sigma_N)$. Because $\sigma_N \neq 0$, we must have that $R^{(1)}(\sigma_1, \sigma_2, \ldots, \sigma_N) = 0$, where the degree of $R^{(1)}$ in σ_N is one less than that of R. The foregoing procedure can be repeated, and eventually will yield $R^{(i)}(\sigma_1, \sigma_2, \ldots, \sigma_{N-1}) = 0$, thus contradicting the assumed independence of $\sigma_1, \sigma_2, \ldots, \sigma_{N-1}$. The uniqueness of (B.4) is easy to

† Cf. Weyl, *op. cit.* p. 33.

see: if $P(\alpha_1, \alpha_2, \ldots, \alpha_N) = C_0(\sigma_1, \sigma_2, \ldots, \sigma_N) = \bar{C}_0(\sigma_1, \sigma_2, \ldots, \sigma_N)$, then the elementary functions would have to be dependent,

$$R(\sigma_1, \sigma_2, \ldots, \sigma_N) \equiv C_0(\sigma_1, \sigma_2, \ldots, \sigma_N) - \bar{C}_0(\sigma_1, \sigma_2, \ldots, \sigma_N) = 0.$$

According to the fundamental theorem on symmetric functions, the power functions $p_1, p_2, \ldots, p_N$ are expressible as polynomials in the elementary symmetric functions $\sigma_1, \sigma_2, \ldots, \sigma_N$. A short, formal proof is as follows.† We take the logarithmic derivative of the product

$$A(\lambda) = \prod_{i=1}^{N} (1 - \lambda\alpha_i) = 1 - \sigma_1\lambda + \sigma_2\lambda^2 - \cdots + (-1)^N\sigma_N\lambda^N,$$

thus
$$-\frac{A'(\lambda)}{A(\lambda)} = \sum_{i=1}^{N} \frac{\alpha_i}{1 - \lambda\alpha_i} = p_i + p_2\lambda + p_3\lambda^2 + \cdots.$$

Comparing equal powers of λ in

$$-A'(\lambda) = A(\lambda) \sum_{i=1}^{N} p_i\lambda^{i-1},$$

we obtain the recursive formulas

$$p_1 = \sigma_1, \quad p_2 = p_1\sigma_1 - 2\sigma_2, \quad p_3 = p_2\sigma_1 - p_1\sigma_2 + 3\sigma_3, \quad \text{etc.,} \tag{B.5}$$

where σ_i must be set equal to zero if $i > N$.

Polynomial-invariants of finite groups

Let us recall that symmetry operations in solids consist of rotations and reflections, described by orthogonal tensors. Moreover, if $\mathbf{S}$ is a symmetry operation, then so is $\mathbf{S}^{-1}$; if $\mathbf{S}$ and $\bar{\mathbf{S}}$ are two symmetry operations, then so are $\mathbf{S}\bar{\mathbf{S}}$ and $\bar{\mathbf{S}}\mathbf{S}$. Consequently, symmetry operations are said to constitute a *group*. An abstract group is a set of elements $A, B, C, \ldots$, and an operation AB, called *multiplication*, with the following properties:

(1) the multiplication is closed, i.e. every product AB is an element of the set,
(2) there exists a "unit" I such that $AI = IA = A$,
(3) each element A has an inverse A^{-1} such that $AA^{-1} = A^{-1}A = I$.

In the case of isotropy, or transverse isotropy, we are dealing with a *continuous group*, the elements depending on one or several continuous parameters (e.g. Euler's angles). Crystal symmetries are described by finite groups; that is, the number of elements is finite, and each of them corresponds to a reflection or a discrete rotation.

† Weyl, *op. cit.*, p. 38.

Let us now investigate the polynomials that are invariant to a finite group $\mathscr{G}:\mathbf{S}^{(k)}$, $k = 1, 2, \ldots, H$, of transformations of the independent variables. A symmetry operation $\mathbf{S}^{(k)}$ maps a "test vector" $\mathbf{x} = [x_1, x_2, \ldots, x_N]$ into the vector $\mathbf{x}^{(k)} = [x_1^{(k)}, x_2^{(k)}, \ldots, x_N^{(k)}]$, thus

$$x_i^{(k)} = S_{ij}^{(k)} x_j. \tag{B.6}$$

If $P(\mathbf{x})$ is a polynomial that is invariant to the transformations (B.6), then $P(\mathbf{x})$ is said to be a *polynomial-invariant of the group* $\mathscr{G}$, and the following must hold:

$$P(\mathbf{x}) = P(\mathbf{x}^{(1)}) = P(\mathbf{x}^{(2)}) = \cdots = P(\mathbf{x}^{(H)}) = \frac{1}{H}\sum_{k=1}^{H} P(\mathbf{x}^{(k)}). \tag{B.7}$$

This means that $P(\mathbf{x})$ is a symmetric polynomial in the variables

$$\begin{aligned} X_1 &= [x_1^{(1)}, x_1^{(2)}, \ldots, x_1^{(H)}], \\ X_2 &= [x_2^{(1)}, x_2^{(2)}, \ldots, x_2^{(H)}], \\ &\cdots\cdots\cdots \\ X_N &= [x_N^{(1)}, x_N^{(2)}, \ldots, x_N^{(H)}]. \end{aligned} \tag{B.8}$$

Let us now take a typical polynomial

$$P(\mathbf{x}) = a + bx_1^{\mu_1} \ldots x_N^{\mu_N} + \cdots + cx_1^{\nu_1} \ldots x_N^{\nu_N},$$

where $a, b, \ldots, c$ are constants. Then, by (B.7),

$$HP(\mathbf{x}) = Ha + bJ_{\mu_1 \ldots \mu_N} + \cdots + cJ_{\nu_1 \ldots \nu_N}, \tag{B.9}$$

where
$$J_{\lambda_1 \ldots \lambda_N} = \sum_{k=1}^{H} \{x_1^{(k)}\}^{\lambda_1} \ldots \{x_N^{(k)}\}^{\lambda_N}, \tag{B.10}$$

i.e. every polynomial-invariant is expressible in terms of the invariants defined by (B.10). To prove the *first main theorem on finite groups*, according to which $P(\mathbf{x})$ can be expressed in terms of a *finite* number of the invariants (B.10), we consider†

$$P_\mu = \sum_{k=1}^{H} (\xi_k)^\mu, \quad \xi_k = u_1 x_1^{(k)} + u_2 x_2^{(k)} + \cdots + u_N x_N^{(k)}.$$

It is not difficult to verify that, except for a numerical factor, the invariants (B.10) are coefficients of terms $u_1^{\mu_1} \ldots u_N^{\mu_N}$ in the expansion of P_μ, μ being given by $\mu = \mu_1 + \mu_2 + \cdots + \mu_N$. Now, because the functions P_μ are symmetric polynomials in the variables ξ_k, they are expressible as polynomials of the elementary symmetric functions $\sigma_1, \sigma_2, \ldots, \sigma_H$ of ξ_k, or, what amounts to the same thing, as

† The proof given here is due to E. Noether [108].

polynomials of the functions $P_1, P_2, \ldots, P_R$ (cf. (B.5)). Therefore, the coefficients of P_μ, $\mu > H$, are polynomials of the coefficients of $P_1, P_2, \ldots, P_H$. Thus we have proved that *the invariants $J_{\mu_1 \ldots \mu_N}$, where $\mu_1 + \cdots + \mu_N \leq H$, provide a complete system of polynomial-invariants of the finite group $\mathscr{G}$:$\mathbf{S}^{(k)}$; the degree of the invariants, μ, does not exceed the order of the group, H.*

The elementary symmetric functions $\sigma_1, \sigma_2, \ldots, \sigma_N$ of $x_1, x_2, \ldots, x_N$ are said to be invariants of the *symmetric group*, which describes the permutations of the subscripts $1, 2, \ldots, N$. In the preceding section it was shown that $\sigma_1, \sigma_2, \ldots, \sigma_N$ are independent; therefore, it is important to remark here that the same is not necessarily true of the invariants of other finite groups. In general there may exist polynomial relations (*syzygies*) among the various invariants.

The equivalent set of invariants $G_{\lambda\lambda_1 \ldots \lambda_N}$ that are coefficients of $\sigma_1, \sigma_2, \ldots, \sigma_H$ is obtained from the "Galois resolvent" G:

$$
\begin{aligned}
G &= \prod_{k=1}^{H} (u + u_1 x_1^{(k)} + \cdots + u_N x_N^{(k)}) \\
&= u^H + \Sigma G_{\lambda\lambda_1 \ldots \lambda_N} u^\lambda u_1^{\lambda_1} \ldots u_N^{\lambda_N},
\end{aligned}
\tag{B.11}
$$

where $\lambda \neq H$, $\lambda + \lambda_1 + \cdots + \lambda_N = H$. In applications we frequently have to deal with the case $H = 2$. Then, letting $\mathbf{x}^{(1)} = \mathbf{x}$, $\mathbf{x}^{(2)} = \mathbf{y}$, we obtain $G = (u + u_1 x_1 + u_2 x_2 + \cdots + u_N x_N)(u + u_1 y_1 + u_2 y_1 + \cdots + u_N y_N) = u^2 + uu_1(x_1 + y_1) + uu_2(x_2 + y_2) + \cdots + uu_N(x_N + y_N) + u_1^2 x_1 y_1 + u_1 u_2(x_1 y_2 + x_2 y_1) + \cdots + u_1 u_N(x_1 y_N + x_N y_1) + u_2^2 x_2 y_2 + \cdots + u_2 u_N(x_2 y_N + x_N y_2) + \cdots + u_N^2 x_N y_N$. Thus a polynomial basis of polynomials that are invariant to replacement of variables $(x_1, x_2, \ldots, x_N)$ by variables $(y_1, y_2, \ldots, y_N)$ is given by

$$
\begin{aligned}
&x_i + y_i, \qquad && i = 1, 2, \ldots, N, \\
&x_i y_k + x_k y_i, && i,k = 1, 2, \ldots, N.
\end{aligned}
\tag{B.12}
$$

Let us take one more example: $\mathbf{x}^{(1)} = [x_1, x_2]$, $\mathbf{x}^{(2)} = [y_1, y_2]$, $\mathbf{x}^{(3)} = [z_1, z_2]$. Then $G = (u + u_1 x_1 + u_2 x_2)(u + u_1 y_1 + u_2 y_2)(u + u_1 z_1 + u_2 z_2)$ yields the following polynomial basis:

$$
\begin{aligned}
&J_1 = x_1 + y_1 + z_1, \quad J_2 = x_2 + y_2 + z_2, \quad J_3 = x_1 y_1 + y_1 z_1 + z_1 x_1, \\
&J_4 = x_1 y_2 + x_2 y_1 + y_1 z_2 + y_2 z_1 + z_1 x_2 + z_2 x_1, \quad J_5 = x_2 y_2 + y_2 z_2 + z_2 x_2, \\
&J_6 = x_1 y_1 z_1, \quad J_7 = x_1 y_1 z_1 + y_1 z_1 x_2 + z_1 x_1 y_2, \\
&J_8 = x_1 y_2 z_2 + y_1 z_2 x_2 + z_1 x_2 y_2, \quad J_9 = x_2 y_2 z_2.
\end{aligned}
\tag{B.13}
$$

Occasionally one needs the polynomial basis of polynomials that are symmetric in the three pairs of variables (X_1, Y_1), (X_2, Y_2), and (X_3, Y_3) (cf. [144]). This basis is obtained by renaming the variables in (B.13) according to

$$\begin{array}{ccc} x_1 x_2 & y_1 y_2 & z_1 z_2 \\ X_1 Y_1 & X_2 Y_2 & X_3 Y_3 \end{array}$$

Then

$$J_1 = X_1 + X_2 + X_3, \quad J_2 = Y_1 + Y_2 + Y_3, \quad J_3 = X_1X_2 + X_2X_3 + X_3X_1,$$
$$J_5 = Y_1Y_2 + Y_2Y_3 + Y_3Y_1,$$
$$J_4 = X_1Y_2 + X_2Y_1 + X_2Y_3 + X_3Y_2 + X_3Y_1 + X_1Y_3, \quad J_6 = X_1X_2X_3, \tag{B.14}$$
$$J_9 = Y_1Y_2Y_3, \quad J_7 = X_1X_2Y_3 + X_2X_3Y_1 + X_3X_1Y_2,$$
$$J_8 = X_1Y_2Y_3 + X_2Y_3Y_1 + X_3Y_1Y_2.$$

To illustrate the application of the theory developed above, let us consider the conditions $W(\mathbf{C}) = W(\mathbf{SCS}^T)$ imposed on the strain-energy function W by the existence of symmetry operations $\mathbf{S}$. The symmetry operations of each crystal class constitute a (proper) subgroup of the orthogonal group. To each group of symmetry operations there corresponds a polynomial basis $J_1(\mathbf{C}), J_2(\mathbf{C}), \ldots, J_K(\mathbf{C})$ such that any polynomial function $W(J_1, J_2, \ldots, J_K)$ is automatically form-invariant to the symmetry operations (the variables $J_1, \ldots$ being "insensitive" to such operations!). Because polynomial bases are also functional bases of general functions,† the problem of obtaining properly invariant functions W reduces to a purely algebraic problem of determining $J_1, \ldots$.

The "most anisotropic" solids belong to the *triclinic* class. Here the representation $W = \overline{W}(C_{11},C_{22},C_{33},C_{12},C_{23},C_{31})$ is invariant simply because there are no symmetry operations (other than the trivial operations $\mathbf{S} = \mathbf{1}$ and $\mathbf{S} = -\mathbf{1}$). As the symmetry operations of the *monoclinic* class we may take $\mathbf{S} = \text{diag}\,(-1, -1, 1)$, or, equivalently, $-\mathbf{1S} = \text{diag}\,(1, 1, -1)$ Considering a model transformation $\mathbf{SCS}^T$ (cf. p. 305), we conclude that $I_1 = C_{11}$, $I_2 = C_{22}$, $I_3 = C_{33}$, $I_4 = C_{12}$ can serve as elements of a polynomial basis, whereas C_{13} and C_{23} can not. Now, to satisfy the condition $W(I_1, \ldots, I_4, C_{13}, C_{23}) = W(I_1, \ldots, I_4, -C_{13}, -C_{23})$, we make use of (B.12), thus obtaining the additional invariants $I_5 = C_{13}^2$, $I_6 = C_{23}^2$, $L_1 = C_{13}C_{23}$.

The invariants are evidently not independent; in fact, $L_1^2 = I_5I_6$. This means that all but the first power of L_1 can be eliminated, so that a *polynomial* strain-energy function can be represented by‡ $W = S_0 + S_1L_1$, where S_0 and S_1 are polynomials in $I_1, I_2, \ldots, I_6$.

Because there are only six components C_{ij}, one might wonder whether it would not be enough to take W as a function of six invariants (of which three can be the

† Wineman and Pipkin [195].
‡ Smith [146].

isotropic invariants I, II, III). The reason why this will not work in general is this: although it is possible that for a particular deformation a polynomial basis containing only six invariants will be sufficient to "span" the appropriate stress space, in general there is no assurance that an arbitrarily selected set of six invariants will do that. Moreover, the use of syzygies to eliminate all but six invariants from the polynomial basis will make W a many-valued function (recall that $L_1 = \pm\sqrt{I_5 I_6}$!). In general, then, one has no choice but to use the full polynomial basis, even though the basis elements may not be functionally independent.

Polynomial bases are equally important in anisotropic plasticity, where it is necessary to obtain representations of yield functions $F(\mathbf{S}) = 0$, $\mathbf{S}$ being the deviatoric stress. In view of $S_{ii} = 0$, one might again be tempted to consider polynomial bases containing only five invariants. This approach, used by von Mises [97] in the case of hexagonal and cubic symmetries, has been shown by Smith [147] to be incompatible with one-valuedness of F.

The basic symmetry operations of the rhombic class are $\underset{2}{z} = \text{diag}(-1, -1, 1)$ and $\underset{2}{x} = \text{diag}(1, -1, -1)$ (note that $\underset{2}{y} = \underset{2}{z}\underset{2}{x}$). The reduction by means of $\underset{2}{z}$ is the same as in the monoclinic case, thus yielding $W = W(C_{11}, C_{22}, C_{33}, C_{12}, C_{13}^2, C_{23}^2, C_{13}C_{23})$. Next, from inspection of $\underset{2}{x}\mathbf{C}\underset{2}{x}$, we obtain the condition $W(C_{11}, C_{22}, C_{33}, C_{12}, C_{13}^2, C_{23}^2, C_{13}C_{23}) = W(C_{11}, C_{22}, C_{33}, -C_{12}, C_{13}^2, C_{23}^2, -C_{13}C_{23})$. Therefore, by (B.12) and the remark made following (B.14), the polynomial basis is given by $I_1 = C_{11}$, $I_2 = C_{22}$, $I_3 = C_{33}$, $I_4^2 = C_{12}^2$, $I_5 = C_{13}^2$, $I_6 = C_{23}^2$, $I_1 = C_{12}\,C_{23}\,C_{31}$.

Anisotropic tensors†

The theory of polynomial bases lends itself to the construction of *anisotropic tensors*, by which we mean tensors that are invariants of some subgroup of the orthogonal group. Thus if $\mathbf{S}$ belongs to the subgroup, and A_{ij} is an invariant of the subgroup, then

$$A_{ij} = S_{ik}S_{jm}A_{km} = S_{ki}S_{mj}A_{km}. \tag{B.15}$$

A bilinear form $P = A_{ij}u_i v_j$ will be form-invariant to the transformations $\bar{u}_i = S_{ij}u_j$, $\bar{v}_i = S_{ij}v_j$ only if A_{ij} satisfy (B.15). Now, each form-invariant polynomial P has a finite polynomial basis made up of invariants $I_1, I_2, \ldots, I_H$ of the group of transformations $\mathbf{S}$. Because P is assumed to be bilinear in $\mathbf{u}$ and $\mathbf{v}$, we can discard all basis elements that are nonlinear functions of $\mathbf{u}$ and $\mathbf{v}$. Denoting the remaining basis elements by $J_1, J_2, \ldots, J_G$, we write

$$P = \sum_{K,L,\ldots,P} B_{KL\ldots P} J_K J_L \ldots J_P. \tag{B.16}$$

Here several observations are in order. First, each constant $B_{KL\ldots P}$ is a scalar with respect to transformations $\mathbf{S}$, because the form-invariance of (B.16) is automati-

† Smith and Rivlin [208].

cally fulfilled by the use of the appropriate polynomial basis. Second, each summand is a product of components of *distinct* vectors, i.e. because (B.16) must define a multilinear function, no two invariants entering into a summand can depend on the same vector. Evidently

$$A_{ij} = \frac{\partial^2 P}{\partial u_i \partial v_i} = \sum B_{KL\ldots P} \frac{\partial^2 J_K J_L \ldots J_P}{\partial u_i \partial v_j}. \tag{B.17}$$

The method for constructing anisotropic tensors of higher rank is exactly the same.

For monoclinic-domatic class of crystals the symmetry operation is $\mathbf{S} = \text{diag}(1, 1, -1)$. With $\mathbf{x} = [u_1^{(1)}, u_2^{(1)}, u_3^{(1)}, u_1^{(2)}, u_2^{(2)}, u_3^{(2)}, \ldots, u_1^{(N)}, u_2^{(N)}, u_3^{(N)}]$ we obtain

$$\mathbf{X} = \mathbf{Sx} = [u_1^{(1)}, u_2^{(1)}, -u_3^{(1)}, u_1^{(2)}, u_2^{(2)}, -u_3^{(2)}, \ldots, u_1^{(N)}, u_2^{(N)}, -u_3^{(N)}].$$

According to (B.12), the polynomial basis is made up of $u_1^{(K)}$, $u_2^{(K)}$, $u_3^{(K)}u_3^{(L)}$, $K \neq L$, the redundant elements having been discarded. Consequently, a basic set of (anisotropic) tensors possessing monoclinic-domatic symmetry can be constructed from

$$\|\partial u_1/\partial u_i\| = \|\delta_{1i}\| = \|1, 0, 0\|, \quad \|\partial u_2/\partial u_i\| = \|\delta_{2i}\| = \|0, 1, 0\|,$$

and $\|\partial^2 u_3 v_3/\partial u_i \partial v_j\| = \text{diag}(0, 0, 1)$.

The rhombic-pyramidal symmetry is described by $\mathbf{S}^{(1)} = \mathbf{1}$, $\mathbf{S}^{(2)} = \text{diag}(-1, 1, 1)$, and $\mathbf{S}^{(3)} = \text{diag}(1, -1, 1)$. The invariants of $\mathbf{S}^{(2)}$ and $\mathbf{S}^{(3)}$ are, respectively, $u_1^{(K)}u_1^{(L)}$, $u_2^{(K)}$, $u_2^{(K)}$, and $u_1^{(K)}$, $u_2^{(K)}u_2^{(L)}$, $u_3^{(K)}$, hence the invariants of the group $\mathscr{J}:\{\mathbf{S}^{(1)}, \mathbf{S}^{(2)}, \mathbf{S}^{(3)}\}$ are $u_1^{(K)}u_1^{(L)}$, $u_2^{(K)}u_2^{(L)}$, $u_3^{(K)}$. Thus a basic set of (anisotropic) tensors possessing rhombic-pyramidal symmetry is given by diag (0, 0, 1), diag(1, 0, 0), diag(0, 1, 0).

The (continuous) group of arbitrary rotations about an axis is said to define *transverse isotropy* about that axis. If the axis of symmetry is taken to be the z axis of the coordinate system, then each element of the group has the representation (4.23). A vector (u_1, u_2, u_3) is transformed by $\mathbf{S}$ into $(u_1 \cos\phi + u_2 \sin\phi, -u_1 \sin\phi + u_2 \cos\phi, u_3)$, i.e. while the symmetry operation places no conditions on u_3, the elements of the polynomial basis which depend on u_1 and u_2 must be invariant to the two-dimensional group of rotations. Adapting the results previously derived in the three-dimensional case (cf. (14.37) *et seq.*) to the present case, we arrive at the following, multilinear polynomial basis:

$$u_3^{(K)}, \quad \varepsilon_{3ij}u_i^{(K)}u_j^{(L)}, \quad u_\alpha^{(K)}u_\alpha^{(L)}, \quad \alpha = 1,2, \quad K \neq L.$$

The basic transversely isotropic tensors can now be constructed from $\partial u_3/\partial u_i$, $\partial^2(\varepsilon_{3ij}u_i v_j)/\partial u_m \partial v_n$, $\partial^2(u_\alpha v_\alpha)/\partial u_i \partial v_j$, hence they are given by

$$\delta_{3i}, \quad \varepsilon_{3ij}, \quad \Delta_{ij} = \|\delta_{1i}\delta_{1j} + \delta_{2i}\delta_{2j}\| = \text{diag}(1, 1, 0).$$

Therefore, a transversely anisotropic tensor G_{ijkm} must be a linear combination of the terms $\Delta_{ij}\Delta_{km}$, $\Delta_{ij}\varepsilon_{3km}$, $\Delta_{ij}\delta_{3k}\delta_{3m}$, $\varepsilon_{3ij}\delta_{3k}\delta_{3m}$, $\delta_{3k}\delta_{3j}\delta_{3k}\delta_{3m}$, and similar terms obtained by permuting the indices. The combination $\varepsilon_{3ij}\varepsilon_{3km}$ need not be considered, because $\varepsilon_{3ij}\varepsilon_{3km} = \Delta_{ij}\Delta_{jm} - \Delta_{im}\Delta_{jk}$. If G_{ijkm} possesses the symmetries $G_{ijkm} = G_{jikm} = G_{ijmk}$, then it is given by†

$$\begin{aligned} G_{ijkm} = {} & \lambda\delta_{ij}\delta_{km} + 2\mu(\delta_{ik}\delta_{jm} + \delta_{jk}\delta_{im}) + (\alpha_2 - \alpha_1)\delta_{ij}\delta_{3k}\delta_{3m} \\ & + (\alpha_3 - \alpha_1)\delta_{km}\delta_{3i}\delta_{3j} + \beta(\delta_{ik}\delta_{3j}\delta_{3m} + \delta_{jk}\delta_{3i}\delta_{3m} \\ & + \delta_{im}\delta_{3j}\delta_{3k} + \delta_{jm}\delta_{3i}\delta_{3k}) + \gamma\delta_{3i}\delta_{3j}\delta_{3k}\delta_{3m} \\ & + \alpha_6(\delta_{ik}\varepsilon_{3jm} + \delta_{jk}\varepsilon_{3im} + \delta_{im}\varepsilon_{3jk} + \delta_{jm}\varepsilon_{3ik}) \\ & + (\alpha_8 - \alpha_6)(\varepsilon_{3ik}\delta_{3j}\delta_{3m} + \varepsilon_{3jk}\delta_{3i}\delta_{3m} + \varepsilon_{3im}\delta_{3j}\delta_{3k} \\ & + \varepsilon_{3jm}\delta_{3i}\delta_{3k}), \end{aligned} \tag{B.18}$$

where $\lambda = \alpha_1$, $2\mu = \alpha_5$. If we impose the additional symmetry $G_{ijkm} = G_{kmij}$, then (B.18) reduces to the form of (14.47), with α being given by $2\alpha = \alpha_2 + \alpha_3 - 2\alpha_1$.

There are two additional subclasses of transverse isotropy, characterized, respectively, by the additional symmetry operations

(1) reflections in planes containing the z axis.

(2) reflections in the xy plane.

In the last case the additional symmetry operation is diag(1, 1, −1), so that the vector $\|\delta_{3i}\| = \|0, 0, 1\|$ is mapped into $-\|\delta_{3i}\| = \|0, 0, -1\|$, but the tensor

$$\|\varepsilon_{3ij}\| = \begin{Vmatrix} 0 & 1 & 0 \\ -1 & 0 & 0 \\ 0 & 0 & 0 \end{Vmatrix}$$

is left unchanged. Because δ_{3i} occur only in pairs, it follows that no further reduction of (B.18) is obtained in this case.

Because of the rotational symmetry, there is no loss of generality if the invariance to reflections in planes passing through the z axis is replaced by invariance to reflections in the yz plane, for instance. The symmetry operation is then diag(−1, 1, 1), and it is easy to verify that δ_{3i} is invariant, but that ε_{3ij} is transformed into $-\varepsilon_{3ij}$. Therefore, it is necessary to set $\alpha_6 = \alpha_8 = 0$.

Isotropic polynomial bases

The recent history of the theory of representations of constitutive equations begins with the work of Rivlin and Ericksen [131] on isotropic stress relations. Rivlin and Ericksen obtained representations of polynomial functions by making use of the idea of linear dependence of sets of tensors. Let us take symmetric second rank tensors **T**, **A**, **B**, . . ., for instance. As was noted in Section 2, these

† Rogers and Pipkin [135], p. 339.

tensors constitute a six-dimensional vector space in which it is possible to introduce representations of the type $\mathbf{T} = T_{ij}\mathbf{e}_{ij}$, where $\mathbf{e}_{ij} = \mathbf{e}_i\mathbf{e}_j$ are base vectors. Now, if **T** is given by

$$\mathbf{T} = \mathbf{f}(\mathbf{A}, \mathbf{B}, \mathbf{C}, \ldots), \tag{B.19}$$

where **f** is an isotropic function, then it must be possible to express **T** in terms of six "base vectors" which are isotropic, linearly independent functions of **A**, **B**, **C** . . . In particular, we may be able to express **T** as a linear combination† of $\mathbf{1}$, $\mathbf{A}$, $\mathbf{B}$, $\mathbf{A}^2$, $\mathbf{AB} + \mathbf{BA}$, $\mathbf{A}^2\mathbf{B} + \mathbf{BA}^2$, provided that these "base vectors" can be shown to be linearly independent. The condition of linear independence gives rise to the following six equations,

$$c_0\mathbf{1} + c_1\mathbf{A} + c_2\mathbf{B} + c_3\mathbf{A}^2 + c_4(\mathbf{AB} + \mathbf{BA}) + c_5(\mathbf{A}^2\mathbf{B} + \mathbf{BA}^2) = 0,$$

which must be satisfied when not all coefficients $c_0, \ldots, c_5$ are zero. However, nontrivial solutions for $c_0, \ldots, c_5$ can exist only if the determinant of the coefficients $\mathbf{1}$, $\mathbf{A}$, $\mathbf{B}$, $\mathbf{A}^2$, $\mathbf{AB} + \mathbf{BA}$, $\mathbf{A}^2\mathbf{B} + \mathbf{BA}^2$ vanishes. In the principal coordinate system of **A**, the vanishing of this determinant can be shown to yield‡

$$D \begin{Vmatrix} B_{23} & B_{23}(A_{22} + A_{33}) & B_{23}(A_{22}^2 + A_{33}^2) \\ B_{31} & B_{31}(A_{33} + A_{11}) & B_{31}(A_{33}^2 + A_{11}^2) \\ B_{12} & B_{12}(A_{11} + A_{22}) & B_{12}(A_{11}^2 + A_{22}^2) \end{Vmatrix} = 0,$$

where

$$D = \begin{Vmatrix} 1 & A_{11} & A_{11}^2 \\ 1 & A_{22} & A_{22}^2 \\ 1 & A_{33} & A_{33}^2 \end{Vmatrix}.$$

Evidently the linear independence of $\mathbf{1}$, $\mathbf{A}$, $\mathbf{B}$, $\mathbf{A}^2$, $\mathbf{AB} + \mathbf{BA}$, $\mathbf{A}^2\mathbf{B} + \mathbf{BA}^2$ requires that, first, the principal values of **A** are distinct, and second, that **A** and **B** have no principal directions in common.

The preceding result illustrates a situation that was pointed out before: a polynomial basis that is selected in a more or less arbitrary way will not be general enough to cover all contingencies.§ A *complete* polynomial basis, on the other hand, will contain more than six elements. Its elements will not always be linearly independent, but they will provide a representation of **T** regardless of what special properties the argument tensors may have.

The subsequent investigations of Rivlin and his co-workers follow a different approach. The reduction of (B.19) is now based on the Cayley-Hamilton equation and various identities that can be derived from it.|| The method is thus quite

† The term *linear* refers to the "base vectors", not to the coefficients multiplying them. The latter will be (nonlinear) scalar-valued functions of the tensors.

‡ [131], Equations (24.1)–(24.5).

§ Rivlin and Ericksen [131] give a detailed analysis of the various possibilities.

|| Rivlin [132].

elementary, although the execution of the reductions is a lengthy task. Starting with the Cayley-Hamilton equation, $-\mathbf{A}^3 + \mathbf{A}^2\,\mathrm{tr}\mathbf{A} - \frac{1}{2}[(\mathrm{tr}\mathbf{A})^2 - \mathrm{tr}\mathbf{A}^2]\mathbf{A} + \mathbf{1}\,\mathrm{det}\mathbf{A} = \mathbf{0}$, we can derive more general identities by replacing $\mathbf{A}$ by $\mathbf{A} + \mathbf{B}$ or $\mathbf{A} + \mathbf{B} + \mathbf{C}$. Thus if the range of indices is from one to two, we obtain from the Cayley-Hamilton equation $\mathbf{A}^2 - \mathbf{A}\,\mathrm{tr}\mathbf{A} + \frac{1}{2}[(\mathrm{tr}\mathbf{A})^2 - \mathrm{tr}\mathbf{A}^2]\mathbf{1} = \mathbf{0}$ that

$$(\mathbf{A} + \mathbf{B})^2 - (\mathbf{A} + \mathbf{B})\mathrm{tr}(\mathbf{A} + \mathbf{B}) + \tfrac{1}{2}[(\mathrm{tr}\mathbf{A} + \mathrm{tr}\mathbf{B})^2 - \mathrm{tr}(\mathbf{A} + \mathbf{B})^2]\mathbf{1}$$
$$= \mathbf{AB} + \mathbf{BA} - \mathbf{A}\,\mathrm{tr}\mathbf{B} - \mathbf{B}\,\mathrm{tr}\mathbf{A} + (\mathrm{tr}\mathbf{A}\,\mathrm{tr}\mathbf{B} - \mathrm{tr}\mathbf{AB})\mathbf{1} = \mathbf{0}.$$

A tensor polynomial in $\mathbf{A}, \mathbf{B}, \mathbf{C}$, for instance, is made up of products $\Pi = \mathbf{M}^{(1)}\mathbf{M}^{(2)} \ldots \mathbf{M}^{(R)}$, where each "cluster" $\mathbf{M}^{(K)}$ is of the form

$$\mathbf{M}^{(K)} = \mathbf{A}^{\alpha_K}\mathbf{B}^{\beta_K}\mathbf{C}^{\gamma_K}.$$

According to the Cayley-Hamilton equation, none of the exponents need be larger than two. The number of such clusters is said to be the *extension* of the product Π. The main task is in fact to reduce the extension of polynomials, i.e. to eliminate terms like $\mathbf{ABABA}$, $\mathbf{A}^2\mathbf{BAB}$, etc. in terms of certain "irreducible" functions of $\mathbf{A}, \mathbf{B}, \mathbf{C}$. For functions of a single tensor $\mathbf{A}$, the irreducible elements are $\mathbf{1}, \mathbf{A}, \mathbf{A}^2$, the Cayley-Hamilton equation being a means for eliminating all other powers in terms of $\mathbf{1}, \mathbf{A}, \mathbf{A}^2$ and the principal invariants of $\mathbf{A}$. To reduce polynomials in $\mathbf{A}, \mathbf{B}, \mathbf{C}$, it is necessary to use the generalized Cayley-Hamilton equation (obtained by replacing $\mathbf{A}$ with $\mathbf{A} + \mathbf{B} + \mathbf{C}$), as well as various identities implied by it. For instance, $\mathbf{ABA}$, which is of extension two, can be replaced by forms of extension one, namely $\mathbf{1}$, $\mathbf{AB} + \mathbf{BA}$, $\mathbf{A}$, $\mathbf{B}$, $\mathbf{A}^2\mathbf{B}$, $\mathbf{BA}^2$. Continuing along these lines, it is possible to show that isotropic functions $\mathbf{f}(\mathbf{A}, \mathbf{B})$ admit the representation†

$$\begin{aligned}\mathbf{f}(\mathbf{A}, \mathbf{B}) = {}& \alpha_0\mathbf{1} + \alpha_1\mathbf{A} + \alpha_2\mathbf{A}^2 + \alpha_3\mathbf{B} + \alpha_4\mathbf{B}^2 + \alpha_5\mathbf{AB} + \alpha_6\mathbf{BA}\\ &+ \alpha_7\mathbf{A}^2\mathbf{B} + \alpha_8\mathbf{BA}^2 + \alpha_9\mathbf{AB}^2 + \alpha_{10}\mathbf{B}^2\mathbf{A} + \alpha_{11}\mathbf{A}^2\mathbf{B}^2 + \alpha_{12}\mathbf{B}^2\mathbf{A}^2 \quad \text{(B.20)}\\ &+ \alpha_{13}\mathbf{ABA}^2 + \alpha_{14}\mathbf{BAB}^2 + \alpha_{15}\mathbf{AB}^2\mathbf{A}^2 + \alpha_{16}\mathbf{BA}^2\mathbf{B}^2.\end{aligned}$$

The coefficients $\alpha_0, \ldots, \alpha_{16}$ are scalar-valued functions of the invariants that can be formed from $\mathbf{A}$ and $\mathbf{B}$. Each invariant must be of the form $J = J_{ijkm\ldots rs\ldots}A_{ij}A_{km} \ldots B_{rs} \ldots$, where $J_{ijkm\ldots rs\ldots}$ are isotropic tensors expressible as free products of Kronecker deltas. It follows, then, that the invariants are products of traces of powers of $\mathbf{A}$ and $\mathbf{B}$. Factoring $\mathbf{A}$, or $\mathbf{B}$, we have that $J = A_{ij}f_{ji}(\mathbf{A}, \mathbf{B})$, or $J = B_{ij}f_{ji}(\mathbf{A}, \mathbf{B})$, where $\mathbf{f}$ admits a representation of the form (B.20). Therefore, the required invariants are obtained from $\mathrm{tr}\mathbf{Af}$ and $\mathrm{tr}\mathbf{Bf}$. Noting that $\mathrm{tr}\mathbf{XY} = \mathrm{tr}\mathbf{YX}$ for any $\mathbf{X}$ and $\mathbf{Y}$, and that $\mathrm{tr}(\mathbf{A}^3\mathbf{B}) = \mathrm{tr}\mathbf{A}\,\mathrm{tr}(\mathbf{A}^2\mathbf{B}) - \frac{1}{2}[(\mathrm{tr}\mathbf{A})^2 - \mathrm{tr}\mathbf{A}^2]\mathrm{tr}\,(\mathbf{AB}) + [\frac{1}{3}\mathrm{tr}\mathbf{A}^3 - \frac{1}{2}\mathrm{tr}\mathbf{A}^2 + \frac{1}{6}(\mathrm{tr}\mathbf{A})^3]\mathrm{tr}\mathbf{B}$, $\mathrm{tr}(\mathbf{A}^3\mathbf{B}^2) = \mathrm{tr}\mathbf{A}\,\mathrm{tr}(\mathbf{A}^2\mathbf{B}^2) - \frac{1}{2}[(\mathrm{tr}\mathbf{A})^2 - \mathrm{tr}\mathbf{A}^2]\mathrm{tr}\mathbf{AB}^2$

† Cf. also the Appendix in [48].

$+ [\frac{1}{3}\,\text{tr}\mathbf{A}^3 - \frac{1}{2}\,\text{tr}\mathbf{A}\,\text{tr}\mathbf{A}^2 + \frac{1}{6}(\text{tr}\mathbf{A})^3]\text{tr}\mathbf{B}^2$, the set of *rationally independent* invariants can be reduced to

$$\text{tr}\mathbf{A},\ \text{tr}\mathbf{B},\ \text{tr}\mathbf{A}^2,\ \text{tr}\mathbf{B}^2,\ \text{tr}\mathbf{A}^3,\ \text{tr}\mathbf{B}^3,\ \text{tr}(\mathbf{AB}),\ \text{tr}(\mathbf{A}^2\mathbf{B}),\ \text{tr}(\mathbf{AB}^2),\ \text{tr}(\mathbf{A}^2\mathbf{B}^2), \quad \text{(B.21)}$$

$$\text{tr}(\mathbf{ABA}^2\mathbf{B}^2), \qquad \text{tr}(\mathbf{BAB}^2\mathbf{A}^2). \quad \text{(B.22)}$$

If the tensors **A** and **B** are symmetric, then (B.20) simplifies to

$$\begin{aligned} f(\mathbf{A}, \mathbf{B}) = \alpha_0\mathbf{1} &+ \alpha_1\mathbf{A} + \alpha_2\mathbf{A}^2 + \alpha_3\mathbf{B} + \alpha_4\mathbf{B}^2 + \alpha_5(\mathbf{AB} + \mathbf{BA}) \\ &+ \alpha_6(\mathbf{A}^2\mathbf{B} + \mathbf{BA}^2) + \alpha_7(\mathbf{AB}^2 + \mathbf{B}^2\mathbf{A}) + \alpha_8(\mathbf{A}^2\mathbf{B}^2 + \mathbf{B}^2\mathbf{A}^2), \end{aligned} \quad \text{(B.23)}$$

and the invariants are given by (B.21) alone.

Because powers of symmetric tensors admit the representations $A_{ij}^K = A_{\underline{a}}^K P_{ai} P_{aj}$, $B_{ij}^M = B_{\underline{b}}^M Q_{bi} Q_{bj}$, it follows that $\text{tr}(\mathbf{A}^K\mathbf{B}^M) = A_{\underline{a}}^K B_{\underline{b}}^M R_{ab} R_{ab}$, where $R_{ab} = P_{ai} Q_{bi}$ are the direction cosines relating the principal coordinate systems of **A** and **B**. It is then easy to see that $\text{tr}(\mathbf{A}^2\mathbf{B}^2)$ is not *functionally* independent of $\text{tr}(\mathbf{AB})$, $\text{tr}(\mathbf{A}^2\mathbf{B})$, and $\text{tr}(\mathbf{AB}^2)$. However, the elimination of $\text{tr}(\mathbf{A}^2\mathbf{B}^2)$ would not be a rational operation (the calculation of principal values requires the solution of a cubic!); in particular, the appearance of plus-minus signs in front of square roots would make $\alpha_0, \ldots, \alpha_8$ many-valued functions of **A** and **B**.

The theory of isotropic tensor polynomials in any number of symmetric second rank tensors has been developed by Spencer and Rivlin [153]. They find that a complete set of invariants of tensors **A**, **B**, **C** is given by $\text{tr}\mathbf{A}$, $\text{tr}\mathbf{A}^2$, $\text{tr}\mathbf{A}^3$, $\text{tr}(\mathbf{AB})$, $\text{tr}(\mathbf{AB}^2)$, $\text{tr}(\mathbf{A}^2\mathbf{B}^2)$, $\text{tr}(\mathbf{ABC})$, $\text{tr}(\mathbf{ABC}^2)$, $\text{tr}(\mathbf{AB}^2\mathbf{C}^2)$, and the terms that can be obtained from these by permutations of **A**, **B**, **C**. The set of invariants so obtained will have redundant elements, however; to eliminate them one should note that $\text{tr}(\mathbf{ABC}) = \text{tr}(\mathbf{BCA}) = \text{tr}(\mathbf{CAB})$, $\text{tr}(\mathbf{AB}^2\mathbf{C}^2) = \text{tr}(\mathbf{AC}^2\mathbf{B}^2)$, $\text{tr}(\mathbf{ABC}^2) = \text{tr}(\mathbf{BAC}^2)$.

Remarks on the general theory of representation†

In the same way that isotropy of the ambient space permits us to replace an orthonormal reference frame $\mathbf{e}_1$, $\mathbf{e}_2$, $\mathbf{e}_3$ by other, equivalent frames $\bar{\mathbf{e}}_1$, $\bar{\mathbf{e}}_2$, $\bar{\mathbf{e}}_3$ related to $\mathbf{e}_k$ by any orthogonal transformation **Q**, the symmetries of the constitution of a material define equivalent orientations of (intrinsic) *material frames* $\mathbf{H}_1$, $\mathbf{H}_2$, $\mathbf{H}_3$ characterizing preferred directions in the material. The mappings **S** that transform one material frame into another, equivalent frame, thus $\hat{\mathbf{H}}_1 = \mathbf{SH}_1$, $\hat{\mathbf{H}}_2 = \mathbf{SH}_2$, $\hat{\mathbf{H}}_3 = \mathbf{SH}_3$, constitute the symmetry group of the material. With the aid of this group we can determine all directions that are indistinguishable, in terms of material properties, from a given direction.

The form-invariance of the strain-energy function, $W(\mathbf{C}) = W(\mathbf{SCS}^T)$, is a case in point. Should the symmetry group $\mathscr{s} = \{\mathbf{S}\}$ be the orthogonal group $\mathscr{o} = \{\mathbf{Q}\}$, then W must be an *isotropic function* of **C**, in which case W can depend

† Pipkin and Rivlin [121], Pipkin and Wineman [120].

only on the isotropic invariants $\text{I} = \text{I}_\text{C}$, $\text{II} = \text{II}_\text{C}$, $\text{III} = \text{III}_\text{C}$, thus $W(\mathbf{C}) = W(\text{I, II, III})$. We also say that I, II, III constitute a *polynomial basis* of isotropic polynomial functions; that is, whereas W as a function of $\mathbf{C}$ is still subject to the invariance requirement $W(\mathbf{C}) = W(\mathbf{QCQ}^T)$, in the representation $W(\mathbf{C}) = \overline{W}(\text{I, II, III})$ the required form-invariance is automatically satisfied, so that, except for any "plausibility requirements" that we may wish to impose on it, $\overline{W}$ is an arbitrary function. This is of course in line with what we try to do everyplace else, namely to satisfy basic requirements once for all by obtaining suitably invariant representations.

More generally, let us take as a typical constitutive equation the following expression: $T_{ij} = f_{ij}(A_{np}, u_q)$ (adding more indices, or more independent variables, will only lengthen the formulas, without any essential gain of generality). If an orthogonal tensor $\mathbf{S}$ represents a symmetry operation of the material, then the response function $\mathbf{f}$ must be form-invariant to $\mathbf{S}$, thus

$$f_{km}(\overline{\mathbf{A}}, \overline{\mathbf{u}}) = S_{ik}S_{jm}f_{ij}(\mathbf{A}, \mathbf{u}), \tag{B.24}$$

where $\overline{A}_{np} = S_{nr}S_{ps}A_{rs}$, $\bar{u}_q = S_{qt}u_t$. Another way of representing the condition of form-invariance of $\mathbf{f}$ is by requiring that the expression $F = M_{ij}f_{ij}(\mathbf{A}, \mathbf{u})$, where $\mathbf{M}$ is an arbitrary tensor, be an invariant of the symmetry group of the material, so that

$$F = M_{ij}f_{ij}(\mathbf{A}, \mathbf{u}) = \overline{M}_{ij}f_{ij}(\overline{\mathbf{A}}, \overline{\mathbf{u}}). \tag{B.25}$$

Because $\mathbf{M}$ is arbitrary, (B.25) clearly implies (B.24), and vice versa.

Assuming that F is a polynomial function, we can express F in terms of the polynomial invariants† of the set of variables $\mathbf{M}, \mathbf{A}, \mathbf{u}$. We denote by $I^{(\alpha)}$, $\alpha = 1, 2, \ldots, M$, the invariants that depend on $\mathbf{A}$ and $\mathbf{u}$, and by $J^{(\beta)}$, $\beta = 1, 2, \ldots, L$, those invariants that are linear in $\mathbf{M}$. The latter are of the form $J^{(\beta)} = M_{ij}f_{ij}^{(\beta)}(\mathbf{A},\mathbf{u})$, where $f_{ij}^{(\beta)}$ are form-invariant functions. We shall call them the *basic form-invariant functions*. Now, because F is a linear function of $\mathbf{M}$, its representation must be of the form

$$F = \sum_{\beta=1}^{L} J^{(\beta)}F^{(\beta)}(I, I_2, \ldots, I_M),$$

from which it follows that

$$M_{ij}f_{ij} = M_{ij}\sum_{\beta=1}^{L} f_{ij}^{(\beta)}F^{(\beta)}(I, I_2, \ldots, I_M),$$

or,

$$f_{ij} = \sum_{\beta=1}^{L} F^{(\beta)}f_{ij}^{(\beta)}. \tag{B.26}$$

† Cf. (B.6) *et seq.*

Consequently, a knowledge of the polynomial invariants $J^{(\beta)}$ provides us with the basic form-invariant functions $f_{ij}^{(\beta)}$ in terms of which any form-invariant function f_{ij} can be expanded. Pipkin and Wineman have shown that the representation (B.26) is valid also if f_{ij} is not a polynomial function. Specifically, if f_{ij} is not a polynomial function, then neither are the coefficients $F^{(\beta)}$; however, the calculation of the basic functions $f_{ij}^{(\beta)}$ from the polynomial invariants $J^{(\beta)}$ remains valid.

To represent a stress relation $\mathbf{T} = \mathbf{Ff(C)F}^T$, we start from $F = f_{ij}(\mathbf{C})M_{ij}$, where $\mathbf{M}$ is an arbitrary tensor. Then the form-invariance of $\mathbf{f}$ requires that

$$F = f_{ij}(\bar{\mathbf{C}})\bar{M}_{ij} = f_{ij}(\mathbf{C})M_{ij}, \quad \bar{\mathbf{M}} = \mathbf{SMS}^T. \tag{B.27}$$

According to (B.27), F is form-invariant with respect to the transformation $\mathbf{S}$, i.e. F is a polynomial invariant, in the variables $\mathbf{C}$ and $\mathbf{M}$, of the group of transformations $\mathbf{S}$. This means that F can be represented in terms of elements of the appropriate polynomial basis in $\mathbf{C}$ and $\mathbf{M}$; moreover, only invariants which are linear in $\mathbf{M}$ need be considered. Therefore, $f_{ij}(C) = \partial F/\partial M_{ij}$.

For example, let us take the monoclinic symmetry. The polynomial basis in $\mathbf{C}$ is then given by

$$C_{11},\ C_{22},\ C_{33},\ C_{12},\ C_{13}^2,\ C_{23}^2,\ C_{13}C_{23}. \tag{B.28}$$

The polynomial basis of F is derived in the same way; we start with the condition

$$\begin{aligned}&F(C_{11}, C_{22}, C_{33}, C_{12}, C_{23}, C_{31}, M_{11}, M_{22}, M_{33}, M_{12}, M_{23}, M_{31})\\ &\quad = F(C_{11}, C_{22}, C_{33}, C_{12}, -C_{23}, -C_{31}, M_{11}, M_{22}, M_{33}, M_{12}, -M_{23}, -M_{31}),\end{aligned}$$

and, using (B.12), obtain a set of invariants that are linear in $\mathbf{M}$: M_{11}, M_{22}, M_{33}, M_{12}, M_{21}, $C_{23}M_{23}$, $C_{23}M_{32}$, C_{23}, M_{31}, $C_{23}M_{13}$, $C_{31}M_{23}$, $C_{31}M_{32}$, $C_{31}M_{31}$, $C_{31}M_{13}$. The invariant F is a linear combination of these invariants, with coefficients depending on the invariants (B.28) only. Thus

$$\|\mathbf{f}\| = \begin{Vmatrix} \alpha_{11} & \alpha_{12} & C_{23}\alpha_{13} + C_{31}\beta_{13} \\ \alpha_{12} & \alpha_{22} & C_{23}\alpha_{23} + C_{31}\beta_{23} \\ C_{23}\alpha_{13} + C_{31}\beta_{13} & C_{23}\alpha_{23} + C_{31}\beta_{23} & \alpha_{33} \end{Vmatrix} \tag{B.29}$$

where α_{ij} and β_{ij} depend on the invariants (B.28).

BIBLIOGRAPHY*

The following abbreviations of titles of journals have been used:

ARMA	Archive for Rational Mechanics and Analysis
JRMA	Journal of Rational Mechanics and Analysis
QAM	Quarterly of Applied Mathematics
ZAMM	Zeitschrift für Angewandte Mathematik und Mechanik
ZAMP	Zeitschrift für Angewandte Mathematik und Physik
PMM	Prikladnaya Matematika i Mehanika
AMS	Archiwum Mechaniki Stosowanej

1. Beatty, M. A., "Some Static and Dynamic Implications of the General Theory of Elastic Stability", *ARMA* **19** (1965), pp. 167–188.

2. Bell, E. T., *Men of Mathematics*, New York: Simon and Schuster (1937).

3. Bernstein, B., "Hypo-Elasticity and Elasticity", *ARMA* **6** (1960), pp. 89–104.

4. Bernstein, B., E. Kearsley and L. Zapas, "Perfect Elastic Fluids", *Trans. Soc. Rheol.* **9** (1965), pp. 27–39.

5. Biot, M. A., "Internal Buckling Under Initial Stress in Finite Elasticity", *Proc. Roy. Soc.* London A**273** (1963), pp. 306–328.

6. Bondi, H., "Some Special Solutions of the Einstein Equations", Vol. I of Lectures on General Relativity, Brandeis Summer Institute in Theoretical Physics, Englewood Cliffs, N.J.: Prentice-Hall (1965), pp. 375–450.

7. Buck, R. C., *Advanced Calculus*, New York: McGraw-Hill Co. (1965).

8. Caldonazzo, B., "Osservazione Sui Tensori Quintupli Emisotropi", *Rend. d. Reale Acad. Naz. dei Lincei* (1932), pp. 840–843.

* With the exception of [196]–[241], the references given throughout the book are listed in alphabetical order.

9. Carslaw, H. S. and J. C. Jaeger, *Conduction of Heat in Solids*, Oxford, Eng.: Clarendon Press, 1959.

10. Chacon, R. V. S. and R. S. Rivlin, "Representation Theorems in the Mechanics of Materials with Memory", *ZAMP* **15** (1964), pp. 444–447.

11. Coleman, B. D. and Walter Noll, "The Thermodynamics of Elastic Materials with Heat Conduction and Viscosity", *ARMA* **12** (1963), pp. 167–177.

12. Coleman, B. D., "Thermodynamics of Materials with Memory", *ARMA* **17**, pp. 1–46, 1964; "On Thermodynamics, Strain Impulses, and Viscoelasticity", *ibid*, pp. 230–254.

13. 13, 17 and 185, originally published in *ARMA*, are now available in *Wave Propagation in Dissipative Materials* (authors: B. D. Coleman, M. E. Gurtin, I. Herrera R., and C. Truesdell), New York: Springer-Verlag (1965).

14. Coleman, B. D. and V. J. Mizel, "Existence of Caloric Equations of State in Thermodynamics", *J. Chem. Phys.* **40** (1964), pp. 1116–1125.

15. Coleman, B. D. and Walter Noll, "Foundations of Linear Viscoelasticity", *Rev. Mod. Phys.* **33** (1961), pp. 239–249.

16. Coleman, B. D. and W. Noll, "An Approximation Theorem for Functionals, with Applications in Continuum Mechanics", *ARMA* **6** (1960), pp. 355–370.

17. See Reference 13.

18. Coleman, B. D. and Walter Noll, "Material Symmetry and Thermostatic Inequalities in Finite Elastic Deformations", *ARMA* **15** (1963), pp. 87–111.

19. Coleman, B. D., H. Markovitz and W. Noll, *Viscometric Flows of Non-Newtonian Fluids*, New York: Springer-Verlag (1966).

20. Condiff, D. W. and J. S. Dahler, "Fluid Mechanical Aspects of Antisymmetric Stress", *Phys. of Fluids* **7** (1964).

21. Courant, R., *Differential and Integral Calculus*, Vol. II, New York: Interscience (1965).

22. Dahler, J. S. and L. E. Scriven, "Theory of structured continua", *Proc. Phil. Soc.* London A**275** (1963), pp. 504–527.

23. Di Francia, G. T., *Electromagnetic Waves*, New York: Interscience (1953).

24. Douglas, W. J., and W. Jaunzemis, "Elastic Response of Prestrained Bodies", *AFOSR Techn. Note*, University Park, Pa.: The Pennsylvania State University (1967).

25. Dunkin, J. W. and A. C. Eringen, "On the Propagation of Waves in an Electromagnetic Elastic Solid", *Int. J. Eng. Sci.* **1** (1963), pp. 461–495.

26. Eckart, C., "The Thermodynamics of Irreversible Processes. IV. The Theory of Elasticity and Anelasticity", *Phys. Rev.* **73** (1948), pp. 373–382.

27. Edelstein, W. S. and M. E. Gurtin, "Uniqueness Theorems in the Linear Dynamic Theory of Anisotropic Viscoelastic Solids", *ARMA* **17** (1964), pp. 47–60.

28. Ericksen, J. L., "Transversely Isotropic Fluids", *Kolloid Z.* **173** (1960), pp. 117–122.

29. Ericksen, J. L., "Kinematics of Macromolecules", *ARMA* **9** (1962), pp. 1–8.

30. Ericksen, J. L., "Conservation Laws for Liquid Crystals", *Trans. Soc. Rheol.* **5** (1961), pp. 23–34.

31. Ericksen, J. L. and C. Truesdell, "Exact Theory of Stress and Strain in Rods and Shells", *ARMA* **1** (1958), pp. 295–323.

32. Ericksen, J. L., *Tensor Fields, Enc. of Physics*, Vol. III/1, New York: Springer-Verlag (1960).

33. Ericksen, J. L. and R. S. Rivlin, "Large Elastic Deformations of Homogeneous Anisotropic Materials", *JRMA* (1955), pp. 281–301.

34. Ericksen, J. L. and R. A. Toupin, "Implications of Hadamard's Conditions for Elastic Stability with Respect to Uniqueness Theorems", *Can. J. Math.* **8** (1956), pp. 432–436.

35. Ericksen, J. L., "Overdetermination of the Speed of Rectilinear Motion of Non-Newtonian Fluids", *QAM* **14** (1956), p. 318.

36. Ericksen, J. L., "Nonexistence Theorems in Linearized Elastostatics", *J. Diff. Equ.* **1** (1965), pp. 446–451.

37. J. L. Ericksen, "Mechanical Theories of Oriented Bodies" (unpublished).

38. Eringen, A. C., "On the Foundations of Electroelastostatics", *Int. J. Eng. Sci.* **1** (1963), pp. 127–153.

39. Eringen, A. C. and R. C. Dixon, "A Dynamical Theory of Polar Elastic Dielectrics—I, II", *Int. J. Eng. Sci.* **3** (1965), pp. 359–398.

40. Eubanks, R. A. and E. Sternberg, "On the Completeness of the Boussinesq-Papkovich Stress Functions", *JRMA* **5** (1956), p. 735.

41. Fisher, G. M. C. and M. E. Gurtin, "Wave Propagation in Linear Theory of Viscoelasticity", *QAM* **23** (1965), pp. 257–263.

42. Flanders, H., *Differential Forms*, New York: Academic Press (1963).

43. Fosdick, R. L., "Remarks on Compatibility in Continuum Mechanics and Deformations which Possess Constant Strain Invariants", *Report, Dept. of Mechanics, Ill. Inst. of Techn.*, Chicago, Ill. (1965).

44. *The Scientific Papers of J. Willard Gibbs*, Vol. II, New York: Dover Publications.

45. Giesekus, H., "Sekundaerstroemungen in viskoelastischen Fluessigkeiten bei stationaerer und periodischer Bewegung", *Rheol. Acta* **4** (1965), pp. 85–101.

46. Grad, M., "Statistical Mechanics, Thermodynamics, and Fluid Dynamics of Systems", Comm. Pure Appl. Math. **5** (1952), pp. 455–494.

47. Green, A. E. and W. Zerna, *Theoretical Elasticity*, Oxford Eng.: Clarendon Press (1954).

48. Green, A. E. and J. E. Adkins, *Large Elastic Deformations*, Oxford, Eng.: Clarendon Press (1960).

49. Green, A. E. and R. S. Rivlin, "Multipolar Continuum Mechanics", *ARMA* **17** (1964), pp. 113–147.

50. Green, A. E. and P. M. Naghdi, "On the Derivation of Discontinuity Conditions in Continuum Mechanics", *Int. J. Eng. Sci.* **6** (1965), pp. 621–624.

51. Green, A. E. and R. S. Rivlin, "On Cauchy's Equations of Motion", *ZAMP* **15** (1964), pp. 290–292.

52. Green, A. E. and P. M. Naghdi, "A Dynamical Theory of Interacting Continua", *Int. J. Eng. Sci.* **3** (1965), pp. 231–241.

53. Green, A. E. and R. S. Rivlin, "The Mechanics of Non-Linear Materials with Memory", Part I, *ARMA* **1** (1957), pp. 1–21.

54. Green, A. E., P. M. Naghdi and W. L. Wainwright, "A General Theory of a Cosserat Surface", *Report No. AM-65-5, Contract Nonr-222(69)*, Institute of Engineering Research, University of California, June 1965.

55. Green, A. E., "Anisotropic simple fluids", *Proc. Roy. Soc.* London A**279** (1964), pp. 437–445.

56. Green, W. A., "The Growth of Plane Discontinuities Propagating into a Homogeneously Deformed Elastic Material", *ARMA* **16** (1964), pp. 79–88; corrections and additional results *ibid*, **17** (1965), pp. 20–23.

57. Gross, B., *Mathematical Structure of the Theories of Viscoelasticity*, Paris, France: Herman and Co. (1953).

58. Guenther, W., "Analoge Systeme von Schalengleichungen", *Ing. Arch.* **30**, (1961), pp. 160–186.

59. Guenther, W., "Zur Statik and Kinematik des Cosseratschen Kontinuums", *Abh. d. Braunschw. Wiss. Ges.* (1958), pp. 195–213.

60. Gurtin, M. E. and E. Sternberg, "A Note on Uniqueness in Classical Elastodynamics", *QAM* **19** (1961), pp. 169–171.

61. Gurtin, M. E. and R. A. Toupin, "A Uniqueness Theorem for the Displacement Boundary-Value Problem of Linear Elastodynamics", *QAM* **23** (1964), pp. 79–81.

62. Gurtin, M. E., "A Generalization of the Beltrami Stress Functions in Continuum Mechanics", *ARMA* **13** (1963), pp. 321–329.

63. Gurtin, M. E., "On Helmholtz's Theorem and the Completeness of the Papkovich-Neuber Stress Functions for Infinite Domains", *ARMA* **9** (1962), pp. 225–233.

64. Gurtin, M. E. and I. Herrera, "On Dissipation Inequalities and Linear Viscoelasticity", *QAM* **23** (1965), pp. 235–245.

65. Gurtin, M. E. and E. Sternberg, "On the Linear Theory of Viscoelasticity", *ARMA* **11** (1962), pp. 291–356.

66. Gurtin, M. E. and E. Sternberg, "A Reciprocal Theorem in the Linear Theory of Anisotropic Viscoelastic Solids", *J. Soc. Indust. Appl. Math.* **11** (1963), pp. 607–613.

67. Hamel, G., *Theoretische Mechanik*, New York: Springer-Verlag (1949).

68. Hayes, M. and R. S. Rivlin, "Surface Waves in Deformed Elastic Materials", *ARMA* **8** (1961), pp. 358–380.

69. Hayes, M. and R. S. Rivlin, "Propagation of a Plane Wave in an Isotropic Elastic Material Subjected to Pure Homogeneous Deformation", *ARMA* (1961), p. 20.

70. Hearmon, R. F. S., *An Introduction to Applied Anisotropic Elasticity*, Oxford, Eng.: Oxford University Press (1961).

71. Hehl, F. and E. Kroener, "Zum Materialgesetz eines elastischen Mediums mit Momentenspannungen", *Zeits. f. Naturf.* **20a** (1965), pp. 336–350.

72. Henniker, J. C., "The Depth of the Surface Zone of a Liquid", *Rev. Mod. Phys.* **21** (1949), pp. 322–341.

73. Herrera, I. and M. E. Gurtin, "A Correspondence Principle for Viscoelastic Wave Propagation", *QAM* **22** (1965), pp. 360–364.

74. Hill, R., "On Uniqueness and Stability in the Theory of Finite Elastic Strain", *J. Mech. Phys. Solids* **5** (1957), pp. 229–241.

75. Hinze, J. O., *Turbulence*, New York: McGraw-Hill (1959).

76. Huang, Chi Lung, "Elastic Anisotropic Materials with Couple-Stresses", Dissertation, New Haven, Conn.: Yale University (1964).

77. Jaunzemis, W. and S. C. Cowin, "Oriented Materials", *Proc. Princeton Conf. on Solid Mechanics*, Nov. 1963.

78. Jones, D. S., *The Theory of Electromagnetism*, New York: The Macmillan Co. (1964).

79. Jordan, N. F. and A. C. Eringen, "On the Static Nonlinear Theory of Electromagnetic Thermoelastic Solids—I, II", *Int. J. Eng. Sci.* **2** (1964), pp. 59–95, 97–114.

80. Kasner, E. and J. Newman, *Mathematics and the Imagination*, New York: Simon and Schuster (1940).

81. Keller, H. B., "Saint-Venant's Procedure and Saint-Venant's Principle", *QAM* **22** (1964), pp. 293–304.

82. Kellogg, O. D., *Foundations of Potential Theory*, New York: Dover Publications.

83. Knowles, J. K. and M. T. Jakub, "Finite Dynamic Deformations of an Incompressible Medium Containing a Spherical Cavity", *ARMA* **18** (1965), pp. 367–378.

84. Kroener, E., *Kontinuumstheorie der Versetzungen und Eigenspannungen*, Springer-Verlag (1958).

85. Lagally, M., *Vorlesungen ueber Vektor-Rechnung*, Akad. Verlagsges., Leipzig (1945).

86. Langlois, W. E., *Slow Viscous Flows*, New York: The Macmillan Co. (1964).

87. Lee, Y. C. and W. Jaunzemis, "Elastic-Plastic Response of a Slab to a Heat Pulse", *AFOSR Techn. Rep. No. 6*, University Park, Pa.: The Pennsylvania State University, March 1963.

88. Lekhnitskii, S. G., *Theory of Elasticity of an Anisotropic Elastic Body*, San Francisco, Calif.: Holden-Day, Inc. (1963).

89. Levi-Civita, T., *The Absolute Differential Calculus*, New York: Hafner (1947).

90. Lodge, A. S., "On the Use of Convected Coordinate Systems in the Mechanics of Continuous Media", *Proc. Cambr. Phil. Soc.* **47** (1951), pp. 575–584.

91. Love, A. E. H., *A Treatise on the Mathematical Theory of Elasticity*, New York: Dover Publications.

92. McSkimin, H. J. and P. Andreatch, Jr., "Measurement of Third-Order Moduli of Silicon and Germanium", *J. Appl. Phys.* **35** (1964), pp. 3312–3319.

93. Meixner, J., "On the Theory of Linear Viscoelastic Behavior", *Rheol. Acta* **4** (1965), pp. 80, 81.

94. Mindlin, R. D., "Second Gradient of Strain and Surface-Tension in Linear Elasticity", *Int. J. Solids Structures* **1** (1965), pp. 417–438.

95. Mindlin, R. D. and H. F. Tiersten, "Effect of Couple-Stresses in Linear Elasticity", *ARMA* **11** (1962), pp. 415–448.

96. Mindlin, R. D., "Microstructure in Linear Elasticity", *ARMA* **16** (1964), pp. 51–78.

97. Von Mises, R., "Mechanik der plastischen Formaenderung von Kristallen", *ZAMM* **8** (1928), pp. 161–185.

98. Von Mises, R., "On Saint-Venant's Principle", *Bull. Am. Math. Soc.* **51** (1945), p. 555.

99. Moon, P. and D. E. Spencer, *Field Theory Handbook*, New York: Springer-Verlag (1961).

100. Morland, L. W. and E. H. Lee, "Stress Analysis for Linear Viscoelastic Materials with Temperature Variation", *Trans. Soc. Rheol.* **4** (1960), pp. 233–263.

101. Mueller, C. H. and A. Timpe, *Die Grundgleichungen* der *Mathematischen Elastizitaets-Theorie, Enc. der Math. Wiss.*, IV/4, Teubner-Verlag (1907–1914).

102. Muki, R. and E. Sternberg, "On Transient Thermal Stresses in Viscoelastic Materials with Temperature-Dependent Properties", *J. Appl. Mech.* (1961), p. 193.

103. Muki, R. and E. Sternberg, "The Influence of Couple-Stresses on Singular Stress Concentrations in Elastic Solids", *ZAMP* **16** (1965).

104. Mura, T., "Continuous Distribution of Dislocations and the Mathematical Theory of Plasticity", *Phys. Stat. Sol.* **10** (1965).

105. Noll, W., "The Equations of Finite Elasticity", *Proc. Symp. Appl. Math.* **17**, Am. Math. Soc., Providence, R. I. (1965).

106. Noll, W., "A Mathematical Theory of the Mechanical Behaviour of Continuous Media", *ARMA* **2** (1958), pp. 197–226.

107. Noll, W., *Tensor Analysis*, course notes prepared by C.-C. Wang, The Johns Hopkins University (1962–1963).

108. Noether, E., *Math. Annalen* **77** (1916), pp. 89–92.

109. Nye, J. F., *Physical Properties of Crystals*, Oxford, Eng.: Clarendon Press (1964).

110. Odeh, F. and I. Tadjbakhsh, "Uniqueness in the Linear Theory of Viscoelasticity", *ARMA* **18** (1964) pp. 244–250.

111. Oldroyd, J. G., "On the Formulation of Rheological Equations of State", *Proc. Roy. Soc.* Lond. A**200** (1950), pp. 523–541.

112. Oshima, N., *Proc. 3rd Japan Nat. Congr. Appl. Mech.*, (1953), p. 77.

113. Panofsky, W. K. H. and M. Phillips, *Classical Electricity and Magnetism*, Appendix I, Mass.: Addison-Wesley (1955).

114. Pearson, C. E., "General Theory of Elastic Stability", *QAM* **14** (1955), pp. 133–144.

115. Phillips, H. B., *Vector Analysis*, New York: John Wiley & Sons (1933).

116. Pipkin, A. C. and R. S. Rivlin, "Electrical Conduction in Deformed Isotropic Materials", *J. Math. Phys.* **1**, pp. 127–130. [Added in proof: cf. also "Electrical, Thermal and Magnetic Constitutive Equations for Deformed Isotropic Materials", *Atti d. Accad. Naz. d. Lincei* **8** (1966), pp. 3–29].

117. Pipkin, A. C. and R. S. Rivlin, "Normal Stresses in Flow Through Tubes of Non-Circular Cross Sections", *ZAMP* **14** (1963), pp. 738–742.

118. Pipkin, A. C., "Annular Effects in Viscoelastic Fluids", *Phys. of Fluids* **7** (1964), pp. 1143–1146.

119. Pipkin, A. C. and R. S. Rivlin, "Electrical Conduction in a Stretched and Twisted Tube", *J. Math. Phys.* **2** (1961), pp. 636–638.

120. Pipkin, A. C. and A. S. Wineman, "Material Symmetry Restrictions on Non-Polynomial Constitutive Equations", *ARMA* **12** (1963), pp. 420–426.

121. Pipkin, A. C. and R. S. Rivlin, "The Formulation of Constitutive Equations in Continuum Physics. I", *ARMA* **4** (1959), pp. 129–144.

122. Pipkin, A. C., "Alternating Flow of Non-Newtonian Fluids in Tubes of Arbitrary Cross-section", *ARMA* **15** (1963), pp. 1–13.

123. Poincare, H., *Science and Hypothesis*, New York: Dover Publications.

124. Post, E. J., *Formal Structure of Electromagnetics*, New York: John Wiley & Sons (1962).

125. Prager, W., *Introduction to Mechanics of Continua*, Boston, Mass.: Ginn and Company (1961).

126. Racah, G., "Determinazione del numero dei tensori isotropi indipendenti di rango n", *Rend. d. Reale Acad. Naz. dei Lincei* (1933), pp. 386–389.

127. Rajagopal, E. S., "The Existence of Interfacial Couples in Infinitesimal Elasticity", *Ann. Phys.* **6** (1960), pp. 192–201.

128. Ricci, G. and T. Levi-Civita, "Methodes de calcul differential absolu et leurs applications", *Math. Annalen*, **54** (1900).

129. Rindler, W., *Special Relativity*, New York: Interscience Publishers (1960).

130. Rivlin, R. S., "The Formulation of Constitutive Equations in Continuum Physics, II", *ARMA* **4** (1959/60), pp. 262–272.

131. Rivlin, R. S. and J. L. Ericksen, "Stress-Deformation Relations for Isotropic Materials", *JRMA* **4** (1955), pp. 323–425.

132. Rivlin, R. S., "Further Remarks on the Stress-Deformation Relations for Isotropic Materials", *JRMA* **4** (1955), p. 690.

133. Rivlin, R. S., "Networks of Inextensible Cords", *Nonlinear Problems of Engineering*, New York: Academic Press (1964), pp. 51–64.

134. Rivlin, R. S. and D. W. Saunders, *Phil. Trans.* A**243** (1951).

135. Rogers, T. G. and A. C. Pipkin, "Asymmetric Relaxation and Compliance Matrices in Linear Viscoelasticity", *ZAMP* **14** (1963), pp. 334–343.

136. Rogers, T. G., "Viscoelastic Stress Analysis", *Proc. Princeton University Conf. on Solid Mechanics* (1963).

137. Rosenfeld, L., *Theory of Electrons*, New York: Interscience (1951).

138. Sackman, J. L., "Creep in Concrete and Concrete Structures", *Proc. Princeton Conf. on Solid Mechanics*, Nov. (1963).

139. Schouten, J. A., *Tensor Analysis for Physicists*, Oxford, Eng.: Clarendon Press (1953).

140. Serrin, J., "Mathematical Principles of Classical Fluid Mechanics", *Enc. of Physics*, Vol. VIII/1, New York: Springer-Verlag (1959).

141. Simmons, G. F., *Introduction to Topology and Modern Analysis*, New York: McGraw-Hill (1963).

142. Singh, Manohar and A. C. Pipkin, "Note on Ericksen's Problem", *ZAMP* **16** (1965), pp. 706–709.

143. Slepian, J., "A Parable on Tensor Analysis", *The Electric Journal* **33** (1936), pp. 541–547; "Tensors and Fruit Salads", *ibid* **34** (1937), pp. 115–119.

144. Smith, G. F., and R. S. Rivlin, "The Anisotropic Tensors", *QAM* **15** (1950), pp. 308–314.

145. Smith, G. F. and R. S. Rivlin, "Stress-Deformation Relations for Anisotropic Solids", *ARMA* **1** (1957), pp. 107–112.

146. Smith, G. F., "Further Results on the Strain-Energy Function for Anisotropic Elastic Materials", *ARMA* **10** (1962), pp. 108–118.

147. Smith, G. F., "On the Yield Condition for Anisotropic Materials", *QAM* **20** (1962), pp. 241–247.

148. Smith, G. F., "On the Minimality of Integrity Bases for Symmetric 3 × 3 Matrices", *ARMA* **5** (1960), pp. 382–389.

149. Smith, G. F. and R. S. Rivlin, "The Strain-Energy Function For Anisotropic Elastic Materials", *Trans. Am. Math. Soc.* **88** (1958), pp. 175–193.

150. Sneddon, I. N., *Fourier Transforms*, New York: McGraw-Hill (1951).

151. Sommerfeld, A., *Partial Differential Equations in Physics*, New York: Academic Press (1949).

152. Spencer, A. J. M. and R. S. Rivlin, "Finite Integrity Bases for Five or Fewer Symmetric 3 × 3 Matrices", *ARMA* **2** (1959), pp. 435–446.

153. Spencer, A. J. M. and R. S. Rivlin, "The Theory of Matrix Polynomials and Its Application to the Mechanics of Isotropic Continua", *ARMA* **2** (1959), pp. 309–336.

154. Spencer, A. J. M. and R. S. Rivlin, "Further Results in the Theory of Matrix Polynomials", *ARMA* **4** (1959), pp. 214–230.

155. Sternberg, E. and R. A. Eubanks, "On the Concept of Concentrated Loads and an Extension of the Uniqueness Theorem in the Linear Theory of Elasticity", *JRMA* **4** (1955), pp. 135–168.

156. Sternberg, E., "On Saint-Venant's Principle", *QAM* **11** (1954), p. 393.

157. Sternberg, E., "On the Analysis of Thermal Stresses in Viscoelastic Solids", *High Temperature Structures and Materials* (editors: A. M. Freudenthal, B. A. Boley, H. Liebowitz), New York: Pergamon Press (1964).

158. Synge, J. L., *Relativity: The Special Theory*, Amsterdam: North-Holland Publ. Co. (1956).

159. Synge, J. L., *The Hypercircle in Mathematical Physics*, Cambridge, Eng.: Cambridge University Press (1957).

160. Synge, J. L. "Elastic Waves in Anisotropic Media", *J. Math. Phys.* (1957), pp. 323–334.

161. Taylor, G. I., "The Plastic Wave in a Wire Extended by an Impact Load", The Scientific Papers of J. I. Taylor, Vol. I (1958), pp. 467–479.

162. Thomson, W. and P. G. Tait, *Natural Philosophy*, 1st ed., Oxford, Eng.: Oxford University Press (1867).

163. Thurston, R. N., "Effective Elastic Coefficients for Wave Propagation in Crystals Under Stress", *J. Acoust. Soc. Am.* **37** (1965), pp. 348–356.

164. Thurston, R. N. and K. Brugger, "Third-Order Elastic Constants and the Velocity of Small Amplitude Waves in Homogeneously Stressed Media", *Phys. Rev.* **133** (1964). pp. A1604–A1610.

165. Toupin, R. A. and B. Bernstein, "Sound Waves in Deformed Perfectly Elastic Materials. Acoustoelastic Effect", *J. Acoust. Soc. Am.* **33** (1961), pp. 216–225.

166. Toupin, R. A., "Saint-Venant's Principle", *ARMA* **18** (1965), pp. 83–96.

167. Toupin, R. A. and D. C. Gazis, "Surface Effects and Initial Stress in Continuum and Lattice Models of Elastic Crystals", *Lattice Dynamics* (edited by R. F. Wallis), New York: Pergamon Press (1965).

168. Toupin, R. A., "A Dynamical Theory of Elastic Dielectrics", *Int. J. Eng. Sci.* **1** (1963), pp. 101–126.

169. Toupin, R. A., "Elastic Materials with Couple-stresses", *ARMA* **11** (1962), pp. 385–414.

170. Toupin, R. A., "Theories of Elasticity with Couple-stress", *ARMA* **17** (1964), pp. 85–112.

171. Truesdell, C., *The Kinematics of Vorticity*, Bloomington, Indiana: Indiana University Press (1953).

172. Truesdell, C., "The Physical Components of Vectors and Tensors", *ZAMM* **33** (1953), pp. 345–355.

173. Truesdell, C., "Stages in the Development of the Concept of Stress", *Problems in Continuum Mechanics, Soc. for Indust. and Appl. Math.*, Philadelphia (1961), pp. 556–564.

174. Truesdell, C., "A Program toward Rediscovering the Rational Mechanics of the Age of Reason", *Arch. Hist. Ex. Sci.* **1**, New York: Springer-Verlag (1960), pp. 3–36.

175. Truesdell, C. and R. Toupin, "Static Grounds for Inequalities in Finite Strain of Elastic Materials", *ARMA* **12** (1963), pp. 1–33. Corrections to this paper are given in **19** (1965), p. 407.

176. Truesdell, C., "Das ungeloeste Hauptproblem der endlichen Elastizitaets-theorie", *ZAMM* **36** (1956), pp. 97–103.

177. Truesdell, C., "The Modern Spirit in Applied Mathematics", *I.C.S.U. Review* **6** (1964).

178. Truesdell, C., *Principles of Continuum Mechanics, Coll. Lect. Pure Appl. Sci. No. 5* (1960), Socony Mobil Oil Co., Dallas, Texas.

179. Truesdell, C., "Whence the Law of Moment of Momentum?", Paris, France: Mélanges Alexandre Koyré (1964).

180. Truesdell, C. (with Appendix by C.-C. Wang), "Fluids of the Second Grade Regarded as Fluids of Convected Elasticity", *Phys. of Fluids* **8** (1965), pp. 1936–1938.

181. Truesdell, C., "The Natural Time of a Viscoelastic Fluid: Its Significance and Measurement", *Phys. of Fluids* **7** (1964), pp. 1134–1142.

182. Truesdell, C., "Reactions of the History of Mechanics Upon Modern Research", *Proc. 4th US Natl. Congr. Appl. Mech.* (1962).

183. Truesdell, C., "The Meaning of Betti's Reciprocal Theorem", *J. of Res., Natl. Bureau of Standards* **67B** (1963), p. 85.

184. Truesdell, C., "Second-Order Theory of Wave Propagation in Isotropic Elastic Materials", *I.U.T.A.M. Symposium on Second-Order Effects in Elasticity, Plasticity, and Fluid Dynamics*, Haifa, Israel (1962).

185. Truesdell, C., "General and Exact Theory of Waves in Finite Elastic Strain", *ARMA* **8** (1961), pp. 263–296.

186. Varley, E., "Acceleration Fronts in Viscoelastic Materials", *ARMA* **19** (1965), pp. 215–225.

187. Varley, E. and J. Dunwoody, "The Effect of Non-Linearity at an Acceleration Wave", *J. Mech. Phys. Solids* **13** (1965), pp. 17–28.

188. Veblen, O., *Invariants of Quadratic Differential Forms*, Cambridge, Mass.: Cambridge University Press.

189. Wang, C.-C., "The Principle of Fading Memory", *ARMA* **18** (1965), pp. 343–365.

190. Wang, C.-C., "On the Radial Oscillations of a Spherical Thin Shell in the Finite Elasticity Theory", *QAM* **23** (1965), pp. 270–274.

191. Wayman, C. M., *Introduction to the Crystallography of Martensitic Transformations*, New York: The Macmillan Co. (1964).

192. Weertman, J. and J. R. Weertman, *Elementary Dislocation Theory*, New York: The Macmillan Co. (1964).

193. Weitsman, Y., "Initial Stresses and Skin Effects in a Hemitropic Cosserat

Continuum", *Techn. Rep. No. 1, ONR Project NR-064-488*, Universty Park, Pa.: The Pennsylvania State University.

194. Weyl, H., *The Classical Groups*, Princeton, N.J.: Princeton University Press (1939).

195. Wineman, A. S. and A. C. Pipkin, "Material Symmetry Restrictions on Constitutive Equations", *ARMA* **17** (1964), pp. 184–214.

Additional References*

196. Truesdell, C., *Six Lectures on Modern Natural Philosophy*, New York: Springer-Verlag (1966).

197. Cohen, H., and C. N. DeSilva, "Nonlinear Theory of Elastic Surfaces," *J. Math. Phys.* **7** (1966), pp. 246–253.

198. Brillouin, L., *Science and Information Theory*, New York: Academic Press (1956).

199. Truesdell, C., "Thermodynamics for Beginners," to appear in the Proceedings of the International Conference on Thermodynamics, Vienna (1966).

200. Green, A. E., and R. T. Shield, "Finite Extension and Torsion of Cylinders," *Phil. Trans. Roy. Soc. Lond.* A**224** (1951), pp. 47–86.

201. Varley, E., "Simple Waves in General Elastic Materials," *ARMA* **20** (1965), pp. 309–328.

202. Fredrickson, A. G., *Principles and Applications of Rheology*, Englewood Cliffs, N.J.: Prentice-Hall (1964).

203. Ericksen, J. L., "A Thermo-Kinetic View of Elastic Stability Theory," *Int. J. Solids Structures* **2** (1966), pp. 573–580.

204. Wang, C.-C., "A Representation Theorem for the Constitutive Equation of a Simple Material in Motions with Constant Stretch History", *ARMA* **20** (1965), pp. 329–340.

205. Sternberg, E., and J. K. Knowles, "Minimum Energy Characterization of Saint-Venant's Solution to the Relaxed Saint-Venant Problem", *ARMA* **21** (1966), pp. 89–107.

206. Volterra, E., *Theory of Functionals*, New York: Dover Publications.

207. Pipkin, A. C., "Small Finite Deformations of Viscoelastic Solids", *Rev. Mod. Phys.* (Oct. 1964), pp. 1034–1041.

208. Hart-Smith, L. J., "Elasticity Parameters for Finite Deformations of Rubber-like Materials", *ZAMP* **17** (1966), pp. 608–625.

209. Zapas, L. J., and T. Craft, "Correlation of Large Longitudinal Deformations with Different Strain Histories", *J. Res. Natl. Bureau of Standards* **69A** (1965), pp. 541–546.

210. Leslie, F. M., "Constitutive Equations for Anisotropic Fluids", *Quart. J. Math. Mech.* (1966), 357–369.

211. Green, A. E., "A Note on Linear Transversely Isotropic Fluids", *Mathematika* **12** (1965), pp. 27–29.

212. Knowles, J. K., "On Saint-Venant's Principle in the Two-Dimensional Linear Theory of Elasticity", *ARMA* **21** (1966), pp. 1–21.

213. Gray, G. W., "*Molecular Structure and the Properties of Liquid Crystals*, New York: Academic Press (1962).

* Not in alphabetical order.

214. Wang, C.-C., "A General Theory of Subfluids", *ARMA* **20** (1965), pp. 1–40.

215. Wang. C.-C. and R. M. Bowen, "On the Thermodynamics of Non-Linear Materials with Quasi-Elastic Response", *ARMA* **22** (1966), pp. 79–99.

216. Lamb, H., *Hydrodynamics*, New York: Dover Publications (1945).

217. Antman, S. S. and W. H. Warner, "Dynamical Theory of Hyperelastic Rods", *ARMA* **23** (1966), pp. 135–161.

218. Thomas, T. Y., *Proc. Natl. Acad. Sci.* **55** (1966), p. 235.

219. Truesdell, C., *The Elements of Continuum Mechanics*, New York: Springer-Verlag (1966).

220. Pipkin, A. C. and R. S. Rivlin, "The Formulation of Constitutive Equations in Continuum Physics", Providence, R.I.: Brown University Report (1958).

221. Gurtin, M. E., "Thermodynamics and the Possibility of Spatial Interactions in Elastic Materials", *ARMA* **19** (1965), pp. 339–352.

222. Truesdell, C., "The Mechanical Foundations of Elasticity and Fluid Dynamics", *JRMA* **1** (1952), pp. 125–300.

223. Kunin, I. A., "Internal Stresses in an Anisotropic Elastic Medium", *PMM* **28** (1964), pp. 612–621.

224. Carlson, D. E., "Stress Functions for Couple and Dipolar Stresses", *QAM* **24** (1965) pp. 29–35.

225. Eshelby, J. D., "The Continuum Theory of Lattice Defects", *Solid State Physics* **3** (1956), New York: Academic Press.

226. Mindlin, R. D. and D. H. Cheng, "Nuclei of Strain in the Semi-Infinite Solid", *J. Appl. Phys.* **21** (1950), pp. 926–930.

227. Treloar, L. R. G., *The Physics of Rubber Elasticity*, Oxford, Eng.: Clarendon Press, 1958.

228. De Wit, R., "The Continuum Theory of Stationary Dislocations", *Solid State Physics* **10** (1960), New York: Academic Press.

229. *Theory of Crystal Defects* (proceedings of the summer school held in Hrazany, Czechoslovakia), New York: Academic Press (1966).

230. *Continuum Mechanics* I, II, III, IV (editor: C. Truesdell), New York: Gordon and Breach, Science Publishers, Inc. (1965).

231. Rivlin, R. S., "Large Elastic Deformations of Isotropic Materials. I, II", *Phil. Trans. Roy. Soc. Lond.*, A**241** (1948), pp. 459–508.

232. Kydoniefs, A. D. and A. J. M. Spencer, "The Finite Inflation of an Elastic Torus", *Int. J. Engng. Sci.* **3** (1965), pp. 173–195.

233. Ralston, T. and W. Jaunzemis, "A Comparison of Lattice and Continuum Theories of Elasticity", *AFOSR Techn. Note*, University Park, Pa.: The Pennsylvania State University, 1967.

234. Fox, N., "A Continuum Theory of Dislocations for Single Crystals", *J. Inst. Math. Appl.* **2** (1966), pp. 285–298.

235. Wozniak, C., "Theory of Fibrous Media. II", *AMS* **17** (1965), pp. 777–799.

236. Singh, M. and A. C. Pipkin, "Controllable States of Elastic Dielectrics" *ARMA* **21** (1966), pp. 169–210.

237. Rivlin, R. S., "Nonlinear Viscoelastic Solids", *SIAM Review* **7** (1965), pp. 323–340.

238. Rivlin, R. S., "Viscoelastic Fluids", *Frontiers of Research in Fluid Dynamics* (editors: G. Temple and R. Seeger), New York: Interscience (1965).

239. Lianis, G. and P. H. DeHoff, Jr., "Studies on Constitutive Equations of First and Second Order Viscoelasticity", *Purdue Univ. Report A & ES* 64-10 (Sept. 1964).

240. Metzner, A. B., J. L. White and M. M. Denn, "Constitutive Equations for Viscoelastic Fluids for Short Deformation Periods and for Rapidly Changing Flows: Significance of the Deborah Number", *A.I.Ch.E. Journal* **12** (1966), pp. 863–866.

241. *Proceedings of the Fourth International Congress on Rheology*, New York: Interscience (1965).

242. Ericksen, J. L., "Instability in Couette Flow of Anisotropic Fluids", *Quart. J. Mech. Appl. Math.* **19** (1966), pp. 455–459.

243. Zorski, H., "Theory of Discrete Defects", *AMS* **18** (1966), pp. 301–371.

Added in proof: Reference [43] is now available in *Modern Developments in the Mechanics of Continua* (Editor: S. Eskinazi), New York: Academic Press (1966).

INDEX